Praise for the Reformation Commentary on Scripture

"Protestant reformers were fundamentally exegetes as much as theologians, yet (except for figures like Luther and Calvin) their commentaries and sermons have been neglected because these writings are not available in modern editions or languages. That makes this new series of Reformation Commentary on Scripture most welcome as a way to provide access to some of the wealth of biblical exposition of the sixteenth and seventeenth centuries. The editor's introduction explains the nature of the sources and the selection process; the intended audience of modern pastors and students of the Bible has led to a focus on theological and practical comments. Although it will be of use to students of the Reformation, this series is far from being an esoteric study of largely forgotten voices; this collection of reforming comments, comprehending every verse and provided with topical headings, will serve contemporary pastors and preachers very well."

Elsie Anne McKee, *Archibald Alexander Professor of Reformation Studies and the History of Worship, Princeton Theological Seminary*

"This series provides an excellent introduction to the history of biblical exegesis in the Reformation period. The introductions are accurate, clear and informative, and the passages intelligently chosen to give the reader a good idea of methods deployed and issues at stake. It puts precritical exegesis in its context and so presents it in its correct light. Highly recommended as reference book, course book and general reading for students and all interested lay and clerical readers."

Irena Backus, *Professeure Ordinaire, Institut d'histoire de la Réformation, Université de Genève*

"The Reformation Commentary on Scripture is a major publishing event—for those with historical interest in the founding convictions of Protestantism, but even more for those who care about understanding the Bible. As with IVP Academic's earlier Ancient Christian Commentary on Scripture, this effort brings flesh and blood to 'the communion of saints' by letting believers of our day look over the shoulders of giants from the past. By connecting the past with the present, and by doing so with the Bible at the center, the editors of this series perform a great service for the church. The series deserves the widest possible support."

Mark A. Noll, *Francis A. McAnaney Professor of History, University of Notre Dame*

"For those who preach and teach Scripture in the church, the Reformation Commentary on Scripture is a significant publishing event. Pastors and other church leaders will find delightful surprises, challenging enigmas and edifying insights in this series, as many Reformational voices are newly translated into English. The lively conversation in these pages can ignite today's pastoral imagination for fresh and faithful expositions of Scripture."

J. Todd Billings, *Gordon H. Girod Research Professor of Reformed Theology, Western Theological Seminary*

"The reformers discerned rightly what the church desperately needed in the sixteenth century—the bold proclamation of the Word based on careful study of the sacred Scriptures. We need not only to hear that same call again for our own day but also to learn from the Reformation how to do it. This commentary series is a godsend!"

Richard J. Mouw, *President Emeritus, Fuller Theological Seminary*

"Like the Ancient Christian Commentary on Scripture, the Reformation Commentary on Scripture does a masterful job of offering excellent selections from well-known and not-so-well-known exegetes. The editor's introductory survey is, by itself, worth the price of the book. It is easy to forget that there were more hands, hearts and minds involved in the Reformation than Luther and Calvin. Furthermore, encounters even with these figures are often limited to familiar quotes on familiar topics. However, the Reformation Commentary helps us to recognize the breadth and depth of exegetical interests and skill that fueled and continue to fuel faithful meditation on God's Word. I heartily recommend this series as a tremendous resource not only for ministry but for personal edification."

Michael S. Horton, *J. G. Machen Professor of Systematic Theology and Apologetics,*
Westminster Seminary, California

"The Reformation was ignited by a fresh reading of Scripture. In this series of commentaries, we contemporary interpreters are allowed to feel some of the excitement, surprise and wonder of our spiritual forebears. Luther, Calvin and their fellow revolutionaries were masterful interpreters of the Word. Now, in this remarkable series, some of our very best Reformation scholars open up the riches of the Reformation's reading of the Scripture."

William H. Willimon, *Professor of the Practice of Christian Ministry, Duke Divinity School*

"The Reformation Scripture principle set the entirety of Christian life and thought under the governance of the divine Word, and pressed the church to renew its exegetical labors. This series promises to place before the contemporary church the fruit of those labors, and so to exemplify life under the Word."

John Webster, *Professor of Divinity, University of St. Andrews*

"Since Gerhard Ebeling's pioneering work on Luther's exegesis seventy years ago, the history of biblical interpretation has occupied many Reformation scholars and become a vital part of study of the period. The Reformation Commentary on Scripture provides fresh materials for students of Reformation-era biblical interpretation and for twenty-first-century preachers to mine the rich stores of insights from leading reformers of the sixteenth century into both the text of Scripture itself and its application in sixteenth-century contexts. This series will strengthen our understanding of the period of the Reformation and enable us to apply its insights to our own days and its challenges to the church."

Robert Kolb, *Professor Emeritus, Concordia Theological Seminary*

"The multivolume Ancient Christian Commentary on Scripture is a valuable resource for those who wish to know how the Fathers interpreted a passage of Scripture but who lack the time or the opportunity to search through the many individual works. This new Reformation Commentary on Scripture will do the same for the reformers and is to be warmly welcomed. It will provide much easier access to the exegetical treasures of the Reformation and will hopefully encourage readers to go back to some of the original works themselves."

Anthony N. S. Lane, *Professor of Historical Theology and Director of Research, London School of Theology*

"This volume of the RCS project is an invaluable source for pastors and the historically/biblically interested that provides unparalleled access not only to commentaries of the leading Protestant reformers but also to a host of nowadays unknown commentaters on Galatians and Ephesians. The RCS is sure to enhance and enliven contemporary exegesis. With its wide scope, the collection will enrich our understanding of the variety of Reformation thought and biblical exegesis."

Sigrun Haude, *Associate Professor of Reformation and Early Modern European History, University of Cincinnati*

"The Reformation Commentary on Scripture series promises to be an 'open sesame' to the biblical exegesis, exposition and application of the Bible that was the hallmark of the Reformation. While comparisons can be odious, the difference between Reformation commentary and exposition and much that both preceded and followed it is laid bare in these pages: whereas others write about the Bible from the outside, Reformation exposition carries with it the atmosphere of men who spoke and wrote from inside the Bible, experiencing the power of biblical teaching even as they expounded it. . . . This grand project sets before scholars, pastors, teachers, students and growing Christians an experience that can only be likened to stumbling into a group Bible study only to discover that your fellow participants include some of the most significant Christians of the Reformation and post-Reformation (for that matter, of any) era. Here the Word of God is explained in a variety of accents: German, Swiss, French, Dutch, English, Scottish and more. Each one vibrates with a thrilling sense of the living nature of God's Word and its power to transform individuals, churches and even whole communities. Here is a series to anticipate, enjoy and treasure."

Sinclair Ferguson, *Senior Minister, First Presbyterian Church, Columbia, South Carolina*

"I strongly endorse the Reformation Commentary on Scripture. Introducing how the Bible was interpreted during the age of the Reformation, these volumes will not only renew contemporary preaching, but they will also help us understand more fully how reading and meditating on Scripture can, in fact, change our lives!"

Lois Malcolm, *Associate Professor of Systematic Theology, Luther Seminary*

"Discerning the true significance of movements in theology requires acquaintance with their biblical exegesis. This is supremely so with the Reformation, which was essentially a biblical revival. The Reformation Commentary on Scripture will fill a yawning gap, just as the Ancient Christian Commentary did before it, and the first volume gets the series off to a fine start, whetting the appetite for more. Most heartily do I welcome and commend this long overdue project."

J. I. Packer, *Retired Board of Governors Professor of Theology, Regent College*

"There is no telling the benefits to emerge from the publication of this magnificent Reformation Commentary on Scripture series! Now exegetical and theological treasures from Reformation era commentators will be at our fingertips, providing new insights from old sources to give light for the present and future. This series is a gift to scholars and to the church; a wonderful resource to enhance our study of the written Word of God for generations to come!"

Donald K. McKim, *Executive Editor of Theology and Reference, Westminster John Knox Press*

"Why was this not done before? The publication of the Reformation Commentary on Scripture should be greeted with enthusiasm by every believing Christian—but especially by those who will preach and teach the Word of God. This commentary series brings the very best of the Reformation heritage to the task of exegesis and exposition, and each volume in this series represents a veritable feast that takes us back to the sixteenth century to enrich the preaching and teaching of God's Word in our own time."

R. Albert Mohler Jr., *President, The Southern Baptist Theological Seminary*

"Today more than ever, the Christian past is the church's future. InterVarsity Press has already brought the voice of the ancients to our ears. Now, in the Reformation Commentary on Scripture, we hear a timely word from the first Protestants as well."

Bryan Litfin, *Professor of Theology, Moody Bible Institute*

"I am delighted to see the Reformation Commentary on Scripture. The editors of this series have done us all a service by gleaning from these rich fields of biblical reflection. May God use this new life for these old words to give him glory and to build his church."

Mark Dever, *Senior Pastor, Capitol Hill Baptist Church, and President of 9Marks.org Ministries*

"Monumental and magisterial, the Reformation Commentary on Scripture, edited by Timothy George, is a remarkably bold and visionary undertaking. Bringing together a wealth of resources, these volumes will provide historians, theologians, biblical scholars, pastors and students with a fresh look at the exegetical insights of those who shaped and influenced the sixteenth-century Reformation. With this marvelous publication, InterVarsity Press has reached yet another plateau of excellence. We pray that this superb series will be used of God to strengthen both church and academy."

David S. Dockery, *President, Trinity International University*

"Detached from her roots, the church cannot reach the world as God intends. While every generation must steward the scriptural insights God grants it, only arrogance or ignorance causes leaders to ignore the contributions of those faithful leaders before us. The Reformation Commentary on Scripture roots our thought in great insights of faithful leaders of the Reformation to further biblical preaching and teaching in this generation."

Bryan Chapell, *chancellor and professor of practical theology, Covenant Theological Seminary*

"After reading several volumes of the Reformation Commentary on Scripture, I exclaimed, 'Hey, this is just what the doctor ordered—I mean Doctor Martinus Lutherus!' The church of today bearing his name needs a strong dose of the medicine this doctor prescribed for the ailing church of the sixteenth century. The reforming fire of Christ-centered preaching that Luther ignited is the only hope to reclaim the impact of the gospel to keep the Reformation going, not for its own sake but to further the renewal of the worldwide church of Christ today. This series of commentaries will equip preachers to step into their pulpits with confidence in the same living Word that inspired the witness of Luther and Calvin and many other lesser-known Reformers."

Carl E. Braaten, *cofounder of the Center for Catholic and Evangelical Theology*

REFORMATION COMMENTARY ON SCRIPTURE

OLD TESTAMENT
VII

PSALMS 1-72

EDITED BY
HERMAN J. SELDERHUIS

GENERAL EDITOR
TIMOTHY GEORGE

ASSOCIATE GENERAL EDITOR
SCOTT M. MANETSCH

IVP Academic

An imprint of InterVarsity Press
Downers Grove, Illinois

InterVarsity Press
P.O. Box 1400, Downers Grove, IL 60515-1426
World Wide Web: www.ivpress.com
E-mail: email@ivpress.com

InterVarsity Press® is the book-publishing division of InterVarsity Christian Fellowship/USA®, a movement of students and faculty active on campus at hundreds of universities, colleges and schools of nursing in the United States of America, and a member movement of the International Fellowship of Evangelical Students. For information about local and regional activities, write Public Relations Dept., InterVarsity Christian Fellowship/USA, 6400 Schroeder Rd., P.O. Box 7895, Madison, WI 537077895, or visit the IVCF website at www.intervarsity.org.

Design: Cindy Kiple
Images: Wooden cross: iStockphoto
> *The Protestant Church in Lyon: The Protestant Church in Lyon, called "The Paradise" at Bibliotheque Publique et Universitaire, Geneva, Switzerland,*
> *Erich Lessing/Art Resource, NY.*

ISBN 978-0-8308-2957-6 (print)
ISBN 978-0-8308-9818-3 (digital)

Printed in the United States of America ♾

Library of Congress Cataloging-in-Publication Data
Psalms 1-72 / edited by Herman J. Selderhuis ; general editor, Timothy George ; associate general, Editor Scott M. Manetsch.
    pages cm.—(Reformation commentary on Scripture. Old Testament ; 7)
    Includes bibliographical references and index.
    ISBN 978-0-8308-2957-6 (hardcover : alk. paper)
    1. Bible. Psalms, I-LXXII—Commentaries. I. Selderhuis, H. J., 1961- editor.
    BS1430.53.P726 2015
    223'.207—dc23
                        2015027321

P	26	25	24	23	22	21	20	19	18	17	16	15	14	13	12	11	10	9	8	7	6	5	4	3	2	1
Y	37	36	35	34	33	32	31	30	29	28	27	26	25	24	23	22	21	20	19	18	17	16	15

Reformation Commentary on Scripture
Project Staff

Project Editor
David W. McNutt

---

*Managing Editor and
Production Manager*
Benjamin M. McCoy

Copyeditor
Linda Triemstra

Assistant Project Editor
Todd R. Hains

Editorial and Research Assistants
David J. Hooper
Ethan McCarthy

Assistants to the General Editors
Le-Ann Little
Jason Odom

Design
Cindy Kiple

Design Assistant
Beth McGill

Content Production
Richard Chung
Kirsten Pott
Maureen G. Tobey
Jeanna L. Wiggins

Proofreader
Ethan McCarthy

Print Coordinator
Jim Erhart

InterVarsity Press

Publisher
Robert A. Fryling

Associate Publisher, Editorial
Andrew T. Le Peau

Senior Editor
Daniel G. Reid

Production Director
Anne Gerth

CONTENTS

ACKNOWLEDGMENTS

This book is only partly mine, since I owe nearly all of its contents to those who studied the Psalms in the Reformation era and wrote down their comments. Besides these colleagues of former times, I wish to thank Brannon Ellis, Timothy George, Mike Gibson, Andy Le Peau, Scott Manetsch, David McNutt and Dan Reid, as well as Todd Hains, David Hooper, Ethan McCarthy, Ben McCoy and many others at IVP for their wonderful help and admirable patience; the various translators, Robert Crellin, André Gazal, James Kellerman, Matthias Mangold, Todd Rester and April Ross for their careful translations; and my assistants at the Theological University Apeldoorn, Martijn de Groot and Mans Raveling, for their help in organizing this project.

Herman J. Selderhuis

ABBREVIATIONS

ACCS	*Ancient Christian Commentary on Scripture.* 29 vols. Edited by Thomas C. Oden. Downers Grove, IL: InterVarsity Press, 1998–2009.
ACW	*Ancient Christian Writers: The Works of the Fathers in Translation.* Mahwah, NJ: Paulist, 1946–.
ANF	*The Ante-Nicene Fathers.* 10 vols. Edited by Alexander Roberts and James Donaldson. Buffalo, NY: Christian Literature, 1885–1896. Available online at www.ccel.org.
AWA	*Archiv zur Weimarer Ausgabe der Werke Martin Luthers: Texte und Untersuchungen.* Cologne: Böhlau, 1981–.
BCP 1549	*The Book of Common Prayer (1549).* In *The Two Liturgies, AD 1549 and AD 1552.* Edited by Joseph Ketley, 9-158. Cambridge: Cambridge University Press, 1844.
BoC	*The Book of Concord: The Confessions of the Evangelical Lutheran Church.* Edited by Robert Kolb and Timothy J. Wengert. Translated by Charles Arand et al. Minneapolis: Fortress, 2000.
BRN	*Bibliotheca Reformatoria Neederlandica.* 10 vols. Edited by S. Cramer and F. Pijper. The Hague: Martinus Nijhoff, 1903–1914. Digital copies online at babel.hathitrust.org.
BSLK	*Die Bekenntnisschriften der evangelisch-lutherischen Kirche.* 12th ed. Göttingen: Vandenhoeck & Ruprecht, 1998.
CHB	*Cambridge History of the Bible.* 3 vols. Cambridge: Cambridge University Press, 1963–1970.
CNTC	*Calvin's New Testament Commentaries.* 12 vols. Edited by D. W. Torrance and T. F. Torrance. Grand Rapids: Eerdmans, 1959–1972.
CO	*Ioannis Calvini Opera quae supersunt omnia.* 59 vols. Corpus Reformatorum 29–88. Edited by G. Baum, E. Cunitz and E. Reuss. Brunswick and Berlin: C. A. Schwetschke, 1863–1900. Digital copies online at archive-ouverte.unige.ch/unige:650.
Creeds	Philip Schaff. *The Creeds of Christendom: With a Critical History and Notes.* 3 vols. New York: Harper & Row, 1877; reprint, Grand Rapids: Baker, 1977. Digital copy online at ccel.org.
CRR	*Classics of the Radical Reformation.* 12 vols. Waterloo, ON, and Scottdale, PA: Herald Press, 1973–2010.
CTS	Calvin Translation Society edition of Calvin's commentaries. 46 vols. Edinburgh, 1843–1855. Several reprints, but variously bound; volume numbers (when cited)

are relative to specific commentaries and not to the entire set. Available online at www.ccel.org.

CWE   *Collected Works of Erasmus.* 86 vols. projected. Toronto: University of Toronto Press, 1969–.

DMBI   *Dictionary of Major Biblical Interpreters.* Edited by Donald K. McKim. Downers Grove, IL: InterVarsity Press, 2007.

DNB   Dictionary of National Biography. Edited by Leslie Stephen and Sidney Lee. 63 vols. London: Smith, Elder, and Co., 1885–1900.

E²   *Dr. Martin Luther's sämmtliche Werke.* 2nd ed. 26 vols. Frankfurt and Erlangen: Heyder & Zimmer, 1862–1885. Digital copies online at babel.hathitrust.org.

EEBO   Early English Books Online. Subscription database, eebo.chadwyck.com.

FC   Fathers of the Church: A New Translation. Washington, DC: Catholic University of America Press, 1947–.

LCC   Library of Christian Classics. 26 vols. Edited by John Baillie et al. Philadelphia: Westminster, 1953–1966.

LSB   *Lutheran Service Book.* Edited by The Commission on Worship for the Lutheran Church–Missouri Synod. St. Louis: Concordia, 2006.

LW   *Luther's Works* [American edition]. 82 vols. projected. St. Louis: Concordia; Philadelphia: Fortress, 1955–86; 2009–.

MO   *Philippi Melanthonis Opera quae supersunt omnia.* 28 vols. Corpus Reformatorum 1–28. Edited by C. G. Bretschneider. Halle: C. A. Schwetschke, 1834–1860. Digital copies online at archive.org and books.google.com.

OER   *Oxford Encyclopedia of the Reformation.* 4 vols. Edited by Hans J. Hillerbrand. New York: Oxford University Press, 1996.

OS   Joannis Calvini Opera selecta. 5 vols. Edited by Peter Barth and Wilhelm Niesel. Munich: Christian Kaiser Verlag, 1970–1974.

NPNF   A Select Library of the Nicene and Post-Nicene Fathers of the Christian Church. 28 vols. in two series, denoted as NPNF and NPNF². Edited by Philip Schaff et al. Buffalo, NY: Christian Literature, 1887–1894. Several reprints; also available online at www.ccel.org.

PG   Patrologia cursus completus. Series Graeca. 161 vols. Edited by J.-P. Migne. Paris, 1857–1866. Digital copies online at books.google.com.

PL   Patrologia cursus completus. Series Latina. 221 vols. Edited by J.-P. Migne. Paris: Migne, 1844–1864. Digital copies online at books.google.com.

PRDL   Post Reformation Digital Library. Online database at prdl.org.

r, v   Some early books are numbered not by page but by folio (leaf). Front and back sides (pages) of a numbered folio are indicated by *recto* (r) and *verso* (v), respectively.

RCS   Reformation Commentary on Scripture. 28 vols. projected. Edited by Timothy George and Scott M. Manetsch. Downers Grove, IL: IVP Academic, 2011–.

SCal   *Supplementa Calviniana: Sermon inédits.* 11 vols. planned. Neukirchen-Vluyn: Neukirchener Verlag; Geneva: Droz, 1961–.

WA   *D. Martin Luthers Werke, Kritische Gesamtausgabe: [Schriften].* 73 vols. Weimar: Hermann Böhlaus Nachfolger, 1883–2009. Digital copy online at archive.org.

WABr   *D. Martin Luthers Werke, Kritische Gesamtausgabe: Briefwechsel.* 18 vols. Weimar: Hermann Böhlaus Nachfolger, 1930–1983. Digital copy online at archive.org.

WADB   *D. Martin Luthers Werke, Kritische Gesamtausgabe: Deutsche Bibel.* 12 vols. Weimar: Böhlaus Nachfolger, 1906–1961. Some digital copies online at archive.org.

WATR   *D. Martin Luthers Werke, Kritische Gesamtausgabe: Tischreden.* 6 vols. Weimar: Hermann Böhlaus Nachfolger, 1912–1921. Digital copy online at archive.org.

ZSW   *Huldreich Zwinglis Sämtliche Werke.* 14 vols. Corpus Reformatorum 88–101. Edited by E. Eglis et al. Berlin: C. A. Schwetschke, 1905–1959; reprint, Zurich: Theologischer Verlag Zürich, 1983. Digital copies online at www.irg.uzh.ch.

BIBLE TRANSLATIONS

CEB	Common English Bible
ESV	English Standard Version
KJV	King James Version
LXX	Septuagint
NASB	New American Standard Bible
NIV	New International Version
NKJV	New King James Version
NRSV	New Revised Standard Version
Vg	Vulgate

A GUIDE TO USING THIS COMMENTARY

Several features have been incorporated into the design of this commentary. The following comments are intended to assist readers in making full use of this volume.

Pericopes of Scripture

The scriptural text has been divided into pericopes, or passages, usually several verses in length. Each of these pericopes is given a heading, which appears at the beginning of the pericope. For example, the first pericope in this commentary on Psalms is "1:1-6 The Two Ways." This heading is followed by the Scripture passage quoted in the English Standard Version (ESV). The Scripture passage is provided for the convenience of readers, but it is also in keeping with Reformation-era commentaries, which often followed the patristic and medieval commentary tradition, in which the citations of the reformers were arranged according to the text of Scripture.

Overviews

Following each pericope of text is an overview of the Reformation authors' comments on that pericope. The format of this overview varies among the volumes of this series, depending on the requirements of the specific book(s) of Scripture. The function of the overview is to identify succinctly the key exegetical, theological and pastoral concerns of the Reformation writers arising from the pericope, providing the reader with an orientation to Reformation-era approaches and emphases. It tracks a reasonably cohesive thread of argument among reformers' comments, even though they are derived from diverse sources and generations. Thus, the summaries do not proceed chronologically or by verse sequence. Rather, they seek to rehearse the overall course of the reformers' comments on that pericope.

We do not assume that the commentators themselves anticipated or expressed a formally received cohesive argument but rather that the various arguments tend to flow in a plausible, recognizable pattern. Modern readers can thus glimpse aspects of continuity in the flow of diverse exegetical traditions representing various generations and geographical locations.

Topical Headings

An abundance of varied Reformation-era comment is available for each pericope. For this reason we have broken the pericopes into two levels. First is the verse with its topical heading. The reformers' comments are then focused on aspects of each verse, with topical headings summarizing the essence of the individual comment by evoking a key phrase, metaphor or idea. This feature provides a bridge by which modern readers can enter into the heart of the Reformation-era comment.

Identifying the Reformation Authors, Texts and Events

Following the topical heading of each section of comment, the name of the Reformation commentator is given. An English translation (where needed) of the reformer's comment is then provided. This is immediately followed by the title of the original work rendered in English.

Readers who wish to pursue a deeper investigation of the reformers' works cited in this commentary will find full bibliographic detail for each reformation title provided in the bibliography at the back of the volume. Information on English translations (where available) and standard original-language editions and critical editions of the works cited is found in the bibliography. The Biographical Sketches section provides brief overviews of the life and work of each commentator, and each confession or collaborative work, appearing in the present volume (as well as in any previous volumes). Finally, a Timeline of the Reformation offers broader context for people, places and events relevant to the commentators and their works.

Footnotes and Back Matter

To aid the reader in exploring the background and texts in further detail, this commentary utilizes footnotes. The use and content of footnotes may vary among the volumes in this series. Where footnotes appear, a footnote number directs the reader to a note at the bottom of the page, where one will find annotations (clarifications or biblical cross references), information on English translations (where available) or standard original-language editions of the work cited.

Where original-language texts have remained untranslated into English, we provide new translations. Where there is any serious ambiguity or textual problem in the selection, we have tried to reflect the best available textual tradition. Wherever current English translations are already well rendered, they are utilized, but where necessary they are stylistically updated. A single asterisk (*) indicates that a previous English translation has been updated to modern English or amended for easier reading. We have standardized spellings and made grammatical variables uniform so that our English references will not reflect the linguistic oddities of the older English translations. For ease of reading we have in some cases removed superfluous conjunctions.

GENERAL INTRODUCTION

The Reformation Commentary on Scripture (RCS) is a twenty-eight-volume series of exegetical comment covering the entire Bible and gathered from the writings of sixteenth-century preachers, scholars and reformers. The RCS is intended as a sequel to the highly acclaimed Ancient Christian Commentary on Scripture (ACCS), and as such its overall concept, method, format and audience are similar to the earlier series. Both series are committed to the renewal of the church through careful study and meditative reflection on the Old and New Testaments, the charter documents of Christianity, read in the context of the worshiping, believing community of faith across the centuries. However, the patristic and Reformation eras are separated by nearly a millennium, and the challenges of reading Scripture with the reformers require special attention to their context, resources and assumptions. The purpose of this general introduction is to present an overview of the context and process of biblical interpretation in the age of the Reformation.

Goals

The Reformation Commentary on Scripture seeks to introduce its readers to the depth and richness of exegetical ferment that defined the Reformation era. The RCS has four goals: the enrichment of contemporary biblical interpretation through exposure to Reformation-era biblical exegesis; the renewal of contemporary preaching through exposure to the biblical insights of the Reformation writers; a deeper understanding of the Reformation itself and the breadth of perspectives represented within it; and a recovery of the profound integration of the life of faith and the life of the mind that should characterize Christian scholarship. Each of these goals requires a brief comment.

Renewing contemporary biblical interpretation. During the past half-century, biblical hermeneutics has become a major growth industry in the academic world. One of the consequences of the historical-critical hegemony of biblical studies has been the privileging of contemporary philosophies and ideologies at the expense of a commitment to the Christian church as the primary reading community within which and for which biblical exegesis is done. Reading Scripture with the church fathers and the reformers is a corrective to all such imperialism of the present. One of the greatest skills required for a fruitful interpretation of the Bible is the ability to listen. We rightly emphasize the importance of listening to the voices of contextual theologies today, but in doing so we often marginalize or ignore another crucial context—the community of believing Christians through the centuries. The serious study of Scripture requires more than the latest

Bible translation in one hand and the latest commentary (or niche study Bible) in the other. John L. Thompson has called on Christians today to practice the art of "reading the Bible with the dead."[1] The RCS presents carefully selected comments from the extant commentaries of the Reformation as an encouragement to more in-depth study of this important epoch in the history of biblical interpretation.

Strengthening contemporary preaching. The Protestant reformers identified the public preaching of the Word of God as an indispensible means of grace and a sure sign of the true church. Through the words of the preacher, the living voice of the gospel (*viva vox evangelii*) is heard. Luther famously said that the church is not a "pen house" but a "mouth house."[2] The Reformation in Switzerland began when Huldrych Zwingli entered the pulpit of the Grossmünster in Zurich on January 1, 1519, and began to preach a series of expositional sermons chapter by chapter from the Gospel of Matthew. In the following years he extended this homiletical approach to other books of the Old and New Testaments. Calvin followed a similar pattern in Geneva. Many of the commentaries represented in this series were either originally presented as sermons or were written to support the regular preaching ministry of local church pastors. Luther said that the preacher should be a *bonus textualis*—a good one with a text—well-versed in the Scriptures. Preachers in the Reformation traditions preached not only about the Bible but also from it, and this required more than a passing acquaintance with its contents. Those who have been charged with the office of preaching in the church today can find wisdom and insight—and fresh perspectives—in the sermons of the Reformation and the biblical commentaries read and studied by preachers of the sixteenth century.

Deepening understanding of the Reformation. Some scholars of the sixteenth century prefer to speak of the period they study in the plural, the European Reformations, to indicate that many diverse impulses for reform were at work in this turbulent age of transition from medieval to modern times.[3] While this point is well taken, the RCS follows the time-honored tradition of using Reformation in the singular form to indicate not only a major moment in the history of Christianity in the West but also, as Hans J. Hillerbrand has put it, "an essential cohesiveness in the heterogeneous pursuits of religious reform in the sixteenth century."[4] At the same time, in developing guidelines to assist the volume editors in making judicious selections from the vast amount of commentary material available in this period, we have stressed the multifaceted character of the Reformation across many confessions, theological orientations and political settings.

Advancing Christian scholarship. By assembling and disseminating numerous voices from such a signal period as the Reformation, the RCS aims to make a significant contribution to the ever-growing stream of Christian scholarship. The post-Enlightenment split between the study

---

[1]John L. Thompson, *Reading the Bible with the Dead* (Grand Rapids: Eerdmans, 2007).
[2]WA 10,2:48.
[3]See Carter Lindberg, *The European Reformations*, 2nd ed. (Malden, MA: Wiley-Blackwell, 2010).
[4]Hans J. Hillerbrand, *The Division of Christendom* (Louisville, KY: Westminster John Knox, 2007), x. Hillerbrand has also edited the standard reference work in Reformation studies, OER. See also Diarmaid MacCulloch, *The Reformation* (New York: Viking, 2003), and Patrick Collinson, *The Reformation: A History* (New York: Random House, 2004).

of the Bible as an academic discipline and the reading of the Bible as spiritual nurture was foreign to the reformers. For them the study of the Bible was transformative at the most basic level of the human person: *coram deo*.

The reformers all repudiated the idea that the Bible could be studied and understood with dispassionate objectivity, as a cold artifact from antiquity. Luther's famous Reformation breakthrough triggered by his laborious study of the Psalms and Paul's letter to the Romans is well known, but the experience of Cambridge scholar Thomas Bilney was perhaps more typical. When Erasmus's critical edition of the Greek New Testament was published in 1516, it was accompanied by a new translation in elegant Latin. Attracted by the classical beauty of Erasmus's Latin, Bilney came across this statement in 1 Timothy 1:15: "Christ Jesus came into the world to save sinners." In the Greek this sentence is described as *pistos ho logos*, which the Vulgate had rendered *fidelis sermo*, "a faithful saying." Erasmus chose a different word for the Greek *pistos—certus*, "sure, certain." When Bilney grasped the meaning of this word applied to the announcement of salvation in Christ, he tells us that "Immediately, I felt a marvellous comfort and quietness, insomuch as 'my bruised bones leaped for joy.'"[5]

Luther described the way the Bible was meant to function in the minds and hearts of believers when he reproached himself and others for studying the nativity narrative with such cool unconcern:

> I hate myself because when I see Christ laid in the manger or in the lap of his mother and hear the angels sing, my heart does not leap into flame. With what good reason should we all despise ourselves that we remain so cold when this word is spoken to us, over which everyone should dance and leap and burn for joy! We act as though it were a frigid historical fact that does not smite our hearts, as if someone were merely relating that the sultan has a crown of gold.[6]

It was a core conviction of the Reformation that the careful study and meditative listening to the Scriptures, what the monks called *lectio divina*, could yield transformative results for *all* of life. The value of such a rich commentary, therefore, lies not only in the impressive volume of Reformation-era voices that are presented throughout the course of the series but in the many particular fields for which their respective lives and ministries are relevant. The Reformation is consequential for historical studies, both church as well as secular history. Biblical and theological studies, to say nothing of pastoral and spiritual studies, also stand to benefit and progress immensely from renewed engagement today, as mediated through the RCS, with the reformers of yesteryear.

Perspectives

In setting forth the perspectives and parameters of the RCS, the following considerations have proved helpful.

---

[5]John Foxe, *The Acts and Monuments of John Foxe: A New and Complete Edition*, 8 vols., ed. Stephen Reed Cattley (London: R. B. Seeley & W. Burnside, 1837), 4:635; quoting Ps 51:8; cited in A. G. Dickens, *The English Reformation*, 2nd ed. (University Park, PA: The Pennsylvannia State University Press, 1991), 102.

[6]WA 49:176-77, quoted in Roland Bainton, "The Bible in the Reformation," in *CHB*, 3:23.

Chronology. When did the Reformation begin, and how long did it last? In some traditional accounts, the answer was clear: the Reformation began with the posting of Luther's Ninety-five Theses at Wittenberg in 1517 and ended with the death of Calvin in Geneva in 1564. Apart from reducing the Reformation to a largely German event with a side trip to Switzerland, this perspective fails to do justice to the important events that led up to Luther's break with Rome and its many reverberations throughout Europe and beyond. In choosing commentary selections for the RCS, we have adopted the concept of the long sixteenth century, say, from the late 1400s to the mid-seventeenth century. Thus we have included commentary selections from early or pre-Reformation writers such as John Colet and Jacques Lefèvre d'Étaples to seventeenth-century figures such as Henry Ainsworth and Johann Gerhard.

Confession. The RCS concentrates primarily, though not exclusively, on the exegetical writings of the Protestant reformers. While the ACCS provided a compendium of key consensual exegetes of the early Christian centuries, the Catholic/Protestant confessional divide in the sixteenth century tested the very idea of consensus, especially with reference to ecclesiology and soteriology. While many able and worthy exegetes faithful to the Roman Catholic Church were active during this period, this project has chosen to include primarily those figures that represent perspectives within the Protestant Reformation. For this reason we have not included comments on the apocryphal or deuterocanonical writings.

We recognize that "Protestant" and "Catholic" as contradistinctive labels are anachronistic terms for the early decades of the sixteenth century before the hardening of confessional identities surrounding the Council of Trent (1545–1563). Protestant figures such as Philipp Melanchthon, Johannes Oecolampadius and John Calvin were all products of the revival of sacred letters known as biblical humanism. They shared an approach to biblical interpretation that owed much to Desiderius Erasmus and other scholars who remained loyal to the Church of Rome. Careful comparative studies of Protestant and Catholic exegesis in the sixteenth century have shown surprising areas of agreement when the focus was the study of a particular biblical text rather than the standard confessional debates.

At the same time, exegetical differences among the various Protestant groups could become strident and church-dividing. The most famous example of this is the interpretive impasse between Luther and Zwingli over the meaning of "This is my body" (Mt 26:26) in the words of institution. Their disagreement at the Colloquy of Marburg in 1529 had important christological and pastoral implications, as well as social and political consequences. Luther refused fellowship with Zwingli and his party at the end of the colloquy; in no small measure this bitter division led to the separate trajectories pursued by Lutheran and Reformed Protestantism to this day. In Elizabethan England, Puritans and Anglicans agreed that "Holy Scripture containeth all things necessary to salvation: so that whatsoever is not read therein, nor may be proved thereby, is not to be required of any man" (article 6 of the Thirty-nine Articles of Religion), yet on the basis of their differing interpretations of the Bible they fought bitterly over the structures of the church, the clothing of the clergy and the ways of worship. On the matter of infant baptism, Catholics and

Protestants alike agreed on its propriety, though there were various theories as to how a practice not mentioned in the Bible could be justified biblically. The Anabaptists were outliers on this subject. They rejected infant baptism altogether. They appealed to the example of the baptism of Jesus and to his final words as recorded in the Gospel of Matthew (Mt 28:19-20), "Go therefore, and make disciples of all nations, baptizing them in the name of the Father, and of the Son, and of the Holy Spirit, teaching them to observe all that I have commanded you." New Testament Christians, they argued, are to follow not only the commands of Jesus in the Great Commission, but also the exact order in which they were given: evangelize, baptize, catechize.

These and many other differences of interpretation among the various Protestant groups are reflected in their many sermons, commentaries and public disputations. In the RCS, the volume editor's introduction to each volume is intended to help the reader understand the nature and significance of doctrinal conversations and disputes that resulted in particular, and frequently clashing, interpretations. Footnotes throughout the text will be provided to explain obscure references, unusual expressions and other matters that require special comment. Volume editors have chosen comments on the Bible across a wide range of sixteenth-century confessions and schools of interpretation: biblical humanists, Lutheran, Reformed, Anglican, Puritan and Anabaptist. We have not pursued passages from post-Tridentine Catholic authors or from radical spiritualists and antitrinitarian writers, though sufficient material is available from these sources to justify another series.

Format. The design of the RCS is intended to offer reader-friendly access to these classic texts. The availability of digital resources has given access to a huge residual database of sixteenth-century exegetical comment hitherto available only in major research universities and rare book collections. The RCS has benefited greatly from online databases such as Alexander Street Press's Digital Library of Classical Protestant Texts (DLCPT) as well as freely accessible databases like the Post-Reformation Digital Library (prdl.org). Through the help of RCS editorial advisor Herman Selderhuis, we have also had access to the special Reformation collections of the Johannes a Lasco Bibliothek in Emden, Germany. In addition, modern critical editions and translations of Reformation sources have been published over the past generation. Original translations of Reformation sources are given unless an acceptable translation already exists.

Each volume in the RCS will include an introduction by the volume editor placing that portion of the canon within the historical context of the Protestant Reformation and presenting a summary of the theological themes, interpretive issues and reception of the particular book(s). The commentary itself consists of particular pericopes identified by a pericope heading; the biblical text in the English Standard Version (ESV), with significant textual variants registered in the footnotes; an overview of the pericope in which principal exegetical and theological concerns of the Reformation writers are succinctly noted; and excerpts from the Reformation writers identified by name according to the conventions of the *Oxford Encyclopedia of the Reformation*. Each volume will also include a bibliography of sources cited, as well as an appendix of authors and source works.

The Reformation era was a time of verbal as well as physical violence, and this fact has presented a challenge for this project. Without unduly sanitizing the texts, where they contain anti-Semitic, sexist or inordinately polemical rhetoric, we have not felt obliged to parade such comments either. We have noted the abridgement of texts with ellipses and an explanatory footnote. While this procedure would not be valid in the critical edition of such a text, we have deemed it appropriate in a series whose primary purpose is pastoral and devotional. When translating *homo* or similar terms that refer to the human race as a whole or to individual persons without reference to gender, we have used alternative English expressions to the word *man* (or derivative constructions that formerly were used generically to signify humanity at large), whenever such substitutions can be made without producing an awkward or artificial construction.

As is true in the ACCS, we have made a special effort where possible to include the voices of women, though we acknowledge the difficulty of doing so for the early modern period when for a variety of social and cultural reasons few theological and biblical works were published by women. However, recent scholarship has focused on a number of female leaders whose literary remains show us how they understood and interpreted the Bible. Women who made significant contributions to the Reformation include Marguerite d'Angoulême, sister of King Francis I, who supported French reformist evangelicals including Calvin and who published a religious poem influenced by Luther's theology, *The Mirror of the Sinful Soul*; Argula von Grumbach, a Bavarian noblewoman who defended the teachings of Luther and Melanchthon before the theologians of the University of Ingolstadt; Katharina Schütz Zell, the wife of a former priest, Matthias Zell, and a remarkable reformer in her own right—she conducted funerals, compiled hymnbooks, defended the downtrodden and published a defense of clerical marriage as well as composing works of consolation on divine comfort and pleas for the toleration of Anabaptists and Catholics alike; and Anne Askew, a Protestant martyr put to death in 1546 after demonstrating remarkable biblical prowess in her examinations by church officials. Other echoes of faithful women in the age of the Reformation are found in their letters, translations, poems, hymns, court depositions and martyr records.

Lay culture, learned culture. In recent decades, much attention has been given to what is called "reforming from below," that is, the expressions of religious beliefs and churchly life that characterized the popular culture of the majority of the population in the era of the Reformation. Social historians have taught us to examine the diverse pieties of townspeople and city folk, of rural religion and village life, the emergence of lay theologies and the experiences of women in the religious tumults of Reformation Europe.[7] Formal commentaries by their nature are artifacts of learned culture. Almost all of them were written in Latin, the lingua franca of learned discourse well past the age of the Reformation. Biblical commentaries were certainly not the primary means by which the Protestant Reformation spread so rapidly across wide sectors of sixteenth-century society. Small pamphlets and broadsheets, later called *Flugschriften* ("flying writings"), with their graphic woodcuts and cartoon-like depictions of Reformation personalities and events, became the means of choice for mass communication in the early age of printing. Sermons and works of

---

[7]See Peter Matheson, ed., *Reformation Christianity* (Minneapolis: Fortress, 2007).

---

devotion were also printed with appealing visual aids. Luther's early writings were often accompanied by drawings and sketches from Lucas Cranach and other artists. This was done "above all for the sake of children and simple folk," as Luther put it, "who are more easily moved by pictures and images to recall divine history than through mere words or doctrines."[8]

We should be cautious, however, in drawing too sharp a distinction between learned and lay culture in this period. The phenomenon of preaching was a kind of verbal bridge between scholars at their desks and the thousands of illiterate or semi-literate listeners whose views were shaped by the results of Reformation exegesis. According to contemporary witness, more than one thousand people were crowding into Geneva to hear Calvin expound the Scriptures every day.[9] An example of how learned theological works by Reformation scholars were received across divisions of class and social status comes from Lazare Drilhon, an apothecary of Toulon. He was accused of heresy in May 1545 when a cache of prohibited books was found hidden in his garden shed. In addition to devotional works, the French New Testament and a copy of Calvin's Genevan liturgy, there was found a series of biblical commentaries, translated from the Latin into French: Martin Bucer's on Matthew, François Lambert's on the Apocalypse and one by Oecolampadius on 1 John.[10] Biblical exegesis in the sixteenth century was not limited to the kind of full-length commentaries found in Drilhon's shed. Citations from the Bible and expositions of its meaning permeate the extant literature of sermons, letters, court depositions, doctrinal treatises, records of public disputations and even last wills and testaments. While most of the selections in the RCS will be drawn from formal commentary literature, other sources of biblical reflection will also be considered.

Historical Context

The medieval legacy. On October 18, 1512, the degree *Doctor in Biblia* was conferred on Martin Luther, and he began his career as a professor in the University of Wittenberg. As is well known, Luther was also a monk who had taken solemn vows in the Augustinian Order of Hermits at Erfurt. These two settings—the university and the monastery—both deeply rooted in the Middle Ages, form the background not only for Luther's personal vocation as a reformer but also for the history of the biblical commentary in the age of the Reformation. Since the time of the Venerable Bede (d. 735), sometimes called "the last of the Fathers," serious study of the Bible had taken place primarily in the context of cloistered monasteries. The Rule of St. Benedict brought together *lectio* and *meditatio*, the knowledge of letters and the life of prayer. The liturgy was the medium through which the daily reading of the Bible, especially the Psalms, and the sayings of the church fathers came together in the spiritual formation of the monks.[11] Essential to this understanding

---

[8]Martin Luther, "Personal Prayer Book," LW 43:42-43* (WA 10,2:458); quoted in R. W. Scribner, *For the Sake of Simple Folk: Popular Propaganda for the German Reformation* (Cambridge: Cambridge University Press, 1981), xi.

[9]Letter of De Beaulieu to Guillaume Farel (1561) in J. W. Baum, ed., *Theodor Beza nach handschriftlichen und anderen gleichzeitigen Quellen* (Leipzig: Weidmann, 1851) 2:92.

[10]Francis Higman, "A Heretic's Library: The Drilhon Inventory" (1545), in Francis Higman, *Lire et Découvrir: la circulation des idées au temps de la Réforme* (Geneva: Droz, 1998), 65-85.

[11]See the classic study by Jean Leclercq, *The Love of Learning and the Desire for God* (New York: Fordham University Press, 1961).

was a belief in the unity of the people of God throughout time as well as space, and an awareness that life in this world was a preparation for the beatific vision in the next.

The source of theology was the study of the sacred page (*sacra pagina*); its object was the accumulation of knowledge not for its own sake but for the obtaining of eternal life. For these monks, the Bible had God for its author, salvation for its end and unadulterated truth for its matter, though they would not have expressed it in such an Aristotelian way. The medieval method of interpreting the Bible owed much to Augustine's *On Christian Doctrine*. In addition to setting forth a series of rules (drawn from an earlier work by Tyconius), Augustine stressed the importance of distinguishing the literal and spiritual or allegorical senses of Scripture. While the literal sense was not disparaged, the allegorical was valued because it enabled the believer to obtain spiritual benefit from the obscure places in the Bible, especially in the Old Testament. For Augustine, as for the monks who followed him, the goal of scriptural exegesis was freighted with eschatological meaning; its purpose was to induce faith, hope and love and so to advance in one's pilgrimage toward that city with foundations (see Heb 11:10).

Building on the work of Augustine and other church fathers going back to Origen, medieval exegetes came to understand Scripture as possessed of four possible meanings, the famous *quadriga*. The literal meaning was retained, of course, but the spiritual meaning was now subdivided into three senses: the allegorical, the moral and the anagogical. Medieval exegetes often referred to the four meanings of Scripture in a popular rhyme:

> The letter shows us what God and our fathers did;
> The allegory shows us where our faith is hid;
> The moral meaning gives us rules of daily life;
> The anagogy shows us where we end our strife.[12]

In this schema, the three spiritual meanings of the text correspond to the three theological virtues: faith (allegory), hope (anagogy) and love (the moral meaning). It should be noted that this way of approaching the Bible assumed a high doctrine of scriptural inspiration: the multiple meanings inherent in the text had been placed there by the Holy Spirit for the benefit of the people of God. The biblical justification for this method went back to the apostle Paul, who had used the words *allegory* and *type* when applying Old Testament events to believers in Christ (Gal 4:21-31; 1 Cor 10:1-11). The problem with this approach was knowing how to relate each of the four senses to one another and how to prevent Scripture from becoming a nose of wax turned this way and that by various interpreters. As G. R. Evans explains, "Any interpretation which could be put upon the text and was in keeping with the faith and edifying, had the warrant of God himself, for no human reader had the ingenuity to find more than God had put there."[13]

With the rise of the universities in the eleventh century, theology and the study of Scripture moved from the cloister into the classroom. Scripture and the Fathers were still important, but they came to function more as footnotes to the theological questions debated in the schools and

---

[12]Robert M. Grant, *A Short History of the Interpretation of the Bible* (New York: Macmillan, 1963), 119. A translation of the well-known Latin quatrain: *Littera gesta docet/Quid credas allegoria/Moralis quid agas/Quo tendas anagogia.*

[13]G. R. Evans, *The Language and Logic of the Bible: The Road to Reformation* (Cambridge: Cambridge University Press, 1985), 42.

brought together in an impressive systematic way in works such as Peter Lombard's *Books of Sentences* (the standard theology textbook of the Middle Ages) and the great scholastic *summae* of the thirteenth century. Indispensible to the study of the Bible in the later Middle Ages was the *Glossa ordinaria*, a collection of exegetical opinions by the church fathers and other commentators. Heiko Oberman summarized the transition from devotion to dialectic this way: "When, due to the scientific revolution of the twelfth century, Scripture became the *object* of study rather than the *subject* through which God speaks to the student, the difference between the two modes of speaking was investigated in terms of the texts themselves rather than in their relation to the recipients."[14] It was possible, of course, to be both a scholastic theologian and a master of the spiritual life. Meister Eckhart, for example, wrote commentaries on the Old Testament in Latin and works of mystical theology in German, reflecting what had come to be seen as a division of labor between the two.

An increasing focus on the text of Scripture led to a revival of interest in its literal sense. The two key figures in this development were Thomas Aquinas (d. 1274) and Nicholas of Lyra (d. 1340). Thomas is best remembered for his *Summa Theologiae*, but he was also a prolific commentator on the Bible. Thomas did not abandon the multiple senses of Scripture but declared that all the senses were founded on one—the literal—and this sense eclipsed allegory as the basis of sacred doctrine. Nicholas of Lyra was a Franciscan scholar who made use of the Hebrew text of the Old Testament and quoted liberally from works of Jewish scholars, especially the learned French rabbi Salomon Rashi (d. 1105). After Aquinas, Lyra was the strongest defender of the literal, historical meaning of Scripture as the primary basis of theological disputation. His *Postilla*, as his notes were called—the abbreviated form of *post illa verba textus* meaning "after these words from Scripture"—were widely circulated in the late Middle Ages and became the first biblical commentary to be printed in the fifteenth century. More than any other commentator from the period of high scholasticism, Lyra and his work were greatly valued by the early reformers. According to an old Latin pun, *Nisi Lyra lyrasset, Lutherus non saltasset*, "If Lyra had not played his lyre, Luther would not have danced."[15] While Luther was never an uncritical disciple of any teacher, he did praise Lyra as a good Hebraist and quoted him more than one hundred times in his lectures on Genesis, where he declared, "I prefer him to almost all other interpreters of Scripture."[16]

Sacred philology. The sixteenth century has been called a golden age of biblical interpretation, and it is a fact that the age of the Reformation witnessed an explosion of commentary writing unparalleled in the history of the Christian church. Kenneth Hagen has cataloged forty-five commentaries on Hebrews between 1516 (Erasmus) and 1598 (Beza).[17] During the sixteenth century, more than seventy new commentaries on Romans were published, five of them by Melanchthon alone, and nearly one hundred commentaries on the Bible's prayer book, the Psalms.[18] There were

---

[14]Heiko Oberman, *Forerunners of the Reformation* (Philadelphia: Fortress, 1966), 284.

[15]Nicholas of Lyra, *The Postilla of Nicolas of Lyra on the Song of Songs*, trans. and ed. James George Kiecker (Milwaukee: Marquette University Press, 1998), 19.

[16]LW 2:164 (WA 42:377).

[17]Kenneth Hagen, *Hebrews Commenting from Erasmus to Bèze, 1516-1598* (Tübingen: Mohr, 1981).

[18]R. Gerald Hobbs, "Biblical Commentaries," *OER* 1:167-71. See in general David C. Steinmetz, ed., *The Bible in the Sixteenth Century* (Durham: Duke University Press, 1990).

two developments in the fifteenth century that presaged this development and without which it could not have taken place: the invention of printing and the rediscovery of a vast store of ancient learning hitherto unknown or unavailable to scholars in the West.

It is now commonplace to say that what the computer has become in our generation, the printing press was to the world of Erasmus, Luther and other leaders of the Reformation. Johannes Gutenberg, a goldsmith by trade, developed a metal alloy suitable for type and a machine that would allow printed characters to be cast with relative ease, placed in even lines of composition and then manipulated again and again making possible the mass production of an unbelievable number of texts. In 1455, the Gutenberg Bible, the masterpiece of the typographical revolution, was published at Mainz in double columns in gothic type. Forty-seven copies of the beautiful Gutenberg Bible are still extant, each consisting of more than one thousand colorfully illuminated and impeccably printed pages. What began at Gutenberg's print shop in Mainz on the Rhine River soon spread, like McDonald's or Starbucks in our day, into every nook and cranny of the known world. Printing presses sprang up in Rome (1464), Venice (1469), Paris (1470), the Netherlands (1471), Switzerland (1472), Spain (1474), England (1476), Sweden (1483) and Constantinople (1490). By 1500, these and other presses across Europe had published some twenty-seven thousand titles, most of them in Latin. Erasmus once compared himself with an obscure preacher whose sermons were heard by only a few people in one or two churches while his books were read in every country in the world. Erasmus was not known for his humility, but in this case he was simply telling the truth.[19]

The Italian humanist Lorenzo Valla (d. 1457) died in the early dawn of the age of printing, but his critical and philological studies would be taken up by others who believed that genuine reform in church and society could come about only by returning to the wellsprings of ancient learning and wisdom—*ad fontes*, "back to the sources!" Valla is best remembered for undermining a major claim made by defenders of the papacy when he proved by philological research that the so-called Donation of Constantine, which had bolstered papal assertions of temporal sovereignty, was a forgery. But it was Valla's *Collatio Novi Testamenti* of 1444 that would have such a great effect on the renewal of biblical studies in the next century. Erasmus discovered the manuscript of this work while rummaging through an old library in Belgium and published it at Paris in 1505. In the preface to his edition of Valla, Erasmus gave the rationale that would guide his own labors in textual criticism. Just as Jerome had translated the Latin Vulgate from older versions and copies of the Scriptures in his day, so now Jerome's own text must be subjected to careful scrutiny and correction. Erasmus would be *Hieronymus redivivus*, a new Jerome come back to life to advance the cause of sacred philology. The restoration of the Scriptures and the writings of the church fathers would usher in what Erasmus believed would be a golden age of peace and learning. In 1516, the Basel publisher Froben brought out Erasmus's *Novum Instrumentum*, the first published edition of the Greek New Testament. Eras-

---

[19]E. Harris Harbison, *The Christian Scholar in the Age of the Reformation* (New York: Charles Scribner's Sons, 1956), 80.

mus's Greek New Testament would go through five editions in his lifetime, each one with new emendations to the text and a growing section of annotations that expanded to include not only technical notes about the text but also theological comment. The influence of Erasmus's Greek New Testament was enormous. It formed the basis for Robert Estienne's *Novum Testamentum Graece* of 1550, which in turn was used to establish the Greek *Textus Receptus* for a number of late Reformation translations including the King James Version of 1611.

For all his expertise in Greek, Erasmus was a poor student of Hebrew and only published commentaries on several of the psalms. However, the renaissance of Hebrew letters was part of the wider program of biblical humanism as reflected in the establishment of trilingual colleges devoted to the study of Hebrew, Greek and Latin (the three languages written on the *titulus* of Jesus' cross [Jn 19:20]) at Alcalá in Spain, Wittenberg in Germany, Louvain in Belgium and Paris in France. While it is true that some medieval commentators, especially Nicholas of Lyra, had been informed by the study of Hebrew and rabbinics in their biblical work, it was the publication of Johannes Reuchlin's *De rudimentis hebraicis* (1506), a combined grammar and dictionary, that led to the recovery of *veritas Hebraica*, as Jerome had referred to the true voice of the Hebrew Scriptures. The pursuit of Hebrew studies was carried forward in the Reformation by two great scholars, Konrad Pellikan and Sebastian Münster. Pellikan was a former Franciscan friar who embraced the Protestant cause and played a major role in the Zurich reformation. He had published a Hebrew grammar even prior to Reuchlin and produced a commentary on nearly the entire Bible that appeared in seven volumes between 1532 and 1539. Münster was Pellikan's student and taught Hebrew at the University of Heidelberg before taking up a similar position in Basel. Like his mentor, Münster was a great collector of Hebraica and published a series of excellent grammars, dictionaries and rabbinic texts. Münster did for the Hebrew Old Testament what Erasmus had done for the Greek New Testament. His *Hebraica Biblia* offered a fresh Latin translation of the Old Testament with annotations from medieval rabbinic exegesis.

Luther first learned Hebrew with Reuchlin's grammar in hand but took advantage of other published resources, such as the four-volume Hebrew Bible published at Venice by Daniel Bomberg in 1516 to 1517. He also gathered his own circle of Hebrew experts, his *sanhedrin* he called it, who helped him with his German translation of the Old Testament. We do not know where William Tyndale learned Hebrew, though perhaps it was in Worms, where there was a thriving rabbinical school during his stay there. In any event, he had sufficiently mastered the language to bring out a freshly translated Pentateuch that was published at Antwerp in 1530. By the time the English separatist scholar Henry Ainsworth published his prolix commentaries on the Pentateuch in 1616, the knowledge of Hebrew, as well as Greek, was taken for granted by every serious scholar of the Bible. In the preface to his commentary on Genesis, Ainsworth explained that "the literal sense of Moses's Hebrew (which is the tongue wherein he wrote the law), is the ground of all interpretation, and that language hath figures and properties of speech, different from ours: These therefore in the first place are to be opened that the natural meaning of the Scripture, being known, the mysteries of godliness therein implied, may be better discerned."[20]

The restoration of the biblical text in the original languages made possible the revival of scriptural exposition reflected in the floodtide of sermon literature and commentary work. Of even more far-reaching import was the steady stream of vernacular Bibles in the sixteenth century. In the introduction to his 1516 edition of the New Testament, Erasmus had expressed his desire that the Scriptures be translated into all languages so that "the lowliest women" could read the Gospels and the Pauline epistles and "the farmer sing some portion of them at the plow, the weaver hum some parts of them to the movement of his shuttle, the traveler lighten the weariness of the journey with stories of this kind."[21] Like Erasmus, Tyndale wanted the Bible to be available in the language of the common people. He once said to a learned divine that if God spared his life he would cause the boy who drives the plow to know more of the Scriptures than he did![22] The project of allowing the Bible to speak in the language of the mother in the house, the children in the street and the cheesemonger in the marketplace was met with stiff opposition by certain Catholic polemists such as Johann Eck, Luther's antagonist at the Leipzig Debate of 1519. In his *Enchiridion* (1525), Eck derided the "inky theologians" whose translations paraded the Bible before "the untutored crowd" and subjected it to the judgment of "laymen and crazy old women."[23] In fact, some fourteen German Bibles had already been published prior to Luther's September Testament of 1522, which he translated from Erasmus's Greek New Testament in less than three months' time while sequestered in the Wartburg. Luther's German New Testament became the first bestseller in the world, appearing in forty-three distinct editions between 1522 and 1525 with upwards of one hundred thousand copies issued in these three years. It is estimated that five percent of the German population may have been literate at this time, but this rate increased as the century wore on due in no small part to the unmitigated success of vernacular Bibles.[24]

Luther's German Bible (inclusive of the Old Testament from 1534) was the most successful venture of its kind, but it was not alone in the field. Hans Denck and Ludwig Hätzer, leaders in the early Anabaptist movement, translated the prophetic books of the Old Testament from Hebrew into German in 1527. This work influenced the Swiss-German Bible of 1531 published by Leo Jud and other pastors in Zurich. Tyndale's influence on the English language rivaled that of Luther on German. At a time when English was regarded as "that obscure and remote dialect of German spoken in an off-shore island," Tyndale, with his remarkable linguistic ability (he was fluent in eight languages), "made a language for England," as his modern editor David Daniell has put it.[25]

[20]Henry Ainsworth, *Annotations Upon the First Book of Moses Called Genesis* (Amsterdam, 1616), preface (unpaginated).

[21]John C. Olin, *Christian Humanism and the Reformation* (New York: Fordham University Press, 1987), 101.

[22]This famous statement of Tyndale was quoted by John Foxe in his *Acts and Monuments of Matters Happening in the Church* (London, 1563). See Henry Wansbrough, "Tyndale," in Richard Griffith, ed., *The Bible in the Renaissance* (Aldershot, UK: Ashgate, 2001), 124.

[23]John Eck, *Enchiridion of Commonplaces*, trans. Ford Lewis Battles (Grand Rapids: Baker, 1979), 47-49.

[24]The effect of printing on the spread of the Reformation has been much debated. See the classic study by Elizabeth L. Eisenstein, *The Printing Press as an Agent of Change* (Cambridge: Cambridge University Press, 1979). More recent studies include Mark U. Edwards Jr., *Printing, Propaganda and Martin Luther* (Minneapolis: Fortress, 1994), and Andrew Pettegree and Matthew Hall, "The Reformation and the Book: A Reconsideration," *Historical Journal* 47 (2004): 1-24.

[25]David Daniell, *William Tyndale: A Biography* (New Haven: Yale University Press, 1994), 3.

Tyndale was imprisoned and executed near Brussels in 1536, but the influence of his biblical work among the common people of England was already being felt. There is no reason to doubt the authenticity of John Foxe's recollection of how Tyndale's New Testament was received in England during the 1520s and 1530s:

> The fervent zeal of those Christian days seemed much superior to these our days and times; as manifestly may appear by their sitting up all night in reading and hearing; also by their expenses and charges in buying of books in English, of whom some gave five marks, some more, some less, for a book: some gave a load of hay for a few chapters of St. James, or of St. Paul in English.[26]

Calvin helped to revise and contributed three prefaces to the French Bible translated by his cousin Pierre Robert Olivétan and originally published at Neuchâtel in 1535. Clément Marot and Beza provided a fresh translation of the Psalms with each psalm rendered in poetic form and accompanied by monophonic musical settings for congregational singing. The Bay Psalter, the first book printed in America, was an English adaptation of this work. Geneva also provided the provenance of the most influential Italian Bible published by Giovanni Diodati in 1607. The flowering of biblical humanism in vernacular Bibles resulted in new translations in all of the major language groups of Europe: Spanish (1569), Portuguese (1681), Dutch (New Testament, 1523; Old Testament, 1527), Danish (1550), Czech (1579–1593/94), Hungarian (New Testament, 1541; complete Bible, 1590), Polish (1563), Swedish (1541) and even Arabic (1591).[27]

Patterns of Reformation

Once the text of the Bible had been placed in the hands of the people, in cheap and easily available editions, what further need was there of published expositions such as commentaries? Given the Protestant doctrine of the priesthood of all believers, was there any longer a need for learned clergy and their bookish religion? Some radical reformers thought not. Sebastian Franck searched for the true church of the Spirit "scattered among the heathen and the weeds" but could not find it in any of the institutional structures of his time. *Veritas non potest scribi, aut exprimi,* he said, "truth can neither be spoken nor written."[28] Kaspar von Schwenckfeld so emphasized religious inwardness that he suspended external observance of the Lord's Supper and downplayed the readable, audible Scriptures in favor of the word within. This trajectory would lead to the rise of the Quakers in the next century, but it was pursued neither by the mainline reformers nor by most of the Anabaptists. Article 7 of the Augsburg Confession (1530) declared the one holy Christian church to be "the assembly of all believers among whom the Gospel is purely preached and the holy sacraments are administered according to the Gospel."[29]

Historians of the nineteenth century referred to the material and formal principles of the

---

[26]Foxe, *Acts and Monuments,* 4:218.
[27]On vernacular translations of the Bible, see *CHB* 3:94-140 and Jaroslav Pelikan, *The Reformation of the Bible/The Bible of the Reformation* (New Haven: Yale University Press, 1996), 41-62.
[28]Sebastian Franck, *280 Paradoxes or Wondrous Sayings,* trans. E. J. Furcha (Lewiston, NY: Edwin Mellen Press, 1986), 10, 212.
[29]BoC 42 (BSLK 61).

Reformation. In this construal, the matter at stake was the meaning of the Christian gospel: the liberating insight that helpless sinners are graciously justified by the gift of faith alone, apart from any works or merits of their own, entirely on the basis of Christ's atoning work on the cross. For Luther especially, justification by faith alone became the criterion by which all other doctrines and practices of the church were to be judged. The cross proves everything, he said at the Heidelberg disputation in 1518. The distinction between law and gospel thus became the primary hermeneutical key that unlocked the true meaning of Scripture.

The formal principle of the Reformation, *sola Scriptura*, was closely bound up with proper distinctions between Scripture and tradition. "Scripture alone," said Luther, "is the true lord and master of all writings and doctrine on earth. If that is not granted, what is Scripture good for? The more we reject it, the more we become satisfied with human books and human teachers."[30] On the basis of this principle, the reformers challenged the structures and institutions of the medieval Catholic Church. Even a simple layperson, they asserted, armed with Scripture should be believed above a pope or a council without it. But, however boldly asserted, the doctrine of the primacy of Scripture did not absolve the reformers from dealing with a host of hermeneutical issues that became matters of contention both between Rome and the Reformation and within each of these two communities: the extent of the biblical canon, the validity of critical study of the Bible, the perspicuity of Scripture and its relation to preaching and the retention of devotional and liturgical practices such as holy days, incense, the burning of candles, the sprinkling of holy water, church art and musical instruments. Zwingli, the Puritans and the radicals dismissed such things as a rubbish heap of ceremonials that amounted to nothing but tomfoolery, while Lutherans and Anglicans retained most of them as consonant with Scripture and valuable aids to worship.

It is important to note that while the mainline reformers differed among themselves on many matters, overwhelmingly they saw themselves as part of the ongoing Catholic tradition, indeed as the legitimate bearers of it. This was seen in numerous ways including their sense of continuity with the church of the preceding centuries; their embrace of the ecumenical orthodoxy of the early church; and their desire to read the Bible in dialogue with the exegetical tradition of the church.

In their biblical commentaries, the reformers of the sixteenth century revealed a close familiarity with the preceding exegetical tradition, and they used it respectfully as well as critically in their own expositions of the sacred text. For them, *sola Scriptura* was not *nuda Scriptura*. Rather, the Scriptures were seen as the book given to the church, gathered and guided by the Holy Spirit. In his restatement of the Vincentian canon, Calvin defined the church as "a society of all the saints, a society which, spread over the whole world, and existing in all ages, and bound together by the one doctrine and the one spirit of Christ, cultivates and observes unity of faith and brotherly concord. With this church we deny that we have any disagreement. Nay, rather, as we revere her as our mother, so we desire to remain in her bosom." Defined thus, the church has a real, albeit relative and circumscribed, authority since, as Calvin admits, "We cannot fly without

---

[30]LW 32:11-12* (WA 7:317).

wings."[31] While the reformers could not agree with the Council of Trent (though some recent Catholic theologians have challenged this interpretation) that Scripture and tradition were two separate and equable sources of divine revelation, they did believe in the coinherence of Scripture and tradition. This conviction shaped the way they read and interpreted the Bible.[32]

Schools of Exegesis

The reformers were passionate about biblical exegesis, but they showed little concern for hermeneutics as a separate field of inquiry. Niels Hemmingsen, a Lutheran theologian in Denmark, did write a treatise, *De methodis* (1555), in which he offered a philosophical and theological framework for the interpretation of Scripture. This was followed by the *Clavis Scripturae Sacrae* (1567) of Matthias Flacius Illyricus, which contains some fifty rules for studying the Bible drawn from Scripture itself.[33] However, hermeneutics as we know it came of age only in the Enlightenment and should not be backloaded into the Reformation. It is also true that the word *commentary* did not mean in the sixteenth century what it means for us today. Erasmus provided both annotations and paraphrases on the New Testament, the former a series of critical notes on the text but also containing points of doctrinal substance, the latter a theological overview and brief exposition. Most of Calvin's commentaries began as sermons or lectures presented in the course of his pastoral ministry. In the dedication to his 1519 study of Galatians, Luther declared that his work was "not so much a commentary as a testimony of my faith in Christ."[34] The exegetical work of the reformers was embodied in a wide variety of forms and genres, and the RCS has worked with this broader concept in setting the guidelines for this compendium.

The Protestant reformers shared in common a number of key interpretive principles such as the priority of the grammatical-historical sense of Scripture and the christological centeredness of the entire Bible, but they also developed a number of distinct approaches and schools of exegesis.[35] For the purposes of the RCS, we note the following key figures and families of interpretation in this period.

Biblical humanism. The key figure is Erasmus, whose importance is hard to exaggerate for Catholic and Protestant exegetes alike. His annotated Greek New Testament and fresh Latin translation challenged the hegemony of the Vulgate tradition and was doubtless a factor in the decision of the Council of Trent to establish the Vulgate edition as authentic and normative. Erasmus believed that the wide distribution of the Scriptures would contribute to personal spiritual renewal and the reform of society. In 1547, the English translation of Erasmus's *Paraphrases*

---

[31]John C. Olin, ed., *John Calvin and Jacopo Sadoleto: A Reformation Debate* (New York: Harper Torchbooks, 1966), 61-62, 77.

[32]See Timothy George, "An Evangelical Reflection on Scripture and Tradition," *Pro Ecclesia* 9 (2000): 184-207.

[33]See Kenneth G. Hagen, "'De Exegetica Methodo': Niels Hemmingsen's *De Methodis* (1555)," in *The Bible in the Sixteenth Century*, ed. David C. Steinmetz (Durham: Duke University Press, 1990), 181-96.

[34]LW 27:159 (WA 2:449). See Kenneth Hagen, "What Did the Term *Commentarius* Mean to Sixteenth-Century Theologians?" in Irena Backus and Francis M. Higman, eds., *Théorie et pratique de l'exégèse* (Geneva: Droz, 1990), 13-38.

[35]I follow here the sketch of Irena Backus, "Biblical Hermeneutics and Exegesis," *OER* 1:152-58. In this work, Backus confines herself to Continental developments, whereas we have noted the exegetical contribution of the English Reformation as well. For more comprehensive listings of sixteenth-century commentators, see Gerald Bray, *Biblical Interpretation* (Downers Grove, IL: InterVarsity Press, 1996), 165-212; and Richard A. Muller, "Biblical Interpretation in the Sixteenth and Seventeenth Centuries," *DMBI* 22-44.

was ordered to be placed in every parish church in England. John Colet first encouraged Erasmus to learn Greek, though he never took up the language himself. Colet's lectures on Paul's epistles at Oxford are reflected in his commentaries on Romans and 1 Corinthians.

Jacques Lefèvre d'Étaples has been called the "French Erasmus" because of his great learning and support for early reform movements in his native land. He published a major edition of the Psalter, as well as commentaries on the Pauline Epistles (1512), the Gospels (1522) and the General Epistles (1527). Guillaume Farel, the early reformer of Geneva, was a disciple of Lefèvre, and the young Calvin also came within his sphere of influence.

Among pre-Tridentine Catholic reformers, special attention should be given to Thomas de Vio, better known as Cajetan. He is best remembered for confronting Martin Luther on behalf of the pope in 1518, but his biblical commentaries (on nearly every book of the Bible) are virtually free of polemic. Like Erasmus, he dared to criticize the Vulgate on linguistic grounds. His commentary on Romans supported the doctrine of justification by grace applied by faith based on the "alien righteousness" of God in Christ. Jared Wicks sums up Cajetan's significance in this way: "Cajetan's combination of passion for pristine biblical meaning with his fully developed theological horizon of understanding indicates, in an intriguing manner, something of the breadth of possibilities open to Roman Catholics before a more restrictive settlement came to exercise its hold on many Catholic interpreters in the wake of the Council of Trent."[36] Girolamo Seripando, like Cajetan, was a cardinal in the Catholic Church, though he belonged to the Augustinian rather than the Dominican order. He was an outstanding classical scholar and published commentaries on Romans and Galatians. Also important is Jacopo Sadoleto, another cardinal, best known for his 1539 letter to the people of Geneva beseeching them to return to the church of Rome, to which Calvin replied with a manifesto of his own. Sadoleto published a commentary on Romans in 1535. Bucer once commended Sadoleto's teaching on justification as approximating that of the reformers, while others saw him tilting away from the Augustinian tradition toward Pelagianism.[37]

Luther and the Wittenberg School. It was in the name of the Word of God, and specifically as a doctor of Scripture, that Luther challenged the church of his day and inaugurated the Reformation. Though Luther renounced his monastic vows, he never lost that sense of intimacy with *sacra pagina* he first acquired as a young monk. Luther provided three rules for reading the Bible: prayer, meditation and struggle (*tentatio*). His exegetical output was enormous. In the American edition of Luther's works, thirty out of the fifty-five volumes are devoted to his biblical studies, and additional translations are planned. Many of his commentaries originated as sermons or lecture notes presented to his students at the university and to his parishioners at Wittenberg's parish church of St. Mary. Luther referred to Galatians as his bride: "The Epistle to the Galatians is my dear epistle. I have betrothed myself to it. It is my Käthe von Bora."[38] He considered his

---

[36]Jared Wicks, "Tommaso de Vio Cajetan (1469-1534)," *DMBI* 283-87, here 286.

[37]See the discussion by Bernard Roussel, "Martin Bucer et Jacques Sadolet: la concorde possible," *Bulletin de la Société de l'histoire de protestantisme français* (1976): 525-50, and T. H. L. Parker, *Commentaries on the Epistle to the Romans, 1532-1542* (Edinburgh: T&T Clark, 1986), 25-34.

[38]WATR 1:69 #146; cf. LW 54:20 #146. I have followed Rörer's variant on Dietrich's notes.

1535 commentary on Galatians his greatest exegetical work, although his massive commentary on Genesis (eight volumes in LW), which he worked on for ten years (1535–1545), must be considered his crowning work. Luther's principles of biblical interpretation are found in his *Open Letter on Translating* and in the prefaces he wrote to all the books of the Bible.

Philipp Melanchthon was brought to Wittenberg to teach Greek in 1518 and proved to be an able associate to Luther in the reform of the church. A set of his lecture notes on Romans was published without his knowledge in 1522. This was revised and expanded many times until his large commentary of 1556. Melanchthon also commented on other New Testament books including Matthew, John, Galatians and the Petrine Epistles, as well as Proverbs, Daniel and Ecclesiastes. Though he was well trained in the humanist disciplines, Melanchthon devoted little attention to critical and textual matters in his commentaries. Rather, he followed the primary argument of the biblical writer and gathered from this exposition a series of doctrinal topics for special consideration. This method lay behind Melanchthon's *Loci communes* (1521), the first Protestant theology textbook to be published. Another Wittenberger was Johannes Bugenhagen of Pomerania, a prolific commentator on both the Old and New Testaments. His commentary on the Psalms (1524), translated into German by Bucer, applied Luther's teaching on justification to the Psalter. He also wrote a commentary on Job and annotations on many of the books in the Bible. The Lutheran exegetical tradition was shaped by many other scholar-reformers including Andreas Osiander, Johannes Brenz, Caspar Cruciger, Erasmus Sarcerius, Georg Maior, Jacob Andreae, Nikolaus Selnecker and Johann Gerhard.

The Strasbourg-Basel tradition. Bucer, the son of a shoemaker in Alsace, became the leader of the Reformation in Strasbourg. A former Dominican, he was early on influenced by Erasmus and continued to share his passion for Christian unity. Bucer was the most ecumenical of the Protestant reformers seeking rapprochement with Catholics on justification and an armistice between Luther and Zwingli in their strife over the Lord's Supper. Bucer also had a decisive influence on Calvin, though the latter characterized his biblical commentaries as longwinded and repetitious.[39] In his exegetical work, Bucer made ample use of patristic and medieval sources, though he criticized the abuse and overuse of allegory as "the most blatant insult to the Holy Spirit."[40] He declared that the purpose of his commentaries was "to help inexperienced brethren [perhaps like the apothecary Drilhon, who owned a French translation of Bucer's *Commentary on Matthew*] to understand each of the words and actions of Christ, and in their proper order as far as possible, and to retain an explanation of them in their natural meaning, so that they will not distort God's Word through age-old aberrations or by inept interpretation, but rather with a faithful comprehension of everything as written by the Spirit of God, they may expound to all the churches in their firm upbuilding in faith and love."[41] In addition to writing commentaries on all four Gospels, Bucer published

---

[39]CNTC 8:3 (CO 10:404).

[40]*DMBI* 249; P. Scherding and F. Wendel, eds., "Un Traité d'exégèse pratique de Bucer," *Revue d'histoire et de philosophie religieuses* 26 (1946): 32-75, here 56.

[41]Martin Bucer, *Enarrationes perpetuae in sacra quatuor evangelia*, 2nd. ed. (Strasbourg: Georg Ulrich Andlanus, 1530), 10r; quoted in D. F. Wright, "Martin Bucer," *DMBI* 290.

commentaries on Judges, the Psalms, Zephaniah, Romans and Ephesians. In the early years of the Reformation, there was a great deal of back and forth between Strasbourg and Basel, and both were centers of a lively publishing trade. Wolfgang Capito, Bucer's associate at Strasbourg, was a notable Hebraist and composed commentaries on Hosea (1529) and Habakkuk (1527).

At Basel, the great Sebastian Münster defended the use of Jewish sources in the Christian study of the Old Testament and published, in addition to his famous Hebrew grammar, an annotated version of the Gospel of Matthew translated from Greek into Hebrew. Oecolampadius, Basel's chief reformer, had been a proofreader in Froben's publishing house and worked with Erasmus on his Greek New Testament and his critical edition of Jerome. From 1523 he was both a preacher and professor of Holy Scripture at Basel. He defended Zwingli's eucharistic theology at the Colloquy of Marburg and published commentaries on 1 John (1524), Romans (1525) and Haggai-Malachi (1525). Oecolampadius was succeeded by Simon Grynaeus, a classical scholar who taught Greek and supported Bucer's efforts to bring Lutherans and Zwinglians together. More in line with Erasmus was Sebastian Castellio, who came to Basel after his expulsion from Geneva in 1545. He is best remembered for questioning the canonicity of the Song of Songs and for his annotations and French translation of the Bible.

The Zurich group. Biblical exegesis in Zurich was centered on the distinctive institution of the *Prophezei*, which began on June 19, 1525. On five days a week, at seven o'clock in the morning, all of the ministers and theological students in Zurich gathered into the choir of the Grossmünster to engage in a period of intense exegesis and interpretation of Scripture. After Zwingli had opened the meeting with prayer, the text of the day was read in Latin, Greek and Hebrew, followed by appropriate textual or exegetical comments. One of the ministers then delivered a sermon on the passage in German that was heard by many of Zurich's citizens who stopped by the cathedral on their way to work. This institute for advanced biblical studies had an enormous influence as a model for Reformed academies and seminaries throughout Europe. It was also the seedbed for sermon series in Zurich's churches and the extensive exegetical publications of Zwingli, Leo Jud, Konrad Pellikan, Heinrich Bullinger, Oswald Myconius and Rudolf Gwalther. Zwingli had memorized in Greek all of the Pauline epistles, and this bore fruit in his powerful expository preaching and biblical exegesis. He took seriously the role of grammar, rhetoric and historical research in explaining the biblical text. For example, he disagreed with Bucer on the value of the Septuagint, regarding it as a trustworthy witness to a proto-Hebrew version earlier than the Masoretic text.

Zwingli's work was carried forward by his successor Bullinger, one of the most formidable scholars and networkers among the reformers. He composed commentaries on Daniel (1565), the Gospels (1542–1546), the Epistles (1537), Acts (1533) and Revelation (1557). He collaborated with Calvin to produce the *Consensus Tigurinus* (1549), a Reformed accord on the nature of the Lord's Supper, and produced a series of fifty sermons on Christian doctrine, known as *Decades*, which became required reading in Elizabethan England. As the *Antistes* ("overseer") of the Zurich church for forty-four years, Bullinger faced opposition from nascent Anabaptism on the one hand and resurgent Catholicism on the other. The need for a well-trained clergy and scholarly resources, including Scripture commentaries, arose from the fact that the Bible was "difficult or obscure to the unlearned, unskillful, unexercised, and malicious or corrupted wills." While forswearing papal claims to infallibility, Bullinger and other leaders of the magisterial Reformation saw the need for a kind of Protestant magisterium as a check against the tendency to read the Bible in "such sense as everyone shall be persuaded in himself to be most convenient."[42]

Two other commentators can be treated in connection with the Zurich group, though each of them had a wide-ranging ministry across the Reformation fronts. A former Benedictine monk, Wolfgang Musculus, embraced the Reformation in the 1520s and served briefly as the secretary to Bucer in Strasbourg. He shared Bucer's desire for Protestant unity and served for seventeen years (1531–1548) as a pastor and reformer in Augsburg. After a brief time in Zurich, where he came under the influence of Bullinger, Musculus was called to Bern, where he taught the Scriptures and published commentaries on the Psalms, the Decalogue, Genesis, Romans, Isaiah, 1 and 2 Corinthians, Galatians and Ephesians, Philippians, Colossians, 1 and 2 Thessalonians and 1 Timothy. Drawing on his exegetical writings, Musculus also produced a compendium of Protestant theology that was translated into English in 1563 as *Commonplaces of Christian Religion*.

Peter Martyr Vermigli was a Florentine-born scholar and Augustinian friar who embraced the Reformation and fled to Switzerland in 1542. Over the next twenty years, he would gain an international reputation as a prolific scholar and leading theologian within the Reformed community. He lectured on the Old Testament at Strasbourg, was made regius professor at Oxford, corresponded with the Italian refugee church in Geneva and spent the last years of his life as professor of Hebrew at Zurich. Vermigli published commentaries on 1 Corinthians, Romans and Judges during his lifetime. His biblical lectures on Genesis, Lamentations, 1 and 2 Samuel and 1 and 2 Kings were published posthumously. The most influential of his writings was the *Loci communes* (*Commonplaces*), a theological compendium drawn from his exegetical writings.

The Genevan Reformers. What Zwingli and Bullinger were to Zurich, Calvin and Beza were to Geneva. Calvin has been called "the father of modern biblical scholarship," and his exegetical work is without parallel in the Reformation. Because of the success of his *Institutes of the Christian Religion* Calvin has sometimes been thought of as a man of one book, but he always intended the *Institutes*, which went through eight editions in Latin and five in French during his lifetime, to serve as a guide to the study of the Bible, to show the reader "what he ought especially to seek in Scripture and to what end he ought to relate its contents." Jacob Arminius, who modified several principles of Calvin's theology, recommended his commentaries next to the Bible, for, as he said, Calvin "is incomparable in the interpretation of Scripture."[43] Drawing on his superb knowledge of Greek and Hebrew and his thorough training in humanist rhetoric, Calvin produced commentaries on all of the New Testament books except 2 and 3 John and Revelation. Calvin's Old Testament

---

[42]Euan Cameron, *The European Reformation* (Oxford: Oxford University Press, 1991), 120.

[43]Letter to Sebastian Egbert (May 3, 1607), in *Praestantium ac eruditorum virorum epistolae ecclesiasticae et theologicae varii argumenti*, ed. Christiaan Hartsoeker (Amsterdam: Henricus Dendrinus, 1660), 236-37. Quoted in A. M. Hunter, *The Teaching of Calvin* (London: James Clarke, 1950), 20.

commentaries originated as sermon and lecture series and include Genesis, Psalms, Hosea, Isaiah, minor prophets, Daniel, Jeremiah and Lamentations, a harmony of the last four books of Moses, Ezekiel 1–20 and Joshua. Calvin sought for brevity and clarity in all of his exegetical work. He emphasized the illumination of the Holy Spirit as essential to a proper understanding of the text. Calvin underscored the continuity between the two Testaments (one covenant in two dispensations) and sought to apply the plain or natural sense of the text to the church of his day. In the preface to his own influential commentary on Romans, Karl Barth described how Calvin worked to recover the mind of Paul and make the apostle's message relevant to his day:

> How energetically Calvin goes to work, first scientifically establishing the text ('what stands there?'), then following along the footsteps of its thought; that is to say, he conducts a discussion with it until the wall between the first and the sixteenth centuries becomes transparent, and until there in the first century Paul speaks and here the man of the sixteenth century hears, until indeed the conversation between document and reader becomes concentrated upon the substance (which must be the same now as then).[44]

Beza was elected moderator of Geneva's Company of Pastors after Calvin's death in 1564 and guided the Genevan Reformation over the next four decades. His annotated Latin translation of the Greek New Testament (1556) and his further revisions of the Greek text established his reputation as the leading textual critic of the sixteenth century after Erasmus. Beza completed the translation of Marot's metrical Psalter, which became a centerpiece of Huguenot piety and Reformed church life. Though known for his polemical writings on grace, free will and predestination, Beza's work is marked by a strong pastoral orientation and concern for a Scripture-based spirituality.

Robert Estienne (Stephanus) was a printer-scholar who had served the royal household in Paris. After his conversion to Protestantism, in 1550 he moved to Geneva, where he published a series of notable editions and translations of the Bible. He also produced sermons and commentaries on Job, Ecclesiastes, the Song of Songs, Romans and Hebrews, as well as dictionaries, concordances and a thesaurus of biblical terms. He also published the first editions of the Bible with chapters divided into verses, an innovation that quickly became universally accepted.

The British Reformation. Commentary writing in England and Scotland lagged behind the continental Reformation for several reasons. In 1500, there were only three publishing houses in England compared with more than two hundred on the Continent. A 1408 statute against publishing or reading the Bible in English, stemming from the days of Lollardy, stifled the free flow of ideas, as was seen in the fate of Tyndale. Moreover, the nature of the English Reformation from Henry through Elizabeth provided little stability for the flourishing of biblical scholarship. In the sixteenth century, many "hot-gospel" Protestants in England were edified by the English translations of commentaries and theological writings by the Continental reformers.

---

[44]Karl Barth, *Die Römerbrief* (Zurich: TVZ, 1940), ii, translated by T. H. L. Parker as the epigraph to *Calvin's New Testament Commentaries*, 2nd ed. (Louisville, KY: Westminster John Knox, 1993).

The influence of Calvin and Beza was felt especially in the Geneva Bible with its "Protestant glosses" of theological notes and references.

During the later Elizabethan and Stuart church, however, the indigenous English commentary came into its own. Both Anglicans and Puritans contributed to this outpouring of biblical studies. The sermons of Lancelot Andrewes and John Donne are replete with exegetical insights based on a close study of the Greek and Hebrew texts. Among the Reformed authors in England, none was more influential than William Perkins, the greatest of the early Puritan theologians, who published commentaries on Galatians, Jude, Revelation and the Sermon on the Mount (Mt 5–7). John Cotton, one of his students, wrote commentaries on the Song of Songs, Ecclesiastes and Revelation before departing for New England in 1633. The separatist pastor Henry Ainsworth was an outstanding scholar of Hebrew and wrote major commentaries on the Pentateuch, the Psalms and the Song of Songs. In Scotland, Robert Rollock, the first principal of Edinburgh University (1585), wrote numerous commentaries including those on the Psalms, Ephesians, Daniel, Romans, 1 and 2 Thessalonians, John, Colossians and Hebrews. Joseph Mede and Thomas Brightman were leading authorities on Revelation and contributed to the apocalyptic thought of the seventeenth century. Mention should also be made of Archbishop James Ussher, whose *Annals of the Old Testament* was published in 1650. Ussher developed a keen interest in biblical chronology and calculated that the creation of the world had taken place on October 26, 4004 B.C. As late as 1945, the Scofield Reference Bible still retained this date next to Genesis 1:1, but later editions omitted it because of the lack of evidence on which to fix such dates.[45]

Anabaptism. Irena Backus has noted that there was no school of "dissident" exegesis during the Reformation, and the reasons are not hard to find. The radical Reformation was an ill-defined movement that existed on the margins of official church life in the sixteenth century. The denial of infant baptism and the refusal to swear an oath marked radicals as a seditious element in society, and they were persecuted by Protestants and Catholics alike. However, in the RCS we have made an attempt to include some voices of the radical Reformation, especially among the Anabaptists. While the Anabaptists published few commentaries in the sixteenth century, they were avid readers and quoters of the Bible. Numerous exegetical gems can be found in their letters, treatises, martyr acts (especially *The Martyrs' Mirror*), hymns and histories. They placed a strong emphasis on the memorizing of Scripture and quoted liberally from vernacular translations of the Bible. George H. Williams has noted that "many an Anabaptist theological tract was really a beautiful mosaic of Scripture texts."[46] In general, most Anabaptists accepted the apocryphal books as canonical, contrasted outer word and inner spirit with relative degrees of strictness and saw the New Testament as normative for church life and social ethics (witness their pacifism, nonswearing, emphasis on believers' baptism and congregational discipline).

We have noted the Old Testament translation of Ludwig Hätzer, who became an antitrinitarian, and Hans Denck that they published at Worms in 1527. Denck also wrote a notable commentary

---

[45]*The New Scofield Reference Bible* (New York: Oxford University Press, 1967), vi.
[46]George H. Williams, *The Radical Reformation*, 3rd ed. (Kirksville, MO: Sixteenth Century Journal Publishers, 1992), 1247.

on Micah. Conrad Grebel belonged to a Greek reading circle in Zurich and came to his Anabaptist convictions while poring over the text of Erasmus's New Testament. The only Anabaptist leader with university credentials was Balthasar Hubmaier, who was made a doctor of theology (Ingolstadt, 1512) in the same year as Luther. His reflections on the Bible are found in his numerous writings, which include the first catechism of the Reformation (1526), a two-part treatise on the freedom of the will and a major work (*On the Sword*) setting forth positive attitudes toward the role of government and the Christian's place in society. Melchior Hoffman was an apocalyptic seer who wrote commentaries on Romans, Revelation and Daniel 12. He predicted that Christ would return in 1533. More temperate was Pilgram Marpeck, a mining engineer who embraced Anabaptism and traveled widely throughout Switzerland and south Germany, from Strasbourg to Augsburg. His "Admonition of 1542" is the longest published defense of Anabaptist views on baptism and the Lord's Supper. He also wrote many letters that functioned as theological tracts for the congregations he had founded dealing with topics such as the fruits of repentance, the lowliness of Christ and the unity of the church. Menno Simons, a former Catholic priest, became the most outstanding leader of the Dutch Anabaptist movement. His masterpiece was the *Foundation of Christian Doctrine* published in 1540. His other writings include *Meditation on the Twenty-fifth Psalm* (1537); *A Personal Exegesis of Psalm Twenty-five* modeled on the style of Augustine's *Confessions*; *Confession of the Triune God* (1550), directed against Adam Pastor, a former disciple of Menno who came to doubt the divinity of Christ; *Meditations and Prayers for Mealtime* (1557); and the *Cross of the Saints* (1554), an exhortation to faithfulness in the face of persecution. Like many other Anabaptists, Menno emphasized the centrality of discipleship (*Nachfolge*) as a deliberate repudiation of the old life and a radical commitment to follow Jesus as Lord.

Reading Scripture with the Reformers

In 1947, Gerhard Ebeling set forth his thesis that the history of the Christian church is the history of the interpretation of Scripture. Since that time, the place of the Bible in the story of the church has been investigated from many angles. A better understanding of the history of exegesis has been aided by new critical editions and scholarly discussions of the primary sources. The *Cambridge History of the Bible*, published in three volumes (1963–1970), remains a standard reference work in the field. The ACCS built on, and itself contributed to, the recovery of patristic biblical wisdom of both East and West. Beryl Smalley's *The Study of the Bible in the Middle Ages* (1940) and Henri de Lubac's *Medieval Exegesis: The Four Senses of Scripture* (1959) are essential reading for understanding the monastic and scholastic settings of commentary work between Augustine and Luther. The Reformation took place during what has been called "le grand siècle de la Bible."[47] Aided by the tools of Renaissance humanism and the dynamic impetus of Reformation theology (including permutations and reactions against it), the sixteenth century produced an unprecedented number of commentaries on every book in the Bible. Drawing from this vast storehouse of exegetical treasures, the RCS allows us to read

---

[47]J.-R. Aarmogathe, ed., *Bible de tous les temps*, 8 vols.; vol. 6, *Le grand siècle de la Bible* (Paris: Beauchesne, 1989).

Scripture along with the reformers. In doing so, it serves as a practical homiletic and devotional guide to some of the greatest masters of biblical interpretation in the history of the church.

The RCS gladly acknowledges its affinity with and dependence on recent scholarly investigations of Reformation-era exegesis. Between 1976 and 1990, three international colloquia on the history of biblical exegesis in the sixteenth century took place in Geneva and in Durham, North Carolina.[48] Among those participating in these three gatherings were a number of scholars who have produced groundbreaking works in the study of biblical interpretation in the Reformation. These include Elsie McKee, Irena Backus, Kenneth Hagen, Scott H. Hendrix, Richard A. Muller, Guy Bedouelle, Gerald Hobbs, John B. Payne, Bernard Roussel, Pierre Fraenkel and David C. Steinmetz. Among other scholars whose works are indispensable for the study of this field are Heinrich Bornkamm, Jaroslav Pelikan, Heiko A. Oberman, James S. Preus, T. H. L. Parker, David F. Wright, Tony Lane, John L. Thompson, Frank A. James and Timothy J. Wengert.[49] Among these scholars no one has had a greater influence on the study of Reformation exegesis than David C. Steinmetz. A student of Oberman, he has emphasized the importance of understanding the Reformation in medieval perspective. In addition to important studies on Luther and Staupitz, he has pioneered the method of comparative exegesis showing both continuity and discontinuity between major Reformation figures and the preceding exegetical traditions (see his *Luther in Context* and *Calvin in Context*). From his base at Duke University, he has spawned what might be called a Steinmetz school, a cadre of students and scholars whose work on the Bible in the Reformation era continues to shape the field. Steinmetz serves on the RCS Board of Editorial Advisors, and a number of our volume editors have pursued doctoral studies under his supervision.

In 1980, Steinmetz published "The Superiority of Pre-critical Exegesis," a seminal essay that not only placed Reformation exegesis in the context of the preceding fifteen centuries of the church's study of the Bible but also challenged certain assumptions underlying the hegemony of historical-critical exegesis of the post-Enlightenment academy.[50] Steinmetz helps us to approach the reformers and other precritical interpreters of the Bible on their own terms as faithful witnesses to the church's apostolic tradition. For them, a specific book or pericope had to be understood within the scope of the consensus of the canon. Thus the reformers, no less than the Fathers and the schoolmen, interpreted the hymn of the Johannine prologue about the preexistent Christ in consonance with the creation narrative of Genesis 1. In the same way, Psalm 22, Isaiah 53 and Daniel 7 are seen as part of an overarching storyline that finds ultimate fulfillment in Jesus

---

[48]Olivier Fatio and Pierre Fraenkel, eds., *Histoire de l'exégèse au XVIe siècle: texts du colloque international tenu à Genève en 1976* (Geneva: Droz, 1978); David C. Steinmetz, ed., *The Bible in the Sixteenth Century* [Second International Colloquy on the History of Biblical Exegesis in the Sixteenth Century] (Durham: Duke University Press, 1990); Irena Backus and Francis M. Higman, eds., *Théorie et pratique de l'exégèse. Actes du troisième colloque international sur l'histoire de l'exégèse biblique au XVIe siècle, Genève, 31 août-2 septembre 1988* (Geneva: Droz, 1990); see also Guy Bedouelle and Bernard Roussel, eds., *Bible de tous les temps*, 8 vols.; vol. 5, *Le temps des Réformes et la Bible* (Paris: Beauchesne, 1989).

[49]For bibliographical references and evaluation of these and other contributors to the scholarly study of Reformation-era exegesis, see Richard A. Muller, "Biblical Interpretation in the Era of the Reformation: The View From the Middle Ages," in *Biblical Interpretation in the Era of the Reformation: Essays Presented to David C. Steinmetz in Honor of His Sixtieth Birthday*, ed. Richard A. Muller and John L. Thompson (Grand Rapids: Eerdmans, 1996), 3-22.

[50]David C. Steinmetz, "The Superiority of Pre-Critical Exegesis," *Theology Today* 37 (1980): 27-38.

Christ. Reading the Bible with the resources of the new learning, the reformers challenged the exegetical conclusions of their medieval predecessors at many points. However, unlike Alexander Campbell in the nineteenth century, their aim was not to "open the New Testament as if mortal man had never seen it before."[51] Rather, they wanted to do their biblical work as part of an interpretive conversation within the family of the people of God. In the reformers' emphatic turn to the literal sense, which prompted their many blasts against the unrestrained use of allegory, their work was an extension of a similar impulse made by Thomas Aquinas and Nicholas of Lyra.

This is not to discount the radically new insights gained by the reformers in their dynamic engagement with the text of Scripture; nor should we dismiss in a reactionary way the light shed on the meaning of the Bible by the scholarly accomplishments of the past two centuries. However, it is to acknowledge that the church's exegetical tradition is an indispensible aid for the proper interpretation of Scripture. And this means, as Richard Muller has said, that "while it is often appropriate to recognize that traditionary readings of the text are erroneous on the grounds offered by the historical-critical method, we ought also to recognize that the conclusions offered by historical-critical exegesis may themselves be quite erroneous on the grounds provided by the exegesis of the patristic, medieval, and reformation periods."[52] The RCS wishes to commend the exegetical work of the Reformation era as a program of retrieval for the sake of renewal—spiritual réssourcement for believers committed to the life of faith today.

George Herbert was an English pastor and poet who reaped the benefits of the renewal of biblical studies in the age of the Reformation. He referred to the Scriptures as a book of infinite sweetness, "a mass of strange delights," a book with secrets to make the life of anyone good. In describing the various means pastors require to be fully furnished in the work of their calling, Herbert provided a rationale for the history of exegesis and for the Reformation Commentary on Scripture:

> The fourth means are commenters and Fathers, who have handled the places controverted, which the parson by no means refuseth. As he doth not so study others as to neglect the grace of God in himself and what the Holy Spirit teacheth him, so doth he assure himself that God in all ages hath had his servants to whom he hath revealed his Truth, as well as to him; and that as one country doth not bear all things that there may be a commerce, so neither hath God opened or will open all to one, that there may be a traffic in knowledge between the servants of God for the planting both of love and humility. Wherefore he hath one comment[ary] at least upon every book of Scripture, and ploughing with this, and his own meditations, he enters into the secrets of God treasured in the holy Scripture.[53]

Timothy George
General Editor

---

[51] Alexander Campbell, *Memoirs of Alexander Campbell*, ed. Robert Richardson (Cincinnati: Standard Publishing Company, 1872), 97.
[52] Richard A. Muller and John L. Thompson, "The Significance of Precritical Exegesis: Retrospect and Prospect," in *Biblical Interpretation in the Era of the Reformation: Essays Presented to David C. Steinmetz in Honor of His Sixtieth Birthday*, ed. Richard A. Muller and John L. Thompson (Grand Rapids: Eerdmans, 1996), 342.
[53] George Herbert, *The Complete English Poems* (London: Penguin, 1991), 205.

INTRODUCTION TO THE PSALMS

Puzzled as to how he should approach and understand the Psalms, Marcellinus requested the aid of his friend Athanasius (c. 295–373). The great bishop of Alexandria willingly obliged him with a lengthy letter, recounting the advice he himself had received:

> My child, *all the books of Scripture*, both old and new, *are inspired by God and useful for instruction*, as it is written. But to those who really study it, the Psalter yields especial treasure. Each book of the Bible has, of course, its own particular message. . . . Each of these books, you see, is like a garden which grows one particular kind of fruit; by contrast, the Psalter is a garden which, besides its particular fruit, grows also those of all the rest.[1]

Here in one holy book, Athanasius asserts, is the entire form and content of God's revelation—creation, exodus, exile and redemption—fixed as praise, inviting our participation. "In the other books of Scripture we read or hear the words of the saints as belonging only to those who spoke them, not at all as though they are our own," Athanasius continues. "With this book, however, . . . it is as if it is our own words that we read; anyone who hears them is pierced to the heart, as though these words voiced for him his deepest thoughts."[2] The Psalms are a mirror that reveals who we really are, instructing us to conform ourselves through the Spirit to the gift and example of Jesus Christ.[3] Only with the guidance of the Holy Spirit—the true Author of these songs—is anyone able to read the Psalms intelligently.[4] Athanasius's letter has influenced more than Marcellinus. Many since, including Martin Luther, John Calvin and other commentators featured in this volume, have included choice phrases from Athanasius's letter in their own works on the Psalms.[5]

For the fathers, the medievals and the reformers, the Words of Christ cannot be interpreted apart from the Spirit of Christ. Thus, praying the Psalms should not only align believers' reason and affections but also conform their will to God's.[6] This is no perfunctory prayer. In a fit of conscience, Augustine worried that he did not pray the Psalms but instead was seduced by their

---

[1]Athanasius, "Letter to Marcellinus," in *On the Incarnation*, ed. and trans. Penelope Lawson (Crestwood, NY: St. Vladimir's Seminary Press, 1993), 97-98* (PG 27:12).

[2]Ibid., 104* (PG 27:21).

[3]Ibid., 105-6 (PG 27:24).

[4]Ibid., 119 (PG 27:45-47).

[5]See LW 35:254-57 (WADB 10,1:99-105); CTS 8:xxxvi-xxxviii (CO 31:15-17). See further, Martin Tetz, "Zum Psalterverständnis bei Athanasius and Luther," *Lutherjahrbuch* 79 (2012): 39-61. Even John Goldingay refers to Athanasius in his *Psalms*, 3 vols., Baker Commentary on the Old Testament Wisdom and Psalms (Grand Rapids: Baker Academic, 2006), 1:23.

[6]Christopher A. Hall, *Worshiping with the Church Fathers* (Downers Grove, IL: IVP Academic, 2009), 89-91.

sweet melodies. He longed to be "moved not by the singing but by the things that are sung."[7] Anything else is to sin grievously. Luther lamented, somewhat hyperbolically, that the Psalms were no longer understood on account of their second-class rank behind legends and histories of saints.[8] Divine things had been exchanged for human things. In the preface to his influential Psalter, Jacques Lefèvre d'Étaples accused himself and his peers of only paying "lip service" to the Psalms and theology.[9] Ignoring the psalmist's word—"Blessed are those who study your testimonies" (Ps 119:2)—they traded heavenly blessings for worldly blessings, pursuing the "literal sense," which left them "utterly sad and downcast."[10]

Christ and the Psalms: What Is the Literal Sense?

But aren't the reformers famous for their insistence on the "literal sense"? Weren't they responsible for freeing biblical interpretation from the chains and restraints of fables and allegories? It depends. What is the literal sense, and what allegories did the reformers disapprove of? Some readers may be surprised to find the reformers saying that certain psalms are literally about Jesus Christ. Today by the "literal meaning of Scripture" we mean its meaning according to the constraints of grammar, history and literary method.[11] It is not uncommon to see contemporaries lambaste our forebears' interpretations as fantasy. And yet specialists trace the revival of the literal sense to Nicholas of Lyra—in some cases even to Thomas Aquinas (1225–1274).[12] Between the early modern period and today there has been a shift in our understanding of the literal sense.[13]

After an interview with monks depressed by their literal reading of Scripture, Lefèvre himself wondered, what do they mean by literal? "Then I began to consider seriously that perhaps this had not been the true literal sense but rather, as quacks like to do with herbs, one thing is substituted for the other, a pseudo sense for the true literal sense."[14] On reflection Lefèvre realized that these monks had been reading Scripture as if there were only a human author. They approached the Psalms considering only David and his context, errantly viewing him not "as a prophet but rather as a chronicler."[15] However, the testimony of the apostles, Evangelists and prophets demonstrates, for Lefèvre, that readers must lift up their hearts and contemplate the intention of a higher Author:

---

[7]Augustine, *The Confessions of St. Augustine*, trans. Rex Warner (New York: Mentor-Omega, 1963), 242.

[8]Preface to the Psalms (1545), LW 35:253 (WADB 10,1:99).

[9]Jacques Lefèvre d'Étaples, "Introduction to Commentary on the Psalms," in Heiko A. Oberman, *Forerunners of the Reformation* (New York: Holt, Rinehart and Winston, 1966), 297.

[10]Ibid., 297-98.

[11]These constraints tend to emphasize the human author—one of the great shifts of exegesis in the history of the church. See further Donald L. Fairbairn, *Life in the Trinity* (Downers Grove, IL: IVP Academic, 2009), 109-16.

[12]Brevard Childs, "The Sensus Literalis of Scripture: An Ancient and Modern Problem," in *Beiträge zur Alttestamentlichen Theologie: Festschrift für Walther Zimmerli zum 70. Geburtstag*, eds. Herbert Donner, Robert Hanhart and Rudolf Sment (Göttingen: Vandenhoeck & Ruprecht, 1977), 80-93; see further Henri de Lubac, *Medieval Exegesis: The Four Senses of Scripture*, 3 vols., trans. Mark Sebanc and E. M. Macierowski (Grand Rapids: Eerdmans, 1998–2009), 1:1-14; 2:41-82.

[13]See Lewis Ayres, *Nicaea and its Legacy: An Approach to Fourth-Century Trinitarian Theology* (Oxford: Oxford University Press, 2004), 31-40.

[14]Lefèvre, "Introduction to Commentary on the Psalms," 298.

[15]Ibid.

[The apostles, Evangelists and prophets] opened the door of understanding of the letter of Sacred Scripture, and I seemed to see another sense: the intention of the prophet and of the Holy Spirit speaking in him. This I call "literal" sense but a literal sense which coincides with the Spirit. No other letter has the Spirit conveyed to the prophets or to those who have open eyes.[16]

For Lefèvre, then, the letter that kills is the letter severed from its true Author, the Holy Spirit. Only by Christ's aid—of one essence with his Spirit—will a reader be able to expound the literal sense of Scripture.[17] "For [Lefèvre] the spiritual, that is, the literal sense is not available through simple grammatical exegesis," Heiko Oberman summarizes. "The unbeliever cannot discover the real meaning because he approaches the text without the most necessary exegetical tool of all, that selfsame Spirit which created Scripture."[18]

So then, Lefèvre intimates a twofold distinction within the literal sense: the simple and the spiritual, or what Richard Muller calls the constructed or compounded.[19] The simple literal sense consists of the immediate grammatical, historical and literary meaning of the very words of Scripture; the spiritual literal sense is the meaning of the very words of Scripture in light of the full form and content of Scripture. The simple and the spiritual literal senses are distinguishable but inseparable. Nevertheless there is a hierarchy: the simple serves the spiritual. Other reformers wholeheartedly affirmed this approach. Luther was particularly insistent that Scripture's substance, Christ, is the interpretive key for *all* its words.[20]

The vast majority of the reformers, not just Luther, affirmed that the concern for textual analysis must be wedded with the rule of faith, which Craig Farmer has tersely defined as "the trinitarian, christological and evangelical scope of Scripture's content and meaning that arises from it and in turn makes sense of the whole and the parts."[21] All biblical interpretation must be ruled. Luther states this with characteristic flourish:

If I were offered free choice either to have St. Augustine's and the dear fathers', that is, the apostles', understanding of Scripture together with the handicap that St. Augustine occasionally lacks the correct Hebrew letters and words—as the Jews sneeringly accuse him—or to have the Jews' correct letters and words (which they, in fact, do not have everywhere) but minus St. Augustine's and the

---

[16]Ibid.

[17]"Let us call that the literal sense which is in accord with the Spirit and is poured out by the Spirit. 'We know,' says Paul, the spokesman of God, 'that the law is spiritual,' and if it *is* spiritual, how could the literal sense, if it is really to be the sense of the law, not be spiritual? Therefore the literal sense and the spiritual sense coincide. This true sense is not what is called the allegorical or tropological sense, but rather the sense the Holy Spirit intends as he speaks through the prophet. It has been our total purpose to draw out of this sense all that the Holy Spirit has put into it" (ibid., 300).

[18]Oberman, *Forerunners of the Reformation*, 288.

[19]Richard Muller, *Dictionary of Latin and Greek Theological Terms* (Grand Rapids: Baker Academic, 1985), 279.

[20]Mickey L. Mattox, "Luther's Interpretation of Scripture: Biblical Understanding in Trinitarian Shape," in *The Substance of Faith: Luther's Doctrinal Theology for Today*, ed. Paul R. Hinlicky (Minneapolis: Fortress, 2008), 11-57, here 46.

[21]RCS NT 4:li. See further Kathryn Greene-McCreight, "Literal Sense" and "Rule of Faith," in *Dictionary for Theological Interpretation of the Bible*, ed. Kevin J. Vanhoozer (Grand Rapids: Baker Academic, 2005), 455-56, 703-704; J. Todd Billings, *The Word of God for the People of God: An Entryway to the Theological Interpretation of Scripture* (Grand Rapids: Eerdmans, 2010), 149-94; Gerald Bray, *Biblical Interpretation: Past and Present* (Downers Grove, IL: InterVarsity Press, 1996), 189-209; Tomas Bokedal, "The Rule of Faith: Tracing Its Origins," *Journal of Theological Interpretation* 7, no. 2 (2013), 233-55; and W. David Buschart and Kent Eilers, *Theology as Retrieval: Receiving the Past, Renewing the Church* (Downers Grove, IL: IVP Academic, 2015), 43-79.

fathers' understanding, that is, with the Jews' interpretation, it can be easily imagined which of the two I would chose.[22]

Luther would rather have a faulty but *ruled* translation than the original text divorced from the church's faith. Even the more restrained Calvin affirms the essential importance of ruled interpretation. Paul, he explains, exhorted "those who prophesied in the church . . . to conform their prophecies to the rule of faith, lest in anything they should deviate from the right line."[23]

The reformers' understanding of the literal sense and the rule of faith helps us understand which allegories they protested against so harshly: those that were not conformed to the rule of faith. Luther is explicit:

> When we condemn allegories we are speaking of those that are fabricated by one's own intellect and ingenuity, without the authority of Scripture. Other allegories which are made to agree with the analogy of faith not only enrich doctrine but also console consciences.[24]

In his *Institutes* Calvin affirms this prescription of Luther: "Allegories ought not to go beyond the limits set by the rule of Scripture, let alone suffice as the foundation for any doctrines."[25] Here we see two giants of the Reformation affirming allegories that present Christ while casting aside all others (e.g., those that affirm papal primacy or purgatory).

Unsurprisingly, the reformers' uses of ruled interpretation in the Psalms are on a spectrum, with Luther as the most ardent, Calvin as the most restrained and Martin Bucer in between.[26] First, Luther and his disciples employ an immediate ruled interpretation.[27] While at times they consider the specific historical data concerning David, generally they quickly venture into Christological details, often reading the Psalms in the person and voice of Christ:

> Every prophecy and every prophet must be understood as referring to Christ the Lord, except where it is clear from plain words that someone else is spoken of. For thus he himself says. "Search the Scriptures! It is they that bear witness to me." Otherwise it is most certain that the searchers will not find what they are searching for. For that same reason some explain very many psalms not prophetically but historically.[28]

---

[22]"Treatise on the Last Words of David (1543)," LW 15:266-70 (WA 54:29-31). See further Mattox, "Luther's Interpretation of Scripture." In this quote we also see an intimation of Luther's definition of "apostolic": whatever presents Christ.

[23]Commentary on Romans 12:6, CTS 38:461 (CO 49:239).

[24]Excursus on Allegory at Genesis 9:12-16, LW 2:151* (WA 42:367-68).

[25]LCC 20:339 (CO 2:246); *Institutes* 2.5.19. See further Luther's comments on Galatians 4:21-31, especially that allegorical interpretations "should not be brought forward with a view to establishing a doctrine of faith" (LW 27:311; WA 2:550).

[26]While many of our commentators applied the *quadriga*, Luther used it very prominently in his pre-Reformational Psalms lectures (1513–1515) but avoided explicit use of it in his incomplete second lecture series on the Psalms (1519–1521). See biographical sketch for the *quadriga* and "General Introduction," pp. xxvii-xxix.

[27]Most early modern Catholic interpreters tended toward this end of the ruled interpretive spectrum. However, some Catholic exegetes, especially Cardinal Cajetan, are at times closer to Calvin's end of the spectrum. For example, Cajetan shrank from publishing commentaries on Song of Songs and Revelation because "I confess that I do not understand Song of Songs according to the true sense," nor did he "know how to expound Revelation according to the literal sense" (Cardinal Cajetan, *Opera Omnia qvotqvot in Sacrae Scripturae Expositionem reperiuntur*, 5 vols [Lyons: Jean and Pierre Prost, 1639], 3:633; 5:400v). John Donne oscillates between Luther and Bucer on the spectrum.

[28]Preface to the First Psalms Lectures (1513–1515), LW 10:7* (WA 3:13); citing Jn 5:39.

Although Luther wholeheartedly affirms the value of history, still, for him, a Christian reading must join the fruit of history to the history itself.[29] Any other reading would be Spirit-less and superficial. The sense of a psalm must be sought "in the Spirit, because superficially it could be understood about David."[30] Yes, "for Christ is the dear origin of the circle; all the histories in Holy Scripture—if they are to be correctly understood—point to Christ."[31] Luther is loath to allow Scripture to be *mere* history. "Take Christ out of the Scriptures and what will you find left in them?"[32]

Due to this Christological immediacy, readers of this volume will notice that from time to time Lutheran exegetes identify the psalmist as Christ without any forewarning. Today we might prefer "the psalmist says here," but for these Lutherans it must be "Christ says here." They would heartily endorse Augustine's statement that "it is Christ's voice which ought by this time to be perfectly known and perfectly familiar to us in all the Psalms—now chanting joyously, now sorrowing, now rejoicing in hope, now sighing in its present state, even as if it were our own. We need not then dwell long on pointing out to you who the speaker here is. Let each one of us be a member of Christ's body and he will be a speaker here."[33] In the Psalms, for these commentators, we learn to recognize and imitate Christ's voice.

The second notch on the ruled interpretative spectrum is Bucer (and most Reformed exegetes).[34] G. Sujin Pak has demonstrated that Bucer is a transitional figure between Luther and Calvin in the field of exegesis.[35] Here we see history more carefully developed as evidence for Christological readings. Bucer, like many of his contemporaries, was well aware of Jewish criticisms of Christian exegesis as too foreign to the biblical text.[36] Therefore, he sought to tie down Christian readings

---

[29]Luther divided many of his postils in this way. He explains this gift-example distinction in "Short Instruction: What Should Be Sought and Expected in the Gospels," LW 75:7-12 (WA 10,1.1:8-18; E² 7:8-13; cf. LW 35:113-24).

[30]Glossa on Psalm 54 (1513–1515), WA 3:299.

[31]Sermon on John 3:14 (1538), WA 47:66 (cf. LW 22:339).

[32]*On the Bondage of the Will* (1525), LCC 17:110 (WA 18:606).

[33]NPNF 8:138*; cf. Peter Brown, *Augustine of Hippo: A Biography* (Berkeley and Los Angeles: University of California Press, 1967), 257-58.

[34]The majority of English Reformed exegetes tend toward Bucer's method of ruled interpretation. However, *The English Annotations*, as a condensed amalgam of continental Reformed comment, fluctuate between Bucer and Calvin on the ruled interpretive spectrum.

[35]G. Sujin Pak, *The Judaizing Calvin: Sixteenth-Century Debates over the Messianic Psalms* (Oxford: Oxford University Press, 2010).

[36]This claim reverberates today, at times even from within the church itself. For example, see John Goldingay, *Do We Need the New Testament?* (Downers Grove, IL: IVP Academic, 2015), esp. 160-76. Goldingay warns that "theological interpretation needs to be wary of being christocentric and being trinitarian and following the formulations of Christian theology and the rule of faith" (p. 174). Few of the reformers would have had nice things to say about such a statement; at the very least they would point out that it is internally incoherent. Who is the God of Scripture but the Trinity? For the reformers, such statements would be like saying, "Try not to think about who God is while reading Scripture." Brevard Childs highlights the naïveté of suggestions like Goldingay's: "It is a common caricature of the relationship between exegesis and theological reflection to suggest that the former is an independent historical and philological exercise which seeks objectively to discover what the text actually says, whereas the latter is a subsequent and subjectively reflective activity, largely of a speculative nature. . . . Rather, I would argue that the relationship between exegesis and theology is a far more complex and subtle one which is basically dialectical in nature. One comes to exegesis already with certain theological assumptions and the task of good exegesis is to penetrate so deeply into the biblical text that even these assumptions are called into question, are tested and revised by the subject matter itself. The implication is also that proper exegesis does not confine itself to registering only the verbal sense of the text, but presses forward through the text to the subject matter (*res*) to which it points." See Brevard S. Childs, "Does the Old Testament Witness to Jesus Christ?" in *Evangelium Schriftauslegung Kirche: Festschrift für Peter Stuhlmacher zum 65. Geburtstag*, eds. Jostein Ådna, Scott J. Hafemann and

by clarifying the historical context. "I am thus able to anchor more solidly in the historical foundation those things that are interpreted of our Savior Christ and of the church."[37] While Bucer acknowledged that even the best historical scholarship apart from the Holy Spirit's illumination was entirely unable to convince Jews of Christian truth, he pilfered rabbinic resources to bolster his historical case.[38]

Some, like Wolfgang Capito, seconded Bucer's suggestion, saying that without historical moorings, Christian interpretation is "a laughingstock with its allegories."[39] Others, while fond of Bucer's efforts, were wary of his brazen use of rabbinic resources; they worried that simpler minds might be confused, thinking that Bucer affirms Jewish theology. This despite Bucer's promise that he would be judicious in his use of the rabbis, as R. Gerald Hobbs summarizes, "None of their materials would be adopted uncritically, for their commentary had been deformed in varying degrees by their inability to penetrate to the heart of Scripture—faith in Christ."[40] This was not enough for Konrad Pellikan. He did acknowledge his debt to Bucer's commentary: "In large part we have followed not only the opinions but even the words of that recent writer Aretius Felinus—whoever he may be, he is certainly a learned, godly and very diligent translator and commentator."[41] However, despite gladly benefiting from the rabbinic resources in Bucer's commentary, Pellikan suppressed all references to the rabbis in his own commentary.[42] He was piqued enough to rebuke Bucer himself:

> I am pained by your labors in searching out and sifting the opinions of the rabbis, which you repeat time and again while they disagree with one another both in grammar and in sense. And I prefer the judgment of Zwingli, yourself and almost all the doctors of the Christian faith to their opinions and Judaic learning, for long ago they have wandered away from the mark and are ignorant of languages other than their own, and seem to have acquired their learning as a birthright; so that I think that you would assuredly have made your way far more quickly and easily by your own judgment into the core sense of Scripture than propped up by the assistance of some of them; save insofar as it concerns the grammatical sense, where they generally have some wisdom, though not always.[43]

Even for the more historically-minded reformers, the Holy Spirit alone reveals the substance of Scripture.

Otfried Hofius (Göttingen: Vandenhoeck & Ruprecht, 1997), 57-64, here p. 60.

[37]Martin Bucer, *Sacrorum Psalmorum libri quinque* (Basel: Johannes Herwagen, 1547), a5v; quoted from R. Gerald Hobbs, "How Firm a Foundation: Martin Bucer's Historical Exegesis of the Psalms," *Church History* 53, no. 4 (1984), 480-81.

[38]Hobbs, "How Firm a Foundation," 481.

[39]Wolfgang Capito, *In Habakuk* (Strasbourg: Wolfgang Köpfel, 1526), 5r; quoted from Hobbs, "How Firm a Foundation," 483.

[40]Hobbs, "How Firm a Foundation," 484; citing Bucer, *Sacrorum Psalmorum*, a5v-a6r.

[41]Konrad Pellikan, *Commentaria Bibliorum*, 7 vols. (Zurich: Christoph Froschauer, 1532–1539), 4:45v; quoted from R. Gerald Hobbs, "Conrad Pellican and the Psalms: The Ambivalent Legacy of a Pioneer Hebraist," *Reformation & Renaissance Review* 1, no. 1 (1999), 88. Aretius Felinus, as Pellikan knew, was a pseudonym for Martin Bucer. Bucer's own Psalms commentary is a revised version of Johannes Bugenhagen's, which Bucer considered somewhat deficient on account of Bugenhagen's unfamiliarity with Hebrew, as well as their differing Eucharistic theologies.

[42]Hobbs, "Conrad Pellican and the Psalms," 93.

[43]Konrad Pellikan to Martin Bucer, August 6, 1529; quoted from Hobbs, "Conrad Pellican and the Psalms," 97-98*.

Finally in Calvin we see the most restrained use of ruled interpretation in the Psalms.[44] He carefully distinguishes the historical David from Jesus of Nazareth, while not separating them. He gives both historical figures exegetical attention, as he also acknowledges their typological connection. Reading his exegesis of the Psalms, we will generally see that he focuses on grammatical and historical considerations, only then moving to Christological or ecclesial interpretations. This was an abrupt enough methodological development that Aegidius Hunnius posthumously called Calvin a "judaizer."[45] That is, Hunnius thought that Calvin suppressed the Christological content of Scripture. Surely Calvin would have been dismayed by such charges. Though he dismissed some of the more imaginative ruled readings as "too forced," he too fully affirmed the use of the rule of faith. Indeed, in the prefatory letter to the *Institutes*, he understands it to be the touchstone of exegesis: "When Paul wished all prophecy to accord with the analogy of faith, he set forth a very clear rule to test all interpretation of Scripture."[46] In fact, Calvin's method has been described as repackaging the *quadriga*, including belief, morality and hope as part of the literal sense.[47]

Like their magisterial counterparts, the Radical reformers also understood Jesus Christ to be the very substance of Scripture.[48] Yet the Radicals do not quite fit on this ruled interpretive spectrum, since they shirked extra-biblical language as best as they could on account of the "dross" of human traditions.[49] Thus, "many an Anabaptist theological tract was really a beautiful mosaic of scriptural texts, an original work only in the exquisite craftsmanship exhibited in the laying and pointing."[50] This style of writing characterized their strictly literal interpretation of Scripture, especially regarding the New Testament. God's Word is so clear, they confessed, that it requires no glosses, let alone detailed interpretation.[51] Some Anabaptists interpreted the New Testament in such a starkly literal way that they preached on rooftops (Mt 10:27), and cooed and cried like infants (e.g., Mt 18:1-6). However, more careful exegetes—like many of the Radicals featured in

---

[44]Moïse Amyraut, Sebastian Münster and Theodore Beza, for example, also tend toward Calvin's style of ruled interpretation.

[45]Pak, *Judaizing Calvin*, esp. pp. 103-24. David Pareus (1548–1622), Calvin's defender, thought that Hunnius misjudged Calvin's exegesis, because he did not understand that Calvin intended his commentaries to be read with *the Institutes*.

[46]LCC 20:12-13 (CO 2:12-13); citing Rom 12:6.

[47]Richard A. Muller, "Biblical Interpretation in the Era of the Reformation: The View From the Middle Ages," in *Biblical Interpretation in the Era of the Reformation: Essays Presented to David C. Steinmetz in Honor of His Sixtieth Birthday*, eds. Richard A. Muller and John L. Thompson (Grand Rapids: Eerdmans, 1996), 11; see further Randall C. Zachman, *John Calvin as Teacher, Pastor, and Theologian: The Shape of His Writings and Thoughts* (Grand Rapids: Baker Academic, 2006), 103-30. See biographical sketch on the *quadriga*, and above, p. xxviii.

[48]Walter Klaassen especially emphasizes this. In fact, he awkwardly claims that the Anabaptists alone taught Christ to be Scripture's substance, while the magisterial reformers were so text-bound "that Jesus Christ becomes for them little more than an incident, albeit an important incident, among other incidents related in the Bible." See Walter Klassen, "Bern Debate of 1538: Christ the Center of Scripture," *Mennonite Quarterly Review* 40, no. 2 (1966), 148-56, here p. 152.

[49]In defending the doctrine of the Trinity, however, Menno Simons resorted to using Nicene language to protect this biblical concept (Timothy George, *Theology of the Reformers*, rev. ed. [Nashville: B & H Academic, 2013], 289). For a more in-depth treatment of Radical hermeneutics, see George H. Williams, *The Radical Reformation*, 3rd ed. (Kirksville, MO: Sixteenth Century Journal Publishers, 1992), 1241-60. Unfortunately, due to the Radicals' exegetical style as well as their focus on New Testament texts, Anabaptist comment in this volume is scarce.

[50]Williams, *The Radical Reformation*, 1247; cf. RCS NT 10:lvi-lvii.

[51]For example, see Michael Sattler, "How Scripture Should Be Discerningly Exposited," in CRR 1:150-77; see further RCS NT 6:l-li.

this volume—guarded against such "erratic literalism."[52] The Old Testament proved more difficult however. While the majority of Radicals did not reject the Old Testament wholesale, they subjected it to the New Testament in such a way—"it is valid 'where Christ has not suspended it'"—that the magisterial reformers regularly charged them as Marcionites.[53]

Despite these various emphases among the confessions of the Reformation, the reformers, like the church fathers, "read Scripture through the prism of Christ's incarnation, crucifixion, resurrection and ascension."[54] The Sun of Righteousness transfigures these interpreters' Bibles. Each one of them would have shuddered at hyper-focused grammatical and historical exegesis, exemplified in commentators like Theodore of Mopsuestia (c. 350–428), who dared to claim that "the subject matter of [Psalm 22] is not about the Lord . . . but about blessed David."[55] Worried that such an assertion potentially divided Christ into two persons—one human and one divine—the Second Council of Constantinople (553) anathematized Theodore's writings.[56] For our forebears the interpretive task could not be severed from theology or, more importantly, worship.[57] The Christian life—in all matters, both thought and deed—should promote the twofold love of God and neighbor; exegesis is no exception.[58]

Sixteenth-Century Pejoratives: What Is "Judaizing"?

The reformers' understanding of the literal sense and the importance of the analogy of faith bore rather foul fruit regarding Judaism. Martin Luther's chilling tract *On the Jews and their Lies* (1543) was especially shrill; however, anti-Judaic[59] sentiment was not unique to him.[60] Disdain for

---

[52]Williams, *The Radical Reformation*, 1257.

[53]Klaassen, "Bern Debate of 1538," 153. The Reformed interlocutors in the Bern Debate of 1538 wielded the equal weight of the testaments as the key to their victory; Heinrich Bullinger also affirmed this. See Heinold Fast and John H. Yoder, "How to Deal with Anabaptists: An Unpublished Letter of Heinrich Bullinger," *Mennonite Quarterly Review* 33, no. 2 (1959), 83-95, esp. pp. 84-88.

[54]Christopher A. Hall, *Reading Scripture with the Church Fathers* (Downers Grove, IL: InterVarsity Press, 1998), 192-94, here p. 192.

[55]PG 66:663-66. Theodore only accepted Psalms 2; 8; 45; 110 as messianic.

[56]Theodore may have suffered from guilt-by-association: his infamous pupil Nestorius (c. 381–c. 451) had indeed improperly distinguished Christ's two natures into two persons. See further Jaroslav Pelikan, *The Christian Tradition*, 5 vols. (Chicago: University of Chicago Press, 1971–1989), 1:243-44, 251-56.

[57]Mahlon Smith has stated this especially eloquently. "Not until the Enlightenment did Christian theology become divorced from the task of clarifying communal ritual. The printing revolution had by this time turned the religious education of westerners—at least those influenced by schools—into reflection on the written Word. But in earlier periods, Christian faith and understanding depended largely on liturgical celebrations, particularly baptism and the Eucharist. In such a context, the coherence of the community so relied upon the common ritual that even the slightest deviation from the traditional format was sufficient to touch off a major theological controversy" (Mahlon H. Smith III, *And Taking Bread...: Cerularius and the Azyme Controversy of 1054* [Paris: Beauchesne, 1978], 29). Thus Smith connects the major theological controversies of the early church to worship: Marcion (fl. 144) challenged the use of the Old Testament in worship; Montanus (fl. 135–170) sought to revive Old Testament prophecy; the Donatists questioned who can participate in worship; Arius (fl. c. 320) challenged prayers that implied the Son to be coeternal; Apollinarius (310–c. 392) and Nestorius rejected the title *theotokos* for Mary.

[58]Augustine famously stated this principle for the interpretive task in his *On Christian Doctrine* 1.39-40; NPNF 2:533.

[59]"Anti-Judaic" is being used to keep historical distance. While most early modern opinions of the Jews are abhorrent today, it is unfair and anachronistic to interpret them through the anti-Semitism of the early twentieth century. This is not to condone such statements, but to put them in context.

[60]Many principalities did not allow this tract to be printed under their jurisdiction on account of its belligerent tone. For the text, see LW 47:121-305 (WA 53:417-552); for a summary of Luther's relationship with Judaism, see Hans-Martin Kirn, "Luther und die

---

Jews permeated medieval and early-modern Europe. Calvin's aside in his Daniel commentary, that "I have never found common sense in any Jew," is typical of the time period.[61]

At times this anti-Judaic sentiment was presented as a sort of Christian chauvinism. "I have preferred the authority of the ancients to the moderns," Pellikan wrote in the preface to his seven-volume commentary of the Bible. "I would rather be in doubt in the company of Jerome and the Seventy Greek translators than to take a stand as if on a sure thing with modern Jews."[62] This ugly interaction between disdain for the Jews and jingoistic Christian pride introduced the pejorative "judaizing" into exegetical discussions.[63] For the reformers and their forbears "judaizers" are those who try to read Scripture without the guidance of the Holy Spirit, who gives it a living voice—that is, those who read Scripture as if only human authorial intention matters. To employ Lefèvre's words, such people were guilty of making the human author a mere chronicler, not a prophet.[64]

Clearly no one wanted this label. And Calvin was not the only person accused of "judaizing"— Luther often harangued Sebastian Münster and his peers.[65] Unfortunately, many of the reformers tried to bolster their Christian allegiance by insulting Jews. Münster, who published a Latin digest of the *Biblia Rabbinica* for those with more rudimentary Hebrew skills, himself wrote vitriol worthy of Luther, calling a Hebrew interpreter "that raw-skinned scoundrel."[66] While the majority of the reformers consulted the rabbinic resources available to them, they seem to present it as a necessary evil. Disguised with barbs, Luther implies how regularly he interacted with Hebrew interpreters. "The blinded Jews . . . have lost all knowledge of the subject matter and confine themselves to grammatical discussions of words. . . . They never arrive at the true meaning."[67] Calvin also highlighted what he saw as Jewish errors, lest anyone be led astray. "I wanted to gather these opinions together, so that you would understand how foolish those Jewish rationalizers are. For they thus make war with God, and furiously rush to assault the clear light of the gospel."[68] Disap-

---

Juden," in *Luther Handbuch*, ed. Albrecht Beutel (Tübingen: Mohr Siebeck, 2005), 217-24; see further Heiko A. Oberman, *The Roots of Anti-Semitism in the Age of the Renaissance and Reformation*, trans. James I. Porter (Philadelphia: Fortress Press, 1984).

[61]Commentary on Daniel 2:44, CTS 24:185 (CO 40:605). See further J. Marius J. Lange van Ravenswaay, "Calvin and the Jews," in *The Calvin Handbook*, ed. Herman J. Selderhuis (Grand Rapids: Eerdmans, 2009), 143-46.

[62]Pellikan, *Commentaria Bibliorum*, 1:B2v; quoted from Hobbs, "Conrad Pellican and the Psalms," 91. While wary of Bucer's use of rabbinic sources, Pellikan heartily endorses his application of the analogy of faith (p. 95).

[63]Denigrating other Christians as Jewish was not unique to the Reformation era. Indeed Jaroslav Pelikan observes that "'to judaize' was long a term for 'to teach false doctrine'" (Pelikan, *Christian Tradition*, 1:71). For example, leading up to the Great Schism (1054), the Eastern Orthodox worried that the Roman Church was "judaizing" by using unleavened wafers. On account of the inclusion of the *Agnus Dei* in the Roman liturgy, some Easterners even thought that their Western counterparts sacrificed a lamb as part of the Eucharist.

[64]Lefèvre, "Introduction to Commentary on the Psalms," 298.

[65]For example, see Luther's introductory comment to Ps 16 below; see further Stephen G. Burnett, "Reassessing the 'Basel-Wittenberg Conflict': Dimensions of the Reformation-Era Discussion of Hebrew Scholarship," in *Hebraica Veritas?: Christian Hebraists and the Study of Judaism in early Modern Europe*, eds. Allison P. Coudert and Jeffrey S. Shoulson (Philadelphia: University of Pennsylvania Press, 2004), 181-201.

[66]Sebastian Münster, *Miqdaš YHWH* (Basel: Michael Isinginius and Henricus Petrus, 1546), 1162. For more on the *Biblia Rabbinica*, see Stephen G. Burnett, "The Strange Career of the *Biblia Rabbinica* among Christian Hebraists, 1517–1620," in *Shaping the Bible in the Reformation: Books, Scholars and Their Readers in the Sixteenth Century*, eds. Bruce Gordon and Matthew McLean (Leiden: Brill, 2012), 63-84.

[67]Lectures on Genesis 16:13-14, LW 3:70-71 (WA 42:599).

[68]Commentary on Daniel 2:44, CO 40:607 (CTS 24:187).

---

pointingly, despite all their interaction with Jewish learning and their love of the Hebrew language, few of the reformers looked on the Jews with tolerance, let alone respect.[69]

The Church's Prayer Book: How Should We Rejoice and Lament?

Reformation-era theologians, pastors and parishioners continued to view the Psalter as the church's prayer book. As monks, many of the reformers had oriented their days around praying the psalms and knew these prayers intimately. Luther, who especially loved music and poetry, exclaimed, "How much more must you imagine me to be affected by the Psalter, the book which has been my companion, my delight and my exercise from my youth."[70] For our forebears, praying the psalms shapes and orders our affections, actions and words.[71]

For early modern commentators and pastors this *for us* aspect has implications for the care of souls and how we praise God. Luther's contemporaries documented one particularly powerful example of how he used this truth to comfort the afflicted. He asked one distressed friend: "How do you like the Psalter? . . . Do you have a sense of joy when you read in it, or of sorrow?" "Sometimes I find comfort in the psalms," the friend quietly answered, "but then Satan intrudes with his argument: 'These things that are written here, what are they to you?'" Luther responded with a simple blessing and exhortation to cling to and trust in the Psalms:

> Very solemnly Doctor Luther made the sign of the cross to banish the evil spirit and at the same time quoted Paul . . . "*Whatever things were written in former days were written for our learning, that we through hope and patience and comfort of the Scriptures might have hope. . . .* So long as the devil holds sway, you hold onto that Psalter and read in it. Trust God who helped David. He will help you too. *For all the promises of God in him are Yes, and in him Amen.*"[72]

The reformers teach that the Psalms are the very words of God for the people of God. By these hymns, the Holy Spirit stirs us up to contemplate the mighty deeds of the Lord and to praise his glory. Indeed, Calvin reminds us, that is why we need this prayer book:

> We must have songs not only honorable but also holy, which are to be like needles to arouse us to pray and praise God, to meditate on his works, in order to love him, fear, honor and glorify him. . . . We will not find better songs nor ones more appropriate for this purpose than the Psalms of David, which the Holy Spirit has spoken to him and made. Therefore, when we sing them, we are certain that God has put the words in our mouth as if they themselves sang in us to exalt his glory.[73]

---

[69]Hobbs, "Conrad Pellican and the Psalms," 96; see further Dean Phillip Bell and Stephen G. Burnett, eds. *Jews, Judaism, and the Reformation in Sixteenth-Century Germany* (Brill: Leiden, 2006); Mark U. Edwards Jr., *Luther's Last Battles: Politics and Polemics, 1531–46* (Ithaca, NY: Cornell University Press, 1983), 115-42.

[70]To Eobanus Hessus (August 1, 1537), WABr 8:107; quoted from H. G. Haile, *Luther: An Experiment in Biography* (Garden City, NY: Doubleday, 1980), 62.

[71]Hall, *Worshiping with the Church Fathers*, 89-90. Athanasius underscores that for this reason we must make the Psalms *ours* (Athanasius, "Letter to Marcellinus," 104-6; PG 27:21-24).

[72]Haile, *Luther*, 187*; citing Rom 15:4; 2 Cor 1:20.

[73]John Calvin, "'The Forms of Prayers and Songs of the Church' (1542): Letter to the Reader," trans. Ford Lewis Battles, *Calvin Theological Journal* 15, no. 2 (1980), 164 (OS 2:17).

As a parent holds and directs their young child's hand while she tries to form letters, so our heavenly Father directs us through the words of the Psalter to express our feelings. By his Spirit our God gives us words when we have none. For this reason each confessional party of the Reformation treasured the Psalms as a regular facet of public worship as well as private meditation; the Reformed, however, are especially well-known for their love of the Psalms in worship. "The Genevan Psalter was not only a staple in public worship," Scott Manetsch writes, "but was sung in the marketplace, intoned by martyrs on their way to the scaffold, and even chanted by armies as they marched into battle. In the decades and centuries that followed, the Genevan Psalter served as the distinguishing mark of Reformed worship and the *cri de coeur* of embattled French Protestantism."[74]

These songs expose human shortcomings and God's steadfast faithfulness; they do not satisfy all our curiosites nor answer all our questions. "The Psalms do not attempt to explain suffering or what mysterious purposes God may have for our pain," Kelly Kapic observes. "Instead they display the character of Yahweh as trustworthy, brimming with compassion for his people."[75] J. Todd Billings goes even further, asserting that there is no biblical answer to the problem evil.[76] Perhaps the reformers would have found this formulation too stark, though they would have approved of the sentiment. Why do bad things happen to good people? We do not know, nor should we presume to try to figure out such mysteries. Nevertheless, the reformers would make at least three points. First, our world is corrupted, thus, evil and suffering are part of our everyday realities (though it is not supposed to be this way).[77] Second, Jesus Christ himself suffered, and he empathizes with our suffering—he was even abandoned by God![78] Third, do not trust appearances. Yes, the wicked may flourish, but that does not mean God approves of them. And the pious might suffer, but that does not mean God disapproves of them. Our Lord knows the heart, and he longs for the repentance of all—he is not a respecter of persons (Ezek 33:11; Acts 10:34; Rom 2:11).

We might be tempted to consider the reformers' statements about corruption, Christ's crucifixion and the upside-down nature of the world as too clinical. "Suffering is complicated!" we say. "People do not want 'answers'; they want you to listen to them." Ronald Rittgers exposes this tendency in Reformation treatises on suffering. "Viewed as a whole, the premodern Christian consolation literature consistently directs believers to accept their suffering patiently and to make no protest against the workings of divine providence. There is no room for lament in this literature."[79]

---

[74]Scott M. Manetsch, *Calvin's Company of Pastors* (Oxford: Oxford University Press, 2012), 234. See further the overview and comment for Psalm 33 below, pp. 258-67.

[75]Kelly M. Kapic, "Faith, Hope and Love: A Theological Meditation on Suffering and Sanctification," in *Sanctification: Explorations in Theology and Practice*, ed. Kelly M. Kapic (Downers Grove, IL: IVP Academic, 2014), 224.

[76]J. Todd Billings, *Rejoicing in Lament: Wrestling with Incurable Cancer and Life in Christ* (Grand Rapids: Brazos, 2015), 17-33, esp. 20-22.

[77]Billings powerfully talks about praying to God as an act of resistance. "We pray with our Savior, 'Thy kingdom come.' In grief. In protest. And in hope. For although the world is in God's hands, things are not the way they are supposed to be" (Billings, *Rejoicing in Lament*, 75-92, here p. 77).

[78]See the commentary on Ps 22, pp. 176-77.

[79]Ronald K. Rittgers, *Reformation of Suffering: Pastoral Theology and Lay Piety in Late Medieval and Early Modern Germany* (Oxford: Oxford University Press, 2012), 258. Rittgers tempers this criticism with the acknowledgment that the reformers took seriously the fact that we suffer in Jesus Christ, who is sovereign over our suffering, see pp. 257-63, esp. 260-61.

This is indeed true of that genre. However, in their interactions with the Psalms in teaching and preaching, the reformers allow room for lament, so long as it is done *before God*. David, Calvin writes, "cries out that he is not cared for by God and yet by this very complaint he testifies . . . that his welfare was secure in the hand of God."[80] Nikolaus Selnecker, following Luther, encourages us to "run to God and cry out to him," we "should hold God to his promises."[81] Yes, we should patiently wait on the Lord, Calvin affirms, "yet God allows the faithful to bewail in prayer the grief which they experience on account of his delay."[82] Luther comforts us that "strength fades, courage fails; God remains firm."[83] These theologians try to hold the psalmist's affirmations in tension: we are in pain; we are seemingly abandoned by God; and God is true to his promises; he is near us. Lament and rejoicing are found side by side throughout the Psalter.

For the reformers, the Psalms allow us to express the heavy and profound affections and afflictions we experience. "Deep calls to deep" (Ps 42:7). Kapic restates Luther's commendation of the Psalms in this way: "We can find words to speak when we become speechless. . . . The community can speak or sing these sacred words when it does not know what to say."[84] Such songs are not to be despised; rather, these are the only songs worth having: "The world should be so well advised that in place of songs of a vain and frivolous sort, some stupid and dull, some coarse and vile, and consequently evil and harmful, used heretofore, it should accustom itself hereafter to sing these divine and heavenly songs with good King David."[85]

Textual Technicalities

Two caveats should be offered before moving on to the commentary proper. First, the text of the Psalms presents difficulties.[86] The precise order of the Psalms has long been a mystery; it seems to be several hymn collections stitched together. Also there are a number of hapax legomena in the Psalms as well as vocabulary used in strange or uncharacteristic ways (it is poetry after all). These words presented troubles for the reformers, and, for the most part, the modern biblical studies guild continues to struggle with these issues. When relevant, references to and sometimes summaries of contemporary critical commentaries have been included, so that interested readers can pursue the question further.

Second, the numbering of the Psalms has been standardized to the Masoretic text (MT); the Septuagint (LXX) and thus the Vulgate are slightly different. Some of the reformers—most notably, Bugenhagen—retained this numbering in their Psalms commentary. LXX Psalm 9 is MT Psalms

---

[80]Commentary on Psalm 13:1, CTS 8:132* (CO 31:132).

[81]Nikolaus Selnecker, *Der gantze Psalter des Königlichen Propheten Davids*, 3 vols. (Nuremberg: Christoph Heußler, 1565–1566), 1:49v.

[82]Commentary on Psalm 35:17, CTS 8:589-90* (CO 31:354).

[83]*Four Comforting Psalms for the Queen of Hungary*, LW 14:237 (WA 19:578). See further Luther's comment on Ps 5, pp. 44-50.

[84]Kapic, "Faith, Hope and Love," 224. On this idea of identifying with words that are not our own, see Benjamin Myers, *Salvation in My Pocket: Fragments of Faith and Theology* (Eugene, OR: Cascade Books, 2013), 94-95.

[85]Calvin, "The Forms of Prayers and Songs of the Church," 165 (OS 2:17-18).

[86]See Robert Alter, *Book of Psalms: A Translation with Commentary* (New York: W. W. Norton, 2007), xiii-xxxviii, esp. xxxv-xxxiii; Goldingay, *Psalms*, 1:24-46; Hans-Joachim Kraus, *Psalms 1–59: A Commentary*, Continental Commentaries, trans. Hilton C. Oswald (Minneapolis: Augsburg, 1988), 13-21.

9–10; LXX Psalm 113 is MT Psalms 114–115; LXX Psalms 114–115 is MT Psalms 116 (vv. 1-9 and vv. 10-19, respectively); LXX Psalms 146–147 is MT Psalm 147 (vv. 1-11 and vv. 12-20, respectively).

The Psalms have always been a book of worship—a service book of sorts. In these songs Israelites learned "the meaning of the testimonies and statutes and rules that the Lord their God commanded them" (Deut 6:20-25). The church also appropriated these hymns as reminders of liberations past, present and future. Medieval monks and nuns measured their days with the Psalms—some even singing the whole Psalter in a day.[87] And the reformers sought to popularize this monastic habit, reorienting Christian worship around the Psalms. For these teachers and preachers, the reading of Scripture could not be bifurcated into study and worship. Studying Scripture objectively without a worshipful posture would have been of no benefit to them indeed, it would have been detrimental to the interpretative process.

The reformers and their parishioners cherished the Psalms as indispensable to that worshipful posture.[88] For them these hymns are not mere words on paper, mere chronicles of past miseries and victories; they are prayers, petitions and promises for the people of God, *for us*. Here with the Spirit as our guide, we are invited into the pain and suffering as well as the victory and triumph of Jesus and his followers. Only in Christ will we learn who we really are. The Psalter offers a dynamic entryway into that relationship. Luther summarizes well how the people of the Reformation felt about this book: "God's Psalms book is the most excellent. How God demonstrates his power in weakness! At no time have I understood the Psalter less than now. It is a great book."[89]

Herman J. Selderhuis

---

[87]Hall, *Worshiping with the Church Fathers*, 89.
[88]"If the poor Genevan citizen had any book, it was just as likely to be a Psalter as a Bible or catechism" (John D. Witvliet and Nathan Bierma, "Liturgy," in *The Calvin Handbook*, ed. Herman J. Selderhuis [Grand Rapids: Eerdmans, 2009], 413).
[89]WATR 4:297, no. 4406.

COMMENTARY ON PSALMS 1–72

OVERVIEW: Our commentators maintain that the chief composer of these hymns, the Holy Spirit, inspired diverse cantors to sing lauds and laments to the Lord so that believers in every age would be strengthened and consoled by the divine promises of Christ, his example and the example of the saints. Here are prophecies of Christ's life, death, resurrection and ascension—even the doctrine of his two natures in the unity of his person is revealed in the Psalms! Here is the full spectrum of human emotion: the highest of highs and the lowest of lows. The Psalms are a précis not only of Scripture—the Bible in miniature, as it were—but also of the soul. Readers of the Psalms learn how their forebears in faith in the context of the divine covenant communicated to God in every event and emotion; they teach us to rue and to rejoice. But, the reformers assert, as with any other part of Scripture, readers of the Psalms must read discerningly: some psalms contain prayers and praises, others instructions and promises, and all contain law and gospel. Each psalm must be read according to its genre; otherwise the church will misunderstand and misapply them. By reading or singing the Psalms in the context of Christ's gift and example, not only will you learn to know Christ and his church but also you will come to know yourself.

Before delving into the commentary proper, the reformers—some explicitly, some implicitly— sketch their methodological approaches to the Psalms. All agree that exegesis apart from the Holy Spirit, the Scripture's ultimate author, is futile. While there are intimations about typology in the Psalms, especially David typifying Christ "our spiritual David," the commentators are not entirely agreed about how to do this typology (keep in mind the different genres; some of the selections are from commentaries, others from sermons). For example, Calvin and other Reformed theologians (e.g., Sebastian Münster and Moïse Amyraut) tend to distinguish carefully the historical David and Jesus of Nazareth, though without separating them. Luther and his disciples as well as Catholic commentators (though Cardinal Cajetan can surprise) demonstrate a more immediate christological interpretation, while not discarding the historical situatedness of David and the other psalmists. Both approaches agree that history is important; however, the Reformed in general would see history as augmenting the spirit of the text, and Lutherans would balk at the idea that any of Scripture's history can be correctly understood without first knowing who Christ is and what he has done. Still, they would agree that these hymns are Christ's and thus they belong to his body, the church. His village rings out with these songs.

Prolegomena: An Anatomy of Scripture and the Soul

THE ANCIENT DIVISION OF PSALMS INTO FIVE BOOKS. THE ENGLISH ANNOTATIONS: This book—cited as "the Psalms" by Christ himself and by Peter, which confirms the antiquity of this inscription, preventing scrupulousness in titles and quotations—has from ancient times by both Jews and Christians been subdivided into five books: the first ends at Psalm 41, the second at Psalm 72, the third at Psalm 89, the fourth at Psalm 106, and the fifth includes all the rest until the end. Most justify this subdivision for this reason: the concluding words in those final psalms are "Amen and Amen" in the first three books, a single "Amen" in the fourth, and a "Hallelujah" in the last. Other reasons are given too, but none of them are very likely or satisfactory. (See the comment on Psalms 41 and 72.) However, being ancient, this division should not be unknown to those who read ancient books. Other divisions according to the order of reading or singing, called *kathismata*, etc., which according to various churches and rites have been different, we here omit. PREFACE TO ANNOTATIONS ON THE PSALMS.[1]

DAVID IS NOT THE SOLE AUTHOR BUT THE PRINCIPAL AUTHOR. THE ENGLISH ANNOTATIONS: The author of this book—we mean the immediate and secondary author beside the original and general author of all true Scriptures, the Holy Spirit—though named in some other passages of Scripture as David . . . is not expressed here in the title. The truth is they are not all David's psalms. Some were composed before him, others long after him—as will be shown later. . . . To make good this title and inscription, it is enough that the greater part of the Psalms were composed by David, and others were collected by him (as is generally believed) into one book and appointed or fitted for public use. PREFACE TO ANNOTATIONS ON THE PSALMS.[2]

THE PSALMS COMPRISE THE ENTIRETY OF SCRIPTURE. MARTIN LUTHER: The Psalter ought to be a precious and beloved book because it promises Christ's death and resurrection so clearly—and depicts his kingdom and the condition and nature of all Christendom—that it might well be called a little Bible. Most beautifully and briefly it contains everything that is in the entire Bible; it is made into a fine enchiridion or handbook. It seems to me that the Holy Spirit

himself wanted to take the trouble to compile a short Bible and example-book of all Christendom or all the saints, so that anyone who could not read the whole Bible would have here almost an entire summary of it, comprised in one dear little book. . . .

Where do we find finer words of joy than in the psalms of praise and thanksgiving? There you look into the hearts of all the saints, as into fine and pleasant gardens, yes, as into heaven—what fine, cordial and merry flowers spring up there from all sorts of beautiful and joyous thoughts toward God because of his good deeds! On the other hand, where do you find deeper, more miserable, more pitiful words of sorrow than in the psalms of lamentation? There again you look into the hearts of all the saints, as into death, yes, as into hell. How dark and gloomy it is there, with all kinds of disturbing glimpses of the wrath of God! So, too, when they speak of fear and hope, they use such words that no painter could so depict fear or hope, and no Cicero or orator could so portray them. . . . This is the reason why the Psalter is the book of all saints. Everyone, in whatever situation he may be, finds in it psalms and words that fit his situation—they fit so precisely, it is as if they were placed there just for his sake, so that he himself could not put it any better, nor could he find or wish for anything better. . . .

In sum, do you want to see the holy Christian church painted in living color and form, comprised in one little picture? Then pick up the Psalter! There you have a fine, bright, pure mirror that will show you what Christendom is. Yes, you will even find yourself in it and the true *gnōthi seauton* ("know yourself"), as well as God himself and all creatures. PREFACE TO THE PSALMS (1545).[3]

THE PSALMS ARE ESSENTIAL FOR THE CHRISTIAN LIFE. RUDOLF GWALTHER: Even though all Scripture—which is from God and is of one Spirit

---

[1]Downame, ed., *Annotations*, 4Z3r*; citing Lk 20:42; Acts 1:20; Lk 24:44.

[2]Downame, ed., *Annotations*, 4Z3r*; citing Mk 12:36; Acts 1:16; 4:25; Lk 20:42.

[3]LW 35:254, 255-57* (WADB 10,1:99-101, 103, 105); cf. Plass, *What Luther Says*, 2:999-1000.

and origin—serves us as manifold teaching, instruction, reproof, correction and consolation, nevertheless in the entire Bible we have no book in which all these parts as well as each individually will be found so bright and clear along with the abundant fruit and powerful assistance of the Holy Spirit as in the Psalter.

Thus, not without reason, some have called the Psalter a brief but complete version and summary of the entire Bible—or even a little Bible. . . . All this we find briefly and simply summarized in this book of Psalms. In it all the secrets of Christ are foreshadowed for us, namely, his eternal divinity, his assumed humanity, the entire course of his life, his teaching and his miraculous deeds—through which, even before he became human, he sustained and protected his church—his suffering and death and burial, his magnificent resurrection from the dead, his kingdom and eternal glory which he possesses eternally with God his Father in one substance. As well, we have numerous examples of true believers in Christ and his chosen servants. In them we can see—through the mediation of the same salvation received in Christ—how they served him, the gratitude they showed him for his gifts and good deeds, how they called on God in their grief, the firm hope they sustained in all suffering, what delight and joy they received in the multiplication of his kingdom and honor, in short how they spoke with God himself in every situation. From this, their spirit, mind and heart can be experienced and known as in a bright mirror.

Here we observe how they were often afflicted under the cross because of human stupidity and with what consolations they reestablished themselves again. These are written for all people as an example, so that they would not be frightened by the same trials; rather, through firm confidence in the divine mercy they would seize strong consolation. And because we human beings have no more precious and essential gift than prayer—through which we come before God and can speak with him about all the things that burden us—the Psalter should be for us a dear and precious treasure indeed! It contains all sorts of prayers and

teaches us with what attitude, words and thoughts we should cry out to God. DEDICATORY LETTER TO WOLFFGANG WEIDNER (1557).[4]

THE PSALMS TEACH US HOW TO SPEAK TO GOD. ANTHONY GILBY: For this purpose this book of Psalms is most necessary for every Christian: not to read them merely for fashion and custom—either in a known or unknown language (which would be to take God's name in vain)—but to meditate on them in our hearts, and so by earnest and continual invocation and heartfelt prayers move the Lord our God to mercy, as his holy servants before us have always found mercy by the same means. While all other Scripture teaches us what God says to us, these prayers of the saints teach us what we should say to God, how we must prepare ourselves to appear before his majesty— both in prosperity and adversity. Therefore they should be used daily with great reverence and humility. . . . Meditate on these psalms by the same Spirit with David, so that you might feel true comfort in all troubles of mind and body (as David did) and so in the end be crowned in the heavens with David and reign forever with Christ our spiritual David in everlasting glory. DEDICATORY EPISTLE TO THE ENGLISH EDITION OF BEZA'S *PSALMES OF DAUID* (1572).[5]

THE PSALMS ARE AN ANATOMY OF THE SOUL. JOHN CALVIN: I have been accustomed to call this book, I think not inappropriately, "An Anatomy of all the Parts of the Soul." For there is not an emotion of which anyone can be conscious that is not here represented as in a mirror. Or rather, the Holy Spirit has presented in a living image all the griefs, sorrows, fears, doubts, hopes, cares, perplexities, in short, all the emotions with which human minds are often disturbed. The other parts of Scripture contain the commandments which God charged his servants to announce to us. But here the prophets themselves are speaking with

---

[4]Gwalther, *Psalter*, 4r-5r; citing 2 Tim 3:16-17.
[5]Gilby, "Dedicatory Epistle," in *Psalmes of Dauid*, a3v, a4v*.

God. They are laying bare all their inner thoughts and feelings. They are calling or compelling each of us to examine ourselves lest one of the many infirmities of which we are guilty and one of the many sins with which we overflow remain secret. It is certainly a rare and remarkable achievement when after every lair is shaken out, the heart is led into the light, purged from that most wicked infection, hypocrisy.

In short, if calling on God is one of the principal means of securing our salvation, then no other better and surer rule can be asked for than from this book. Thus, anyone who grows in understanding it will attain a good part of heavenly doctrine. Genuine prayer proceeds first from our sense of need, then from faith in God's promises. So here in this book, readers will become very conscious of their wicked feelings, and they will be admonished how to seek their cure. Truly whatever is able to encourage us whenever we pray to God is demonstrated in this book. Not only are there promises here, but between God's invitation and the flesh's impediments, there stands One in the middle for us; he prepares himself for prayer. Thus, if various doubts ever attack us, let us learn to struggle until our mind soars unhindered to God. And not only this, but in any doubt, fear and panic let us labor in prayer until, consoled, it no longer disturbs us. PREFACE TO THE READER.[6]

OBSERVATIONS FOR THE PRUDENT READER OF THE PSALMS. PHILIPP MELANCHTHON: In Ephesians 4, it is written that by divine help the ministry of heavenly teaching is to be preserved and that constantly prophets, pastors and doctors be raised up lest the light of heavenly teaching, true invocation of God and true worship be extinguished, and that the whole human race would not rush into darkness, error and eternal

destruction. And a succession of times in the church of God henceforth shows examples of this vast gift of God all the way from our first parents. Immediately leaders and doctors of the church were raised up: after Seth, Enoch, then Noah, Shem, Abraham, Joseph, Moses, then Samuel. Nathan succeeded Samuel, followed by David and many others. For that age was the most prosperous of all, and most greatly ornamented with wisdom and victories. Then followed Elijah, and Elisha whom Isaiah saw, and Jeremiah saw Isaiah. Daniel followed Jeremiah. All of these were doctors through whom God by their testimony published his revelations, illuminated his doctrine and wanted his law and promises to be interpreted against the judgments of hypocrites. He wanted them to be witnesses of the correct interpretation. Thus God bestows on the church his own Word and the gift of interpretation.

Therefore as often as we think about the writing of a particular prophet, the whole government of the church should be contemplated by the mind, the call of the prophets should be considered, so that we may know the sermons of the prophets to be the voice of God by which he revealed himself to the human race, and that the prophet is the preacher or governor called directly by God, confirmed by reliable miracles and a witness of the correct interpretation of the law and divine promises concerning Christ the Mediator. And the miraculous testimonies of each prophet are their teachings. Let us thus therefore hear David's sermons as the voice of God singing from heaven with which God truly and certainly reveals himself to the church, and by these sermons may we strengthen faith and prayer in us and give thanks to God for this revelation and for this doctrine. May this therefore be the foundation of exposition, that the Psalms are truly the teachings of God, as it is said in 2 Peter 1 concerning the prophets.

Then you must distinguish the subject matter. As the whole teaching of the church is distributed into two parts—namely, law and gospel—so also are the Psalms distinguished. Some contain more

---

[6]CTS 8:xxxvi-xxxviii* (CO 31:15-17). In the preface to his Psalms commentary, Calvin wrote his most extensive and candid autobiographical statement, in which he identified with David and emphasized the power of God to overcome all obstacles. See further Alezandre Ganoczy, *The Young Calvin*, trans. David Foxgrover and Wade Provo (Philadelphia: Westminster, 1987), 241-66.

of the teaching of the law, that is, commandments and exhortations. Others are better interpreted as the proper promise of the gospel concerning Christ. Others belong entirely to the didactic[7] or demonstrative genre, like Psalm 110, which is an interpretation of the promise concerning Christ. For it is the special office of prophets to be witnesses concerning the coming Messiah and interpreters of the promises. Other psalms are of the persuasive type, such as those that preach about good works, console the pious in their afflictions or contain prayers, like Psalm 51, "Have mercy on me, O God."

These types must be distinguished so that they are understood as the guidelines for the Psalms, that is, so that the readers may understand what the Holy Spirit wants to teach and accomplish in each psalm and may accommodate their hearts and minds to that movement which is set forth, embrace the teaching by faith, be frightened by reading the threats, be sustained by the promises, pray ardently and truly expect the mitigation of their calamities, remember the manifest testimonies taught to the church for nourishing and strengthening faith, as the apostle confirms the resurrection of Christ from Psalm 16. This distinction in type brings a great amount of light to the Psalms so that the prudent reader may easily understand them. PROLEGOMENA TO THE PSALMS.[8]

ALL SCRIPTURE IS LITERALLY ABOUT JESUS. MARTIN LUTHER: Every prophecy and every prophet must be understood as referring to Christ the Lord, except where it is clear from plain words that someone else is spoken of. For thus he himself says: "Search the Scriptures! it is they that bear

witness to me." Otherwise it is most certain that the searchers will not find what they are searching for. For that reason some explain very many psalms not prophetically but historically. . . . No wonder, because they are far away from Christ (that is, from the truth). "But we have the mind of Christ," the apostle says.

Whatever is said literally concerning the Lord Jesus Christ as to his person must be understood allegorically of a help that is like him and of the church conformed to him in all things. And at the same time this must be understood tropologically of any spiritual and inner person against the flesh and the outer person. PREFACE TO THE FIRST PSALMS LECTURES (1513–1515).[9]

HEBREW TRANSCENDS EVERY OTHER LANGUAGE. MARTIN LUTHER: The Hebrew language is so rich that no other language is able to capture its sense satisfactorily. It has so many words for singing, praising, worshiping, honoring, rejoicing, mourning, etc., for which we hardly have one! And especially in divine and holy matters it is rich with words—indeed it has ten names by which it calls God, while we have no more than the single word "God," so that it should clearly be called a holy language. On account of this no translation can be so free as it sounds in the Hebrew itself without additional flowery words which we call *figures*—in which Hebrew also transcends every language. PREFACE TO THE PSALTER (1524).[10]

THE PSALMS ARE THE MUSIC OF CHRIST'S VILLAGE. JAKOB DACHSER: All people in all their fears and needs should only have God through Christ as their one refuge, as Psalm 51 teaches; for he is able to act, help and give abundantly—mercy, help, comfort and salvation in all that we ask. Thus it is surely right that all people also thank, praise and worship God for manifest and demonstrated good deeds, as David sings and teaches in Psalm 118. But neither can happen in a more salutary way

---

[7]Melanchthon added this type of speech (*genus didaskalikon*) to the three Aristotelian rhetorical types (i.e., deliberative, forensic and epideictic). This genus focused on basic, simple information of a subject matter. See further Volkhard Wels, "Melanchthon's Textbooks on Dialectic and Rhetoric as Complementary Parts of a Theory of Argumentation," in *Scholarly Knowledge: Textbooks in Early Modern Europe*, ed. Emidio Campi (Geneva: Droz, 2008), 151-53.
[8]MO 13:1017-18; citing Eph 4:11-16; 2 Pet 1:21; Acts 13:35-37 (cf. Acts 2:22-28); 16:10.

[9]LW 10:7* (WA 3:13); citing Jn 5:39; 1 Cor 2:16.
[10]WADB 10,1:94.

than when we cry out to, praise and worship God with such pure, salutary and believing affections, attitudes and thoughts as those that the Holy Spirit has exemplified for us in holy Scripture, especially in the psalms of David. . . .

And so in their sermons the holy men of God—who remained true to the church of Christ, even in their time—diligently exhorted Christians to these songs of praise and deterred them from impure, indecent, devilish love songs. . . . And thus Saint Jerome . . . said: "In the dear village of Christ, there we sing nothing other than the psalms—whichever way you turn. The farmer, when he takes the plough in his hands, praises God and sings a joyous *Alleluia*. A reaper with sweat running down his face refreshes himself with a joyous psalm. And a vinedresser, as he cuts the vines, sings something blessed and comforting from the psalms of David. *These*," he says, "are our hymns and songs." Preface to the Christian Congregation (1557).[11]

The Vivifying and Salvific Music of the Psalter. John Fisher: All we Christian people are bound by very duty to give great and immortal thanks to the holy prophet David who so diligently has left in writing his Psalms, most godly to be read by us and our posterity. And he did this, it seems to me, for three reasons. First, by these holy Psalms the minds of sinners might be raised up and excited, as by a sweet melody, to receive and take the study and learning of virtue. Second, if any have fallen to great and abominable sins, yet they should not despair but put their whole and steadfast hope of forgiveness in God. Third, they might use these holy Psalms as letters of supplication and speedful prayers for remission and forgiveness to be purchased of Almighty God.

The Pythagoreans . . . were accustomed every morning when they should rise from their beds to hear the sound of a harp, by which their spirits

might be more quick and ready to receive their studies; thinking nothing more profitable than it to the free and noble exciting of their minds. For doubtless their sluggish and slothful minds by that melody were made quick and merry. . . . Let us therefore turn again to these sweet melodies of our prophet David, which he sometimes sang with his godly harp, by which we may chase and put away all sluggishness and sloth put into us by wretched spirits. In these sweet sounds we shall hear such an abundance and diversity of tunes as ever was heard before. For sometimes he speaks of God, sometimes of the devil, sometimes of holy angels, sometimes of damned spirits, now of hell pains and sometimes of the pains of Purgatory, other times the righteousness of God, sometimes of his great mercy, now of dread, then of hope, sometimes of sorrow and weeping, sometimes of gladness and comfort, sometimes of the soul, sometimes of the cursing of vices and sins, sometimes of the praising of virtues, other times of good and righteous people and then of the wicked and unrighteous. By this diversity of melody, if sinners cannot be raised up from the sleep of sin and excited to godly watchings, they are to be thought as very dead. The Third Penitential Psalm.[12]

Teach Us to Sing Thy Praise! John Donne:

> Eternal God, (for whom whoever dare
> Seek new expressions, do the circle square,
> And thrust into strait corners of poor wit
> Thee, who art cornerless and infinite)
> I would but bless thy Name, not name thee
>   now;
> (And thy gifts are as infinite as thou)
> Fixe we our praises therefore on this one,
> That, as thy blessed Spirit fell upon
> These Psalms first Author in a cloven tongue;
> (For 'twas a double power by which he sung
> The highest matter in the noblest form)
> So thou hast cleft that Spirit, to perform
> That work again, and shed it, here, upon

---

[11]Dachser, *Gsang büchlin*, A1r, A2r-v; citing Chrysostom, Homily 9 on Colossians, NPNF 13:300-303; Jerome, "To Marcella," Letter 46, NPNF² 6:64-65.

[12]Fisher, *Commentary on the Seven Penitential Psalms*, 1:60-61*.

Two, by their bloods and by thy Spirit one;
A brother and a sister made by thee
The organ where thou art the Harmony.
Two that make one John Baptist's holy voice,
And who that Psalm, *Now let the isles rejoice,*
Have both translated, and apply'd it too,
Both told us what, and taught us how to do.
They show us islanders our joy, our King,
They tell us *why,* and teach us *how* to sing;
Make all this All, three choirs, heaven, earth
    and spheres;
The first, heaven, hath a song, but no man hears,
The spheres have music, but they have no tongue,
Their harmony is rather danc'd than sung;
But our third choir, to which the first gives ear,
(For angels learn by what the church does here)
This choir hath all. The organist is he
Who hath tun'd God and Man, the organ we:
The songs are these, which heavens high holy
    Muse
Whisper'd to David, David to the Jews:
And David's successors in holy zeal,
In forms of joy and art do re-reveal
To us so sweetly and sincerely too,
That I must not rejoice as I would do
When I behold that these Psalms are become

So well attir'd abroad, so ill at home,
So well in chambers, in thy church so ill,
As I can scarce call that reform'd until
This be reform'd; Would a whole state present
A lesser gift than some one man hath sent?
And shall our church, unto our Spouse and
    King
More hoarse, more harsh than any other, sing?
For *that* we pray, we praise thy name for *this,*
Which, by this Moses and this Miriam, is
Already done; and as those Psalms we call
(Though some have other Authors) David's all:
So though some have, some may some Psalms
    translate,
We thy Sydnean Psalms shall celebrate,
And, till we come th'Extemporal song to sing,
(Learn'd the first hower, that we see the King,
Who hath translated those translators) may
These their sweet learned labors, all the way
Be as our tuning; that, when hence we part,
We may fall in with them, and sing our part.

UPON THE TRANSLATION OF THE PSALMS BY
SIR PHILIP SYDNEY AND THE COUNTESS OF
PEMBROKE, HIS SISTER.[13]

---

[13]Donne, *Poems of John Donne,* 348-50.

1:1-6 THE TWO WAYS

[1] Blessed is the man[a]
　　who walks not in the counsel of the wicked,
nor stands in the way of sinners,
　　nor sits in the seat of scoffers;
[2] but his delight is in the law[b] of the LORD,
　　and on his law he meditates day and night.

[3] He is like a tree
　　planted by streams of water
that yields its fruit in its season,
　　and its leaf does not wither.

In all that he does, he prospers.
[4] The wicked are not so,
　　but are like chaff that the wind drives away.

[5] Therefore the wicked will not stand in the
　　judgment,
　　nor sinners in the congregation of the
　　　righteous;
[6] for the LORD knows the way of the righteous,
　　but the way of the wicked will perish.

a The singular Hebrew word for *man* (*ish*) is used here to portray a representative example of a godly person　b Or *instruction*

OVERVIEW: For our Reformation commentators, this brief psalm serves as a significant introduction to the whole Psalter, and it thus establishes the appropriate attitude with which one should approach the Psalms. By pointing to the blessings of God's law, this psalm encourages believers to take delight in, meditate on and cherish the law of the Lord, which for the reformers corresponds with their emphasis on the Word of God, as expressed by the principle of *sola Scriptura*. In addition, they point out, this opening psalm lays before the reader the two paths of life—and their respective consequences—very clearly: the pious will be blessed, and the impious will receive God's just punishment. These exegetes wield christological interpretation throughout the Psalms—and the whole of Scripture—and the introductory psalm is no exception.[1] Here they understand Christ as the blessed man and the water that refreshes and sustains life. Although the worldly condition of believers may not always reflect God's blessing, and although the reality of sin persists, by God's grace and faith in Jesus Christ they will delight in God's Word and follow God's way.

WHY IS THERE NO TITLE? FELIX PRATENSIS: The first psalm has no title because, according to the teaching of a great number of men, it is an introduction to all the psalms; according to some of them, not David but Ezra himself composed this psalm. THE HEBREW PSALTER.[2]

PSALM 1 AS RULE AND GUIDE TO ALL PSALMS. JOHN CALVIN: Whoever collected the Psalms into one volume, whether Ezra or some other person, appears to have placed this psalm at the beginning by way of preface, in which he admonishes all believers to meditate on the law of God. The sum and substance of the whole is, blessed are those who focus on the pursuit of heavenly wisdom; but the profane despisers of God, although for a time they may consider themselves happy, shall eventually come to a most miserable end. COMMENTARY ON THE PSALMS.[3]

THE SCOPE OF SCRIPTURE. NIKOLAUS SELNECKER: This psalm is an appropriate entrance into the whole Psalter, for it has the true scope of all the holy Scriptures, namely, it preaches about

---

[1]The reformers did not apply christological interpretation in a uniform manner; see the Introduction to the Psalms above, *xlviii-lii*.

[2]Pratensis, *Psalterium*, 1r.
[3]CTS 8:1* (CO 31:37).

the Word of God and admonishes us that we should cherish and love it, and we should gladly listen to and learn from it. The Word of God alone is the beautiful garden of delight and paradise in which we are able to have all our joy, delight and refreshment in this life, and should bear our fruits and live.

Here the prophet also makes a fine, clear distinction between what is godliness and what is an ungodly character and life. Ungodly character is described in the first verse and is called "a counsel of the ungodly," "a way of sinners" and "a seat of scoffers." Godliness and the fear of God are called, first, avoiding false teaching and coarse living, second, having delight in the law of the Lord, and third, freely and without reserve confessing and talking about the same out loud. Whoever possesses such godliness, to that person the Holy Spirit promises all blessing from God, happiness and well-being, victory over all temptation of the devil, the flesh, the world and whatever else can be mentioned. The others, however, who despise, slander or persecute God's Word, he threatens all harm, their final demise and destruction in body and soul. THE WHOLE PSALTER.[4]

THE REWARD, GLORY AND JOY OF THIS PSALM.
DESIDERIUS ERASMUS: Despite its extreme brevity, this psalm deals with vital and universal themes. It begins by offering a great reward, bliss; it appeals to everyone to shun vice and turn to the pursuit of virtue, and by obeying divine law to be renewed, to flower again in Christ, in whom they are already engrafted through baptism. Second, it enhances the glorious destiny of the pious by contrasting it with the very different lot of the impious, even in this mortal life. Finally, it reveals the happiness which awaits the pious in the Last Judgment and the punishment which awaits the impious. EXPOSITION OF PSALM 1.[5]

1:1-2 *Shun the Wicked, Choose the Law*

CHRIST IS THIS BLESSED MAN. MARTIN LUTHER: The first psalm speaks about Christ—literally—thus: *Blessed is the man.* He is the only blessed One and the only Man from whose fullness they have all received that they might be blessed and men and everything that follows in this psalm. He is "the firstborn among many brothers," "the firstfruits of those who have fallen asleep," so that he might also be the firstfruits of those who are awake, namely, in the Spirit. For it is also written in the roll of this book concerning him, to do the will of God. He is a man in a threefold sense: first, because he is a man of manly virtue; second, because he is not a boy to be educated but is manly in grace; third, because he has a bride. This is the Man whom a woman has embraced, because as a bridegroom he went forth not only after but also from his chamber, having his own bride from the beginning. FIRST PSALMS LECTURES (1513–1515).[6]

UNITED TO CHRIST, ALL BLESSING AND UNDERSTANDING IS OURS. JOHANNES BUGEN-HAGEN: The blessed man, who is here described, is first, Christ the Lord, who, on account of us, was made human, second, any person who is in Christ. But neither with this do we say that you should consider excluded those believers who died before Christ's incarnation: for these also were in Christ, who all expected that seed of the woman which would crush the serpent's head (Gen 3) and the seed of Abraham in whom all the kindred of the earth would be blessed (Gen 22). Christ proposed this aim to you, as it is said in Luke 2. See that you do not oppose this sign. He has this desire for the law of God day and night, that is, ceaselessly, and that is necessary for you if you want to be a blessed person. May God give you, by the Spirit of Christ, this desired and continued meditation and delight in the Word of God (because it is in a spiritual person alone), which will increase as long

---

[4]Selnecker, *Der gantze Psalter*, 1:1r. Selnecker often reused the arguments of the Psalms from Luther's *Summaries of the Psalms* (1531–1533); see WA 38:18-69. They will be included as part of the three new volumes of Luther's Psalms work, LW 64–66.
[5]CWE 63:11-13.

---

[6]LW 10:11* (WA 3:15); citing Jn 1:16; Rom 8:29; 1 Cor 15:20; Ps 40:8; 19:6.

as you live here, so that you may never in this life cease to thirst and hunger for righteousness. Otherwise you will be destitute of all blessedness, according to Matthew 5, "Blessed are those who hunger and thirst after righteousness." And according to the Magnificat, "He filled those who were hungry with good things, and the rich he sent away empty." In Christ is perfection, in you, imperfection, and what you have is from God, and you have it through Christ. Learn through Christ to hunger after righteousness and then you will see how much you still lack from that blessedness. Meanwhile, human creatures do not understand the things which are of God, for they cannot. "For they are fools and cannot understand." For whoever does not believe himself to be one with Christ, that person will never understand the Psalms. INTERPRETATION OF THE PSALMS.[7]

WOMEN ARE NOT EXCLUDED FROM THIS PROMISE. DESIDERIUS ERASMUS: The psalm uses the word *man*, but does this exclude woman from a share in bliss? Not at all. In the kingdom of heaven sex and status count for nothing. In Christ there is no master or slave, no man or woman, no rich or poor, but a new creature. It is true that in mystical writing the superior part of the mind, which the philosophers call reason and Paul the spirit, is often described symbolically as "man"; similarly, the word *woman* describes the weaker part of our mind, which the philosophers call instinct and Christians the flesh.[8] It is relevant to this that at the world's beginning woman was ordered to obey her husband and to follow him in acts of worship, as she had led him by her example into sin. . . . It requires a true man to scorn all that is terrifying in this world, to reject and trample underfoot all that is stimulating or tempting and to approach Christ along the narrow path of virtue. Believe me, this is no task for the soft or the unwarlike. If nothing can separate you from the love of Christ, be it the

glitter of gold, the snares of pleasure, the affection of friends, disgrace in the eyes of men, or indeed the sword, hunger, death, life or angels: then, clearly, you are a true man—even if you are a woman. EXPOSITION OF PSALM 1.[9]

FLEE THE COMPANY OF UNBELIEVERS! JOHN CALVIN: He starts with a declaration of his abhorrence of the wicked in order to teach us how impossible it is for anyone to apply his mind to meditation on God's laws who has not first withdrawn and separated from the society of unbelievers. Such an admonition surely is needed. We see how thoughtlessly human beings will throw themselves into the snares of Satan—how few guard against the enticements of sin! In order not to be caught unaware, it is necessary to remember that the world is fraught with deadly corruption, and that the first step to living well is to renounce the company of unbelievers; otherwise it is sure to infect us with its own pollution. COMMENTARY ON THE PSALMS.[10]

THE WICKED ARE DRIVEN BY PAIN. RUDOLF GWALTHER: The godless are called *rĕšāîm* ["wicked"] by the Hebrews, because they are of a distressed, unstable disposition—without the fear of God they are ruled only by their afflictions. For this reason no one—who longs for salvation and peace of conscience—should follow their advice. THE PSALTER.[11]

TRUE BLESSING IS ONLY IN THE WORD. HIERONYMUS WELLER VON MOLSDORF: The world preaches that the blessed are those who flourish in this life and abound in all life's comforts. The Holy Spirit, however, proclaims that those who are truly blessed and forever joyous are those who embrace the Word of God in earnest and count it among their delights, and who regard it as

---

[7]Bugenhagen, *In librvm Psalmorvm interpretatio*, IV; citing Gen 3:15; 22; Lk 2:8-20, 28-32; Mt 5:6; Lk 1:53; 1 Cor 2:14.
[8]See RCS OT 1:53-54.
[9]CWE 63:14-15*. Luther and Cajetan also insist women are included in this promise; see WA 5:27; Cajetan, *In Sacrae Scripturae Expositionem*, 3:6.
[10]CTS 8:2* (CO 31:37).
[11]Gwalther, *Der Psalter*, IV.

their greatest treasure. They love to hear God's Word! The reason for this he gives below: the Word of God provides relief in every kind of affliction and trouble. That is, it brings a sure and steadfast consolation; human traditions do the opposite. BRIEF COMMENT ON PSALM 1.[12]

GOD'S LAW DOES NOT IMPRISON US BUT FREES US. CARDINAL CAJETAN: Now, know that the Hebrew term translated here as "instruction" truly means "instruction," because the psalmist is considering what should be taught. And among the Hebrews this term was used to indicate the divine law [tôrāh] whenever it is said "instruction of the Lord." Thus, not by the act of being bound or being read to but by the act of being taught do they mean "law." And this is very fitting on account of the distinguishing mark of human laws which do not teach but bind, for divine law went forth not for the human race to be bound but to be taught by the divine light.

Accordingly, "instruction" or "law of the Lord" can be taken in two ways. First, it can be understood as what is simply and absolutely the law of the Lord. This also is twofold: the law of nature and the law of grace. The former is introduced to us; the latter is poured into our soul by the Holy Spirit, as Jeremiah and the apostle say. By the former they observe the precepts of natural law; by the latter the precepts of faith, hope and love. Second, it can be taken as the law of the Lord which was given by the Lord for a time. And these too are twofold: the law of the Old Testament, written by Moses and the prophets, and the written law of the New Testament, handed down to us through the apostles and Evangelists, by which the apostles and Evangelists observe the precepts about baptism, the Eucharist, etc., just as how by the law of the Old Testament Moses and the prophets observed ceremonial precepts, etc., for that time. COMMENTARY ON PSALM 2.[13]

PLEASURE IN SACRED LITERATURE. DESIDERIUS ERASMUS: By "law" the psalm means all the holy Scriptures; earnest study of them will assist greatly in keeping us from sin. To avoid finding pleasure in the sins of the flesh, take pleasure in the study of literature (of Sacred Literature, of course, because literature unconnected with Christ scarcely deserves the name). The one sure bulwark against all the assaults of the demons is that a person should be thoroughly and wholeheartedly imbued with the Scriptures. In them the righteous man "takes delight" each time that, scorning and rejecting all others, he gazes with wonder and love on this one true pearl; as the Gospel says: "Where your treasure lies, there will your heart be also." . . . The human heart is naturally disposed toward love and cannot remain empty of it; moreover, the lover himself becomes like the thing he loves. If someone loves the holy Scriptures, he is enraptured, changed, transfigured into God. EXPOSITION OF PSALM 1.[14]

TRUE DELIGHT COMES BY FAITH IN CHRIST. MARTIN LUTHER: Here "delight" stands, first of all, neither for ability nor for the indolent habit which was introduced from Aristotle by the new theologians in order to subvert the understanding of the Scriptures, nor for the action out of which, as they say, that ability or habit proceeds. All human nature does not have this delight, but it must necessarily come from heaven. For human nature is intent and inclined to evil, as the divine authority says. The law of the Lord is truly good, holy and just. Then it follows that human desire is the opposite of the law—even hating it and fleeing from it. When now and then human beings out of fear of punishment or desire for its promise pretend to love the law, there nevertheless remains an inward hatred of the law. Human beings cannot love it freely, for they do not love the law, because it is good, but because it profits them. . . .

This desire comes from faith in God through Jesus Christ. On the other hand, a desire which has

---

[12]Weller, *Enarratio Psalmorum*, 2.
[13]Cajetan, *In Sacrae Scripturae Expositionem*, 3:6; citing Jer 31:31-34; Heb 8:8-13; 1 Cor 13:13.

[14]CWE 63:25*; citing Mt 6:21 (cf. Lk 12:34).

been extorted through fear of punishment is servile and impetuous, while what is induced through a desire for reward is mercenary and false. However, that other desire is free, voluntary and cheerful—thus, Christ's people are called *nĕdābōt* in Hebrew, that is, willing, voluntary, free. SECOND PSALMS LECTURES (1519–1521).[15]

MEDITATING AND THINKING ARE NOT THE SAME. MARTIN LUTHER: Meditating is an exclusive trait of human beings, for even beasts appear to fancy and to think. Therefore the ability to meditate belongs to reason. There is a difference between meditating and thinking. To meditate is to think carefully, deeply and diligently, and properly it means to muse in the heart. Hence to meditate is, as it were, to stir up in the inside, or to be moved in the innermost self; therefore, one who thinks inwardly and diligently asks, discusses, etc. Such a person meditates. But one does not meditate on the law of the Lord unless one's delight was first fixed in it. For what we want and love, on that we reflect inwardly and diligently. But what we hate or despise we pass over lightly and do not desire deeply, diligently or for long. Therefore let delight be first sent into the heart as the root, and then meditation will come of its own accord. It is for this reason that the unbelievers do not meditate on the law of the Lord, because as false plants they did not take root. Instead they meditate on other things, namely, on things in which their delight is rooted, things they themselves desire and love, such as gold, honor and flesh. FIRST PSALMS LECTURES (1513–1515).[16]

MEDITATE ON THE ONE GOSPEL OF CHRIST. VALENTIN WEIGEL: To hear God's Word is not to stroll to church for the sermon on Sunday, and out of habit let the preacher give a sermon, running out before it is half-finished. Nor is it to hear five sermons in a day—as early as 5 a.m. the first, at 7 a.m. the second, at 8 a.m. the third, at 12 p.m. the

fourth and at 2 p.m. the fifth—as I myself have seen in some places and have myself experienced without knowing it. And after hearing such sermons, in the evening to go to parties or friends, to raucous celebrations or feasts. Or sometimes to read to yourself with the mouth but not with the heart, that is not God's Word. Instead to hear God's Word is to hear an internal sermon in the heart and to meditate on it with wonder for an entire week, an entire month! Yes, not to forget it for our entire life—that's how deeply it should be rooted into our heart, as David says in Psalm 1. . . . Namely, to hear, to receive, to be amazed at, to contemplate, to reflect on an article, saying or speech of Christ with great diligence and sincerity and to grasp so deeply in our heart that we are never able to forget.

Yet, you say: "There are many gospels, there are even more sermons! How can I retain such a heap and contemplate it?" Answer: There is only one possible gospel. And if you can only grasp correctly one teaching about Christ or take one saying for yourself, the same are so rich and abundant that everything else will be included with it for you. For what Christ says has hands and feet, that is, Spirit and life; he is the Second Person in the Trinity. Now whatever you take for yourself from Christ and contemplate gladly and joyously and with a good heart, you will be brought to life and illumined and justified. For his Word is life and light and penetrates into your spirit. As an iron rod lying among the coals in the furnace becomes united with the fiery heat, so also a good person is united with Christ through contemplation, reflection, and is born from God; a child of God is thus made alive, justified and holy. This power we have from the Almighty Creator and from our Redeemer, so that we are able to transform ourselves through faith, from the old creature into the new. HOUSE OR CHURCH POSTIL: FIFTH SUNDAY IN LENT.[17]

OBEDIENCE IS A MATTER OF THE HEART. JOHN CALVIN: From his characterizing the godly as

---

[15]LW 14:295* (WA 5:33); citing Gen 8:21; Ps 110:3.
[16]LW 10:17* (WA 3:19).

[17]Weigel, *Sämtliche Schriften*, 12,1:182-83.

delighting in the law of the Lord, we may learn that forced or servile obedience is not at all acceptable to God, and that only those are worthy students of the law who come to it with a cheerful heart and are so delighted with its instructions as to account nothing more desirable or delicious than to make progress therein. From this love of the law flows their constant meditation, which the prophet mentions in the last clause of the verse. For you cannot feel pleasure in the diligent study of the law unless you are truly touched by the love for it. COMMENTARY ON THE PSALMS.[18]

1:3 The Righteous Are Mighty Trees

DRINK FROM THE DEEP, CAVERNOUS CISTERN OF SCRIPTURE. DESIDERIUS ERASMUS: What will be the result? If he has done all this, this teacher of mine, says the psalm, "will be like a tree planted beside streams of water, because he will give in his season the fruit" of salutary doctrine. He will be a tree that will not bend to the buffets of fortune, a living tree, a tree watered by the abundant stream of heavenly grace, forever standing by the sacred river of Scripture. Ezekiel entered this river long ago and was amazed to find that it could not be crossed; it is immeasurably deep, and no human mind can reach to the bottom. You must be satisfied to drink from it as much as is permitted. EXPOSITION OF PSALM 1.[19]

THIS TREE NEVER WITHERS. RUDOLF GWALTHER: This tree could be taken as a palm or olive tree, whose foliage or leaves never fall. For this reason, also in Psalm 92, it stands: "The pious will be green like a palm," etc. THE PSALTER.[20]

CHRIST IS THE FOUNTAIN. HENRY AINSWORTH: In hot countries they used to plant gardens near wellsprings of water, from which farmers derived many little becks or rivers, to run on the roots of the trees set in a row, whereby

they are moistened and made fruitful (see Ezek 31:3-4; Eccl 2:6). According to this, Christ is called the "fountain of the gardens," that is, of the churches. Also, in Jeremiah 17:8 the godly person is likened to a tree planted by water, which thrusts out its roots by the river, and does not feel when the heat comes, and does not worry about the year of drought, nor ceases from yielding fruit. ANNOTATIONS ON PSALM 1:3.[21]

NO CREATURE LIVES FOR ITSELF. MARTIN LUTHER: A tree does not bear fruit for itself, but it gives its fruit to others; in fact, no creature lives for or serves only itself except human beings and the devil. The sun does not shine for itself, water does not flow for itself, etc. Thus, every creature serves the law of love, and its whole substance is in the law of the Lord. And even the members of the human body do not serve only themselves. Only the passions of the heart are wicked. The wicked heart not only gives no one what is his, serves no one, is kind to no one, but even snatches absolutely everything for itself, looking for what is its in everything, even God himself. Thus, you can correctly say that this tree is a thornbush or a wild shoot which no one cultivates, nor does it rejoice to be by streams of water. It brings forth nothing but thorns, with which it sticks, tears and chokes the fruit of all surrounding trees—even the trees themselves. It grasps, plucks and tears the clothes, hide, skin, flesh and whatever else of all who pass by. SECOND PSALMS LECTURES (1519–1521).[22]

1:4 The Wicked Are Dust

MORE WORTHLESS THAN DUNG. DESIDERIUS ERASMUS: What is more worthless than dust? What is more despicable? What is nearer to nothing? And yet, as if it were not enough to call them dust, the psalm adds: "Which the wind drives away." Nothing is more contemptible than dung, and yet a use is found for it, as manure for the

---

[18]CTS 8:4-5* (CO 31:39).
[19]CWE 63:43-44*.
[20]Gwalther, Der Psalter, iv-2r; citing Ps 92:12.

[21]Ainsworth, Annotations, 2:409*; citing Song 4:15.
[22]LW 14:300-301* (WA 5:38).

fields. But what is the value, what is the use, of dust flying through the air? EXPOSITION OF PSALM 1.[23]

THE WICKED ARE NOT IN CONTROL. THOMAS WILCOX: But what are the wicked like? They are like chaff. That is, light, unprofitable for anything and void of fruit. (It is normal in Scripture to compare the wicked with chaff.) The wind drives it away. Chaff cannot withstand the violence of the wind, but it tosses it to and fro and drives it wherever it pleases. So shall the wicked be before God's judgment—no matter how great, mighty and strong they seem before human beings.... This verse not only contains judgment against the wicked, but also by showing their punishment it teaches, yes, spurs forward the godly to a more careful life. And because the Holy Spirit compares the wicked with chaff tossed before the wind, he teaches us that although the wicked think that they are glorious and longlasting, nevertheless they are neither the one nor the other. EXPOSITION UPON PSALM 1.[24]

THE VAIN DREAMS OF THE IMPIOUS. TILEMANN HESSHUS: This is an antithesis. By this simile against the impious, the iniquitous and hypocrites—despisers of the divine Word—it threatens every kind of curse and eternal destruction. Epicureans promise themselves only happiness and the most favorable outcomes. For they rely on their own talent, power, cunning and trickery. Nor do they suppose that there is any force able to hinder their plans. Accordingly they arrogantly and audaciously proclaim their future plans. Sennacherib absolutely did not doubt that he would seize Jerusalem. Antiochus Epiphanes thought nothing was more certain than that he would annihilate the Jewish nation. Julian the Apostate convinced himself that it was already in his power to uproot the Christian religion. Such frenzied promises as they made are commonly used among the impious, but the results teach the impious that their hopes are completely futile. Therefore, lest they trust in their impiety, David warns them that although they accomplished great things, obtained victories and enlarged their empires . . . however, because they guarded themselves against the knowledge of God and did not respect God's Word, they were cursed and all their efforts were foolish and ineffective. COMMENTARY ON PSALM 1.[25]

1:5-6 The Lord's Justice

THE COMING JUST JUDGMENT OF THE REPROBATE. KONRAD PELLIKAN: In the judgment of divine justice and in the great general council of the saints . . . the wicked and licentious will not stand at all, but will fall condemned on account of their own impiety and faithlessness; they will stand before the judgment seat of Christ, the supreme Judge. And they will soon receive the sentence pronounced on them; more correctly, they will be violently dragged off into eternal fire and punishment prepared for the devil and his angels. COMMENTARY ON PSALM 1:5.[26]

DIVINE AND NATURAL JUSTICE COMPARED. JACQUES LEFÈVRE D'ÉTAPLES: The way of the just is the faith and commandments of God. . . . And the just are defined by faith and the fulfillment of divine commandments. The unjust, the opposite: who either do not keep the faith and are impious or who violate the commandments and who are sinners. And justice is faith and the preservation of divine commandments. However, injustice is not only infidelity but also the transgression of the commandments of God. And although there may be something, which philosophers define as

---

[23]CWE 63:53.
[24]Wilcox, *Godly Exposition upon the Psalmes*, 3*; citing Ps 35:5; Is 17:13; Mt 3:12.

[25]Hesshus, *Commentarius in Psalmos*, 8r. Antiochus IV Epiphanes (215–164 B.C.) was responsible for the desecration of the temple; see further 1 Macc 1; RCS OT 12:399-404. Julian the Apostate was a Roman emperor (331–363) who tried to revive paganism, against the policies of previous emperors who, since Constantine, had promoted Christianity.
[26]Pellikan, *Commentaria Bibliorum*, 4:46r.

justice—namely, "to render to each what is their own,"[27] which they further divide into distributive justice, which pertains to the duties of public officers and must be dispensed by geometric reckoning, and commutative justice, which deals with the commutation of property and is dispensed by arithmetic reckoning—nonetheless this matter is very small if you wish to compare to that which was defined before.[28] For the latter [the justice of the philosophers] is the justice of nature, but the former [the justice of the psalmist] is divine justice. Therefore as much as the divine excels over nature, so much so do justice and the just man, whom the holy declarations mention, excel over the justice and the just man with whom the philosophers are familiar. However, the vestige of divine justice is noble; it is natural and human justice. If you violate it, you will also violate divine justice, for the divine commands that the former be observed. And [divine justice] encloses it in itself, as a certain limb or part. However, if you preserve natural justice, you will not automatically have divine justice. And as the light is the formal cause of colors, so is faith the formal cause of the works of divine justice. Remove light, and even if color is present in its raw substance, it is not useful for vision. Remove faith, and all the works will be useless for eternal salvation but will remain in perpetual darkness. Therefore let Christ the Lord, who alone is truly blessed and truly just, grant to us that we may at last be revived through true justice to the true light, and we may walk on the path which he who is blessed above all things knows. Amen. FIVEFOLD PSALTER: ANNOTATIONS ON PSALM 1:5.[29]

REFLECT BLESSEDNESS IN YOUR MANNER OF LIFE. DESIDERIUS ERASMUS: The psalm did not say that the impious would be destroyed, but rather "the path of the impious"; they themselves will survive the punishment but will be thwarted of their desires; they will not obtain what they turned everything upside down to achieve, and, in fact, completely the opposite will happen. Therefore, if we wish to acquire that most blessed title of "blessed man" let us ensure that it is not only in our confessions and our acts of worship, but also in our lives and our deeds, that we reflect the only source of bliss, Christ, to whom be praise and glory without end. Amen. EXPOSITION OF PSALM 1.[30]

THINGS ARE NOT ALWAYS AS THEY SEEM. JOHN CALVIN: According to all outward appearance, the servants of God may derive no advantage from their uprightness; but as it is the special office of God to defend them and take care of their safety, they must be happy under his protection. And from this we may also conclude that, as he is the sure avenger of wickedness, although, for a time, he may seem to hide himself, yet in the end he will visit the unbelievers with destruction. Therefore, instead of allowing ourselves to be deceived with their imaginary felicity, let us, in circumstances of distress, always have before our eyes the providence of God, to whom it belongs to settle the affairs of the world and to bring it back to the right order. COMMENTARY ON THE PSALMS.[31]

GOD'S HIDDEN RIGHTEOUSNESS. MARTIN LUTHER: The way of the impious, he says, is beautiful so that among human beings they seem to stand tall in judgment and council. But whoever is

---

[27]See Plato, *Republic* 1.331e; Cicero, *Laws* 1.15.

[28]For the distinction between distributive justice (which deals with justice between the community as a whole) and commutative justice (which deals with justice between two individuals) see Aristotle, *Nichomachean Ethics*, book 5, esp. 5.4.3, where Aristotle clarifies the difference between the geometric and arithmetic versions of justice. Thomas Aquinas adopted this distinction; see his *Summa Theologica*, 2.2.q.61.

[29]Lefèvre, *Quincuplum Psalterium*, 5v-6r. To answer the question "Why?", Aristotle distinguishes four causes through which the nature of things can be understood: the material cause—the

material of which a thing consists; the formal cause—the form of the thing, encompassing its basic attributes; the efficient cause—the thing which brings about motion or change; and the final cause—the reason for which a thing is done. For a statue, the material cause is the stone from which it is made; the formal cause is the shape that it takes once it has been crafted; the efficient cause is the sculptor carving it; and the final cause may be to preserve a memory, to make money or to represent beauty.

[30]CWE 63:62-63*.

[31]CTS 8:8* (CO 31:41).

not deceived knows their ways. He knows them to be impious, and before him they do not belong to any church. He knows only the just, not the unjust; that is, he does not commend them. So then, because they believe least of all, their way will perish. I say it will perish even though it flourishes to such an extent that it would seem to be eternal. Notice how the psalmist frightens us away from the appearance of good fortune and recommends to us various trials and adversities. For this way of the righteous, human beings reject entirely, imagining that God disregards it. Because this is the wisdom of the cross, therefore God alone knows the way of the righteous. It is hidden even from the righteous themselves; for his right hand leads them miraculously, so that it is not the way of feeling or of reason but of faith alone, which is able to see through the darkness and behold the invisible. SECOND PSALMS LECTURES (1519–1521).[32]

SANCTIFY ME IN YOUR SPIRIT. NIKOLAUS SELNECKER: Almighty and eternal God, Father of our Lord Jesus Christ, from my heart I ask that you through your Holy Spirit would create and maintain in me a longing and love for your holy Word—to pray and cry out to you always. For I am certain of this: aside from your Word there is no comfort, faith, life or salvation, instead everything is only the way of sinners, the seat of scoffers, and it must, like chaff, be blown away by the wind! Sanctify me in your truth; your Word is the truth. Let me have and sustain true faith and a good, peaceful conscience, so that I would remain eternally green and fruitful like a palm tree by water and that my leaves—either in this life or in eternal life—would not wither. Lord God, hear me and let me be and remain yours. Amen. THE WHOLE PSALTER.[33]

---

[32]LW 14:309* (WA 5:45).

[33]Selnecker, *Der gantze Psalter*, 1:9r.

2:1-12 THE REIGN OF THE LORD'S ANOINTED

¹ *Why do the nations rage*^a
and the peoples plot in vain?
² *The kings of the earth set themselves,*
and the rulers take counsel together,
against the LORD and against his Anointed,
saying,
³ *"Let us burst their bonds apart*
and cast away their cords from us."

⁴ *He who sits in the heavens laughs;*
the Lord holds them in derision.
⁵ *Then he will speak to them in his wrath,*
and terrify them in his fury, saying,
⁶ *"As for me, I have set my King*
on Zion, my holy hill."

⁷ *I will tell of the decree:*

The LORD said to me, "You are my Son;
today I have begotten you.
⁸ *Ask of me, and I will make the nations your*
heritage,
and the ends of the earth your possession.
⁹ *You shall break*^b *them with a rod of iron*
and dash them in pieces like a potter's vessel."

¹⁰ *Now therefore, O kings, be wise;*
be warned, O rulers of the earth.
¹¹ *Serve the LORD with fear,*
and rejoice with trembling.
¹² *Kiss the Son,*
lest he be angry, and you perish in the way,
for his wrath is quickly kindled.
Blessed are all who take refuge in him.

a Or *nations noisily assemble*   **b** Revocalization yields (compare Septuagint) *You shall rule*

OVERVIEW: The church has long employed a variety of hermeneutical methods that have led to different interpretations of Scripture, including literal, allegorical (of which typology is a common example) and tropological (or ethical) readings. Following this heritage, the reformers also point to several ways to read this psalm, but collectively emphasize a christological interpretation. Thus, although the establishment of David's kingdom and the subsequent Davidic line provide a historical context by which to interpret this psalm, our commentators perceive it to be a clear prophecy concerning Jesus Christ.

Such christological interpretation is evident not only, as one might expect, with regard to the identification of God's Son in verse 7, which is quoted in the baptismal narratives in the Synoptic Gospels, but also with regard to the entire psalm. For example, according to our interpreters' allegorical readings, the setting of God's king in Zion is a reference to the incarnation, Zion itself is equated

with the church, the rod of iron refers to God's Word or the Holy Spirit, and the command to "kiss the Son" is symbolic of embracing Christ by faith. Several of our commentators address the question of how the Son's eternal generation relates to the affirmation "today I have begotten you," concluding that the psalmist affirms the eternal and temporal generation of the Son. Thus, our commentators affirm that although followers of Christ will encounter adversaries and hardships, they can take comfort in the power and eternal reign of Jesus Christ, who is the true King.

PSALM 2 REITERATES THE CONTENT OF THE PSALMS. FELIX PRATENSIS: Psalm 2 has no title, because in it our harpist narrates the Son of God's eternal and temporal generation, his passion and victory. Anxious to make clear his intention and the subject and substance of the entire book of Psalms—not without the greatest kindness and attention for his students—he shows that he wants to talk about so lofty and so difficult a matter as the Son of God's incarnation, death and resurrection, and his triumphant bride. THE HEBREW PSALTER.[1]

A CLEAR AND OBVIOUS WITNESS TO JESUS' PERSON AND WORK. SEBASTIAN MÜNSTER: Not one Christian after the time of the apostles could not suppose that this psalm must be interpreted about Christ, the Savior of the human race. It so clearly mentions his nativity, passion and resurrection that the Jews almost confess it, too, even if they firmly deny our interpretation about Christ. THE TEMPLE OF THE LORD: PSALM 2.[2]

HISTORICALLY AND ALLEGORICALLY THIS PSALM IS ABOUT OUR DAVID, THAT IS, CHRIST. DESIDERIUS ERASMUS: In many psalms, the theme is twofold: the historical, which underlies it like the foundations of a building, and the allegorical or anagogical, which, beneath the cloak of historical events, conceals, or rather reveals, the gospel story, instruction in true piety or an image of eternal bliss. There is almost no passage of Scripture which cannot be interpreted in the tropological sense.

Let us now see whether there lies beneath this psalm too a historical meaning on which the allegory may rest; the evidence of the apostle Paul and of Luke in the Acts of the Apostles confirms that the whole psalm is a prophecy of Christ. . . . It is therefore clear that this psalm is a prophecy of Christ, as indeed are many others, which are quoted by the apostles in various places as prophecies of the gospel story. . . . However, it cannot be established by the heading whether this psalm could apply, in the historical sense, to somebody other than Christ. . . . So I shall not waste any time in considering how individual parts of the psalm may be applied to history; let us investigate instead the extent to which it applies

to our David, that is, Jesus Christ, about whom it was unquestionably written.

In fact this one psalm embraces not merely a part of the gospel story but the whole subject of the redemption of humankind: how the Son of God assumes a human body; how, overflowing with heavenly grace, he used the gospel teaching as a torch to dissipate the darkness of Moses' law, to lighten the yoke of ritual, to undermine the ungodly cults of the Gentiles and to overthrow the haughty pride of the philosophers; how he accomplished all this, not with the weapons of this world, but by a new and unprecedented application of that divine wisdom against which all humankind's ingenuity struggles in vain. The whole world conspired together to attack the gospel with all its might, but he turned all the scheming of the Pharisees, high priests, kings and princes into an ornament and a testimony of his victory, thwarting human cunning with heavenly wisdom, conquering godless violence by invincible gentleness, and by his death absolving death's tyranny. In descending to hell, he opened up the kingdom of heaven, and in plumbing the depths of humiliation he rose to the heights of glory; at the same time he showed us all the path by which we may overcome the prince of this world: distrustful of our own resources, we must rely entirely on Christ, as he relied entirely on the Father. Even princes and high priests, whose influence towers above the rest, must fear to offend against Jesus Christ, the ruler of all, and must not dare to ignore his laws, ever mindful of the eternal judgment whose sentence no one, however humble, however mighty, can escape. COMMENTARY ON PSALM 2.[3]

THE TRUE NATURE OF THE KINGDOM IS DESCRIBED. MARTIN LUTHER: Now Psalm 2, as we learn from Acts, supplied the first prayers and words of thanksgiving to God in the church of the new covenant. . . . It is also a prophetic psalm, in which we too will praise God, and with the apostles we will pray against the raving of the world, and certainly we will receive with the

---

[1]Pratensis, *Psalterium*, IV.
[2]Münster, *Miqdaš YHWH*, 1161.

[3]CWE 63:78-80*; citing Acts 13:32-33; Acts 4:24-27; Heb 1:4.

apostles the consolation which he promises abundantly and describes in fine words and thoughts. For David treats this subject in order to console and teach the church about the expansion of Christ's kingdom in spite of the powers of the world and of the air. Therefore, it serves especially to confirm the article concerning the new covenant or the kingdom of Christ: it will be a spiritual kingdom, Christ is an eternal King who will have no successor, he is also a Priest who teaches the church, who is indeed God by nature and brings us eternal righteousness and wisdom.

When all of this is explained, it is full of comfort. Nevertheless, the prophet shows that this kingdom would appear to be so weak that one might think it would fall at any moment. For it does not have any visible foundation or strength as have the kingdoms of the world, which depend on power, riches, the size of their population or the extent of their territories. This kingdom, lacking all of these defenses, without foundation, clings to the simple Word as a drop of water clings to a small pitcher. The present psalm contains just about all these things. It is, accordingly, useful for teaching the church so that we may learn all the circumstances of this kingdom, what kind of king Christ is, when, where and how he will rule his kingdom, what things are in harmony with this kingdom and what things are contrary to it, what the fruits or effects of it are, how it looks to the world, how it looks to God and in the Spirit. Those who know these facts have a sure and true conception of this kingdom.

It, then, can serve as a consolation also for us. For we are forewarned that the devil and the world will oppose this kingdom and that whatever is highly esteemed in the world, whether because of sanctity or eminent wisdom, all this, the prophet foretells, will assail the kingdom by common counsel. But, you will ask, will these warnings not terrify rather than console? Not in the least! For it is added that Satan and the world with all their powers and might can achieve nothing more than to move God to laughter and finally stir up in him such indignation that for opposing this kingdom they must perish. Knowing this is useful and comforting and belongs to a proper conception of this kingdom, lest we, troubled by the offenses with which this kingdom is assaulted, become despondent and dispirited. COMMENTARY ON PSALM 2 (1532).[4]

2:1-3 *The Treachery of the Powerful*

THE PROPHET IS BAFFLED BY THEIR RAGE.
DESIDERIUS ERASMUS: He was the Promised One, mild and gentle, generous to all, the Savior of all, freely taking on himself the sins of the world and lifting the harsh yoke of Moses' law; offering through evangelical faith and grace to the people of every nation—kings and commoners, scholars and simpletons, slaves and free—the status of God's children and the bliss of life everlasting. . . . We had been promised someone so remarkable that all the nations of the earth should, by rights, have opened their arms to him, and when he arrived, he was all that had been promised. Wealth often creates envy; he neither had nor wanted riches. Power often causes hatred; he declared he wanted nothing to do with the kingdoms of this world. The least show of kindness can win people's gratitude; he spared no effort to help everyone, swiftly and without asking a reward. He fed the hungry, cured the sick, restored the crippled and the weak; he gave eyes to the blind, ears to the deaf, tongues to the dumb; and in his wholesome teaching, gently and patiently, he showed all human beings the path to eternal bliss.

Thus the prophet has every reason to be astonished that the Gentiles should rebel, the peoples conspire, the kings rise and the leaders take arms against a man like this, so full of lovingkindness. They all conspire to destroy a single man, who had come, alone, to save them all; they unite to direct all their plots against him, who gave his whole being for them all. Why this frenzy? Why this mad conspiracy? Because, of course, there was no common ground between the world and Christ. And so the world turned from him, as from a

---

[4]LW 12:5-6* (WA 40,2:195, 196-97); citing Acts 4:25.

person summoning them to leave all that the stubborn children of that age held dear.

Did not that proud and godless world shudder at the very birth of Christ? . . . Later, when Christ began to win fame by performing miracles, to dispel the shadows of the Pharisees teaching with his heavenly doctrine and to show some tiny sparks, as it were, of his divine nature, how often did the people rage against him, running to pick up stones, or taking him to the brow of the hill to fling him headlong? COMMENTARY ON PSALM 2.[5]

THE PROPHET'S QUESTION IS AN ACCUSATION. CARDINAL CAJETAN: The prophet seeks the ultimate cause. This is not because the prophet asks out of ignorance or doubt; rather, he is charging and condemning them. Through this manner of speech he places before the eyes of the people and the king their error. He indicates through this how vainly they fight, striving to act against the Lord and his Christ. Indeed, similarly, we have been accustomed to scold the lowly who try to fight against the powerful: "Why do you fight against him—against the one whom you are unable to defeat?" COMMENTARY ON PSALM 2.[6]

WHY DOES THE PROPHET USE THE PAST TENSE HERE? CARDINAL CAJETAN: "Why did they throng together" [*rāgšû*]. The prophet uses the past tense for the future because of the certainty of the prophecy. Among them, what they will do is as certain as if it had already happened. Remember this rule in similar circumstances; it is not necessary to repeat it again and again. COMMENTARY ON PSALM 2.[7]

GOD REFASHIONS AND SUBVERTS THE PLANS OF THE WICKED. MARTIN LUTHER: Thus God permits the impious to raise their roaring counsel and striving against the godly. Yet these are all like swollen streams of water which with their swelling beat against the shore as if they would overwhelm

it; and before the waves reach the shore, they collapse and fade away or are dashed against the shore with empty noise. For the righteous, as a strong bulwark of faith in Christ, confidently despises these weak threats and quickly collapsing commotions. . . . With this cross the ungodly are quite fittingly tormented, because it is a particular torment when one wants to do harm in all things and yet cannot harm anything. . . . By God's counsel their torment and their vain plots must serve most of all to promote what they seek to prevent. Thus the friends of Christians are really not as useful to them as their enemies. SECOND PSALMS LECTURES (1519–1521).[8]

EXTERNAL ANOINTING IS USELESS WITHOUT THE HOLY SPIRIT. DESIDERIUS ERASMUS: The prophet, in naming the Father, called him simply "Lord," to show that he is the Lord of all, whereas he qualified "kings" with "of the earth," but he did not simply call the Son "Christ," intending no doubt to emphasize his status as the only being to have been specially anointed by God. This world too has its anointed ones, kings and priests; many of them are anointed outwardly, but their hearts are untouched by the oil. Human beings anoint the head, then the shoulder, the breastbone and the chest, right down to the navel even, but it is futile for one person to anoint another's body unless the heavenly Spirit has anointed his heart. Thus we often see princes who have been anointed time and again but who are nonetheless intolerable to the people in their cruelty, ambition and greed. COMMENTARY ON PSALM 2.[9]

HOW TO UNDERSTAND CHRISTOLOGICAL TYPOLOGY. JOHN CALVIN: It is now high time to come to the substance of the type. That David prophesied concerning Christ is clearly manifest from this, that he knew his own kingdom to be merely a shadow. And in order to learn to apply to Christ whatever David sang in times past concern-

---

[5]CWE 63:82-83*.
[6]Cajetan, *In Sacrae Scripturae Expositionem*, 3:9.
[7]Cajetan, *In Sacrae Scripturae Expositionem*, 3:9.
[8]LW 14:317* (WA 5:50-51).
[9]CWE 63:89*.

ing himself, we must hold this principle, which we meet with everywhere in all the prophets, that he, at the head of his posterity, was made king, not so much for his own sake but to be a type for the Redeemer. We will often have occasion to return to this later, but right now I want to inform my readers briefly, that as David's temporal kingdom was a kind of pledge to God's ancient people of the eternal kingdom, which at length was truly established in the person of Christ, those things which David declares concerning himself are not violently, or even allegorically, applied to Christ but were truly predicted concerning him. If we attentively consider the nature of the kingdom, we will perceive that it would be absurd to overlook the end or scope, and to rest in the mere shadow.

That the kingdom of Christ is here described by the spirit of prophecy is sufficiently attested to us by the apostles, who arm themselves in prayer with this doctrine when they see the unbelievers conspiring against Christ. But to place our faith beyond the reach of all cavils, it is plainly made manifest from all the prophets that those things which David testified concerning his own kingdom are properly applicable to Christ. Let this, therefore, be held as a settled point, that all who do not submit themselves to the authority of Christ make war against God. Because it seems good to God to rule us by the hand of his own Son, those who refuse to obey Christ himself deny the authority of God, and it is in vain for them to profess otherwise. For it is a true saying, "Whoever does not honor the Son does not honor the Father who sent him." And it is of great importance to hold fast this inseparable connection, that as the majesty of God has shone forth in his only-begotten Son, so the Father will not be feared and worshiped except in Christ's person. COMMENTARY ON THE PSALMS.[10]

CHRIST'S BONDS AND CORDS. RUDOLF GWAL-THER: The bonds here are the laws of Christ, with which he binds his faithful and maintains them in

obedience. The cords, however, are his power and might with which he compels and leads his enemies—even against their will—wherever he chooses. THE PSALTER.[11]

SATAN RAGES AGAINST THE WORD AT ALL COSTS. MARTIN LUTHER: Here the Holy Spirit explains the cause of the raging, what kind of counsels they take and what the kings and rulers discuss among themselves, namely, how with all their powers and efforts they may break the chains of Christ and of the Father. For Satan does this not only to humble us, not only to slay us who teach and believe, but to exterminate and destroy the Word, the name of Christ, baptism, and whatever our religion contains. As a result, because we teach Christ with the greatest confidence, he begins to rage, he lays hold of the wills of the princes, of kings, of the wise, the powerful, finally of the multitude. Here by common counsel all apply themselves to breaking these bonds, that is, to extinguishing the Word and protecting idolatry. COMMENTARY ON PSALM 2 (1532).[12]

REJECTING THE AUTHORITY OF CHRIST. WOLFGANG MUSCULUS: Notice this grumbling of the ungodly against the kingdom of Christ, this universal opposition and this planning and consulting of adversaries to form a rebellion of subjects against a higher power. Not every subterfuge has a rebellious aspect; however, this subterfuge by which the ungodly oppose the kingdom of Christ is particularly guilty of the crime of rebellion. For when they say, "Let us break their chains in pieces, and throw off their bonds from us," they mean nothing other than, "We reject the authority of this Christ. We do not bear it so that we may be subjected to his yoke. Let us be masters ourselves. Let him be subject to us; let us not serve him. It is shameful for so many kings, princes, nations and people to serve the Son, the Creator of the world." The disobedience of the Israelite people, by which

---

[10]CTS 8:11-12* (CO 31:43); citing Acts 4:24; Jn 5:22.

[11]Gwalther, *Der Psalter*, 3r.
[12]LW 12:14-15* (WA 40,2:207-8).

they continually rejected the Holy Spirit, is treated with a similar metaphor in Jeremiah 5.... Therefore, it has been predicted that the world would be rebellious to the kingdom of Christ and that the world would not endure his yoke. Next, it must be noted that they do not say, "Let us break God's chains in pieces, and let us throw off his bond from us," but "Let us break *their* chains in pieces, and let us throw off *their* bonds from ourselves." It is sufficiently indicated by these words that the ungodly pay attention only to those few weak people, to whom the Lord entrusts the ministry of his own kingdom and gospel in this world. For in this way, the ungodly only regard outward appearances. If ministers seem weak, the ungodly think that they can easily be broken. COMMENTARY ON PSALM 2.[13]

HOW TO BE SURE YOU BELONG TO THE LORD. JOHN BOYS: We may know from the following whether we are the Lord's anointed or not. The world loves its own. If then it hates Christ in us, it is an infallible sign that we are good soldiers of the Lord, and not servants of the world. The way to heaven is to sail by hell. If you will embrace Christ in his robes, you must not scorn him in his rags; if you will sit at his table in the kingdom, you must first abide with him in his temptations; if you will drink from his cup of glory, you must not forsake his cup of ignominy. Can the chief cornerstone be rejected, and the other more base stones in God's building be set by? You are one of God's living stones, and therefore be content to be hewn and snagged, so that you might be made more suitable to be joined to your fellows, suffering the snatches of Satan and the wounds of the world. EXPOSITION OF PSALM 2.[14]

2:4-6 God Laughs at Their Plans

GOD IN HEAVEN REIGNS. MARTIN LUTHER: To strengthen our hope the psalmist represents God as both a quiet and a wonderfully hidden Judge.

He who concerns himself about us dwells there secure and calm; and if we are disturbed, he who cares for us is not disturbed. We are tossed about, but he is calm; he will not let the righteous be eternally restless. But this all takes place in such a hidden manner that you would not know it unless you were in heaven. You suffer on the earth, in the sea and among all creatures. All hope of aid is denied to you everywhere and in all things, until by hope and faith you leap over everything and grasp him who dwells in heaven. Then you also dwell in heaven, but through faith and hope. Here we must throw out the anchor of our heart in all tribulations. In this way the evils of the world will be not only light but even laughable. SECOND PSALMS LECTURES (1519–1521).[15]

THIS LAUGHTER IS ONLY TEMPORARY. JOHN CALVIN: David attributes laughter to God for two reasons. First, so that we would know that he does not need great armies to restrain wicked people's uprisings, as if this were an arduous and difficult matter; instead he could do this trick as often as he pleases. Second, David shows that God is not inactive whenever he allows the kingdom of his Son to be troubled—either because he is busy with something else or because he is unable to help or because he despises his Son's honor—but he intentionally delays his vengeance until the right time, namely, once he has exposed their rage as a laughingstock.

Let us, therefore, understand that if God does not immediately stretch out his hand against the unbelievers, it is now his time of laughter. And although, in the meantime, we feel like crying, yet let us assuage the bitterness of our grief, yes even wipe away our tears, with this reflection, because God does not ignore his enemies' impudence, as if out of laziness or weakness, but because for the time he is willing to dishearten them with quiet contempt. COMMENTARY ON THE PSALMS.[16]

---

[13]Musculus, *In Psalterium Commentarii*, 21–22; citing Jer 5:5.
[14]Boys, *Exposition of Psalmes*, 82-83*; citing Jn 15:19; 2 Tim 2:3; Ps 118:22-23 (cf. Mt 21:42).

[15]LW 14:321-22 (WA 5:54).
[16]CTS 8:14* (CO 31:44).

How Reason Understands This Clause.
Martin Luther: Reason proclaims that either
God does not see such things and hence carries out
all things by chance, or if he sees and does not
suppress the wicked, he is weak. For to see and to
allow unworthy things, which you are able to
prohibit, reason believes, shows an unjust and
unfair mind. This is the honor that reason grants
to God: it judges him either to be foolish, because
he does not see or know many things, or wicked,
because he does not prevent the evil which he sees.
Against these blasphemies the Holy Spirit here
warns us, lest we think that God does not see the
attempts of the wicked because he turns a blind
eye to them. Commentary on Psalm 2 (1532).[17]

God Speaks to Us in Word and Deed.
Desiderius Erasmus: God addresses us in two
different ways: through his Scriptures and
through events themselves. We must therefore
spend much time studying the sacred books to
hear what God says to us there—and let us be
sure that his words do not fall on deaf ears. In
addition, he often speaks to the unlearned through
events, and here the inward ear must be kept open
so that we do not miss the Lord's voice. If some
good fortune comes our way, we must not act like
the man described by the psalmist elsewhere: "The
beloved grew fat and unruly; he grew sleek and
bloated. He forsook God who made him, and
abandoned the God of his salvation." If we know
that we have sinned, we should give thanks for
God's mercy, which, although we deserve punishment, still urges us by kindness to mend our ways;
on the other hand, if we are sure that we have
done no wrong, we must strive to increase still
further our previous devotion to God. If illness or
some other calamity befalls us, we should give
thanks for God's goodness, which calls us to
reform when we forget ourselves, scourging his
children here and now to keep them from eternal
death. Commentary on Psalm 2.[18]

Zion Represents the Church. Rudolf
Gwalther: Mount Zion also includes Jerusalem,
which on account of the kingly throne and temple
there was an intimation of the holy Christian
church. The Psalter.[19]

**Always Remember the Sweet Voice of
the Father.** Tilemann Hesshus: This is the
most important statement in this psalm. For here
the eternal Father himself gives birth, and he
plainly affirms that he will establish his King over
all his clamoring enemies and that he will defend
him against the gates of hell. This affirmation not
only was placed to check his enemies but more
importantly to confirm pious minds. In order that
we would certainly stand firm, God desires this to
be his eternal and unchangeable will, that the
only-begotten Son of God, our Lord Jesus Christ
would be an eternal King who not only defends us
against our enemies' violence but who also blots
out all our adversaries, namely, death, sin, Satan,
the condemnation of the law, the wrath of God
and hell. So to us he lavishes peace of conscience
and every good eternal thing: life, righteousness,
friendship with God, joy, light and eternal
salvation. The Father affirms that he has established this kind of kingdom; that is, by his sure
and unchangeable will he decreed the gathering of
his church through his Son.

When he calls the church his holy mountain, he
promises that through his Son in this kingdom he
will blot out sin and restore righteousness. He also
demonstrates in this passage where his Son is going
to establish this kingdom, namely, in Zion. By this
he teaches that his Son is going to assume human
nature and, according to the promises given to the
patriarchs, live among the Jewish people, proclaim
his teaching, perform miracles and fulfill his royal
duties. Therefore, this unchangeable decree of the
eternal Father should always be before us. And we
should always stand firm; wherever empires fall,
nevertheless the kingdom of Christ—the church—
will remain. We should know that God is always

---

[17]LW 12:23* (WA 40,2:219).
[18]CWE 63:116; citing Deut 32:15 (Vg).

[19]Gwalther, Der Psalter, 3r.

near the assembly of the pious and that in the kingdom of the Son he works through the voice of his ministers. We should know that this is the unchangeable and eternal will of God, that through this King, the Son of God, we would be sanctified. Thus, this voice of the eternal Father, containing in it the sum of gospel teaching, will be the most efficacious consolation against all temptations. COMMENTARY ON PSALM 2.[20]

2:7-9 The Son of God

THE GOSPEL MUST BE PREACHED. PHILIPP MELANCHTHON: What kind of kingdom will it be? It will not be governed like others—by laws, courts and arms—but it will be ruled by the new Word concerning the will of God, who has been placated through the Son. Thus he says, "I will preach about the commandment, you are my Son." He speaks about this new decree that he will preach about the Son. And because he affirms that he will preach, he establishes the ministry of the gospel: it must be taught and therefore learned. And according to this dictum we should reflect on our studies: God affirms that he wills to establish this kingdom by preaching; therefore, he defends study and teaching; he will not allow churches, schools and houses of teaching to be entirely destroyed. COMMENTS ON THE PSALMS.[21]

GRAMMATICAL EVIDENCE OF CHRIST'S DEITY. CARDINAL CAJETAN: In this sense he is addressed as Son and is the living one who has been brought forth through his life-giving activity from a living being from his own proper [*proprius*][22] substance in likeness of his particular nature. And although these conditions cannot be found in created

spiritual substances and for this reason none of them has the Father or the Son (because none of them could beget from their own proper [*proprius*] substance a substance like themselves), still according to his divine nature the Word—because it is said by God—is his Son properly speaking, because he is a living person, and from a living being he was brought forth from God's substance through a life-giving act of generation into the same nature; therefore, because of the power of his bringing forth he is similar to the one who brought him forth. Therefore, the bringing forth of this sort is called generation in the active voice; however, in the passive voice it is called birth. So, truly and rightly to this esteemed filiation it is added: "I have begotten you." For here not only is the person of the Messiah distinguished from the person of the Father (because no one begets himself and a difference of persons is indicated by the pronouns *I* and *you*; it is evident that these pronouns reveal the persons), but also it indicates their distinction from both the Holy Spirit and all creatures. For the Holy Spirit is not begotten by God.[23] And creatures are not properly speaking begotten by God; rather, they are made, as that verse says: "He spoke and they were made; through him all things were made." Therefore, by the fact that he is called my Son, a Son according to nature is indicated. For this reason his true nature is shown, because "today I have begotten you."

And see how finely the complex perfection of his generation is indicated. His generation, as far as according to spirit and intellect, is indicated through "to say—the Lord has said." As far as according to nature and substance, it is indicated through "to beget—I have begotten." As far as in perfect likeness, it is indicated through filiation—"My Son." As far as it is completed, it is indicated through past tense verbs—"I have said; I have begotten." As far as it is eternal, it is indicated

---

[20]Hesshus, *Commentarius in Psalmos*, 16v-17r.

[21]MO 13:1020.

[22]Those attributes that belong to a substance itself are called *proprius*; those borrowed from another substance, *alienus*. For example, wetness is proper to water, not a cloth; if a cloth is wet this attribute is alien, borrowed from water. Here Cajetan emphasizes that Christ was begotten from God, thus God's substance is properly his own substance. The Nicene Creed puts it this way: *God from God, Light from Light, true God from true God.*

[23]The Spirit cannot be begotten, for that would threaten the uniqueness of the Son. Instead, according to the Western tradition the Spirit proceeds eternally from the Father and the Son through "spiration" or "breathing forth" (the Eastern tradition does not affirm the *filioque*).

through the present adverb—"today"—which is not the present time but rather the present tense which implies what is always standing still, apart from any kind of succession. By saying "today I have begotten you," he indicates that not yesterday (that is, in the past) but *today*—that is, in an eternity unaware of the past or future—"I have begotten you"; I have completed your generation. And it is necessary to combine "I have begotten" with "today." For as far as those begettings that are among us are concerned, if they are in the present, they are not yet completed. And if they are completed, they are not in the present but in the past. Christ's—the Son of God's—birth is always completed and always present. And that is indicated through "today I have begotten."

Therefore the Messiah responds directly to the world that is thinking vain thoughts about his deity, that he did not make himself to be God, that human opinions did not make him to be God, but that the Lord "said to me, you are my Son" according to nature, for "today I have begotten you." COMMENTARY ON PSALM 2.[24]

THE ETERNAL SON OF GOD. JOHN CALVIN: Let us understand "God's Son" here not as one son among many but as his only-begotten Son, as he alone will be preeminent in heaven and on earth. When God proclaims to have begotten him, he must refer to human understanding or knowledge. For David was begotten by God when his election as king became clear. The word *today*, therefore, denotes the time of this manifestation; because after it became known that he was made king by divine appointment, he came forth as one who had recently been begotten of God, because so great an honor could not belong to a private person. The same explanation is to be given of the words as applied to Christ. He is not said to be begotten in any other sense than as the Father bore testimony to him as being his own Son. This passage, I am aware, has been explained by many as referring to

the eternal generation of Christ; and from the word *today*, they have reasoned ingeniously as if they denoted an eternal act without any relation to time. But Paul, who is a more faithful and a better qualified interpreter of this prophecy, in Acts 13 calls our attention to the manifestation of the heavenly glory of Christ of which I have spoken. This expression, "to be begotten," does not therefore imply that he then began to be the Son of God but that his being so was then made manifest to the world. COMMENTARY ON THE PSALMS.[25]

MUCH GOSPEL IN A BRIEF DOCTRINE. MARTIN LUTHER: The teaching of this king is to be distinguished from all other teachings, even from the law itself, which, nevertheless, regarding works or what we should do is most perfect. But this king's teaching does not teach about works but about the person to whom the Lord says: "You are my Son." A brief doctrine, presented pure and simple, without elaborations, without details! But if you reflect on these few words correctly, they suggest spontaneously their own amplifications, which the gospel reveals. This person it depicts most clearly, and teaches that by the Holy Spirit he was conceived, by Mary, a virgin mother, he was born, under Pontius Pilate he suffered, died, rose again from death by his own power, and sits at the right hand of the Father. And we have been commanded from heaven to listen to him, so that we should fix our eyes on him alone, as the Jews in the desert fixed their eyes on the bronze serpent; in no way should we turn away from his words. We should know that not only whatever he says, but also whatever he does, all pertains to our salvation. For the gospel is always concerned with this. Therefore, it so diligently reveals not only the miracles of Christ but also his sermons, so that it commends him to us in order to invite us to embrace, follow and obey him. If we do this, we never wander astray but remain on the right path to salvation. COMMENTARY ON PSALM 2 (1532).[26]

---

[24]Cajetan, *In Sacrae Scripturae Expositionem*, 3:11; citing Ps 148:5; Jn 1:3.

[25]CTS 8:17-18* (CO 31:46-47); citing Acts 13:33.
[26]LW 12:45* (WA 40,2:248).

**CHRIST ETERNALLY AND TEMPORALLY BEGOT-
TEN.** SEBASTIAN MÜNSTER: "The Lord," he says,
"said to me: 'You are my Son,' and this word I will
repeat and recount again and again to others, just as
the statute and command about this matter were
given to me." Thus, Rabbi Salomon exegetes this
passage as follows. . . . "'The decree has been established concerning me.' Thus, I will explain it as
follows: 'Certainly the Lord said to me, You are my
Son.'" And here the author of *Sefer Nizahon*—as is
his custom—attacks and argues against Christians. . . .
I omit . . . his blasphemy which that raw-skinned
scoundrel writes about this passage. Nevertheless he
thinks that he writes most sensibly who ignores that
Christ has a twofold generation, eternal and temporal,
according to his two natures. Nevertheless there are
those who think that in this passage this return is
intimated by the prophet, that the regenerated Christ
rose again from the grave to immortal life, because it
is added, "Ask from me," etc. And Christ says in
Matthew 28: "All power in heaven has been given to
me," etc. THE TEMPLE OF THE LORD: PSALM 2.[27]

**HOW CAN IT BE THAT THIS PERSON DOES
WHAT GOD ALONE DOES?** MARTIN LUTHER:
Learn, then, to apply this verse against the Arians.
Christ accepts dominion over the nations, but he
accepts it in such a way that he himself is Lord,
that through him the nations should receive
"righteousness and justice, love and faithfulness," as
Psalm 89 testifies. These are not the kind of things,
however, which are in the hands of angels. But
God alone forgives sins and justifies. God alone
liberates from death and eternal damnation. God
alone gives the Holy Spirit. God alone is also
truthful. Because the Son is commanded to pour
out these gifts on the nations, who does not see
that he is God by nature? For these are not the
deeds of a creature, and yet this person, to whom
these things are given from God the Father himself,
is the seed of David and possesses the seat of his
father David. COMMENTARY ON PSALM 2 (1532).[28]

PRESENT AND FUTURE CONSIDERATIONS.
CARDINAL CAJETAN: "Demand" is said in the
present tense and "I will give" in the future, so that
you understand how to consider a petition according
to the time when Christ was a traveler present in this
world. "To give the nations" should be considered
according to the time of future immortality which
Christ obtained by his rising again. Now the nations
are promised to Christ who was first described as
King over Zion, so that you understand that those
who are under the law of Moses and those who are
outside of the law are made subject to Christ by God.
COMMENTARY ON PSALM 2.[29]

THE WORD IS LIKE IRON. MARTIN LUTHER: Just
as iron crushes and breaks all things, as Daniel 2
says, so the Word of Christ does all this. It crushes
the great, that is, humbles the proud. It straightens
the crooked, that is, corrects the disorderly. It
bends the straight, that is, bows down the exalted.
It levels the rough, that is, soothes the angry. It
extends the short, that is, encourages the timid. It
shortens the long, that is, terrifies the presumptuous.
It widens the narrow, that is, makes the stingy
generous. It narrows the wide, that is, makes the
spendthrift economical. It sharps the blunt, that is,
gives knowledge to the unlearned. It blunts the
sharp, that is, makes the wise ignorant. And it
repels rust, that is, banishes laziness. In short, it
destroys every faulty form and changes it into one
that is pleasing to God. And, as the apostle says,
"All Scripture has been inspired by God and made
profitable for teaching, for reproof, for correction,
and for training in righteousness, so that a person
of God may be complete, equipped for every good
work." SECOND PSALMS LECTURES (1519–1521).[30]

THE WORD WILL WEAR THEM DOWN. JOHN
CALVIN: It may be asked, what is that iron scepter
which the Father has placed in the hand of Christ,
with which he shatters his enemies? I answer:
instead of any other weapon the breath of his

---

[27]Münster, *Miqdaš YHWH*, 1161-62; citing Mt 28:18.
[28]LW 12:55-56* (WA 40,2:261-62); citing Ps 89:14.
[29]Cajetan, *In Sacrae Scripturae Expositionem*, 3:11.
[30]LW 14:338* (WA 5:66); citing Dan 2:40; 2 Tim 3:16-17.

mouth is enough for him. . . . Therefore, even if Christ does not move a finger, by speaking he thunders powerfully enough against his enemies, and the staff of his lips alone reduces them to nothing. They may fret, kick and resist him with wild fury, but they will eventually be compelled to see that the one whom they refuse to honor as their King is their Judge. In short, by various methods they are worn down until they become his footstool. COMMENTARY ON THE PSALMS.[31]

2:10-12 Kiss the Son

WITHOUT CHRIST AS TEACHER ALL ARE FOOLS. MARTIN LUTHER: The Holy Spirit indicates that even if kings and judges have the law and a zeal for excellence, still unless they listen to this Teacher and let themselves be taught, they are idiots and fools. For if they lack knowledge of Christ, all their wisdom is foolishness, all their righteousness is iniquity and sin. In fact, their life is actually death. In this verse, then, the Holy Spirit draws together the whole world and subjects all things to Christ. He speaks to kings as though they were locusts and to the wise people of the world as though they were schoolchildren. For he sees what will eventually happen if they will not listen to this Teacher, namely, that with all their wisdom, righteousness and power, they will be cast into the eternal flames. COMMENTARY ON PSALM 2 (1532).[32]

HOW TO SERVE AND PRAISE GOD. JOHANNES BUGENHAGEN: "Serve the Lord" not in the hypocrisy of an outward worship of God, which today or only for the present is called holiness, but in fear, that is, so that you may tremble at his Word. Thus be kings and guardians that you may acknowledge that you are the servants of God. Then you will serve the Lord not when you expend your money on the pomp of ceremonies and luxury of clerics and monks but whenever you diligently pursue those things which pertain to your duty in the fear of God,

knowing also that you yourselves have a judge in heaven. Again, let not your service be coerced.

"Exult him" or about him, as about a benign father, who rejects no one no matter with what dignity with respect to this age he may shine, if only he would acknowledge the ministry approved by God and not his own dignity. But in order that this exultation may not produce neglect, he adds again: "in trembling." For the spirit (if I may call it that) seems greatly to fear princes and the rest who are in charge. And here you see fear mixed with exaltation, which truly is faith—to fear at the Word of God and its scolding—and at the same time to rejoice at the promises of God and be secure concerning one's salvation on account of the Word of God. Such faith is demanded here from judges, for they cannot rightly execute their office, so as to seem most prudent to themselves, unless they do all things according to faith in God through Jesus Christ, our Lord, especially when whatever is not of faith is sin. INTERPRETATION OF THE PSALMS.[33]

THE CULTURAL UNDERSTANDING OF "KISS." RUDOLF GWALTHER: Among the ancients, the kiss was a sign of love and willing obedience or submission—like in our time a kiss of the hand among Spaniards, Italians and the French. THE PSALTER.[34]

LOVE GOD'S SON! FELIX PRATENSIS: Truly we interpret "kiss the Son" as the salvation of everyone through his peace—in agreement with the opinion of a great number of Hebrew authors and in agreement with the truth. For *našqû* means "to kiss," as it is clear in Song of Songs. Because when we kiss someone's hand, we are said to adore that person, therefore "kiss!" will also mean "adore!"—as most of the Hebrew expositors say here. Sometimes, however, it means "desire!" or "love!"—actually it rarely means something other than "love!" THE HEBREW PSALTER.[35]

---

[31]CTS 8:21* (CO 31:48-49).
[32]LW 12:69* (WA 40,2:280).
[33]Bugenhagen, *In librvm Psalmorvm interpretatio*, 7.
[34]Gwalther, *Der Psalter*, 3v.
[35]Pratensis, *Psalterium*, iv-2r.

SEIZE CHRIST WHOLEHEARTEDLY, EVEN AGAINST REASON. MARTIN LUTHER: There is great force, then, in the word *kiss*; for it indicates that we should embrace this Son with our whole heart and see or hear nothing else than Christ and him crucified. But whoever looks for something else in religion or seeks something higher will deceive himself and wander from the way of salvation. We should use our reason and wisdom for other things, for managing the household, doing our jobs, for buying and selling. But when it comes to the worship of God, you should deny all access to reason and cling to this Son alone. COMMENTARY ON PSALM 2 (1532).[36]

JESUS IS BONE FROM MY BONE! JOHN DONNE: There is no person so near of kin to you as Christ Jesus. Christ Jesus your father created you; he is your brother because he took your nature. He is your father because he provided an inheritance for you; he is your brother because he divided this inheritance with you. And because he died to give you possession of that inheritance, he is the Nourishing One, your foster father who has nursed you in his house, in the Christian church. He is your twin brother, so similar to you that his Father and yours in him, will not know you from one another but will mingle your conditions: he finds your sins in him and his righteousness in you. "Kiss this Son" as your kinsman. SERMON 39: PREACHED ON TRINITY SUNDAY.[37]

THE SWEETNESS OF GOD'S GRACE. JOHN CALVIN: The concluding sentence of the psalm qualifies what was formerly said concerning the severity of Christ; for his iron rod and the fiery wrath of God would strike terror into all people without distinction, unless this comfort had been added. Therefore having spoken the terrible judgment which hangs over the unbelieving, the psalmist now encourages God's faithful and devout servants to entertain good hope, by setting forth

the sweetness of his grace. Paul likewise observes the same order, for having declared that vengeance was in readiness against the disobedient, he immediately adds, addressing himself to believers: "When your obedience is fulfilled." Now, we understand the meaning of the psalmist. As believers might have applied to themselves the severity of which he makes mention, he opens to them a sanctuary of hope whither they may flee, in order not to be overwhelmed by the terror of God's wrath; just as Joel also after having summoned the unbelievers to the awful judgment seat of God, which of itself is terrible to people, immediately subjoins the comfort, "Whosoever shall call on the name of the Lord shall be saved." COMMENTARY ON THE PSALMS.[38]

WHAT THIS PSALM TEACHES US. NIKOLAUS SELNECKER: From this psalm we are to learn the following. First, we should not let ourselves be afflicted so severely even when pagans and all the world rage against the Lord Christ and desire to eradicate him along with all his people. Indeed they will not accomplish anything; instead, they will vanish and be brought to nothing—however smart, learned and mighty they may be. Second, we look to our Lord Christ, know him and understand that he is eternal God and true man, our King and Priest, the eternal Son of God, who is begotten today—that is, continually from eternity—by God the Father, and chosen to be the true Son and the beloved Child Jesus. He will also make others—if they believe in him—children of God through his obedience, suffering, death and resurrection. His kingdom will be without end forever and ever. Third, we also serve this Lord and King with fear and trembling and rejoice in him. Namely, we despair of ourselves and know that we cannot on our own deliver ourselves from God's wrath and condemnation. All is lost for us and our works. Instead the Son of God must make us righteous and holy, so that we rejoice solely in God and have peace with God, because through faith for the sake

---

[36]LW 12:88 (WA 40,2:306)*.
[37]Donne, *Works*, 2:195*.

[38]CTS 8:26* (CO 31:51-52); citing 2 Cor 10:6; Joel 2:32.

of the Lord Christ we became righteous and holy. As a result, the fruits of faith should not be absent, so that we serve the Lord Christ with body, honor and goods, with true confession and promotion of doctrine, with preservation of churches and schools, with prayer and true diligence in holiness, discipline and honesty, unity and peace. For this is also called "kissing the Son," when we embrace him with faith and the fruits of faith are not absent. But the manner that we pursue and perform such kissing has unfortunately come to light. In all classes it has totally ceased, so that is correctly written: "He will be angry, his wrath soon will be kindled, there is no doubt, and you will perish on the way, in your sins you will die and perish." Now then, may God be gracious to us and help many people, so that they might trust in him and rely on him and be saved and blessed. Amen. THE WHOLE PSALTER.[39]

APPLYING THE MYSTERY OF CHRIST FOR US. DESIDERIUS ERASMUS: Let me demonstrate that the mystical sense of this psalm can be extended more widely, to various people and various times, so that even today it applies to every one of us. First, although the historical meaning is often rather dull when set beside the allegorical, still it sometimes sheds much light on the mystical meaning and adds not a little to it. . . . Nor is it essential that every part of a prophecy should fit perfectly into either a historical or an allegorical reading, because often certain elements are included to ensure chronological coherence while others, which are out of place in the historical context, compel us to have recourse to allegory.

The next step is to accommodate the prophecies to Christ and to demonstrate that already long ago these oracles of the prophets foretold what the Gospels narrate openly and without a veil as history. This level of meaning, particularly in the Psalms, is almost inexhaustible and has indeed been shown to be irrefutable on the authority of Scripture. . . . Christ is the truth of the gospel, the

world is the cause of its own impermanence; in the end Christ suffers or is revived in his limbs.

The final step remains, when the meaning of Scripture is applied personally to each one of us and the deeds ascribed to various groups in the other readings are applied to a single individual. For example, whenever anger, lust, ambition or avarice distract our thoughts to those things that are contrary to the teachings of the gospel, then, so to speak, "the nations rage and the peoples carry through their futile plots." Again, if reason gives way to unbridled passions, then "the kings of the earth stand ready, and the leaders conspire together against the Lord and his anointed." But whenever our minds are restored and, sickened by the harsh bondage which our sins have imposed, we remember our former freedom; then we cry out: "Let us break their fetters, let us throw off their yoke from us." Moreover, the Lord assists our efforts from heaven by mocking and laughing us to scorn; he allows us to be swayed by our passions for a while until we are taught by our misfortunes that the very things in which we placed our hopes of wondrous bliss have brought us total ruin. Next, he speaks to us in his wrath, exposing to our eyes the terrors of eternal torment and filling us with the horror of the life we have led. Then, in our terror and confusion, he shows us the source of our hopes of salvation; he sets his Son before us, who says to us all: "Come to me, all you who labor." He warns us that our instincts must be made to obey his laws, that human reason must conform to his decree and that we must so serve this single ruler of us all that we must both rejoice in his boundless goodness towards us and yet be always fearful. That is, we must mistrust our own deeds and our own strength, because we are not our own judges but must place all hope and trust in his inestimable kindness, through which eternal salvation is won by those who turn to him for help with all their heart. To him be praise and thanksgiving, with the Father and the Holy Spirit, for all eternity. COMMENTARY ON PSALM 2.[40]

---

[39]Selnecker, Der gantze Psalter, 1:13v-14r; citing Heb 1; 5.

[40]CWE 63:144-46*; citing Mt 11:28.

3:1-8 SAVE ME, O MY GOD!

A Psalm of David, when he fled from Absalom his son.

¹ O LORD, how many are my foes!
  Many are rising against me;
² many are saying of my soul,
  there is no salvation for him in God.   Selah^a

³ But you, O LORD, are a shield about me,
  my glory, and the lifter of my head.
⁴ I cried aloud to the LORD,
  and he answered me from his holy hill.
                                    Selah

⁵ I lay down and slept;
  I woke again, for the LORD sustained me.
⁶ I will not be afraid of many thousands of
    people
  who have set themselves against me all around.
⁷ Arise, O LORD!
  Save me, O my God!
For you strike all my enemies on the cheek;
  you break the teeth of the wicked.

⁸ Salvation belongs to the LORD;
  your blessing be on your people!   Selah

a The meaning of the Hebrew word *Selah*, used frequently in the Psalms, is uncertain. It may be a musical or liturgical direction

OVERVIEW: Many of the reformers—especially the Radicals—lost property, were divided from their families, persecuted, exiled and martyred for their faith. They understood this psalm to reflect both the lament that is rightly expressed in such situations as well as the trust and confidence that believers should have in God's mercy and providence. While the particular historical setting for this psalm was David's flight from Jerusalem during the rebellion against him led by his son, Absalom (2 Sam 13:23–17:29), from the reformer's perspective it is meant as a model for those who find themselves in similar circumstances, as many of the reformers did. Thus, the overriding emphasis of this Davidic psalm, which is sometimes referred to as an "evening" or "night" psalm, is not the reality of night but God's promise of the morning and salvation through Jesus Christ.

CROSSBEARING IS SURE TO FOLLOW CHRIST'S CHILDREN AND LOVERS. NIKOLAUS SELNECKER: David serves God, kisses his Son and trusts in him. But on account of this he must have the entire world as an enemy—even his flesh and blood, his dear son Absalom! Absalom harasses him, hounds him and shatters his heart. All David's subjects turn away from him and—as Scripture says—"Absalom stole their hearts." What great misery this must have been, fathers and mothers can easily discern.

But still it is certain, indeed, it is definitively decided that whoever wants to serve Christ the Lord and the Son of God, to kiss him and to trust in him, to believe in him and remain with him, will be subjected to crossbearing and many and diverse sorrows. That person has or is able to keep almost no friends, either by blood or by any other way. Now, therefore, true Christians should surrender themselves to this reality and protect themselves with diligence from this stumbling block, so that they are not rattled by such raging of the devil, the world and death; instead, they should cling to God and to his Word, and so in God's name they should risk body and life, honor and goods. . . .

Now Psalm 3 follows this and in fine order follows Psalm 2. We serve God, but what do we have on account of this in this world other than envy, hatred, disdain and unrest, yes often enough sickness and death? But what does that matter? A true Christian says, "I will turn to God through assiduous prayer and say to him, *O Lord, how is it that my enemies are so many and that so many stand against me?*" THE WHOLE PSALTER.[1]

LEADERS MUST TRUST IN GOD'S PRESENCE DURING TRIALS. RUDOLF GWALTHER: This psalm serves every oppressed and troubled servant of God—especially rulers and leaders who are assailed by their own subjects in a rebellious manner. These people learn here with what firm faith they should trust God and long for help from him with sure confidence that he will never abandon them. THE PSALTER.[2]

Superscription: *From, For or To David?*

THE HOLY SPIRIT COMPOSED THESE PSALMS FOR DAVID. MARTIN LUTHER: In all titles the name of David is preceded by the particle of the dative case, but the Jews say that it is the genitive in superscriptions and titles. I do not agree with that. I maintain that it is the dative, as always elsewhere, so also in the title of psalms. Then it means that the psalm is not properly "of David" but "for David" or "to David." This gives expression to the movement of the Holy Spirit who produced the psalm and revealed it for David or to David. FIRST PSALMS LECTURES (1513–1515).[3]

DAVID WROTE MORE PSALMS THAN THOSE WITH HIS NAME. THE ENGLISH ANNOTATIONS: It is not to be trusted that, as a general rule, that only those psalms are David's that bear his name in the title or beginning, because—beside other reasons—we find some in other passages of Scripture directly ascribed to David, which do not have his name prefixed, like Psalm 2 in Acts 4:25. PREFACE TO ANNOTATIONS ON THE PSALMS.[4]

3:1-2b *Multitude of Foes*

THIS LAMENT IS ROOTED IN THE HOLY SPIRIT. ROBERT ROLLOCK: The beginning of this complaint clearly manifests the source of this familiar manner of dealing with God. . . . For such a familiar fashion of dealing with God shows that this complaint did not come from the spirit of a human being. For the spirit of a human being would not dare to appear before God and his judgment seat. For although in other ways it appears to be fierce, it trembles and shakes at the sight of God. Therefore it must be that so familiar a complaint proceeds from the Spirit of God himself. They call this Spirit the Spirit of adoption, which as Paul says in Romans 5:5 pours out into the hearts that fatherly love of God, testifying by this that we are the children of God and therefore opening our mouth so that we cry, "Abba! Father!" and in our affliction we complain to God. EXPOSITION UPON PSALM 3.[5]

THE VOICES OF SIN. DESIDERIUS ERASMUS: Sins, too, have speeches to make, but of a different kind; their voices are soft and persuasive as they tempt our souls. How persuasive, for example, was ambition's voice when it said: "You shall not die, but shall be like gods, with the knowledge of good and evil"! Unchastity speaks in this way: what could be sweeter? So does intemperance: what could be more attractive? And the mania for power: what could be more dazzling? And avarice: what could be more satisfying? But when the soul has drunk the sweet poison, there is a change of tone, and it hears these bitter words: "Your sin is too great to deserve pardon." God is just; you can expect nothing except punishment. The sentence is harsh enough when passed on us for a single crime; who could bear it if all our many crimes, adultery, robbery, murder, theft, were to cry out together to our souls: "There is no salvation for you in your God"? Hard words, bitter words indeed! PARAPHRASE OF PSALM 3.[6]

---

[1]Selnecker, *Der gantze Psalter*, 1:14r-v; citing 2 Sam 5:16.
[2]Gwalther, *Der Psalter*, 3v.
[3]LW 10:44* (WA 3:41). For contemporary discussions of *lĕdāwid*, see Kraus, *Psalms 1–59*, 22-23; Goldingay, *Psalms*, 1:25-30.
[4]Downame, ed., *Annotations*, 4Z3r*.

[5]Rollock, *Exposition upon Some Psalmes*, 7-8*.
[6]CWE 63:160.

3:2c *How to Understand* Selāh?

DIVERSE UNDERSTANDINGS OF *SELĀH*. FELIX PRATENSIS: Various authors expound the word *selāh* in various ways. Some say it means "in eternity" or "always"; others say it means nothing, rather it is some sign of sighing and praying for some stress and excessive emotion over a matter or event. THE HEBREW PSALTER.[7]

HEBREW INSCRIPTIONS PROVE THAT *SELĀH* MEANS "IN ETERNITY." SEBASTIAN MÜNSTER: There are those who explain this term as *adî ad*, "in eternity"—it is used this way in Psalm 84: *yĕhallûkā selāh*, "They will praise you forever and ever." And so also the Jews finish their epitaphs in this way, as here in Basel I found written in stone:

נשמתה תהא צרורה בגן עדן א א א סלה

That is, "May his soul have been united into paradise, Amen, Amen, Amen, in eternity." And there is a stone in Heidelberg, carved before the year 243 whose inscription ends with these words:

מנוחתה בצרור החיים עם
שאר צדקניות א א א סלה

That is, "May her rest be in eternal life together with all the other righteous women, Amen, Amen, Amen, in eternity." Abraham Ibn Ezra explains this word *selāh* as *ĕmet*, "truth" or "true." And David Kimchi says *selāh* is a lifting up of the voice, which he deduces from the fact that this word is found nowhere else than in psalms and songs.... He thinks the root word is *sll* which means "to lift up." THE TEMPLE OF THE LORD: HABAKKUK 3.[8]

SELĀH IS A LITURGICAL MARKER. RUDOLF GWALTHER: The Hebrews placed *selāh* in songs as a sign that we should lift up both our voice and heart and meditate on the intoned phrase with particular diligence and focus. THE PSALTER.[9]

DAVID LIFTS HIS SPIRITS BY SINGING *SELĀH*. JOHN CALVIN: It must be observed that the music was adapted to the sentiment, and so the harmony was connected with the character or subject matter (as they say). For example, after David complained that his hope was shamefully scorned—as if nothing would help him be protected by God—he endures this blasphemy, which severely wounded his heart, by singing *selāh*. And then a little after, when he has exposed a new ground of confidence, he repeats this same word again. COMMENTARY ON THE PSALMS.[10]

SELĀH IS PROBABLY A MUSICAL TERM. CARDINAL CAJETAN: *Selāh* is a Hebrew term. Including the three occurrences in this psalm there are seventy occurrences in this Psalter. It is not repeated anywhere else in all holy Scripture, except in the song of Habakkuk, where it occurs three times. There is a big question concerning this term, whether it is best understood as a meaningful term—such that it should be part of the psalm's body like the other meaningful terms. It means "always" or "eternity" or "lifted up"; for that reason many interpreters have "always" in place of *selāh*; others "everlasting." Or whether it does not hold meaning but is a technical term for indicating or changing tone or meter, or for a pause in the song, or something else like that. And the translators of the LXX seem to have embraced this approach. In place of *selāh* they have *diapsalma* ["pause"] in Greek....

The Hebrews think this term is technical. They have a point, because it is not found except in meter. I agree with this opinion. And so, I will mention nothing further about this term in my commentary—in the text I will always be careful that it be written in red. If I discovered other experts to ascend into the Hebrew meters of the Psalms, the truth would be readily apparent, whether this term is part of the meter or not—because it could be discerned by the length of the meter. If you want to see the various opinions, read Jerome's epistle to Marcella. COMMENTARY ON PSALM 3.[11]

---

[7]Pratensis, *Psalterium*, 2r.

[8]Münster, *Miqdaš YHWH*, 1121.

[9]Gwalther, *Der Psalter*, 4r.

[10]CTS 8:30* (CO 31:54).

[11]Cajetan, *In Sacrae Scripturae Expositionem*, 3:14; citing Hab 3; Jerome's letter 28 to Marcella (see PL 22:433-35; cf. NPNF[2] 6:44). Instead of placing *selāh* in red, some publishers italicized it.

SELĀH INDICATES THE MYSTERY OF THE SPIRIT'S MOVEMENT. MARTIN LUTHER: What the translators of the LXX wanted *diapsalma* to mean grammatically, I do not know. I will guess the mystery. For by their habit they seem to have indicated a mystery, because they dared to translate it as a division, pause or delay—which *selāh* does not mean in Hebrew. Nor are they moved lightly; it is certain that neither an iota nor a "squiggle" is written for nothing in Sacred Literature.

So, this pause I suppose according to my temerity to mean some sign of mood by which the psalmist is affected according to the Spirit's movement. The Spirit is not in our power. He is not able to be contained by us in every psalm or every verse—but only as the Holy Spirit allows us to be stirred. Therefore *selāh* is placed in psalms in such a haphazard manner, without any reason, because by this it reveals something secret and unknown to us. It is not possible to foresee the Spirit's movement. When this movement comes, by disregarding the psalm's words the Spirit demands the soul be quiet and pause, which is capable of either the illumination or the emotion that is offered. So in this verse—because it is about that extraordinary trial of spirit when [the idea of] a wrathful God, even a wrathful creation, is bolstered—the prophet was stirred to experience and acknowledge [this trial] in deep emotion. SECOND PSALMS LECTURES (1519–1521).[12]

3:3-6 The Lord Defends and Sustains His People

DAVID'S CONFIDENCE IS IN THE LORD. JOHN CALVIN: Convinced that he was not utterly cut off from God's favor and that God's selection of him to be king remained unchanged, David encourages

himself to hope for a favorable outcome to his present trials. And, first, by comparing God with a shield he means that he was defended by his power. Thus, he also concludes that God was his glory, because he would be the Champion and Guardian of the royal dignity which he had been pleased to confer on David. And on this account, he became so confident that he dares to advance with his head held high. COMMENTARY ON THE PSALMS.[13]

WHY TAKE REFUGE IN GOD? PHILIPP MELANCHTHON: He begins the petition by an argument from the power and will of God whom he calls on: "Consider the person, that is, God, and his commandments, promises and examples. Thus, I call on you only, because you are my shield, that is, you have commanded that you are to be called on, you have given promises that you are willing to hear and help, and you have declared this so many times by your deeds, save me, the one who calls on you." He encompasses all these points when he signifies the reasons why he takes refuge in God. Moreover, it is evident from the petitions that the chief arguments are taken up from the means: "You are able and willing to help me, and you have often saved me previously; therefore, to you alone do I flee." These are ardent passions when in true sorrows we raise ourselves by this consolation, namely, that when this light still remains in our heart, we are not cast away from God but are truly received, heard and will experience divine help, comfort and liberation. COMMENTS ON THE PSALMS.[14]

WHAT DOES "HOLY MOUNTAIN" SIGNIFY? RUDOLF GWALTHER: Through the "holy mountain" we could understand either heaven itself or the mercy cover on the ark of the covenant which was in the tabernacle on Mount Zion. By these God reveals his will, etc. THE PSALTER.[15]

ASCENDING TO PREDESTINATION. ROBERT ROLLOCK: God's presence is perceived by his

---

[12]WA 5:81. Prior to this section, Luther summarizes and compares the opinions of Cassiodorus, Jerome's letter to Marcella, Origen, Paul of Burgos, Jacque Lefèvre d'Étaples, Johannes Reuchlin and the Septuagint (pp. 79-81). The meaning of *selāh* remains a mystery. There are numerous conjectures—including all those that the reformers offer here—but no consensus. See Kraus, *Psalms 1–59*, 27-29; Goldingay, *Psalms*, 1:599.

[13]CTS 8:31* (CO 31:54).
[14]MO 13:1022.
[15]Gwalther, *Der Psalter*, 3v.

powerfulness in calling, justifying and glorifying us, so that any persons who would know whether God be present with them or not, they must see whether they be called, whether they be justified and by these, as by the means, they must ascend to the predestination and foreknowledge of God, which were from everlasting. Then lest any should doubt these benefits, by which he declares the Lord himself to be present with us, he brings us to that gift of his Son of Christ, chiefest of all gifts. EXPOSITION UPON PSALM 3.[16]

A PROVERB AMONG THE HEBREWS. THE ENGLISH ANNOTATIONS: Though the words "I lay down and sleep; I awoke again" simply taken, give a good sense of what they mean, still that sense will be fuller if it is observed that this was a proverbial saying among the Hebrews, meaning to set out great confidence and security. . . . That is, he troubles himself no more about it, he takes no further thought, but rests himself with all confidence and security. ANNOTATIONS ON PSALM 3:5.[17]

THE SAFETY OF THE CHURCH. JOHN CALVIN: These words not only preserve the office and praise appropriate to God alone, tacitly opposing his power to all human support, but also declare that although a thousand deaths hang over his people, yet this cannot render God unable to save them or prevent him from speedily sending forth without any effort the deliverance which he is always able to impart. In the end of the psalm, David affirms that this was not so much given to him as an individual but to the whole people, that the universal church, whose welfare depended on the safety and prosperity of his kingdom, might be preserved from destruction. For this reason, David recognizes that the wicked conspiracy was destroyed because the oversight of God protects the church. From this passage we learn that the church will always be delivered from the calamities which befall it, because God who is able to save it will never withdraw his grace and blessing from it. COMMENTARY ON THE PSALMS.[18]

3:7 Lord, Come Quickly!

REMEMBER THE LORD'S PAST ASSISTANCE. WOLFGANG MUSCULUS: Here we observe how the prophet nourishes and strengthens the trust in obtaining help by calling to remembrance past deliverances, by which he had been divinely snatched from the hand of all his enemies. Let us also recollect from God's acts of kindness which we have enjoyed even to the present day how much divine goodwill, kindness and providence exists toward us that we may shout more confidently to obtain this divine aid. Here he approaches the heart to deplore our diffidence, that is, the crookedness of our hearts. By this crookedness it happens that we are not led by God's acts of kindness—not even his daily ones—to acknowledge certainly and clearly the divine providence and goodness toward us and to entrust our whole selves to him, although even the cow and donkey recognize the manger of their own Master and today seek food in the place where they were fed on a former day. COMMENTARY ON PSALM 3.[19]

GOD PROMISES THE DEFEAT OF OUR ENEMIES. DIRK PHILIPS: Holy Scripture thus comforts all those saved by God who suffer persecution here and says that the godless threaten the righteous and gnash their teeth over them, that they draw out the sword, stretch the bow and nock poisonous arrows to shoot the pious secretly. But their sword will go into their own heart, their bow will break, the Lord will break in pieces the teeth of the godless, and it is only a little time more until the godless are no more and their place will be nowhere to be found. But the righteous will live in eternity; they will grow like palm trees and stand

---

[16]Rollock, *Exposition upon Some Psalmes*, 21*.
[17]Downame, ed., *Annotations*, 5Zr*; citing Prov 3:24; Job 11:18; Mk 4:27.
[18]CTS 8:36* (CO 31:57).
[19]Musculus, *In Psalterium Commentarii*, 46.

like olive trees in the court of the Lord. THE ENCHIRIDION: THREE ADMONITIONS.[20]

3:8 Salvation Is God's

GOD'S PEOPLE DELIGHT IN BLESSING, NOT IDOLATRY. WOLFGANG MUSCULUS: The blessing of God has been appointed for the people of God, in order that that people whose God is the Lord may truly become blessed. It turns out differently, however, for those people who are subjected to tyrants in this age; whose delights are not in blessing but in cursing; and who have been repaid with calamities of every kind. Truly, the people of God must also be careful, so that they may persevere by a solid and sincere faith in obedience to the Word of God, and so that no idolatry may repay this alien kindness of God to themselves. COMMENTARY ON PSALM 3.[21]

BLESS YOUR PEOPLE WITH THEIR INHERI-TANCE. DESIDERIUS ERASMUS: Bless your people, as in the beginning. Let our enemies curse us, if only you will bless us. We care nothing for human blessings, which lead simple hearts astray, when "the sinner is praised for his soul's desires, and the unjust is given blessing." Such blessings are cursed by you. There will always be people who will hire Balaam to curse your people, but your Son declared that those whom human beings cursed for his sake would be blessed. David patiently endured Shimei's curses, and we too bless those who curse us, we speak well of those who revile us, we pray for those who revile us, following both the example and the teaching of your Son, so that your blessing shall always rest on your people. Grant that we may always remain your people; we trust that we shall never lose your blessing. Meanwhile we in turn shall bless your holy name, which is blessed forevermore, until we hear your final blessing from the lips of your blessed Son Jesus: "Come, you who are blessed by my Father, and possess the kingdom prepared for you since the beginning of the world." PARAPHRASE OF PSALM 3.[22]

---

[20]CRR 6:424* (BRN 10:458); citing Ps 37:10, 12-15; 92:12-13. [21]Musculus, *In Psalterium Commentarii*, 48. [22]CWE 63:168*; citing Deut 26:15; Ps 10:3; Num 22:6; Deut 23:4; Mt 5:11 (cf. Rom 12:14; 1 Cor 4:12); 2 Sam 16:5-12; Mt 25:34.

4:1-8 ANSWER ME WHEN I CALL!

To the choirmaster: with stringed instruments.
A Psalm of David.

¹ Answer me when I call, O God of my
    righteousness!
  You have given me relief when I was in distress.
  Be gracious to me and hear my prayer!
² O men,ᵃ how long shall my honor be turned
    into shame?
  How long will you love vain words and seek
    after lies?   Selah
³ But know that the LORD has set apart the
    godly for himself;
  the LORD hears when I call to him.

⁴ Be angry,ᵇ and do not sin;
  ponder in your own hearts on your beds,
    and be silent.   Selah
⁵ Offer right sacrifices,
  and put your trust in the LORD.

⁶ There are many who say, "Who will show us
    some good?
  Lift up the light of your face upon us, O
    LORD!"
⁷ You have put more joy in my heart
  than they have when their grain and wine
    abound.

⁸ In peace I will both lie down and sleep;
  for you alone, O LORD, make me dwell in
    safety.

a Or O men of rank   b Or Be agitated

OVERVIEW: As with Psalm 3, the historical context for the lament that opens this psalm could well be Absalom's rebellion against his father, David. Our Reformation commentators find significance not only in the psalmist's cry of distress but, more importantly, in the peace and trust in the Lord that he affirms by the end of this "evening" psalm. Several commentators point to the role of the Holy Spirit, not only in David's composition of the psalm but also in our understanding of the text and in shaping followers of Jesus Christ, whose lives are meant to be true sacrifices to God. Moreover, the anthropomorphic imagery concerning God's face in verse 6 provides them with an opportunity to discuss the use of metaphorical language within Scripture as well as the significance of the fact that God, who is incorporeal by nature, took on flesh—including a human face—in Jesus Christ. Finally, some commentators reflect on the meaning of the psalm's superscription, which—although ambiguous and disputed—seems to imply its use within corporate worship, which further indicates that both the psalmist's lament as well as his ultimate confidence in God could be expressed and shared by others.

READING AND HEARING SCRIPTURE REQUIRE DILIGENCE. DESIDERIUS ERASMUS: Dear brothers in the Lord: interpretation of this psalm is fraught with difficulties, and we must therefore give it all our attention; if not, you will be deprived of much pleasure and profit, and I shall have labored in vain to instruct you. In order to enjoy the kernel of a nut, you do not begrudge the small effort involved in removing the hard shell and bitter rind. You should not therefore be reluctant to concentrate your thoughts for a while, in order to feed them with the wholesome and delicious nourishment which this psalm offers you. The Holy Spirit inspired the composer of this psalm and will honor both you and me with his presence if we can show that our minds are ready and eager to learn. SERMON ON PSALM 4.[1]

---

[1]CWE 63:175*.

Superscription: *How Are These Words to Be Understood?*

THE SUPERSCRIPTION REVEALS THE WORK OF THE HOLY SPIRIT. MARTIN LUTHER: Because this title is often used in the Psalms and is here given for the first time, we should look at it a little more closely.... Let us, then, speak to the first word *lamnaṣēaḥ*. It is derived from the verb *nāṣaḥ*, which means to urge, to incite, to provoke, to arouse, as the soldier is stirred up to battle by the drum and the horse by the sound of the trumpet.... It is the function of music to arouse the sad, sluggish and dull spirit. Thus Elisha summoned a minstrel so that he might be stirred up to prophesy. Hence, *měnaṣēah* properly means stimulus, incitement, challenge, and, as it were, a spur of the spirit, a goad and an exhortation.... For in all these the listless mind is sharpened and kindled, so that it may be alert and vigorous as it proceeds to the task. But when these are at the same time sung to artistic music, they kindle the mind more intensely and sharply. And in this manner David here composed this psalm *lamnaṣēaḥ*, that is, as something inciting, stirring and inflaming, so that he might have something to arouse him to stir up the devotion and inclination of his heart, and in order that this might be done more sharply, he did so with musical instruments. Thus in ancient times the church used to read psalms before Mass as an incentive....

As to the second word *bingînôt*, it does not denote a specific instrument but is a common name for any instrument whatever.... The sense of the title is: A psalm of David as an incitement with musical instruments. This is according to Johannes Reuchlin. FIRST PSALMS LECTURES (1513–1515).[2]

A COMMON SUPERSCRIPTION IN THE PSALMS. CARDINAL CAJETAN: The title is "To the conquering one in modulations, a psalm for David." In this notice once and for all that in many titles this term is translated as "to the conquering one." It has been read as "to the conquering one," "to the victor," "according to victory"—nevertheless they correctly say it is a participle, so it is of course "to the conquering one." And there are various opinions about what that means in this sort of title. Some think it means a type of song or note, which is sung simultaneously by rivals trying to outdo one another. Others think it is the director for musical instruments or a specific song or note, as would be denoted by "the one directing" to whom such a song or way of singing was assigned.... For we will frequently find something similar in the titles of psalms. And it seems by this that a director should always be appointed for such a song or note or instrument.

Now that it is said "in modulation," you should not understand to be a special Hebrew term used in this passage. For there is a question about this term: whether it is the name of a musical instrument or the name of a special type of music whose style is modulation.... Now this too has been said once and for all for the many titles which have "in modulations." COMMENTARY ON PSALM 4.[3]

THE SUPERSCRIPTION REVEALS CHRIST'S SACRIFICE. FELIX PRATENSIS: The title of Psalm 4 has two terms that are not a little ambiguous in meaning. Regarding the first term, so far I have not found a single author who has correctly exegeted it. This word *měnaṣēah* is a participle from the verb *nṣḥ*.... It has numerous meanings. The noun *nēṣaḥ*, according to the testimonies of Hebrew authors, sometimes means "eternity," sometimes "victory," sometimes "strength," sometimes "blood"—as is apparent in Isaiah 63: "Their blood was spattered on my garments." ... Of course, I would not want you to believe me without a reason that this is its meaning. For because David, filled with the Holy Spirit, sang about Christ's life in his melodies, not without reason did he use such a term portraying Christ's passion, victory and resurrection in the first word of this psalm's title.... So, David—when

---

[2]LW 10:43-44* (WA 3:40-41); citing Job 39:25; 2 Kings 3:15; 1 Chron 15:21; Johannes Reuchlin, *In septem psalmos poenitentiales hebraicos* (Tübingen: Thomas Anselm, 1512), unpaginated. Later Luther rejected this conjecture about *lamnaṣēaḥ* in favor of "choir director"; see LW 12:199-200 (WA 40,2:475-76).

[3]Cajetan, *In Sacrae Scripturae Expositionem*, 3:16.

he began to narrate Christ's passion, not his own persecution—said to shedding blood or bleeding, or to granting eternity, or to conquering or to overcoming, that is, in praise of shedding blood or conquering, etc.

Now the second term, *nĕgînôt*, sometimes means "choir," sometimes a song accompanied by musical instruments. Thus, David intimates that we should rejoice, conduct the choir and offer praise in honor of our Redeemer who redeemed us with his very own blood. THE HEBREW PSALTER.[4]

THE SUPERSCRIPTION PROVIDES MUSICAL INFORMATION. JOHN CALVIN: Concerning the words which are contained in this verse, I will only touch on them very briefly. Some translate *lamnaṣēaḥ* as "forever," as if this psalm were composed to the tune of an ordinary song; I reject this as too strained. Others more correctly believe *mĕnaṣēah* to mean someone who excels and surpasses all others. But because there is not agreement among everyone about what kind of excellence and rank it would be, let it suffice for us that by this word, the choir director is meant. I do not approve of rendering this word as "victor." Although it fits the argument of this psalm, still in other passages where we will find it again it is not at all suitable. Now *nĕgînôt*, I derive from *nāgan* which means "to beat." Therefore, I do not doubt that it was a musical instrument. From this it follows that this psalm was meant to be sung not only with a high voice but also to be accompanied with musical instruments, which were directed and guided by the choir director, whom we just mentioned. COMMENTARY ON THE PSALMS.[5]

4:1-3 The Lord Hears and Answers My Prayers

WHAT IS RIGHTEOUSNESS? WHOSE IS IT? DESIDERIUS ERASMUS: Someone may ask why he

is called "the God of righteousness" in the psalm. It is because no one is righteous unless God makes him righteous, or justified, by faith. But why then does the psalm say "of *my* righteousness"? Because nothing is more truly our own than God's gifts to us, because he puts no conditions on them and never asks for them back, unless we are ungrateful; "his gifts are irrevocable." As I have said, human righteousness consists in trusting in God's promises while acknowledging that we ourselves have earned nothing but damnation. God's righteousness lies in fulfilling his promises, not because humanity deserves it but because it was he who made them. Nevertheless, the ability to confess our wrongdoing and, distrusting ourselves, to trust in God's promises is in itself a gift from God. SERMON ON PSALM 4.[6]

PLEA FOR MERCY. DESIDERIUS ERASMUS: Our lives are subject to constant alternation between joy and sorrow; they are never free from dangers and cannot be lived entirely without sin. Therefore, just as we must always give thanks to God for whatever he may send us, so we must constantly cry out: "Have pity on me." All God's gifts to us may be called God's pity or mercy, since he freely bestows them on us when we need his aid. Sometimes he shows his mercy in greatest measure when he sends us troubles; in that case, we must beg him, in his mercy, to grant us patience. In times of prosperity we must again beg him, in his mercy, to save us from corruption. Without God's mercy, adversity and prosperity are equally dangerous to us. But ordinary people only cry, "Have mercy on me!" when they are beset by troubles; the Pharisee, who thinks himself righteous, never cries, "Have mercy on me!" but merely gives thanks. But just as true Christians always give thanks for everything, so they always add a fresh plea for mercy, because we know, first, that God's gifts need protection against theft by the unworthy, and, second, that we must prepare to receive still greater gifts; neither can be achieved without God's mercy to help us. A SERMON ON PSALM 4.[7]

---

[4] Pratensis, *Psalterium*, 2v-3r.
[5] CTS 8:37* (CO 31:57-58). The precise meaning of these terms continues to evade commentators; see Kraus, *Psalms 1–59*, 29-30, 26-27 for *lamnaṣēaḥ* and *nĕgînôt*, respectively.
[6] CWE 63:220*; citing Rom 11:29.
[7] CWE 63:236*; citing Lk 18:11.

WHAT DOES "YOU ENLARGED ME"[8] MEAN?

MARTIN BUCER: This translation in the Scriptures, and especially in the Psalms, is quite frequent. For while we are afflicted and pressed by adversities, as if confined to a close and narrow space, then indeed when we are freed, it is as if we are sent out into a broad place and given space for moving about at our leisure. For those go wherever they please ought to be under their own authority and impaired by no one. And so when Absalom threatened David so that he was scarcely allowed to escape his hand, he was distressed, and, just as if he was constrained in a tight corner, no place was open to him in any jurisdiction of Israel. Moreover, when Absalom died and the people again asked for the true king, it was as if he were led from a narrow space into the broadest one: then nothing hindered him and nothing stood in his way. He is permitted to turn about and go where he wants; God had made space for him. HOLY PSALMS.[9]

RECONCILING TEXTUAL AND INTERPRETIVE DISAGREEMENTS. DESIDERIUS ERASMUS:

Where the Septuagint translates "children of humankind," Jerome translates, from the original Hebrew, "children of the man." . . . Some take "the man" to mean Abraham, that outstanding hero in whose name the Israelites glory. . . . Others take "the man" to mean Adam, but in the sense in which the Hebrews use it, it is more likely that this word should be understood to refer to Abraham, whose name is the most renowned of all among the Hebrews. . . . In the Gospels the Lord thus upbraids the Jews because, although they took pride in the name of their father Abraham, they fell far short of his achievements; they behaved rather as if their father were the devil, and a liar and a murderer, because they opposed the truth and plotted the death of an innocent. Such a reading thus produces the following: "How long will you take pride in the names of your patriarchs yet fall short in their faith and piety, tarnishing your ancestor's glory, loving vanity instead of the things necessary for salvation, seeking out falsehood instead of truth?" The alternative reading . . . produces: "Children of Abraham, how long will you dishonor my name among the Gentiles, turning my glory into shame? You are the chosen people, you are called the children of God, but because of your unholy way of life, I am reviled among the Gentiles, who think that a deity must resemble his people. Your showy titles are vain unless accompanied by piety in your lives; to call yourselves the children of God is to lie, because by your deeds you proclaim yourselves the children of the devil." . . .

The large number of different readings here should surprise no one. There can be no doubt that what the psalmist wrote, at the behest of the Holy Spirit, was simple and unambiguous; but God allowed these variations, the work of copyists and translators, to appear in the holy books, so that these extra difficulties would rouse us from our torpor. Salvation is not imperiled by a slight departure from the original sense of Scripture, so long as the new reading conforms to piety and truth; even if our interpretation does not entirely fit into its original context, our labors will have been worthwhile if our reading contributes to moral improvement and fits in with other Scriptural texts. SERMON ON PSALM 4.[10]

THE SHIELD OF A GOOD CONSCIENCE. JOHN

CALVIN: Now, from this passage, we ought to take up a shield of invincible steadfastness as often as we see ourselves overmatched in skill and guile by the wicked. For with whatever schemes they assault us, yet if we have the testimony of a good conscience, God will remain on our side, and against him they shall not prevail. They may greatly excel in ingenuity and possess much power of hurting us, and have

---

[8]Here Bucer, as well as most of his peers, renders *rāḥab* literally. Most English translations—except KJV and NRSV—translate this more idiomatically as "relieve" or "give relief" (ESV, NIV, NASB). Contemporary commentators seem to prefer a more literal "you have made room," though they disagree whether *hirḥabtā* should be emended to an imperative. Kraus and Alter are against the emendation; Goldingay is for it. See Kraus, *Psalms 1–59*, 144-45, 147-48; Alter, *Book of Psalms*, 10; Goldingay, *Psalms*, 1:116, 118-19.
[9]Bucer, *Sacrorum Psalmorum*, 35r.

[10]CWE 63:237-40*; citing Jn 8:33.

their plans and subsidiary aid in the greatest readiness and be very shrewd in discernment, yet whatever they may invent, it will be but lying and vanity. COMMENTARY ON THE PSALMS.[11]

THE CROSS IS PART OF FAITH. NIKOLAUS SELNECKER: This is comfort. God sends crosses and yet saves those who are his. Therefore humble yourselves under the mighty hand of God so that he would save you in his time. Learn to submit to God's way. He deals wondrously with those who are his. Whenever we think that he is very far from us and wants to let us perish, he helps us. Yes, once all human help comes to an end, then God's help truly begins. But we are the sort who want instead for God to help us from the very moment on, not wondrously but in our way, as it pleases us. But that cannot be. If he is to help, it has to be such help that no one would expect. For when he loves someone, he presents himself as if he were that person's enemy and sends various crosses. In the same way a pious housefather does not give his son as much to eat as a pig; he keeps his child under discipline and under the rod. The pig he lets wallow in its own filth and muck—not because he loves the pig more than his child. This is God's way, too; we must learn to adjust ourselves to this and not become impatient during crosses. That is, believe, suffer and pray. THE WHOLE PSALTER.[12]

THE COMFORT OF GOD'S FAITHFULNESS. JOHN CALVIN: He infers that he would be heard by God as often as he called on him. For God principally proves his faithfulness in this, that he does not forsake the work of his own hands but continually defends those whom he has once received into his favor. Hence, we are taught to proceed fearlessly in our path, because whatever we may have undertaken according to his will shall never be ineffectual. Let this truth then obtain a fixed place in our minds, that God will never withhold his assistance from those who go

on sincerely in their course. Without this comfort every moment, the faithful will inevitably perish. COMMENTARY ON THE PSALMS.[13]

4:4-5 Be Angry but Trust in the Lord

MURDER TRANSFORMED INTO SELF-REPENTANCE. DESIDERIUS ERASMUS: Anger is the first step toward murder, wounding words are the second, and, when anger is well established, the final step toward murder is to plan how to kill the object of your hatred. The Jews sacrificed by slaughtering cattle; Christians sacrifice by slaughtering the "former self" and all its ways. Thus sinners, inspired by the change in their brother, first become angry with themselves. Anger is followed by self-reproach as they scold themselves in their heart; then they conceive an infallible plan for killing the former self: they strike it down by repentance, bury it in baptism, and then lay the new self, born to replace the old, on the altar of faith, there to be consumed by the divine fire, the Holy Spirit. SERMON ON PSALM 4.[14]

THE UPRIGHT ARE STILL AFFLICTED WITH SIN. HIERONYMUS WELLER VON MOLSDORF: This is very good counsel, that is, to put out the first flames of anger, hate and vengeance, and any desires of a similar kind. For those who give in to them both increase the evil and pile sin on sin. The prophet then teaches with the words, "Be angry and do not sin," that among the saints there are still wicked desires, albeit the remnant of sin and manifold infirmity, and that they are inflamed with rage, envy, lust for vengeance, impatience, lack of faith, in just the same way as the wicked are. For him the difference is that the wicked give in to the crooked impulses of their heart and slacken the bridle, while the upright vigorously reject these impulses and diligently set about putting their own earthly bodies—that is, their flesh with its desires—to death. And because they are always in Christ

---

[11]CTS 8:41-42* (CO 31:60).
[12]Selnecker, *Der gantze Psalter*, 1:17r.

[13]CTS 8:43* (CO 31:61).
[14]CWE 63:256-57*.

and he is in them, God does not impute this remnant of sin, their own sins and errors to them, according to Psalm 32: "Blessed are they whose wickedness has been forgiven, and whose sins are covered." So the mind of the upright should not be troubled when they feel the immensity of their own weakness and various flames of anger, hate, envy, desire, impatience. However, they should not give approval to these feelings or give in to them. BRIEF COMMENT ON PSALM 4.[15]

CHAMBER OF THE HEART. DESIDERIUS ERASMUS: I imagine that you understand that prophet's figure of speech here. He is not referring to a room in a house but to the innermost chamber of the heart. The heart is in fact the most inaccessible organ of the human body, a sort of inner room where secrets are stored, but there is a still more secret place within the heart, which is here called the private chamber. It is well known that the heart has various recesses and chambers, and the image of the heart is used in two different ways, in that people are said to speak both "in their hearts" and "from the heart." But we can only search our consciences properly *in* the inner chamber of the heart where we speak to God and not to other people. A SERMON ON PSALM 4.[16]

EXAMINE YOURSELF. JOHN CALVIN: "To speak on one's bed" is an expression taken from common human practice and experience. We know that in everyday life dealing with people, our thoughts are distracted, and we often judge rashly, being deceived by the external appearance. But when we are alone, we can give to any subject closer attention, and shame does not hinder persons from reflecting on their own faults. David, therefore, exhorts his enemies to withdraw from witnesses and spectators, so that they can examine themselves honestly and candidly. And this exhortation is significant for us all; for there is nothing to which human beings are more prone than to

deceive one another with empty applause, until each person descends into himself, and speaks with himself. COMMENTARY ON THE PSALMS.[17]

THROUGH FORGIVENESS THE LORD BUILDS HIS LIVING TEMPLE. DESIDERIUS ERASMUS: Just as there is no forgiveness of sins outside the church, so no sacrifice is acceptable to God unless it is offered within that temple which the Lord, its foundation and cornerstone, fashioned from living rocks. David therefore added: "Let it be your pleasure, Lord, to favor Zion, that the walls of your Jerusalem may be built anew." Without your good will this building cannot rise, nor can this temple be preserved without your mercy, for among people nothing can be found except decay, collapse and ruin. "Only then will you accept the sacrifice of righteousness, gifts and burnt offerings; only then will people lay their calves on your altar." Such sacrifices are made every day on our Zion, which spreads throughout the world, in the form of the confession of sins, thanksgiving and the kind of incense which is most pleasing to God, heartfelt prayer. God takes no delight in the slaughter of cattle, the reek of burning flesh or the heavy fumes of incense. SERMON ON PSALM 4.[18]

SACRIFICE YOURSELF TO GOD. MARTIN LUTHER: A "sacrifice," he says, not of cattle and of calves but of "righteousness" (that is, what is denoted by them). That is: slaughter and cut to pieces and crucify and put to death the bestial and living members, so that they may not serve sin and for sin but that by the fire of love they may be completely consumed and changed by the Spirit, so that they might serve the living God. This is what it means to burn the animals with a perpetual fire, as Romans 12 says: "Present your bodies as a living sacrifice, holy and acceptable to God." Such is assuredly the sacrifice of righteousness "for a pleasing odor to the Lord." What else does "sacrifice" mean but to make sacred, and a sacrifice something

[15]Weller, *Enarratio Psalmorum*, 24; citing Ps 32:1.
[16]CWE 63:254-55*.

[17]CTS 8:44* (CO 31:61-62).
[18]CWE 63:193*; citing 1 Pet 2:5-6; Ps 51:18.

made holy and offered and set apart for sacred purposes? But all of us ought to be such a sacrifice, at the same time one and each one his own. LECTURES ON PSALMS (1513–1515).[19]

4:6-8 Joy in the Lord Is Not Dependent on Material Goods

REQUEST FOR THE WEAK. RUDOLF GWALTHER: This should be understood concerning the weak in faith, who suppose it will never again happen that they might recover their former good fortune. For this reason David asks that for their sake God would act quickly, so that they do not completely despair. THE PSALTER.[20]

HOW DOES GOD TURN HIS FACE? DESIDERIUS ERASMUS: The Israelites could not look on God's face or bear the words he spoke. But when the age of the gospel's grace arrived, God put on his other face, which is not only bearable but lovable. He took on human form, so that all might be saved and none perish. He freely forgave us all our sins through trust in his Son Jesus. But to return to the point: of course, God is by nature incorporeal and does not have a face which he turns this way and that, sometimes calm and smiling, sometimes grim and stormy; rather, he views everything, both good and evil, past and future as well as present, in the same way. But the holy Scriptures say metaphorically that he "gazes down" when he bestows his favor and that he "turns away his face" when he withdraws his mercy—when this occurs, a deep and numbing terror takes possession of us. Sometimes he does so when offended by our sins; sometimes he even turns his face from good people for a while, to remind them that they can do nothing for themselves unless they are constantly upheld by God's favor. A SERMON ON PSALM 4.[21]

GOD'S FATHERLY COUNTENANCE. JOHN CALVIN: "The light of God's face" denotes his serene countenance, just as, on the other hand, the face of God seems to us dark and clouded when he shows any sign of anger. This light, by a beautiful metaphor, is said to be lifted up, when, shining in our hearts, it produces trust and hope. It would not be enough for us to be beloved by God, unless the sense of this love came home to our hearts; but, shining on them by the Holy Spirit, he cheers us with true and solid joy. This passage teaches us that those are miserable who do not, with full resolution, repose themselves wholly in God. The faithful, although they are tossed amid many troubles, are truly happy, were there no other ground for it but this, that God's fatherly countenance shines on them, which turns darkness into light, and, as I may say, quickens even death itself. COMMENTARY ON THE PSALMS.[22]

DESPITE APPEARANCES—AND IDIOMS—ALL THINGS ARE FROM GOD. CARDINAL CAJETAN: Notice here that if the pronoun *their* (repeated, too) did not oppose this interpretation, the sense of the letters would be obvious: that this season should be expected when God lifts up the light of his face on us, like how crops and wine abound in their season—provided that the crops, vines and grapes grow in their seasons. But the pronoun *their* . . . and similarly the following verse, that everything is given by God alone, oppose this sense. It is indeed clear that the prophet intends to distinguish between himself and those from one group and others from another group. To say that others increase their "crops and wine in season" or that others' crops and wine abound in season— the meaning is the same—their goods are not expected from the time of season but from God alone. And he intends this by means of the abundance of crops and riches of wine. Indeed this is metaphorical speech, asserting that others' wealth abounds as a result of the season, like crops and wine, that is, like the enjoyment of vegetables:

[19]LW 10:67 (WA 3:56); citing Rom 12:1; Lev 6:21.
[20]Gwalther, *Der Psalter*, 5v.
[21]CWE 63:203*.

[22]CTS 8:48* (CO 31:63).

our wealth should not be expected from the season but from God alone.

And the prophet intends by this according to the letter to respond to their grumbling, when they said that he himself had not made use of the season when Saul had been delivered into his hands. For at that time they said, "Look, the day about which the Lord said to you: 'Look, I will hand over your enemy to you, so that you will do with him what is pleasing in your eyes.'" To this he responds directly that others' advantage results from the season, whether just or unjust (for this reason he said *their*), but my advantage depends on God alone. COMMENTARY ON PSALM 4.[23]

THE GIFT OF DEATH. DESIDERIUS ERASMUS: Only those can lie down and sleep in peace together who wage war against sin, who bear no ill will toward anyone, and, as far as they can, show good will to all; only those who lie down to sleep in this way can find peace of mind in this life. . . . We are dealing here with the death of the passions not of the body. Nonetheless, although this interpretation can be applied to every part of Christian life, it is true that death provides a particularly striking example of this kind of peace, for death represents the final battle between the flesh and the spirit. I need not point out the obvious fact that in Holy Writ death is often called sleep. . . . Because of the comparison between death and sleep, this psalm is sung, according to church custom, before the time for sleep, and thus it may be sung still more appropriately at the hour of death; the pagans call death eternal sleep, whereas we, who are to live again, may more correctly call it "the long sleep," but not eternal. SERMON ON PSALM 4.[24]

---

[23]Cajetan, *In Sacrae Scripturae Expositionem*, 3:18-19; citing 1 Sam 24:4.

[24]CWE 63:272*.

5:1-12 LEAD ME INTO YOUR TEMPLE

To the choirmaster: for the flutes. A Psalm of David.

¹ Give ear to my words, O LORD;
  consider my groaning.
² Give attention to the sound of my cry,
  my King and my God,
  for to you do I pray.
³ O LORD, in the morning you hear my voice;
  in the morning I prepare a sacrifice for you[a]
  and watch.

⁴ For you are not a God who delights in
  wickedness;
  evil may not dwell with you.
⁵ The boastful shall not stand before your eyes;
  you hate all evildoers.
⁶ You destroy those who speak lies;
  the LORD abhors the bloodthirsty and
  deceitful man.

⁷ But I, through the abundance of your
  steadfast love,
  will enter your house.

I will bow down toward your holy temple
  in the fear of you.
⁸ Lead me, O LORD, in your righteousness
  because of my enemies;
  make your way straight before me.

⁹ For there is no truth in their mouth;
  their inmost self is destruction;
  their throat is an open grave;
  they flatter with their tongue.
¹⁰ Make them bear their guilt, O God;
  let them fall by their own counsels;
  because of the abundance of their transgressions
  cast them out,
  for they have rebelled against you.

¹¹ But let all who take refuge in you rejoice;
  let them ever sing for joy,
and spread your protection over them,
  that those who love your name may exult
  in you.
¹² For you bless the righteous, O LORD;
  you cover him with favor as with a shield.

a Or I direct my prayer to you

OVERVIEW: This exemplary psalm of prayer provides the reformers the opportunity to develop two propositions that they will repeat and thicken throughout their comments on the Psalms: appearances on earth are deceiving, and human emotions are valid but must be shared with God. First, how things appear before human beings is not how they appear before God. In fact, we should know that there is an inverse relationship between human and divine perceptions, so that living in faith often means living upside down compared with the world around us. Thus, often it is the wicked who are mighty and esteemed, while the godly are poor and oppressed. Whenever we are tempted to doubt how things really are—that is,

before the eyes of God—we must turn to him in prayer through the Word. Believers are defended by worship, not weapons.

Second, despite how the reformers are sometimes stereotyped—stern and stoic regarding suffering—here they validate the fears and doubts that people experience; however, they command us to direct these emotions to God himself. Whether we are angry or elated, hesitant or faithful, the Lord longs to hear us. In the same way that we do not hide how we are feeling from close friends, so also we should not falsify how we feel before God. And we should not forget that Christ suffers with us and sustains us by his grace and faithfulness, not by our own ability and actions. From the rising to the setting of the sun, we should orient ourselves to the Sun of Righteousness, the true temple of God, communing with him as a dear and intimate friend. Despite how things seem and how we feel, God is able to hit straight blows with crooked sticks.

Also, our exegetes' debate concerning this polyvalent or ambiguous title (*lamnaṣēaḥ el-hannĕḥîlôt*) is typical of such discussions. Some commentators often focus on these christologically, understanding their ambiguity as pointing to the mystery of Christ. Others, particularly Calvin, find this too speculative. Such commentators either prefer to profess their ignorance or to apply a more concrete, low-risk interpretation, usually that the term is a musical instrument or melody. The former commentators connect *neḥilôt* to the psalm's subject matter concerning the inheritance of those who are in Christ and those who are not.

FOCUS ON GOD'S GLORY IN PRAYER. THEODORE BEZA: This psalm is also a prayer. It rightly teaches those rules of prayer for when someone is unjustly afflicted. Clearly, we must pray earnestly and oppose all doubt of God's goodwill toward us or of his power with this truth: he is our God and our King. Our impatience is to be bridled with this consideration, that the nature of God cannot suffer the wicked to go unpunished, and therefore the more ferocious that our enemies appear, the more near and more certain is their destruction. Finally, in our prayers we should not consider our enemies' punishment or our own interests but only God's glory—for this reason he will not cease to bless us. PARAPHRASE OF PSALM 5.[1]

Superscription: *Flutes, Inheritances or Mysteries?*

THE MYSTERIOUS MEANING OF NEḤILÔT IS FITTING. FELIX PRATENSIS: *Neḥilôt* has not a few explanations. Some say it means a certain musical instrument with which they say David sang this psalm; others, "weakness" or "injury";

others, "congregations" or "friends"; others, "inheritances for the heirs." Others interpret it as "near brooks" or "above brooks." All these meanings are appropriate for this term, because it is highly ambiguous—indeed, this manner of speaking David uses in almost all his titles. This is not without great and divine mystery.

For, as we said in the previous psalm, David wants to embrace all the mysteries of Christ in a few words. As a matter of fact, near the brook Kidron our Savior prayed to the Father; the Jews also wounded him; and the powerful weakness by which he received no redemption; on behalf of his congregation or his friends or his disciples or anyone else—both good and bad—he asks the Father for the inheritance which the Father gave him. For he says, "I myself intercede for them. . . . Holy Father, keep them in your name, all those whom you gave to me." The rest you will understand as in the previous psalm. THE HEBREW PSALTER.[2]

NEḤILÔT PROBABLY HAS NOTHING TO DO WITH THE PSALM'S SUBJECT MATTER. CARDINAL CAJETAN: This Hebrew term has so many meanings that it is uncertain whether it is placed in the title to indicate instruments or some other musical things, or whether to touch on the subject matter of the psalm. For on the one hand it means musical instruments, on the other, it means congregations or inheritances or valleys. Neither from what precedes or follows of the title is the correct choice of meaning intimated. Still the first word implies that it is the name of a musical instrument or the name of a melody. COMMENTARY ON PSALM 5.[3]

NEḤILÔT INDICATES THE PSALM'S SUBJECT MATTER. PHILIPP MELANCHTHON: The title indicates the argument. For David prays for his heirs, that is, for the church: this is without a doubt the point of this psalm. For the whole

---

[1]Beza, *Psalmes of Dauid*, 6* (*Psalmorum Davidis*, 12).

[2]Pratensis, *Psalterium*, 3v; citing Jn 18:1; Jn 17:9-11.
[3]Cajetan, *In Sacrae Scripturae Expositionem*, 3:20.

prayer is full of sorrow and indignation against the impious teachers who, with their authority, ordinary succession (as it is called), power, titles and wealth, prevail over the miserable assembly of those who teach rightly, such that they commend, establish and defend errors. Against these, it is necessary that the pious are strengthened by both doctrine and the invocation of God. So beginning at once David and the church ardently pray that it is ruled and defended against impostors. This proposition is repeated beginning in the first three verses of this psalm. COMMENTS ON THE PSALMS.[4]

THIS PSALM IS ABOUT THE INHERITANCE OF THE GOOD AND BAD. NIKOLAUS SELNECKER: The title of this psalm indicates its content and what it encompasses.[5] It talks about the inheritance—that is, about the fruit and reward or wage—of both the blessed and the godless. For this word, *inheritance*, is often used this way in Scripture: as a reward, benefit and fruit, or gift—as in Psalm 127: "See, children are an inheritance or gift from the Lord." Now this psalm also deals with the inheritance of the pious and the wicked in this world and also in the next.

In this life, things generally go well for the wicked; they flutter about in great honor. They are powerful and rich; they also possess such names and titles that intimate that they are holy, pious and honorable people. The pious, however, and in fact, the whole church of God, must suffer in this life and are subject to crosses on every side. They must also continue to bear such names that intimate that they are unruly rebels and heretics among whom no peace or order can be maintained. Now this is painful. And it causes great offense to and grieves the hearts and conscience of many pious, godfearing people and teachers. Against this, we must arm and prepare ourselves not only with the Word or with teaching with which we confront the godless, but also with somber, incessant prayer to God, that he would rule and protect his inheritance—that is, his church and believers—against false teachers, fanatical spirits and tyrants.... We learn from this psalm how we should confront false teachers and brothers, tyrants and all enemies of God, namely, with prayer. Not with violence, with swords and pikes or with Saint Peter's dagger, but instead with true worship which a true Christian should offer: teaching, praying, thanking, lamenting, comforting and confessing. Prayer makes us sure and confident in our vocation and in our life. THE WHOLE PSALTER.[6]

IT IS A WASTE TO SPECULATE ABOUT PSALM TITLES. JOHN CALVIN: Some translate the Hebrew word *neḥilôt* as "inheritances"; others as "armies." The former give this reason for their opinion: David prayed for the welfare of the twelve tribes. But the latter give this reason: being besieged by a mighty multitude of people, he turned to his guardian, God; thus, the word *above* can mean "against." But because I do not approve of such enigmatic conjectures about these inscriptions, I gladly subscribe to the opinion of those who teach that it was either a musical instrument or tone—however, I am not at all troubled to figure out what particular sort. COMMENTARY ON THE PSALMS.[7]

---

[4]MO 13:1024.

[5]That is, *lamnaṣēaḥ el-hannēḥilôt*. The meaning of both these words is uncertain, though generally modern translations render them as "to the choirmaster for the flutes." Most early modern commentators—excluding Calvin and Cajetan, who both agree with Alter—translated this as "in praise of inheritance" (e.g., Luther, Selnecker, Gwalther). Because of *neḥilôt*'s obscurity Alter transliterates it, while Kraus draws connections to 1 Kings 1:40 and 1 Sam 10:5, asserting that this is indeed likely a flute. See further Alter, *Book of Psalms*, 12; Kraus, *Psalms 1–59*, 27.

[6]Selnecker, *Der gantze Psalter*, 1:18v; citing Ps 127:3.

[7]CTS 8:51* (CO 31:65). This is Calvin's default explanation of mysterious terms in psalm superscriptions, perhaps following Cajetan. This possibilty is intimated by the similarity between Calvin and Cajetan's exegesis. It could be supported by the fact that the Genevan Academy's library collection—built on Calvin's own library—owned many of Cajetan's commentaries; see Alexandre Ganoczy, *La Bibliothèque de l'Académie de Calvin* (Geneva: Droz, 1969).

PSALM TITLES ARE VALUABLE. MOÏSE AMY-
RAUT: Those who consider the prefixed titles for
many psalms to be unimportant, dream wildly. For
they are very ancient, and the person who gathered
these songs into one volume and who was a
prophet understood them as authoritative.
ANNOTATIONS ON PSALM 3:1.[8]

5:1-3 Hear My Cry

**ROUSE YOURSELF IN PRAYER THROUGH GOD'S
MANY TITLES.** JOHN CALVIN: If, then, we are
slothful in prayer or our devout affections easily
waver, here is a spur to urge us on. By calling God
his King and his God, he intended zealously to stir
up himself to greater trust. Let us learn to apply
these titles to a similar use, namely, for the purpose
of making ourselves more familiar with God. At the
close, he testifies that he does not sullenly gnaw the
bit, as unbelievers are accustomed to do, but directs
his groaning to God. For those who, disregarding
God, either fret inwardly or utter their complaints
to human beings are not worthy of being regarded
by him. COMMENTARY ON THE PSALMS.[9]

**KNOW THAT GOD LONGS TO HEAR YOU AND
TO ENSURE YOUR WELL-BEING.** NIKOLAUS
SELNECKER: The godly, whenever they call out to
God in their times of need, generally according to
the flesh have these two afflictions and doubts: they
think that God will not hear them right away, or
they imagine that their crossbearing not only came
out of God's infliction but also that God desires for
them to be plagued by their enemies for an even
longer amount of time. "It is God's will," they say,
"that such miserable things happen to me now."
Against such afflictions the Holy Spirit himself
consoles us and desires that we would not imagine
that God does not want to hear us; rather, he
desires that we would persist diligently in prayer
and cry out to God, so that he would hear us early
in the morning. That is, he does not want to leave

us mired in our distress; instead, he longs to come
to our help with his timely deliverance.

And this is a fine and lovely explanation that
several teachers give: these words should be divided
in this way. "Lord, in the morning you will hear my
voice": these are the words of the one calling on
God and shouting for help. The other words that
follow—"In the morning I will send myself to you
and watch"—should be understood as God's words,
who answers those who call on him, because he
wants to hear them and wants to send himself to
them. That is, he wants everything to be ordered
and even, so that there would be no distresses, just
like how we order and set a table so that we can eat.
THE WHOLE PSALTER.[10]

5:4-6 No Rest for the Wicked

THE LORD IS A GOD OF FAITH AND GRACE.
MARTIN LUTHER: God is not a respecter of
persons. It is as if he were saying, "My salvation is
in faith and grace, and not in the law or physical
descent." Otherwise God would be unjust if he
were to receive all who are children of Abraham
according to the flesh and his heirs, even though
many among them are ungodly and evil. Therefore,
to choose and receive them thus without distinction would be a manifest injustice. But now the
Lord "comes to judge the earth," and he rules in
judgment, because he receives neither according to
the flesh nor according to the person. Instead
"whoever believes will be saved." FIRST PSALMS
LECTURES (1513–1515).[11]

**GOD USES THE WICKED BUT DOES NOT
AUTHORIZE THEIR WICKEDNESS.** JOHN
CALVIN: Again, we may infer from this passage the
common doctrine, that although he works by Satan
and by the unbelievers and makes use of their
malice for executing his judgments, God is not, on
this account, the author of sin, nor is he pleased
with it because the end which he purposes is always

---

[8]Amyraut, *Paraphrasis in Psalmos Davidis*, 13.
[9]CTS 8:53* (CO 31:66).

[10]Selnecker, *Der gantze Psalter*, 19r.
[11]LW 10:76* (WA 3:67); citing Ps 98:9; 1 Chron 16:33; Mk 16:16.

righteous. And he justly condemns and punishes those who, by his hidden providence, are driven just as he pleases. COMMENTARY ON THE PSALMS.[12]

GOD IS NOT NEUTRAL. TILEMANN HESSHUS: Above all God hates untroubled people's impiety. Their impiety destroys all religion and is the root of all wickedness. Because God in his Word so stringently demands that we fear him, it is impossible that however much the impious glorify him, God would stand on the side of the impious. Truly God is not neutral in the battles of the church; therefore, he stands on the side of the pious, however much they may seem to be deserted. COMMENTARY ON PSALM 5.[13]

BAPTISM APART FROM WORKS IS NOT ENOUGH. MARTIN LUTHER: In saying, "All who work iniquity," and "You will destroy all," he is using that expression to strike those who with foolish confidence think that they are saved because they are numbered with the people of God, are baptized and believing, and without works. So there are some who say, "Because there are so many heathen who will perish, we must hope that few Christians will perish," as if Christians must necessarily be saved because the heathen perish. But here he says *all*, without any exception whatever. The Lord makes the same point: "Do you think that only these above others were sinners in Jerusalem, because they suffered this? Truly, I say to you, unless you repent, you will all likewise perish." For on the Day of Judgment he will say to those who have this kind of confidence: "Depart from me, all you workers of evil," namely, whoever they were. The same is said in Romans 11. FIRST PSALMS LECTURES (1513–1515).[14]

5:7-8 I Will Worship in Your Spirit

ORIENTED TOWARD THE TEMPLE, THAT IS, JESUS. RUDOLF GWALTHER: The ancients either performed their prayers in the temple and tabernacle or, if they were unable to go there, they turned themselves toward it—as you find with Daniel, that he prayed toward Jerusalem. But such was done on account of the great promises that God has given, and so Christ was depicted through the temple and its sacrifices. THE PSALTER.[15]

THE TEMPLE WAS AN EXTERNAL SIGN FOR INTERNAL UNITY. MARTIN BUCER: What he calls "the house of the Lord" he understands to mean the same as "holy temple," for the Hebrew word *hêkal* can mean "palace," "inner sanctum" or "especially hallowed royal court." In each instance he means the place where the tabernacle of the covenant was, for the temple of Solomon had not yet been built. Moreover he seeks these things not because David was making such a big deal of a place, for God is everywhere present for his people and must be adored, although at that time he desired to have a specific place for his own worship, so that the people might more conveniently preserve the unity of religion. No, he seeks these things because it greatly pained him to dwell among wicked idolaters, and the greatest desire afflicted him for a holy fellowship with those who feared God. For those who truly love God have no greater torment than not publicly praising and proclaiming him with some enjoyment of piety, just as in the same manner they delight in nothing other than in being united with the children of God. HOLY PSALMS.[16]

WE NEED DIVINE GUIDANCE. VIKTORIN STRIGEL: The petition for divine guidance stands in contrast to the Gentile verse, "Fortune rules the way, not wisdom." Here it is as if he were saying, "Do not allow us to be led astray by the devil to impiety and other wickedness. Defend us against the treacheries of the devil, guide us with your light, by your counsels, and do not permit us to come to ruin, deceived by our errors and incited by the weakness of the flesh." The wisdom and virtue of

---

[12]CTS 8:56* (CO 31:68).
[13]Hesshus, *Commentarius in Psalmos*, 34r.
[14]LW 10:77* (WA 3:68); citing Lk 13:2-5; Ps 6:8; Mt 7:23; Lk 13:27.
[15]Gwalther, *Der Psalter*, 6v-7r; citing Dan 6:10.
[16]Bucer, *Sacrorum Psalmorum*, 43r.

David was great and admirable; still, we see him sometimes incited, now by the devil, now by human error, as when he orders the people to be counted. Therefore, because everyone's weakness is great, you, God the Father of our Lord Jesus Christ, guide us always and show to us your wholesome counsels in private and public affairs, and strengthen our hearts with your Holy Spirit, so that they might submit to you, and so that we might not be instruments of wrath but instruments of mercy and useful for the church. HYPONĒMATA IN ALL THE PSALMS.[17]

RIGHTEOUSNESS IS FAITHFULNESS. JOHN CALVIN: The righteousness of God, therefore, in this passage, as in many others, is to be understood of his faithfulness and mercy which he shows in defending and preserving his people. Consequently, "in your righteousness" means the same thing as "for" or "according to your righteousness." David, desiring to have God as the guide of his path, encourages himself in the hope of obtaining his request, because God is righteous; as if he had said, Lord, as you are righteous, defend me with your help, that I may escape from the wicked plots of my enemies. Of the same import is the last clause of the verse, where he prays that the way of God may be made straight before his face, in other words, that he might be delivered by the power of God from the distresses with which he was so completely surrounded, that, according to the judgment of the flesh, he never expected to find a way of escape. And thus he acknowledges how impossible it was for him to avoid being entangled in the snares of his enemies, unless God both gave him wisdom and opened up for him a way where no way is. It becomes us, after his example, to do the same thing; so that distrusting ourselves when counsel fails us, and the malice and wickedness of our enemies prevail, we may betake ourselves speedily to God, in whose hands are the issues of death, as we shall see afterwards. COMMENTARY ON THE PSALMS.[18]

5:9-12 The Wicked Descend, the Righteous Ascend

DEATH AND WICKEDNESS POUR FROM THEIR MOUTHS. SEBASTIAN MÜNSTER: Their innermost being, he says, and their heart is full of wickedness, and therefore their throat is exactly like a fetid grave. Thus, nothing is able to flow from their mouth other than the most rank wickedness. THE TEMPLE OF THE LORD: PSALM 5.[19]

GOD IS NOT VENGEFUL BUT PATIENT. WOLFGANG MUSCULUS: We are admonished in this passage that this prayer must not be prayed too soon against any transgressors. It is not simply said, "on account of transgressions" but "on account of the multitude of their transgressions." He notes the rashness of the ungodly, by which they join transgression to transgression without ceasing, and thus they stir up the anger of God against themselves. For God is not inclined to vengeance because of his own patience; nevertheless, being angered, he punishes more severely. Therefore, let us first beware, lest we should fall into this infinite multitude of transgressions; second, let us learn against which transgressors we must pray this prayer to God, and against which transgressors we may not. COMMENTARY ON THE PSALMS.[20]

REBELLION AGAINST GOD IS A GRAVE SIN. WOLFGANG MUSCULUS: Let us also notice that he does not say this, "because they sin against you," but, "because they rebel against you." It is one thing to sin against God, and another to rebel against God. They sin, because they do not do what is instructed. This definition is true of everyone, even the godly. Those who try to throw off authority itself rebel. So it is one thing not to obey the Word of God in all matters, but it is another for heretics to condemn the teaching and Word of God and to shake off the yoke completely.

---

[17]Strigel, Hyponēmata, 16.
[18]CTS 8:59* (CO 31:69-70); citing Ps 69:1.
[19]Münster, Miqdaš YHWH, 1163.
[20]Musculus, In Psalterium Commentarii, 74.

The latter is true of the ungodly, and they are worthily destroyed and cast off from his grace. COMMENTARY ON THE PSALMS.[21]

WHAT TRUE BLESSING AND RIGHTEOUSNESS ARE. JOHN CALVIN: The psalmist teaches us that there is no true and right joy but what is derived from the sense of God's fatherly love. The Hebrew word "to bless" (when spoken regarding human beings) means to pray for someone's well-being; but when it refers to God, it means the same thing as to strengthen a person or to make him abundantly fortunate—as they say—or accumulate every good thing. For because the favor of God is efficacious, his blessing of itself produces an abundance of every good thing. The noun *righteous* is not restricted to one person but indicates in general all worshipers of God. Those, however, whom Scripture calls righteous, are not those who are judged as such by the merit of their works, but those who aspire to righteousness. Because after God has received them into his favor, by not imputing their sins to them, he accepts their virtuous zeal as perfect righteousness. COMMENTARY ON THE PSALMS.[22]

HEIRS WITH CHRIST, WE SUFFER TOGETHER. NIKOLAUS SELNECKER: We are heirs of God and coheirs with Christ. Accordingly we should persevere with prayer and know that God wants to sustain us in the true knowledge and confession of his truth—free will in us will neither do nor cause this. Without Christ we are able to do nothing. Without the Holy Spirit we are powerless. As Leonhard Kaiser—who was burned in Bavaria in 1527 on account of the truth of the gospel—said, "O Lord Christ, you must suffer with me! You must carry me! With me it's over. I have firmly decided that I want to remain with you, but it is not by my own action or ability; your grace is my foundation and strength. Give what you command, and do what you will." David speaks in the same way in this psalm against bare free will: "Lord, direct your way before me." Bless us and crown us. Be our shield and shelter, strength and power. Without you we are lost. THE WHOLE PSALTER.[23]

---

[23]Selnecker, *Der gantze Psalter*, 1:20v; citing Rom 8:17. Leonhard Kaiser (c. 1480–1527) was defrocked and burned to death near Passau, having been convicted of heresy (i.e., as a Protestant). Luther published a *Flugschrift*—from which Selnecker here quotes—in Kaiser's defense after Johann Eck published a scathing explanation of Kaiser's heresy. See Johann Eck, *Warhafftige handlung wie es mit herr Lenhart Käser zu Schärding verbrent ergangen ist: Wider ain falsch erdicht unnd erlogen büchlin* (Ingolstadt: Apian, 1527); Martin Luther, *Von Er Lenhard keiser ynn Beyern umb des Euangelii willen verbrandt: Eine selige geschicht* (Wittenberg: Hans Lufft, 1528), esp. D4r.

---

[21]Musculus, *In Psalterium Commentarii*, 74.
[22]CTS 8:63-64* (CO 31:72).

6:1-10 O LORD, DELIVER MY LIFE

To the choirmaster: with stringed instruments; according to The Sheminith.[a] A Psalm of David.

¹ O LORD, rebuke me not in your anger,
    nor discipline me in your wrath.
² Be gracious to me, O LORD, for I am languish-
    ing;
  heal me, O LORD, for my bones are troubled.
³ My soul also is greatly troubled.
    But you, O LORD—how long?

⁴ Turn, O LORD, deliver my life;
    save me for the sake of your steadfast love.
⁵ For in death there is no remembrance of you;
    in Sheol who will give you praise?

⁶ I am weary with my moaning;
    every night I flood my bed with tears;
    I drench my couch with my weeping.
⁷ My eye wastes away because of grief;
    it grows weak because of all my foes.

⁸ Depart from me, all you workers of evil,
    for the LORD has heard the sound of my
        weeping.
⁹ The LORD has heard my plea;
    the LORD accepts my prayer.
¹⁰ All my enemies shall be ashamed and greatly
        troubled;
    they shall turn back and be put to shame in
        a moment.

a Probably a musical or liturgical term

OVERVIEW: In their comment on the first of the seven penitential psalms (i.e., Pss 6; 32; 38; 51; 102; 130; 143) the reformers focus on the relationship between repentance and suffering. David's poetic imagery deeply moves our commentators: his affliction must have been profound! Seemingly at a loss for words, he repeats himself; his laments are choked off mid-sentence on account of his weeping and wailing. His internal turmoil affects his body; however, it does not thus earn his repentance. Instead his tears and tremors demonstrate his repentance. Again, the reformers remind their readers that the Lord desires that they would exhibit emotion and empathy—like the Son of God himself; however, they should not let their feelings overwhelm their faith, steering them away from confidence in God. Instead, they are to feel *and* trust in God's will.

The reformers observe that when we are mired in such misery, we often make the mistake of assuming we are being punished by God or that God has forsaken us, but that is not necessarily so. Instead through suffering the Lord desires that

people would realize the inverted order of reality: his ways are not ours, his wisdom seems like foolishness to the world. These pains, Donne claims, are medicinal, not viral. We suffer so that we might be like Christ, so that we might be made whole by participating in his promises and the love of the Father and the Son. Just as the Father never forsook his Son, so also he will not forsake his people.

The extended aside on the Tetragrammaton from Luther and Donne merits some background on the name of God during the Reformation. Many people allege the reformers to be the inventors of the name Jehovah, which resulted from their putative Hebraic ignorance by conflating the *Qere* (i.e., what is spoken) with the *Kethib* (i.e., what is written). According to Hebrew tradition the divine name YHWH is unspeakable and therefore whenever it occurs in the Hebrew Bible—more than sixty-eight hundred times—the word *ădōnāy* ("Lord") is usually said in its place, though sometimes *ʾēl* ("God") is used. As a reminder of this custom the vowels for *ădōnāy* are placed on the consonants YHWH. However,

Donne here shows that he knows that tradition.[1] In fact, Nicholas of Lyra, a commentator most of the reformers would have referenced, gives a lengthy treatment about the Tetragrammaton in his comment on Exodus 6:2 in which he explains the *Kethib-Qere*. "Because that name among the Hebrews is considered so holy that it should not be pronounced except by the high priest and only then during the blessings in the temple, thus, this name *ădōnāy* is said in place of that name."[2]

So then, if Donne and others knew this, why do they use "Jehovah"? In light of the revelation of the gospel, these believers thought it unfitting and superstitious that God's name should be unpronounceable. Some commentators thus used Jehovah, the use of which dates back at least to the thirteenth century.[3] Others used the Tetragrammaton (e.g., Luther). Still others tried different solutions. Johannes Reuchlin claimed that the Tetragrammaton had become pronounceable in the Pentagrammaton, that is, Jesus; Bucer used *Autophyes*, that is, "Self-Existent One," to translate YHWH in his commentary on Psalms; Folengo used Jove. Some printers, following Luther, tried a typographical solution: LORD or GOD indicated YHWH; LOrd or GOd indicated *ădōnāy*.[4]

Christ Delivers His Own from the Depths of Hell. Nikolaus Selnecker: Few people understand this psalm except the sad and afflicted hearts, who feel their sin and the wrath of God against their sin. It preaches about the true fear of hell, in which the saints are thrust, when they feel and lament their sin in their conscience. And this is a truly spiritual plague, known to few

people and is called in Scripture "the cords of hell" and "pangs of hell," along with a number of other names. It is a temporal hell in the hearts of those who are weary of their sins and have God's wrath placed right before their eyes—just as Christ himself was also in this hell, when he cried out on the cross in his deepest suffering: "My God, my God, why have you forsaken me?" Thus, it often seems to us that God does not want to accept us, he is our enemy, he wants to surrender us to the devil right now. As the good Jacob says, "I must rush into hell to my son." And this suffering is above all suffering, horrifying the mind, reason, heart and soul....

Out of this temporal hell those for whom Christ conquered hell are saved.... For the blessed burst out of this with Christ, and they again see Christ with joy, so that they do not despair in the end like the godless. These rightly sing—and it is composed and intended for them—"You have come, O Long-Anticipated One, for whom we in darkness have waited."[5] He lets the glimmer of divine mercies settle again in the heart and illuminates it with new joy. Some people rightly call these trials true purgatory. And they are truly the very mouth and courtyard of hell, from which the fathers and still more pious people are saved daily. The Whole Psalter.[6]

Superscription: *What Does the Šĕmînît Mean?*

Šĕmînît Could Mean Three Things. Felix Pratensis: The title of Psalm 6 has a term, *šĕmînît*, that is not a little ambiguous in meaning. Some say it is the name of a certain musical instrument with eight strings, called the *octochordus*; therefore, it is also known as the eighth. However, others say it is not the name of an instrument, but "eighth" is taken for eight days or

---

[1]Luther does, too, but not in what is excerpted here; see, for example, his lectures on Exodus (1524), WA 16:99.29-30.

[2]*Biblia Sacra cum Glossa ordinaria, novisque additionibus*, 6 vols. (Venice: Magna Societas, 1603), 1:533-35, here 533.

[3]See "Jehovah," in *Catholic Encyclopedia*, 15 vols. (New York: Robert Appleton, 1907–1912), 8:329-31. The preferred contemporary pronunciation "Yahweh" is also speculative.

[4]See further R. Kendall Soulen, *The Divine Name(s) and the Holy Trinity* (Louisville, KY: Westminster John Knox, 2011); Christine Helmer, "Luther's Trinitarian Hermeneutic and the Old Testament," *Modern Theology* 18, no. 1 (2002): 49-73, esp. 56.

[5]This is the beginning of the second verse for *Canticum Triumphale*, an ancient Easter hymn sung in celebration of Christ's victory over hell (cf. 1 Pet 3:18-19).

[6]Selnecker, *Der gantze Psalter*, 1:21r; Ps 18:5; 116:3; Mt 27:46 (cf. Ps 22:1); Gen 37:35.

years or ages. And others, like the Kabbalists, want it to be understood as the eighth *sefirah*[7] which they attribute to the Messiah himself. You will have to adapt these options to your own understanding. As we have said, we are not focusing on the exegete's office but the translator's task. THE HEBREW PSALTER.[8]

FREEDOM TO SPECULATE ABOUT THE MEANING OF ŠĔMÎNÎT. JOHN CALVIN: Now concerning the word *eighth*, because we have said elsewhere that *nĕgînôt* is a musical instrument, I do not know whether it would be fitting to call it a harp of eight strings. Therefore, I readily allow it to refer to the tone, so that it indicates the particular song to which the psalm was to be sung. Nevertheless in such an obscure matter—and of trivial importance—I leave each person free to form his own conjecture. COMMENTARY ON THE PSALMS.[9]

6:1-3 Lord, I Am Troubled

ACCEPT GOD'S DISCIPLINE BOTH AS HIS CHILD AND HIS DEFENDANT. MARTIN LUTHER: To explain this psalm several things must be noted. First, in all suffering and affliction human beings should first of all run to God; they should realize and accept the fact that everything is sent by God, whether it comes from the devil or from human beings. This is what the prophet does here. In this psalm he mentions his suffering, but first he hurries to God and accepts this suffering from God; for this is how to learn patience and the fear of God. But whoever looks to human beings and does not accept these things from God becomes impatient and a despiser of God.

Second, God disciplines in two ways. At times he does so in grace as a good Father—and temporally. At other times he does so in wrath as a stern

Judge—and eternally. Now when God seizes human beings, their nature is so weak and disheartened, because they do not know whether God seizes them out of wrath or mercy. And in fear of his wrath they lift up their voice and cry out: "O God, do not discipline me in your wrath! Let me be disciplined in your mercy—and temporally. Be my Father and not my Judge." As Saint Augustine also says, "O God, raze this, hack that, strike here and spare our life to come!" Thus, he implores here, not that he wants to go entirely undisciplined, for this would not be a good sign, but that we would be disciplined as a child by his father. THE SEVEN PENITENTIAL PSALMS (1525).[10]

GOD'S CHILDREN ACKNOWLEDGE HIM AS THE SOURCE OF ALL THINGS; THE REPROBATE DO NOT. JOHN KNOX: In this especially the children of God differ from the reprobate: the children of God know both prosperity and adversity to be the gifts of God alone.... And therefore in prosperity commonly they are not insolent nor proud, but even in the day of joy and rest they look for trouble and sorrow. And yet, in the time of adversity, they are not altogether left without comfort; but by one way or another, God shows to them that their trouble will have an end. While, on the other hand, the reprobate, either taking all things of chance or else making an idol of their own wisdom, in prosperity are so puffed up that they forget God, without any care that trouble should follow. And in adversity they are so dejected that they look for nothing but hell. A FORT FOR THE AFFLICTED.[11]

DAVID FLEES TO GOD BY NAME. JOHN DONNE: The name then of Jehovah, which is here translated "Lord," is agreed by all to be the greatest name by which God has declared and manifested himself to human beings. This is that name which the Jews falsely but peremptorily—for falsehood lives by peremptoriness and feeds and arms itself with

---

[7]Medieval Kabbalists believed that God reveals himself through ten *sefirot* (sg. *sefirah*), that is, divine attributes: the crown (i.e. creation), wisdom, understanding, lovingkindness, strength, beauty, eternity, glory, foundation and kingship.
[8]Pratensis, *Psalterium*, 4r.
[9]CTS 8:65* (CO 31:73).

[10]LW 14:140-41* (WA 18:480-81): citing Augustine, *Confessions* 4 passim.
[11]Knox, *A Fort for the Afflicted*, A3r-v*.

peremptoriness—deny ever to have been attributed to the Messiah in the Scriptures. This is that name in whose virtue and use those calumniators of our Savior's miracles do say that he did his miracles, according to a direction and schedule, for the true and right pronouncing of that name, which Solomon in his time had made, and Christ in his time had found, and by which, say they, any other person might have done those miracles, if he had had Solomon's directions for the right sounding of this name, Jehovah. This is that name, which out of a superstitious reverence the Jews always forebore to sound or utter, but ever pronounced some other name, either *ădōnāy* or *ĕlōhîm*, in its place, wherever they found Jehovah. But now their rabbis will not so much as write that name, but still express it in four other letters. So that they dare not, not only not sound it, not say it, but not see it.....

But however this name is to be sounded, what falls into our consideration at this time is that David in his distress fled presently to God, and to God by name, that is, in consideration and commemoration of his particular blessings; and to a God who had that name, the name Jehovah, the name of Essence and Being, which name carried a confession, that all our well-being, and the very first being itself, was, and was to be derived from him. SERMON 48: PREACHED UPON THE PENITENTIAL PSALMS.[12]

THE TETRAGRAMMATON FORESHADOWED THE TRINITY. MARTIN LUTHER: Now because all these things happened in figures so that neither an iota or squiggle could be believed to be written in vain, I do not deny that in the name Tetragrammaton a different and unique name beyond all other names was figured and designated to be revealed clearly in the New Testament. And so at that time it was considered ineffable.... We should believe that the name Tetragrammaton is a symbol of the name of the Holy Trinity, and the now revealed name of the Father and the Son and the Holy Spirit was then foreshadowed under these four

letters. In order to understand this truth, we will babble about the very letters ... and their meaning.

The meaning of the Tetragrammaton is this: *yodh* ("origin"), *he* ("this"), *waw* ("and"), *he* ("this"). Were these to be constructed grammatically and in Latin, this sentence will result: "The Origin of This and This." And this fits with the name of the Holy Trinity in all respects, because the Father in his divinity is "the Origin of This," that is the Son, "and This," that is the Holy Spirit. For these pronouns, "this and this," rather obscurely represent the Son and the Holy Spirit, as was suitable to that Testament in which the mystery of the Holy Trinity was not to be revealed but merely intimated. Still the Father's name is not clearly expressed, even though as the name of origin it is more noticeable than the Son and Holy Spirit. And by this it is indicated that, as Christ says in Matthew 11, "No one knows the Father or the Son unless it has been revealed to him." Accordingly today the mystery of the Holy Trinity is not known, despite the name being clearly displayed, unless it is taught by the Spirit of faith.

Thus, it is clear that under the name of the Tetragrammaton the number of divine persons and their nature was not outlined any differently to those in the Old Testament than it is to us under this name "Trinity." As the word *Trinity*, if it is analyzed will mean the Father and the Son and the Holy Spirit; thus, the Tetragrammaton will render "the Origin of This and This," which is indeed rather obscure but nevertheless the same. So also the three persons and two processions are also designated in the name of the Father and the Son and the Holy Spirit. SECOND PSALMS LECTURES (1519–1521): ON THE NAME OF GOD, TETRAGRAMMATON.[13]

JESUS IS OUR JEHOVAH. JOHN DONNE: Now what Jehovah was to David, Jesus is to us. Human beings in general relate to God, as he is Jehovah, Being; we have relation to Christ, as he is Jesus, our

---

[12]Donne, *Works*, 2:381-82*.

[13]AWA 2:334-35 (cf. WA 5:184-85; Soulen, *Divine Name[s]*, 90-92); citing 1 Cor 10:11; Mt 5:18; 11:27.

salvation; salvation is our being, Jesus is our Jehovah. Sermon 48: Preached upon the Penitential Psalms.[14]

Misery Begs for Mercy. Robert Rollock: David, in this passage, in order to move God to mercy, sets down his misery before God and amplifies it, so that he would see it. Mercy presupposes misery. Now for God to be merciful, we must first be miserable. Therefore, if anyone fervently craves God's mercy, he must declare before God that he is miserable. Everyone can truly say that he is by nature miserable. This confession, above all things, is most acceptable to God. It is not to our advantage to display our supposed free will—even if it were under our own power—before God. It is better to consider what is pleasant and acceptable to God. For [the display of our supposed free will] would only detract from the grace of God in Christ Jesus. By his grace alone do we have any power to think rightly, to desire rightly and to act rightly. Nor should we enter God's presence thinking of our merits and good deeds. Those who seek to be justified through these things will be greatly disappointed. Exposition upon Psalm 6.[15]

God's Wrath; God's Blessings. John Donne: This is the miserable condition, or danger, that David abhors and depreciates in this text, "To be rebuked in anger," without any purpose in God to amend him, and "to be chastened in his hot displeasure"; so, we can find no interest in the gracious promises of the gospel, no conditions, no power of revocation in the severe threatenings of the law, no difference between those torments which have attacked us here and the everlasting torments of hell itself. We have lost all our joy in this life and all our hope in the next; we would fain die, though it were by our own hands, and though that death do but unlock us a door to pass from one hell into another. This is "your anger, O Lord,

and your hot displeasure." When it comes to be "your anger and your hot displeasure," as David did, so let every Christian find comfort, if he is able to say this verse faithfully.... For as long as one can pray against it, that person is not yet so fallen under it but that he still has a part in all God's blessings, which we shed on the congregation in our sermons and which we seal to every soul in the sacrament of reconciliation. Sermon 48: Preached upon the Penitential Psalms.[16]

A Redundant Prayer. Viktorin Strigel: The repetition of the complaint shows in some way the magnitude of his grief and consternation. And although the power of those emotions cannot be described by words, still this seems to be the sense of the third verse: "Because you are very truly a faithful God, and you do not permit anyone to be tempted beyond their abilities, grant that with no further delay I experience your presence and aid, the mitigation of evils and liberation from them. 'He gives twice who gives quickly.' Therefore, lest I be wanting in such great weakness, and lest I be overcome by a fierce enemy, come and be close by my side and supply me with strength, and do it quickly." Obviously, many are broken and made weak by the long duration of tribulations. Hyponēmata in All the Psalms.[17]

Weeping Sullies Mind and Speech. John Calvin: "And you, Jehovah, how long?" This broken speech express more strongly the vehemence of anguish, which not only holds the mind bound up, but also the throat, so that it overwhelms our speech in the middle of a sentence. Commentary on the Psalms.[18]

The Timelessness of Suffering. Martin Luther: To all suffering people time seems long, and ... to the joyous it seems short. But it seems especially and immeasurably long to those who have this internal hurt of the soul, the feeling of

[14]Donne, *Works*, 2:383-84*.
[15]Rollock, *Exposition*, 49-50*.
[16]Donne, *Works*, 2:395*.
[17]Strigel, *Hyponēmata*, 29.
[18]CTS 8:69* (CO 31:75).

being forsaken and rejected by God, as we say, one hour in purgatory is more bitter than a thousand years of temporal, bodily torment. Thus there is no greater pain than the gnawing pangs of conscience, which occur when God withholds truth, righteousness, wisdom, and nothing remains but sin, darkness, pain and woe. This is a sip or foretaste of the hellish pains and eternal damnation; therefore, it pierces the very bones, strength, blood, marrow and whatever there is in human beings. THE SEVEN PENITENTIAL PSALMS (1525).[19]

6:4-5 Spare and Save Me!

IN SUFFERING GOD SEEMS ABSENT BUT STILL THE HOLY SPIRIT WORKS IN US. JOHN KNOX: It seems to David—being in the extremity of his pain—that God has altogether departed from him. For the flesh, indeed the whole person, always judges in this way when trouble continues for any duration of time. David had sustained trouble many days; he had prayed and yet was not delivered. And therefore he judges that God, being offended by his sins, had left him. And yet it is plain that God was with him, working repentance in his heart by his Holy Spirit, expressing forth those sobs and groans, as well as the desire he had to be restored to that comfort and consolation which sometimes he had felt through the familiarity which he had with God. All these motions, I say, were the operations of God's Holy Spirit, and yet David could perceive no comfort or presence of God in his trouble but lamentably complains. . . . By this it is plain that even the elect themselves sometimes are without all feeling of consolation, and that they think themselves altogether destitute. . . . But David in his anguish remembers that God had formerly been familiar with him. For he says, "Turn again, O Lord," indicating that before he had felt the sweetness of God's presence, but now he was left to himself without comfort or consolation. A FORT FOR THE AFFLICTED.[20]

IN THE SACRAMENT GOD IS HERE WITH US. JOHN DONNE: The first step in this prayer . . . implies a former presence, a present absence and a confidence for the future. Whosoever says, "O Lord, return" says all this: "Lord, you were here; Lord, you are presently departed; but still, Lord, may you return here again." . . . But can God return in a sense such as this? Can we find an *ubi* for God? A place that is his place? Yes. And an earth which is his earth. "Surely the vineyard of the Lord of hosts is the house of Israel, and the men of Judah are his pleasant plant." So the church, which is his vineyard, is his *ubi*, his place, his center, to which he is naturally affected. And when he calls us here and meets us here, on his sabbaths, and sheds the promises of his gospel on the congregation in his ordinance, he returns to us here, as in his *ubi*, as in his own place. And as he has a place of his own here, so he has an earth of his own in this place. Our flesh is earth, and God has invested our flesh, and in that flesh of ours, which suffered death for us, he returns to us in this place, as often as he makes us partakers of his flesh, and in his blood, the blessed sacrament. SERMON 50: PREACHED UPON THE PENITENTIAL PSALMS.[21]

PASTORAL ENCOURAGEMENT IN TRIALS. JOHN KNOX: Turn and consider, dearly beloved, in what state David was when he had no other comfort except the remembrance of God's former benefits to him. And therefore, do not marvel, do not despair—even when you find yourself in the same state as David! I am certain that your own heart must confess that you have received similar benefits from the hand of God as David did. He has called you from a more vile office than from keeping sheep to as great a dignity—including eternal inheritance—as he did David. For from the service of the devil and sin, God has anointed us priests and kings by the blood of his only Son Jesus. He has given you courage and boldness to fight against more cruel, more subtle, more dangerous enemies, even against enemies that are

---

[19]LW 14:142* (WA 18:481).
[20]Knox, *A Fort for the Afflicted*, Cr-v*.

[21]Donne, *Works*, 2:426-27*; citing Is 5:7.

nearer to you than either the lion, the bear or Goliath was to David! I mean against the devil and his assaults, against your own flesh and most inward affections, against the multitude of those who were—and remain—enemies to Christ's religion. Yes, against some of your natural friends who appear to profess Christ with you—and in that the battle is even more vehement.

What boldness I have seen with you in all such conflicts I need not rehearse! I write this to the praise of God: I have wondered at that bold constancy which I have found in you at times when my own heart was faint. I am certain that flesh and blood could never have persuaded you to have condemned and set at naught those things that the world esteems most. You have tasted and felt God's goodness and mercies in such measure that not only are you able to reason and speak but also by the Spirit of God working in you to give comfort and consolation to those who are in trouble. And therefore, most dear mother, do not imagine that God will leave his own mansion forever. No, it is impossible that the devil shall occupy God's inheritance or yet that God shall leave and forsake his holy temple in such a way that he would not also sanctify it. A FORT FOR THE AFFLICTED.[22]

DEATH HERE IS DESCRIBED WITHOUT THE GOSPEL. MOÏSE AMYRAUT: This has been taken from nature's economy. For the end of physical creation of human beings is already appointed. Some vestiges of that economy during the dispensation of the law still survive. Under the dispensation of the gospel, death—whenever it happens to the faithful—has been joined with the experience of God's grace. And because of this, death does not bring any divine curses, that came with a sudden death under the economy of the law. ANNOTATIONS OF PSALM 6:5.[23]

IN THE MISERY OF DEATH THERE IS NO PRAISE. JOHN CALVIN: From this passage some conclude that the dead have no feeling and that it is wholly extinct in them; but this is a rash and unwarranted conclusion, for nothing is here treated but the mutual celebration of the grace of God, in which human beings engage while they continue in the land of the living. We know that we are placed on the earth to praise God with one mind and one mouth, and that this is the end of our life. Death, it is true, puts an end to such praises, but it does not follow from this that the souls of the faithful, when divested of their bodies, are deprived of understanding or touched with no affection toward God. It is also to be considered that, on the present occasion, David dreaded the judgment of God if death should befall him, and this made him dumb as to singing the praises of God. It is only the goodness of God sensibly experienced by us which opens our mouth to celebrate his praise. Therefore, whenever joy and gladness are taken away, praises also must cease. So it does not really surprise that the wrath of God, which overwhelms us with the fear of eternal destruction, is said to extinguish in us the praises of God. COMMENTARY ON THE PSALMS.[24]

GOD'S FAVOR AND DISFAVOR. MARTIN LUTHER: Hell, where your lovingkindness is not, does not praise you; actually it desecrates and blasphemes your justice and truth. This is by far the noblest thought which the saints have in their suffering, by which they are also sustained. Otherwise they are in every way like the damned. . . . However, the difference is that the saints retain favor toward God—they are more concerned about losing God's favor, praise and honor than about being damned. For David does not say, "In hell there is no joy and pleasure," but rather, "There is no praise and honor." Therefore here he inserts that God shows his favor toward no one in hell, and should David go to hell, he, like the condemned, would be in God's disfavor. This

---

[22]Knox, A Fort for the Afflicted, C2v-C3r*.
[23]Amyraut, Paraphrasis in Psalmos Davidis, 24.

[24]CTS 8:71* (CO 31:76). Calvin is refuting here the theory of soul sleep, the idea that the soul sleeps between death and the day of final judgment. See RCS NT II:lii-liii, 30.

would be more unwelcome and painful to him than the pain itself. Therefore we read in the Song of Solomon that the love of God is as strong as death and as firm as hell, because it remains even in deathly and hellish pain. THE SEVEN PENITENTIAL PSALMS (1525).[25]

6:6-7 Drowning in Grief

WHY DO BAD THINGS HAPPEN TO GOOD CHRISTIANS? HIERONYMUS WELLER VON MOLSDORF: It seems that this psalm was composed by David in his old age, after his fall, when all the strength of his body had been exhausted, so much so that he was not able to keep warm even when covered with clothes. But someone might say, "Why should God allow only those who are upright in this life to be terribly tormented by the feeling of sin and the anger of God, while the wicked are allowed to flourish and live free from care?" The answer is clear and straightforward: the upright should resemble the likeness of Christ. These things happen, then, so that the world, that is, unholy and impenitent people, come to understanding, and realize how abominable is the ruin that awaits them. If God so intensely attacks the pious, what will become of the unbelievers? Therefore, may unholy people and all who are free from care know that they are condemned and will suffer these hellish punishments forever in the age to come. BRIEF COMMENT ON PSALM 6.[26]

HYPERBOLE THAT CLEARLY COMMUNICATES DAVID'S SORROWS. JOHN CALVIN: These forms of expression are hyperbolical, but it must not be imagined that David, after the manner of poets, exaggerates his sorrow; but he declares truly and simply how severe and bitter it had been. It should always be kept in mind that his affliction was not so much from his having been severely wounded with bodily distress; but regarding God

as greatly displeased with him, he saw, as it were, hell open to receive him. And the mental distress which this produces exceeds all other sorrows. Indeed, the more sincerely a person is devoted to God, that person is just so much the more severely disquieted by the sense of his wrath. Thus, it happens that saints—who are otherwise gifted with rare strength—have exhibited the greatest fragility and weakness in this matter. And nothing prevents us at this day from experiencing in ourselves what David describes concerning himself but the stupidity of our flesh. Those who have experienced, even in a moderate degree, what it is to wrestle with the fear of eternal death will be satisfied that there is nothing extravagant in these words. Let us, therefore, know that here David is represented to us as being afflicted with the terrors of his conscience, and feeling within him torment of no ordinary kind, but such as made him almost faint away, and lie as if dead. COMMENTARY ON THE PSALMS.[27]

TRUE REPENTANCE REQUIRES AN EXTERNAL RESPONSE. JOHN DONNE: Human concupiscences are naturally dry powder, easily apt to take fire; but tears damp them and give them a little more leisure, and us intermission and consideration. David had labored hard. First . . . as physicians advise, to a redness, to a blushing, to a shame of his sin, and now . . . he labored to a sweat. . . . Tears are the sweat of a laboring soul, and that soul that labors as David did, will sweat, as David did, in the tears of contrition. Until then, until tears break out and find a vent in outward declaration, we pant and struggle in miserable convulsions and distortions and distractions and earthquakes and uncertainties of the soul. I can believe that God will have mercy on me, if I repent. But I cannot believe that that is repentance if I cannot weep or come to outward declarations. . . . These tears carry up our soul, as the flood carried up the ark, higher than any hills; whether hills of power, and so above the oppression of potent adversaries, or hills of our

---

[25]LW 14:143-44* (WA 18:482); citing Song 8:6.
[26]Weller, *Enarratio Psalmorum*, 37.

[27]CTS 8:72-73* (CO 31:77).

own pride and ambition. True holy tears carry us above all. SERMON 52: PREACHED UPON THE PENITENTIAL PSALMS.[28]

GOD DOES NOT DESPISE EMOTION. MARTIN BUCER: Now what the sacred letters relate concerning David clearly show that he had a fine arrangement of nature, with an uncommonly sharp disposition and exceedingly ardent affections. Accordingly, in whatever way he was influenced, he showed himself to be sharp and vigorous, even if he allowed nothing to be done beyond decorum or by weakness, with the exception of what was done to Uriah. God does not want apathy among his own; for this reason not even the Savior exhibited this trait. The saints have it in their power to be sufficiently attentive so that they are not snatched away in some direction by the force of their affections contrary to God's will. God does not demand that they be unaffected. Moreover, if that sorrow would be removed, what, I ask, would they suffer which would be a cross for them? Therefore, it is necessary that they are crucified and grieve. Complaining about it before God and praying for his help is the heart of having God as a Father. Nothing more indulgent happens than with him; nothing equally merciful occurs than with him; he is delighted by requests of this kind and is not offended. In fact, his Spirit always chimes in with requests of this kind: "But not my will, but yours be done." HOLY PSALMS.[29]

IN THE MIDST OF OUR SUFFERING WE THINK WE ARE ALONE. NIKOLAUS SELNECKER: Here David repeats his secret suffering, in which he has become worn out from groaning and weeping. His whole body is decayed; his face has become old and unsightly, because he is full of grave thoughts and temptations. For it happens in this way, that heavily afflicted people swelter in fear from day to day and continually lie in dying sweats, do not have any true rest, and are in fear and anxiety as if they

were in the midst of death and hell, cast away from God's face. And they think that they are the only ones who are cast off by God, as Psalm 31 says: "I said in my trepidation, I am cut off from before your eyes." And Jacob, in Genesis 37 says the same: "In mourning I will rush down into hell, to my son." Which is to say as much as: God hates me and wants to cast me from this temporal heartbreak into eternal heartbreak, to my son, into hell and condemnation. For in this and in other passages the word *hell* does not mean the grave, in which we lay the dead—as many have interpreted it—but truly, condemnation. THE WHOLE PSALTER.[30]

6:8-10 *The Lord Brings Shame on My Enemies*

GOD GRACIOUSLY ALLOWS DAVID TO AVOID SIN. JOHN DONNE: That David could command them away, whose errand was to blaspheme God and whose staying in a longer conversation might have given him occasion of new sins, either in distrusting God's mercy toward himself, or in murmuring against God's patience towards them or perhaps in being uncharitably offended with them and expressing it with some bitterness, but that in respect of himself and not of God's glory only, this *Discedite*—"Depart from me all such people who sin in yourselves, and may cause me to sin, too"—was an act of heavenly courage and a thankful testimony of God's gracious visiting of his soul, enabling him so resolutely to tear himself from such people who might lead him into temptation. SERMON 53: PREACHED ON THE PENITENTIAL PSALMS.[31]

THE CONSOLATION OF GOD'S NEARNESS. PHILIPP MELANCHTHON: This part is now an act of thanksgiving and shows us this consoling teaching. For this reason, the consolation is recited so that we may know that God truly hears the prayers of the church and the members of the

---

[28]Donne, *Works*, 2:457-58*.
[29]Bucer, *Sacrorum Psalmorum*, 50v.

[30]Selnecker, *Der gantze Psalter*, 1:22v; citing Ps 31:22; Gen 37:35.
[31]Donne, *Works*, 2:484*.

church. As well, this promise must be restricted to us. For David as a member of the church declares that there is one true God who reveals himself among this people and has given his promise of mercy to them. In considering this promise, he seeks a kindness and speaks to God who has delivered his promise with certain testimonies. Therefore, David calls on him even by his personal name, YHWH, so this invocation in the true church of God is different from a pagan invocation. Additionally, this example of the deliverance of David is a testimony of the promise. So in our own dangers and distresses, we should read these examples and believe that we too are heard, and obtain more lenient punishments *and* deliverance. And those who cry out with true groans and in this sort of faith, without a doubt, experience relief, just as another psalm says, "The Lord is near to all those who call on him in truth." COMMENTS ON THE PSALMS.[32]

DAVID BLESSES HIS ENEMIES. JOHN DONNE: In the second phrase—"Let them be sore vexed"— he wished his enemies no worse than he himself had been. For he had used the same word of himself before—"My bones are vexed, my soul is vexed"—and considering, that David found this vexation to be his way to God, it was no malicious curse to wish that enemy—who was more sick of the same disease than he was—the same medicine that he had taken.

This is like a troubled sea after a tempest. The danger is past, but the billow still great; the danger was in the calm, in the security or in the tempest by misinterpreting God's corrections to our obduration and to a remorseless stupidity. But when a person has come to this holy vexation: to be troubled, to be shaken with a sense of the indignation of God, the storm is past and the indignation of God has blown over. That soul is in a fair and near way of being restored to a calmness and to a reposed security of conscience that has come to this holy vexation....

A troublesome spirit and a quiet spirit are far asunder; but a troubled spirit and a quiet spirit are near neighbors. And therefore David means them no great harm when he says, "Let them be troubled." Let the wind be as high as it will, so I sail before the wind; let the trouble of my soul be as great as it will, so it direct me on God, and I have calm enough. SERMON 53: PREACHED ON THE PENITENTIAL PSALMS.[33]

THE PSALMIST CONFRONTS THE WICKED WITH LAW. MARTIN LUTHER: God's enemies stand so noxiously and menacingly in their prosperity and boast of themselves as if all were well with them. O God, they do not know how cursed they are! It would be good for them if they came to their senses and realized how very shameful and miserable they are before God. For the very "spiritual" and the wise cannot but be satisfied with themselves, be secure, esteem themselves highly, never feel foolish, say everything well, do the right thing, have holy intentions, stand out among others and acknowledge few as their equals. This is the greatest blindness on earth. However much they think, esteem and consider themselves great in these things, so they are despised and dishonored before God. And the psalmist wants them to recognize this, for they would be different if they came to their senses and were terrified at themselves. THE SEVEN PENITENTIAL PSALMS (1525).[34]

REST IN THE SALVE OF THE CROSS. JOHN KNOX: Now, dearly beloved in our Savior Christ Jesus, the spiritual cross is proper to the children of God. It is given to us a most efficacious medicine to remove diseases and to plant in our souls the most notable virtues, such as humility, mercy, contempt of ourselves and continual remembrance of our own weakness and imperfection. And you have had most evident signs that this same medicine has wrought in you a part of all the promises. There-

---

[32]MO 13:1027; citing Ps 145:18.

[33]Donne, *Works*, 2:498-99*; citing Ps 6:10.
[34]LW 14:146* (WA 18:484).

fore, receive it thankfully from your Father's hand—no matter what trouble it brings with it. The flesh may begrudge it, but let the spirit rejoice, steadfastly looking for deliverance, and assuredly you will obtain it according to the goodwill and promise of him who cannot deceive, to whom be glory forever and ever before his congregation. Amen. A FORT FOR THE AFFLICTED.[35]

[35]Knox, *A Fort for the Afflicted*, D3v-D4r*.

7:1-17 IN YOU I TAKE REFUGE

A Shiggaion[a] of David, which he sang to the
Lord concerning the words of Cush, a Benjaminite.

[1] *O* Lord *my God, in you do I take refuge;*
  save me from all my pursuers and deliver me,
[2] *lest like a lion they tear my soul apart,*
  rending it in pieces, with none to deliver.

[3] *O* Lord *my God, if I have done this,*
  if there is wrong in my hands,
[4] *if I have repaid my friend[b] with evil*
  or plundered my enemy without cause,
[5] *let the enemy pursue my soul and overtake it,*
  and let him trample my life to the ground
  and lay my glory in the dust. Selah

[6] *Arise, O* Lord, *in your anger;*
  lift yourself up against the fury of my enemies;
  awake for me; you have appointed a
    judgment.
[7] *Let the assembly of the peoples be gathered*
    about you;
  over it return on high.

[8] *The* Lord *judges the peoples;*
  judge me, O Lord, *according to my*
    righteousness
  and according to the integrity that is in me.

[9] *Oh, let the evil of the wicked come to an end,*
  and may you establish the righteous—
  you who test the minds and hearts,[c]
  O righteous God!
[10] *My shield is with God,*
  who saves the upright in heart.
[11] *God is a righteous judge,*
  and a God who feels indignation every day.

[12] *If a man[d] does not repent, God[e] will whet his*
    sword;
  he has bent and readied his bow;
[13] *he has prepared for him his deadly weapons,*
  making his arrows fiery shafts.
[14] *Behold, the wicked man conceives evil*
  and is pregnant with mischief
  and gives birth to lies.
[15] *He makes a pit, digging it out,*
  and falls into the hole that he has made.
[16] *His mischief returns upon his own head,*
  and on his own skull his violence descends.

[17] *I will give to the* Lord *the thanks due to his*
    righteousness,
  and I will sing praise to the name of the
    Lord, *the Most High.*

a Probably a musical or liturgical term   b Hebrew *the one at peace with me*   c Hebrew *the hearts and kidneys*   d Hebrew *he*   e Hebrew *he*

OVERVIEW: David's bold assertion of his innocence—had he sinned, he asks that the Lord would erase all memory of him from the earth—prompts the reformers to examine more closely what David means by his innocence. All our commentators reject out of hand the idea that David is sinless. He is of course a sinner, they tell us, as he himself admits: "I was conceived in sin" (Ps 51:3-6). David means that he is being falsely accused and therefore turns to God in faith through earnest prayer. Here David exemplifies how we are to use our good conscience.

For medieval and early modern theologians the conscience is the faculty that determines and assesses moral action. This faculty involves three steps: (1) an abstract command ("Thou shalt"), (2) an assessment of the particular circumstances, and (3) a conclusion of how to act. To act against conscience—to go against what your conscience says you should or should not do—is always to sin. This is what to have a bad conscience means. To act in agreement with conscience, however, does not ensure that you will not sin. Theologians agreed that the first step—provided by the "spark" that was left of the image of God—was inerrant, while the second step could err, depending on what informed it: human instruction or God's Word. For the reformers, David's bold assertion of innocence is an acknowledgment that his conscience might be in error. If he is in error, he is asking that God would instruct and discipline him; if he is not, he is holding God to his promises to protect and preserve his people for his name's sake. A good conscience informed by God's Word and gospel is a powerful defense and consolation.

A Model for Us in the Midst of False Accusations. Theodore Beza: When human beings become accustomed to being harassed with reproachful slanders, so that it is difficult for them to bridle their rage and its consequent evils—especially when there is no protection left for us in the lawful investigation of the magistrate—we are taught in this psalm to seek defense in the presence of God and to oppose human beings. But even so, without any wild feelings, let us entrust our innocence to God alone, the most severe punisher of slanderous tongues. Now the reasons for and circumstances of this psalm's composition are to be considered diligently—whether it refers to Saul himself or to Shimei (see 2 Sam 16) or to someone else from Saul's family—so that we may learn how in the most grave slanders, in which both our reputation and our very life are attacked, to maintain this moderation of our mind. And this lesson especially concerns the church herself and her leaders, whom Satan and his ministers prefer to pierce with these darts before anyone else. Paraphrase of Psalm 7.[1]

Superscription: *The Melody or Content of the Psalm?*

What Does Šiggāyôn Mean? Sebastian Münster: The first term in the title, namely,

šiggāyôn, we did not translate, because it is uncertain what it means in this passage. Some think it is אחד ממיני הניגון, that is, some type of melody or a musical instrument to which the psalm would have been sung. The Temple of the Lord: Psalm 7.[2]

The Psalm Title Fitted to Christ. Felix Pratensis: Various authors explain the first term in the title of Psalm 7, šiggāyôn, in various ways.... Some say it means "err"; others, "anxiety" or "anguish" from the verb šgh. Others assert that it means "interpretation" because, according to their opinion, David composed this psalm through an interpreter. However, we will adjust all these to Christ our Redeemer. For he had the greatest anguish and anxiety, and he suffered under the Jews themselves who were called Cush and of the son of my right hand [i.e., Benjamin]. For they were sons of God's right hand; all other nations are sons of his left hand. What is indicated by "right hand" if not God's lovingkindness, and by "left hand" if not God's wrath? However, they are also Cush, that is, the darkest Ethiopians; these dark ones, since blinded minds and hearts nailed the Lord himself to a cross. For this reason, the Jews' delusion will be revealed when they say Cush represents Saul, who is found nowhere; Saul himself represents all Christ's enemies. The Hebrew Psalter.[3]

7:1-5 *If I Am Guilty, Let Justice Happen*

The Humility of a Good Conscience. Nikolaus Selnecker: This is the proper beginning to an earnest prayer. He does not start like the Pharisee: "I thank you, God, that I am not like other people. I fast twice a week." Instead, he starts concerning the grace and help of God: "You are my God, I trust in you. So now prove to me your goodness. For you are ... God, that is, you are good. I will do what I must. I trust in you. Do

---

[1] Beza, *Psalmorum Davidis*, 18 (cf. *Psalmes of Dauid*, 9); citing 2 Sam 16:5-14.

[2] Münster, *Miqdaš YHWH*, 1164-65. Kraus posits that šiggaāyôn is drawn from an Akkadian word for "lamentation"; see Kraus, *Psalms 1–59*, 26.

[3] Pratensis, *Psalterium*, 4r, 4v.

what you must and help me." In this way the three men in the fiery furnace were delivered, and their persecutors had to acknowledge that the true God preserved such men.

If we take such refuge in God, the result should be a good, cheerful conscience. . . . Therefore David says, "Lord, my God, if I have done such, and it is wrong, then may my enemy persecute my soul." That is, I am innocent and have a good conscience. In other things I am guilty before you and have sinned greatly. But here, in this matter of which I am accused, you know, Lord, that I am righteous. For you chose me to be king in Saul's place. I did not cast him out, as Shimei blames me. I did not pursue it by means of deceit and violence. I am not that ambitious. If I have done so, however, I am willing to suffer whatever I should suffer. If I deserve it, I am willing to be subject to my enemy. He should capture, martyr, kill and completely annihilate me."

Here we see both how a clear conscience is cheerful and bold and yet is at the same time weak and hardly able to trust itself. A good conscience is the best life in the worldly and spiritual estates, before God and all creatures. If someone knows he is just, and an injustice happens to him, even if it hurts badly, still he can console himself and say, "I have a good conscience, let God be my witness." Now the most precious treasure in this world is a good conscience; it is surely not too be valued as insignificant. . . . The pious are not too bold, so that they do not also consider whether they might have been too brazen to someone, like we see here with David. The conscience of a pious person, therefore, is a frail and weak thing, so that, even if he is surely right, still he is afraid and worries if he was too brazen with someone, if he is not as right as he thinks. David is certain that he was chosen and appointed by God to be king, but still he debates here and argues with himself and passes judgment on himself in case he might have done wrong. The Whole Psalter.[4]

Hold Firm the Key of Faith. John Calvin: David does not boast of a confidence from which he had now fallen but of a confidence which he constantly cherished in his afflictions. And this is a genuine proof of our faith, when, having been afflicted by our adversaries, we, nevertheless, do not abandon hope in God. From this passage, we also learn that the door is shut to our prayers, unless it is opened by the key of faith. Nor is it superfluous that he calls Jehovah his God; instead this, like a rampart, repels waves of temptations, lest they overwhelm his faith. Commentary on the Psalms.[5]

All People Are Tempted by Iniquity. Wolfgang Musculus: We see in this passage how important the confidence of an innocent mind before God is! Although before the Lord, David is a sinner—as also he says elsewhere, "Do not enter into judgment with your servant, O Lord!"—nevertheless he boldly calls on the Lord his God against Saul's wickedness, and he asserts his innocence. "If I did this," he says, "if there is such iniquity in my hands." So then, this passage should serve all those who are cast down by injustice and are forced to endure unjust power, so that they themselves, although in other matters are guilty before God, nevertheless in that case in which they are pursued unjustly, flee to their God and place their innocence against the wickedness of the impious. Nor should they doubt that their status of innocence before God is sound and undiminished. . . .

Notice that he does not say, "If iniquity tempted my heart," but, "If there is iniquity in my hands." Because he was a human being, there is no doubt that he was often tempted by wicked thoughts. But because he was a devout person, he did not give way to temptations, nor did he allow iniquity to come into his hands. Thus we read that he said to Saul: "Look, today your own eyes have seen that the Lord has given you into my hand in this cave, and I considered that I could kill you"—see the temptation in his heart!—"but my eyes spared you. For I said, 'I will not stretch out my hand against

---

[4]Selnecker, *Der gantze Psalter*, 1:25v-26r; citing Lk 18:11-12.

[5]CTS 8:77* (CO 31:80).

my lord, because he is the Lord's anointed [*Christus*]." You see here that there was no iniquity in his hands—as he also adds a little later. Thus, it is one thing for people to be tempted in their heart, and another, to bring it to completion in their hand. The first matter concerns all human beings; in the second matter, the impious and reprobate are separated from the pious. The pious do not allow iniquity to come into their hands—even if they were offered the opportunity to bring it to completion—but the impious have crammed their hands full of iniquity. COMMENTARY ON THE PSALMS.[6]

How Are We to Understand David's Curse?

CARDINAL CAJETAN: This way of speaking is metaphorical, indicating that Saul would reduce David's honor to nothing. According to this simile, those who lie in the dust are considered to be nothing, because they could be trampled by everyone. Because all this is conditional language, accordingly it is quite clear that David justifies his petition before God by presenting it as a curse. If he has conducted himself wickedly toward Saul, may he fall into Saul's hands, may Saul destroy the honor of David's kingdom (which was promised to him by God), may Saul destroy David's life. COMMENTARY ON PSALM 7.[7]

7:6-11 *Arise, O Just Judge!*

Thy Will Be Done on Earth As in Heaven.

JOHN CALVIN: David asks nothing but the command of God. And this is the rule which ought to be observed by us in our prayers: we should in everything conform our requests to the divine will (as John also instructs us). And, indeed, we can never pray in faith unless we attend, in the first place, to what God commands, so that our minds may not rashly and at random start aside in desiring more than we are permitted to desire and pray for. David, therefore, in order to pray correctly, reposes

himself on the Word and promise of God; and the import of his exercise is this: "Lord, I am not led by ambition, or foolish headstrong passion or depraved desire, inconsiderately to ask from you whatever is pleasing to my flesh; but it is the clear light of your Word which directs me, and on it I securely depend." COMMENTARY ON THE PSALMS.[8]

The Goal of Good Governance Is to Promulgate Knowledge of God.

TILEMANN HESSHUS: Seditious people were disrupting the blessed state of his government. Therefore, David asked that the Lord would rise up in his wrath, that is, that he would demonstrate his presence and power and restrain the seditious. He uses two arguments. First, he takes up the efficient cause. "You, O Lord," he says, "have appointed judgment to me." That is, by your mandate and authority I have been established as king. Therefore it is not lawful for private citizens to cast me out of the kingdom. For it has not been based on human will but it is God's will to establish kingdoms, to lift up and to depose kings. And God threatens all seditious people harshly. Indeed I have committed a serious crime and have provoked your anger, and I rightly endure your punishment. But my subjects do not have a just cause to be disappointed by me, and the entire kingdom will be disrupted and will nearly be overthrown! Therefore it is just for you to restore me, so that my subjects would understand that you condemn seditious plans.

Second, he takes up the final cause, that "the assembly of the people would gather around you," that is, that the church would be assembled by God. For this is the principle end why God establishes and preserves governments, so that people should learn about God and the Mediator Jesus Christ, so that they would be called to repentance by the ministry of the Word, instructed about the things pertaining to eternal life—moreover the church is gathered in such a way that its victory is always with God. Isaiah says, "The nation and kingdom that is unwilling to serve Christ will

---

[6]Musculus, *In Psalterium Commentarii*, 93-94; citing Ps 143:2; 1 Sam 24:10-11.
[7]Cajetan, *In Sacrae Scripturae Expositionem*, 3:28.
[8]CTS 8:81* (CO 31:82); citing 1 Jn 5:14.

be destroyed, and such nations will be completely laid waste." On account of this, "return on high," that is, on account of the church, show your power, justice and majesty; give me victory from heaven and restrain seditious and duplicitous people.

Here David teaches to what end God establishes and preserves governments: surely not so that human beings may indulge in leisure and pleasures, but so that the church would be gathered in Christ. And therefore, all governance should be directed toward this, so that intimate knowledge of God would be propagated among human beings and the light of the gospel would radiate far and wide, not merely to amass wealth, enlarge empires and grant external peace to citizens. Commentary on Psalm 7.[9]

The Power of a Good Conscience.

Viktorin Strigel: We all know by the voice of nature and written law that no one is permitted to pass judgment on another when they themselves are involved in a dispute. Therefore, David does not demand for himself the power of judging in regard to this controversy, nor does he allow it for his enemies, but he calls forth to the Judge, in whom there is no bias and who looks through to the hidden places of the human heart deep within. And he adduces in this forum the righteousness, not really of his person but of the case, and to the charges he opposes the testimony of a good conscience as if it were Gorgon.[10]

Furthermore, there are many reasons which encourage us to guard the integrity of the conscience. First, there is the command of God in 1 Timothy 1: "Fight the good fight, keeping the faith and a good conscience." Again, "The end of the commandment is love from a pure heart and a good conscience and a faith that is real." Let these words be fixed in our hearts, and let them rule us,

lest we act against our conscience, that is, unknowingly violate the law of God. The second reason is so that faith might be preserved. For there are two contradictory acts of the will, to want knowingly to act against God and to want to repent from wrongdoing. By no means, therefore, are an evil conscience and faith able to exist simultaneously in the heart. Third, that a true prayer might be offered up. For the person who harbors an evil intent in vain prays to God; in fact, that person is not even able to pray, because without penitence and faith one does not approach God. Now think about how miserable it is to live without God, that is, not to be able to seek and to hope for God's help, but to be deserted by God and held prisoner by the devil. The fourth is the hope of divine aid and protection. This reason arises from the prior ones. For the one who relies on a good conscience, to this one there is always present good hope, which is the sweet nourishment of old age. The fifth reason is the tranquility of the heart. Concerning this reason regard the very pleasant saying of Nazianzus: "Nothing brings us as much joy as a pure conscience and a good hope." The sixth is mitigation and liberation in times of trouble. For it is certainly something "in great misfortunes to be free from crime."[11] For these reasons and the like effort must be given so that the conscience in all our actions is congruent with the Word of God, and that nothing is done or approved of that goes against the conscience, and when the integrity of the conscience is preserved by such things, the mind is at rest, it keeps the faith and remains in grace. Hyponēmata in All the Psalms.[12]

Diligently Contemplate God Our Judge.

Nikolaus Selnecker: God is also a strict Judge: he mercifully helps the innocent and frightfully punishes the guilty. These are serious words which we too in our time must consider carefully. If we do not repent, God has whetted his sword, stretched and aimed his bow—and he will not shoot stalks

---

[9]Hesshus, *Commentarius in Psalmos*, 44r; citing Is 60:12.
[10]Gorgons—the three sisters, Stheno, Euryale and Medusa—are fierce and ugly mythological creatures whose sight could turn people into stone. They are commonly depicted with living snakes for hair, fangs and scaled skin. Images of a gorgon were used in ancient Greece to protect people or places from evil.

[11]Ovid, *Metamorphoses* 1.486.
[12]Strigel, *Hyponēmata*, 35; citing 1 Tim 6:12; 1:5.

of straw! This is a matter of body and life as well as of the soul. He will come with war, pestilence, inflation and with the plundering of his Word. But who believes our sermons? We do not ask about it. It helps neither to threaten nor to exhort nor to scream. Yes, if the trees and stones were to speak, then we would forget immediately and would be as much as nothing. The Whole Psalter.[13]

Patient Punishment. John Calvin: Now it is asked: How does the psalmist present God as judging every day, when we see that he often postpones punishment for a long time? And certainly Scripture does not proclaim his forbearance without reason, but, although he does not immediately execute his judgments, yet there is no time, yes, not even a day passes, in which he does not furnish sure evidence that while they are mixed on earth, he discerns between the righteous and the wicked. It remains sure that he never ceases to execute his office. For those who will lift up their eyes to consider the government of the world will distinctly see that the patience of God is very different from turning a blind eye. Surely, then, the faithful will take refuge in him every day undaunted. Commentary on the Psalms.[14]

7:12-17 Wickedness Curves Back on Itself

What Are the Lord's Sword, Bow and Arrows? Martin Luther: These are comprehensive terms and they are properly used in a more prophetic sense concerning the last destruction of the Jews by the Romans, where for forty years the Lord "brandished" and "made ready" and "prepared his weapons" against them and threatened them. However, these words can also be interpreted in multiple ways. First, as they sound. For the sword of the Romans was the sword of the Lord, that is, used by his will, as Job 40 says: "He who has made him will wield his sword." And without a doubt the Romans at that time had and prepared hot and

even fiery arrows. Allegorically, however, the sword, bow, arrows—the whole world—are to the present day against the same people, for in a metaphorical sense the Jews are constantly being shot at by arrows, vexed and killed, even by "burning ones," that is, by sometimes angry and sharp people who are filled with indignation against them. For secular powers are like bows in the hand of God, from which ministers are sent against them like arrows and spears. And some of them are set on fire and full of anger. Tropologically it means this: The sword and bow are their pestilent teachers who wound them with "arrows" that are sharp and "burning," that is, with bitter blasphemies and instigations against Christ and Christians. And in a similar way such a sword or bow is the Lord's, that is, dispatched against them by the Lord. There are, however, such bows in the hand of the devil, who by means of them dispatches such evil words, burning and sulfur, into the midst of those people that they stab each other with their extremely evil teachings. But anagogically this psalm is still prophecy. For to the present day God threatens with the dreadful arrows of his judgment, where he will thunder against the unbelievers and the whole world and every creature will be struck down, as Wisdom of Solomon 5 most beautifully describes. Thus the "sword" is the power of judgment by which he separates the unbelievers, the "bow" is the power of imposing penalties, and the "arrows" and spears are the torments and punishments themselves. First Psalms Lectures (1513–1515).[15]

Saul Is Pregnant with Murderous Threats. Wolfgang Musculus: These three verses also pertain to the threatening of death against the malicious attempts of ungodly Saul. . . . He explains the unremitting attempts of Saul in the likeness of a pregnant woman, as if she appeared before one's eyes. By these attempts, Saul was plotting against David's very life. The prophet compares the plans of Saul's heart with conception.

---

[13]Selnecker, *Der gantze Psalter*, 1:26v; citing Lk 19:40; Hab 2:11. [14]CTS 8:86-87* (CO 31:85).

[15]LW 10:85-86* (WA 3:78); citing Job 40:19; Gen 27:40; 1 Sam 14:20; Judg 7:22; Wis 5:15-23.

He calls the persecution he was enduring an affliction. He compares the attempts of death which Saul had conceived in his mind with giving birth. He calls those attempts iniquity. You see, iniquity itself was to seek the death of a man who was not only harmless but also was well-deserving in his deeds and was Saul's son-in-law. He calls the proposed work "birth." Because it had not been accomplished, he attributed a lie to it. He will give birth, he says, to a lie. That is, he will not complete what he conceived in his mind, and he has given birth to so many perverse attempts. Therefore, this does not only produce the same iniquity which he was bringing forth, but also a lie, which is another matter entirely; he will give birth to what he has thought and proposed, namely, his own destruction of himself. Commentary on the Psalms.[16]

Those Who Live by the Sword Die by the Sword. John Calvin: Here David not only says that their impious machinations were without success but that, by the wonderful providence of God, the result of their machinations was the opposite of their expectations. First, he sings this metaphorically, by using the figure of a pit and a ditch. Then without figures he expresses the same thing in simple words, that this iniquity returns on the head of its author. There is no doubt that it was a common proverb among the Hebrews—"whoever had dug the pit falls into it"—when they wanted to say that the deceitful are caught in their own snares and traps, or that skilled murderers perish by their own skill. There is a twofold use of this doctrine. First, however powerful in the craft of injury our enemies may be, we must trust in the outcome that God promises here, that they will fall by their own sword. Nor does this happen by accident, but the evil that they intended for the innocent, God, by the secret guidance of his hand, twists back on their own heads. Second, if at any time the lust of the flesh incites us to wound our neighbors or to commit some other wicked deed, let this retribution of God help us. Those who prepare a ditch for others are cast into it themselves. Thus, it will happen, that as far as anyone is willing to consider his own welfare, he will restrain himself from all injustice. Commentary on the Psalms.[17]

God's Righteousness Shields Us. John Calvin: In this passage, the righteousness of God is to be taken as faithfulness which he accomplishes for his servants by protecting their lives. Nor does God conceal his righteousness within himself, but he advances it for our benefit when he defends us against all unjust violence, liberates us from oppression, and whenever we are assaulted by infamous human beings he nevertheless preserves us unharmed. Commentary on the Psalms.[18]

God Is Our Refuge. Philipp Melanchthon: This whole psalm reminds us that what is set forth is for the sake of an example. It is difficult for the wise to endure accusations. Therefore, this psalm teaches what must be done and from where we should seek and expect a defense when the judgments of the world are unjust. It teaches us that the righteousness of a good conscience must be upheld and that a defense and deliverance must be sought and expected from God. By his own example, David testifies that God does in fact refute accusations and deceit, just as David was restored and Shimei was punished. Because we have been encouraged by this teaching, let us now also seek and expect our defense and deliverance from God against poisonous tricksters, who falsely accuse us of crimes, heresies, seditions, ambitions and many other things. This psalm is a useful teaching and a sweet consolation to a good mind, which is often opposed by unjust hatreds, false suspicions and invented accusations, as often occurs. Comments on the Psalms.[19]

---

[16]Musculus, *In Psalterium Commentarii*, 102.

[17]CTS 8:90-91* (CO 31:86-87); citing Prov 26:27.
[18]CTS 8:92* (CO 31:87).
[19]MO 13:1030; citing 2 Sam 16:5-13; 1 Kings 1:8; 2:8-9, 36-44.

8:1-9 HOW MAJESTIC IS THE CREATOR'S NAME!

To the choirmaster: according to The Gittith.[a] A Psalm of David.

[1] O Lord, our Lord,
how majestic is your name in all the earth!
You have set your glory above the heavens.
[2] Out of the mouth of babies and infants,
you have established strength because of your foes,
to still the enemy and the avenger.

[3] When I look at your heavens, the work of
your fingers,
the moon and the stars, which you have set
in place,
[4] what is man that you are mindful of him,
and the son of man that you care for him?

[5] Yet you have made him a little lower than the
heavenly beings[b]
and crowned him with glory and honor.
[6] You have given him dominion over the works
of your hands;
you have put all things under his feet,
[7] all sheep and oxen,
and also the beasts of the field,
[8] the birds of the heavens, and the fish of the
sea,
whatever passes along the paths of the seas.

[9] O Lord, our Lord,
how majestic is your name in all the earth!

a Probably a musical or liturgical term   b Or than God; Septuagint than the angels

---

OVERVIEW: This psalm, for our commentators, sings the praises of God's name purely, untarnished by human troubles; here believers are revived by contemplating the mysterious and mighty deeds of the Lord. The reformers go to work at the node of grammar and Christ. This psalm draws together creation and redemption in the incarnation of Jesus Christ through whom the vestiges of uncorrupted human nature that remain after the fall are refurbished and restored. The psalmist gives subtle grammatical clues to indicate to the reader that by the direction of the Holy Spirit he intended this psalm—according to the literal sense—to be about Christ. For example, Christ is both man and a son of man, unlike our ancient father, Adam, who was not born of a human being but was made. Thus, for these exegetes verse 4 indicates the mystery of Christ, who as both man *and* son of man is nearer and dearer to us than Adam and Eve.[1] The reformers' debate concerning the use of *ĕlōhîm* and the citation of this psalm in

Hebrews 2 provide us with an interesting sample of how commentators in the past employed grammar as theology's helpmate rather than its taskmaster.

GOSPEL REFRESHMENT FOLLOWS CROSS-BEARING. NIKOLAUS SELNECKER: After great heat, it is proper for refreshment to follow. And after great rain and storm, it is also proper for the beloved sun to shine again. Because so far in the seven psalms—one after another—there was only crossbearing and misery, now Psalm 8 follows as a refreshment, deliverance and consolation, for it talks about the Lord Christ and his kingdom, in which there is only pure joy and peace. And the heavens are opened and everything in heaven and earth is subjected to the Lord Christ. However, it also preaches about the suffering and humiliation of the Lord Christ, that he was abandoned by God for a little while, emptied himself of his divinity and became a worm and curse for humankind, as we will hear. THE WHOLE PSALTER.[2]

---

[1]See Luther's comments on the ascension (Lk 24:50-53), RCS NT 3:500.

[2]Selnecker, *Der gantze Psalter*, 1:27r.

ALWAYS BE THANKFUL FOR GOD'S MERCY.
RUDOLF GWALTHER: In this psalm, God's surpassing love and friendliness, which he shows toward us human beings, are praised. From this we see that he does not shame the low and unworthy state that human beings are in; instead, he accepts us with fidelity and grants us the highest honor and glory.

Some posit that David appointed this psalm for autumn, so that the people would not give themselves over to improper and fleshly celebration, but rather through such remembrance of the manifold mercies of God they would be stirred up to true thankfulness—which is the proper use of this psalm at all times. THE PSALTER.[3]

CREATION AND REDEMPTION ARE DRAWN TOGETHER IN THIS PSALM. THEODORE BEZA: This psalm gives thanks to God for two excellent benefits bestowed on humankind: creation in Adam and restoration in Christ. Although that man, Adam, by his own fault tarnished that preeminence in which he was created, still vestiges of that dignity survive. In that he is preeminent over all beasts and has a certain power of life and death over them, and also in that special providence by which God embraces humankind. But in that second state, the eternal Son of God has exalted human nature—having been assumed in the unity of his person—after all human infirmity had been laid on him, so that he would make all believers partakers of his dignity. To them alone he grants that in this life they should have the light of true wisdom and that they may enjoy all created things in this world with good conscience. That is the true goal of this psalm, as interpreted by the Holy Spirit himself. PARAPHRASE OF PSALM 8.[4]

Superscription: *According to the* Gittît

WHAT DOES *GITTÎT* MEAN? SEBASTIAN MÜNSTER: Some think that *mîn haggittît* is a type of musical instrument. According to others, it indicates that this psalm was composed in the Philistine city of Gath. THE TEMPLE OF THE LORD: PSALM 8.[5]

GITTÎT IS A TYPE FOR THE GENTILES. FELIX PRATENSIS: The third term in this psalm's title is somewhat obscure. Some explain this term as a winepress, with which the saying of the prophet fits indeed: "I alone have trampled the winepress." But others say that it is the name of an instrument of a certain type of music named for the Philistine city of Gath, which the Jews had brought from there. But we do not at all doubt that it should be interpreted as the Gentiles. For such a word, *gittît*, is a patronymic name, derived from the word *Gath*, because it is well-known among those who know the Hebrew language that as David signifies Christ, so the Philistines will signify the Gentiles. When the prophet David considered the conversion of all the Gentiles to faith in Christ, filled with the Holy Spirit he burst out with these words: "O Lord, our Lord." THE HEBREW PSALTER.[6]

WHAT *GITTÎT* MEANS IS NOT IMPORTANT. JOHN CALVIN: Whether *gittît* means a musical instrument or some particular tune or the beginning of some famous and familiar song, I leave undetermined. Those who think that the psalm is called this because it was composed in the city of Gath give a strained and far-fetched explanation. Of the other three opinions, which I have selected, it is not very important which is adopted. However, what the psalm itself contains and what its purpose is, are to be diligently considered. COMMENTARY ON THE PSALMS.[7]

GOD'S PRAISE IS A VITAL MATTER. MARTIN LUTHER: The statement in the title "to be sung upon *haggittît*" should be taken to mean that a priest or a Levite sang this psalm and another one played the harp or violin. David had ordained four

---

[3]Gwalther, *Der Psalter*, 10r.
[4]Beza, *Psalmes of Dauid*, 10-11 (*Psalmorum Davidis*, 22); citing Mt 21:16; 1 Cor 15:27; Heb 2:6-8.
[5]Münster, *Miqdaš YHWH*, 1165.
[6]Pratensis, *Psalterium*, 5r; citing Is 63:3.
[7]CTS 8:23* (CO 31:87-88).

thousand singers to praise the Lord and divided these into four groups, to worship, thank and praise God on all sorts of stringed instruments before the ark of the covenant. Therefore there must have been constant singing and ringing all year—cymbals, lyres and harps, as we can see from 1 Chronicles 25. David himself wrote the songs they had to use for worshiping and praising God in his works. Hence this book is called *sēfer tĕhillīm*, that is, a book of praise or a book of thanks. Therefore it has so many psalms of thanks, which worship and praise God for all sorts of blessings; mingled with these there are many prophecies and promises for the pious as well as warnings against the ungodly. The priests and the Levites were ordained to sing and to accompany on stringed instruments such songs of thanks written by David. SERMON ON ALL SAINTS DAY (1537).[8]

8:1-2 Our Lord's Majesty

PRAISE OF THE NAME. CARDINAL CAJETAN: We sometimes say, "Your voice is so strong that, if you speak in the town square, it will be heard at the farthest reaches of the city." And similarly, "So strong is your reign that, if you make a command in the east, it will be obeyed in the west." Here the prophet uses a similar expression as he praises God: "How majestic is your name in all the earth that, display your glory above the heavens," and "from the mouth of infants and nursing babes you established strength." In other words, as you display your glory in the heavens, also in the earth small children and nursing babes will resound with the majesty of your name. . . .

And so here the prophet begins to declare the majesty of the divine name in terms of its resulting fruit, and then in terms of intermediary things. . . . The fruit of the divine name is the glory of the divine name and the praise of it in heaven and on earth; this is the fruit of the incarnation of the

Word of God. Thus the angels say in his nativity, "Glory to God in the highest." This resulting fruit, then, is described here. It is described in heaven in terms of glory, which, speaking strictly in terms of its working out, began to be fulfilled in the day of the ascension of Christ. For he gave his glory above the heavens, both when he placed his Messiah full of glory above the heavens and when God was glorified because of the mystery of the Messiah without ambiguity in the heavens, and not through faith, as in our praise on earth. And he is glorified deservedly in the holy life of Christ. COMMENTARY ON PSALM 8.[9]

GOD'S NAME REVEALS HIS ECONOMY, NOT HIS ESSENCE. JOHN CALVIN: The name of God is placed here, I understand, as honoring the knowledge of God, insofar as he reveals himself to us. The foolish speculations of some do not please me; they imagine the name of God is nothing other than God himself. His name should refer to the works and properties by which he is known rather than to his essence. The earth therefore is full of God's wonderful glory, David says, so that his renown ascends far beyond the heavens. COMMENTARY ON THE PSALMS.[10]

A PROPHECY ABOUT THOSE WHO PROMULGATE CHRIST. RUDOLF GWALTHER: By "children and sucklings" some understand preachers of the divine Word through whom God wields his power against our common enemy, the devil, who ceaselessly tries to conquer us. Through a higher understanding Christ applies this passage to the young children who were crying out in the temple "Hosanna to the Son of David." That event fulfilled this passage according to the literal sense. THE PSALTER.[11]

UNDERSTAND "INFANTS" AND "SUCKLINGS" ALLEGORICALLY. MARTIN LUTHER: By "infants" he does not mean young children who cannot talk

---

[8]LW 12:98* (WA 45:206-7). Contemporary commentators are still unsure about this term, *ʿāl-haggittît*; they speculate that it might be a tune, instrument or person. See Kraus, *Psalms 1–59*, 31; Alter, *Psalms*, 1:154; Alter, *Book of Psalms*, 22.

[9]Cajetan, *In Sacrae Scripturae Expositionem*, 3:31.
[10]CTS 8:94* (CO 31:88).
[11]Gwalther, *Der Psalter*, 11r; citing 1 Pet 5:8; Mt 21:15-16.

(for if they are to speak and preach the Word, they must be able to talk), but plain, simple, unsophisticated people, who are like infant children in that they set aside all reason, grasp and accept the Word with simple faith and let themselves be led and directed by God like children. Such people are also the best students and teachers in Christ's kingdom, as he himself says. . . .

By "sucklings" he does not mean those who lie at their mother's breast and suck, but those who are like sucklings in that they cling to the pure, unmixed Word without the addition of human dreams and thoughts. For just as a suckling newborn child is satisfied with mother's milk, so these people do not seek any other food for their soul than the pure and unadulterated gospel of Christ. Thus Saint Peter says, "Long for the reasonable,[12] pure milk like newborn babes." He calls the gospel "reasonable," that is, spiritual milk, which we must obtain with the soul; and "pure" milk, which we must grasp not with the senses but with pure faith. Therefore the word *infants* excludes all human reason in matters of faith; the word *sucklings* excludes all adulteration of the Word and false addition of human thoughts. SERMON ON ALL SAINTS DAY (1537).[13]

"INFANTS" AND "SUCKLINGS" SHOULD NOT BE UNDERSTOOD ALLEGORICALLY. JOHN CALVIN:
God, in order to commend his providence, has no need of the powerful eloquence of rhetoricians, nor even of distinct and formed language, because the tongues of infants, although they do not as yet speak, are ready and eloquent enough to celebrate it. But it may be asked: In what sense does he speak of children as the proclaimers of the glory of God? In my judgment, those reason very foolishly who think that this is done when children begin to articulate, because then also the intellectual faculty

of the soul shows itself. Granting that they are called babes, or infants, even until they arrive at their seventh year, how can such people imagine that those who now speak distinctly are still hanging on the breast? Nor is there any more propriety in the opinion of those who say that the words for babes and sucklings are here put allegorically for the faithful, who, being born again by the Spirit of God, no longer retain the old age of the flesh. What need, then, is there to torture David's words, when their true meaning is so clear and suitable? He says that babes and sucklings are advocates sufficiently powerful to assert the providence of God. Why does he not entrust this to adults, unless to show that the tongues of infants, even before they are able to pronounce a single word, proclaim loudly God's generosity toward the human race? How is it that nourishment is ready for them as soon as they are born, but because God wonderfully changes blood into milk? How, also, do they have the skill to suck, but because the same God has, by a mysterious instinct, fitted their tongues for doing this? David, therefore, has the best reason for declaring that although the tongues of all who have arrived at the age of adulthood should become silent, the speechless mouth of infants is sufficiently able to celebrate the praise of God. COMMENTARY ON THE PSALMS.[14]

THE LORD'S POWER IS THROUGH WEAKNESS.
MARTIN LUTHER: The power from the mouths of babes and sucklings slashes through and obtains the victory. Emperors, kings and the mighty on the earth must hang their heads and confess that they cannot defend against it. . . . The prophet is amazed at this: the Lord and Ruler ordains a strength, that is, a mighty, powerful, well-established and eternal kingdom, and does so in a way that looks foolish to all reason. What then is his method? Through what does he ordain this strength? Through the Word, from the mouths of babes and sucklings. How does this fit with such infinite, eternal might that is supposed to stand up

---

[12]Luther translates λογικὸν here as *vernünfftig* ("reasonable" or "rational"). The ESV—with the NIV and NRSV—renders this as "spiritual"; the CEB, KJV, NASB and NKJV use "of the word."
[13]LW 12:109-10* (WA 45:218); citing Mt 11:25; Ps 19:7; Ps 119:130; 1 Pet 2:2. This sermon was later expanded for publication in 1572; see LW 12:ix.

[14]CTS 8:95-96* (CO 31:89).

against death, the devil and the world? Let it fit however it pleases! The Lord, our Ruler, does not use sword, rifle or armor to establish this strength, but the Word—and a word that comes out of the mouths of infants and sucklings. . . .

The Lord knows the art of being strongest when he looks weak. With weakness and feebleness he begins and lets his Word be preached, which the world regards as childish, foolish and silly. But through such weakness and feebleness he is so powerful that he destroys every other word, power and wisdom in the world. This is the way the Lord, our Ruler, establishes his kingdom, through the external spoken Word which the apostles preached and which now, by God's grace, we also preach, hear, accept and believe. SERMON ON ALL SAINTS DAY (1537).[15]

8:3-4 Why Do You Care About Human Beings?

THE TESTIMONY OF CREATION. THE ENGLISH ANNOTATIONS: That is, "You are the maker of such glorious creatures, so pure, so bright, so beautiful! How can you stoop so low as to take care of human beings, so vile, so frail, so wretched in comparison?" Or, "What are human beings to you, or what are human beings in themselves, that you should have created and provided for their use such glorious creatures? Not to be used for their enjoyment only after their death, but also for their use in the present life: for the contentment of their contemplation and for the benefits which they receive from them—not only light but also the seasons of the year and the fruits of the earth, which would not be produced without the influence of heaven." Some of the pagans have acknowledged as much, and from this inferred both the goodness of God and the value of human beings above all other creatures.

This verse and the words following are interpreted as referring to Christ by the apostle. From this, it may well be inferred that Christ is indeed

the principal aim in the intention of the Holy Spirit who dictated to David. . . . However, David may well have had a more immediate and obvious aim also: to set out the goodness and providence of God to humankind. And while it is true that human beings since their rebellion against God—from whom they had received it—have lost much of the sovereignty over the creatures insisted on in the following verses. That it still remains to this day in great measure is evidently true and acknowledged by ancient pagans. . . . From this they fetch excellent arguments for providence. ANNOTATIONS ON PSALM 8:4.[16]

THE MAJESTY OF THE HEAVENS SURPASSED IN THE INCARNATION. CARDINAL CAJETAN: Here the strength of the divine name is described with respect to the means by which the divine name has overcome not only enemies but also everyone. And because those means depend on the Messiah, therefore, such an exaltation of human generation the prophet is going to understand as in the person of the Messiah. He describes it with marvel: "Look at the worthlessness of human beings compared with the heavens!" Of course, it seems remarkable to him that by subordinating the heavenly bodies— far more noble than human beings!—God has exalted human beings above everything. . . .

According to this sense, notice that although the heavenly bodies (as it is said principally in Aristotle's *Ethics*) clearly reveal that human beings are less noble, still the prophet mentions that the nobility of the heavenly bodies is on account of their nearness to God, appealing to "your heavens" as if they were God's proper dwelling place. For the heavens, according to everyone's opinion, are God's proper habitation, namely, in which the divine work of perfectly ordered movement shines brightly. And for this reason, it is said in Sunday prayer: "Our Father who art in heaven." Second, the heavenly bodies are called "the work of God's fingers": according to this simile of artistry, they are

---

[15]LW 12:III, 113, 114* (WA 45:221-22, 223, 225).

[16]Downame, ed., *Annotations*, 5Z2r*; citing Heb 2:6-8; 1 Cor 15:27; Eph 1:22.

the work of the Artist's fingers. Accordingly, those whom the Artist makes through the hands of his ministers are less noble than those made by his very own hand. And again, more noble and without fault are those things which the Artist distinguishes, shapes and completes by his fingers than those things for which the guidance of his very own hand is enough. Of course, this distinction of fingers reveals greater precision in the work. Third, the heavenly bodies are made noble because of the stars, "the moon and the stars." For because of the stars the nobility of the heavens is powerfully experienced and revealed; the stars are the more noble part of the heavens. Fourth, they are made noble by preserving their order, because it is said "which you yourself have planned" or set in place. For all the stars preserve their arrangement which God has arranged from the beginning. From this the heavens' nobility is apparent in not transgressing the arrangement made by God.

"Because," he says, "I will see these things, therefore I say with marvel: What is man or a son of man?" Man is the name of the nature; son of man is the name of generation. And indeed, the first man Adam was a man, while not the son of man; however, anyone born from him is both a man and a son of man. Therefore, lest you thought that the prophet is speaking about the dignity of the first man, he used both phrases so that you should understand that he is speaking about the worthlessness and consequently the exaltation of human generation. For the Messiah was not only going to be a man but also a son of man. And therefore it is indicated that not only human nature but also human generation will be exalted. It is even said in the future tense: "Because you will call him to mind, because you will visit him." For from this it is manifestly clear that this word is a prophecy and that it proclaims the future: God will call man to mind, and he will visit the Son of man. According to the letter the future tense indicates the mystery of the incarnation by which God has called to mind human generation to exalt it, and he has visited the Son of man, because the Word became a Son of *Ādām*, that is, a Son of man.

Ādām among the Hebrews is the name of human nature as *homo* ["man"] is among us. And we often deviate from this in the work of translation; it does not have a plural. COMMENTARY ON PSALM 8.[17]

8:5 Lower Than Ĕlōhîm[18]

Ĕlōhîm Here Means Gods. SEBASTIAN MÜNSTER: In Hebrew the word is *ĕlōhîm*, that is, "gods." Nevertheless here it is understood as "angels" [mal'ākîm], because we have translated it according to the Hebrews' interpretation. Now those who claim this verse mentions Christ strain *ĕlōhîm* as meaning "God" here. THE TEMPLE OF THE LORD: PSALM 8.[19]

To Render Ĕlōhîm Here as "Angels" Is Absurd. JACQUES LEFÈVRE D'ÉTAPLES: For how should it say "than the angels" when this passage is understood everywhere to be about Christ? . . . When he introduced his firstborn on earth, it says, "And all the angels of God adored him." How, therefore, must it be read: "you have made him a little less than the angels"? But because while "he was in the form of God, he did not consider it robbery for himself to be the equal of God, he himself laid it aside, accepting the form of a servant." Therefore he is correctly said to be made a little lesser than God. In addition: speaking to the Ephesians about the Father and him, Paul

---

[17]Cajetan, *In Sacrae Scripturae Expositionem*, 3:32; citing Aristotle, *Nichomachean Ethics* 6.7; Mt 6:9. In the final paragraph, Cajetan uses *homo* and *filius hominis* for what we have rendered "man" and "son of man." Unfortunately this translation flattens Cajetan's original, more gender-inclusive language.
[18]This is notoriously difficult to translate. Among modern translations, "heavenly beings" (ESV), "angels" (KJV, NIV), and "God" (NASB, NRSV) are used to render *ĕlōhîm*. Contemporary scholars do not warrant a messianic interpretation of this verse based on current guild hermeneutics. Most of our commentators would balk at such a notion (see above Introduction to the Psalms, pp. xlvi-lii). See Goldingay, *Psalms*, 1:154, 160-61; Alter, *Book of Psalms*, 23; Kraus, *Psalms 1–59*, 183.
[19]Münster, *Miqdaš YHWH*, 1165. Gwalther agrees with Münster, translating this as "angels" without further comment; Beza paraphrases this as "lower than the angels" but translates it as "below God." See Gwalther, *Der Psalter*, 10v; Beza, *Psaltorum Davidis*, 23.

said, "setting him on his right in heaven above all principality and power and authority and dominion." How, therefore, is it rightly written that he is made less than the angels, who was established over all principality and power and authority and dominion? FIVEFOLD PSALTER: ANNOTATIONS ON PSALM 8:5.[20]

HOW SHOULD ĔLŌHÎM BE TRANSLATED?

CARDINAL CAJETAN: The Hebrew term is ĕlōhîm, which is used in the beginning of Genesis, when it is said: "In the beginning God created the heaven and the earth." When it is in the plural, either—as it generally is in Scripture—it means "God," or sometimes it is said to be used as "angels." It has produced all sorts of different interpretations. If we had Paul's epistle to the Hebrews in the Hebrew language, perhaps in that it would be clear if the apostle understood this passage about angels by using the word angels [mal'ăkîm] or whether he would have used the word ĕlōhîm.

Whatever the answer to that question would be, it seems that it would be said that this clause can be explained in two ways. First, in order to show conformity to the preceding and following verses—the exaltation of man in the person of the Messiah—it should undoubtedly be read as "than God." For the exaltation of man is indicated by this because they fall far short of God. And this is confirmed in the mystery of the incarnation. Because when "the Word became flesh," God became man through the grace of the personal union. And thus he falls far short of God by nature. The Word, of course, is God by nature; God is man in Christ Jesus through the grace of the personal union. And this is that "far" by which the Messiah, the man, falls short of God. Here the sense fits powerfully with the text, because ĕlōhîm is used as "God" as it is generally used in Scripture. And it fits powerfully with the context, because the preceding verse as much as the following verse indicates that they are about exaltation. Therefore, it is part of

this section, so that also this middle clause should indicate exaltation, and it should explain what the recollection of man and the visitation of the Son of man is, of course, to make him to fall far short of God.

Nor does it contradict the sense that the apostle in Hebrews 2 connects such a lowering to Christ's suffering, saying: "But we see him who for a little while was made lower than the angels, that is Jesus, crowned with glory and honor because of the suffering of death." Also because the letters of the apostle could be pointed this way: "But we see him who for a little while was made lower than the angels, that is, Jesus." Either the point is made there or afterwards he is subjected. "Crowned with glory and honor because of the suffering of death." Therefore, because of the suffering of death, he does not finish with his lowering but with the merit of his coronation. For a crown should be given to Christ because of the merit of his suffering, as the same is said in Philippians 2: "Because of that God has exalted him." And understand by this supposed ignorance, whether the apostle would use angels [mal'ăkîm] or the word ĕlōhîm in Hebrew. Also because it is not unsuitable to the apostle's use for there to have been a second sense. For holy Scripture is capable of many senses as well as the literal.

The second sense is that in this phrase the manner is indicated by which the Messiah has conquered by the divine name being glorified and has deserved to be exalted. And so, it should be read as "lower than the angels," for it is signified by that "lower" the entire condition of his journey. For in this short time that the Messiah was going to be a traveler capable of suffering [passibilis viator] who was more inferior than the angels. Here the sense fits the letters of the epistle to the Hebrews, as the Greeks and we have it. And the truth is found, because they observe that except for his suffering, the Messiah was going to be greater than the angels, namely, he will be worshiped by the angels. And here that "far" is his status of traveler, namely, considered the least among man . . . and enduring for the least time (that is, thirty-three

---

[20]Lefèvre, Quincuplum Psalterium, 13v; citing Heb 1:6 (cf. Deut 32:43; Ps 97:7); Phil 2:6-7; Eph 1:20-21; Jn 3:31, 35.

years), so that it is rightly said: "And you made him fall short for a little while," that is, since it is a short time, "lower than the angels." COMMENTARY ON PSALM 8.[21]

BOTH "ANGELS" AND "GOD" ARE APPROPRIATE TRANSLATIONS OF ĔLŌHÎM. JOHN CALVIN: The Septuagint renders *ĕlōhîm* by "angels," of which I do not disapprove, because this name, as is well known, is often given to angels, and I explain the words of David as meaning the same thing as if he had said that the condition of people is nothing less than a divine and celestial state. But as the other translation seems more natural, and as it is almost universally adopted by the Jewish interpreters, I have preferred following it. Nor is it any sufficient objection to this view that the apostle, in his epistle to the Hebrews, quoting this passage, says, "little less than the angels," and not "than God"; for we know what freedoms the apostles took in quoting texts of Scripture; not, indeed, to wrest them to a meaning different from the true one but because they reckoned it sufficient to show, by a reference to Scripture, that what they taught was sanctioned by the Word of God, although they did not quote the precise words. Accordingly, they never had any hesitation in changing the words, provided the substance of the text remained unchanged.

There is another question which it is more difficult to solve. While the psalmist here discourses concerning the excellency of human beings, and describes them, in respect of this, as coming near to God, the apostle applies the passage to the humiliation of Christ. In the first place, we must consider the propriety of applying to the person of Christ what is here spoken concerning all humanity; and, second, how we may explain it as referring to Christ's being humbled in his death, when he lay without form or beauty, and as it were disfigured under the reproach and curse of the cross. What some say—what is true of the members may be properly and suitably transferred to the head—

might be a sufficient answer to the first question; but I go a step farther, for Christ is not only the first begotten of every creature but also the Restorer of humanity. What David here relates belongs properly to the beginning of the creation, when human nature was perfect. But we know that, by the fall of Adam, all humanity fell from its primeval state of integrity, for by this the image of God was almost entirely effaced from us, and we were also divested of those distinguishing gifts by which we would have been, as it were, elevated to the condition of demigods. In short, from a state of the highest excellence, we were reduced to a condition of wretched and shameful destitution. In consequence of this corruption, the liberality of God, of which David here speaks, ceased, so far, at least, as that it does not at all appear in the brilliancy and splendor in which it was manifested when humanity was in its unfallen state. True, it is not altogether extinguished; but, alas! How small a portion of it remains amid the miserable overthrow and ruins of the fall. But as the heavenly Father has bestowed on his Son an immeasurable fullness of all blessings, that all of us may draw from this fountain, it follows that whatever God bestows on us by him belongs to him in the highest degree; yes, he himself is the living image of God, according to which we must be renewed, on which depends our participation of the invaluable blessings which are here spoken of. If any person objects that David first put the question, What is man? because God has so abundantly poured forth his favor on a creature so miserable, contemptible and worthless; but that there is no cause for such admiration of God's favor for Christ, who is not an ordinary man but the only-begotten Son of God. The answer is easy, and it is this: What was bestowed on Christ's human nature was a free gift; nay, more, the fact that a mortal man, and the son of Adam, is the only Son of God, and the Lord of glory and the Head of angels, affords a bright illustration of the mercy of God. At the same time, it is to be observed that whatever gifts he has received ought to be considered as proceeding from the free grace of God, so much the more for this reason, that

---

[21]Cajetan, *In Sacrae Scripturae Expositionem*, 3:32-33; citing Gen 1:1; Heb 2:9; Phil 2:9.

they are intended principally to be conferred on us. His excellence and heavenly dignity, therefore, are extended to us also, seeing that it is for our sake he is enriched with them.

What the apostle therefore says in that passage concerning the abasement of Christ for a short time is not intended by him as an explanation of this text; but for the purpose of enriching and illustrating the subject on which he is discoursing, he introduces and accommodates to it what had been spoken in a different sense. The same apostle did not hesitate, in Romans 10, in the same manner to enrich and to employ, in a sense different from their original one, the words of Moses in Deuteronomy 30: "Who shall go up for us to heaven and bring it to us, that we may hear it and do it?" The apostle, therefore, in quoting this psalm, had not so much an eye to what David meant; but making an allusion to these words, "You have made him a little lower," and again, "You have crowned him with honor," he applies this diminution to the death of Christ, and the glory and honor to his resurrection. COMMENTARY ON THE PSALMS.[22]

CHRIST'S SUFFERING AND ITS FRUIT ARE PRESAGED HERE. MARTIN LUTHER: In this verse David describes how miserably Christ will be forsaken. No human words can describe this as clearly, briefly and simply as it is here. He is not speaking of the physical suffering of Christ, which was also great and difficult, but of his sublime spiritual suffering, which he felt in his soul, a suffering that far surpasses all physical suffering. . . . What this is, no human being on earth understands, and no human being can reach or express it in words. For to be forsaken by God is far worse than death. . . .

It is as if David wanted to say: "Sin and death are conquered, the enemy is destroyed, the kingdom of heaven is won. It happened in this way. The Lord, our Ruler, true man and Son of Man, labored with body and soul in his tender humanity.

He underwent such need and anguish that he sweat blood and felt nothing so much as that he was forsaken by God. In his soul he had to quench and extinguish the temptation of being forsaken by God, the devil's flaming darts, hellish fire, anguish and everything that we had earned by our sins." By this the kingdom of heaven, eternal life and salvation were secured for us, as Isaiah also says: "So, because his soul has labored, he will see his delight and have its fullness." His body and soul, he says, labor in deep and difficult suffering. But he does this for our great benefit and for his own great joy. For he conquers his enemies and triumphs, and by his knowledge he makes many righteous. SERMON ON ALL SAINTS DAY (1537).[23]

CROWNED WITH GLORY AND HONOR. HENRY AINSWORTH: This may be understood of all human beings as first made in God's image, and Lord of the world, but since the transgression, it is peculiar to Christ and to Christians who have their dignity restored by Christ. To them the apostle applies this psalm: "We see Jesus crowned with glory and honor, which was a little made lesser than the angels, through the suffering of death, that by the grace of God he might taste death for all." Glory refers to inward virtues, like wisdom and holiness, and honor to his outward estate in ruling over the creatures. ANNOTATIONS ON PSALM 8:5.[24]

8:6-9 Total Dominion Over the Earth

MARVEL AT GOD'S MERCY. THOMAS WILCOX: This passage sets forth the graces and blessings that God has bestowed on human beings, not so that human beings become proud and grin smugly because of these gifts, but to compel them to be thankful to the Giver, to use these gifts rightly for themselves and others and to humble themselves always (see 1 Cor 4:7). A word or two concerning this matter: let us consider what excellence we have lost through Adam's fall, and

---

[22]CTS 8:102-5* (CO 31:92-93); citing Heb 2:7; Rom 10:6; Deut 30:12.

[23]LW 12:124, 127* (WA 45:237, 240); citing Eph 6:16; Is 53:11 (Vg).
[24]Ainsworth, *Annotations*, 2:425*; citing Gen 1:26; Heb 2:9.

mourn our misery. Let us also value the grace bestowed on us in Christ, and be joyful and thankful for his mercy. Know that if the creatures are not now subject to us, it is because of the flesh and relics of sin, which still remain in us. Therefore, if we desire to rule over the creatures, we must first have victory over sin, or else we will never profit! If anyone would object and say, "Many creatures are subdued to many people who are without God in the world and who remain in their sin," I answer that God's mercy with our iniquity or other people's is no charge against the truth of this doctrine. No, instead it should encourage us even more, not only to be thankful to him for his goodness but also to combat our iniquity valiantly and bravely—even to blood. For in his mercy we have—without any effort or fighting—half the victory . . . the rest, no doubt, he will graciously supply . . . especially if there is a willing mind. Now all this belongs to the faithful—who are indeed heirs of the world—and to no one else. EXPOSITION UPON PSALM 8.[25]

GOD SEASONS HUMAN BEINGS THROUGH JUSTIFICATION. HANS HUT: All animals are subject to human beings. If we want to use an animal, it must first be dealt with according to human will; it must be prepared, cooked and roasted. That is, the animal must suffer. God does the same thing with human beings! If God is to have use of us or enjoyment of us, we must first be justified and made pure by him, both inwardly and outwardly—inwardly from greed and lust, outwardly from injustice in our way of living and our misuse of the creatures. KUNSTBUCH: BEGINNING OF A TRUE CHRISTIAN LIFE.[26]

VARIOUS OPINIONS ABOUT ʿŌBĒR ʾĀRḤŌT YAMMÎM. FELIX PRATENSIS: We should direct our attention to some of the words in the second to last verse of this psalm, which are explained in diverse ways by diverse expositors. For some say that the participle "crossing over," which in Hebrew is ʿōbēr, refers to animals, either to say "you have placed under his feet the sparrows of the heavens and the fish of the sea" or "all those things that pass through the paths of the sea." But a few others (particularly the Chaldean exposition) say that these words refer to leviathan. Certainly, in what way leviathan passes through the paths of the sea and what leviathan would be is not—for now—my task in the least! Others say that it refers to the nature of human beings and their ability. And they say, "You have given them such ability and nature, so that they are able to pass through the paths of the sea." This participle is given in the singular, though we have translated it in the plural, so that it retains a more harmonious sense, lest it seem to be confused speech. THE HEBREW PSALTER.[27]

GRAMMATICAL CONSIDERATIONS REVEAL CHRIST'S UBIQUITOUS POWER. CARDINAL CAJETAN: This clause is obscure. The Hebrew text sounds like a singular participle without marking the case. And therefore it cannot be construed with "fish" [i.e., dāgîm], which is in the plural. It is uncertain with which word it should be construed. Nor do they lack construals with the pronoun "him." Thus, this is the sense: You will tame him who passes through the paths of the seas. . . . And, thus, it was indicated that Christ's power penetrates under the sea, too, in the same way that the phrase "all the earth" includes not only the earth's surface but also what is under the waters. Perhaps it is better to say that it is placed in the singular for a plural because of the meter, so that "the one who passes through" has been said for "those who pass through." And so it is construed with the earlier clause "fish of the sea." Now this construction agrees with regular usage in this sort of text; we often come across similar constructions below. Plus, the Hebrews expound it this way: "fish passing through," that is, whatever passes through. COMMENTARY ON PSALM 8.[28]

---

[25]Wilcox, *Godly Exposition upon the Psalmes*, 19-20*.
[26]CRR 12:126; citing Gen 1:28; 2 Tim 2:21.
[27]Pratensis, *Psalterium*, 5v.
[28]Cajetan, *In Sacrae Scripturae Expositionem*, 3:33.

CONTEMPLATION LEADS TO WORSHIP. JOHN CALVIN: God, in creating human beings, demonstrated his infinite grace and more than fatherly love toward them, which ought justly to strike us with amazement. And although, by the fall of humankind, that happy condition has been almost entirely ruined, yet there is still in people some remains of the liberality which God then displayed toward them, which should suffice to fill us with admiration. In this mournful and wretched overthrow, it is true, the legitimate order which God originally established no longer shines forth, but the faithful whom God gathers to himself, under Christ their Head, enjoy so much of the fragments of the good things which they lost in Adam, as may furnish them with abundant matter of wonder at the singularly gracious manner in which God deals with them. David here confines his attention to God's temporal benefits, but it is our duty to rise higher, and to contemplate the invaluable treasures of the kingdom of heaven which he has unfolded in Christ, and all the gifts which belong to the spiritual life, that by reflecting on these our hearts may be inflamed with love to God, that we may be stirred up to the practice of godliness and that we may not suffer ourselves to become slothful and remiss in celebrating his praises. COMMENTARY ON THE PSALMS.[29]

THANK THE LORD AND SING HIS PRAISE! MARTIN LUTHER: Let us respond in singing to this singer of praises as he calls to us. The Lord is our Ruler, too, and his kingdom is established and founded out of the mouths of infants and sucklings. We were placed into it through baptism, and we are called to it daily through Word and gospel. With David we also hope to come to where we will see the heavens, the work of his fingers, the moon and the stars which he will prepare. He won the kingdom with great trouble and anguish. Now he is crowned with honor and adornment and has everything under his feet. For this we give God our praise and thanks, but especially for the fact that he has brought us to such light and knowledge that does not spring up out of human reason but out of Christ. He is our Sun, who died for us and was raised from the dead, lives and reigns, so that through him we would be saved. To this end may God help us all. SERMON ON ALL SAINTS DAY (1537).[30]

THIS PSALM REVEALS THE MESSIAH'S MISSION. CARDINAL CAJETAN: Here the first verse is repeated word for word, so that by this you would understand that this verse is the substance of the psalm, and that the purpose of the Messiah is to magnify the divine name throughout all the earth. And truly for this reason the Word became flesh, so that the name of God would be glorified throughout the entire universe. Amen. COMMENTARY ON PSALM 8.[31]

---

[29]CTS 8:108* (CO 31:95).

[30]LW 12:136* (WA 45:249-50).
[31]Cajetan, *In Sacrae Scripturae Expositionem*, 3:33.

9:1-20 I WILL RECOUNT YOUR WONDERFUL DEEDS

^aTo the choirmaster: according to Muth-labben.^b
A Psalm of David.

¹ I will give thanks to the LORD with my whole
heart;
I will recount all of your wonderful deeds.

² I will be glad and exult in you;
I will sing praise to your name, O Most High.
³ When my enemies turn back,
they stumble and perish before^c your presence.
⁴ For you have maintained my just cause;
you have sat on the throne, giving righteous
judgment.

⁵ You have rebuked the nations; you have made
the wicked perish;
you have blotted out their name forever
and ever.
⁶ The enemy came to an end in everlasting ruins;
their cities you rooted out;
the very memory of them has perished.

⁷ But the LORD sits enthroned forever;
he has established his throne for justice,
⁸ and he judges the world with righteousness;
he judges the peoples with uprightness.

⁹ The LORD is a stronghold for the oppressed,
a stronghold in times of trouble.
¹⁰ And those who know your name put their
trust in you,
for you, O LORD, have not forsaken those
who seek you.

¹¹ Sing praises to the LORD, who sits enthroned
in Zion!
Tell among the peoples his deeds!
¹² For he who avenges blood is mindful of them;
he does not forget the cry of the afflicted.

¹³ Be gracious to me, O LORD!
See my affliction from those who hate me,
O you who lift me up from the gates of death,
¹⁴ that I may recount all your praises,
that in the gates of the daughter of Zion
I may rejoice in your salvation.

¹⁵ The nations have sunk in the pit that they
made;
in the net that they hid, their own foot has
been caught.
¹⁶ The LORD has made himself known; he has
executed judgment;
the wicked are snared in the work of their
own hands.   Higgaion.^d Selah

¹⁷ The wicked shall return to Sheol,
all the nations that forget God.

¹⁸ For the needy shall not always be forgotten,
and the hope of the poor shall not perish
forever.

¹⁹ Arise, O LORD! Let not man prevail;
let the nations be judged before you!
²⁰ Put them in fear, O LORD!
Let the nations know that they are but men!
Selah

a Psalms 9 and 10 together follow an acrostic pattern, each stanza beginning with the successive letters of the Hebrew alphabet. In the Septuagint they form one psalm   b Probably a musical or liturgical term   c Or *because of*   d Probably a musical or liturgical term

OVERVIEW: This psalm is today widely recognized as an acrostic that originally included Psalm 10 in a single composition, ordered according to the Hebrew alphabet. Reformation commentators wrestle with the rare terminology in the psalm's superscription, which remains opaque to translators today. Luther affirms traditional theological options—believers as virgins—maintaining that this psalm should be interpreted in a spiritual, not a literal, sense.

The opening praise is followed by a familiar biblical pattern of movement from divine conquest, or rebuke, of the nations to divine enthronement. While the reformers attend to the theme of glorifying God in praise and thanksgiving, they also observe how God discloses his enemies wickedness through the rebuke of the law. The psalmist's meditation on divine enthronement and justice prompts questions about the apparent lack of justice in this life. These commentators remind us that we can only inquire into the revealed will of God. Our Lord does not desire the death of a sinner; our God is also a God of justice. Divine inaction teaches us patience and mercifully allows for the wicked to turn to repentance. Meanwhile, we should look to the throne of God, pleading for his deliverance and mercy.

SALVATION BY GOD'S HELP ALONE. PHILIPP MELANCHTHON: From this psalm and similar ones let us especially learn thanksgiving, that is, the confession of a soul thinking rightly, because we are not helped and saved accidentally or by human strength but by the help of God, because God is in fact the effective one, which is not an empty expression. He is not idle, he is not bound by second causes, but he truly cares for us, hears us, is near us, helps us, even when we lack second causes. God desires to be known in this way; he desires this praise to be attributed to him. Indeed, the blind nature of human beings frequently either by chance or by human work attempts to produce deliverance for itself. Against this blindness, the divine testimonies of the prophets everywhere must be brought together, which affirm that the church is ruled and saved by God, just as other psalms say elsewhere: human salvation is vain. Second, we should also fix in our hearts the promise of help, and we should add examples to the promise, first recited in the psalms of David, then to be sure, others, such as examples of Abraham and the rest. By these promises and examples, faith and prayer are illuminated. These are, as it is often called, the particular worship of God. COMMENTS ON THE PSALMS.[1]

Superscription: *Victory, Virginity or Vague?*

HOW TO UNDERSTAND 'ALMÛT? SEBASTIAN MÜNSTER: The Chaldean translator separates this term into two words. He translates the title in this way: "Concerning the death of the man who had gone out from the middle of camp"—of course, meaning that Goliath the Philistine would be *labbēn*.... Others think that *bēn* in *labbēn* is the name of the singer to whom the singing of this psalm was assigned. And others believe that "Laben" was the name of a certain Philistine leader; this psalm was composed for the victory which followed after he was killed. THE TEMPLE OF THE LORD: PSALM 9.[2]

IN CHRIST WE ARE 'ALMÛT. MARTIN LUTHER: The Hebrew word *'almāh* in the singular denotes, first, a virgin or young girl, second, a hidden girl or secretive girl. Therefore *'almût*, the plural of the same word, means "virgins" or "hidden ones" or "youth" in a collective sense. Thus, putting both meanings together into one, *'almût* is nothing else than mystic or hidden youth, or spiritual virgins and young girls, who are all the faithful of Christ, as Psalm 45 says: "Virgins shall be brought to the king."... However, they are called "mystic," "secret" or "hidden" virgins to distinguish them from outward and physical virgins, because they are in the tabernacle of faith, as Psalm 31 says: "You will hide them in your hidden tabernacle," that is, in the faith of your church, "from the contradiction of human beings." But here it is better taken in the second meaning, "secrets," because in this psalm almost all the words must be understood in a spiritual sense, not in a literal one. And thus they are of the spirit, not of the letter. Thus the sense of the title is: This psalm was revealed to David as a victory song or song of triumph, or it is an exhortation of mystical youth, spiritual virgins of the Son of God, Christ. For faith is the spiritual virginity by which we are betrothed to Christ, as

---

[1] MO 13:1033.

[2] Münster, *Miqdaš YHWH*, 1166.

the Lord says in Hosea: "I will betroth you to me in faith." For that reason . . . bad Christians are always accused of fornication, that is, unbelief in the writings of the prophets. FIRST PSALMS LECTURES (1513–1515).[3]

THE MEANING OF 'ALMÛT HERE IS OBSCURE AND UNIMPORTANT. JOHN CALVIN: This inscription is variously explained. Some translate it "On the death of Laben" and are of opinion that he was one of the chief captains of David's enemies. Others are inclined to think it was a fictitious name—they think that Goliath is spoken of in this psalm. Others think it was a musical instrument. But to me it seems more correct, or, at least—as is customary in this obscure matter— more probable that it was the beginning of some popular song, to the tune of which the psalm was composed. The disputes of interpreters as to what victory David here proclaims, in my judgment, are vain. COMMENTARY ON THE PSALMS.[4]

9:1-6 Thanks to the Lord

PRAISE GOD FOR GOD'S GLORY. JOHN CALVIN: David, with good reason, affirms that he is unlike the children of this world, whose hypocrisy or fraud is discovered by the wicked and dishonest distribution which they make between God and themselves, arrogating to themselves the greater part of the praise which they pretended to ascribe to God. He praised God with his whole heart, which they did not; for certainly it is not praising God with the whole heart when a mortal human being dares to appropriate even the smallest portion of the glory which God claims for himself. God cannot bear seeing his glory appropriated by the creature in even the smallest degree, so intolerable to him is the sacrilegious arrogance of those who, by praising themselves, obscure his glory as far as they can. COMMENTARY ON THE PSALMS.[5]

UNDERSTAND THIS PASSAGE THROUGH THE SPIRIT OF LOVE. MARTIN LUTHER: "I will tell of all your wonders," he says, which is not possible. But such is the nature of love and strong emotion that it is extremely eager and, as far as eagerness is concerned, it lacks nothing to do the impossible. To one in love nothing is difficult; yes, the impossible seems possible. So the learned teachers say about Mary Magdalene that she wanted to carry the Lord away from the gardener all by herself. Also Psalm 6 above used such language: "I will wash my bed every night," that is, I am completely ready to do this, if it should be possible. "The spirit is willing, but the flesh is weak," that is, it cannot do as much as the spirit is ready to do, because these things go beyond its nature. And there are many things in the Psalter and the Bible that must be understood in this manner. Some interpret these things hyperbolically according to the killing letter, but according to the life-giving Spirit they are completely true.

Those things are the "wonders" because the Lord has destroyed what is strong by what is weak, the wisdom of the world by the folly of the cross, the things that are by the things that are not, glorious things by base things. . . . Thus, because this psalm is in the mouth of spirits and of mystical youth, its historical meaning is altogether spiritual. FIRST PSALMS LECTURES (1513–1515).[6]

GOD IDENTIFIES WITH US. WOLFGANG MUSCULUS: This verse is a great consolation in which God is set forth as a just judge who will vindicate the cause of the innocent and of the oppressed by sitting at a tribunal against whatever powers, whatever armed foes, and those gathered for war and those already attacking. Meanwhile, let

---

[3]LW 10:91* (WA 3:88-89; cf. 5:284-86); citing Ps 45:14; Song 1:3; 6:8; Ps 31:20; Hos 2:20.
[4]CTS 8:109* (CO 31:95-96). No one is sure what 'almût labbēn means; the LXX renders the phrase as huper tōn kruphiōn tou huiou ("according to the secrets of youth"—or "sons"). While most assume that it is some sort of musical instrument, Goldingay also allows for the options Luther mentions. See Goldingay, *Psalms*, 1:162, 170; Kraus, *Psalms 1–59*, 31; Alter, *Book of Psalms*, 25.

[5]CTS 8:111* (CO 31:96-97).
[6]LW 10:92* (WA 3:89); citing Jn 20:15; Ps 6:6; Mt 26:41; 2 Cor 3:6; 1 Cor 1:27-28.

us nevertheless see that our cause is such that it can be defended against our enemies by a just judge.

Second . . . he calls the cause of the people of God his own cause, and the judgment of Israel, his own judgment. For he is not being entreated by the person of David alone, but by all of Israel regarding the enemies who encircle them. Therefore, David speaks here as king and head of the people of God and transfers the cause of the people onto himself, in whose name he also waged war. Thus our cause is in fact that of Christ, our David and King, on account of which we are attacked by the children of this age in various ways: not only whenever the whole church is afflicted but also if one or the other members of the church is unjustly oppressed. COMMENTARY ON THE PSALMS.[7]

BE GRATEFUL FOR THE LORD'S GENEROSITY. NIKOLAUS SELNECKER: That we are and live, that we have, hear, read your Word, that we are sustained and still have a seed of your church among us, this is your doing, mercy and gift. Therefore, everyone who knows you should thank you. What is good comes from you and not from us. . . . This is a great consolation and beautiful promise: God is always our protection, but especially in times of need. Who then will fear if God is for us? If we poor and miserable, it does not matter. We hope in the name of God. We know the name of God and know that he gladly and freely gives us everything. He will not abandon us, if we would only knock, desire and acknowledge his goodness, and thank him for it. THE WHOLE PSALTER.[8]

THE REBUKE OF GOD'S JUDGMENT IS A DEVAS-TATING WEAPON. TILEMANN HESSHUS: David expresses how God revealed his judgment. God does not need a large army or many weapons; merely by rebuke does he wipe out his enemies and the church's. And God rebukes his enemies mainly with the voice of the law with which he discloses their impiety, their false teaching, their idolatry,

their blindness and all their other misdeeds. He threatens them with the severest punishments. But the impious are hardly moved by this rebuke—yes, on account of this voice of the law which the church utters, they stoke their fury even more. Then, God rebukes them by hurling dreadful panic by which the impious are tortured with curses. . . . Finally God rebukes his enemies by imposing punishment from heaven. By the might of his judgment he makes himself known throughout the whole world. COMMENTARY ON PSALM 9.[9]

9:7-14 *Tell Everyone What the Lord Has Done*

JUSTICE REQUIRES JUDGMENT. VIKTORIN STRIGEL: The combination of human weakness and divine punishment is common in the Psalms. Therefore, because he said in a verse above that the shifting of human affairs is more erratic than that of a fly as it darts about, now he weaves in the second part of the contrast: "The Lord," he said, "together with his Word and his church, can never be made to waver by any force or dislodged from his place." It is safer, therefore, and preferable to trust in God alone than to place one's confidence in a thousand of the best people, whose will or fortune or life is subject to change. But those things which are said about God's judgment can be related foremost to the ministry of the Word, in which the Holy Spirit teaches the world about sin, righteousness and judgment.

Second, these words can be applied to the Last Judgment, in which the minds of all the impious will be revealed, all their evil plans and deeds will be brought into the light, and they will be condemned and cast out into eternal torture. The testimonies of this judgment are inscribed in our minds and testify to what God is, what his nature is, and the fact that he will one day stand as Judge. For in vain God would have established a differentiation between what is pure and impure in human minds, unless afterwards followed punishment for what is out of order.

---

[7]Musculus, *In Psalterium Commentarii*, 115.
[8]Selnecker, *Der gantze Psalter*, 1:32r-v.

[9]Hesshus, *Commentarius in Psalmos*, 52r.

Also, it is impossible, because he is God, that there is no providential care for and separation of the wicked and the good. Here the wicked flourish while the good are oppressed. Therefore, it must be that there awaits another life, in which there will be a separation. For, because God showed to Abel, Jonathan, Isaiah and Jeremiah that he cared for them before they died, if he neglected them later, that would not fit with his providential care or righteousness. It is obvious, therefore, that those who deny that after death there awaits any judgment remove from God providential care and justice in regard to a great part of the human race, or, more precisely, those who persevere in righteousness. For if God neglects his own both now and then later, immortality does not await, and I do not at all understand how either providential care or righteousness could be attributed to God. HYPONĒMATA IN ALL THE PSALMS.[10]

FOCUS ON GOD AS JUDGE. JOHN CALVIN: This contrast between the power of the enemies of God and his people, and the work of God in breaking up their proceedings, very well illustrates the wonderful character of the help which he granted to his people. The unbelievers had set to themselves no limit in the work of doing mischief, save in the utter destruction of all things, and at the commencement complete destruction seemed to be at hand. However, when things were in this state of confusion, God seasonably made his appearance for the help of his people. As often, therefore, as nothing but destruction presents itself to our view, to whatever side we may turn, let us remember to lift up our eyes to the heavenly throne, from where God sees all that is done here below. In the world our affairs may have been brought to such extremes that there is no longer hope in regard to them; but the shield with which we ought to repel all the temptations that assail us is this: God sits as Judge in heaven. Yes, when he seems to take no notice of us and does not immediately remedy the evils which we suffer, it becomes us to realize by faith his secret providence. . . .

Although he does not immediately save and help those who are unrighteously oppressed, there is not a moment in which he ceases to take a deep interest in them. And when he seems for a time to take no notice of things, the conclusion to which we should come most assuredly is not that he deserts his office but that he wishes hereby to exercise the patience of his people, and that, therefore, we should wait the issue in patience and with tranquility of mind. COMMENTARY ON THE PSALMS.[11]

PRAISE AND PROCLAIM GOD'S FAVOR. WOLFGANG MUSCULUS: David demands these two things from the church of God—which through divine kindness has been freed from the hands of the impious tyrants—first to praise and second to proclaim. He requires these two things together from the people of God. First, that they sing praise to the Lord, that is, that they sing his praises to the end with a grateful heart and give him thanks. Second, that they proclaim and thoroughly preach his deeds among the people, among those who have no knowledge of the true God. Therefore, the church should sing psalms and worship by lifting up their hearts to their Liberator, that is, to offer the sacrifice of praise. Then to proclaim his wonderful deeds to all nations with zeal for the propagation of his glory and for devotion to the salvation of mortals. These are two things which the church of the redeemed should do without ceasing. COMMENTARY ON THE PSALMS.[12]

SACRAMENTS ELEVATE OUR HEARTS AND MINDS TO HEAVEN. JOHN CALVIN: God, indeed, gave real tokens of his presence in that visible sanctuary, but not for the purpose of binding the senses and thoughts of his people to earthly elements. No, instead, he wanted these external symbols to serve as ladders, by which the faithful might ascend even to heaven. The design of God from the initiation of the sacraments, and all the outward exercises of piety, was to advise the

---

[10]Strigel, *Hyponēmata*, 45.

[11]CTS 8:116-18* (CO 31:99-100).
[12]Musculus, *In Psalterium Commentarii*, 121.

coarseness of his people. Accordingly, even today, the true and proper use of them is to assist us in seeking God spiritually in his heavenly glory and not to occupy our minds with the things of this world or keep them fixed in the vanities of the flesh. . . . And as the Lord, in ancient times, when he called himself "he who dwells in Zion," intended to give his people full and solid ground of trust, tranquility and joy; so even now, after the law has come out of Zion and the covenant of grace has flowed to us from that fountain, let us know and be fully persuaded that wherever the faithful, who worship him purely and in due form, according to the appointment of his Word, are assembled together to engage in the solemn acts of religious worship, he is graciously present and presides in the midst of them. COMMENTARY ON THE PSALMS.[13]

GOD DEMONSTRATES HIS POWER THROUGH THE LOWLY. HANS HAS VON HALLSTATT: When those whom God loves have sunk deep down, God often lets them swim a long time until they are about to go under and drown in their suffering. Then he comes to them at the last minute and helps, showing himself to be God and a gracious, loving Father. For he helps most when no other help can be found, when all creaturely comfort and hope is completely gone. When the proper time comes for help, then he comes forth. For he is called "a help in times of trouble," that is, a helper at an opportune, convenient and appropriate moment. When no other comfort and help are available, he shows himself to be a strong, mighty and powerful God, who is the Lord of heaven and earth, and that all creatures are in his hand. Through such help God pours out his grace into the chosen, so that they might increase and dwell all the more in the truth and trust completely in God, so that God may do with them whatever his will deems proper. Thus they set their hope on him.

For that reason he sets up mighty and powerful people before us who have formidable reputations of strength in the eyes of the world, and not a simple, lesser, weak people of no value. Why is this? So that he can demonstrate his might and strength through the least of creatures against the great and mighty. The least overcome the mighty with their patience, so that it becomes known that God is even more mighty and powerful than all powers on this earth. KUNSTBUCH: CONCERNING THE COMFORT OF CHRISTIANS.[14]

THREE SENSES OF "GATES." MARTIN LUTHER: "Gates" literally is the name given to the residence of the authority and rulers in the republic, or senators. In Proverbs 31 we read: "Her husband is honorable in the gates, when he sits among the senators of the land." There are, however, senatorial "gates of death," first of the synagogue and also of the Gentiles. And this because there the killing letter is defended and the power of demons is exerted. For that reason the Lord in the Gospel calls them "the gates of hell," which fight against the church but will not prevail. But they lead all who sit in them to death. On the contrary, the "gates of Zion" are the powers in the church through whose authority they enter into life and whose function it is to judge and to sit in behalf of the causes of the church. In a tropological sense, however, "the gates of death" are the inclinations of the flesh, through which death by means of a mortal inducement of sin gains access to the soul. On the contrary, the gates of Zion are the same inclinations disciplined, through which the works of life go out and the words and examples of life go in. . . . Here is also another allegory: it is faith and the articles of faith. Another one: It is every bishop or teacher over his people, a person who ought to be for them a door and an entrance-way to life, like Christ, whose representative he is. FIRST PSALMS LECTURES (1513–1515).[15]

CONFIDENCE IN DAVID'S REQUEST FOR SALVATION. MARTIN BUCER: Because he had said that the Lord has not forgotten the outcry of the afflicted, and because he wanted to show that it

---

[13]CTS 8:122* (CO 31:100).

[14]CRR 12:442-43*; citing Mt 11:27.
[15]LW 10:95-96 (WA 3:91); citing Prov 31:23; Mt 16:18.

was true in his own case, he inserts among these praises of the Lord a prayer which he poured out when he was in danger, when it was especially unclear how it would turn out, by which he asked that he would be lifted up from the gates of destruction and the jaws of death. Moreover, he had prayed that God would have mercy on him, look on his affliction that he endured from those by whom he was hated and raise him from the gates of death, by which expression he indicated that he had approached death, all the way to its threshold. Then he prayed that he would celebrate his praises in the gates and gatherings of Zion, in the church of the people of God, and openly testify of his happiness concerning the salvation received from God. So the saints only ask to live for the glory of God. Holy Psalms.[16]

Zion's Gates Are Life. Henry Ainsworth: These are opposed to the former "gates of death" and mean the public places where God's people come together at Zion—gates, where God sat and which he loved most. The daughter of Zion signifies the church or congregation there gathered . . . for every chief city was counted as a mother—thus, the apostle calls Jerusalem "the mother of us all"—the villages that were near and pertained to such cities are called daughters, and the inhabitants there seated or assemblies of people resorting there are also named daughters, because they were bred, born, nourished and governed there. Annotations on Psalm 9:14.[17]

9:15-20 *Judgment Prepared and Executed*

The Wicked Are Cast Away from God's Affection. David Dickson: As the devices of the wicked come from hell, so they return there and draw the devisers with them, and although they cry, Peace, peace, and put the fear of hell far from them, yet "all the wicked shall be turned into

hell." As they who give themselves to sin, and especially enemies to peace, cast away the knowledge of God out of their mind and affection, so shall God cast them away far from his presence: "All the nations that forget God shall be turned into hell." Commentary on Psalm 9.[18]

Perhaps Through Threats They Will Learn Salvation. Nikolaus Selnecker: Here he starts to threaten, and nevertheless wishes at the same time that—wherever possible—the godless might be converted. "I do *not* desire," he says, "that they should utterly and eternally perish in body and soul. From my heart I long for the salvation of their souls. However, they lack one thing: they do not repent, so that they would not be led into hell." That is, they live in security, lechery and peace, and it is impossible for them to understand the Word of God, because it is a word of the cross. A person must be mired in misery; otherwise he thinks that faith is merely an invented illusion, which only stands on the tongue. For this reason he says, "I wish they would come to the same school where I was, to the gates of death; then they would perhaps change their mind." The Whole Psalter.[19]

Meditate on the Depths of God's Works. Sebastian Münster: *Higgāyôn*, that is, "meditation." God's elect discover, the psalmist says, in his works much to meditate on. They are stunned how God, for a time, permits the wicked to dig pits, to hide their snares and to prepare ambushes for the pious, and yet it is the wicked themselves who, by divine judgment, fall into them. For God, in the end, never forsakes his own but at the right time brings salvation. The Temple of the Lord: Psalm 9.[20]

---

[16]Bucer, *Sacrorum Psalmorum*, 62r.

[17]Ainsworth, *Annotations*, 2:428*; citing Ps 87:2; 2 Sam 20:19; Gal 4:26; Josh 15:45; 2 Chron 13:19; Ps 48:12.

[18]Dickson, *First Fifty Psalms*, 41*.

[19]Selnecker, *Der gantze Psalter*, 1:34v; citing Ps 83.

[20]Münster, *Miqdaš YHWH*, 1166. Modern commentators derive *higgāyôn* from *hāgâ*, which can refer to an animal making noise or a human being groaning as well as meditating (cf. Is 16:7; 31:4; 38:4; Ps 1:2; 19:14; 92:3). Goldingay is uncertain what it means here; Kraus prefers to understand it as a musical interlude, though he wonders if Münster's suggestion might be correct. See Goldingay, *Psalms*, 1:163; Kraus, *Psalms 1–59*, 27.

ŠĔʾÔL IS MORE THAN MERE DEATH. JOHN
CALVIN: The meaning of the Hebrew word *šĕʾôl*, is
doubtful, but I have not hesitated to translate it
"hell." I do not find fault with those who translate it
"the grave," but it is certain that the prophet means
something more than common death; otherwise he
would here say nothing else with respect to the
wicked than what would also happen to all the
faithful in common with them. Although then he
does not speak in explicit terms of eternal destruction but only says, "They shall be turned into the
grave," still, under the metaphor of the grave, he
intimates that all unbelievers shall perish and that
the presumption with which, by every unlawful
means, they raise themselves on high to trample
righteousness under foot and to oppress the
innocent, shall bring on them ruin and perdition.
The faithful, also, it is true, descend into the grave,
but not with such fearful violence as plunges them
into it without hope of coming out again. So far is
this from being the case that even when shut up in
the grave, they dwell already in heaven by hope.
COMMENTARY ON THE PSALMS.[21]

**ŠĔʾÔL REVEALS THE FOOLISHNESS OF WORLDLY
DESIRES.** THE ENGLISH ANNOTATIONS: Some
understand "sepulcher" here by "hell" and translate it
accordingly; others "the place of torments." For
otherwise, they say, who is a person—good or
bad—who can escape the grave? As for the Hebrew
word *šĕʾôl* (about which so much has been written)
it is certain that it means both. But besides these
two meanings *šĕʾôl* (like *hadēs* in Greek) sometimes
also gives the idea of simple non-existence or
annihilation as in Isaiah 5:14.... Here some also
expound it this way: they will be reduced to nothing.
Not because they will be annihilated in every way by

death—which is the error of many Jewish interpreters, who teach that the wicked and ungodly will be
totally extinct and never rise again, contrary to
Christ's plain teaching and the apostle's—but
because this word serves well to set out more fully
the vanity of the worldly, in both their lives and
actions. ANNOTATIONS ON PSALM 9:17.[22]

THE FEAR OF THE LORD. JOHN CALVIN: Now, it
is to be considered of what kind of fear David
speaks. God commonly subdues even his chosen
ones to obedience by means of fear. But as he
moderates his severity toward them, and, at the
same time, softens their stony hearts so that they
willingly and quietly submit themselves to him, he
cannot be properly said to compel them by fear.
With respect to the reprobate, he takes a different
way of dealing. As their obduracy is inflexible, so
that it is easier to break than to bend them, he
subdues their desperate obstinacy by force; not,
indeed, that they are reformed, but, whether they
will or no, an acknowledgment of their own
weakness is extorted from them. They may gnash
their teeth and boil with rage, and even exceed in
cruelty wild beasts, but when the dread of God
seizes on them, they are thrown down with their
own violence and fall with their own weight. Some
explain these words as a prayer that God would
bring the nations under the yoke of David and
make them tributaries to his government; but this
is a cold and forced explanation. The word *fear*
comprehends in general all the plagues of God, by
which is repulsed, as by the heavy blows of a
hammer, the rebellion of those who would never
obey him except by compulsion. COMMENTARY
ON THE PSALMS.[23]

---

[21]CTS 8:129* (CO 31:106).

[22]Downame, ed., *Annotations*, 5Z2v*; citing Jn 5:28-29; 2 Cor 5:10.
[23]CTS 8:131-32* (CO 31:107).

10:1-18 WHERE ARE YOU, LORD? DRAW NEAR!

¹ Why, O LORD, do you stand far away?
  Why do you hide yourself in times of trouble?

² In arrogance the wicked hotly pursue the poor;
  let them be caught in the schemes that they
    have devised.
³ For the wicked boasts of the desires of his soul,
  and the one greedy for gain curses^a and
    renounces the LORD.
⁴ In the pride of his face^b the wicked does not
    seek him;^c
  all his thoughts are, "There is no God."
⁵ His ways prosper at all times;
  your judgments are on high, out of his sight;
  as for all his foes, he puffs at them.
⁶ He says in his heart, "I shall not be moved;
  throughout all generations I shall not meet
    adversity."
⁷ His mouth is filled with cursing and deceit
    and oppression;
  under his tongue are mischief and iniquity.
⁸ He sits in ambush in the villages;
  in hiding places he murders the innocent.
His eyes stealthily watch for the helpless;
⁹ he lurks in ambush like a lion in his thicket;
he lurks that he may seize the poor;
  he seizes the poor when he draws him into
    his net.

¹⁰ The helpless are crushed, sink down,
  and fall by his might.
¹¹ He says in his heart, "God has forgotten,
  he has hidden his face, he will never see it."

¹² Arise, O LORD; O God, lift up your hand;
  forget not the afflicted.
¹³ Why does the wicked renounce God
  and say in his heart, "You will not call to
    account"?
¹⁴ But you do see, for you note mischief and
    vexation,
  that you may take it into your hands;
to you the helpless commits himself;
  you have been the helper of the fatherless.
¹⁵ Break the arm of the wicked and evildoer;
  call his wickedness to account till you find none.

¹⁶ The LORD is king forever and ever;
  the nations perish from his land.
¹⁷ O LORD, you hear the desire of the afflicted;
  you will strengthen their heart; you will
    incline your ear
¹⁸ to do justice to the fatherless and the
    oppressed,
  so that man who is of the earth may strike
    terror no more.

a Or and he blesses the one greedy for gain   b Or of his anger   c Or the wicked says, "He will not call to account"

OVERVIEW: Contemporary Psalm studies identify this psalm as originally being united with Psalm 9 and framed together on an acrostic pattern. Gwalther acknowledges the Septuagint tradition; however, he thinks that this was because Psalm 10 lacks a title rather than that it reflects an earlier textual tradition. The reformers, while showing some interest in the ancient horizon and the meaning of Hebrew terms, freely weld that horizon with their own. The psalm moves from questioning where God is in the midst of opposition and meditating on the wiles of the wicked to calling on God to arise and fight. It concludes on a note of confidence in God's rule and care for the weak and vulnerable.

From our modern context, language of God being "far off" and the wicked thinking "there is no God" catches our attention as a note of divine absence. But for the reformers atheism was not so much an intellectual persuasion as a lack of true knowledge of God. Calvin reminds us that the psalmist's language here is figurative. Our commentators do not fret over characterizing their own enemies in the style of the psalmist. The reformers gladly thicken the figures of this psalm against the backdrop of their contemporary conflicts: Selnecker conflates the traits of the psalmist's enemies with his own; Luther understands these wicked people to be opponents of Christ's church and kingdom; Musculus, in contrast, meditates on a godly mindset. As the psalm closes with the theme of the orphan and the oppressed, Hesshus sees the church as the afflicted orphan.

The Septuagint Conflates Psalm 9 and Psalm 10. RUDOLF GWALTHER: Because this psalm does not have a specific title, the Greeks did not separate it from Psalm 9. And so it happened that the psalm numbers used until now in the church did not agree with the Hebrew numbers. However, that this is itself a separate psalm is easily inferred from its content. THE PSALTER.[1]

Though Ferocious, the Church's Enemies Are Impotent. THEODORE BEZA: In this psalm the belligerence of the church's enemies is graphically described, as well as their savage carelessness. They are like those monsters, the Cyclops, described by the poets. Nevertheless all their plans are rendered vain in the end—God will not let them go unpunished, nor will he forsake his church. PARAPHRASE OF PSALM 10.[2]

Psalm of Consolation Against Christ's Enemies and Their Actions. MARTIN LUTHER: This is a psalm of prayer. It bemoans the archenemy of the kingdom of Christ, that is, the antichrist who disturbs Christianity both with violence and with trickery on account of his avarice and arrogance. He directs both the sword of worldly tyranny against the body and the net of false doctrine against the soul. As it says here, "His mouth is full of cursing, lies and deceit." He cannot do anything more than curse; that is, punish and damn; lie, that is, establish false doctrine and worship; and deceive, that is, hoodwink and fool the world for its possessions, honor, power, body and soul. But at the end the psalm grants the consolation that such horrors will be uprooted with the end of the world. SUMMARY OF PSALM 10 (1531–1533).[3]

10:1 *Where Is God?*

The Psalmist Describes God Familiarly but Not Strictly Accurately. JOHN CALVIN: It is in an improper sense, and by anthropopathy,[4] that the psalmist speaks of God as standing far off; nothing can be hidden from his eyes. But because God permits us to speak to him as we do to one another, these forms of expression do not contain anything absurd, provided we understand them as applied to God not in a strict sense but only figuratively, according to the judgment which mere sense forms from the present appearance of things. It is possible that a righteous person may not restrain an injury done to a poor person before his eyes, because he lacks power; but this cannot be the case with God, who is always armed with invincible power. If, therefore, he conceals himself, it seems as if he withdrew himself far away. COMMENTARY ON THE PSALMS.[5]

God Is Omnipresent but Distinct from Creation. THE ENGLISH ANNOTATIONS: God, according to his essence, is in all places equally *intra omnia sed non inclusus*, that is, "within all things but not included, outside all things but not excluded," "whole and entire in the whole and in every part of the whole," as the schoolmen say

---

[1]Gwalther, *Der Psalter*, 13v. See above, pp. *lvi-lvii*.
[2]Beza, *Psalmorum Davidis*, 28 (cf. *Psalmes of Dauid*, 13-14).
[3]WA 38:21.
[4]That is, ascribing human feelings to God.
[5]CTS 8:134-35* (CO 31:108-9).

and the Scriptures (David himself!) teach. However, he is frequently said to be or to dwell where his glory is most visible, as in the heavens or in his church or wherever he manifests himself in an extraordinary manner by any effects of his power or grace. Now . . . nothing is more proper and natural (if we may speak this way) to God than to be just and righteous. ANNOTATIONS ON PSALM 10:1.[6]

10:2-11 *Deceit! Murder! Oppression!*

DAVID HERE SUMMARIZES THE MARKS OF THE FALSE CHURCH. TILEMANN HESSHUS: In Psalm 10:2-11 a long description of the wickedness of the impious follows; by these they waylay the church. By recounting these evil deeds David tries to stir God up in order to bring forth his aid; he also strengthens himself in faith. . . . And he warns all people that they should avoid the company of the impious, lest they partake in their wickedness. COMMENTARY ON PSALM 10.[7]

GOD IS JUDGE. JOHN CALVIN: The beginning of well-doing in a person's life is inquiry; in other words, we can only begin to do well when we keep ourselves from following, without choice and discrimination, the dictates of our own fancy, and from being carried away by the wayward propensities of our flesh. But the exercise of inquiring proceeds from humility, when we assign to God, as is reasonable, the place of Judge and Ruler over us. The prophet, therefore, very properly says that the reason why the unbelievers, without any regard or consideration, presume to do whatever they desire is because, being lifted up with pride, they leave to God nothing whatever of the prerogative of a judge. COMMENTARY ON THE PSALMS.[8]

ADVERSARIES OF THE GOSPEL SNORT AND SPIT. NIKOLAUS SELNECKER: Here a little Hebrew word stands, *yāpîaḥ*, that is, to speak impudently and recklessly, to be rude and unashamed, to act freely without thinking it through. Anyone who does not immediately obey them, they berate, damn, persecute and call heretics and apostates. Anything that does not please them must be driven away and damned. And such a manner is now—God have mercy!—among us, too. And this word describes a great security and impudence like that in Thomas Müntzer and Andreas Karlstadt. Again, this word also means to be puffed up, so that a person on account of rage and pride will break out against his enemies; he snorts and spits, curses and wants to tear up everything with roots. THE WHOLE PSALTER.[9]

THE DIFFERENCE BETWEEN THE GODLY AND UNGODLY. JOHN CALVIN: The faithful promise themselves security in God and nowhere else, yet while they do this, they know that they are exposed to all the storms of affliction and patiently submit to them. There is a very great difference between a despiser of God—who enjoying prosperity today is so forgetful of the condition of human beings in this world, as through a distempered imagination to build his nest above the clouds, and who persuades himself that he will always enjoy comfort and repose—and the godly person. The godly person knows that his life hangs only by a thread, that he is encompassed by a thousand deaths, he is ready to endure any kind of afflictions which shall be sent on him. That person lives in the world as if he were sailing on a tempestuous and dangerous sea; nevertheless, he bears patiently all his troubles and sorrows and comforts himself in his afflictions, because he leans wholly on the grace of God and entirely confides in it. COMMENTARY ON THE PSALMS.[10]

---

[6]Downame, ed., *Annotations*, 5Z2v*; citing Augustine, *On the Literal Meaning of Genesis* 8.26 (ACW 42:67); *On the Trinity* 6.6 (NPNF 3:101); Ps 139.
[7]Hesshus, *Commentarius in Psalmos*, 56v.
[8]CTS 8:139* (CO 31:111).
[9]Selnecker, *Der gantze Psalter*, 1:38r.
[10]CTS 8:143* (CO 31:112).

THE LABOR OF A WICKED MOUTH. MARTIN LUTHER: "Mouth" means open speech and what goes forth to human beings publicly. But "under his tongue there is toil and grief" means that with toil and anxious care they contrive a disguise for their own lie. On top of the tongue there is honey, but under the tongue there is poison, and thus they teach evil and their own pernicious teachings disguised to look like piety and truth. But falsehood always needs many things to look like truth, according to blessed Jerome. Therefore this attempt, this design by which pestilent fellows try to establish their error, is called "toil," as in another psalm, "The labor of their lips shall overwhelm them," that is, catch and oppress them. Therefore blessed Augustine says on this verse of the psalm, "Nothing is more toilsome than ungodliness," especially when it must defend and adorn itself. Similarly "grief" is the jealousy that arises from that ungodly toil. Observe, then, how very clearly Scripture speaks: "under their tongue is toil and grief," that is, an anxious and envious concern for glossing over error. FIRST PSALMS LECTURES (1513-1515).[11]

HOW SHOULD ḤĂṢĒRÎM BE TRANSLATED? THE ENGLISH ANNOTATIONS: Ḥăṣērîm, understood by some rabbis as "inner courts," is here translated "villages," that is, open courts, public halls and the like. We know that the word itself includes both senses, and some interpreters—besides the rabbis—prefer the latter, as if by this word David aimed not at petty thieves who rob in obscure places, but at the grand ones. Those who, in open courts and public places of commerce, do the same as petty thieves, with as bad a conscience, by perverting justice, by horrible—though tolerated and allowed—extortions and exactions and the like; but with more credit and allowance. And here some inveigh greatly against merchants, as people usually guilty of this kind of theft. For my part, I do not think so ill of that profession, and even among them I believe that people of great integrity and generosity may be found. Nor do I think so well of any other profession that is a *quaestvosa professio*—that is, whose chief end is gain and profit—that a store of such thieves will not be found. But how shall "lurking places" agree with open courts and common halls? It may be answered, I know that the original word may be translated (as it is by some) "in ambushes" as well as "in lurking places." And ambushes may be laid in public places, there is no question. But then it follows immediately, *bamistārîm*, "in secret places," which is directly opposite to public. Something may be said to that as well, but when all is done, I must profess that I conceive "villages," as it is here, the more warranted translation of the two. ANNOTATIONS ON PSALM 10:8.[12]

THE REPROBATE ARE BLOODTHIRSTY BUTCHERS. TILEMANN HESSHUS: It is not enough for the impious to badger and burden the pious. They are not able to be satisfied by interrogating and torturing them; no indeed, they even drain out the blood of the pious, so that they become even more frenzied. And with all their strength they strive not only to blot out utterly any memory of the pious but even any memory of all true religion. David also reminds us here that God sometimes allows pious and innocent ministers not only to be badgered but even cruelly butchered, so that the tremendous odium of the impious may be seen and the true steadfastness of the pious may become even clearer. Like those criminal cardinals at the Council of Constance who accused, struck down and burned the poor and pious Jan Hus. COMMENTARY ON PSALM 10.[13]

THE RELATIONSHIP BETWEEN THE WEALTHY AND THE POOR. THE ENGLISH ANNOTATIONS: Wealthy people, if good and just and truly generous, are a great support to the poor, and so it commonly

---

[11]LW 10:97* (WA 3:92); citing Jerome, Epistle 34 to Marcella (PL 22:450); Ps 140:9; Augustine, Exposition on Psalm 10 (NPNF 8:38).

[12]Downame, ed., *Annotations*, 5Z3r*. See Münster, *Miqdaš YHWH*, 1167.

[13]Hesshus, *Commentarius in Psalmos*, 58r.

is in a well-governed state. But otherwise, if they are of themselves wicked and ungodly and the times are licentious, it is no wonder they prove great oppressors. ANNOTATIONS ON PSALM 10:10.[14]

THE WICKED THINK GOD DOES NOT SEE THEIR ACTIONS. MARTIN BUCER: This sets forth the cause of all the things which were set before it. In this way with all their strength, the wicked strive to trap, ensnare, defraud, despoil, overturn and extinguish whoever cannot resist their devices and force, so that in this zeal for harming and destroying the poor, they surpass the rapacity of thugs, the ferocity of lions and the trickery of fowlers. This is because among themselves they constantly think that God does not have any regard, any concern for present affairs, that he has turned his face away, such that he does not see what they have done. . . . For this reason they might reluctantly listen to something from God to a certain extent and then atrociously persecute and mock the true religion as well as whoever admires the providence of God. HOLY PSALMS.[15]

10:12-15 Act, Lord, Lest the Wicked Think They Are Free to Do Evil

DOUBT TROUBLES ALL HUMAN BEINGS. JOHN CALVIN: By speaking of God according to human manner, the prophet declares that the same error which he has just now condemned in the despisers of God had gradually creeped into his own mind. But he immediately corrects it, and resolutely struggles with himself, and restrains his mind from forming such conceptions of God as would reflect dishonor on his righteousness and glory. It is therefore a temptation to which all human beings are naturally prone, to begin to doubt the providence of God when his hand and judgment are not seen. The godly, however, differ widely from the wicked. The former, by means of faith, check this apprehension of the flesh, while the latter indulge

themselves in their perverse imagination. Thus David, by the word *Arise*, does not so much stir up God as he awakens himself, or tries to awaken himself, to hope for more of the assistance of God than he presently experienced. COMMENTARY ON THE PSALMS.[16]

THE GODLY CONTRADICTS THE UNGODLY. WOLFGANG MUSCULUS: Note here how different the character of the ungodly and the godly are. The ungodly say in their own heart, "God does not see." On the contrary, the godly say, "God sees, and he considers trouble and fury." Therefore, just as the ungodly speak out of what is in their heart, "God does not see," and they blaspheme God and continue into their own wickedness and oppress the innocent, so also the godly are persuaded from what they believe—that God sees and observes the plans and deeds of mortal human beings—and they glorify God and strengthen themselves in eagerness for piety. They are fully refreshed, continuing in the afflictions bestowed on them by the ungodly. . . .

It was not enough for the prophet to have said, "You see"; plainly he added, "Because you see trouble and fury." This was so that the verse might signify that God does not simply see what is done here on earth, as if those events seem to happen by great chance and incidentally, but he observes and considers all things by his plan.

Second, note that he does not simply say, "Because you consider," but, "because *you* consider trouble and fury." The emphasis on the pronoun "you" signifies that God alone is the one who carefully considers how the ungodly oppress the innocent. And the prophet seeks consolation from this: where the minds of the afflicted see that none of the magistrates observe and restrain the wickedness of the ungodly or look on the enslaved and free them, they are revived and encouraged in God, the just Judge and most vigilant observer of all.

Finally . . . he joins fury together with trouble, that is, the affliction and distress by which the

---

[14]Downame, ed., *Annotations*, 5Z3r*.
[15]Bucer, *Sacrorum Psalmorum*, 67v-68r.

[16]CTS 8:149-50* (CO 31:116).

innocent are oppressed by the ungodly. Fury is an attack of passion in the mind of a person. Therefore, the ungodly are insane, while they afflict the innocent and say in their heart, "God does not see." Let us learn here what we ought to feel about the violence and tyranny of the wicked, by which they think that they chiefly look after their own affairs and their own glory. Of course, it is insane fury, which they themselves think is the highest prudence. What prudent person does not understand that he is hardened and continually unable to proceed, because he is governed by fury? COMMENTARY ON THE PSALMS.[17]

WAIT PATIENTLY FOR GOD. JOHN CALVIN: It is, however, our duty to wait patiently until vengeance will be brought about by the hand of God, until he stretches forth his arm to help us. Therefore, it is immediately added, "To you the poor will entrust themselves." By these words David means that time should be entrusted to the providence of God, so that the pious, when they are wretchedly afflicted, may cast their cares into his bosom and then commit themselves to his protection. They should not rush into vows, but, now unburdened, they should enjoy respite until God declares that the right time has come. Therefore, whoever entrusts himself to God, to his protection, and is fully persuaded that he is a faithful trustee, calmly anticipates the seasonable time of his deliverance. COMMENTARY ON THE PSALMS.[18]

10:16-18 Our God Protects the Fatherless and the Oppressed

HOPE IS NOT IN VAIN. JOHN CALVIN: It is not in vain that God directs the hearts of his people and leads them in obedience to his command, to look to himself and to call on him in hope and patience. It is

not in vain, because his ears are never shut against their groaning. Thus the mutual harmony between two religious exercises is commended here. God does not allow the faith of his servants to faint or fail, nor does he let them cease praying; rather, he keeps them near him by faith and prayer, until it actually appears that their hope has been neither vain nor ineffectual. COMMENTARY ON THE PSALMS.[19]

THE LORD PROMISES TO CARE FOR THE FATHERLESS AND TO RESTRAIN THE WICKED. TILEMANN HESSHUS: Finally he adds these two reasons why he so anxiously asks for a favorable answer to his prayer. First, because God helps orphans and the oppressed. The church dwells in the midst of the greatest dangers. It is without any protection; it is like an orphan and fatherless child. Therefore, it will be glorious when God comes to the help of his deserted church, as he promised. Second, because the pride, insolence and ferocity of the impious is restrained, lest the impious' good fortune be so great that others are troubled by their pride, haughtiness and immodesty. But finally the impious should be restrained and should understand that they are miserable human beings who are able to think of nothing more ridiculous, when they oppose the omnipotent God. COMMENTARY ON PSALM 10.[20]

THE WICKED CREEP OUT OF THEIR HOLES TO ASSAULT GOD AND HIS PEOPLE. JOHN CALVIN: The phrase "who is of the earth" contains a tacit contrast between the low abode of this world and the height of heaven. For from where will they come forth to assault the children of God? From the earth, of course, just like maggots creeping up out of crevices in the ground. But in this way, they attack God himself who promises help to his servants from heaven. COMMENTARY ON THE PSALMS.[21]

---

[17]Musculus, *In Psalterium Commentarii*, 140-41.
[18]CTS 8:152* (CO 31:117).
[19]CTS 8:156* (CO 31:119).
[20]Hesshus, *Commentarius in Psalmos*, 59r.
[21]CTS 8:157* (CO 31:120).

11:1-7 THE MIGHTY AND RIGHTEOUS LORD REIGNS FROM HEAVEN

To the choirmaster. Of David.

[1] *In the LORD I take refuge;*
how can you say to my soul,
　"Flee like a bird to your mountain,
[2] *for behold, the wicked bend the bow;*
　they have fitted their arrow to the string
　to shoot in the dark at the upright in heart;
[3] *if the foundations are destroyed,*
　what can the righteous do?"ᵃ

[4] *The LORD is in his holy temple;*
　the LORD's throne is in heaven;

his eyes see, his eyelids test the children of
　man.
[5] *The LORD tests the righteous,*
　but his soul hates the wicked and the one
　who loves violence.
[6] *Let him rain coals on the wicked;*
　fire and sulfur and a scorching wind shall be
　the portion of their cup.
[7] *For the LORD is righteous;*
he loves righteous deeds;
　the upright shall behold his face.

a Or *for the foundations will be destroyed; what has the righteous done?*

OVERVIEW: The movement of this psalm of confidence is from faith in the midst of despair to a renewed assurance in the Lord. The psalm pivots on this question: "If the foundations are destroyed, what can the righteous do?" The response is that the Lord is in his holy temple, enthroned in heaven. For Selnecker, the psalm "belongs to our time" and speaks of faithful ministry of the Word amid human and satanic opposition. Our commentators search out the meaning of the "foundations" that are destroyed; Gwalther suggests that they are the common laws and covenants that make government and peace possible. Calvin observes that the psalmist enlarges the holy temple by speaking of God's throne in heaven, evoking his heavenly rule. Faith is a lamp that discerns God's reign even in the midst of chaos. The psalm's vivid imagery of the fate of the wicked evokes two options: a future of eternal pain and torment in hell, or metaphorical language, symbolizing a sulfurous disgrace and a cup of affliction in this world. For those who are righteous and precious to God, the "fierce hammer of adversity" is the training of the cross.

THIS PSALM'S COMFORT PAIRS WITH PSALM 10'S PROPHECY. NIKOLAUS SELNECKER: This is a glorious, beautiful psalm, and it belongs to our time. For it speaks about the comfort of pious teachers and all Christians, which they are to have against all tyrants, persecutors, heretics and other enemies. And this psalm follows the previous one nicely. Before he prophesied about the antichrist—how he will disturb Christianity both with violence and trickery and swindle all the world for its possessions, honor, body and soul—thus, now in this psalm he sets down a true comfort, with which we are able to withstand the antichrist and all his disciples as well as other fanatical spirits, in such a way that we trust in the Lord alone and remain directly, simply, purely and truly in his Word. We do not let ourselves be forced away from this by violence, honor, trickery, favor, peace or anything else. Nor will we be horrified even if all the world, all schools and churches, all the mighty, learned and wise people should stumble over and get riled up by the same Word of God. THE WHOLE PSALTER.[1]

---

[1] Selnecker, *Der gantze Psalter*, 1:39r.

PSALMS ARE FOR SPIRITUAL VICTORIES.
CARDINAL CAJETAN: The title is "To the Conqueror, to David." Notice here that unless there is a technical term or type of music in a psalm title, the title itself shows David as a conqueror, no doubt in a spiritual victory for which he will rely on God—as in 1 John 5, "This is the victory that has conquered the world: our faith"—or he has dedicated the psalm to God on account of a spiritual victory. COMMENTARY ON PSALM 11.[2]

11:1-7 *Flee to the Lord!*

THE LORD IS HIS ONLY HOPE. SEBASTIAN MÜNSTER: "Fly from your mountain!" This is what David's enemies said to him when they pursued him hard so that he withdrew from Judah. There was no safe place remaining among the people of God; even in the wilderness and the surrounding mountains—that terrain only navigable for the ibex!—they sought David. There was no hope for him except in the Lord alone. (Here "mountain" also includes the entire land of Judah.) THE TEMPLE OF THE LORD: PSALM 11.[3]

DOES DAVID FLEE OUT OF FEAR OR FAITH?
JOHN CALVIN: But as David seems to intimate that it would be a sign of distrust were he to place his safety in flight, it may be asked whether or not it would have been lawful for him to flee. And yes, we know that he was often forced to retire into exile and driven about from place to place, and that he even sometimes hid himself in caves. I answer: it is true that he was unsettled like a poor fearful bird which leaps from branch to branch, and had to change course through many turns to avoid the snares of his enemies; yet still his faith continued so steadfast that he never alienated himself from the people of God. Others considered him a lost man, and one whose affairs were in a hopeless condition, setting no more value on him than if he had been a rotten limb, yet he never

separated himself from the body of the church. COMMENTARY ON THE PSALMS.[4]

WE ARE RESPONSIBLE FOR PREACHING, NOT FOR HOW OTHERS RESPOND. NIKOLAUS SELNECKER: Whatever the situation, we must cling to God's Word and throw out all human cleverness and favor if we want to stand before God. For they cannot and will not coexist; God's grace and human favor are far apart from each other, yes much farther than heaven from earth. Therefore it is written in Psalm 116: "I believe, therefore I speak. But I am greatly afflicted. I said in my trepidation, All human beings are liars." That is, whoever wants to confess Christ must devote himself neither to have nor keep any favor if he really wants to remain simple and true in his faithfulness to his word in all matters of faith. When he preaches the law, nobody wants to suffer it, even if he speaks the truth sparingly. Townspeople and peasants would rather listen to a swineherd calling together the swine than hear God's Word in church with just their ears—they will be dumbfounded should they be expected to do so with their hearts. And there is hardly a village or little town that still wants to be corrected and directed by its pastor. If then we preach the gospel and cast beautiful pearls before swine, surely it is not appropriate. And this hurts pious teachers, makes their hearts ache, because they must cast such beautiful, divine teaching into the air and preach to stony hearts. Nevertheless, be that as it may, the gospel must be spoken and preached, even if on account of it the world should burst and break. For whoever wants to serve the world cannot serve God. Surely we are in the world, and we deal with people in the world, and we need to meditate on the fact that we desire to promote the glory of God in the world. But we should also remember that our life is in heaven and that the devil is a prince of this world and that among devils we are learning, teaching, writing, living and preaching; we are faced daily on all sides with the devil's infidelity and the world's infidelity, their bow

---

[2]Cajetan, *In Sacrae Scripturae Expositionem*, 3:41; citing 1 Jn 5:4.
[3]Münster, *Miqdaš YHWH*, 1168.

[4]CTS 8:160-61* (CO 31:121-22).

and arrows. For the devil does not rest but walks about like a roaring lion, seeking whom he may devour. THE WHOLE PSALTER.[5]

WHAT DO THE FOUNDATIONS OF THE TEMPLE SYMBOLIZE? SEBASTIAN MÜNSTER: This verse is explained variously by the Hebrew interpreters. By "foundations" Kimchi understands "thinking and clever plans." Rabbi Salomon [i.e., Rashi] understands the just priests slain by Saul. It could also be that by "foundations" the conditions of peace and the sacraments themselves are to be understood, which Saul violated so many times. Therefore, David protests this injustice to God who, though he remains seated in the heights of heaven, nevertheless sees everything which happens here below. THE TEMPLE OF THE LORD: PSALM 11.[6]

THE FOUNDATIONS SYMBOLIZE A SOCIETY'S LEGAL AGREEMENTS. RUDOLF GWALTHER: The statutes, common law, treaties and covenants should be understood by "foundation"; such things are like a foundation and groundwork of all government. For where there is neither court nor law, letter and seal, treaty and assembly are invalid, and it is not possible for a people to exist. Now the Scriptures show that Saul had broken all this apart. He hounded David completely contrary to the law! In violation of all treaties and assemblies, he acted with open tyranny. Therefore, David opens his mouth and says, "If neither court nor law helps, how is a pious, upright citizen to comfort himself? What should he do? Should he not doubt, too? No, indeed, he should not. For God still lives and reigns! He will protect him." Others set it out this way: "Even if the godless rage and rave against this figure as if they wanted to tear the entire world from its foundation, nevertheless the pious person who is comforted in God should be undaunted." THE PSALTER.[7]

DO NOT COMPLAIN THAT THE WORLD HATES YOU. MARTIN BUCER: In fact, let us consider and

examine these things with an attentive mind. David was a man formed after God's own heart, divinely chosen and anointed for being king over his people. Therefore, he was the one to whom the Spirit was given, so that he would be more fully obligated to the noblest deeds rather than to crimes, as well as every one of the kings. Still, however much God loved him most, he so willed to exercise him, to cast him here and there and to snatch him a thousand times from the brink of death before he would allow him the quiet administration of the kingdom. Likewise, our Savior came into the same use, whose type the former one bore. For although he was the uniquely beloved Son of God, yet he could not advance into the glory of his kingdom except through countless afflictions and the most dreadful death. Now if we are his disciples, his brothers and his members, why do we complain? Indeed should we not be strengthened with a good hope, when whatever circumstances surround us, when friends abandon us, and those bound to us by our acts of kindness partly abandon and partly persecute us, while there is not any refuge accessible anywhere? This certainly was the path for our Lord and Savior to his own glory; in this way David arrived at his own kingdom. With what impudence shall we desire for ourselves a better lot than what befell each of the two men formed according to the will of the Lord, or than what the only-begotten of God experienced? Or shall we think another fate to be more desirable? The blessed Paul thought nothing was equally glorious than to have approached most closely to this lot, just as no one else was endangered as frequently, no one was rejected more often and no one suffered more from false friends as much as from enemies. But who is like this one who helped the church so much, and who now in glory should be remembered among the saints? And so when the world rages against us, it is not proper for us to be dismayed but rather to fear if the world befriends us and if it flatters us. For the world does not love any but its own; however, it hates and persecutes those who have escaped from it to Christ when the Father draws them. HOLY PSALMS.[8]

[5]Selnecker, *Der gantze Psalter*, 1:40r-v.
[6]Münster, *Miqdaš YHWH*, 1168; citing 1 Sam 22.
[7]Gwalther, *Der Psalter*, 16v.

[8]Bucer, *Sacrorum Psalmorum*, 72v.

GOD REIGNS FROM HEAVEN. JOHN CALVIN: He does not simply say that God dwells in heaven but that he reigns there, as it were, in a royal palace, and has his throne of judgment there. Nor do we indeed render to him the honor which is his due unless we are fully persuaded that his judgment seat is a sacred sanctuary for all who are in affliction and unrighteously oppressed. When, therefore, deceit, craft, treachery, cruelty, violence and extortion reign in the world—in short, when all things are thrown into disorder and darkness by injustice and wickedness—let faith serve as a lamp to enable us to behold God's heavenly throne, and let that sight suffice to make us wait in patience for the restoration of things to a better state. "The temple of his holiness or his holy temple," which is commonly understood as Zion, doubtless here signifies heaven. And this is clearly shown by the repetition in the next clause—"Jehovah has his throne in heaven"—for it is certain David expresses the same thing twice. COMMENTARY ON THE PSALMS.[9]

THE FAITHFUL ARE TESTED LIKE GOLD. THOMAS WILCOX: God will often afflict his own, not because he hates them but because he will by that fiery trial scourge away their dross and make them pure gold unto himself. EXPOSITION UPON PSALM 11.[10]

THE BURNING TEMPESTS OF FUTURE JUDGMENT. THE ENGLISH ANNOTATIONS: All expressions of terrible judgments and calamities shall befall, by God's special order and appointment, those wicked ungodly people—though great pretenders of godliness—who did or do boast so greatly their flourishing condition and great success in this world. Now because it often happens that those who have been great oppressors of the church and God's people often enjoy their peace and prosperity to the last and die quietly to the world on their beds, it is very likely that by these expressions, David especially intended that the judgments of God on such people take place in

another world. The Old Testament speaks sparingly and obscurely about these matters—according to the tradition of those times—while in the New, we read plentifully, so that all execution of justice and judgment seems almost to be referred to that time—to that time at least, if not as the only, still the proper time. . . .

Indeed, from this observation—beside the revelation of Scripture—many learned people have inferred the necessity of a future judgment, because we often see things happen in this world that are so contrary to what we understand of God's justice. We may sooner be convinced to believe that by these words David intended eternal pains and torments, because hell in the New Testament is not only described by fire generally, but also by fire and brimstone in Saint John's Apocalypse more than once. Although the original expression in Saint John's Apocalypse is derived from that particular fire and brimstone which was the destruction of Sodom and Gomorrah (as we read in Genesis 19 and is further confirmed by our Savior), still it is possible that it alluded to this very passage of David. ANNOTATIONS ON PSALM 11:6.[11]

METAPHORICAL SPEECH DESCRIBING THE WICKED AND THEIR PUNISHMENT. HIERONYMUS WELLER VON MOLSDORF: Some explain this verse in this way. Fire symbolizes that raging zeal of idolatry and wicked doctrine. Sulfur symbolizes a bad reputation or disgrace—a bad name—by which someone smells foul before God and the church. That name, like a most noxious stench, God and human beings will loathe. The cup symbolizes their horrible punishment. Now young people should know that the word *cup* symbolizes two things in Scripture. First, it can mean teaching and thanksgiving, by which we glorify God—like Psalm 116: "I will take the cup of salvation, and I will call on the name of the Lord." Second, it can mean cross and afflictions like those Christ experienced: "Father, remove this cup from me."

---

[9]CTS 8:164* (CO 31:123).
[10]Wilcox, *Godly Exposition upon the Psalmes*, 30*.

[11]Downame, ed., *Annotations*, 5Z3v*; citing Ps 37:1; Rev 20:7-10; Gen 19:23-29; Lk 17:28-30; 2 Thess 1:5-9.

Also, Psalm 75: "Because in the hand of the Lord there is a cup of wine—stained red—well-mixed, and he pours out from it. Surely all the wicked of the earth will gulp it down and drink it." BRIEF COMMENT ON PSALM 11.[12]

GOD'S JUDGMENT IS AS PREDICTABLE AS A TEMPEST. JOHN CALVIN: He appropriately compares the punishments that God inflicts with rain. Rain is not constant, but the Lord sends it forth when he pleases; when the weather is calmest and very serene, suddenly he raises a storm of hail or violent showers of rain. In the same way, it is intimated here that the vengeance which will be inflicted on the wicked will come suddenly—while they are indulging in mirth and intoxicated with their pleasures, and "while they are saying, 'There is peace and safety,' sudden destruction will come over them." COMMENTARY ON THE PSALMS.[13]

NEVER FORGET THE LORD'S JUSTICE. GIOVANNI BATTISTA FOLENGO: This last verse of the psalm gives the reason why the Lord customar-ily tests and perfects the good by their adversaries but detests the wicked and scourges them in their death and destruction. Because God is just, he is not able not to love righteousness, that is, according to the Hebrew phrase, "worshipers of righteous-ness." So, it is not without reason that it was said that he loves justice and his face sees righteousness. It is the same as if David would say, "He considers righteousness and favors it." For those who want to show favor to someone usually demonstrate their friendliness not only with words and nods of assent but also with gestures and cheerful expres-sions, in order to show their appreciation for that person. Now, who presently reading this can become weary of their zeal for righteousness, no matter with what evil gift the world reward them? It should be enough, I pray, that we who are refined under the fierce hammer of adversity are precious to God. It should be enough, I say, that so fair a Judge considers our case with a cheerful and friendly face. Let the bitterness of bad fortune not strike us down from this firm foundation, because, as long as they live, God has determined that those of his household should be trained continually under the cross. KING DAVID'S PSALTER.[14]

---

[12]Weller, *Enarratio Psalmorum*, 55; citing Ps 116:13; Lk 22:42; Ps 75:8. Compare with Luther's comments on Ps 16, p. 122.
[13]CTS 8:166* (CO 31:124); citing 1 Thess 5:3.

[14]Folengo, *In Psalterium Davidis*, 33v.

12:1-8 WHY DO THE WICKED FLOURISH AND THE FAITHFUL VANISH?

To the choirmaster: according to The Sheminith.[a] A Psalm of David.

¹ Save, O LORD, for the godly one is gone;
  for the faithful have vanished from among
    the children of man.
² Everyone utters lies to his neighbor;
  with flattering lips and a double heart they
    speak.

³ May the LORD cut off all flattering lips,
  the tongue that makes great boasts,
⁴ those who say, "With our tongue we will prevail,
  our lips are with us; who is master over us?"

⁵ "Because the poor are plundered, because the
    needy groan,
  I will now arise," says the LORD;
  "I will place him in the safety for which he
    longs."
⁶ The words of the LORD are pure words,
  like silver refined in a furnace on the ground,
    purified seven times.

⁷ You, O LORD, will keep them;
  you will guard us[b] from this generation forever.
⁸ On every side the wicked prowl,
  as vileness is exalted among the children of
    man.

a Probably a musical or liturgical term   b Or *guard him*

OVERVIEW: In a movement from lament to confidence, the psalmist first notes how godliness is vanishing and the enemies of truth prevail. Their lips, tongues and lies register their impudence. Thus our commentators focus on the power of words, fusing the psalm to their own day, identifying the opponents as heretics and teachers of innovative doctrine amidst the righteous struggle for purity of truth. Responding to the groans of the afflicted, God arises to deliver them and place them in safety. Musculus cautions that this is anthropopathic language, dramatizing God's long patience with the hard hearts of the adversaries and God's responsiveness to the cries of the righteous. God will certainly—though not necessarily immediately—rescue the oppressed and needy. In contrast to the lies, flattery and doublespeak of the opponents, the words of the Lord are like purest silver refined of its dross. The reformers remind us that these precious words are the gospel, which makes those who bear it "sonorous and eloquent." The psalm closes in the confidence that the Lord will guard his people from the vileness of humankind.

WITHOUT THE WORD OF THE LORD THE PIOUS PERISH. SEBASTIAN MÜNSTER: This psalm teaches that among humankind faith and justice have perished but deceitful human beings have grown strong. Now, unless the Lord through his word comes to the aid of the afflicted, it is over for them. THE TEMPLE OF THE LORD: PSALM 12.[1]

A NECESSARY PRAYER FOR PURE TEACHING. NIKOLAUS SELNECKER: This is a lamentation about fanatical spirits and heretics, who distort doctrine. David prays to God that he would fell such scoundrels, frauds and hypocrites, and protect and preserve the true teachers and Christians. At the same time it is also a comforting promise that God will surely defend his Word and pure doctrine and wipe out all enthusiasts

---

[1]Münster, *Miqdaš YHWH*, 1168.

and distorters, as he dealt with Cerinthus, Ebion, Arius and many others.[2] The truth shall and must remain and triumph in the end, even if it might from time to time be contested, covered up for awhile and oppressed.

We should consider this psalm often, pray it and meditate on it, especially if we want God to preserve his Word against all human doctrines and new innovations. It is very necessary in our present time that we pray this psalm often, because great barrels full of human doctrines are brought forth from all sides—there is no limit, no ceasing, no end. Everyone wants to be a master and do it better than it was previously done and confirmed by God's grace. Therefore there emerge so many new innovations, such strange discourses, allegories, bizarre thoughts and interpretations of the clear and bright Word of God; poor consciences are needlessly confused, made to error, burdened and tricked. Therefore we must pray this psalm and take comfort in it, that God will awaken his salvation, namely, his Word, which confidently storms such straw work of human doctrine and frees captive consciences. Without crossbearing, danger and agony, however, it does not happen, but rather in the same way as silver is purified by fire, we must suffer because of it and as a consequence become more refined, and know the truth more clearly.

As the two previous psalms talk about tremendous public idolatry and false doctrine that is maintained without reserve, this psalm, too, talks about secret, creeping innovations and heresies that are peddled without shame among those who have the Word of God, pure and perfect, until at last, when they gain the upper hand, they dash everything to the ground, as it has unfortunately happened to us who are called Lutheran. THE WHOLE PSALTER.[3]

12:1-8 *The Lord Preserves His People*

ZEAL FOR GOSPEL PURITY. PHILIPP MELANCHTHON: The complaint is about corrupt doctrine and the prayer is that God would restrain imposters and flatterers and restore pure doctrine, as well as govern and save those who think better. He mixes this with a passionate saying that the Word of God would be more well-known in confession, although the impious oppose it, and the glory of God would be seen, which conquers and does not allow the truth to be extinguished but instead destroys errors and brings relief to the truth, and acts so that the true church, which professes and embraces the gospel, upholds "the true teaching for all eternity." In this way, when the Ebionites, Arians and Manichaeans were destroyed, the true teaching conquered only by the help of God, just as the psalmist here teaches us here to pray: "You, O Lord, will guard them." And it ought to be frequently recited when we pray that God would check impious teachers and would kindle and preserve the light of true doctrine. COMMENTS ON THE PSALMS.[4]

BE READY TO LISTEN. MARTIN LUTHER: You must never be so learned that you should not always be ready to hear also the opinion of others, even if you have spoken the truth, but especially when you have spoken doubtful things. From this arise heresies and strife, and in their midst even the truth itself is lost, because truth is not contentious: "Be not wise in your own conceits." As a result of this people become incorrigible. . . . And the apostle says, "If a revelation is made to another sitting by, let the first be silent." For "God is wonderful in his saints," and in a remarkable way he has the proud and the contentious in derision. FIRST PSALMS LECTURES (1513–1515).[5]

ANTHROPOPATHIC LANGUAGE. WOLFGANG MUSCULUS: From this verse all the way to the end

---

[2]Cerinthus, Ebion and Arius denied one or the other of Christ's two natures: Cerinthus denied the human nature; Ebion, the divine nature; Arius taught that Jesus was the first created being. Many doubt the historicity of a person named Ebion.
[3]Selnecker, *Der gantze Psalter*, 1:42r-v.

[4]MO 13:1036.
[5]LW 10:102* (WA 3:97); citing Rom 12:16; 1 Cor 14:30; Ps 68:35; 2:4.

of the psalm, the prophet consoles the afflicted and devastated. He, however, consoles them by the surest and strongest consolation of all: not out of human beings or chances or events or power but out of the unspeakable goodness, faithfulness and truth of God, who is unable to despise the groans of infants and afflicted and who cannot enter a stubborn heart. Therefore, when he had said, "The Lord will destroy all deceitful lips," lest a prayer of this sort appear bare and incapable of having the vow of an unworthy heart, he has presented God as one who is unable to bear any longer the devastation of the afflicted and the groans of the poor but has determined within himself to help the afflicted, as powerful people are wont to do, and is aroused to vindicate them after a long period of patience from the depravity of their adversaries.

He uses anthropopathism, because he does not simply say, "On account of the devastation of the afflicted the Lord arises," but he presents God as if he were angry and indignant, and bursting the chains of patience, and grumbling to himself in this manner: "Now the time of arising has come; the needy are devastated and the devastated infants groan to me. I am unable to bear their groans and devastation. I shall bring salvation to those people. I shall give them strength according to my heart, by which I shall snatch them from the hands of the ungodly, and rule and protect them in good faith." COMMENTARY ON THE PSALMS.[6]

CRY OUT TO GOD. JOHN CALVIN: David now sets before himself, as matter of consolation, the truth that God will not permit the wicked to make havoc without end and measure. The more effectually to establish himself and others in the belief of this truth, he introduces God himself as speaking. The expression is more emphatic when God is repre- sented as coming forward and declaring with his own mouth that he has come to deliver the poor and distressed. There is also great emphasis in the adverb *now*, by which God intimates that, although our safety is in his hand, and therefore in secure

keeping, yet he does not immediately grant deliverance from affliction; for his words imply that he had been, as it were, lying still and asleep, until he was awakened by the calamities and the cries of his people. When, therefore, the injuries, the extortions and the devastations of our enemies leave us nothing but tears and groans, let us remember that now the time is at hand when God intends to rise up to execute judgment. This doctrine should also serve to produce in us patience and prevent us from taking it ill that we are reckoned among the number of the poor and afflicted, whose cause God promises to take into his own hand. COMMENTARY ON THE PSALMS.[7]

THE SHIELD OF GOD'S WORD. JOHN CALVIN: Whenever he delays his assistance, we question his fidelity to his promises and murmur just as if he had deceived us. There is no truth which is more generally received among human beings than that God is true, but there are few who frankly give him credit for this when they are in adversity. It is, therefore, highly necessary for us to cut off the occasion of our distrust, and whenever any doubt concerning the faithfulness of God's promises creeps into us, we should immediately lift up this shield against it, that the words of the Lord are pure. COMMENTARY ON THE PSALMS.[8]

IDIOMS ABOUT THE LORD'S TRUTHFULNESS. JOHANNES BUGENHAGEN: The words of the Lord are pure, not mixed with false opinions; such glory cannot be granted to any human teaching. In human teaching there are opinions, errors and lies; in the words of God there is sure knowledge, an honest way and truth. For they are "silver refined in a furnace on the ground, purified seven times," that is, in numerous ways and perfectly, according to the idiom of the Hebrews, who understand the number seven as perfect. Silver signifies the Word, just as gold signifies love. . . . What we read—"tested of the earth"—is a Hellenism for purged from the earth,

---

[6]Musculus, *In Psalterium Commentarii*, 156.

[7]CTS 8:174-75* (CO 31:128).
[8]CTS 8:177* (CO 31:129).

so that the silver is entirely pure. Among the Hebrews they understood this to mean "in earthen vessels" in which the silver is tested by fire. "And we," says Paul, "carry that treasure in earthen vessels" in such temptations the Word of God is tested by fire—whether it is pure and present in us by pure faith, which in itself is pure and cannot deceive. . . . The Lord cannot lie. And so these things are understood concerning the promises of God. INTERPRETATION OF THE PSALMS.[9]

FAITH PURIFIED LIKE SILVER. VIKTORIN STRIGEL: Just as the silver remains when the impurities are burned off in the fire, and the more it is put through the fire, the purer it is, so in temptation human habits vanish. . . . But faith—which relies on the Word of God—conquers fears and doubts and hardships; like an oak cut by double-edged axes, it brings forth riches and life from the very blade. HYPONĒMATA IN ALL THE PSALMS.[10]

HOW PRECIOUS THE GOSPEL IS. MARTIN LUTHER: The gospel is called "silver," first, because it is precious, not according to the flesh, but because it makes the soul precious in the sight of God; second, because it is solid, that is, because it makes people solid and full, not like an empty reed and a carnal letter; third, because it is heard far and wide. Thus the sound of the gospel has gone out through all the world, and it makes the disciples sonorous and eloquent. Fourth, it is weighty, because it does not contain fables or superficial things, and it makes human beings serious and mature, as stated below, "I will praise you in a strong people." Fifth, it is white and shining, because it is modest and chaste and teaches modesty; it speaks modestly. Therefore, because of this characteristic, when he had said, "The promises of the Lord are pure," he immediately called it "silver" altogether. Keep in mind what Psalm 68 says, "The wings of a dove covered with silver" and

understand what that means. Nevertheless, this "trying" and "testing" of his seems to demonstrate that it is rather clarified and strengthened by the controversies of the heretics. But the preacher of the Word of God should also be like this: valuable and genuine, solid and full of knowledge instead of empty opinions, eloquent, sober and steadfast, shining and reproving without malice and rage. FIRST PSALMS LECTURES (1513–1515).[11]

ENDURE STEADFASTLY AND DAILY. JOHN CALVIN: The word $l\check{e}^c\hat{o}l\bar{a}m$, which means "forever," is added, so that we may learn to extend our confidence in God far into the future, because he commands us to hope for deliverance from him, not only once or for one day but as long as the wickedness of our enemies continues its work of mischief. We are, however, from this passage also admonished that war is not prepared against us for a short time only, but that we must daily engage in the conflict. And if the guardianship which God exercises over the faithful is sometimes hidden and is not manifest in its effects, let them wait in patience until he arises. And the greater the flood of calamities which overtakes them, let them keep themselves so much the more in the practice of godly fear and solicitude. COMMENTARY ON THE PSALMS.[12]

LET THE WORD OF GOD FEED YOUR CONSCIENCE. NIKOLAUS SELNECKER: Through crossbearing the Word should increase, grow, be sustained, scattered and safeguarded. And this we should learn from this psalm, cherish it as a consolation and inscribe it in our heart. Whoever will not rest, let them brawl, rave, rage, howl and huff! But you, remain in the Word of God and do not let yourself be driven away from it. What it validates should be enough for you. Your conscience will be excellent, quiet and still. For the Word of God is pure and perfect and also makes our hearts excellent, pure and perfect, so that they

---

[9]Bugenhagen, *In librvm Psalmorvm interpretatio*, 29r; citing 2 Cor 4:7.
[10]Strigel, *Hyponēmata*, 58.

[11]LW 10:103 (WA 3:97-98); citing Ps 19:4; 35:18; 68:13.
[12]CTS 8:180* (CO 31:131).

are able to be sure and quiet. May God give us his mercy and blessing so that we would maintain and remain, in thought and deed, in the Word. THE WHOLE PSALTER.[13]

LET US PRAY TO THE LORD FOR MERCY.
NIKOLAUS SELNECKER: Almighty and eternal God, you see how your saints are so few and indeed how rarely and infrequently they seek or promote your honor. And now, as unfortunately you can see, in churches and worldly governments as well as in common life there is a great sense of security, pride, discord and dissension. Thus, dear Lord, we ask you that you would mercifully turn away, or, even as a father, temper our well-deserved punishments and leave us a true seed, so that we would not become like Sodom and Gomorrah. Send faithful workers into your vineyard who do

not speak of useless matters and made-up fables, who are not hypocrites, who are not proud, arrogant and lazy and self-assured. Ensure that they teach from unity of heart and that they are united in you; grant them humble hearts. O Lord God, it is dearly needed! Bring your help, so that we would be consoled and teach rightly and remain in our Christian walk and life, that we would not be a stumbling block for others nor would we continue in sins against conscience. Protect us from sluggish people who do not observe your Word; sustain us by your Word which is pure, perfect and clear. Grant us endurance in suffering and crossbearing and rule us with your Holy Spirit, so that we would not fall into error and vice but instead would be and remain your dwelling and temple. Amen. THE WHOLE PSALTER.[14]

---

[13]Selnecker, *Der gantze Psalter*, 1:46v.

[14]Selnecker, *Der gantze Psalter*, 1:47r; citing 1 Tim 4:7; Jn 17:21.

13:1-6 I REMEMBER THE LORD

To the choirmaster. A Psalm of David.

[1] *How long, O* LORD? *Will you forget me
forever?*
How long will you hide your face from me?
[2] *How long must I take counsel in my soul
and have sorrow in my heart all the day?*
How long shall my enemy be exalted over me?

[3] *Consider and answer me, O* LORD *my God;
light up my eyes, lest I sleep the sleep of death,*
[4] *lest my enemy say, "I have prevailed over him,"
lest my foes rejoice because I am shaken.*

[5] *But I have trusted in your steadfast love;
my heart shall rejoice in your salvation.*
[6] *I will sing to the* LORD,
because he has dealt bountifully with me.

OVERVIEW: This psalm of lament in the face of God's silence opens with a stepped repetition of the characteristic cry, "How long?" After an entreaty for God to reply and save his righteous servant from being shamed by his enemies, the psalmist's hope is restored. The psalm concludes on a note of confidence and rejoicing in God's steadfast love and salvation. Our commentators find in this psalm an occasion for pastoral counsel. Gwalther recommends it as a template for the Christian's prayer in the midst of anguish. Strigel comments on the successive stages of despair but ultimately finds the devil at work. And although the text does not mention this spiritual adversary, the reformers do see Satan behind all physical and spiritual attacks. Calvin notes that even in the psalmist's crying out, faith is present. For Luther this song is itself evidence that the psalmist has robbed the devil of his own song of triumph. Even when we have not yet fully obtained our freedom from trials, the reformers teach, this psalm inspires faith in God's promises and a singing that defies the devil.

A PRAYER FOR TIMES OF DESPAIR. RUDOLF GWALTHER: This is a completely grave and anxious prayer that David prayed when, in the midst of deep distress, God had withdrawn his help from him for a long time, so that he began to think that God had totally forgotten him. . . . So

then, this psalm is a general template according to which we can model our prayers to God in the midst of the deepest anguish and anxiety. In such times, by this psalm, we might strengthen our faith. THE PSALTER.[1]

13:1-6 *Answer Me In My Distress, O Faithful God!*

THE THREEFOLD LAMENT "HOW LONG?"
VIKTORIN STRIGEL: The complaint "How long," repeated so many times, shows well enough the bitterness of the grief and the difficulty of the struggle. The man's grief follows a threefold succession: first, toward God; second, toward himself; third, toward others, whether friends or enemies. Thus he describes three very painful experiences, in the first of which he bemoans the fact that he is neglected and cast out by God. For the act of forgetting and the turning away of one's face are undeniable signs of neglect and indignation. And as often as consolation and deliverance are delayed, we resort to this opinion, that we think that we are deserted and rejected by God. Second, he wrestles with himself, entertaining various plans in his soul, but he cannot be helped and restored by these. For the wounds of the heart cannot be healed without divine help. Finally, he meets with

---

[1]Gwalther, *Der Psalter*, 17v-18r.

the enemy the devil, who throws up such specters that it seems he will soon overthrow and triumph over him as he struggles. . . . Both in the reading of the Psalms and the prophetic narratives the pious should, in times of their own grief, look at these extreme examples; there the descriptions of such sorrows exist to teach and console us. HYPONĒMATA IN ALL THE PSALMS.[2]

SOMETIMES IT SEEMS LIKE WE ARE FORSAKEN BY GOD.

JOHN CALVIN: To acknowledge in the midst of our afflictions that God really cares about us is not the usual way with human beings or what the feelings of nature would prompt, but by faith we apprehend his invisible providence. Thus, it seemed to David, so far as could be judged from beholding the actual state of his affairs, that he was forsaken by God. At the same time, however, the eyes of his mind, guided by the light of faith, penetrated even to the grace of God, although it was hidden. And so, discerning no good hope anywhere—as much as the capacity of human nature is able to judge—constrained by grief, he cries out that he is not cared for by God. And yet by this very complaint he testifies that faith enabled him to rise higher and to conclude, contrary to the judgment of the flesh, that his welfare was secure in the hand of God. COMMENTARY ON THE PSALMS.[3]

IN AFFLICTION WE SEEK OUT EVERYTHING BUT THE WORD OF GOD.

HIERONYMUS WELLER VON MOLSDORF: Here the psalmwriter teaches by his own example how, after we have dismissed the Word of God, we are accustomed to wander in our minds to seek counsel, partly from ourselves, partly from others, so that we would get out of our present troubles. Yet this accomplishes nothing, except toil and pain, which we amass for ourselves, as well as the various deadly thoughts in which we become entangled. Psalm 42 says that we fall from one tumult headlong into another: "Deep calls to deep in the voice of your waterfalls." BRIEF COMMENT ON PSALM 13.[4]

WHILE MIRED IN MAZES DO NOT FORGET GOD'S PROMISES.

JOHN CALVIN: The Lord, indeed, promises to give to believers "the spirit of counsels," but he does not always supply this at the very first moment of need, but as if in a winding maze he allows them to run in circles for a time or to hesitate entangled among thorns. COMMENTARY ON THE PSALMS.[5]

THE LORD IS NOT THE AUTHOR OF ANGUISH BUT OF LIFE.

HIERONYMUS WELLER VON MOLSDORF: Here the prophet proclaims and confesses that the devil himself is the author of his anguish. For God is not the author of anguish but rather of joy and life, as in Psalm 30, "Life is his will." But the devil is accustomed to hurl the pious into anguish either when he places before their eyes the monstrosity of their sins and the immensity of God's wrath, or when he torments them with the fear of death. For that sly old fox knows many ways to make death more terrifying than it really is. And he is preeminent in this craft, so that with deadly thoughts he so tortures the minds of the pious that they lose their voice and are unable to take a breath, as Psalm 77 testifies: "I am so troubled that I cannot speak." For this reason God promises that he will open up the choked-up breathing of the pious who are afflicted, as in Isaiah 57: "I will make the breath of life." BRIEF COMMENT ON PSALM 13.[6]

WHY DOES DAVID PRAY FOR HIS EYES TO BE LIT UP?

THE ENGLISH ANNOTATIONS: As when the body is exhausted through sickness or otherwise, it appears most in the eyes, which are like a glass through which we may look into the inward temper and disposition of the whole. Thus, if the body be revived and receive comfort, it will appear first in the quickness and cheerfulness of

---

[2]Strigel, Hyponēmata, 60.
[3]CTS 8:182* (CO 31:132).

[4]Weller, Enarratio Psalmorum, 59; citing Ps 42:7.
[5]CTS 8:183* (CO 31:133); citing Is 11:2; 19:20.
[6]Weller, Enarratio Psalmorum, 59-60; citing Ps 30:5; 77:4; Is 57:16.

the sight. . . . Therefore, when David prays here that God would lighten his eyes, he is praying for his whole body, that God would raise it from the pining condition into which perpetual grief and danger had brought it. And so he prays that God will deliver him from those crosses and persecutions that had been the occasion of his grief. ANNOTATIONS ON PSALM 13:3.[7]

VIGILANTLY PRAY TO BE VIGILANT. MARTIN BUCER: He has complained that God has forsaken him, that God has hidden his face from him. Now therefore he prays that he would consider him and pay attention to his affliction. He has complained in this way that he is wrenched and afflicted by anxious thoughts, that he could not find any refuge. On the contrary, he prays that God would favor him and respond to him, and that he would have a path to follow by which he would finally escape from the crisis in which he was constrained. At the same time, what he asks for also occurs, namely, for his eyes to be enlightened, that is, be awakened and made vigilant, lest he fall asleep, lest he neglect something and imprudently come into the hands of his enemies, sleeping the sleep of death. . . . "Let me not sleep death" is a synecdoche, a figure of speech by which another phrase is concealed. For he ought to have said, "let me not sleep the sleep of death." For among Hebrews, as among other races, the majority of nouns are taken from verbs, as Abraham Ibn Ezra says. So here the verb "let me sleep" includes the noun "sleep." We have spoken about this in Psalm 6:8 that they beg so much for relief from the insult of their enemies. Because in the enemies' victory and insult the godly man saw the blasphemy and insult of God conjoined, he therefore recoiled from it, not from his own degradation. In fact, from these things we must learn that as long as God does not lead us by his own Spirit, affliction can be heaped on our plans and our mind can be vainly consumed by foolish cares, while right counsels cannot be useful and received. Therefore above all we must pray that

God would regard us and direct us by his divine Word. If he should abandon us, no vigilance, circumspection or precaution is sufficient; in fact those persons would be caught napping, taken flat on their backs in sleep, as doubtless ruin follows such sleep like a companion. For however much we try to extricate ourselves from evil when we are devoid of the Spirit of God, the more we entangle ourselves: just as happened to Pharaoh, Saul and the people of Israel who daily fled to other things than to the protection of God. And those who try to look after and provide for themselves or try to set themselves free from the dangers that encircle them have experienced daily. Certain commentators make this psalm a prayer against Satan but this takes places by *anagoge*, while preserving the truth of the history: just as David asked to be saved from his own visible enemies, so we should ask to be saved from the force and cunning of Satan. An interpretation of this sort is much closer to the mind of the psalmist than that of the Jews, who want this psalm to be a complaint about their own exile, and because the "How long?" is repeated four times they strive to answer that those four repetitions correspond to the oppression that they endured from the Chaldeans, Persians, Greeks and Romans. HOLY PSALMS.[8]

THE DEVIL WILL NEVER GET TO SING THIS SONG. MARTIN LUTHER: O God, do not allow the devil to have the victory and triumph. He might say, "He's on the ground. What's he going to do now, this David?" . . . Do not allow this to happen; he might make a little song out of it. Do not let him rejoice and boast that I am suffering because he knocked me down. . . . God allows us to be weak, to be beaten into sand. But the devil is not able to sing his little song; we fight with him and he beats us, but he will not bury us, as this psalm teaches. "Not only does he gladly beat me but he rejoices over me because he has defeated me." Then David goes forth again and beats down the devil and his adversaries and sings a little song

---

[7]Downame, ed., *Annotations*, 5Z4r*, citing 1 Sam 14:29.

[8]Bucer, *Sacrorum Psalmorum*, 78v-79r.

about it—the devil cannot sing his song. SERMON ON PSALM 13 (NOVEMBER 1, 1533).[9]

WHAT CAN WE GIVE BUT A SACRIFICE OF PRAISE? WOLFGANG MUSCULUS: The prophet desires to recompense the Lord for the promised salvation. And what else could a needy person, who lacks everything, render or would God, who does not lack anything demand, than a service of thanksgiving, praise and song? So then Moses in Exodus 15, Deborah in Judges 5, David here and Ezekiel—all of whom bestowed these in the divine services—sang to the Lord. Thus, the well-known custom of singing and playing instruments to the Lord obtained in the churches.

Also observe from where David's song to the Lord arises: from the heart, of course, that has been touched with true joy and a sense of God's kindness. He said, "My heart will exult in your salvation," and immediately he added, "I will sing to the Lord because he recompensed me," so that we may understand that the song of divine praise in the mouth of the pious is an exultation of the heart rejoicing in the salvation of God and giving thanks to its benefactor. He did not say, "I will sing to the Lord so that he will recompense me," . . . but "I will sing to the Lord because he recompensed me." COMMENTARY ON THE PSALMS.[10]

CELEBRATE THE GRACE OF GOD EVEN IN TIMES OF SORROW. JOHN CALVIN: David, it is true, had not yet obtained what he earnestly desired, but being fully convinced that God was already at hand to grant him deliverance, he pledges himself to give thanks to him for it. And surely it becomes us to engage in prayer in such a frame of mind as at the same time to be ready to sing the praises of God—a thing which is impos-

sible, unless we are fully persuaded that our prayers will not be ineffectual. We may not be wholly free from sorrow, but it is nevertheless necessary that this cheerfulness of faith rise above it and put into our mouth a song on account of the joy which is reserved for us in the future although not yet experienced by us; just as we see David here preparing himself to celebrate in songs the grace of God, before he perceives the end of his troubles. COMMENTARY ON THE PSALMS.[11]

IMITATE DAVID'S EXAMPLE HERE IN TIMES OF TRIAL. NIKOLAUS SELNECKER: Now whenever Christians are afflicted and tormented by the devil on account of their sins or whatever else, they should run to God and cry out to him. They should hold God to his promises. And they should comfort and refresh themselves with the Word of God, knowing that they certainly are God's children no matter how much the devil roars otherwise! Heartfelt thanksgiving should follow such faith, consolation and hope, as David here demonstrates with his example and says, "I will sing to the Lord, because he deals so bountifully with me!" This is the triumph and victory of believers. They sing merrily of their merciful redemption, they laud and praise God and thank him because he saves, sustains and protects his people. In this way we too should act in our times of need. We should direct our needs and concerns to God. Then we should ask for his help and deliverance—and all this for the sake of his honor and his name. Third, we should firmly believe and hope that he will not abandon us but instead will hear us and will deliver us. Finally, we should thank him for his merciful counsel, help and assistance. To this may God the Father, Son and Holy Spirit help us! THE WHOLE PSALTER.[12]

---

[9]WA 37:187.
[10]Musculus, *In Psalterium Commentarii*, 168.

[11]CTS 8:187* (CO 31:134-35).
[12]Selnecker, *Der gantze Psalter*, 1:49v.

14:1-7 THE FOOL SAYS THERE IS NO GOD

To the choirmaster. Of David.

¹ The fool says in his heart, "There is no God."
　They are corrupt, they do abominable deeds,
　there is none who does good.

² The LORD looks down from heaven on the
　　children of man,
　to see if there are any who understand,ᵃ
　who seek after God.

³ They have all turned aside; together they have
　　become corrupt;
　there is none who does good,
　not even one.

⁴ Have they no knowledge, all the evildoers
　who eat up my people as they eat bread
　and do not call upon the LORD?

⁵ There they are in great terror,
　for God is with the generation of the righteous.
⁶ You would shame the plans of the poor,
　butᵇ the LORD is his refuge.

⁷ Oh, that salvation for Israel would come out
　　of Zion!
　When the LORD restores the fortunes of his
　　people,
　let Jacob rejoice, let Israel be glad.

a Or *that act wisely*　b Or *for*

OVERVIEW: The psalm confronts those who assert that "there is no God." Reformation commentators understand this foolishness as a de facto atheism. Here the reformers with the psalmist echo Proverbs' indictment of such "a rude heap of fools" who worship their desires. Selnecker finds the psalm speaking of the wickedness of the entire world, though Calvin limits it to Israel alone, excluding a remnant that is saved. But our interpreters are aware that Paul cites the beginning of this psalm in Romans 3:10-12, where he enlists biblical witnesses in an indictment of all humankind. Viewing Scripture as a seamless whole, the comments disclose a view of original sin sharpened by Pauline acuity. The psalm goes on to speak of all who have turned aside from true knowledge of God and devour God's people. Here Selnecker too sees the focus narrowing to Israel, and Calvin comments on the disheartening wickedness that prevails even within the church. Finally, the psalmist cries out for Israel's salvation, that it might break forth from Zion and restore the fortunes of Israel. And Selnecker, capturing the prophetic overtones of the Psalms, finds here an expression of messianic longing.

A PSALM OF REBUKE. NIKOLAUS SELNECKER: This is one of the psalms which repudiates and rebukes the whole world with all its teaching, wisdom and holiness. And it teaches how all human teaching and life without faith are a complete abomination to God, and their best worship is nothing but bellyworship, by which they fatten themselves and devour people's goods. Not one, however, knows or understands right worship although they teach and praise the law of God. Indeed, they defile and blaspheme the Word of God; when they are rebuked, they do not want to hear anything about confidence or faith in God.

Now this psalm has three parts. First, David teaches that all people are dolts and fools; they do not have any right knowledge of God but are mired in darkness. Their understanding and reason are entirely ignorant and their heart and will wholly disobedient, full of evil lust and desire and indecent passions against God and their neighbor. Thus, there is no one who does good, not even one. The second part is an earnest rebuke and threat against godless teachers, who do not seek God's honor but only focus on their own temporal benefit, so they can fill and fatten their belly and gut and live in all kinds of lust, riches and worldly honor, without fear of God. The third part is a prayer and heartfelt request that God would bring into reality his prophecy and promise about the Lord Christ, so that the gospel would be preached. THE WHOLE PSALTER.[1]

THE CHURCH'S DOMESTIC, NOT FOREIGN, ENEMIES. JOHN CALVIN: The structure of the psalm very clearly shows that David means domestic tyrants and enemies of the faithful rather than foreign ones—a point which is very necessary for us to understand. We know that it is a temptation which pains us exceedingly, to see wickedness breaking forth and prevailing in the midst of the church, the good and the simple unrighteously afflicted, while the wicked cruelly domineer according to their pleasure. This sad spectacle almost completely disheartens us. And, therefore, the example which David here sets before us is of no little use to strengthen us, so that, in the church's miserable catastrophes, we may endure having confidence in God's deliverance. COMMENTARY ON THE PSALMS.[2]

14:1-7 *The Words and Deeds of Fools*

NUANCE TO NĀBĀL. RUDOLF GWALTHER: The little word *nābāl* really does not mean a fool or a dolt as the world understands them; rather, it is someone who lacks the general knowledge of God. Such a person is like an uprooted trunk or stalk: It no longer has physical strength and therefore cannot bear any fruit. THE PSALTER.[3]

THESE FOOLS LIVE LIKE SWINE. MARTIN LUTHER: Those who despise God's Word . . . are fools. This is the chief characteristic of all the impious: they are fools and dolts in Scripture, unwise people who have no knowledge about God, they are able to say nothing about God. This pains the pious, holy children—the patri-

archs and apostles and us—because these people toss the Word of God into the wind as if it is less than nothing. A rude heap of fools—nobility, citizens, farmers, the learned—who do not at all care whether God exists or not; they live like pigs. As long as they gorge themselves and get drunk and have enough money, etc., they do not care at all about heaven. SERMON ON PSALM 14 (November 8, 1533).[4]

THESE FOOLS DENY GOD BY HOW THEY LIVE. JOHN CALVIN: Not that they maintain, by drawn-out arguments or formal syllogisms—as they call them—that there is no God. For to render them so much the more inexcusable, God from time to time causes even the most wicked people to feel secret pangs of conscience, so that they may be compelled to acknowledge his majesty and sovereign power. Whatever right knowledge God instills into them they partly stifle by their malice against him, and partly corrupt it, until religion in them becomes torpid and finally dead. They may not plainly deny the existence of a God, but they imagine him to be shut up in heaven and divested of his righteousness and power, which is to fashion an idol in the place of God. As if the time would never come when they will have to appear before him in judgment, they endeavor, in all the transactions and concerns of their life, to remove him to the greatest distance and to efface from their minds all apprehension of his majesty. And when God is dragged from his throne and divested of his character as Judge, impiety has come to its utmost height. Therefore, we must conclude that David has most certainly spoken according to the truth in declaring that those who give themselves liberty to commit all manner of wickedness, in the flattering hope of escaping with impunity, deny in their heart that there is a God. COMMENTARY ON THE PSALMS.[5]

---

[1]Selnecker, *Der gantze Psalter*, 1:50r.
[2]CTS 8:189* (CO 31:136).
[3]Gwalther, *Der Psalter*, 19r-v.

[4]WA 37:190-91.
[5]CTS 8:190-91* (CO 31:136; cf. *Institutes* 1.4.2).

HUMAN BEINGS WORSHIP THEMSELVES RATHER THAN GOD. HIERONYMUS WELLER VON MOLSDORF: The entire human race not only does not care about God but even blasphemes him and persecutes his Word. Thus, by disregarding God, in fact we seek and adore another god, the specter of our own heart, that is, worship devised and instituted by us. This is true idolatry. BRIEF COMMENT ON PSALM 14.[6]

NO ONE DOES ABSOLUTE GOOD. CARDINAL CAJETAN: Even if one person has at some point done some intrinsically good deed (for example, honoring one's parents), still that person has committed so many wicked deeds that it cannot, in simple and absolute terms, be affirmed that that person is one who does good, only one who does good in this instance. For the person who is does good absolutely is described as absolutely good; that cannot be stated about someone committing innumerable wicked deeds while doing one mere good deed. And therefore the prophet says, "There is not one who does good," speaking about moral good in simple and absolute terms. COMMENTARY ON PSALM 14.[7]

ORIGINAL SIN INFECTS EVERYONE UNTIL GOD'S GRACE RECREATES US. JOHN CALVIN: But it might be asked how David makes no exception, how he declares that no righteous person remains, not even one, when, nevertheless, he informs us, a little after, that the poor and afflicted put their trust in God? Again, it might be asked, if all were wicked, who was that Israel whose future redemption he celebrates in the end of the psalm? Indeed, as he himself was one of the body of that people, why does he not at least exclude himself? I answer: It is against the carnal and degenerate body of the nation of Israel that he here inveighs, and the small number constituting the seed which God had set apart for himself is not included among them. This is the reason why Paul,

in his epistle to the Romans, extends this sentence to all humanity. David, it is true, deplores the disordered and desolate state of matters under the reign of Saul. At the same time, however, he doubtless makes a comparison between the children of God and all who have not been regenerated by the Spirit but are carried away according to the inclinations of their flesh. Some give a different explanation, maintaining that Paul, by quoting the testimony of David, did not understand him as meaning that human beings are naturally depraved and corrupt; and that the truth which David intended to teach is that the rulers and the more distinguished of the people were wicked, and that, therefore, it was not surprising to behold unrighteousness and wickedness prevailing so generally in the world. This answer is far from being satisfactory. The subject on which Paul there reasons is not what is the character of the greater part of human beings, but what is the character of all who are led and governed by their own corrupt nature. . . .

Therefore, when David places himself and the small remnant of the godly on one side and puts on the other the body of the people, in general, this implies that there is a manifest difference between the children of God who are created anew by his Spirit, and all the posterity of Adam, in whom corruption and depravity exercise dominion. From this it follows that all of us, when we are born, bring with us from our mother's womb this folly and filthiness manifested in the whole life, which David here describes, and that we continue such until God make us new creatures by his mysterious grace. COMMENTARY ON THE PSALMS.[8]

FAITH AND PRAYER ARE NOT MUTUALLY EXCLUSIVE. NIKOLAUS SELNECKER: Thus far David has generally preached about all people, that they are by nature godless and idolaters. Yet now he attacks teachers and their teaching; he calls them evil, harmful seducers and evildoers. They do, he says, evil work and teach falsehood, and seduce many souls with their lies, and defraud the poor of

[6]Weller, *Enarratio Psalmorum*, 71.
[7]Cajetan, *In Sacrae Scripturae Expositionem*, 3:49.

[8]CTS 8:194-95* (CO 31:138); citing Rom 3:10.

body and soul and of all they have. And when they are gently rebuked, they will not suffer it; they grumble, complain, yell and even kill faithful teachers. They are full of ambition, pride, lust, fornication and other such vices. . . . And in addition to promoting false teaching, they devour and consume the sweat and blood of the poor and suck them dry spiritually and physically, wanting to have absolutely everything. They always give precedence to their god, who is called Dagon and Mammon, that is, wealth and lust, filled belly and gluttony in their churches and schools. . . . Therefore this psalm says here: "They do not call on the Lord, they do not put their trust in God, they do not believe the gracious promise of God, and no one has good confidence in our Lord God." Now where there is no true faith, there also cannot be true prayer, even if we tally up Our Fathers all day and night, babbled, screamed and sung with the mouth one after the other. It is nothing but hypocrisy and comes out of an evil heart, which is full of unbelief, doubt and suspicion. THE WHOLE PSALTER.[9]

THE WORD OF GOD IS THE ONLY TRUE COUNSEL WE NEED. HIERONYMUS WELLER VON MOLSDORF: By "counsels of the poor" the psalmist means the teaching and admonishing of the pious; these the impious disfigure, that is, they condemn them and call them heretical.

Therefore, the Word of God is called "counsel" because in all dangers, afflictions, temptations and tribulations it is able to bring counsel and solace. For in matters which are impossible for human counsel to untangle—like the anguish of death and the fear of hell—the Word of God alone is able to instruct the conscience rightly, to lift up afflicted minds and to console their hearts. BRIEF COMMENT ON PSALM 14.[10]

THE FUTURE PROMISE OF CHRIST WE TOO SHOULD CLAIM. NIKOLAUS SELNECKER: Here David desires that Christ, the promised seed of the woman, would become flesh and redeem his people who lie captive under the devil, sin, law and death. "Oh, we have preached so long," he says. "May the true Savior come soon, who will bring the gospel, the good news and who will be our true Immanuel, God With Us, because otherwise there is no consolation, faith or confidence in the entire world." True living joy is in the Lord Christ alone; otherwise everything is vanity and nothingness. And we too in our time should often pray this beautiful verse and heartfelt desire, that God would come with his Last Day and mercifully redeem us who lie captive here in this world, so that we would be joyous in all eternity, praising and thanking God the Lord for all his wonderful deeds! Amen. THE WHOLE PSALTER.[11]

---

[9]Selnecker, *Der gantze Psalter*, 1:52r.

[10]Weller, *Enarratio Psalmorum*, 83.
[11]Selnecker, *Der gantze Psalter*, 1:53r; citing Gen 3:15.

15:1-5 WHO SHALL DWELL ON YOUR HOLY HILL?

A Psalm of David.

[1] O LORD, who shall sojourn in your tent?
   Who shall dwell on your holy hill?

[2] He who walks blamelessly and does what is
    right
   and speaks truth in his heart;
[3] who does not slander with his tongue

and does no evil to his neighbor,
   nor takes up a reproach against his friend;
[4] in whose eyes a vile person is despised,
   but who honors those who fear the LORD;
who swears to his own hurt and does not change;
[5] who does not put out his money at interest
   and does not take a bribe against the innocent.
He who does these things shall never be moved.

OVERVIEW: While the reformers believe this psalm originally speaks to priests and Levites, they also acknowledge that it foreshadows the reality that came in Christ, our David. For Christians the church is Christ's temple, the holy mountain represents the heights of Christian teaching, and the psalmist as prophet contemplates with spiritual eyes the majesty and sanctity of the church. This psalm instructs the true citizens of God's kingdom. These magisterial reformers—in contrast to the Radicals—teach that while the church inevitably contains hypocrites and evildoers, it will not be purified until the Last Day. Nevertheless, the faithful are enjoined to pursue holy lives and the church's purity. An important corollary is that we are not to regard people by social and outward appearances but by discerning those who love God's Word and do not harm their neighbors.

Our commentators briefy discuss usury on account of the psalmist's implicit condemnation of lending money at interest (*nešek*).[1] The Council of Nicaea (325) forbade usury to clergy; later the church extended this ban to the laity. Some of the reformers revised church teaching concerning money lending and usury. Calvin understood the problem with usury to be that it exploited the poor and allowed effortless gain to the rich. Were money lent without inflicting such harm, it could be

legitimate. Thus, Calvin and the Genevan magistrates allowed for interest up to five percent; abusing this freedom could result in temporary excommunication from the Lord's Supper.[2] Luther, like Calvin, thought usurers should be excommunicated; they should only be reinstated to Communion, if, like Zacchaeus, they return all their ill-gotten gains.[3]

THIS PSALM TEACHES THE FRUITS OF FAITH.
RUDOLF GWALTHER: Some think that David wrote this song when he led God's ark of the covenant into Jerusalem, so that he could promulgate to the entire people what they should do if they long to remain in God's protection and to enjoy the presence of his mercy at all times. However, he presents a general lesson which demonstrates what true good works are. All who want to be true members of God's church and in the end to possess the heavenly fatherland should diligently strive to do such good works. And notice that here he does not talk about the first cause and basis for our salvation—which is the mercy of God, in which we have become participants through

---

[1]In some ancient Near Eastern cultures interest rates could be as high as fifty percent; see further Kraus, *Psalms 1–59*, 230-31.

[2]See W. Fred Graham, *The Constructive Revolutionary: John Calvin and His Socio-Economic Impact* (Richmond, VA: John Knox Press, 1971), 116-27; Scott M. Manetsch, *Calvin's Company of Pastors: Pastoral Care and the Emerging Reformed Church, 1536–1609* (Oxford: Oxford University Press, 2012), 193-95.
[3]For example, see LW 54:369, no. 4875 (WATR 4:565-66); 398, no. 5216 (5:12).

faith in Christ—rather, he talks about the fruits of faith which all who present themselves as believers should bear. THE PSALTER.[4]

SINCERE AND TRUE GOOD WORKS. NIKOLAUS SELNECKER: This is a psalm of doctrine. It teaches us to understand the law correctly: a sincere, good life and sincere, good works are the fruits of the Spirit and of faith. We should walk before God by sincere faith and sincere deeds toward our neighbors and should avoid the evil character of the godless and their hypocrisy who serve God with foolish works and neglecting sincere works. . . . This psalm does not talk about the forgiveness of sins and how human beings become righteous before God, but rather, about a new obedience and about a good conscience, about which also Paul talks in 1 Timothy 1 when he says, "Embrace a good soldier's struggle, holding faith and a good conscience." Again, "Because the salvific grace of God has appeared to all people, disciplining us so that we would renounce ungodly character and worldly desires, and to live chaste, righteous and godly lives in this world, waiting for the blessed hope and appearance of the glory of our great God and Savior Jesus Christ, who gave himself for us to redeem us from all unrighteousness and to purify for himself a people for his possession who are diligent for good works." THE WHOLE PSALTER.[5]

15:1-5 Holy Life on the Holy Hill

TYPES FOR OUR COUNTRY IN HEAVEN. RUDOLF GWALTHER: Through the Lord's tent and holy mountain we should understand the heavenly fatherland which in the Old Testament is portrayed through the external tabernacle or tent (which is described in the second book of Moses) as well as through Mount Zion, both of which God chose as a court for his temple and external worship. THE PSALTER.[6]

THE PRIESTLY MINISTRY TYPIFIES CHRIST. DESIDERIUS ERASMUS: According to the most basic meaning, the tabernacle which Moses had constructed at God's command stood in Jerusalem on Mount Zion until the time when Solomon, once again in accordance with an oracle from God, built on the same spot that most splendid, impressive and celebrated temple which was also venerated by the pagan nations. . . . And just as the Jews took pride in Abraham and David, whose descendants they boasted that they were, so they prided themselves on the city of Jerusalem. We gather from the gospel that they used to swear by it as a holy object; in fact, they put too much confidence in the temple and the altar, which is why the prophet reproached them thus: "The Temple of the LORD, the Temple of the LORD, the Temple of the LORD" and so on. They believed that God lived there, and they thought that this was the place where they had to worship him; this was where they had to placate him by means of sacrifices; this, they believed, was where they had to seek religious guidance and where the mercy seat stood from which God made his prophetic utterances. There lay the tablets written with the finger of God, there lay Aaron's rod, and there stood the ark of the covenant, the sacred table, the jar of manna and the cherubim. There was the Holy of Holies, which only the high priest was allowed to enter, and even he only once a year. This was the cause of the Jewish people's arrogance and pride and the reason why they scorned all other nations. Indeed, so great was their pride and their reverence for the temple that they brought a most shocking charge of blasphemy against Christ, because he had said, "Destroy this temple, and I will restore it in three days." The hidden meaning of his words was that he must be put to death by the Jews and within three days he would come back to life.

And so, in my opinion at any rate, the literal meaning of this psalm applies particularly to the Levites and the priests whose duty it was to reside in the tabernacle for which they were responsible and to take their rest in the temple. For the utmost purity and exceptional holiness were demanded of these men, but the ordinary Jews believed that this

---

[4]Gwalther, *Der Psalter*, 19v; citing 1 Sam 6; 1 Chron 16.
[5]Selnecker, *Der gantze Psalter*, 1:53v; citing 1 Tim 1:18-19; Tit 2:11-14.
[6]Gwalther, *Der Psalter*, 20r; citing Ex 36; Heb 8–9.

consisted in the performance of outward rites. This was why they performed that scrupulous consecration of their head, hands and garments and those frequent ritual washings. The priests were not permitted to assist at a funeral or to touch a corpse; they were not allowed to eat unconsecrated bread or to visit women and children or to step outside the temple, at least not on those days when they were engaged in sacred rites, in case they should be infected by some impurity from any source whatsoever.

However, all these things were merely shadows or types of far greater things. For Christ is our true David: to him has been promised a kingdom extending to the farthest corners of the earth which will endure as long as the sun and the moon, and to him has been granted all power in heaven and on earth. He is Christ, anointed not with the oil of priests but with heavenly grace before all humankind. His royal palace is the church, which the Lord himself sometimes refers to as the kingdom of heaven; his power is the freedom of the spirit; his tabernacle the association of believers of all nations; his Jerusalem is that mystical city which Saint John beheld, according to Revelation 21, built of living stones with Christ himself as the cornerstone. The holy mountain corresponds to the sublime heights of Christian teaching and the inviolable truth on which the temple structure rests, and it is also mentioned in another psalm: "Whoever trusts in the Lord is like Mount Zion; whoever lives in Jerusalem will never be moved." The prophet, therefore, is contemplating with spiritual eyes the wonderful majesty and sanctity of the church to which those types refer. For the glory of the church has eclipsed all those things which the Jews considered so glorious and has deprived them of honor according to the interpretation of Paul. EXPOSITION OF PSALM 15.[7]

THOUGH A MIXED BODY THE CHURCH IS CALLED TO BE PURE. JOHN CALVIN: David saw the temple crowded with a great multitude of people who all professed the same religion and presented

themselves before God according to external ceremonies. Therefore, assuming the perspective of someone wondering at this spectacle, he directs his discourse to God, who, in such a confusion and medley of characters, could easily distinguish his own people from strangers. There is a threefold use of this doctrine. In the first place, if we really wish to be reckoned among the number of the children of God, the Holy Spirit teaches us that we must show ourselves to be such by a holy and an upright life; for it is not enough to serve God by outward ceremonies, unless we also live uprightly and without doing wrong to our neighbors. In the second place, as we too often see the church of God defaced by much impurity, to prevent us from stumbling at what appears so offensive, a distinction is made between those who are permanent citizens of the church and strangers who are mingled among them only for a time. This is undoubtedly a highly necessary warning, in order that when the temple of God happens to be tainted by many impurities, we may not contract such loathing and disgust as will make us withdraw from it.

By impurities I understand the vices of a corrupt and polluted life. For religion is pure as long as doctrine and worship are strong; it is inappropriate for us to be so offended by human failings that for this reason we rend the unity of the church. Yet the experience of all ages teaches us how dangerous a temptation this is. The church of God—which should glisten brightly, cleansed from every stain—cherishes in its bosom many impious hypocrites or wicked people. Formerly the Cathars, Novatians and Donatists used this pretext to separate themselves from the fellowship of the godly.[8] The Anabaptists today renew the same

---

[7]CWE 65:228-30*; citing Jer 7:4; Jn 2:19; Ps 125:1; 2 Cor 3:7-11.

[8]Each of these movements sought to distinguish the elect and reprobate here on earth. Cathars were a dualist sect in Southern France. Novatians demanded rebaptism for lapsed Christians; responding to this Pope Stephen decreed that valid baptism required water and the Triune Name. Donatists had a similar split with the African Catholics concerning the surrender of Scriptures to the authorities during persecution—although Donatism is more subtle and nuanced than this; see Peter Brown, *Augustine of Hippo* (Berkeley and Los Angeles: University of California Press, 1967), 212-25; W. H. C. Frend, *The Donatist Church*, 3rd ed. (Oxford: Clarendon, 1985).

schisms, because it does not seem to them that a church in which vices are tolerated can be a true church. But Christ justly claims it as his own peculiar office to separate the sheep from the goats and thus admonishes us that we must bear with the evils which it is not in our power to correct, until all things become ripe and the proper season of purging the church arrive.

At the same time, the faithful are here enjoined, each in their own sphere, to use their endeavors that the church of God may be purified from the corruptions which still exist within it. And this is the third use which we should make of this doctrine. God's sacred threshing floor will not be perfectly cleansed before the Last Day, when Christ at his coming will cast out the chaff; but he has already begun to do this by the doctrine of his gospel, which on this account he terms a fan. We must, therefore, by no means be indifferent about this matter; on the contrary, we ought rather to exert ourselves in good earnest, that all who profess themselves Christians may lead a holy and an unspotted life. But above all, what God here declares with respect to all the unrighteous should be deeply imprinted on our memory; namely, that he prohibits them from coming to his sanctuary and condemns their impious presumption, in irreverently thrusting themselves into the society of the godly. David makes mention of the tabernacle, because the temple was not yet built. In sum, none have access to God unless they are genuine worshipers. Commentary on the Psalms.[9]

Know and Do Righteousness. Wolfgang Musculus: He does not say, "and he knows righteousness," but "he does righteousness." It is easily learned what is just, what is unjust, what ought to be done and what ought not to be done. Indeed, the pursuit of righteousness is not situated in knowledge, alone and bare, but also in practice. Let us not reject knowledge of righteousness but require that it must be living and effective. For a pious person, to know righteousness is not simply to know what it is but to express it in action. And righteousness must be done in this way, that first it is rendered to whomever is among our own household. In general, we owe nothing to anyone except that we love our neighbor as ourselves—which not only the law of the Old Testament requires but also the law of the New. Commentary on the Psalms.[10]

God's Honor Is Not Like Human Honor. Nikolaus Selnecker: Verse four is the most beautiful verse of this psalm. It indicates that those who fear God do not consider the person as the godless do. If a person is powerful and wealthy, it does not matter if he is a wicked scoundrel; we court him and honor him, even if he does not care about God, is an Epicurean, usurer, adulterer, robber and full of other sins and vices. But whoever fears God does not consider how wealthy, powerful or learned someone is but simply says, "Whoever loves the Word of God and does not harm his neighbor is honorable, even if he is a beggar. Whoever has no concern for the Word of God and does not care about his neighbor but only looks out for his own benefit and deceives his neighbor contrary to God and law is a godless person and is not honorable, no matter how powerful, wealthy, learned and high-ranking he may be." This is the characteristic of a person who fears God: that he clears away all worldly circumstances, does away with the mirrors and masks and does not consider what this or that person is, but instead considers God's glory alone. . . . But this art belongs to true Christians alone; it is a gift of the Holy Spirit about which "all-talk Christians" [*Maulchristen*] know nothing. The Whole Psalter.[11]

Usurers Ignore Love of Neighbor. John Calvin: With respect to usury, it is scarcely possible to find in the world a usurer who is not at the same time a robber, and addicted to unlawful

---

[9]CTS 8:203-5* (CO 31:143-44); citing Mt 25:32.

[10]Musculus, *In Psalterium Commentarii*, 195; citing Rom 13:8-10.
[11]Selnecker, *Der gantze Psalter*, 1:56v. *Maulchrist* is a descriptive pejorative for a nominal Christian; it is someone who "talks the talk but can't walk the walk."

and dishonorable gain. Accordingly, Cato of old[12] justly placed the practice of usury and the killing of human beings in the same rank of criminality, for the object of this class of people is to suck the blood of other human beings. It is also a very strange and shameful thing that, while all other human beings obtain the means of their subsistence with much toil, while farmers fatigue themselves by their daily occupations, and artisans serve the community by the sweat of their brow, and merchants not only employ themselves in labors but also expose themselves to many inconveniences and dangers, that moneymongers should sit at their ease without doing anything and receive tribute from the labor of everyone else. Besides, we know that generally it is not the rich who are exhausted by their usury, but the poor, who ought rather to be relieved. It is not, therefore, without reason that God has forbidden usury, adding this reason, "And if your brother becomes poor and falls into debt with you, then you will relieve him; take no usury or profit from him." We see that the purpose for which the law was framed was that people should not cruelly oppress the poor, who ought rather to receive sympathy and compassion. This was, indeed, a part of the judicial law which God appointed for the Jews in particular; but it is a common principle of justice which extends to all nations and to all ages, that we should keep ourselves from plundering and devouring the poor who are in distress and need.

From this it follows that the gain which the one who lends his money on interest acquires, without doing injury to anyone, is not to be included under the head of unlawful usury. The Hebrew word *nešek*, which David employs, is derived from another word which means to bite, and sufficiently shows that usurers are condemned insofar as they involve in them or lead to a license of robbing and plundering our fellow human beings. Ezekiel (indeed, Ezekiel 18 and Ezekiel 22) seems to condemn the taking of any interest whatever on money lent; but he doubtless

has an eye to the unjust and crafty arts of gaining by which the rich devoured the poor people. In short, provided we had engraved on our hearts the rule of equity, which Christ prescribes in Matthew 7— "Therefore, whatever you wish to be done to you, do to your neighbor"—it would not be necessary to enter into lengthened disputes concerning usury. COMMENTARY ON THE PSALMS.[13]

WE ARE RESPONSIBLE TO THE INNOCENT.
DESIDERIUS ERASMUS: Even the pagans considered despicable anyone who accepted a bribe to condemn someone who was not guilty or who received money to incriminate an innocent person through false testimony, or an advocate who, for the sake of profit, defended a guilty person against someone whom he knew to be innocent. For the persecutor used to clear himself of calumny under oath, while the advocate used to take an oath as to his good faith. If only this practice were not so frequently detected among Christians!

This statement can of course be given a wider application: anyone who, for the sake of some benefit to himself, does not assist an innocent person when he has the opportunity to do so accepts a bribe against the innocent. For example, if you see your neighbor being wronged and you pretend not to notice in order to oblige someone or another, then you are accepting a bribe against the innocent. If a person reflects thus: "If I defend this person, his oppressor will withdraw his assistance although up to now he has been generous to me," then the benefits which he usually receives are a bribe taken against the innocent. EXPOSITION OF PSALM 15.[14]

CHRIST'S EXAMPLE AND THE LAW OF LOVE COMPEL COMPASSION. MARTIN LUTHER: Many will address a miser like this: "Dear friend, I am a poor citizen, a poor craftsman. I sorely need you to lend me ten or twenty gulden for food." "Yes," the skinflint replies, "but I am not obliged to lend

---

[12]Cato the Younger (95–46 B.C.) was a Roman politician and Stoic.

[13]CTS 8:212-14* (CO 31:147-48); citing Lev 25:35-36; Ezek 18:17; 22:12.
[14]CWE 65:258*.

to you, and there is no law you can use to compel me to lend or let to you." Yes, dear brother, it is true—if you want to judge by the common law of the empire, land or city—that no judge will condemn you for not wanting to lend anything to me. Neither can he punish you for that. But if you want to be a Christian, answer me on the basis of this example of Christ. Christ laid down his body and life on the cross and shed his blood for you, just as for your sake he came down from heaven, was born, circumcised, purified and submitted himself to the law. Yes, all of that he did for you, to deliver you from eternal destitution and distress, though he surely owed absolutely nothing to you, whereas you lay in eternal debt, under his eternal wrath, condemned to hell. This debt he has forgiven you and, moreover, made you blessed and rich by his divine grace and gifts. And you did not want to do even so much for him out of love and honor—quite apart from being obliged to do so—as to help your neighbor with a little of what God has richly bestowed on you. Thus you are obligated both by the law of love—that you do for your neighbor what you would want done for you in the same need—and by the excellent example of Christ your Lord, who has done such great service for your sake, not counting cost to himself, that he has given all of his divine honor, wealth, body and life for you, sparing nothing. SERMON FOR THE FEAST OF THE PRESENTATION OF CHRIST IN THE TEMPLE (1546).[15]

---

[15]LW 58:436-37* (WA 51:169-70); citing Lev 19:18; Lk 10:25-28.

16:1-11 YOU WILL NOT ABANDON MY SOUL

A Miktam[a] of David.

[1] *Preserve me, O God, for in you I take refuge.*

[2] *I say to the LORD, "You are my Lord;*
I have no good apart from you."

[3] *As for the saints in the land, they are the*
excellent ones,
in whom is all my delight.[b]

[4] *The sorrows of those who run after[c] another*
god shall multiply;
their drink offerings of blood I will not
pour out
or take their names on my lips.

[5] *The LORD is my chosen portion and my cup;*
you hold my lot.

[6] *The lines have fallen for me in pleasant places;*
indeed, I have a beautiful inheritance.

[7] *I bless the LORD who gives me counsel;*
in the night also my heart instructs me.[d]

[8] *I have set the LORD always before me;*
because he is at my right hand, I shall not
be shaken.

[9] *Therefore my heart is glad, and my whole*
being[e] rejoices;
my flesh also dwells secure.

[10] *For you will not abandon my soul to Sheol,*
or let your holy one see corruption.[f]

[11] *You make known to me the path of life;*
in your presence there is fullness of joy;
at your right hand are pleasures forevermore.

a Probably a musical or liturgical term   b Or *To the saints in the land, the excellent in whom is all my delight, I say:*   c Or *who acquire*   d Hebrew *my kidneys instruct me*   e Hebrew *my glory*   f Or *see the pit*

OVERVIEW: In this psalm's movement from cry for help to affirmation of God's rule and blessings, the reformers, propelled by Peter's apostolic warrant in Acts 2, find the acts of Christ's passion, death and resurrection. Even the psalm's title—for all our exegetes except Calvin—authorizes this view: *miktām*, that is, "a golden jewel," clearly indicates that the psalm's content is about Jesus. Nevertheless there is some variance in how these commentators apply christological interpretation. Münster holds David and Christ together, confirming that these experiences were true of David's life while also asserting these things—and similar Old Testament events and prophecies—to be fulfilled in Christ. Cajetan, in contrast, understands this psalm to be about Christ literally, rather than typologically, because these words are too great for any mere human being. And Luther reminds his students and readers that exegesis and theology are inseparable. As Mickey Mattox

summarizes concerning Luther's methodology, "The knowledge of God, given in authentic Christian faith could not be bracketed out of properly Christian biblical study, reflection and exegesis. To put the matter in terms Luther himself used, the 'substance of Scripture' (*res Scripturae sacrae*) holds the key to the 'words of Holy Scripture' (*verba Scripturae sacrae*)."[1] Without Christ as its master, for Luther and many of his peers, grammar is a blind and false tyrant.

---

[1]Mickey L. Mattox, "Luther's Interpretation of Scripture: Biblical Understanding in Trinitarian Shape," in *The Substance of Faith: Luther's Doctrinal Theology for Today*, ed. Paul R. Hinlickey, 11-57 (Minneapolis: Fortress, 2008), here 46; cf. Luther, "Treatise on the Last Words of David (1543)," LW 15:266-70 (WA 54:29-31). See further Stephen G. Burnett, "Reassessing the 'Basel-Wittenberg Conflict': Dimensions of the Reformation-Era Discussion of Hebrew Scholarship," in *Hebraica Veritas?: Christian Hebraists and the Study of Judaism in Early Modern Europe*, ed. Allison Coudert and Jeffrey S. Shoulson (Philadelphia: Universtiy of Pennsylvania Press, 2004), 181-201.

THE APOSTLES HAVE PROVEN THAT THIS PSALM—AND ALL SUCH PSALMS—IS LITERALLY ABOUT CHRIST.

CARDINAL CAJETAN: The chief apostles, Peter and Paul, have informed us of this psalm's subject matter. For Peter in Acts 2 uses several verses from this psalm to reveal Christ's resurrection, affirming that David is not talking about himself but about Christ when he said, "You will not abandon my soul to hell, nor will my flesh see corruption," because David's body was in the grave all those years. Similarly Paul in Acts 13 quotes the same words and by the same reasoning affirms that David said Christ's body would not see corruption.

From this not only do we see this psalm's subject matter to be Christ's resurrection, etc., but we also pick up a general rule for how to understand the psalms when they speak of David: surely because these psalms, which are said to be about David, do not fit David himself, they are understood about Christ. For by this reasoning, maintaining that the truth of these words—"do not let your Holy One see corruption"—concerning David is not possible, each apostle asserted that David's words were about Christ's promise. And note this: because we follow these rules in the literal exposition of the psalms, such expositions are founded on apostolic authority. COMMENTARY ON PSALM 16.[2]

GRAMMAR ALONE IS INSUFFICIENT FOR THE TASK OF TRANSLATION.

MARTIN LUTHER: On March 27, 1538, Dr. Luther mentioned Sebastian Münster and other Hebraists who scourged him concerning his translation of the Bible for not following the rules of grammar: "Indeed grammar is necessary for declining words, conjugating verbs and construing syntax, but for the proclamation of the meaning and the consideration of the subject matter, grammar is not needed. For grammar should not reign over the meaning. As in Psalm 16 they scourge me: 'Preserve me, O Lord.' The entire psalm is in the person of Christ and this is its meaning: *O Lord God, see I am dying not on account of my sin but on account of the people's sin.* 'Preserve,' that is, let me rise again, because I hope in you. 'I said,' that is, my confession is in you, that you are my Lord, for I do not lack goods. We translate it this way: 'I suffer for your sake,' as if he would say, because I am dying for sin, I am not able to have any good. For the Hebrew words are *tôbātî bal-ʿālêkā*, that is, on account of you there is no good for me. Certainly with the greatest care we consider the subject matter and the meaning, before we decide how to translate. Nevertheless we are scourged." TABLE TALK: ANTON LAUTERBACH (1538).[3]

Superscription: *What Does* Miktām *Mean?*

MIKTĀM COULD MEAN SEVERAL THINGS.

FELIX PRATENSIS: There is not a little ambiguity among Hebrew authors concerning *miktām*. Some say it is the name of some musical instrument. Others posit that it means either a musical instrument or a healed wound: when this kind of word is placed before the word *David*, it means musical instrument; but when it is placed after "David," they assert, it means "healed wound." Others interpret it as an emblem. For the word from which it seems to be derived is *ketem*, which means "a lump of the finest gold." And they say that it indicated David's own military rank, as in those days cavalry who achieved some illustrious feat were accustomed to wear gilded armor. THE HEBREW PSALTER.[4]

MIKTĀM IS A TYPE OF TUNE.

JOHN CALVIN: Concerning the word *miktām* the Hebrew expositors are not agreed. Some derive it from *ketem*, as if it were a golden emblem. Others think it is the beginning of a popular and well-known song. To

---

[2]Cajetan, *In Sacrae Scripturae Expositionem*, 3:53; citing Acts 2:25-33; 13:35-39.

[3]WATR 3:619, no. 3794.

[4]Pratensis, *Psalterium*, 9r. Kraus rejects the translation of *miktām* as "golden jewel" (Abraham Ibn Ezra) out of hand; he prefers "stelographic publication" (στηλογραφία, cf. LXX)—though he admits this too is speculative. See Kraus, *Psalms 1–59*, 24-25.

others it seems rather to be some kind of tune. This last opinion I approve of. COMMENTARY ON THE PSALMS.[5]

MIKTĀM APPLIES TO DAVID. MARTIN LUTHER: *Miktām* could be understood about David in this way: this psalm was revealed to David himself as golden—that is, by a prophet according to divine illumination—because gold symbolizes knowledge of the new grace and law, silver the old. And he understood the mystery and spirit of the letter. So this title is happy boasting, like in 2 Samuel 23: "The eminent man, the psalmist of Israel said." So also here: this psalm is a *miktām*, that is, from one more excellent than other prophets and from one more eminent than other psalmists, like gold among other metals. GLOSSA ON PSALM 16 (1513–1515).[6]

MIKTĀM INTIMATES THE GOLDEN CONTENT: CHRIST. RUDOLF GWALTHER: This psalm David called "a golden jewel." For in it he describes his highest good and only treasure. . . . Now because David was a figure and depiction of Christ, several things are indicated here which according to the letter cannot be understand about anyone other than Christ—as the holy apostles interpreted it, too. THE PSALTER.[7]

16:1-4 Worship the True God

CLOTHED WITH CHRIST. ROBERT ROLLOCK: The first part of this psalm is a petition. He also seeks his own preservation which indicates he had come into some trouble and that he was exposed to some peril, either through idolatry or through something else. For this reason he has recourse to God as a suppliant. He craved for God to save him. . . . The reason for this petition is his confidence in God, whereby surely he embraced God, in this present danger in his heart, in Christ Jesus. David, therefore, who was about to present himself before that judgment seat of God and who was about to

seek his salvation and preservation, dare not be so bold as to come forth in God's sight unless he first be clothed over with Christ and with his righteousness. For this is to believe in God or that he had his recourse to God. For there was no other way at any time to appear before God, no not to the best kings themselves, except by faith in Jesus Christ, without which no entry was ever yet made to God. EXPOSITION UPON PSALM 16.[8]

WHAT IS GOOD FOR ME? PHILIPP MELANCH-THON: I understand this verse most simply in this way: "It is not for me a good," that is, "I am afflicted on account of you," that is, "On account of your wondrous and secret counsel concerning redeeming humankind I have passed under these horrible penalties, not on account of any of my sins. Therefore, because you are my God and you desire to preserve for yourself your own inheritance and my members, you would not allow me to succumb to these sorrowful afflictions but would console and deliver me." I have thought that this simple exposition must be surveyed, which is not absurd and does not render the psalm rather obscure. However, if anyone may show me a more neatly arranged interpretation, I would freely follow them. COMMENTS ON THE PSALMS.[9]

LOVE OF GOD IS NOT NATURAL FOR US. ANDREAS VON KARLSTADT: Love of God (to speak in terms of performed works) is a strong and intense longing for God; the soul does not find itself in this state, nor is it inclined to this. The prophet speaks about it this way: "Long for God" and "I am not well without you." In God David was well; without God, unwell. David had full satisfaction in God and complete anguish without God, and he abhorred everything that was not of God. But he loved his neighbor for God's sake, as the history of Saul demonstrates. REGARDING THE TWO GREATEST COMMANDMENTS.[10]

---

[5]CTS 8:215* (CO 31:149).
[6]WA 3:102; citing 2 Sam 23:1.
[7]Gwalther, *Der Psalter*, 20v.

[8]Rollock, *Exposition upon Some Psalmes*, 81-82*.
[9]MO 13:1041.
[10]CRR 8:236* (*Von den zweyen höchsten gebotten*, b3r-v); citing Ps 37:34; 16:2.

WE MUST APPROACH GOD IN HUMILITY. JOHN CALVIN: Human beings may strive ever so painstakingly to devote themselves to God, yet they are unable to offer him anything. Because, of course, whatever is in our hand cannot reach all the way to him, not only because he does not need anything—content in himself alone—but because we are empty and destitute of all honor and have nothing with which we could be more generous toward him. Still from this doctrine it will follow . . . that it is impossible by any merits for God to be bound, so that he would be a debtor to human beings. The main point is that when we come before God, we must lay aside all presumption. For if we imagine that anything belongs to us, because we diminish the principal part of honor which he deserves, it is no surprise if he rejects us. If, however, we acknowledge that our obedience in itself is nothing and is not worthy of any reward, this humility goes up like a sweet fragrance, which will procure for us acceptance with God. COMMENTARY ON THE PSALMS.[11]

I BELIEVE IN THE HOLY CATHOLIC CHURCH. NIKOLAUS SELNECKER: But who the saints are we should learn to understand correctly. For Christ does not talk about such saints, who before God through their own works are pious and righteous and who have no sins, because no person is righteous before God—otherwise Christ should not have had to suffer for the human race. Rather, he speaks about real sinners and children of death, whom the Lord Christ has saved from God's wrath and eternal damnation through his suffering and death. And he has made them all, as many as believe in him, children of God, righteous and blessed. On account of this he calls them saints. Not because they are holy and pious by nature—just as little as the thief on the cross—but because he has reconciled these poor, miserable, great sinners and enemies of God with his heavenly Father through his sacrifice given on the cross, and through his suffering, death and resurrection he has redeemed them from sin, God's wrath and

eternal damnation. He has made them righteous, holy and blessed, as the Lord himself intercedes for them to his Father in John 17: "Sanctify them in your truth; your word is the truth." And shortly afterwards: "I sanctify myself for them, so that they also might be sanctified in the truth." . . . From this we now understand what the holy Christian church is, namely, a congregation or assembly who are gathered by the Holy Spirit through the gospel of Christ. In this assembly . . . they still have much weakness and sin in them and must endure much crossbearing and misery; nevertheless they have the forgiveness of sin, righteousness, the Holy Spirit and eternal life on account of the Mediator Christ Jesus. They are his holy and living members. THE WHOLE PSALTER.[12]

THE FANATICISM OF THE WICKED FOR IDOLATRY. HIERONYMUS WELLER VON MOLSDORF: So far Christ has preached about his members, that is, those who believe in him; he has also described them. Now in this verse he starts to preach about hypocrites, that is, those . . . who deny, despise and persecute Christ; these he also depicts in their true colors. First he says that in these people there is the darkest zeal to cultivate idolatry. For they are much more roused, diligent and passionate for idolatry in their own zeal and worship than worshipers of the truth, who maintain the true worship of God. Therefore in Jeremiah they are compared with a camel that runs here and there, itching and inflamed with desire. . . . And elsewhere, in Jeremiah 8, they are compared with a wild horse in battle. The pious do not thrust forward their own teaching and worship so fiercely as the hypocrites. This is because of the devil and the corruption of human nature. BRIEF COMMENT ON PSALM 16.[13]

16:5-8 *The Lord Is Near*

GLORYING IN GOD. ROBERT ROLLOCK: First, David glories in his heritage and calls Jehovah

---

[11]CTS 8:217-18* (CO 31:150).

[12]Selnecker, *Der gantze Psalter*, 1:65r; citing Jn 17:17, 19; 1 Cor 1:30.
[13]Weller, *Enarratio Psalmorum*, 117-18; citing Jer 2:23-25; 8:6-7.

himself his heritage. For it is necessary that we first partake of God himself, according to the promise in the covenant: "I will be your God." Then all God's benefits in Christ Jesus may be communicated to us, as are the remission of sins, righteousness and eternal life. Second, he glories in the assurance of his heritage, yes, and even by speaking to God. By this we are indeed warned that when we glory, we should turn our eyes often to God, so that the confidence which proceeds from the sight and presence of God alone might increase. Third, he glories in the pleasantness of his heritage. . . . Finally, he glories in the fairness agreeable with his heritage. . . . All these words of David are great and heavy; they manifest a very strong feeling of God in Christ and of eternal life which hidden under these words was in David's soul, yes, surely they contain a greater sense than just what is contained in the words themselves. For that joy of faith, as Peter thinks, is unutterable and glorious. Thus, the feeling was greater than the words, but the matter itself and the substance of rejoicing are greater than all sense. . . . David's words declare that joy which we shall feel in the life to come and which indeed shall be wonderful.

Therefore, we must travel diligently, so that when we read those things which are uttered here by David in this psalm, we feel some similar sense of joy in ourselves. Let us reason with ourselves by these same words, so that our joy shall be incomprehensible which we one day shall full attain to when our Lord Jesus Christ shall be made manifest to us in his second coming. When we shall see him, how glorious he is in himself! Exposition upon Psalm 16.[14]

The Spirit and Letter of "Cup" in the Scriptures. Martin Luther: Because of the frequent use of the word *cup* in the Scriptures, let us speak about it in a little more detail. The cup is altogether the holy Scripture, or the book of Scripture, especially of the Old Testament. In Scripture there is a twofold sense, namely, the veil and clarity, the letter and the spirit, the figure and the truth, the shadow and the form. In Psalm 75 there is reference to a cup "full of mixture," and yet it is "pure wine." For truly, if this is understood spiritually, it is pure wine. Otherwise the cup has the dregs of the letter mixed in with it. Therefore this cup has two parts: The one is the letter, the other is the spirit. Thus he says now, "The Lord is the portion of my cup," that is, for me Scripture is understood as speaking about Christ. Then he says below, "I will bless the Lord who has given me understanding."

But for the unbelievers the "portion of the cup" is snow, ice, brimstone, that is, the letter. This is what it is for them in the soul, just as it is pure wine in the soul for the righteous. But now, because Scripture approves of mercy and judgment (spiritually understood, so that it becomes the same as the gospel), it thus also has two parts in the spirit. For it gives souls mercy to drink in the spirit and peace and salvation and altogether the best wine and nothing but good things and delightful things in the spirit.

But together with this it gives the flesh the cross to drink and judgment and the sufferings of Christ. For that reason it correctly says, "The Lord is" not the whole cup but "a portion of my cup." For at the same time he has Christ as salvation, and he drinks his benefits. Nevertheless he also drinks the evils of the world. And he has both from Scripture, for he is taught to have the benefits and to bear the evils. Thus Jeremiah says, "Those who do not deserve it will drink it." . . . Therefore to drink the cup is to accept the Word of Christ for the salvation of the soul and the torments of the flesh. But this is hard to accept, and it is offered first. But while you drink, you must say, "The Lord is the portion of my cup," for it is not only a cross, but at the same time it is salutary for the soul for the sake of the Lord who is imbibed in it in connection with the drinking of the cross and of the inheritance. First Psalms Lectures (1513–1515).[15]

---

[14]Rollock, *Exposition upon Some Psalmes*, 94-97*; citing Ex 6:7; 1 Pet 1:8.

[15]LW 10:109-10* (WA 3:108); citing Ps 75:8; Jer 49:12.

NO JOY WITHOUT GRACE. WOLFGANG MUSCU-
LUS: It must be observed how effective that faith of
divine grace and of a heavenly inheritance is in the
elect. He is contented with his own extraordinarily
dear inheritance, always aspiring and striving for
fuller things. But the spirit of the elect is not only
content in its own inheritance, but also with
respect to that inheritance, he may boast in
whatever situation, in tribulations and afflictions of
this age, just as is apparent in this example of
David. Therefore, it cannot happen that a person's
heart may be truly and solidly filled and exhilarated
unless it acquires this inheritance of the heavenly
kingdom with David for which the apostle in
Colossians 1 writes to us who have been called,
saying "with joy giving thanks to God, and to the
Father, who has made us worthy for the part of the
inheritance of the saints in the light."

Those who have the spirit of this world declare
themselves to be blessed and judge that their
inheritance has fallen in pleasant places, which they
have regarded as riches, glory and power in this age,
just as you see in Psalm 144. They have called the
people who have these things blessed. Indeed, the
Holy Spirit also declares the felicity of the elect of
God to such a degree, saying, "Blessed are those
people whose God is the Lord." They do not
acknowledge this unless they are the ones who
possess it. Moreover, they acknowledge it by the
certainty of faith, which the followers of the
Antichrist ignore—indeed they impugn it—setting
forth a doctrine of doubt for the church of God.
COMMENTARY ON THE PSALMS.[16]

**"KIDNEYS" MUST BE UNDERSTOOD FIGURA-
TIVELY.** SEBASTIAN MÜNSTER: By "kidneys
instruct me," understand a hidden goad, spurring
each person to do good. For the Hebrews
understood the kidneys [kĕlāyôt] to be the
workshop of counsel. THE TEMPLE OF THE
LORD: PSALM 16.[17]

**THE SUFFICIENCY OF THE HOLY SPIRIT'S
ILLUMINATION.** JOHN CALVIN: David confesses
that it was entirely due to the pure grace of God that
he had come to possess so great a good and that he
had been made a partaker of it by faith. It would be
of no advantage to us for God to offer himself freely
and graciously to us if we did not receive him by
faith, seeing he invites to himself both the reprobate
and the elect in common; but the former, by their
ingratitude, defraud themselves of this inestimable
blessing. Let us, therefore, know that both these
things proceed from the free liberality of God: first,
his being our inheritance, and second, our coming to
the possession of him by faith.

The counsel which David mentions is the
inward illumination of the Holy Spirit, by which
we are prevented from rejecting the salvation to
which he calls us, which we would otherwise
certainly do, considering the blindness of our flesh.
From this we gather that those who attribute to
human free will the choice of accepting or
rejecting the grace of God basely mangle that
grace and show as much ignorance as impiety.
That this discourse of David ought not to be
understood of external teaching appears clearly
from the words, for he tells us that he was
instructed in the night when he was removed from
the sight of human beings. Again, when he speaks
of this being done "in his kidneys," he doubtless
means secret inspirations. Further, it ought to be
carefully observed that, in speaking of the time
when he was instructed, he uses the plural number,
saying it was done "in the nights." By this manner
of speaking, he not only ascribes to God the
beginning of faith but also acknowledges that he is
continually making progress under his tuition;
and, indeed, it is necessary for God, during the
whole of our life, to continue to correct the vanity
of our minds, to kindle the light of faith into a
brighter flame and by every means to advance us
higher in the attainments of spiritual wisdom.
COMMENTARY ON THE PSALMS.[18]

---

[16]Musculus, *In Psalterium Commentarii*, 221; citing Col 1:11-12; Ps
144:15.
[17]Münster, *Miqdaš YHWH*, 1170.

[18]CTS 8:226-27* (CO 31:154-55).

WHAT DOES IT MEAN TO SET THE LORD BEFORE OUR EYES? NIKOLAUS SELNECKER:

To have the Lord always before our eyes is nothing other than to know and trust confidently that God is merciful to us; he is well-pleased with us and presents himself in a friendly manner to us in his Word and in the holy sacraments. God will never turn away from us in any affliction.... The dear word *set* points to a sure, sturdy faith which is not based and built on sand but on a strong rock and a firm foundation. It cannot be moved or knocked over by any wind or storm. Such a foundation is the Lord Christ himself as well as his Word, as it is written: "No other foundation can be laid than the Lord Christ Jesus alone who is the true cornerstone and rock on which faith must be built." And whoever builds on it will not be put to shame. But a hypocrite will be tossed here and there by the wind and has nothing sure either to believe or to say—as we experience today with the Sacramentarians.[19] Next follows the dear word *Lord* which indicates on what and to what faith is directed, namely, only to the mercy-rich lovingkindness of God which is promised and gifted to us in Christ. And here all the world's saints and human merit fall away, for everything depends only on God's grace and lovingkindness. Third, the dear word *always* indicates that faith must not be idle or inconsistent and it should never let itself be turned away from God but instead should remain constantly with God, as it is written in Psalm 123: "I lift my eyes to you who sit in heaven." See how the eyes of his servants look to the hands of the Lord, like the eyes of maidens look to the hands of their ladies. In this way our eyes look to the Lord our God until he is merciful to us. THE WHOLE PSALTER.[20]

16:9-11 *I Rejoice in Body and Soul*

THE IMPORTANCE OF A PEACEFUL MIND AND CONSCIENCE. JOHN CALVIN: The psalmist

commends the inestimable fruit of faith, which Scripture mentions everywhere, in that, by placing us under the protection of God, it makes us not only to live in the enjoyment of mental tranquility, but, what is more, to live joyfully and cheerfully. The essential part of a happy life, as we know, is to possess tranquility of conscience and mind. For, on the contrary, there is no greater infelicity than to be tossed amid a multiplicity of cares and fears. But the unbelievers, however much intoxicated with the spirit of thoughtlessness or stupidity, never experience true joy or serene mental peace. They rather feel terrible agitations within, which often come on them and trouble them so much as to constrain them to awake from their lethargy.

In short, to rejoice calmly is the lot of no one but of the one who has learned to place his confidence in God alone and to commit his life and safety to his protection. Therefore, when encompassed with innumerable troubles on all sides, let us be persuaded that the only remedy is to direct our eyes toward God; and if we do this, faith will not only pacify our minds but also replenish them with fullness of joy. COMMENTARY ON THE PSALMS.[21]

"HOLY ONE" TEACHES THE ENTIRETY OF THE GOSPEL. THEODORE BEZA: Now when David calls the Messiah *ḥāsîd* ("Holy One")—that is, as I interpret it, the human being on whom the Father has poured out most abundantly all his grace and gifts which we drink in from him alone by faith—in one word he seems to have embraced the sum of the doctrine of the gospel. PARAPHRASE OF PSALM 16.[22]

DAVID PROPHESIES JESUS' DEATH AND RESURRECTION. SEBASTIAN MÜNSTER: This passage can also be translated in this way: "You will not abandon my soul to the grave, nor will you let your Holy One see the pit." Again, to see the pit is to be concealed in the pit until corruption. And this passage has been fulfilled in our Savior, as also

---

[19]Lutherans pejoratively called "Sacramentarians" those who rejected the bodily presence of Christ in the Eucharistic elements and asserted instead his spiritual presence.
[20]Selnecker, *Der gantze Psalter*, 1:78r-v; citing Mt 7:24-27; Eph 2:19-21; Ps 123:1.

[21]CTS 8:229* (CO 31:155-56).
[22]Beza, *Psalmes of Dauid*, 21* (cf. *Psalmorum Davidis*, 43).

the apostles cite it in Acts. For although Christ died and was buried, nevertheless he did not remain in the grave like other mortals. For that reason, it is written here that he did not see the grave, because immediately, after three days, he rose again from the grave. Now when the prophet wrote this about himself, it should not be doubted that in fact at that time his mind was lifted up in Christ and he recognized himself to be a type for Christ. Many other such things are written typologically about the patriarchs, yet they were all fulfilled in Christ. THE TEMPLE OF THE LORD: PSALM 16.[23]

AN OBVIOUS PROPHECY OF CHRIST'S RESUR-RECTION. WOLFGANG MUSCULUS: By the authority of the apostle Peter, the prophet says this about the resurrection of Christ, under whose person he prophesied these things. For more concerning this matter, see Acts 2. . . . Peter said these things by the instinct of the Holy Spirit and opened the meaning of the passage to those present: the prophet had clearly spoken about the resurrection of Christ and predicted the future, namely, that his soul would not remain in hell, nor would his flesh see corruption in the tomb. These things especially pertain to Christ so that they are not able to be attributed to David, although the remaining things are common to both. COMMENTARY ON THE PSALMS.[24]

DID CHRIST NOT ROT IN THE GRAVE? JOHN CALVIN: The question, however, may be asked, because Christ descended into the grave, was not he also subject to corruption? The answer is easy. The etymology or derivation of the two words here used to express the grave should be carefully attended to. The grave is called šĕʾôl, being as it were an insatiable gulf which devours and consumes all things, and the pit is called šāḥat, which means corruption. These words, therefore, here denote not so much the place as the quality and condition of the place. . . . Besides, we know

that the grave of Christ was filled, and as it were embalmed with the life-giving perfume of his Spirit, that it might be to him the gate to immortal glory. Both the Greek and Latin fathers, I confess, have strained these words to a meaning wholly different, referring them to the bringing back of the soul of Christ from hell. But it is better to adhere to the natural simplicity of the interpretation which I have given, so that we may not make ourselves objects of ridicule to the Jews; and further, so that one subtlety, by engendering many others, may not involve us in a labyrinth. COMMENTARY ON THE PSALMS.[25]

THE ARTICLE OF CHRIST'S DESCENT INTO HELL IS ROOTED IN SCRIPTURE. NIKOLAUS SELNECKER: In these words the article of the Lord Christ's descent into hell is based. This article has been disputed by many who say that the ancients did not have this little phrase—"descended into hell"—in their symbol or in their Creed. Such errors should be diligently refuted with God's Word. For we believe and confess truthfully that he descended into hell and released all Christians captive to the devil, and removed all the devil's power so that he can no longer harm us. For us he went below, so that we would not enter hell and remain there forever.

So, the words of this psalm are clear: "You will not leave my soul in hell." For from this it follows undeniably that the Lord descended into hell, as also Psalm 30 says: "Lord, you have led my soul out of hell." And Psalm 86: "Your goodness is great over me, and you have saved my soul from the depths of hell." So also Saint Paul says in Ephesians 4 "that Christ ascended, what is this other than that earlier he descended into the lower regions of the earth?" Therefore it is a harmful error that the Papists pretend that this article of faith—"descended into hell"—has no basis in Scripture but that it is merely a tradition of the church. And with this they agree who say that the word šĕʾôl, "hell," in Scripture means nothing other

[23]Münster, *Miqdaš YHWH*, 1170; citing Acts 2:25-33; 13:35-39.
[24]Musculus, *In Psalterium Commentarii*, 223.

[25]CTS 8:231-32* (CO 31:157); citing Acts 2:30; 13:33.

than the grave. As a result of this clever trick the articles of faith will be weakened and in the end not one will be affirmed. . . . What would we be able to say about eternal damnation? And many other horrid errors would follow if the word šĕ'ôl should mean a grave every time in Scripture. The Whole Psalter.[26]

Christ Freed the Captives of Hell. Peter Riedemann: In order that he might fulfill all things, we confess that Christ went down to the lowest parts of the earth, that is, to the place of captivity where those are kept who formerly did not believe the word spoken to them. Christ proclaimed to those spirits that the word of salvation had now been sent. God had previously planned this word of salvation and had promised it to humanity, so that all who believed it in their hearts should be set free. Now, in accordance with the Father's promise, Christ through his death had destroyed the power of death, hell and the devil, which for so long had betrayed human beings and led them astray.

We confess that after Christ had destroyed death's power through his own death, he rose from the dead through the power of the Father. He became the firstborn of those who are to inherit salvation, for death could not hold him. Confession of Faith.[27]

Keep Us in Your Grace. The Book of Common Prayer (1549): Almighty God, through your only-begotten Son Jesus Christ you have overcome death and opened to us the gate of eternal life. We humbly beseech you, that as by your special grace, going before us, you would put in our minds good desires, so that by your continual help we may bring the same to good effect, through Jesus Christ our Lord who lives and reigns with you in the unity of the same Spirit, one God, world without end. Collect for Matins on Easter.[28]

---

[26]Selnecker, *Der gantze Psalter*, 1:80v-81r; citing Ps 30:3; 86:13; Eph 4:9. See further *Formula of Concord*, Article 9.

[27]CRR 9:70-71; citing Eph 4:8-10; 1 Pet 3:18-21; 1:3-5; Gen 3:14-15; 12:1-4; Heb 2:14-15; Is 25:6-9; Hos 13:14; 1 Cor 15:53-58; Acts 2:33-39.
[28]BCP 1549, 54*.

17:1-15 IN THE SHADOW OF THE LORD'S PROMISES

A Prayer of David.

¹ Hear a just cause, O Lord; attend to my cry!
Give ear to my prayer from lips free of deceit!
² From your presence let my vindication come!
Let your eyes behold the right!

³ You have tried my heart, you have visited me
by night,
you have tested me, and you will find nothing;
I have purposed that my mouth will not
transgress.
⁴ With regard to the works of man, by the word
of your lips
I have avoided the ways of the violent.
⁵ My steps have held fast to your paths;
my feet have not slipped.

⁶ I call upon you, for you will answer me, O God;
incline your ear to me; hear my words.
⁷ Wondrously show[a] your steadfast love,
O Savior of those who seek refuge
from their adversaries at your right hand.

⁸ Keep me as the apple of your eye;
hide me in the shadow of your wings,

⁹ from the wicked who do me violence,
my deadly enemies who surround me.

¹⁰ They close their hearts to pity;
with their mouths they speak arrogantly.
¹¹ They have now surrounded our steps;
they set their eyes to cast us to the ground.
¹² He is like a lion eager to tear,
as a young lion lurking in ambush.

¹³ Arise, O Lord! Confront him, subdue him!
Deliver my soul from the wicked by your
sword,
¹⁴ from men by your hand, O Lord,
from men of the world whose portion is in
this life.[b]
You fill their womb with treasure;[c]
they are satisfied with children,
and they leave their abundance to their
infants.

¹⁵ As for me, I shall behold your face in
righteousness;
when I awake, I shall be satisfied with your
likeness.

a Or Distinguish me by   b Or from men whose portion in life is of the world   c Or As for your treasured ones, you fill their womb

---

OVERVIEW: The reformers commend this psalm as an exhortation to persevere in prayer, despite the circumstances, against false teachers and tyrants. We hear the familiar refrain that earthly and heavenly statuses are not to be equated: evildoers might be wealthy and powerful on earth and the pious might be poor and weak; however, this mirage will dissipate when they both behold God's face at judgment. The intimate image of God as mother of his people elicits poetic and pastoral praise of God from the reformers: "It is absolutely the sweetest figure of speech." Christ our mother hen, as it were, covers us his chicks with his wings when vultures appear. Paradoxically he does this by spreading out his hands on the cross, providing us with the cover of his promises which we must nestle into for salvation and safety.

A PRAYER FOR FAITHFUL PREACHERS AND TEACHERS. NIKOLAUS SELNECKER: This is a beautiful, glorious psalm of prayer; it is very necessary in our time. For it laments the false teachers and shows the way, manner and moderation for pious, faithful teachers: how they are to behave in their office, namely, that they do not become timid but rather steadily continue to call on God, and in temptation to maintain true comfort and protection—such protection is God himself and his Word. For however things may go, still this saying remains true: "The name of the Lord is the strongest tower." Therefore this psalm should be pleasant and well-known to all faithful teachers as well as their listeners. When they see how so many bad things happen in the church and everywhere strife, envy, hatred, heresy and corruption of the right, true doctrine creeps in, they should not despair but rather cry to God and sing with heart and mouth: "Lord, keep us steadfast in your Word; Lord, pagans have invaded your inheritance; outside of you, Lord Jesus Christ, there is no hope on earth." Faithful teachers can and should sincerely do such by day and night if they are serious about the doctrine and honor of God. For those who look after their gut, greed, lust, honor, fame, name and title do not achieve anything and are mute hounds, more harmful than useful. So, pious teachers should always consider carefully their office—which indeed is difficult and vast—which is essential in order for a teacher to be found faithful, as Paul says in 1 Corinthians 4: "We do not require anything more of stewards than that they be found faithful." The faithfulness required of teachers, however, is stirred up and increased when they meditate on whom they serve, what kind of office they have and to what their office is directed. Whoever is mindful of these three things will surely be found faithful. . . .

The office is not a human office but God's office and deals with the mysteries of God, which are hidden to human reason and understanding, and consist in the forgiveness of sins, God's grace and the doctrine of eternal life. And such an office is to be executed solely to the glory of God and to the salvation of the hearers. From these parts we see and recognize that the preaching office is a very serious and high office. THE WHOLE PSALTER.[1]

17:1-5 Hear My Prayer, Bring Justice!

BE ATTENTIVE IN PRAYER. JOHN CALVIN: By this form of prayer the Holy Spirit teaches us that we should diligently do our best to live an upright and innocent life, so that, if there are any who give us trouble, we may be able to boast that we are blamed and persecuted wrongfully. Again, whenever the wicked assault us, the same Spirit invites us to pray. And if anyone who trusts on the fact that he enjoys a good conscience and yet neglects the exercise of prayer, he defrauds God of the honor which belongs to him, in not referring his cause to him and in not leaving him to judge and determine it. Let us learn, also, that when we present ourselves before God in prayer, it is not to be done with the ornaments of an artificial eloquence, for the finest rhetoric and the best grace which we can have before him consists in pure simplicity. COMMENTARY ON THE PSALMS.[2]

NEVER ARROGATE RIGHTEOUSNESS TO YOURSELF EXCEPT IN PERSECUTION. JOHANNES BUGENHAGEN: Pay attention that believers never allege their own righteousness before God (otherwise they are hypocrites) unless they are in persecution: for in that case they are certain that they suffer on account of their righteousness and their adversaries have an unjust case. Therefore they do not arrogate righteousness to themselves but embrace Christ's way of thinking that they are pronounced blessed. INTERPRETATION OF THE PSALMS.[3]

AFFLICTIONS TOO GREAT FOR A MERE HUMAN BEING. MOÏSE AMYRAUT: What this verse holds is more magnificent than if it were possible for someone else beside Christ alone to measure up exactly. For that reason David's words here extend somewhat beyond his own conduct. ANNOTATION ON PSALM 17:3.[4]

THE LONELINESS OF NIGHT IS OPPORTUNE FOR TEMPTATION. JOHN CALVIN: The time when he declares God to have visited him is during the night, because, when a person is withdrawn from

---

[1]Selnecker, *Der gantze Psalter*, 1:83r-v; citing 1 Cor 4:2.

[2]CTS 8:236* (CO 31:159).
[3]Bugenhagen, *In librvm Psalmorvm interpretatio*, 37.
[4]Amyraut, *Paraphrasis in Psalmos Davidis*, 59-60.

the presence of his fellow creatures, he sees more clearly his sins, which otherwise would be hidden from his view; just as, on the contrary, the sight of human beings affects us with shame, and this is, as it were, a veil before our eyes, which prevents us from deliberately examining our faults. It is, therefore, as if David had said: "O Lord, because the darkness of the night discovers the conscience more fully, all coverings being then taken away, and because, at that moment, the affections, either good or bad, according to human inclinations, manifest themselves more freely, when there is no person present to witness and pronounce judgment on them; if you would then examine me, there will be found neither disguise nor deceit in my heart." COMMENTARY ON THE PSALMS.[5]

17:6-9 God's Motherly Care

GOD PROTECTS THROUGH MIRACULOUS AND MUNDANE MEANS. JOHN CALVIN: David, in my judgment, perceiving that he could be delivered from the perilous circumstances in which he was placed only by special and extraordinary means, turns to the miraculous power of God. Those who think he desires God to withhold his grace from his persecutors do too great violence to the scope of the passage. By this circumstance the extreme danger is expressed, because otherwise it would have been enough for him to have been aided in the ordinary and common way in which God is accustomed to favor and protect his own people every day. The grievousness of his distress, therefore, constrained him to request that God miraculously deliver him. The title with which he honors God here—"O Savior of those who seek refuge"— confirms his hope of obtaining his requests. Because God takes on himself the charge of saving all who confide in him, David, who was one of them, was therefore able to assure himself of deliverance. Therefore as often as we approach God, let this be the first thought to enter our minds. Because God is not called in vain the Preserver of

those who hope in him, if only our faith rests in his grace, we have no reason at all to fear that he is not ready to help us. If all paths are barricaded, let this also enter our minds, that he possesses incredible ways of helping us which magnify his power even more. COMMENTARY ON THE PSALMS.[6]

THE SWEETEST CONSOLATION. HIERONYMUS WELLER VON MOLSDORF: This little verse teaches that God cares for his church like the pupil of his eye. Indeed nothing sweeter or more gracious can be proclaimed to the minds of the pious than this consolation. God loves his church even more tenderly than any—even the gentlest—mommy loves the child of her womb. It is absolutely the sweetest figure of speech. BRIEF COMMENT ON PSALM 17.[7]

GOD IS LIKE A MOTHER BIRD. RUDOLF GWALTHER: The wings of God are his shield and shelter. And through this God is compared with a hen that covers and shelters her young chicks with her wings. This comparison Christ also uses in the Gospel. THE PSALTER.[8]

CHRIST IS OUR HEN AND WE ARE HIS CHICKS. NIKOLAUS SELNECKER: The Holy Spirit has wonderfully outlined and depicted Christ and the Christian church under this figure which is the dearest and most blessed: the Holy Spirit compares Christ with a hen. For as a hen protects and shelters her young from vultures, so also Christ Jesus, the Son of God, guards, nourishes and defends his Christian church from the savage power of the devil. And as the young chicks, when vultures circle overhead, rush to their mother and seek protection and tuck themselves under her wings, so also all pious Christians flee to and seek protection with Christ their Lord as often as they are afflicted and plagued by the devil and the world; they crawl under his wings and rest in his promises. THE WHOLE PSALTER.[9]

---

[5]CTS 8:238* (CO 31:160).

[6]CTS 8:243-44* (CO 31:162-63).
[7]Weller, *Enarratio Psalmorum*, 149.
[8]Gwalther, *Der Psalter*, 23r-v; citing Mt 23:37; Lk 13:34.
[9]Selnecker, *Der gantze Psalter*, 1:86v.

THE MYSTICAL SHADOW OF CHRIST'S WINGS.
MARTIN LUTHER: "The shadow of your wings" in a mystical sense is faith in Christ, which in this life is mysterious and shadowy. But the wings of Christ are his hands stretched out on the cross. For just as the body of Christ on the cross produces a shadow, so it casts a spiritual shadow on the soul, namely, faith in his cross, under which every saint is protected. Second, the shadow of the wings is the protection and watch of the holy angels or of the contemplative, who are the wings of God, for in them he soars and dwells in affectionate and encaptured minds. Third, the shadow of the wings is the learning of the Scriptures, in which there is rest for those who devote themselves to this learning. Thus the bride says: "I sat down under his shadow, whom I desired." FIRST PSALMS LECTURES (1513–1515).[10]

17:10-15 *Vindicate the Faithful from the Wicked Who Prowl as Predators*

STAY WITH CHRIST, THE SHEPHERD.
WOLFGANG MUSCULUS: He notes that Saul was the leader and head of the others, even the author of all the persecution which he endured. Here Saul bore the image of Satan, who is the head of all the reprobate, just as Christ is the head of the pious and the elect. This is what we read about in 1 Peter 5: "The devil," he says, "circles about like a roaring and ravenous lion seeking whom he may devour." He does not circle about alone but with an innumerable entourage of both experienced, wicked spirits and persons. Therefore we must take care that we may be continuously held fast under the protection and custody of the true David, namely, Christ our Shepherd. For in this way he guards his flock so that they cannot be snatched by anyone from his hands (Jn 10).

Let us not wander far from his custody. For we could not be safe from the attack of these infernal lions, those horrible ones who not only run about with an open mouth and manifest roaring but also through ambush overwhelm the incautious. For

which reason the prophet also says here, "And like young lions hiding in ambush." For as a matter of fact Satan transfigures himself into an angel of light so that he can seduce the ignorant and simple. Therefore not only on those who manifestly are impious and exercise an open tyranny but also in false prophets, false priests, hypocrites and heretics, in whom he lurks as if in a certain lair, he must be feared and taken heed to with the greatest diligence. COMMENTARY ON THE PSALMS.[11]

NOT ALL THE CHURCH'S ENEMIES ARE THE SAME. NIKOLAUS SELNECKER: Here a common question occurs: Whether we too may pray against the enemies and persecutors of the holy gospel? It is however a correct answer that there are two types of enemies of the Christian church. Some oppose the church unknowingly and think that they have a correct zeal, like Paul before his conversion. For such people we should pray that God would enlighten, convert and, yes, defend them. Others persecute the teaching of the gospel knowingly, like, in past times, the Pharisees, high priests and scribes and today the Roman papal mob. Such people we should pray that God would topple and bring to shame, allowing them to become completely errant and wild. THE WHOLE PSALTER.[12]

THE TEMPTATION TO EQUATE EARTHLY AND HEAVENLY BLESSINGS. JOHN CALVIN: When he says, "Their portion is in life," I explain it as meaning that they are exempted from all troubles and abound in pleasures; in short, that they do not experience the common condition of other human beings; as, on the contrary, when a person is oppressed with adversities, it is said of him that his portion is in death. David therefore intimates that it is not a reasonable thing that the unbelievers should be permitted to go around only in joy and cheerfulness without having any fear of death, and to claim for themselves, as if by hereditary right, a peaceful and happy life.

---

[11]Musculus, *In Psalterium Commentarii*, 245; citing 1 Pet 5:8; Jn 10:25-29.
[12]Selnecker, *Der gantze Psalter*, 1:87r.

[10]LW 10:111 (WA 3:111-12); citing Song 2:3.

What he adds immediately after, "God stuffs their bellies with his hidden goods," is of the same import. We see these persons not only enjoying, in common with other people, light, breath, food and all other commodities of life, but we also see God often treating them more delicately and more bountifully than others, as if he fed them on his lap, holding them tenderly like little babes and fondling them more than all the rest of humankind. Accordingly, by "the secret goods of God" we are here to understand the rare and more exquisite privileges of life which he bestows on them. Now, this is a severe temptation, if a human being estimates the love and favor of God by the measure of earthly prosperity which he bestows; and, therefore, it is not to be wondered at, though David was greatly afflicted in contemplating the prosperous condition of unbelievers. But let us remember that he makes this holy complaint to console himself and to mitigate his distress, not in the way of murmuring against God and resisting his will. Let us remember this, I say, that, according to his example, we may learn also to direct our groanings to heaven. COMMENTARY ON THE PSALMS.[13]

LOOKING INTO GOD'S FACE TEACHES US MANIFOLD DOCTRINES. NIKOLAUS SELNECKER: That is, I will gladly let the godless have all the world's lusts and joys, honors, happiness and riches, and I will not fume or mumble about it.... Instead I will entrust myself to God and will wait.... This is a beautiful, dear verse, and it holds it in a great deal of beautiful teaching: the image of God, how human beings were created by God; our righteousness, how the Son of God makes us righteous and holy; the resurrection of the dead and eternal life and the complete restitution and restoration of the right, true image of God. And it would be necessary to handle all of these articles here, but that would surely be too long. THE WHOLE PSALTER.[14]

DAVID FINISHES THE PSALM WITH HEAVENLY JOY. JOHN CALVIN: Having with anguish of heart declared before God the troubles which afflicted and tormented him, that he might not be overwhelmed with the load of temptations which pressed on him, David now takes, as it were, the wings of faith and rises up to a region of undisturbed tranquility, where he may behold all things arranged and directed in due order. In the first place, there is a tacit comparison here between the well-regulated state of things which will be seen when God by his judgment shall restore to order those things which are now embroiled and confused, and the deep and distressing darkness which is in the world, when God keeps silence and hides his face. In the midst of those afflictions which he has recounted, the psalmist might seem to be plunged in darkness from which he would never obtain deliverance. When we see the ungodly enjoying prosperity, crowned with honors and loaded with riches, they seem to be in great favor with God. But David triumphs over their proud and presumptuous boasting; and although, to the eye of sense and reason, God has cast him off and removed him far from him, yet he assures himself that one day he will enjoy the privilege of familiarly beholding him.

The pronoun *I* is emphatic, as if he had said, The calamities and reproaches which I now endure will not prevent me from again experiencing the fullness of joy from the fatherly love of God manifested toward me. We ought carefully to observe that David, in order to enjoy supreme happiness, desires nothing more than to have the taste and experience of this great blessing always that God is reconciled to him. The wicked may imagine themselves to be happy, but so long as God is opposed to them, they deceive themselves in indulging this imagination. "To behold God's face" is nothing else than to have a sense of his fatherly favor, with which he not only causes us to rejoice by removing our sorrows but also transports us even to heaven. COMMENTARY ON THE PSALMS.[15]

---

[13]CTS 8:251-52* (CO 31:166).
[14]Selnecker, *Der gantze Psalter*, 1:88r-v.
[15]CTS 8:253-54* (CO 31:167).

18:1-50 THE LORD IS MY ROCK AND MY FORTRESS

To the choirmaster. A Psalm of David, the servant of the LORD, who addressed the words of this song to the LORD on the day when the LORD rescued him from the hand of all his enemies, and from the hand of Saul. He said:

¹ I love you, O LORD, my strength.
² The LORD is my rock and my fortress and my
  deliverer,
  my God, my rock, in whom I take refuge,
  my shield, and the horn of my salvation, my
  stronghold.
³ I call upon the LORD, who is worthy to be
  praised,
  and I am saved from my enemies.

⁴ The cords of death encompassed me;
  the torrents of destruction assailed me;ᵃ
⁵ the cords of Sheol entangled me;
  the snares of death confronted me.

⁶ In my distress I called upon the LORD;
  to my God I cried for help.
From his temple he heard my voice,
  and my cry to him reached his ears.

⁷ Then the earth reeled and rocked;
  the foundations also of the mountains
    trembled
  and quaked, because he was angry.
⁸ Smoke went up from his nostrils,ᵇ
  and devouring fire from his mouth;
  glowing coals flamed forth from him.
⁹ He bowed the heavens and came down;
  thick darkness was under his feet.
¹⁰ He rode on a cherub and flew;
  he came swiftly on the wings of the wind.
¹¹ He made darkness his covering, his canopy
    around him,
  thick clouds dark with water.
¹² Out of the brightness before him
  hailstones and coals of fire broke through his
    clouds.

¹³ The LORD also thundered in the heavens,
  and the Most High uttered his voice,
  hailstones and coals of fire.
¹⁴ And he sent out his arrows and scattered
    them;
  he flashed forth lightnings and routed them.
¹⁵ Then the channels of the sea were seen,
  and the foundations of the world were laid
    bare
at your rebuke, O LORD,
  at the blast of the breath of your nostrils.

¹⁶ He sent from on high, he took me;
  he drew me out of many waters.
¹⁷ He rescued me from my strong enemy
  and from those who hated me,
  for they were too mighty for me.
¹⁸ They confronted me in the day of my
    calamity,
  but the LORD was my support.
¹⁹ He brought me out into a broad place;
  he rescued me, because he delighted in me.

²⁰ The LORD dealt with me according to my
    righteousness;
  according to the cleanness of my hands he
    rewarded me.
²¹ For I have kept the ways of the LORD,
  and have not wickedly departed from my
    God.
²² For all his rulesᶜ were before me,
  and his statutes I did not put away from me.
²³ I was blameless before him,
  and I kept myself from my guilt.
²⁴ So the LORD has rewarded me according to
    my righteousness,
  according to the cleanness of my hands in
    his sight.

²⁵ With the merciful you show yourself merciful;
  with the blameless man you show yourself
    blameless;

²⁶ with the purified you show yourself pure;
  and with the crooked you make yourself
    seem tortuous.
²⁷ For you save a humble people,
  but the haughty eyes you bring down.
²⁸ For it is you who light my lamp;
  the Lord my God lightens my darkness.
²⁹ For by you I can run against a troop,
  and by my God I can leap over a wall.
³⁰ This God—his way is perfect;ᵈ
  the word of the Lord proves true;
  he is a shield for all those who take refuge
    in him.

³¹ For who is God, but the Lord?
  And who is a rock, except our God?—
³² the God who equipped me with strength
  and made my way blameless.
³³ He made my feet like the feet of a deer
  and set me secure on the heights.
³⁴ He trains my hands for war,
  so that my arms can bend a bow of bronze.
³⁵ You have given me the shield of your salvation,
  and your right hand supported me,
  and your gentleness made me great.
³⁶ You gave a wide place for my steps under me,
  and my feet did not slip.
³⁷ I pursued my enemies and overtook them,
  and did not turn back till they were consumed.
³⁸ I thrust them through, so that they were not
    able to rise;
  they fell under my feet.
³⁹ For you equipped me with strength for the
    battle;

you made those who rise against me sink
    under me.
⁴⁰ You made my enemies turn their backs to
    me,ᵉ
  and those who hated me I destroyed.
⁴¹ They cried for help, but there was none to
    save;
  they cried to the Lord, but he did not
    answer them.
⁴² I beat them fine as dust before the wind;
  I cast them out like the mire of the streets.

⁴³ You delivered me from strife with the people;
  you made me the head of the nations;
  people whom I had not known served me.
⁴⁴ As soon as they heard of me they obeyed me;
  foreigners came cringing to me.
⁴⁵ Foreigners lost heart
  and came trembling out of their fortresses.

⁴⁶ The Lord lives, and blessed be my rock,
  and exalted be the God of my salvation—
⁴⁷ the God who gave me vengeance
  and subdued peoples under me,
⁴⁸ who delivered me from my enemies;
  yes, you exalted me above those who rose
    against me;
  you rescued me from the man of violence.

⁴⁹ For this I will praise you, O Lord, among
    the nations,
  and sing to your name.
⁵⁰ Great salvation he brings to his king,
  and shows steadfast love to his anointed,
  to David and his offspring forever.

a Or terrified me   b Or in his wrath   c Or just decrees   d Or blameless   e Or You gave me my enemies' necks

Overview: A close variant of this lengthy psalm appears in 2 Samuel 22, where it is also attributed to David. It is a victory psalm, celebrating the king's triumph over his enemies by the power of God. The movement begins with a declaration of love for God, the psalmist's rock and refuge. After a brief remembrance of distress and a cry for help, God's rescue is recounted in powerful and vibrant storm imagery that resonates with other biblical accounts of God's warring might (e.g., Ps 29; Hab 3). The reformers marvel at the eloquence and power of the poetry, which plants the readers in the very midst of the scene. The psalm then extols the righteousness of David and the favor God sheds on him. The Lord trains the king's hand for war as he pursues his enemies and he is established over the nations. The psalm ends with praise for God's favor on David and his offspring forever.

This psalm offers Reformation commentators several opportunities for christological interpretation. When the psalmist speaks of the "cords of sheol," or "ropes of death" (Ps 18:4-5), Luther takes it to be a clear allusion to Christ's descent into Hades. But as he notes, the psalm speaks of despair, which poses a problem for attributing it to Christ. When the psalm depicts the king subduing the world (Ps 18:44-45), Calvin sees a type of Christ conquering the Gentiles and establishing his reign by the preaching of the gospel. And Melanchthon understands the afflictions and triumphs of David as a type of the passion and victory of Christ. As pastors, our commentators offer these examples to stir up believers to faith in God's promises, despite all appearances.

Our commentators also find numerous opportunities to draw out pastoral applications from the psalm. Calvin, for instance, notes that even when David is ensnared by death, he prays to the Lord as his God and is a model of faith's full persuasion. And when the psalmist speaks of God being merciful to the merciful, blameless to the blameless and pure to the pure, Calvin reminds us not to prejudge God but to wait until the end.

CHRIST'S KINGDOM PROCLAIMED THROUGH MASTERFUL POETRY. THEODORE BEZA: The occasion for which David composed this song of victory [*epinikion*] is clear from 2 Samuel 22 as well as the plain and evident title of this psalm. After he had conquered all his enemies and not only was his kingdom established in his own nation but it even extended far and wide beyond his nation, he was focused on this one thing alone: to proclaim that he did not reign to promote himself but to promote God's glory alone. And we must grant this, that we have no writing extant from the poets that flourishes with greater talent and eloquence when compared with this psalm—even if we only consider the phrasing! Now concerning the meaning itself, he describes his momentous perils in such a way that whoever reads them feels like he is in the very midst of them, whirling around him. In addition he depicts the glory of God in executing judgment and his divine majesty with such lofty style, it is as if we can feel the heavens and earth tremble while we are still reading! Finally, he narrates his victories in such a way that we seem to see his triumphs with our very eyes. These things he attributes to God alone in such way that he accepts absolutely no praise for himself. Likewise, on account of the Spirit of prophecy, he is certain that this kingdom—flourishing so well—is merely an image and likeness of that eternal kingdom of the Messiah who will be born of him. Thus, he marches right up to that and prophesies that all the people of the earth will welcome this King—like Paul's interpretation in Romans 15. PARAPHRASE OF PSALM 18.[1]

18:1-3 *I Love and Laud the Lord My Savior*

LET US BIND OURSELVES TO GOD WITH A CHAIN OF LOVE. JOHN CALVIN: Love to God is here laid down as constituting the principal part of true godliness. For there is no better way of serving God than to love him. No doubt, the service which we owe him is better expressed by the word *reverence*, that thus his majesty may prominently stand forth to our view in its infinite greatness. But as he requires nothing so expressly as to possess all the affections of our heart and to have them going out toward him, so there is no sacrifice which he values more than when we are bound fast to him by the chain of a free and spontaneous love. On the other hand, there is nothing in which his glory shines forth more conspicuously than in his free and sovereign goodness. Moses, therefore, when he meant to give a summary of the law, says, "And now, Israel, what does the Lord God ask from you but to love him?"

So in this way, David also intended to show that his thoughts and affections were not so intently fixed on the benefits of God as to be

---

[1]Beza, *Psalmorum Davidis*, 50-51 (cf. *Psalmes of Dauid*, 24-25); citing Rom 15:9-12.

ungrateful to him who was the author of them—a sin which has been too common in all ages. Even today we see how the greater part of humanity enjoy wholly at their ease the gifts of God without paying any regard to him, or, if they think of him at all, it is only to despise him. David, to prevent himself from falling into this ingratitude, in these words makes as it were a solemn vow: "Lord, because you are my strength, I will continue united and devoted to you by sincere love." COMMENTARY ON THE PSALMS.[2]

DAVID'S METAPHORIC LANGUAGE FOR GOD. SEBASTIAN MÜNSTER: In this psalm God is called a rock, a hilltop, a fortress, a barracks, a shield, a refuge, a *miśgab*, that is, a high place or asylum—and many other such names—because those who flee to him are absolutely secure. And "he has lifted up a horn of salvation among the Hebrews" in Luke's saying, and it is used for salvation and a sign of victory. For as the horn is the crown of horned animals, so also the highest divine deliverance is called the horn of salvation. THE TEMPLE OF THE LORD: 2 SAMUEL 22.[3]

PRAISE FOR SECURITY IN THE LORD. CARDINAL CAJETAN: He praises the Lord's blessings and at the same time expresses loudly his love toward God in this and in the following blessings. . . . "The Lord is my rock and my fortress." That is, my firm security, the source of both my steadfastness and my security, because fortresses render people secure, but only if they are on a rock. And therefore, it is set on a rock because rocks are steadfast, and it is likened to a fortress because fortresses are secure; this is so that you may understand that God is his source of strength not only on the inside but also on the outside, a rock, so to speak, and an edifice built on a rock. . . . The end result of both the strength and the rock and fortress is safety. COMMENTARY ON PSALM 18.[4]

"HORN" IS A MARTIAL METAPHOR. GIOVANNI DIODATI: "The horn," namely, my strength, valor, defense, and victory. A frequent phrase in Scripture, taken from horned beasts, or from the ancient custom of wearing horns made of iron or some other metal on their helmets, for a crest or military ornament; the raised horn was a sign of victory, and the horn beaten down a sign of being overcome. ANNOTATIONS ON PSALM 18:2.[5]

GOD'S TITLES ARE STRONG MEDICINE. JOHN CALVIN: Let us, therefore, learn from David's example, to apply for our own use those titles which are here attributed to God, and to apply them as an antidote against all the perplexities and distresses which may assail us. Or rather, let them be deeply imprinted on our memory, so that we may be able at once to repel to a distance whatever fear Satan may suggest to our mind. I give this exhortation, not only because we tremble under the calamities with which we are presently assailed, but also because we groundlessly conjure up in our own imaginations dangers as to the time to come and thus needlessly disquiet ourselves by the mere creations of fancy. COMMENTARY ON THE PSALMS.[6]

18:4-6 Snares of Sin, Death and the Devil

DO NOT TRUST APPEARANCES OR AFFECTIONS BUT THE WORD. NIKOLAUS SELNECKER: The cords of death are every trick and deceit by which some want to ensnare the pious, like what Saul and Absalom did to David, just as we lay out snares and booby traps for birds and game. All such things must be thwarted and the pious must remain safe. Therefore, he says, "My fear is indeed great, but I call on the Lord—beside him there is no comfort. To hope in human beings will accomplish nothing; to hope in God accomplishes everything. He answers me, although my heart says nothing but no. I do not respect what my flesh and

---

[2]CTS 8:260* (CO 31:170-71); citing Deut 10:12.
[3]Münster, *Miqdaš YHWH*, 619; citing Lk 1:69.
[4]Cajetan, *In Sacrae Scripturae Expositionem*, 3:62.

[5]Diodati, Pious Annotations, Ss2r*.
[6]CTS 8:262* (CO 31:171).

blood say to me, but instead what I hear in his temple. And I respect his Word, to which I adhere and by which I abide. I experience that I am unable to lack anything, no matter what my reason or the world, enemies, heretics or fanatics may say. Everything depends on his Word. On it I trust and will not be put to shame. God be praised. Amen." THE WHOLE PSALTER.[7]

CHRIST EXPERIENCED GRIEF. MARTIN LUTHER: Some take this in the literal sense of the words, "the ropes of death," that is, the bonds that held Christ three days in death, and "the ropes of hell," that is, the bonds that held his soul in hell for three days. This seems to be the sense of Psalm 16, which says that his soul was in hell. But here he says that he endured even the sorrows of death, which is what the aforementioned psalm also seems to be affirming when it says, "You will fill me with joy," as if to say: "I am now in the sorrow of death, or, at any rate, as the doctors say, I am rejoicing and grieving at the same time. But when you shall have made the ways of life known to me by resurrecting me, then you will altogether fill me with joy, even by removing those sorrows." Peter, too, bears witness to this in Acts when he says, "God raised him up, having loosed the pangs of death," or hell.

Therefore he even sorrowed in death, and God loosed these sorrows by raising him. For it does not seem that the sorrows of this life should be spoken of as the sorrows of death. And according to them this is what it means: "The ropes of death have surrounded me (that is, they have held me and were stronger than I), and the torrents of Belial, or the devil, confounded me (that is, strong devils have utterly terrified me in death), the ropes of hell have surrounded me (behold, it was not only death that vanquished and held him, but also hell with its ropes) and the snares of death confronted me." That is to say, concerning the ropes of which he states above that they had surrounded him, he here confesses that they have vanquished him, because they held him as one

who has no power to withstand, which is, nevertheless, what he wanted. And I do not know how anyone could explain this statement. I firmly believe that Christ did not feel the punishments and grief of the damned, who are the children of despair, but that Christ always hoped. Nevertheless, these words testify that he was not altogether without grief. And if there had been no other grief, yet because he was held by the ropes and in the power of death and hell, this in itself was without doubt loathsome and irksome to his most noble soul, for without putting off the substance he desired freedom and his own brilliant glorification. Yet it is exceedingly rash to deny that his soul was held captive in hell and to go against so clear a Bible passage. FIRST PSALMS LECTURES (1513–1515).[8]

DAVID'S POETIC DESCRIPTION OF HIS ANGUISH. SEBASTIAN MÜNSTER: This expression— "the torrents of destruction"—is metaphorical. By it, tyrants' violent persecution is to be understood; such persecution is compared with a flood of waters. Almost the same idea follows: "The sorrows of hell enveloped me." The sense is this: "Such sorrows weaken me in every way, so that they could take my life and put me in the grave. Nowhere is the snare and noose of death not set for me. But God alone is my refuge; he will deliver me from all these things." David's enemies' fury is so insufferable that when he fights them, it seems that heaven and earth reel because of them. THE TEMPLE OF THE LORD: 2 SAMUEL 22.[9]

LIKE DAVID, LET NOTHING HINDER YOUR PRAYER. JOHN CALVIN: It was a very evident proof of uncommon faith in David, when, being almost plunged into the gulf of death, he lifted up his heart to heaven by prayer. Let us therefore learn that such an example is set before our eyes so that no calamities, however great and oppressive, may hinder us from praying or create an aversion to it.

---

[7]Selnecker, _Der gantze Psalter_, 1:94v.

[8]LW 10:115-16* (WA 3:121); citing Ps 16:10, 11; Acts 2:24.
[9]Münster, _Miqdaš YHWH_, 620.

It was prayer which brought to David the fruits or wonderful effects of which he speaks a little after, and from this it appears still more clearly that his deliverance was effected by the power of God.

In saying that he cried, he means the ardor and earnestness of affection which he had in prayer. Again, by calling God "his God," he separates himself from the gross despisers of God, or hypocrites, who, when constrained by necessity, call on the divine Majesty in a confused and tumultuous manner but do not come to God familiarly and with a pure heart, as they know nothing of his fatherly favor and goodness. When, therefore, as we approach God, faith goes before to illumine the way, giving us the full persuasion that he is our Father. Then is the gate opened, and we may converse freely with him and he with us. COMMENTARY ON THE PSALMS.[10]

18:7-19 God Descends in Mystery and Tumult

MYSTERIOUS MATTERS REQUIRE MYSTERIOUS SPEECH. THE ENGLISH ANNOTATIONS: This verse inclusive to verse 15 is not to be taken as a simple or historical account of what happened, but as a poetic description of God's presence and—in his powerful help and assistance—concurrence in David's conquests. The Scripture—even where no poetry is otherwise suspected—is full of such poetic, or more properly, sublime descriptions and expressions, far above the strain of either the most sublime poets or orators. In this way, the prophets speak often of Christ, the Son of God, and his coming into the world—a high subject indeed, and well-deserving of the highest expressions, although in the manner of its execution, in outward appearance, a deep mystery of humiliation. And they do this in many other passages. This is not understood by the Jews and has been a great occasion of their—and many others'—unbelief. ANNOTATIONS ON PSALM 18:7.[11]

THE MAJESTY OF THE AUTHOR OF NATURE. JOHN CALVIN: David, convinced that the aid of God, which he had experienced, was of such a character that it was impossible for him to extol it sufficiently and as it deserved, sets forth an image of it in the sky and the earth, as if he had said, "It has been as visible as the changes which give different appearances to the sky and the earth." If natural things always flowed in an even and uniform course, the power of God would not be so perceptible. But when he changes the face of the sky by sudden rain or by loud thunder or by dreadful tempests, those who before were, as it were, asleep and insensible must necessarily be awakened and be tremblingly conscious of the existence of a presiding God. Such sudden and unforeseen changes manifest more clearly the presence of the great Author of nature.

No doubt, when the sky is unclouded and tranquil, we see in it sufficient evidences of the majesty of God, but as human beings will not stir up their minds to reflect on that majesty until it comes nearer to them, David, the more powerfully to affect us, recounts the sudden changes by which we are usually moved and dismayed and introduces God at one time clothed with a dark cloud; at another, throwing the air into confusion by tempests; now rending it by the boisterous violence of winds; now launching the lightning; and darting down hailstones and thunderbolts. In short, the object of the psalmist is to show that the God who, as often as he pleases, causes all parts of the world to tremble by his power, when he intended to manifest himself as the deliverer of David, was known as openly and by signs as evident as if he had displayed his power in all the creatures both above and beneath. COMMENTARY ON THE PSALMS.[12]

THESE WORDS ARE TO BE CONTEMPLATED, NOT CALCULATED. MOÏSE AMYRAUT: This is indeed poetry; nevertheless, it is the sort that no poet would have thought to use or dared to write, unless stirred up by some extraordinary breath and

---

[10]CTS 8:266* (CO 31:173).
[11]Downame, ed., *Annotations*, 6A2v*.
[12]CTS 8:267-68* (CO 31:174).

inspiration of God's Spirit. And concerning the verses that follow the same judgment should be made. Because the universe consists of heaven and the elements, and here both heaven and the elements are said to tremble, the confusion of the entire universe is indicated. Now this is not like what we observe in a proof, which should be examined very diligently and scrupulously . . . but instead this should be considered more thickly as proceeding from poetic and prophetic inspiration. ANNOTATION ON PSALM 18:9.[13]

BY "CHERUB" DAVID ALLUDES TO THE TEMPLE AND GOD'S PRESENCE AMONG HIS PEOPLE. JOHN CALVIN: David does not, however, simply represent God as the governor of the winds, who drives them by his power wherever he pleases; he at the same time tells us that he rides on a cherub, to teach us that the very violence of the winds is governed by angels as God has ordained. We know that the angels were represented under the figure of the cherubim. David, therefore, I have no doubt, here intended to make an allusion to the ark of the covenant. In proposing for our consideration the power of God as manifested in the wonders of nature, he does it in such a manner as all the time to have an eye to the temple, where he knew God had made himself known in a peculiar manner to the children of Abraham. He therefore celebrates God not only as creator of the world, but as he who entered into covenant with Israel and chose for himself a holy dwelling place in the midst of that people. COMMENTARY ON THE PSALMS.[14]

THE DREADFUL POWER OF THE LORD GIVES DAVID JOY. WOLFGANG MUSCULUS: Let us have this understanding, whenever David makes mention of this storm with such joy that he has exulted over it with his whole heart, because the subject matter itself compels him and it was done for his own liberation. Let us have this understanding then, because the enemies were not beginning

any undertaking without the highest rashness, as if there were no one in heaven who is able and willing to resist their attempts and evil plots. For what more pleasant thing could happen to the faithful slave running a risk for the sake of the glory of his own master than if he should be freed from that risk by a powerful hand, especially because it is not so much by his own name but on account of the revealed power and declared majesty of his own master? I do not doubt that such people are also found in these most recent times, those who, crying at other times because of the incorrigible impiety of mortals and the impunity of the wicked, exult in a wonderful way in tempests that arise, and suddenly setting aside their tears, call on the power of God that is despised more than is right, although meanwhile the rest are almost scared out of their wits by anxiety. Therefore, let us also live in such a way in this age, so that the declaration of the power of God, however dreadful it may be in itself, may be a joy to us, not a horror. Then we may compare the universal power of all the princes of this age with the one power of this sort, and whatever is admired by this world may disappear. COMMENTARY ON THE PSALMS.[15]

18:20-30 The Lord Is Merciful with the Merciful but Crooked with the Crooked

THE PIOUS ARE NEVER ABANDONED. MARTIN BUCER: In these verses, he piously declares his own blamelessness and zeal for righteousness, by which he would show in himself that God by no means forsakes those zealous for righteousness and in due time recompenses with the desired reward. HOLY PSALMS.[16]

DOES DAVID MEAN THAT GOD'S FAVOR IS MERITED? JOHN CALVIN: David might seem at first sight to contradict himself; for, while a little before he declared that all the blessings which he possessed were to be traced to the good pleasure of

---

[13]Amyraut, *Paraphrasis in Psalmos Davidis*, 65-66.
[14]CTS 8:271-72* (CO 31:176).

[15]Musculus, *In Psalterium Commentarii*, 263.
[16]Bucer, *Sacrorum Psalmorum*, 113; citing Ps 4:2.

God, he now boasts that God rendered to him a just recompense. But if we remember for what purpose he connects these commendations of his own integrity with the good pleasure of God, it will be easy to reconcile these apparently conflicting statements. He has before declared that God was the sole author and originator of the hope of coming to the kingdom which he entertained and that he had not been elevated to it by the suffrages of human beings, nor had he rushed forward to it through the mere impulse of his own mind but accepted it because such was the will of God. Now he adds, in the second place, that he had yielded faithful obedience to God and had never turned aside from his will.

Both these things were necessary. First, God should previously show his favor freely toward David in choosing him to be king. Second, David, on the other hand, should, with an obedient spirit and a pure conscience, receive the kingdom which God thus freely gave him; and further, that whatever the wicked might attempt, with the view of overthrowing or shaking his faith, he should nevertheless continue to adhere to the direct course of his calling. Thus, then, we see that these two statements, so far from disagreeing with each other, admirably harmonize. COMMENTARY ON THE PSALMS.[17]

THE LORD INVERTS THE AFFLICTIONS OF THE PIOUS AND THE CELEBRATIONS OF THE IMPIOUS. MARTIN LUTHER: "With the holy you will be holy" can be understood in this way. God, in dealing with the perverse person who perverts everything, also perverts him by turning everything for him into the opposite of what he hoped for. Even so, in dealing with the saints, God turns everything to good contrary to what they feared, so that what seemed evil and unfavorable to the saints will be proved to have been the very best, and what is propitious and choice to the wicked, God subsequently turns into the most unfavorable thing and the opposite of what they hoped

for. . . . For such a person despises spiritual goods and loves the physical. He is perverse who substitutes the letter for the spirit, like . . . carnal people; he is holy who puts the spirit in place of the letter, like spiritual people. FIRST PSALMS LECTURES (1513–1515).[18]

GOD GOES TO DRASTIC MEASURES TO ROUSE SINNERS. JOHN CALVIN: The last clause of verse 26—where it is said that God behaves perversely with the perverse—although it seems to be harsh, it nevertheless does not imply anything absurd. Indeed not without the best reason does the Holy Spirit use this manner of speaking, in order to rouse hypocrites and crass despisers of God from their torpor. For we see that whenever Scripture proclaims the stern and dreadful judgments of God, whenever God himself warns of his terrible vengeance, how securely all such people ignore these proclamations. Therefore, this brutish and quasi-monstrous stupidity forces God to fashion new forms of speech and, as it were, to clothe himself with a different character. COMMENTARY ON THE PSALMS.[19]

MAINTAIN A GOOD CONSCIENCE. NIKOLAUS SELNECKER: Until now, the prophet has preached about a good conscience. And we are to remember such a sermon to be sure, so that we may learn what a good conscience is and when it manifests itself, namely, in faith, in vocation, in life, in persistence and during anxieties of death. When it comes to faith or doctrine, we must always be sure that we have correct doctrine concerning God's nature and will and our salvation, so that we do not get mixed up with blasphemous errors and heresies. The conscience cannot be quiet or good where there is false doctrine. We should also pursue our vocation with diligence and faithfulness; otherwise our conscience is good for nothing, even if it seems to be satisfied and peaceful and quiet for a while. In life we should always guard ourselves against

---

[17]CTS 8:279* (CO 31:179-80).

[18]LW 10:123-24* (WA 3:127).
[19]CTS 8:286* (CO 31:183).

offensive and public vices: gluttony, whoring, greed, pride, usury, adultery and other sins that are against conscience. We should serve our neighbor as much as possible, according to the measure of the second table of the Ten Commandments.

Because, however, a good conscience is not only to be maintained for one, two or three hours but for the time of our whole life, a truly Christian *constantia* or persistence is needed with respect to doctrine, vocation and life. Such persistence is eventually needed the most in the anxieties of death, so that the person, although he cannot boast of anything before God, nevertheless shall say with beloved David: "I have a good conscience. I am not godless before my God. His commandments I do not reject." As Luther of blessed memory said on his deathbed: "Lord Jesus Christ, I sought your glory, this you know, and I did not begin or defend anything against you and your Word. In this I take comfort. You have I preached and praised, you know it well. I was concerned about you and nothing else." Such a conscience is glorious to God and all angels and keeps true, right faith and comfort in mind and heart, while a doubtful, evil conscience cannot have a confident, persistent comfort, as we not only see in the example of flagrant persecutors of true doctrine and all great heretics, but also we occasionally experience this with naive people, who fall somewhat willfully. THE WHOLE PSALTER.[20]

DO NOT PREJUDGE ANYONE OR ANYTHING. JOHN CALVIN: This verse contains the correction of a mistake into which we are very ready to fall. As experience shows that the merciful are often severely afflicted and the sincere involved in troubles of a very distressing description, to prevent any from regarding the statement as false that God deals mercifully with the merciful, David admonishes us that we must wait for the end. For although God does not immediately run to rescue the good, yet, after having exercised their patience for a time, he lifts them up from the dust on which

they lay prostrate and brings effectual relief to them, even when they were in despair. From this it follows that we ought only to judge the issue by how God shows himself merciful toward the merciful and pure toward the pure. If he did not keep his people in suspense and waiting long for deliverance from affliction, it could not be said that it is his prerogative to save the afflicted. And it is no small consolation, in the midst of our adversities, to know that God purposely delays to communicate his assistance, which otherwise is quite prepared, that we may experience his goodness in saving us after we have been afflicted and brought low. Nor ought we to reckon the wrongs which are inflicted on us too bitter, because they excite God to show toward us his favor which brings salvation. COMMENTARY ON THE PSALMS.[21]

18:31-45 The True Rock Establishes and Equips Me

DAVID DESIRES JUSTICE BUT NOT BLOOD-SHED. JOHN CALVIN: We are likely to think that David here speaks too much after the manner of a soldier, in declaring that he will not cease from the work of slaughter until he has destroyed all his enemies, or rather that he has forgotten the gentleness and meekness which ought to shine in all true believers and in which they should resemble their heavenly Father. But, as he attempted nothing without the command of God, and as his affections were governed and regulated by the Holy Spirit, we may be assured that these are not the words of a man who was cruel and who took pleasure in shedding blood, but of a man who faithfully executed the judgment which God had committed to him. And, indeed, we know that he was so distinguished for gentleness of disposition as to abhor the shedding of even a single drop of blood, except insofar as duty and the necessity of his office required. We must, therefore, take into consideration David's vocation and his pure zeal,

---

[20]Selnecker, *Der gantze Psalter*, 1:99r-v. [21]CTS 8:287-88* (CO 31:184).

which was free from all the flesh's agitation. Moreover, it should be particularly attended to that the psalmist here calls those his enemies whose indomitable and infatuated obstinacy merited and called forth such vengeance from God. As he represented the person of Christ, he inflicted the punishment of death only on those who were so inflexible that they could not be reduced to order by the exercise of a mild and humane authority. And this in itself shows that there was nothing in which he more delighted than to pardon those who repented and reformed themselves. He thus resembled Christ, who gently allures all people to repentance but breaks in pieces, with his iron rod, those who obstinately resist him to the last. COMMENTARY ON THE PSALMS.[22]

THE CALL OF THE NATIONS. NIKOLAUS SELNECKER: We should always consider what David in the Spirit especially respected, namely, that he, with these words here, mainly looked to and prophesied about the Lord Christ and his kingdom. For surely the Spirit of God spoke about Christ, whom his own people opposed and whom they did not want as their king. But they would be rejected and Christ would become a Head and King of all the Gentiles in the whole world. This happened after his resurrection and ascension, when through the gospel he was proclaimed, confessed and accepted as King in all the world. . . .

Whenever the call of the Gentiles is proclaimed in holy Scripture there are three things which we learn. First, the promise of grace belongs to all people—no one is excluded, as it is written, "In your seed all the people or Gentiles of the earth will be blessed." For God shows no partiality. Second, the kingdom of Christ is no worldly kingdom but rather a spiritual one; it is not bound to Mosaic ceremonies, laws, nation, place or temple but rather wherever and whenever we honor God in the confession of his Son, there true worship takes place. Third, the lovingkindness of God is recognized which gathers a church to him out of

the poor human race, of Jews and Gentiles, without any partiality. . . . "For those who are baptized into Christ have put on Christ, and here there is neither Jew nor Greek, neither servant nor free, neither man nor woman, but rather we are all one in Christ Jesus." For if the dear sun daily rises and shines both on the pious and the wicked, how much more will Christ—who is the true Sun and true eternal light, the radiance of his Father—rise in his dear church and shine, lifted up on high, and illuminate all human beings? Thus he came into the world, especial because he is the true heavenly manna that should be collected by us all, great and small, young and old. These three things we should always consider as often as anything is said about the call of the Gentiles. THE WHOLE PSALTER.[23]

TYPOLOGICALLY THIS VERSE DEMONSTRATES CHRIST'S CONQUEST THROUGH PREACHING. JOHN CALVIN: This applies more truly to the person of Christ, who, by means of his Word, subdues the world to himself, and, at the simple hearing of his name, makes those obedient to him who before had been rebels against him. As David was intended to be a type of Christ, God subjected to his authority distant nations, and such as before had been unknown to Israel insofar as familiar intercourse was concerned. But that was only a prelude, and, as it were, preparatory to the dominion promised to Christ, the boundaries of which must be extended to the uttermost ends of the earth. Similarly, David had acquired to himself so great a name by arms and warlike prowess that many of his enemies, subdued by fear, submitted themselves to him. And in this God exhibited a type of the conquest which Christ would make of the Gentiles, who, by the preaching of the gospel alone, were subdued and brought voluntarily to submit to his dominion; for the obedience of faith in which the dominion of Christ is founded "comes by hearing." COMMENTARY ON THE PSALMS.[24]

---

[22]CTS 8:294-95* (CO 31:187-88).

[23]Selnecker, *Der gantze Psalter*, 1:106r, 106v-107r; citing Gen 22:18; Acts 10:34; Gal 3:27-28; Mt 5:45; Mal 4:2; Heb 1:3.

[24]CTS 8:300-301* (CO 31:190-91); citing Rom 10:17.

18:46-50 *God Delivers Me from Violence*

VENGEANCE ONLY AGAINST THE OBSTINATE.
JOHN CALVIN: It may seem at first sight strange that
God should arm his own people to execute vengeance; but as I have previously shown you, we ought
always to remember David's vocation. He was not a
private person, but being endued with royal power
and authority, the judgment which he executed was
enjoined on him by God. If a person, on receiving
injury, breaks forth to avenge himself, he usurps the
office of God. Therefore, it is rash and impious for
private individuals to retaliate the injuries which have
been inflicted on them. With respect to kings and
magistrates, God, who declares that vengeance
belongs to him, in arming them with the sword
constitutes them the ministers and executioners of
his vengeance. David, therefore, has put the word
vengeance for the just punishments which it was
lawful for him to inflict by the commandment of
God, provided he was led under the influence of a
zeal duly regulated by the Holy Spirit, and not under
the influence of the impetuosity of the flesh.

Unless this moderation is exemplified in performing the duties of their calling, it is in vain for kings to
boast that God has committed to them the charge of
taking vengeance; seeing it is not less unwarrantable
for a person to abuse, according to his own fancy and
the lust of the flesh, the sword which he is allowed to
use, than to seize it without the command of God.
The church militant, which is under the standard of
Christ, has no permission to execute vengeance,
except against those who obstinately refuse to be
reclaimed. We are commanded to try to overcome
our enemies by doing them good and to pray for
their salvation. It becomes us, therefore, at the same
time, to desire that they may be brought to repentance and to a right state of mind, until it appear
beyond all doubt that they are irrecoverably and
hopelessly depraved. In the meantime, in regard to
vengeance, it must be left to God, that we may not be
carried headlong to execute it before the time.
COMMENTARY ON THE PSALMS.[25]

EVEN THE CONDEMNED SERVE GOD'S GLORY.
HANS HAS VON HALLSTATT: Though they have
nothing good in them, he works in the same way
through the damned to his honor and glory. For
they have been ordained to demonstrate God's
justice on themselves, just as we have been
ordained to demonstrate his fatherly mercy on us.
For he is God, who must be acknowledged as
mighty and powerful. Because these things must
be revealed, it is necessary that something must
be available to demonstrate them. Thus the great
powers and strengths of this world exist, against
which God's might and omnipotence should be
shown. God brings forth his vessels of wrath,
which he ordained as a means to exercise his
justice on them. When he chooses to reveal this,
he has a servant, Satan, whom he uses through
his omnipotence in order to awaken such things
in the damned, which then erupt from within
them. KUNSTBUCH: CONCERNING THE COM-
FORT OF CHRISTIANS.[26]

**DAVID DIRECTS US TO CHRIST'S SUFFERING
AND VICTORY.** PHILIPP MELANCHTHON: The
afflictions and victories of David are a type of the
passion and victory of Christ; thus the psalm
itself does not speak about David alone but
simultaneously signifies both the afflictions and
victory of Christ. And its proper end reveals
Christ, whom the priests, princes and especially
the multitude persecutes with an awful fury and
acts so that he will be killed. And like these
treacherous citizens, the church is collected and
joined to him from the Gentiles; he truly is the
head of the Gentiles, that is to say, of the entire,
gathered church from the seed of Abraham and
the Gentiles, bestowing the eternal life which
David could not bestow. Therefore even when we
recite this psalm for the deliverances which
happened for us, just as God performed many
deliverances in every age, yet we should simultaneously think about Christ's afflictions and
victories that are signified: indeed, we should

---

[25]CTS 8:304-5* (CO 31:192-93). [26]CRR 12:444-45*; citing Rom 9:15, 22.

know that our calling on him and thanksgiving pleases God because it is joined to Christ's calling on him and thanksgiving, who suffered for us and gives us the benefits of his victories. When Paul was delivered when he was struggling with beasts, the kindness stems from the victory of Christ, that is, because Christ conquered so that he may redeem and gather the eternal church; thus he helps Paul and others who call on him by faith. Even though David recites these things concerning himself, nevertheless he was looking toward the coming of Christ, whom he thought would have similar afflictions and glorious victories. Thus immediately after the recitation of this psalm in the history of David, David's last words follow, as the text says, in which he prophesies as clearly as possible concerning the coming of Christ. COMMENTS ON THE PSALMS.[27]

RELENT, O GOD, FOR THE GLORY OF YOUR NAME. NIKOLAUS SELNECKER:

> Priest: *Call on me in times of distress.*
> Response: *And I will save you and you will praise me.*

Almighty Lord God, we see and hear your omnipotence and your wrath. We acknowledge and confess that we are poor, miserable sinners, and we ask you that you would forgive us our iniquities for the sake of your Son Jesus Christ our Lord—yes, and count neither old nor new guilt. For wherever you enter into judgment with your servants, we are ruined not only in health, harvest, grain, goods and temporal wellbeing, but also entirely and completely in body and soul. Spare us, O Lord God, for the sake of your name, so that we might still laud and praise you for a long time to come in this life. Give us good weather and our daily bread for the preservation of your church in this land, for the sake of your Son Jesus Christ our Lord, Amen. THE WHOLE PSALTER: A COLLECT FOR PSALM 18.[28]

---

[27]MO 13:1044; citing 2 Sam 22; 23:1-7.

[28]Selnecker, *Der gantze Psalter,* 1:108v.

19:1-14 THE LAW OF THE LORD IS PERFECT

To the choirmaster. A Psalm of David.

¹ The heavens declare the glory of God,
　　and the sky above[a] proclaims his handiwork.
² Day to day pours out speech,
　　and night to night reveals knowledge.
³ There is no speech, nor are there words,
　　whose voice is not heard.
⁴ Their voice[b] goes out through all the earth,
　　and their words to the end of the world.
In them he has set a tent for the sun,
⁵ which comes out like a bridegroom leaving
　　　his chamber,
　　and, like a strong man, runs its course
　　　with joy.
⁶ Its rising is from the end of the heavens,
　　and its circuit to the end of them,
　　and there is nothing hidden from its heat.

⁷ The law of the LORD is perfect,[c]
　　reviving the soul;
the testimony of the LORD is sure,
　　making wise the simple;
⁸ the precepts of the LORD are right,
　　rejoicing the heart;

the commandment of the LORD is pure,
　　enlightening the eyes;
⁹ the fear of the LORD is clean,
　　enduring forever;
the rules[d] of the LORD are true,
　　and righteous altogether.
¹⁰ More to be desired are they than gold,
　　even much fine gold;
sweeter also than honey
　　and drippings of the honeycomb.
¹¹ Moreover, by them is your servant warned;
　　in keeping them there is great reward.

¹² Who can discern his errors?
　　Declare me innocent from hidden faults.
¹³ Keep back your servant also from presump-
　　　tuous sins;
　　let them not have dominion over me!
Then I shall be blameless,
　　and innocent of great transgression.

¹⁴ Let the words of my mouth and the medita-
　　　tion of my heart
　　be acceptable in your sight,
　　O LORD, my rock and my redeemer.

a Hebrew *the expanse*; compare Genesis 1:6–8　　b Or *Their measuring line*　　c Or *blameless*　　d Or *just decrees*

OVERVIEW: The reformers focus on three things in this psalm: God's glory as revealed through nature, God's names and the relation between law and gospel. First, all our commentators agree that nature, especially the celestial movements, witness magnificently to God's glory. While this is enough to indict human beings of ingratitude toward their Creator, it is not enough to proclaim the fullness of the divine relationship with humanity. The office of the Word must add the command to repent and the promise of forgiveness and life. Second, this psalm—as in so many other places in Scripture—is full of names and epithets for God. These various names (e.g., Sun) comfort grieved consciences and oppressed believers, reminding them of various facets of Christ's person and office in whom the love of the Father is openly revealed. Finally, the question of the relationship between the law and the gospel lurks beneath the surface of our commentators' considerations of this psalm. Implicit for each of these exegetes is their commitment to the distinguishable but inseparable union of law and gospel. To sever this tension would be to corrupt and lose them both. Together they work the Lord's purposes in human beings, convicting them of their sin and re-forming them in Christ's image through union with him in his death, resurrection and ascension.

THE HOLY SPIRIT SCHOOLS US IN GOD'S WORD. RUDOLF GWALTHER: This psalm is composed to laud and praise God's law and Word.... So, here the Holy Spirit teaches us what great good deeds God demonstrates through his Word. In contrast to this, he causes us to recognize our ungratefulness, through which we despise these good deeds. And he tells us how we should hear, read and contemplate God's Word. THE PSALTER.[1]

THE HEAVENS AND SCRIPTURES DECLARE GOD'S MAJESTY. THEODORE BEZA: This psalm teaches us the sum of all true divinity, whose purpose is for us to be acquainted with both God himself and his divine worship, by which we become partakers of eternal life. Thus, he says that human beings are taught God's glory and majesty, that is—as Paul interprets it—his eternal power and divinity, by observing the heavens, by the succession of days and nights and especially by the golden splendor of the sun, which shines over the whole world with an indescribable course, so that no one can pretend to be ignorant of it.... The prophet adds that human beings require a far more perfect declaration which will clearly declare those same things as well as God's will. Finally, this should calm our consciences—ill from the deadly wounds of our sins—as the apostle eloquently teaches in 1 Corinthians 1. Now these things are taught to us in no other way, Paul affirms, than by that heavenly doctrine which was passed down to us by the apostle himself, sealing our souls with that true wisdom, not only with words but also with the very thing itself, so that it would gladden us with eternal joy. And this power belongs entirely to the gospel. It is clear that David speaks principally of this part of the written Word of God, and he addresses the free forgiveness of sins which at that time was merely silhouetted by the legal ceremonies but now has been exhibited to us quite lavishly and

clearly, both by Christ himself and by the apostolic writings. PARAPHRASE OF PSALM 19.[2]

19:1-6 *Creation Proclaims God's Glory*

DAVID USES COMMON IDIOMS, NOT PRECISE SCIENTIFIC LANGUAGE. THE ENGLISH ANNOTATIONS: Now what is spoken here about the sun is not said according to the precision of astronomy—no more than many other things in Scripture—but instead according to external appearances and common judgments. Though the motion or conversion of it—if astronomically considered—be equal and constant, still to us, when the sun first appears, it seems first to rise and move across the sky which presupposes a resting place, if not a new birth (as some used to think). ANNOTATIONS ON PSALM 19:1-6.[3]

ALL CREATION KNOWS AND PROCLAIMS ITS EXISTENCE IS FROM GOD ALONE. JACOBUS ARMINIUS: God is called "Being itself," because he offers himself to the understanding as an object of knowledge. But all beings, both visible and invisible, corporeal and incorporeal, proclaim aloud that they have derived the beginning of their essence and condition from something other than themselves. They do not have their own proper existence until they have it from another. All of them utter speech, according to the saying of the royal prophet: "The heavens declare the glory of God and the firmament shows his handiwork." That is, the firmament sounds aloud as with a trumpet and proclaims that it is "the work of the right hand of the Most High." Among created objects you may discover many signs indicating "that they derive from some other source all that they themselves possess," more strongly than "that they have an existence in the number and scale of beings." Nor is this matter surprising, because created things are always nearer to nothing than to their Creator, from whom they

---

[1]Gwalther, *Der Psalter*, 28v.

[2]Beza, *Psalmes of Dauid*, 29-30* (*Psalmorum Davidis*, 62); citing Rom 1:19-20; 1 Cor 1:21-25.
[3]Downame, ed., *Annotations*, 6A3v* (cf. CTS 8:315-16; CO 31:198).

are removed to a distance that is infinite and separated by infinite space. While, by properties that are only finite, they are distinguished from nothing, the primeval womb from which they sprung and into which they may fall back again, but they can never be raised to a divine equality with God their Maker. Therefore it was rightly said by the ancient pagans, "Of Jove all things are full." ORATION 2: THE OBJECT OF THEOLOGY.[4]

WITHOUT GOD'S WORD NATURAL OBSERVATION INSUFFICIENTLY DECLARES GOD'S GLORY. PHILIPP MELANCHTHON: If ideas have been obtained from the celestial motions' order without the Word of God, it does not give birth to the church; the voice of the gospel must be added to these movements. For those philosophical ideas are even known by the Gentiles, even as far as the smallest particle of God's law, but this does not include the gospel about the forgiveness of sins. Therefore, let us firmly uphold this belief about the propagation of the gospel and the advent and victories of Christ that this psalm proclaims. . . . These verses must be understood as "the heavens declare the glory of God," that is, everywhere the voice of the gospel is scattered. Likewise, "day to day they pour forth speech," that is, the voice of the gospel abides through all eternity, nor is it suppressed by any power of the impious. There is no utterance or speech in which their voices are not heard, that is, the gospel resounds in all languages scattered among all peoples. And why has this preaching been established? To display Christ the Son of God. For this, a tent is placed in the church like for the sun in the sky. Here Christ is made known—here is the fountain of light as the sun is the fountain of bodily light. COMMENTS ON THE PSALMS.[5]

WITHOUT GOD'S WORD NATURAL OBSERVATION SUFFICIENTLY PROCLAIMS GOD'S GLORY. JOHN CALVIN: If, indeed, we were as attentive as

we ought to be, even one day would suffice to witness to God's glory for us, and even one night would be enough to perform the same office for us. But when we see the sun and the moon performing their daily revolutions—the sun by day appears over our heads and the moon follows in its successions, the sun ascends by degrees, while at the same time it comes nearer to us, and then it changes its course so as to slip away from us little by little—and from this we see that the length of days and nights is regulated and that the variation of their length is arranged according to a law so uniform that they return at the same time every year. This is a far clearer testimony to the glory of God. David, therefore, not unjustly, declares that even if God should not speak a single word to human beings, nevertheless the orderly and proper succession of days and nights eloquently proclaims the glory of God. Nor is there now any pretext for ignorance available to human beings. For because the days and nights discharge the teaching office so well, we are able to acquire sufficient knowledge of God's glory from their instruction. COMMENTARY ON THE PSALMS.[6]

HUMAN UNDERSTANDING REQUIRES REPETITION. CARDINAL CAJETAN: In the succession of days and nights, an idea about the heavens is generated in us. Because one day or one night is not sufficient. But what is seen in one night about the stars is only the beginning of understanding another night; what is seen in one summer is only the beginning of understanding others; what is seen in one eclipse is only the beginning of understanding another—so it is concerning similar heavenly motions, appearances, events and effects. COMMENTARY ON PSALM 19.[7]

SPIRITUAL INTERPRETATION OF THESE VERSES. DIRK PHILIPS: This is a prophecy of the gospel that went out through the apostles and is preached in the whole world, as Paul testifies. Therefore these

[4]Arminius, *Works*, 1:58-59*.
[5]MO 13:1045-46.
[6]CTS 8:310-11* (CO 31:195-96).
[7]Cajetan, *In Sacrae Scripturae Expositionem*, 3:69-70.

heavens, which declare the glory of God in which the sun has a tabernacle or dwelling and shines over everything, are the apostles and all true teachers and Christians who proclaim God's Word and in whom God has his dwelling. Here is also the new moon, and it illuminates these new heavens, namely, that firm word of prophecy that shines there in a dark corner. Here are also the new stars, the righteous ones, who instruct others to salvation, who shine as the brightness of the heavens and as the stars eternally. Here through the brightness of the divine Word and hereafter through the glory of Christ in the heavenly beings. . . .

Thus the creation of the heavens and the earth is spiritually restored in Christ until the time that the perfect transformation out of the perishable into that eternal imperishable and glorified state takes place, and all believers shall inherit and possess the new heavens and new earth—which God will create and we await and in which righteousness shall dwell. THE ENCHIRIDION: CONCERNING SPIRITUAL RESTITUTION.[8]

CHRIST IS THE TRUE SUN. MARTIN LUTHER: It is David's habit that he usually speaks first with veiled and vague words and then with plain words. Here he explicitly teaches that it will come to be that God's grace will be preached everywhere. . . . Here David returns to the vague description and he mixes—as we love to do in joyous poems—the vague and veiled words together wonderfully. And with the sun, in a veiled manner, he wants to reveal and indicate Christ, for he previously made the heavens. Thus, he now calls the Prince of heaven the sun and reveals by this that his kingdom should thrive under the entire heavens. Now he says that "for the sun a tent has been made in the heavens." That is, that Christ will reign and rule in every land that will believe in Christ. The holy Christian church will be as wide as the world is. EXEGESIS OF PSALM 19.[9]

CHRIST THE BRIDEGROOM EAGERLY DESIRES US. TILEMANN HESSHUS: This is a digression by which the psalmist illustrates the glory of the Son of God's indwelling in the church, so that this boundless good can be considered more closely. . . . This simile concerning the bridegroom—without a doubt, the Mediator, the Son of God, Jesus Christ in his assumed office and in the church redeemed and liberated from the wrath of God and Satan's power—demonstrates his eagerness and enthusiasm as well as his boundless love toward the church which, redeemed by an eternal covenant, he united to himself. COMMENTARY ON PSALM 19.[10]

CHRIST IS OUR SUN, BRIDEGROOM AND HERO. NIKOLAUS SELNECKER: Here, the Lord Christ is given three beautiful, sweet titles and names: namely, he is called the Sun, the Bridegroom and a Hero. He is called the sun . . . because, as the sun in the sky with its light illuminates all the other stars and the whole firmament, so also Christ, the true Sun of Righteousness (as Malachi calls Christ) illuminates all apostles and teachers with his light. And he is always present with them, he rules, sustains and strengthens them, so that their teaching is powerful and by it other people will be enlightened. . . .

Second, Christ is called the Bridegroom. . . . As the love of a bridegroom toward his bride is great and fervent, so also Christ's heart and love toward his church is great and immeasurable. And even though we are still mired in many defects and sins, nevertheless Christ loves us, so that he does not see our deficiencies. His spirit and mind toward us is like what we say about a new bridegroom: "Anyone who loves a frog thinks that frog to be Diana." As Dr. Johann Forster says, "Beloved, Christ cherishes us in this way and promises this about us."[11] . . . In marriage, between husband and wife there are many beautiful, magnificent images and likenesses of Christ's love and faithfulness toward his

[8]CRR 6:318-19* (BRN 10:343-44); citing Rom 10:18; Eph 3:5; 1 Cor 3:16; 2 Cor 6:16; 2 Pet 1:19; Dan 12:3; 1 Cor 15:41; Phil 3:20; 2 Pet 3:13.
[9]WA 31,1:582.

[10]Hesshus, *Commentarius in Psalmos*, 89r.
[11]A student of Johannes Reuchlin, Johann Forster (1498–1556) taught Hebrew at Wittenberg and Tübingen. Forster composed an influential Hebrew-Latin lexicon.

church—as Paul therefore calls marriage a "mystery," a secret or sacrament. And we should always focus on these five things in marriage. First, *mutual love*, that is, true love among married couples. Second, *marital fidelity*, that is, faithfulness and trust for which both praise one another and which both promise to one another; they are accountable and responsible for this before God and before the world. Third, *friends in every good and hardship*, that is, husband and wife have and share with one another all their goods, undivided, all their burdens in joy and sadness. Fourth, *begetting*, that is, to bear and raise children. Fifth, *defense*, that is, to protect and shield one another. Now these five things reveal to us the true secret of God. . . . Only in this way should we understand the words of Hosea 2, when God says, "I will betroth myself to you in eternity; I will entrust myself to you in righteousness and justice, in mercy and lovingkindness, yes, in faith I will betroth myself to you, and you will come to know the Lord."

Third, Christ is called a Hero in this psalm for the following reasons. First, his highest desire and joy is to redeem the human race. Thus, he runs confidently with the Word like a courageous and manly hero who longs to meet his enemies and to protect his people from tyranny. And such a desire Christ has also poured into his members. . . . All true teachers run forward boldly and undaunted with the truth; they fear nothing, remaining steadfast and unshaken. . . . Also, as a true hero is not idle but always strives against his enemies, so also Christ is *never* idle, he strives against Satan, against whom he battles, wrestles and wins. And through Christ all who believe in him are victorious over Satan.

The Holy Spirit also gives Christ such names in Isaiah 9, calling him Wonderful—according to his person and office—Counselor, Mighty, Hero, eternal Father and Prince of Peace. Now the Lord Christ has these beautiful names and runs through the entire world with his Word. . . . This teaching is a powerful consolation to the pious. They know, if they only have the Word of God that Christ is always with them and they are always with him.

They comfort themselves in his presence; they call on him and are heard and sustained. They desire his Word through which the Holy Spirit works in their hearts. THE WHOLE PSALTER.[12]

19:7-11 *The Law of the Lord Is Perfect, Pure and True*

THE CORRUPTED SOUL REQUIRES THE MEDICINE OF THE LAW. JOHN CALVIN: I admit that the soul is not restored by the law of God without being at the same time renewed to righteousness. But David's single meaning should be considered, that as the soul invigorates the body, so also the law is the life of the soul. He also says that the soul is restored, alluding to the miserable state in which we are all born. For even though remnants of our first creation indeed survive, still because no part of us remains pure from impurity and fault, the corrupted condition of our soul differs little from death and it altogether leads to death. It is, therefore, necessary that God should employ the law as medicine—not that the letter of the law can do this by itself . . . but because God uses his Word as an instrument for restoring our souls. COMMENTARY ON THE PSALMS.[13]

DAVID COMMENDS GOD'S LAW TO GUARD FROM THE IDOLATROUS WORSHIP OF CREATION. THE ENGLISH ANNOTATIONS: What follows here in commendation of the law could be entirely—or for the most part—interpreted with some reference or allusion to the aforementioned sun and its proprieties. Like when he says that it is pure, that it enlightens, that it brings joy. But I do not find that any interpreters go about it this way, so I will instead imitate their sobriety rather than be an example of too much subtlety. . . .

So, having commended the sun and set out its glory—which for the very reason of its glorious appearance to human eyes had been transformed

---

[12]Selnecker, *Der gantze Psalter*, 1:111r, 111v-112r, 112v; citing Mal 4:2; Eph 5:31-33; Hos 2:19-20; Is 9:6.
[13]CTS 8:319* (CO 31:200).

by most human beings into an object of idolatry and worshiped as a god, indeed not by a few as the only god—lest David might seem to say anything that might unadvisedly be turned into idolatry . . . he immediately and abruptly . . . commends the law of God. For all idolatry is strictly and frequently forbidden by the law of God, especially the worship of the sun and moon and stars. . . .

Because the sun is the light of our eyes and the chief comfort of our natural lives, we should gather from this parallel of praises that what the sun is to the body, the law and the Word of God is to the soul: its only true light and life. Without it the soul is in darkness and destitute of life. ANNOTATIONS ON PSALM 19:7.[14]

SIX TRAITS OF GOD'S WORD. TILEMANN HESSHUS: Here the prophet returns to the description and commendation of the ministers of the gospel and gospel teaching which is proper to the church of God, unknown to foreign nations and detested by the world. And by this bright and shining reference to distinguishing traits—as it were, by the proper marks by which this prophetic teaching is recognized and distinguished from impious dogmas fashioned by the curse of human origin—so also by the list of noble effects and benefits which it brings to the conscience, he wonderfully proclaims this ministry of the Word, in order to encourage us to embrace it with a sincere and firm heart. Now he names six distinguished marks or proper distinguishing traits of the divine Word by which he wonderfully unites each effect or fruit with its sweetness. Law, testimony, commandments, precepts, fear and judgments are synonyms which indicate the prophetic doctrine or Word of God that resounds in the church. COMMENTARY ON PSALM 19.[15]

EXPOSITION OF THIS PSALM'S GOSPEL EPITHETS. HIERONYMUS WELLER VON MOLSDORF: Now David preaches about the *energeia* and

power or effect of the gospel. The teaching of the gospel he calls "law" through hypallage,[16] so that he admonishes the reader by antithesis, because he knows that the teaching of the gospel is quite different from the law of Moses. This manner of speaking can be seen in Paul when he says, "Through the law I died to the law, so that I might live to God." The law of Moses is not able to render human beings immaculate, whole and perfect. . . . But this new law of the gospel will excel at what was impossible for the law, that is, it will render human beings immaculate, whole and perfect. Through this they will be regenerated. New selves will be made from them; before God they will be without fault and blemish. Because all who embrace the teaching of the gospel and believe in Christ are righteous, holy, immaculate and irreproachable before God. That—the law of the Lord is perfect—is the first epithet of the gospel. . . .

Another praise of the gospel is that it is sure. That is, it makes our conscience more sure about God's will toward us. Because it reveals the will and love of God the Father to us in Christ. In sum, it teaches that "all the treasure of wisdom and knowledge have been hidden in Christ." See Colossians 2. The Father established this Son as a Mediator and Reconciler for us, so that all who have believed in him will be certain of the love and favor of God toward them and will be made inheritors of eternal life. . . . A person is certain and sure in Christ and near Christ. This collage of antitheses makes that clearer. See! The law renders the conscience uncertain, doubtful, hesitant, hopeless. But here someone might say, "If the law makes the conscience uncertain, then how should it teach?" I respond that it should be acknowledged that the law makes the conscience uncertain and troubled only if the conscience does not have the gospel preached to it. But Christ commands that the teaching of the gospel be joined with the teaching of the law. . . .

---

[14]Downame, ed., *Annotations*, 6A4r*.
[15]Hesshus, *Commentarius in Psalmos*, 89r.

[16]Hypallage is a technical term meaning interchange or exchange; it is a figure of speech in which there is an interchange of two elements of a proposition, the natural relations of these being reversed.

Another epithet of the gospel is that it is right. It frees the conscience from all its weight; it removes every nettling doubt from the conscience. From every fear, trouble, perplexity, ambiguity and doubt. Clearly the gospel treats the conscience in a different manner than the law which causes the conscience to doubt and to be guilt-stricken—always teaching but never arriving at knowledge. But here in the gospel it goes correctly. It is a fine, beautiful, upright teaching that makes people joyous. . . .

Another epithet of the gospel is that it enlightens the eyes of the heart. That is, it removes that darkness and fog from the mind that original sin brings into every human heart: the ignorance of God. Because it births a new movement of the heart, human beings are truly able to acknowledge, worship, honor and call on God. For after the Word of God has been heard, the Holy Spirit drives out that inborn darkness from our nature and lifts a new light of knowledge, fear and love of God in us. Certainly the law is not able to furnish such a benefit. For it is not able to enlighten our eyes—indeed, it dulls them even more! "For through the law comes the knowledge of sin." . . .

Another epithet of the gospel is that it births worship that is true, sincere, perfect, fine and pleasing to God. For all the works of believers are the most pleasing sacrifices to God. . . . And this is another praise of the gospel that it makes the sort of worshipers of God who are without hypocrisy; they are truthful who honor God in spirit and truth. In sum both their teaching and life are true, sober and sincere. It makes upright people and servants of God. It accomplishes what was impossible for the law, that out of their soul and their strongest desire, human beings worship, honor and obey God. And so, David calls the gospel "judgment," because it judges and damns all human wisdom, justice and holiness. Brief Comments on Psalm 19.[17]

How Do We Fear the Lord? Wolfgang Musculus: Here it must be asked how we should regard the fear of the Lord with respect to the observance of those commandments, which in the preceding verse he said gladden the heart. These verses do not seem to agree with each other, that is to say, the heart's joy and fear are in the same thing and toward the same Lawgiver. Thus it holds in human affairs that those who feel pangs of conscience for sin in the heart are especially fearful of the law; those who do the things commanded with joy love the law. But here we see not only that the pious—whose hearts are gladdened by the commandments of God—love it but also fear it. To indicate the nature of this fear, it is added that it is clean, distinguishing it from the unclean kind of fear, that is servile, which has entirely no place in the heart which is delighted by the observance of the commandments of God. . . .

Second, it also must be explained why he says this fear remains perpetually. Again, a distinction should be made between a servile fear and this one which he calls pure. The one who fears in a servile way fears as long as and until the consideration of the danger and penalty remains. In fact whenever he thinks no further of the danger, he soon sets aside his fear and partakes of a certain kind of preposterous security. Whoever does not fear in a servile way but is endowed with a pure, chaste and sincere fear—the sort that a chaste wife has toward her husband and noble children have toward their parents—that person fears not because of a fear of punishment but from a spirit of love toward God. The fear of that sort of person is constant and wholesome. Thus the people of God through the ages fear their God in prosperous times as well as in adversities. That is, they worship and obey him. Commentary on Psalm 19.[18]

Christians Must Hunger and Thirst for Righteousness. Dirk Philips: If it is now a fact that the prophet has tasted such sweetness in the law. . . . It is always right that a Christian tastes

---

[17]Weller, *Enarratio Psalmorum*, 176-81; citing Gal 2:19; Col 2:3; Rom 3:20.

[18]Musculus, *In Psalterium Commentarii*, 303-4.

and finds such sweetness in the gospel of Jesus Christ. In it God reveals to us all grace and love, all friendliness and goodness. And if it were possible for the figurative bread of heaven to give everyone what they desire and for everyone according to his taste to make of it what he would like . . . how much more is it possible for the true bread of heaven to give to all hungry souls who are hungry and thirsty after righteousness every desire and taste of the divine sweetness! But this sweetness and power of the true heavenly bread no one can taste except those who hunger and thirst after righteousness. THE ENCHIRIDION: CONCERNING THE TRUE KNOWLEDGE OF JESUS CHRIST.[19]

HUMAN BEINGS RECEIVE THE LAW'S REWARDS THROUGH GOD'S GRACE. JOHN CALVIN: It is no lowly commendation of the law when it is said that in it God enters into covenant with us, and, so to speak, brings himself under obligation to reward our obedience. In requiring from us whatever is contained in the law, he demands nothing but what he has a right to; yet such is his free and underserved generosity that he promises to his servants a reward, which he does not owe to them. The promises of the law, it is true, are rendered ineffective, but it is through our fault. Even those who are most perfect among us fall far short of full and complete righteousness; human beings cannot expect any reward for their works until they have perfectly and fully satisfied the requirements of the law. Thus these two doctrines completely harmonize. First, eternal life will be given as the reward of works to those who fulfill the law in all points; second, the law nevertheless denounces a curse against all people, because the whole human family are destitute of the righteousness of works. . . . As in the covenant of adoption there is included the free pardon of sins, on which depends the imputation of righteousness, God bestows a recompense on the works of his people, although it is not due to them. What God promises in the law to those

who perfectly obey it, true believers obtain by his gracious liberality and fatherly goodness, inasmuch as he accepts for perfect righteousness their holy desires and earnest attempts to obey. COMMENTARY ON THE PSALMS.[20]

19:12-13 *Purge All My Sin, Seen and Unseen*

HUMAN BEINGS ARE UNABLE NOT TO SIN. SEBASTIAN MÜNSTER: Here the prophet teaches that however diligent we might be to avoid stumbling, nevertheless we are unable to guard ourselves sufficiently. In fact, we fall in many different ways, we sin unconsciously, and there are many sins in us which are able to deceive our conscience—even if we are unaware of it! Therefore, the prophet prays that he would be purged of these secret faults and passions. THE TEMPLE OF THE LORD: PSALM 19.[21]

WHAT SHOULD WE LEARN FROM DAVID'S CONFESSION OF UNKNOWN SIN? NIKOLAUS SELNECKER: This is a severe objection to the previous teaching about the holy gospel. "Although I have the doctrine right," he says, "by which I will be righteous and saved, still I feel and experience that in this life I am never so devout, strong and righteous that sin, impurity, confusion, evil passions and inclinations of the heart, desire to evil and all sorts of vices do not also remain in me beyond measure. Everything in me is full of sin, conscious and unconscious, original sin and actual sin." Therefore, no one may feel secure, no matter how holy and devout he may be. Nobody can rightly see and know his own heart. Indeed, often the heart is our greatest enemy. And each one has enough to do for himself, whoever he may be, in order to tame and silence his heart and steer it away from evil even a little. In this way all saints live and lament until in their grave. When we hear the beautiful doctrine of the forgiveness of sins,

---

[19]CRR 6:168* (BRN 10:173).

[20]CTS 8:326* (CO 31:203-4).
[21]Münster, *Miqdaš YHWH*, 1175.

most people generally become confident and proud, thinking now there will be no further struggles; however, the doctrine of the gospel should lead us to the acknowledgment of our weakness and prevent all security and presumptuousness in us.

Here, we are to learn the following. First, our vice, we abuse the doctrine of the gospel through our security and presumptuousness and in this way lose the true faith and the Holy Spirit and pay no attention to how we can subdue the remaining sin in our life. Second, in all saints there still remains much sin, pride, ambition, envy, doubt, impatience and other confusion. Third, no one can search out the amount of his sin, for "the human heart is wicked and unfathomable," says Jeremiah. . . . Fourth, from our heart we are to ask God for forgiveness even of the hidden, secret sins, which he knows better than we can ever know. Like Osiander, when he was still in Nuremberg, often used to say: "God knows many more casks full of sins hidden away in us, while we hardly recognize those worth three pennies." Fifth, we are also diligently to ask God that he would keep us in his Word in such a way that we would steadily increase in faith, grow and become righteous, especially since without his grace, gift and Spirit we are neither able nor capable of doing anything. . . . Sixth, we are to be confident that if we repent, acknowledge and confess our sin—like David does here—and believe in the Son of God, our sin will not be credited to us and will no longer reign in us nor condemn us. For we are no longer under the curse of the law, but under grace. Thus David consoles himself here and knows that his hidden faults will be forgiven him and will not harm him with respect to his salvation, unless sin against the conscience is added to them. THE WHOLE PSALTER.[22]

PRAYER IS THE ONLY REMEDY AGAINST SIN. CARDINAL CAJETAN: Because it is impossible for human frailty to observe divine law down to the smallest details, after the observance of the law is described, this medicine for human weakness—for both the intellect and the affections—is added. The medicine is to run back to God for grace and protection. Here, note that the request for grace refers to sins unknown to us, so from this you should understand how much more ardently we must seek pardon for sins which we know that we have committed. COMMENTARY ON PSALM 19.[23]

THE ARMOR OF GRACE. JOHN CALVIN: No doubt, David could have wished to feel in his heart no stirrings of corruption, but knowing that he would never be wholly free from the remnants of sin, until in death when he put off this corrupt nature, he prays to be armed with the grace of the Holy Spirit for combat, so that iniquity might not reign victorious over him. COMMENTARY ON THE PSALMS.[24]

19:14 Cleanse My Mind, Mouth and Heart

PRAY WITHOUT WORDS! HIERONYMUS WELLER VON MOLSDORF: This is a great comfort, which should be brought to those who are cast down in spirit, when they bewail their inability to pray or their inability to utter cogent prayers and are greatly troubled by this. These people should know that they are praying most profoundly and with a passionate heart when they utter such sighs before the Lord and bring such feeble groans from the depths of their hearts. BRIEF COMMENT ON PSALM 19.[25]

PRAY WITH FOCUS AND ATTENTION. WOLFGANG MUSCULUS: David does not simply say, "And the thoughts of my heart," but "the *meditations*," he says, "of my heart." It is one thing to think simply, in passing and just once about something—that is what usually happens in the human heart, the sort of thinking that soon vanishes, which in German we call "fleeting thoughts"—and another to

---

[22]Selnecker, *Der gantze Psalter*, 1:114r; citing Jer 17:9.

[23]Cajetan, *In Sacrae Scripturae Expositionem*, 3:71.
[24]CTS 8:331-32* (CO 31:206).
[25]Weller, *Enarratio Psalmorum*, 189.

meditate on it. Meditation is when we turn over a certain matter sincerely, for an extended length of time and repeatedly, we speak out with our mouth and if possible, we even eagerly express it with motions and actions. These meditations should be entrusted to God; we want him to approve of them. By no means are those prayers born of vanishing and passing thoughts that gush out into prayer able to please him. Instead those prayers that seem to be prayed very sincerely and, as it is said, zealously, please him. COMMENTARY ON PSALM 19.[26]

THE PSALM ENDS IN A CONFESSION OF FAITH IN CHRIST. HIERONYMUS WELLER VON MOLSDORF: He now brings the psalm to an end with an exclamation, which contains both a prayer and a confession of faith. He also teaches where all doctrine, prayer and worship of God are directed, that is, to Christ, in whom God the Father placed every single treasure of wisdom, knowledge, favor and grace. He attributes two beautiful titles to Christ. First he calls him "Helper."[27] In the German translation this word is rendered more accurately and better expresses the emphasis of the Hebrew word: ṣûrî properly means "rock" or "refuge." Christ then is that rock, on whom his church is established through the Word and the sacraments, and on whom the church rests secure against all the raging of the devil and the world.

Second he calls him "Redeemer," who frees believers from sin, the wrath of God, the devil and eternal death. So we see that there is almost no psalm in which there is no mention of Christ—if it is not expressed explicitly, surely it is in mystical language, but clear enough. Let us give thanks with our whole heart to God the eternal Father of our Lord Jesus Christ, because he has given us such a great light in his most holy Word, so that we can hear, learn from and hand on to others the true and full meaning not only of this psalm but also of all holy Scripture. To him be praise, honor and glory forever and ever. Amen. BRIEF COMMENT ON PSALM 19.[28]

---

[26]Musculus, *In Psalterium Commentarii*, 308.
[27]This is how the Vg renders ṣûrî.

[28]Weller, *Enarratio Psalmorum*, 189-90.

20:1-9 TRUST IN THE NAME OF THE LORD OUR GOD

To the choirmaster. A Psalm of David.

¹ May the LORD answer you in the day of
    trouble!
    May the name of the God of Jacob protect you!
² May he send you help from the sanctuary
    and give you support from Zion!
³ May he remember all your offerings
    and regard with favor your burnt sacrifices!
                     Selah

⁴ May he grant you your heart's desire
    and fulfill all your plans!
⁵ May we shout for joy over your salvation,

and in the name of our God set up our
    banners!
May the LORD fulfill all your petitions!

⁶ Now I know that the LORD saves his anointed;
    he will answer him from his holy heaven
    with the saving might of his right hand.
⁷ Some trust in chariots and some in horses,
    but we trust in the name of the LORD our God.
⁸ They collapse and fall,
    but we rise and stand upright.

⁹ O LORD, save the king!
    May he answer us when we call.

OVERVIEW: At first glimpse this psalm might seem to be merely a prayer for a temporal ruler who is now long dead. But our commentators are not fooled; this psalm's lofty language can only be said of YHWH's Messiah, who is his Son *and* the Son of David. This psalm teaches that all things come from God: he alone grants success and victory; any efforts without his help will surely come to nothing. Still we too must act. None of our commentators tries to untangle the knot of divine sovereignty and human responsibility. Each is happy to grant that God is wholly in control *and* that we too are accountable. Human beings cannot ignore or despise the means at their disposal for their protection and preservation. Even so, these reformers exhort us to pray for church and country, trusting that his will be done.

A key theme of this psalm for our exegetes is the upside-down nature of God's kingdom. Citizens of the kingdom do not trust in physical, tangible items, which shield them or which they use to bludgeon and beat back their enemies; instead, they trust in the name of the Lord, letting out a small and quiet wind from their mouth in the midst of palpable temptation and terror. The Lord's protection and assurance may not always seem real or present, these commentators remind us. We might continue to cry, "How long, Lord?" But when we look to the cross—the banner of God's victory over sin, death and the devil—we are reminded that Jesus Christ too has suffered. United to him we are nourished and consoled by his Word and Spirit, tasting crumbs of the wedding feast that is to come.

THE CONTENT OF THIS PSALM IS TOO GREAT FOR A MERE HUMAN KING. CARDINAL CAJETAN: Observe, prudent reader, that if the exact history that is treated here were sought, none would be found written in which all these details are confirmed—as it is generally accessible to any time since the ark of the Lord was in Zion. But if the proper truth of this prophecy is sought, no king would be found except the Messiah of whom this could be true. It is abundantly obvious that this is only true of the Messiah alone: "He will fulfill all your plans and all your petitions." As well there is no king except the Messiah about whom David prophesies that this same King will answer us in our day of trouble, especially because David counts himself among those crying out, saying, "Answer us when we call." So, because the words in this psalm surpass David—and how much more the other kings, indeed even the people!—they fit the Messiah. It must be concluded according to the rule of the apostle Peter, that this psalm according to the letter is about the Messiah.[1] And as far as it is apparent from the development of the psalm, it is about the exaltation of the Messiah as a result of the merit of his passion by which he subjected the world to the yoke of faith. COMMENTARY ON PSALM 20.[2]

20:1-3 The Blessing, Benefit and Bulwark of the Lord Our God

BECAUSE GOD IS TRANSCENDENT, HE HAS GIVEN US HIS NAME AS A COMFORT. JOHN CALVIN: "The name of God" is here put for God himself, and not without good reason. For because the essence of God is incomprehensible to us, to the extent that his grace and power are made known to us, it is fitting for us to trust in him. From his name, therefore, proceeds confidence in calling on him. The faithful desire that the king would be protected and aided by God.... For it was part of their adoption to live under the guardianship of a king set over them by God himself. From this, by anagogy, we should understand what I have elsewhere mentioned briefly. Because Christ our King, as eternal Priest, never ceases to intercede with God, the whole body of the church should join in his prayers. In the same way, we have no hope of being heard unless he goes before us. And this—no small means of assuaging our sorrows—is our comfort that our difficulties with which we are afflicted Christ considers to be his own. But he also should come to mind in the midst of tribulation to bring us peace, because the Holy Spirit here prophesies that the kingdom of Christ would experience dangers and troubles. COMMENTARY ON THE PSALMS.[3]

THE SANCTUARY IS THE PROMISE OF GOD'S PRESENCE. RUDOLF GWALTHER: Those who say this—"May he send you help from the sanctuary"—do not think God's help is bound to a certain location; rather, they say this on account of the promise of God, who gave them the tabernacle and ark of the covenant as a guarantee of his presence. THE PSALTER.[4]

PRAYERS OF THE CHURCH AND HUMAN RESPONSIBILITY. HIERONYMUS WELLER VON MOLSDORF: This request is either a repetition or a tautology, as if to say: "It is not right for you to seek human protection from any people or wait for it, but let the Lord bring help to you from Zion," that is, seek help from the throne where God dwells by his Word, by his promise and his sacraments— with regard to the church, pray with a passionate heart on behalf of pious magistrates. For God will not be called on or hear prayers except in the church, the congregation of the pious. The prophet teaches therefore that God hears the prayers of the church and of the pious, and that by these prayers he is moved to bring help for pious magistrates, and that he might grant them victory against their enemies. The prayer of Christians must do [this]; human power and might cannot do it alone. Nevertheless weapons are not to be abandoned, nor are human means of defense to be ignored, lest we tempt God. A middle course is needed, so that we do not allow ourselves to be taken too far to the right or left. If we have at our disposal great force of arms, we should not put our trust in them, nor if they fail, should we lose hope. BRIEF COMMENT ON PSALM 20.[5]

THE MERIT OF CHRIST'S WORSHIP, THE SACRIFICE OF HIS WORK. CARDINAL CAJETAN: The reason for God's help is described as the worship presented to God by the Messiah in the temple in Zion. In fact, according to the letter,

---

[1]Cajetan obliquely refers to 2 Pet 1:16-21 by "the rule of the apostle Peter"; see further Henri de Lubac, *Medieval Exegesis: The Four Senses of Scripture*, 3 vols., trans. Mark Sebanc and E. M. Macierowski (Grand Rapids: Eerdmans: 1998–2009), 1:27.
[2]Cajetan, *In Sacrae Scripturae Expositionem*, 3:73.
[3]CTS 8:334-35* (CO 31:208).

[4]Gwalther, *Der Psalter*, 31v (cf. p. 31r for Gwalther's translation of Ps 20:2).
[5]Weller, *Enarratio Psalmorum*, 197-98.

Christ the human being worshiped God in the temple that was in Zion. And for this reason the prophet says that "he will send his help from his holiness," that is, concerning the merit of the worship presented to God in his house of holiness and on Mount Zion. For because of this Christ deserved both to be sustained and helped. Although, as God, he did not need these things.

And to the reason of merit he adds the reason of sacrifice. "He will remember all your offerings, and your burnt offerings he will burn to ashes." According to this simile of physical offerings, which happened in the old law, and burnt sacrifices, which were offered to God, he describes the burnt sacrifice of Christ's body on the cross and the Messiah's spiritual offerings for the salvation of souls. . . . Just as in the case of material burnt sacrifice, sometimes the fire from heaven was cast down so violently that it reduced the sacrifice to ashes, in the same way the fire of the Holy Spirit accepted Christ's entire most-pleasing passion. COMMENTARY ON PSALM 20.[6]

SACRIFICES DO NOT INDEBT GOD TO US; THEY DEMONSTRATE OUR FAITHFULNESS. THE ENGLISH ANNOTATIONS: The commemoration of David's sacrifices is not performed as though the oblation of such things is of itself pleasing to God or meritorious with him. The idolatrous heathens believed that about their own gods—though reproved for it by many of their own philosophers—which therefore emboldened them in their prayers and supplications to these gods, to remind these gods of the cost and charges in their oblations. . . . The drift and scope of this commemoration here is but this: to set out David's piety and fear of God by those outward solemn performances, appointed then by the law of God, and in reference to his commandment and institution, not to be omitted but performed with all reverence and devotion. And because they prayed at the same time, David's prayers which he made are also included in the mention of these

sacrifices, as if he said, "Remember your prayers" and so on. ANNOTATIONS ON PSALM 20:3.[7]

20:4-5 *Joy for the Fulfillment of God's Plans*

LET YOUR WILL BE CONFORMED TO GOD'S. NIKOLAUS SELNECKER: In the previous verse David prayed that God the Lord would make him a true theologian. Now he prays that God would also make a pious jurist out of him, that he would not begin anything in his office without God, and that whatever he begins with God, God would grant his blessing so that everything would progress well. For whatever we begin with God goes happily. Like when a prince says, "Lord God, I'm planning this offensive or opposition. If it is pleasing to you, then help; if it is not pleasing to you, then oppose it and govern me as pleases you." But where does that happen? . . . Just like how now at the Council of Trent they are defining, discerning, anathematizing, damning and doing whatever they want, and they granted God so little honor that they did not say, "Lord God, if it pleases you, then help, so that we do it correctly; if it does not please you, then oppose it." And in this way, almost all the world acts—doing everything without God's counsel, fear and supplication. But it is well for those who follow the beloved David and say, "Lord, help! It is your honor. May your will be done." For when we do this, then nothing else is necessary and we can say, "The Lord helps us and our weapons, might, power and strength stand on the name of the Lord. The Lord is with us in the midst of the field, yes, at the very tip of our swords."

O, what greater glory, triumph and majesty is there in which we can boast than that God will help us? As we now boast against the Sacramentarians: "God is with us; Christ—true God and human being—will not abandon us. He helps us. The victory comes from him. He is the Truth; all human beings are liars." THE COMPLETE PSALTER.[8]

---

[6]Cajetan, *In Sacrae Scripturae Expositionem*, 3:73.

[7]Downame, ed., *Annotations*, 6A4r*.
[8]Selnecker, *Der gantze Psalter*, 1:116v. In the final paragraph,

LIFT HIGH THE CROSS OF CHRIST, THE BANNER OF VICTORY! CARDINAL CAJETAN: This exaltation is also prophesied in the first person plural, so that David includes himself in the joy of it: "We will rejoice in your salvation." He himself says "we will rejoice" by singing and we will sing by rejoicing—in fact the Hebrew term sounds like singing joined with rejoicing—"in your salvation" that has been revealed to us. "And in the name of our God"—not another god, not a new god—"we will be adorned by his banner." This Hebrew term means—if it can be said—"we will be bannered." It is passive; translators render it "we will be adorned by his banner." And it means according to the letter that in the name of God we will raise up the banner of victory. Without a doubt this is the banner of the cross. For David himself along with his people— that is, along with the Jews—were the first people to praise and raise up the banner of the cross's victory in the time of the Messiah. This is about that prophecy. COMMENTARY ON PSALM 20.[9]

20:6-8 Trust in the Name Alone

THE METAPHOR OF THE CHURCH AS HEAVEN. HIERONYMUS WELLER VON MOLSDORF: The psalmist accords three attributes to the church: first, he calls it the Lord's holy possession, second Zion and third the holy heaven of God. . . . Scripture calls the church "heaven" as a metaphor. As our heaven encompasses the earth and everything in it in its very broad circuit, so indescribable is the mercy and grace of God shown in Christ. It encompasses all those who are in the church, that is, in the congregation of the pious. It cherishes them and does not allow anyone to be lost from this heaven of grace, if they earnestly embrace the teaching of the gospel and seize Christ in faith. BRIEF COMMENT ON PSALM 20.[10]

LIFT UP YOUR HEARTS TO THE LORD'S HEAVENLY PRESENCE! JOHN CALVIN: Here the psalmist mentions another sanctuary, namely, a heavenly one. As God saw fit to descend to the people through the ark of the covenant to reveal himself more intimately to them, so also he wanted to draw the minds of his people upward to himself, lest they might have formed fleshly and earthly ideas about him, and to teach them that he is far superior to the whole world. Thus, under the visible sanctuary—made with hands—God's fatherly graciousness is commended. He has intimate relationship with his people—under the heavenly sanctuary, his infinite power, dominion and majesty are revealed. COMMENTARY ON THE PSALMS.[11]

THE SOVEREIGN MIGHT OF THE LORD. MARTIN BUCER: Now each one was saying, "After the Self-Existent One[12] helped our king in such an amazing act of kindness, he made them turn in flight and caused an army of such great magnitude to fall, I clearly recognize that God helped David by the power of his right hand. For the enemies were so numerous and so powerful that unless by the present help of God and by a brilliant miracle of divine power, our king could not have conquered them." Accordingly, it is abundantly evident that his prayer was poured out on Mount Zion, which was heard by the Lord in the heavenly Holy of Holies; that is, God truly brought heavenly help to him and by himself has overthrown David's enemies. He is

---

Selnecker flattens Reformed Eucharistic theology—which he pejoratively labels as "Sacramentarian"—and turns it against them, claiming that because they do not believe Christ to be *bodily* present with them in the Eucharist, they cannot say that he is present with them at all. For a nuanced treatment of the various confessional understandings of the Eucharist, see "Eucharist," *OER* 2:71-81.

[9]Cajetan, *In Sacrae Scripturae Expositionem*, 3:73. Scholars continue to debate the meaning of the Hebrew word *nidgōl* which Cajetan woodenly renders as "we will be bannered." Kraus amends the text to "we shall rejoice," following the LXX. See Kraus, *Psalms 1–59*, 278; Alter, *Book of Psalms*, 66.

[10]Weller, *Enarratio Psalmorum*, 215-16.

[11]CTS 8:339* (CO 31:210).

[12]That is, *Autophyes*; Bucer attempted to demystify the unpronounceable Tetragrammaton with this epithet; Pellikan questioned it as "unusual and novel." See Hobbs, "Conrad Pellican and the Psalms," 98; R. Gerald Hobbs "Pluriformity of Early Reformation Scriptural Interpretation," in *Hebrew Bible, Old Testament: The History of Its Interpretation*, 3 vols., ed. Magne Sæbø (Göttingen: Vandenhoecht & Ruprecht, 1996–2015), 2:469.

said to dwell in heaven on account of their immortal substance and their force greater than all lesser things, by which fact he reveals in those his own power and divinity. Holy Psalms.[13]

Theologians Must Rely on God. Martin Luther: Some—that is, doctors—trust in chariots; others—that is, lawyers—trust in horses; but we—that is, theologians—trust in the name of the Lord. Table Talk: Konrad Cordatus.[14]

The Impious Trust in What They Can See; the Pious Trust in God Alone. Tilemann Hesshus: By a contrast of dissimilar things the psalmist illustrates the confidence of the church. It is obvious in what things people in the world trust: no doubt, in strength of body, in abundance of wealth, in size of empire, in well-trained troops, in a great number of friends and in other similar things which meet the eye.

Now because God has forbidden us to trust in these worldly things and commands us to place all our hope in him alone, not only is this foolish confidence mistaken, but also it is punished by God most grievously. Thus, Apries the Egyptian,[15] Sennacherib, Xerxes and innumerable others placed their confidence in their armies and strength, but they were disappointed in their expectation. The church, therefore, separates itself from profane people and does not profess to trust in weapons and armies but instead to place all hope in the name, that is, in calling on the true God. He mercifully heeds his people who are in danger and who call on him, he rescues them by divine power, and he mightily defends them against all their enemies. Theodosius, in the midst of the greatest danger and completely surrounded by various enemies, took refuge in calling on God, and he obtained a glorious victory. Commentary on Psalm 20.[16]

The Name of the Lord Will Lift Us Up. David Dickson: What terrifies believers in the first assault of a temptation—before they go to their refuge—is condemned by believers when they look to the Lord, their true defense. Chariots and horses when they are invading God's people are terrible, but now when the Lord is remembered they become nothing in comparison. The condition of the worldly and the enemies of God's people seems to be better—at first—and the condition of the church worse. But soon a reversal comes, which determines the question in the end: the standing of the ungodly is followed with a fall, and the low condition of the godly has a better condition following it. The worldly and the enemy are brought down and fall, but the godly are made to say, "We rise and stand upright." Commentary on Psalm 20.[17]

20:9 The Lord's Victory Through the King

This Psalm Stirs Us Up to Pray for Good Government and Peace. Philipp Melanchthon: At the end an exclamation has been added, because God certainly is the one who hears those who call on him; let us who have been strengthened by this promise stir up our faith and call on him. And this psalm will be more clear and sweet to us if we will recite it frequently, praying for the government and thinking about the great dangers that face all pious governors. And we should remember the commandment of God, so that we would seek him from the heart. May he rule and help all who are in command. May he grant tranquil political orders, which would be respectable promoters of churches and education. May he restrain villainy, pillaging and the dissolution of discipline. Comments on the Psalms.[18]

---

[13]Bucer, *Sacrorum Psalmorum*, 116v-117r.
[14]WATR 3:323, no. 3459.
[15]Apries, an Egyptian pharaoh who reigned 589–570 B.C., tried—and failed—to defend Judah against the Babylonian invasion of Nebuchadnezzar II.
[16]Hesshus, *Commentarius in Psalmos*, 94r; citing 2 Kings 19 (cf. Is

37). Hesshus is referring to the prayer of Emperor Theodosius I (347–395) during the Battle of the Frigidus (394). See Theodoret, *Ecclesiastical History* 24 (NPNF² 3:149-50).
[17]Dickson, *First Fifty Psalms*, 110-11*.
[18]MO 13:1047-48.

Know That Salvation Always Comes from God. John Calvin: In short, this is a prayer that God, by blessing the king, would reveal himself as the preserver of all the people. The means of this salvation are expressed in this way: the people pray that the king would be furnished with power from God to deliver them whenever they are in distress and cry to him for help. "Let the king hear us when we call on him." God had not promised that his people would be saved in any other way than by the hand and conduct of the king whom he had given

them. Today—now that Christ has been revealed— let us learn to yield him this honor: to renounce all hope of salvation from any other quarter and to trust only in that salvation which he will bring to us from God his Father. Now we will only become partakers of this, if we are all gathered under our Head into one body, we should care for one another mutually, not considering our own well-being alone. Commentary on the Psalms.[19]

---

[19]CTS 8:342-43* (CO 31:212).

21:1-13 THE KING REJOICES IN
THE LORD'S STRENGTH

To the choirmaster. A Psalm of David.

¹ O LORD, in your strength the king rejoices,
　and in your salvation how greatly he exults!
² You have given him his heart's desire
　and have not withheld the request of his lips.
　　　　　　　　　　　　　　　Selah

³ For you meet him with rich blessings;
　you set a crown of fine gold upon his head.
⁴ He asked life of you; you gave it to him,
　length of days forever and ever.
⁵ His glory is great through your salvation;
　splendor and majesty you bestow on him.
⁶ For you make him most blessed forever;ᵃ
　you make him glad with the joy of your
　　presence.
⁷ For the king trusts in the LORD,
　and through the steadfast love of the Most
　　High he shall not be moved.

⁸ Your hand will find out all your enemies;
　your right hand will find out those who hate
　　you.
⁹ You will make them as a blazing oven
　when you appear.
The LORD will swallow them up in his wrath,
　and fire will consume them.
¹⁰ You will destroy their descendants from the
　　earth,
　and their offspring from among the children
　　of man.
¹¹ Though they plan evil against you,
　though they devise mischief, they will not
　　succeed.
¹² For you will put them to flight;
　you will aim at their faces with your bows.

¹³ Be exalted, O LORD, in your strength!
　We will sing and praise your power.

a Or make him a source of blessing forever

OVERVIEW: In continuity with the previous psalm, these commentators contend, this psalm typifies Christ and his kingdom. One exegete underscores that we must always approach the Psalter with the knowledge that David and his peers describe spiritual realities—which we cannot see or understand—with physical realities. Thus, both the internal and external affairs of the heavenly kingdom are revealed: its citizens are filled with joy in the presence and blessing of their King Messiah; its enemies shake in terror at its defenses and military prowess. Our commentators encourage us to meditate on this reality, receiving consolation in it and strengthening our faith which is the only entry into this kingdom—unlike all others which are gained through violence, influence or wealth. The subjects of the kingdom are to imitate their King, Savior and Brother, Jesus Christ, whose eternal victory grants them life.

THIS PSALM CONTINUES PSALM 20'S THEME. THEODORE BEZA: This psalm depends on the former. It contains a thanksgiving for a distinguished victory which the church attributes to the bountiful clemency of God alone who promises the church the same help in all other distresses. PARAPHRASE OF PSALM 21.[1]

THIS PSALM MUST BE UNDERSTOOD ABOUT THE MESSIAH. CARDINAL CAJETAN: Concerning the subject matter of this psalm it is quite evident that it treats a king. And because what is described about this king far surpasses David and any other king

---

[1]Beza, *Psalmes of Dauid*, 33* (*Psalmorum Davidis*, 69).

besides the Messiah alone, this psalm therefore treats the Messiah according to the letter. The psalmist shows that verse 4 fits the Messiah alone: "He asked for life from you, you gave him length of days, forever and always." Verse 6 also strengthens this: "Because you will establish him as an eternal blessing." These conditions are proper to the Messiah. Thus even among the Hebrews of old, this psalm was expounded about the Messiah. And the Targum says this explicitly: "O God! In your strength, King Messiah will reign!"[2] Accordingly, without a doubt, the subject of this psalm according to the letter is the kingdom of the Messiah or to what extent the Messiah will be king. COMMENTARY ON PSALM 21.[3]

21:1-7 The Lord Has Blessed the King's Requests

THE OMNIPOTENCE OF CHRIST OUR KING. NIKOLAUS SELNECKER: Christ is the king, as he is also therefore called *Christus*, an anointed king and high priest. This king God the Father raised up from the dead and made him an eternal king through divine power, as Psalm 2 says: "I have established my king on my holy hill Zion." That is, he will be the Head of the church, as Paul says, to him all things are subjected in heaven and earth. And this is a great and inexpressible consolation, that we now have such a king and brother who reigns in joy and has overcome death and rejoices in the power of God his Father. That is, he is almighty God and man, as he himself says in Matthew: "From now on you will see the Son of Man seated at the right hand of power." . . . That is, at the right hand of the omnipotence of God, so that wherever God is with his power and omnipotence there too is the human being Christ. O Lord God, sustain us in this faith and consolation, protect us from the devil in these last days, so that we too will be joyous for your help and hold fast to the victory! Amen. THE WHOLE PSALTER.[4]

THIS FIRST VERSE IS THE PSALM'S HEART. TILEMANN HESSHUS: Almost the entire psalm is this one continuous proposition, explaining what kind of kingdom the Messiah's is and what kind of success it will have. The beginning of the psalm speaks of the Messiah and his kingdom generally. First, he demonstrates that Jehovah, the eternal God and Father of our Lord Jesus Christ, is the Founder of this kingdom. The Messiah will not aspire to or invade a spiritual kingdom by his own audacity, but rather according to his divinity he is summoned to this and by the authority of the eternal God he is confirmed in this office. God himself is the Founder, Defender and Preserver of this kingdom. Second, he names the Messiah the King in order to teach us that he was established by the Father as all-powerful Savior, so that he would restrain his enemies' rage, annihilate sin, death and hell, and bestow his eternal righteousness, life and joy to his subjects. Third, he prophesies about the success of this kingdom. "In your power he will rejoice," that is, the Messiah will not be overcome by the enemy. He has not been downcast and broken in spirit. He will not wage war without victory. Neither the world's rage nor Satan's savage power nor death's ferocious force will overwhelm Christ; instead, he will have prosperous success. The victory will be obtained from heaven. And in every vocation God's presence and help will be experienced. In the end, after every enemy is annihilated and death is defeated, he will gather the church in the human race. And he will uphold the church forever and transfer it to eternal blessedness. COMMENTARY ON PSALM 21.[5]

CROWNS REPRESENT KINGDOMS. THE ENGLISH ANNOTATIONS: Therefore, as a crown in ordinary use is taken metaphorically for a kingdom, so "a crown of pure gold" must here be taken metaphorically for a choice kingdom—such as the kingdom of Israel. ANNOTATION ON PSALM 21:3.[6]

---

[2]TgPss 21:2; see further David Stec, trans., *The Targum of Psalms* (Collegeville, MN: Liturgical Press, 1987).

[3]Cajetan, *In Sacrae Scripturae Expositionem*, 3:75.

[4]Selnecker, *Der gantze Psalter*, 1:118r; citing Ps 2:6; Eph 1:22-23; Mt 26:64 (cf. Lk 22:69).

[5]Hesshus, *Commentarius in Psalmos*, 95r.

[6]Downame, ed., *Annotations*, 64Av*; citing 2 Sam 12:30.

CROWNED WITH GLORY AT THE RIGHT HAND OF THE FATHER. GIOVANNI BATTISTA FOLENGO: It is as if the psalmist wanted to say, "You made him king, giving him all power in heaven and on earth." For the crown is a special sign and splendor of the king by which honor—due to such high rank—is expressed. A gold crown—the Spirit confirms in another passage—on his head is an explicit sign of holiness, glory, honor and mighty deeds. These are truly qualities with which it is appropriate for a king to be adorned and which in pure gold—surely the most purely refined gold—are seen mystically. According to the prophet's custom, he traces out spiritual matters with worldly words. Indeed I frequently emphasize this, so that those who by nature are slower in spiritual things would no longer imagine these matters to be corporeal. Thus, this is the sum of it: you should understand that the Son of God received royal power from the Father. It was an especially excellent gift and favor—among countless others—with which he was adorned before his peers, and "whose glory we have seen," John said, "glory as of the only-begotten of the Father, full of grace and truth." KING DAVID'S PSALTER.[7]

WHY DOES THE PSALMIST REPEAT "JOY"? CARDINAL CAJETAN: Notice that the word *joy* is repeated—"you will make him joyful in joy"—to indicate the fullness of joy. And "of your presence" is added, so that you would understand that the reason for his complete joy is the divine presence. Make sure that you consider all these things that are about the salvation of the Messiah himself . . . not in the state of his humility but in the state of his royal power. COMMENTARY ON PSALM 21.[8]

JOY CAN BE FLESHLY OR SPIRITUAL. WOLFGANG MUSCULUS: The psalmist considers a twofold kind of joy in this passage: one of the flesh, another of the spirit. By the joy of the flesh, we rejoice in many kindnesses and great affection. About this joy the pious do not speak here. The other is the joy by which the pious rejoice, not because of kindness alone but rather because of a sense of the grace and favor of God. At such joy these singers gaze, because they do not say, "You have made him joyful with your kindnesses," but "You have made him joyful in the joy of your countenance." All those who love sincerely are affected by this kind of joy, and they care for nothing more than gaining the favor of him whom they love. COMMENTARY ON PSALM 21.[9]

A KINGDOM LIKE NO OTHER. TILEMANN HESSHUS: After he has described the glory, magnificence, happiness and favor of Christ's kingdom, in this verse he teaches the reason he moved God to establish this kingdom and how we are able to become participants in it. Not by weapons or military strength is this kingdom seized, nor by works or merits is it obtained, but rather by faith or confidence in the Lord is it obtained and maintained. For as the King himself, the Messiah, obtained all things from the Father through faith and hope by which he united himself to the Lord, in the same way there is no other way to enter into this kingdom except through true faith in Christ. Nor are riches of this kingdom granted on account of anyone's merits, but instead only by God's lovingkindness does he give us the Messiah himself, raised him from the dead and offers all benefits of this kingdom to believers. COMMENTARY ON PSALM 21.[10]

21:8-12 *The Consuming Power of the Lord*

THE KINGDOM'S POWERFUL DEFENSES. JOHN CALVIN: So far the internal happiness of the kingdom has been described. Now its invincible strength against its enemies, as was necessary, is added. It is just as important as if the king were proclaimed the victor over all his enemies. . . . It would not have been enough for the kingdom to have flourished internally and to have overflowed

---

[7]Folengo, *In Psalterium Davidis*, 68v-69r; citing Rev 14:14; Jn 1:14.
[8]Cajetan, *In Sacrae Scripturae Expositionem*, 3:75.
[9]Musculus, *In Psalterium Commentarii*, 323.
[10]Hesshus, *Commentarius in Psalmos*, 96r.

with peace, riches and abundance of all good things unless it also had been well-fortified against external violence. This particularly applies to the kingdom of Christ, which is never without enemies in the world. Although it is not always assailed by open war but is sometimes allowed a period of respite, nevertheless the ministers of Satan never cast aside their malice and longing to cause harm. Therefore, they never abandon to struggle to overthrow Christ's kingdom. It is fitting that our King, who lifts up his hand to protect us, is far stronger than all things. . . .

Also a dreadful kind of vengeance is added here, from which we gather that he does not speak of every kind of enemy in general but of the impious and frantic despisers of God who rise up against his only-begotten Son like giants [nephilim]. The severity of the punishment shows the gravity of their wickedness. Some think that David alludes to the kind of punishment which he inflicted on the Ammonites—which the sacred history narrates— but it is more probable that he here expounds metaphorically the dreadful destruction which awaits all Christ's adversaries. Although they may burn with rage against the church and set the world on fire by their cruelty, nevertheless when their impiety will have reached its pinnacle, this is the reward which God has in reserve for them: he will cast them into his burning furnace to consume them. COMMENTARY ON THE PSALMS.[11]

ONLY THOSE WHO PARTICIPATE IN IMPIETY ARE DESCENDANTS OF IMPIETY. WOLFGANG MUSCULUS: Let us consider here how great is the wrath of God toward the impious. It destroys not only them but also their posterity. The abomination of the impious is great in the sight of God, and so it happens that not even on earth and among humankind does any place remain for them, much less in heaven. This truth is not included so that we should anxiously inquire whether it is fair that the seed of the impious are blotted out on account of the impiety of their

parents' evil deeds. Instead the Holy Spirit is speaking about the seed corresponding to its root, that is, about those descendants who follow the great impiety of their parents; such are rightly called the seed of the impious. Scripture does not call those who are the posterity of the impious only according to the flesh but not according to their impiety by this name. Because truly children do not bear the iniquity of the parent if they do not participate in it. COMMENTARY ON PSALM 21.[12]

THE ACTIONS OF THE IMPIOUS DO NOT GO UNPUNISHED. TILEMANN HESSHUS: The psalmist shows the efficient cause of the obstruction of the plans of the impious. Clearly because God almighty opposes them, he casts various hindrances at them, he oppresses them with heavy burdens, and finally he defeats them by sending a volley of arrows from heaven at them. "You will turn them into shoulders."[13] That is, you overwhelm your enemies with various hindrances, difficulties and calamities. Pharaoh tried to blot out the people of God, but he was oppressed with innumerable calamities so that in the end he rejoiced to see the people leave. Antiochus Epiphanes was opposed by various hindrances and calamities; in the end he died falling from his chariot. Thus Diocletian and Maximian were burdened with such a great number of hardships that they resigned the emperorship. "You will stretch your bowstring." That is, in the end you will send a volley of arrows from heaven and annihilate them. Sennacherib experienced a volley of arrows from heaven when he was run through in a temple by his sons. Decius drowned in a swamp in Thrace, Diocletian drank poison, Maximian was strangled, Julian the Apostate was killed by a spear and Valens was burned in his house. COMMENTARY ON PSALM 21.[14]

---

[11]CTS 8:350-52* (CO 31:216-17); citing Gen 6:1-7.

[12]Musculus, *In Psalterium Commentarii*, 326-27; citing Ezek 18:20-21.

[13]Hesshus has woodenly translated the difficult Hebrew, which many understand to mean "you will turn them back." See Alter, *Book of Psalms*, 70; Goldingay, *Psalms*, 1:311; Kraus, *Psalms 1–59*, 283, 288.

[14]Hesshus, *Commentarius in Psalmos*, 97r; citing 2 Macc 9:7; 2 Kings 19:37. All the examples Hesshus cites of God's judgment are infamous oppressors of God's people: Antiochus Epiphanes

God's Orderly Orchestrated Punishment. Wolfgang Musculus: Here the metaphor of shooting arrows is used; they sing that God guides the path of their flight against his enemies and those who are accustomed to aim their arrows at them, trying to destroy and capture them. It seems that the enemies of God are compared with those who are bound to stakes and pinned there with javelins so that it is impossible for them to deflect or avoid the incoming volley of arrows. To this it is added that the chorus sing, "You will aim your bowstrings at their faces." Therefore, they will not be struck unexpectedly, but they will openly experience the wrathful hand of God raging against them, and they will not be able to escape. Commentary on Psalm 21.[15]

21:13 Praise God's Power

The Messiah's Might Causes Us to Sing. Cardinal Cajetan: The prophet prays to the finishing line, as was fitting, after an entirely excellent prophecy, so that he reaches only the good. "Be exalted," he says, "Lord in your strength," by which you have conquered the world and the rulers of this world. For "we will praise" and "we will sing psalms," that is, we will celebrate "your strength." To indicate the fullness of singing he repeats it again, so that you would understand the strength of the Messiah to be the subject matter of and reason for human singing. Commentary on Psalm 21.[16]

Petition and Praise for the Messiah's Eternal Power. Tilemann Hesshus: A prayer—that the Lord of the Messiah would

continually demonstrate his power against his enemies—and a repetition of thanksgiving for the benefit of the Messiah's works conclude the psalm. It is as if he wanted to say, "You, O Lord and King Jesus Christ, gifted with divine power and seated at the right hand of the eternal Father, exalt, reveal and proclaim throughout the world examples of your power! Blot out sin, death, Satan and hell. Gather to yourself the church through Word and sacraments. Give life and salvation to believers. Restrain all tyrants and heretics who oppose your name. Assist us your saints so that we would celebrate your righteousness, lovingkindness, power, truth, wisdom and immeasurable, gracious benefits for all eternity." Commentary on Psalm 21.[17]

Contemplate This Psalm Typologically in Christ. Wolfgang Musculus: Both parts of this psalm have an eminent type for the kingdom of Christ. For he is truly that king whose desires and petitions are accomplished by God the Father. On him the Father has heaped the highest blessings. The Father has inaugurated him with the crown of the heavenly kingdom. He has given him eternal life. He has illuminated him with glory and splendor. For this reason, he has been made an eternal blessing for all mortals. In eternal joy he gladdens him with his face and in this way strengthens him so that for all eternity he cannot be moved. Finally this is his lot, that all his enemies accomplish nothing with their scheming, devising, planning and striving against him, except that by this they make themselves guilty of extreme, sure and eternal destruction. The mind gifted with the spirit of faith will reflect on this most beautifully in Christ according to the prefigured type which David contains in himself and will receive powerful consolation. Commentary on Psalm 21.[18]

---

famously desecrated the temple; Sennacherib, king of Assyria, invaded Judah; Diocletian, Maximian, Decius and Valens instigated imperial persecutions of Christians; and Julian the Apostate (331–363) tried to reestablish Roman paganism in place of Christianity.
[15]Musculus, *In Psalterium Commentarii*, 325.
[16]Cajetan, *In Sacrae Scripturae Expositionem*, 3:76.

[17]Hesshus, *Commentarius in Psalmos*, 97r.
[18]Musculus, *In Psalterium Commentarii*, 327-28.

22:1-31 MY GOD, MY GOD,
WHY HAVE YOU FORSAKEN ME?

To the choirmaster: according to The Doe of
the Dawn. A Psalm of David.

¹ My God, my God, why have you forsaken
    me?
    Why are you so far from saving me, from
      the words of my groaning?
² O my God, I cry by day, but you do not answer,
    and by night, but I find no rest.

³ Yet you are holy,
    enthroned on the praises[a] of Israel.
⁴ In you our fathers trusted;
    they trusted, and you delivered them.
⁵ To you they cried and were rescued;
    in you they trusted and were not put to shame.

⁶ But I am a worm and not a man,
    scorned by mankind and despised by the
      people.
⁷ All who see me mock me;
    they make mouths at me; they wag their
      heads;
⁸ "He trusts in the LORD; let him deliver him;
    let him rescue him, for he delights in him!"

⁹ Yet you are he who took me from the womb;
    you made me trust you at my mother's breasts.
¹⁰ On you was I cast from my birth,
    and from my mother's womb you have been
      my God.
¹¹ Be not far from me,
    for trouble is near,
    and there is none to help.

¹² Many bulls encompass me;
    strong bulls of Bashan surround me;
¹³ they open wide their mouths at me,
    like a ravening and roaring lion.

¹⁴ I am poured out like water,
    and all my bones are out of joint;
my heart is like wax;

it is melted within my breast;
¹⁵ my strength is dried up like a potsherd,
    and my tongue sticks to my jaws;
    you lay me in the dust of death.
¹⁶ For dogs encompass me;
    a company of evildoers encircles me;
they have pierced my hands and feet[b]—
¹⁷ I can count all my bones—
they stare and gloat over me;
¹⁸ they divide my garments among them,
    and for my clothing they cast lots.

¹⁹ But you, O LORD, do not be far off!
    O you my help, come quickly to my aid!
²⁰ Deliver my soul from the sword,
    my precious life from the power of the dog!
²¹ Save me from the mouth of the lion!
You have rescued[c] me from the horns of the
    wild oxen!

²² I will tell of your name to my brothers;
    in the midst of the congregation I will praise
      you:
²³ You who fear the LORD, praise him!
    All you offspring of Jacob, glorify him,
    and stand in awe of him, all you offspring of
      Israel!
²⁴ For he has not despised or abhorred
    the affliction of the afflicted,
and he has not hidden his face from him,
    but has heard, when he cried to him.

²⁵ From you comes my praise in the great
      congregation;
    my vows I will perform before those who
      fear him.
²⁶ The afflicted[d] shall eat and be satisfied;
    those who seek him shall praise the LORD!
    May your hearts live forever!
²⁷ All the ends of the earth shall remember
    and turn to the LORD,

and all the families of the nations
  shall worship before you.
²⁸ For kingship belongs to the LORD,
  and he rules over the nations.

²⁹ All the prosperous of the earth eat and worship;
  before him shall bow all who go down to the
  dust,

even the one who could not keep himself alive.
³⁰ Posterity shall serve him;
  it shall be told of the Lord to the coming
  generation;
³¹ they shall come and proclaim his righteousness to a people yet unborn,
  that he has done it.

a Or *dwelling in the praises*   b Some Hebrew manuscripts, Septuagint, Vulgate, Syriac; most Hebrew manuscripts *like a lion* [they are at] *my hands and feet*
c Hebrew *answered*   d Or *The meek*

OVERVIEW: At the Second Council of Constanti-nople (553), Theodore of Mopsuestia (c. 350–428) was anathematized for asserting that the subject of this psalm was David. Aligned with this tradition, most early modern commentators understand this psalm to be a literal prophecy of Christ, if not the work of Christ himself; David recedes into the background. Even in the writings of those such as Calvin and Münster, who seek to distinguish more clearly between the historical David and the prophesied Christ, christological interpretation predominates. And so this psalm is seen to speak primarily of Christ, his suffering for his church, his exaltation to the state of glory and the worldwide expansion of his kingdom. For the church, then, this psalm serves as a depiction of her participation in Christ, granting encouragement, consolation and comfort as she is united to him in his suffering, death and victory.

THIS IS NOT JUST ABOUT DAVID; IN CHRIST WE CLAIM ITS CONTENT FOR US. NIKOLAUS SELNECKER: Now the Holy Spirit through David—almost 1,230 years before Christ's suffering and death—proclaimed this exact suffering, death and resurrection of Christ with the same words that were used in Christ's suffering concerning Christ himself and his enemies.[1] This is a special

teaching and proof that divine prophecy must precisely correspond with its end and fulfillment. . . . Nicholas of Lyra writes that a person with the name Theodore had wanted to exegete this psalm word for word about David, and on account of that he was condemned and excommunicated by upright doctors at the Council of Toledo. Now let them rave who want to rave! We give thanks to God the Lord that we teach and know truly and simply that this psalm is the Lord Christ's song, lament and mourning, which he composed because he had to suffer and die for our sin. And now with God's help we too want to take this psalm for us. THE WHOLE PSALTER.[2]

DAVIDIC HISTORY AND MESSIANIC PROPHECY. SEBASTIAN MÜNSTER: Now we do not deny that all these things happened to David and that in a specific situation and tribulation he was driven to

---

[1] It is unclear how Selnecker calculated that Psalm 22 was composed "almost 1,230 years" before Christ's crucifixion. Luther, for example, dated the "first edition" of the Psalter to 1057 B.C. and Christ's crucifixion and resurrection to A.D. 34—thus, at most, 1,091 years between them. See Luther's *Supputatio annorum mundi*

(1541), WA 53:22-184, here, pp. 81-82, 124-25. The modern biblical studies guild generally agrees that David's reign was c. 1010–970 B.C.; see further Bill T. Arnold and H. G. M. Williamson, eds., *Dictionary of the Old Testament: Historical Books* (Downers Grove, IL: InterVarsity Press, 2005), 198-206.
[2] Selnecker, *Der gantze Psalter*, 1:120v, 121r. Selnecker's information about Theodore of Mopsuestia (c. 350–428) is slightly distorted, as were Nicholas of Lyra's comments. Theodore and his work were indeed condemned, but at the Second Council of Constantinople (553). His strong preference for historical-grammatical exegesis strictly limited christological interpretation and intertextual resonance (he accepted only four psalms as messianic: Pss 2; 8; 45; 110). The council saw this as potentially dividing Christ into two persons—one human and one divine—which Theodore's infamous pupil Nestorius later did. See above "Introduction to the Psalms," pp. *xlvi-lii.*

these laments, but still while he composed this psalm, recognizing he was a type for Christ, he especially turned his spirit to that. THE TEMPLE OF THE LORD: Psalm 22.[3]

CONTINUALLY MEDITATE ON THIS PSALM. THEODORE BEZA: Since we can never sufficiently meditate on that battle of Christ on which our own victory depends—and in it we may plainly behold not only how horrible it is to fall into the hand of God, our Judge, but also how great the lovingkindness of God is toward his church and finally how sublime the mystery of God's wisdom is—surely this psalm among others is worthy never to be put out of our hands and memory. For it depicts the self-emptying of the Son of God in such a way that his body hanging on the cross and those most sorrowful groans that he uttered in his wrestling with Satan, our sin and death—as if he were forcing his way out of the very bottom of a whirlpool—we almost see with our very eyes and hear with our very ears. Even besides that, this psalm describes brilliantly and clearly the illustrious victory of his resurrection, his perpetual and eternal office as high priest and teacher which Christ will execute until the end of the world through his ambassadors, gathering his church from all nations and preserving it for his sake. In this way the four Evangelists interpret this psalm in the history of the passion as well as the apostle in the epistle to the Hebrews. PARAPHRASE OF PSALM 22.[4]

SCRIPTURE'S UNANIMITY PROVES ITS DIVINITY. JACOBUS ARMINIUS: The agreement between each and every part of the Scriptures proves, with sufficient evidence, their divinity, because such an agreement of its many parts can be ascribed to nothing less than the divine Spirit. To confirm this it will be useful to consider: (1) The immense span of time which it took to write it—from the age of Moses to the age of Saint John, to whom the last

authentic revelation was entrusted; (2) the multitude of writers or amanuenses and of books; (3) the great distance of the places in which the books were variously written, which made it impossible for the authors to confer together; (4) finally and most importantly, a comparison between the teaching of Moses and the latter prophets as well as between the teaching of the Old and New Testaments.

Just the predictions of Moses concerning the Messiah, the calling of the Gentiles and the rejection of the Jews, when compared with the interpretations and addition of particular circumstances which are found in the Prophets and Psalms, will prove that the perfect agreement that exists between the various writers is divine. To the divinity of the agreement between the writings of the Old and New Testaments, abundant testimony will be afforded even solely by that sudden, unexpected and miraculously unanimous accommodation and befitting aptitude of all the predictions about the Messiah: the gathering of the Gentiles to him, the unbelief and rejection of the Jews and finally concerning the abrogation of the ceremonial law—first by it being fulfilled and then by it being forcibly removed. Whether these predictions were foretold in words or types of things, persons, facts and events, their accommodation to the person, advent, state, offices and times of Jesus of Nazareth is unanimous even to a miracle!

If the Old Testament alone or only the New Testament were now extant, some doubts could be indulged concerning their divinity. But their agreement together excludes all doubt concerning the divinity. Both of them are so completely in agreement! Thus, it is impossible for such a perfect agreement to have been fabricated by an angelic or human mind. DISPUTATION 1: ON THE AUTHORITY AND CERTAINTY OF THE SACRED SCRIPTURES.[5]

---

[3]Münster, *Miqdaš YHWH*, 1177.
[4]Beza, *Psalmes of Dauid*, 34-35* (*Psalmorum Davidis*, 72).

[5]Arminius, *Works*, 1:405-6*; citing Mal 4:4; Jer 28:8; Jn 5:46; Gen 49:10; Deut 32:21; Dan 9:25-26; Mal 1:10-11; Pss 2; 22; 110; 132; Mt 1-2; 24; 27; Lk 1:55, 70; 24:27, 44; Ps 118:22-23; Mt 21:42; Is 65:1; Acts 11:18; Ps 40:7-8; Dan 9:25-26.

Superscription: *Doe of the Dawn?*

WHAT DOES "DOE OF THE DAWN" MEAN?
SEBASTIAN MÜNSTER: It is uncertain—even among the Hebrews, not to mention the Latins!—what this phrase means. Some think that it is a musical instrument, others the morning star, others strength, others a doe—which metaphorically means Israel, as in Song of Songs Israel is compared with a gazelle. Those who interpret it as "morning star" suppose Christ, who illuminates the world through his radiance, is signified by this. For all the Evangelists testify that this psalm was written about Christ our Savior; it so explicitly mentions his passion, exaltation and kingdom, promulgating it to the ends of the earth. THE TEMPLE OF THE LORD: PSALM 22.[6]

THE INSCRIPTION PROPHESIES THE GOD-
MAN. MARTIN LUTHER: Christ is called the doe because he (1) slaughters and devours serpents, that is, the devil, (2) easily and swiftly travels the way, that is, cheerfully and willingly, and (3) easily births his fawns, that is, his children. Dawn applies to Christ because he is God. The deity of Christ is the morning; his humanity is the evening. And as evening and morning are one day, so also human and God have become one Christ. Therefore, this is the meaning of the title: Psalm for the God-Man who slaughters the devil. This is Christ who through his cross destroyed that ancient serpent. GLOSSA ON PSALM 22 (1513–1515).[7]

BELIEVE AND EAT THE TRUE VENISON,
CHRIST. WOLFGANG MUSCULUS: In this reading, which gives "Doe of the Dawn," not only should we reflect historically on the persecution, suffering and death of Christ but also to what end this reading was foreordained by God. For in the same way that the doe of the dawn is not captured and killed for

the sake of capturing and killing—as wolves usually kill—but so that it would become pleasing sustenance for these hunters and killers, so also Christ was not destined to this end by the Father merely to be killed, but so that he would become the sustenance of life for his killers and hunters, so long as they eat of him by faith. . . .

Thus, like venison, Christ's flesh is seasoned and cooked for us by God as the pleasing food of life—so excellent, of course, that without it no one has life. Oh! the true Venison, Christ's flesh, for the faithful soul is far more savory than what this world's nobility have in their delicacies. And lest that food be lacking exquisite flavor and taste, our Deer was not simply killed but first was highly sought after—just like how royalty are accustomed to hunt and pursue before they capture and kill, rendering their venison more sweet, more tender and more exquisite. For he was not simply strangled but was pierced with a spear, so that by spilling blood his body was rendered more pleasing to eat and less distasteful. For this also is usually done with deer to prepare it as food for royalty. Oh, but whose palate, teeth and stomach are worthy of this Venison? "Believe," Augustine says, "and chew." COMMENTARY ON PSALM 22.[8]

THE INSCRIPTION HAS NOTHING TO DO
WITH THE PSALM ITSELF. JOHN CALVIN: Although this inscription is obscure, nevertheless interpreters, in order to torture themselves needlessly, have sought after I know not what sublime mystery in such a small thing. . . . Now because it is a prophecy about Christ—as the apostles splendidly testify—the ancients thought that Christ's excellence was not sufficiently honored, unless through an allegorical interpretation of the word *doe* they shifted its meaning to his sacrifice (so also those who preferred to render the word as "morning star"). But because I find nothing solid in these word games, it will be better to choose what is simpler and more natural. To me it is surely believable that it was the beginning of a

---

[6]Münster, *Miqdaš YHWH*, 1177.
[7]WA 3:134 (cf. 5:598-601). Cajetan interprets "dawn" similarly; see Cajetan, *In Sacrae Scripturae Expositionem*, 3:78. That deer ate snakes was a common ancient and early modern conception; see Pliny the Elder, *Natural History* 8.50; 28.42.

[8]Musculus, *In Psalterium Commentarii*, 330-31; citing Jn 6:52-56.

popular song. How the inscription corresponds to the psalm's subject matter, I do not see. COMMENTARY ON THE PSALMS.[9]

CHRIST—THROUGH DAVID'S LIPS—SPEAKS.
PHILIPP MELANCHTHON: The person speaking is Christ. Even though David speaks about himself and undergoes similar things, still he knows that his own afflictions and deliverances are portraits of the afflictions and victories of Christ, which the propagation of the gospel and the gathering of the church would follow. David recites this psalm, indicating that the coming Christ would undergo similar things and after having liberated and triumphing, would propagate the gospel, give eternal life and gather his church from among the Gentiles, and so forth. Therefore, the recitation of the psalm fits David as a type signifying the coming of Christ, but it also fits Christ, as the chief member of the church, indeed him whose passion truly surpasses the miseries of all the ancestors and whose victory restored eternal life.

Many words are more fitting for the history of Christ than for the history of David. But nevertheless David also suffers almost similar things: and I do not dispute exceedingly meticulously over the accommodation of every individual word. It is enough to hold this in sum, namely, that here the passion of Christ and his victories are described. And David must not be excluded because he is a type of Christ. They are the most sorrowful sufferings because he asks why he has been abandoned by God, and because he is not delivered as the fathers—like Abraham, Jacob and Joseph— were delivered so that they were not killed. COMMENTS ON THE PSALMS.[10]

22:1-2 Why Do You Ignore My Cries?

CAREFULLY EXPOUND THESE WORDS FOR THE SIMPLE. MARTIN LUTHER: Now in order to indicate a rather remarkable condition and sense in

these words . . . the Evangelists intentionally repeated this verse in the Hebrew as a sign of emphasis. I cannot think of another passage in Scripture where this word is repeated like this, "My God, my God." That it is said by others that he was not forsaken in the sense that his humanity was not separated from his divinity, but rather in the sense that divine help was removed, is said most correctly, but for the unlearned, on account of their capacity, it is good to wrap up such a lofty statement in simpler words. In fact, this was said quite obscurely, that his humanity was forsaken by God's help—which is what these words mean, of course that he was forsaken by God. . . .

I see that there are some very cantankerous people who as soon as they have just formulated or heard something remarkable and enigmatic, they immediately go and show it off everywhere before everyone, as if they alone could appear to produce something new and strange. They have absolutely no discernment or consideration for either subjects or listeners or places. Their unseasonable wisdom—as long as it has no sense of sobriety—offends a great many people for no reason and begets not a little reproach for our word and ministry. If they served Christ in proportion to their gifts, they would have more than enough that they could teach profitably, and they would honor God's manifold grace as good stewards. Yes, these same people tried, as I began to fear and tire of, to engage in matters which surpass their ordinary ability, especially in matters which require no common knowledge.

We know indeed that theology should be common to all believers, but we also know that some are only partakers of milk, others are ready for solid food, and we know that only one truth is seized by these various methods. It is not possible for all people, at once, to be accommodated according to their ability while at the same time not robbing them of the truth. Paul also did not want to offend the weak—who were troubled with the scruples of ceremonies—with the example and teaching of the strong in faith. But why am I going on about this? The long journey through lessons has a shortcut, love, which easily has taught us all in all things.

---

[9]CO 31:219 (cf. CTS 8:356-57).
[10]MO 13:1049-50.

Nevertheless I will not say nothing, lest we completely pass over so rich a verse! First, what it is to be forsaken by God we do not understand well, unless we already know who God is. Now God is life, light, wisdom, truth, justice, goodness, power, happiness, glory, peace, blessedness and every good thing. Therefore, to be forsaken by God is to be in death, darkness, foolishness, falsehood, sin, wickedness, weakness, sadness, confusion, disorder, despair, damnation and in every evil thing. So, what follows? Can it be that we would make Christ a fool, a liar, a sinner, an evil man, a hopeless man, a cursed man? That, as I have said, would be enigmatic and remarkable. However, see for yourself! It is acknowledged by everyone that in Christ there was both the greatest happiness and the greatest sadness, both the greatest weakness and the greatest power, both the greatest glory and the greatest confusion, both the greatest peace and the greatest disorder, both the greatest life and the greatest death. This verse shows this adequately when, as if he were contradicting himself, he declares that he has been forsaken by God and nevertheless calls God *his* God and through this he confesses that he has not been forsaken. For no one who has been entirely forsaken says to God, "My God." If, therefore, any "part" of God—if I might speak in this way—forsook Christ, why is it not said that God completely and wholly forsook him? For here there is no difficulty besides the use and sense of common people. Otherwise, what was absurd to the Gentiles before belief prevailed than what I said, that the same person both lived the greatest life and died the greatest death? Therefore, what should we say? That Christ is both the greatest righteous person and the greatest sinner, both the greatest liar and truth teller, both the most glorious and the most hopeless, both the most blessed and the most cursed? For unless we say this, I do not see in what way he has been forsaken by God, because many saints—Job, David, Hezekiah, Jacob—have been forsaken in this way, how much more so therefore Christ, the Head of the saints, who bore all our weakness in himself.

Here my mind prophesies: Christ, in fact, was and remained righteous who neither committed sin, nor was any deceit found in his mouth. For this reason he wanted to be conceived and born of the Virgin by the Holy Spirit, so that he was without all sin; otherwise how could he have been able to free us from sin? But for this reason, for a time, when he suffered, he therefore accepted all our sin as if in fact it had been his very own. He suffered on account of these our sins—on account of which we should have rightly suffered. These our sins allowed him to be cursed as Paul, from Psalm 69, says, "The reproaches of those who reproached you fell on me." SECOND PSALMS LECTURES (1519–1521).[11]

CHRIST SAVES EXCESSIVELY, NOT SUFFICIENTLY. CARDINAL CAJETAN: If you can believe this surprised lament—"My God, why have you forsaken me?"—proceeded from the condition of his divine state and mind, that is false. And in order to remove such a possibility he says that "these words" are "my bellowing." That is, not from his divine but his natural condition. Bellowing in fact is the natural voice of a lion suffering from hunger or sadness. Here notice that Christ's expression, "My God, my God"—because it is mournful—reveals the natural condition of his fleshly sense, which strives against the nails, the whips and such, as being harmful to itself; similarly it reveals the natural condition of his rational mind, which strives against disgrace, derision and such. But because the expression is surprised, it reveals the excess[12] of his suffering which surpasses human reason, even taking into account the salvation of the human race that was accomplished through this suffering. For human reason imagines

---

[11]WA 5:601-3; citing 1 Cor 3:1-2; Ps 69:9 (cf. Rom 15:1-7); Is 52:13–53:12. Patristic and medieval understandings of the relationship between Christ's two natures in his person (via *communicatio idiomatum in concreto*) inform Luther's comment here. See further David J. Luy, *Dominus Mortis: Martin Luther on the Incorruptibility of God in Christ* (Minneapolis: Fortress, 2014), esp. 178-94.

[12]Here Cajetan creatively interprets *excessum* (Lk 9:31 Vg) to mean "excess," though, as he himself acknowledges in his commentary on Lk 9:31 itself, *exodos* in Greek means "departure," that is, in context, "death." See Cajetan, *In Sacrae Scripturae Expositionem*, 4:212.

that Christ would save the human race by sufficient means, not by excessive means. But while Christ could have saved the human race sufficiently with one drop of his blood, nevertheless he suffered so excessively that it surpasses all human reason. Thus, Moses and Elijah at Christ's transfiguration "spoke of his excess which he was about to accomplish in Jerusalem" (Lk 9). Therefore, the sense is this: "Because you keep yourself far away, not from me but from my salvation, on account of such a withdrawal these words, which I have spoken, are not mine according to my divine mind, instead they are 'my bellowing'—my natural and rational condition according to my human mind." Commentary on Psalm 22.[13]

Believers: Between God and Devil. John Calvin: That David sustained the assaults of temptation, without being overwhelmed or swallowed up by it, may be easily gathered from his words. He was greatly oppressed with sorrow, but notwithstanding this, he breaks forth into the language of assurance, "My God! My God!" which he could not have done without vigorously resisting the contrary apprehension that God had forsaken him. There is not one believer who does not daily experience the same thing. According to the judgment of the flesh, believers think themselves cast off and forsaken by God, while by faith they embrace a hidden grace. Thus it happens that in their prayers opposing affections are mingled and interwoven. Fleshly sense and reason cannot but conceive of God as being either favorable or hostile, based on the current condition of things as they appear. When, therefore, he suffers us to lie long in sorrow, and as it were to pine away under it, we must necessarily feel, according to the apprehension of the flesh, as if he had quite forgotten us. When such anxiety captures the entire human mind, it overwhelms believers in profound unbelief, so that they no longer long for a remedy. But if faith comes to their aid against such a temptation, these same persons who, judging from the outward

appearance of things regarded God as enraged against or estranged from them, beholds in the mirror of his promises the hidden and withdrawn grace of God. Between these two contrary affections believers fluctuate; Satan throws before them the signs of God's wrath, drives them to despair and strives to cast them down headlong. However, faith, which calls them back to God's promises, teaches them to wait patiently and to rest in God, until he again shows them his fatherly countenance. Commentary on the Psalms.[14]

Christ's Love for Us Strengthened Him Through Unprecedented and Unequaled Trial. Hieronymus Weller von Molsdorf: Here he magnifies his suffering through comparison, as if he were to say, "I look around for an example to keep myself going. I want to find one, but none comes to mind. I see no saint who has been tormented by my same trial and affliction." For the examples of those who have experienced the same suffering that we are currently experiencing strengthens our mind wonderfully. In addition to that it is a joy for those in misery to have companions in affliction. And there is no doubt that Satan has magnified this evil with the most dreadful thoughts. Not only did the devil bluster and try to goad him to despair, but also he could call to mind no example fitting his own suffering. For no saint has ever fallen into such misfortune or affliction who has not found companions in his misfortune as examples. There is no temptation for which there cannot be found an example in sacred literature and history. For although our first parents had no example in their sight by which they could keep themselves going when Cain killed his own brother, nevertheless their suffering is in no way to be compared with the suffering of Christ, because they themselves were strengthened by God.

Through this passage we should engage in pious meditation. So great was this flame of love toward the human race in Christ that he endured numerous and great sorrows and torments on

---

[13]Cajetan, *In Sacrae Scripturae Expositionem*, 3:79.

[14]CTS 8:358-59* (CO 31:220).

account of our sins. This we should learn well and imprint on our hearts! But how few meditate on the magnitude of Christ's love? For some are devoted to zeal for amassing wealth, others are slaves to marks of honor and have minds overtaken with profane worries and cares, still others keep busy with philosophical studies, while others not only scorn but even persecute this doctrine about the suffering of Christ.

Therefore the meaning of this verse is "I am compelled to cry out to you day and night as if to a relentless and unyielding God; in short I feel that I pour out useless prayers." By these words Christ shows that he was thoroughly and truly well acquainted with such a trial from an angry and estranged God who averts and avoids our groans and prayers. The saints before him, however, barely tasted this trial. BRIEF COMMENT ON PSALM 22.[15]

22:3-8 Remember How You Remembered Your People Before

GOD FORSAKES NO ONE AND THUS FORSOOK HIS SON. TILEMANN HESSHUS: This is an argument from God himself, illumined by the church's witness. Not only does Christ testify to his faith but also reveals that in many things he was much more horribly oppressed by God than any of the patriarchs or prophets were burdened by God. He glorifies God's holiness and remembers that his name will be preached by the whole church. "You," he says, "are holy, O God," that is, "You are gracious, merciful, just, truthful, loving, immeasurably good and eager to keep your promises. You have forsaken no one. You have cheated no one of your promise. You act unjustly toward no one." Why, therefore, does he not listen to Christ, his only-begotten Son, in such extreme need? It was declared that the Mediator would be humbled and this was that time when Christ must pay the penalty for the sins of the world. Therefore, although God is most holy, nevertheless he does not listen to the Messiah in

this moment but plunges him into death. By completing this time of humiliation and by paying *lutron* ["ransom"] God exalted the Messiah with glory and honor. "Dwelling in the praises of Israel," that is, "your church, the people of Israel, in which you have revealed yourself, sing your praises. The church preaches that you are omnipotent, wise, just, merciful, gracious, loving; you are the Father. All the orphans who call out to you, you rescue. These praises and *enchōmia* are most surely true, however, I am now in that very place in which your wisdom, justice, truth and goodness are not seen. For I was destined to be sacrificed." Christ does not deny what the church rightly celebrates, but he was afflicted in this particular way by God.

Another amplification of the misfortune and agony which the Messiah experienced is constructed by a juxtaposition of dissimilar examples. For the Messiah wants to teach that he does not experience ordinary misery and distress, like the sort that the rest of the patriarchs—Adam, Noah, Shem, Abraham, Jacob, David—endured. Instead he endured a far more difficult struggle, for he experienced the full wrath of God, kindled against all human sin. "He is the Lamb of God who bears the sin of the world."

God tested the patriarchs by various distresses and dangers, but the fullness of his wrath he did not pour out on them, nor did he forsake them; instead he always consoled them in every need. He confirmed them through the Holy Spirit and in the end snatched them out of every distress. But Christ was the most wretched of all human beings; on him God poured out the fullness of his wrath. Satan and the world spewed out all their venom and hatred into him. "But I am a worm," that is, "I am experiencing such horrible distress that I am not even like a human being." "He is despised," Isaiah says, "and the most hated of men." And Pilate, loathing Christ's squalor, said, "Behold the man!" As if he were to say, "Indeed he is not at all like a human being." Now here let us consider the immeasurable love of the Son of God who suffered; for the

---

[15]Weller, *Enarratio Psalmorum*, 225-26.

sake of our salvation he was despised in this way. "The reproach of human beings and despised by the masses," that is, "the world judges me to be *katharma peripsēma* ["scum and filth"], the plague and defect of the human race. People fear that even my shadow might harm them." So they cried out, "Away with him! Away with him! Crucify him! Crucify him!" Thus, the most savage condemnation followed the greatest calamity. Commentary on Psalm 22.[16]

Consolation Lies Underneath the Surface of This Lament. Nikolaus Selnecker: In this lament of the Lord Christ there is also this to consider: it is not only a complaint and lament but also at the same time a hidden consolation: "You helped the patriarchs so mercifully, surely you will not leave me, your Son, entangled." That is a true consolation, that we can turn every sorrow and heartache into true hope and joy and thus bring Satan with his trickery and raging to nothing. Even so the devil wants to terrify us and to make us despair; we should console ourselves as the Lord Christ himself does here. If you are a sinner, if you are afraid of the wrath of God, if the devil whispers continually in your thoughts that you should not pray and call on God, because sinners will not be heard by God, then hold him against the suffering of Christ and say, "Even so, despite that I am a poor sinner, I should cry out and know that I will be heard on account of the Son of God who came into the world to save sinners of whom I am the greatest. For 'the healthy require no doctor.' Thus Christ himself calls to me and says, 'Come to me all who are weary and burdened, I will refresh you.' But I am weary and burdened. Thus, I come to the Lord Christ and am certain that he will refresh my body and soul." With such consolation we conquer the devil in the midst of fears of death and hell. A few years ago a sick man, while he lay in bed alone, and saw the evil enemy visibly come

to him. He sat down next to the bed and demanded the sick man tell his sins—of which he was conscious—one after the other. For the devil wanted to record all of them in a register which he had. In such a frightful situation, the poor man answered, "I will tell as many as I know of, but first write at the beginning: 'The woman's seed will crush the snake's head.'" As soon as the sick man said that, the evil enemy stood up and retreated, leaving behind him a nasty stench in the whole house. This is a true and consoling history. The Whole Psalter.[17]

Shield Yourselves Against Satan Through Prayer. John Calvin: How severe a temptation this must have been, everyone can judge from his own experience. But by the remedy that David used he proved the sincerity of his confidence. For unless he had had God as his sure witness, he would never have dared to bring his complaint to God. Therefore, whenever people charge that our works should be labeled as hypocrisy, the inward sincerity of our hearts may answer for us before God. And whenever Satan with his snarling and sneering strives to dislodge faith from us, let this be our sacred anchor: to summon God as witness, so that, beholding it, he would assert his righteousness by defending us. For his holy name can suffer no viler blasphemy than to say that those who put their hope in him are puffed up with false confidence and that those who are convinced that God loves them deceive themselves with a groundless fancy. Now because the Son of God was assailed with this same dart, surely Satan will not spare believers who are his members. Therefore, they should defend themselves with this shield: although they are despised among human beings, nevertheless, if they cast their cares on God, their prayers will not be useless. Commentary on the Psalms.[18]

---

[16]Hesshus, *Commentarius in Psalmos*, 100v-101r; citing Mt 20:28; Jn 1:29; Is 53:3; 1 Cor 4:13; Jn 19:15.

[17]Selnecker, *Der gantze Psalter*, 1:130v; citing 1 Tim 1:15; Mt 9:12; 11:28; Gen 3:15.

[18]CTS 8:367-68* (CO 31:225).

22:9-15 *Protect Me from These Violent Tribulations*

CHRIST'S CONCEPTION AND BIRTH ARE UNIQUE TO HIM BUT BENEFICIAL TO ALL. NIKOLAUS SELNECKER: In these ... verses the Lord Christ consoles and encourages himself; he lifts up his heart again. . . . "You have taken me," he says, "out of my mother's womb," that is, I was not conceived and born like any other person. Other persons must say of themselves: "I am born from sinful seed, and my mother conceived me in sin." . . . However, it belongs to Christ alone and to absolutely no other person, that transcendent of and contrary to the nature of things he was conceived and born from the body of the pure Virgin Mary, just like how a tiny bee sucks the best juice out of a plant or flower and yet the plant or flower remains unharmed.

Such belongs to our faith, in which it stands written: "I believe in Jesus Christ who was conceived by the Holy Spirit, born of the Virgin Mary." That is, I believe that Jesus Christ, God's only Son, for my benefit and the benefit of every human being, was conceived by the Holy Spirit without any human love and fleshly work, without a fleshly father and man's seed, and was born of a pure virgin, Mary, without any harm to her fleshly and spiritual virginity, so that he—according to the mandate of fatherly lovingkindness—would bless and purify me and every human being who believes in him from our sinful, fleshly, impure and condemned conception and birth.

So, in the conception and birth of the Lord Christ unspeakably great mysteries transcendent of nature are brought together, as Saint Bernard of Clairveaux wrote very beautifully, saying: "God did three great things when he wanted to assume our flesh—nothing like it had ever happened before nor will ever happen again—namely, he made God and man one person, mother and virgin one person, and he united faith and the human heart." The first mystery is the eternal Word, the Son of God who put on our flesh and became one person from the Word, from the soul and the flesh; these three are

one thing and the one thing is three. The second mystery is mother and virgin united in one person. It cannot happen according to nature that a virgin would become pregnant and give birth, thus becoming a true mother, and yet remain a virgin. The third mystery is the union of faith and the human heart. Yes, it is a great mystery that human beings are able to believe such high things which cannot be gauged and grasped with reason—God is human, a mother is a virgin. Such faith the Holy Spirit must work and prepare in us, because it is above all reason! As the ancient teachers said in the words of Isaiah 53, "Who will declare his birth?" Here they turned and declared that it is impossible for us to be able to understand the mystery of such a birth. Here we must let go of all understanding. Here every tongue and voice must be silent—not only the tongues and voices of human beings but also of angels. For it remains that the Lord Christ was conceived by the Holy Spirit and born of the Virgin Mary, that is, as he himself says in this psalm: God has taken him out of his mother's womb. . . .

Now we should also contemplate that Christ was conceived by the Holy Spirit, so that we know what the Son says that is the will of the Father, because the Holy Spirit is himself the very love between the Father and the Son. And this is a powerful consolation in all the promises of the teaching of the gospel, that we actually know that the Son brought and revealed to us the wonderful counsel of redemption from his Father's bosom, and that the Father wants to hear us because of his Son in whom he has his heart's joy and delight. And what he says is the very holy, eternal and omnipotent Trinity's mind, will and word. THE WHOLE PSALTER.[19]

GOD'S GRACE SURROUNDS AND SUSTAINS INFANTS—EVEN IN UTERO. JOHN CALVIN: Although it is by natural causes that infants come into the world and are nourished with their mother's milk, nevertheless in this God's wonderful providence brightly shines forth. This miracle, it is true, because of its ordinary occurrence, is reviled.

---

[19]Selnecker, *Der gantze Psalter*, 1:132v-133r; citing Ps 51:5; Is 53:8.

But if ingratitude did not veil our eyes with stupidity, we would be ravished with admiration at every childbirth in the world. What prevents the child from perishing, as it might, a hundred times in its own corruption, before the time for bringing it forth arrives, but that God, by his secret and incomprehensible power, keeps it alive in its grave? And after it is brought into the world, seeing it is subject to so many miseries and cannot stir a finger to help itself, how could it live even for a single day if God did not take it up into his fatherly bosom to nourish and protect it? It is said, therefore, with good reason, that the infant "is cast on him," for, unless he fed the tender little infants and watched over all the offices of the nurse, even at the very time of their being brought forth, they are exposed to a hundred deaths, by which they would be suffocated in an instant. COMMENTARY ON THE PSALMS.[20]

THE FAITH NEEDED IN TEMPTATIONS. WOLFGANG MUSCULUS: Because after that huge and gravest testing of a struggling hope, in which it seems that not only all human beings but even God himself is averse and opposed to him, and thus it seems that his most anxious and daily cries are in vain; when he has grasped hope anew, he prays to God himself and does not flee to any other. He does this in a most beautiful example of what such faith can be in all kinds of temptations. This is the faith by which the saints most firmly believe that the God that is true, unique, omnipotent, the best, and the Savior of his own people is their God.

First, in the greatest period of testing, which we have heard about up to this point in time, in which not only in the presence of all people but also in his own presence it seems that he has been abandoned by God, and in vain has hoped so much in God and implored help from him, so that not only does he not receive any help but receives pure mockery and derision. What raised his wavering hope in the midst of that temptation, what repelled his desperation except that unique faith which we have now brought to mind?

Second, in the matter of that tribulation which was from external enemies, of which the speaker reminds us here, "Because tribulation is near" (which he expounds on in the following verses), we see how the one deserted—as he thought—flees to God himself and implores him for help, saying, "Do not depart from me, because tribulation is near." For what reason does he think this except from the kindness of a roused hope? Moreover, from where is this hope roused except through that faith by which God would be his God? Therefore in this passage we have a splendid exercise of faith in temptations depicted as a virtue, which forces the matter on him as David, contrary to his own opinion of himself and of all others flees in those greatest temptations to the very God who seemed angry and withdrawn to him, and thus entreats him, whose help certainly seems antithetical to all because nothing is evident except the anger of God and even destruction itself.

Let us compare this sort of faith with our non-faith, what could be called rather our frigidity and stupidity, or at least our most frigid faith. This faith generally is so faint that even at that time when it does not appear that God is angry and hostile toward us, but well-disposed, we will not even dare to seek those things with confidence that God himself offers voluntarily by his own free will, even ordering us to seek them and adding that he will give us what we ask. When, I ask, will we flee to a God who appears angry and withdrawn in temptations of this sort? When will we cry out to one who has stopped-up ears? When will we seek those things which not only seem not to offer themselves before both our eyes and those of others but whose complete opposites will be observed? Therefore we see how far distant we stand at this point from faith of this sort, and then how the idea that true faith should be displaced by the trials caused by adverse things stands from the idea that it should be strengthened and become evident all the more through them. COMMENTARY ON PSALM 22.[21]

---

[20]CTS 8:369* (CO 31:226).

[21]Musculus, *In Psalterium Commentarii*, 354-55.

THE MESSIAH SPEAKS ELOQUENTLY OF HIS SUFFERING. TILEMANN HESSHUS: He returns to remembering and heaping up his extreme misfortune. He says that he is surrounded by oxen and fat bulls—that is, by strong and Epicurean tyrants—so that he is incapable of escaping. He is talking about the priests, Pharisees, Sadducees and elders in Jerusalem. These Epicureans—as if it were a matter of a herd of pigs—did not care for the church or its ministry but only fattened themselves by it. The more powerful they became, the greater they raged against the pious. Next, to depict their brutality he compares them with a lion opening wide its jaws and roaring, threatening to devour. Cows surrounded Christ when the Pharisees gathered in Caiaphas's house to accuse, charge and condemn him to death; then they covered up this sham trial before Pilate and Herod the tetrarch.

The magnitude of his misfortune he amplifies by its effect on him, and he illustrates its effect on him by similes. "I am poured out like water," that is, my strength has become weakness. The strength of my heart has been consumed by the magnitude of my anguish, because my heart has been burdened beyond human might by an enormous weight of sin. "And my bones are out of joint"; they barely hold together under my skin. I am entirely consumed by mourning and anxiety. "My heart has melted like wax." For mourning and sadness incapacitate and gradually consume my heart's spirit and strength. Here the Son of God testifies that he truly put on human flesh like our nature in all things but sin. And because the heart of Christ was burdened with the sin of the entire world and experienced the full wrath of God, he would not have been able to stand in such a battle, lest at the same time he was omnipotent and eternal God. Therefore, both of these similes teach and testify that he indeed experienced immeasurable anguish in his heart on account of the wrath of God, but nevertheless his divine power overcame them.

He continues with his description and remembrance of his remarkable misery. By choosing a simile of an earthen vessel, he shows that he was emptied of all his strength. The anguish of a bad conscience is the greatest of all anguish. It obsesses with its inadequacy and feels God's dreadful wrath. All the world's sins had already been placed on Christ's shoulders. And he experienced the full wrath of God poured into him, aflame on account of my sin, your sin and every single person's sin. Thus, Christ's anguish was immeasurable. His heart was scorched like an earthen vessel scorched in fire. Thus, in the Gospel he says, "My soul is very sorrowful, even to death." For in fear and sorrow the heart throbs and is forced into distress by the blood returning so quickly to the heart, and thus the heart steams with blood and air rushing about like boiling water, and dries up, exhausted by air. Therefore Christ testifies that he was truly—and from the soul—grieved that God was offended by the world's great number of iniquities. In severe weakness and faintness, his voice was obstructed by a withered throat and a paralyzed tongue. So also by this measure Christ bitterly lamented what was happening to him. His troubles are spoken of glibly, he says, but they should be quite astonishing. Christ speaks eloquently. He is publicly laid in the dust of death; therefore, here the Spirit prophesies that the Messiah is going to suffer death. COMMENTARY ON PSALM 22.[22]

WORDS TOO GREAT FOR DAVID'S SUFFERING. JOHN CALVIN: Here David speaks of himself hyperbolically in order to lead us beyond himself to Christ. The dreadful encounter of our Redeemer with death, by which blood instead of sweat was forced from his body; his descent into hell, by which he tasted of the wrath of God which was due to sinners; and, in short, his emptying himself, could not be adequately expressed by any of the ordinary forms of speech. And David speaks of death as those who are in trouble are accustomed to speak of it, who, struck with fear, can think of nothing but being reduced to dust and to destruction. Whenever the minds of the saints are surrounded and oppressed with this darkness, there is always some unbelief mixed with their exercise which prevents them from emerging all at once

---

[22]Hesshus, *Commentarius in Psalmos*, 101v-102r; citing Mt 26:38.

from it to the light of a new life. But in Christ these two things were wonderfully conjoined, namely, terror, proceeding from a sense of the curse of God, and endurance, arising from faith, which calmed all emotions, so that they were calmed under God's authority. We who are not endued with equal power, if at any time we see nothing but destruction, for a time we are sunk in dismay, nevertheless we should climb little by little to the hope which gives life to the dead. COMMENTARY ON THE PSALMS.[23]

REMEMBER THAT WE SUFFER NO DIFFERENTLY FROM HOW CHRIST SUFFERED.

JOHANNES BUGENHAGEN: Indeed, you should not only think about the history but you should also understand all these things as the prophecy about the body of Christ, which is the church. For what happened to Christ also happens to us in trials and persecutions. When that does happen to us, then it both can and must be called to mind in turn as a solace. Consider the particulars carefully, from the beginning of the psalm all the way even to when the trial occurs so that it proceeds to inwardly extinguish all vigor of faith and causes whatever spiritual fatness there is to wither up, and what is more, it leads to desperation and death. What occurs is much more dangerous by far: while we speak of ourselves as Christians, not sensing the worst temptation, we are seduced by the doctrines of human beings and anti-Christians under a show of piety, so that not even the least drop of divine unction remains on us, so that even antichrist quietly encamps in our consciences with a confirmed reign—indeed as a true, quiet tyrant, but our consciences are not quiet. In our conscience it is right that God alone sits there as in his own temple. If only we would cry out rightly acknowledging that very fact, as God now at last shows mercy, until the praise of Christ rising from the dead (concerning which we will hear soon) may be heard in the great assembly [ecclesia] of the Gentiles! INTERPRETATION OF THE PSALMS.[24]

22:16-21a Save Me from These Wild Beasts!

CHRIST IS HOUNDED.

HIERONYMUS WELLER VON MOLSDORF: He continues with a metaphor, comparing himself with a deer and his persecutors with dogs vigilantly pursuing a deer. Clearly he says many dogs, as if he were to say, "You are not afflicting and pursuing me, but dogs are! That is, my enemies, who with doggish fury and savagery pursue me and rage against me." From these words it is clear that Christ obtained some relief from his fears, and that he nearly [propemodum] conquered that most terrible trial: abandonment. It became more bearable for him, for he turns his thoughts to the evil of his adversaries, that is, he reproaches them but praises God, and in this way comforts himself. He teaches that God is not the author of hellish fear and trepidation, but the devil and his minions. And though God permits it and prescribes certain limits, it is the devil and his minions who afflict the pious. Just as hunting dogs harass and mangle the terrified deer with their barking and biting, so the enemies of the gospel harass the upright with their barking, that is, with their most bitter invective, and mangle them with their biting, that is, with sword, fire and imprisonment. BRIEF COMMENT ON PSALM 22.[25]

THE SUBSTANCE OF SCRIPTURE INTERPRETS THE WORDS OF SCRIPTURE.

MARTIN LUTHER: To us, who believe in Christ—we hold that this entire psalm spoke about Christ with gospel authority—it is easy to prove that the reading should be "they pierced," not "like a lion." For we do not explain the substance according to Scripture's mysteries, but we explain Scripture's mysteries according to the substance. That is, we illuminate the ancient Scriptures with the gospel, not the other way around.... Therefore because we are certain that Christ's hands and feet were nailed to the cross, nor are we less certain that this psalm fits Christ, moreover, the sense marvelously agrees and

---

[23]CTS 8:372-73* (CO 31:228).
[24]Bugenhagen, In librvm Psalmorvm interpretatio, 54r.
[25]Weller, Enarratio Psalmorum, 239-40.

absolutely demands that "they pierced" be read, especially because no grammarian's rigidity opposes it, without controversy and hesitation we read "they pierced." But their absurdity will urge the first sense ["like a lion"] on our adversaries.... None of their nonsense will drown out our understanding, but everything fits most appropriately, so that even if neither *caari* nor *caru* had been placed there, still the substance would clearly teach what it means....

The only grammar that remains should yield to theology. For the words yield and are subjected to the substance, not the substance to the words. And the expression rightly follows the sense and the letter, the Spirit. SECOND PSALMS LECTURES (1519–1521).[26]

THE HEBREW TEXT HAS BEEN CORRUPTED.

JOHN CALVIN: According to the text the phrase here is "like a lion at my hands." Now, because all the Hebraica resources agree in this reading, to depart from such a consensus would have been taboo to me, except that the scope of the passage compels such a departure and there are credible reasons for conjecturing that this passage has been fraudulently corrupted by the Jews. At any rate there is no doubt that the Greek translators [LXX] read the letter *wāw* where the text now has a *yôd*. That the Jews jabber that the literal sense has been deliberately turned upside down by our rendering ["they have pierced"] has absolutely no justification. For what need was there to trifle so audaciously in an unimportant matter? But suspicion of falsehood—not at all trivial—falls on them, who with focused zeal seek to strip the crucified Jesus of his marks, lest he be found to be the Christ and Redeemer.

If we accept what they want to be the reading, the sense will be greatly confused and obscured. First, it will be ungrammatical speech. To complete the phrase they say that it is necessary to supply the word *besieging*. But what is that? "To surround hands and feet"? For a siege considers not just these members but the entire person. Recognizing this, they flee to deluded fables—according to their

custom—saying that when a lion comes across some prey, it makes a circle around it with its tail before it falls on its pray. From this it is clear enough that they have no reason for their translation. Even so, because David used the simile of a lion in the verse before, its repetition here would be superfluous. I omit what some of our expositors have observed, that this word when the letter for similes [*kāp*] is attached, should almost surely be pointed differently. Still, I am not striving to convince the Jews, whose obstinacy in disputes is untameable. I only wanted to show briefly how wickedly they attack Christians on account of their different reading of this passage. COMMENTARY ON THE PSALMS.[27]

THESE WORDS ARE ONLY ABOUT JESUS.

MOÏSE AMYRAUT: Because these words—"My hands and my feet they have pierced"—have no basis in David's life, and because they are wonderfully fulfilled in Christ's crucifixion, they should be referred to Christ alone. ANNOTATIONS ON PSALM 22:16.[28]

CHRIST CRUCIFIED ACCORDING TO ROMAN CUSTOM, NOT HEBREW LAW. MARTIN

LUTHER: The Jews clearly ridiculed the idea that this text was about the Christ's crucifixion; indeed they even asserted that the Christ would not be crucified. For neither Moses nor the prophets indicated that sort of torture to have been practiced among the Jews—instead they practiced stoning or burning. To them, I respond that the Romans executed Christ not according to the laws of the Jews but according to the Gentiles' customs; just as today in Syria people are executed by hanging and in Hungary they are impaled. Therefore, such Jewish arguments that Christ was not crucified because this sort of torture—except being

---

[26]WA 5:633, 634.

[27]CO 31:228-29 (cf. CTS 8:373-75). Finding the Hebrew text unintelligible, Alter and Kraus amend "like a lion" to "they bound"; Goldingay accepts "like a lion." See Alter, *Book of Psalms*, 74; Kraus, *Psalms 1–59*, 291-92, 297; Goldingay, *Psalms*, 1:321, 333.

[28]Amyraut, *Paraphrasis in Psalmos Davidis*, 88; citing Mt 27:35; Mk 15:24; Lk 23:33; Jn 19:18.

hanged on a tree—that is, the piercing of hands and feet, is not found in Moses, are not strong. TABLE TALK: ANTON LAUTERBACH (1538).[29]

ALL THIS JESUS SUFFERED FOR US. DIRK PHILIPS: By this the righteousness of God is now fully revealed in that he has so severely beaten and humbled his only-begotten Son on account of the sins of his people. For how very much God hates sins is revealed from this: because of the disobedience and transgression of one man—through whom we all have become sinners—he did not allow himself to be reconciled (for his righteousness endures forever) before he allowed his beloved only-begotten Son to be so miserably handled by the godless and the pagans. His pure and holy body he also allowed to be wounded, his head to be crowned with a crown of thorns and finally to suffer the bitter and most shameful death for us on the cross.

Oh, what the only-begotten Son of God, Jesus Christ our Lord and faithful Savior, has suffered for us all! He who is the eternal wisdom and truth of God, he who cannot lie or fail—him they have reproached as a liar and deceiver of the people. He who is the righteousness and holiness of all believers and the innocent Lamb of God who knows no sin, indeed, who takes away the sin of the world—him they have numbered among the transgressors. He who is the peace of all Christians and the reconciliation of all that is in heaven and on earth—him they have accused and deplored as a revolutionary sectmaker. He who is the appearance of eternal light, an unblemished mirror of divine purity and the image of the invisible God, in whose face the angels in heaven rejoice and in whose purity all believers on earth are reflected—before him they have hidden their faces and cried before Pilate: "Away! Away! Crucify him!"

He who is the Lord of the whole world they have rejected and refused to accept as their King. He who clothes all true believing and baptized Christians with the garment of righteousness and

with the mantle of salvation—him they stripped and afterward nailed naked to the cross and divided his clothes among themselves and cast lots over his robe. He who gives the water of life to all thirsty souls—him they have given vinegar to drink in his thirst. And he who is the pioneer of life—him they have killed.

Nevertheless, this the heavenly Father, the almighty God laid on his only-begotten Son, Jesus Christ, because of our sins. And yet this, alas, is so little reflected on by the whole world! There are indeed many people today who boast the merits of Jesus Christ, his death and blood, but few are found who with true zeal reflect on the suffering of the Lord and take it to heart so that through this they become better, die to sin and live to righteousness. THE ENCHIRIDION: CONCERNING THE TRUE KNOWLEDGE OF JESUS CHRIST.[30]

THE LORD IS OUR STRENGTH, TOO. NIKOLAUS SELNECKER: He calls the Lord his strength. This is a great comfort to every distressed, afflicted heart, if that person too can say: "Dear God, I'm not well and soon I will surely lapse. O Lord, may you be my strength! If you do not help, then I'm finished. Yes, you are my life, my comfort, my might and strength. Hurry to help me!" With such words we secure God's fatherly heart. THE WHOLE PSALTER.[31]

OUR PRAYERS MUST BE FOCUSED AND CONFIDENT. JOHN CALVIN: We should remember all that David has said about himself so far. Because there was nothing missing from the heap of his miseries—nor did even a spark of hope for future deliverance glimmer—that he not only endured patiently but also that he rose up from the abyss of despair to call on God is a remarkable lesson in faith. Let us, therefore, observe that David

---

[29]WATR 4:170, no. 4150; citing Deut 21:22-23.

[30]CRR 6:163-64* (BRN 10:168-69); citing Rom 5:12; Mt 27; Jn 19; 3:16; 7:12; 1 Cor 1:30; Jn 1:29; Mt 27:38; 2 Cor 5:19; Eph 1:10; Col 1:20; Wis 7:26; 2 Cor 4:4; Col 1:15; Heb 1:3; 1 Pet 1:12; 2 Cor 3:18; Mt 27:22; Gal 3:27; Mt 27:35; Jn 4:10; 7:38; Rev 22:1; Ps 69:21; Jn 19:29; Heb 12:2. [31]Selnecker, Der gantze Psalter, 1:140r-v.

did not scatter his lamentations as if they were empty and useless—like anxious people who often blurt out their groans randomly—because his prayers show sufficiently that he trusted that the outcome he desired would happen. Indeed when he calls God "his strength," by this epithet he gives clearer evidence of his confidence. He does not pray doubtingly; instead he promises himself that assistance which he cannot yet see. COMMENTARY ON THE PSALMS.[32]

THE GOSPEL'S ENEMIES ARE THE FIERCEST BEASTS ON EARTH. HIERONYMUS WELLER VON MOLSDORF: All this is written for us, so that we would truly imitate Christ in this way. Whenever we are assailed by similar trials, certainly it will be necessary that we do not cease to bring our prayers before God, magnifying our feebleness and our enemies' fury and savagery while also exalting God's power and lovingkindness. And we must not pray as if God would disregard the dangers and evils we live in the midst of, but instead we stir up our minds to implore him.

An amplification follows. He repeats and magnifies his peril with four similes: the first is taken from a sword, the second from angry and rabid dogs, the third [from lions, the fourth][33] from unicorns—which furiously attack terrified deer with their horns. Indeed they say that the unicorn is the fiercest wild beast: it can be killed, but it cannot be caught. Thus, Christ compares his enemies with these monstrous wild beasts to show that no wild beast, however monstrous, rages as fiercely against other animals as the enemies of Christ are accustomed to roar and rage against him and his members. Accordingly through these similes the Holy Spirit wanted to depict the fury and savagery of the enemies of the gospel.

That none of the most monstrous wild beasts are as savage as the enemies of the gospel is proven by the history of every generation. Now it is

enough for lions, bears and similar monstrous wild beasts to mangle human beings. But the enemies of the gospel cannot sate their passion with just any kind of torture; they must devise extraordinary torments with which to torture Christians. Yet they are not even content with this! They even try to obliterate the memory of Christians entirely. That the enemies of the gospel can surpass even the wildest beasts in fury, the examples of the martyrs prove—many of whom, when they were thrown to lions, bears and similar wild beasts, remained unharmed. When Euphemia was thrown to an angry lion in the theater, the lion calmly approached her, gently and calmly frisking its tail, just as fawning dogs do. It brushed its body against hers and licked the shins and hands of the astonished girl. . . . God wanted by this kind of example to show that people possessed by the devil far exceed the fiercest wild beasts in brutality and ferocity.[34] BRIEF COMMENT ON PSALM 22.[35]

22:21b *The Horns of the* Rĕᵉēm[36]

THE DEVIL IS KING OVER THE UNICORNS. CARDINAL CAJETAN: There is no doubt that when the demons heard Christ saying, "My God, My God, why have you forsaken me?" they dared to devise an attack on Christ's soul, as he says, "the

---

[32]CO 31:230 (CTS 8:377).

[33]Weller—or his printer—omits the example of lions, giving three similes despite having promised four.

[34]In 303, Euphemia was martyred in an arena by wild beasts after refusing to recant her faith under torture.

[35]Weller, *Enarratio Psalmorum*, 248-50.

[36]The LXX rendered *rĕᵉēm* as *monokerōtos*, thus, the Vg used *unicornes*. Almost all the reformers either translated *rĕᵉēm* as *unicornes* or transliterated the LXX, resulting in *monocerotes* (though Beza did paraphrase it as "very ferocious beasts" [*Psalmorum Davidis*, 74]). Though this translation today is universally rejected, this Hebrew term continues to give interpreters trouble—especially because the best options (wild ox and buffalo) are tamable. The standard Hebrew dictionaries render the word as "wild ox" with a reference to the extinct auruchs, though Goldingay assumes it to be "buffalo." Kraus admits the word is uncertain and intimates that perhaps it could be a mythological reference, though he also uses "buffalo" in his translation. See Goldingay, *Psalms*, 1:334-35; Kraus, *Psalms 1–59*, 291, 298. For a potential method to determine animals in the Old Testament, see Edward R. Hope, "Animals in the Old Testament—Anybody's Guess," *Bible Translator* (*Ja, Jl Technical Papers*) 42, no. 1 (1991): 128-32.

prince of this world is coming." Now that under the names of lions and unicorns these demons come is obvious. For the devil is king over every child of pride, even the animal that is called the "unicorn"—because it has one horn on its forehead—which would rather be killed than captured. This trait is common to all demons. Peter the apostle also declared that the devil is like a roaring lion seeking someone to devour. And I know what Pliny writes about the unicorn: "The fiercest animal, the unicorn has a body like a horse, a head like a deer, feet like an elephant, a tail like a boar; it has a deep bellow, a single black horn two cubits long projecting from the middle of its forehead. It is impossible to capture this wild animal alive." COMMENTARY ON PSALM 22.[37]

THIS ANIMAL IS A TYPE FOR UNBELIEVERS.
MARTIN LUTHER: We will talk about the nature of unicorns more than enough in another passage (Ps 92), where it is said in a good way, "My horn will be exalted like a unicorn's." Here it is enough to know that it is a beast of unquenchable anger, like both a roaring lion and a hunting dog. In addition it is untamable; no unicorn has ever been captured alive. In fact, that is what is written in Job 39: "Is a rhinoceros willing to serve you? Or will it stay in your stall? Can you bind a rhinoceros with reins to plow your field? Or will it break up the soil of the valleys after you? Can you have confidence in its great strength? And will you leave your labor to it? Will you have faith in it that it will gather your crops? And will it convene at your threshing floor?"

All this that was said in the law of the people is a dreadful mystery. For by this the synagogue is shown to be untamed. Its righteousness is thus puffed up, so that it consented neither to serve Christ nor to stay in its stall and hear his word, nor plow and teach under him and to cultivate the valleys. And despite abounding in many mighty deeds and in works of the law, nevertheless Christ has no confidence in it, nor does he unite his substance to it.

For it neither gathers his crops nor convenes at his threshing floor, that is, it absolutely does not grow into the church or out of the church. These unicorns are indeed savage beasts, Christ here remembers. I will not discuss here that some think they are different animals, either a rhinoceros or a unicorn. The former, they say, has a little horn on its nose, the latter a large horn on its forehead. It is certain that our interpreter considered them to be the same. SECOND PSALMS LECTURES (1519–1521).[38]

RĔ̌ĒM IS AN UNKNOWN BUT VICIOUS BEAST.
THE ENGLISH ANNOTATIONS: As for the unicorn mentioned here in the translation, it is certain that the Hebrew word *rĕ̌ēm* is the name of a wild beast similar to the nature of a rhinoceros—but different from it. . . . But what creature it should be is not known with certainty. Pliny and some other ancients mention *monoceros* [i.e., "unicorn"], which is commonly taken for the *rĕ̌ēm*, not here only but often in Scripture. And yet whether there be any such creature as what we commonly call the "unicorn"—with that shape and those properties as are commonly ascribed to it—is much doubted and decried by not a few (both travelers and others). The unicorn's horn also—so esteemed—is thought by many to be a mere mistake or imposture. It may suffice us to know—leaving the further search to naturalists—that *rĕ̌ēm* (whatever it may be called in English or Latin) undoubtedly is the name of a wild beast, very fierce and furious, and of great strength. It is an apt emblem of unjust, violent, tyrannical people or princes. ANNOTATIONS ON PSALM 22:21.[39]

DESPITE THIS STRANGE PHRASE ABOUT UNICORNS THE MEANING IS CLEAR. JOHN
CALVIN: When it is said, "Answer me," or, "Hear me from the horns of the unicorns," although this

---

[37]Cajetan, *In Sacrae Scripturae Expositionem*, 3:81; citing Jn 14:30; 1 Pet 5:8; Pliny the Elder, *Natural History* 8.31.

[38]WA 5:656; citing Ps 92:10; Job 39:9-12. In the First Psalms Lectures, following the *Glossa Ordinaria*, Luther glosses that "unicorns are princes and prelates—their horns are their power and tyranny" (WA 3:137).
[39]Downame, ed., *Annotations*, B2r*; citing Job 39:9-12; Pliny the Elder, *Natural History* 8.31.

Hebrew phrase is not a little obscure to Latin ears, nevertheless the sense is not at all ambiguous, because the cause is merely presented instead of the effect. Thus, liberation happens because God hears us. If someone were to ask how this can be applied to Christ, whom the Father did not deliver from death, I answer, in one word, that he was more powerfully delivered than if he had been prevented from meeting death. How much greater is it to rise again from the dead than to be healed of a serious disease? Death, therefore, did not prevent Christ's resurrection in the least from testifying that he had been heard. COMMENTARY ON THE PSALMS.[40]

22:22-26 I Will Proclaim Your Name and Deeds to Israel

THE PSALMIST PRAYS IN DISTURBANCE AND CALM. CARDINAL CAJETAN: Now he adds to this petition that he has heard the first fruits of the resurrection, so that from this you should understand the difference between prayer proceeding from natural affection (in which he said, "I cry out and you do not respond!") and prayer proceeding from the mind's focused counsel. COMMENTARY ON PSALM 22.[41]

THE PREACHING OFFICE IS CHRIST'S KINGDOM ON EARTH. NIKOLAUS SELNECKER: In these few words—"I will glorify you in the congregation"—stands what the Christian church is, what the preaching office is, who maintains it and who the true preachers and teachers are. For the church is nothing other than a dear group of true Christians, teachers and hearers of Christ's Word. In this church Christ, God's Son, is in its midst, he adorns the pulpit and the use of the most blessed sacrament, so that everything is correctly and ably cared for, and God is rightly confessed and honored. As he himself says, "Where two or three are gathered in my name, there I am in their midst." And here he says, "In the midst of the church I will glorify you."

Now the preaching office truly is the kingdom of Christ in this life. For Christ, through his external Word whenever it is preached in his church, works faith and true comfort in the hearts of pious listeners, and he gives his Holy Spirit, who makes a dwelling place and temple for God out of believing human beings. And Christ himself maintains this preaching office and will continue to maintain it, as he has promised and said, "I will be with you to the end of the world." Thus, the true teachers are those who cling to Christ's Word simply and truly, and confess Christ freely and publicly, without shame, without fear—risking body, honor, goods, possessions and their life.

So much is said in the tersest manner by this verse! "I will glorify you in the congregation." In it there is much important teaching which merely has been told; however, it has not been explained sufficiently. And we ask that all pious Christians would meditate further on this magnificent consolation and that they would apply it in their own life. THE WHOLE PSALTER.[42]

PURE PRAISES FROM A PURE HEART STIR UP THE CHURCH. JOHN CALVIN: Here the psalmist expresses more distinctly . . . the fruit of public thanksgiving. By this practice each person rouses the church by his own example to praise God. For this purpose believers proclaim that he will praise the name of God in the assembly in order to encourage his brothers to do the same. But because many hypocrites force themselves into the church, and because on the Lord's threshing floor the chaff is mingled with the wheat, he addresses by name believers and those who fear God. And surely though the impure might roar God's praises with a full throat, still they do nothing but profane his sacred name. Indeed it should be desired that people from every status in the world would sing in harmony, but because the principal part of this harmony flows from a sincere and pure affection of heart, there will never be a genuine herald of God's

[40]CTS 9:377-78* (CO 31:230-31).
[41]Cajetan, *In Sacrae Scripturae Expositionem*, 3:81.
[42]Selnecker, *Der gantze Psalter*, 1:143v; citing Mt 18:20; 28:20.

glory, except those who worship in holy fear. COMMENTARY ON THE PSALMS.[43]

THE LORD WHO IS ALWAYS MERCIFUL IS ALWAYS TO BE PRAISED. TILEMANN HESSHUS: He adds a reason for this sudden praise. Rightly, he says, the whole church celebrates God's immeasurable goodness. God did not abandon the Messiah in death, nor did he cast him into damnation on account of the sins of the human race. Instead God established the Messiah as the Head and Lord of the entire church. Through him he offers the forgiveness of sin, righteousness and eternal life. And the eternal Father did not cast Christ down oppressed with the entire bulk of sin; instead he saved him. Placed in extreme difficulty he did not abandon him but mercifully delivered him. Because of these facts, it is very clear that God will neither abandon nor cast down anyone bent over by so great a bulk of sin or anyone in such extreme dangers, if only through confidence in the Mediator they ask for favor and help from God. COMMENTARY ON PSALM 22.[44]

SATISFIED AND CONSOLED BY CHRIST'S BODY AND BLOOD. NIKOLAUS SELNECKER: Because in the previous verse the kingdom of Christ is preached—what sort of kingdom it is—now the effect follows: what we should seek and find in such a kingdom, namely, true consolation or refreshment and eternal life. The consolation stands in the words that the miserable will eat and be full. That is, they will be richly consoled through the gospel; thus, they richly satisfy their spiritual hunger and thirst in the gospel and in the sacraments.

The miserable are sluggish and fearful consciences that are subject to the law in such a way that they feel and see their sin and God's wrath against their sin so acutely that they know no consolation. Instead they are weary and burdened, as Christ says. They hunger and thirst,

that is, they have no strength and might, no vitals; they languish in their misery like human beings and cattle when they have nothing to eat and to drink.

Such hunger and thirst—that is, an evil and frightened conscience that sees its sin and feels God's wrath—requires not physical food or drink. Instead it requires God's Word and true Christian teaching. Just as a hungry belly longs for food and a thirsty heart pants to be restored and refreshed, so also a frightened heart longs for divine consolation. . . . Such a frightened heart will be consoled and sustained only through God's Word; it does not receive a creature's help but instead only help through the Son of God, our Lord Christ Jesus. . . . There is nothing in heaven or on earth that is able to or will appease the conscience's hunger and thirst, aside from faith in Christ, who is God's bread who came from heaven and gives the world life. We must eat him, that is, believe in him, as he himself says: "Truly, truly, I say to you, if you do not eat the flesh of the Son of Man and drink his blood, then you have no life in you." . . .

Thus, we see how hungry and thirsty consciences can appease their hunger and thirst and become satisfied: not through Moses or the law or their works but only through the Lord Jesus Christ, whom the Word of God holds out to us. And God has appointed him, so that he would refresh us by giving us his blood to drink and would nourish us and sustain us in eternity by feeding us with his body. THE WHOLE PSALTER.[45]

EAT CHRIST'S PREACHING. JOHANNES BUGENHAGEN: It follows that their hearts live eternally, that is, they do not die eternally. Is this not what it is to be filled, and likewise to eat so that eternal life remains? Is this not what it is to be one with the immortal Christ, that is, immortal? You see how the chewing of the preaching of Christ should lead the poor into the church, that is, faith in the Word of God preached to both Jews and Gentiles. Christ speaks specifically about this chewing in John 6.

---

[43]CTS 8:380* (CO 31:232).
[44]Hesshus, *Commentarius in Psalmos*, 103v.
[45]Selnecker, *Der gantze Psalter*, 1:146r-v; citing Mt 11:28; Jn 6:53-58.

INTERPRETATION OF THE PSALMS.[46]

22:27-31 The Lord's Deeds and Words Yesterday, Today and Tomorrow

THE PSALMIST PROCLAIMS THE CALL OF THE GENTILES. MOÏSE AMYRAUT: The contents of these verses can be understood in no other way than about the call of the Gentiles. They should be explained in comparison with the meager number of those who worshiped the true God under the dispensation of the law. For that juxtaposition presents an opportunity for eloquent and universal words. And this should be explained according to the gospel. These verses wonderfully fit with what is said about Christ's kingdom in Philippians 2:9-10. ANNOTATIONS ON PSALM 22:27-29.[47]

REMEMBER GOD'S MERCY, GRACE AND KINGDOM. VIKTORIN STRIGEL: Three things should come to mind regarding the calling of the nations. First, we should think about the greatness of God's mercy by which he gathered the eternal church to himself, not only from the people of Israel but also from the nations which were polluted by idols, passions and disgraces of every kind. Second, we should consider the witness of the promise of the gospel, which is both free and universal. For the nations have offered no merits or virtues to God. Instead, on account of the Son of God they are received into grace and called to the fellowship of eternal and immortal life. Third, we should understand that the words spoken about the calling of the nations repeal the law and refute that fantasy that the Jews had about a political kingdom of Moses. HYPONĒMATA IN ALL THE PSALMS.[48]

JESUS IS LORD OF RICH AND POOR. RUDOLF GWALTHER: The fat here are the rich and noteworthy, and by those lying in the dust the psalmist understands the poor and oppressed. Thus, Christ is a Savior of the rich and the poor. However, some understand the dead by those lying in the dust, so that the meaning would be: the dead too will hear the voice of Christ, will rise again, will bow before him and will acknowledge him to be the Lord of the living and the dead. THE PSALTER.[49]

PREACHING GOD'S GRACE PRESERVES THE CHURCH. JOHN CALVIN: The psalmist confirms what I have said before: because parents will transmit (as if from hand to hand) the knowledge of this benefit to their children, God's name will always be renowned. From this we also gather this additional truth: it is by the preaching of God's grace alone that the church never perishes. Likewise, the care and diligence of propagating true doctrine are entrusted to us, so that it would continue to stand after our deaths. Because the Holy Spirit prescribes this as a duty common to all believers—to be diligent in instructing children, so that a new shoot would follow after us to worship God—sluggishness is condemned. Their idleness by which they bury God's remembrance in eternal silence is no religion; through them God's remembrance does not stand; it is not kept from being forgotten. COMMENTARY ON THE PSALMS.[50]

CHRIST'S ONE CHURCH BORN THROUGH HIS BAPTISM AND SPIRIT. CARDINAL CAJETAN: Here the unity of the church [is stated]. "It will be accounted to the Lord's birth." Everyone—however different their merits—will be judged according to their birth alone, that is, their baptismal birth, by the Lord, not by a human being. And this is how this one birth of all will happen: the apostles and Christ's other disciples will come and will announce and preach God's righteousness to a people not yet born of water and spirit, because the Lord has accomplished it, that is, his righteousness through his suffering, his death and his resurrection. For this is the righteousness of God which God accomplished, which Christ's disciples preach. This is how

---

[46]Bugenhagen, *In librvm Psalmorvm interpretatio*, 56v; citing Jn 6:22-40.
[47]Amyraut, *Paraphrasis in Psalmos Davidis*, 90.
[48]Strigel, *In omnes Psalmos*, 105; citing Is 53.
[49]Gwalther, *Der Psalter*, 364.
[50]CTS 8:388-89* (CO 31:237).

we are all reborn in the unity of the church by the Lord. Amen. COMMENTARY ON PSALM 22.[51]

IN CHRIST PUT TO DEATH OUR SIN AND GIVE US LIFE. BOOK OF COMMON PRAYER (1549): Christ, having risen again from the dead, now does not die. Thus, death no longer has any power over him. For in that he died, he died but once to put away sin, but in that he lives, he lives to God. And so likewise, count yourselves dead to sin but living to God in Christ Jesus our Lord. Alleluia, Alleluia. Christ is risen again, the first fruits of those who sleep, for seeing that by one man came death, by one man also comes the resurrection of the dead. For as by Adam all human beings do die, so by Christ all human beings will be restored to life. Alleluia.

Show forth to all nations the glory of God. And among all people his wonderful works. Let us pray. O God, who for our redemption gave your only-begotten Son to the death of the cross, and by his glorious resurrection have delivered us from the power of our enemy, grant us to die daily from sin, so that we may eternally live with him in the joy of his resurrection, through the same Christ our Lord. Amen. COLLECT FOR EASTER DAY.[52]

---

[51]Cajetan, *In Sacrae Scripturae Expositionem*, 3:82.

[52]BCP 1549, 53*.

23:1-6 THE LORD IS MY SHEPHERD

A Psalm of David.

[1] The LORD is my shepherd; I shall not want.
  [2] He makes me lie down in green pastures.
He leads me beside still waters.[a]
  [3] He restores my soul.
He leads me in paths of righteousness[b]
  for his name's sake.

[4] Even though I walk through the valley of the
  shadow of death,[c]
  I will fear no evil,

for you are with me;
  your rod and your staff,
  they comfort me.

[5] You prepare a table before me
  in the presence of my enemies;
you anoint my head with oil;
  my cup overflows.
[6] Surely[d] goodness and mercy[e] shall follow me
  all the days of my life,
and I shall dwell[f] in the house of the LORD
  forever.[g]

a Hebrew *beside waters of rest*   b Or *in right paths*   c Or *the valley of deep darkness*   d Or *Only*   e Or *steadfast love*   f Or *shall return to dwell*   g Hebrew *for length of days*

OVERVIEW: Unlike the previous psalm, our interpreters bring David to the foreground in this meditation on God's generous provision and sovereign care for his people. Alongside the supernatural guidance and protection of the divine Shepherd, many exegetes give the holy Scriptures—preached, heard, read and believed—particular prominence as the pasture of this metaphor; in both prosperity and adversity these sheep wholly depend on their Shepherd. Luther's exegesis of the first three verses of this psalm is particularly powerful, as he moves from the temporal implications of earthly shepherding to the eternal, spiritual shepherding of Christ, who guides his sheep and keeps them from perishing. While not all the interpreters—in agreement with contemporary biblical scholars—read the shepherding metaphor as extending through the final two verses of the psalm, the continuities with what goes before are nevertheless made clear, as the sustenance of the Lord and the benefits he pours out on his people are understood to be at the center of this passage as well.

ALL THINGS COME FROM GOD'S GRACE.
THEODORE BEZA: Out of a shepherd, David

became a most powerful king. Contrary to the error of the Epicureans—who dream that what they have comes to them either by chance or by their diligence, and thus they misuse every good thing, transforming each into the most filthy thing—David attributes everything that he has received to God's generosity alone. . . . He teaches us that we should lift up our minds from these perishable goods to those eternal and heavenly blessings, because piety holds the promises of both this present life and that future life. PARAPHRASE OF PSALM 23.[1]

A SONG WRITTEN TO PROCLAIM GOD'S PROTECTION. JOHN HOOPER: On account of the marvelous and wonderful description and explanation of the almighty God by the prophet and king David in this psalm, it should be clear that he was inflamed with the Holy Spirit—having been delivered from all his enemies—to declare to all the world how faithful and mighty a defender and keeper God is of all who put their trust in him. David was in great danger, especially in the wars

---

[1]Beza, *Psalmorum Davidis*, 79 (cf. *Psalmes of Dauid*, 37-38).

that he waged against the Ammonites, whose events, it seems according to Psalm 20, his subjects greatly feared; so they commended their king—as true subjects always do—with earnest prayer to God. That battle and many other dangers now ended—in which the godly king always found the protection and defense of the heavenly Father ready and at hand—now being at peace, he wanted everyone else to know about this merciful defense of God, so that as he in all his adversities put his trust in the Lord and had overcome all his enemies, in the same way, by his example, all other people should learn to do the same and assure themselves to find—as he found—the Lord of heaven to be the helper and defender of the troubled, and their keeper from all evil. THE ARGUMENT OF PSALM 23.[2]

THIS PSALM IS FULL OF DELIGHTFUL IMAGERY. NIKOLAUS SELNECKER: This psalm is a very beautiful and lovely psalm, a true thanksgiving to God, who himself teaches, preserves, protects, comforts and strengthens those who are his through his holy Word. David compares himself with a sheep that a faithful shepherd grazes with fresh grass and by cool waters. . . . Now the Word of God, which is a pasture for poor little sheep, he calls lush, green grass, fresh waters, a true highway or straight path, a rod and staff or scepter, a table, a balm or oil of joy, a full cup and a refreshing draught. For he wants to make God's Word joyous, dear, beautiful and excellent to us so that we would hold it high as well as love and delight in it. Thus, he uses such fine and playful words and parables. He sings this psalm as a beautiful spring song when everything blossoms, there are many little flowers, fresh brooks babble, the little birds sing, and all creatures are merry. THE WHOLE PSALTER.[3]

23:1-3 I Trust My Shepherd's Guidance

PASTORAL IMAGERY AND JESUS CHRIST. VIKTORIN STRIGEL: This image set forth by the

verses of Virgil delighted the prophets so that they would often set it before the church many times. "Just as the shepherd will feed his flock, he will gather together his lambs in his arms and will lift them to his breast, he will carry his offspring" (Is 40). "I will raise up over them one shepherd, who will feed them, my servant David: He will feed them, and he will be to them as a shepherd" (Ezek 34). Moreover, my flocks, the flocks of my pasture, you are my people. But if one should ask who would be Jehovah's shepherd of the church, we could not answer more easily. For the Son of God in John 10 repeated several times this strong affirmation: "I am the good shepherd." And Peter in his first epistle, chapter 2, says eloquently: "You at times wandered like sheep. But you returned to the Shepherd and Bishop of your souls, Jesus Christ." The same conviction can be confirmed by a skilled comparison of sections from the prophetic sermons. For Isaiah 40 without any doubt prophesies about John the Baptist as a precursor of Christ and about Christ. Concerning the Baptist it says: "A voice of one crying in the wilderness, make straight the way of the Lord." Concerning Christ it says: "As a shepherd he will feed his sheep." Ezekiel undoubtedly names David Christ, a phrase used in the prophetic sermon. But what is manifest is not used in the longer oration. But the established hypothesis is that this Shepherd and Jehovah is the Son of God our Mediator. *HYPOMNĒMATA IN ALL THE PSALMS.*[4]

THE METAPHOR OF SHEEP AND SHEPHERD OPENS THE MEANING OF SCRIPTURE. MARTIN LUTHER: This metaphor is one of the most beautiful and comforting and yet most common of all in Scripture, when it compares his divine Majesty with a pious, faithful or—as Christ says—"good Shepherd," and compares us poor, weak, miserable sinners with sheep. We can, however, understand this comforting and beautiful picture best when we consider the creature

---

[2]Hooper, *Certain Comfortable Expositions*, 9r*.
[3]Selnecker, *Der gantze Psalter*, 1:149r.

[4]Strigel, *Hypomnēmata*, 107-8; citing Is 40:11; Ezek 34:23; Jn 10:1-18; 1 Pet 2:25; Is 40:3 (cf. Mt 3:3).

itself—out of which the Prophets have taken this and similar images—and diligently learn from it the traits and characteristics of a natural sheep and the office, work and diligence of a pious shepherd. Whoever does this carefully will not only readily understand this comparison and others in Scripture concerning the shepherd and the sheep but also will find the comparisons exceedingly sweet and comforting.

A sheep must live entirely by its shepherd's help, protection and care. As soon as it loses him, it is surrounded by all kinds of dangers and must perish, for it is quite unable to help itself. The reason? It is a poor, weak, simple little beast that can neither feed nor rule itself, nor find the right way, nor protect itself against any kind of danger or misfortune. Moreover, it is by nature timid, shy and likely to go astray. When it does go a bit astray and leaves its shepherd, it is unable to find its way back to him; indeed, it merely runs farther away from him. Though it may find other shepherds and sheep, that does not help it, for it does not know the voices of strange shepherds. Therefore it flees them and strays about until the wolf seizes it or it perishes some other way.

Still, however weak and small an animal a sheep may be, it nevertheless has this trait about it: it is very careful to stay near its shepherd, take comfort in his help and protection and follow him however and wherever he may lead it. And if it can only so much as be near him, it worries about nothing, fears no one and is secure and happy; it lacks absolutely nothing. It also has this virtue—and this is to be marked well, because Christ praises it especially in his sheep—that it very carefully and surely hears and knows its shepherd's voice, is guided by it, does not let itself be turned away from it, but follows it without swerving. On the other hand, it pays no attention to all the voices of strange shepherds. Though they may tempt and lure it in the most friendly manner, it does not heed them, much less does it follow them.

It is the function of a faithful shepherd not only to supply his sheep with good pasture and other related things but also to keep them from suffering harm. Moreover, he takes good care not to lose any of them. But if one of them should go astray, he goes after it, seeks it and returns it. He looks after the young, the weak and the sick very carefully, waits on them, lifts them up and carries them in his arms until they are grown and strong and well.

It is just so in spiritual shepherding, that is, in Christendom. As little as a natural sheep can feed, direct, guide itself or guard and protect itself against danger and misfortune—for it is a weak and quite defenseless little animal—just so little can we poor, weak, miserable people feed and guide ourselves spiritually, walk and remain on the right path or by our own power protect ourselves against all evil and gain help and comfort for ourselves in anxiety and distress. . . . As little as a natural sheep can help itself in even the slightest degree but must simply depend on its shepherd for all benefits, just so little—even much less—can human beings govern themselves and find comfort, help and counsel in themselves in the things that pertain to salvation. They must depend on God, their Shepherd, for all of that. And God is a thousand times more willing and ready to do everything that is to be done for his sheep than is any faithful human shepherd.

This Shepherd, however, whom the prophet foretold so long before, is Christ our dear Lord, who is a shepherd much different from Moses. Moses is harsh and unfriendly toward his sheep. He drives them away into the desert, where they will find neither pasture nor water but only want. Christ, however, is the good, friendly Shepherd who goes after a famished and lost sheep in the wilderness, seeks it there and, when he has found it, lays it on his shoulder rejoicing. He even "gives his life for his sheep." He is a friendly Shepherd. Who would not be happy to be his sheep?

The voice of this Shepherd, however, with which he speaks to his sheep and calls them, is the holy gospel. It teaches us how we may win grace, forgiveness of sins and eternal salvation, not by the law of Moses—which makes us even more shy, unstable and discouraged, though even in times past we were excessively timid, shy and frightened—but by Christ who is "the shepherd and bishop of our souls." For Christ has sought us miserable, lost sheep and has brought us back from the wilderness. That is, he has redeemed us from the law, sin, death, the power of the devil and eternal damnation. By giving his life for us he has obtained for us grace, forgiveness of sin, comfort, help, strength and eternal life against the devil and all misfortune. To the sheep of Christ this is a dear, sweet voice. They are sincerely glad to hear it, for they know it well and let themselves be guided by it. But a strange voice they neither know nor hear, because it sounds unfamiliar; they avoid it and flee from it.

The pasture with which Christ feeds his sheep is also the dear gospel by which our souls are fed and strengthened, preserved from error, comforted in all temptations and sorrows, protected against the devil's wile and power and finally saved from all need. But his sheep are not all equally strong; in part they are still lost, scattered all about, wounded, sick, young and weak. He does not reject them for that reason but gives more attention to them and also cares for them more diligently than he does for the others who have no faults. As the prophet Ezekiel says . . . he seeks the lost, brings back the strayed, binds up the crippled, strengthens the sick. And the young lambs that have just been born, Isaiah says, he will gather in his arms and carry them so that they may not grow tired and will gently lead those who are with young. All of this, Christ our dear Shepherd effects through the office of preaching and the holy sacraments. . . .

But here at once you hear the opposite, namely, that you lost sheep cannot find your way to the Shepherd yourself but can only roam around in the wilderness. If Christ your Shepherd did not seek you and bring you back, you would simply have to fall prey to the wolf. But now he comes, seeks and finds you. He takes you into his flock, that is, into Christendom, through the Word and the sacrament. He gives his life for you, keeps you always on the right path, so that you may not fall into error. You hear nothing at all about your powers, good works and merits—unless you would say that it is strength, good works, merit when you run around in the wilderness and are defenseless

and lost. No, Christ alone is active here, merits things and manifests his power. He seeks, carries and directs you. He earns life for you through his death. He alone is strong and keeps you from perishing, from being snatched out of his hand. And for all of this you can do nothing at all other than pay attention, listen and with thanksgiving receive the inexpressible treasure and learn to know well the voice of your Shepherd, follow him and avoid the voice of the stranger. . . .

From what has been said until now one can, I hope, easily understand these words, "The Lord is my shepherd," and indeed the whole psalm. The words "the Lord is my shepherd" are brief but also impressive and apt. The world glories and trusts in honor, power, riches and the favor of human beings. Our psalm, however, glories in none of these, for they are all uncertain and perishable. It says briefly, "The Lord is my shepherd." Thus speaks a sure, certain faith that turns its back on everything temporal and transitory, however noble and precious it may be, and turns its face and heart directly to the Lord, who alone is Lord and is and does everything. EXEGESIS OF PSALM 23 AT TABLE (1536).[5]

IN CHRIST WE OBEY THROUGH WORD AND SPIRIT. RUDOLF GWALTHER: This green pasture is the divine Word which turns green without interruption and gives the healthy, holy food that souls need. The still waters are the consolation of the Holy Spirit who alone can calm every unrest of our consciences (see Jn 7). The path of righteousness is the obedience of faith through which we put on Christ's righteousness and direct our lives according to his commands. THE PSALTER.[6]

THE SOVEREIGNTY OF GOD'S GRACE DOES NOT FREE US FROM OBEDIENCE TO HIM. JOHN HOOPER: Now as King David in this text has wonderfully set forth the miserable nature of all God's sheep and made himself an example, that the

---

[5]LW 12:153-57* (WA 51:272-76); citing Jn 10:14, 4; Lk 15:4; Is 40:11; Ex 3:1; Jn 10:12; 1 Pet 2:25; Jn 10:5; Ezek 34:16; Jn 10:28. For more on this metaphor, see RCS NT 4:367-95, esp. 392-93.
[6]Gwalther, *Der Psalter*, 37v; citing Jn 7:37-39.

nature and condition of all human beings is corrupt, wicked and damnable, so that it cannot be a partaker of God's blessings and eternal grace unless it is born again, amended, restored and instructed, so also he shows that no one converts a person's soul but the heavenly Father, the great Shepherd who both sees the lost state of his sheep and by his mercy wills to save and call home the sheep again. David goes even further and shows what the heavenly Shepherd will do with his sheep. He says, "He will lead them into paths of justice." In which the prophet declares that it is not only God who converts the person from evil but also he alone who keeps him in goodness and virtue. Thus, an incredible misery and wretchedness in the soul and body of human beings is revealed; we can neither begin nor even continue in a life acceptable to God unless God wholly works the same himself in us.

And as it declares the incredible wretchedness of human beings, it also reveals and proclaims an incredible and unspeakable mercy and compassion of God toward human beings: he so marvelously and graciously cannot be content to help and save his enemy and adversary. And this is required of everyone the Lord converts from iniquity and sinful living, that they walk in the same law and life in equity and justice as is fitting for obedient men and women redeemed with the Shepherd's most precious blood.

For the Lord does not teach his sheep the truth so that they can live in falsehood. Nor does he give them the remission of their sins so that they can return to them again. Rather, he does this so that they would studiously apply and diligently exercise themselves in virtuous works to the honor of almighty God. EXPOSITION UPON PSALM 23.[7]

OUR CONFIDENCE IS THE HOLY NAME.

DESIDERIUS ERASMUS: The great confidence which the church has derived from this: whatever her spouse offers her or has promised her is not attributed to her own merits—of which she has none, or if she has any she does not acknowledge

them, or if she acknowledges them she does not count them either as originating in herself or as worthy of reward. But because that good Shepherd gives everything to his chosen ones for the sake of his name's glory—that is, to confer renown on his wonderful mercy toward the human race—there is no danger that he will change his mind, because in a sense it is his own business which is being transacted. His name remains forever. EXPOSITION OF PSALM 23.[8]

23:4 My Shepherd Is Present Even in the Midst of Death

THE SHADOW OF DEATH. JOHN CALVIN: We thus see how, in his prosperity, David never forgot that he was a human being but even then seasonably meditated on the adversities which afterward might come on him. And certainly, the reason why we are so terrified, when it pleases God to exercise us with the cross, is because every person, so that he may sleep soundly and undisturbed, wraps himself up in carnal security. But there is a great difference between this sleep of stupidity and the repose which faith produces. Because God tries faith by adversity, it follows that no one truly confides in God, but whoever is armed with invincible constancy for resisting all fears with which he may be assailed. Yet David did not mean to say that he was devoid of all fear, but only that he would surmount it so as to go without fear wherever his shepherd should lead him.

This appears more clearly from the context. First, he says, "I will fear no evil," but immediately adds why. He openly acknowledges that he seeks a remedy against his fear in contemplating and focusing on the staff of his shepherd. "For your staff and your crook comfort me." What need would he have had of that consolation, if he had not been disquieted and agitated with fear? Therefore, it should be remembered that when David reflected on the adversities which might befall him, he became victorious over fear and temptations, in no

---

[7]Hooper, *Certain Comfortable Expositions*, 21v-22r*.

[8]CWE 64:158*.

other way than by casting himself on the protection of God. This he had also stated before, although a little more obscurely, in these words, "For you are with me." This implies that he had been afflicted with fear. Had this not been the case, why would he long for the presence of God? Besides, it is not against the common and ordinary calamities of life only that he opposes the protection of God, but against those which distract and confound human minds with the darkness of death.

For the Jewish grammarians think that ṣalmāwet—which we have translated "the shadow of death"—is a compound word, as if one should say "deadly shade." David here makes an allusion to the dark recesses or dens of wild beasts. When a person approaches such he is suddenly seized at his first entrance with an apprehension and fear of death. Now, because God, in the person of his only-begotten Son, has exhibited himself to us as our Shepherd much more clearly than he did in ancient times to the ancestors who lived under the law, we do not render sufficient honor to his protecting care if we do not lift our eyes to behold it, and keeping them fixed on it, tread all fears and terrors under our feet. COMMENTARY ON THE PSALMS.[9]

SEE WITH EYES OF FAITH, NOT EYES OF REASON. MARTIN LUTHER: Here you must not be guided by your eyes or follow your reason, as the world does. The world cannot see this rich, splendid comfort of the Christians, that they lack nothing. Yes, the world considers it quite certain that the opposite is true, namely, that on earth there are no poorer, more miserable and more unhappy people than these same Christians. And it helps very faithfully and boldly in having them most cruelly persecuted, exiled, reviled and killed. And when the world does this, it thinks that by this it has offered service to God. Outwardly, then, it appears as if the Christians were the scattered sheep, forsaken by God and surrendered to the very jaws of the wolves, and that they lack abso-

lutely everything. . . . Therefore, I say, do not follow the world in this matter, nor your own reason which, because it judges according to outward appearances, becomes a fool and considers the prophet a liar for saying "I shall not want." You, however, cling to God's Word and promise. . . . Listen to your Shepherd, however, and whatever he says to you. Judge according to his voice and not according to what your eyes see and your heart feels. Then you have gained the victory. EXEGESIS OF PSALM 23 AT TABLE (1536).[10]

HIS ROD AND STAFF: INSTRUMENTS OF GOD'S CARE. THOMAS WILCOX: He puts the instruments that the shepherds used while caring for their flocks, for the care that God had over him, and he joined the rod and staff together, because some shepherds used a rod and others a staff, but God used both. It is as if he were to say, "The care that you have over me, which far exceeds the care of a most watchful and diligent shepherd, means that in the greatest dangers, I neither doubt nor despair but am wonderfully comforted." I make this the difference between the rod and staff: the rod is put for some small goad, with which shepherds drive their sheep, to strike them but not hurt them, and staff is put for the shepherd's staff that has his hook on it, by which he catches and rules the ones that sometimes go astray. EXPOSITION UPON PSALM 23.[11]

23:5-6 *The Feast of the Lord*

WE ARE WELCOME AT THE LORD'S TABLE. JOHN HOOPER: By the name of a table he sets forth the familiar and, in a way, friendly love that the omnipotent God has toward his sheep, whom he treats not only with friendship but also with familiarity; he does not disdain—though the King of kings—to admit and receive to his table vile and beggarly sinners, scabbed and rotten sheep. That friendship and familiarity is marvelously set forth

---

[9]CTS 8:395-96* (CO 31:240).

[10]LW 12:167-68* (WA 51:285); citing Jn 16:2.
[11]Wilcox, *Godly Exposition Upon the Psalmes*, 56*.

in this, that he made a table for David. It is as if David had said, "Who can hurt me, when the Lord of lords not only loves me but always admits me to be in his company?" . . . This word *table* is used in many different ways in Scripture, but in this passage it is nearest to the mind of King David to take it in this signification that I have noted. And our Savior Christ takes it in the same signification in Saint Luke's Gospel, where he says his disciples shall eat with him at his table in the kingdom of God. EXPOSITION UPON PSALM 23.[12]

THE LORD'S TABLE SUSTAINS BELIEVERS AND SHAMES UNBELIEVERS. DESIDERIUS ERASMUS: The table is prepared in the presence of those who persecute Christ's sheep; it refreshes the pious and gives pain to the wicked. The good cheer which the faithful possess is something secret, it is true, and yet it appears most plainly in their speech and shines out in their faces. And so it happens that when the wicked hurl abuse at the pious, and the pious are not disturbed but return blessings for curses, the wicked grow more enraged than if these had been insults—particularly those who are incorrigible. But others, observing the constant calm and cheerful aspect of the pious amid all these insults and tortures, realize that the Spirit of God is at work in them and are themselves converted to a pious life. For this reason the table is prepared for those who cling with complete trust to Christ their Shepherd in the sight of the wicked, so that as the sheep begin here their enjoyment of the delights of heaven, those who are lost begin to feel here the tortures of hell, their final destination. Tyrants have devoted all their mental resources to seducing the faithful from Christ by inhuman punishments, but when they perceive that all their power, their bluster and their threats are despised and that the martyrs continue with a serene expression in the midst of torture and fire and the most cruel butchery, their own mental suffering is greater than the martyrs' physical torment. EXPOSITION OF PSALM 23.[13]

THE SUSTAINING POWER OF CHRIST'S BODY AND BLOOD. MARTIN LUTHER: How is it that Christendom in such utter weakness is able to withstand the trickery and tyranny of the devil and the world? The Lord is its Shepherd; therefore it does not want. . . . Before it the Lord has prepared a table or Easter lamb, in order to destroy its enemies completely whenever they rage greatly, gnash their teeth against it, become wild, insane, raging and raving, and draw to their aid all their trickery, strength and power. Thus, the dear bride of Christ sits down at the table of her Lord, eats from the Easter lamb, drinks from the fresh water, is joyous and sings: "The Lord is my Shepherd, I shall not want." These are her cannons and rifles, with which she has defeated and conquered all her foes so far. And with these she will continue to obtain victory until Judgment Day. EXEGESIS OF PSALM 23 AT TABLE (1536).[14]

THE POWER OF GOD'S WORD. NIKOLAUS SELNECKER: The oil or precious balm with which they anointed kings and priests is the Word of God through which the Holy Spirit anoints us, sanctifies us, purifies us, strengthens us, gladdens us and makes us rested and radiant. So also, the cup which they used for offerings of thanksgiving is nothing other than the Word of God through which we become joyous and inebriated in the Holy Spirit.

Now when the world uses armor, pikes, rifles, walls and swords against its enemies, look! Faithful, pious Christians use the table of God, balm or a beautiful little rosary and a good fresh drink, that is, they commend their matter to God and trust in his Word. THE WHOLE PSALTER.[15]

DAVID STIRS UP OUR GRATITUDE BY HIS EXAMPLE. JOHN CALVIN: All people, it is true, are not treated with the same generosity with which David was treated, but there is not an individual

---

[12]Hooper, *Certain Comfortable Expositions*, 34r-v*.
[13]CWE 64:167*; citing 1 Pet 3:9.

[14]LW 12:174* (WA 51:291). As a result of his belief that the church has existed since Adam and Eve, Luther regularly referred to Israelite feasts and festivals by their "Christian" names.
[15]Selnecker, *Der gantze Psalter*, 1:151r.

who is not under obligation to God by the benefits which God has conferred on him, so that we are constrained to acknowledge that he is a kind and generous Father to all his people. Let us stir up ourselves to gratitude to God for his benefits, and the more abundantly these have been bestowed on us, our gratitude ought to be the greater. If one is ungrateful who, having only a coarse loaf, does not acknowledge in that the fatherly providence of God, how much less can the stupidity of those be tolerated who glut themselves with the great abundance of the good things of God which they possess, without having any sense or taste of his goodness toward them?

David, therefore, by his own example, admonishes the rich of their duty, so that they may be the more ardent in the expression of their gratitude to God, the more delicately he feeds them. Further, let us remember that those who have greater abundance than others are bound to observe moderation not less than if they had only as much of the good things of this life as would serve for their limited and temperate enjoyment. We are too much inclined by nature to excess. Therefore, when God is, concerning worldly things, bountiful to his people, it is not to stir up and nourish in them this disease. All people ought to attend to the rule of Paul, so that they "may know both how to be abased and how to abound." So that want may not sink us into despondency, we need to be sustained by patient endurance; also, so that too great abundance may not elate us above measure, we need to be restrained by the bridle of temperance. COMMENTARY ON THE PSALMS.[16]

GOD PURSUES THOSE WHO ENTRUST THEM-SELVES TO HIM. MARTIN BUCER: In fact there is a noteworthy rhetorical amplification in the phrase "they follow." People pursue happiness, but happiness pursues the saints and those who entrust themselves to God himself. And yet they do not seek him with such zeal that it may be well for themselves, as much as God seeks that he may do

good to them. And he does that not for some brief period of time, as human beings customarily do, but for all time: just as they also do not withdraw themselves from that divine providence but sit eternally in the house of the Lord, that is, leading their lives among his sheep, in his church, with a sincere faith and an attentive love. That the psalmist is speaking about this house of the Lord is sufficiently shown from the fact that he says that he would dwell in it for length of days, that is, for the greatest amount of time. However, because it was fitting that the church of God would then come together at the tabernacle of the covenant and there would be a public place for preaching the name of God and for learning his law, the psalmist was also frequently present in that place, just as whoever truly loves God attends most zealously the sacred assemblies. HOLY PSALMS.[17]

THE POLYVALENCE OF "THE LORD'S HOUSE." RUDOLF GWALTHER: Sometimes the Lord's house means the people of God, as in Hebrews 3; sometimes the temple, as when Christ says, "My house shall be a house of prayer"; sometimes heaven itself. And all these meanings serve this word. For a believer always remains a member of the people of God, diligently participates in the common assembles and will possess the kingdom of heaven eternally. THE PSALTER.[18]

THE IMMEASURABLE BENEFITS OF DWELLING IN THE LORD'S HOUSE, THE CHURCH. TILEMANN HESSHUS: Another benefit is communion with the true church of God, in which—because God himself dwells in it and is always present—access to God is always granted to believers. We are allowed to hear God speak with us. We are allowed to enjoy the sacraments established by the Son of God. We are allowed to receive counsel from the mouth of God, to be present in divine worship, to ask for consolation from the Word, to delight in the habits of the saints, to mature in knowledge of

---

[16]CTS 8:397-98* (CO 31:241); citing Phil 4:12.

[17]Bucer, *Sacrorum Psalmorum*, 133v; citing Ps 24:7.
[18]Gwalther, *Der Psalter*, 37v; citing Heb 3:6; Mt 21:13.

God, to hear and to see the astonishing works of God which happen in the church, to sing praises, to honor the name of God, to cherish the sure hope of eternal life. These immeasurable advantages they obtain who dwell in the house of the Lord, as it is written elsewhere, "In the house of the Lord, in our God's courtyard, they will flourish." Therefore, we rightly give thanks for these immeasurable benefits. COMMENTARY ON PSALM 23.[19]

THE HOLY SPIRIT TEACHES US TO ASK GOD FOR HIS MERCY. PHILIPP MELANCHTHON: David seeks his defense so that afterwards he may serve in the house of the Lord, learn heavenly doctrine, adorn the church by the propagation of salvific doctrine and train the young and the entire population in the knowledge of God. Here the goal of the pious governor is set forth. When the victor returns home from the battle line, a greater concern for his soul is observed than there was previously a concern for waging war, namely, how he would rightly govern the church. To this end, all the other labors from all peoples must be brought to bear so that each and every one may serve the church according to his vocation and apply some work to upholding and adorning doctrine. Thus even in other psalms he seeks the propagation of life on account of this reason: "It is not the dead that will praise you, O Lord." For in order that there may be teachers, it is necessary that some people live who have been rightly taught and strengthened by life experience.

This is the sum of the psalm, which we ourselves will now understand more plainly when we recite it with this very intention, so that we too would give thanks to God for our nourishment, defense and governance—all these benefits we should seek from God. For these songs are written not for the sake of David but for the sake of the whole church. The Holy Spirit through the prophet teaches all the pious that these are the benefits of God and the promises of God. And these thoughts are taken from those first promises delivered to Abraham, as in Genesis 15: "Do not fear, Abraham! I am your protector; your reward will be great." COMMENTS ON THE PSALMS.[20]

I, A HAPPY SHEEP, AM CHRIST'S TO KEEP. RICHARD CRASHAW:

Happy me! O happy sheep!
Whom my God vouchsafes to keep;
Even my God, even he it is
That points me to these ways of bliss;
On whose pastures cheerful spring
All the year doth sit and sing,
And, rejoicing, smiles to see
Their green backs wear his livery.
Pleasure sings my soul to rest,
Plenty wears me at her breast,
Whose sweet temper teaches me
Nor wanton nor in want to be.
At my feet the blubb'ring mountain,
Weeping, melts into a fountain,
Whose soft silver-sweating streams
Make high noon forget his beams.
When my wayward breath is flying
He calls home my soul from dying,
Strokes and tames my rabid grief,
And does woo me into life:
When my simple weakness strays,
Tangled in forbidden ways,
He, my Shepherd, is my guide,
He's before me, at my side,
And behind me, he beguiles
Craft in all her knotty wiles:
He expounds the giddy wonder
Of my weary steps, and under
Spreads a path clear as the day,
Where no churlish rub says nay
To my joy-conducted feet,
Whilst they gladly go to meet
Grace and Peace, to meet new lays
Tuned to my great Shepherd's praise.
Come now all ye terrors, sally,
Muster forth into the valley,

---

[19]Hesshus, *Commentarius in Psalmos*, 107v; citing Ps 92:13. [20]MO 13:1051; citing Ps 115:17 (cf. Ps 6:5; Is 38:18); Gen 15:1.

Where triumphant darkness hovers
With a sable wing, that covers
Brooding horror. Come thou, Death,
Let the damps of thy dull breath
Overshadow even the shade,
And make Darkness' self afraid;
There my feet, even there shall find
Way for a resolvèd mind.
Still my Shepherd, still my God,
Thou art with me; still thy rod
And thy staff, whose influence
Gives direction, gives defense.
At the whisper of thy word
Crown'd abundance spreads my board:
While I feast, my foes do feed
Their rank malice, not their need;
So that with the selfsame bread
They are starved, and I am fed.
How my head in ointment swims!
How my cup o'erlooks her brims!

So, even so still may I move
By the line of thy dear love;
Still may thy sweet mercy spread
A shady arm above my head,
About my paths; so shall I find
The fair center of my mind,
Thy temple and those lovely walls
Bright ever with a beam that falls
Fresh from the pure glance of thine eye,
Lighting to eternity.
There I'll dwell for ever, there
Will I find a purer air.
To feed my life with, there I'll sup
Balm and nectar in my cup,
And thence my ripe soul will I breathe
Warm into the arms of death.

STEPS TO THE TEMPLE.[21]

---

[21]Crashaw, *Complete Works of Richard Crashaw*, 33-35*.

24:1-10 THE KING OF GLORY

A Psalm of David.

[1] The earth is the LORD's and the fullness
thereof,[a]
the world and those who dwell therein,
[2] for he has founded it upon the seas
and established it upon the rivers.

[3] Who shall ascend the hill of the LORD?
And who shall stand in his holy place?
[4] He who has clean hands and a pure heart,
who does not lift up his soul to what is false
and does not swear deceitfully.
[5] He will receive blessing from the LORD
and righteousness from the God of his
salvation.

[6] Such is the generation of those who seek him,
who seek the face of the God of Jacob.[b]
Selah

[7] Lift up your heads, O gates!
And be lifted up, O ancient doors,
that the King of glory may come in.
[8] Who is this King of glory?
The LORD, strong and mighty,
the LORD, mighty in battle!
[9] Lift up your heads, O gates!
And lift them up, O ancient doors,
that the King of glory may come in.
[10] Who is this King of glory?
The LORD of hosts,
he is the King of glory! Selah

a Or and all that fills it   b Septuagint, Syriac, and two Hebrew manuscripts; Masoretic Text Jacob, who seek your face

OVERVIEW: While the historic restoration of the ark to Zion is not ignored in the interpretation of this psalm, the reformers have nevertheless given primacy to christological readings that envision the entrance of Christ into his true temple, the church. Thus, these exegetes interpret most of the psalm as speaking primarily of the ascent of the true Israel, the church, to Christ, where the Lord will dwell continuously with her. While there is general agreement over the framework for interpreting this psalm, Lutheran commentators in particular draw out its political implications, recognizing the need for earthly powers to humble themselves before Christ and to fulfill the calling to which they have been ordained, assisting in the propagation of the gospel and maintaining discipline.

THIS PSALM TEACHES US TO CLAIM THE ASCENDED CHRIST AS OUR OWN. ALEXANDER ALESIUS: We will interpret this psalm as an encomium for the church gathered from all nations, scattered throughout the entire globe after the resurrection and ascension of Christ into heaven. And it is evident that Christ considered this psalm when, after his resurrection and before his ascension into heaven, he said to the apostles, "All power in heaven and earth has been given to me; as you go throughout the entire world, preach the gospel to all creation," as if he had said, "At that time this prophecy—that stands in this psalm—has been fulfilled." Therefore, this psalm is a prophecy about Christ, and it is characterized as an epideictic speech [genus demonstratiuum], because it testifies that Christ will come. . . . The use of this psalm is that we should know that we should accept and acknowledge this King, that he will bring us blessing from God, grant us his righteousness and eternal life. We should learn that this King is by nature God and our Savior, that is, a true human being, and that those who have innocent hands and a pure heart will ascend to his throne on the mountain of the Lord, that is, they belong to the true church. And the princes of the world will not receive this King but will oppose him and will persecute his church. FIRST BOOK OF PSALMS: ARGUMENT OF PSALM 24.[1]

THE TASK OF MAGISTRATES. PHILIPP MEL-ANCHTHON: This passage must be heeded for teaching political magistrates that they should know that a concern for helping the propagation of the gospel and protecting true churches of God pertains to them. Let us not suppose that polities are thus ordained by God only for the reason that we may seek goods for our belly. A magistrate should not think that he is only a herdsman, that is, a guardian of external peace, as many say, but much more a guardian of discipline, prohibiting all the external sins against the first and second table. And he should know first that he ought to adorn the glory of God, who conjoined people in political society for that reason, that some may teach others about the will of God and the gospel be propagated among people. Therefore, the impiety of princes and magistrates must be cursed, who tolerate the confusion of whatever sects there are or oppress the gospel, by this false pretext, as if it did not pertain to the magistrate to care about the propagation of the gospel. COMMENTS ON THE PSALMS.[2]

24:1-2 All Creation Is the Lord's

GOD'S GRACE IS GENERAL AND SPECIAL. THE ENGLISH ANNOTATIONS: Before he speaks of the church and the people of God particularly, which he does afterward, he first begins with the generality of God's sovereignty over all the world, over all human beings, as Creator of all, to let us know, first, that although the church of God has a particular relation to him, to be called his people and so forth, God is still the God of all human beings and cares for all. Second, that although God, by right of creation, administration, sustenance and so forth, is the God of all human beings in general, there is a select people (called the

church) who have a more particular right to and interest in his love, favor and protection; whom he describes by certain marks and properties, external and visible. ANNOTATIONS ON PSALM 24:1.[3]

"FULLNESS" INTIMATES HUMAN BEINGS. JOHN CALVIN: With respect to the word *fullness*, I admit that under it all the riches with which the earth is adorned are comprehended (as is proved by the authority of Paul), but I have no doubt that the psalmist intends by the expression human beings themselves, who are the most illustrious ornament and glory of the earth. If they should fail, the earth would exhibit a scene of desolation and solitude, not less hideous than if God should despoil it of all its other riches. To what purpose are there produced so many kinds of fruit, and in so great abundance, and why are there so many pleasant and delightful countries, if it is not for the use and comfort of human beings? COMMENTARY ON THE PSALMS.[4]

GOD'S CAREFUL CREATION AND PRESERVATION OF EARTH INTIMATES HIS CARE FOR US. CARDINAL CAJETAN: The prophet gives an explanation for God's care over the abundance and welfare of the whole earth. "Because he himself," that is, God, "founded it on the seas" when he made the waters gather into one place and dry land to appear. And truly "on the seas," because he made the lands that were once underwater rise up above the seas. Obviously, the seas do not flow on the earth, for, because the natural motion of water is to flow into a more downward sloping space, if the sea were higher than the earth, its motion would be toward covering up the earth. For this reason, just as he wrote, "on the seas," so he also wrote, "and on the rivers he will establish it," in other words, he will make it continue to be stable. Firmness in its foundation and continuing stability, both a past and ongoing action, is signified by the past and future tense. And he is trying to show that, in view of the

---

[1]Alesius, *Primus Liber Psalmorvm*, 103v-104r; citing Mt 28:18-20; Mk 16:15-16.
[2]MO 13:1053-54; citing Ps 2:10-12.
[3]Downame, ed., *Annotations*, 6B3v*.
[4]CTS 8:402* (CO 31:244).

fact that he exhibited such great care in preparing a dwelling place for the inhabitants of the earth, it is no wonder, then, if he cares for its general welfare and abundance. COMMENTARY ON PSALM 24.[5]

THIS VERSE IS TO BE UNDERSTOOD ABOUT THE CHURCH, NOT SCIENCE. NIKOLAUS

SELNECKER: These words about earth and water have been greatly disputed in the schools—and they continue to dispute on what the earth stands. But this matter does not concern us here. Earth and water are next to one another, so that they even make a sphere. So we are not at all able to understand, as the wise pagan Pindar said, "water is the best element of all."[6] . . . But this psalm does not speak of philosophical thoughts and disputes but instead how it is part of the kingdom of the Lord Christ, of his church and the gospel. The gospel is like an ocean and water that is always flowing, as we heard in the psalm before when he says, "He leads me to fresh waters." Again, in Psalm 1, "A godly person is like a tree planted by water." Thus, the earth, that is, the church or people of Christ, is established on the ocean and on water, namely, on the teaching of the gospel or on the Word of the Lord Christ. As Paul says, "No other foundation can be laid than what has been laid, Christ Jesus." THE WHOLE PSALTER.[7]

24:3-6 The Lord's Messiah Will Bring Righteousness and Salvation

BY FAITH WE ASCEND THIS HOLY MOUNTAIN.

KONRAD PELLIKAN: Who will stand in this holy place? . . . This place is free of all sin and misery; not only is there real righteousness but also the righteous participate in the total joy of the Godhead. Those who are true Jews and have circumcised hearts will ascend this mountain. For Mount Moriah was a certain shadow of the true mountain of God and the holy place, which no one enters

except by true faith in God. Those who are gifted with this will be inhabitants and citizens of this mountain wherever they are physically. For in them God is present, lives and works. They are the only true Israelites. COMMENTARY ON PSALM 24:3.[8]

THE PROMISED BLESSING BELONGS ONLY TO

TRUE ISRAELITES. JOHN CALVIN: The more effectually to move the minds of the Israelites, David declares that nothing is more desirable than to be numbered among the flock of God and to be members of the church. We must here consider that there is an implied contrast between true and degenerate Israelites. The more lawlessness the wicked indulge in, the more boldly they allege the name of God as justification, as if they held him bound by an oath, because they are adorned with the same symbols as believers. Accordingly, the demonstrative pronoun *this*, in the following verse, is not without weight, for it eloquently excludes all that adulterous generation which gloried only in the mask of ceremonies. And now, when he speaks of blessing, he means that not all who boast the label "God's worshipers" will be participants in the promised blessing but only those who answer to their calling from their heart. COMMENTARY ON THE PSALMS.[9]

THE TRUE TEMPLE IS JESUS CHRIST. PETER

RIEDEMANN: God built and established a temple for himself, a temple separate from all abominations. Christ is the first stone and foundation, and we must all be built on him. He was delivered up for us and was raised from the dead on the third day, in order that we too might walk in a new life. . . . This building is not earthly and human, but heavenly and of God. Therefore, it is the duty of the builders to learn their skill in heaven from the Father of all grace, from whom flow all good gifts, and not from human beings, even if they are called doctors or masters. Christ himself says, "They must all be taught by the Lord. Everyone who hears and

[5]Cajetan, *In Sacrae Scripturae Expositionem*, 3:86.
[6]Pindar (518–438 B.C.) was a Greek poet; this famous quote is from the opening line of his *Olympian Ode 1*.
[7]Selnecker, *Der gantze Psalter*, 1:152r; citing Ps 23:2; 1:3; 1 Cor 3:11.

[8]Pellikan, *Commentaria Bibliorum*, 4:69r.
[9]CTS 8:407* (CO 31:247).

learns from my Father comes to me." Therefore we must first of all go to this school, and with Moses we must climb up to the mount to see the tabernacle, in order to take note of its form and all its decorations. We should observe the command given by the Lord to Moses. "Take care and observe," he says, "that you create it according to the design I showed you on the mountain."

Woe indeed to the foolish workers who have never been to the mountain and still less have seen the example of the tabernacle! What kind of work can they do, since they have remained in the valley and in the encampment? They have never gone outside the camp to Christ and know nothing of the size and design of the tabernacle. How can they work when they do not know how to go about it, or what is needed for the task? If they bring thornbushes instead of firs, dross instead of silver and gold, what kind of house will that be? Who will enjoy living in it? . . .

Therefore, before the foundation of the world, Christ the caretaker of the holy tabernacle was assigned by the Father to reveal to us the Father's eternal will and to raise and rebuild again the fallen structure. He does not come from Mount Sinai, as did Moses, but from heaven itself. However, he climbs the mount at the Father's bidding, as God had appointed him to do. CONFESSION OF FAITH.[10]

WE ARE BLESSED THROUGH CHRIST ALONE BY GRACE ALONE. NIKOLAUS SELNECKER: This part of this psalm talks about the goods that Christ gives to his church, namely, blessing and righteousness. Christ is the God of our salvation; therefore he is called Jesus, a Savior and Redeemer, Jehovah. In him all peoples and Gentiles on earth are blessed, as the promise says. The blessing, however, is nothing else but true reconciliation with God

and redemption from the curse and malediction of the law or from eternal death and eternal condemnation. Righteousness means that through Christ's obedience we are acquitted of our sins and are dead to them, and have the forgiveness of sins for free, by grace, without the works of the law, solely for the sake of Christ's benefit.

And what is written here is particularly beautiful. We receive blessing and righteousness from God. Therefore our works cannot achieve anything and our free will is of no avail. If we want to think and talk about the righteousness by which we shall stand before God and about those divine things that pertain to our faith in Christ and to the salvation of our souls, our own works have to be completely swept out of the way and may not be thought about, but rather we must look solely to the Lord Christ; otherwise we are utterly lost.

If we do not do such, but instead ascribe something to our works that would pertain to salvation, we are thieves and rob the Lord Christ of his glory and are enemies of the cross of Christ and finally must perish. If we, however, believe in the Lord Christ, that he alone and no one else, neither in heaven nor on earth, makes us righteous and blessed, and that we take and receive all our blessing and righteousness from him as the God of our salvation and leave to him his glory, which belongs solely to him, then we are his bride and true church and, as it is written here, the generation that seeks him, that is, his people, which shall always remain and live, as it seeks your face, O Jacob, and it is the real and true church of Christ forever more.

The face of Jacob means God's presence with his church and the revelation whereby God reveals himself to us in his Word, in baptism and in the right use of the sacrament of the altar, as he made himself known to his people in the fire and the pillar. Jacob is the father of the people of Israel, which is therefore called the house of Jacob, that is, his household, generation and descendants or his seed, which believes in Christ and abides by the promise of the seed of the woman. THE WHOLE PSALTER.[11]

---

[10]CRR 9:172-73; citing Gen 12:1-3; 2 Cor 6:1-2; Amos 9:11-15; Acts 15:16-17; Is 52:1; 1 Pet 2:1-5; 1 Cor 3:11; Eph 2:19-22; Mt 26:47-56; Mk 14:43-50; Lk 22:47-53; 1 Cor 11:23-26; Jn 2:18-22; 20:11-18; Mt 28:1-10; Mk 16:1-7; Lk 24:1-15; Rom 6:4; 1 Cor 3:9; Ex 31:1-6; Jas 1:17; Is 54:13; Jn 6:45; Ex 24:12-18; 25:40; Acts 7:44; Heb 8:1-5; Ps 2:4-6; 15:1-5; 24:3-6; Heb 13:10-13; 1 Cor 2:11-16; Jer 8:4-12; Ezek 13:1-12; Heb 8:1-2; 1 Pet 1:18-20; Jn 16:13-15; Amos 9:11; Acts 15:15-18; Ex 32:15-16; Jn 3:3-8; 6:28-40.

[11]Selnecker, *Der gantze Psalter*, 1:153v.

24:7-10 *Open Wide the Gates for the Lord*

Here the Temple Is Dedicated as the House of the Ark of the Covenant.
Sebastian Münster: This is said to the temple itself, so that it would open for the Lord of majesty and become his continuous dwelling. For first the ark of the Lord had no permanent residence; instead, for a while it had remained in Gilgal but was brought to Shiloh. Then after it was brought back from the Philistines, it resided in Beth-Shemesh, in Kiriath-Jearim, as well as in the house of Obed-Edom until finally with great solemnity David led it onto Mount Zion into the Mosaic tabernacle where it remained until through Solomon the house of the Lord was built. The Temple of the Lord: Psalm 24.[12]

The Powers of the World Must Give Way to Christ. Nikolaus Selnecker: David exhorts the gates of the world, that is, kings, princes, lords and all rulers that they should give way to the kingdom and church of Christ; open windows, doors and gates for the King of glory; yield to the strong and mighty Lord, yes, the God of Sabaoth, the Creator of heaven and earth. As he says in Psalm 2: "O you kings, be wise, and you judges of the earth be warned; serve the Lord with fear and rejoice with trembling; kiss the Son."

For those who are the great and powerful gates and pillars in the world—emperors, kings, princes and lords—are the ones who rage the most against Christ and his Word, they devise treachery and rebel together with one another against the Lord and his anointed Christ, saying, "Who is this King

of glory?" It is as if they should say, "This beggar, yes, this heretic, this thief, this whore's child, this insurrectionist is supposed to be a King? He's supposed to reform us and we're supposed to yield to him and obey him? We don't want to do that. Let's spread a net for him with cords; let's set snares for him! Away! Away with him! Crucify him! Crucify him!" Thus, David proclaims that God's Word must be condemned and persecuted. They can rave and rage as much as they want; thus David repeats these words as consolation. The Whole Psalter.[13]

The Lord Has Literally Entered His Temple, the Church. John Calvin: This repetition teaches us that believers cannot be too constant and diligent in this meditation. The Son of God, clothed with our flesh, has now appeared as the King of glory and Jehovah of hosts; he has not entered his temple merely by shadows and figures but truly, so that he may dwell in the midst of us. Nothing, therefore, hinders us from boasting that we will be invincible by his power. Although neither Mount Zion today is appointed as the place for the sanctuary, nor is the ark of the covenant any longer the image of God dwelling between the cherubim, nevertheless because we share this with the patriarchs, that, by the preaching of the Word and sacraments, we may be united to God, it is fitting for us to embrace these aids reverently. Because nothing else can happen, if we despise with impious arrogance these aids, than that God would finally withdraw himself completely from us. Commentary on the Psalms.[14]

---

[12]Münster, *Miqdaš YHWH*, 1179; citing 1 Sam 4–7; 2 Sam 6:1-15.

[13]Selnecker, *Der gantze Psalter*, 1:154r; citing Ps 2:10-12; 140:5; Jn 19:15.
[14]CTS 8:412-13* (CO 31:249).

25:1-22 TEACH ME YOUR PATHS

ªOf David.

[1] To you, O Lord, I lift up my soul.
[2] O my God, in you I trust;
    let me not be put to shame;
    let not my enemies exult over me.
[3] Indeed, none who wait for you shall be put
       to shame;
    they shall be ashamed who are wantonly
       treacherous.

[4] Make me to know your ways, O Lord;
    teach me your paths.
[5] Lead me in your truth and teach me,
    for you are the God of my salvation;
    for you I wait all the day long.

[6] Remember your mercy, O Lord, and your
       steadfast love,
    for they have been from of old.
[7] Remember not the sins of my youth or my
       transgressions;
    according to your steadfast love remember me,
    for the sake of your goodness, O Lord!

[8] Good and upright is the Lord;
    therefore he instructs sinners in the way.
[9] He leads the humble in what is right,
    and teaches the humble his way.
[10] All the paths of the Lord are steadfast love
       and faithfulness,
    for those who keep his covenant and his
       testimonies.

[11] For your name's sake, O Lord,
    pardon my guilt, for it is great.
[12] Who is the man who fears the Lord?
    Him will he instruct in the way that he
       should choose.
[13] His soul shall abide in well-being,
    and his offspring shall inherit the land.
[14] The friendshipᵇ of the Lord is for those who
       fear him,
    and he makes known to them his
       covenant.
[15] My eyes are ever toward the Lord,
    for he will pluck my feet out of the net.

[16] Turn to me and be gracious to me,
    for I am lonely and afflicted.
[17] The troubles of my heart are enlarged;
    bring me out of my distresses.
[18] Consider my affliction and my trouble,
    and forgive all my sins.

[19] Consider how many are my foes,
    and with what violent hatred they hate me.
[20] Oh, guard my soul, and deliver me!
    Let me not be put to shame, for I take
       refuge in you.
[21] May integrity and uprightness preserve me,
    for I wait for you.

[22] Redeem Israel, O God,
    out of all his troubles.

a This psalm is an acrostic poem, each verse beginning with the successive letters of the Hebrew alphabet   b Or *The secret counsel*

OVERVIEW: Many of the reformers understood this psalm to be exegetically straightforward; thus, they extol it as a paradigm for Christian prayer. The words of David provide a model of repentance and submission to God's sovereignty and guidance. Our exegetes also draw attention to the didactic elements of the psalm. They comment on both the pedagogical tools employed by the psalmist and the model of teaching set forth by the Lord. The final verse is given a predictable typological interpretation, as the Israel that David prays for is understood as a reference to the church, the true Israel gathered by Christ.

PRAYER FOR FORGIVENESS. PHILIPP MELANCH-
THON: This whole psalm is a prayer in which the
obvious petition is for the remission of sins. Therefore it testifies that the remission of sin is given; it is
the voice of the gospel teaching the whole church
about this article, that is, about the sure and free
remission of sins, given through lovingkindness.
This cannot be sure from the voice of the law,
because the law always demands the condition of
perfect obedience. But here the remission of sin is
asked for, although we feel great weakness, gloom,
doubts, deformed affections and various flames of
sins dwelling in us. And by name it is the sin that is
born with us, that we call the sin or disease of our
origin. For we call that sin of childhood, that is, that
we always carry it within ourselves from birth on;
we cannot set it aside, namely, the infirmity of mind,
doubts, deformed inclinations of the will and heart.

Now it is a long prayer—amplified by the
circumstances—so that it may be distinguished
from the Gentiles, and so that it not seem to be
dull or feigned babble but a true prayer proceeding
from the heart. COMMENTS ON THE PSALMS.[1]

A PATTERN FOR DAILY PRAYER. THEODORE
BEZA: This psalm presents a model for the daily
prayers of the church and every saint. In it three
things are requested, and indeed from faith focusing
on the promises already revealed to us and confirmed
by past experiences. The first is the free forgiveness of
sin. The second is that we would be governed by the
Holy Spirit in the remaining course of our life. The
third is protection against our enemies' injustices.
These three things correspond to the petitions of the
Lord's Prayer in which we request to have our sins
forgiven, not to be led into temptation and to be
delivered from evil. PARAPHRASE OF PSALM 25.[2]

25:1-3 Do Not Put Us to Shame

KEEP ME FROM SHAME. MENNO SIMONS:
O Lord of hosts, my flesh is weak; my misery and

necessities are great! Nevertheless, I do not fear the
fleshly scoffing of my enemies, but I do fear greatly,
lest I deny your adored and revered name and
depart from your truth; lest they rejoice over my
weakness and my transgression of your will, and
mock me and say, "Where is your God now?
Where is your Christ?"; lest your divine honor be
thus reproached through me. O Lord, preserve me!
Keep me, O Lord! For my enemies are strong and
many; indeed, more numerous than the hairs of
my head and the spears of grass in the fields. My
unclean flesh is never at rest. Satan encompasses
me like a roaring lion, so that he may devour me.
The bloodthirsty, revengeful world is determined
on my life. They also hate, persecute, burn and
murder those who seek your praise. Wretched man,
I know not where to go! Misery, tribulation, fear
and dread are on every side; strife within and
persecution without. I say with king Jehoshaphat,
"If I know not where to go, I lift my eyes to you and
depend only on your grace and mercy, as Abraham
in Gerar, Jacob in Mesopotamia, Joseph in Egypt,
Moses in Media, Israel in the wilderness, David in
the mountains, Hezekiah in Jerusalem, the young
men in the fiery furnace, Daniel in the lion's den—
yes, as all the pious fathers trusted in you, and were
not ashamed." MEDITATION ON PSALM 25.[3]

**IN PRAYER, FOCUS ON GOD ALONE AND LET
THE WORLD FADE.** JOHN CALVIN: The psalmist
declares right away that he is not driven here and
there like the habit of unbelievers; instead he directs
all his hopes and prayers to God alone. Nothing is
more opposed to true and sincere prayer to God
than to waver and look around—as profane people
are accustomed to do—whether some help from
the world will run to them. Meanwhile, they
disregard God, or they do not turn immediately to
his faithfulness and guardianship. Those who
imagine that David here testifies that he had
devoted himself entirely to God, as if he had offered
himself up as a sacrifice, do not pay enough
attention to the context. The meaning rather is that

---

[1]MO 13:1054.
[2]Beza, *Psalmes of Dauid*, 40* (*Psalmorum Davidis*, 84).

[3]Simons, *Complete Works*, 215*.

in order to strengthen the hope of obtaining his request, he declares, what is of the greatest importance in prayer, that he had his hope fixed in God and that he was not ensnared by the allurements of the world or prevented from lifting up his soul fully and unfeignedly to God. Therefore, let us duly observe this rule of prayer: not to distract our minds by various and uncertain hopes, nor to depend on worldly help, but to yield to God the honor of lifting up our hearts to him in sincere and earnest prayer. COMMENTARY ON THE PSALMS.[4]

25:4-10 Teach Me and Lead Me in Your Truth

A MARITIME METAPHOR. MOÏSE AMYRAUT: Here I believe I can use an allegory from navigating shipping lanes to apply the meaning of David's words. By such a metaphor David asks for guidance in our earthly journey. ANNOTATIONS ON PSALM 25:4.[5]

REPETITION AS A PEDAGOGICAL TOOL. JOHN CALVIN: Although the psalmist frequently repeats the same thing, asking that God would make him know his ways and instruct him in them and lead him in his truth, there is no redundancy in these forms of speech. Our adversities are often like mists which darken the eyes, and everyone knows from experience how difficult a thing it is—while these clouds of darkness continue—to discern in what way we ought to walk. But if David, so distinguished a prophet and endued with so much wisdom, stood in need of divine instruction, what shall become of us if, in our afflictions, God does not dispel from our minds those clouds of darkness which prevent us from seeing his light? As often, then, as any temptation may assail us, we ought always to pray that God would make the light of his truth to shine on us, lest, by having recourse to sinful devices, we should go astray and wander into devious and forbidden paths. COMMENTARY ON THE PSALMS.[6]

REMEMBER YOUR PAST MERCY. MENNO SIMONS: Yes, dear Lord, how many did you accept in grace, who, according to your strict justice, merited otherwise. Adam departed from you and believed the counsel of the serpent; he broke your covenant and was found a child of death before you; your paternal kindness did not reject him, but you sought him graciously, you called and reproved him, and his nakedness you covered with coats of skin, and so graciously comforted him with the promised seed. Paul, your chosen vessel, raved like a roaring lion and a devouring wolf on your holy mountain; nevertheless, your grace shone around him in his blindness and illuminated him; you called him from heaven and chose him as a holy apostle and as a servant of your house. I also, dear Lord—the greatest of all sinners and the least among all the saints—am called your child or servant, for I have sinned against heaven and before you. Although I resisted your precious Word and your holy will with all my powers, before this with open eyes and with full understanding I disputed, taught and lived after the ease of the flesh, and sought my own praise more than your righteousness, honor, Word and truth. Nevertheless, your fatherly grace did not forsake me, a wretched sinner. Instead you received me in love, converted me to another mind, led me with your right hand and taught me by your Holy Spirit, until I voluntarily fought against the world, the flesh and the devil, renounced all my pleasure, peace, glory, lust and the ease of the flesh, and willingly submitted to the pressing cross of our Lord Jesus Christ, so that I may inherit the promised kingdom with all the valiant of God and the disciples of Christ. MEDITATION ON PSALM 25.[7]

"SINS OF MY YOUTH" IS SYNECDOCHE FOR "ALL MY SINS." RUDOLF GWALTHER: David remembers his youth not because he wants to minimize his [later] sins, but rather because youth by nature is inclined to every evil. By this phrase he includes *all* his sins, which he committed from his youth until now. He wants it to be understood that his

---

[4] CTS 8:413-14* (CO 31:250).
[5] Amyraut, *Paraphrasis in Psalmos Davidis*, 98.
[6] CTS 8:417* (CO 31:252).

[7] Simons, *Complete Works*, 217*.

sins displease him and on account of them he would surely be damned if God wanted to judge them. THE PSALTER.[8]

BEGGING FORGIVENESS SHOULD BE THE FIRST ACT OF EVERY PRAYER. JOHN CALVIN: Because our sins are like a wall between us and God, which prevents him from hearing our prayers or stretching forth his hand to help us, David now removes this obstruction. It is indeed true, in general, that human beings pray incorrectly and in vain, unless they begin by seeking the forgiveness of their sins. There is no hope of obtaining any favor from God unless he is reconciled to us. How shall he love us unless he first freely reconciles us to himself? The right and proper order of prayer therefore is, as I have said, to ask, at the very outset, that God would pardon our sins. David here acknowledges, in explicit terms, that he cannot in any other way become a partaker of the grace of God than by having his sins blotted out. In order, therefore, that God may be mindful of his mercy toward us, it is necessary that he forget our sins, the very sight of which turns away his favor from us. COMMENTARY ON THE PSALMS.[9]

THE POWER OF THE LORD'S INSTRUCTION. MENNO SIMONS: You sent forth your faithful servant, Moses, who gave Israel the law by the disposition of angels; also your servants and prophets who preached the way of repentance and broke the bread of life for the people. Sin they reproved earnestly; proclaimed your grace far abroad and taught the truth; your sharp piercing Word was in their mouth, their light shone as the golden lights; they were as flowering olive trees, as a sweet smell of costly perfumery, yes, as the fair mountain strewn with roses and lilies. Nevertheless, they did not desire them but thrust them out furiously, derided, persecuted and delivered them to death. Still the wells of your mercy flowed; you sent your beloved Son, the dear pledge of your grace, who preached your Word, fulfilled your

righteousness, accomplished your will, bore our sins, blotted them out with his blood, and brought about reconciliation; conquered the devil, hell, sin and death, and obtained grace, mercy, favor and peace for all who truly believe on him. His command is eternal life; he sent out his messengers, ministers and apostles of peace, who spread this grace abroad through the whole world; who shone as bright, burning torches before all, that they might lead me and all erring sinners into the true way. MEDITATION ON PSALM 25.[10]

CHRIST'S GOSPEL IS ONLY FOR THOSE WHO ARE DESPISED AND HUMBLE. MARTIN LUTHER: Here David adds "the miserable." Christ in Matthew 11 says, "Tell John what you see and hear"—the poor hear the gospel. Now this word *poor* or *miserable*, in Hebrew is "poor" and with us, "miserable." It means a despised and miserable person, as Mary sings, "He cared for the miserable." For us, it is misery when someone has enemies and sins which make him miserable. These are true students who are in turmoil—to them belongs the gospel. We do not preach to the rich. "I have not come to build a kingdom in which we should flaunt our wealth and thus become 'holy!' But I," God says, "I am a preacher for sinners and the miserable." Works are not your physician! Therefore, whoever begs, grieves and needs God encounters this preaching whenever that hour of misery comes. The Word of God teaches the poor, miserable sinners because they receive it. Others, who seek the kingdom of heaven here on earth, do not care about this doctrine. To such the gospel is not preached; their ears drink it in but not their hearts. But God preaches not only externally but internally by the Holy Spirit, and he gladly considers the miserable, as Mary sings. The poor and miserable—that is, those who sigh and pine for grace, lovingkindness and consolation—he draws to himself. For that reason, whenever they pray, through the Word they obtain what they pray for and thus are sustained. It is the office of God to

---

[8]Gwalther, *Der Psalter*, 41r.
[9]CTS 8:419-20* (CO 31:253).

[10]Simons, *Complete Works*, 218*.

preach to sinners who experience misery and grumble, to those who are starving and naked. With the rich and proud nothing can come of it. The little band of fishermen, Mary Magdalene, Zechariah are those to whom God preaches. So it is today. The same doctrine produces nothing in those who consider the world; it is effective only among the miserable. SERMON AT THE CASTLE CHURCH (MAY 3, 1536).[11]

RUN TO GOD WITH CONFIDENCE. NIKOLAUS SELNECKER: God can and will forgive me my sins. For he is good and holy, friendly and merciful to all who flee to him. He mercifully receives sinners and teaches them how they will become righteous and holy. First, he directs them to the right path through his Son. Second, he correctly guides the miserable in doctrine and life, in crossbearing and death, in everything according to his goodness and not his wrath. Third, he teaches them through crossbearing that they would recognize the fatherly lovingkindness of God. Fourth, all his ways are completely good and true to all who cling tightly to his grace which he has displayed to us in his Son. I will rely on this and be certain. THE WHOLE PSALTER.[12]

WHAT DOES "COVENANT" MEAN? HENRY AINSWORTH: "His testamental bond" or "league," called in Hebrew *bĕrît*, indicates brotherly or friendly parting, and it explains the conditions of agreement. For at the making of solemn covenants, beasts were killed and parted asunder, and the covenant makers went between the parts. From this comes the phrase of "cutting (or striking) a covenant." The apostles in Greek call it *diathēkē*, a testament, a testamental covenant or disposing of things. And there are two principal covenants or testaments. First, the one God made with our ancestors when he brought them out of Egypt; the sum of which is contained in the Ten Commandments written by the finger of God and the other

laws written by Moses in his book, called the book of the covenant. The second covenant is that New Testament bond which God has made with us in Christ, established in better promises and confirmed by the blood and death of Christ the testator, as the first was by the blood and death of beasts. ANNOTATIONS ON PSALM 25:10.[13]

LIVE AND PRAY THIS VERSE. MARTIN LUTHER: "All their paths are pleasing, which are called mercy and truth." This is a most beautiful verse which especially commends the Christian life, and we live accordingly. Although it is still childish and impure, nevertheless let us pray, "I am covered with scabs; lead me, O Lord! The devil, flesh and world obstruct my way." Now if in your life God's goodness and truth are not apparent to you and to hypocrites, then to pray one Our Father in faith is better than to pray the entire Psalter. SERMON AT THE CASTLE CHURCH (MAY 3, 1536).[14]

THE WAY OF THE LORD IS BLESSING AND PEACE. MENNO SIMONS: O Lord, the one who rules, your path is the path of peace; blessed is he who walks in it; for we find mercy, love, righteousness, humility, obedience and patience in her ways. Peace clothes the naked, feeds the hungry, gives drink to the thirsty, entertains the needy, reproves, threatens, comforts and admonishes; she is sober, honest, chaste and upright in all her ways; none takes offense at her; her goings forth are to eternal life, but few there are that find her. MEDITATION ON PSALM 25.[15]

25:11-15 *The Fear of the Lord*

SIN MAY ALWAYS BE WITH US BUT SO IS THE GOSPEL. NIKOLAUS SELNECKER: David still remains a sinner—even in his old age! For who is able to know how often he sins? "I am an old fool.

---

[11]WA 41:571-72; citing Mt 11:4; Lk 1:48; Mt 25:34-40.
[12]Selnecker, *Der gantze Psalter*, 1:155v.

[13]Ainsworth, *Annotations*, 2:464*; citing Gen 15:9-10, 17; Jer 34:18; Ps 1:5; 83:6; 89:4; Heb 8:8 (cf. Jer 31:31); Deut 4:13; Ex 24:8; 1 Kings 8:21; 2 Kings 23:2; Ex 24:4, 7; Lk 22:20; Heb 8:6, 8; 9:16-18.
[14]WA 41:572-73.
[15]Simons, *Complete Works*, 220*.

I've been taught," he says, "nevertheless I still do not do what I should. Sin always clings to me—even when I am sleeping it is awake in me." This is the lament of all the saints: half saint, all sinner. Sin sticks to us like muck on a wheel. Now when there is no further help, then we acknowledge and confess our sin and ask forgiveness as David does here. We exist and live under grace. Grace takes away and tolerates our sin. . . .

Neither the work-righteous nor self-assured people know or believe this doctrine, but only those who fear the Lord and know the truth which is hidden and the secret wisdom of the redemption of the human race. For this is the best path on which believers travel and are certain in eternity, as it stands here: "Their soul will abide in well-being." That is, they will have enough in eternity—eternal life. . . . Why? For they know the secret or secret word of the Lord, namely, every secret in Scripture: the teaching of the gospel—not only its history but also its fruit and use, consolation and joy. And they are a temple of the Holy Spirit. This the godless neither know or believe. They do not acknowledge their sin and do not want to be sinners. . . . They have the hull and not the kernel, the letter and not the spirit. THE WHOLE PSALTER.[16]

HIS SOUL SHALL DWELL AT EASE. MENNO SIMONS: They are released from hell, sin, the devil and death, and they serve before you in peace and joy of heart through life. They repose without fear, for you are their strength and shield. They rest under the shadow of your wings, for they are yours. They do not fear, for you warm them with the beams of your love; they do not hunger, for you feed them with the bread of life; they do not thirst, for you give them the waters of your Holy Spirit to drink; they do not want, for you are their treasure and their kingdom. They dwell in the house of your peace, in the tabernacles of righteousness, and in sure peace. They have pleasure in your law and speak of your word day and night among all the people. They wash their souls in the clear waters of your truth. They

view their consciences in the clear mirror of your wisdom; their thoughts are upright, their words are words of grace, seasoned with salt. Their works are faithful and true. The light of their piety shines around them; what they seek they find; what they desire they obtain; their souls dwell in the fullness of your goodness; the dew of your grace has been sprinkled on them; the soil of their consciences bears wine and oil without measure, and although they must endure, in their flesh for a time, much misery, suffering and trouble, yet they know well that the way of the cross is the way of life. They are not ashamed of the way of the cross and the weapons of the Lord. They patiently go with Christ to the conflict and contend valiantly, till they have reached the boundary of life and have received the crown. Nothing can hinder them, because they have become partakers of your Spirit and have tasted of your sweetness. They neither waver nor turn aside; their house stands firmly on a rock; they are as the pillars of the holy temple; they have eaten of your hidden manna. MEDITATION ON PSALM 25.[17]

GOD SPEAKS TO HIS FRIENDS. RUDOLF GWALTHER: The Word and law of God are called a secret, because it is hidden from our reason— God alone reveals it to those he considers his friends (as Christ testifies). THE PSALTER.[18]

THE SECRET OF THE LORD. THE ENGLISH ANNOTATIONS: The phrase "the secret of the Lord" is not always used in one sense, for when Job uses it . . . he means God's secret favor and providence toward him in temporal things, blessing the works of his hands and whatever belonged to him, whereby many insensibly thrive in this world, as to the admiration of others, so beyond their own expectation. . . . This cannot be the meaning here. Some understand by it a particular assurance of God's favor, whereby happiness is secured to us,

---

[16]Selnecker, *Der gantze Psalter*, 1:155v-156r.

[17]Simons, *Complete Works*, 220-21*.

[18]Gwalther, *Der Psalter*, 41r; citing Jn 15:12-17. Goldingay admits the Hebrew here is strange but prefers "counsel" instead of "friendship," which he sees as too distant to parallel Ps 25:12. See Goldingay, *Psalms*, 1:374.

both present and future. But this does not seem to agree so well with the scope of the words, neither here nor elsewhere where the expression is used. Besides, it is a doctrine subject to many restrictions and limitations, without which many are deceived by it or deceive themselves. Others therefore understand by it the doctrine of God, and particularly the Law before Christ, a secret not only to all the nations other than the Jews but even among the Jews, although commonly professed, yet hidden except to the godly, who earnestly applied themselves to the search and study of it. . . . Before Christ, then, the Law, after Christ, the gospel, of which Christ spoke to his disciples, "To you it is given to know the mysteries of the kingdom of heaven, but to them it is not given." . . . All this is granted as pertinent and probable, yet by the secret of the Lord, I conceive it . . . more particularly to be understood as a certain knowledge and acknowledgment of God's providence, and manifold dispensations not obvious to carnal judgement, and indeed many times contrary to it, in which those who in all humility fear God and heartily desire and endeavor to submit to him in all things attain it in time by long observation and God's special favor. Annotations on Psalm 25:14.[19]

We Learn God's Covenant Through the Spirit in Fear and Worship. Wolfgang Musculus: The covenant of the Lord does not pertain to anyone except those who fear and worship the Lord. Indeed, no one even acknowledges the good of the divine covenant except those whom he himself causes to acknowledge it. He does not teach that to anyone except those who fear him. And we Christians should take note of this! Today many people argue about the mysteries and signs of the covenant and the New Testament, in which there is no fear of the Lord, as if knowledge of the mysteries of God has been explained to just anyone. What do the secret things of the Lord and the covenant of the Lord have to do with the impious? The covenant of the

Lord is that he is our God and the God of our seed; we are his people. Now what kind of person cannot be among the people of God but will have a part in the covenant of God? This knowledge of the secret things of God and the covenant of God cannot be taken from the letter but from a lively and most certain experience of all of the goodness and truth of God, summarized in the covenant of God—no impious person has even had a taste of this. Because if the secret things of God and the knowledge of his covenant can be grasped from the letter, why was it necessary for David to cry out daily to the Lord, "Teach me your ways and your will"? And why was it necessary for Christ to open the apostles' minds to understand the Scriptures? Commentary on the Psalms.[20]

True Teachers Do What They Say and Say What They Do. Tilemann Hesshus: David includes his example as an exhortation to show that he not only warns others but also that he is willing to lead them into the pursuit of piety. Human beings do not want only commands but also examples. And his command or warning has the great weight of authority because it is immediately established and illustrated by the example of the teacher. "My eyes always look to the Lord. Immediately I run to the Lord in sincere prayer in every need. For he snatches me out of every difficulty and danger. If you also desire this same joy, follow my example in the pursuit of piety!" Commentary on Psalm 25.[21]

25:16-21 Turn to Me In the Midst of My Afflictions

Consider My Enemies and My Faithfulness. Menno Simons: But now that I love the world with a godly love, I have sought from my heart their welfare and happiness; I rebuked, admonished and instructed them with your Word, pointing out to them Jesus Christ and him

---

[19]Downame, ed., *Annotations*, 6B4r*, citing Job 29:4; Mt 13:11.

[20]Musculus, *In Psalterium Commentarii*, 430.
[21]Hesshus, *Commentarius in Psalmos*, 115v-116r.

crucified, they have become to me as a grievous cross and as the gall of bitterness. So fiendlike is their hatred that not only I myself but all those who love me and show me favor and mercy must . . . look for imprisonment and death. O blessed Lord! I am more despicable in their eyes than a notorious thief and murderer. I am like a lost sheep in the wilderness of the world, chased, tormented and pursued to death by ravenous wolves. Am I not like a person without hope, forsaken and comfortless like a ship in the depth of the ocean, without mast, sail and helm, tossed about by every wave and every tempest? My flesh had almost said: "I am betrayed because I find the unrighteous, disobedient nation enjoying riches, honor and prosperity, and reposing in quietude and peace, while the godly must endure so much hunger, thirst, affliction and violence; their habitation is insecure, they must toil and labor for their bread; they are accursed, defamed, persecuted and hated by all people, as the filth of the world, and as an abomination." O blessed Lord! My enemies are many and great, their heart roars like the furious lion, their words are as deadly arrows, their tongues are always against me; at one time I am reviled by them as a false seducer, at another reproached as an accursed heretic, although by your grace I possess nothing but unyielding truth. Thus am I their mortal enemy, because I instruct them in the way of righteousness.

O Lord! I am not ashamed of my doctrine before you and your angels, much less before this rebellious world, for I know assuredly that I teach your Word. I have taught, throughout, a true repentance, a dying to our sinful flesh and the new life that comes from God. I have taught a true, sincere faith in you and in your beloved Son, that it might be made powerful through love. I have taught Jesus Christ and him crucified, true God and true man, who, in an incomprehensible, inexpressible and indescribable manner, was born of you from all eternity, your eternal Word and Wisdom, the brightness of your glory and the express image of your person, and that in fullness of time, through the power of your Holy Spirit, he became, in the womb of the unspotted virgin, Mary,

real flesh and blood, a visible, tangible and mortal man, like Adam and his posterity in all things, yet without sin; born of the seed or lineage of Abraham and David, dead and buried, arose again, ascended into heaven, and thus became before you our only and eternal Advocate, Mediator, Intercessor and Redeemer.

If all the prophets, apostles and Evangelists have not taught this with the greatest clearness from the beginning, I will gladly bear my shame and reproof. I have taught no other baptism, no other supper, no other ordinance than that sanctioned by the unerring Word of our Lord Jesus Christ, and the declared example and usages of his holy apostles, to say nothing of the superabundant evidence of the historians and learned of both the primitive and the present church. Since then, I substantiate my doctrine by the evidence of your plain, ineffable Word and by the ordinance of your Son, who can reprove me and show with the argument of truth that I am an imposter? Does not the whole Scripture teach that Christ is the truth and shall abide forever? Is not the apostolic church the true Christian church? We know that all human doctrines are chaff and froth, and that antichrist has spoiled and corrupted the doctrine of Christ. Why then do they hate me, because out of pure zeal I teach and propound the doctrine of Christ and his apostles unadulterated? No one, however, hates the opposers of antichrist but those who are his members. If I did not have the Word of Christ, how cheerfully would I be taught it, for I seek it with fear and trembling; in this I can not be deceived. I have by grace, through the influence of thy Holy Spirit, believed and accepted your holy truth as the sure word of your pleasure. It will, also, never deceive me. Let them write and vociferate, threaten and dispute, boast, extirpate, persecute and destroy as they please, still your Word will triumph and the Lamb will gain the victory. Indeed, I rest assured that with this my doctrine, which is your Word, I shall, at the coming of Christ, judge and condemn not only human beings but also angels. And though I and my beloved brethren were totally extirpated and taken from the earth, yet your Word would remain eternal truth. We are no better than our coworkers who preceded us. Yet the time will arrive when they shall exalt your power, and look, perhaps too late, on him whom they have pierced.

O Lord! With what cruel hatred they hate me! Whom have I slandered in a single expression? Whom have I curtailed a penny's worth? Whose gold, silver or cattle have I desired? I have loved them with a pure love, even to death; I have taught them your Word and will, and with earnest diligence have I shown them, by your grace, the way that leads to felicity. Therefore my enemies are many, and hate me with cruel hatred. MEDITATION ON PSALM 25.[22]

25:22 Redeem Israel

ISRAEL REPRESENTS ALL BELIEVERS IN ALL TIMES. MOÏSE AMYRAUT: This gesture of piety is not restricted to the Israelite people who were pious to a certain extent. Instead it considers them under the idea of the church and so extends to believers in every age. ANNOTATIONS ON PSALM 25:22.[23]

PRAY FOR THE CHURCH. JOHN CALVIN: By the word *redeem*, which he uses here, we may infer that the church was at that time oppressed with hard bondage. And, therefore, I have no doubt that in this psalm he alludes to Saul and others who reigned with him in a tyrannical manner. At the same time, he shows that he considers not merely his own benefit, but that he comprehends in his prayer the state of the whole realm, just as the mutual communion and connection which subsist among the saints require that every individual, deeply affected by a sense of the public calamities which befall the church at large, should unite with all the others in lamentation before God. This contributed in no small degree to confirm the faith of David, when, regarding himself as in all things connected with the whole body of the faithful, he considered that all the afflictions and wrongs which he endured were common to himself with them. And we ought to regard it as of the greatest importance that in accordance with this rule, every one of us, in bewailing his private miseries and trials, should extend his desires and prayers to the whole church. COMMENTARY ON THE PSALMS.[24]

THE LORD SENT HIS SON FOR US. MENNO SIMONS: You sent forth your beloved Son, anointed with your Holy Spirit, to preach the gospel to the poor, to heal the brokenhearted, to preach deliverance to the captives and recovery of sight to the blind, to set at liberty those who are bruised, to proclaim the acceptable year of the Lord, to comfort all who mourn, to appoint to those who mourn in Zion, to give to them beauty for ashes, the oil of joy for mourning, the garment of praise for the spirit of heaviness. He preached ransom to all who are heavy laden and with faithful hearts come to him. He invites all the thirsty to the waters of life. He bore all our sins on the cross in his own body, and our debt he blotted out by his blood, even as Moses did before, through types and shadows, when he sprinkled unclean Israel with the blood of oxen and rams and with the ashes of the heifer—under the law nearly all things were purified by the shedding of blood. If the figurative blood had such virtue that it could purify the flesh to sanctification, how much more shall the blood of the beloved Son, who offered himself unspotted through the eternal Spirit, purify our consciences from dead works! MEDITATION ON PSALM 25.[25]

---

[22]Simons, *Complete Works*, 224-26*.
[23]Amyraut, *Paraphrasis in Psalmos Davidis*, 101.
[24]CTS 8:436* (CO 31:262).
[25]Simons, *Complete Works*, 223-24*.

26:1-12 I WILL BLESS THE LORD

Of David.

¹ *Vindicate me, O LORD,*
  for I have walked in my integrity,
  and I have trusted in the LORD without
    wavering.
² *Prove me, O LORD, and try me;*
  test my heart and my mind.[a]
³ *For your steadfast love is before my eyes,*
  and I walk in your faithfulness.

⁴ *I do not sit with men of falsehood,*
  nor do I consort with hypocrites.
⁵ *I hate the assembly of evildoers,*
  and I will not sit with the wicked.

⁶ *I wash my hands in innocence*
  and go around your altar, O LORD,
⁷ *proclaiming thanksgiving aloud,*
  and telling all your wondrous deeds.

⁸ *O LORD, I love the habitation of your house*
  and the place where your glory dwells.
⁹ *Do not sweep my soul away with sinners,*
  nor my life with bloodthirsty men,
¹⁰ *in whose hands are evil devices,*
  and whose right hands are full of bribes.

¹¹ *But as for me, I shall walk in my integrity;*
  redeem me, and be gracious to me.
¹² *My foot stands on level ground;*
  in the great assembly I will bless the LORD.

a Hebrew *test my kidneys and my heart*

OVERVIEW: In contrast to the patristic tendency—Augustine excepted—toward reading this psalm as a literal prayer of Christ, the reformers understand it to be literally a prayer of David and figuratively of Christ and the church. In their exegesis they underscore the importance of integrity and good conscience. Believers must meditate on the grace of God and respond to the activity of the Holy Spirit through the ministry of the Word. This also leads the reformers to consider how believers should relate to unbelievers and hypocrites in their daily lives and as they worship.

A COMMON PRAYER. NIKOLAUS SELNECKER: The ancients interpreted this psalm as a prayer of the Lord Christ as he hung on the cross. (Augustine argued that it talks about David and not about Christ.[1]) However, it is a common psalm of prayer which belongs to all the saints and to the Lord

Christ himself. In it the pious lament the false saints and their slanderers; they ask God to intervene and protect the pious against their enemies and persecutors. And it is indeed a truly beautiful psalm against the false accusations and false accusers, against the envious, evil slanderers and liars who desire to strip the pious of their honor—both in doctrine and in life—with spectacular schemes and tactics, in secret and in public. Against this there is no better advice and help than this alone: Lament to the Lord your God, and be sure that you are innocent and have a good conscience. THE WHOLE PSALTER.[2]

26:1-3 Redeem and Re-form me

THE MINISTRY OF THE WORD IS A SACRIFICE PLEASING TO GOD. PHILIPP MELANCHTHON: Enormous dangers and struggles always follow confession. Thus defense must be sought, as he seeks it here, "Judge me, O Lord," that is, defend me by your

---

[1] NPNF 8:63. This psalm "may be attributed to David himself, not the Mediator, the man Christ Jesus, but the whole church now perfectly established in Christ."

[2] Selnecker, *Der gantze Psalter*, 1:156r.

judgment. Next he adds the cause: "Because I profess true doctrine and I do not collude with your enemies." He recites this cause not so that he may oppose his merit but so that the cause of the danger is demonstrated: "Defend me, because I am sustaining a huge burden of confession. And in such danger you have especially promised defense on account of your glory and the propagation of your doctrine." This is the simplest interpretation. And yet I do not entirely cast merit aside, but in such a way that first the person is understood to be just by faith through mercy on account of the Mediator. Next, these works—diligence in vocation, constancy in confession and crossbearing, toil in teaching and refuting adversaries—these are sacrifices pleasing to God and are compensated by the greatest rewards. Now there are many of the sweetest amplifications: I avoid the doctrine of the enemies of the gospel, their guidance and their sacrifices. On the contrary, in fact, I hear and teach the expression of your praise, that is, true doctrine. And I tell others, and I love your church, that is, I give my studies, counsels and labors to cherishing, assisting and protecting her. For just as the first commandment is, "You shall love the Lord your God with all your heart," so the greatest of all works is to learn the Word of God, and that so everyone in his own place may help in its propagation, adorn and defend the ministry of true doctrine, cherish the harmony of the true church, defend her and restrain her adversaries. COMMENTS ON THE PSALMS.[3]

PURGE OUR HEART, O LORD! MARTIN LUTHER: Now David wants to be winnowed so that the old Adam might collapse and not arise again. He says, "Prove me, O Lord, and try me; purify my kidneys and my heart." He wants God to purify him as a goldsmith lets gold run through fire, melts it and makes it pure and clean. The human heart has been so powerfully poisoned that it does not feel itself. Therefore he says, "Lord, you feel my heart; I do not see it. Let it be then that I would be shaken and wrung out, that everyone would spit on me and despise me. If I become despondent and languid

and if it upsets me that people fall away from me, that is bad; if, however, I laugh when people despise me, that is good." I know many preachers who stand there and preach comfortably, for many affirm their teaching, so they preach comfortably. But if their listeners fell away from their teaching, they would quit preaching and fall away from their own teaching. Their heart isn't in it. They say "Christ" well enough with their mouths, but they do not mean it. A Christian says, "I hope in God, let them praise or despise me, let them fall here or there. That I preach, I do not do it for my sake; I don't need to preach. On my account I would rather stay quiet, but I do it out of service to you. If you accept the sermon, good for you; but, if you fall away from it, you have a Judge over you. And as I do not preach on my account, nor should you accept it on my account." Whenever we see accepting and rejecting, and God sends persecution, then we first see our heart. If you can dispense with popularity, honor, support and acceptance, that is good. But it is born in us and clings in us deeply, so that we like to see that people favor us. On the other hand, if they fall away, that upsets us. This truly shows that our heart is impure, as if he should say, "Just purge it thoroughly for me!" SERMON ON FRIDAY AFTER THE THIRD SUNDAY IN EASTER (1525).[4]

MEDITATE ON AND REFLECT GOD'S LOVINGKINDNESS. THE ENGLISH ANNOTATIONS: He shows what kept him from repaying evil for evil. Or, "Because your lovingkindness is before my eyes, I have therefore walked in truth," that is, in the way of your commandments; I have therefore applied myself faithfully to perform what you have commanded. ANNOTATIONS ON PSALM 26:3.[5]

26:4-10 *I Am Innocent*

AVOID HYPOCRITES BUT DO NOT SPURN PUBLIC WORSHIP ON THEIR ACCOUNT. JOHN CALVIN: When the psalmist denominates them

---

[3]MO 13:1057-58.

[4]LW 12:190-91* (WA 17,1:236-37).
[5]Downame, ed., *Annotations*, 6B4v*.

as the assembly of unbelievers, we may unquestionably conclude that their number was not few; indeed, it is likely that they flaunted about at that time, as if they alone were exalted above the people of God and were lords over them. Still this did not prevent David from coming as usual to the sacrifices. Public care, indeed, is to be used so that the church is not defiled by such wickedness, and everyone should work privately on this, in his own place, lest forgiveness and leniency toward these vices foster sicknesses. Nevertheless because this severity should not be too vigorous, no corruption hinders any believer from remaining piously and justly in the fellowship of the church. Meanwhile notice what David preserved, namely, participation in sacred matters. COMMENTARY ON THE PSALMS.[6]

PUBLIC INTERACTION WITH SINNERS IS UNAVOIDABLE. MARTIN LUTHER: But how should we do this? How can we avoid [the company of evildoers]? Physically I must be among them. This we must consider, but we should not accept their teaching. So this is a spiritual avoiding or fleeing when we separate ourselves from them with our heart, even though with our body we remain near them. If a Christian who adheres to the true, pure and divine Word hears a preacher who does not preach the divine Word, that Christian does not agree with him—even though he may be a good friend—if he uses the Word of God falsely, as a sham or mask. Hence the Christian says, "Either preach otherwise and correctly, or, if you refuse, I will not go along with you." We cannot avoid external association, for we must eat and drink with one another, buy and sell; but we should not receive their doctrine into our hearts or support it. In the same way they do not accept my doctrine, and I have no hopes that the whole world will accept the gospel. SERMON ON FRIDAY AFTER THE THIRD SUNDAY IN EASTER (1525).[7]

THE HEIGHT OF HUMAN EXPERIENCE IS LIFE IN THE WORD. TILEMANN HESSHUS: The Lord's anointed shows for what purpose he gathers the true church to himself and on what he especially focuses. I do not seek riches, power, glory, pleasures, but on this alone am I focused, that I would be able to enjoy your Word of salvation, that daily I would be instructed by sacred Scripture, that your divine promises would ring in my ears, that I would always quaff true consolations—moreover that with other believers I would celebrate the immeasurable benefits of God that have been granted to me. As this is the particular purpose of all human beings, so also it is the highest happiness of all human beings in this life. COMMENTARY ON PSALM 26.[8]

READ THIS ABOUT DAVID AND HIS SON. MOÏSE AMYRAUT: Verse 8 can very correctly be accommodated to Christ; nevertheless it cannot be denied that this fits David, too. ANNOTATIONS ON PSALM 26:8.[9]

ENTER WORSHIP IN DEVOTION. JOHN CALVIN: David confirms what he had said before, that he did not enter into the sanctuary in a careless manner but with serious devotion. Irreligious people, although they often resort to the sacred assemblies, frequent them merely as lurking places, where they may escape the eye of God. On the contrary, the truly pious and pure in heart resort to them not for the sake of vain ostentation, but as they are sincerely focused on seeking God, they willingly and affectionately employ the aids which he there affords them and the advantage which they derive from them creates love for them in their hearts and longing after them. This declaration further shows that however David excelled others in faith, yet he was not without fear lest the violence of his enemies might deprive him of the ordinary means of instruction which God had conferred on his church. He felt his need of the church's common discipline and order, and he

---

[6]CTS 8:443* (CO 31:266-67).
[7]LW 12:193* (WA 17,1:241-42).

[8]Hesshus, *Commentarius in Psalmos*, 118r.
[9]Amyraut, *Paraphrasis in Psalmos Davidis*, 104.

therefore anxiously labored to retain his enjoyment of them. From this we infer the impious pride of those who look with contempt on the services of religion as unnecessary, although David himself could not live without them.

Another consideration, indeed, existed in those days, I confess, while the law, like a schoolmaster, held the ancient people in a state of servitude compared with ours. Our case, however, is one with theirs in this respect, that the weakness of our faith requires help as well as theirs. And as God for this purpose has appointed the sacraments, as well as the whole order of the church, woe to the pride of those who recklessly desert the services which we perceive to have been held in such high esteem by the pious servants of God. COMMENTARY ON THE PSALMS.[10]

A DESCRIPTION OF THE GODLESS. NIKOLAUS SELNECKER: David describes the doctrine and the life of the godless. First, they are godless in their hearts; they do not at all care about God's honor. Second, they are bloodthirsty; they cannot and will not suffer true teachers and pious Christians. Whenever they are able, they chase them away or even kill them. Third, they treat others with wicked treachery, are full of envy, hatred, evil practices, trickery and deceit, and do it all for their own benefit, for their own esteem—even if they do something good. Fourth, they like to take presents. Everything is welcome, be it honor, wealth, pride, pomp or money. Their belly is their god, as Saint Paul says. They grasp whatever they can, be it just or unjust. THE WHOLE PSALTER.[11]

26:11-12 *I Walk in Integrity*

DAVID DEMONSTRATES INTEGRITY. MARTIN BUCER: He repeats his profession of blamelessness and reverence, and for this reason he prays that God would redeem him from evil things, which deservedly threaten the reprobate, and furthermore

that there would be the hope (as I have oftentimes taught) that God would strengthen him henceforth. That phrase, "my foot stands in the right," certain interpreters take it for this: "he is in the right path." Abraham Ibn Ezra, however, takes it for what is public before the churches. It seems to me that he is mentioning that he has planted his feet where he ought to, where it is most fitting for him to do so, namely, in preaching and in the assembly of the saints, to which he dedicates himself, having given himself over entirely to proclaiming God. Likewise it must also be observed what true saints chiefly desire or what is especially suitable for sacred assemblies. Certainly there is nothing of greater importance than that the goodness of God be duly preached and acknowledged; all the children of God rightly have the duty of lifting this up with a whole heart. Accordingly, from this source, faith in and love of God, who is the source of all virtues, are both originated and nourished: but without a life worthy of God, the name of God is disparaged rather than preached. . . . Now let each person see what is done in our assemblies, how the name of God is glorified, so that first one's own and then another's faith may be renewed. For God is mocked and not praised when words are poured out thoughtlessly, as well as when ceremonies are employed for the sake of promoting either only one small offering or public habit or even one's own private advantage. HOLY PSALMS.[12]

DAVID DRINKS FROM THE FOUNTAIN OF GOD'S GRACE. JOHN CALVIN: In this repetition the circumstance should be noted—it better illustrates David's righteousness—namely, that, in the midst of so many temptations, he firmly continued on his way. He witnessed many suddenly become wealthy, as today whoever represents the government in a brief amount of time accumulates a great abundance of wealth, they build costly palaces, they stretch their estates far and wide. Because he was not persuaded by any allurement

---

[10]CTS 8:445-46* (CO 31:268).
[11]Selnecker, *Der gantze Psalter*, 1:157r; citing Phil 3:19.

[12]Bucer, *Sacrorum Psalmorum*, 146v.

to imitate this behavior, he demonstrates rare and heroic strength. Therefore he rightly affirms that although the world regarded such people as blessed, he had not been seduced away from his customary integrity. From this it is clear that he ascribed more to the providence of God than to evil practices. He, therefore, prays to be redeemed, because, oppressed by injustices and tempted in various ways, he relied only on God, trusting in his Redeemer. From this we may gather that at the time he was shackled with inflexible difficulties. Again he drinks this redemption, as it were, from the proper fountain, from God's grace. We have seen that the cause is not placed before the effect. COMMENTARY ON THE PSALMS.[13]

DAVID LONGS TO BE SAVED ON ACCOUNT OF THE OFFICE OF THE WORD. VIKTORIN STRIGEL: In the last verse the final cause is added why he asks to be saved, namely, so that he might bless the Lord in the church. This cause must be considered diligently. For God wants the ministry of the gospel to be public; he does not want the gospel message to be kept imprisoned in secret lairs, like the Eleusinian mysteries, but instead he wants it to be heard clearly by the whole human race, he wants to be acknowledged and called on.[14] Therefore, he wants congregations to be public and honest, and in them he wants the gospel message to resound; he wants to be called on and celebrated there. He also wants these very congregations to be witnesses to the separation of the church of God from other peoples' sects, factions and beliefs. *HYPONĒMATA IN ALL THE PSALMS.*[15]

MAY THE LOVE OF GOD BE POURED INTO OUR HEARTS. THE BOOK OF COMMON PRAYER (1549): O Lord, you teach us that all our deeds without charity are worth nothing. Send your Holy Spirit and pour into our hearts that most excellent gift of charity, the very bond of peace and all virtues, without which whoever lives is counted dead before you. Grant this for the sake of your only Son Jesus Christ. THE COLLECT FOR THE SUNDAY CALLED QUINQUAGESIMA.[16]

---

[13]CTS 8:448-49* (CO 31:270).

[14]The cult of Demeter and Persephone annually held secret initiatory rites in Eleusis known as "the Eleusinian mysteries"; see further Erasmus, *Adages*, 2.5.66 (CWE 33:207).

[15]Strigel, *Hyponēmata*, 127.

[16]BCP 1549, 48*.

27:1-14 THE LORD IS MY LIGHT AND SALVATION

Of David.

¹ The LORD is my light and my salvation;
　　whom shall I fear?
The LORD is the stronghold[a] of my life;
　　of whom shall I be afraid?

² When evildoers assail me
　　to eat up my flesh,
my adversaries and foes,
　　it is they who stumble and fall.

³ Though an army encamp against me,
　　my heart shall not fear;
though war arise against me,
　　yet[b] I will be confident.

⁴ One thing have I asked of the LORD,
　　that will I seek after:
that I may dwell in the house of the LORD
　　all the days of my life,
to gaze upon the beauty of the LORD
　　and to inquire[c] in his temple.

⁵ For he will hide me in his shelter
　　in the day of trouble;
he will conceal me under the cover of his tent;
　　he will lift me high upon a rock.

⁶ And now my head shall be lifted up
　　above my enemies all around me,
and I will offer in his tent

sacrifices with shouts of joy;
　　I will sing and make melody to the LORD.

⁷ Hear, O LORD, when I cry aloud;
　　be gracious to me and answer me!
⁸ You have said, "Seek[d] my face."
My heart says to you,
　　"Your face, LORD, do I seek."[e]
　　⁹ Hide not your face from me.
Turn not your servant away in anger,
　　O you who have been my help.
Cast me not off; forsake me not,
　　O God of my salvation!
¹⁰ For my father and my mother have
　　　　forsaken me,
　　but the LORD will take me in.

¹¹ Teach me your way, O LORD,
　　and lead me on a level path
　　because of my enemies.
¹² Give me not up to the will of my adversaries;
　　for false witnesses have risen against me,
　　and they breathe out violence.

¹³ I believe[f] that I shall look upon the goodness
　　　　of the LORD
　　in the land of the living!
¹⁴ Wait for the LORD;
　　be strong, and let your heart take courage;
　　wait for the LORD!

a Or refuge　b Or in this　c Or meditate　d The command (seek) is addressed to more than one person　e The meaning of the Hebrew verse is uncertain
f Other Hebrew manuscripts Oh! Had I not believed

OVERVIEW: In reading this psalm of comfort, the reformers exhort believers to maintain their trust in the powerful presence of God, who lovingly guides his people and protects them from their enemies. The interpretation of this psalm reveals significant conformity across confessional divides. Most understand the house of the Lord as pointing typologically to the church; they emphasize the ministry of the Word and the practice of pure worship. The doctrine of justification by faith alone (*sola fide*) is directly linked to the promises of God preached in the church; through the inspiration and grace of the Holy Spirit, the believer is expected to respond to the gracious acts of the Lord with thanksgiving, trust and obedience.

Preserve and Protect the Ministry of the Word. Nikolaus Selnecker: This is a beautiful psalm of thanksgiving and comfort. In it David, indeed Christ himself with all his faithful, gives thanks to God the Father for the good, true comfort by which he is strengthened in his crossbearing and misery and preserved and protected against his enemies and false teachers. Second, he prays and desires that God would preserve him in right faith and in the true church, where God's Word is purely and sincerely taught and learned. Third, he prays against all false teachers, whom he calls false witnesses. They commit iniquities without shame, for they are quite mad and presumptuous saints, who testify about God self-assuredly and brazenly—especially those without a command to do so. As we see daily that the madder and the more unlearned the people are, the more presumptuous and brazen they are in their preaching. And they teach all the world that no one is capable of anything; they alone know everything. Indeed they also direct war and turmoil against the true saints and God-fearers. The Whole Psalter.[1]

Three Fountains for Believers. Theodore Beza: Whether we say that David wrote this psalm already delivered or still whirling in the midst of dangers is of no concern. However, in this psalm are opened to us—even when everything seems hopeless—three perpetual and inexhaustible fountains from which we may drink sure comfort. The first fountain is to seize God's power by true faith against all our enemies' menaces. The second fountain is a perpetual zeal for the glory of God, always preserving a good conscience and diligently seizing the means by which our faith may be confirmed, namely, the hearing of the divine Word and the use of the sacraments if they are granted to us; if not, we should meditate on them continually. The third fountain is earnest prayer in faith and endurance. Paraphrase of Psalm 27.[2]

27:1-5 *Whom Shall I Fear?*

The Lord's Covenant Lovingkindness. David Dickson: God by virtue of the covenant has obliged himself to give direction, comfort and deliverance in trouble. From this David infers that he did not need to fear his enemies. . . . We should wrestle in prayer against the doubts which trouble and try our hearts to mar our confidence in prayer. It is wisdom to arm ourselves by faith against these doubts before we pray as the prophet's example teaches us. Whoever is in covenant with God has solid grounds to expect from God direction, comfort and deliverance in every trouble. By virtue of the covenant of grace, David says, "The Lord is my light and my salvation." When we have fastened our faith on God, then we may with reason defy our enemies and say with the prophet, "Of whom shall I be afraid?" When our enemies appear strong and we know that we are weak, we should place the Lord's strength against our temptations, so that we may resist all fear, as David teaches, "The Lord is the strength of my life, of whom shall I be afraid?" Commentary on Psalm 27.[3]

Trust in God's Power. John Calvin: Let us learn, therefore, to put such a value on God's power to protect us as to put to flight all our fears. Not that the minds of the faithful can, by reason of the infirmity of the flesh, be at all times entirely devoid of fear, but immediately recovering courage, let us, from the high tower of our confidence, look down on all our dangers with contempt. Those who have never tasted the grace of God tremble because they refuse to rely on him and imagine that he is often incensed against them, or at least far removed from them. But with the promises of God before our eyes and the grace which they offer, our unbelief does him grievous wrong, if we do not with unshrinking courage boldly set him against all our enemies. When God, therefore, kindly invites us to himself and assures us that he will take care of our safety, because we have embraced his promises or

---

[1]Selnecker, *Der gantze Psalter*, 1:157v.
[2]Beza, *Psalmes of Dauid*, 44* (*Psalmorum Davidis*, 93).

[3]Dickson, *First Fifty Psalms*, 181-82*.

because we believe him to be faithful, it is fitting that we highly extol his power, so that it may ravish our hearts with admiration of him. COMMENTARY ON THE PSALMS.[4]

LOVE FOR THE HOUSE OF THE LORD. CARDINAL CAJETAN: Here he elaborates on that phrase, "my salvation," from the first verse. Here notice that the whole rationale of this psalm on the part of David is explained in his devoted love for the house of the Lord. He implies by this that it was so perfect that he did not count the assumption of power to be equal to the attainment of his wish for the home of the Lord. . . . In this is clearly evident his past and continuing devotion. As for what is the thing that he is seeking, he adds, "my dwelling," that is, my abiding, my resting place "in the home of the Lord all the days of my life." And he did not say, "That I might find rest in power," but, "That I might find rest in the splendor of the Lord." And literally David tried to accomplish this immediately, establishing his home next to the home of the Lord. This he did according to the example of Moses, the leader of the people, to whom it was charged by God in Numbers 2 that he dwell next to the entrance of the house of the Lord. COMMENTARY ON PSALM 27.[5]

THE CHURCH IN EVERY AGE PRAYS THIS PRAYER. MOÏSE AMYRAUT: The tabernacle and the temple, into which it was converted, were types for the Christian church, both the church militant on earth and the church triumphant in heaven. On account of this, these prayers of David can be accommodated by believers to every age. ANNOTATIONS ON PSALM 27:4.[6]

THE BEAUTY OF THE TEMPLE REFLECTS SPIRITUAL REALITIES. JOHN CALVIN: As the fashion of the temple was not framed according to human wisdom but was an image of spiritual things, the prophet directed his eyes and all his affections to this object. The madness is, therefore,

truly detestable of those who wrest this passage in favor of pictures and images, which, instead of deserving to be numbered among temple ornaments, are rather like dung and filth, defiling all the purity of holy things. We should now consider whether the faithful are to be like-minded under the Christian or gospel dispensation. I state, indeed, that we are in very different circumstances from the ancient fathers, but as far as God still preserves his people under a certain external order and draws them to himself by earthly instructions, temples still have their beauty, which deservedly ought to draw the affections and desires of the faithful to them. The Word, sacraments, public prayers and other helps of the same kind cannot be neglected without a wicked contempt of God, who manifests himself to us in these ordinances, as in a mirror or image. COMMENTARY ON THE PSALMS.[7]

MINISTERS OF THE TEMPLE. THE ENGLISH ANNOTATIONS: The servants of God seek to know God's will in God's house: from his Word read and preached, or interpreted, by God's lawful ministers, who, if they mislead, woe be to them! It is very possible that they may mislead, I confess, especially if they are ignorant or parties in a faction—and even in the best times, wicked practices and unconscionable prelates are found. However, if those who are lawfully ordained and appointed mislead, those who are misled may be able to plead for themselves. . . . Nevertheless, godly people must not overly trust their ministers, but those who are able must embrace all good opportunities to further satisfy themselves when an occasion presents, as those noble Bereans did. ANNOTATIONS ON PSALM 27:4.[8]

FAITH COVERS THE CHURCH. MARTIN LUTHER: The tabernacle is the church or the body of Christ, which, however, in a mystical sense is also the church. And in it is hidden every believer. This hiding must not be understood in a physical sense,

---

[4]CTS 8:451* (CO 31:271).
[5]Cajetan, *In Sacrae Scripturae Expositionem*, 3:96.
[6]Amyraut, *Paraphrasis in Psalmos Davidis*, 106-7.

[7]CTS 8:454-55* (CO 31:274).
[8]Downame, ed., *Annotations*, 6C1r*; citing Mt 23:2-3; Acts 17:11.

because the saints are certainly placed on the candlestick. This does not mean, however, that all his glory is in his soul alone, but rather because human beings are called inward and hidden in that they do not live in a worldly and carnal fashion, that is to say, he withdraws himself from the life, the customs and the activity of the world. Indeed, as the apostle says, that even though they live in the flesh, they do not wage war according to the flesh. And 1 Peter 4 says, "They are surprised that you do not join them." Therefore to be hidden is nothing else than not running with those who live carnally, something carnal people certainly see plainly. Yet they do not live like those who live spiritually.

The cover therefore is the church's faith, or spirit, which is the same. For they live by faith and in spirit, that is, by the recognition and love of what is invisible. So the carnal do not live by faith but empirically, not in spirit but in the flesh. Hence they are not "under the cover" but out in the open, and they are involved in visible things. And note that the church is protected, not in the open and in visible things—no, in these the church is abandoned to the will of tyrants and the wicked. . . . But the church is defended in spiritual things, so that they cannot be taken away from it or it be harmed in them, for they are the invincible and eternal spiritual benefits of faith. First Psalms Lectures (1513–1515).[9]

Take Shelter in the Word and in Christ.
Nikolaus Selnecker: The tent is the Word of God with which God wonderfully rules and leads his saints; by it he protects them against every misfortune that the devil or the world are able to direct at and send to them. The rock is true strength and power with which God consoles and emboldens his people in the Word, so that they show neither misery nor anguish but instead are joyous and strong in their Lord Christ, who is their true rock, foundation and cornerstone on which they cast themselves and are lifted up. There they remain until the end in true confession, that Christ is the Son of the living God of whom it stands

written, "On this Rock I will build my church." The Whole Psalter.[10]

No Safer Place Than in the Lord's Hands.
Tilemann Hesshus: He adds the reason for this supplication by a final cause. "Therefore, I ask above all else this one benefit, because there is no safer place, no surer protection, no surer salvation—every human aid is uncertain—but in the house of the Lord, God miraculously and divinely protects his people by his hand and he always demonstrates his presence." The shelter of the tabernacle is what he calls God's secret wisdom and power by which he marvelously protects his people even though they are thrashed about in the hands of the impious. David had been surrounded by Saul's soldiers, nevertheless he was rescued; Athanasius almost fell into the hand of his enemy, Julian the Apostate, nevertheless he was protected; Luther at the Diet of Worms was in the hands of the pontifical curia, nevertheless, he was divinely kept safe. Commentary on Psalm 27.[11]

27:6-10 With Shouts of Joy I Seek the Face of the Lord

David Demonstrates His Confidence in God. John Calvin: By making a vow of thanksgiving that he will perform after he has been rescued from this crisis, he confirms himself again in the hope of deliverance. We know that under the law the faithful, whenever they had experienced any remarkable blessing from God, performed their vows by a solemn rite. Here, therefore, David in his exile where he was prohibited from approaching the temple boasts that he will again come to the altar to offer God the sacrifice of praise. Still it seems that the holy jubilation and songs—in which he promises to give thanks to God—he implicitly opposes to the world's profane triumphs. Commentary on the Psalms.[12]

---

[9]LW 10:125* (WA 3:150); citing Mk 4:21; 2 Cor 10:3; 1 Pet 4:4.

[10]Selnecker, *Der gantze Psalter*, 1:109r; citing Mt 16:18.
[11]Hesshus, *Commentarius in Psalmos*, 121r. Julian the Apostate (331–363) sent Athanasius (296–373) into exile.
[12]CTS 8:456* (CO 31:274-75).

FIRMLY FIX YOUR STARE ON GOD AND HIS COMMAND. TILEMANN HESSHUS: This is a very distinguished verse in which David claims God's command, on which his faith in prayer depends. "My heart," he says, "constantly dwells on you, O God, by remembering your precepts, which you have decreed so that we would pray. You have said, 'Seek the Lord and his strength! Seek his face always!' Again, 'Call out to me in the day of tribulation.' Therefore whenever we obey your command, you are not able to spurn our prayers." It is impossible to say how greatly God's command strengthens us in prayer. For however great our vileness is, God's command should be placed before it and it should be submitted to God. Therefore, God's command should always be before us, by which we are commanded to seek good things from God. Nor should we allow ourselves to think that God stands at a distance from our prayers because of our vileness or because of the magnitude of his punishments.

Remarkable, various and indescribable emotions have been established in the heart of the pious in profound times of need—by begging for both assistance and deliverance in faith. For not only should we consider the splendid benefits of God and the various ways he has delivered his saints, but our soul should also exult for joy. Not only should our eyes be firmly fixed on the command and promise of God, but we should also ask for assistance in steadfast faith. On the other hand, if the danger is great in which our soul is trapped, which it stares at, in which it is disturbed and afraid of destruction, then more than anything else the memory of our sin is fixed before our eyes and we fear God's wrath and eternal rejection. Therefore, in this verse David turns his eyes away from his sins and prays that God not abandon him in his wrath, but instead that he would consider him mercifully and defend him. COMMENTARY ON PSALM 27.[13]

GOD NEVER ABANDONS HIS PEOPLE. NIKOLAUS SELNECKER: David ascribes everything to God and removes all power from himself, for he sees that there is nothing in a person without God's grace and gift. "Without me, you can do nothing," Christ says. Because neither free will, nor human strength, nor human works count for anything—before God's court these are not of any worth. It is all too weak and vain, impure and unfitting. Therefore, David says, "My father and mother abandon me," that is, all human advice, help, favor, ability and work is nothing, if God does not shelter us and rule us. For this reason I rejoice, that the Lord has adopted me to grace through his Son. For he will not abandon me, even if father and mother abandon and forget me. As it is written in Isaiah, "And even if your mother forgets you, still I will not forget you, says the Lord Sabaoth." This is an excellent and powerful comfort in all our conflicts. O, you of little faith!

The great prophet Dr. Luther of blessed memory, when there was tumult in every street and one fire after the other went up, friend and foe fell away from him, and he never had a hideout or protection, he said these words, too, to his brothers in Wittenberg with whom he amused himself: "Father and mother abandon me, but the Lord takes me in." THE WHOLE PSALTER.[14]

THE LORD IS INSEPARABLY NEAR HIS PEOPLE. DAVID DICKSON: The bands between God and a believing soul are more direct, more intimate and stronger than any civil or natural band between a person and any creature. And they are appointed to hold fast when natural bands fail. COMMENTARY ON PSALM 27.[15]

27:11-14 Guide Me in Your Strength

IN THE WORD THERE IS NO DARKNESS AT ALL. HIERONYMUS WELLER VON MOLSDORF: The psalmist teaches that this is the means by which God rules and governs us, by which we are less ruined by the devil and that all our plans and

---

[13]Hesshus, *Commentarius in Psalmos*, 121r.

[14]Selnecker, *Der gantze Psalter*, 1:159v-160r; citing Jn 15:5; Is 49:15.
[15]Dickson, *First Fifty Psalms*, 1:185*.

the business of our vocation are blessed—whether in the estate of the church, politics or the home—it is the Word of God that God places in the mouths of the church's ministers. Therefore, wherever the Word of God shines, there is that way and path by which God leads us, governs us, defends us and helps us. . . .

In this passage the prophet also teaches that all human beings who are without the Word of God wander about in the thickest darkness, rushing headlong into every kind of sin, error and calamity. And absolutely no counsel or help can possibly come to those who have been crushed by these as well as internal fears, unless that true light and lamp, that is, the Word of God, has shone on them. For just as the rising sun gladdens and illuminates heaven and earth and all that is in them with the sweetest light, so the Word of God, as it begins to dawn in their hearts, gladdens them, brings them to life and brings them sure and steadfast consolation, so that they are able to fear God, to love and trust in God, seeking and expecting all blessings from him. Finally, they regard God as their greatest good—their greatest pleasure and joy is in God. BRIEF COMMENT ON PSALM 27.[16]

LET US ALSO PRAY DELIVER US NOT. DAVID DICKSON: The godly have reason to pray with submission that they would not fall into the hands of other mortals, because of their cruelty, and to say, "Do not deliver me to the will of my enemy." Because it is easy for the Lord to mitigate the enemies' fury or to break their power or to elude their trickery and might. Let us pray "Deliver," and let God chose the way of deliverance. When the good cause of the godly and the godly themselves are left to suffer, know that God in that case will interpose himself in due time. For this is David's reason of hope to be helped, because false witnesses resolved to oppress

him and "breathers of violence" set to take his life, continually "rising against him." And here he is a clear type and example of the suffering of Christ and his followers. COMMENTARY ON PSALM 27.[17]

HEAVEN IS TRUE LIFE; HELL IS TRUE DEATH. MARTIN LUTHER: The "land of the living" is the church; the world is the land of the dying. Now heaven is not the land of the living—that is, of those beginning to live—rather, it is the land of those who are truly alive or have been made perfectly alive, just as hell is not the land of the dying but of the dead, "a land that is covered with the darkness of death." And it is called a land on account of human bodies which are of the earth but live forever. FIRST PSALMS LECTURES (1513–1515).[18]

DAVID IS OBEDIENT AND GOD IS SOVEREIGN. JOHN CALVIN: Now because David was incapable of standing up to so great a struggle, he borrows strength from God by prayer. If he had only said "Act like a man," he would have seemed to allege the agency of his own free will, but because he immediately adds, by way of correction, that God would be near to supply strength, he plainly enough shows that when the saints strive vigorously, they fight in another person's strength. For David does not hurl his own efforts onto the battlefield, as the papists imagine, and afterward summon God's aid. Instead he has been incited to that duty, because he acknowledged that he lacked any strength, he seeks the remedy for this shortcoming in the Spirit's grace. Now because he knew that war must be waged all his life, that new conflicts would arise constantly, that often the saints' troubles are drawn out for a long time, he repeats again what he had said about looking for God. COMMENTARY ON THE PSALMS.[19]

---

[16]Weller, *Enarratio Psalmorum*, 296, 298.

[17]Dickson, *First Fifty Psalms*, 1:186*.
[18]LW 10:126* (WA 3:151); citing Job 10:21.
[19]CTS 8:464-65* (CO 31:280).

28:1-9 THE LORD IS MY STRENGTH AND SHIELD

Of David.

[1] *To you, O LORD, I call;*
my rock, be not deaf to me,
lest, if you be silent to me,
I become like those who go down to the pit.
[2] *Hear the voice of my pleas for mercy,*
when I cry to you for help,
when I lift up my hands
toward your most holy sanctuary.[a]

[3] *Do not drag me off with the wicked,*
with the workers of evil,
who speak peace with their neighbors
while evil is in their hearts.
[4] *Give to them according to their work*
and according to the evil of their deeds;
give to them according to the work of their hands;
render them their due reward.

[5] *Because they do not regard the works of the*
LORD
or the work of his hands,
he will tear them down and build them up no
more.

[6] *Blessed be the LORD!*
For he has heard the voice of my pleas for
mercy.
[7] *The LORD is my strength and my shield;*
in him my heart trusts, and I am helped;
my heart exults,
and with my song I give thanks to him.

[8] *The LORD is the strength of his people;*[b]
he is the saving refuge of his anointed.
[9] *Oh, save your people and bless your heritage!*
Be their shepherd and carry them forever.

a Hebrew *your innermost sanctuary*   b Some Hebrew manuscripts, Septuagint, Syriac; most Hebrew manuscripts *is their strength*

OVERVIEW: The primary interpretation of this psalm is straightforward. Our commentators agree that its central message is that God protects and delivers his people. Reading it primarily of David, but with some interpreters adapting it to Christ, the reformers exhort their readers to confidence and patience while awaiting the powerful intervention of the Lord. A number of interesting exegetical directions are also followed on the periphery, as Calvin considers the significance of raised hands in worship and addresses the difficult question of praying for vengeance, while Luther considers the nature of David's piety and the troubles that he faces.

A PSALM OF SURE CONFIDENCE IN GOD'S PROTECTION. THEODORE BEZA: David in this psalm—not as a private citizen but in the public office of king, appointed by God himself—prays for himself and for God's people with such

confidence that although as a private citizen he was unable to live safely in Saul's kingdom, he gives thanks for his already granted petition. Beside this, he adds clearly prophetic prayers against all those who persecute the church, not by ignorance or some sudden affection but with resolute and stubborn malice. Those matters written in 1 Samuel 23–24 pertain to this psalm. PARAPHRASE OF PSALM 28.[1]

28:1-2 *Listen to Me, My Rock!*

THE UNITY OF WORD AND DEED. KONRAD PELLIKAN: Scripture everywhere employs speaking for doing, just as God said, "Let there be," and it was done. Thus, being silent is also understood as neglecting; resting as doing nothing. And so David prays that God would not cease to help him in the

---

[1]Beza, *Psalmes of Dauid,* 46* (*Psalmorum Davidis,* 98).

midst of danger. He does not run to the generals of his armies, to the bravest of his soldiers or to the dead patriarchs, but to the Lord his God in whom alone he trusts, whom he called on with his whole heart, without hesitation. Also he demonstrates what great danger he was in, because he complains that he will be like those who descend into the grave—that is, dead—and that would surely happen to him unless God would bring help. Sacred history teaches that this did not happen rarely. COMMENTARY ON PSALM 28:1.[2]

UNDERSTANDING GOD'S SILENCE. THE ENGLISH ANNOTATIONS: As for God being silent when we call again and again, it is either because our prayers are not acceptable to him . . . or because he has further plans for our good and his glory, such as to make us examples of patience to others and the like. And whatever flesh and blood—that is, natural sense and judgment—suggest to us, God is *makrothymōn*, long, very long sometimes, before he hears us and executes justice, yet Scripture says positively that he will do it *en tachei*, speedily, because many years are but as a moment of time to eternity, which should therefore always, in out sharpest extremities or longest trials, prevent the assaults of impatience on our faith and confidence and be in our thoughts before our eyes. ANNOTATIONS ON PSALM 28:1.[3]

THE INNERMOST SANCTUARY TYPIFIES GOD'S PRESENCE. RUDOLF GWALTHER: In the innermost sanctuary was the ark of the covenant, an external testimony to the presence of God. For this reason, the ancients lifted up their hands in prayer toward the sanctuary. THE PSALTER.[4]

LIFTED HANDS ARE A PROPER EXTERNAL SIGN OF TRUE WORSHIP. JOHN CALVIN: It has been a common practice in all ages for people to lift up their hands in prayer. Nature has extorted this gesture even from pagan idolaters as a visible sign

that they directed their minds to God alone. The great majority, it is true, when they perform this ceremony, it vanishes into their own inventions. Still the lifting up of hands, when there is no hypocrisy and deceit, is an aid to pious and true prayer. COMMENTARY ON THE PSALMS.[5]

28:3-5 *Give the Wicked What They Deserve*

THE HEART OF DAVID'S REQUEST IS TO BE PROTECTED FROM HYPOCRISY. VIKTORIN STRIGEL: This is the main proposition of the psalm, in which he asks with the most passionate vows and with all his heart that he would not be injured by the infection of hypocrisy—which performs a tragedy with a comic mask—or be caught up in the punishments of the hypocrites. Consider with what colors he depicts these extremely lethal beasts! He explicitly calls them "impious," because hypocrisy is a sin committed against the first table. For, even if hypocrites are not defiled by external idols, nevertheless in their hearts they lack a genuine fear of God, they lack faith and they influence leaders with their own opinions about religion.

Second, they commit iniquity, because they attempt to use slanders to disgrace and crush those who disagree with them even slightly and who do not approve all their contradictions. For they do not dissent from others with moderation, but they do zealously what the ancient saying warns, "The serpent does not become a dragon unless it devours many serpents."[6] But even though they engage in these great evils, still they speak of peace with their neighbor, that is, they clothe themselves and their deeds with a friendly and believable appearance. Thus they claim that they are moved by righteous zeal to defend the glory of God and to be concerned with and to be looking out for people's eternal salvation. By this kind of talk they win over to themselves the devotion of the crowd

---

[2]Pellikan, *Commentaria Bibliorum*, 4:73r; citing Gen 1.
[3]Downame, ed., *Annotations*, 6Civ*; citing Lk 18:7-8.
[4]Gwalther, *Der Psalter*, 45r.

[5]CTS 8:466* (CO 31:281).
[6]See Erasmus, *Adages* 3.3.61 (CWE 34:272).

and those who prefer severity and inflexibility to constancy, and persistence in wrongheaded endeavors seems more respectable than repentance.

Therefore, just as David prays that he not be dragged down with the impious, so I pray with my whole heart that the eternal God, the Father of our Lord Jesus Christ, never permit me to become associated with such hypocrites, and not remove from my mouth the word of truth but direct my steps according to his Word, and keep me in perpetual simplicity and uprightness, which is the bane of a hypocrite. *Hyponēmata in All the Psalms.*[7]

Is David Praying for Vengeance? John Calvin: Here again occurs the difficult question about praying for vengeance, which, however, I shall dispatch in just a few words. In the first place, then, it is unquestionable that if the flesh moves us to seek revenge, the desire is wicked in the sight of God. He not only forbids us to utter evil curses on our enemies for private injuries, but it cannot be otherwise than that all those desires which spring from hatred must be disordered. David's example, therefore, must not be claimed by those who are driven by their own intemperate passion to seek vengeance. The holy prophet is not inflamed here by his own private sorrow to devote his enemies to destruction, but laying aside the desire of the flesh, he gives judgment concerning the matter itself. Therefore, before a person can denounce vengeance against the wicked, he must first shake himself free from all improper feelings in his own mind.

In the second place, prudence must be exercised, that the heinousness of the evils which offend us do not drive us to intemperate zeal, which happened even to Christ's disciples when they desired that fire might be brought from heaven to consume those who refused to entertain their Master. They pretended, it is true, to act according to the example of Elijah, but Christ severely rebuked them and told them that they did not know by what spirit they were being urged on. In particular we must observe

this general rule, that we cordially desire and labor for the welfare of the whole human race. Thus it will come to pass that we shall not only give way to the exercise of God's mercy but shall also wish the conversion of those who seem obstinately to rush headlong into their own destruction. In short, David, free from every evil passion and also endued with the spirit of discretion and judgment, pleads here not so much his own case as the case of God. And by this prayer he further reminds both himself and the faithful that although the wicked may give themselves loose reins in the commission of every kind of vice with impunity for a time, they must at length stand before the judgment seat of God. *Commentary on the Psalms.*[8]

28:6-9 Blessed Lord, You Are the Strength of Your People

Follow the Path of Faith to Praise God. Wolfgang Musculus: Faith tested in tribulations—because it believes the promise of God that says, "Call on me in the day of tribulation and I will deliver you"—calls on God. Then, by calling on God he is heard, having been heard he is helped, having been helped he acknowledges that God is the shield and strength of those who hope in him, and from that he is enraptured by ardent affections to praise God, because he too has the promise of God— "I will deliver you and you will glorify me." Let us learn that path of faith by whose steps we may ascend to sing the praise of God....

We also see in this passage how the minds of the pious, while praying, are reminded both of the divine goodness and of the receipt of the benefits of God and soon are stirred up to praise the Lord. Therefore why are our prayers so frigid that we feel none of these things? Often in church by prayer we are reminded to sing to the Lord. But I ask why are there so few who sing from the heart? *Commentary on Psalm 28.*[9]

---

[7]Strigel, *Hyponēmata*, 132.

[8]CTS 8:469-70* (CO 31:283); citing Lk 9:54.
[9]Musculus, *In Psalterium Commentarii*, 441-42; citing Ps 50:15.

ADAPT THIS PSALM TO CHRIST. MOÏSE
AMYRAUT: What this song is about the prophet
said in the previous verse. The rest of the psalm,
therefore, pertains to him and to the Israelite
people, so that it should be applied to Christ and
to his church as to the substance that was figured
which David and the Israelite people foreshadowed.
ANNOTATIONS ON PSALM 28:8-9.[10]

**ALL GOD'S THINGS ARE OURS THROUGH
CHRIST.** JOHANNES BUGENHAGEN: Some boast
about their own strength, righteousness and good
works without confidence in God, but the people
of the Lord know that it is true what Christ says,
"Without me you can do nothing." And the Lord is
their protector, or, as Felix has it, "the strength of
his Christ's deliverances," that is, the things
accomplished through his Christ. The deliverances
of his Christ by which we are saved are God's
strength, might and power; nothing is left to us
here, all things of God are through Christ —unless you understand it in such a way that the Lord
is the strength of deliverances, by which he
himself established the Savior, his Christ, that is,
his Messiah, his Anointed One, the King. Nevertheless I do not understand this concerning one
person but about the entire kingdom, as the next
verse indicates. "Save," he says, "your people, O

Lord!" For when we read about the salvation of
Christ, we read about our salvation, who we are in
Christ, as it is said in Psalm 20. INTERPRETATION
OF THE PSALMS.[11]

**IF DAVID REALLY IS SO GODLY, WHY DID HE
EXPERIENCE SO MUCH TROUBLE?** MARTIN
LUTHER: A psalm was read at dinner: "Save your
people, O Lord." . . . It was asked how then did it
happen that David—the king who by divine
ordination had replaced another king—had had so
many offenses and scourges? As also his psalms
indicate which are full of complaints—he must
not have had many good days! Luther answered,
"He was disturbed by impious teachers, saw a
rebellious people and suffered many rebellions.
That taught him well how to pray. Without
temptation he was quite free and ready to sin, as
he betrays in the murder of Uriah and his adultery.
O, dear Lord God! That you let such great people
fall! This David had six wives. . . . Beside these six
David had two concubines. But he still became an
adulterer! Indeed we all desire to rule. But when
we come into control, it's toil and labor. May our
Lord God help us, so that those who have begun
the contest would finish well!" TABLE TALK:
ANTON LAUTERBACH (1539).[12]

---

[10]Amyraut, *Paraphrasis in Psalmos Davidis*, 112.

[11]Bugenhagen, *In librvm Psalmorvm interpretatio*, 68r; citing Jn
15:5; Pratensis, *Psalterium*, 15v.
[12]WATR 4:241-42, no. 4344; citing 2 Sam 11; 1 Sam 25.

29:1-11 ASCRIBE GLORY TO GOD

A Psalm of David.

[1] *Ascribe to the LORD, O heavenly beings,[a]*
  ascribe to the LORD glory and strength.
[2] *Ascribe to the LORD the glory due his name;*
  worship the LORD in the splendor of
    holiness.[b]

[3] *The voice of the LORD is over the waters;*
  the God of glory thunders,
  the LORD, over many waters.
[4] *The voice of the LORD is powerful;*
  the voice of the LORD is full of majesty.

[5] *The voice of the LORD breaks the cedars;*
  the LORD breaks the cedars of Lebanon.

[6] *He makes Lebanon to skip like a calf,*
  and Sirion like a young wild ox.

[7] *The voice of the LORD flashes forth flames of*
  fire.
[8] *The voice of the LORD shakes the wilderness;*
  the LORD shakes the wilderness of Kadesh.

[9] *The voice of the LORD makes the deer give birth[c]*
  and strips the forests bare,
  and in his temple all cry, "Glory!"

[10] *The LORD sits enthroned over the flood;*
  the LORD sits enthroned as king forever.
[11] *May the LORD give strength to his people!*
  May the LORD bless[d] his people with peace!

a Hebrew *sons of God*, or *sons of might*   b Or *in holy attire*   c Revocalization yields *makes the oaks to shake*   d Or *The LORD will give. . . . The LORD will bless*

OVERVIEW: The psalmist praises God's voice, which creates and redeems. Contemporary Old Testament studies focuses on the psalm's putative polemical reappropriation of texts about the Canaanite storm god Baal to demonstrate YHWH's superiority. Our commentators, unfamiliar with the trove of Canaanite lore accessible to us now, focus on the poetic storm language in a straightforward manner, augmenting their exegesis through their own experience of nature's frightening wonders (Luther wasn't the only one to make rash vows to God in the midst of tempests!). For the reformers, and many of our forebears, bad weather was a reminder of God's wrath, a warning of his pending judgment. Pastors would call their congregations to a time of fasting, repentance and reflection. The terrible power of nature should awaken us from our slumber, and from the illusion that we are in control of our lives. In the midst of this terror we scurry to find assurance, which can only be found in God's revelation of himself in Jesus Christ, our brother and Lord. All creation must serve its Creator, and in this way our Lord employs nature to urge us to hear the preached Word.

A GOSPEL PSALM. MARTIN LUTHER: The voice of the gospel says this, "Ascribe to the Lord." Clearly this is a prophetic psalm. TABLE TALK: JOHANNES SCHLAGINHAUSEN (1532).[1]

BAD WEATHER AND BAPTISM PROCLAIM GOD'S MIGHT. NIKOLAUS SELNECKER: This psalm the Jews interpreted about the weather. Thus, they kept the people in the fear of God, so that whenever they heard or saw bad weather— thunder and downpours—from it they would learn to acknowledge God's might and wrath and would reform themselves. Dr. Moibanus, pastor in Breslau, also expounded this psalm in the city of Olste when there was terrible weather in Silesia in 1535; with it he exhorted the people to repentance. . . . This psalm, however, is a prophecy of the gospel, as the saints—like Basil, Augustine and others—understood it, namely, how the gospel should be trumpeted throughout all the world and should put to shame the

---

[1]WATR 5:137, no. 1570.

wisdom, reason, holiness and glory of all kings, princes, lords and nations. The Lord Christ alone should be the one true King whom we must serve and glorify with true wisdom and holiness. In addition it points to the flood of baptism, in which the old Adam drowns and the new self is born. It is truly quite a prophetic psalm! It demolishes all philosophical and human arts and works; it only glorifies the righteousness of faith. THE WHOLE PSALTER.[2]

AN EXHORTATION AGAINST GODLESS RULERS. GENEVA BIBLE: The prophet exhorts the princes and rulers of the world, who for the most part think that there is no God, at least to fear him because of the thunders and tempests, which cause all creatures to fear. While God thereby threatens sinners, he is always merciful to his people and moves them thereby to praise his name. PSALM 29: ARGUMENT.

29:1-2 Ascribe Glory, Splendor and Strength to the Lord

GOD'S THUNDER REMINDS RULERS HOW LITTLE CONTROL THEY HAVE. THE ENGLISH ANNOTATIONS: He exhorts the proud tyrants to humble themselves under God's hand and not to have the high opinion of their own power and greatness as most people in such high places have. This exposition I like very well . . . because we read of so many great princes, both good and bad—especially the bad and cruel—who have been fearful of thunder (like Augustus, Caligula and many others), which is the subject of this psalm. ANNOTATIONS ON PSALM 29.[3]

EVERYTHING MUST PRAISE THE LORD. SEBASTIAN MÜNSTER: "The sons of nobles." Based on the Chaldean translation, Kimchi exegetes this as "the company of angels"; that is a Hebraism for "the sons of gods." There are some among the Hebrews who explain it as the stars, because they are summoned to praise God, as also in Job 38 they are called "the sons of gods." Still there is nothing here that forbids "the sons of gods" from being accepted as "the sons of the powerful and important." No matter which rendering you might accept, in this passage the prophet intended to say that there is nothing so lofty and so magnificent that it is not required to praise and glorify God, its Creator. THE TEMPLE OF THE LORD: PSALM 29.[4]

NATURE IS AWESOME, BUT ONLY GOD CAN BE WORSHIPED. JOHN CALVIN: By "the brightness of God's sanctuary" is to be understood not heaven, as some think, but the tabernacle of the covenant, adorned with the symbols of the divine glory, as is evident from the context. And the prophet deliberately recalls this place, in which the true God had manifested himself, so that all people, saying farewell to superstition, would focus on the pure worship of God. It would not be sufficient to worship any heavenly power, but the one and unchangeable God alone must be worshiped, which cannot happen until the world has been reclaimed from every foolish invention. COMMENTARY ON THE PSALMS.[5]

29:3-9 The Power of the Voice of the Lord

THUNDER AND STORMS PROMULGATE GOD'S POWER AND PRESENCE. AMBROSE MOIBANUS: That in this psalm the phrase "the voice of the Lord, the voice of the Lord," is repeated so often happens because the psalmist wants us to imagine the power of God which is seen and heard everywhere. It is as if he wanted to say: "Now listen you princes, listen you powerful, listen to the ancient voice of

---

[2]Selnecker, *Der gantze Psalter*, 1:161v-162r. The Sunday after the feast of Saint Margaret lightning struck the church, killing two women. Moibanus published a report of the extreme weather of that year and his expanded sermon on Ps 29. See Ambrose Moibanus, *Wie in Schlesien zur Olsen über die Stadt ein unerhört, wunderbarlich und grawsam ungewitter mit feür regnen und erschrocklichem wunderwürckenden wind kommen ist* (Augsburg: Philipp Ulhart, 1536).
[3]Downame, ed., *Annotations*, 6C2r*.

[4]Münster, *Miqdaš YHWH*, 1182; citing Job 38:7.
[5]CTS 8:476-77* (CO 31:287).

God through which he brought all creatures into being! Listen to this voice alone! Listen to this peal and boom of thunder in the air! It breaks out over the entire earth; it cannot be hidden from any person. Contemplate and consider who is this Lord who comes with such a great roar of his drums and his trumpets in the clouds? Truly it must be no other lord than God himself who is your Lord and Creator. With his voice and drums he wants to wake you up from your sleep and unbelief, to hear the Word and the voice of salvation which powerfully resound in the holy gospel." This is like how in the previous age of the law the people were brought together with the blast of horns, so that they could hear the Word of God; and like how today we use bells, so that people would come to hear the preaching of the gospel; or even like how a prince who wants to be seen and heard in his majesty and might . . . so that his subjects would recognize him as their lord and prince, indeed also that they would be ready to hear his command and order, trumpets blast, bugles sound far and wide, so that the people would run quickly and gather to hear and see their prince.

So too God has his triumphant horns, his bells, drums, trumpets and bugles which he lets resound in the air over the entire world—and many times a year at that—so that through this he would move us, tear us away from our vanity and arrogance and bring us to the preaching of the gospel. And these are certainly the true bells of God, namely, thunder and lightning in the air, by which he wakes up the powerful and drives them to his preaching, because they so reluctantly come to it otherwise. PSALM 29: THE POWER OF THE VOICE OF GOD.[6]

POETIC DESCRIPTIONS OF GOD'S MIGHT.

MOÏSE AMYRAUT: This description is poetic. These similitudes are very noble and elegant, although perhaps less familiar among Greek and Latin poets. ANNOTATIONS ON PSALM 29:6-8.[7]

JEWS AND GENTILES ARE EQUAL BEFORE GOD'S WORD.

TILEMANN HESSHUS: David continues to explain the efficacy of the divine Word. He teaches that every human heart should submit itself to the doctrine of Christ. Indeed, the Israelites had the law, circumcision and sacrifices; many strove to obey the law, and by its glory they towered above the Gentiles like a cedar planted on the summit of Mount Lebanon, but, accordingly, before God they had no righteousness because of their priority over the Gentiles. The Mosaic law accuses, condemns and curses the Jews no less because of their sin than the Gentiles. And this is more terrible than thunder. "All are cursed who do not abide in everything that is written in the book of the law. . . . Whoever is under the law is under the curse of the law." Again, "For there is no distinction: all have sinned and fall short of the glory of God."

"The voice of the Lord shatters the cedars of Lebanon," that is, the arrogant and exalted Pharisees among the Jewish people. The Pharisees were bloated by their belief in their own righteousness, and on account of their observance of the law they bore a haughty brow. . . . They rage against and disdain Christ and the apostles, but they accomplish nothing, except that they wear themselves out and increase their consciences' terror and trepidation. Not only the Pharisees and priests but all Lebanon and Sirion, that is, the entire people of Israel are roused by the doctrine of Christ and the apostle Paul, so that they tremble and raise a tumult, because they are made equal with the Gentiles and sinners. COMMENTARY ON PSALM 29.[8]

GOD'S TERRIFYING POWER SHOULD BE MEDITATED ON.

SEBASTIAN MÜNSTER: There is no animal so savage and hardhearted in that very vast desert that it does not become frightened and tremble with fear at the terrifying voice of the Lord, just like how certain animals when they are having trouble giving birth are shocked by the peal of

---

[6]Moibanus, _Der xxix. Psalm Dauids_, C2v-C3v.
[7]Amyraut, _Paraphrasis in Psalmos Davidis_, 114.

[8]Hesshus, _Commentarius in Psalmos_, 125v-126r; citing Gal 3:10 (cf. Deut 27:26); Rom 3:22-23.

thunder and immediately discharge their offspring. And struck by lightning, forests are laid bare. In all these events, the pious fix their attention on the power of God. They speak glory and praise to God in his temple, that is, the entire earth which God fills. THE TEMPLE OF THE LORD: PSALM 29.[9]

GOD'S VOICE ECHOES THROUGHOUT THE WORLD BUT IS CELEBRATED ONLY BY THE FAITHFUL. JOHN CALVIN: God's voice fills the whole world and spreads itself to its farthest limits; but the prophet declares that his glory is celebrated only in his church, because God not only speaks intelligibly and distinctly there, but also there gently allures the faithful to himself. His terrible voice, which thunders in various ways in the air, strikes on the ears and causes the hearts of human beings to beat in such a manner as to make them shrink from rather than approach him, not to mention that a considerable portion turn a deaf ear to its sound in storms, rains, thunder and lightning. Because human beings, therefore, profit not so much in this common school as to submit themselves to God, David wisely says that the faithful sing the praises of God in his temple, because, being familiarly instructed there by his fatherly voice, they devote and consecrate themselves wholly to his service. No one proclaims the glory of God aright but one who worships him willingly. COMMENTARY ON THE PSALMS.[10]

29:10-11 *The Lord Enthroned as King*

GOD SAVES THE PIOUS AND CONDEMNS THE IMPIOUS. MARTIN LUTHER: The flood I gladly understand about baptism, although it is ambiguous. God will cause a new flood, namely, salvation. For the flood signifies baptism. Now more have been baptized than those who perished in the flood. Since then, twenty generations have transpired in which many have been baptized. Or if you prefer to understand the negative consequences, then you

will admit that the Lord will continue as King, overthrowing and destroying all the impious. TABLE TALK: JOHANNES SCHLAGINHAUSEN (1532).[11]

OUR GOD IS A MIGHTY FORTRESS OF BLESSING AND PEACE. JOHN CALVIN: Although God exhibits his visible power to the view of the whole world indiscriminately, yet he exerts it in a special way for his elect. Now the psalmist describes him here not as one who overwhelms with fear and dread those to whom he speaks but as one who upholds, cherishes and strengthens them. By the word *strength* is to be understood the whole condition of humankind. And thus he intimates that everything necessary to the preservation of the life of the godly depends entirely on the grace of God. He amplifies this by the word *bless*, for God is said "to bless with peace" those whom he treats graciously and kindly, so that they lack nothing for a prosperous life and complete happiness. From this we may learn that we revere God's majesty, so that we would still look to him for all prosperity. Because his power is infinite, let us surely be persuaded that we are defended by an invincible fortress. COMMENTARY ON THE PSALMS.[12]

THE WORD IS A TWO-EDGED SWORD. JOHANNES BUGENHAGEN: In this psalm, every power is challenged so that each would be subjected to the Word of the Lord and give glory to God. God by his most powerful and efficacious Word created all things. By his Word he terrifies, punishes, devours, slays, consumes by fire and even plunges into hell alive the proud who resist God and the people of God. Some he even puts to flight, trembling, because of his appearance and his saints' appearance. . . . On the other hand, the Word of God makes it so that there is nothing inaccessible to his saints; in fact, those who rely on the power of the Word of God can pass through anything, even opposing the gates of hell. Thus, the Word of God or the voice of the Lord is so

---

[9]Münster, *Miqdaš YHWH*, 1182. [10]CTS 8:481-82* (CO 31:290).

[11]WATR 5:137, no. 1570. [12]CTS 8:483-84* (CO 31:291).

effective that it functions differently in different circumstances. The arrogant and despisers of the Word perish by it. And the people of God are also challenged by the Word and strengthened to worship God and praise his glory. Indeed this people cannot perish in mighty waters and the shadow of death! Their King and Governor is the eternal Lord: he comforts them against all the powers of both the world and hell—I even add the powers of heaven—so that they can receive the promises of God. In short, this blessing—that is, his eternal grace and peace—he lavishes on them. INTERPRETATION OF THE PSALMS.[13]

[13]Bugenhagen, *In librvm Psalmorvm interpretatio*, 68r.

30:1-12 JOY COMES WITH THE MORNING

A Psalm of David. A song at the dedication of the temple.

¹ I will extol you, O LORD, for you have drawn
    me up
    and have not let my foes rejoice over me.
² O LORD my God, I cried to you for help,
    and you have healed me.
³ O LORD, you have brought up my soul from
    Sheol;
    you restored me to life from among those
    who go down to the pit.ᵃ

⁴ Sing praises to the LORD, O you his saints,
    and give thanks to his holy name.ᵇ
⁵ For his anger is but for a moment,
    and his favor is for a lifetime.ᶜ
Weeping may tarry for the night,
    but joy comes with the morning.

⁶ As for me, I said in my prosperity,
    "I shall never be moved."

⁷ By your favor, O LORD,
    you made my mountain stand strong;
you hid your face;
    I was dismayed.

⁸ To you, O LORD, I cry,
    and to the Lord I plead for mercy:
⁹ "What profit is there in my death,ᵈ
    if I go down to the pit?ᵉ
Will the dust praise you?
    Will it tell of your faithfulness?
¹⁰ Hear, O LORD, and be merciful to me!
    O LORD, be my helper!"

¹¹ You have turned for me my mourning into
    dancing;
    you have loosed my sackcloth
    and clothed me with gladness,
¹² that my glory may sing your praise and not
    be silent.
    O LORD my God, I will give thanks to you
    forever!

a Or to life, that I should not go down to the pit   b Hebrew to the memorial of his holiness (see Exodus 3:15)   c Or and in his favor is life   d Hebrew in my blood   e Or to corruption

---

OVERVIEW: In this psalm of thanksgiving the psalmist reflects a reorientation from loss and lament to newness of life. Our commentators muse on whether to read the superscription literally or metaphorically, because it indicates the psalm was for the dedication of the temple, an event that did not take place under David. The psalmist extols God for his healing, for bringing him up from the grave, which Calvin and others develop in its broadly figurative sense. When the psalmist turns to sing praise to God, it is for God's enduring favor in contrast with God's momentary anger. Weeping lasts but for a night and is followed by joy in the morning. Here our commentators find pastoral counsel rooted in God's ways now revealed in the

pattern of the cross and resurrection. The psalm closes with the image of mourning turned to dancing, and Calvin notes that this is not "wanton or profane leaping." For Hesshus the praise that follows deliverance prompts us to join the angels in our eternal vocation of celebrating the divine name.

Superscription: *David's House or God's?*

DAVID COMPOSED THIS PSALM FOR HIS NEW HOME. SEBASTIAN MÜNSTER: Formerly the Israelites under the law of Moses used this psalm for certain ceremonies: when they wanted to live in new houses as well as for the solemn dedication of the house of the Lord which Solomon had built. It was consecrated to God, and God was given praise by this sort of initiation. . . . So therefore when David had built a new house in Jerusalem, as it is written in 2 Samuel 5, it is believed that, the first time he entered it singing praises to God as well as this psalm—although the principal argument of this psalm seems to be thanksgiving for being restored to health after sickness, as the first three verses testify. THE TEMPLE OF THE LORD: PSALM 30.[1]

GRAMMAR AND HISTORY INTIMATE THAT THE HOUSE IS DAVID'S. JOHN CALVIN: Interpreters are uncertain whether this psalm was composed by David or by some of the prophets after the return of the Jews from the Babylonian exile. For "house" means, in their opinion, "the temple." But because the title explicitly mentions David's name, it seems more probable that the word refers to David's private dwelling. Also, that some hypothesize that David, when he wanted to dedicate his palace, was seized with a grave sickness, is based on no solid reason. Rather, we should conjecture from that sacred history that as soon as he had built his palace, he dwelled in it quietly and at his ease. COMMENTARY ON THE PSALMS.[2]

"HOUSE OF DAVID" MEANS CHRIST'S BODY. MARTIN LUTHER: A psalm to be sung for the dedication of the restored house of David, that is, the body of Christ. It is not written anywhere that David restored and dedicated his house; therefore this word *house* is metaphoric here. GLOSSA ON PSALM 30 (1513–1515).[3]

WE ARE CHRIST'S BODY. NIKOLAUS SELNECKER: We are the temple, the house and dwelling place of God, if God dwells in us through faith and through true consolation, takes us and redeems us. For this we say and sing a "thanks be to God" [*Deo gratias*]. And we should surrender and commend ourselves

to God the Lord wholly and completely. Concerning this dedication it stands written, "Blessed are those who dwell in the house of the Lord; they will praise you eternally!" THE WHOLE PSALTER.[4]

30:1-3 Brought Back from Sheol

IN SICKNESS DAVID PRAISES GOD'S PAST DELIVERANCES. RUDOLF GWALTHER: It seems, according to all the circumstances, as if David, before he dedicated his new house, lay in a severe illness, so severe that he examined his life. Thus, he first and foremost praises God because he helped him up against his enemies' hopes who would have much rather seen him dead. THE PSALTER.[5]

GOD AUTHORS ALL DELIVERANCE, NOT JUST FROM DISEASE. JOHN CALVIN: Because David had been brought, as it were, from the grave to the life-giving air, he promises to exalt the name of God. It is God who lifts us up with his own hand when we have been plunged into a profound gulf; and therefore it is our duty, on our part, to sing his praises with our tongues. . . . He concludes that he was preserved by the favor of God, alleging in proof of this that when he was at the very point of death he directed his supplications to God alone, and that he immediately felt that he had not done so in vain. When God hears our prayers, it is a proof which enables us to conclude with certainty that he is the author of our salvation, and of the deliverance which we obtain. As the Hebrew word *rāfāʾ* means "to heal," interpreters have been led, from this consideration, to restrict it to sickness. But as it is certain that it sometimes means "to restore" or "to set up again" and is also applied to an altar or a house when they are said to be repaired or rebuilt, it may properly enough mean here any deliverance. The life of a person is in danger in many other ways than merely from disease; and we know that it is a form of speech which occurs everywhere in the Psalms, to say that David was restored to life

---

[1]Münster, *Miqdaš YHWH*, 1183-84; citing 2 Sam 5:11; Deut 28:30.
[2]CTS 8:484* (CO 31:291-92); citing 2 Sam 7:2.
[3]WA 3:161. Goldingay states that the psalm's content fits a house dedication better; based on the intertestamental use of this psalm, Kraus accepts a temple context. See Goldingay, *Psalms*, 1:425; Kraus, *Psalms 1–59*, 354.

---

[4]Selnecker, *Der gantze Psalter*, 1:163v; citing Ps 84:4.
[5]Gwalther, *Der Psalter*, 48r.

whenever the Lord delivered him from any grievous and extreme danger.

For the sake of amplification, accordingly, he immediately adds, "You have brought back my soul from the grave." He reckoned that he could not sufficiently express in words the magnitude of the favor which God had conferred on him, unless he compared the darkness of that period with a grave and pit, into which he had been forced to throw himself hastily, to protect his life by hiding, until the flame of insurrection was quenched. As one restored to life, therefore, he proclaims that he had been marvelously delivered from present death, as if he had been restored to life after he had been dead. And assuredly, it appears from sacred history how completely he was overwhelmed with despair on every side. COMMENTARY ON THE PSALMS.[6]

30:4-7 I Shall Not Be Moved

ONE MOUTH IS INSUFFICIENT! DAVID DICKSON: Dwelling on the consideration of the mercies shown to us should bring with it rejoicing in God and a singing disposition, which—once we are wakened and warmed to—we will think that one mouth to praise God is too little, as we see here in David, who not only praises God himself but also commands all the saints to do the same. COMMENTARY ON PSALM 30.[7]

OUR PAIN WILL CEASE ONE DAY. HIERONYMUS WELLER VON MOLSDORF: Although it would be satisfactory enough to expound this verse according to the letter, nevertheless the allegorical sense pleases me more. Accordingly the verse is understood concerning that continual cycle of affliction and deliverance which the pious always experience. Thus, the sense is this: "However hard, bitter, fierce and intolerable the affliction or testing may be which oppresses and tortures the pious, yet it will not last forever but before God is momentary. For in the end God will miraculously rescue them from

it." Meanwhile, however, while the testing or afflicting oppresses them, the Father of mercies and the God of all comfort will grant them the ability to be able to endure it. For he will strengthen their hearts, and he will fortify them by his Holy Spirit, so that they can endure the throng of their afflictions. BRIEF COMMENT ON PSALM 30.[8]

GOD'S PATIENCE TEMPERS HIS WRATH. JACOB ARMINIUS: Longsuffering, gentleness, readiness to pardon and clemency are the moderators of anger and punishments. Longsuffering suspends anger, lest it should hasten to drive away the evil as soon as ever such an act was required by the iniquities of the creature. We call that gentleness or leniency which tempers anger, lest it should be of too great a magnitude—indeed lest its severity should correspond with the magnitude of the wickedness committed! We call that readiness to pardon which moderates anger, so that it may not continue forever, as sinners' merit deserves. Clemency is that by which God tempers the deserved punishments that by their severity and constancy they may be far inferior to what our sin deserves and may not exceed the strength of the creature. DISPUTATION 4: ON THE NATURE OF GOD.[9]

UNDERSTAND THIS VERSE AS THE PROMISE OF GOD'S COMING LIGHT AND DELIVERANCE. JOHN CALVIN: David does not simply mean that the affliction would be only for one night, but that if the darkness of adversity should fall on the people of God, as it were, in the evening or at the setting of the sun, light would soon after arise on them, to comfort their sorrow-stricken spirits. This is the point of David's counsel, that were we not too headstrong, we would acknowledge that the Lord, even when he appears to hide from us for a time in the darkness of affliction, always seasonably grants the substance of joy, just as the morning arises after the night. COMMENTARY ON THE PSALMS.[10]

---

[6]CTS 8:485-86* (CO 31:292-93).
[7]Dickson, *First Fifty Psalms*, 196-97*.
[8]Weller, *Enarratio Psalmorum*, 311.
[9]Arminius, *Works*, 1:459-60*; citing Ex 34:6; Is 48:8-9; Ps 103:9-10; Jer 3:5; Joel 2:13; 2 Sam 7:14; Ps 103:13-14.
[10]CTS 8:490* (CO 31:295).

JOY IN THE MORNING OF THE TRUE SUN OF RIGHTEOUSNESS. MARTIN LUTHER: "Weeping will continue for the evening," because through the many tribulations of this life it is fitting for us to enter eternal life. The tribulations of this life are figured by the evening. In the evening Christ died, and early in the morning he rose again. For during that entire evening until the morning the disciples grieved, while the world rejoiced; after that morning the disciples rejoiced to see their Lord, while the Jews were saddened. In this same way the saints grieve, the world rejoices until its end and death, but in the resurrection the saints will rejoice and the world will grieve. GLOSSA ON PSALM 30 (1513–1515).[11]

THE PENDULUM SWING OF EMOTIONS. HIERONYMUS WELLER VON MOLSDORF: Those who are especially inexperienced in spiritual warfare imagine that after their deliverance—that is, once they have been delivered from very bitter temptations and afflictions by the aid of the Word of God and faith—they have at last surmounted their difficulties, that the battle is now completely finished. They seem to believe that the strength of their faith is such that they are able to resist and despise easily the devil, the flesh, the world and every kind of temptation. However, to these same novices, whenever God has hidden his face, that is, whenever he appears to withdraw from them and leave them alone to wrestle and fight with the devil, sin, death and dark thoughts, they feel how great human nature's weakness is, and how far they still are from that perfection which they believed they had achieved—indeed they know that without the help of God they are unable to conquer even the most trifling temptation. With the psalmwriter they pray, saying, "Deliver me, O Lord, from my persecutors!" BRIEF COMMENT ON PSALM 30.[12]

ALWAYS TAKE REFUGE IN PRAYER TO GOD. JOHN CALVIN: How indeed should those flee to God who have no sense of their need to instigate or move them to that? The children of God have also a pious security of their own, which preserves their minds in tranquility amid the troublesome storms of the world; like David, who, although he had seen the whole world made to shake, yet leaning on the promise of God, was bound to hope well concerning the continuance of his kingdom. But although the faithful, when raised aloft on the wings of faith, despise adversity, yet, as they consider themselves liable to the common troubles of life, they lay their account with enduring them, they are every hour prepared to receive wounds, they shake off their sluggishness and exercise themselves in the warfare to which they know that they were appointed, and with humility and fear they put themselves under God's protection. And they do not consider themselves safe anywhere else than under God's hand. COMMENTARY ON THE PSALMS.[13]

ALL OUR EFFORTS ARE VAIN WITHOUT GOD'S GRACE. CARDINAL CAJETAN: From this, O wise reader, you understand that it is not sufficient for us to persevere in the good grace of our strength, but the grace of the divine will is required. That is, we need God's gracious protection which preserves a person lest he squander the grace of his strength. For this gracious will is what the Lord said to Paul, "My grace is sufficient for you." COMMENTARY ON PSALM 30.[14]

THE ABUNDANT LIFE IS THE LIFE OF THE RESURRECTION. MARTIN LUTHER: This can also be understood in the manner of that apostolic word: "Christ, rising from the dead, dies no more." And thus "abundance" signifies the glory of resurrection, where every kind of salvation beyond the prior life has abounded in him. And because of this abundance he says that he will not be moved in eternity, that is, he will not die again. And this is because the Lord God in his good will "gave to my beauty"—that is, beauty to humanity through the

[11]WA 3:162.
[12]Weller, *Enarratio Psalmorum*, 311-12.
[13]CTS 8:491-92* (CO 31:296).
[14]Cajetan, *In Sacrae Scripturae Expositionem*, 3:104-5; citing 2 Cor 12:9.

glory of the resurrection—"strength" not to die. As in Psalm 93: "The Lord has reigned, clothed with beauty; the Lord is clothed with strength." First Psalms Lectures (1513–1515).[15]

30:8-10 *Can Dust and Death Praise You?*

David Worries That His Premature Death Would Imply God's Wrath. Moïse Amyraut: This seems to be said out of the economy of nature, in which, because human life is given to be devoted to the glory of its Creator, thus, a lengthy life is considered a blessing from God, while a reckless and hasty death is considered a testimony of God's wrath and vengeance. Annotations on Psalm 30:9.[16]

Our Purpose Is to Praise God's Glory. John Calvin: David does not mean that the dead are altogether deprived of power to praise God (as I have already shown in Psalm 6).[17] If the faithful, while encumbered with a burden of flesh, exercise themselves in this pious duty, how should they desist from it when they are unencumbered and set free from the restraints of the body? It ought to be observed, therefore, that David does not professedly treat of what the dead do or how they are occupied but considers only the purpose for which we live in this world, which is this, that we may mutually show forth to one another the glory of God. Having been employed in this exercise to the end of our life, death at length comes on us and shuts our mouth. Commentary on the Psalms.[18]

30:11-12 *Mourning Transformed into Dancing*

Like the Saints Before Us, We Too Will Be Heard. Philipp Melanchthon: Prayer is always necessary for our deliverance. All these

things are written down for our use. . . . The Psalms become clear and, therefore, sweet when we learn faith and prayer in these examples. . . . In this prayer faith is kindled so that we may firmly believe that we are heard. And because we know that the promise pertains to us—"All who call on the name of the Lord will be saved"—we will be saved. Thus, let us know that these examples have been recorded so that we would believe we too will be heard. For "God is rich toward all those who call on him." Comments on the Psalms.[19]

David Begins and Ends the Psalm with Thanksgiving. John Calvin: David concludes the psalm as he had begun it, with thanksgiving. He affirms that it was by the help and blessing of God that he had escaped safely. And he then adds that the final object of his escape was that he might employ the rest of his life in celebrating the praises of God. He also shows us that he was not insensible or obdurate under his afflictions but mourned in sorrow and grief, and he also shows that his very mourning had been the means of leading him to pray to God for relief from his wrath. Both these points are most worthy of our observation, in order, first, that we may not suppose that the saints are guilty of stoical insensibility, depriving them of all feeling of grief, and, second, that we may perceive that in their mourning they were exercised to repentance.

The latter he denotes by the word *sackcloth*. It was a common practice among the ancients to clothe themselves with sackcloth when mourning, for no other reason, indeed, than that like guilty criminals, they might approach their heavenly Judge, imploring his forgiveness with all humility and testifying by this clothing their humiliation and dissatisfaction with themselves. We also know that people in the east—more so than others—were especially prone to ceremonies. We perceive, therefore, that David, although he patiently submitted himself to God, was not free from grief. We also see that his

---

[15]LW 10:138* (WA 3:163); citing Rom 6:9; Ps 93:1.
[16]Amyraut, *Paraphrasis in Psalmos Davidis*, 118.
[17]See Calvin's comment on Ps 6:4-5, p. 57 above.
[18]CTS 8:495* (CO 31:297).

[19]MO 13:1063; citing Joel 2:32 (cf. Acts 2:21; Rom 10:13); Rom 10:12.

sorrow was "a godly grief," as Paul says, for to demonstrate his penitence he clothed himself with sackcloth.

By the term *dancing*, he does not mean any wanton or profane leaping but a sober and holy exhibition of joy like what sacred Scripture mentions when David brought the ark of the covenant to its place. . . . David therefore means that, laying aside his mourning apparel, he turned from squalor and humiliation to joy. Ascribing this to God's grace alone he testifies that God was his Deliverer. COMMENTARY ON THE PSALMS.[20]

OUR SOLE PURPOSE IS TO PRAISE THE NAME OF THE LORD. TILEMANN HESSHUS: David obliges himself by this vow to God to celebrate perpetually the divine name. For *that* reason, God preserves us in life and delivers us from many grave dangers—not so that we would do whatever we want, but rather so that we would proclaim his goodness and truth throughout the world. For this reason, human beings have been preserved, so that they would serve the glory of God. And we should proclaim this gratitude to God after we are rescued from grave dangers, so that we would nourish and strengthen our faith, as well as invite others to faith and prayer, that they would always praise the benefits of God. No other office should delight us more! The holy angels delight in nothing more than they do in the celebration of the divine name. It is right for us to imitate them. In the heavenly life to come will we be occupied in any other matter but the praise of the divine name? My glory is my voice and musical instruments by which I glorify and celebrate you. COMMENTARY ON PSALM 30.[21]

---

[20]CTS 8:495-97* (CO 31:299); citing 2 Cor 7:10; 2 Sam 6:16.

[21]Hesshus, *Commentarius in Psalmos*, 129v.

31:1-24 INTO YOUR HANDS, FATHER, I COMMIT MY SPIRIT

To the choirmaster. A Psalm of David.

¹ In you, O LORD, do I take refuge;
   let me never be put to shame;
   in your righteousness deliver me!
² Incline your ear to me;
   rescue me speedily!
Be a rock of refuge for me,
   a strong fortress to save me!

³ For you are my rock and my fortress;
   and for your name's sake you lead me and
      guide me;
⁴ you take me out of the net they have hidden
      for me,
   for you are my refuge.
⁵ Into your hand I commit my spirit;
   you have redeemed me, O LORD, faithful God.

⁶ I hate*ᵃ* those who pay regard to worthless idols,
   but I trust in the LORD.
⁷ I will rejoice and be glad in your steadfast love,
   because you have seen my affliction;
   you have known the distress of my soul,
⁸ and you have not delivered me into the hand
      of the enemy;
   you have set my feet in a broad place.

⁹ Be gracious to me, O LORD, for I am in
      distress;
   my eye is wasted from grief;
   my soul and my body also.
¹⁰ For my life is spent with sorrow,
   and my years with sighing;
my strength fails because of my iniquity,
   and my bones waste away.

¹¹ Because of all my adversaries I have become
      a reproach,
   especially to my neighbors,
and an object of dread to my acquaintances;
   those who see me in the street flee from me.

¹² I have been forgotten like one who is dead;
   I have become like a broken vessel.
¹³ For I hear the whispering of many—
   terror on every side!—
as they scheme together against me,
   as they plot to take my life.

¹⁴ But I trust in you, O LORD;
   I say, "You are my God."
¹⁵ My times are in your hand;
   rescue me from the hand of my enemies and
      from my persecutors!
¹⁶ Make your face shine on your servant;
   save me in your steadfast love!
¹⁷ O LORD, let me not be put to shame,
   for I call upon you;
let the wicked be put to shame;
   let them go silently to Sheol.
¹⁸ Let the lying lips be mute,
   which speak insolently against the
      righteous
in pride and contempt.

¹⁹ Oh, how abundant is your goodness,
   which you have stored up for those who
      fear you
and worked for those who take refuge in you,
   in the sight of the children of mankind!
²⁰ In the cover of your presence you hide them
   from the plots of men;
you store them in your shelter
   from the strife of tongues.

²¹ Blessed be the LORD,
   for he has wondrously shown his steadfast
      love to me
   when I was in a besieged city.
²² I had said in my alarm,*ᵇ*
   "I am cut off from your sight."
But you heard the voice of my pleas for mercy
   when I cried to you for help.

²³ Love the LORD, all you his saints!
  The LORD preserves the faithful
  but abundantly repays the one who acts in pride.

²⁴ Be strong, and let your heart take courage,
  all you who wait for the LORD!

a Masoretic Text; one Hebrew manuscript, Septuagint, Syriac, Jerome *You hate*   b Or *in my haste*

OVERVIEW: While our commentators cannot avoid the intertestamental resonance of this psalm in Christ's Lukan prayer from the cross, they are not entirely agreed as to how to understand this resonance. Did Christ understand this psalm as prophecy, prayer or type? Unsurprisingly many of the Lutheran exegetes underscore that this psalm is a prophecy of Christ's death *and* resurrection, an outline of his victory over that ancient serpent. In submission to authorial intent—that is, of the Holy Spirit—they focus on these words as the very words of Christ our Lord. Because Christ emended verse 5, Cajetan staunchly asserts that this psalm should not be understood as prophecy but as a prayer of David, whose petitions and promises Jesus of Nazareth rightly fitted to his own circumstances. Amyraut and other Reformed expositors pave a middle route via typology, affirming the historical circumstances of David while also intimating a *sensus plenior* (i.e., "fuller sense") concerning Jesus Christ.

The key theme in the reformers' commentary here is God's sure and steadfast providential care—even in the midst of suffering. Together these commentators seize and embrace the prophet's affirmation, "You are my God!" This is the reality in which believers are to live. They are not their own, and their Master is faithful, not fickle. Whether we are to die or to live, we are God's, and he has not forgotten us. Yes, there are times when we will hesitate, perhaps even lose hope—despite these faults, the reformers remind us, the Lord's care is unchanged. Seize his promises with faith, enter that strong city walled with the Lord's salvation, and revel in the treasury of God's goodness. Christ suffered. And just as he was delivered, so too our future deliverance—temporal and eternal—is as sure as if it had already hap-pened. Hidden in Christ, these commentators boast, we participate in the very life of God. All other hope is vanity.

CHRIST SINGS THIS PSALM. TILEMANN HESSHUS: The particular person speaking in this psalm is the Son of God, our Lord Jesus Christ, who while hanging on the cross on account of our sins and breathing his last, used and spoke words from this psalm in the greatest agony of death: "Into your hand I commit, O Lord, my spirit." Nothing is more certain than that in this psalm Christ prophesies about his passion and death—that he is going to surrender his life for the life of the world—as well as about his resurrection.

I do not deny that this psalm can be accommodated rightly to the entire church and each believer. Often believers are brought into such difficulties that they are forced to despair of their lives; nevertheless, they are sustained and defended. But as the Son of God Jesus Christ is not only their Leader through every affliction and misery, but he even undertakes all misery in himself. The entire wrath of God he bore alone. And on account of our sins he was placed under the most sorrowful agony and finally suffered death. Thus there is no doubt that the Holy Spirit especially considered Christ's suffering when he uttered this psalm. COMMENTARY ON PSALM 31.[1]

CHRIST ADAPTED THIS PSALM ABOUT DAVID TO HIMSELF. CARDINAL CAJETAN: Concerning the subject matter of this psalm, notice that it is found neither by the title nor is it determined by the authority of sacred Scripture in another passage. In fact, that the Lord while on the cross

---

[1]Hesshus, *Commentarius in Psalmos*, 130r.

prayed the fifth verse of this psalm—"into your hands I will commit my spirit"—does not mean that this psalm treats Christ according to the letter. Moreover, the words spoken by Christ are different from those of this psalm. For Christ said "into your hands," but the psalm says "into your hand." From this difference it can be discerned that by transposition the Lord accommodated his words to the proposition from this passage. Also, because in this psalm so much of the material is proper to David himself—as the psalm itself confirms—according to the letter it speaks of David. COMMENTARY ON PSALM 31.[2]

THE CIRCUMSTANCES AND CONFESSIONS OF THIS PSALM. THEODORE BEZA: Because there are various circumstances of misfortunes by which the Lord either tests or disciplines his people, it is useful when reading the Psalms—which contain prayers spoken by the Spirit of the Lord—to consider what is common among all of them and what is particular to each one, so that we would use them agreeably and appropriately. This psalm was written by David—as is quite obvious—regarding that time when, before his glory and authority blossomed and before he took Saul's place as king, suddenly by the unjust hatred of the king and by the fury stirred up by the envy of some, he was brought into extreme misery. It is well known that by this sort of unexpected fickleness a countless number of people have been struck down; even some of the most steadfast people have seized on the most disgraceful counsels and, in the end, have shamefully fallen. In contrast, David, confessing two errors—namely, in his prosperity he forgot about this kind of inconstancy and in the midst of the threatening storm he almost gave up hope—prays all the more diligently to God, relying on what he knew from Samuel as well as his good conscience. In short, he places before himself those famous promises of God, confirmed by a great number of very sure examples, by which God proves that he takes the

greatest care of his people even when things seem quite hopeless. Finally, so that his example would teach the pious that such prayers are heard, he gives thanks to God—whether because he was so utterly confident that his prayer would be answered . . . or because he wrote this psalm after his deliverance. PARAPHRASE OF PSALM 31.[3]

31:1-5 Into Your Hands, My Rock and Fortress, I Commit My Spirit

TYPE AND THING TYPIFIED: THIS PSALM IS ABOUT DAVID AND CHRIST. MOÏSE AMYRAUT: Everything that is contained in this verse as well as all the rest can be about both David, as the type, and Christ, as the substance that the type foreshadows. ANNOTATIONS ON PSALM 31:1-5.[4]

BOAST IN HOLY CONFIDENCE. KONRAD PELLIKAN: For the majority of David's life he was full of anxieties—either on account of enemies or consciousness of sins—from the beginning of his kingdom and before, more correctly even to his last breath; thus all his psalms are easily understood. For they always recall great calamities but not without confidence and consolation in God, with the confusion of his enemies and the exhortation of the pious, not in the least distrusting the Lord. He often mixes in the mystery of Christ his own Son according to the flesh, who, as the head of all the elect, is thus a model of crossbearing, for all those who desire and strive to live piously in this calamitous life, full of fear, and in the midst of the greatest difficulties. Now, because the chief consolation in every affliction is to feel in his own conscience confidence in God, without hesitation, therefore he boasts in an especially holy way, and for that reason he nevertheless does not cease to pray that God would rescue him. For we should never cease to pray—even offering our prayers with full confidence in God's grace. Moreover he adds a prayer against confusion, for the sake of the glory

---

[2]Cajetan, *In Sacrae Scripturae Expositionem*, 3:107; citing Lk 23:46.

[3]Beza, *Psalmorum Davidis*, 108 (cf. *Psalmes of Dauid*, 50-51).
[4]Amyraut, *Paraphrasis in Psalmos Davidis*, 119-20.

of God, which might seem to be misrepresented, if God would desert and destroy the person boasting of divine power and righteousness as well as so many of his good promises. He implores through the righteousness of God, by which God should not or cannot destroy his Word and any of his promises. COMMENTARY ON PSALM 31:1.[5]

GOD'S RIGHTEOUSNESS IS HIS FAITHFULNESS.

JOHN CALVIN: David desires "to be delivered in the righteousness of God," because God proves his righteousness by fulfilling his promise to his servants. They philosophize far too shrewdly who say that David fled to that righteousness that God freely lavishes on his people, because his own righteousness of works were of no use. Even more foolish are those who imagine that God preserves his saints according to his righteousness, because they merited it, equity requires that they be compensated with a reward. For from the frequent use of this term in the Psalms, it can be gathered that the righteousness of God should be understood as his faithfulness, by which he defends all his people who commit themselves to his guardianship and protection. Therefore, by considering the nature of God, David confirms his hope, because God cannot contradict himself. COMMENTARY ON THE PSALMS.[6]

THE FIRST COMMANDMENT: I AM THE LORD YOUR GOD.

TILEMANN HESSHUS: As God in the first commandment demands faith and hope from us, so also God obliges himself to us, that he is willing to be our Lord, that is, our protector, defender, deliverer, safe refuge, firm consolation and most certain salvation. And God offers every spiritual and corporal blessing to us when he says, "I am your God." Therefore, out of the first commandment he weaves this argument into his petition. Now when David calls God his rock and fortress, he shows God that he abandons all confidence in human things: he does not trust in

his works, his power, his kingdom, his friends, his fortresses; instead he depends on God alone. Because this is the most difficult in the midst of pressing dangers, so nothing is more pleasing to God than if we show him such obedience. COMMENTARY ON PSALM 31.[7]

GOD IS PRESENT THROUGH HIS NAME.

GIOVANNI BATTISTA FOLENGO: Wherever the name of God is—as we have reminded you elsewhere—there God himself is. To be led for the sake of God's name is to be led and guided by God himself for the sake of God himself, not for the sake of our merits. KING DAVID'S PSALTER.[8]

OUR HAVEN IN THE MIDST OF STORMS OF AFFLICTION.

JOHN CALVIN: David again declares his faith to God and affirms that he had such high thoughts of his providence as to cast all his care on it. Whoever commits himself into God's hand and to his guardianship not only establishes him as the arbiter of life and death but also calmly depends on him for protection amid all dangers. . . . As various tempests of grief disturb us, and even sometimes throw us down headlong or drag us from the direct path of duty, or at least remove us from our post, the only remedy which exists for setting these things at rest is to consider that God, who is the Author of our life, is also its Preserver. This, then, is the only means of lightening all our burdens and preserving us from being swallowed up of too much sorrow. Seeing, therefore, that God condescends to undertake the care of our lives and to support them, although they are often exposed to various sorts of death, let us learn always to flee to this asylum. Indeed, the more that anyone is exposed to dangers, let him exercise himself the more carefully in meditating on it. In short, let this be our shield against all dangerous attacks—our haven amid all trials and tempests—that, although our safety may be beyond all human hope, God is the faithful guardian of it. Let this again stir us up

---

[5]Pellikan, *Commentaria Bibliorum*, 4:75r-v.
[6]CTS 8:499* (CO 31:301).

[7]Hesshus, *Commentarius in Psalmos*, 131r; citing Ex 20:2.
[8]Folengo, *In Psalterium Davidis*, 111r.

to prayer, that he would defend us and ensure our deliverance. COMMENTARY ON THE PSALMS.[9]

PART OF THIS VERSE FITS CHRIST BETTER THAN DAVID. MOÏSE AMYRAUT: In certain ways this—"Into your hand I commit my spirit"—can be uttered by David, but it fits Christ much better. That is why he, while he hung on the cross, accommodated it to himself. But he omitted that phrase—"You have redeemed me"—as if it were strange to him, appropriate only for human beings. ANNOTATIONS ON PSALM 31:5.[10]

THE TERRIBLE WORDS OF CHRIST'S DEATH. NIKOLAUS SELNECKER: These words the Lord our Redeemer and Savior Christ Jesus spoke on the beam of the cross. And these words are certainly very fervent and full of pain as well as full of joy. I contend that these words—"My soul is very sorrowful even to the point of death"; "My God, My God why have you forsaken me?"; "Father, if it is possible, remove this cup from me"; and "Into your hands I commit my spirit"—are the most severe, sorrowful, fervent and terrible words which the Son of God for our sake could have ever uttered, to show the burden of our sins and the severity of his suffering. We acknowledge that we must always be completely silent before these words. We are not able to understand these words with our thoughts. If we are silent, we will be able to understand them only a little.

Yes, the Son of God—who was without sin and not subject to death—did not utter these words for his sake but for mine. Because he suffered for me. Because he experienced and suffered death so that I could obtain life. Now it is wretched and miserable, tragic and terrifying that the eternal Son of God should see his Father as his enemy who poured out the fullness of his wrath on his Son on account of the sins of the entire human race—whom the Son of God assumed in his person. And this was the truly terrible and deadly struggle of the Lord

Christ. In it he wrestled with death in no other way than as if he must be overcome by the wrath of God, by sin, by the curse of the law, by the devil, by death, by the world and by all the gates of hell—knocked to the ground and completely annihilated. But because he is true God and because he became human, so that through his obedience, suffering, death and resurrection he would destroy the works of the devil, he would crush the serpent's head and in this way he would redeem the human race from death and eternal damnation, thus he must not be defeated but instead must remain strong and obtain victory and triumph against death, hell, the world and the devil. However, only the first step, as it were, of this victory is described here, that the Son of God did not doubt the mercy and grace of his eternal heavenly Father but instead placed all his trust in him. THE WHOLE PSALTER.[11]

GOD'S HANDS CRAFT AND CARE FOR OUR BODIES AND SOULS. THE ENGLISH ANNOTATIONS: God is the Creator of both body and soul, or spirit.... We may therefore commit and commend our bodies to God, who takes care of them too, but our souls especially; they are God's primary care and should be ours on all occasions ... but especially at the point of death, when ready to give up our spirit, as seen in Christ's example. ANNOTATIONS ON PSALM 31:5.[12]

OUR REDEMPTION IS THROUGH CHRIST; HIS IS THROUGH THE FATHER. JACQUES LEFÈVRE D'ÉTAPLES: This phrase "You have redeemed me" should be taken one way concerning Christ, another concerning us. For the Father redeemed Christ through himself; Christ begotten free from original sin, according to Isaiah's oracle: "Thus says the Lord, he who created you, O Jacob, and he who formed you, O Israel, 'Do not be afraid, because I have redeemed you, and I have called you by your name, you are mine.'" That prophecy is about

---

[9]CTS 8:501, 502* (CO 31:302-3).
[10]Amyraut, *Paraphrasis in Psalmos Davidis*, 120.

[11]Selnecker, *Der gantze Psalter*, 1:166v; citing Lk 23:46; Mt 26:38; 27:46 (cf. Mk 15:34); Lk 22:42.
[12]Downame, ed., *Annotations*, 6C3r*; citing Lk 23:46.

Christ the Lord, but he redeemed us through his own Son, who "surely bore our weaknesses and carried our sufferings," and by whose "bruising we are healed." FIVEFOLD PSALTER: ANNOTATIONS ON PSALM 31:5.[13]

31:6-13 *Look on My Affliction in Mercy*

DAVID HATES ANYTHING THAT DISTRACTS HIM FROM THE TRUE GOD. JOHN CALVIN: In order the better to express that his faith was firmly fixed on God, he affirms that he was free from the vile affections which usually turn away our minds from God and under which unbelievers, for the most part, labor. For by contrasting opposites, as we know, he better illustrates the subject. To restrict the Hebrew word *hebel*—here rendered as "vanities"—to magical arts, as some interpreters do, is absurd. I confess, indeed, that the easterners were so addicted to these counterfeits that it was a common evil among them. But because Satan ensnares human minds by innumerable deceits and turns them away from God by just as many enticements, it is not at all probable that the prophet mentions one type alone. Whatever empty hopes, therefore, we invent for ourselves, which might draw us away from our confidence in God, David generally calls "vanities," indeed, false or lying vanities. For, although they feed us for a time with magnificent promises, in the end they dupe and disappoint us. He testifies, therefore, that having thrown away the vanities which human beings usually invent to support their hopes, he relies solely on God. And because human beings not only intoxicate themselves with the deceitful enticements of the world but also deceive one another, the prophet explicitly declares that he hates all who manufacture such lies, because we should carefully avoid them, lest we willfully desire to be entangled in their criminal deceptions.

The second clause, "I have trusted in Jehovah," must be read in connection with the first, because it both assigns the cause of his hatred of lying vanities and shows that it is impossible for human beings to have any true faith in God, unless they abhor whatever would draw them away from him. COMMENTARY ON THE PSALMS.[14]

EVEN IN SORROW WE HAVE JOY IN THE SPIRIT. TILEMANN HESSHUS: He illustrates his confidence by the efficient cause and its effect. He does not say, "I depend on my righteousness, works and worthiness," but "on your lovingkindness and goodness which you have revealed in your Word. And in this faith I feel joy kindled in my heart through the Holy Spirit." As long as there is faith in the midst of sorrow, nothing is felt other than the joy of the Holy Spirit, but the struggle does not end without difficulty, without labor, sweat, pain—rather, whenever we endure in faith and do not withdraw our hand from the plow but press on in the Word and are sustained constantly in the brief time of sorrow, it was said incredibly how faith would beget a passionate joy in our heart. For we see that we have been brought back from the underworld and transported into heaven. From this and in this passage Christ confesses that God has considered his affliction. This confession of the Spirit should be placed against the doubts of our heart and the blasphemous clamor of the Epicureans and the hopeless. COMMENTARY ON PSALM 31.[15]

NOW DELIVERED, DAVID RECALLS HIS SORROW. MARTIN BUCER: Everything fits. The more simply the words of Scripture are taken, the more certainly one arrives at the thought of the Spirit, if nothing else should hinder. Accordingly, lest it be necessary to twist anything in these two verses, I take them as a sudden and abrupt exclamation, in which the prophet broke forth out of consideration of such wonderful and stupendous power by which the Lord truly saved him from such a present death.

---

[13]Lefèvre, *Quincuplum Psalterium*, 47v; citing Is 43:1; 53:4, 5.

[14]CTS 8:504-5* (CO 31:304).
[15]Hesshus, *Commentarius in Psalmos*, 132r.

In fact, it is evident in these ways that he had composed this psalm after he had escaped the dangers, and indeed as was especially his custom, recalled his own feelings in the dangers that he was embroiled. But rarely does he not also mix in his current affections that he was experiencing at that time when he wrote holy songs of this sort. This is why there is so much rejoicing and joy even in those songs which are otherwise sung most sorrowfully. Although by a remarkable and incredible imitation of speech he set forth in front of his eyes in songs of this sort the disturbance of his soul with which he was afflicted in adversities, he nonetheless was by no means either willing, able or obligated to lie about how joyful he was at that time about the salvation he had already received, when in the song he recalled those sorrowful matters.

This therefore would seem to be the case in the present psalm. With the most ardent emotions he recited from the beginning of the psalm so that the one caught up in the crisis would have revived himself and sought the help of God. From this point, sometimes in the verses which follow the previous ones, he interwove complaints of the most afflicted and greatest disturbances of his soul. However, in these verses what else could be done than that his soul would therefore more fully exult with joy in the salvation that he had received—a joy with which he considered inwardly the danger from which the goodness of God had snatched him and that faith which God had preserved in him in whatever incomparable anxiety? Therefore because he remembers his faith so magnificently, by which he not only would not bend his ear to vain wiles but even had detested them and had prayed, although despairing of all deliverance yet hoping against hope for salvation from God, he blazed with an admiration of the divine goodness toward him. But also desiring to provoke a similar faith in God and zeal for God in others, he now begins to preach about the salvation that he received, not delaying because the order of the ode now would demand that he mention now how he would have been affected in the crisis, either what he would have prayed for or what he would have complained about. HOLY PSALMS.[16]

HYPERBOLIC AMPLIFICATION OF DAVID'S SORROWS. MOÏSE AMYRAUT: This description is surely poetic and hyperbolic—nevertheless it undoubtedly depends on the truth. But still this truth is poetically exaggerated. ANNOTATIONS ON PSALM 31:9.[17]

RULE FOR TROPOLOGY. MARTIN LUTHER: From verses 9 to 12, there is, tropologically, a beautiful prayer of a conscience that is fearful and acknowledges it has sinned. . . . Indeed, this is the rule for tropology: Wherever in the Psalms Christ complains and prays in bodily affliction according to the letter, there, in the same words, every faithful soul, born and trained in Christ, complains and prays, confessing that it has been tempted to sin or has fallen into sin. For Christ, even to today, is spat on, killed, scourged, crucified in us ourselves. Even now they crouch hidden, waiting to ambush him. FIRST PSALMS LECTURES (1513–1515).[18]

ALLEGORICALLY THIS VERSE IS ABOUT THE MINISTRY OF THE WORD. MARTIN LUTHER: Everything can be understood as referring to Christ literally as well as mystically. . . . Allegorically the "eye" of Christ is the order of teachers and leaders, whose task it is to supervise and direct and by the eye of others. . . . The "soul" is the order of those who administer the sacraments and the Word of God, who give life to the church as the soul does to the body, yes, who are the life of the church, giving it life through the Holy Spirit. "Belly" is the whole order of the people in whom the faithful are begotten, or also the priests themselves and common people, who are pregnant and carry them in their womb until they form Christ in them. Concerning this womb it is written in Song of Songs: "Your belly is like a heap of wheat." All of these things [i.e., the eye, the soul and the belly] are

---

[16]Bucer, *Sacrorum Psalmorum*, 159v-160r.
[17]Amyraut, *Paraphrasis in Psalmos Davidis*, 121.
[18]LW 10:139* (WA 3:167); citing Ps 6.

troubled with the wrath of God. For an angry God seems to allow these things today to be for nothing and without efficacy, because they are given a false meaning, so that they do what is not proper. They do not give direction as an eye, but they make themselves blind. Nor do they give life as their soul, but they kill by the influence of a death-dealing life. By their example they do not cause life to flow in but death. Then they care about nothing less than conceiving and begetting them. So then the same order can be said to involve all three because of the diversity of churchly functions. Indeed any person can be eye, soul and belly to another, when he guides him, gives life to him and preserves him in life and carefully bears him in the womb. FIRST PSALMS LECTURES (1513–1515).[19]

I AM A MAN OF CONSTANT SORROW. DAVID DICKSON: The consciousness of sin joined with trouble is greater than any burden, able to break a person's strength more than any other trouble. For David says, "My strength fails because of my iniquity, and my bones are consumed." When the godly have many and powerful enemies, then their acquaintance and neighbors and most people will readily believe that all the false reports about them are true, and this makes the grief of the godly the greater. As here, "I was a reproach among all my enemies, but especially among my neighbors." When the godly fall under persecution and trouble, their worldly friends, for fear of danger of burden by them, will turn their back on them and forget acquaintances, yes, and natural bands with them also; and then the godly must lean on God and expect comfort from him. This is held forth in this type of Christ and the example of believers under trials: "I am an object of dread to my acquaintances." Long lying in trouble will cause a person to be forgotten by his friends, as if he were dead, and make him lose all estimation at their hands, as if there were no worth in him at all. COMMENTARY ON PSALM 31.[20]

JESUS BECAME A VESSEL OF WRATH SO THAT WE WOULD BE VESSELS OF MERCY. NIKOLAUS SELNECKER: Above in Psalm 22, he spoke in this way: "My strength is dried up like a potsherd, and my tongue sticks to the roof of my mouth." For in suffering and in deep, difficult sorrow our strength dries up and everything becomes dull and weak. However, Christ, without a doubt, wanted to indicate by these words—"a broken vessel"—his wounds in his hands and feet as well as his side which had been opened and pierced by a spear; from it, as from a broken vessel, flowed blood and water.

In Hebrew it reads as "a vessel cast out," a vessel which we should throw away; it is no longer useful. Holy Scripture also uses this phrase this way, so that it often calls the entire person a vessel; for example, Paul is a chosen vessel or instrument. For that reason we say "a vessel of God's mercy," that is, a believing, justified and holy person, as well as "a vessel of God's wrath," namely, an unbelieving, unrepentant, unjustified and damned person. Christ understands such a vessel here, on which the weight and burden of sin and the wrath of God against humanity had been placed—for us he became a curse and guilt offering. "I have become," he says, "like a vessel of wrath that must be cast away and damned, as if all mercy and fatherly grace is gone." Indeed this great lament and word we should contemplate with true focus. On account of this meditation we should acknowledge the filthiness of our nature and our sin and the bitter suffering of Christ because of our sin—we should heartily thank him for his love and benefits.... What is said in the person of the Lord Christ all believers should claim for themselves. In suffering and crossbearing everything is fear and terror, so that we often think that we are abandoned by God and that we are vessels of wrath. Enemies and friends are against us. There is absolutely no help anywhere. "There is the trouble, there is the toil."[21] So then, be consoled and undaunted; wait on the

---

[19]LW 10:142, 143* (WA 3:170); citing Gal 4:19; Song 7:2.
[20]Dickson, *First Fifty Psalms*, 204*.

[21]Virgil, *Aeneid* 6.129 (*The Aeneid*, trans. Robert Fitzgerald [New York: Vintage Classics, 1990], 164).

Lord. Trust in God and say, "You are my God, my time is in your hands." Everything is based on this consolation. Blessed is the one who relies on this consolation. The Whole Psalter.[22]

31:14-20 *My Trust Is in the Lord and His Steadfast Love*

Trusting God Is Not Easy in the Face of Worldly Derision. John Calvin: In these words he intimates that he was so entirely persuaded of this truth, that God was his God, that he would not admit even a suggestion to the contrary. And until this persuasion prevails so as to take possession of our minds, we shall always waver in uncertainty. It is, however, to be observed that this declaration is not only inward and secret—made rather in the heart than with the tongue—but that it is directed to God himself, as to him who is the only witness of it. Nothing is more difficult, when we see our faith derided by the whole world, than to direct our speech to God only and to rest satisfied with this testimony which our conscience gives us, that he is our God. And certainly it is an undoubted proof of genuine faith, when, however fierce the waves are which beat against us, and however sore the assaults by which we are shaken, we hold fast this as a fixed principle, that we are constantly under the protection of God and can say to him freely, "You are our God." Commentary on the Psalms.[23]

In the Firm Grasp of God. Nikolaus Selnecker: These words—"My time is in your hands"—belong to the devout, believing Christians of whom Christ said that not even a hair should fall from their head apart from the will of God. And such words do not belong to those selfsure and crude people who have so often made a mockery out of such comforting words. . . . But these words are a true consolation for the pious

and fearful conscience. They should know that they are under the protection of God and so whenever they experience crossbearing, they should be certain that God will not abandon them or forget them, even if they are in the midst of death. Yes, he has counted all their hair, and they are inscribed on his hand as it is written in Isaiah. Therefore the devout should not be afraid of tyrants, who are only able to destroy the body but not the soul; instead they should trust in the Lord and not allow this consolation to be taken from them, that they can say, "You are my God, My Lord and my God, you have saved me, you faithful God!" Tyrants and heretics and all our enemies must pass away. *Were they to take our life, goods, honor, child and wife, let everything go; they have no profit so, the kingdom ours remaineth.* The Whole Psalter.[24]

God Is for Us. Martin Bucer: Here it must be observed how much hope he nourished in that greatest dejection of his soul that he described in the prior verses. In his soul and body an incredible force of anxiety, sickness and indignation raged, devoured blood, consumed his bones and made every part of his body to waste away. At this point his spirit, relying on the testimony of the divine Spirit, thought, "You are my God," that is, no matter how you have overwhelmed me with bad things and tortured me with terror, grief, lamentation and wrath, still you are my God, I trust in your goodness, you by no means carry me away into these things, I have entrusted myself to your faith, you could not abandon me by any means. Now my days and the length of my life are in your hands, not those of my enemies. So then no matter to what extent I am surrounded by enemies and there is no way of escape that remains; even at this point you could save me. Therefore shine your face on your servant, that is, bring your power, by which you support me, and witness that you consider me with a benevolent countenance. . . .

---

[22]Selnecker, *Der gantze Psalter*, 1:168v-169r; citing Ps 22:15; Acts 9:15.
[23]CTS 8:511* (CO 31:307-8).

[24]Selnecker, *Der gantze Psalter*, 1:169r; citing Lk 21:16; Mt 10:30; Is 49:16; Mt 10:28. The last sentence of this selection is the latter half of stanza four from Luther's "A Mighty Fortress Is Our God"; see LW 53:285; (WA 35:457); below, p. 355.

The summary of this entire consolation that must be considered is: the Lord is God for us, and our times, that is, our whole life, are in his hand. Those who have been persuaded of this easily will refresh themselves against every danger. If the Lord God is acknowledged as being for us, we cannot doubt that we are his concern. Now while we carefully considered that all things are placed in his hand, who among us would believe that all things end best, when our God who rules all things arranges them? HOLY PSALMS.[25]

CONSIDER GOD'S PROMISES, NOT TEMPORAL AFFLICTIONS. TILEMANN HESSHUS: He repeats the prayer and emphasizes that he is accustomed to being in severe temptation. Christ, experiencing the Father's wrath and having been made a curse for our sake on the cross, looks at the stern face of the Father and his very terrible anger at the sins of human beings. Therefore, he prays that he would lay aside his wrath and turn his cheerful and kind face toward his Son. He prays that he would rescue him from this current catastrophe and most bitter struggle, revive him from death and establish him as the head of the church. Now he appeals to the lovingkindness of God. For this is the sole cause of the redemption of the entire human race, accomplished through Christ, that God would show us mercy according to his immeasurable goodness.

[In verse 17] he demonstrates by what means he obtains his prayer and deliverance from God; what he prays, he declares more strongly. "By true prayer," he says, "I flee to God. Therefore it is certain that I will not be oppressed, nor will I be destroyed forever. For God commands that we pray to him. He has bound himself to us, because he is surely willing to rescue and deliver those who call on him. Therefore, although I now seem to be forsaken by God himself—I am nailed to the cross, I am sinking into death—nevertheless I am not ruined forever. I will not be destroyed, but instead I will rise again from death and I will glorify God. The impious blush for shame," he says. Here what will

happen to the impious is not only prayed but also prophesied.... This verse teaches us not to consider the brief moment of time when the impious exult and boast over their iniquities but to wait until God reveals his judgment. For it is necessary that the impious, in the end, are put to shame, that is, to show the world that they furiously opposed the truth, unjustly afflicted the innocent, were enemies of God and therefore deserve eternal torment. This shaming and humiliation God will announce before all creatures—the immeasurable suffering of the impious on the Day of Judgment. COMMENTARY ON PSALM 31.[26]

FAITH AND EXPERIENCE. JOHANNES BUGENHAGEN: Believe here the experienced teacher—but you will not believe unless you also experience it. The person freed from grave temptation knows how to proclaim the sweetness of divine mercy, which nevertheless always aids those who fear God more than people, yet in that affliction it hides itself and seems to be absent. In its own time it also becomes plain to those who believe in both temporal and future judgment, when the righteousness of the pious and the iniquity of the impious are revealed. INTERPRETATION OF THE PSALMS.[27]

THE INEXHAUSTIBLE STOREHOUSE OF GOD'S GOODNESS. WOLFGANG MUSCULUS: It should be noted in this passage how the prophet, from the private kindnesses of God, enters into and is seized by contemplation and commendation of the goodness of God in general, which extends toward whoever fears him. It is as if he were saying, "That you are good to me to such an extent does not happen on account of my merit but on account of you, immeasurably good to all those who worship and fear you." Such contemplation is the most pious and the most fitting of all; it is not only for the glory of God's goodness but also for the consolation of the pious. The amplification of the goodness of God must also be observed in this

[25]Bucer, *Sacrorum Psalmorum*, 162r.

[26]Hesshus, *Commentarius in Psalmos*, 133v-134r.

[27]Bugenhagen, *In librvm Psalmorvm interpretatio*, 73v.

verse when he says, "How great is your goodness, which you have stored up for those who fear you." By these words he teaches that the goodness of God toward his own is an example of the richest treasury which cannot be exhausted. And this is why it has been stored up, so that it may serve the necessities and salvation of the pious. For this use of treasuries is like what either parents put away for their children or kings for their kingdom or a republic for its citizens, so that in a time of need it is within reach; from this treasury all necessities may be sought. COMMENTARY ON THE PSALMS.[28]

WE ARE SAFE IN CHRIST'S CHURCH. MARTIN LUTHER: Faith in the deity protects from all persecution. In this verse the persecution of tyrants is mentioned. "You will protect them in your tabernacle from the plots of human beings," that is, in the church from heretics. Therefore whoever wants to avoid heresy should remain in the tabernacle, and that person will overcome and be protected. Whoever wants to overcome persecutors should hide himself in the faith of Christ's divinity. FIRST PSALMS LECTURES (1513–1515).[29]

31:21-24 God Proved His Faithfulness to Me

THE LORD IS OUR SURE ROCK AND SALVATION. NIKOLAUS SELNECKER: Now he thanks God for mercifully hearing his prayer. This wonderful goodness, however, is nothing other than what he said in Psalm 4. "The Lord leads his saints wonderfully," namely, through crossbearing and back again, and he mightily rescues them whenever every human aid is gone. Human reason is unable to grasp this; indeed, it is contrary to all human reason and understanding. For example, the disciples of Christ did not understand that Christ must suffer and in this way enter his glory.

For that reason the Lord scolded them and called them fools and unbelievers.

"Strong city" means the congregation and church of God, the house of the Lord about which we have commented above in Psalm 27. Whoever lives in it remains safe, sure and free in God. It is the true heavenly and spiritual Jerusalem; it is shielded and sheltered by God, as Isaiah 26 sings, "We have a strong city; the Lord sets up salvation like walls and bulwarks." Cast yourself on the Lord eternally, for God the Lord is a rock eternally. THE WHOLE PSALTER.[30]

DO NOT LET DOUBT ROB GOD'S GRACE FROM YOU. JOHN CALVIN: David here confesses that for his distrust he deserved to be deserted by God and left to perish. It is true that to confess this before people he felt to be a shameful thing; but that he may the more fully illustrate the grace of God to him, he hesitates not to publish the shame of his fault.... Now if peevish hastiness of thought could drive this holy prophet of God—a man who was adorned with so many excellencies—to despair, how much reason do we have to fear, lest our minds should fail and fatally ruin us? This confession of David . . . serves to magnify the grace of God, but at the same time he sufficiently shows, in the second clause of verse [22], that his faith, although severely shaken, had not been altogether eradicated, because he did not cease meanwhile to pray. The saints often wrestle in this manner with their distrust, that partly they may not despond, and that partly they may gather courage and stimulate themselves to prayer. Nor does the weakness of the flesh, even when they are almost overthrown, hinder them from showing that they are unwearied and invincible champions before God. But although David stoutly resisted temptation, he nevertheless acknowledges himself unworthy of God's grace, of which he in some measure deprived himself by his doubt. COMMENTARY ON THE PSALMS.[31]

---

[28]Musculus, *In Psalterium Commentarii*, 455.
[29]LW 10:144* (WA 3:171).

[30]Selnecker, *Der gantze Psalter*, 1:171r; citing Ps 4:3; 27:4; Is 26:1.
[31]CTS 8:517, 518* (CO 31:311, 312).

THE SURE REALITY OF GOD'S FUTURE JUSTICE.
PHILIPP MELANCHTHON: An exhortation is added
which demonstrates the application of the example.
"Just as I have been heard and liberated, so also you
will be heard. Therefore, act courageously, do not let
your spirit fall, do not cast away the promise of true
doctrine; rouse and strengthen your mind in the
hope and the expectation of divine help." And the
sweetest promise is added, "The Lord preserves the
faithful," that is, those who are true and steadfast,
who embrace the truth of God and teach true
doctrine without hypocrisy. On the contrary, indeed
the Lord destroys the proud, who very audaciously
and arrogantly condemn God, relying on human
power, so that now many Epicureans slay the pious
very cruelly, audaciously condemning God. But
God will restrain their raging at any moment.
COMMENTS ON THE PSALMS.[32]

WAIT ON THE LORD! NIKOLAUS SELNECKER:
Therefore Christ closes with the exhortation
that we should love and laud God. "Love the
Lord for all his benefits!" Thank the Lord, for he
is indeed friendly. He protects those who believe
in him and have their confidence in him. He
punishes the proud and arrogant. Be comforted
and undaunted all of you who wait on the Lord!
Wait on the Lord! He will not abandon you; you
will see and experience this. Wait on the Lord
alone, even if it seems too long to flesh and
blood. . . . Praise and thanks be to God the Lord
for this beautiful psalm! Grant that his Christians would take it, study it and meditate on it
well to the glory of God and to the reformation,
consolation and salvation of their lives, Amen.
THE WHOLE PSALTER.[33]

---

[32]MO 13:1064.

[33]Selnecker, *Der gantze Psalter*, 1:171r; citing Ps 27:14.

32:1-11 BLESSED ARE THE FORGIVEN

A Maskil[a] of David.

[1] Blessed is the one whose transgression is
    forgiven,
    whose sin is covered.
[2] Blessed is the man against whom the LORD
    counts no iniquity,
    and in whose spirit there is no deceit.

[3] For when I kept silent, my bones wasted away
    through my groaning all day long.
[4] For day and night your hand was heavy
    upon me;
    my strength was dried up[b] as by the heat of
      summer.   Selah

[5] I acknowledged my sin to you,
    and I did not cover my iniquity;
I said, "I will confess my transgressions to the
    LORD,"
    and you forgave the iniquity of my sin. Selah

[6] Therefore let everyone who is godly
offer prayer to you at a time when you may
    be found;
surely in the rush of great waters,
    they shall not reach him.
[7] You are a hiding place for me;
    you preserve me from trouble;
    you surround me with shouts of deliverance.
            Selah

[8] I will instruct you and teach you in the way
    you should go;
    I will counsel you with my eye upon you.
[9] Be not like a horse or a mule, without
    understanding,
    which must be curbed with bit and bridle,
    or it will not stay near you.

[10] Many are the sorrows of the wicked,
    but steadfast love surrounds the one who
      trusts in the LORD.
[11] Be glad in the LORD, and rejoice, O righteous,
    and shout for joy, all you upright in heart!

a Probably a musical or liturgical term b Hebrew *my vitality was changed*

OVERVIEW: In this penitential psalm, the reformers teach, David offers believers a catechism in the forgiveness of sins: we are made righteous by nothing else than the freely given blood of Christ our Mediator. While affirming the need for Christ's righteousness and our repentance, our exegetes are eager to steer their audience away from the twin errors, common to every age, of Pelagianism and semi-Pelagianism—that is, that we are without original sin and are capable of achieving perfection in this life, and that we are able to reach out to God first unaided, unprovoked by him; then he responds with his grace—toward the grace-infused tradition of the church catholic.[1] Some do this more explicitly, like Calvin: our repentance does not cause us to receive God's grace; repentance itself is a gift of God's grace. Others do so more implicitly, like Selnecker: because of God's Son our debt has been cancelled from God's ledger; now we must live in light of that triumph. Thus, it is the

---

Pelikan has memorably stated how unhelpful and anachronistic—it was coined in the sixteenth century—the label semi-Pelagian is: "The penchant for tagging every doctrinal position with a party label has led to the invention of the name Semi-Pelagianism, which is even less useful than most such designations" (Pelikan, *Christian Tradition*, 1:318). Examining the writings of so-called semi-Pelagians such as John Cassian (365–435), Vincent of Lérins (d. c. 445) and Faustus of Riez (c. 405–490) reveals a less clearly "heretical" formulation of the relationship between grace and nature. Cassian, in particular, is unafraid to say that grace saturates every part of creation and redemption; see his *Conferences* 13.3, 11 (NPNF[2] 11:423, 427-28).

---

[1]This is the abstract definition of semi-Pelagianism, which was condemned by the Second Council of Orange (529). Jaroslav

very faith and grace of God that enables us to repent. Donne frames this discussion within the typology of the ark and baptism (1 Pet 3:18-22): we cannot swim our way to salvation; we require the raft of God's sacraments.

Nevertheless human responsibility is not ignored or dismissed by these exegetes; the Lord must be sought while he is near. Yes, the relationship between human responsibility and God's sovereignty is mysterious! We are neither relieved of the requirement of our obedience, nor should we be deceived about our continued imperfection while on earth. Here these commentators affirm the need for law and gospel in everyone's life. With the young Luther they assert that "the entire life of believers is repentance," and *all* solace is rooted in the gospel of Genesis 3:15: "The woman's seed will crush the serpent's head."[2]

THE CHRISTIAN'S GREATEST DOCTRINE: OUR RIGHTEOUSNESS IN CHRIST. NIKOLAUS SELNECKER: David calls this psalm an instruction—it is the greatest knowledge that a person is able to know and possess. He teaches from his own experience what true salvation and righteousness is, and how the same righteousness, peace of conscience toward God, joy and comfort of the heart in God is brought about—not by our free will, good works or merit, but rather solely by the grace and pure mercy of God. For the sake of the Son of God, our sins are not credited to us but rather are forgiven by grace on account of the Lord Christ Jesus, and we are purified and redeemed from all eternal misery solely by the blood of Christ....

In this psalm we learn what our righteousness is, namely, nothing other than the forgiveness of our sins.... This is also the greatest knowledge and instruction of Christians, that they know how they shall be loosed and liberated from their sins. Works do not do it. The very righteousness of God condemns us. We are incapable of changing this. It stands on this alone: Faith looks to Jesus Christ, who has done enough for us all. He has become

our Mediator. This is the knowledge of true Christians that will never pass away. Next to this everything else must be considered less than nothing. Blessed is he who has this knowledge....

Therefore this is an excellent, beautiful psalm of instruction, in which the Christian's highest teaching and knowledge stands. For even if we were to know everything else—everything that is perishable in heaven and on earth—nevertheless it is not even worth mentioning, if we do not know this: how we may be redeemed from this misery and may become righteous before God, although we are all sinners and under the wrath of God who must be thrust into eternal damnation. THE WHOLE PSALTER.[3]

Superscription: *A Psalm of Instruction*

WHAT IS A *MAŚKÎL*? SEBASTIAN MÜNSTER: "Instruction" or "superior understanding." Thus, as it is said below, "I will make you more prudent," or "I will give you understanding and teach you in the way." On account of this Abraham Ibn Ezra believes that this psalm has been labeled with this title. Others think other things. THE TEMPLE OF THE LORD: PSALM 32.[4]

THE ANCIENT SUPERSCRIPTIONS ARE PART OF SCRIPTURE. JOHN DONNE: There belongs more to the first verse than I have read. For in all those translators and expositors who apply themselves exactly to the original—to the Hebrew—the title of the psalm is part of the first verse of the psalm. Saint Augustine gives a somewhat strange reason why the Book of Enoch—cited by Saint Jude in his epistle—and some other similar ancient books were never received into the body of canonical Scriptures:

---

[2]*Ninety-Five Theses* (1517), LW 31:83* (WA 1:233).

[3]Selnecker, *Der gantze Psalter*, 1:171v.
[4]Münster, *Miqdaš YHWH*, 1185. Even Calvin agrees that *maśkil* indicates the subject matter of the psalm; see CTS 8:521-22 (CO 31:314). Until recently contemporary scholars affirmed Münster's understanding of *maśkil*; however, Kraus rejects this, preferring "art song" instead; Alter leaves it untranslated. See Kraus, *Psalms 1–59*, 25-26; Alter, *Book of Psalms*, 110.

"The church suspected them, because they were too ancient," says Saint Augustine.[5] But that reason alone is far from being enough to exclude anything from being part of the Scriptures, because we justly make it an argument for the reception of the titles of the Psalms into the body of canonical Scriptures: they are as ancient as the Psalms themselves.

So then the title of this psalm enters into our text as a part of the first verse. And the title is *Davidis Erudiens*, where we need not insert—as our translators in all languages and editions have conceived it necessary to do so—any word to clarify the text more than the text itself does. (Therefore, Tremellius has inserted that phrase, "An Ode of David"; we, "A Psalm of David"; others, other things.[6]) For the words themselves yield a perfect sense in themselves, *lĕdāwid maśkîl* is *Davidis Erudiens*, that is, *Davidis Eruditio*, David's Instruction, David's Catechism. And so our text . . . in all accounts is now David's catechism: "Blessed is he whose transgression is forgiven." SERMON 54: PREACHED UPON THE PENITENTIAL PSALMS.[7]

32:1-5 The Relief and Restoration of Forgiveness

CHRIST IS OUR SHELTER AND PAYMENT. RUDOLF GWALTHER: Christ is the cover on account of which God does not credit our sins to us, because he gave us Christ, so that he would be our payment and righteousness. THE PSALTER.[8]

ALL GOD'S PROMISES ARE TRUE BECAUSE OF JESUS ALONE. NIKOLAUS SELNECKER: Although the prophet does not mention Christ explicitly, nevertheless he indicates that only through Christ are we granted our righteousness and salvation when he says, "God wants to be gracious and not impute guilt but instead to give gifts." Such happens only through Christ. Whoever does not have him has no grace—indeed, no God, no comfort, no life, but rather condemnation, despair and eternal death. And here we must observe this true and firm rule: Everything Scripture says to comfort us about God is based solely on the promise of the woman's Seed, that is, on our beloved Lord Christ, who will crush the serpent's head and destroy the works of the devil and redeem us from eternal death. THE WHOLE PSALTER.[9]

FORGIVEN AND JUSTIFIED IN CHRIST ALONE BEFORE GOD. GALLIC CONFESSION: We believe that all our justification rests on the remission of our sins, in which also is our only blessedness, as the psalmist says. We therefore reject all other means of justification before God, and without claiming any virtue or merit, we rest simply in the obedience of Jesus Christ, which is imputed to us as much to blot out all our sins as to make us find grace and favor in the sight of God. And, in fact, we believe that in falling away from this foundation, however slightly, we could not find rest elsewhere but should always be troubled. For we are never at peace with God until we resolve to be loved in Jesus Christ, for of ourselves we are worthy of hatred. ARTICLE 18.[10]

DAILY LIVE OUT LIVES OF REPENTANCE. JOHN CALVIN: When David was taught that he was blessed through the mercy of God alone, he was not an alien from the church of God; on the contrary, he had profited above many in the fear and service of God, and in holiness of life, and had exercised himself in all the duties of godliness. And even after making these advances in religion, God so exercised him that he placed the Alpha and Omega of his salvation in his gratuitous reconciliation to God. Nor is it without reason that Zechariah, in his song, represents "the knowledge of salvation" as consisting in knowing "the remission of

---

[5]Augustine, *City of God* 18.38 (NPNF 2:383); however, Augustine affirms *maśkîl* as "understanding"; see Augustine, Exposition on Psalm 32 (NPNF 8:70).
[6]See Immanuel Tremellius, *Testamenti Veteris Biblia Sacra sive Libri Canonici priscae Iudaeorum Ecclesiae a Deo traditi* (London: Henry Middleton, 1580), 81; Geneva Bible (1560), in loco.
[7]Donne, *Works*, 2:502*.
[8]Gwalther, *Der Psalter*, 52r.

[9]Selnecker, *Der gantze Psalter*, 1:173r; citing Gen 3:15.
[10]*Creeds* 3:369-70*.

sins." The more eminently that anyone excels in holiness, the farther he feels himself from perfect righteousness, and the more clearly he perceives that he can trust in nothing but the mercy of God alone. Hence it appears that those are grossly mistaken who conceive that the pardon of sin is necessary only to the beginning of righteousness. As believers are every day involved in many faults, it will profit them nothing that they have once entered the way of righteousness, unless the same grace which brought them into it accompany them to the last step of their life. Does anyone object that they are elsewhere said to be blessed "who fear the Lord," "who walk in his ways," "who are upright in heart"? The answer is easy, namely, that as the perfect fear of the Lord, the perfect observance of his law and perfect uprightness of heart are nowhere to be found, all that the Scripture anywhere says concerning blessedness is founded on the free favor of God, by which he reconciles us to himself. COMMENTARY ON THE PSALMS.[11]

HUMAN HISTORY IS A WARDROBE OF SIN.
JOHN DONNE: Sin has that pride that it is not content with one garment; Adam covered first with fig leaves, then with whole trees. "He hid himself among the trees." Then he covered his sin with the woman, "She provoked him," and then with God's action, "The woman whom you gave to me." And this was Adam's wardrobe. David covers his first sin of uncleanness with soft stuff, with deceit, with falsehood, with soft persuasions to Uriah to go in to his wife; then he covers it with rich stuff, with scarlet, with the blood of Uriah and of the army of the Lord of hosts; and then he covers it with strong and durable stuff, with an impenitence and with an insensibleness, a year together; too long for a king, too long for any man to wear such a garment. This was David's wardrobe.

But beloved, sin is a serpent, and whoever covers sin does but keep it warm, that it may sting the more fiercely and disperse its venom and malignity the more effectually. Adam has patched up an apron to cover him; God took none of those leaves; God wrought not on his beginnings, but he covered him all over with durable skins. God ensured that David's several coverings weighed on him rather than cover the sin, and therefore he took all away, sin and covering. For the coverings were as great as sins, as the radical sin that was to be covered—indeed even greater, as the arms and boughs of a tree are greater than the root. Now to this extension and growth and largeness of sin, no lesser covering serves than God in his church. It was the prayer against those who hindered the building of the temple, "Do not cover their iniquity or let their sin be put out of your presence." Our prayer is, "Lord, do not look on our sins, so that you may look on us." And because among ourselves it is the effect of love to cover "the multitude of sins," indeed to cover all sins, "Love covers all sins," much more shall God, who is love itself, cover our sins so, as he covered the Egyptians in a Red Sea, in the application of his blood, by visible means in his church. SERMON 54: PREACHED UPON THE PENITENTIAL PSALMS.[12]

WE OVERFLOW WITH TRANSGRESSION, SIN AND INIQUITY.
NIKOLAUS SELNECKER: Three kinds of sins are mentioned here: transgression, sin and iniquity. Transgressions are forgiven. Sins are covered. Iniquity is not credited. By this it is indicated that in human beings there are many, various and great sins, and our whole nature is thoroughly corrupted. As we sing in the beautiful song:

> Through Adam's fall is corrupted
> Human nature and essence
> This poison we inherited
> Unable to mend its illness.[13]

"Transgression" means all kinds of sin: internal and

---

[11]CTS 8:525-26* (CO 31:316-17); citing Lk 1:77.

[12]Donne, *Works*, 2:523-24*; citing Gen 3:1-13; Neh 4:5; 1 Pet 4:8; Prov 10:12.
[13]This is the first half of the opening stanza to Lazarus Spengler's (1479–1534) *Durch Adams Fall*. The common English translation, which necessarily takes some poetic license, is "All mankind fell in Adam's fall / One common sin infects us all / From one to all the curse descends / And over all God's wrath impends." See LSB no. 562.

external, inborn, original and actual, deadly, known and unknown.[14] Such sins are forgiven by grace to those who repent, for Christ takes it on himself and pays for it. "Sin" is actually original sin, about which Psalm 51 preaches, "In sin I was conceived and born." And this sin condemns us just as much as any other sin. For we all fell in Adam and with him not only by imitation and descent but by participation of our flesh and nature. But God wants to cover it with his hand and cloak our sin with the garment of his Son's purity. For the Son of God is the golden plate that lay on top of the ark of the covenant and covered it. That is, he covers our sin, of which we are accused by the law, which was placed inside the ark, so that God the Lord will not see sin. Otherwise no one could stand before God, as Psalm 130 says: "If you, O Lord, should credit sin, O Lord, who could stand?" "Iniquities" are all actual, deadly sins against conscience: blasphemy, whoring, disobedience, adultery, murder, gluttony, theft, usury and the like. Whoever lives in such sins is judged by God to damnation. But whoever turns and repents, his iniquities are not credited to him—yet such turning must be without pretense. . . .

The word "to credit" is a particular parable, which Christ uses in Matthew 18, and Paul, too, in Colossians 2. And this, now, is the sense: We are all sinners, not only by nature, but we even multiply our sin daily throughout our entire life, so that it is recorded, as it were, like a debt into God's ledger. On account of such debt—like the servant who owed his lord ten thousand pounds or sixty tons of gold—we should have had to have been cast into an eternal debtor's prison and to have perished there. That would have been the case were it not that God out of pure grace on account of his Son

had crossed out our debt from his ledger, now counting us loosed and liberated from it. The Whole Psalter.[15]

Seek God's Mercy Honestly. Rudolf Gwalther: By "deceit" he means those feignedly repressed and renounced sins which are found among those who do not want to acknowledge that they are such great sinners but instead believe that on their own they can be righteous and saved. Thus, he wants to say that it stands well with those who acknowledge who they are and thus do not feign to be someone they are not before God but rather without pretense and deceit confess to God that they are miserable and broken, like the poor sinner in Luke 18. The Psalter.[16]

The Wicked Silence of Buried Sin. John Donne: And properly this was David's silence. He confesses his silence to have been out of a spirit in which was deceit. And David did not hope, directly and determinately to deceive God, but by endeavoring to hide his sin from others and from his own conscience, he buried it deeper and deeper, but still under more and more sins. He silences his adultery, but he smothers it, he buries it under a turf of hypocrisy, of dissimulation with Uriah, so that he might have gone home and covered his sin. He silences this hypocrisy—but that must have a larger turf to cover it. He buries it under the whole body of Uriah, treacherously murdered. He silences that murder, but no turf was large enough to cover that except the defeat of the whole army, and in the end, the blaspheming of the name and power of the Lord of hosts in the ruin of the army. That sin—which, if he would have carried it upward toward God, in confession, would have vanished away and evaporated—by silencing, by suppressing, by burying, as corn buried in the earth, multiplies into many ears. Sermon 55: Preached upon the Penitential Psalms.[17]

---

[14]In medieval theology, original sin (the hereditary guilt and corruption inherited from Adam) is distinguished from actual sin (the exercise of the sinful nature). Actual sins can be categorized as follows: voluntary and involuntary sins, sins of commission and omission, mortal sins (which lead to eternal death), and venial sins (which are forgivable). See further Richard A. Muller, *Dictionary of Latin and Greek Theological Terms: Drawn Principally from Protestant Scholastic Theology* (Grand Rapids: Baker Academic, 1985), 219-21.

[15]Selnecker, *Der gantze Psalter*, 1:173-74; citing Ps 51:5; 130:3; Mt 18:21-35; Col 2:8-15.
[16]Gwalther, *Der Psalter*, 52r; citing Lk 18:13.
[17]Donne, *Works*, 2:540*.

Three Reasons Why God Afflicts His People.

MARTIN BUCER: There are three reasons why God sends adversities on his own. First, he does this namely so that he may thereby bring forth into the open the power of the Spirit given to his saints (who, in their testimony and praise of the divine goodness on the elect, most boldly condemn all earthly things in view of heavenly things, whose heirs they have become) as he shows that power first for the sake of confounding the impious and then for strengthening the weaker ones of the pious and causes a certain triumph over the prince of this world. By this rationale, he customarily subjects his own saints to the ferocious lust of the world and ferocity of the sinful, who also are thus called martyrs because they present a testimony to the world by their own blood concerning internal as well as future goods of the saints. . . .

Second, in fact in adversities, God tries to call his own away from the love of the world, from which they experience only trouble and adversity. That point is outlined in this, because at one time he willed that all their neighbors would be enemies to the people of Israel, so that by which custom the people blending together with those nations would not be contaminated by their sins. Accordingly the Savior pronounced them blessed who were poor and afflicted in spirit in grief and a desire for righteousness because they would be fit for the kingdom of heaven, that is, for the gospel and heavenly consolation. This is also why he called the ones of this sort that are laboring and burdened to himself with the promised heavenly rest for their souls.

Finally he causes his own to be crucified so that they may descend deeply into themselves and acknowledge the treachery of their own hearts. For hardly does any other evil lie in ambush for the holiest people in the same manner as hypocrisy, nor are any more difficult to cut off. In a fine way, at first they seem quite frequently to pursue the honorable things of life both in that they are zealous for God and love their neighbors, whereas in the meantime they in general live for themselves. God, however, is jealous and desires to be loved and worshiped in earnest with the whole heart. Therefore for careless saints (not to mention passive ones and those who seek their own glory) when they seem to want only the glory of God and seek the salvation of their brethren, God frequently and customarily sends on them diseases and other calamities, and he shows himself to be angry: accordingly the fatness of their souls is cut through and their senses are opened, and they see how far they are from loving him with their whole heart and their neighbors as themselves, so that they may die to themselves and live only for the glory of God. Here the deceit is fraud, dissimulation, hypocrisy, passivity, torpor, a wrong-headed security and a secret contempt of God. HOLY PSALMS.[18]

Whatever the Misfortune It Led David to Repent.

RUDOLF GWALTHER: Some think that by striking him with a severe sickness the Lord led David to acknowledge his sin. Others understand it only about a severe temptation which he felt in his conscience. However, both expositions could indeed be seen as relating to each other, so that through misfortune God very often leads us to acknowledge our own sin. THE PSALTER.[19]

Withered Under the Hand of the Lord.

KONRAD PELLIKAN: The heat of his emotions and anxieties—having been multiplied within his innermost being—consume and destroy all his vitality and render him more withered than someone scorched in the midst of summer heat. It seems that he experiences such emotions and anxieties whenever he compares the magnitude of his sin with the kindnesses of God, conveyed to him alone above all mortals: that ingratitude, like the most troublesome burden threatening his conscience, he considers to be the hand of the Lord, on account of which he is always unable not to fear that the righteous judgment of God is also threatening him. For this reason, the Lord permits believers and their friends to sin, so that humbled they would grow in the fear of God, think frequently and carefully about the Lord, learn to be compassionate to others and

---

[18]Bucer, *Sacrorum Psalmorum*, 164r-v; citing Phil 1:20; 1 Pet 4:14.
[19]Gwalther, *Der Psalter*, 52v.

not to jump to rash judgment. Moreover, the *selāh* is added to insinuate the weight of guilt after sin has been committed as well as perpetual repentance. COMMENTARY ON PSALM 32:4.[20]

A METAPHOR FOR CONFESSION. JOHN DONNE: It is but a homely metaphor, but it is a wholesome and a useful one: Confession works like vomiting.[21] It shakes the frame, and it breaks the bed of sin; and it is an ease to the spiritual stomach, to the conscience, to be disburdened in this way. It is an ease to the sinner, to the patient, but what makes it absolutely necessary is that it is a glory to God. For in all my spiritual actions, appreciations or depreciations, whether I pray for benefits or against calamities, still my Alpha and Omega, my first and last motive, must be the glory of God. SERMON 56: PREACHED UPON THE PENITENTIAL PSALMS.[22]

CONFESSION DOES NOT MERIT FORGIVENESS. JOHN CALVIN: Should anyone infer from this that repentance and confession are the cause of obtaining grace, the answer is easy, namely, David is not speaking here of the cause but of the manner in which the sinner becomes reconciled to God. Confession, no doubt, intervenes, but we must go beyond this and consider that it is faith which, by opening our hearts and tongues, really obtains our pardon. It is not admitted that everything which is necessarily connected with pardon is to be reckoned among its causes. Or, to speak more simply: David obtained pardon by his confession, not because he merited it by the mere act of confession but because, under the guidance of faith, he humbly implored it from his judge. COMMENTARY ON THE PSALMS.[23]

32:6-9 The Instruction and Example of the Saints

THE TIME OF MERCY. RUDOLF GWALTHER: The Hebrew, according to the very letters, is this, "at the time of finding," that is, "at the time of mercy," when we may still find his mercy, and this time is not yet barred to us through persistent repentance. Here the proverb from Isaiah is applicable: "Seek the Lord while he may be found." THE PSALTER.[24]

THE MEANING OF "WATERS." THE ENGLISH ANNOTATIONS: By waters, great tribulations and calamities are often set out in the Scriptures.... The meaning, according to most expositors, should be that in the time of greatest danger and most threatening destruction, whether public or private, no evil shall reach those who fly to God for succor. ANNOTATIONS ON PSALM 32:6.[25]

THROUGH CHRIST'S BLOOD AND FLOOD WE BECOME THE CHURCH. JOHN DONNE: Those are the holy ones whom God will hear, who are of the household of the faithful, of the communion of the saints, matriculated, engrafted, enrolled in the church, by that initiatory sacrament of baptism. For the house of God, into which we enter by baptism, is the house of prayer; and, as out of the ark, whosoever swam best was not saved by his swimming, no more is any mortal person, out of the church, by his praying. He who swam in the flood, swam but into more and more water; he who prays out of the church, prays but into more and more sin, because he does not establish his prayer in that: Grant this for our Lord and Savior Christ Jesus' sake. It is true then, that these holy ones, whose prayer is acceptable, are those of the Christian church; only them. But is it all of them? Are all their prayers acceptable? There is a second concoction necessary too: not only to have been sanctified by the church in baptism, but a sanctification in a worthy receiving of the other sacrament too; a life that pleads the first seal, baptism, and claims the other seal, the body and blood of Christ Jesus....

Maintain therefore a holy patience in all God's visitations: accept your waters, though they come

---

[20]Pellikan, *Commentaria Bibliorum*, 4:77r-v.
[21]Origen, *De Principiis* 3.1.13 (ANF 4:314).
[22]Donne, *Works*, 2:558*.
[23]CTS 8:531-32* (CO 31:320).

[24]Gwalther, *Der Psalter*, 52v; citing Is 55:6.
[25]Downame, ed., *Annotations*, 6C4r*.

in tears; for he who sends them, Christ Jesus, had his flood, his inundation in blood; and whatever you suffer from him, you suffer for him and it glorifies him in that constancy. . . . We consider three waters in our blessed Savior. He wept over Jerusalem; as you should, over your sinful soul. He sweat in the garden; as you should, in eating your bread in the sweat of your brow, in laboring sincerely in your calling. And then he sent water and blood out of his side, being dead, which was . . . the springhead of both Sacraments. You should also refresh in your soul the dignity which you received in the first sacrament of baptism, and thereby come worthily to the participation of the second, and therein the Holy Spirit shall give to you the seal of that security. SERMON 57: PREACHED UPON THE PENITENTIAL PSALMS.[26]

ENCOMPASSED BY DIVINE GRACE. CARDINAL CAJETAN: After expounding on the necessity for prayer, there is added this particular utterance of a righteous person, containing three things. First, he professes that he must be hidden away lest he sin: "You are my hiding place." Second, by his petition he underscores the function of the hiding place: "You will guard me from the troubles" of a demon. Third, he asks for deliverance from the dangers of sinning which surround him on every side: "You will surround me with the praises of deliverance." The praises of deliverance are the expressions of thanksgiving through singing and praising God for deliverance from the dangers of sinning. More importantly, however, he says, "You will surround me": an indication that he is attributing his deliverance completely and totally to divine grace. For, if he had escaped some danger apart from divine grace, he would not be surrounded by the praises of deliverance. But because he imputes to the grace of God whatever is not a moral failing on his part, therefore, acknowledging this blessing by praying, he says, "You will surround me with the praises of deliverance." Look closely at this prayer and you will find that it is full of the profession of

divine grace, which protects the righteous under its shadow, by providing protection from spiritual enemies and from other opportunities for sinning. COMMENTARY ON PSALM 32.[27]

THE PRECIOUS DOCTRINE OF GOD'S GRACIOUS FORGIVENESS. PHILIPP MELANCHTHON: Even among the saints, sin remains, but it is forgiven to those who ask. . . . The saints do not satisfy the law, they are not justified because they fulfill the law, but still, they are surrounded by many internal vices, doubts, unbelief, carelessness and other evils which hypocrites excuse, but the saints acknowledge that they are sinners, seek forgiveness and rest in the teaching of this psalm, they know that human beings are justified in this way, because their sin is covered and is not imputed. . . . Whoever ignores this teaching concerning the gracious remission of sins judges that they are hurled into calamities by God on account of their sins, as Cain says, "My sin is worse than what can be forgiven." But this teaching calls the soul back from hell because it certainly shows that sins are graciously forgiven and God instructs us to seek the remission of our sins by faith. COMMENTS ON THE PSALMS.[28]

HOW TO SEEK THE LITERAL SENSE OF SCRIPTURE. JOHN DONNE: This then expresses God's daily care of us, that he teaches us the way. But then, even that implies that we are all out of our way; still all bends, all conduces to that, a humble acknowledgment of our own weakness, a present recourse to the love and power of God; the first thing I look for in the exposition of any Scripture, and the nearest way to the literal sense of it, is, what may most deject and vilify humankind, what may most exalt and glorify God. SERMON 59: PREACHED UPON THE PENITENTIAL PSALMS.[29]

[26]Donne, *Works*, 2:573*, 587-88*.
[27]Cajetan, *In Sacrae Scripturae Expositionem*, 3:114.
[28]MO 13:1065-66; citing Gen 4:13.
[29]Donne, *Works*, 3:29*.

Surrender Everything to the Lord, and Gain More Than Everything. Martin Luther: [It is as if the Lord were saying] "This is where I want you to be. You ask that I deliver you. Then do not be uneasy about it; do not teach me, and do not teach yourself; surrender yourself to me. I am competent to be your Master. I will lead you in a way that is pleasing to me. You think it wrong if things do not go as you feel they should, but your thinking harms you and hinders me. Things must go not according to your understanding but above your understanding. Submerge yourself in a lack of understanding, and I will give you my understanding. Lack of understanding is real understanding; not knowing where you are going is really knowing where you are going. My understanding makes you without understanding. Thus Abraham went out from his homeland and did not know where he was going. He yielded to my knowledge and abandoned his own knowledge; and by the right way he reached the right goal. See, that is the way of the cross. You cannot find it, but I must lead you like a blind person. Therefore not you, not a human being, not a creature, but I through my Spirit and my Word will teach you the way you must go. You must not follow the work which you choose, not the suffering which you devise, but what comes to you against your choice, thoughts and desires. There I call. There you must be a pupil. There it is the time. There your Master has come. There you must not be a horse or irrational animal. If you follow me and forsake yourself, then, I will counsel you with my eye on you. I will not leave you. You shall not fall and perish. I will not forget you. Your eyes shall be closed because my eyes are open over you." The Seven Penitential Psalms (1525).[30]

The Horse and Mule. The English Annotations: The one noted for lasciviousness and stubbornness, the other for stupidity and dullness. In general, do not be like brutes. Annotations on Psalm 32:9.[31]

32:10-11 *Rejoice in the Lord*

Sorrows Without the Limitation of Time. John Donne: And here his sorrows are multiplied, "many sorrows."... [These sorrows are] great in their own weight, great in themselves and great also in the apprehension and tenderness and impatience of the sufferer—great to him. And then all these heavy-laden circumstances, as the dregs and lees of this cup of malediction, meet in the bottom, in the center of all. These sorrows are determinable by no time ... lest the wicked say, "Let it go as it came, if I know how it came, what occasioned the sorrow, I know how to overcome it."... Although it implies a continuance once it comes, yet the wicked might say, "It has not come yet, and why should I anticipate sorrow or execute myself before the executioner be sent?" But it is without limitation of time, and so it includes all parts of time—is, was and will be—the wicked are not, never were or will be without sorrows, many sorrows, great sorrows, everlasting sorrows....

For when we conceive of sorrow in the mind, without any real and external cause, without pain or shame or loss, this is but a melancholy, but an abundance of distempered humor, but a natural thing, to which some in their constitutions are born, and to be considered but so. But when God lays his hand and his crosses on us, the sorrow of the wicked, conceived on that impression, is the sorrow. For this word, which we translate as "sorrows" here, is according to the Septuagint, scourges and whips. God shall scourge them, and that shall work only to a sorrow; so far, and no farther. As a startled horse, they shall avoid a shadow and fall into a ditch; they shall be sorrowful and murmur at their afflictions in this life and fall sooner for that into the eternal. Sermon 61: Preached upon the Penitential Psalms.[32]

---

[30]LW 10:152* (WA 18:489); citing Gen 12:1-9.

[31]Downame, ed., *Annotations*, 6C4r*.
[32]Donne, *Works*, 3:61, 62-63*.

THE ROOT OF THE RIGHTEOUS. JOHN DONNE: Now as three great sums of gold put into one bag, these three branches of this portion of the righteous are fixed in one root, raised on one foundation, "Mercy shall surround him." But then this mercy, this surrounding mercy, reaches not so far as that you shall have no affliction, though you trust in God. David would have been an unfit person to have delivered such a doctrine, who says of himself, "Daily have I been punished and chastened every morning." He had it every day, it was his daily bread; and it was the first thing he had, he had it in the morning. Here it is mentioned of a morning, early sorrows, even to the godly; and mention of a day, continuing sorrows, even to the godly, but he speaks of no night here: the Son of grace, the Son of God, does not set in a cloud of anger on him. The martyrs that abounded with this trust in God, and this righteousness, and this uprightness of heart, abounded with these afflictions too. . . .

It is not then that the godly shall have no afflictions, no sorrows; but "they who wait on the Lord shall renew their strength," our translators say in the body of their translation, but in the margin—and nearer to the original—"They shall change their strength." They who have been strong in sinning, who have sinned with a strong hand, when they feel a judgment on them and find that it is God's hand, and God's hand for their sins, they do not faint, they do not lose their strength, but they change their strength, they grow as strong in suffering as they were in sinning and invest the prophet's resolution, "I will bear the indignation of the Lord, because I have sinned against him." . . .

When prosperity and adversity, honor and disgrace, profit and loss, the Lord's giving and the Lord's taking, do all concur to make this beam that must encompass us; when we acknowledge that there must be nails in the beam as well as stakes, there must be thorns in the hedge as well as fruit trees; crosses as well as blessings; when we leer not over the beam, neither into the common; that is, to the Gentiles and nations, and begin to think that we might be saved by the light of nature, without this burden of Christianity: nor leer over into the pastures and corn of our neighbors; that is, to think that we are not well in our own church but must listen to the doctrine or discipline of another; when we see all that comes, to come from God, and are content with that, then every piece serves to make this beam, and "his mercy surrounds us." SERMON 61: PREACHED UPON THE PENITENTIAL PSALMS.[33]

OUR JOY IS THE LORD, OUR CREATOR AND REDEEMER. NIKOLAUS SELNECKER: The true joy of the blessed is in the Lord himself. Temporal goods accomplish nothing. Our joy is only in God, as Jeremiah also says: "Whoever wants to boast should boast in the Lord who is gracious to us on account of Christ his Son and who has made us eternally blessed." May God the Father, Son and Holy Spirit help us all accomplish this! Amen. THE WHOLE PSALTER.[34]

---

[33]Donne, *Works*, 3:76-80*; citing Ps 73:14; Is 40:31; Mic 7:9; Ps 34:8.
[34]Selnecker, *Der gantze Psalter*, 1:178v; citing Jer 9:24 (cf. 1 Cor 1:31; 2 Cor 10:17).

33:1-22 THE STEADFAST LOVE OF THE LORD

[1] Shout for joy in the LORD, O you righteous!
  Praise befits the upright.
[2] Give thanks to the LORD with the lyre;
  make melody to him with the harp of ten
    strings!
[3] Sing to him a new song;
  play skillfully on the strings, with loud shouts.

[4] For the word of the LORD is upright,
  and all his work is done in faithfulness.
[5] He loves righteousness and justice;
  the earth is full of the steadfast love of the
    LORD.

[6] By the word of the LORD the heavens were
    made,
  and by the breath of his mouth all their host.
[7] He gathers the waters of the sea as a heap;
  he puts the deeps in storehouses.

[8] Let all the earth fear the LORD;
  let all the inhabitants of the world stand in
    awe of him!
[9] For he spoke, and it came to be;
  he commanded, and it stood firm.

[10] The LORD brings the counsel of the nations
    to nothing;
  he frustrates the plans of the peoples.

[11] The counsel of the LORD stands forever,
  the plans of his heart to all generations.
[12] Blessed is the nation whose God is the LORD,
  the people whom he has chosen as his heritage!

[13] The LORD looks down from heaven;
  he sees all the children of man;
[14] from where he sits enthroned he looks out
  on all the inhabitants of the earth,
[15] he who fashions the hearts of them all
  and observes all their deeds.
[16] The king is not saved by his great army;
  a warrior is not delivered by his great strength.
[17] The war horse is a false hope for salvation,
  and by its great might it cannot rescue.

[18] Behold, the eye of the LORD is on those who
    fear him,
  on those who hope in his steadfast love,
[19] that he may deliver their soul from death
  and keep them alive in famine.

[20] Our soul waits for the LORD;
  he is our help and our shield.
[21] For our heart is glad in him,
  because we trust in his holy name.
[22] Let your steadfast love, O LORD, be upon us,
  even as we hope in you.

OVERVIEW: The reformers reiterate the Augustinian assertion that all human beings—elect and reprobate—depend on God's grace and providence for their very existence. On account of this, the psalmist, according to these commentators, gives the imperative to praise the Lord, our Creator. All human beings must pray "thy will be done." Whether we orient ourselves toward God's will or not, it will be accomplished; let it be done for our salvation rather than our condemnation!

In this straightforward psalm of praise there are two loci for the reformers that might surprise contemporary readers: the question of instruments in worship and the Trinity. The Genevan Reformed church under Calvin adapted a radical but simple discontinuity with the medieval liturgy: only psalms were to be sung, and only a cappella.[1] Calvin and his venerable company of pastors did not

---

[1] See further Selderhuis, *Calvin's Theology of the Psalms*, 207-10; Manetsch, *Calvin's Company of Pastors*, 31-37. According to Calvin's "regulative principle," unless specifically sanctioned by Scripture a practice is to be proscribed; Lutherans argued that unless specifically prohibited by Scripture a practice received in faith could be sanctioned.

condemn instrumental music altogether; indeed they delighted in it. And that was the issue. If instruments were used in Christian worship, Calvin worried, the joy from that music might not only be indistinguishable from the joy of the gospel preached—worse, it might supersede it. In Genevan worship, nothing was to distract congregants from the Word, which is sullied not supported by further external adornment aside from the human voice. Lutherans and Catholics suffered no pangs of conscience about the use of instruments in worship. For them, these external aids augment the power of the Word and accommodate God's voice to ours; indeed, for Luther music's sole purpose is to be the handmaiden of God's Word.[2] Of course, all parties of the Reformation would have agreed that God alone in Christ is to be praised.

According to church tradition verse 6—"By the word of the Lord the heavens were made, and by the breath[3] of his mouth all their host"—is a classic locus for the doctrine of the Trinity. While all the reformers affirmed the church's teaching about the Trinity as scriptural, not all of them received this tradition concerning verse 6. Calvin shirks expositing this passage explicitly in light of the Trinity, saying that "breath of his mouth" is an anthropomorphic idiom, not a reference to God's Spirit. However, he implicitly acknowledges the doctrine of the Trinity in this verse by stating that the eternal Word participated in creation—each person of the Trinity together creates and redeems as true God in himself.[4] Amyraut refuses to weigh in on the discussion, but Lutheran exegetes storm these

trinitarian gates happily! They agree with the fathers, that this verse intimates the Trinity. Yes, the Old Testament prophets knew and confessed the Trinity, these reformers teach, but they did not insist on the highest article of faith because they had so many other struggles with God's people. All these exegetes would agree that there are better verses for building the doctrine of the Trinity; however, Hesshus, Selnecker and Luther, unlike Calvin, gladly placed it in their exegetical quiver.

THE LORD IS OUR GOD. NIKOLAUS SELNECKER: We want to present the summary as the blessed Dr. Luther outlined it. "This psalm is a psalm of thanksgiving, which generally gives God thanks for the blessing that he helps his believers in all their needs and does not leave them stuck there. For he is able to help, because he created everything, and still accomplishes everything with a word; to him nothing is impossible. Thus he is also benevolent and faithful, so that he wants to help, and does so gladly, as he promised in the first commandment: 'I will be your God.' That is, I will be your comfort, help, salvation, life and everything that is good, against everything that will cause you harm. That is what it means to be God. Now he especially gives thanks for and praises the mighty deeds of God, namely, that he directs all the world—even the hearts, thoughts, plans, wrath and rage of kings and princes—not as they will but as he wills, and finally renders all their plots void, so that they cannot accomplish what they wanted to do, and what they planned to do against the righteous, he immediately turns back on them, and he puts them to shame. This is a special joy and comfort for his saints against the haughty and inordinate threatening, opposing and menacing of the wrathful nobles and raging tyrants, who think that they can devour all of God's saints and drag God down from heaven merely with threats. But before they are even halfway done they lie in the muck [kot]." THE WHOLE PSALTER.[5]

---

[2]Steven Ozment argues that Cranach influenced Luther powerfully concerning art and theology, namely, that to destroy images was not to destroy idolatry but to create it. See Steven E. Ozment, *The Serpent and the Lamb: Cranach, Luther and the Making of the Reformation* (New Haven, CT: Yale University Press, 2011).

[3]That is, *rûach*, which can also mean "spirit" or "Spirit."

[4]The God of Jesus Christ is the God of both redemption and creation. He is not the author of sin, nor are human beings created in the image of the devil but instead, contrary to the Manicheans, the image of God. Concerning the aseity of the persons of the Trinity, see further Brannon E. Ellis, *Calvin, Classical Trinitarianism and the Aseity of the Son* (Oxford: Oxford University Press, 2012).

[5]Selnecker, *Der gantze Psalter*, 1:179r; citing Ex 6:7 (cf. Ex 20:2). This is a verbatim citation of Luther's summary for Ps 32; see WA 38:28-29. See also Luther's comments above on Ps 22:1-2, pp. 169-70.

GOD'S GRACE AND OUR EFFORT. PHILIPP MELANCHTHON: This psalm teaches that this true God, who reveals himself in the church by the promises that have been given, must be called on. And he affirms this, that he cares for human beings—great and small—and hears the prayers of those who call on him, and even desires that each undertake the works of his own calling, so that teachers should teach, senators should rule in the council of the republic, generals should do battle, heads of families should instruct their children and everyone should strive to avoid transgressions and direct their work to adorning the church and guarding the common peace. But still we know that even if we are not lazy and strive with an honest conscience, nevertheless for these efforts to be successful, blessed and salvific is from God. Thus let us learn to fit together, in every good deed, the help of God and our efforts, just as it is usually said, "When grace precedes, the will follows." COMMENTS ON THE PSALMS.[6]

33:1-5 *Sing a New Song to the Lord*

ISRAEL WORSHIPED GOD WITH VOICE AND INSTRUMENT. MOÏSE AMYRAUT: These words are said according to the custom of the church at that time. According to the order established by David, singing in the tabernacle was accompanied by many different types of musical instruments. ANNOTATIONS ON PSALM 33:1-3.[7]

IN CHURCH INSTRUMENTS ARE UNFITTING FOR GOD'S WORSHIP. JOHN CALVIN: The psalmist here expresses the vehement and ardent affection which the faithful ought to have in praising God, when he says that musical instruments should be employed for this purpose. He would have nothing omitted by believers which tends to animate the minds and feelings of human beings in singing God's praises. The name of God, no doubt, can,

properly speaking, be celebrated only by the articulate voice, but it is not without reason that David adds to this those aids by which believers were accustomed to stimulate themselves the more to this exercise; especially considering that he was speaking to God's ancient people. There is a distinction, however, to be observed here, that we may not indiscriminately consider as applicable to ourselves everything which was formerly enjoined on the Jews. I have no doubt that clanging cymbals, singing with the harp and the psaltery,[8] and all that kind of music, which is so frequently mentioned in the Psalms, was a part of their education; that is to say, the instruction of the law—I speak of the stated service of the temple. For even now, if believers choose to cheer themselves with musical instruments, they should, I think, make it their object not to dissever their cheerfulness from the praises of God. But when they frequent their sacred assemblies, musical instruments in celebrating the praises of God would be no more suitable than the burning of incense, the lighting of lamps and the restoration of the other shadows of the law. COMMENTARY ON THE PSALMS.[9]

MUSIC MUST SERVE THE WORD OF GOD. MARTIN LUTHER: Here it must suffice to discuss the benefit of this great art. But even that transcends the greatest eloquence of the most eloquent, because of the infinite variety of its forms and benefits. We can mention only one point—which experience confirms—namely, that next to the Word of God, music deserves the highest praise. She is a mistress and governess of those human emotions—to pass over animals—which as masters govern human beings or more often overwhelm them. No greater commendation than this can be found—at least not by us. For whether you wish to comfort the sad, to terrify the happy, to encourage the despairing, to humble the proud, to calm the passionate or to appease those full of hate—and who could number all these masters of the human

---

[6]MO 13:1067. The final sentence is Melanchthon's summary of part of Augustine's letter 186.3 (PL 33:819); see further E. P. Meijering, *Melanchthon and Patristic Thought: The Doctrines of Christ and Grace, the Trinity and the Creation* (Leiden: Brill, 1983), 27-28. [7]Amyraut, *Paraphrasis in Psalmos Davidis*, 130.

[8]An ancient stringed musical instrument. [9]CTS 8:538-59* (CO 31:324-25).

heart, namely, the emotions, inclinations and affections that impel human beings to evil or good? What more effective means than music could you find? The Holy Spirit himself honors her as an instrument for his proper work when in his holy Scriptures he asserts that through her his gifts were instilled in the prophets, namely, the inclination to all virtues, as can be seen in Elisha. On the other hand, she serves to cast out Satan, the instigator of all sins, as is shown in Saul, the king of Israel.

Thus it was not without reason that the fathers and prophets wanted nothing else to be associated as closely with the Word of God as music. Therefore, we have so many hymns and Psalms where Word and voice join to move the listener's soul, while in other living beings and instruments music remains a language without words. After all, the gift of language combined with the gift of song was only given to human beings to let them know that they should praise God with both word and music, namely, by proclaiming the Word of God through music and by providing sweet melodies with words. For even a comparison between different people will show how rich and manifold our glorious Creator proves himself in distributing the gifts of music! . . . No two can be found with exactly the same voice and manner of speaking. . . .

But the subject is much too great for me briefly to describe all its benefits. . . . Let this noble, wholesome and cheerful creation of God be commended to you. By it you may escape shameful desires and bad company. At the same time you may by this creation accustom yourself to recognize and praise the Creator. Take special care to shun perverted minds who prostitute this lovely gift of nature and of art with their erotic rantings; and be quite assured that none but the devil goads them on to defy their very nature which would and should praise God its Maker with this gift, so that these bastards purloin the gift of God and use it to worship the foe of God, the enemy of nature and of this lovely art. PREFACE TO GEORG RHAU'S *SYMPHONIAE IUCUNDAE* (1538).[10]

MYSTICALLY, THE HARP IS CHRIST. MARTIN LUTHER: The harp is a musical instrument that differs from the psaltery in this way. Both have the same shape—the letter delta, and like the delta a triangle—but the harp is a vertical delta and has its resonance from the lower part, that is, this is curved, and the strings are attached to it. The psaltery, on the other hand, is an inverted delta and has the same things from the upper part and sounds louder and better than the harp. Both instruments can be taken in a literal sense in this passage, because God is to be praised by Christians, and he is praised today with both and with many other musical instruments. Yet it is more appropriate to take the instruments in a mystical sense, so that God alone, and not human beings, can be praised by them. But the mysteries of both are endless.

In the first place, the harp is Christ himself according to his human nature, who was stretched on the cross for us like a string on the harp. Thus to confess with the harp means to think about the acts and sufferings of Christ according to the flesh, for such meditation has its resonance from below, from humanity to divinity. The fingers of the harpists are the thinking forces and powers in the soul. The psaltery is the very same Christ according to divinity, as he dwells among the ten choirs of angels. And thus to confess with the psaltery means to think about divine and heavenly things and about the angels. And this meditation sounds down from above. Therefore in one and the same person of Christ there takes place by way of meditation a descent from divinity to humanity, and an ascent from humanity to divinity, just as the angels ascend on Jacob's ladder in Genesis 28.

Therefore to confess with harp and psaltery means in short to believe, to confess and to praise Christ as being both God and human being. With that thought in mind it is quite easy to find allegory and tropology, according to Augustine, such as the soul, church, the heaven of angels, furthermore, faith, holy Scripture and the whole world. Indeed, whatever there is in the world is for

---

[10]LW 53:323-24* (WA 50:370-74); citing 2 Kings 3:15; 1 Sam 16:23.

the saints harp and psaltery and all things in Christ. First Psalms Lectures (1513–1515).[11]

An Ancient Kabbalistic Interpretation of Iota. Nikolaus Selnecker: Now we do not want to neglect to show how the ancient scribes in the Greek language here understand the Lord Christ in a wonderful manner and through a particular kabbalah, when David says, "We should sing praises on the psaltery of ten strings." For the letter *iota* among the Greeks meant as much as ten. The dear word *Jesus* begins with an *iota*. Thus, our praises consist only in the name Jesus at which every knee must bow in heaven and on earth. But concerning this method, the learned will know how to judge it. The Whole Psalter.[12]

New People and New Songs. Martin Luther: Only a new person can sing a new song. But the new person is person of grace, a spiritual and inner person before God. The old person, however, is the person of sin, the carnal and outer person before the world. The newness is grace, the oldness, sin. Therefore the devil is called the "old serpent," and Christ "a new thing which the Lord created on the earth," through whom God the Father made all things new, according to Revelation 21. It is clear, then, that this "new song" is so called not because of time but because of the new holy thing, for Scripture is holy, and it speaks of the holy. Thus also the harp is holy and the psaltery is holy.

Corollary: Old songs are all shameful, scurrilous, carnal and worldly songs, even if they should first be sung or composed today. New songs, however, are all psalms, honorable, holy, godly and spiritual songs, even if they dated back to the time of the first human being; indeed, these are the newest songs. Thus says the Lord: "The last will be first, and the first last." Thus the songs of our time are surely extremely old, even though in point of time they are the latest. Second, the newer or more recent a person is in the soul, the newer and more recent that person can make one and the same song. And the same applies to the old. Third, the songs that are neutral in character, in congregations or in figural music, can be drawn to either, as a good or an evil situation exists. First Psalms Lectures (1513–1515).[13]

The Highest Good of God's Providence. Konrad Pellikan: He begins to preach about the Lord from his deeds and works, which are all by necessity right. Nothing proceeds from the highest good except what is good. He establishes, does and manages all things with the greatest equity and faithfulness. The order of divine providence is irreproachable in all things, so the law of falsity would refute whoever tries to disparage the works of God, whose will cannot be turned aside, so that it cannot be impeded, so also it cannot deceive or be deceived. All his works are faithful, stable, true and useful for the progress of the elect—even those without knowledge—and thus ought to be welcomed by believers, and without doubt considered holy and faithful. Commentary on Psalm 33:4.[14]

Righteousness of Believers and Judgment of Nonbelievers. Thomas Wilcox: I make this difference here between these two terms, righteousness and judgment. "Righteousness" should be referred to the good people, understanding by it the faithful performance of all his promises made to them, and "judgment" to the ungodly, meaning the punishments that he will lay on them. And yet—I do not think this should be forgotten in this passage—that judgment consists of two parts, that is, of acquitting and clearing the innocent, and of condemning the guilty. Thus, "judgment" may be referred to the faithful also. Exposition upon Psalm 33.[15]

---

[11]LW 10:152-53* (WA 3:181-82); citing Gen 28:12.
[12]Selnecker, *Der gantze Psalter*, 1:179v; citing Phil 2:10.
[13]LW 10:154* (WA 3:182); citing Rev 12:9; Jer 31:22; Rev 21:6; Mt 20:16.
[14]Pellikan, *Commentaria Bibliorum*, 4:78r.
[15]Wilcox, *Godly Exposition upon the Psalmes*, 73-74*.

33:6 *By the Lord's Word and Spirit*

THE ANCIENTS UNDERSTOOD THIS VERSE ABOUT THE TRINITY. TILEMANN HESSHUS: All the ancients expounded this verse concerning the three divine persons and from this passage proved that the Father, Son and Holy Spirit simultaneously established heaven and earth. Basil, Augustine, Epiphanius of Salamis and others expounded this passage in this way. And this exposition agrees with the testimonies of the New Testament. For Christ said, "My Father is working still, and I am working." And Paul in Corinthians 12 says, "All these things one and the same Spirit accomplishes." There is no doubt that David considered here Moses' narration in Genesis 1, "God said, 'Let there be light.' And the Spirit of the Lord hovered over the water." COMMENTARY ON PSALM 33.[16]

THE ANCIENTS WERE CLEVER BUT WRONG. JOHN CALVIN: In saying that the heavens were created by "the word of God," he greatly magnifies his power, because by his nod alone, without any other aid or means, and without much time or labor, he created so noble and magnificent a work. But although the psalmist sets "the word of God and the breath of his mouth" in opposition both to all external means and to every idea of painful labor on God's part, yet we may truly and certainly infer from this passage that the world was framed by God's eternal Word, his only-begotten Son. Ancient interpreters have, with considerable ingenuity, employed this passage as a proof of the eternal deity of the Holy Spirit against the Sabellians. But it appears from other places, particularly from Isaiah 11, that by "the breath of the mouth" is meant nothing else but speech. For it is there said concerning Christ, "He shall smite the earth with the rod of his mouth, and with the breath of his lips shall he slay the wicked." As powerful and effective speech is there allegorically denominated "the rod of his

mouth," so in a similar way, for another purpose it is denominated in the immediately succeeding clause "the breath of his mouth," to mark the difference that exists between God's speech and the empty sounds which proceed from the mouths of people. In proving the divinity of the Holy Spirit, therefore, I may not press this text against Sabellius. Let us account it sufficient that God has formed the heavens by his Word in such a manner as to prove the eternal deity of Christ.

Should any object that these divine persons would not appear distinct if the terms "Word" and "Breath" are synonymous; I answer that the term "breath" is not employed here simply as in other passages, in which there is evidently a distinction made between the Word and the Spirit; but "the breath of his mouth" is used figuratively for the very utterance of speech, as if it had been said, "As soon as God uttered the breath of his mouth, or proclaimed in word what he wished to be done, the heavens were instantly brought into existence and were furnished, too, with an inconceivable number and variety of stars." It is indeed true that this similitude is borrowed from human beings; but the Scriptures often teach in other passages that the world was created by that eternal Word, who, being the only-begotten Son of God, appeared afterwards in flesh. COMMENTARY ON THE PSALMS.[17]

A CONFIRMATION OF THE TRINITY. NIKOLAUS SELNECKER: Here the prophet begins to explain the mighty deeds of God, namely, that he created everything—angels, the heavens, the elements, animals and human beings—out of nothing. And here the article of creation, as it is described by Moses, is clearly exposited, and the three persons of the Godhead are named in a distinguishable manner as the LORD, God the Father, the Word, God the Son and the Holy Spirit. Thus, the pious ancient teachers have always used these words to confirm the great, high article of the eternal, divine and almighty Trinity against the Jews and Arians

---

[16]Hesshus, *Commentarius in Psalmos*, 147r; citing Jn 5:17; 1 Cor 12:12; Gen 1:1-3. See ACCS OT 7:249-51.

[17]CTS 8:542-43* (CO 31:327); citing Is 11:4.

and other such blasphemers, like, in our days, the Turks or Muhammadans, Servetians and the like.

However, the eternal Son of God is called "the Word" according to the words of Genesis 1, "And God spoke." For such speaking of God is the Son of God himself. Thus, David and John call the Lord Christ "the Word," as John says, "In the beginning was the Word." Again, "We have heard, seen, looked on and touched the Word of Life." For through him all things were created and through him we have the Word and teaching of our redemption which he himself brought forth from the loins of his Father. And it is certainly this title that the Son of God is called "the Word." In the Old Testament it was well-known, thus, that the Word has also come to the Gentiles, as we can understand from Plato, who explicitly calls the Son of God "the Word," through whom all things are made and adorned. THE WHOLE PSALTER.[18]

THIS VERSE MAY OR MAY NOT AFFIRM THE TRINITY. MOÏSE AMYRAUT: Whether through "the Word" he understood the second person of the Trinity, as in John in the first chapter of his Gospel, I am prepared neither to affirm nor deny. For that mystery concerning the three persons was finally clearly revealed in the times of the gospel. But in the time of David it had begun to be not altogether obscurely intimated. And to that Wisdom which is the Word, the creation of things is attributed in Proverbs 8. ANNOTATIONS ON PSALM 33:6.[19]

THE PROPHETS CONFESSED THE TRINITY. MARTIN LUTHER: Such an article the prophets in the Old Testament also believed and understood well. On account of the stiff-necked, unbelieving, wicked people they did not come out with it as clearly as the New Testament does; nevertheless they forcefully indicated it. THE THREE SYMBOLS OR CONFESSION OF FAITH IN CHRIST (1538).[20]

33:7-12 *The Lord Creates and Sustains the World and Its Inhabitants*

OUR CREATOR ESTABLISHED ALL THINGS BY HIS WORD. MARTIN BUCER: The power of God declared in the founding and construction of the heavens, the restraining of the sea, by which he willed to excite the soul and that it may carefully observe the miracles of the rest of things which he completed with a word, and at this point now one is encouraged to a fear of such great majesty. For by nature we are disposed that we would esteem the one with greater power, even more that we would defer and zealously perform the order of such a person. Therefore because God infinitely exceeds every other power, as he is the one who spoke and caused all things, we deservedly ought to fear, worship and reverence him above all things. And plainly the matter is such that if we were truly persuaded of what we all discussed in agreement concerning him, of course that he created with the Word and preserves all things. Therefore, rightly the author of the epistle to the Hebrews wrote, "By faith we understand that the ages were established by the Word of God." HOLY PSALMS.[21]

FEAR THE LORD WITH JOY: AN EXHORTATION TO THE PIOUS AND IMPIOUS. WOLFGANG MUSCULUS: But here it could be asked how this admonition concerning fearing God fits with the beginning of the psalm, where we are commanded to exult in the Lord. What is suitable for joy and fear? Although nothing impedes someone from both fearing and rejoicing in the same person, as in Psalm 2, "Exult him with trembling," still it seems to me that in this verse David now addresses not the same people whom he previously called the righteous and upright in heart, but rather those who ignore and despise God's power, and thus do not worship this God. He exhorts all such people to fear and worship the true God, on account of his omnipotence. For this sort of person is more accustomed to being terrified by

---

[18]Selnecker, *Der gantze Psalter*, 1:180r; citing Gen 1; Jn 1:1; 1 Jn 1:1. Selnecker may be referring to *Timaeus* 29a.
[19]Amyraut, *Paraphrasis in Psalmos Davidis*, 131.
[20]WA 50:278 (cf. Plass, *What Luther Says*, 3:1383, no. 4455; LW 34:223).

[21]Bucer, *Sacrorum Psalmorum*, 171r; citing Heb 11:3.

force and power than won over by goodness. And thus rightly he exhorts the righteous and upright in heart to exult in the Lord and to praise the Lord on account of his faith, truth, justice, goodness and omnipotence. For the latter only rejoice that God is so just and of course omnipotent, on account of which the impious grieve more. Indeed he calls the rest to fear the Lord. COMMENTARY ON THE PSALMS.[22]

CONTEMPLATE THE REVEALED COUNSEL OF GOD. JOHN CALVIN: Let us learn to look at God's counsel in the mirror of his Word; and when we have satisfied ourselves that he has promised nothing but what he has determined to perform, let us immediately call to mind the steadfastness of which the prophet here speaks. And as many, or rather whole, nations sometimes try to impede its course by innumerable hindrances, let us also remember the preceding declaration, that when people have imagined many devices, it is in God's power, and often his pleasure, to bring them to naught. The Holy Spirit unquestionably intended to have our faith exercised in this practical knowledge; otherwise what he here says of the counsel of God would be but cold and fruitless. But when we shall have once persuaded ourselves of this, that God will defend his servants who call on his name, and rid them of all dangers; whatever mischief the wicked may practice against them, their endeavors and attempts shall in nowise terrify us, because, so soon as God sets himself in opposition to their machinations, no treachery on their part will be able to defeat his counsel. COMMENTARY ON THE PSALMS.[23]

THE MYSTERIES OF PREDESTINATION ARE FOR GOD TO KNOW. KONRAD PELLIKAN: After the complicated and inscrutable mysteries of predestination and universal providence have been cast aside, believers may consider generally and most certainly that that people alone are blessed

and happy in this age and in the age to come who are the sort who in the end, wherever they are, do not worship another God than the omnipotent Creator of everything who governs everything by his providence in a most holy way—even if the reasons for his works cannot be ascertained. Formerly almost the only nation like this was the nation of Israel or that one descended from Abraham which the Lord chose as his very own. Moreover, such people were specially chosen by God at that time so that now all nations or peoples which have been drawn by God's grace might know that all things are governed by God and accomplished according to his will. And they have been persuaded that God considers them his children. Therefore they do not doubt at all that whatever may happen, in the end all things work together for their salvation. Concerning such people, David says, "Blessed is that nation" to which God reveals himself as their Teacher, Savior and Highest Good. Blessed is that nation which he honors as his inheritance and treasured possession. Such are the children of Israel, not only those born according to the flesh but also whoever, in any place and in every age, are endowed with the faith of Abraham. Whoever, whatever sort, whenever and wherever they may be, those who learn to know God, with however much faith in God they have been given, by however much of God's grace they have been granted and justified, God knows. It is our responsibility to be concerned with ourselves so that we may worship and follow the Lord as worthily as possible. COMMENTARY ON PSALM 33:12.[24]

33:13-19 The Might of the Lord's Steadfast Love Saves

GOD SEES EVERYTHING. WOLFGANG MUSCULUS: The reason why there are so many evils in human lives should not be curiously examined in the providence of God. For God says that in all things he sees, knows, has power over, governs and

---

[22]Musculus, *In Psalterium Commentarii*, 465.
[23]CTS 8:547* (CO 31:329-30).

[24]Pellikan, *Commentaria Bibliorum*, 4:79r.

forms every person's heart according to his will. But if those evil things which you see trouble you, march on and consider again whence every good thing arises—even from the wicked efforts of the wicked, whether Satan wills or not. Indeed, from that, learn that it is God who governs the direction of all things. It is not fitting to consider such things individually and separately; instead you should consider the whole thing itself and the scope and substance of all things. If you see evil things, attribute those things to Satan, attribute them to you yourself or to the evil intent of human beings; good things, however, ascribe to God. COMMENTARY ON PSALM 33.[25]

PRIMARY AND SECONDARY CAUSES. THE ENGLISH ANNOTATIONS: All he means is this, that no secondary means, neither multitude of people nor horses and the like can do anything, where God has otherwise determined it, and therefore although means are used and had, as good as they may be it is God who must be trusted and thought on for the issue, and in case means cannot be had, such as our present case may seem to require, and there may be a need to fight, then we should (but without presumption) trust God and the goodness of our cause. To God, I say, who can save with few as well as with many, as well without means as with, if he pleases. ANNOTATIONS ON PSALM 33:16.[26]

ORIGINAL SIN IS NOT THE SUBSTANCE OF HUMAN BEINGS. TILEMANN HESSHUS: This testimony of the Holy Spirit refutes the delirium of the Manichaeans. They imagine that the very heart of human beings or their soul is the result of original sin; from this it must follow that God is the author of sin. God shapes each and every heart, but in no way should this opinion be accepted that God in any way is the author of sin. For that reason the Manichaean dogma that original sin is the substance of human beings is worthily

condemned with its author and defenders. COMMENTARY ON PSALM 33.[27]

HOW WOULD WE LIVE IF WE ALWAYS BELIEVED THIS? WOLFGANG MUSCULUS: Whoever believes that he lives before the eyes of the Lord his God—everything he contemplates and considers—when will he, I ask, rashly do something which he knows offends those omniscient and always watchful eyes? COMMENTARY ON PSALM 33.[28]

GOD'S WARD AND WATCH, CONSOLATION TO THE WEAK. JOHN CALVIN: In saying that the eye of God is bent on those who fear him to save them, he expresses more than if he had said that his hand and power were sufficient to preserve them. A doubt might creep into the minds of the weak, whether God would extend this protection to every individual, but when the psalmist introduces him as keeping watch and ward, as it were, over the safety of the faithful, there is no reason why any one of them should tremble or hesitate a moment longer, because it is certain that God is present with him to assist him, provided he remain quietly under his providence. From this, also, it appears still more clearly how truly he had said a little before, that "the people are blessed whose God is Jehovah," because, without him, all the strength and riches which we may possess will be vain, deceitful and perishing, whereas with a single look he can defend his people, supply their wants, feed them in a time of famine and preserve them when they are appointed to death. The whole human race, no doubt, is maintained by the providence of God, but we know that his fatherly care is specially vouchsafed to none but his own children, that they may feel that their necessities are truly regarded by him. . . .

---

[27]Hesshus, *Commentarius in Psalmos*, 148v. Manichaeism asserts a complicated, if not convoluted, myth of origins. For the church fathers its chief fault, which Hesshus here condemns, was that it separated creation and redemption, as if the God who creates is not the God who redeems. See further the discussion of original sin below, pp. 382-84.
[28]Musculus, *In Psalterium Commentarii*, 469.

[25]Musculus, *In Psalterium Commentarii*, 469.
[26]Downame, ed., *Annotations*, 6C4v*.

The psalmist characterizes believers by two marks, which comprehend the whole perfection of our life. The first is that we reverently serve the Lord; and the second, that we depend on his grace. Hypocrites may loudly boast of their faith, but they have never tasted even a little of the divine goodness, so as to be induced to look to him for what they need. On the contrary, when the faithful give themselves with their whole heart to the service and fear of God, this affection springs from faith. Or rather the principal part of right worship, which the faithful render to God, consists in this, that they depend upon his mercy. COMMENTARY ON THE PSALMS.[29]

33:20-22 Our Hope Is in the Lord

HOPE AND MERCY. KONRAD PELLIKAN: In the name of the whole people of God he prays that God's goodness would continually be planted in them according to their hope, so that likewise God would consider those who trust in him and who expect all things from him. He, of course, teaches that God is continuously present to help and to defend them, to comfort and restore them in all circumstances, so that they may rejoice in him and according to their hope, enjoy his eternal goodness. However, this is not the fate of everyone, but only of the elect and those who depend on God's providence in all things. Nevertheless the comparison must not be understood in such a way that he only has mercy on us when we hope, but instead he wants to say, "Because it is our habit to hope, you always deign to be present with us by your infinite grace." COMMENTARY ON PSALM 33:22.[30]

WE ARE TAUGHT TO HOPE FOR NO OTHER HELP THAN THE LORD. JOHN CALVIN: The Spirit, by dictating to us this rule of prayer by the mouth of the prophet, teaches us that the gate of divine grace is opened for us when salvation is neither sought nor hoped for from any other quarter. This passage gives us another very sweet consolation, namely, that if our hope faint not in the midst of our course, we have no reason to fear that God will fail to continue his mercy towards us, without intermission, to the end of it. COMMENTARY ON THE PSALMS.[31]

---

[29]CTS 8:552-53* (CO 31:332-33). [30]Pellikan, *Commentaria Bibliorum*, 4:79v. [31]CTS 8:555* (CO 31:334).

34:1-22 TASTE AND SEE THE LORD'S GOODNESS

[a]Of David, when he changed his behavior before Abimelech, so that he drove him out, and he went away.

1 I will bless the LORD at all times;
   his praise shall continually be in my mouth.
2 My soul makes its boast in the LORD;
   let the humble hear and be glad.
3 Oh, magnify the LORD with me,
   and let us exalt his name together!

4 I sought the LORD, and he answered me
   and delivered me from all my fears.
5 Those who look to him are radiant,
   and their faces shall never be ashamed.
6 This poor man cried, and the LORD heard him
   and saved him out of all his troubles.
7 The angel of the LORD encamps
   around those who fear him, and delivers them.

8 Oh, taste and see that the LORD is good!
   Blessed is the man who takes refuge in him!
9 Oh, fear the LORD, you his saints,
   for those who fear him have no lack!
10 The young lions suffer want and hunger;
    but those who seek the LORD lack no good
    thing.

11 Come, O children, listen to me;
    I will teach you the fear of the LORD.

12 What man is there who desires life
    and loves many days, that he may see good?
13 Keep your tongue from evil
    and your lips from speaking deceit.
14 Turn away from evil and do good;
    seek peace and pursue it.

15 The eyes of the LORD are toward the
    righteous
    and his ears toward their cry.
16 The face of the LORD is against those who
    do evil,
    to cut off the memory of them from the earth.
17 When the righteous cry for help, the LORD
    hears
    and delivers them out of all their troubles.
18 The LORD is near to the brokenhearted
    and saves the crushed in spirit.

19 Many are the afflictions of the righteous,
    but the LORD delivers him out of them all.
20 He keeps all his bones;
    not one of them is broken.
21 Affliction will slay the wicked,
    and those who hate the righteous will be
    condemned.
22 The LORD redeems the life of his servants;
    none of those who take refuge in him will be
    condemned.

a This psalm is an acrostic poem, each verse beginning with the successive letters of the Hebrew alphabet

---

OVERVIEW: The reformers commend this acrostic poem, which Mary excellently improvised into the Magnificat, to their readers for daily meditation and proclamation. By treading this well-worn path, as it were, we should call to mind the gifts of God's goodness and grace as well as the magnificent and mundane examples of how he has delivered his saints and his Son. These recollections give us confidence in the Lord's intervention in and governance over our own lives, but more importantly they cause praise to brim over and burst out of our mouths. The Lord does not need our praise, our commentators state; rather, human beings require it, so that they can recall who he is and what he has done and continues to do.

For much of the church's life this psalm has been read with special reference to the life-giving, soul-nourishing Eucharist. Surprisingly our commentators skirt this reading, agreeing instead that the psalmist focuses on spiritual eating. We should pray for a proper palate, these commentators exhort, so that by correctly tasting spiritual matters we might see these realities. Through the feast of God's Word and by the movement of the Holy Spirit believers are made participants in the divine nature.

WRITE THESE ABCs ON YOUR HEART. NIKOLAUS SELNECKER: There is no doubt that this psalm must have been very dear to the beloved David, because he placed and began every verse according to the order of the Hebrew alphabet, which he otherwise did relatively seldom. He did this, for example, above with Psalm 25, which is also very beautiful, majestic and comforting, and it is indeed worthy that we meditate on it daily along with Psalm 34, and were it possible, we should seal it and inscribe it into our hearts with gold letters. THE WHOLE PSALTER.[1]

BELIEVERS SHOULD BE EXAMPLES OF GOD'S MERCY TO OTHERS. JOHANNES BUGENHAGEN: All believers who have been delivered from all their tribulations give thanks, urging others also so that by their own example they may believe in God, so that they may taste the sweetness of his mercy, so that they may fear him alone, who with such fatherly concern provides for his people so that they lack nothing either for the salvation of their body or their soul—but the impious he drives back from himself. If you would rightly examine it, this psalm strengthens our faith not a little. INTERPRETATION OF THE PSALMS.[2]

SURE SIGNS OF A CHRISTIAN. DESIDERIUS ERASMUS: Clearly, this is the sign that distinguishes a Christian mentality: to give thanks in the midst of afflictions and to pray that those responsible for one's sufferings may repent. You may find many who fast, who give to the poor, who pray frequently, who go about in lowly attire, but very few who in the

midst of a constant stream of adversities give thanks to God, who do not plot revenge, who even do not return evil for evil. These are the infallible signs by which you may recognize a mind that is truly pious and Christian. Other signs are easy to feign but I doubt whether anyone could simulate this for long. EXPOSITIONS OF PSALM 34.[3]

WHY IS KING ACHISH CALLED "ABIMELECH"? NIKOLAUS SELNECKER: The title of the psalm indicates what moved David to compose this psalm of thanksgiving. The history stands in 1 Samuel 21 when David came to Gath, to King Achish. . . . However, that King Achish here is called Abimelech happens on account of the general title of all kings. For "Abimelech" means as much as a king who is his people's father. And in this way they called their kings with a very beautiful and lovely name: Abimelech, "my father the dear king," as Romans called Augustus *Patrem patriae*, "a father of the fatherland." For a king, prince and lord should bear a fatherly heart toward his subjects. The Egyptians called their kings *Pharaoh*, that is, Defender, True Protector. We call our high secular magistrate *Caesar Augustos*, that is, majestic and beautiful. THE WHOLE PSALTER.[4]

34:1-3 I Exalt in the Lord and His Name

PRAISE IS THE PRIVILEGE AND DUTY OF GOD'S PEOPLE. DAVID DICKSON: Whatever our condition, matters about which to glorify God shall never be lacking for believers; this glorifying is a duty and point of praising God. "My soul shall boast in the Lord." Only humble souls who are aware of their

---

[1]Selnecker, *Der gantze Psalter*, 1:181v-182r.
[2]Bugenhagen, *In librvm Psalmorvm interpretatio*, 79v.

[3]CWE 64:308*.
[4]Selnecker, *Der gantze Psalter*, 171v; citing 1 Sam 21:10-15. This insight is probably from Jerome—Alter says that the rabbinical commentators thought this, too (Alter, *Book of Psalms*, 117). Calvin's comment as well as Luther's resonate with Selnecker here; see CTS 8:555-57 (CO 31:334-35); LW 12:158-59 (WA 3:188-89). Modern commentators tend to understand "Abimelech" as a redactor's mistake, though Golidingay sees this as thickening the message of the psalm by helping us to imagine the fear of Abraham, Isaac and David. See Goldingay, *Psalms*, 1:477-78; Kraus, *Psalms 1–59*, 383.

own weakness are the people who reap the benefit of God's mercies, bestowed on others and themselves. COMMENTARY ON PSALM 34.[5]

GOD EXALTS THOSE WHO HAVE BEEN CAST DOWN. JOHN CALVIN: The term "soul" in this place signifies not the vital spirit but the seat of the affections; as if David had said, I shall always have ground of boasting with my whole heart in God alone, so that I shall never suffer myself to fall into forgetfulness of so great a deliverance. In the second clause he specifies this as the fruit of his thanksgiving, that the afflicted and miserable shall derive from it ground of hope. The Hebrew word 'ănāwim—which we have rendered "humble"—does not mean all the afflicted in general but those who, being humbled and subdued by afflictions, instead of breathing the spirit of pride are cast down and ready to abase themselves to the very dust. These, he says, shall be partakers of his joy; but not, as some have coldly explained it, simply from a feeling of sympathy but because, being persuaded that in the example of David, God had given them a general testimony of his grace, their hearts would recover from sorrow and would be lifted up on high. Accordingly, he says that this joy shall spring from hope, because, having received a pledge of their deliverance, they shall cheerfully have recourse to God. COMMENTARY ON THE PSALMS.[6]

THE MAGNIFICAT IS DERIVED FROM THIS PSALM. NIKOLAUS SELNECKER: The pious gladly desire that all creatures would constantly praise God, indeed, even that the leaves on the trees and the grass on the earth would have tongues to praise God and hallow his name! And it seems that dear Mary in Luke 1 drew her beautiful Magnificat from this psalm—not only the meaning but even the very words: "My soul magnifies the Lord and my spirit rejoices in God my Savior." THE WHOLE PSALTER.[7]

CHRIST'S BODY SINGS OUT IN WORD AND DEED. DESIDERIUS ERASMUS: The most beautiful harmony is when all the members of Christ sing the same song as their Head; the sweetest music is when voices differ but the intent is the same. The Hebrew sings, the Greek sings, the Scythian sings, the Thracian sings, the Indian sings, the Frenchman sings, the German sings, the Briton sings—the whole world sings, singing in harmony with Christ its Shepherd, magnifying its Lord and exalting his name "in itself" or "in unity." . . . In a scriptural text with a mystical application, this word usually denotes the wonderful concord proper to Christ's disciples, who as they are one body so also they are animated by one Spirit. . . . The world has its concords, its groups and societies, heretics have their associations, but that "in itself" exists nowhere except among those joined together by the Spirit of Christ, and nowhere is there true peace or rest except where that "in unity" exists. . . .

The Lord is not made greater by human praise, but his glory among humankind becomes greater. He wants renown for his glory, not because this adds anything to him but because we become better as we contemplate his sublimity, goodness and wisdom. As we turn our mind's eye to gaze at the supreme good which is himself, everything the world admires and pursues through good and evil grows cheap and mean. . . .

It is not enough to magnify the Lord with our mouths. . . . Magnify the Lord with your tongue, but magnify him more with your spirit. You will do this if you go down into yourself and consider how in yourself you are nothing, how lost and how wretched you are; then, turning your eyes to God, think how utterly good, utterly wise and utterly powerful he is; think over what he has done for you, how mercifully he sought you out, how kindly he gave to you; and finally compare his goodness with your wickedness. EXPOSITION OF PSALM 34.[8]

---

[5]Dickson, *First Fifty Psalms*, 220*.
[6]CTS 8:558* (CO 31:336-37); see Luther's comment on 'ănāwim above in Ps 25:4-10, pp. 204-5.
[7]Selnecker, *Der gantze Psalter*, 1:182v; citing Lk 1:46-55.

[8]CWE 64:321, 322-23*; citing Ps 133:1.

34:4-7 *The Lord Delivers*

WE PRAISE GOD FOR HIS DELIVERANCE.
NIKOLAUS SELNECKER: Why should we praise
God? Because he delivers us from all times of
need, however they may be called. To seek the
Lord means to allow ourselves to be comforted by
the Word of God and firmly cling to the promises
of God and call on him and invite him or, as it
stands here, look to him and run to him and
besiege and beleaguer him with diligent prayer—
as the begging widow overcame the unjust judge
through her persistence, and as the Canaanite
woman convinced Christ to deliver her daughter
from the devil. Therefore David also says here:
"When there was absolutely no human counsel
and help left for me, I turned my heart and
tongue to God, looked toward heaven and
conquered God's ears with my prayer, which went
up and ran through the clouds and was a sweet
savor before God." THE WHOLE PSALTER.[9]

EXAMPLES OF THE SAINTS. HIERONYMUS
WELLER VON MOLSDORF: Above he remembered
his own example; now he lays out the examples
of all kinds of pious people and commands us to
look at them. They show how gloriously and
wonderfully God has rescued them from the
bitterest testing and the greatest dangers and
ruin. Sacred history is full of such examples.
How often did God snatch Abraham, Isaac,
David and others from the gates of death? ... It
is fitting for the one whom the Lord saves to be
poor, that is, deprived of all human aid. For those
who lack all human aid and comfort are likely to
flee to God. ... We should not give up in the face
of pain and disaster, but we should rather run to
prayer and pour everything that torments us out
into the bosom of God. BRIEF COMMENT ON
PSALM 34.[10]

WHAT ABOUT THE "SHAME" OF MARTYRDOM?
DESIDERIUS ERASMUS: At this point a reflection
on the human level may occur in some minds, that
if those who are not delivered are put to shame,
then all those martyrs who breathed their last
amidst terrible tortures were shamed, as even today
are numerous devout people whose troubles leave
them only with their life. My reply is this: only the
defeated are put to shame, while the victor receives
glory however many weapons wound him. It is
those who in their agonies deserted Christ who
were really put to shame, for they in truth were
defeated, even if they gained their lives. But those
who in the midst of appalling martyrdoms are
buoyed up by hopes of a life in heaven, and with
their last words courageously confess Christ, are
neither deserted nor abandoned, nor are they put
to shame, but through their glorious deaths they
pass to the triumph of everlasting glory. Rather it is
the tyrants who are defeated and shamed, and in
the tyrants, Satan. The tortured gives thanks while
the torturer rages: which of the two is vanquished?
EXPOSITION OF PSALM 34:5.[11]

LEGIONS OF ANGELS PROTECT GOD'S PEOPLE.
JOHN CALVIN: The power of God alone would
indeed be sufficient of itself to perform this; but in
mercy to our infirmity he decided to employ angels
as his ministers. It serves not a little for the confirmation of our faith to know that God has innumerable
legions of angels who are always ready for his service
as often as he is pleased to aid us; indeed, more, that
the angels too, who are called principalities and
powers, are ever intent on the preservation of our life,
because they know that this duty is entrusted to
them. God is indeed designated with propriety the
wall of his church, and every kind of fortress and
place of defense to it; but in accommodation to the
measure and extent of our present imperfect state, he
manifests the presence of his power to aid us through
the instrumentality of his angels.

Moreover, what the psalmist here says of one
angel in the singular number should be applied to

---

[9]Selnecker, *Der gantze Psalter*, 1:183r; citing Lk 18:1-8; Mt 15:21-28
(cf. Mk 7:24-30); Ps 141:1-2; 34:6; 2 Chron 20:6-12.
[10]Weller, *Enarratio Psalmorum*, 322.

[11]CWE 64:329-30.

all the other angels, for they are distinguished by the general appellation of "ministering spirits sent forth to minister to those who shall be the heirs of salvation." And the Scriptures in other passages teach us that whenever it pleases God, and whenever he knows it to be for their benefit, many angels are appointed to take care of each one of his people. In short, however great the number of our enemies and the dangers by which we are surrounded may be, yet the angels of God, armed with invincible power, constantly watch over us and array themselves on every side to aid and deliver us from all evil. COMMENTARY ON THE PSALMS.[12]

ENCIRCLED BY PATIENT AND FRIENDLY ANGELS. NIKOLAUS SELNECKER: God helps us out of every dire situation and protects us with his dear holy angels who are around and among us day and night. They guard us against all the wrath of the devil and the world and against all other dangers. For otherwise it would be impossible that we would live and stay secure before the raging of the devil—even for the blink of an eye—if the dear angels were not our protectors, custodians, wardens and guardians. We huddle together as in a great, big siege in which the devils with their heavy artillery shoot at us day and night; they also shoot poisoned and fiery arrows with which they want to pierce our hearts. But the dear and mighty heroes of God's army, our captains and wardens, are there. These beautiful, ministering spirits set up their camp around us, they do not rest, they shield us and watch. Whenever we sleep, indeed often, whenever we go about in security and should die and perish in our sins, become and remain the devil's own, these spirits mercifully, kindly, steadfastly and diligently care for us, that they still protect and sustain our body and life. And they patiently wait for reformation and conversion with us. "They rejoice," as Christ himself said, "over one sinner who repents." THE WHOLE PSALTER.[13]

34:8-10 *Given for You*

CHEW AND RELISH GOD'S GOODNESS! JOHN CALVIN: In this verse the psalmist indirectly reproves human beings for their dullness in not perceiving the goodness of God, which ought to be to them more than a matter of simple knowledge. By the word *taste* he shows that they are without taste, and at the same time he assigns the reason for this, that they devour the gifts of God without relishing them, or through a vitiated loathing ungratefully conceal them. He, therefore, calls on them to stir up their senses and to bring a palate endued with some capacity of tasting, that God's goodness may become known to them, or rather, be made manifest to them. COMMENTARY ON THE PSALMS.[14]

ONE DAY WE WILL SEE WHAT WE TASTE. DESIDERIUS ERASMUS: Of all the senses two are the most reliable: feeling and sight. Taste is a kind of feeling peculiar to the tongue and palate, a most refined sense of feeling which distinguishes not only hard and soft, harsh and smooth, hot and cold, but thousands of different flavors. . . . But to taste signifies more than to touch, for what is tasted gives life and nourishment, while this is not true of things that are touched by hands. The Jews approached Jesus, they touched and saw him, but they did not taste him, because they chose to revile what they heard, not to believe it.

In physical terms, we see before we taste, but in spiritual concerns the opposite is true. We look at the bread that feeds our body before we put it in our mouth. But no one can look at the Word of the Lord, which is bread for the soul, without first believing it. . . . Thus we seek the Lord when we turn from our sins to repentance. We approach with faith, and when we receive the firstfruits of the Spirit, like a pledge, we taste; when we enjoy his presence as we think of his extraordinary love for us and hope that we may experience the eternal bliss of gazing on his face, we see. Here we see through a

---

[12]CTS 8:562-63* (CO 31:339); citing Heb 1:14; 2 Kings 6:15; Ps 91:11; Lk 16:22.
[13]Selnecker, *Der gantze Psalter*, 1:183r-v; citing Lk 15:10.

[14]CTS 8:563* (CO 31:339).

glass darkly, but there we shall see him as he is. Then there will be no more seeking, no more approaching, because there is no faith where experience is complete. There will be no more tasting, because there is no need for a pledge to sustain hope where promises are fulfilled in their entirety. Only sight will remain and continue forever. The one happiness, the one pleasure of the whole army of heaven is to know—that is, to gaze on— the true God and Jesus Christ whom he has sent.

Our world has dainty pleasures and distractions, but they fail to satisfy in full measure, and sometimes they bore us by their abundance. This is the only food which satisfies the soul without bloating. Every object is at rest when it achieves its end, and human beings are born for the purpose of knowing and of enjoying their Creator. This is the bread of angels that comes down from heaven to become the bread of human beings. The Word was made flesh—that is, the Son of God became human so that he might become the food of human beings. Those who hunger for this bread are happy, but happier are those who eat it in the kingdom of God. Some commentators interpret this passage as referring to the consumption of the Lord's body and blood, but the reference to spiritual consumption gives a reverent sense. It is true that the Lord is sweet in this way also, but as he himself says, "The flesh is of no avail without the Spirit who gives life." EXPOSITION OF PSALM 34.[15]

UNITED WITH CHRIST WE TASTE THE DIVINE NATURE. TILEMANN HESSHUS: God himself is present with the pious in troubles and adversities. "I am with him in tribulation, I will rescue him and I will glorify him." God does not allow us to be tempted beyond our strength but mitigates our troubles so that we are able to endure them. The Holy Spirit also supplies divine and distinguished promises which vigorously gladden our hearts in our misery and bolster our hope. According to these promises the Holy Spirit strengthens us, so that we would be children of God and sure heirs of

eternal life, because by an indescribable joy he pours over our hearts the sure hope of eternal blessedness. For this reason, God mercifully and generously lavishes on believers in Christ not only spiritual and eternal necessities but also physical and temporal necessities. He cares for them as a most gentle Father. He governs and nourishes them. He defends and protects them against all their enemies. And daily he answers their prayers. This happiness of the pious is a taste of eternal life and communion with God. Indeed the Holy Spirit, dwelling in their hearts, stirs up in us joy for God, unites us most intimately with God and makes us participants of the divine nature. COMMENTARY ON PSALM 34.[16]

GOD GIVES US SO MANY EXAMPLES OF HIS GOODNESS. NIKOLAUS SELNECKER: Tasting belongs especially to us; seeing refers to other people. By ourselves we are to taste and with others we are to see. The prophet wants to say: "You pious not only have me and others like myself as examples of the goodness of God but also you yourselves. You experience daily how God leads, nourishes, preserves, protects and saves you out of many dangers. You also see how God together with his beloved angels preserves others, your companions and brothers—indeed the whole Christian church—from all evil, against the tyrants, in a way that transcends reason. Blessed is the one who sets his hope in God. Such hope will not be put to shame, even if it leads through much crossbearing and misery, is chastened and tested."

Yes, there is no one, who, when he thinks back over his life, must not say and confess that he, being in a state of destitution, was preserved by God in many a great danger and saved out of it. Whoever takes this to heart will truly be able to taste the goodness of God and say, "O, how God is such a friendly Lord!" And he can thank him for it and trust in him for all of his life. But the secure, godless and ungrateful people know nothing of it. THE WHOLE PSALTER.[17]

---

[15]CWE 64:336-37*; citing Is 7:9; Jn 6:63.

[16]Hesshus, *Commentarius in Psalmos*, 152v; citing Rom 5:5.
[17]Selnecker, *Der gantze Psalter*, 1:186r; citing Rom 5:1-5.

THE PROMISE OF THE LORD'S PROVISION.
THE ENGLISH ANNOTATIONS: The godly who
trust God, even the poor and needy, should be
more content—which is accounted great riches—
in their estate, whatever it be, than rich people
who trust their wealth. ANNOTATIONS ON
PSALM 34:10.[18]

34:11-14 *Enter the School of the Lord*

OBEY GOD'S PREACHING LIKE CHILDREN.
JOHN DONNE: The text does not call children
simply, literally, but such men and women who
are willing to come with the simplicity of children; such children as Christ spoke of: "Unless
you become like little children, you will not enter
the kingdom of heaven." Come such children,
come such children. Nor does the text call such as
come and would fain be gone again. It is come to
listen; not such as wish themselves away, nor such
as wish another person here; but such as value
God's ordinance of preaching, though it be, as the
apostle says, but the foolishness of preaching, and
such as consider the office, and not the person,
however lowly they be....

To every minister and dispenser of the Word of
God and to every congregation belong these words;
and therefore we will divide the text between us; to
you one, to us appertains another part. You must
come, and you must listen; we must teach, and
teach to edification. There is your part and our part.
From each part, these branches flow out naturally;
in yours first, the capacity, as children; then the
action, you come; then your disposition here, you
listen; and lastly, your submission to God's
ordinance, you listen even to me, to any minister of
his sending. In our part, there is first a teaching; for,
otherwise, why should you come, or listen to me, or
any? It is a teaching, it is not only a praying; and
then, there is a catholic doctrine, a circular doctrine,
that walks the round and goes the whole compass
of our whole lives, from our first to our last
childhood, when age has made us children again,

and it is the art of arts, the root and fruit of all true
wisdom, "the true fear of the Lord." SERMON 127:
PREACHED AT SAINT DUNSTAN'S (1624).[19]

**BE STUDIOUS IN LEARNING THE FEAR OF THE
LORD.** DESIDERIUS ERASMUS: There can be no
doubt that so great a teacher, who calls us so
lovingly, has something important to offer—so
what is it? "I will teach you the fear of the Lord." He
has already commended the fear of the Lord to us
in glowing terms. What are these terms? Those
who fear the Lord are protected by angels from all
dangers. And further? Those who fear God are
untouched by any kind of want. The rewards are
outstanding, but in order to fear the Lord in the
correct way you need instruction. How many rules
must you learn to become skilled in dialectic? Yes
dialecticians do not immediately gain happiness.
How many precepts do you need to learn the art of
painting? But how slender are the wages! How
much more studious, then, we should be in learning
the art of fearing the Lord. Let us approach eagerly,
for this teacher gives us the very thing that he
commends. Teach us, then, best of teachers, we are
attentive. EXPOSITIONS OF PSALM 34.[20]

GLIMPSES OF THE LIFE TO COME. MARTIN
BUCER: Seeing that God is jealous for his own, he
so guards them, so cherishes them, and in general
bestows every kind of good on them, it is now
fitting that the psalmist exhorts us to a life pleasing
to God. He calls them children because disciples
and hearers are customarily called such by their
teachers. For this reason, Solomon in Proverbs says
the exact same thing, "my son," when he directs his
speech toward someone suited to holy teaching. So
also the sons of the prophets are called their
disciples. The term for one welcoming and
exhorting is the Hebrew *lekhah*. In fact he understands the accustomed fear of the Lord, to which
he promises to lead his own disciples, as the true
worship of God and the religious life which is

---

[18]Downame, ed., *Annotations*, 6D1r*.

[19]Donne, *Works*, 5:270-71*; citing Mt 18:3; 1 Cor 1:21.
[20]CWE 64:346.

approved by God, whose foundation and beginning is the fear and obedience of God.

Therefore, to render this sort of life more alluring, he indicates in the following verse that life—and that of a long time—and an abundance of every good thing is to be expected from that source. For God is the author of these things; to whom would he rather give these things than to his own? And certainly he would amply supply these things to those who truly worship him, not only to the ancients, who were in the likeness of children, who were being gently drawn by these enticements to piety, but also to the New Testament saints who (because they are like adults in the life of God) so customarily experienced the favor of God toward them in more ample goods, namely, heavenly ones. For what is life and what is happiness for the essence of the soul other than to enjoy and abound in a soul always rejoicing in all things? What other longevity is there than the one replete with life transported to heaven? . . .

Certainly from this God rescues most before the duties of this present life touch them: but he has destined for their enjoyment those of the future life, not of this present life. Accordingly those whom he calls in the middle course, as they are few, so that becomes an example of quickly and boldly exchanging this life with the future one. However, concerning the distinction between the saints of the old and new covenants and the more ardent desire for this life in the former, as they had a rather slender knowledge of the future life I have spoken more fully in Psalm 8. . . . Furthermore, the fear and worship of God that this psalm teaches, he established in this, that you should harm no one in word or deed, that you should be exceedingly eager for kindness and religiously cultivate peace with all. HOLY PSALMS.[21]

TURN FROM EVIL! DESIDERIUS ERASMUS: He says "turn from evil" rather than "avoid evil." In this life everything is full of evils, and so no one can avoid evil, but one may turn aside from it to avoid

injury. One turns aside to avoid a weapon by bending one's body—so whenever an opportunity for sin is hurled and evil rushes down on us, let us turn aside and move our thoughts in another direction. If you ask where, the answer is prayer, charitable gifts, reading the Bible, the torments of hell and the reward of eternal life. But if we are to turn aside from evil whenever it seeks us out, what can we hope for those who deliberately acquire the raw material of sin for themselves? EXPOSITIONS OF PSALM 34.[22]

GOOD CHRISTIANS MUST PURSUE SELF-DENIAL. KONRAD PELLIKAN: Just as rooting out the tares precedes sowing, so also withdrawing from evil and repenting of sin precedes doing good and the propagation of virtues. Nor is one sufficient without the other. Not whoever has omitted evil but whoever does good will be praised. To stand in the path of virtues and not to move forward is to retreat. Whoever will not shun evil will not train himself in good works. The tree that does not produce good fruit in season is not good. What the psalmist says must be observed, "Seek peace and pursue it." For unless you diligently seek to live in peace with your neighbor and strive with all your might when the opportunity presents itself, you will not be allowed to enjoy these things for long. So many offenses occur daily among mortals and so different are the characters and judgments of human beings that a Christian should diligently seize every opportunity for peace and hold onto it most boldly. For this reason, a Christian's own self-denial is necessary—the sort that does not always seek what is its own, does not understand lofty things, can be content with little, as much with honors as with wealth, considering nothing more venerable than to do good to everyone and to bear the weakness of everyone: in the end this is to deny oneself. Such a person can enjoy perpetual peace. It is only for these who through Christ know that they are among the number of the children of God, busying themselves with nothing other than

---

[21]Bucer, *Sacrorum Psalmorum*, 174v-175r; citing Ps 4:6-8.

[22]CWE 64:353.

being thankful to their Father, emulating his goodness like good children. COMMENTARY ON PSALM 34:14.[23]

34:15-18 *The Eyes of the Lord Are Watching*

THE GODLY AND THE UNGODLY CONTRASTED. DAVID DICKSON: It is a good means to keep our hearts in the fear of God to consider the gain of godliness and the damage and danger of wickedness, as they are here set in opposition. Those who have their eyes on God and his Word for righteousness and life may be sure of the watchful eye of God on them for their direction in their way, their consolation in their grief and deliverance from the trouble. For "the eyes of the Lord are on the righteous." As the righteous lend their ears to God's Word, to his promises and precepts, so the Lord lends his ear to their supplication and desires: "His ears are open to their cry."

On the other hand, the wicked, who do not fear God, set their face to do evil and to disobey God's commands; thus God will set his face against them and avenge himself. "The face of the Lord is against those who do evil." The only happiness which the wicked seek is to have riches, honor and pleasure on earth and to have their own name esteemed among human beings after their death. And these things, beside the loss of heaven, will be taken from them as well as their temporal life. For "the face of the Lord is against them, to cut off their remembrance from the earth." COMMENTARY ON PSALM 34.[24]

THE TERROR OF GOD'S FACE. MARTIN LUTHER: This is a terrible word. If we believed it to be true, as it is completely true, who would doubt that we would go about far more carefully? We truly lack much as to faith with regard to that statement. Because all things are bare before his eyes, he is most immediately present also to the evildoers, not only with the hand or the foot or the back but also with the face. Even so we are most immediately

present when we turn to a face or threaten someone with the face. It is frightful to contemplate that the divine Majesty has his face extended and hostile against those who do evil and that he knows all their works, because he sees all humankind. But we think that he either has his back turned toward us or a veil over his face, so that we go our way secure, like those about whom Isaiah says: "Woe to those who are deep of heart, who say, 'Who sees us? Who knows us?'" That is what we say in fact, if not in words, because our hearts are so deep in sins. Therefore Scripture often admonishes us to live in the sight of God. . . .

Therefore the beginning of the psalm is full of the example of humility, for no one blesses the Lord except the one who is displeased with himself and curses himself and to whom God alone is pleasing. So Job cursed the day of his birth. One who regards himself as anything but completely detestable clearly has praise of himself in his mouth, and the praise of God is not "continually in my mouth." Therefore the confession of sin glorifies and praises God, and we never praise God correctly unless we first disparage ourselves. For he does not permit something else to be praised alongside himself, nor does he want anything else to be loved beside himself. And thus our ugliness is God's beauty, our blushing is God's glory, our shame is his dignity, our sin is the excellence of his grace. FIRST PSALMS LECTURES (1513–1515).[25]

THE LORD HEARS OUR CRIES. JOHN CALVIN: This is a doctrine applicable to all times; and David does not merely relate what God has done once or twice but what he is accustomed to do. It is also a confirmation of the preceding sentence, where he had said that the ears of the Lord are open to the cry of the righteous; for he now demonstrates by the effect that God is not deaf when we lay our complaints and groaning before him. By the word *cry* we are taught that although God defends the righteous, they are not exempt from adversity. He

---

[23]Pellikan, *Commentaria Bibliorum*, 4:80v.
[24]Dickson, *First Fifty Psalms*, 224*.

[25]LW 10:161-62* (WA 3:190); citing Is 29:15; Ps 68:3; 5:8; 16:8; 2 Cor 4:2; 8:21; Job 3:1.

regulates the protection which he affords them in such a wonderful manner as that he notwithstanding exercises them by various trials. Similarly, when we here see that deliverance is promised only to those who call on God, this ought to prove no small encouragement to us to pray to him; for it is not his will that the godly should so regard his providence as to indulge in idleness but rather that, being firmly persuaded that he is the guardian of their safety, they should direct their prayers and supplications to him. COMMENTARY ON THE PSALMS.[26]

GOD IS NEAR. CARDINAL CAJETAN: Since in human terms, our ears and eyes must be nearby in order to help—for the more distant the less we hear and see to offer assistance—therefore the prophet includes a reference to God's nearness with regard to the righteous. "The Lord is near to the brokenhearted," that is, to those who fear God; "and the contrite in spirit"—not those who are swollen with conceit and self-importance—"he will save." COMMENTARY ON PSALM 34.[27]

34:19-22 Affliction and Affirmation of the Righteous

THE NECESSITY OF TRIALS. JOHN CALVIN: That the temptations by which we are continually assailed may not shake our belief in the providence of God, we ought to remember this lesson of instruction, that although God governs the righteous and provides for their safety, they are nevertheless subject and exposed to many miseries, so that, being tested by such trials, they may give evidence of their invincible constancy and experience all the more that God is their deliverer. If they were exempted from every kind of trial, their faith would languish, they would cease to call on God and their piety would remain hidden and unknown. It is, therefore, necessary that they should be exercised with various trials, and especially for this reason, that they may acknowledge that they

have been wonderfully preserved by God amid innumerable deaths. If this should seldom happen, it might appear to be fortuitous or the result of chance. But when innumerable and interminable evils come on them in succession, the grace of God cannot be unknown, when he always stretches forth his hand to them. David, therefore, admonishes the faithful never to lose their courage, whatever evils may threaten them, because God, who can as easily deliver them a thousand times as once from death, will never disappoint their expectation. COMMENTARY ON THE PSALMS.[28]

BONES, SINEWS AND FLESH. DESIDERIUS ERASMUS: This can be simply accepted as a parallel to our Lord's saying to the apostles in the Gospel: "Not a hair of your heads shall be lost." This hyperbole is a promise that the whole person will rise again, even though from this earth the body may perish by fire or by sword. How many hairs fall from our head in our lifetime? They have nothing to do with our resurrection, any more than our nail clippings have. But perhaps the word *bones* conceals some more inward sense. In Exodus we come across the prohibition on breaking the bones of the Passover lamb, and the Evangelist shows that this is a prophesy referring to the Lord, because in historical fact the bones of Christ were not broken on the cross—even though it is remarkable that his hands and feet should have been pierced by nails without breaking any bones. So let us grant that in Christ's body no bone was broken—but this very fact shows us a higher truth which bears out the figure, because it is not plausible that no bone was broken among those who were thrown to lions and leopards and torn to pieces, or sawn in half, cut with axes, stoned to death or thrown off cliffs. Rather, just as our inner person has his own eyes and ears, his head and face, his belly, feet and hands, so he also has his bones. When then you hear, "The wise man's eyes are in his head" obviously you take this to mean his mental powers, and when you hear, "The Lord's law is clear, and lights up the eyes" you think of the intellect....

---

[26]CTS 8:570-71* (CO 31:343).
[27]Cajetan, *In Sacrae Scripturae Expositionem*, 3:122.

[28]CTS 8:572* (CO 31:344).

So what do "bones" mean? In the body of a living creature there is nothing more solid than the bones. They are connected with each other by sinews and thus support and move the body's whole bulk, and in their inmost parts, like a precious store of treasure, nature has hidden the marrow. If you inquire what it is that most strengthens human beings in every temptation, you will know what the bones of the righteous are. Without prejudice to those devout people who have spent so much ingenuity on this passage—or who might have done so—it seems to me that bones indicate the strength of faith. . . . As long as faith remains in us, complete and unimpaired, our enemy cannot defeat us, and if it should ever happen that we lose our footing and come crashing down, we can easily right ourselves again and return more keenly to the battle. But when the bones are broken, no one can rise up and fight. . . .

If bones are faith, what are sinews and flesh? The sinews are love, which links member to member, so that each can perform its proper function. The flesh is good works, which are inseparable from faith and love and also form its ornament and safeguard. But because the faith of all pious people is one, how does it happen that it says, "He guards all their bones, not one of them shall be broken"? Faith is indeed one, but you could say that there are as many faiths as there are articles of faith. Someone whose legs are whole can still have a broken arm. Heretics seem to have some bones which are not broken, because there are many articles of faith which they confess along with us. . . . Yet the Lord safeguards the bones of the righteous; he does not allow the righteous to depart from the truth of the Catholic faith at any point, for no one can be saved if even one of his bones is broken. It does not help the Jew that he believes in one God if he denies the Son and Holy Spirit. It is useless to admit that Christ suffered for our sake if one denies the resurrection of the body. So what are we to say of those who died in some heretical error? . . . A wounded or dislocated bone is one thing, but a broken bone quite another. A wounded bone can be healed, a bone out of joint can be put back in place, but a broken bone is scarcely curable. There are very few examples of a confirmed heretic's return to the church. But those whose error is a merely intellectual one and whose emotions have not been seduced are easily brought back to the path. This was the case with Paul, and so when he received a warning he at once returned to the path. EXPOSITION OF PSALM 34.[29]

PRAY FOR SINNERS. DESIDERIUS ERASMUS: But if the death of sinners is terrible, and no one's life is free from sin, who will be saved? The prophet does not here mean any and every sin, for not every sin leads to hell. So what kind of sin is he talking about? Anticipating the question, he makes this clear: "And those who hate the righteous will do wrong." But whom does he mean by the righteous man? Primarily, he means him who through faith makes righteous everyone who comes into this world. Those who reject him and refused to believe him hear the words "You will die in your sins." Such a death is terrible. But the verse can also correctly be understood to refer to anyone at all. "Do not be surprised if the world hates you, because it hated me before you." People full of the spirit of this world will hate all those in whom they see the image of Christ. There is scarcely hope for such people; but those who sin from time to time, who hate themselves for it but who love the modesty in others which they themselves lack, who love the restraint which they do not possess, who give their resources to help the righteous when in need and who ask for their prayers—for them, if they do these things without hypocrisy, there is hope, because they have not gone so far in sin as to hate the righteous person, but rather they hate themselves for their lack of righteousness. We must pray that such people make progress, because to love another's righteousness and to hate one's own lack of it is already a step on the road to righteousness. EXPOSITIONS OF PSALM 34.[30]

---

[29]CWE 64:365-68*; citing Lk 21:18; Eccl 2:14; Ps 19:8.
[30]CWE 64:369*; citing Jn 15:18-19.

35:1-28 GREAT IS THE LORD

Of David.

[1] *Contend, O LORD, with those who contend*
    with me;
    fight against those who fight against me!
[2] *Take hold of shield and buckler*
    and rise for my help!
[3] *Draw the spear and javelin[a]*
    against my pursuers!
Say to my soul,
    "I am your salvation!"

[4] *Let them be put to shame and dishonor*
    who seek after my life!
Let them be turned back and disappointed
    who devise evil against me!
[5] *Let them be like chaff before the wind,*
    with the angel of the LORD driving them away!
[6] *Let their way be dark and slippery,*
    with the angel of the LORD pursuing them!

[7] *For without cause they hid their net for me;*
    without cause they dug a pit for my life.[b]
[8] *Let destruction come upon him when he does*
    not know it!
And let the net that he hid ensnare him;
    let him fall into it—to his destruction!

[9] *Then my soul will rejoice in the LORD,*
    exulting in his salvation.
[10] *All my bones shall say,*
    "O LORD, who is like you,
delivering the poor
    from him who is too strong for him,
    the poor and needy from him who robs him?"

[11] *Malicious[c] witnesses rise up;*
    they ask me of things that I do not know.
[12] *They repay me evil for good;*
    my soul is bereft.[d]
[13] *But I, when they were sick—*
    I wore sackcloth;
    I afflicted myself with fasting;
I prayed with head bowed[e] on my chest.

[14] *I went about as though I grieved for my*
    friend or my brother;
as one who laments his mother,
    I bowed down in mourning.

[15] *But at my stumbling they rejoiced and gathered;*
    they gathered together against me;
wretches whom I did not know
    tore at me without ceasing;
[16] *like profane mockers at a feast,[f]*
    they gnash at me with their teeth.

[17] *How long, O Lord, will you look on?*
    Rescue me from their destruction,
    my precious life from the lions!
[18] *I will thank you in the great congregation;*
    in the mighty throng I will praise you.

[19] *Let not those rejoice over me*
    who are wrongfully my foes,
and let not those wink the eye
    who hate me without cause.
[20] *For they do not speak peace,*
but against those who are quiet in the land
    they devise words of deceit.
[21] *They open wide their mouths against me;*
they say, "Aha, Aha!
    Our eyes have seen it!"

[22] *You have seen, O LORD; be not silent!*
    O Lord, be not far from me!
[23] *Awake and rouse yourself for my vindication,*
    for my cause, my God and my Lord!
[24] *Vindicate me, O LORD, my God,*
    according to your righteousness,
    and let them not rejoice over me!
[25] *Let them not say in their hearts,*
    "Aha, our heart's desire!"
    Let them not say, "We have swallowed
        him up."

[26] *Let them be put to shame and disappointed*
    altogether
who rejoice at my calamity!

Let them be clothed with shame and dishonor
   who magnify themselves against me!
²⁷ Let those who delight in my righteousness
   shout for joy and be glad
     and say evermore,

"Great is the LORD,
   who delights in the welfare of his servant!"
²⁸ Then my tongue shall tell of your righteousness
   and of your praise all the day long.

a Or *and close the way*   b The word *pit* is transposed from the preceding line; Hebrew *For without cause they hid the pit of their net for me; without cause they dug for my life*   c Or *Violent*   d Hebrew *it is bereavement to my soul*   e Or *my prayer shall turn back*   f The meaning of the Hebrew phrase is uncertain

OVERVIEW: Our commentators treat this long psalm in a somewhat cursory fashion, saying it replicates themes common throughout the Psalter: be constant in prayer; trust the Lord no matter what you see but look with the eyes of faith and experience God's help and presence; we must always praise the Lord. In addition to these typical loci, the reformers address how we should pray concerning our enemies. They feel obliged to explain how such harsh curses could be uttered against other imagebearers. Did Jesus not teach us to love our enemies? To love others in a manner that surpasses the love of the world (Mt 5:43-48; Lk 6:27-36)? We must always pray for God's righteousness in our enemies' lives, these exegetes remind us: for the repentant that it will be manifested in conversion; for the unrepentant in condemnation. Who is repentant and who is not is for God to judge. We, however, must pray for all our sisters and brothers who bear his image.

A PSALM FOR THE AFFLICTED. NIKOLAUS SELNECKER: This psalm is easy to understand by itself—it has neither difficult words nor senses. We can and should pray this psalm whenever we, without cause, are despised, hated, persecuted, trampled, opposed and afflicted—whether at court or somewhere else, especially against open enemies and Epicureans. Such people are not at all worried about God's honor. They are liars, ungrateful, volatile, hypocritical, greedy and jealous people—just as they are depicted in this psalm. They are a rebellious, bloodthirsty crowd that rejoices over misfortune. . . .

O how many such people there are everywhere! But God will find them in his time. Those who do not convert from the heart, in the meanwhile, limp along—like geese waddling back and forth—with their teaching, life, prayers, yes, even with their gestures, heads and false, hypocritical intentions, as long as they are able. They are volatile and fickle as the weather. Only let us not be sluggish and lazy in prayer, but rather praise the name of God, speak of his righteousness, as the end of the psalm says. Then there should be no time of need with us, if there were a thousand more mockers, liars, hypocrites, false accusers, ticklers of ears, bellyservants and envious people, yes, even if the world were full of devils, we would not be very afraid—it must turn out well. THE WHOLE PSALTER.[1]

35:1-10 The Lord Is My Salvation

MILITARY METAPHORS. MOÏSE AMYRAUT: The things contained in these first three verses, especially the second, are shaped by and selected from military matters. These things cannot be said about God except by anthropopathy, and thus they fit with a poetic style. ANNOTATIONS ON PSALM 35:1-3.[2]

GOD ACCOMMODATES HIMSELF TO US. JOHN CALVIN: These words certainly cannot be applied, in the strict and proper sense, to God, who has no need of the spear or buckler, for by the breath of his mouth alone, or merely with his nod, he is able to overthrow all his enemies. But although such figures at first sight appear rude, yet the Holy Spirit employs them in accommodation to the weakness

---

[1]Selnecker, *Der gantze Psalter*, 1:188v.
[2]Amyraut, *Paraphrasis in Psalmos Davidis*, 142. Anthropopathy is the attribution of human feelings to God.

of our understanding, for the purpose of impressing more effectually on our minds the conviction that God is present to aid us. When troubles and dangers arise, when terrors assail us on every side, when even death presents itself to our view, it is difficult to realize the secret and invisible power of God, which is able to deliver us from all anxiety and fear; for our understandings, which are gross and earthly, tend downward to the earth. So that our faith, therefore, may ascend by degrees to the heavenly power of God, he is here introduced armed, according to human custom, with sword and shield. COMMENTARY ON THE PSALMS.[3]

PERSECUTORS WILL BE PERSECUTED. DAVID DICKSON: Though the enemies of Christ and the godly advance in the prosecution of their hurtful devices, yet they shall be forced to retire with shame.... As the enemy has pursued, so shall God's wrath pursue him, chase him and drive him to perdition. COMMENTARY ON PSALM 35.[4]

DAVID'S PRAYERS, EVEN HIS CURSES, ARE DIRECTED BY THE HOLY SPIRIT. JOHN CALVIN: These sorts of curses which the psalmist here employs can be explained only by bearing in mind what I have elsewhere said, namely, that David pleads not simply his own cause, nor utters rashly the dictates of passion, nor with unadvised zeal desires the destruction of his enemies, but under the guidance of the Holy Spirit he entertains and expresses against the reprobate such desires as were characterized by great moderation and which were far removed from the spirit of those who are impelled either by desire of revenge or hatred or some other inordinate emotion of the flesh. COMMENTARY ON THE PSALMS.[5]

HOW SHOULD WE PRAY AGAINST OUR ENEMIES? NIKOLAUS SELNECKER: How we should pray against enemies has been indicated elsewhere, namely, that when possible, pray that

they would come to convert. But if they persist in their stubbornness, pray that they would be punished by God as an example and horror for other tyrants, as here David—or Christ himself—prays. THE WHOLE PSALTER.[6]

OUR EVIL DEEDS HARM US FIRST. MARTIN LUTHER: According to Augustine this snare is each person's own iniquity by which he attempts to harm others. And, because sin is darkness, it inevitably follows that by that very iniquity by which he attacks another he unknowingly harms himself. So it happened to the Jews. For the Lord overcame their iniquity, but they were overcome by their own iniquity. He rose from the death which they had prepared for him, but they are dead in themselves and will not rise. For every iniquity first harms its originator, as a torch burns itself before it kindles something else. It can happen that your evil deed may not harm someone else, but it cannot happen that it will not harm yourself. FIRST PSALMS LECTURES (1513–1515).[7]

PRAY FOR GOD'S GLORY. DAVID DICKSON: It is a good reason to strengthen our hope to be heard, when our comfort and God's glory may both be promoted by the granting of our desire, as we find it here. The destruction of the enemies of the church is not a matter of rejoicing in the destruction of human beings but of rejoicing in the Lord and in his wise manner of delivering his people. COMMENTARY ON PSALM 35.[8]

35:11-16 The Malicious Joy of My Oppressors

THE THEATER OF A GOOD CONSCIENCE. JOHN CALVIN: David then was not only spoiled of his worldly goods and basely driven into exile but was also accused and loaded with infamy under the appearance of justice. Being involved in such distress,

---

[3]CTS 8:575-76* (CO 31:346).
[4]Dickson, First Fifty Psalms, 228-29*.
[5]CTS 8:579* (CO 31:348).

[6]Selnecker, Der gantze Psalter, 1:188r; see Selnecker's above comment on Ps 17:10-15, p. 130.
[7]LW 10:167* (WA 3:197).
[8]Dickson, First Fifty Psalms, 230*.

he resorted directly to God, hoping that he would maintain his innocence. So ought the children of God to walk through good and bad report and patiently suffer reproach, until he asserts and declares their innocence from on high. In ancient times, it was a common proverb among the heathen, "There is no theater more beautiful than a good conscience."[9] And in this they uttered a noble sentiment; but no one can be sustained and supported by the purity of his conscience unless he has recourse to God. COMMENTARY ON THE PSALMS.[10]

FASTING AND SIGNS OF HUMILITY. JOHN CALVIN: With respect to "sackcloth and fasting," he used them as helps to prayer. The faithful pray even after their meals and do not observe fasting every day as necessary for prayer or consider it necessary to put on sackcloth whenever they come into the presence of God. But we know that those who lived in ancient times resorted to these exercises when any urgent necessity pressed on them. In the time of public calamity or danger they all put on sackcloth and gave themselves to fasting, so that by humbling themselves before God and acknowledging their guilt, they might appease his wrath. In like manner, when anyone in particular was afflicted, in order to stir himself up to greater earnestness in prayer, he put on sackcloth and engaged in fasting, as being the signs of grief. When David then, as he here tells us, put on sackcloth, it was the same as if he had taken on himself the sins of his enemies, in order to implore from God mercy for them, while they were exerting all their power to accomplish his destruction. Although we may reckon the wearing of sackcloth and sitting in ashes among the number of legal ceremonies, yet the exercise of fasting remains in force among us today as well as in the time of David. When God, therefore, calls us to repentance by showing us signs of his displeasure, let us bear in mind that we should not only pray to

him in the ordinary manner but also to employ such means as are fitted to promote our humility. In conclusion, the psalmist says that he behaved and acted toward them as if each of them had been his brother. COMMENTARY ON THE PSALMS.[11]

BROTHERLY AFFECTION FOR OUR ENEMIES. DAVID DICKSON: "My prayer," he says, "returned into my bosom," which is as much as "my expressions in prayer, in sighs, affectionate words and tears affected my heart with new earnest desires to intercede for them." True Christians' affection toward their enemies is able to affect their soul as much as to seek their welfare and commiserate their misery, as the natural affection of natural persons can affect them toward friends and family in the closest natural relation to them. COMMENTARY ON PSALM 35.[12]

WHO ARE "PROFANE MOCKERS AT A FEAST"?[13] RUDOLF GWALTHER: These people are lackeys and parasites and freeloaders, who for the sake of their own benefit always affirm powerful lords in every matter. Such people often serve in the courts of princes. THE PSALTER.[14]

MĀʿÔG STILL MEANS BREAD. JOHN CALVIN: As to the meaning of the word *māʿôg*, which follows, interpreters are not agreed. Properly, it means bread baked on the hearth on the embers. Some, however, because they could not elicit from it a meaning suitable to the passage, have thought that it should be taken for talkative jesting or idle speech. Others, presuming to give a still wider range to their fancy, have supposed the meaning of the psalmist to be that the scoffing of such people was as bread to them, because they take pleasure in scoffing and jesting. To me, it appears that we ought to retain the proper meaning of the word, while, at the same time it may be understood in a twofold sense. Some who understand *māʿôg* as a

[9]Cicero, *Tusculan Disputations*, trans. J. E. King, Loeb Classical Library 141 (Cambridge: Harvard University Press, 1927), 219.
[10]CTS 8:583* (CO 31:350-51).
[11]CTS 8:584* (CO 31:351).
[12]Dickson, *First Fifty Psalms*, 231*; citing Lam 3:49-51.
[13]Gwalther renders this clause as "for the sake of their bellies"; so does Luther (WADB 10,1:209).
[14]Gwalther, *Der Psalter*, 59v.

cake or tart are of the opinion that David here censures people of delicate taste, who seek fine and dainty fare, many of whom are always to be found in the courts of princes. Others rather suppose that he rebukes people of a servile and sordid spirit, who, for the most trifling consideration, would employ their tongues in reviling others, just as in all ages there have been found people who, for a bit of bread, as we say, put their tongues up for sale. When I carefully consider other passages in which David describes the nature and character of his enemies, I am disposed to think that those who indulged in jesting and scoffing at feasts, and who, in sitting over their cups, plotted about how to kill David, are here referred to. He therefore complains that even in the midst of their feasting and banqueting, the ungodly, who had shaken off all shame, plotted how they might take away his life. Commentary on the Psalms.[15]

35:17-26 Quit Your Silence, and Judge Swiftly

Is God Watching? John Calvin: The meaning of the word which I have translated "how long" is ambiguous among the Hebrews. In Latin it means, "How long will you see it, and delay silently?" But a second translation will be equally appropriate, "After having seemed not to notice what is happening for a long time, when will you finally begin to see it?" The meaning, however, is the same, for David complains of God's long forbearance, declaring that while the wicked are running to every excess, God seems to turn a blind eye to them and delays too long to take vengeance. And although God inculcates on the faithful the duty of quietly and patiently waiting until the time arrives when he shall judge it proper

to help them, yet he allows them to bewail in prayer the grief which they experience on account of his delay. Commentary on the Psalms.[16]

Orient Your Life to God's Glory and Name. Tilemann Hesshus: Our Lord Jesus Christ prophesies that after he has been delivered from his enemies and has risen from the dead, he will gather his church through his ministers and will multiply the name and glory of God far and wide. And according to this goal we should worthily order all our activities and counsels. Commentary on Psalm 35.[17]

The Strong in Faith. Martin Luther: Here the word strong is not taken in its proper sense, though it could be taken as mature and without frivolity, as manly and steady. In our time jesting or witty remarks, which the apostle calls "levity which is to no purpose," are doing much to sap the spirit in the church and to pour out our hearts, as Reuben was poured out like water, so that they can make no progress. But according to Augustine a "strong people" are people who are in the church by a living faith, like grain on the threshing floor, where others, whose faith is empty, are like the light chaff. First Psalms Lectures (1513–1515).[18]

The Wicked Enemies of the Church. David Dickson: It multiplies the grief of the godly to see the wicked take advantage of their trouble and to see mockers of religion to rejoice over their suffering in a good cause. They should heartily pray against this evil that it would at least not last long. . . . The enemies of the church are a base generation, taking pleasure and sport in the miseries of the godly, who do not injure them; indeed they are a vain and insolent generation, triumphing over the weakness of the innocent when they are in a low condition, and in the case of suffering, which is common to humanity and ordinary generosity abhors, "They opened their

---

[15]CTS 8:589* (CO 31:353-54); citing 1 Kings 17:12. Calvin translates this clause as "Among treacherous mockers gathered for feasts." Commentators continue to debate solutions for māʿôg here. Although Kraus and Goldingay both understand the root here to be ʿûg ("to be twisted"), they propose different solutions: Kraus, "like mockers of the refuge"; Goldingay, "As the most profane twisted mockers." Alter accepts Kimchi's suggestion that māʿôg means "empty talk." See Kraus, Psalms 1–59, 390-91; Goldingay, Psalms, 1:488; Alter, Book of Psalms, 124.

[16]CTS 8:589-90* (CO 31:354).
[17]Hesshus, Commentarius in Psalmos, 159r.
[18]LW 10:168* (WA 3:198); citing Eph 5:4; Gen 49:4.

mouth wide against me and said 'Aha, aha, our eyes have seen it!'" COMMENTARY ON PSALM 35.[19]

A TRUE AND ACCURATE PORTRAIT OF THE WICKED. JOHANNES BUGENHAGEN: And so you see, reader, how the Spirit—who knows the hearts of people—has depicted the enemies of the gospel in their true colors. INTERPRETATION OF THE PSALMS.[20]

APPEAL TO GOD BY HIS RIGHTEOUSNESS. JOHN CALVIN: Having been for a time subjected to suffering as one who had been forsaken and forgotten, he sets before himself the righteousness of God, which forbids that he should altogether abandon the upright and the just. It is, therefore, not simply a prayer but a solemn appeal to God, that because he is righteous, he should manifest his righteousness in defending his servant in a good cause. And certainly, when we seem to be forsaken and deprived of all help, there is no remedy which we can employ more effectually to overcome temptation than this consideration, that the righteousness of God, on which our deliverance depends, can never fail. COMMENTARY ON THE PSALMS.[21]

TRUST YOUR CONSCIENCE. GIOVANNI BATTISTA FOLENGO: Surely there is nothing more delightful than a conscience's pure testimony; nothing more miserable than an impure testimony.... Whence, not unjustly, that most wise king asserted that "the wicked flee when no one pursues them, but the righteous will be as confident as lions." Therefore relying on his conscience a good person is not afraid to appeal to divine judgment. KING DAVID'S PSALTER.[22]

CONFIDENCE IN AFFLICTIONS. WOLFGANG MUSCULUS: In these verses we see what confidence and hope the saints are provided with in the midst

of their afflictions, above all when they pray to God. The psalmist trusts that he will not be forsaken but will be delivered eventually, so that by the great rejoicing of his soul he is going to sing praises and proclaim the goodness and righteousness of God. And also the psalmist trusts that those who believed God to be and to love kindness and righteousness would rejoice over his innocence and will be glad and will praise the goodness of God, who does not forsake his people.... All these things are plain and they occur repeatedly in the Psalms, which is why we have here considered them so briefly, lest this commentary grow too large. COMMENTARY ON PSALM 35.[23]

35:27-28 Praise Righteousness

WHAT IS OUR PEACE?[24] KONRAD PELLIKAN: The success of all things is usually signified by the word *peace* in the Scriptures. The greatest peace and salvation of God's servants is in this, that they know God to be favorable to them. And daily may God's glory be magnified, may true piety do good in the world—whatever our adversaries threaten our body with, only that God's glory would be unharmed and our conscience holy. COMMENTARY ON PSALM 35:27.[25]

DAILY PRAISE. TILEMANN HESSHUS: The psalmist promises that he will join with those who will praise the Lord.... This worship is most pleasing to God, as the psalm testifies, "Call on me in the day of tribulation, and I will rescue you and you will glorify me." Every day the praise of God should resound from our mouths, that is, knowledge of the divine goodness should always glimmer in us, and we should do everything for the glory of God. COMMENTARY ON PSALM 35.[26]

---

[19]Dickson, *First Fifty Psalms*, 233, 234*.
[20]Bugenhagen, *In librvm Psalmorvm interpretatio*, 84r.
[21]CTS 8:590* (CO 31:357).
[22]Folengo, *In Psalterium Davidis*, 139v; citing Prov 28:1.
[23]Musculus, *In Psalterium Commentarii*, 484.
[24]Unlike most English translations—except the CEB—our commentators render *šālôm* here literally as "peace."
[25]Pellikan, *Commentaria Bibliorum*, 4:82v-83r.
[26]Hesshus, *Commentarius in Psalmos*, 160v; citing Ps 50:15.

36:1-12 HOW PRECIOUS IS YOUR STEADFAST LOVE

To the choirmaster. Of David, the servant of the LORD.

¹ Transgression speaks to the wicked
    deep in his heart;[a]
there is no fear of God
    before his eyes.
² For he flatters himself in his own eyes
    that his iniquity cannot be found out and
    hated.
³ The words of his mouth are trouble and
    deceit;
he has ceased to act wisely and do good.
⁴ He plots trouble while on his bed;
he sets himself in a way that is not good;
he does not reject evil.

⁵ Your steadfast love, O LORD, extends to the
    heavens,
    your faithfulness to the clouds.

⁶ Your righteousness is like the mountains of God;
    your judgments are like the great deep;
    man and beast you save, O LORD.

⁷ How precious is your steadfast love, O God!
    The children of mankind take refuge in the
    shadow of your wings.
⁸ They feast on the abundance of your house,
    and you give them drink from the river of
    your delights.
⁹ For with you is the fountain of life;
    in your light do we see light.

¹⁰ Oh, continue your steadfast love to those who
    know you,
    and your righteousness to the upright of heart!
¹¹ Let not the foot of arrogance come upon me,
    nor the hand of the wicked drive me away.
¹² There the evildoers lie fallen;
    they are thrust down, unable to rise.

a Some Hebrew manuscripts, Syriac, Jerome (compare Septuagint); most Hebrew manuscripts *in my heart*

OVERVIEW: In this psalm, for the reformers, the astonishing lovingkindness of God toward all people—even all creatures—is commended. Again nature is called to testify against human beings; the heavens and earth proclaim God's lordship over all creation, but do we listen? How we receive God's goodness and lordship reveals our heart. His sun and rain benefit the good and the bad. Yet it is not only the wicked who ignore these simple necessities; some are so focused on the benefits of the life to come that they are blind to the benefits of this life. Our commentators remind us that God deserves praise and thanksgiving for both spiritual and corporeal blessings. They commend this psalm as a pattern of prayer and a guard against human teaching and fanaticism. The wicked may flourish for now, but the pious must remember the immoveable and unassailable faithfulness and righteousness of God. He is indeed their mountain of refuge!

THE KINGDOM OF GOD IS UNASSAILABLE.

NIKOLAUS SELNECKER: This is a glorious, beautiful psalm of doctrine in which David praises the hidden and wonderful righteousness of God, which cannot be comprehended by human reason. That is, how God is gracious and merciful toward all human beings and longsuffering even toward wicked, godless people in such a way that in this life hardly any difference can be noted between the pious and the wicked—indeed, often the wicked have it much better than the pious. Now this also grieves the saints.... Therefore, David teaches here how we should orient our attitude, so that we do not become irritated by the good fortune of the godless—nor should we run and compete with them. Instead we should first remember that although these rotten rogues experience much good fortune and welfare, nevertheless their heart and soul are filled with nothing but filth and vices. . . . God's mercy stretches out very widely. He is the one who causes his sun to rise on the wicked as well as on the pious; he is patient and waits for us to come to repentance. . . .

But we should use this psalm against the common offense, to guard us against false teachers, heretics, fanatical spirits and other godless people, and to comfort us, that God's Word and kingdom will not be overthrown by their rabble-rousing but rather will continue to stand firm in all the world, like the mountains God himself set in place and like the deep chasms that are inexhaustible. THE WHOLE PSALTER.[1]

36:1-4 The Treachery of the Wicked

THE SYNTAX OF VERSE I IS DIFFICULT. JOHN CALVIN: Commentators are not agreed about the interpretation of the first verse. Literally it is, "The speech of transgression," or rather, "Transgression says to the wicked." As, however, the letter *lāmed* in Hebrew is sometimes used for *min* ["out of"], some translate it thus, "Ungodliness or transgression speaks of the wicked in my heart," as if the prophet had said, "I clearly perceive from the wickedness which the ungodly commit that they are not influenced by the fear of God." But as there is no need to depart from the proper signification of the words, I rather agree with others in supposing that the language of the prophet is to this effect: "The malice of the wicked, though seemingly hidden and unknown, speaks aloud in my heart, and I am a sure witness of what it says or suggests." COMMENTARY ON THE PSALMS.[2]

WHENCE COMES INIQUITY? RUDOLF GWALTHER: These words—"In my heart sin says to me about the godless,'there is no fear of God before

their eyes'"—indicate that David, having witnessed the common depravation of the godless world, ruminated over this with great bewilderment: Whence is its origin? And in the end he noted that all this originated from the false and errant opinion through which human beings have persuaded themselves that there either is no god at all or if there is one, he surely does not burden human beings on account of that fact—so, we should not be very worried about him, as if he might punish someone! THE PSALTER.[3]

THOSE WHO FEAR GOD COMPARED WITH THOSE WHO DO NOT. DAVID DICKSON: As those who fear God are watchful over their ways and censorious of themselves, so those who do not fear God are secure and well-pleased with their own actions. "They flatter themselves in their own eyes." As those who fear God labor to inform their conscience well, so that they would not commit iniquity, so those who do not fear God dupe and deceive their own conscience until they have accomplished the iniquity and it is fully revealed in its own colors. . . . As those who fear God will discern the sin in themselves of which they are in danger before others perceive it, so those who do not fear God will not see their own sin, no, not even when others look on it. . . . As those who fear God by all means strive to grow wiser and holier, so those who do not fear God will disregard and cast aside the means of wisdom and holiness. COMMENTARY ON PSALM 34.[4]

NO REST FOR THE WICKED. TILEMANN HESSHUS: The impious teacher repeatedly devises new deceits and crimes. Indeed in the night he is unable to sleep; instead in his bed he forms and hunts new paths of crimes, so that he might destroy uncorrupted doctrine and overthrow the

---

[1]Selnecker, *Der gantze Psalter*, 1:189r; citing Lk 9:51-56; Mt 5:45. [2]CTS 9:2* (CO 31:358-59).

[3]Gwalther, *Der Psalter*, 61r. Verse 1 is very difficult. Alter sees this as a personification of "crime" within the wicked; Kraus emends the verse to read "pleasing is transgression to the ungodly deep within his heart." See Alter, *Book of Psalms*, 126; Kraus, *Psalms 1–59*, 296-98; Goldingay, *Psalms*, 1:505, 507-8. [4]Dickson, *First Fifty Psalms*, 237-38*.

true church.... Therefore, from this their impiety and malice is discerned. The pious in their beds sleep, after praying; they commit themselves and the church to God. But the impious incessantly fatigue themselves by devising new deceits. Therefore not by a state of confusion or human weakness do they bring their crimes to completion accidentally, but instead by diligence, practice, attentiveness they assiduously seek out crimes and deceits. COMMENTARY ON PSALM 36.[5]

36:5-9 Praise for the Nourishment of the Lord's Steadfast Love

PRAISE FOR GOD'S LOVINGKINDNESS. NIKO-LAUS SELNECKER: Here David praises the lovingkindness of God. He is so longsuffering toward the godless; he lets rain fall on the pious and wicked alike. Whatever we look at—heaven, clouds, sun, moon, stars, water, earth, animals, fire and everything else—we see everywhere the goodness of God, as it was said more expansively above in Psalm 19. So also, the truth of God, namely, his Word, is preached everywhere, so that no one can be excused. It has filled the entire wide world and been in every place. Thus, God's righteousness also stands like the mountain—firm and undisturbed—and his justice is like great deeps, so that we all must say with dear Paul, "O what a depth of wealth and wisdom and knowledge of God! How totally unfathomable are his judgments and unsearchable his paths!" THE WHOLE PSALTER.[6]

"YOUR JUSTICE IS LIKE THE MAJESTIC MOUNTAINS." SEBASTIAN MÜNSTER: In Hebrew it is "the mountains of God," but this is a familiar Hebraism, that whatever is majestic is called divine. For the same reason, he also calls that justice and those judgments divine by which God rules over everything, governs everything and sustains everything—especially preserving human beings and animals in life, indeed, not individually

but as a species. Some take "beasts of burden" as sinners whom the Lord saves just as he saves human beings who live rightly, that is, who do good in this world; "the Lord makes his sun rise over the good and the bad." THE TEMPLE OF THE LORD: PSALM 36.[7]

THE UNFATHOMABLE DEPTHS OF GOD'S CARE. JOHN CALVIN: By these words the psalmist teaches us that to whatever side we turn our eyes, and whether we look upward or downward, all things are disposed and ordered by the just judgment of God. This passage is usually quoted in a sense quite different, namely, that the judgments of God far exceed our limited capacity and are too mysterious for us to be able to comprehend them, and, indeed, in this sense the similitude of an abyss is not inappropriate. It is, however, obvious from the context that the language of the psalmist is to be understood in a much more extensive sense, and as meaning that however great the depth of wickedness which there is among human beings, and though it seems like a flood which breaks forth and overflows the whole earth, yet still greater is the depth of God's providence, by which he righteously disposes and governs all things. Whenever, therefore, our faith may be shaken by the confusion and disorder of human affairs, and when we are unable to explain the reasons of this disorder and confusion, let us remember that the judgments of God in the government of the world are with the highest propriety compared with a great depth which fills heaven and earth, that the consideration of its infinite greatness may ravish our minds with admiration, swallow up all our cares and dispel all our sorrows. COMMENTARY ON THE PSALMS.[8]

---

[7]Münster, *Miqdaš YHWH*, 1188; citing Mt 5:45. Most modern commentators agree with Münster that ʾ*el* here is a superlative, although Kraus still uses "the mountains of God" here. See Kraus, *Psalms 1–59*, 396, 399; Alter, *Book of Psalms*, 127; Goldingay, *Psalms*, 1:509-10. The ESV is the only modern English translation to translate ʾ*el* as "God" here. [8]CTS 9:9-10* (CO 31:362).

[5]Hesshus, *Commentarius in Psalmos*, 162r-v. [6]Selnecker, *Der gantze Psalter*, 1:189v; citing Rom 11:33.

RECONCILIATION THROUGH JESUS. DAVID DICKSON: The Lord, without exception of any to whom he sends the gospel, and without exception of any within the visible church, offers everyone to be reconciled through Christ Jesus who shall fly into the mercy seat erected in Jesus Christ, who is God incarnate, as he was foreshadowed in the figure of the golden ark of the covenant and the stretched-forth wings of the cherubim. COMMENTARY ON PSALM 36.[9]

THE ABUNDANCE OF CHRIST. NIKOLAUS SELNECKER: They feast and refresh themselves with the Word of God or with the pure teaching of the holy gospel—even if they do not have full bellies—and quench their thirst with the Word, yes, with the blood of the Son of God, which he poured out for us, and revive their body and soul with true consolation and life. For with God there is the living wellspring, the fountain of life; without God, there is only death. THE WHOLE PSALTER.[10]

GIVE THANKS FOR GOD'S SPIRITUAL AND CORPOREAL GOODNESS. WOLFGANG MUSCULUS: Accordingly, let us also learn to consider and glorify that goodness of God, especially when we see, either in ourselves or in others, that his goodness does not destroy us for our wicked and shameful acts. Let us also learn, I say, to be astonished by considering this. And let us not believe it to be ill-fitting for us, because we see that it is so greatly commended in so many passages of holy Scripture. Let us acknowledge him who gives life, light, nourishment, and who cares for the whole world under the shadow of his wings, lest, with the impious, we use his goodness to our condemnation. O Christian! how many pious people strain for heavenly and spiritual gifts in such a way that those corporeal and temporal things which they gladly enjoy in the meanwhile, they do not deem worthy of thanksgiving and value! COMMENTARY ON THE PSALMS.[11]

36:10-12 Never Cease Your Steadfast Love

FOLLOW DAVID'S EXAMPLE. DAVID DICKSON: The true mark of a godly person stands in the conjunction of faith in God with sincere zeal for obedience to him, for "he is the one who knows God and is upright in heart." Albeit what the believers have found in God by experience, they may expect it to be continued to them, both for their entertainment by God, and defense and deliverance in their righteous cause from their enemies; yet they must follow their confidence with prayer. "Oh continue your lovingkindness to those who know you, and your righteousness to the upright in heart." As we have no right to any benefit, but insofar as we are of the number of upright-hearted believers, so should we seek every benefit we would have, as being of this number, and as seeking that others may be participants with us, as David does here. It is the Lord alone who can divert proud persecutors, that they do not hurt his children in the course of faith and obedience, when the wicked employ their power against them. COMMENTARY ON PSALM 36.[12]

CONFIDENCE IN GOD'S FUTURE JUDGMENT. JOHN CALVIN: Here he derives confidence from his prayer, not doubting that he has already obtained his request. And thus we see how the certainty of faith directs the saints to prayer. Beside, to confirm his confidence and hope in God even more, he shows, as it were, by pointing to it with the finger, the certain destruction of the wicked, even though it lay as yet concealed in the future. In this respect, the adverb *there* is not superfluous, for while the ungodly boast of their good fortune and the world applauds them, David beholds by the eye of faith, as if from a watchtower, their destruction and speaks of it with as much confidence as if he had already seen it realized. That we also may attain a similar assurance, let us remember that those who would hasten prematurely the time of God's vengeance on the wicked, according to the

[9]Dickson, *First Fifty Psalms*, 240*.
[10]Selnecker, *Der gantze Psalter*, 1:190r.
[11]Musculus, *In Psalterium Commentarii*, 487.

[12]Dickson, *First Fifty Psalms*, 241*.

ardor of their desires, do indeed err, and that we should leave it to the providence of God to fix the period when, in his wisdom, he shall rise up to judgment. COMMENTARY ON THE PSALMS.[13]

PRAYER FOR PERSEVERANCE AND PRESERVATION. NIKOLAUS SELNECKER: Grant that we steadfastly persist in your Word and not be led astray; do not let us stumble because of your truth. Let us not be proud or tread underfoot by the proud (Ps 19), but rather be merciful to us; support and sanctify us in your truth. Your Word is the truth. Direct and restrain all proud spirits of falsehood that seek neither your honor nor your truth; shove them into the grave. Preserve your Christians! THE WHOLE PSALTER.[14]

---

[13]CTS 9:14-15* (CO 31:364-65).

[14]Selnecker, *Der gantze Psalter,* 1:190r.

37:1-40 THE LORD WILL NOT FORSAKE HIS SAINTS

^aOf David.

¹ Fret not yourself because of evildoers;
  be not envious of wrongdoers!
² For they will soon fade like the grass
  and wither like the green herb.

³ Trust in the LORD, and do good;
  dwell in the land and befriend faithfulness.^b
⁴ Delight yourself in the LORD,
  and he will give you the desires of your heart.

⁵ Commit your way to the LORD;
  trust in him, and he will act.
⁶ He will bring forth your righteousness as the
    light,
  and your justice as the noonday.

⁷ Be still before the LORD and wait patiently for
    him;
 fret not yourself over the one who prospers in
    his way,
  over the man who carries out evil devices!

⁸ Refrain from anger, and forsake wrath!
  Fret not yourself; it tends only to evil.
⁹ For the evildoers shall be cut off,
  but those who wait for the LORD shall
    inherit the land.

¹⁰ In just a little while, the wicked will be no more;
  though you look carefully at his place, he
    will not be there.
¹¹ But the meek shall inherit the land
  and delight themselves in abundant peace.

¹² The wicked plots against the righteous
  and gnashes his teeth at him,
¹³ but the Lord laughs at the wicked,
  for he sees that his day is coming.

¹⁴ The wicked draw the sword and bend their
    bows
 to bring down the poor and needy,
  to slay those whose way is upright;

¹⁵ their sword shall enter their own heart,
  and their bows shall be broken.

¹⁶ Better is the little that the righteous has
  than the abundance of many wicked.
¹⁷ For the arms of the wicked shall be broken,
  but the LORD upholds the righteous.

¹⁸ The LORD knows the days of the blameless,
  and their heritage will remain forever;
¹⁹ they are not put to shame in evil times;
  in the days of famine they have abundance.

²⁰ But the wicked will perish;
 the enemies of the LORD are like the glory of
    the pastures;
  they vanish—like smoke they vanish away.

²¹ The wicked borrows but does not pay back,
  but the righteous is generous and gives;
²² for those blessed by the LORD^c shall inherit
    the land,
  but those cursed by him shall be cut off.

²³ The steps of a man are established by the
    LORD,
  when he delights in his way;
²⁴ though he fall, he shall not be cast headlong,
  for the LORD upholds his hand.

²⁵ I have been young, and now am old,
 yet I have not seen the righteous forsaken
  or his children begging for bread.
²⁶ He is ever lending generously,
  and his children become a blessing.

²⁷ Turn away from evil and do good;
  so shall you dwell forever.
²⁸ For the LORD loves justice;
  he will not forsake his saints.
 They are preserved forever,
  but the children of the wicked shall be cut off.
²⁹ The righteous shall inherit the land
  and dwell upon it forever.

³⁰ The mouth of the righteous utters wisdom,
     and his tongue speaks justice.
³¹ The law of his God is in his heart;
     his steps do not slip.
³² The wicked watches for the righteous
     and seeks to put him to death.
³³ The LORD will not abandon him to his power
     or let him be condemned when he is brought
          to trial.

³⁴ Wait for the LORD and keep his way,
   and he will exalt you to inherit the land;
     you will look on when the wicked are cut off.
³⁵ I have seen a wicked, ruthless man,
     spreading himself like a green laurel tree.ᵈ

³⁶ But he passed away,ᵉ and behold, he was
          no more;
     though I sought him, he could not be found.

³⁷ Mark the blameless and behold the upright,
     for there is a future for the man of peace.
³⁸ But transgressors shall be altogether destroyed;
     the future of the wicked shall be cut off.

³⁹ The salvation of the righteous is from the
          LORD;
     he is their stronghold in the time of trouble.
⁴⁰ The LORD helps them and delivers them;
   he delivers them from the wicked and saves them,
     because they take refuge in him.

a This psalm is an acrostic poem, each stanza beginning with the successive letters of the Hebrew alphabet   b Or *and feed on faithfulness*, or *and find safe pasture*   c Hebrew *by him*   d The identity of this tree is uncertain   e Or *But one passed by*

OVERVIEW: Like the psalmist, who laments the prosperity of the wicked and the affliction of the weak, our Reformation commentators confront the reality that Christians live in a world in which sometimes evildoers flourish and the righteous suffer. However, the overriding interest of the reformers, as for David, is the affirmation that believers should not fear or worry, even though the impious may prosper for a time. To be overly worried about such earthly struggles demonstrates, in their eyes, a lack of faith. Instead, despite their sufferings, Christians should trust in God, take comfort in divine providence, be at peace through the presence of the Holy Spirit and endure in faithfulness through prayer, patience and meditation on the Word of God. In addition, while acknowledging that the original promises regarding the inheritance of the land refer to the Promised Land of Canaan, several of our commentators interpret the land as a type for the heavenly inheritance that awaits followers of Jesus Christ, whose pilgrimage takes them through this life to their true home.

THE WICKED PROSPER FOR A TIME; THE GODLY SUFFER FOR A TIME. GENEVA BIBLE: This psalm contains exhortation and consolation for the weak, who are grieved at the prosperity of the wicked and the affliction of the godly. However prosperously the wicked live for a time, he affirms their felicity to be vain and transitory, because they are not in the favor of God, but in the end they are his enemies. And however miserably the righteous seem to live in the world, their end is peace and the favor of God, as they are preserved and delivered from the wicked. ARGUMENT: PSALM 37.

CLING TO FAITH NO MATTER THE TEMPORAL CIRCUMSTANCES. RUDOLF GWALTHER: It seems as if David composed this psalm concerning the difficult trials which he experienced within himself as he was stalked by godless Saul and therefore in his deep misery he must have seen his enemies' good fortune and affluence. For in this he takes hold of a salutary teaching, that we should become neither enraged nor resentful because of the prosperity of the godless; instead, we should steadfastly endure by faith in God, in innocence and piety—whatever objections we encounter that our flesh introduces. THE PSALTER.[1]

---

[1] Gwalther, *Der Psalter*, 61v.

THIS PSALM IS LIKE A STRING OF PEARLS.
MOÏSE AMYRAUT: There are two things especially
worth mentioning about the structure of this
psalm, one of which depends on the other in a
certain way. The first is that David observed almost
no order in this psalm. None of the parts cohere,
except that one and the same thing changes into
different expressions and considerations, all of
which generally result in the same meaning;
nevertheless each and every [petition] blossoms
with its own charm. Second, at the beginning of
the verses the author seems to have heeded a
particular method, for, as in several other psalms, it
follows the order of the alphabet, except that
between *aleph* and *beth*, for example and so on, he
inserts a verse whose first letter is such that the
prophet seems to put down his pen at random.

We have already noted elsewhere that zeal
which some observe with regard to the order of
the letters, out of which they take account of
each sentence in order to reveal the mind of the
author or that they were very much among them.
Unrestrained because of a totally impassioned
enthusiasm and to such a degree that they
shamelessly tromp into the discussion of the
material as if they were masters, and were lords
as well as judges of the authors' thoughts. On
account of this, I will not be troubled to find a
connection between the verses, so that I might
weave them together as a whole. Now, you are
easily able to observe that there are certainly
some passages in the Old Testament which were
joined together by this exact method and which
are united, as it were, in one physical body. But it
is no less certain that there are others in which
the way of thinking is like flowers in a bouquet,
which have been gathered together, and a
common bond holds them together or restrains
them, as they depend on one another no more
than many jewels or pearls which, strung
together on the same thread, make one necklace.
ARGUMENT OF PSALM 37.[2]

37:1-7 Do Not Fear but Trust in the Lord

THE PSALM'S THESIS IS VERSE 1. TILEMANN
HESSHUS: This is the argument of the whole
psalm: Do not become angry or let your inability
to endure be kindled, even though you see that the
impious flourish and the wicked succeed and
prosper in their wickedness. Do not let yourself be
disturbed so that you would abandon your zeal for
piety or abandon your vocation or associate with
the impious or participate in the world's usual
trickery and deceits. But whatever should happen,
always endure in knowledge and confession of the
truth, in zeal for piety, in the labor of your vocation
and in keeping a pure conscience.

David saw in the court of Saul that the
impious and wicked prospered and acquired
great wealth and honor, not by virtue but by
false accusations, denunciations, flattery, lies
and iniquities—but he, on account of his virtue
and piety was forced into exile, poverty and
misery. Here David's heart is troubled by this
inequity but is encouraged by the Holy Spirit,
lest he become languid, lest his inability to
endure be shattered, lest he imitate Doeg's
impiety; instead, he should endure continually
in piety and should anticipate God's judgment.
COMMENTARY ON PSALM 37.[3]

**GRASS, A FITTING METAPHOR FOR THE
WICKED.** MARTIN LUTHER: This is a fine
illustration; it is frightening to the hypocrites and
comforting to the suffering. How wonderfully he
takes us out of our own sight and puts us before
the sight of God! Before our own sight the mob
of hypocrites grows green, blooms and increases
until it covers the whole world; they only seem to
amount to anything, as the green grass covers and
adorns the earth. But in God's sight, what are
they? Hay that is soon to be harvested. The
higher the grass grows, the closer are the scythes
and pitchforks. Thus the faster the wicked grow
and the higher they soar, the closer is their

---

[2]Amyraut, *Paraphrasis in Psalmos Davidis*, 153.

[3]Hesshus, *Commentarius in Psalmos*, 166v-167r.

downfall. FOUR COMFORTING PSALMS FOR THE QUEEN OF HUNGARY (1526).[4]

FAITH PRECEDES GOOD WORKS. JOHN CALVIN: The inspired writer now goes on to say in the third verse that everything in the end shall be well with the righteous, because they are under the protection of God. But because there is nothing better or more desirable than to enjoy the nourishing and protecting care of God, he exhorts them to put their trust in him and at the same time to follow after goodness and truth. It is not without good reason that he begins with the doctrine of faith or trust in God, for there is nothing more difficult for human beings than to preserve their minds in a state of peace and tranquility, undisturbed by any disquieting fears, while they are in this world, which is subject to so many changes. On the other hand, while they see the wicked becoming rich by unjust means, extending their influence and acquiring power by unrestrained indulgence in sin, it is no less difficult for them steadily to persevere in a life of piety and virtue.

Nor is it sufficient merely to disregard those things that are commonly sought after with the greatest eagerness. Some of the philosophers of antiquity were so noble-minded that they despised riches unjustly acquired and abstained from fraud and robbery; indeed, they held up to ridicule the vain pomp and splendor of the wicked, which the common people look on with such high admiration. But because they were destitute of faith, they defrauded God of his honor, and so it happened that they never knew what it was to be truly happy. Now, David places faith first in order to show that God is the author of all good and that by his blessing alone prosperity is to be looked for; so it should be observed that he connects this with a holy life. For those who place their whole confidence in God and give themselves up to be governed by him will live uprightly and innocently and will devote themselves to doing good. COMMENTARY ON THE PSALMS.[5]

THE FRUIT OF PIETY. MARTIN BUCER: He declares that the primary fruit of piety, namely, to be delightful to God, who is known now as the most bountiful Father and source of all goods, who is disposed to the benefit of all who have faith in and lean on him. Therefore in this sense the topic for the prior verses is this: Do not worry because the wicked delight in those matters that are prone to decay; depend on God and please him, the Originator of all good things. He will show you how to delight in him, for he will give you whatever you ask of him. And in fact they receive whatever they want of this kind. For they want and desire only those things that work toward the displaying of God's glory, which are also those sorts of things that are good to them. HOLY PSALMS.[6]

THE LORD IS OUR CONFIDANT. HIERONYMUS WELLER VON MOLSDORF: Entrust your whole cause to God, disclose all your thoughts and plans to God, and as it is said, pour out all the feelings of your heart into his bosom and say with the prophet David in Psalm 139: "Test me, God, and search out my heart; examine me and know my paths. See if there is any evil way in me, and direct me in the way everlasting." For God delights in this confidence of ours toward him, when we flee to him and disclose all the needs and worries of our minds to him, acknowledging the feebleness of our mind and the weakness of our faith. BRIEF COMMENT ON PSALM 37.[7]

GOD'S PROVIDENCE DRAWS US OUT OF THE ABYSS AND FREES US FROM THE LABYRINTH. JOHN CALVIN: Why does it happen that the children of God are envious of the reprobate, often seethe or stagger, indulge immoderately in their sorrow and sometimes even growl and rage? Is it not because they immoderately entangle themselves in worries and, rashly preferring to provide for themselves without God, they plunge themselves, as it were, into an abyss? Anyhow, they heap up a mass of cares for themselves to which, in the

---

[4]LW 14:211 (WA 19:554).
[5]CTS 9:18* (CO 31:366-67).

[6]Bucer, *Sacrorum Psalmorum*, 185v.
[7]Weller, *Enarratio Psalmorum*, 339; citing Ps 139:23-24.

end, they are forced to surrender. Desirous to provide a remedy for this evil, David warns us that in presuming to take on us the government of our own life and to provide for all our affairs—as if we were able to bear so great a burden—we are greatly deceived, and that, therefore, our only remedy is to fix our eyes on the providence of God and to draw from it consolation in all our sorrows. Those who obey this counsel shall escape that horrible labyrinth in which all human beings labor in vain. Once God shall have taken the management of our affairs into his own hand, there is no reason to fear that prosperity shall ever fail us. Why does he desert and disappoint us? Is it not because we have barricaded the road against him, thinking we are far wiser than we are? If, therefore, we would only permit him to act, he will execute his office and will not disappoint our expectations, which he sometimes does as a just punishment for our unbelief. COMMENTARY ON THE PSALMS.[8]

DO NOT TRUST APPEARANCES. MARTIN LUTHER: This is the greatest worry of those who are weak in faith: they are vexed that the wickedness of the evil should put on such a fine appearance and have such a good reputation. They are afraid that their own cause will be beaten down and obscured, because they see how high and handsome the raging of their opponents is. Therefore he brings this comfort and says, "Dear child, it does not matter that they beat you and your cause down with clouds and rain, minimize your reputation in the sight of the world and bury you in darkness, while their cause is soaring and shining like the sun. If you commit your business to God, hope and wait for him; then you may be sure that your right and vindication will not remain in the darkness. It will have to come forth and become as evident to everyone as the brightness of noonday. All those who have beaten you down and obscured you will come to naught. All you have to do is to wait, so that by your raging, discontent and vexation you do not hinder God in

this undertaking." FOUR COMFORTING PSALMS FOR THE QUEEN OF HUNGARY (1526).[9]

GOD DELAYS FOR THE SAKE OF OUR FAITH. HIERONYMUS WELLER VON MOLSDORF: It is not enough to entrust your cause to God and to ask him to rule and govern you in all your affairs, but you must also persevere in faith, prayer and suffering and not let anything oppose your hope or break your spirit when you see the help and protection of God delayed. For by delaying his help and vindication God wants you to practice your faith and prayer. God wants you to be sustained by the rule and governance of his hand, just as a fetus in its mother's womb is sustained by God's creating hand. BRIEF COMMENT ON PSALM 37.[10]

37:8-26 Though the Lord's Justice Delays, It Never Fails

ANGER ACCELERATES WICKEDNESS. MARTIN LUTHER: See how diligently he warns us not to repay evil with evil or to follow the example of the wicked because of their success, as our nature continually urges us to do. What does such anger accomplish? It does not make things better; it only mires you down even deeper. And even if everything went as well as possible and you came out on top and were the winner, what would you have won? You would have hindered God, lost his grace and favor and become like the wicked evildoers, whose fate you would share. FOUR COMFORTING PSALMS FOR THE QUEEN OF HUNGARY (1526).[11]

CANAAN IS A TYPE FOR OUR HEAVENLY INHERITANCE. MOÏSE AMYRAUT: All such promises concerning the possession of the land obviously are about the promise of the land of Canaan—on this hope the covenant of the law was established. But their meaning is about the heavenly Palestine. ANNOTATIONS ON PSALM 37:9.[12]

---

[8]CTS 9:21-22* (CO 31:367).

[9]LW 14:213* (WA 19:555).
[10]Weller, *Enarratio Psalmorum*, 342.
[11]LW 14:214* (WA 19:557).
[12]Amyraut, *Paraphrasis in Psalmos Davidis*, 156-57.

ANTICIPATE THE AGE TO COME. DAVID DICKSON: It is not the present condition in which people are which is to be looked to, but what shall become of them in the end; for all the prosperity of the wicked is blasted with this one sentence of the supreme Judge: "Evildoers shall be cut off." Although the godly are kept in some hardships for a time, as young heirs in their minority, yet their inheritance in heaven—represented by the land of Canaan—will be reserved to them. And, in the meantime, by being heirs in Christ, they have solid right to what portion in this world God allows them, they have the use of such with a good conscience and remain on the earth as long as God has service for them. However the wicked would thrust them out of the world as unworthy of it. And if they are banished out of one country, they know that "the earth is the Lord's, and the fullness thereof." And they live more contentedly in that condition than the wicked in their nest, for "those that wait on the Lord shall inherit the earth." COMMENTARY ON THE PSALMS.[13]

OUR SURE FORTRESS. PHILIPP MELANCHTHON: There are also many, amazing deliverances in this life of individual saints, like Joseph, David and Daniel. It is better therefore for the righteous because they always have a sure fortress—God, of course—who is present, sustains them through affliction, alleviates their troubles and often delivers them entirely. He always gives eternal rewards, proves our case and preserves the church's body. Yes, on the contrary, although blasphemers flourish for a time, yet in the end they are overthrown and destroyed. COMMENTS ON THE PSALMS.[14]

THE SOLACE OF DRAWN SWORDS AND STRETCHED BOWS. WOLFGANG MUSCULUS: These verses as well as some that follow after them . . . are prepared, as it were, as remedies to console and strengthen those who pursue righteousness. Now it is no average temptation that the impious perpetu-

ally persecute the righteous with hatred, snares and every kind of evil, so that you could rightly say that the hatred of the impious against the righteous is deadly and inextinguishable. Accordingly, in order to oppose these temptations the prophet says, "Do the impious plot against the righteous, do they gnash their teeth at them, do they draw their sword against them, do they bend their bows in order to strike down the afflicted and the poor? It is true that in this way the reprobate are roused against the righteous. But it is no reason for you to be disturbed or frightened. For all the efforts of the impious against the righteous are useless and vain—no indeed, not only are they useless and vain but even fatal to the impious themselves. For the Lord laughs at them, because he sees their day approaching. In fact, he punishes them in this way, that the destruction that they intend for the righteous they turn back on themselves."

There are those who would expound by "sword" here the open assault and manifest rage of the impious against the righteous, and by "bow" a ready and taut hidden snare, as in Psalm 11. "See, sinners stretched their bows, nocked their arrows, to shoot in the dark at the upright in heart." Although it is completely true that the impious attempt to destroy the righteous in both ways, first through snares, then through open violence, or if at first they accomplish nothing by violence, in the end they attempt to destroy the righteous by secret and cunning machinations. Nevertheless, to me, in this passage this seems to be more fitting, to declare how the deceptive efforts of the impious against the upright in heart come to nothing—even when they already seem to be overthrown and destroyed. That is what the prophet wanted to indicate through drawn swords and stretched bows. COMMENTARY ON PSALM 37.[15]

WEEP PATIENTLY. JOHN CALVIN: David, therefore, teaches us that it is not fitting that God, who sees the destruction of the wicked to be at hand, should rage and fret according to the custom of

---

[13]Dickson, *First Fifty Psalms*, 246*; citing Ps 24:1.
[14]MO 13:1076.

[15]Musculus, *In Psalterium Commentarii*, 493; citing Ps 11:2.

human beings. There is then a tacit distinction here made between God and human beings, who, amid the troubles and confusions of the world, do not see the day of the wicked coming, and who, oppressed by cares and fears, cannot laugh, but because vengeance is delayed, rather become so impatient that they murmur and fret. It is not, however, enough for us to know that God acts in a manner altogether different from us, unless we learn to weep patiently while he laughs, so that our tears may be a sacrifice of obedience. In the meantime, let us pray that he would enlighten us by his light, for by this means alone will we, by beholding with the eye of faith his laughter, become partakers of it, even in the midst of sorrow. COMMENTARY ON THE PSALMS.[16]

IN THE LORD'S HANDS. MARTIN LUTHER: Human nature is also irked because the wicked are wealthy, numerous and mighty, while the righteous are poor and lonely. They have very little to begin with, and the wicked take even this away from them and keep them from making a living. Therefore the Holy Spirit comforts his dear children and says, "Do not let it irk you that you have so little and they have so much. Let them be rich and sated here. It is better for you to have a little with the favor of God than to have a big pile of goods not only from one wicked person but from all of them, with God's disfavor, as they do. Listen, too, to the judgment on your poverty and their riches, 'For the arms of the wicked shall be broken, but the Lord upholds the righteous.'"

The "arm" or hand is the entourage of the wicked. They are so great, mighty and powerful because there are so many of them sticking together. Thus the arm of the pope today is the kings, princes, bishops, scholars, priests and monks on whom he relies but about whom God does not care. Every wicked person has the crowd of the mighty on his side, for riches and might have never—or at least very seldom—stood on the side of the righteous. But what does it matter? Only trust in God, for it

must all be broken. You should not become excited about it or let it irk you. God is holding you up; you will not sink. His arm and his hand are over you and have a firm grip on you. FOUR COMFORTING PSALMS FOR THE QUEEN OF HUNGARY (1526).[17]

OUR DAYS ARE NUMBERED. JOHN CALVIN: Nothing is more profitable for us than to have our eyes continually set on the providence of God, which alone can best provide for us everything we need. On this account, David now says that "God knows the days of the righteous," that is to say, he is not ignorant of the dangers to which they are exposed, and the help which they need. This doctrine we should accommodate to every vicissitude which threatens us with destruction. We may be harassed in various ways and distracted by many dangers, which every moment threaten us with death, but this consideration ought to prove to us a sufficient ground of comfort, that not only are our days numbered by God, but that he also knows all the vicissitudes of our lot on earth. Because God then so carefully watches over us for the maintenance of our welfare, we ought to enjoy, in this our pilgrimage on earth, as much peace and satisfaction as if we were put in full possession of our paternal inheritance and home. COMMENTARY ON THE PSALMS.[18]

LIKE FAT ON THE ALTAR. RUDOLF GWALTHER: This comparison is taken from the sacrifices in which the lard or fat of the animals was burned on the altar. And this is its meaning: As the fat is consumed all over by fire, so that even no ash remains but instead everything blows away in smoke, in the same way the godless will be executed through the strict judgment of God, so that they do not leave behind even a sign or memory of their former glory and power. THE PSALTER.[19]

UP IN SMOKE. HIERONYMUS WELLER VON MOLSDORF: This contrast to the pious contains a very serious warning, that God in the end is going

---

[16]CTS 9:29* (CO 31:372-73).

[17]LW 14:217* (WA 19:560).
[18]CTS 9:33* (CO 31:375).
[19]Gwalther, *Der Psalter*, 64v-65r.

to punish the impious very harshly, nor will he allow them to escape unpunished, though for a time he may allow them to flourish. Now this is a most beautiful simile, which compares the fortune of the wicked with the greenest meadow and smoke, to show that indeed the impious have astonishing success for a time and flourish most beautifully, but suddenly their fortune, like smoke, vanishes. For their lives have a kind of stunning grandeur which overwhelms the eyes of human beings, in the same way that the greenest meadow wonderfully lures and holds the attention of those passing by. BRIEF COMMENT ON PSALM 37.[20]

THOSE WHO ARE FULL GIVE; THE EMPTY TAKE.[21] MARTIN LUTHER: This is a comforting difference among possessions. Not only are the possessions of the wicked perishable and transitory, but also they are evil and damnable possessions, because they have only been heaped up and have not been distributed to those in need. This violates the nature of possessions.

The possessions of the righteous, on the other hand, not only have no end—because they trust in God and wait for their possessions from him—but they are truly useful possessions which are distributed to others and are not just heaped up. Thus they have enough, even sufficient temporal reserves, and give enough to others too. This is a genuine possession. Even though you may not have much, it is pleasing to God and useful. The wicked have a great deal, but it is unchristian and useless.

When he says, "The wicked borrows," this is not to be taken to mean that the rich take possessions away from people. It is used as a parable or proverb. The person who borrows much and does not pay back is heading for the time when he will be dispossessed. So the rich and wicked receive much from God and borrow from him, but they do not pay him back by distributing to those in need (which is why they received the possessions in the first place).

Therefore their possessions will come to an evil end and vanish like smoke. This interpretation is substantiated by his comparison of the wicked with the righteous: one gives, and the other does not, even though they both receive from God. Therefore the receiving of the wicked is compared with borrowing and not paying back, while the possessions of the righteous are not a loan or a debt but a free gift from God, put to a good use for themselves and for their neighbor. FOUR COMFORTING PSALMS FOR THE QUEEN OF HUNGARY (1526).[22]

TWO CONSOLATIONS ESPECIALLY FOR THE TIMID. HIERONYMUS WELLER VON MOLSDORF: This verse has two senses. First, even if the pious have fallen into some misfortunes and troubles, nevertheless the Lord does not allow them to perish in them but will support them with his hand and rescue them, as Paul testifies in 2 Corinthians 4. "We are afflicted but are not crushed, we suffer anguish but do not surrender to it, we suffer persecution but are not forsaken, we are struck down but not destroyed."

This is the second sense. Although the upright are from time to time taken captive by the flesh and, deceived by the devil, fall into sin, nevertheless the Lord will not reject them but instead will restore them and will pardon their sins. And this sense is better. This is the richest consolation, which should be placed before afflicted and fearful minds. For this sort of consolation does not pertain in the least to careless and defiant minds. For people like that should be terrified by the teaching of the law and the most severe threats of God. BRIEF COMMENT ON PSALM 37.[23]

HOW IS THIS CONSISTENT WITH SCRIPTURE AND EXPERIENCE? JOHN CALVIN: Here there arises a question of some difficulty, for it is certain that many righteous people have been reduced to beggary. And what David here declares as the result of his own experience pertains to all ages. Addition-

[20]Weller, *Enarratio Psalmorum*, 354.
[21]See Donald L. Fairbairn, *Life in the Trinity* (Downers Grove, IL: IVP Academic, 2009), 214.

[22]LW 14:219* (WA 19:561-62).
[23]Weller, *Enarratio Psalmorum*, 359; citing 2 Cor 4:8-9.

ally he refers in this verse to the writings of Moses, for in Deuteronomy 15, begging is reckoned among the curses of God, and the law, in that passage, expressly exempts from it those who fear and serve God. How then can these fit together? That none of the righteous were beggars although Christ considered Lazarus among the humblest beggars? I answer that we must remember what I have said previously about this: with respect to the temporal blessings which God confers on his people, no certain or uniform rule can be established.

There are various reasons why God does not manifest his favor equally to all the believers in this world. He chastises some, while he spares others. He heals the secret maladies of some and passes by others, because they have no need of a similar remedy. He exercises the patience of some as he has given them the spirit of fortitude. And, finally, he sets forth others by way of example. But in general, he humbles all of them by signs of his wrath, so that by secret warnings they may be brought to repentance. In sum he leads them, by a variety of afflictions, to fix their thoughts in meditation on the heavenly life; and yet it is not a vain or imaginary thing, that, as is set forth in the law, God grants earthly blessings to his servants as proofs of his favor toward them. I confess that it is not in vain, or for naught, that an abundance of earthly blessings, sufficient for the supply of all their wants, is promised to the godly.

This, however, is always to be understood with this limitation, that God will bestow these blessings only insofar as he shall consider it expedient. Accordingly, it may happen that the blessing of God may be manifested in the life of human beings in general, and yet some of the godly be pinched with poverty, because it is for their good. But if it happens that any of the faithful are brought to beggary, they should lift up their minds on high, to that blessed state in which God will largely recompense them for all that is now wanting in the blessings of this transitory life. COMMENTARY ON THE PSALMS.[24]

37:27-40 *Shun Evil, Do Good!*

THE LORD LOVES JUSTICE. MARTIN LUTHER: You must not fear that the justice of your cause is being defeated, for that is impossible. God loves justice; therefore it must be preserved, and the righteous must not be forsaken. If he were an idol who loved injustice or hated justice, as the wicked do, then you would have reason to worry and to be afraid. But now that you know he loves justice, why do you worry? Why are you afraid? Why do you doubt? His saints are preserved not only temporally but eternally; and the wicked, with their children and everything they have, are cut off.

Here "saints" does not mean those who are in heaven, about whom the Scriptures speak only rarely, but more generally those who live on earth, who believe in God and by their faith have the grace of God and the Holy Spirit. This is why they are called "saints," as we all are if we truly believe. FOUR COMFORTING PSALMS FOR THE QUEEN OF HUNGARY (1526).[25]

THE FRUIT OF THE WORD PLANTED IN OUR HEART. HIERONYMUS WELLER VON MOLSDORF: The wicked also have the Word of God, but not in their hearts. Let us learn here, therefore, that it is not enough if someone has the Word of God, because the devil and his minions have the Word, but in the end only in their mouths. But it is necessary that the Word be given to us, so that we implant it into our heart. We should teach, hear and learn God's Word so that it becomes part of our nature. And those who have the Word of God in their hearts will experience by it an increase in fruits. For they will be able to teach and console others correctly from the Word of God. Then they will judge correctly concerning all sorts of doctrinal and spiritual issues. Finally they will have been strengthened against every deceit and mockery of the devil and his minions. Thus, they will not easily be driven to sin, nor will they be overthrown, like those who are accustomed to being driven and

---

[24]CTS 9:39-40* (CO 31:378-79); citing Deut 15:4; Lk 16:20.

[25]LW 14:222 (WA 19:565).

overthrown by the devil, that is, those who do not have the Word of God in their hearts but only in their mouths. BRIEF COMMENT ON PSALM 37.[26]

VARIATION ON PSALM I. JOHANNES BUGENHAGEN: Here you see what I have often taught, that cause of hatred, whence it occurs that the impious who flash and flourish as saints in name only, with hatred conceived, they finally reveal themselves to be people of blood. "The mouth of the righteous will meditate on, speak of and preach the wisdom" that God judges to be wisdom, not the wisdom of the world and according to human inventions as well as counterfeit religions and fabricated worship of God, which the wisdom of God condemns as foolishness and impiety. For he desires that we would not follow what seems right to us but what he himself judges to be right according to his wisdom, that is, according to his Word, as we rightly pray, "Thy will be done on earth as it is in heaven."

"And his tongue will speak of his judgment," that is, what is justice, by which he judges and condemns as useless and reveals and declares as harmful according to the Word of God for salvation, everything and anything that carnal people—who do not have the Spirit of God—judge to be best. But whence does it come that the righteous speak of God's wisdom and righteousness? He responds: "This comes from the root of the heart." "From the abundance of the heart the mouth speaks." They can do nothing other than confess the truth, because the law of God, the Word of life, is in their heart (Ps 1). Just as no one can understand the law, so also no one can rightly preach it unless he has it in his heart, that is, if he loves it and lives according to it—and this only faith in God accomplishes. This is the law of the spirit of life written on their hearts by God, according to the prophet Jeremiah. The impious and hypocrites have it only in books; they only have it, but they do not speak it from the heart. They are ignorant about what they are affirming. Therefore, he says, "Their step will not be tripped up," that is, they will not wander, they will not fall from the path of righteousness.

Here the impious watch the righteous, as it was said above, and strive in the desire of their heart to kill the righteous. They are not willing to be righteous; they are not willing to admit the truth that they hear to be truth. They are not willing thus to meditate on Sacred Literature. Does this not seem to be the reason why he above addresses the enemies of the Lord? Such impious people and hypocrites hated God; for the world they abandoned his truth which they did not think fit very well with their lusts. But although the righteous are judged by the impious—they are proclaimed to be blasphemers and heretics, condemned six hundred times by excommunications and in addition are killed—as a welcome and favorable Father, nevertheless, the Lord will not condemn them. Indeed the righteous boast because they have all been gathered by the Holy Spirit and are formed in the name of the Lord. Not the Holy Spirit but the spirit of the devil and the kingdom of Satan is there where they strive to kill the righteous (Ezek 13). INTERPRETATION OF THE PSALMS.[27]

THE BLINDNESS AND ILLUSION OF THE WICKED. JOHN CALVIN: David adds that the wicked will perish before the eyes of the godly. If their end were not very different from that of the righteous, the state in which the reprobate now rejoice for a time would easily allure even the best of people to evil. And, indeed, God would make us daily to behold such sights if we had eyes to behold his judgments. And yet, although the whole world were blinded, God does not cease to render a just reward to the wickedness of human beings; but by punishing them in a more private manner, he withdraws from us that fruit of which our own dullness deprives us. . . .

David here confirms from his own experience what I have just said, namely, that although the wicked are intoxicated with their prosperity and held in admiration by all on account of it, yet their happiness is perishable and transitory, and,

---

[26]Weller, *Enarratio Psalmorum*, 365.

[27]Bugenhagen, *In librvm Psalmorvm interpretatio*, 92r-v; citing Mt 12:34; Ps 1; Jer 31:31-34.

therefore, nothing other than a mere illusion. [In verse 35] he tells us that it is no strange or unusual thing for the ungodly, puffed up with their prosperity, to spread themselves far and wide and to give occasion of terror to the innocent. Then he adds that their greatness, which had been regarded with so much wonder, disappears in a moment. Commentary on the Psalms.[28]

Whether Abstract Concepts or Concrete Examples, the Meaning Is the Same. Cardinal Cajetan: With respect to what he had said above—"And keep his way"—he supplements it by proclaiming, "Keep the perfect and behold the upright." These two work together for the care of God's way: to behold, to discern the upright from the crooked (for it is necessary to walk down the straight path) and to take care of perfection, that it be whole and complete, lest it happens that the road runs out halfway. And whether by "perfect" and "upright" you understand perfection and uprightness, or whether, as in a mirror, you understand a perfect person and an upright person, it amounts to the same opinion. Yet the second sense resonates better with the letters, including, as a mirror and an example, the difference in outcome for the righteous, who accomplish uprightness, and the outcome for the wicked. For this reason, it is added, as an example of a reward: "Because the end for the man is peace." By the term "peace" understand the tranquility of order that brings with itself all other good things. And he means that those who hope in God care for uprightness and perseverance by the example of upright and perfect people, because the end of an honest person will be peace, and salvation will be at rest. Commentary on Psalm 37.[29]

This Consolation Is Ours, If Only We Would Believe. Martin Luther: Look, look, what a rich promise, what a great consolation, what an abundant admonition, if only we trust and believe! First, God helps them in the very midst of evil. He does not leave them lying there but stands by them, strengthens them and preserves them. Second, he not only helps them but also delivers them and enables them to escape. For the precise meaning of this Hebrew word is "to escape misfortune and to get away from it." And as a vexation to the wicked he mentions them by name and says, "He delivers them from the wicked." They may not like it; but their rage will not do them a bit of good, though they believe that the righteous will not escape them and will surely be destroyed. Third, he not only delivers them but goes right on helping them, so that they do not remain in any trouble, no matter when it comes. And he does all this because they have trusted in him. Thus he also says in Psalm 91: "Because he cleaves to me in love, I will deliver him; I will protect him, because he knows my name. When he calls to me, I will answer him; I will be with him in trouble, I will rescue him and honor him. With long life I will satisfy him, and show him my salvation."

O, such shameful disloyalty, mistrust and damnable unbelief! We refuse to believe these rich, powerful and comforting promises of God. When we hear a few threatening words from the wicked, we begin to tremble at the slightest threat. May God help us to obtain the true faith which we see the Scriptures demanding everywhere! Amen. Four Comforting Psalms for the Queen of Hungary (1526).[30]

[28]CTS 9:50* (CO 31:384).
[29]Cajetan, *In Sacrae Scripturae Expositionem*, 3:135.

[30]LW 14:228-29* (WA 19:571); citing Ps 91:14-16.

38:1-22 DO NOT FORSAKE ME, O LORD

A Psalm of David, for the memorial offering.

¹ O LORD, rebuke me not in your anger,
 nor discipline me in your wrath!
² For your arrows have sunk into me,
 and your hand has come down on me.

³ There is no soundness in my flesh
 because of your indignation;
there is no health in my bones
 because of my sin.
⁴ For my iniquities have gone over my head;
 like a heavy burden, they are too heavy for me.

⁵ My wounds stink and fester
 because of my foolishness,
⁶ I am utterly bowed down and prostrate;
 all the day I go about mourning.
⁷ For my sides are filled with burning,
 and there is no soundness in my flesh.
⁸ I am feeble and crushed;
 I groan because of the tumult of my heart.

⁹ O Lord, all my longing is before you;
 my sighing is not hidden from you.
¹⁰ My heart throbs; my strength fails me,
 and the light of my eyes—it also has gone
  from me.
¹¹ My friends and companions stand aloof from
 my plague,
and my nearest kin stand far off.

¹² Those who seek my life lay their snares;
those who seek my hurt speak of ruin
 and meditate treachery all day long.

¹³ But I am like a deaf man; I do not hear,
 like a mute man who does not open his
  mouth.
¹⁴ I have become like a man who does not hear,
 and in whose mouth are no rebukes.

¹⁵ But for you, O LORD, do I wait;
 it is you, O Lord my God, who will answer.
¹⁶ For I said, "Only let them not rejoice over me,
 who boast against me when my foot slips!"

¹⁷ For I am ready to fall,
 and my pain is ever before me.
¹⁸ I confess my iniquity;
 I am sorry for my sin.
¹⁹ But my foes are vigorous, they are mighty,
 and many are those who hate me wrongfully.
²⁰ Those who render me evil for good
 accuse me because I follow after good.

²¹ Do not forsake me, O LORD!
 O my God, be not far from me!
²² Make haste to help me,
 O Lord, my salvation!

OVERVIEW: The original context for this penitential psalm may have been a severe illness that David was suffering. For our commentators, however, it is far more significant that the psalm reveals not just the physical pain of the psalmist, but his intense emotional and spiritual suffering as well. They highlight his awareness of his own sin and his desire not only for physical healing but also for spiritual healing. For our interpreters, this points to the condition of all who lament their sins. Moreover, several commentators interpret the text as a prophetic revelation of Christ, who like the psalmist was pursued by enemies, abandoned by friends and experienced suffering. Overall, then, the reformers view this psalm as an affirmation of both the wretched condition of humanity, which so desperately needs God's grace, and the redemptive power of God, who alone can restore the soul and the body, bringing not just temporal health on earth but also eternal life in heaven.

IN CHRIST THIS PRAYER IS OURS. NIKOLAUS SELNECKER: The rabbis understand this psalm to be about a dangerous and deadly illness in which David lay bedridden and composed this psalm. But this is an uncertain thing; it must remain undecided. Blessed Jerome wanted to understand it about the suffering and agony of Christ Jesus, and he says that he actually hears and sees his Lord Christ being cornered and hung on the cross, as often as he reads these words: "My lovers and my friends stand against me, seek after my life, lay snares for me," at the end of this psalm. Because the death of Christ is of particular significance, yes, it is the beginning and perfection of all agony which the saints also suffer, especially when they acknowledge and feel their sin and want to mortify it. This psalm belongs to all believers and saints who lament their sins, which cause their conscience to be disheartened and sorrowful and see nothing but God's arrow, that is, threats, wrath, agony, death and hell.

Thus this psalm is an earnest, devout prayer in which the pious ask God out of his mercy to forgive them their sins and to take away their punishment, crossbearing, affliction and great distress—or at least to mitigate these things and grant them patience, so that they would not be cast out by God, or be overcome and oppressed by their enemies and persecutors or be carried off and chastised with the godless. THE WHOLE PSALTER.[1]

Superscription: *What Does* Lĕhazkîr *Mean?*

DIVERSE POSSIBILITIES FOR LĔHAZKÎR.
FELIX PRATENSIS: Some say *lĕhazkîr* means a certain musical instrument. But several others say it means "to recall or to remember what has been done," that is, so that he would impel others to remember the goodness of God or to reveal his tribulation before God. And according to others it means "for confession." According to the Chaldean translation, it means "for burning incense" or "for fumigation." THE HEBREW PSALTER.[2]

LĔHAZKÎR REMINDS US OF OUR UNITY OF PERSON WITH JESUS. MARTIN LUTHER: The title is "a psalm of David for remembrance or for commemoration"; in Hebrew "to remember what has been done," that is, "for confession of our sins." As in Isaiah 36: "I will meditate on you all my years in the bitterness of my soul." Therefore he does not say "for confession," because to confess also means to praise. Here he only recites his sins. Because according to the apostle, "Christ became a curse for us" and sin; "he himself bore our sin." Therefore this psalm is said in his person. In it he recalls and confesses our sins for us to God the Father and intercedes for his people's liberation—that is, us, through himself and in himself. Therefore whoever desires to pray this psalm fruitfully should not pray it in himself but in Christ, as if he hears this prayer—feeling this way and saying "amen." For as he consecrated our baptism and for us or in our person was willing to be baptized, so also he confesses for us. And according to Augustine, Christ and the church are one flesh as husband and wife. How wonderful it is that they have one tongue, the same words, since they are of one flesh, one body and, of course, one head! GLOSSA ON PSALM 38 (1513–1515).[3]

THE TITLE IS NOT FROM A POPULAR SONG. JOHN CALVIN: The title of this psalm refers to its subject. Some suppose that it is the beginning of a common song, because in other psalms the beginning of the song, to the tune of which they were set, is commonly prefixed, but such an interpretation is unnatural and without foundation. Instead of this, I rather think that the title indicates that David composed this psalm as a memorial for himself, as well as others, lest he should too soon forget the chastisement by which God had afflicted him. He knew how easily and speedily the chastisements with which God visits us, and which ought to serve as a means of instruction to us all our life, pass away from the mind. He was also

---

[1]Selnecker, *Der gantze Psalter*, 1:194r; citing Ps 38:11-22.
[2]Pratensis, *Psalterium*, 20r.

[3]WA 3:211; citing Is 38:15; Gal 3:13; 2 Cor 5:21; Is 53:12; Augustine's comment on Psalm 38:3, NPNF 8:104.

mindful of his own high calling; for, as he was appointed master and teacher over the whole church, it was necessary that whatever he had himself learned in particular by divine teaching should be made known and appropriated to the use of all, that all might profit thereby. Thus we are admonished that it is a very profitable exercise often to recall to remembrance the chastisements with which God has afflicted us for our sins. COMMENTARY ON THE PSALMS.[4]

38:1-2 I Am Pierced with Your Arrows

WHAT ARE THE LORD'S ARROWS? SEBASTIAN MÜNSTER: He calls that intolerable power of sickness—whatever it was, a plague or an ulcer, that caused his lameness—"arrows and the heavy hand of the Lord," that is, misfortune. THE TEMPLE OF THE LORD: PSALM 38.[5]

GOD'S THREATS ARE HIS ARROWS. MARTIN LUTHER: The words with which God rebukes and threatens in Scripture are arrows. Whoever feels them cries out: "O Lord, rebuke me not in your anger." However, only he feels them into whose heart they are thrust and whose conscience is terrified. It is the sensitive into whose heart God shoots the arrows. From the smug, who have become hardened, the arrows glance off as from a hard stone. And this continues as long as the words are spoken by human preaching without the cooperation and the interpenetration of God. THE SEVEN PENITENTIAL PSALMS (1522).[6]

ARROWS ARE A METAPHOR FOR GOD'S INDIGNATION. JOHN DONNE: David in a rectified conscience finds that he may be admitted to present reasons against further corrections, and that this may be received as a reason, "that God's arrows are on him." For this is a phrase or a metaphor in which God's indignation is often expressed in the Scripture. . . . It is an idiom of the Holy Spirit, expressing God's anger in that metaphor of shooting arrows. In this passage, some understand by these arrows foul and infectious diseases in his body, derived by his incontinence.[7] Others, the sting of conscience, and that fearful choice, which the prophet offered him, war, famine or pestilence. Others, his passionate sorrow in the death of Bathsheba's first child, or in the incest of Amnon on his sister, or in the murder of Amnon by Absalom; or in the death of Absalom at the hand of Joab; or in many other occasions of sorrow that surrounded David and his family: more, perhaps, than any such family in the body of history.

But these psalms were made not only to vent David's present holy passion but to serve the church of God to the world's end. And therefore, change the person, and we shall find a whole quiver of arrows. Extend this man to all humankind; carry David's history up to Adam's history, and consider us in that state, which we inherit from him, and we shall see arrows fly about our ears, the anger of God hanging over our heads, in a cloud of arrows; and our own consciences shooting poisoned arrows of desperation into our souls; and human beings multiplying arrows of detraction and calumny and contumely on our good name and estimation. Briefly, in that wound, as we were all shot in Adam, we bled out impassibility, and we sucked in impossibility; there we lost our immortality, our impassibility, our assurance of paradise, and then we lost the possibility of good, Saint Augustine says, that is, all possibility of recovering any of this by ourselves.

So that these arrows which are lamented are all those miseries which sin has cast on us: labor and its child, sickness, and its offspring, death; security of conscience and terror of conscience; the searing of conscience and overtenderness of conscience. God's quiver, the devil's quiver, our own quiver and our neighbor's quiver afford and furnish arrows to

---

[4]CTS 9:53* (CO 31:386). *Lĕhazkîr* only occurs here and in Ps 70:1; commentators continue to struggle with its meaning, connecting it with a simple act of commemoration or worship (see, e.g., Lev 2:2, 9). Kraus, *Psalms 1–59,* 29; Alter, *Book of Psalms,* 134.
[5]Münster, *Miqdaš YHWH,* 1191.
[6]LW 14:156-57 (WA 18:492).

[7]That is, lack of self-control and failure to restrain sexual appetite.

gall and wound us. These arrows then in our text, proceeding from sin and sin proceeding from temptations and inducing tribulations, it shall advance your spiritual edification most to fix your consideration on those fiery darts, as they are temptations and as they are tribulations. Sermon 100: Preached at Lincoln's Inn.[8]

God Afflicts Us. John Calvin: This rule is always to be observed in our prayers: to keep God's promises present to our view. But God has promised that he will chastise his servants, not according to what they deserve but as they are able to bear. This is the reason why the saints so often speak of their own weakness when they are severely oppressed with affliction. David very properly describes the malady under which he labored by the terms *the arrows* and *the hand*, or the chastisement of God. Had he not been persuaded that it was God who thus afflicted him, he could never have been brought to seek from him deliverance from his affliction. We know that the great majority of human beings are blinded under the judgments of God and imagine that they are entirely the events of chance; and scarcely one in a hundred discerns in them the hand of God. Commentary on the Psalms.[9]

38:3-8 I Am a Walking Corpse

We Provoke God's Affliction. John Calvin: He has here attributed to his own sins as the cause the weight of the wrath of God which he felt; and, as we shall find in the following verse, he again acknowledges that what he is now suffering was procured by his own foolishness. Although, then, in bewailing his own miseries, he may seem in some measure to quarrel with God, yet he still cherishes the humble conviction (for God afflicts not beyond measure), that there is no rest for him but in imploring the divine compassion and forgiveness; whereas unbelievers, although

convicted by their own consciences of guilt, murmur against God like the wild beasts, which, in their rage, gnaw the chains with which they are bound. Commentary on the Psalms.[10]

Drowning in the Waters of Sin. John Donne: We consider this plurality, this multiplicity of habitual sins that have gotten over our head, as waters, especially in this, that they have stupefied us and taken from us all sense of reparation of our sinful condition. The organ that God has given the natural person is the eye; he sees God in the creature. The organ that God has given the Christian is the ear; he hears God in his Word.[11] But when we are under water, both senses and organs are vitiated and depraved, if not defeated. The habitual and manifold sinner sees nothing aright; he sees a judgment and calls it an accident. He hears nothing aright; he hears the ordinance of preaching for salvation in the next world, and he calls it an invention of the state, for subjection in this world. And as under water everything seems distorted and crooked to a person, so does a person to God, who sees not his own image in that person, in the form as he made it. . . . Keep low these waters, as waters signify sin, and God shall keep them low, as they signify punishments; and his dove shall return to the ark with an olive leaf, to show you that the waters are abated; he shall give you testimony of the return of his love, in his oil and wine and milk and honey, in the temporal abundances of this life. And if he does fill all your vessels with water, with water of bitterness, that is, fill and exercise all your patience and all your faculties with his corrections, yet he shall do that but to change water into wine, as he did there, he shall make his very judgments, sacraments, conveyances and seals of his mercy to you, though those manifold sins be over your heads, as a roof, as a noise, as an overflowing of waters: and that which

---

[8]Donne, *Works*, 4:314-16*.
[9]CTS 9:55* (CO 31:387).

[10]CTS 9:57* (CO 31:388).
[11]Possibly a reference to Luther: "The ears alone are the organs of a Christian, for he is justified and declared to be a Christian, not because of the works of any member but because of faith" (Lectures on Hebrews [1517–1518], LW 29:224; WA 57,3:222).

is the heaviest of all; and our last consideration, as a lord, as a tyrant, as an usurper. SERMON 102: PREACHED AT LINCOLN'S INN.[12]

WICKEDNESS BENDS US TO THE GROUND.
KONRAD PELLIKAN: This is the manifest misery of human wickedness, by which David has been bent down toward the ground like a beast of burden. He does not think about divine judgments; instead he diverts his thoughts to the soil—rolling around only in earthy, fleshly and shameful things in his mind, omitting any thoughts of heavenly things. Now he spent many days troubled in this way in his mind. He was more worried about concealing and hiding his sin with an even more grave sin than about repenting of his sin. For this reason, he called Uriah back to his house, so that he might burden the pious man with the illegitimate offspring. However, because he did not succeed, he turned to betrayal; in the end he took his wife whom he had polluted with adultery. Now truly penitent, he accuses himself of his sin for many days, that is, he spent the entire day in sorrow, not knowing how to rest on account of his dire straits. COMMENTARY ON PSALM 38:6.[13]

38:9-14 *Longing for the Lord in the Midst of My Affliction*

FAIRWEATHER FRIENDS. JOHANNES BUGENHAGEN: So far, David has spoken about the judgment of God which he felt internally, but now he speaks about that internal anguish through those who are external to us—both friends and enemies—so that despair would be unavoidable, unless the kind Father's hand preserved the righteous person, so that although he falls, he is not cast headlong—as was said in the above psalm. Who does not know that this touches on Christ? Friends attack in this way: "You think that you alone have the truth, that you alone understand? So many learned and wise people and good people also long to be saved, like

you! Why do you bring everyone's hatred on yourself? We are grieved by your plight. Is this not Cineas's piety?[14] To think contrary to everyone? That is not Christian modesty." Yes, when they see and hear that you are hated by everyone—condemned and damned by the powerful, the wise and holy ones, afflicted by evils—they stand at a distance, saying: "We told him, but he doesn't want to listen to anyone. If only he would come to his senses! But he understands these matters contrary to everyone; he has now brought this on himself." Indeed some are willing not to know that the righteous suffer such things; instead they dare not open their mouths—even against such things. For they fear human beings more than God; they fear more for their possessions and honor than the truth. Such people are friends until there are enemies who wickedly long to inflict violence against the Word of God, seeking their soul, that is, to destroy their life.

I say "life" not only of the flesh but also of the spirit. For these people strive for the former instead, so that by their frenzied and violent teaching—which, diverted from the right path, is not according to the Word of God—we might agree with them. Here they behave with all sorts of tricks and deceits. "Do you imagine that the holy fathers did not understand Scripture? Do the words seem to sound so completely different than how the fathers interpreted them? The long tradition of time, the great number of wise people who hold these opinions as well as the devotees of the worship of God everywhere—do these mean nothing to you? Should our ancestors in faith not be obeyed, among whom the authority to command was granted as representatives of God? See this and that passage of Scripture which are against you according to the interpretation of the teachers who interpreted Scripture mystically according to the Spirit! For the letter, according to Paul, kills—nevertheless you follow it." What mental affliction this causes! Certainly without the grace of God no one would

---

[12]Donne, *Works*, 4:377-78*.
[13]Pellikan, *Commentaria Bibliorum*, 4:86v.

[14]In Greek antiquity, Cineas was advisor to King Pyrrhus (318–272 B.C.); he pressed Pyrrhus to consider the costs of his ambition.

be able to persevere in this. If they stand firm, already other vicious things will be said, condemning the truth, cursing, blaspheming, concocting every evil. Such people commonly foist sham charges against the righteous because they cannot do so truthfully. All this is said here: "Those who seek my life do violence to me." INTERPRETATION OF THE PSALMS.[15]

38:15-22 I Am Waiting, O Lord; Do Not Abandon Me

REASONS FOR DAVID'S PATIENCE. MARTIN BUCER: David gives four reasons for his clemency, on account of which, however greatly tormented by a most savage disease and forsaken by his friends, nevertheless he would not answer his enemies' sham charges. He kept his silence like a mute and deaf person. The first and foremost reason is that he inwardly depended on God. And he did not doubt that in time he would be heard while praying for the pardon of his sins. Therefore while awaiting that the pardon he turned a deaf ear to all the slanders of the wicked. (He sings this in verse 16.)

The second reason flows from the first, namely, that while praying he had said—that is, he had desired in his heart—"Do not let my enemies boast over me, my enemies who insult me, when my foot had slipped," that is, when he was bent toward ruin. He knew that however much God was angry with him, he is loved; although his enemies hate him, they do not try to destroy him so much as the glory of God. Thus he correctly said, "I have become silent as a result of however many are all the false accusations and defamations of my enemies. For I spoke and prayed in my heart, 'Let them not gain the victory over me, in which they would not delight in my sins but fight against my piety and righteousness: I know that in the end God will provide. Therefore I restrain myself and do not respond, although they should say many false and dreadful things against me.'" (This is verse 17.)

The third reason is the vehemence and length of the disease. Accordingly he was persuaded that God would not oppress him forever with such great evils. And so the anger of God had continuously ravaged him so that plainly he already had been made lame and was being tormented with a continuous sorrow, so that there was hope that the Lord would also immediately declare his forbearance, so becoming mute to all things, while the most loving, kindly disposed Father was standing ready so that he might personally drive away all evil things. Accordingly in fact it must be said that truly the chastisement of the Lord would humble the saints and lead them into the greatest trouble as well as clemency.

The fourth reason of clemency was that, because he had already entirely acknowledged and confessed his own sin, truly sorrowing over it, he would no longer torture himself so severely on account of these things, because those sins were by far the greatest torment to him. Moreover, when he is so dejected and contrite in heart, God cannot postpone consolation and help for so long. For this reason he also addressed this reason first out of his own clemency and patience, then out of hope and confidence. It would be in a short time that God would respond and answer favorably. HOLY PSALMS.[16]

GOD CREATES EX NIHILO; THUS WE MUST BECOME NOTHING. MARTIN LUTHER: It is God's nature to make something out of nothing; hence out of one who is not yet nothing God cannot make anything. Human beings, however, make something else out of what already exists; but this has no value whatever. Therefore God accepts only the forsaken, cures only the sick, gives sight only to the blind, restores life only to the dead, sanctifies only the sinners, gives wisdom only to the unwise. In short, he has mercy only on those who are wretched, and gives grace only to those who are not in grace. THE SEVEN PENITENTIAL PSALMS (1525).[17]

---

[15]Bugenhagen, *In librvm Psalmorvm interpretatio*, 95r-v; citing Ps 37:24; 2 Cor 3:6.

[16]Bucer, *Sacrorum Psalmorum*, 190r-v; citing Ps 32:5.
[17]LW 14:163 (WA 18:497-98).

THESE ARE POWERFUL WORDS. JOHN FISHER: John Cassian says that "these words are of great virtue and always to be held in remembrance," which also the church uses very often in the service of God, and at all times asks his help in the beginning of it. Let us, therefore, wrapped and closed in all these miseries . . . go by prayer to our best and merciful Lord God, with steadfast hope and true penance, and meekly beseech him for his help, because he alone is able to defend us from our enemies. May he vouchsafe to deliver us from them, and not to go away nor forsake us, but always give heed unto our help. Why? Because, "he is God and Lord of our health," giving temporal health to our bodies and to our souls the health of grace in this life, and in the general resurrection to come— which we trust verily—everlasting health both to body and soul. To which may our Lord by his ineffable mercy bring us. Amen. THE THIRD PENITENTIAL PSALM.[18]

---

[18]Fisher, *Commentary on the Seven Penitential Psalms*, 1:78*.

39:1-13 WHAT IS THE MEASURE OF MY DAYS?

To the choirmaster: to Jeduthun. A Psalm of David.

¹ I said, "I will guard my ways,
    that I may not sin with my tongue;
I will guard my mouth with a muzzle,
    so long as the wicked are in my presence."
² I was mute and silent;
    I held my peace to no avail,
    and my distress grew worse.
    ³ My heart became hot within me.
As I mused, the fire burned;
    then I spoke with my tongue:

⁴ "O Lord, make me know my end
and what is the measure of my days;
    let me know how fleeting I am!
⁵ Behold, you have made my days a few
        handbreadths,
    and my lifetime is as nothing before you.
    Surely all mankind stands as a mere
            breath!   Selah
    ⁶ Surely a man goes about as a shadow!
Surely for nothingᵃ they are in turmoil;

a Hebrew Surely as a breath

man heaps up wealth and does not know
    who will gather!

⁷ "And now, O Lord, for what do I wait?
    My hope is in you.
⁸ Deliver me from all my transgressions.
    Do not make me the scorn of the fool!
⁹ I am mute; I do not open my mouth,
    for it is you who have done it.
¹⁰ Remove your stroke from me;
    I am spent by the hostility of your hand.
¹¹ When you discipline a man
    with rebukes for sin,
you consume like a moth what is dear to him;
    surely all mankind is a mere breath!   Selah

¹² "Hear my prayer, O Lord,
and give ear to my cry;
    hold not your peace at my tears!
For I am a sojourner with you,
    a guest, like all my fathers.
¹³ Look away from me, that I may smile again,
    before I depart and am no more!"

OVERVIEW: In this psalm, Reformation-era interpreters confronted the pleading lament of David, who earnestly calls on God in the midst of an existential crisis as he reflects upon the fleeting life of humanity. They see this as an opportunity to discuss how Christians should respond to such moments of doubt by comparing the uncertainties and vagaries of human life with the assurance found in the mercy and constancy of God. Hence, they encourage Christians not to focus on the things of this world but rather to trust in God, turn their eyes to him and cling to his Word. In this way, David's prayer in the midst of suffering becomes a source of encouragement and a model for Christian faithfulness. As with other psalms, some of our commentators apply an allegorical or spiritual interpretation to this text, equating David's anguish variously to the persecution of the early church, the challenges faced by Paul and the suffering of Christ. Thus, although David's lament rightly points to the fact that human life may be brief and filled with anguish, for our interpreters, it also reveals that Christians can trust in the promises of God.

To Whom Can This Psalm Be Applied?

DESIDERIUS ERASMUS: In my opinion there is nothing to prevent one applying this psalm to Christ, or to the church itself, the mystical body of

Christ, or to the prophets, apostles and bishops who are the pillars and leaders of the church, or to any one individual fighting under the banner of Christ. We can imagine people who are wearied by the ingratitude and malice of the wicked and who consider abandoning their desire to do good. At last, when their mental agonies become overpowering, in their weariness with life they seek an end to their suffering in death; but they recover from this state of despair, partly by reflecting on the nature of human existence (which, despite being so miserable, is at least very short and cannot torment us for long) and partly by a consideration of divine mercy, which does not allow people to be tempted beyond their strength, although it sometimes uses terrible sufferings to test its subjects; with the temptation God also provides the means to endure it. We know that Christ was thoroughly tested and tempted in every way, and it is well known, too, that Paul was troubled by so many misfortunes that he was occasionally overcome with weariness of this life. We are also aware of the violent disturbances suffered by the church in the past and even today; in fact, it would altogether cease to exist without Christ's powerful support. Finally, anyone can experience within himself the truth of the apostle's words: "Those who wish to lead a godly life in Christ Jesus must suffer persecution" from those who love this world. EXPOSITION OF PSALM 39.[1]

DAVID PRAYS FOR AN EMPATHETIC SPIRIT. NIKOLAUS SELNECKER: This psalm is, as it were, an answer to Psalm 37 in which we were taught how we should conduct ourselves when things go well for the godless and poorly for the pious. We should not grumble and be impatient toward the godless who, as it stands here, live so self-assuredly and stockpile goods, as if they would never die. Instead we should commend everything to God and trust him; in his good time he will make it well. Now based on such teaching this psalm responds and says: David placed God before him. He will follow him and be patient and no longer seethe against the godless but instead

will cling to the word and promise of God. He prays that God would cause him to remember how short, miserable and uncertain all people's lives are, and how for the pious everything depends on this: that they have the forgiveness of sins and a merciful God. THE WHOLE PSALTER.[2]

Superscription: *What Does* Jeduthun *Mean?*

JEDUTHUN COULD MEAN MANY THINGS. FELIX PRATENSIS: The title of this psalm has a unique term which has been ambiguous for some time, namely, "Jeduthun." Some say it signifies a type of musical instrument. Others say that it is the name of a certain singer who sang this psalm in the temple. Others allege it to signify the law; they say that this psalm was composed on account of legal troubles which are going to plague the Israelite people. But we will assert instead that the term is composed from the word *idh*, which means "to cast" or "to lift up" or "to exalt and confess." The other option means either "severity" or "devastation" or "retribution" or "lawsuit" and "contention." Or we could say that it is derived from the word *iādāh*— the *he* changed to a *taw*, for we find this form very often in holy Scripture. Adapt the meaning which pleases you! It is the office of the expositor to determine the meaning. THE HEBREW PSALTER.[3]

MYSTICALLY JEDUTHUN **INDICATES CHRIST AND THE CHURCH.** MARTIN LUTHER: Of course, by "Jeduthun" the singer, who was one of those who sang to the lyre, is meant. This word also signifies Christ and his people who sing this psalm as a new and spiritual song. According to his name, *Jeduthun*, he is called "one who leaps," in which the despisers and leapers of this world and lovers of heaven are signified. Whence it is also said in this psalm: "My hope is the Lord, and my substance is as nothing before you." Therefore, *Jeduthun* signifies the one people of the church. These agree

---

[1]CWE 65:39*; citing 2 Tim 3:12.

[2]Selnecker, *Der gantze Psalter*, 1:196r.
[3]Pratensis, *Psalterium*, 20v-21r.

with those who understand this psalm mystically—like Psalm 9, "According to 'almût," so also here "According to *Jeduthun.*" GLOSSA ON PSALM 39 (1513–1515).[4]

39:1-3 Inner Torment

HUMAN LIFE IS BRIEF AND VAIN. JOHANNES BUGENHAGEN: If we follow the world we are condemned by God; if we follow God, whatever is worldly persecutes us. Therefore wherever we turn, whether to sweetness or bitterness, this life is a vanity of vanities and an affliction of our spirit, just as the preacher said: "How brief, O Lord, is my life and the measure of my days! Form and teach me, so that I would acknowledge this brevity, so that I would know that my time is nothing, that whatever I am or could be is nothing, that human beings are only vanity and a ghost or shadow over the earth. Here human beings are cast into many sorrows, clinging to and treasuring the things of this age, as if they would live here for a long time—even forever. Why else does the world persecute me so?" It is proper to see here how holy persecution is to the saints, whereas also the world urges us to God, which this whole psalm clearly teaches. INTERPRETATION OF THE PSALMS.[5]

THE DIFFICULT NECESSITY OF ENDURING SHAM CHARGES. MARTIN LUTHER: This is very hard to do when we suffer injury from those whom we have benefited, because we are generally quick to exaggerate and magnify the good we have done and the ingratitude of those people, and so we make accusations on a grand scale. And then grief is renewed, because it is a particularly sharp sorrow to receive injury and malice from one whom we have helped and at the same time to keep silent about the good we have done him and let it be construed as something evil. This is what happened to Christ. In another way we are silent from

the good by teaching and persuading them that they are unteachable and impossible to discipline. And so again there is sorrow for jealous souls. Third, I am silent from the good, that is, my own, when I do not justify myself and do not cite my own righteousness and goodness. Because it is simply stated, "from the good," it makes a great deal of sense by dividing it into particulars. FIRST PSALMS LECTURES (1513–1515).[6]

EMOTIONS LIKE THE WEATHER. JOHN CALVIN: If, therefore, at any time we feel ardent emotions struggling and raising a commotion in our breasts, we should remember this conflict of David, so that our courage may not fail us, or at least so that our infirmity may not drive us headlong to despair. The dry and hot exhalations which the sun causes to arise in summer, if nothing occurred in the atmosphere to obstruct their progress, would ascend into the air without commotion; but when intervening clouds prevent their free ascent, a conflict arises, from which the thunders are produced. It is similar with respect to the godly who desire to lift up their hearts to God. If they would resign themselves to the vain imaginations which arise in their minds, they might enjoy a sort of unrestrained liberty to indulge in every fancy; but because they try to resist their influence and seek to devote themselves to God, obstructions which arise from the opposition of the flesh begin to trouble them. Whenever, therefore, the flesh shall put forth its efforts and shall kindle up a fire in our hearts, let us know that we are exercised with the same kind of temptation which occasioned so much pain and trouble to David. COMMENTARY ON THE PSALMS.[7]

39:4-6 Human Life Is Merely a Breath

FOLLOW THE EXAMPLE OF CHRIST! DESIDERIUS ERASMUS: And so, whenever God allows the storm of temptation to create in us a similar feeling, let us

---

[4]WA 3:218; citing 1 Chron 15:17; 1 Chron 16:42; Ps 39:2; 9:1. See Kraus, *Psalms 1–59*, 30; Alter, *Book of Psalms*, 137.
[5]Bugenhagen, *In librvm Psalmorvm interpretatio*, 96v; citing Ps 39:4-6.

[6]LW 10:184 (WA 3:222).
[7]CTS 9:75-76* (CO 31:398).

not give up hope completely or take refuge in the assistance which the world provides; instead let us turn our eyes to God, who will alleviate our suffering so that we can endure it. We do not have the capacity to prevent the mind from being agitated by possible problems but we can try to support it with the hope of speedy relief. The Lord accepted this distress when the torment of the cross was imminent, to provide us with an example which might prevent us from being similarly affected and rushing headlong into revenge or despair; instead we should lie prostrate: in other words, not trust in our own resources but follow the Lord's example and pray at length, begging for divine support. EXPOSITION OF PSALM 39.[8]

Life's Vanity Causes Us to Seek God's Deliverance.

Wolfgang Musculus: David reprehends the vanity of his life, which until that time he did not continue to acknowledge. He acknowledges and approves the reprimand and instruction of divine providence. These are two things which will be noted through this exposition. If these opinions do not please you, it should be expounded simply just as a prayer by which he asks to be instructed how quickly we should be taken from this life and are going to be overcome by its vanity. And so we see portrayed an example of those affected by a grave and lasting disease; it makes them weary of this life, and they long to depart from it as quickly as possible. Thus it is apparent what the advantage of afflictions is. They possess this advantage in themselves: they declare to us and expose right before our eyes the vanity of this life; they carry with them the desire for death. Otherwise, we are so secure that if our will and longing to live are granted, we would never long to depart this forsaken age for our heavenly homeland. Therefore, although God has ordained the course of our life in this way—not only is it brief but also we do not want to want it to hasten to the end at a constant speed—and nevertheless he adds this: that it is full of vanity and affliction so much so

that, affected by its weariness, we begin to sigh and beg for deliverance. We see this here in David. . . . The pious know that it has been divinely established thus, that the death of all is certain, but the hour of death is uncertain. And this is far better than if the hour of death were actually known. Commentary on the Psalms.[9]

Human Beings Themselves Are Vanity.

Henry Ainsworth: Or, "a mere vapor, all manner vanity, and nothing else." Whatever is vanity in the world can be seen entirely in human beings. The Hebrew *hebel* is a soon vanishing vapor, like the breath of one's mouth. To this the apostle refers, saying, "What is your life? It is even a vapor that appears for a little time and afterwards vanishes away." . . . Adam named his second son *Hebel*, that is, vanity. And here David says, that "all Adam" [i.e., every person] is *hebel*, vanity. Solomon in Ecclesiastes declares this at large. Annotations on Psalm 39:5.[10]

Ambition Alone Does Not Bring Peace.

Desiderius Erasmus: The word *treasure* refers not only to gold, jewels and such but also to anything which a person values highly and which he expects to be a source of happiness and comfort to him in this life. Think of all the things which some people do and put up with in order to complete their education. They learn one language after another, study one subject after another, always adding something to their treasure. Death, however, often puts an unexpected end to all their efforts; there and then all those sleepless nights of hard work over the years are wasted once and for all. The same is true of those who seek high office, for it often happens that they are disappointed of what they seek to gain through great hardships and at enormous expense. Thus it happens that what they expected would provide them with a peaceful life turns out to be a source of disaster;

---

[8]CWE 65:76.

[9]Musculus, *In Psalterium Commentarii*, 513.
[10]Ainsworth, *Annotations*, 2:492*; citing Jas 4:14; Gen 4:2; Ps 62:10.

what they hoped would provide them with pleasures brings with it extreme suffering instead. EXPOSITION OF PSALM 39.[11]

39:7-11 *What Am I Waiting For?*

DIVINE CONSTANCY, HUMAN INCONSTANCY.
VIKTORIN STRIGEL: Up until this point he laid out nicely the earlier consolation, employing words and figures that were particularly suited. Now he adds a second consolation about the difference between human assistance and divine help. "I know," he says, "that nothing is more uncertain than human assistance, nothing more deceptive. For the will of human beings is changeable, their fortune is inconstant, and their life is brief. But the will of God is fixed and unyielding, his power is immense and infinite, and he is eternal life itself. Therefore, it is better to hope in God than in any person, who is as likely to change as quickly as the flight of a fly." But because this consolation is often repeated elsewhere in the Psalms, I will be very brief here. *HYPONĒMATA IN ALL THE PSALMS.*[12]

OUR GREAT AND MERCIFUL GOD. NIKOLAUS SELNECKER: Here he indicates what the very best thing is, namely, to have forgiveness of sins and a merciful God. "I will," he says, "gladly grant others their power and welfare and remain silent and not grumble. Lord God, let me be yours alone, forgive me my sin, protect and vindicate me; let me not be put to shame, and do not let my enemies rejoice over me, who indeed are nothing but fools who neither seek your Word nor your glory." THE WHOLE PSALTER.[13]

ACKNOWLEDGE AND CONFESS YOUR SINS.
JOHN CALVIN: He is now no longer carried away by the violence of his grief to murmur against God, but, humbly acknowledging himself guilty before God, he has recourse to his mercy. In asking to be delivered from his transgressions, he ascribes the praise of righteousness to God, while he charges on himself the blame of all the misery which he endures; and he blames himself, not only on account of one sin but acknowledges that he is justly chargeable with manifold transgressions. By this rule we must be guided, if we would wish to obtain an alleviation of our miseries; for, until the very source of them has been dried up, they will never cease to follow one another in rapid succession. COMMENTARY ON THE PSALMS.[14]

GOD, THE SKILLED SURGEON. DESIDERIUS ERASMUS: A person ought therefore to commit himself with all confidence to the hand of God who chastises him. God is his Father and does not inflict more blows than are necessary. God is a wise and omnipotent doctor and will not inflict wounds which cause death. Even if he drives the knife in quite deeply, he does not do so with the intention of killing but in order to cure the patient more quickly. Even if he does kill, by killing he restores to life. Thus he cast the persecuting Paul down so that he might rise up as a preacher; he threw the wolf to the ground that he might rise again as a lamb. Those who have mortified their desires and who live for Christ are fortunate in their death. EXPOSITION OF PSALM 39.[15]

THE FITTING SIMILE OF GOD AS A MOTH.
JOHN CALVIN: At first view the comparison of God with a moth may seem absurd. For what relation is there, it may be said, between a small moth-worm and the infinite majesty of God? I answer: David has with much propriety made use of this simile that we may know that although God does not openly thunder from heaven against the reprobate, yet his secret curse does not cease to consume them away, just as the moth, though unperceived, wastes by its secret gnawing a piece of cloth or wood. At the same time, he alludes to the excellence of human beings, which he says is destroyed as it were by corruption, when God is

---

[11]CWE 65:93*.
[12]Strigel, *Hyponēmata*, 196.
[13]Selnecker, *Der gantze Psalter*, 1:197v.
[14]CTS 9:82* (CO 31:401).
[15]CWE 65:111; citing Acts 9. See RCS NT 6:104, 119-25.

offended, even as the moth destroys the most precious clothes by wasting them. The Scriptures often very appropriately employ various similitudes in this way and are wont to apply them sometimes in one view and sometimes in another. COMMENTARY ON THE PSALMS.[16]

39:12-13 *Hear My Sojourner's Prayer*

WE SOJOURN ON EARTH AS GOD'S VASSALS. RUDOLF GWALTHER: This word [*sojourner*] can be interpreted as "vassal." For we human beings here on earth have nothing that is our own. Instead, as God's vassals, we are established in this temporal life and are sustained in it so long as it pleases him. THE PSALTER.[17]

THE RULE OF THE SPIRIT. ROBERT ROLLOCK: These words declare the shortness of this present life, as if he should say, so long as the short light continues, or, so long as I enjoy this short light. . . . Mark first in David a certain memorable change and prayers, greatly disagreeing among themselves.

Before indeed he had prayed with a troubled mind, but now he prays with a more quiet and settled heart. For sometimes the flesh rules the prayers of the faithful more than the spirit does. In this change you have also an instruction on the final victory of the Holy Spirit. For although in this present life the victory appears to be often on the flesh side, nevertheless by that same thing, that after the movement of the flesh, the Holy Spirit raises up in us that operation, which starts the motion of the Spirit, and we are then reminded that once the victory shall be perfect and full on the Spirit's side. EXPOSITION UPON PSALM 39.[18]

DAVID IS NOT LOST. THE ENGLISH ANNOTATIONS: Some people might be scandalized by the expression "and be no more" as an intimation of utter abolishment. God forbid. The original word, very elegant, might have borne a more favorable translation of "and be no more seen or found" among human beings. This has been said of Enoch, and the same phrase is used by Daniel concerning the Messiah. ANNOTATIONS ON PSALM 39:13.[19]

---

[16]CTS 9:85-86* (CO 31:403).
[17]Gwalther, *Der Psalter*, 69r.

[18]Rollock, *Exposition upon Some Psalmes*, 225-26*.
[19]Downame, ed., *Annotations*, 6E1r*; citing Gen 5:24; Dan 9:26.

40:1-17 MY HELP AND DELIVERER

To the choirmaster. A Psalm of David.

¹ I waited patiently for the LORD;
    he inclined to me and heard my cry.
² He drew me up from the pit of destruction,
    out of the miry bog,
and set my feet upon a rock,
    making my steps secure.
³ He put a new song in my mouth,
    a song of praise to our God.
Many will see and fear,
    and put their trust in the LORD.

⁴ Blessed is the man who makes
    the LORD his trust,
who does not turn to the proud,
    to those who go astray after a lie!
⁵ You have multiplied, O LORD my God,
your wondrous deeds and your thoughts
        toward us;
    none can compare with you!
I will proclaim and tell of them,
    yet they are more than can be told.

⁶ In sacrifice and offering you have not delighted,
    but you have given me an open ear.ᵃ
Burnt offering and sin offering
    you have not required.
⁷ Then I said, "Behold, I have come;
    in the scroll of the book it is written of me:
⁸ I delight to do your will, O my God;
    your law is within my heart."

⁹ I have told the glad news of deliveranceᵇ
    in the great congregation;
behold, I have not restrained my lips,
    as you know, O LORD.

¹⁰ I have not hidden your deliverance within
        my heart;
    I have spoken of your faithfulness and
        your salvation;
I have not concealed your steadfast love and
        your faithfulness
    from the great congregation.

¹¹ As for you, O LORD, you will not restrain
    your mercy from me;
your steadfast love and your faithfulness will
    ever preserve me!

¹² For evils have encompassed me
    beyond number;
my iniquities have overtaken me,
    and I cannot see;
they are more than the hairs of my head;
    my heart fails me.
¹³ Be pleased, O LORD, to deliver me!
    O LORD, make haste to help me!
¹⁴ Let those be put to shame and disappointed
        altogether
    who seek to snatch away my life;
let those be turned back and brought to dishonor
    who delight in my hurt!
¹⁵ Let those be appalled because of their shame
    who say to me, "Aha, Aha!"

¹⁶ But may all who seek you
    rejoice and be glad in you;
may those who love your salvation
    say continually, "Great is the LORD!"
¹⁷ As for me, I am poor and needy,
    but the Lord takes thought for me.
You are my help and my deliverer;
    do not delay, O my God!

a Hebrew ears you have dug for me b Hebrew righteousness; also verse 10

OVERVIEW: This psalm offers a clear affirmation of God's grace and power to deliver. For these com- mentators, it is therefore appropriate to interpret the muck and mire from which David was pulled as our sinfulness. And the rock on which David was set is read as a reference to the certainty of divine deliverance and the hope that believers have in God's promises, or as an allusion to Christ, who is the foundation of the church. In this way, the song that David sings points not only to his own thanksgiving but also represents humanity's gratefulness for God's mighty rescue. Our interpreters debate whether the difficult Hebrew of verse 6—which most of them translate as "you have bored through or pierced my ears"—is a reference to Exodus 21. However, they agree that the phrase intimates the importance of hearing the Word rightly interpreted and preached. Finally, in light of what seems to be a rather abrupt shift in tone at verse 11, some of our commentators point out that God's promises do not remove the reality of suffering here and now, but Christians, who have received God's mercy, are now able to show mercy to others.

WE PERFORM SACRIFICES BY IMITATING CHRIST. JOHANNES BUGENHAGEN: These are the words of Christ, Hebrews 10 teaches us, proving now that there is no longer any external sacrifice unless if by Christ's example you perform the will and law of God, not with external offerings but in your very heart. This is the law of the spirit, that is, faith in your heart which does not act wickedly, which also causes you not to remain silent about God's righteousness, truth, salvation and loving-kindness in the great congregation or among the multitudes. . . . The beginning of the psalm is an act of thanksgiving for God's astonishing deliverance. INTERPRETATION OF THE PSALMS.[1]

40:1-5 God's Abundant Mercy

DAVID'S EXEMPLARY ENDURANCE. JOHN CALVIN: The beginning of this psalm is an expression of thanksgiving, in which David relates that he had been delivered not only from danger but also from present death. Some are of the

opinion, but without good reason, that it should be understood of sickness. Instead it should be supposed that David here comprehends a multitude of dangers from which he had escaped. He had certainly been more than once exposed to the greatest danger, even of death, so that, with good reason, he might be said to have been swallowed up in the gulf of death and sunk in miry clay. It nevertheless appears that his faith had still continued firm, for he did not cease to trust in God, although the long continuance of the calamity had well nigh exhausted his patience. He tells us not merely that he had waited but by the repetition of the same phrase, he shows that he had been a long time in anxious suspense. In proportion then as his trial was prolonged, the evidence and proof of his faith in enduring the delay with calmness and equanimity of mind was so much the more apparent. The meaning in short is that although God delayed his help, yet the heart of David did not faint or grow weary from delay; but that after he had given, as it were, sufficient proof of his patience, he was finally heard. COMMENTARY ON THE PSALMS.[2]

SIMILES OF SIN AND SALVATION. NIKOLAUS SELNECKER: The terrible grave and muck is nothing other than our sins, transgressions and iniquities, the tyranny of the devil and death and every human misfortune. Concerning this, it stands in Zechariah: "In the blood of your covenant you have led out the prisoners from the grave, in which there was no water." That is, the Son of God emptied himself of his divinity and took on the form of a servant. He became human and through his suffering and death led us out of hell, redeemed us from death and saved us from all the muck of sin.

"Rock" means sure consolation, faith, hope, protection and divine help. And it is placed in opposition to the grave and muck in which we cannot stand or step. However, on the rock we remain sure. For Christ, the Son of God, this rock is God the Father himself; our rock is Christ, true

---

[1]Bugenhagen, *In librvm Psalmorvm interpretatio*, 98r; citing Heb 10:5-7.

[2]CTS 9:89-90* (CO 31:405-6).

God and true man, the Son of the living God. He leads us with his Holy Spirit. We believe in him; thus we are able to tread securely. As above in Psalm 32, God himself says, "I will instruct you and show you the way you should go; I will lead you with my eyes." The Whole Psalter.[3]

A New Song for the Lord, from the Lord. Cardinal Cajetan: Here the new covenant's grace is described by the author, because a human being does not give the song, but God. By revelation, because believers not only believe in their heart but also confess with their mouth. "In my mouth." By sweetness, because it is a song and through this is delicious. By wonder, because it is new and truly new because it sings that the Word was made flesh. The restoration of human beings is as much internal as external. Indeed, it sings about the restoration of all creation. "See, I am making all things new." By service, it is "praise to our God," so that you should understand that this song about the new covenant is God's praise no differently than our people who worshiped him in the old covenant. Commentary on Psalm 40.[4]

Do Not Restrict God's Agency to External Means. John Calvin: While some are in constant pain because of their own anxiety and discontent, or quake at the slightest breeze that blows, and others work hard to fortify and preserve their life by means of earthly succors— all this proceeds from ignorance of the doctrine that God governs the affairs of this world according to his own good pleasure. And as the great majority of people, measuring the providence of God by their own understanding, wickedly obscure or degrade it, David, placing it on its proper footing, wisely removes this impediment. The meaning of the sentence, therefore, amounts to this, that in the works of God human beings should reverently admire what they cannot comprehend by their reason; and when-

ever the flesh moves them to contradiction or murmuring, they should raise themselves above the world. If God ceases to work, he seems to be asleep, because, binding up his hands to the use of outward means, we do not consider that he works by means which are secret. We may therefore learn from this passage that although the reason of his works may be hidden or unknown to us, he is nevertheless wonderful in his counsels. Commentary on the Psalms.[5]

40:6 Why Does God Pierce the Psalmist's Ears?

To Demonstrate Obedience. Rudolf Gwalther: "You have bored through my ear." . . . That is, "You have opened my ears and heart, so that I can hear your Word and gain a desire to obey it." Now he takes these words from the Law according to whose command servants would have their ears punctured and pierced on the doorpost as a sign that they are no longer under their own power but rather should be obedient and attentive to their lord. The Psalter.[6]

To Hear the Word. The English Annotations: It is common among all expositors of our time and of the former age to understand that David, by these words, is alluding to the law concerning servants. . . . It is true, however, that the Law speaks of only one ear being bored through by the awl, and that here we have the plural. From the context, we may also infer that David had a further aim and meaning, as God prepared him for hearing by opening not one of the two, but both his ears (because believing comes especially from hearing). Annotation on Psalm 40:6.[7]

---

[3]Selnecker, *Der gantze Psalter*, 1:198r; citing Zech 9:11; Phil 2:7; Ps 32:8.

[4]Cajetan, *In Sacrae Scripturae Expositionem*, 3:146; citing Rev 21:5.

[5]CTS 9:96* (CO 31:409).

[6]Gwalther, *Der Psalter*, 69v, 71r; citing Ex 21:5-6. See the note on verse 6 in the ESV text above. Goldingay includes this interpretation as possible but less likely; other commentators understand *ear* as a contrast to sacrifices (cf. 1 Sam 15:22). See Goldingay, *Psalms*, 1:573; Kraus, *Psalms 1–59*, 426-27; Alter, *Book of Psalms*, 142.

[7]Downame, ed., *Annotations*, 6E1r*; citing Ex 21:6.

To Commend Faith and Obedience. Martin Luther: Why not the eyes or the tongue? In the first place, he commends obedience and, second, faith. Faith comes by hearing, not by seeing. And here is a golden word that we might learn to have ears.... We have two ears, first, so that we may be more apt to learn than to teach, to hear than to be heard, to yield to one speaking rather than to speak. For we have only one tongue, and this is enclosed by twenty-eight teeth, of which the first four are sharp, and also by two lips, while the ears are out in the open....

This is said against the disobedient, because they do not hear, as if they had no ears, or at least, as in the case of a statue, they have ears that are not pierced but rather stopped up, and therefore they do not hear. For this reason it is the highest praise of Christ and of all Christians to have ears perfected and pierced.... As an example of this, it is commanded in Exodus 21 that when a Hebrew slave has voluntarily given himself over, his master shall pierce his ear with an awl at the door. This happens when anyone dedicates himself to Christ and renounces his freedom so that he may be a slave of righteousness....

"Earrings" are the same as piercing the ear with an awl, namely, the decrees of holy Scripture. With these the ears are adorned. First Psalms Lectures (1513–1515).[8]

To Signify Pure Interpretation of the Law. John Calvin: Some think that in using this form of expression, David refers to the ordinance under the Law which we read in Exodus 21.... But this interpretation seems too forced and refined. Others more simply consider that it is of the same meaning as to render fit or qualify for service, for David mentions not one ear only, but both. Human beings, we know, are naturally deaf, because they are so dull that their ears are stopped until God pierces them. By this expression, therefore, is denoted the docility to which we are brought and molded by the grace of the Holy Spirit.

I, however, apply this manner of expression more closely to the scope of the passage before us and explain it in this sense: David was not slow and dull of hearing, as human beings usually are, so that he could discern nothing but what was earthly in the sacrifices, but his ears had been cleansed, so that he was a better interpreter of the Law and able to refer all the outward ceremonies to the spiritual service of God. He encloses the sentence, "You have pierced my ears," as it were, in parenthesis, because he is discussing sacrifices.... If, however, it is objected that sacrifices were offered by the express commandment of God, I have just said that David here distinguishes between the spiritual service of God and what consisted in outward types and shadows. And in making this comparison, it is no great wonder to find him saying that the sacrifices are of no value, because they were only helps designed to lead human beings to true piety and tended to a far higher end than what was at first apparent. Seeing, then, God made use of these elements, only to lead his people to the exercises of faith and repentance, we conclude that he had no delight in being worshiped by sacrifices. We must always bear in mind that whatever is not pleasing to God for its own sake but only insofar as it leads to some other end, if it be put in the place of his true worship and service is rejected and cast away by him. Commentary on the Psalms.[9]

40:7-10 I Will Promulgate the Lord's Kindnesses

Consolation and Exhortation. Wolfgang Musculus: When verses 7-10 are considered, they serve a double use for us: one for consolation, the other for doctrine. It has consolation as it pertains to Christ, who obeys the Father to the point of death, redeemed us by his obedience and freed us from the curse of our disobedience, so that we may have in him life and remission of our sins. They are for doctrine so that we may learn how to be grateful to God in whatever circumstance. The true worship of God is situated in this circumstance, so

---

[8]LW 10:188-89* (WA 3:227-28); citing Ex 21:5-6.

[9]CTS 9:99-100* (CO 31:410-11); citing Ex 21:5-6.

that we also may serve God the Father according to his will with our Head, Christ, especially because we have been sanctified for this through Christ in the Holy Spirit. Two things are set forth by the prophet: one is that he offers himself as one who is obedient and ready to yield to the divine will; the other which promises the attentive and public preaching of the divine praise, which is nothing other than the sacrifice of praise, which is proper to the New Testament, granted that God would require those two from us perpetually. . . .

For obedience there are four things necessary which are also contained in these verses. The first is that the divine work in sanctification is necessary, which instructs us for this obedience. . . . The second is that it demands a ready heart and mind. For one neither obeys God nor is thankful without a ready mind. . . . The third is that it is effective in its operation. . . . Fourth, it is necessary that obedience is accommodated to the will of God, which is expressed in his law. Let us not think that God is served if we do what pleases ourselves. This pertains to what he reminds us of the law and will of God. COMMENTARY ON THE PSALMS.[10]

Be Diligent in Your Calling. The English Annotations: As public citizens, in relation to the salvation of others, we must not hide the Word. As private citizens, in relation to our own, we must. Or to speak more distinctly and properly: In the first expression, to hide is to conceal, and that must not be: it is a fault in any person. In the second, to hide is to cherish, to often think and ruminate on . . . something that should be done by all people who make use of the Word of God to their own salvation. ANNOTATION ON PSALM 40:10.[11]

40:11-17 The Lord Does Not Restrain His Mercy

Disturbed in the Heart. Konrad Pellikan: The psalmist amplifies the greatness of God's goodness by the mass of evils from which God had liberated him. In this way they surrounded him not only once, so that, to the judgment of the flesh, it would seem impossible to escape; even if he had ever emerged from one calamity, another calamity, frequently more serious, immediately threatened and overwhelmed him. . . . And when external foes ceased their raging, immediately a great many sins disturbed his conscience, and not light ones but also the sins of his children, which he was surely not able to foresee or prevent. For in this way the Lord had decided to test his eminent friend, as an example to all believers, so that he would be a suitable type of Christ the Lord, who endured far greater things—even the cross of death itself for the sake of the elect. COMMENTARY ON PSALM 40:12.[12]

God Will Punish Our Enemies. John Calvin: We are here taught that when our enemies shall have persecuted us to the uttermost, a recompense is also prepared for them; and that God will turn back and cause to fall on their own heads all the evil which they had devised against us; and this doctrine ought to act as a restraint on us, that we may behave compassionately and kindly toward our neighbors. COMMENTARY ON THE PSALMS.[13]

Share the Joy of God's Mercy. David Dickson: As every mercy to every believer gives proof of God's readiness to show the same mercy to all believers when they are in need, so should any mercy shown to any of the number, when it becomes known to others, be the matter and occasion of magnifying the Lord. COMMENTARY ON PSALM 40:16.[14]

[10]Musculus, *In Psalterium Commentarii*, 522; citing Jer 31:31-34.
[11]Downame, ed., *Annotations*, 6E iv*.
[12]Pellikan, *Commentaria Bibliorum*, 4:89v.
[13]CTS 9:109* (CO 31:416).
[14]Dickson, *First Fifty Psalms*, 275*.

41:1-13 LORD, BE GRACIOUS TO ME

To the choirmaster. A Psalm of David.

[1] Blessed is the one who considers the poor![a]
　　In the day of trouble the LORD delivers him;
[2] the LORD protects him and keeps him alive;
　　he is called blessed in the land;
　　you do not give him up to the will of his
　　　　enemies.
[3] The LORD sustains him on his sickbed;
　　in his illness you restore him to full health.[b]

[4] As for me, I said, "O LORD, be gracious to me;
　　heal me,[c] for I have sinned against you!"
[5] My enemies say of me in malice,
　　"When will he die, and his name perish?"
[6] And when one comes to see me, he utters
　　　　empty words,
　　while his heart gathers iniquity;
　　when he goes out, he tells it abroad.

[7] All who hate me whisper together about me;
　　they imagine the worst for me.[d]
[8] They say, "A deadly thing is poured out[e] on him;
　　he will not rise again from where he lies."
[9] Even my close friend in whom I trusted,
　　who ate my bread, has lifted his heel
　　　　against me.
[10] But you, O LORD, be gracious to me,
　　and raise me up, that I may repay them!

[11] By this I know that you delight in me:
　　my enemy will not shout in triumph over me.
[12] But you have upheld me because of my
　　　　integrity,
　　and set me in your presence forever.

[13] Blessed be the LORD, the God of Israel,
　　from everlasting to everlasting!
　　Amen and Amen.

a Or weak   b Hebrew you turn all his bed   c Hebrew my soul   d Or they devise evil against me   e Or has fastened

---

OVERVIEW: The reformers wanted to reform not only the church's faith according to the Scriptures but also the church's practice according to its faith. Thus several of our commentators reflect on the duties of all Christians, who are themselves in need of God's grace, toward the poor. Such outward activity should reflect, in their view, the fact that life in Christ should bring about both internal and external transformation. Unsurprisingly, given many of our commentators' strong emphasis on a christological reading of the Psalms, some understand the reference to poverty in light of Christ's becoming poor and caring for the poor. In addition, they read David's anguish over a close friend who has eaten bread with him and now stands against him as a prophetic reference to Judas's betrayal of Jesus.

THIS PSALM PROPHESIES JUDAS'S TREACHERY.
NIKOLAUS SELNECKER: Some people have

expounded this psalm about good works—we have dealt with this above in Psalm 15.[1] About whom, however, this psalm should particularly be understood, Christ indicates in John 13. There he says of his betrayer Judas to his disciples: "The Scripture must be fulfilled. He who eats my bread tramples me with his feet." These words stand in this psalm. So also the end of the previous psalm indicates that Christ himself speaks here and laments his betrayer, Judas, as well as his compatriots by whom he will be crucified. And Christ prays that God would resurrect him from the dead and raise him up to his right hand. THE WHOLE PSALTER.[2]

THIS PSALM IS LITERALLY ABOUT CHRIST.
CARDINAL CAJETAN: Christ said that this

---

[1]See above, p. 113.
[2]Selnecker, Der gantze Psalter, 1:200r; citing Jn 13:18 (cf. Ps 41:9);
　Ps 40:11-17.

Scripture is fulfilled in Judas the traitor; consequently he made known that the context of this psalm treats his suffering. Therefore, according to the letter the subject matter of this psalm is the suffering of Christ for the human race as well as his resurrection. Commentary on Psalm 41.[3]

41:1-3 *The Lord Cares for and Cures the Sick*

Poverty and Providence. The English Annotations: This translation is defective. *Maśkîl* is not simply "one who considers" but "one who wisely considers." . . . Neither is it "that considers the poor," but *'el dāl,* "concerning the poor," that is (according to the best expositors), a person who does not rashly judge that he is poor and afflicted because he is wicked and hated by God. This (the sufferings and calamities of good and godly people in this world) is a mystery of God's providence, which those who do not understand are scandalized by, and they either conclude that there is no God or that those who are afflicted are not godly. But wise people make good use of it. For knowing by sense (through the sight of his works) that there is a God, and, if there is a God, then by common sense and reason, he must be a good and just God (which has been acknowledged by ordinary pagans and philosophers), then their faith of a future judgment and of another world after this is further confirmed because in this world they do not see the good or the bad fare according to their deserts and according to the dictates of ordinary justice and providence. Annotation on Psalm 41:1.[4]

Christ Identifies with the Poor. Martin Luther: The Hebrew does not have the word *needy*; it has only the word *poor*. And this addition does not take away one bit of the dignity and weight from the majesty of the statement. In

Zechariah 9, Christ is called poor. And all Christians are poor, according to Psalm 72, for only the poor have the gospel preached to them. And "blessed are the poor in spirit, for theirs is the kingdom of heaven." But we must not understand this as applying only to the internal act but also to the external, so that we act in public toward Christ and the poor as we feel and think inwardly. Otherwise such a person will be regarded as one who does not understand, and he will be the fool who says in his heart, there is no God. First Psalms Lectures (1513–1515).[5]

Our Charity Should Draw Beggars Out of Poverty. Andreas von Karlstadt: In short, then, let me say that I receive certain clues when I enter a city from seeing people running about for bread. It suggests that there are no Christians or else very few, dispirited ones. A change is needed, therefore, so that we do not act like those (hapless sophists) who open their hands when a needy person is in extreme need or on his last breath and is no longer aware of their help, when nothing can nourish or refresh him. These detestable people say that the Scripture passage "blessed is the one who considers the weak and the poor" is to be understood as meaning "blessed is the one who gives heed to the poor in his extreme and last hunger," that is, when he no longer suffers pangs of hunger, as if we were not obligated to prevent begging by gracious assistance and by forestalling the pangs of hunger.

I have said, and will continue to say without ceasing, that beggars are a sure indicator that there are no Christians, or else very few dispirited ones, in any town in which beggars are seen. In short, you may understand this as follows: beggars are those who must run from place to place looking for bread or who sit in the streets, in front of houses or churches, asking for bread. We should not tolerate having such people, but should rid ourselves of them—not in an unreasonable or despotic way, but

---

[3]Cajetan, *In Sacrae Scripturae Expositionem,* 3:149; citing Jn 13:18.
[4]Downame, ed., *Annotations,* 6E2r*. For more on *maśkîl,* see above, pp. 249-50.

[5]LW 10:190-91* (WA 3:231); citing Zech 9:9; Ps 72:2; Mt 11:5; 5:2; Ps 14:1.

by the giving of well-intentioned help. As Christians we are not to let anyone descend into such poverty and need that they are driven and forced to cry and search for bread. ON THE REMOVAL OF IMAGES. THAT THERE SHOULD BE NO BEGGARS AMONG CHRISTIANS.[6]

WE ARE IN THE HANDS OF GOD. WOLFGANG MUSCULUS: The grace of consolation must be noted, because although every affliction and sickness comes from the Lord, nothing less than this is ascribed to the Lord, that he guards and sustains his own people in tribulations sent by himself. What, I ask, is that guarding and sustaining? Namely, he preserves them, lest they forfeit their souls and perish; lest tribulation creep along more slowly than is suitable and useful. What else does this guarding and sustaining indicate than that every affliction of the godly is a sign of the affection of God, by which he instructs and chastises his own people? . . .

We see here that the desire of the ungodly is vain and useless, by which they seek the destruction of the godly, unless the Lord should give the godly into their hands. Therefore, all our salvation is in the hand of the Lord, just as destruction is also, and not in the hand of our enemies. In fact, we are also taught here that God does not give his own to the desire of their enemies themselves, however much they seem to lack any help of God in the eyes of the world. COMMENTARY ON THE PSALMS.[7]

GENERAL AFFLICTION, NOT JUST SICKNESS. JOHN CALVIN: What follows concerning the bed of sorrow has led some to form a conjecture, which, in my opinion, is not at all probable. What David says of affliction in general, without determining what kind of affliction, they regard as applicable exclusively to sickness. But it is no uncommon thing for those who are sorrowful and grieved in their minds to throw themselves on their bed and to seek

repose; for the hearts of human beings are sometimes more distressed by grief than by sickness. It is certainly highly probable that David was at that time afflicted with some very heavy calamity, which might be a token that God was not a little displeased with him. In the second clause of the verse there is some obscurity. Some understand the expression "turning the bed" in the same sense as if God, in order to give some alleviation to his servant in the time of trouble, had made his bed and arranged it, as we are wont to do to those who are sick that they may lay themselves more softly. Others hold, in my opinion more correctly, that when David was restored to health, his bed, which had formerly served him as a sick couch, was turned, that is to say, changed. This the sense would be that although he now languishes in sorrow while the Lord is chastening him and training him by means of affliction, yet in a little while he will experience relief by the hand of the same God and thus recover his strength. COMMENTARY ON THE PSALMS.[8]

41:4-10 *My Friends and Enemies Deride Me Because of My Illness*

THE LORD IS MOVED BY OUR CONFESSION. WOLFGANG MUSCULUS: The wonderful reason for obtaining health must be noted, in which he says, "because I have sinned against you." Who, I ask, so asks for a work of some powerful person, so that he should say, "Help me, for I have sinned against you"? Does not this reason, by the judgment of the world, result in a greater impediment to obtaining health? So what, therefore, does he mean? Does God love the sins of mortals so that he may be induced by them to well-doing? By no means! Rather, he loves the confession of sinners and the complaint of their evil deeds, which overtake the pious on account of their sins. From which it is also that infirmity of soul which the prophet prays is healed by the added confession of his sins. And thus we are taught in this place that above all things we acknowledge and deplore the infirmity of

---

[6]CRR 8:120-21*.
[7]Musculus, *In Psalterium Commentarii*, 525.

[8]CTS 9:116* (CO 31:419-20).

our souls which is due to sins, and having been humbled through confession of our failings before God, we would pray that it is cured. Indeed, let us deplore those things that have been neglected, either alone or in the presence of all, and seek to be cured of those things which afflict our bodies. COMMENTARY ON THE PSALMS.[9]

SHARED HATRED OF CHRIST. TILEMANN HESSHUS: Although the impious disagree among themselves about many things and are devoted to various and opposing religions—indeed, they contend among themselves with hatred and deceit, and they do not set aside these feelings, except for hope of profit or pleasure, or for violence—nevertheless they are like a monster in oppressing Christ and exterminating the church, his bride. Enticed by neither profit nor pleasure, nevertheless they easily come to agreement, stop all their conflicts, conspire, join together their plans and resources in order to obliterate this common enemy. Thus, the Pharisees and Sadducees—bitter enemies—conspired to destroy Christ. COMMENTARY ON PSALM 41.[10]

THE BITTERNESS OF BETRAYAL. VIKTORIN STRIGEL: Although Jacob has many enemies, nevertheless the most dangerous is his brother Esau, who by nature is closest to him and brought up by paternal instruction to the same profession and invocation of God and to the observance of all virtues. Thus because it is common to see in the church dissension between relatives and friends, our minds must be prepared and strengthened ahead of time so that we might bear wisely this enormous pain, which their bitterness creates, who were once very close to us. For it is arrogant for us not to be willing to endure those things which other, better people, endured, such as Abel, Isaac, Jacob, Joseph and others. *HYPONĒMATA* IN ALL THE PSALMS.[11]

CHRIST INTERPRETS THIS VERSE FOR US. SEBASTIAN MÜNSTER: "Man of my peace."[12] In John 13 Christ states that this verse has been fulfilled in him who, pretending to be a disciple, betrayed him to the Judeans and handed him over to death. But we have already often said that the prophet David in many ways prefigured Christ, as is clear above in Psalm 22. Now some Jews make this the end of the first book of Psalms. THE TEMPLE OF THE LORD: PSALM 41.[13]

DAVID TYPIFIES CHRIST'S COMING BETRAYAL. JOHN CALVIN: Christ, in quoting this passage, applies it to the person of Judas. And certainly we ought to understand that, although David speaks of himself in this psalm, yet he speaks not as a common and private person but as one who represented the person of Christ, inasmuch as he was, as it were, the example after which the whole church should be conformed. . . . Each of us should prepare himself for the same condition. It was necessary that what was begun in David should be fully accomplished in Christ. Therefore, it must of necessity come to pass that the same thing should be fulfilled in each of his members, namely, that they should suffer not only from external violence and force but also from internal foes, ever ready to betray them, even as Paul declares that the church shall be assailed not only by "fighting from without" but also by "fears within." COMMENTARY ON THE PSALMS.[14]

NEVERTHELESS THIS PSALM IS ABOUT CHRIST AND DAVID. RUDOLF GWALTHER: However, there is a great difference between the Lord Christ and David. For Christ experienced this not unknowingly, because he already knew Judas and never placed any hope on him. Thus, we should note that whenever several phrases of the psalms, on account of figures and images, are to be

---

[9]Musculus, *In Psalterium Commentarii*, 517.
[10]Hesshus, *Commentarius in Psalmos*, 190r.
[11]Strigel, *Hyponēmata*, 206-7.
[12]Münster, like other reformers, here renders the Hebrew literally: *ʾiš šělōmî*. Kraus and Goldingay flesh out how intimate this phrase is; see Kraus, *Psalms 1–59*, 432; Goldingay, *Psalms*, 1:586.
[13]Münster, *Miqdaš YHWH*, 1194.
[14]CTS 9:122* (CO 31:422); citing Jn 13:18; 2 Cor 7:5.

pointed to Christ, we should not therefore force the entire psalm onto him. THE PSALTER.[15]

ON REVENGE. THE ENGLISH ANNOTATIONS: This open profession of David's intended revenge has troubled interpreters, both Jewish and Christian. While Jewish interpreters for the most part allow revenge and even think of it as a virtue, they are troubled in reconciling these words with those of Psalm 7:4. They have devised many ways of reconciliation, avoiding the literal sense and saying that I may render to them good for evil, which indeed may be deemed a good and godly way of revenge commended to us, nay commanded, by Christ and his apostles, and even some ancient heathens approved of this. I found some very learned Christian expositors willing to embrace this sense, yet as one may see by their words, it is their good will rather than their good judgment that leads them. . . . I must profess against this interpretation. The tenor of the words is against it, and objections may be raised from other places in the psalms as well as in the content of other interpreters. . . . So that neither Jews nor Christians need to take offense at these words, we can say that David speaks as a king and not a private man. But it is added that he also speaks as a prophet, by a particular warrant from God himself. And following this, it must be added that while private revenge was denounced and forbidden by the old law, . . . it is not so clearly and generally forbidden to us as Christians by Christ our lawgiver. As we have no reason therefore to expect such preciseness of words in this case from those that lived under the law, so neither can we draw any conclusions from their examples, if they offer themselves to us, that can justify us or excuse us against the clear dictates and decisions of the gospel, without doing great injury to the name whereby we are called, and for which, if we rightly understand the worth of it, nothing should be hard or grievous to us. ANNOTATION ON PSALM 41:10.[16]

41:11-13 *Blessed Be the Lord God*

GOD NEVER FORGETS. JOHN CALVIN: By these words, then, he bears testimony to his patience, because, when sorely vexed and tormented, he had not forsaken the path of uprightness. If this meaning should be adopted, it must be observed that this benefit, namely, that David continued invincible and boldly sustained these assaults of temptation, is immediately after ascribed to God, and that for the future, David looked for preservation by no other means than by the sustaining power of God. If the language should be understood as referring to his external condition, this will be found to suit equally well the scope of the passage, and the meaning will be this: that God will never cease to manifest his favor until he has preserved his servants in safety, even to the end. As to the form of expression, that God establishes them before his face, this is said of those whom he defends and preserves in such a manner that he shows by evident tokens the paternal care which he exercises over them; as, on the other hand, when he seems to have forgotten his own people, he is said to hide his face from them. COMMENTARY ON THE PSALMS.[17]

WHY DOES DAVID SAY "AMEN" TWICE? RUDOLF GWALTHER: "Amen" means as much as "truthfully" and "firmly" or "surely." Now with the repetition of this little word he intends us to understand the heartfelt longing which he has toward God's honor, which he wants to increase and lift up. THE PSALTER.[18]

THE END OF BOOK ONE. THE ENGLISH ANNOTATIONS: Here ends the first book of the Psalms. Of these divisions see above on Psalm 1. Some take no notice of it. Others do, who—like [Franciscus] Junius, Bucer—prefix a new title before the next psalm, "The Second Book of Psalms," and also after Psalm 72, "The Third Book

---

[15]Gwalther, *Der Psalter*, 72v.
[16]Downame, ed., *Annotations*, 6E2r*.
[17]CTS 9:126* (CO 31:424).
[18]Gwalther, *Der Psalter*, 72v.

of Psalms." The word *amen* at the end of the prayers—as of blessings and curses, Numbers 5:22 and elsewhere—implies a concurrence of wishes and affections and is also an expression of confidence that it shall come to pass accordingly. Twice repeated, as here, it makes the speech more emotional. But at the beginning of sentences, as Matthew 24:47 and elsewhere, it stands for an asseveration and is as much as "verily, verily." ANNOTATIONS ON PSALM 41:13.[19]

---

[19]Downame, ed., *Annotations*, 6E2r-v*.

42:1-11 WHY ARE YOU CAST DOWN, O MY SOUL?

To the choirmaster. A Maskil[a] of the Sons of Korah.

[1] As a deer pants for flowing streams,
  so pants my soul for you, O God.
[2] My soul thirsts for God,
  for the living God.
  When shall I come and appear before God?[b]
[3] My tears have been my food
  day and night,
while they say to me all the day long,
  "Where is your God?"
[4] These things I remember,
  as I pour out my soul:
how I would go with the throng
  and lead them in procession to the house of
    God
with glad shouts and songs of praise,
  a multitude keeping festival.

[5] Why are you cast down, O my soul,
  and why are you in turmoil within me?
Hope in God; for I shall again praise him,
  my salvation[c] [6] and my God.

My soul is cast down within me;
  therefore I remember you
from the land of Jordan and of Hermon,
  from Mount Mizar.
[7] Deep calls to deep
  at the roar of your waterfalls;
all your breakers and your waves
  have gone over me.
[8] By day the LORD commands his steadfast love,
and at night his song is with me,
  a prayer to the God of my life.
[9] I say to God, my rock:
  "Why have you forgotten me?
Why do I go mourning
  because of the oppression of the enemy?"
[10] As with a deadly wound in my bones,
  my adversaries taunt me,
while they say to me all the day long,
  "Where is your God?"
[11] Why are you cast down, O my soul,
  and why are you in turmoil within me?
Hope in God; for I shall again praise him,
  my salvation and my God.

a Probably a musical or liturgical term   b Revocalization yields *and see the face of God*   c Hebrew *the salvation of my face*; also verse 11 and 43:5

OVERVIEW: The image of a deer yearning to quench its thirst points to the psalmist's desire to be in God's presence, for he seems to be in exile, separated from the people of God and therefore from the cultic life of the temple. According to these reformers, this image points to humanity's thirst and hunger for God's grace and righteousness. It also affirms the importance of the church in the Christian life, for it is within the community of faith that Christians are encouraged and nourished in the faith by listening to the Word of God and receiving the sacraments. Rather than viewing the psalmist's repeated plea in the midst of suffering as problematic, they interpret it as a Spirit-led petition of God, who alone can bring peace to such turmoil and who alone can fulfill the hope for salvation. Regarding more technical matters, our commentators disagree whether the psalms with "sons of Korah" in the superscription were composed by them or for them by David.

WORD AND SACRAMENT MINISTRY IS IMPERATIVE FOR HUMAN BEINGS. THEODORE BEZA: This psalm exhibits a singular example of true faith united with an extraordinary zeal for piety. For David testifies—as an exile, deprived not only of his honor but also surrounded by his most cruel enemies who sought to murder him—that nevertheless his soul did not despair in the least. He then says that he considers nothing else as so great a loss compared with this one thing, that although he had been accustomed to enter the tabernacle before others, now he was forced to go without those aids of faith prescribed by God. For that most holy man understood that although he had God present with him wherever he had gone and had succeeded in the knowledge of God and his office as no one else had before, nevertheless there is the greatest benefit in the public and sacred assemblies, and there is not one person who does not need to hear the Word and receive the sacraments. Therefore, mark this, especially those who, because they think themselves wise enough, wantonly despise the holy assemblies and sacraments, and even more so those who for the benefit of transitory things ward off the sacrifice of the holy ministry, and finally those who prefer to lie in the filth of idolatry rather than to attend church. PARAPHRASE OF PSALM 42.[1]

Superscription: *The Sons of Korah*

WHO WERE THE SONS OF KORAH? MARTIN LUTHER: After the destruction of their father, as recorded in Numbers 16, who was of the tribe of Levi and the house of Kohath, related to Moses and Aaron, the sons of Korah were excellent and outstanding prophets, and they composed some very excellent psalms, as will become clear below, and these were almost always songs and instructions [*maśkillim*]. FIRST PSALMS LECTURES (1513–1515).[2]

SEE AUGUSTINE'S DISCUSSION OF KORAH. FELIX PRATENSIS: The title of this psalm or the last word of the title, namely, "Korah," I think, requires not very much explanation—especially among those who carefully study Augustine's exposition of the Psalms.[3] Of course, I do not wish to hide from

you that this name means either "baldness" or "crystal" or "ice." THE HEBREW PSALTER.[4]

MYSTICAL INTERPRETATIONS OF "KORAH." MARTIN LUTHER: In a mystical sense Korah is interpreted as "baldhead" or "baldness," and it denotes the synagogue which was short of the priesthood and the kingdom, as Isaiah prophesied: "Instead of curled hair there will be baldness," that is, instead of the chosen princes, leaders and priests. . . . The apostles are sons of this baldness, because the synagogue came down and was swallowed up alive in the earth, that is, they perished in the dead letter and earthly wisdom. In the same manner the apostles are also called the sons of those who have been shaken, according to Psalm 127, because the synagogue was shaken and swallowed up.

However, others, like Jerome and Augustine, interpret mystically in this way, that the bald one is Christ, because he was crucified on Mount Calvary.[5] Therefore the sons of Korah are all Christians, children of their father Christ. But tropologically all saints—that is, the poor in spirit—should be bald, for luxuriant hair signifies the craving for riches and other pleasures that are fleeting, transitory and temporary. FIRST PSALMS LECTURES (1513–1515).[6]

REVELATION OF HIDDEN MATTERS. CARDINAL CAJETAN: The sense of the title is that this psalm understands secret things; it is attributed to the sons of Korah as revelation that happened to them—at least as singers. For the sons of Korah not only were doorkeepers, as it is said in 1 Chronicles 26, but also singers, as 2 Chronicles 20 shows. COMMENTARY ON PSALM 42.[7]

SONGS ARE COMPOSED BY ONE AUTHOR. RUDOLF GWALTHER: The children of Korah were singers whom David had ordained for the worship of God; he prepared several psalms especially for

[1]Beza, *Psalmes of Dauid*, 86* (*Psalmorum Davidis*, 172).
[2]LW 10:194* (WA 3:235). On *maśkil*, see above, pp. 249-50.
[3]Augustine understands "Korah" as the Hebrew for *Calvaria*; see NPNF 8:132.
[4]Pratensis, *Psalterium*, 22r.
[5]See NPNF 8:132.
[6]LW 10:194* (WA 3:235-36); citing Is 3:24; 7:20; Mic 1:16; Ps 127:4.
[7]Cajetan, *In Sacrae Scripturae Expositionem*, 3:152; citing 1 Chron 26:1-19; 2 Chron 20:19.

them. Some claim that these children of Korah composed this psalm in David's name. But it does not make sense that so many people should compose a psalm together. THE PSALTER.[8]

DAVID WROTE THIS PSALM. JOHN CALVIN: The name of David is not expressly mentioned in the inscription of this psalm. Many conjecture that the sons of Korah were the authors of it. This, I think, is not at all probable. As it is composed in the person of David, who, it is well known, was endued above all others with the spirit of prophecy, who will believe that it was written and composed for him by another person? He was the teacher generally of the whole church and a distinguished instrument of the Spirit. He had already delivered to the company of the Levites, of whom the sons of Korah formed a part, other psalms to be sung by them. What need, then, had he to borrow their help or to have recourse to their assistance in a matter which he was much better able of himself to execute than they were? To me, therefore, it seems more probable that the sons of Korah are here mentioned because this psalm was committed as a precious treasure to be preserved by them, as we know that out of the number of the singers, some were chosen and appointed to be keepers of the psalms. That there is no mention made of David's name does not of itself involve any difficulty, because we see the same omission in other psalms, of which there is, notwithstanding, the strongest grounds for concluding that he was the author. COMMENTARY ON THE PSALMS.[9]

42:1-4 *Longing, Thirsting, Hungering for God's Presence*

THE UNITED VOICE OF CHRIST AND THE CHURCH. MARTIN LUTHER: Because the voice of Christ and the church is one, therefore it is also

possible to understand this, in the person of the church, about those who pray to Christ. And perhaps this understanding about Christ is better as well as easier. Therefore we accept it about the church, and it can likewise be expounded about any believer. GLOSSA ON PSALM 42 (1513–1515).[10]

DAVID EXCLUDED FROM EXTERNAL WORSHIP. JOHN CALVIN: The meaning of the first two verses is simply that David preferred over all worldly enjoyment, riches, pleasures and honors the opportunity to access the sanctuary, so that in this way he might cherish and strengthen his faith and piety by the exercise prescribed in the law. When he says that he cried for the living God, we are not to understand it merely in the sense of a burning love and desire toward God; rather, we should remember how God allures us to himself and by what means he raises our minds upward. He does not demand that we ascend straight into heaven, but, consulting our weakness, he descends to us. David, then, considering that the way of access was shut against him, cried to God, because he was excluded from the outward service of the sanctuary, which is the sacred bond of communion with God. I do not mean to say that the observance of external ceremonies can of itself bring us into favor with God, but they are religious exercises which we cannot bear to miss by reason of our infirmity. David, therefore, being excluded from the sanctuary, is no less grieved than if he had been separated from God himself. He did not, it is true, cease in the meantime to direct his prayers toward heaven, and even to the sanctuary itself; but conscious of his own infirmity, he was specially grieved that the way by which the faithful obtained access to God was shut against him. This is an example which may well suffice to put to shame the arrogance of those who without concern can bear to be deprived of those means, or rather, who proudly despise them, as if it were in their power to ascend to heaven in a moment's flight, yes, even as if they surpassed David in zeal

[8]Gwalther, *Der Psalter*, 74r.
[9]CTS 9:127* (CO 31:425). Musculus and Amyraut agree with Calvin about Davidic authorship; see Musculus, *In Psalterium Commentarii*, 528; Amyraut, *Paraphrasis in Psalmos Davidis*, 180-81.
[10]WA 3:232-33.

and alacrity of mind. COMMENTARY ON THE PSALMS.[11]

WITHOUT THE GRACE OF GOD HUMAN BEINGS ARE WITHERED AND DEAD. ROBERT ROLLOCK: By nature all human beings ... are dry and withered, burned up by that fire of sin and the wrath of God. But few feel their drought whereby it comes to pass that few are moved with the thirst of grace. For no human being is thoroughly touched with the thirst of the grace of God unless God first by his Spirit has provoked him, especially by the preaching of the law. But now, when once it is provoked, except new grace follow on, whereby the thirsty are continually led forward to that pure fountain of the water of life, Jesus Christ, presently they will seek to themselves foul puddles. And for clean and living water, they will drink in filthy and stinking waters, for the only merit of Jesus Christ and his blood, they will drink up the merits of human beings, and such poisons which the papists this day offer to miserable people. EXPOSITION UPON PSALM 42.[12]

A TRINITARIAN WELLSPRING. MARTIN LUTHER:

	God:	the Father
"The mighty,[13] living God" is three fountains of water	Mighty:	the Son
	Living:	the Holy Spirit

GLOSSA ON PSALM 42 (1513–1515).[14]

HUNGER AND THIRST FOR RIGHTEOUSNESS! DIRK PHILIPS: This sweetness and power of the true heavenly bread no one can taste except one who hungers and thirsts after righteousness and says with David, "As the deer longs for fresh water, so my soul thirsts for you, O God; my soul thirsts for the living God." ... Whoever is now thirsty for

the living God, hungry for the bread of heaven and desirous for the water of life, they shall without doubt be well satisfied, as Christ said, "Blessed are those who hunger and thirst for righteousness, for they shall be satisfied." ... These are now those who believe in Jesus Christ, who live by every word that goes out of the mouth of God and are nourished with the bread of heaven. Here these shall not lack the food of life and hereafter shall be eternally satisfied, as God shall be all in all.

Contrary to this, those who have now tasted the sweetness of the divine Word and the power of the coming world and have received the Holy Spirit and again turn away and sin willfully, according to the known and accepted truth, despise Christ and his Word out of pride—these may not, according to the word of the apostle, be renewed through repentance. For they themselves have crucified the Son of God and made mockery of it. Yes, they trample the Son of God with their feet and regard the blood of the covenant through which they are sanctified as impure, and outrage the Spirit of grace. Therefore, no sacrifice is left for their sins, but a strong and fearful fire is prepared for them which shall consume the adversary, that is, those who set themselves against Christ and his Word, "for our God is a consuming fire." THE ENCHIRIDION: CONCERNING THE TRUE KNOWLEDGE OF JESUS CHRIST.[15]

42:5-10 "Why Are You Cast Down, O My Soul?"

REFUGE IN GOD. JOHN CALVIN: We ought to learn from this that although we are deprived of the helps which God has appointed for the edification of our faith and piety, it is nevertheless our duty to be diligent in stirring up our minds, that we may never suffer ourselves to be forgetful of God. But, above all, this is to be observed, that as in the preceding verse we have seen David contending courageously against his own affections, so now we

---

[11]CTS 9:128-29* (CO 31:426).
[12]Rollock, *Exposition upon Some Psalmes*, 231-32*.
[13]The Hebrew is *lēʾlōhîm lēʾel ḥāi*; as he does elsewhere (e.g., Is 9:6) Luther has rendered *ʾel* as "mighty" (*fortem*).
[14]WA 3:233.

[15]CRR 6:168-69* (BRN 10:173-74); citing Ps 42:1-2; 63:1; Mt 5:6; Jn 6:35; Rev 7:14-17; Mt 4:4; 1 Cor 15:28; Heb 6:5-6; 10:29, 27-28.

here see by what means he steadfastly maintained his ground. He did this by having recourse to the help of God and taking refuge in it as in a holy sanctuary. And, assuredly, if meditation on the promises of God does not lead us to prayer, it will not have sufficient power to sustain and confirm us. Unless God imparts strength to us, how shall we be able to subdue the many evil thoughts which constantly arise in our minds? The human soul serves the purpose, as it were, of a workshop of Satan in which to forge a thousand methods of despair. And, therefore, it is not without reason that David, after a severe conflict with himself, has recourse to prayer and calls on God as the witness of his sorrow. COMMENTARY ON THE PSALMS.[16]

DAVID CRIES OUT TO GOD HIS FATHER.

ROBERT ROLLOCK: As he had first turned himself to his soul, now he turns himself to his God, and he lifts up his eyes and sighs, as it were, to him, opening up to him the sorrow of his soul. And he pours out his carefulness and solicitude on his bosom. Whosoever is endued with the Holy Spirit, will, as this man, sigh to God in his affliction and sorrow. But he who is endued with a human spirit only, that person will never sigh to God, for he supposes God to be angry with him, especially when there lies any affliction on him. For he thinks that this whole misery proceeds from the wrath of God. But he who has the Spirit of God, that Spirit of adoption by whom we cry, "Abba, Father," this person comes without fear to God, because indeed that Spirit is always with some feeling of God's mercy and fatherly love. Wherefore as a son who has his father well-willing to him, in his sorrow, he takes his way straight to his father. Even so the child of God passes in his sorrow and misery to God his Father, and makes his complaint to him. EXPOSITION UPON PSALM 42.[17]

SEAS OF EVIL. MARTIN BUCER: He compares the present calamity, which was continuously piling up,

to the prior blessedness which he had enjoyed also on other occasions, but chiefly in the holy festivals. For he counted it his highest joy to see the preaching of God filled and passionate with reverence. Now there was a calamity that was in its own right the very greatest, and not of the sort he had experienced before, namely, that he should be most miserably cast out from the kingdom so miraculously majestic and peaceful and be shamefully banished from the royal city, into which he had transferred the tabernacle of the covenant with such great pomp, where he had most splendidly established all things not only of religion but also of the kingdom. In addition to these problems, there was no safe place to flee, with a meager band of soldiers which would escort him while he was fleeing. Meanwhile his most beloved wives were bedded in the whole sight of Israel as a certain sign that he had been thoroughly rejected by God, and that was believed to such an extent that he was thrown out by the whole people. Besides, he did not suffer these things from foreigners but specifically from his own beloved son, and therefore by the force of the entire kingdom, for the peace and safety of which he had suffered such great dangers. Likewise, he suffered by the counsels of those who were of first authority in the kingdom. Finally he suffered the insults most impudently given by any of the most wicked persons. And after all these things, when this great enemy had been destroyed and the people now desired to take back their king, another son of Belial, the author of a new rebellion, was stirred up. These things were as if the sluice gates of heaven were opened, as if certain seas of evil in vast waves and storms flooded him, tossed him about and vexed him, and led him near to death. HOLY PSALMS.[18]

A METAPHOR OF DEEP DISTRESS. JOHN

CALVIN: These words express the grievousness, as well as the number and long continuance, of the miseries which he suffered; as if he had said, I am oppressed not only with one kind of misery, but

---

[16]CTS 9:137* (CO 31:430).
[17]Rollock, *Exposition upon Some Psalmes*, 246-48*.
[18]Bucer, *Sacrorum Psalmorum*, 206r-v.

various kinds of distress return one after another, so that there seems to be neither end nor measure to them. In the first place, by the term *depth*, he shows that the temptations by which he was assailed were such that they might well be compared with gulfs in the sea; then he complains of their long continuance, which he describes by the very appropriate figure, that his temptations cry out from a distance and call to one another. In the second part of the verse, he continues the same metaphor, when he says that "all the waves and floods of God have passed over his head." By this he means that he had been over-whelmed, and as it were swallowed up by the accumulation of afflictions. It ought, however, to be observed, that he designates the cruelty of Saul and his other enemies "floods of God," that in all our adversities we may always remember to humble ourselves under the mighty hand of God which afflicts us. But it is of importance to go beyond this and to consider that if it should please God to rain with violence on us, as soon as he shall have opened his sluices or "waterspouts," there will be no termination to our miseries till he is appeased; for he has in his power means marvelous and unknown for executing his vengeance against us. Thus, when once his anger is kindled against us, there will be not only one depth to swallow us up, but depth will call to depth. And as the insensibility of people is such that they do not stand in awe of the threaten-ings of God, to the degree in which they ought, whenever mention is made of his vengeance, let us recall this verse to our recollection. COMMENTARY ON THE PSALMS.[19]

GOD'S MERCY IS GREATER THAN OUR MISERY. GIROLAMO SAVONAROLA:

Deep calls to deep: The deep of misery calls to the deep of mercy; the deep of transgression calls to the deep of grace. Greater is the deep of mercy than the deep of misery. Therefore let deep swallow deep. Let the deep of mercy swallow up the deep of misery. AN EXPOSITION OF THE PSALM *MISERERE*.[20]

THE NOISE OF THE WATERSPOUTS. THE ENGLISH ANNOTATIONS:

By waterspouts, or cataracts, David understands the clouds, from which (at such times) water falls on the earth with such violence and precipitancy as it runs from great waterspouts and sluices, where the current is strong of itself, and the fall great. By "noise" the cracks of thunder are intended, which break forth out of the clouds and are usually followed by fierce and mighty showers. ANNOTATION ON PSALM 42:7.[21]

LORD, CONTROL AND CONSOLE US DAY AND NIGHT. NIKOLAUS SELNECKER:

"By day you allow your goodness to be proclaimed and promised," that is, at the time of grace you allow your lovingkindness to be revealed. I should console myself and others with this truth, and let myself depend on it when it is night, that is, when tribulation, crossbearing and floods come. For "it is a precious thing to thank the Lord and to sing praises to your name, you, O Most High, and to proclaim your mercy in the morning and your truth in the night" (Ps 92). In short, day or morning means consolation and mercy, life and salvation; the night, however, means crossbearing and suffering, in which we should remember the promises of God and should cry out to our living God and pray with David: "Lord God, my rock, why have you forgotten me? Be merciful to me, do not let me be put to shame, nor to die in my time of need." . . .

This prayer we should also contemplate well in our time, when the pious, in various ways, are hated, persecuted and despised; they must suffer much crossbearing and misery, hunger, poverty, sickness, hatred and sorrow. Blessed are they who do not stumble but persevere to the end! May God help us accomplish this, and may he rule and sustain us in this confessed and acknowl-edged truth until our last sigh. Amen. THE WHOLE PSALTER.[22]

---

[19]CTS 9:138-39* (CO 31:431).
[20]Savonarola, *An Exposition of the Psalm Miserere Mei Deus*, 8*.
[21]Downame, ed., *Annotations*, 6E2v*.
[22]Selnecker, *Der gantze Psalter*, 1:206r; citing Ps 92:1-2.

WOUNDED BONES. VIKTORIN STRIGEL: Fierce temptations suck out the marrow of the bones. Therefore, it is not without good reason that these temptations are compared with a band of robbers lying in ambush in the very marrow of the bones. Those mentioned here, moreover, are the most bitter of temptations. One has to do with the forgetfulness of God: "Why did you forget me?" The other concerns God's desertion: "Where is your God?" For when the heart grieves, imagining that it is being neglected by God, the ears resound with the blasphemous shouts of the enemies: "Where is your God? Where is your fortress and your protection?" But what Paul said is very true, which I cited above in the summary: "We are tormented in our spirit, but we are not disheartened; we are shaken, but we do not perish." Therefore, there is soon added the happy exclamation of one emerging victoriously from the waves of fear and trepidation. HYPONĒMATA IN ALL THE PSALMS.[23]

42:11 Hope in the Lord!

THE CAST-DOWN SOUL. CARDINAL CAJETAN: Then at length he apostrophizes again to his own soul: "Why are you disturbed, my soul?" And again the verses from above are repeated, but with three important differences. The first is that here the interrogative "why" is reiterated: "And why are you troubled within me?" And this has the effect of intensifying the rebuke of his soul. The second is that here the pronoun "my" is used: "the deliverance of *my* countenance"; in the previous verse he says, "the deliverance of *his* countenance." He does this so that you understand that he will proclaim the well-being and security both of the divine presence, that is, its presence in the house of God, and of his own presence in the house of God. In this there seems to be an indication that he himself will see these two instances of deliverance. And also he is showing that there is not much difference between the two. And truly, as has been

said, many of those who had seen the earlier temple were present for the foundation of the second temple. And the third is that here is added "and my God," as an expression of worship.

Recall and notice that in this psalm the prophet is speaking in the persona of a dispersed people, and for this reason, when he turns and addresses his own soul, it seems that the passage is metaphorical, that is to say, just as in the case of a singular individual, a person, according to his higher part, namely, his mind, strengthens himself in regard to his lower part (which the term *soul* denotes based on its function of animating the body, and which is indicated by the fact that it looks to the lower functions), so in one people, as if in one mystically joined body, the higher part, which is wiser in the matters of God, strengthens the weaker part, whose wisdom lies in matters of the carnal disposition. And in accord with this comparison, we understand that this psalm is spoken by the people in the persona of spiritual individuals who are thinking about and expecting with a steady hope the arrival into Jerusalem, desiring it with the utmost eagerness: such as were Daniel, Zechariah, Haggai, and so on. And these are induced to strengthen the weak, those who possess less hope and murmur more. And so that you might understand that these were strengthened through coaxing, he describes them as ones called "my soul" by the higher parts. COMMENTARY ON PSALM 42.[24]

THIS PSALM IS OURS IN FAITH. PHILIPP MELANCHTHON: To this extent, insofar as we display the sort of sorrows that David endures and how he consoles himself, then these things are not written for his sake alone but also for ours. Many in the church have enormous sorrows—some more, some less severe. Also let us all learn that the will of God is that we would not succumb to such sorrows but that we rouse ourselves in faith and hope. And it is necessary to lean on this faith and hope, not on our righteousness or dignity, but

---

[23]Strigel, *Hyponēmata*, 211.

[24]Cajetan, *In Sacrae Scripturae Expositionem*, 3:154.

on the mercy of God alone revealed in the promises. Even when the most sorrowful waves crash on us so that we are terrified at the sight of our sins and of the wrath of God, and we fear being eternally cast away, yet let us rouse ourselves by this expression in which David here sustains himself: "Hope in God." You should not faint from God but believe that by his mercy on account of the Son, the Mediator, you are truly received by God, even if you do not bring any merits. Thus, this thought must be accommodated to the doctrine concerning the righteousness of faith. Comments on the Psalms.[25]

---

[25]MO 13:1087-88.

43:1-5 SEND OUT YOUR LIGHT AND TRUTH

¹ Vindicate me, O God, and defend my cause
  against an ungodly people,
from the deceitful and unjust man
  deliver me!
² For you are the God in whom I take refuge;
  why have you rejected me?
Why do I go about mourning
  because of the oppression of the enemy?

³ Send out your light and your truth;
  let them lead me;

let them bring me to your holy hill
  and to your dwelling!
⁴ Then I will go to the altar of God,
  to God my exceeding joy,
and I will praise you with the lyre,
  O God, my God.

⁵ Why are you cast down, O my soul,
  and why are you in turmoil within me?
Hope in God; for I shall again praise him,
  my salvation and my God.

OVERVIEW: This psalm of lament is today recognized as having been originally joined with Psalm 42 as one psalm, evidenced in features such as the repeated refrain, "Why are you cast down, O my soul, and why are you in turmoil within me? Hope in God; for I shall again praise him, my salvation and my God." Our commentators also recognize a relationship between the two psalms, but based on subject matter rather than literary details. The psalmist's cry, "Send out your light and truth," elicits pastoral reflection from our interpreters: the Lord illuminates believers' lives through his Word. Without this illumination we are in utter darkness. God's Word purely taught consoles the afflicted, brings blessing and salvation to the miserable and dispels the darkness. For the reformers, our unbelief and discouragement must be overcome by Scripture's logic.

THIS PSALM IS FOCUSED AND SIMPLE. SEBASTIAN MÜNSTER: This psalm has an argument no different from the one before it, when the prophet protests the injustice which he suffered from his people—cast out of the temple and the holy city. Some think that this psalm, just like the one before it, was composed during David's flight from Absalom. THE TEMPLE OF THE LORD: PSALM 43.[1]

THIS PSALM CONTINUES PSALM 42. NIKOLAUS SELNECKER: This psalm is connected to the previous psalm with regard to words and subject and explains these words: "In the night I sing and pray to the God of my life." What and how he prays stand here, namely, that God himself would be his judge and would sustain the right cause or teaching against the godless, so that the true light and truth would remain and constantly shine in the house of God. That is, that God's Word would always be rightly and purely taught. Through this the miserable are consoled and refreshed. They praise and thank God. They are joyful and of good cheer in God, and they stand firm against all misfortune that comes their way. THE WHOLE PSALTER.[2]

43:1-5 Hope in God

LIGHT AND TRUTH. JOHN CALVIN: The term *light* is to be understood as denoting favor; for as adversities not only obscure the face of God but also overcast the heavens, as it were, with clouds and fogs, so also, when we enjoy the divine blessing which makes us rich, it is like the cheerful light of a serene day shining around us; or rather the light of life, dispelling all that thick obscurity which

---

[1]Münster, *Miqdaš YHWH*, 1195.

[2]Selnecker, *Der gantze Psalter*, 1:206v; citing Ps 42:9; 33:17-19.

overwhelmed us in sorrow. By this word the psalmist intimates two things. First, all our miseries arise from no other source than this: God withdraws from us the tokens of his fatherly love. And, second, as soon as he is pleased to manifest toward us his serene and gracious countenance, deliverance and salvation also arise to us. He adds truth, because he expected this light only from the promises of God. The unbelieving desire the favor of God, but they do not raise their eyes to his light; for the natural disposition of human beings always tends toward the earth, unless their mind and all their feelings are raised up on high by the Word of God. In order, then, to encourage himself in the hope of obtaining the grace of God, David rests with confidence in this, that God, who is true and cannot deceive any, has promised to assist his servants.

We must therefore explain the sentence thus: Send forth your light, that it may be a token and testimony of your truth, or that it may really and effectually prove that you are faithful and free from all deceit in your promises. The knowledge of the divine favor, it is true, must be sought for in the Word of God; nor has faith any other foundation on which it can rest with security except his Word; but when God stretches out his hand to help us,

the experience of this is no small confirmation both of the Word and of faith. COMMENTARY ON THE PSALMS.[3]

WRESTLE DOUBTS FROM GOD'S PERSPECTIVE. DAVID DICKSON: To argue unbelief to the door and to dispute ourselves out of the dumps by reasons taken from the Lord's Word is a sanctifying means for wrestling out discouragement. It takes wisdom to get the conscience to be our friend, and when it is the case that the mind and the heart are in the wrong temper, it is necessary to take God's part against doubt and unwarrantable disquiet and to dispute both his cause and our own against temptation. COMMENTARY ON PSALM 43:5.[4]

BE OUR BULWARK, O LORD! THE BOOK OF COMMON PRAYER (1549): We beseech you, almighty God, look on the heartfelt desires of your humble servants and stretch forth the right hand of your majesty, to be our defense against all our enemies: Through Jesus Christ our Lord. Amen. COLLECT FOR THE THIRD SUNDAY IN LENT.[5]

---

[3]CTS 9:145-46* (CO 31:434-35).
[4]Dickson, *First Fifty Psalms*, 290*.
[5]BCP 1549, 50*.

44:1-26 COME TO OUR HELP

To the choirmaster. A Maskil[a] of the Sons of Korah.

[1] O God, we have heard with our ears,
  our fathers have told us,
what deeds you performed in their days,
  in the days of old:
[2] you with your own hand drove out the nations,
  but them you planted;
you afflicted the peoples,
  but them you set free;
[3] for not by their own sword did they win the land,
  nor did their own arm save them,
but your right hand and your arm,
and the light of your face,
  for you delighted in them.

[4] You are my King, O God;
  ordain salvation for Jacob!
[5] Through you we push down our foes;
  through your name we tread down those
    who rise up against us.
[6] For not in my bow do I trust,
  nor can my sword save me.
[7] But you have saved us from our foes
  and have put to shame those who hate us.
[8] In God we have boasted continually,
  and we will give thanks to your name
    forever.   Selah

[9] But you have rejected us and disgraced us
  and have not gone out with our armies.
[10] You have made us turn back from the foe,
  and those who hate us have gotten spoil.
[11] You have made us like sheep for slaughter

and have scattered us among the nations.
[12] You have sold your people for a trifle,
  demanding no high price for them.
[13] You have made us the taunt of our neighbors,
  the derision and scorn of those around us.
[14] You have made us a byword among the nations,
  a laughingstock[b] among the peoples.
[15] All day long my disgrace is before me,
  and shame has covered my face
[16] at the sound of the taunter and reviler,
  at the sight of the enemy and the avenger.

[17] All this has come upon us,
though we have not forgotten you,
  and we have not been false to your covenant.
[18] Our heart has not turned back,
  nor have our steps departed from your way;
[19] yet you have broken us in the place of jackals
  and covered us with the shadow of death.
[20] If we had forgotten the name of our God
  or spread out our hands to a foreign god,
[21] would not God discover this?
  For he knows the secrets of the heart.
[22] Yet for your sake we are killed all the day long;
  we are regarded as sheep to be slaughtered.

[23] Awake! Why are you sleeping, O Lord?
  Rouse yourself! Do not reject us forever!
[24] Why do you hide your face?
  Why do you forget our affliction and
    oppression?
[25] For our soul is bowed down to the dust;
  our belly clings to the ground.
[26] Rise up; come to our help!
  Redeem us for the sake of your steadfast love!

a Probably a musical or liturgical term   b Hebrew *a shaking of the head*

OVERVIEW: The psalmist rehearses the victories of God over Israel's enemies in days of old and in days not long past. Yet, despite Israel's faithfulness, God seems to have now abandoned his people to defeat by the nations. Now, like sheep being led to the slaughter, they call on God to awaken, rise up and come to their aid. Münster, appealing to Paul, sets the hermeneutical tone in seeing the psalm as speaking of Christians, true Israelites. The appeal to God's former acts for his covenant people reminds these interpreters of God's eternal covenant across the generations; God will act in accordance with this promise. Trust and wait patiently on him. The source of trouble, whether we brought it on ourselves or it is the work of the devil, is under the sovereignty of God. We should use it as an opportunity to meditate on his providence and judgment and continue to serve him. Nevertheless, with the psalmist, the reformers invite us to unburden our hearts before God, to purge ourselves of fleshly sentiments so that we would reflect untarnished and true faith.

CONTEMPORARY JEWS UNDERSTAND THIS PSALM ABOUT THEM. NIKOLAUS SELNECKER: The Jews exegete this psalm concerning their miserable situation and imprisonment in which they are now; they do not have a certain place or dwelling in the entire world. But such exegesis is false, because they cannot say the following words truthfully: "All this has come over us, but we have not forgotten your works nor have we acted unfaithfully in your covenant or testament." Yes, these words are very much against the Jews, who have acted so unfaithfully with the testament of Christ Jesus, the Son of God. THE WHOLE PSALTER.[1]

PAUL TEACHES US THIS PSALM'S INTERPRETATION. SEBASTIAN MÜNSTER: Blessed Paul teaches in Romans 8 that this psalm should be understood about true Israelites who are Christians, who by the time of the early church had been tested in every way, which is predicted in this psalm. Therefore, the Judeans lie who demand that this psalm should be expounded concerning their modern captivity [i.e., exile]. THE TEMPLE OF THE LORD: PSALM 44.[2]

EVERYTHING IS FROM GOD. JOHANNES BUGENHAGEN: In this psalm, our work, our strength, our wisdom and righteousness are entirely rejected, and all things which are for our salvation are attributed to God's activity, to God's strength, to God's illumination and mercy, which the Lord shows to us not for any other reason than that he loves us and is merciful. Thus, the one who boasts should boast in the Lord. INTERPRETATION OF THE PSALMS.[3]

44:1-8 God, We Remember!

WHY DOES DAVID ADD "WITH OUR EARS"? MARTIN LUTHER: Why does the psalmist say, "O God, we have heard with our ears"? Can anyone hear without ears? And without his own ears? Was the prophet afraid that the people might be thought to have heard with nostrils or eyes, or not with their own ears, so that he found it necessary to add "with our ears"? We ask the same question about these: "I spoke with my tongue"; "My mouth spoke"; and "David played with his hand." Can any member other than the tongue or mouth speak? Or did David sometimes play the harp with his feet or mouth? I answer: therefore mysteries are touched on here.

The first one is that to hear with the ears is to hear only things subject to the senses, and to hear can be applied in an absolute sense to both. Here, then, for the purpose of distinguishing the hearing of spiritual things he adds "with the ears," with which spiritual things cannot be heard, because in the psalm he intends to talk about the tangible benefits shown to the patriarchs.

Second, to express promptness and obedience and perfection.... We should not feel that we want to hear God only inwardly, but we should also humbly hear openly with our ears, so that the ministry of the church is not despised. As Moses says in Deuteronomy 32: "Ask your father, and he will tell you." Thus these faithful ones through obedience rely more on the words of others than on

---

[1]Selnecker, *Der gantze Psalter*, 1:207r.
[2]Münster, *Miqdaš YHWH*, 1196; citing Rom 8:31-39.
[3]Bugenhagen, *In librvm Psalmorvm interpretatio*, 107r.

their own feelings. They prefer to learn rather than be teachers themselves. Therefore they listen to others. Similarly humility is also commended here, in that it adduces nothing of its own but only what comes from elsewhere, namely, from the fathers. . . .

Third, it is not enough for any virtue to be internal unless it also proceeds into the open to a work of the senses. This is what he wants, that they hear with the ears, speak with the mouth, play the harp with the hand, see with the eyes. For with the heart we believe to righteousness; with the mouth we confess for salvation. Many hear inwardly and speak and deal with themselves, but they do not want to show it openly. FIRST PSALMS LECTURES (1513–1515).[4]

GOD REMAINS THE SAME. JOHN CALVIN: I freely admit that the more we think of the benefits which God has bestowed on others, the greater is the grief which we experience when he does not relieve us in our adversities. But faith directs us to another conclusion, namely, that we should assuredly believe that we shall also in due time experience some relief, because God continues unchangeably the same. There can be no reason to doubt that the faithful now call to remembrance the things which God had formerly done for the welfare of his church, with the view of inspiring their minds with stronger hope. They do not simply state the comparison, which would tend to draw a line of separation between those who have in former times been preserved by the power of God and those who now labor and groan under afflictions; but they rather set forth the covenant of God as the bond of holy alliance between them and their ancestors, that they might conclude from this that whatever amount of goodness the church had at any time experienced in God pertained also to them. COMMENTARY ON THE PSALMS.[5]

GOD SUSTAINS THE CHURCH. NIKOLAUS SELNECKER: God himself protects and sustains his church against bloodthirsty tyrants and heretics. . . . Now God will sustain his church for two reasons. First, because he has chosen them to be his people, indeed, his children and heirs in his Son Christ Jesus; he is their Father and King. Second, because he has promised help for the church in his Word. His Word is true, and what he promises, he will surely keep. . . . For such grace of God all of us, who are members of the true church, should thank God from our heart and say with David: "We daily want to praise God and thank your name forever. For he has, in so many great dangers and changes, wondrously sustained his churches and schools by and among us; contrary to and above all human reason he has protected and increased them. He continues to do this every hour. We thank you God, we thank you and proclaim your wonders, that your name is so near." THE WHOLE PSALTER.[6]

CONFIDENCE IN GOD. KONRAD PELLIKAN: This verse is full of holy doctrine and teaches here the whole confidence with which believers ought to cast themselves on God, not taking hold of a bow or swords when God has not been consulted, and if we would have taken hold of them by a command, nevertheless we do not do so as those who hope in them but as those who hope in the Lord. Yet if that is the case, we would not have an enemy except for our faithlessness and impious life. An especially just cause is necessary in a war for believers. Also it is necessary that it should be begun according to the law. The Lord will not be tested; prayers should not be absent. COMMENTARY ON PSALM 44:6.[7]

44:9-16 *You Have Abandoned and Disgraced Us*

JUDGE ACCORDING TO THE SPIRIT, NOT FLESH AND BLOOD. NIKOLAUS SELNECKER: Until now David spoke in the Spirit according to

---

[4]LW 10:205-6* (WA 3:248); citing Ps 39:3; 66:14; 1 Sam 18:10; Deut 32:8; Is 53:1; Rom 10:10.
[5]CTS 9:151-52* (CO 31:437-38); citing Ps 22:3-6.

[6]Selnecker, *Der gantze Psalter*, 1:207v; citing Ps 33; 105:8; 111:7; 75:1.
[7]Pellikan, *Commentaria Bibliorum*, 4:92r-v.

the Word of God concerning the grace and help of God. Now he begins to examine his own as well as all the saints' flesh and senses, and he speaks as his flesh and blood are disposed and inclined. For the flesh grumbles constantly against God, as if he would judge and reign wickedly according to reason, as if he would let the pious—whom he should help—suffer and raise up the wicked, whom he should punish....

In short, there is nothing more difficult for the flesh to learn than to wait on and expect God's help.... The flesh always wants the experience to be over in the blink of an eye; it wants to be untormented and, as the youth say, "unvexed." Now in this way, according to the manner of the flesh, David speaks here and complains very bitterly about the crossbearing of God's church in which, according to reason, it seems as if God had cast them away, as if God were far off, as if he did not at all care about the pious, whenever they are persecuted, hated, pursued, martyred and killed by the world, as one apostle after the other were slaughtered, so also the prophets. Isaiah was sawed in two with a saw by the command of King Manassah. Jeremiah was stoned in Egypt by the Jews by the command of King Apries (whom Jeremiah called Pharaoh Hophra). Many others had to suffer and be tormented. All the apostles, except for John, had to be sacrificed one after the other.... Whoever is a true Christian will surely discover this judgment according to his reason in his flesh and blood, that he must think and say, "God does not care about us. He lets us be put to shame." THE WHOLE PSALTER.[8]

LESSONS LEARNED FROM CALAMITIES. DAVID DICKSON: Having thus fastened a resolution to believe constantly in God, the psalmist lays forth the lamentable condition of the church before God, with the temptation that assaults his people in their sufferings. Whence we learn: First, it can happen with the constant love of God for his people, to put them to such hard exercises by a variety of troubles

that he may seem not only to break off his former course of kindness towards them but also to cast them off and turn against them, by sending sore judgments on them, which ordinarily speak to human sense wrath, and utter wrath....

Second, as God's presence, manifested among his people, and for them in the sight of the world, makes them the most famous, wise, courageous, prosperous and blessed people in the world, so when God being provoked by the wicked behavior of his professed people leaves them, withdraws his protection from them and shows himself angry at them, they become foolish and feeble sheep, a despicable and a disdained people above all others. "We turn back from the enemy. You have given us as sheep appointed for food, a reproach, a scorn, a byword."

Third, whatever calamity might come over us—whatever the reason—we may safely understand God to be the worker of all our woe. Even though we bring it on ourselves, God inflicts the calamity, for there is no trouble in the city which the Lord does not confess himself to have inflicted. COMMENTARY ON THE PSALMS.[9]

GOD'S PROMISES STRENGTHEN OUR HEART. JOHN CALVIN: Thus the faithful mean that they were cast out as being altogether worthless, so that their condition was worse than that of any slave. And as they would rather appeal to God than turn to their enemies, of whose pride and cruelty they had just cause to complain, let us learn from this, that there is nothing better or more advantageous for us in our adversity than to give ourselves to meditation on the providence and judgment of God. When human beings trouble us, it is no doubt the devil who drives them to it, and it is with him we have to do; but we must, notwithstanding, raise our thoughts to God himself, that we may know that we are proved and tried by him, either to chastise us, or to exercise our patience, or to subdue the sinful desires of our flesh or to humble us and train us to the practice of self-denial. And when we hear that the ancestors who lived under the Law were treated

---

[8]Selnecker, *Der gantze Psalter,* 1:208r, 208v; citing Jer 44:30.

[9]Dickson, *First Fifty Psalms,* 295-96*.

so ignominiously, there is no reason why we should lose courage by any outrage or ill treatment, if God should at any time see fit to subject us to it. It is not here said simply that God sold some people, but that he sold his own people, as if his own inheritance were of no estimation in his sight. Even today, we may in our prayers still make the same complaint, provided we, at the same time, make use of this example, for the purpose of supporting and establishing our faith, so that, however much afflicted we may be, our hearts may not fail us. COMMENTARY ON THE PSALMS.[10]

44:17-22 We Continue to Remember You and Suffer for It

A HOLY RESTRAINT. JOHN CALVIN: We see how the great majority of people murmur and obstinately fret against God, like untamed horses which rage furiously against their masters and strike them with their feet. And, therefore, we know that the person who, in affliction, imposes a holy restraint on himself, that he may not by any impatience be carried away from the path of duty, has made no inconsiderable attainments in the fear of God. It is an easy matter even for hypocrites to bless God in the time of their prosperity; but as soon as he begins to deal sternly with them, they break forth into a rage against him. Accordingly, the faithful declare that although so many afflictions as they endured tended to turn them aside from the right path, they did not forget God but always served him, even when he did not show himself favorable and merciful toward them. COMMENTARY ON THE PSALMS.[11]

THEY DID NOT CAPITULATE. THE ENGLISH ANNOTATIONS: With these words, they intend to justify themselves from the heinous sin of idolatry. Professing that God seems to have, in a manner, forsaken them, having delivered them into the hands of idolaters from whom they have

suffered all kinds of persecutions, yet they have not forsaken him in kind, so as to be proven idolaters, but have submitted to all manner of torments and cruel deaths rather than be drawn into it. ANNOTATIONS ON PSALM 44:17.[12]

SUGGESTIONS OF THE DEVIL. JOHN CALVIN: And this is an artifice of the devil, who, because he cannot at once eradicate from our hearts all sense of religion, endeavors to overthrow our faith by suggesting to our minds these devices: that we must seek another God, or that the God whom we have hitherto served must be appeased after another manner or that the assurance of his favor must be sought elsewhere than in the law and the gospel. Because, then, it is a much more difficult matter for human beings, amid the tossing and waves of adversity, to continue steadfast and tranquil in the true faith, we must carefully observe the protestation which the holy fathers here make, that even when reduced to the lowest extremity of distress by calamities of every kind, they nevertheless did not cease to trust in the true God. COMMENTARY ON THE PSALMS.[13]

THE SHADOW OF DEATH. KONRAD PELLIKAN: He calls the same difficulties the shadow of death, for it is harder than death that he has been exposed to all the desires of the impious ... for all piety to be condemned: this is what it is to be covered in mortal darkness and to be covered completely with the shadow of death. COMMENTARY ON PSALM 44:19.[14]

HATRED OF GOD AND THE CHURCH. PHILIPP MELANCHTHON: The church is not in heavy suppression, as the empires of the world, on account of their idols, tyrannies and desires, for these are the chief causes why they are in a process of change, but because the devil hates God, he provokes impious princes so that they may rage against the church. Therefore because the devil

---

[10]CTS 9:160* (CO 31:441-42).
[11]CTS 9:163-64* (CO 31:444).

[12]Downame, ed., *Annotations*, 6E3r*.
[13]CTS 9:166-67* (CO 31:445).
[14]Pellikan, *Commentaria Bibliorum*, 4:93r.

attempts to destroy the true knowledge of God, the church in its supplications opposes him with a true confession; thus our afflictions become testimonies of doctrine and sacrifices pleasing to God. . . .

Therefore this psalm teaches that confession must be given in our supplications, and likewise it shows why the world advances against the church, namely, from hatred of God and of true doctrine. But because we know that God will not permit true doctrine to be destroyed, likewise we are sustained by this consolation, that God will be with us in this contest. COMMENTS ON THE PSALMS.[15]

44:23-26 Awake, O Sleeper, and Redeem Us!

UNBURDEN YOUR HEART. JOHN CALVIN: We must, indeed, firmly believe that God does not cease to regard us, although he appears to do so. Yet as such an assurance is of faith and not of the flesh—that is to say, it is not natural to us—the faithful familiarly come before God and unburden themselves from this contrary sentiment, which they conceive from the state of things as it is presented to their view. And in doing so, they discharge from their breasts those morbid affec-

tions which belong to the corruption of our nature, in consequence of which faith then shines forth in its pure and native character. COMMENTARY ON THE PSALMS.[16]

METAPHOR OF CONTRITION. MARTIN LUTHER: In the first place, this is a metaphor, as is shown in the gloss.[17] In the second place, it denotes the mortification of the flesh, for as the belly living in pleasures and opulence is in sins, so on the contrary, it sticks to the ground when it is deprived of these things; and so also the soul is humiliated in the dust, which otherwise would be proud in glory and riches and bask in the well-being of the flesh. Therefore Isaiah says, "Come down and sit in the dust, O daughter of Babylon." . . . And thus it means to be in contrition, for that is dust. This, nevertheless, befalls the saints according to the flesh. In the third place, blessed Augustine explains it in a contrary mystery as referring to those who are involved with the earth by the pleasure of the body, for the belly is gluttony itself or the craving for eating. FIRST PSALMS LECTURES (1513–1515).[18]

---

[15]MO 13:1090.

[16]CTS 9:171-72* (CO 31:448).

[17]WA 3:247.

[18]LW 10:207 (WA 3:249); citing Is 47:1; Is 26:19; Augustine's comment on Psalm 44:25, NPNF 8:145.

45:1-17 THE MAGNIFICENT, ETERNAL REIGN OF THE LORD

To the choirmaster: according to Lilies. A Maskil[a] of the Sons of Korah; a love song.

¹ My heart overflows with a pleasing theme;
  I address my verses to the king;
  my tongue is like the pen of a ready scribe.

² You are the most handsome of the sons of men;
  grace is poured upon your lips;
  therefore God has blessed you forever.
³ Gird your sword on your thigh, O mighty one,
  in your splendor and majesty!

⁴ In your majesty ride out victoriously
  for the cause of truth and meekness and
    righteousness;
  let your right hand teach you awesome deeds!
⁵ Your arrows are sharp
  in the heart of the king's enemies;
  the peoples fall under you.

⁶ Your throne, O God, is forever and ever.
  The scepter of your kingdom is a scepter of
    uprightness;
⁷ you have loved righteousness and hated
    wickedness.
Therefore God, your God, has anointed you
  with the oil of gladness beyond your
    companions;
⁸ your robes are all fragrant with myrrh and
  aloes and cassia.

From ivory palaces stringed instruments make
    you glad;
⁹ daughters of kings are among your ladies
    of honor;
  at your right hand stands the queen in gold
    of Ophir.

¹⁰ Hear, O daughter, and consider, and incline
    your ear:
  forget your people and your father's house,
¹¹ and the king will desire your beauty.
Since he is your lord, bow to him.
  ¹² The people[b] of Tyre will seek your favor
    with gifts,
  the richest of the people.[c]

¹³ All glorious is the princess in her chamber,
    with robes interwoven with gold.
  ¹⁴ In many-colored robes she is led to the king,
    with her virgin companions following
      behind her.
¹⁵ With joy and gladness they are led along
    as they enter the palace of the king.
¹⁶ In place of your fathers shall be your sons;
    you will make them princes in all the earth.
¹⁷ I will cause your name to be remembered in
    all generations;
  therefore nations will praise you forever
    and ever.

a Probably a musical or liturgical term b Hebrew *daughter* c Or *The daughter of Tyre is here with gifts, the richest of people seek your favor*

OVERVIEW: Our Reformation commentators find this psalm redolent with messianic and christological meaning concerning the union of Christ with his church. The kingly warrior who rides out to victory in majesty is the victorious Christ, who with the sharp arrows of his words convicts sinners. While God has imprinted the king with a mark of his glory that points to a higher kingdom and glory, the reformers assert that these royal attributions— the eternal throne and righteous scepter—do not pertain to Solomon "truly and perfectly," but to Christ. The queenly bride is the church, a metaphor Paul develops in Ephesians 5; the rich imagery of ivory, gold, precious stones and spices is

Scripture's style of speaking of the spiritual wealth of the church. The royal offspring of bride and groom suggest for Melanchthon the perpetuity of the church and its gospel ministry.

A PROPHECY ABOUT THE PROMISED MESSIAH.
PHILIPP MELANCHTHON: This whole psalm is a prophecy about the promised Messiah, telling who he is, what kind of kingdom he has and what advantages he will furnish the people of God. Second, it also speaks about the church and teaches it that it should heed this king. It reminds it that it would have remarkable glory, but likewise that the impious will advance against it, but also that this Messiah will be the victor and will have an eternal kingdom. This is the summary of this psalm, which is for the most part a narration pertaining to a demonstrative genre: and as it is customarily more brilliantly said in a demonstrative genre, thus there are many ornaments, figures and reproofs, almost as in a lover's or reveler's song, as they call it. COMMENTS ON THE PSALMS.[1]

Superscription: *How to Understand "To the Lilies; A Song of Loves"?*

LEARN THE MIGHTY HEBREW LANGUAGE WELL. MARTIN LUTHER: I have often advised you to learn the Hebrew language and not to neglect it so. For even if this language were otherwise useless, we should still learn it out of thankfulness. It is a part of religion and divine worship to teach or learn this language through which alone we can learn anything at all of the divine. In it we hear God speak, we hear how the saints call on God and achieve the mightiest deeds; thus study directed toward learning this language might rightly be called a kind of Mass or worship of God. Therefore I earnestly admonish you not to neglect it. There is a danger that God may be offended by this ingratitude and deprive us not only of the knowledge of this sacred language but of Greek, Latin and all religion. For how easy it would be for him

to stir up some savage people who might eradicate these languages in one fell stroke!

In addition to the fact that this study is a part of the worship of God, it is also eminently useful. If there are to be any theologians—as there must necessarily be, because not everyone can study law or medicine—they must be armed against the papacy and the whole troop of hateful people who, once they have learned to pronounce one Hebrew word, immediately consider themselves masters of this sacred language. Then, if we do not hold fast to the language, they will ridicule and abuse us as though we were asses. But if we also are fortified with a knowledge of the language, we shall be able to stop their impudent mouths. For this is the way we must resist the devil and his servants. I am of the opinion, however, that we shall have as enemies of our religion the Spaniards, French, Italians and the Turks, too; then certainly there will be need for a knowledge of the Hebrew language. I know how useful it has been to me against my enemies. For that reason I would not be without this knowledge—however small it is—for infinite sums of gold. You, too, as future teachers of religion, should apply yourselves to the task of learning this language, unless you want to be taken for wild beasts and uninstructed rabble who somehow teach the Sunday Gospels and the catechism with the help of books published in German [i.e., postils].[2] We need theological leaders, we must have fighters who stand on the battlefront against people of other nations and languages, people who are teachers, judges and masters in this language. LECTURE ON PSALM 45 (1532).[3]

---

[2]Although Luther's postils were among his favorite and most successful works, he later regretted how pastors used them, reading them from the pulpit verbatim rather than as an aid to interpreting Scripture. "There are some lazy, no-good pastors and preachers," he fumed, "who depend on these and many other good books that they can take a sermon out of. They don't pray, study or read, pondering nothing in Scripture, just as if we need not read the Bible, using such books as a template and calendar to earn their living" (Preface to Johann Spangenberg's *Postilla Teütsch* [1543], WA 53:218; cf. LW 60:281-85). Such people came to be known as *Postillenreiter*, "postil riders." See further John M. Frymire, *The Primacy of the Postils* (Leiden: Brill, 2010), 195-216.
[3]LW 12:198-99* (WA 40,2:474-75).

[1]MO 13:1091.

THE HEBREWS ALSO CALL THIS A MESSIANIC PSALM. SEBASTIAN MÜNSTER: According to the Hebrews as much as Christians this psalm handles the Messiah—even if it seems to be expounded by some about Solomon, who was a type for Christ. Whence the title has "song of loves" because the Lord loved Solomon, supplied him with complete peace and indescribable wealth, made him super-abundant in luxuries and expanded the boundaries of his empire. In all these things the kingdom of Christ—the only beloved of God—was prefigured, through whom all good things are granted to us, too. But the word *šōšanîm* that is written in the title, the Hebrews believe to indicate a musical instrument. THE TEMPLE OF THE LORD: Psalm 45.[4]

LILIES ARE A FIGURE FOR BELIEVERS. RUDOLF GWALTHER: The Hebrews usually expound "lilies" as a zither to which this psalm should have been sung. Thus some understand this word to mean that this psalm was intended for the joyful time of spring. But because it comprises the mysteries of Christ and his church, we may expound these lilies simply about them. For Christ himself calls the church a flower and lily in the Song of Solomon. And he says that his bride, the church, is like a lily among thorns. And the bride says that her bridegroom grazes among the lilies—understand by this each and every believer. THE PSALTER.[5]

A LOVE SONG FOR CHRIST AND HIS BRIDE. JOHN CALVIN: This psalm is called "a song of loves" not, as some suppose, because it illustrates the fatherly love of God, as to the benefits which he had conferred in such a distinguished manner on Solomon, but because it contains an expression of rejoicing on account of his happy and prosperous marriage. Thus the words "of loves" are put for a descriptive epithet and denote that it is a love song. Indeed, Solomon was called *Yĕdîdyah*, which

means "beloved of the Lord." But the context, in my opinion, requires that this term *yĕdîdōt*, that is to say, "loves," be understood as referring to the mutual love which husband and wife ought to cherish toward each other. But as the word *loves* is sometimes taken in a bad sense, and as even conjugal affection itself, however well regulated, has always some irregularity of the flesh mingled with it, this song is at the same time called *maśkîl*, to teach us that the subject here treated of is not some obscene or unchaste amours but that, under what is here said of Solomon as a type, the holy and divine union of Christ and his church is described and set forth.

As to the remaining part of the inscription, interpreters explain it in various ways. *Šûšan* properly means "a lily," and Psalm 60 has in its inscription the same term in the singular number. Here, and in Psalm 80, the plural number is employed. It is therefore probable that it was either the beginning of a common song or else some instrument of music. But as this is a matter of no great consequence, I give no opinion but leave it undecided; for, without any danger to the truth, everyone may freely adopt on this point whatever view he chooses. COMMENTARY ON THE PSALMS.[6]

45:1-5 Praise for the King's Beauty and Might

HEAR AND BE READY. THOMAS WILCOX: This verse teaches us first to take heed that we utter nothing but good things, knowing that we must account not only for every evil but for every idle word we speak, and second, to do that willingly and readily as well, lest we be prevented by death or some other occasion, as also because in every duty God loves and looks for cheerfulness; third, to dispose ourselves with all the power we have, to set forth holy marriage, especially that which is between Christ and his church. EXPOSITION UPON PSALM 45.[7]

---

[4]Münster, *Miqdaš YHWH*, 1197. Scholars still are unsure of the meaning of *šōšanîm* here; it literally means "lilies," but most, like Münster, assume it is some sort of instrument, possibly with six strings. See Kraus, *Psalms 1–59*, 30; Alter, *Book of Psalms*, 158.
[5]Gwalther, *Der Psalter*, 79v; citing Song 2:1-2; 6:2-3.

[6]CTS 9:173-74* (CO 31:449); citing 2 Sam 12:25.
[7]Wilcox, *Godly Exposition upon Some Psalmes*, 130*.

CHRIST'S SWEET LIPS. MARTIN LUTHER: So here, too, after describing his person and unequaled beauty, the psalm demands the same sort of wisdom that he possessed. This is "the wisdom of grace poured on his lips." It seems that Luke was looking back at this verse when he said that as Christ was teaching, all eyes were fixed on him because of the gracious Word which the good will of his hearers occasioned in him. . . . He glances here at Moses, too, who also had lips, but thick, ineloquent, heavy, wrathful ones, on which there was no gracious Word but words of anger, death and sin. Gather together all the wisdom of Moses, the heathen and the philosophers, and you will find that in God's sight they are either idolatry or a false wisdom or, in civil government, a wisdom of wrath. Only the beauty of this King, Christ, is beauty. So only his wisdom is wisdom, for it is the wisdom of grace, that is, of promise; and his Word is sweet, full of consolation and trust. Thus the poet has diligently read the prophecies and promises regarding Christ and has seen that his lips are the sweetest and loveliest lips, which attract the hearts of all the weak. So Christ should not be depicted with gall or a sword in his mouth, as they always portray him, unless it is to be understood spiritually. He should be depicted in such a way that his lips seem to be pure sugar or honey. LECTURE ON PSALM 45 (1532).[8]

THE WORD REVEALS CHRIST'S MAJESTY. RUDOLF GWALTHER: He calls the sword of the divine Word the honor and splendor of Christ, because he displays and reveals his honor and splendor though it, in the same imagery as princes of this world are accustomed to do with their weapons and their flamboyant suit of armor. THE PSALTER.[9]

CHRIST'S CAVALRY, THE APOSTOLIC MINISTRY. SEBASTIAN MÜNSTER: Here the prophet preaches about Solomon and in Solomon about Christ's kingdom, increasing happily; as you can see, it spread to the very ends of the earth. How? He mounted the apostles like horses and stormed the globe with the word of truth, clemency and righteousness, as you have more clearly in Zechariah 6. THE TEMPLE OF THE LORD: PSALM 45.[10]

A METAPHOR FOR CHRIST'S VICTORY. RUDOLF GWALTHER: Christ rides and proceeds forward on the word of the gospel, which teaches us the truth and offers us the mercy of God and true righteousness. And with this word he succeeds, because through it he has conquered every people. This he also understands soon after with arrows. Through the same imagery the preaching of the gospel is depicted. THE PSALTER.[11]

ARROWS IN THE HEART. HENRY AINSWORTH: "Your arrows," that is, your words by which you convict and beat down sin and sinners. So the rider on the white horse has a bow when he goes to conquer. . . . Understand that "they pierce the heart of the king's enemies." And this shows the efficacy of these words or judgments, as elsewhere he says, "I will send all my plagues on their heart." ANNOTATIONS ON PSALM 45:5.[12]

TRAIN FOR BATTLE. MARTIN LUTHER: You see here what kind of king we have. After he has taught us and poured out his promises on us, and by his Word has transferred us into his kingdom, Satan is immediately there and crucifies us. For "all who wish to live a godly life in Christ must endure persecution"; similarly "through many tribulations we must enter the kingdom of God." But our King will not forsake us. He is present and fights in us against the power of tyrants and against the lies of the devil. Indeed, he renders us invincible against the lying teachers and secure against the power of tyrants.

You, therefore . . . who someday will administer the affairs of the churches, should be armed and trained not only to teach and instruct the good who think correctly in the faith but also to combat

---

[8]LW 12:210-11* (WA 40,2:489-90); citing Lk 4:20, 22.
[9]Gwalther, *Der Psalter*, 79v.

[10]Münster, *Miqdaš YHWH*, 1197.
[11]Gwalther, *Der Psalter*, 79v-80r.
[12]Ainsworth, *Annotations*, 2:504*; citing Rev 6:2; Ps 64:4; Deut 32:23; Ex 9:14; Heb 4:12; 2 Cor 10:4-5.

and reprove the adversaries. Otherwise the churches will soon be scattered if there are not people who fight at the battlefront and refute the adversaries, people who expound the passages and ideas of Scripture that the enemies have stolen and defend the truth. Therefore he says here: "The Lord is mighty in battle, because by his patience he conquers every power and tyranny of the world and makes us (as he says in Jer 1) 'fortified cities, an iron pillar and a bronze wall,' and 'faces of flint' (Is 50). Thus we can bear up against all blows, against prisons, chains and death. In short, whatever the world and the devil wish to do in their most bitter anger, we shall overcome through him who lives in us. So first we vanquish the power of tyrants. Then, if we fight the deceptions of the devil, he conquers in us, too. This is our war; no matter how dangerous and difficult it may be, it is still most joyous because the victory remains ours." LECTURE ON PSALM 45 (1532).[13]

45:6-12 Worship the Lord Who Has Anointed You

HIGHER THAN AN EARTHLY KINGDOM. JOHN CALVIN: Although he is called "god," because God has imprinted some mark of his glory in the person of kings, yet this title cannot well be applied to a mortal human being; for we nowhere read in Scripture that a human being or an angel has been distinguished by this title without some qualification. It is true, indeed, that angels as well as judges are called collectively 'elōhîm, "gods"; but not individually, and no one person is called by this name without some word added by way of restriction, as when Moses was appointed to be a god to Pharaoh. From this we may naturally infer that this psalm relates, as we shall soon see, to a kingdom higher than any earthly kingdom....

Now, there is nothing of all this that applies literally to the kingdom of Christ, which is separated from the pomp of this world. But as it

was the design of the prophets to adapt their instruction to the capacity of God's ancient people, so in describing the kingdom of Christ and the worship of God which ought to be observed in it, they use figures taken from the ceremonies of the law. If we bear in mind this mode of statement, in accordance with which such descriptions are made, there will no longer be any obscurity in this passage. COMMENTARY ON THE PSALMS.[14]

CHRIST'S KINGDOM ENDURES FOREVER! WOLFGANG MUSCULUS: These verses prove these things which are said, for they do not pertain to Solomon truly and perfectly, but to Christ. They do not refer to the mundane king and kingdom but must refer to the heavenly king and the heavenly kingdom. The first is his phrase, "Your throne, O God," which calls this king God. The title of God is sometimes also ascribed to the princes of people in Scripture, just as it is read about Moses, "I have established you as the god of Pharaoh." ... Although these passages admonish those who have power over affairs on earth about how they ought to act toward the people subject to themselves, nevertheless the circumstances of the kingdom in this psalm convincingly indicate that what will come to pass is about Christ, not about Solomon. This man, not Solomon, is true God, because he is the Word of the Father, about whom John 1 speaks. Still, he is also the Son of Man, inaugurated by the Father into divine majesty and seated together at the right hand of the Father, God-blessed beyond all things forever. The Holy Spirit also speaks here about this matter. So then he adds, "Because of these things, God, your God, has anointed you with the oil of gladness." The one who anoints is God; and, the one who is anointed is God. And nevertheless there is one divinity, one kingdom, one power.

Second, he says that the seat of this king is perpetual and eternal. If any kingdom of the world lasts for a thousand years, it is called great. Truly, the kingdom in this psalm is eternal. Solomon has already died, long ago. Therefore, it is right that

---

[13]LW 12:216-17* (WA 40,2:497-98); citing Col 1:13; 2 Tim 3:12; Acts 14:22; Jer 1:18; Is 50:7.

[14]CTS 9:178, 182* (CO 31:451, 453); citing Ex 7:1.

this kingdom be heavenly, not earthly. Luke 1 refers to this kingdom of Christ: "And the Lord God will give to that One the seat of David his father, and he will reign in the House of Jacob forever, and his kingdom will have no end." . . . This also must be understood about the kingdom of Christ, as if he receives that kingdom from the Father as the Son of Man, not as the Word of the Father, whose power does not have a beginning. . .

Third, he says, "the scepter of this king is a straight scepter"; that is, his kingdom is a kingdom of equity and justice. Even the king himself is a just king, truly a lover of justice and hater of impiety. By this statement, the prophet deprives the king of any acceptance of persons, because he has established that such a king loves nothing except justice and hates nothing except impurity. And because the example seen here belongs to a perpetual kingdom, then the perpetuity of no earthly kingdom is able to be ascribed to the beginning of the world. Evidently it follows that the righteousness of the scepter cannot pertain to any of those kingdoms and plainly it is fitting with respect to the kingdom of Christ. COMMENTARY ON THE PSALMS.[15]

I LOVE WHAT IS CONTRARY TO GOD. MARTIN LUTHER: The word *righteousness* . . . must be taken very generally, to mean believing in Jesus Christ and loving God and our neighbor. That is, it should be taken as standing for the righteousness both of faith and of works, serving God and the neighbor, in the household and civil society and in all the other offices that God commands. This righteousness—both of faith and of works—is governed by the scepter; and he loves it and has a passion for it. We all hate it by nature, for I would rather have a merciful God without faith, by my own merit. I often dispute with myself regarding this matter, because it seems to me a most difficult thing. I cling to invisible things and esteem them so highly that I can rejoice in them and comfort myself. I neither see nor hear them; in fact,

according to the dictates of reason, they are altogether nothing. Yet I should permit myself to be killed and be willing to lose everything, if only I may have Christ! Whoever has not experienced such things thinks it is an easy matter to believe, but I often murmur against this righteousness and love godlessness. That is, I do not believe that I am acceptable to God through grace, without any works of my own. I dread the divine judgment. I murmur and am impatient at the chastisement of God. So I love what is contrary to God. Christ does not do this. He has loved righteousness with an altogether pure love and has done all these things for us. And now that he is sitting in his kingdom, he plans to instill that same hatred of godlessness in us, that we may be righteous in keeping with his example. Meanwhile that righteousness is implanted daily by the Word, and God bears with us and for the sake of Christ regards us as people who love righteousness. LECTURE ON PSALM 45 (1532).[16]

OPHIR MIGHT BE IN THE AMERICAS. THE BISHOPS' BIBLE: Ophir is thought to be the land to the west recently found by Christopher Columbus. At this time, the most fine gold is brought from here. ANNOTATION ON PSALM 45:9.[17]

THIS PASSAGE MUST BE UNDERSTOOD FIGURATIVELY. JOHN CALVIN: In the first place, let us remember that what is spiritual is here described to us figuratively—just like how the prophets, on account of human dullness, were under the necessity of borrowing similitudes from earthly things. When we bear in mind this style of speaking, which is quite common in the Scriptures, we will not think it strange that the sacred writer here makes mention of ivory palaces, gold, precious stones and spices; for by these he means to intimate that the kingdom of Christ will be replenished with a rich abundance and furnished with all good things. The glory and excellence of the spiritual gifts, with

---

[15]Musculus, *In Psalterium Commentarii*, 541-42; citing Ex 7:1; Gen 6:1-5; Ps 82:6; Jn 1:1-18; Lk 1:32-33; Dan 6:25-27; Is 11:16.

[16]LW 12:244-45* (WA 40,2:534).
[17]*Bishops' Bible*, Part III, XVr*.

which God enriches his church, are indeed held in no estimation among human beings; but in the sight of God they are of more value than all the riches of the world. At the same time, it is not necessary that we should apply curiously to Christ every particular here enumerated, as for instance, what is here said of the many wives which Solomon had. If it should be imagined from this that there may be several churches, the unity of Christ's body will be rent in pieces. I admit that as every individual believer is called "the temple of God," so also might each be named "the spouse of Christ," but properly speaking, there is only one spouse of Christ, which consists of the whole body of the faithful. COMMENTARY ON THE PSALMS.[18]

CHRIST AND HIS QUEEN ARE WED. JACOBUS ARMINIUS: It will be, therefore, a connubial tie that will unite Christ with the church. The espousals of the church on earth are contracted by the agency of the bridesmen of Christ, who are the prophets, apostles and their successors, and particularly the Holy Spirit, who is in this affair a mediator and arbitrator. The consummation will then follow, when Christ will introduce his spouse into his bridechamber. From such a union as this, there arises not only a communion of blessings but a previous union of the persons themselves; from which the possession of blessings is likewise assigned, by a more glorious title, to her who is united in the bonds of marriage. The church comes into a participation not only of the blessings of Christ but also of his title. For, being the wife of the King, she enjoys it as a right due to her to be called Queen, which dignified appellation the Scripture does not withhold from her. ORATION 3: THE AUTHOR AND THE END OF THEOLOGY.[19]

CHRIST'S BRIDE IS DRAWN AND UNIFIED FROM ALL SORTS OF PEOPLE. MARTIN LUTHER: He calls the bride "the queen," his spouse. She stands as though all in gold. This bride is the

church and the entire body, particularly what was taken over from the synagogue. . . . The bride is one, gathered from all these members of kings and princes, the weak and the poor, virgins and married people—and from all of these is formed one bride, the church. This is common usage, that Christ is called the bridegroom and the church, the bride, as in Ephesians 5 and other passages. He calls her through holy baptism and the word of the gospel, and adorns and clothes her with mercy, grace and the remission of sins. That is what he means when he says, "She stands at your right hand." It is a magnificent compliment, and it is also appropriate that no one be nearer the bridegroom than the bride herself. But the principal thing is that the church has everything that is Christ's and that two bodies have become one, so that what belongs to the church is Christ's and in the same way what belongs to Christ is the church's. LECTURE ON PSALM 45 (1532).[20]

BETROTHED TO CHRIST WE ARE DAUGHTERS OF KINGS. JOHANNES BUGENHAGEN: So far the psalmist has described the Bridegroom and King; now he also describes the Bride and Queen who reigns with Christ at his right hand. This is indeed so now, but at the end of the world it will be seen plainly, "when the sheep will be placed on his right." As also Paul says in Ephesians 2: "He made us alive with him and seated us with Christ in the heavenly places." Therefore, we are one with Christ, because we are his bride—therefore kings and priests as well. But this Bride and chaste Queen is a Virgin composed of many members, that is, from many virgins, which are called here "daughters of kings and the nearest brides." When you hear "virgins" here, you should not imagine that this speaks about the body's virginity which has been cast aside out of paradise because it had betrayed faith's chastity and trusted that adulterer, the serpent. . . . Rather, you should take the subject matter to be about the uncorrupted mind which preserves the Word of

---

[18]CTS 9:187-88* (CO 31:456); citing 1 Cor 3:17; 6:19.
[19]Arminius, *Works*, 1:105*.

[20]LW 12:259-60* (WA 40,2:555-56); citing Eph 5:22-33 (cf. Col 3:18-19; 1 Pet 3:1-7).

God—pure and unmixed. God considers this alone to be virginity, as Jeremiah says, "O Lord, your eyes consider faith!" And thus Paul interprets it when he writes to the Corinthians, "I have betrothed you all to one husband, to present you to Christ as a chaste virgin, but I fear that as the serpent seduced Eve by his cunning, so your thoughts will be corrupted and fall away from the simplicity which is in Christ Jesus." We fall away from this simplicity when we depart from the faith and simple doctrine of Christ for confidence in works and human traditions. For in this passage Paul stands against the false apostles who taught people to rely on the works of the law. These daughters of kings and these virgins who belong to the Bride, are drawn to Christ by the good fragrance which permeates and flows from his garments—that is, the word of grace and the abundance from which we all receive, as it was said above. INTERPRETATION OF THE PSALMS.[21]

CHRIST IS OUR BEAUTY. MARTIN LUTHER: Our beauty does not consist in our own virtues or even in the gifts we have received from God, by which we exercise our virtues and do everything that pertains to the life of the law. It consists in this: if we apprehend Christ and believe in him, we are truly lovely, and Christ looks at that beauty alone and at nothing besides. Therefore it is nonsense to teach that we should try to be beautiful by our own chosen religiousness and our own righteousness. To be sure, among human beings and at the courts of the wise these things are brilliant, but in God's courts we must have another beauty. There this is the one and only beauty: to believe in the Lord Jesus Christ. He removes all spots and wrinkles and makes us acceptable to God. This faith is an all-powerful matter and the greatest beauty, besides which there is no beauty. For without and outside Christ we are damned and lost with everything we have and are. LECTURE ON PSALM 45 (1532).[22]

UNEXPECTED DEFENSE OF THE CHURCH. JOHN CALVIN: In our own day we realize some happy fruits of this prophecy when God has so ordered it that some of the great people of this world, although they themselves refuse to submit to the authority of Christ, act with kindness toward the church, maintaining and defending it. COMMENTARY ON THE PSALMS.[23]

45:13-17 The Glory and Fruitfulness of This Bride

EXTERNAL MAGNIFICENCE REPRESENTS INTERNAL BEAUTY. THE ENGLISH ANNOTATIONS: Of the mystical sense or application of this psalm I have no question, either to the church in general—oftentimes in the sight of God and his angels, both in its living saints by their holy conversation and in its dying martyrs by their patient deaths and sufferings in several kinds, most glorious when most oppressed and trampled by people—or to every individual member of it whose beauty and excellency is not external but internal, in the several endowments and qualifications of the soul, both natural and divine or infused. This interpretation is very common and ordinary in all writers, both ancient and late. But because I make this in the secondary sense, not immediately intended by the prophet (whoever he was) and holy penman, though foremost in the intention of the Holy Spirit, we must inquire into the literal, of which there is more question among interpreters. . . . How ordinary is it, even among profane poets and authors, to compare mental perfections with external beauty, and to prefer those that are more considerable and lasting. So this sacred poet, though he sets out the external glory of this bride with all imaginable magnificence, her chiefest glory and beauty he ascribes to her soul, her better part. ANNOTATIONS ON PSALM 45:13.[24]

---

[21]Bugenhagen, *In librvm Psalmorvm interpretatio*, 112r; citing Mt 25:31-46; Eph 2:4-8; 1 Cor 7:25-40; Jer 5:3; 2 Cor 11:2-3; 1 Cor 4:15 (cf. Gal 4:19).
[22]LW 12:280* (WA 40,2:583); citing Eph 5:22-33.

[23]CTS 9:190* (CO 31:457-58).
[24]Downame, ed., *Annotations*, 6E4r*.

THE UNIVERSAL CHURCH. PHILIPP MELANCH-THON: The last two verses contain the promise of the perpetuity of the church and of the evangelical ministry as the church has gathered from the named fathers (Adam, Jacob, Moses, Samuel, David). Thus I gather the church by the children called from the seed of the ancestors and from the Gentiles. And these engaged in the evangelical ministry were guardians and propagators of the gospel in all regions, not only in Palestine. Through the ministry of these, Christ will be effective and will gather the eternal church that will glorify God and his Son, our Lord Jesus Christ, throughout all eternity. Therefore this king will give righteousness and eternal life to his people who heed him. COMMENTS ON THE PSALMS.[25]

WORDS FOR THE BRIDE ALSO. THE ENGLISH ANNOTATIONS: It is generally conceived that these words are directed to Solomon himself, not to his bride, because of the masculine affixes, or pronouns, in the original, with its sense being that his posterity shall not degenerate but be equal to their fathers in wisdom, prudence, piety and all true nobility. Indeed, if the words are directed to Solomon, I do not know what else to make of them. But because it is not without example that a masculine should be substituted for a feminine, as is observed in this place by some, it is better, perchance, to take these words as directed to the same subject addressed in verse 10, or at least, in this way, as belonging to the bride. In this case, the

meaning would be—which I conceive would fit the context much better—to persuade her not to take too much to heart (which many women in this case are apt to do, and sometimes it is the cause of much trouble to them and their people), that she is brought away from her kindred and parents, and that all these she must now forsake, because instead of them, she shall have children, from whom she may expect as much and more comfort than from any parents. ANNOTATIONS ON PSALM 45:16.[26]

THE GLORY OF THE CHURCH. JOHN CALVIN: In the estimation of the world, the hideousness of the cross obscures the glory of the church; but when we consider how wonderfully it has increased and how much it has been distinguished by spiritual gifts, we must confess that it is not without cause that its glory is in this passage is celebrated in such sublime language. It ought, however, to be observed that the sovereignty, of which mention is here made, does not consist in the character of human beings but refers to the Head. According to a frequent mode of expression in the Word of God, the dominion and power which belong properly to the Head and are applicable peculiarly to Christ alone, are in many places ascribed to his members. We know that those who occupy eminent stations in the church and who rule in the name of Christ do not exercise a lordly dominion, but rather act as servants. COMMENTARY ON THE PSALMS.[27]

---

[25]MO 13:1094.

[26]Downame, ed., *Annotations*, 6E4r*.
[27]CTS 9:192-93* (CO 31:458-59).

46:1-11 A MIGHTY FORTRESS IS OUR GOD

To the choirmaster. Of the Sons of Korah. According to Alamoth.[a] A Song.

¹ God is our refuge and strength,
  a very present[b] help in trouble.
² Therefore we will not fear though the earth
    gives way,
  though the mountains be moved into the
    heart of the sea,
³ though its waters roar and foam,
  though the mountains tremble at its swelling.
                                    Selah

⁴ There is a river whose streams make glad the
    city of God,
  the holy habitation of the Most High.
⁵ God is in the midst of her; she shall not be
    moved;

God will help her when morning dawns.
⁶ The nations rage, the kingdoms totter;
  he utters his voice, the earth melts.
⁷ The LORD of hosts is with us;
  the God of Jacob is our fortress.   Selah

⁸ Come, behold the works of the LORD,
  how he has brought desolations on the
    earth.
⁹ He makes wars cease to the end of the earth;
  he breaks the bow and shatters the spear;
  he burns the chariots with fire.
¹⁰ "Be still, and know that I am God.
  I will be exalted among the nations,
  I will be exalted in the earth!"
¹¹ The LORD of hosts is with us;
  the God of Jacob is our fortress.   Selah

a Probably a musical or liturgical term   b Or *well proved*

OVERVIEW: This psalm of confidence centers on Zion, the "city of God" and symbol of God's presence and dominion over the nations. The habitation of the Most High is a secure fortress guarded by the divine warrior. The psalm's imagery of trembling mountains and roaring seas, raging nations and tottering kingdoms resonates with the reformers' understanding of the world, the flesh and the devil. Against them the city of God, the church, is a bulwark indwelt by God and nourished by flowing streams of doctrine. This is how a people, not defined by land or fixed location, find their security and protection. The God of Jacob roots this confidence in the continuity of the covenant promises. The pastoral message is one of confident trust in the presence of almighty God among his people and his ultimate victory over every enemy. The peace and rest of the people of God is granted by the victory of God in Christ. The themes of this psalm are

memorably sounded in Luther's hymn, "A Mighty Fortress Is Our God."

THE CHURCH IS A LIVING FOUNTAIN. MARTIN LUTHER: Psalm 46 is a psalm of thanks, sung by the people of Israel for the mighty deeds of God, that he protected and preserved the city of Jerusalem—where his dwelling was—against the ranting and raging of every king and heathen, and he maintained peace against all wars and weapons. According to Scripture's custom, the psalmist calls the commonwealth of the city a dear spring, like a small rivulet, that shall not recede into the great waters, seas and oceans of the heathens, that is, the great kingdoms, principalities and dominions, which must dry up and die.

We, however, sing this psalm in praise to God, that he is with us and wonderfully sustains his Word and Christendom against the gates of hell, against the raging of all the devils, fanatical spirits, the world, flesh, sin and death. Our dear spring also remains a living fount, while those swamps, puddles and bogs must become foul and fetid and dry up. SUMMARIES OF THE PSALMS (1531–1533).[1]

AUGUSTINE UNDERSTOOD THIS PSALM TO BE ABOUT THE GENTILES. NIKOLAUS SELNECKER: Augustine exegetes this psalm concerning the conversion of the Gentiles. The ocean, he says, is the Gentiles or the world. The mountains are the apostles. The teaching of the gospel spread among the Gentiles, and from this arose great uproar and discord, war and bloodshed, as it still happens according to the word of Christ, when he says, "I did not come to bring peace but a sword." THE WHOLE PSALTER.[2]

Superscription: *A Song According to the ʿAlāmôt*

WHAT DOES ʿALĀMÔT MEAN? SEBASTIAN MÜNSTER: Many claim ʿalāmôt to be *kĕlê hanîgôn*, a musical instrument; others are pleased with other conjectures. However, this psalm is a song of thanks for some remarkable relief brought to the holy city of Jerusalem. THE TEMPLE OF THE LORD: PSALM 46.[3]

THE SUPERSCRIPTION POINTS TO THE EARLY CHURCH. MARTIN LUTHER: Here is a certain word which occurred above in Psalm 9, namely ʿalmût, which is the plural of ʿalmāh. It means "hidden or secret girls," that is, mystic young women, which are of the faithful souls in the early church, for at that time the church was a young woman. GLOSSA ON PSALM 46 (1513–1515).[4]

UNSURE WHAT ʿALĀMÔT MEANS. RUDOLF GWALTHER: ʿAlāmôt by some is expounded as a zither. Others think that it was a particular melody or manner of singing among the Hebrews. However, because it is entirely uncertain, we have let the Hebrew word remain. THE PSALTER.[5]

46:1-3 *God Is Our Immovable Rock*

STAND STRONG, FOR GOD IS WITH YOU. DAVID JORIS: Yes, let [our opponents] do what they will; the Lord will be a surety and shelter for his people in the time of need. And he gives them strength in their heart and strengthens their weakness. A heart will not become faint when it is strengthened in the midst of the fight. It is in necessity that the supply appears, so that the holy faith and the kingdom are upheld, for it must be full of temptation and disturbances. Also, it is for God's praise and wonder. Yes, I know what I see and confess, regarding all such power and life. For I advise no one that he seek to keep his own life here, or that he run from or be frightened of death or his enemy, but that he willingly come against it. Yes, wake up, for this is the basis of the Spirit, for the Lord desires that we be submissive in this manner, completely trustworthy and prepared, according to the will of God, ready to be delivered up as sheep to the slaughter.

Also, I am able to testify of this deed because it is well known to me, beloved. See it and believe in the name of our Lord, in his saints and great works of love. Pray and be awake; suffer and fight and win, so that you might sit and reign from eternity to eternity with Christ our Lord Jesus, eternally blessed. Amen. LETTER CONCERNING MARTYRDOM (1539).[6]

GOD IS A PRESENT HELP. KONRAD PELLIKAN: Certainly the church of believers in this world always suffers many things, as also do all those who desire to live piously—consider especially the

---

[1]WA 38:35.
[2]Selnecker, *Der gantze Psalter*, 1:216v; citing Mt 10:34. See NPNF 8:155-60, esp. 156-57.
[3]Münster, *Miqdaš YHWH*, 1198. Scholars are still uncertain about what sort of musical term ʿalāmôth is. See Kraus, *Psalms 1–59*, 31; Alter, *Book of Psalms*, 162.
[4]WA 3:265; citing Ps 9:1. See the comment on the superscription of Ps 9 above, pp. 81-82.

[5]Gwalther, *Der Psalter*, 81v.
[6]CRR 7:266.

example of Christ. Yet because our God and Lord—who wills to be the only hope of believers—knows and arranges all things, he also commands them to call on him in all their anxieties. Additionally, he is their very strength, whom no one can resist, as he is thus understood by the pious to will and be able to help, so he must always be called on in all circumstances, in whatever great difficulties occur. In fact, he is a present help, either for delivering from difficulties or by giving the grace to bravely sustain. COMMENTARY ON PSALM 46:1.[7]

THE PROMISE OF CONSOLATION. VIKTORIN STRIGEL: Nature leads us all to conclude that no society of people is able to last unless it has some fixed locale and designated rulers by which it is defended. The church has neither a fixed locale, nor is it defended with the consent of its leaders but rather is oppressed and abused. And the society of people is wretched, as the troubles of the apostles and our own daily miseries attest. Amid these spectacles, what else is human reason to think but that true doctrine and the studies of this doctrine will soon be wiped from the face of the earth?

But contrary to this human logic, the psalmist consoles us by saying, "God is our refuge and fortress." For, although powers of this world do not defend us, nevertheless God protects us and keeps us from harm. The church of God needs this consolation so that we may know that it will endure, even if it does not have a fixed locale or the defense of powerful leaders. Therefore, this consolation bears repeating often, as in Isaiah 51: "I placed my words in your mouth, and with the shadow of my hand I covered you, so that I might plant the heavens." That is, "I am establishing the ministry of the gospel. It will not be defended by earthly powers, but rather it will be savagely attacked. Therefore, I myself promise your defense; I will protect the ministers of the gospel, the churches, the schools, devout studies, even though the world in its madness tries to destroy the gospel." Therefore, although we have no human protectors

to speak of—as in the psalm it is written, "My father and mother have abandoned me"—nevertheless, let us keep these words before us, by which, if we will rouse our faith, we will feel that God is truly with us, that we are helped, guided and defended. HYPONĒMATA IN ALL THE PSALMS.[8]

TEMPTATIONS SO GREAT THE MOUNTAINS RETREAT. JOHN CALVIN: And what will this affliction be? He does not say that they will have their refuge in God when they are at ease, when their enemies never say a word to them, nor go about once to accost them. Instead, he says, it will be when temptations will be so great and so horrible that people will think that the mountains might run headlong into the bottom of the sea! Now, I ask you, how shameful is it if we were amazed that three or four people move or stir in such circumstances? It is true that the prophet used here a manner of speech which we call, in common language, "excessive," but it is not without reason: that is, to instruct our faith well. Thus, the psalmist brings us to a confusion so fearful that we no longer can tell the difference between heaven and earth. It is as if, he says, there were not only open war—they beat the drum for soldiers everywhere, mount artillery, make all preparations, assemble cavalry and foot soldiers—not only is this done, but also there is much more than this, that is, the mountains retreat, and it seems that they will fall and perish, and there is nothing but gaping gulfs everywhere to swallow us up! Still we must be strong, assured even then that God will help us.

Now then, when it is said that we will not fear, it is not that we will be unfeeling—nor would that be good. For what would become of our faith that we have in God, if we had no danger? So we must fear. Instead he speaks of the sort of bewilderment that the unbelieving have. For because they do not rest in God, nor have they tasted the value of his promises, nor prayed to him as they should, he treats them as they have merited, that is, only a leaf from a tree must fall, and look, they vanish! There is neither sense, memory nor courage in them, and

[7]Pellikan, *Commentaria Bibliorum*, 4:95r.

[8]Strigel, *Hyponēmata*, 225; citing Is 51:16; Ps 27:10.

no one can mitigate their sorrows at all. This then is what the prophet means: to know that in the midst of our fear we will not be oppressed with fear, because we have sheltered ourselves in God and have our refuge in the help he has promised us. AFTERNOON SERMON ON MAY 12, 1561.[9]

46:4-7 The Kingdom of God

THE CITY OF GOD IS THE CHURCH. RUDOLF GWALTHER: Through the city of God we can understand the entire Christian church in which God dwells with his Word and Spirit, with which he sanctifies it. THE PSALTER.[10]

FIGURES AND ALLEGORIES FOR THE OFFICE OF THE WORD. PHILIPP MELANCHTHON: Thus another part of the comparison follows in the fourth verse, "The rivulets of the river will water the city of God," as if he should say, "Even if elsewhere the earth and sea are overturned, shaken into a spectacular chaos, yet the sources and rivulets will not be disturbed which water this city, which is the chief seat of the doctrine of God, established by the commandment of God; it rightly discharges the prophetic ministry and has prophets rightly teaching the Word of God."

Customarily, sources and rivulets are allegories for doctrine and the office of teaching. This is also customary in the Psalms, because first something is said by a figure. Afterwards in short the same thing it speaks more clearly without a figure—as is done in the fifth and sixth verses, where it states clearly that the church is protected because God dwells in it and assists it. Indeed, other nations and religions are destroyed, just as many nations and lands on the whole globe have been horribly destroyed—the Egyptians, Syrians, Chaldeans, Asiatics, Greeks and Romans. The polities and religions of all these have perished with their nations. COMMENTS ON THE PSALMS.[11]

COMFORT FOR ALL THE UPRIGHT. HIERONY-MUS WELLER VON MOLSDORF: This comfort was not just for the citizens of Jerusalem but also for all the upright at all times. Let us eagerly take hold of this comfort, fixing it in our heart of hearts, so that we are able to call on it in our time of affliction. Let us use it against the devil, the world, the flesh and every one of our enemies. When powers persecute us because of the gospel, when the devil and indeed our own hearts torment us with deathly thoughts, let our only thought be that God lives within us. Indeed, when we sense we are in the grip of the flesh, when we feel we are wandering amid the demons, that is the time when we should take hold of this sweetest of thoughts and meditate on it, trampling on the devil, the powers and the flesh. Though I may feel I have been utterly rejected by God, things are not the way I feel them to be. It is certain that God lives in me, and that I live in God. For this reason I will not be moved, nor will I perish, even if the gates of hell rush on me in all their might and attempt to devour me. May Christ's words—"I live and you live," and also, "I will not abandon you as orphans," be stronger in me than all the passions of the flesh.

It does, however, require great effort and wisdom to encourage one's soul with comforts from Scripture and to trample on our enemies in this way. So let all provinces, authorities, cities and individual Christians who are attacked, afflicted and endure suffering from powers because they preach the gospel sing this verse. BRIEF COMMENT ON PSALM 46.[12]

GOD AND HIS CHURCH. JOHN CALVIN: Because the church of God is never without enemies, and because these enemies are very powerful and consequently fight against it with cruel and unbridled fury, the prophet now confirms from experience the doctrine which he had advanced concerning the impregnable character of the divine protection. He then deduces from it this general ground of consola-

---

[9]SCal 7:75-76*.
[10]Gwalther, *Der Psalter*, 81v-82r.
[11]MO 13:1095-96.

[12]Weller, *Enarratio Psalmorum*, 379-80; citing Jn 14:18.

tion, namely, that it belongs continually to God to restrain and quell all commotions, and that his arm is strong enough to break all the efforts of the enemy. This passage, I admit, might be understood in a more general sense, as meaning that the city of God is liable to be assailed by many storms and tempests, but that by the favor of God it is, nevertheless, always preserved in safety. It is, however, more probable . . . that the psalmist is here speaking of some notable deliverance, in which God had given a striking proof of the power and favor which he exercises in the constant preservation of the church. COMMENTARY ON THE PSALMS.[13]

INTERPRET AND APPLY SCRIPTURE. JOHN CALVIN: The prophet, after having celebrated the power of God by calling him "the Lord of hosts," immediately adds another epithet, "the God of Jacob," by which he confirms the covenant made of old with Abraham, that his posterity, to whom the inheritance of the promised grace belongs, should not doubt that God was favorable to them also. . . . From this we learn that those persons err miserably in the interpretation of Scripture who leave the application of all that is said concerning the power of God floating in the air, and who conclude that as they are of his flock, he will be a Father to them and that they are partakers of the adoption. COMMENTARY ON THE PSALMS.[14]

46:8-11 Peace and Rest Established by the Lord

GOD'S MAGNIFICENT SALVATION. NIKOLAUS SELNECKER: We are admonished to recognize the marvelous deliverance of God's church and contemplate well how God so wonderfully preserves and protects his Word, above and contrary to all human reason. When God makes himself known with one word only—for instance, with a peal of thunder or something else—every-

one must hide and submit to his power. In Acts 2, for example, three thousand people were converted by a sermon of Peter. Paul had to fall to the ground when Christ spoke to him: "Saul, Saul, why are you persecuting me?" David did not know what to do when Nathan said, "Behold, you are the man!" Julian the Apostate, struck by thunder and wounded, had to confess and say, "You have prevailed."[15] Therefore we should carefully observe how God acts among kings, princes, heretics and even among his saints, until he rightly directs and converts them, and how Christ destroys and brings to naught all his enemies. This still happens. Such examples are before the eyes of those who will only pay attention. THE WHOLE PSALTER.[16]

CHRIST'S TRIUMPH. HIERONYMUS WELLER VON MOLSDORF: This verse is to be understood first as describing the victories of God which he pursued once the enemies of God had been destroyed. Second, it is to be taken as describing the victories of Christ which he claimed against his enemies who were crushed: the devil, the world, sin, death and hell. For when the preaching of the gospel reached all the ends of the earth and once his enemies were slain, Christ began to lead magnificent triumphs with his apostles and servants. In this way Christ is said to become supreme and to triumph whenever we defeat our enemies—sin, the flesh, the devil, the world, death—by word, faith and prayer. This then is what Christ the King of glory is saying: "I will make all people in all the earth recognize and worship me; I will make my name glorious in every single place throughout the earth. I will make my precepts resound, and I will be truly worshiped." BRIEF COMMENT ON PSALM 46.[17]

CONSIDER GOD AT ALL TIMES. PHILIPP MELANCHTHON: After God has commanded us to

---

[15] The supposed dying words of Julian, according to Theodoret (*Historia Ecclesiastica* 3.25).
[16] Selnecker, *Der gantze Psalter*, 1:217r; citing Acts 2:14-41; Acts 9:1-9; 2 Sam 12:1-14.
[17] Weller, *Enarratio Psalmorum*, 392-93.

---

[13] CTS 9:201* (CO 31:463).
[14] CTS 9:202* (CO 31:464).

restrain our curiosity, he places divine help in opposition to it. He shows the object of faith and commands us to stir up true confidence in God's presence. Indeed he teaches that we should pray to and acknowledge the true God who has revealed himself in Israel by giving his Word; nor should we be partial to false gods.

Therefore, he says: "Know that I am God; I will be exalted among the nations, and I will be exalted on earth!" That is, whenever you are in danger, do not fear, do not seek unlawful refuges, as if there is no God, or as if he does not care for you! But, first of all, your minds should look to God, who revealed himself in this people, Israel; ask him for help and expect it according to his promises! And surely know that this worship pleases him and is special to him, because he does not reveal himself for nothing, nor does he make promises for nothing, but he wants to be acknowledged, and he wants the testimonies about him to be visible in his church and before his enemies.

Therefore, he says, "I will be exalted among the nations, and I will be exalted on earth! I do not just want to hide in this, my light, unknown to my creatures, but I go forth! I want to be acknowledged, seen, loved and invoked; I want help to be sought and expected from me; I want to be glorified by my people and to be feared by those who refuse to embrace my Word." This sweet consolation is displayed in his Word. "I will be exalted in the nations, and I will be exalted on earth!" For God promises that he will reveal himself according to his testimonies, so that he would be invoked and so that his benefits would be celebrated on earth among us miserable human beings. COMMENTS ON THE PSALMS.[18]

BATTLE HYMN OF THE REFORMATION.
MARTIN LUTHER:

A mighty fortress is our God,
A trusty shield and weapon;

He helps us free from ev'ry need
That hath us now o'ertaken.
The old evil foe
Now means deadly woe;
Deep guile and great might
Are his dread arms in fight;
On earth is not his equal.

With might of ours can naught be done,
Soon were our loss effected;
But for us fights the Valiant One,
Whom God himself elected.
Ask ye, Who is this?
Jesus Christ is,
Of Sabaoth Lord,
And there's none other God;
He holds the field forever.

Though devils all the world should fill,
All eager to devour us,
We tremble not, we fear no ill;
They shall not overpow'r us.
This world's prince may still
Scowl fierce as he will,
He can harm us none.
He's judged; the deed is done;
One little word can fell him.

The Word they still shall let remain
Nor any thanks have for it;
He's by our side upon the plain
With his good gifts and Spirit.
And take they our life,
Goods, fame, child and wife,
Though these all be gone,
Our vict'ry has been won;
The kingdom ours remaineth.

A MIGHTY FORTRESS IS OUR GOD.[19]

---

[18]MO 13:1097-98.

[19]LSB no. 656 (WA 35:455-57; cf. LW 53:284-85).

47:1-9 THE LORD'S ASCENSION AS KING OVER ALL THE EARTH

To the choirmaster. A Psalm of the Sons of Korah.

¹ *Clap your hands, all peoples!*
  Shout to God with loud songs of joy!
² *For the* L*ORD, the Most High, is to be feared,*
  a great king over all the earth.
³ *He subdued peoples under us,*
  and nations under our feet.
⁴ *He chose our heritage for us,*
  the pride of Jacob whom he loves.   Selah

⁵ *God has gone up with a shout,*
  the L*ORD with the sound of a trumpet.*
⁶ *Sing praises to God, sing praises!*
  Sing praises to our King, sing praises!
⁷ *For God is the King of all the earth;*
  sing praises with a psalm![a]

⁸ *God reigns over the nations;*
  God sits on his holy throne.
⁹ *The princes of the peoples gather*
  as the people of the God of Abraham.
For the shields of the earth belong to God;
  he is highly exalted!

a Hebrew *maskil*

OVERVIEW: While the reformers recognize the possibility of a distinct original setting, such as the processional entrance of the ark of the covenant, they focus on Christ's ascension after his victory. God's throne was symbolized within Jerusalem's temple, but at a mystical level heaven is in view. Luther contrasts God's descending at Sinai and his ascending here as a contrast between law and gospel. The psalmist enjoins the people to sing psalms of praise to the king, and so the church is now to sing wisely and with full understanding.

CHRIST'S VICTORY. RUDOLF GWALTHER: According to the opinion of some this psalm was sung as Solomon dedicated the temple and placed God's ark of the covenant in it. Consequently it contains a comforting prophesy: how Christ will extend his kingdom throughout the entire world. Thus, the Holy Spirit also exhorts each and every nation that they should rejoice in God and should laud and praise him. He also explains the reasons why such should happen.

Here it is good for us to notice the order in which these psalms are set. In Psalm 45 the psalmist described the union of Christ and his church. In Psalm 46 he announced the church's misfortunes in which God will nevertheless sustain the church. Now here follows the victory of Christ, in which our salvation is accomplished, on account of which all of us should rejoice and show our thanks to him. THE PSALTER.[1]

PRAISE FOR THE KINGDOM OF CHRIST. NIKOLAUS SELNECKER: This is a thanksgiving for the kingdom of Christ and his spiritual, eternal benefits. For it prophesies about the Lord Christ and rejoices that God, through the promised Messiah, his Son, gathers a church and eternal seed for him and redeems us from death, sin, wrath, the devil and hell. It further talks about the ascension of Christ to heaven and about his glory, how he is a King and Lord over all creatures and rules by his Word without any violence, solely through rejoicing, singing and trumpets, that is, through the cheerful proclamation of the gospel. THE WHOLE PSALTER.[2]

---

[1]Gwalther, *Der Psalter*, 82v.
[2]Selnecker, *Der gantze Psalter*, 1:218r.

47:1-4 *Clap Your Hands and Sing Your Praises to the Most High God*

CELEBRATE GOD'S TRIUMPH! DAVID DICKSON: Our joy and our victory over all our enemies, which Christ has purchased and brings to all believers in every nation, are the matter of Christ's praise and declare that he is God, who, having in his humanity suffered, and wrestled against sin, Satan, death, hell and the curse of the law, did, by the power of his divinity, prevail before he brought joy to the Gentiles. . . . His triumph presupposes his victory, and his victory presupposes his battle before he overcame, and the commanding of the Gentiles "to clap their hands and shout," and to shout "with the voice of triumph," presuppose their interest in the victory, for while they are bidden to shout to God the triumphant, who, in this entire psalm, is the Redeemer, Christ. . . . It indicates that the Redeemer is God. And he is God inseparably from the Father and the Holy Spirit, yet here he is distinctly to be praised for this his work of victorious redemption of sinners. Therefore it is said with distinct relation to his person, "shout to God with the voice of triumph." COMMENTARY ON THE PSALMS.[3]

THE GRACE OF ELECTION. KONRAD PELLIKAN: The Israelites recognize the grace of election, by which God used them to magnify the glory of the divine name all over the world before all other nations. By the grace of election he made known the judgments of his righteousness and revealed his will by words, deeds and the Scriptures. He glorified himself through victories and miracles, so that all the nations would know the grace of the omnipotent God toward the Israelites, whenever they would rest in their vows; his righteousness and judgment, whenever they violated their vows. Therefore this was the pride and splendor of Jacob, by which he was exalted by the Lord God in his descendants, and by which he was loved more than Esau: the Lord God chose Jacob's descendants to trumpet his glory through his divine and mighty deeds. Out of the Israelites he was born according to the flesh, and among the Israelites he wanted to dwell on earth and to preach the will of the Father and to perform miracles, so that with good reason *selāh* was added to encourage contemplation. COMMENTARY ON PSALM 47:4.[4]

47:5-7 *The Lord's Triumphant Shout*

VOICE OF THE GOSPEL. MARTIN LUTHER: This is the argument in this psalm which speaks of the ascension. At Sinai he descended; here he ascended. There he shoved them into hell; here he leads them out to heaven. He ascends and takes others with him. There he went forth with fire and destruction; here he goes up in pure joy. Therefore this psalm contains the difference between gospel and law. For he ascended because he conquered death, sin and hell, and he reigns in life. . . . This goes with rejoicing, that is, the voice of the gospel. Therefore everywhere you hear in the Psalms or the prophets' voice: "Praise," then we should always go to the gospel. Also, whenever you hear, "all the nations." TABLE TALK: VEIT DIETRICH (1532).[5]

GOD'S PRESENCE IN THE ARK. JOHN CALVIN: The name Jehovah is here applied to the ark; for although the essence or majesty of God was not shut up in it, nor his power or operation fixed to it, it was nevertheless not a vain or idle symbol of his presence. God had promised that he would dwell in the midst of the people so long as the Jews worshiped him according to the rule which he had prescribed in the law, and he actually showed that he was present with them and that it was not in vain that he was called on among them. COMMENTARY ON THE PSALMS.[6]

THE ARK IS A FIGURE OF CHRIST. THE ENGLISH ANNOTATIONS: This verse refers to the ark of God, as God is said to arise when the ark is carried. For this reason, most interpreters agree that this psalm was penned on an occasion of solemnity, such as bringing the ark in or settling it someplace.

---

[3]Dickson, *First Fifty Psalms*, 320*.

[4]Pellikan, *Commentaria Bibliorum*, 4:96r.
[5]WATR 1:166, no. 386.
[6]CTS 9:211* (CO 31:469).

Spiritually and mystically, Christ in his glorious ascension into heaven is foretold. For this conclusion, we have the authority of the apostle who applies to Christ the same words of the psalmist which were literally intended and spoken concerning the ark. ANNOTATIONS ON PSALM 47:5.[7]

SING WISELY. PHILIPP MELANCHTHON: My worship is commanded as often as these words are repeated, "Rejoice in God! Sing psalms! Sing psalms wisely!" These words command that we should acknowledge and glorify him, indeed, and do so wisely, as if he should say, "It concerns the honors due to a king and to other kings. Other kings are honored by external duties; here he must be honored in wisdom, that is, by hearing his word and rightly as well as wisely understanding, embracing, profiting by and preaching it."

The Jews did not sing psalms of the Messiah wisely, because they imagined a political king and one who would die; because they were fascinated with this persuasion, they crucified the Messiah. By no means did they glorify and wisely sing of him. We should also conclude in this way concerning the rest of impious teachers of all times. Monks who teach only the law and command us to doubt do not wisely sing psalms, and thus they destroy the gospel and the teaching about faith. COMMENTS ON THE PSALMS.[8]

WORSHIP IS DEBASED BY IGNORANCE. THE ENGLISH ANNOTATIONS: The psalmist required that understanding be joined with singing, lest the name of God be profaned with vain crying. ANNOTATIONS ON PSALM 47:7.[9]

47:8-9 God Is Enthroned Over All People

IN HEAVEN OR ON EARTH. JOHN CALVIN: The second clause of verse 8, "God sits on his holy throne," can be interpreted in two ways, as this expression is often understood as the tabernacle or temple, and other times it is used to signify heaven. If any are inclined to explain it of the temple, the meaning will be that while God reigns over the whole world, and all nations are encompassed by his dominion, he has established his chief seat in Jerusalem, and it was from there that the doctrine of the gospel flowed, by which he has brought all people under his dominion. We may, however, also very properly take this expression as being spoken of heaven. In this case, the meaning will be that God, in stretching forth his hand to subdue people and bring them to submit to his authority, evidently shows that he reigns over people from his heavenly throne. COMMENTARY ON THE PSALMS.[10]

ZEAL FOR TRUE RELIGION. KONRAD PELLIKAN: Wherever he, the Lord our God, reigns, there the saints possess eternal life, real righteousness and whatever is completely desirable. His kingdom's boundaries [*pomeria*] are celebrated here to be the guardians and governors of all the earth, including those who are highborn and lowborn, who are indicated by "princes" and "shields" as the shields or guardians of the earth. Therefore, they ought to defend their people, to drive the wicked away from them and to place themselves against their enemies on behalf of the people. As shields repel javelins, and protect those whom they cover, in the same way also David often calls God "his shield." But how rare are such princes! Nevertheless they are found in the kingdom of Christ, namely, the holy apostles and bishops who make themselves vulnerable on behalf of their churches. Many such princes are always found in the church of the nations, who preach the faith of Abraham's God, and expose themselves to death on behalf of their holy teaching. By their great zeal and faith, true religion has always caused faith in the one God; today too it does and will continue to do so. COMMENTARY ON PSALM 47:9.[11]

---

[7]Downame, ed., *Annotations*, 6E4v*; citing Num 10:35; Eph 4:8.
[8]MO 13:1099.
[9]Downame, ed., *Annotations*, 6E4v. Downame borrowed this from the Geneva Bible.

[10]CTS 9:213-14* (CO 31:470).
[11]Pellikan, *Commentaria Bibliorum*, 4:96r.

48:1-14 ZION, THE CITY OF OUR GOD

A Song. A Psalm of the Sons of Korah.

¹ Great is the LORD and greatly to be praised
    in the city of our God!
His holy mountain, ² beautiful in elevation,
    is the joy of all the earth,
Mount Zion, in the far north,
    the city of the great King.
³ Within her citadels God
    has made himself known as a fortress.

⁴ For behold, the kings assembled;
    they came on together.
⁵ As soon as they saw it, they were astounded;
    they were in panic; they took to flight.
⁶ Trembling took hold of them there,
    anguish as of a woman in labor.
⁷ By the east wind you shattered
    the ships of Tarshish.
⁸ As we have heard, so have we seen
    in the city of the LORD of hosts,

in the city of our God,
    which God will establish forever.   Selah

⁹ We have thought on your steadfast love, O God,
    in the midst of your temple.
¹⁰ As your name, O God,
    so your praise reaches to the ends of the earth.
    Your right hand is filled with righteousness.
¹¹ Let Mount Zion be glad!
Let the daughters of Judah rejoice
    because of your judgments!

¹² Walk about Zion, go around her,
    number her towers,
¹³ consider well her ramparts,
    go through her citadels,
    that you may tell the next generation
¹⁴ that this is God,
our God forever and ever.
    He will guide us forever.[a]

a Septuagint; another reading is (compare Jerome, Syriac) *He will guide us beyond death*

OVERVIEW: This psalm and the gospel story resonate with the prophetic imagery of God's word—law and gospel—radiating from Zion, God's church, and drawing all nations to the Lord. With the psalmist, the reformers marvel at Zion's beauty, emblematic of God's presence: by her beauty she preserves and protects her citizens; by her beauty she terrifies and trounces her enemies. Zion's beauty is the gospel message, that on this mountain Christ our Lord was crucified and resurrected, he ascended into heaven and sent his Spirit to dwell among and lead his people in all nations. No worldly confederation can succeed against Zion; the Lord our God will protect and vindicate his church. And we too are called to consider the church's ramparts and citadels, to love, adorn, protect and defend the church.

48:1-3 Holy Mount Zion

SEVEN IS SYMBOLIC AND MYSTERIOUS.
MARTIN LUTHER: According to the letter the church starts on Mount Zion, which is in the north; whence it gets its name. Thus, he here calls the church by seven names—many and great mysteries are contained in sevens. GLOSSA ON PSALM 48 (1513–1515).[1]

AN EFFICACIOUS REMEDY. VIKTORIN STRIGEL: The distinct glory of the church . . . is the true recognition of God, prayer and worship. The psalmist describes this glory with magnificent and splendid words. For he compares the church to a city and a mountain, in which God is praised and

---

[1]WA 3:268.

worshiped, in part with the doctrine which he himself handed down, and in part by the obedience that he demands. Furthermore, he compares the church with a shoot that produces the wondrously medicinal balsam, which heals wounds without pain. For the word of the gospel, which the church proclaims aloud in the world, is an efficacious remedy, removing sin and death. But why does he so often mention the mountain of Zion? Because in Jerusalem the Son of God was crucified and resurrected, and from there his gospel spread throughout the whole world, as Isaiah and Micah predicted: "From Zion will come the Law, and the Word of the Lord from Jerusalem." To this mountain all nations will gather, that is, they will embrace the doctrine that spread from Zion. Therefore, those who either reject and spurn this Word, whose preaching began in Zion . . . or corrupt it impiously and foully, as do the heretics of all periods . . . we know that they are not the church but enemies of the Son of God and chaff destined for eternal fire. HYPONĒMATA IN ALL THE PSALMS.[2]

NO JOY WITHOUT GOD. JOHN CALVIN: The psalmist calls Mount Zion the joy of the whole earth, and he does so not because, as Jewish interpreters foolishly talk, that country was healthy on account of the mildness of the climate, or because it produced sweet and excellent fruits, which might gratify and yield delight to foreign nations—for this also is a cold and unsatisfactory speculation—but because from there salvation was to issue forth to the whole world. Yes, all nations have received from there the light of life and the testimony of heavenly grace. If the joy which human beings experience and cherish is without God, the issue of their joy at length will be destruction, and their laughter will be turned into gnashing of teeth. But Christ appeared with his gospel out of Zion, to fill the world with true joy and everlasting felicity. In the time of the prophet, the knowledge of the gospel, it is true, had not yet reached foreign nations, but he makes use of this

manner of expression with the highest propriety, to teach the Israelites that true blessedness was to be sought for only from the gracious covenant of God, which was deposited in that holy place.

At the same time also, he has foretold what was at length fulfilled in the Last Day by the coming of Christ. From this we may learn that to cause the hearts of the godly to rejoice, the favor of God alone abundantly suffices. On the other hand, when it is withdrawn, all people must inevitably be thrown into a state of wretchedness and sorrow. What is added immediately after, concerning the city of the great King, is intended to show that Mount Zion was not only holy itself, but that this high prerogative had been conferred on it to render sacred the whole city, where God had chosen his seat, so that he might rule over all people. COMMENTARY ON THE PSALMS.[3]

HOLY WORSHIP THRIVES IN JERUSALEM ONLY. CARDINAL CAJETAN: The first [description] relates to the city's beauty. It is a "beautiful bride," in the sense that the city has a beauty like that of a lovely bride. For this reason it is also commended by love, just as a beautiful spouse is loveable and much desired, and so on.

The second description is this: "Bringing joy to the whole earth." Among parts of the earth the city has shared its beauty. Moreover, it is a source of joy for the remaining parts of the earth. This is what lies behind Lamentations 2. Jeremiah introduces these two descriptions when he speaks about the ruins of Jerusalem: "Is this the city of perfect beauty, the joy of the whole earth?" The Hebrews say that truth of this second description lies in the city's wholesome air that it shares with all nations, saying that people who come from all parts of the world are kept in good health in Jerusalem, whereas we see that people who cross over into remote climates are weakened. I think that the city is called the joy of the whole earth because holy worship thrives in Jerusalem alone. COMMENTARY ON PSALM 48.[4]

---

[2]Strigel, *Hyponēmata*, 231; citing Is 2:3; Mic 4:2.

[3]CTS 9:219-20* (CO 31:473-74).
[4]Cajetan, *In Sacrae Scripturae Expositionem*, 3:172; citing Lam 2:15.

48:4-8 *You Have Struck Terror in the Hearts of Kings*

VENI, VIDI, VICI. JOHN CALVIN: The language should be resolved thus: As soon as they saw the city they marveled. It is related of Caesar in ancient times that, when speaking of the ease with which he subdued Egypt, he made use of the laconic saying: "I came, I saw, I conquered." But the prophet here states, on the contrary, that the ungodly were struck with amazement at the mere sight of the city, as if God had dazzled their eyes with the splendor of his glory. COMMENTARY ON THE PSALMS.[5]

THE LORD CANNOT BE OUTFLANKED. DAVID DICKSON: One work of the Lord's justice and power against his enemies, and one experience of his merciful defense of his church, should lead his people to acknowledge his sovereign power and omnipotence over all. Having all creatures at his disposal, he can secure his people from all quarters and destroy all those that rise up against him. He who scattered the armies of kings who invaded us has all the power in the world, by sea and land, to overtake your enemies. COMMENTARY ON PSALM 48:7.[6]

A MIGHTY CONSOLATION. NIKOLAUS SELNECKER: "The ships of Tarshish" are a certain sort of ship in the ocean. For the psalmist wants to say, "Whether we are attacked by land or by sea, we will remain unharmed, for we have God as our protection." God can knock down and drown with a mere wind every power, every ship and everything in them. This is a truly powerful consolation. THE WHOLE PSALTER.[7]

48:9-14 *Contemplate the Steadfast Love of the Lord*

UNDISTURBED TRANQUILITY. JOHN CALVIN: Now, if this symbol of the presence of God, which was only a shadow, ought to have had such influence on the minds of true believers under the former dispensation as to make them hope for life in the midst of death, surely when Christ has now descended among us, to unite us much more closely to his Father, we have sufficient ground for continuing in a state of undisturbed tranquility, even if the world should be embroiled in confusion and turned upside down. Only it must be our endeavor that the service of God may flourish purely and wholly among us. And thus the glory of his temple may shine forth in our midst. COMMENTARY ON THE PSALMS.[8]

HEBREW IDIOM, CHRISTIAN ALLEGORY. RUDOLF GWALTHER: The Hebrews called cities "daughters." Here we can understand every Christian people and congregation. THE PSALTER.[9]

JERUSALEM IS THE CHURCH. KONRAD PELLIKAN: The considering of every side of Jerusalem—its walls and palaces, of course its external and internal magnificence—is taught because it is so great that its memory ought never to pass away. Who is the sort of person that understands this about that earthly city that was totally leveled so long ago? Therefore here a type is disclosed, of the church of Christ: no one can marvel enough at its walls and palaces, that is, its unconquered fortifications against whatever sorts of enemies, or its ornaments for the virtues of an honored life. COMMENTARY ON PSALM 48:12.[10]

CHERISH THE CHURCH. PHILIPP MELANCHTHON: A command is added concerning loving, adorning, protecting and defending the church. Just as he says elsewhere, "Ask for those things which pertain to the peace of Jerusalem," therefore he commands here, "Faithfully build up her walls," that is, love and cherish the church in all offices. Teachers should rightly teach and not wall in the church with depraved opinions and destructive, noisome disputes. It is the concern of princes to preserve the ministry of the gospel for all

[5]CTS 9:222-23 (CO 31:475).
[6]Dickson, *First Fifty Psalms*, 328*.
[7]Selnecker, *Der gantze Psalter*, 1:221r.

[8]CTS 9:228* (CO 31:478).
[9]Gwalther, *Der Psalter*, 84v.
[10]Pellikan, *Commentaria Bibliorum*, 4:97r.

posterity and not to exercise cruelty against the pious who rightly understand it, but to protect them and not to allow true doctrine to be extinguished. Youths should love their necessary study of the church, and the people should protect both the studies of doctrine and the public ministry [of the gospel]. He commands these and similar duties in this verse so that we who have been admonished should love both the church and the study of doctrine more. COMMENTS ON THE PSALMS.[11]

NO UNKNOWN GOD. JOHN CALVIN: We have not an uncertain God, or a God of whom we have only a confused and an indistinct apprehension, but one of whom we have a true and solid knowledge. When the faithful here declare that God will continue unchangeably steadfast to his purpose in maintaining his church, their object is to encourage and strengthen themselves to persevere in a continued course of faith. COMMENTARY ON THE PSALMS.[12]

---

[11]MO 13:1103; citing Ps 122:6.

[12]CTS 9:232-33 (CO 31:480).

49:1-20 WHY SHOULD I FEAR IN TIMES OF TROUBLE?

To the choirmaster. A Psalm of the Sons of Korah.

¹ Hear this, all peoples!
　Give ear, all inhabitants of the world,
² both low and high,
　rich and poor together!
³ My mouth shall speak wisdom;
　the meditation of my heart shall be
　　understanding.
⁴ I will incline my ear to a proverb;
　I will solve my riddle to the music of the lyre.

⁵ Why should I fear in times of trouble,
　when the iniquity of those who cheat me sur-
　　rounds me,
⁶ those who trust in their wealth
　and boast of the abundance of their riches?
⁷ Truly no man can ransom another,
　or give to God the price of his life,
⁸ for the ransom of their life is costly
　and can never suffice,
⁹ that he should live on forever
　and never see the pit.

¹⁰ For he sees that even the wise die;
　the fool and the stupid alike must perish
　and leave their wealth to others.
¹¹ Their graves are their homes forever,ᵃ
　their dwelling places to all generations,
　though they called lands by their own names.

¹² Man in his pomp will not remain;
　he is like the beasts that perish.
¹³ This is the path of those who have foolish
　　confidence;
　yet after them people approve of their
　　boasts.ᵇ   Selah
¹⁴ Like sheep they are appointed for Sheol;
　death shall be their shepherd,
and the upright shall rule over them in the
　　morning.
　Their form shall be consumed in Sheol, with
　　no place to dwell.
¹⁵ But God will ransom my soul from the power
　of Sheol,
　for he will receive me.   Selah

¹⁶ Be not afraid when a man becomes rich,
　when the glory of his house increases.
¹⁷ For when he dies he will carry nothing away;
　his glory will not go down after him.
¹⁸ For though, while he lives, he counts himself
　　blessed
　—and though you get praise when you do
　　well for yourself—
¹⁹ his soul will go to the generation of his fathers,
　who will never again see light.
²⁰ Man in his pomp yet without understanding
　is like the beasts that perish.

a Septuagint, Syriac, Targum; Hebrew *Their inward thought was that their homes were forever*　b Or *and of those after them who approve of their boasts*

OVERVIEW: Our commentators demonstrate general agreement on the basic meaning of this psalm: it is a message of comfort to God's people and an exhortation to remember his promises. The reformers expend little energy identifying the particular historical occasion on which this psalm was composed. Instead, they focus on the psalmist's antithesis between worldly things and eternal things, encouraging believers to resist the temporal temptations that satisfy mortal desires and to trust in the Lord for their deliverance while they await eternal rest.

RIGHTEOUS BEFORE GOD, I CAN ENDURE ALL TRIALS. NIKOLAUS SELNECKER: This is a psalm of comfort for the church and for all believers, that they will not be exasperated when the godless prosper, and are wealthy and mighty, and all have their bellies filled, trusting in and depending on themselves; they too must die and out of all their goods and passions they can't take anything more with them than a linen cloth or sheet in which they are sewed and buried.... This psalm teaches us that we should commend ourselves to the eternal and to look to eternal salvation, so that we will be able stand at the Last Judgment and inherit eternal glory and joy....

Since, however, everyone pays attention to the external and bodily fortune of human beings—which is wrong and against God and great foolishness—therefore the prophet begins to cry out as if he wanted to say, "You fools who live in the world, listen to me! I want to say it quite differently than you think. Your thoughts, words and curiosities are foolish. When you see a rich, mighty person, you fear him, coddle him and honor him, while you disregard a poor, pious person. When a strong, barbaric meathead becomes your enemy, you think it is all over with you and you do not have a place in the world any longer. But listen to me! I want to teach you something quite different and to present you with an enigma or little riddle. Here is the little riddle: 'I am not afraid in days of evil, when the iniquity of my oppressors surrounds me.' That is, I may be poor, sick, miserable and forsaken—however it can be in this life—if I only would have a merciful God, then I am not afraid. Let heaven and earth suddenly come crashing down, and whoever might be against me—the devil, the world, tyrants, heretics, false brothers, unfaithful people—let them trample me with their feet or bite my heel, as they did to my Lord Christ. All their attacks, thoughts, words and gestures are sins and iniquities. But I am righteous before God through the bitter suffering and death of Christ Jesus my Savior! Why then should I be afraid?" The Whole Psalter.[1]

49:1-4 *Listen and Become Wise*

The Holy Spirit's Philosophy. John Calvin: Whoever composed this psalm discusses one of the

most important principles in divine philosophy. There is a propriety in the elevated terms designed to awaken and secure attention, with which the psalmist announces his purpose to talk about things of a deep and momentous nature. To a superficial view, indeed, the subject might seem trite and commonplace, treating, as it does, the shortness of human life and the vanity of those objects in which worldly people confide. But the real scope of the psalm is to comfort the people of God under the sufferings to which they are exposed, by teaching them to expect a happy change in their condition, when God, in his own time, shall intervene to rectify the disorders of the present system.

There is a higher lesson still inculcated by the psalmist. As God's providence of the world is not presently apparent, we must exercise patience and rise above the suggestions of carnal sense in anticipating the favorable outcome. That it is our duty to maintain a resolute struggle with our afflictions, however severe they may be, and that it were foolish to place happiness in the enjoyment of such fleeting possessions as the riches, honors or pleasures of this world, may be precepts which even the heathen philosophers have enforced, but they have uniformly failed in setting before us the true source of consolation. However admirably they talk about a happy life, they confine themselves entirely to commendations on virtue and do not bring prominently forward to our view that God governs the world, and to him alone we can repair with confidence in the most desperate circumstances.

But slender comfort can be derived on this subject from the teaching of philosophy. If, therefore, the Holy Spirit in this psalm introduces to our notice truths which are sufficiently familiar to experience, it is so that he may raise our minds from them to the higher truth of the divine government of the world, assuring us of the fact that God sits supreme, even when the wicked are triumphing most in their success, or when the righteous are trampled under the foot of the insolent, and that a day is coming when he will dash the cup of pleasure out of the hands of his enemies and bring joy to the hearts of his friends by delivering them out of their

---

[1]Selnecker, *Der gantze Psalter*, 1:222r; citing Ps 4; Ps 36; Ps 37.

most severe distresses. This is the only consideration which can impart solid comfort under our afflictions. Formidable and terrible in themselves, they would overwhelm our souls if the Lord did not lift on us the light of his countenance. Were we not assured that he watches over our safety, we could find no remedy from our evils and no quarter to which we might resort under them. COMMENTARY ON THE PSALMS.[2]

THREE HEBREW TERMS FOR *HUMAN BEING*.
MARTIN LUTHER: In Hebrew there are three designations for "human being." The first is *ʾādām*. This, strictly speaking, refers to the bodily nature of human beings and the external human being, according to which he was shaped from the clay of the earth. *ʾĀdām* properly denotes earth, especially reddish earth. And so the apostle says very aptly that Adam was a type of the One who was to come, for the earthly and physical human being is a type of the heavenly (that is, the spiritual). Hence he says, "If we have borne the image of the earthly."

The second is *ʾĕnôš*. This is interpreted as one who forgets or one who has given up. It properly speaks of human beings according to the rational nature, according to which they have been steeped in the body of sin and have become desperate and forgetful. Therefore Psalm 8 beautifully combines these two names when it says, "What is *ʾĕnôš* that you are mindful of him, or the son of *ʾādām* that you visit him?" As if to say, "God, why are you mindful of those who are totally desperate and have been consigned to forgetfulness? And why do you visit those who are the lowest earth?" God's regard is astounding, that he is mindful of the despairing and that he visits the vile earth, choosing the weak things and the things that are not.

The third is *ʾîš*. It denotes the male human being, while *ʾiššāh* denotes the female. It properly designates the one who is the head or the one who excels among others, as hero and chief. Accordingly we have here: "All who are *ʾādām* and sons of *ʾîšîm*," that is, "all of you who are of the earth and

very lowly as well as those who are chiefs and nobles among you." Nothing can follow this characteristic of the Hebrew language. FIRST PSALMS LECTURES (1513–1515).[3]

INSTRUCTIONS FOR TEACHERS. WOLFGANG MUSCULUS: Here it must be noted what is fitting for those who desire to instruct others in wisdom and understanding. First, all the hearts of those who want to teach others both speak with their mouth and are struck by a sense that what they teach did not merely originate in their mouth but has been pondered in their hearts. Not because all the meditations of the human heart are good, but because those things which in general are good in themselves are mentioned with much greater profit if they affect the soul of the one teaching. . . . The second is that those who teach others should not think that they therefore teach others as if what they teach does not pertain to themselves at all. Instead they should also know that their ears must be alert to proper doctrine. . . . To incline one's ear is to listen diligently with the purpose of the mind and to learn what has been said: "They incline ears which hear" is a metaphor selected by those living at the time; thus they declare that they listen diligently. COMMENTARY ON THE PSALMS.[4]

PARABLES EXCITE CURIOSITY AND THUS DILIGENCE. HULDRYCH ZWINGLI: If God wants his Word to be understood, why does he speak in parables and riddles? . . . The fact that in times past God taught by parables but in these last days has revealed himself fully by the Lord Jesus Christ indicates to us that God wished to give his message to human beings in a gentle and attractive way. For it is of the nature of what is presented in parables and proverbs and riddles that it appeals to the understanding of human beings and brings them to knowledge and indeed increases that knowledge. . . . For when the parable or proverb has provoked

---

[2]CTS 9:234-36* (CO 31:481-82).

[3]LW 10:224* (WA 3:273); citing Rom 5:14; 1 Cor 15:49; Ps 8:4; 1 Cor 1:27-28.
[4]Musculus, *In Psalterium Commentarii*, 562.

us to search out its hidden meaning, once we have found it we value it more highly than if it had been presented to us plainly. So then as it says in Psalm 49: "My mouth shall speak of wisdom, and the meditation of my heart shall be of understanding; I will incline my ear to a parable, I will open my dark saying on the sweet harp." The heavenly and divine wisdom reveals its will to human beings in the form of sweet parables, so that those who might otherwise be dull and unwilling are persuaded to listen, and the truth which is discovered is received the more firmly and valued the more highly, and the divine lesson is busy and active all the longer in the understanding, and its roots sink deeper into the heart. OF THE CLARITY AND CERTAINTY OF THE WORD OF GOD.[5]

A COMFORTING RIDDLE. THE ENGLISH ANNO-TATIONS: A "parable" in the Scripture, and *ḥîdātî* as well (here translated "dark saying") is sometimes taken for a sententious speech or excellent doctrine, though otherwise neither very obscure nor parabolical. And such is the doctrine of this psalm, which very well deserves the solemnity of this extraordinary prefacing: a doctrine of as much comfort and consequence to people as any can be, delivered here more plainly than in any other part of Scripture until Christ's time, Daniel excepted. The sum is this: that we should not be troubled at the prosperity of the wicked and ungodly, because this world and all its delights are things so transitory, and God has provided better things for those that live in his fear in another world. ANNOTA-TIONS ON PSALM 49:4.[6]

ALL SCRIPTURE'S RIDDLES ARE SOLVED IN CHRIST. MARTIN LUTHER: Through Christ the mysteries placed in the Psalter concerning him were opened. Second, here in the Psalter, that is, in this psalm, Christ teaches what he later taught in the gospel. And thus his propositions, which he

later opened in the gospel, he opens here, too, prophetically. . . . Therefore "to uncover on the psalter" means to bring forth the spirit and the mystical sense in parable and shadow—such as the letter is. But it is certain that this is how Christ acted. FIRST PSALMS LECTURES (1513–1515).[7]

49:5-9 Human Impotence in the Face of Trouble

EVIL DAYS WILL COME. DAVID DICKSON: Here the psalmist presupposes that evil days will come. He presupposes that every sinful or iniquitous action he has committed during the passage of his life leaves behind an impression of guiltiness to be taken notice of thereafter—like a person's footprint when he lifts his heel and walks forward. He presupposes that, after the repeated, daily exercise of repentance and the remission of sin, in the day of trouble a person may be brought back and held to account, and old reckonings may be raked up again by the troubled conscience and by the accuser of the believers. God will be ruling over this business for the further glory of the riches of his grace, and the further good of his exercised child. Here the psalmist foresees and speaks of his looking for days of evil, and the iniquity of his heels compassing him about, as what shall or may befall him. COMMENTARY ON PSALM 49:5.[8]

THE INIQUITY OF MY HEELS SURROUNDS ME. THE ENGLISH ANNOTATIONS: There are only two interpretations of this verse worthy of consideration, because this is a point of high consequence. First (as in most ancients) there are those who by "heels" understand the last of a person's life, or the day of his death, to this purpose: Why should I commit anything that I should need to fear when that dreadful day comes, when sentence, in private first and in public afterwards, must be passed on me? The principal cause of fearing is the possibility of it emerging that at the end and close of my life I

---

[5]LCC 24:72-73* (ZSW 1:358-59); citing Sir 39:3; Ps 49:3.
[6]Downame, ed., *Annotations*, 6Fir*. The ESV uses "proverb" and "riddle," respectively, for the KJV's "parable" and "dark saying."
[7]LW 10:228, 229* (WA 3:276, 277).
[8]Dickson, *First Fifty Psalms*, 334*.

am encircled with sins, especially those where, in gaining wealth for myself, I have made no conscience to oppress others. But because it is in my power, through God's grace, to prevent this, or in the case that I have sinned, to repent in time through his mercy and obtain pardon, why should I fear so much? . . . The second interpretation, therefore, which I reckon considerable, is to take 'āwōn, "iniquity," for wicked people, the abstract for the concrete, which is usual enough, for this effect: Why should I fear, when wicked, unjust people (encouraged by their success and worldly prosperity) pursue me closely on every side? Either I fear and am dismayed, or I put my trust in God. ANNOTATIONS ON PSALM 49:5.[9]

DEATH COMES FOR EVERYONE. NIKOLAUS SELNECKER: No one can save himself from death, however mighty and rich, beautiful and strong he may be. "We each hasten to the end, one after another."[10] We all must die, be it sooner or later. Nor can someone free another person from death. It costs too much. It cost the pure, precious blood of Jesus Christ with which we have been loosed and freed from eternal death. Human works, holiness, power, violence, riches—all these do nothing in this matter! And even if someone lives for a long time, keeps good spirits, never thinks about death, is without worry, still he has to get in line. Death pulls up a stool whenever the hourglass or clock has run out. "For each his day waits; his time is brief and irretrievable."[11] Wise, sensible, clever, knowledgeable, learned, well-known people must die too, just like dolts and fools. "Philosophers, sophists, theologians, jurists, doctors and the wealthy, the diseased and poor, lords and their subjects, the low, the high, old men and fathers, infants and mothers—absolutely no one is excluded, they all are forced thither," the children in school recite. Everyone must approach it, like dying cattle, however wise, manly or learned they may be

considered by others. And if they have walked without God's fear, in self-assured security and an unrepentant life, then they must walk to Ceres's son and the black pyre, that they would lie in hell like sheep, that they would be slaughtered and killed by eternal death. Death and the abominable wolf devours them, as Isaiah 14 preaches about the mighty kingdom Babylon: "Your pomp is brought down into hell; maggots are your bed and worms your blankets."

But for the pious it is very different: they are redeemed and inherit eternal life. Thus, David exhorts us that we should not let ourselves err, even if the godless become rich, like the rich usurer and glutton (Lk 16). Pay attention to the end! They are pitifully brought down to their old ancestors who were also godless—without cross and without light—like cattle. However, pay attention to yourself, trust in God, wait on his call, believe in Christ, pray and commend your spirit into the hands of God day and night and in every moment. Then there is no time of need—neither with your body nor with your soul. That we would do this zealously and from the heart, O Lord Jesus Christ, help me and others to this! Amen. THE WHOLE PSALTER.[12]

49:10-15 All Human Beings Must Perish

THE CHIEF ANTITHESIS: WORLDLY AND HEAVENLY WEALTH. PHILIPP MELANCHTHON: Human wisdom is greatly offended by this scandal, that it sees the just treated wickedly. God himself with his own voice explains this dispute, which human reason is not able to explain. He states the things which afflict the just, and he says that another judge remains over this life. This is the heart of this psalm—everyone agrees on account of this antithesis. They err who place power, wealth and the desires of this mortal life ahead of God, and on account of those present goods neglect the confession of true doctrine and the other duties owed to God. For even if they should flourish now,

---

[9]Downame, ed., *Annotations*, 6F1r*.
[10]Ovid, *Metamorphoses* 10.33.
[11]Virgil, *Aeneid* 10.467.

[12]Selnecker, *Der gantze Psalter*, 1:223v; citing Is 14:11.

yet after their death they will fall into eternal destruction, from which no wealth or human protection can rescue them. But in contrast, the pious, even if they are now in great affliction, yet in their death God will deliver them and will adorn them with eternal goods—life, wisdom, righteousness, joy—in that eternal experience of the church. Therefore, this psalm contains the article concerning eternal life and future judgment. COMMENTS ON THE PSALMS.[13]

THE PUNISHMENT OF THE WICKED. VIKTORIN STRIGEL: This verse describes the very last level of the punishment of the impious, namely, eternal misery, which is a worm constantly gnawing away at the conscience, and a fire that will never cease but will torture their bodies without end, as Isaiah says in his last chapter: "Their worm will not die, and their fire will not be extinguished." Just as "the eye has not seen, nor has the ear heard, nor is the heart of a person able to comprehend the good things which God has prepared for those that love him," so no one, either in thought or in speech, is able to exhaust the magnitude of eternal punishment.

But here someone will object, "I do not see how Paul, who was killed by Nero, is the lord of Nero." I respond: Although Paul was killed by a most cruel tyrant, nevertheless he is not reduced to nothing, nor is he abandoned in destruction and death, as Nero was, but is adorned with eternal rewards and in the Last Day of the world, together with Christ, will judge Nero and all the impious. "Now our life," as it is written in Colossians 3, "is hidden away with Christ in God. But when Christ, who is our life, will be made manifest, then we also will be manifest with him in glory." Then the impious will have in their mouths and in their minds those words in Proverbs 5. *HYPONĒMATA* IN ALL THE PSALMS.[14]

IGNORANT OF HISTORY, WE ARE DOOMED TO REPEAT IT. JOHN CALVIN: If human beings reflect at all on the judgments which God executes in the world, we might expect that they would particularly consider his dealings with their immediate predecessors. When, wholly insensible to the lessons which should be learned from their fate, they precipitate themselves into the same courses, this convincingly demonstrates their brutish folly. COMMENTARY ON THE PSALMS.[15]

CHRIST OUR SUN. GIOVANNI DIODATI: The elect are partakers of Christ's eternal kingdom in the blessed resurrection, which is called the great daybreak. They shall obtain a full victory and have quiet dominion over the world and the worldly. ANNOTATIONS ON PSALM 49:14.[16]

BELIEVERS ARE COREGENTS WITH CHRIST. RUDOLF GWALTHER: These words hold a magnificent consolation, namely, after the darkness of this world will follow a joyous morning. And the godless will be plunged into hell's anguish and the pious believers will be exalted before all the world. For Christ promised his kingdom to them, so that they would reign with him. THE PSALTER.[17]

LIFE BEYOND THE GRAVE. JOHN CALVIN: The prophet does not deny his liability to death, but he looks to God as the one who will defend and redeem him from it. We have here a convincing proof of that faith in which the saints under the law lived and died. It is evident that their views were directed to another and a higher life, to which the present was only preparatory. Had the prophet merely intended to intimate that he expected deliverance from some ordinary emergency, this would have been no more than what is frequently done by the children of the world, whom God often delivers from great dangers. But here it is evident that he hoped for a life beyond the grave,

[13]MO 13:1105.
[14]Strigel, *Hyponēmata*, 236; citing Is 66:24; 1 Cor 2:9 (cf. Is 64:4); Col 3:3-4; Prov 5:11-14.

[15]CTS 9:247* (CO 31:488).
[16]Diodati, *Pious Annotations*, Tt3v*; citing Song 2:17; 7:12; 2 Pet 1:19.
[17]Gwalther, *Der Psalter*, 86v.

that he extended his glance beyond this sublunary sphere and anticipated the morning which will introduce eternity. From this we may conclude that the promises of the law were spiritual, and that our ancestors who embraced them were willing to confess themselves pilgrims on earth and sought an inheritance in heaven. . . .

The despairing fears which so many entertain when descending to the grave spring from the fact that they do not commend their spirit to the preserving care of God. They do not consider it in the light of a precious deposit which will be safe in his protecting hands. Let our faith be established in the great truth that our soul, though it appears to vanish on its separation from the body, is in reality only gathered to the bosom of God, there to be kept until the day of the resurrection. COMMENTARY ON THE PSALMS.[18]

THE MYSTERY OF GOD'S REDEMPTION. MARTIN BUCER: He foretells with these verses that God gives immortality to his own, the rest only enjoy their goods in this age. But, he says, "God will redeem my soul from the hand of the pit," that is, of death, he will also restore the life and happiness of the body, with the soul enjoying the blessed comfort of God while the body that has been committed to the ground is wormfood. In fact from the cause which he supplies of his happiness, he declares that the same is common to all believers. He says "Because God supports me." . . . Moreover he supports those whom he elects to life, to whom he gives his own Spirit; all these, as the Savior said, will never taste death. He will raise them up on the very Last Day, and in the meantime he will give their souls his joy in heaven. And this is a mystery because flesh and blood can by no means understand it, and thus the *selāh* is added. HOLY PSALMS.[19]

A MOST APPROPRIATE *SELĀH*. THE ENGLISH ANNOTATIONS: If *selāh* is a note—as many think it is—of exaltation or elevation of mind, I do not know of a place in the whole book that better deserves or requires it. Here is a clear testimony for the immortality of the soul and for a better life after this: without this assurance we might say with the apostle, "Let us eat and drink, for tomorrow we must die." ANNOTATIONS ON PSALM 49:15.[20]

49:16-20 *Pomp and Pride Are Vain*

BEASTS THAT PERISH. THE ENGLISH ANNOTATIONS: Before, in the twelfth verse, to be like the beasts that perish was to be subject to mortality like them, which is the condition of all people, both good and bad. Now that he has distinguished and speaks of the wicked only, to be like the beasts that perish must be to die without hope of any further good or happiness, which is the case for all brutes. Or, like brutes in their life, in that they take care only of the present, to fare well and pass time merrily, not considering what will become of their souls, as creatures that had no souls except for that which perishes with the body. But in very deed, the psalmist in this psalm may seem to set out the case of the wicked at the point of death as being in no way different from brutes. ANNOTATIONS ON PSALM 49:20.[21]

MAKE US ONE. THE BOOK OF COMMON PRAYER (1549): Almighty God, you have knit together your elect in one communion and fellowship in the mystical body of your Son Christ our Lord; grant us grace so to follow your holy saints in all virtues and godly living, that we may come to those unspeakable joys which you have prepared for all those who unfeignedly love you, through Jesus Christ. COLLECT FOR ALL SAINTS DAY.[22]

---

[18]CTS 9:251, 252-53* (CO 31:491).
[19]Bucer, *Sacrorum Psalmorum*, 223r; citing Mt 16:28.

[20]Downame, ed., *Annotations*, 6F1v*; citing 1 Cor 15:32. See above comment on *selāh* at Ps 3:2c, pp. 32-33.
[21]Downame, ed., *Annotations*, 6F1v*.
[22]BCP 1549, 75*.

50:1-23 THEOPHANY OF THE DIVINE JUDGE

A Psalm of Asaph.

¹ The Mighty One, God the LORD,
　　speaks and summons the earth
　　from the rising of the sun to its setting.
² Out of Zion, the perfection of beauty,
　　God shines forth.

³ Our God comes; he does not keep silence;^a
　　before him is a devouring fire,
　　around him a mighty tempest.
⁴ He calls to the heavens above
　　and to the earth, that he may judge his people:
⁵ "Gather to me my faithful ones,
　　who made a covenant with me by sacrifice!"
⁶ The heavens declare his righteousness,
　　for God himself is judge!　　　　　Selah

⁷ "Hear, O my people, and I will speak;
　　O Israel, I will testify against you.
　　I am God, your God.
⁸ Not for your sacrifices do I rebuke you;
　　your burnt offerings are continually before
　　me.
⁹ I will not accept a bull from your house
　　or goats from your folds.
¹⁰ For every beast of the forest is mine,
　　the cattle on a thousand hills.
¹¹ I know all the birds of the hills,
　　and all that moves in the field is mine.

¹² "If I were hungry, I would not tell you,
　　for the world and its fullness are mine.

¹³ Do I eat the flesh of bulls
　　or drink the blood of goats?
¹⁴ Offer to God a sacrifice of thanksgiving,^b
　　and perform your vows to the Most High,
¹⁵ and call upon me in the day of trouble;
　　I will deliver you, and you shall glorify me."

¹⁶ But to the wicked God says:
　　"What right have you to recite my statutes
　　or take my covenant on your lips?
¹⁷ For you hate discipline,
　　and you cast my words behind you.
¹⁸ If you see a thief, you are pleased with him,
　　and you keep company with adulterers.

¹⁹ "You give your mouth free rein for evil,
　　and your tongue frames deceit.
²⁰ You sit and speak against your brother;
　　you slander your own mother's son.
²¹ These things you have done, and I have been
　　silent;
　　you thought that I^c was one like yourself.
But now I rebuke you and lay the charge
　　before you.

²² "Mark this, then, you who forget God,
　　lest I tear you apart, and there be none to
　　deliver!
²³ The one who offers thanksgiving as his
　　sacrifice glorifies me;
　　to one who orders his way rightly
　　I will show the salvation of God!"

a Or May our God come, and not keep silence　b Or Make thanksgiving your sacrifice to God　c Or that the I AM

OVERVIEW: The reformers gladly utilize this psalm's description of the Lord's power and majesty in judgment as an opportunity to contemplate God's glory; they especially focus on the nature of true worship. They understand this psalm to reinterpret the Old Testament ceremonial and sacrificial system as a religion of the heart: our beliefs and attitudes affect the effectiveness of our actions before God. Here David teaches that in all dispensations, true worship is spiritual and the external provisions must reflect internal truths. To separate internal conviction from external worship is hypocritical; but also, to imagine that human beings can worship without external expressions is to deceive ourselves. Our actions should reflect Christ's sacrifice for us. Only by orienting our wills to God's are we able to worship in truth, power and grace.

THE GLOBAL CALL OF THE GOSPEL. SEBASTIAN MÜNSTER: Now this psalm teaches, according to our interpreters, how God has called all the nations of the earth to the gospel. He has protected his people from the hand of the mighty; he prefers acts of thanks and praise to all sacrifices. The rabbis also understand this psalm to be about judgment, which they state is to come at the time of the Redeemer; for this reason they expound the beginning of this psalm, 'el 'elohim, as Judge of judges. THE TEMPLE OF THE LORD: PSALM 50.[1]

Superscription: *Who Is Asaph?*

THE PSALMS OF ASAPH. NIKOLAUS SELNECKER: Asaph was one of the foremost singers and musicians under David, just as today the court of a great lord includes a choir director. To this man and his associates David gave several psalms with which to praise God, to thank him and to laud his name. Thus, we call these "psalms of Asaph," as also Psalms 73–[83]. THE WHOLE PSALTER.[2]

50:1-6 *The Transcendent Lord Is Judge*

GOD'S GLORY BURSTS FORTH IN CHRIST. NIKOLAUS SELNECKER: The beginning of this psalm is quite magnificent and grand. God the Lord the Mighty One, the Lord of all lords, Creator and Sustainer of heaven and earth, our God, Father and Judge converses with and calls to the world with his voice, yes, with his eternal Word through his Son: "Out of Zion breaks forth the beautiful glory of God." Not from the mountain of

law, Sinai, which is full of rocks, stones and is wilderness and is where the law was given with thunder and lightning. Even the word *Sinai* in itself is petrifying and prickly, because it means a thornbush and hedge, a thicket, by which the law's manner and curse, terror and wrath are indicated. Instead it comes from Zion, which was in the beautiful city of Jerusalem, a bright mountain and towering summit in the land, on which one could clearly see all the surrounding area and would not remain and dwell in the dark valley. This indicates the manner of the holy gospel, through which we are illuminated and are on the mountain of God, which is often contemplated in the Psalms (as in Pss 2–3; 15; 20; 24; 36; 43; 48; 61; 68; 72; 74; 78; 87; 99; 121; 125; 133). For Zion is the true mountain of God. Zion represents any specific place where the teaching of the gospel—which first broke out from Zion and was preached by the Son of God—is taught and kept purely and clearly. There God is and dwells, the beautiful glory of God is there, namely, the eternal Son of God, Christ Jesus, the glory of his Father, light from light, the true Ḥašmal [Radiance], with his Word and gospel.

Our God, namely, Christ Jesus, our Lord and Savior, who comes to us, became a true human being and is not silent but fulfills the will of God his Father, proclaims and preaches the same, punishes the world and consoles poor consciences. A devouring fire goes forth from him, that is, he consumes and burns up everything that will not obey him or will not believe in him—all work-righteousness, idolatry, unrepentance, and stiffnecked and militant self-assurance, tyrants, heretics and anything else that is contrary to him or his gospel. All around him is a mighty tempest, thunder and lightning against all his enemies. He thunders with his Word, strikes with lightning and casts everything to the ground, as he did in Paul's conversion. He secures the victory in his Word. He calls to heaven and earth, to angels and human beings, that they should serve and follow him. For he will judge, rule, help and save his people from the devil, death, sin and hell. This involves great toil and labor. Such work of redemption is indeed great, and it costs a great deal—not the

---

[1] Münster, *Miqdaš YHWH*, 1201.
[2] Selnecker, *Der gantze Psalter*, 1:224r; citing 1 Chron 15:17, 19; 16:4-7, 37-38. Selnecker fails to include Ps 83 among the psalms of Asaph.

blood of oxen and calves, but instead the precious and worthy blood of our God and Brother Jesus Christ. THE WHOLE PSALTER.[3]

CONCERNING THE ISLAMIC INTERPRETATION OF THIS PSALM. THE ENGLISH ANNOTATIONS: Because it has been thought fit that the Turkish (so-called, though it is written in Arabic) Qur'an, a book full of blasphemies in matters of religion and often senseless absurdities in points of human reason, should be communicated to the people in the vulgar English tongue, it will not be thought amiss to take notice that in all of the Scriptures, either of the Old or New Testament, there are two places in particular that Muslims take hold of, and are wont to object to Christians. This is one of them. I have lately seen a letter from one of that sect to a Christian in Rome, as I remember (the letter is printed) where those two places are much pressed and insisted on. They quote the words of this verse thus: "God has shown out of Zion *Gelilan Mahmudan*," that is, a "glorious or renowned" crown. By which crown, they would have a kingdom, and they take *renowned* (*mahmudan* in Arabic) to mean "Muhammad," because of the affinity, or rather the identity, of the letters. But granting that it has been found as such in some Arabic translations of the Psalms (even though it is yet to be seen by some who are very learned and well-versed in these languages and books and have seen many other printed texts), what does it matter, unless it were so in the original Hebrew as well? Here, we find neither letters nor sense to this purpose. The words which they press in the Hebrew are *miklal yōpî*. In the first indeed, *miklal*, for the letters (not that it will serve their argument), there is affinity enough, but for the second (*yōpî*), there is none at all. Yet were it indeed so, even in the original text, would this justify their impostures and forgeries—not to be refuted or maintained by carnal allusions—or affinities of bare words and letters,

but by evidences of truth, reason and history? ANNOTATIONS ON PSALM 50:2.[4]

INTIMATIONS OF GOD'S TRANSCENDENCE. MOÏSE AMYRAUT: These clouds pertain to the secret majesty of God whose revelation creatures are not able to sustain. ANNOTATIONS ON PSALM 50:3.[5]

CREATED ORDER TESTIFIES AGAINST OUR IGNORANCE. RUDOLF GWALTHER: The heavens and earth will be brought forth as witnesses, that our dear God has many witnesses against us in heaven and on earth. Through all created things we should learn obedience and gratitude, because we see how they hold so surely their order to which God created them. THE PSALTER.[6]

TRUE MEMBERS OF CHRIST WORSHIP TRULY. JOHN CALVIN: The passage defines those who are to be considered the true members of the church. They are those who are characterized by the spirit of meekness, practicing righteousness in their inter-action with the world, and who exercise a genuine faith with in compliance with the covenant of adoption which God has bestowed on them. This forms the true worship of God, as he has himself delivered it to us from heaven. But those who decline from it are excommunicated from the church by the Holy Spirit, whatever pretensions they may make to be considered a church of God. As to sacrifices or other ceremonies, they are of no value, except insofar as they seal to us the pure truth of God. From this it follows that all rites which do not depend on God's Word are impure, and all worship which is not drawn from Scripture is nothing other than a corruption of piety. COMMENTARY ON THE PSALMS.[7]

OUR LORD IS THE JUDGE OF JUDGES. MARTIN LUTHER: The apostles have declared this new word,

---

[3]Selnecker, *Der gantze Psalter*, 1:224r; Is 9:1-2. Ḥašmal, translated in the ESV as "gleaming metal," occurs in Ezek 1:4, 27; 8:2.

[4]Downame, ed., *Annotations*, 6F1v-6F2r*.
[5]Amyraut, *Paraphrasis in Psalmos Davidis*, 212.
[6]Gwalther, *Der Psalter*, 89r.
[7]CTS 9:264* (CO 31:498).

namely, that one day God himself, not a man in the place of God, will judge. It is therefore necessary that such judgment be universal and all-inclusive, because it is God's judgment. His representatives deal only in a partial way, but because he is supreme and most exalted, it is necessary that he himself judge all things. Therefore to declare that God is Judge is to announce a universal judgment and that someone else's righteousness, which a person might have before human beings, is not enough, but the righteousness of God is needed so that a person might be righteous before God. And this is required for the reason that a person will be judged not by a human being but by God, because God is the Judge. First Psalms Lectures (1513–1515).[8]

50:7-15 All Creation Is Mine! Do I Need You to Feed Me?

I Am Your God. Philipp Melanchthon: This address, "I am God, your God," calls the minds of all people back to the first commandment, to true works of the first commandment and to the knowledge of the promise which this phrase, "your God," declares. That is, the one who truly receives you, cares for you and gives you not only temporal goods—nourishment and governance—but also gives you eternal goods—the ministry of teaching, righteousness and eternal life on account of the Mediator. Thus, "I desire that I who rage against sins am truly feared, and likewise I demand to be believed in. I desire to be called on by faith, to be sought and looked to for a defense of this present life and for eternal goods." This phrase contains this entire teaching in "I am your God." Comments on the Psalms.[9]

If God Legislated Sacrifices, Why Does He Not Want Them? Nikolaus Selnecker: Here David teaches what the true worship of God is and what true sacrifice is, not the performance of works, that is, works or ceremonies in themselves.

As also in Isaiah God says, "Hear the word of the Lord, you princes! What is this heap of your sacrifices to me? I am fed up with your burnt offerings of rams and the fat of well-fed beasts; I have no delight in the blood of bulls." . . . Now here a Jew or someone else might wonder and ask, "If God himself introduced and commanded the sacrifices in the old covenant, why then does he say they do not please him?" This is the clear, correct answer: "All sacrifices in the old covenant were nothing other than a shadow and portent or figure for the new covenant and for Christ, who redeems us with his true sacrifice on the cross and has atoned for our sin." The Whole Psalter.[10]

External Ceremonies Are Fleeting Shadows. Martin Bucer: There is nothing more senseless than carnal striving while the concern for piety is a lie. . . . No one—no one who acknowledges that the more mature form of life is that we should be conformed to Christ and thus also to God himself, no one so equipped and instructed that all that we have done and said in every time and place are for the glory of God and for the salvation of mortals—could doubt that childish elements are whatever pertains to the corporeal rites and external ceremonies. . . . They were figures, types and shadows of the sacrifice of Christ, so also prefiguring the sacrifice of all Christians that we may offer ourselves now to God, just as Christ did. There will be at this time no more sacrificing of sheep or offering anything else. Holy Psalms.[11]

All Worship Is Praise and Prayer. John Calvin: Faith, self-denial, a holy life and patient endurance of the cross are all sacrifices which please God. But as prayer, the offspring of faith born of God, is uniformly accompanied with suffering and mortification of sin, praise, where it is genuine, indicates holiness of heart. We need not wonder that these two points of worship

---

[8]LW 10:234* (WA 3:283).
[9]MO 13:1111.

[10]Selnecker, Der gantze Psalter, 1:225r; citing Is 1:10-11.
[11]Bucer, Sacrorum Psalmorum, 226v.

should here be mentioned to represent the whole. Praise and prayer are set in opposition to ceremonies and mere external observances of religion, to teach us that the worship of God is spiritual. COMMENTARY ON THE PSALMS.[12]

THE PRESUPPOSITIONS OF THANKSGIVING.

DAVID DICKSON: The way of salvation and the worship of God is spiritual, and while it may possibly be mirrored and furthered by external bodily exercises, they do not stand on things external. More particularly, God will accept both a person and his service, insofar as he understands his want of every good thing and his inability to furnish anything to himself that he lacks. Further, he must acknowledge that God alone is the all-sufficient fountain of grace and every good gift, and must seek all he needs from God, depending on his grace when he has sought it and returning praise to God for his free and gracious gift when he has received it. This is presupposed in this offering of thanks. COMMENTARY ON PSALM 50:14.[13]

ACKNOWLEDGE GOD'S GOODNESS! NIKOLAUS

SELNECKER: How beautiful and consoling is this word! God tells us to call on him and to pray to him; he promises us his help. And all he asks for from us is a simple, lowly *Deo gratias* ["thanks be to God"]. O unbelief! O doubt! O melancholy and apathy! We are not worthy of this magnificent promise. Cry out, whoever can cry out! God will answer and pronounce the benediction, "You are blessed." We should thank him. No time of distress should be too difficult; God will help. Whom has he ever once failed? To him be all praise and thanks. Amen. THE WHOLE PSALTER.[14]

50:16-21 *The Lord Accuses Us Hypocrites*

REBUKE AGAINST HYPOCRITES. PHILIPP

MELANCHTHON: The remainder of this psalm . . .

is a rebuke of hypocrites, who try to suppress the true light of the teaching about faith and true invocation as well as exercise their ferocity against the true church so that they may retain their own rites and opinions, whether on account of superstitions or profit, so that they may not undermine the cords of power, as the papists, canonists and monks now defend their own ceremonies with great cruelty. If anyone will consider that example, he would understand more clearly why it is said here, "You who encamp against your brother," and so forth. Teaching about the distinction between true and false worship has always excited the greatest struggles, as the contentions of the prophets, Christ and the apostles demonstrate. For this reason, the cruelty of hypocrites is reprimanded here at the end of the psalm. COMMENTS ON THE PSALMS.[15]

OUR CORRUPT HUMANITY REFUSES TO OBEY.

JOHN CALVIN: The psalmist points out also the cause of perversity, which lies in the unwillingness of corrupt humanity to bear the yoke of God. They have no hesitation in granting that whatever proceeds from the mouth of God is both true and right. This honor they are willing to concede to his Word, but insofar as it proposes to regulate their conduct and restrain their sinful affections, they dislike and detest it. Our corruption makes it impossible to receive correction but makes us stand up against the Word of God. And it is also not possible that we can ever listen to it with true docility and meekness of mind until we have been brought to give ourselves up to be ruled and disciplined by its precepts. COMMENTARY ON THE PSALMS.[16]

WORD AND DEED CANNOT BE SEPARATED.

CARDINAL CAJETAN: Although in human conventions, a contradiction between what one says and how one lives is tolerable—given that human beings praise good mores and yet live badly—it is

---

[12]CTS 9:270* (CO 31:501).
[13]Dickson, *First Fifty Psalms*, 347*.
[14]Selnecker, *Der gantze Psalter*, 1:226v.

[15]MO 13:1112.
[16]CTS 9:276* (CO 31:505).

intolerable, however, to someone aspiring to Christian things, specifically, that people should represent themselves as holy by preaching, praising and giving precepts which are from God, while in another part of life conducting themselves badly. The reason is, such people hold themselves out as ministers of Christ, while doing everything in their power to weaken the faith and the Christian ministry. On the one hand—namely, by their tongue and the execution of their office—they magnify Christian precepts, and on the other, they despise them with their life. For people who are influenced more by examples than words think that what they hear from such teachers is not true, because, if it were true, those who teach it would abide by it. From this arises a greater downfall, because they think that such also were the old preachers, that they were all just seducers. So the Messiah here says in regard to such a great transgression: "You have judged," that is, you made it a matter of judgment, "that I am essentially like you," that is, that I will say and not do, like a seducer.... Although I am silent now, nevertheless "I will reprove you," in death. And "I will lay out in order" your faults, by applying penalties before "your eyes," in other words, so that you can find no excuse for yourself. COMMENTARY ON PSALM 50.[17]

A DIFFICULT BUT NEEDED WORD FOR PREACHERS AND TEACHERS. NIKOLAUS SELNECKER: This is a difficult and terrifying sermon, which all teachers in schools and churches should take to heart. They should be led truly, seriously and passionately by the Word of the divine, almighty Majesty, live irreproachably and should not shy away from punishing vice.... May God, full of mercy and lovingkindness, rule and guide us, teachers and students, with his Holy Spirit, be gracious to us on account of his name and protect us from false teaching, self-assurance, pride, greed and troublesome living.

Epiphanius writes that Origen, who lived about 189 years after Christ's birth and who transcribed

all the books of the Bible and expounded all of them, once was supposed to read at his school in Alexandria. He opened the book and came to the words: "To the godless, God says, what right do you have to recite my law?" And at these words he immediately began to weep bitterly, so that he was unable to read anything more. For he thought, what a great thing it is to proclaim God's Word, law and covenant while at the same time being a poor, miserable human being and sinner. Our mad, impudent wailers can pull a sermon out of their sleeve and let it be preached with wine at parties, often still drunk; besides they live in so many great sins against conscience. If they—I say—were to think about this, just what is in these words here, and how they cut old Origen to the heart as well as all pious, faithful teachers, it would make their hair stand on end. All their impudence, pride and audacity would fall away. But enough of this. "Not to us, O Lord, not to us, but to your name give the glory." THE WHOLE PSALTER.[18]

50:22-23 True Worship and Sacrifice Is a Thankful Heart

GOD'S GRACE DESPITE OUR LETHARGY. JOHN CALVIN: Hypocrites, until they feel the hand of God against them, are ever ready to surrender themselves to a state of security, and nothing is more difficult than to awaken their apprehensions. By this alarming language the psalmist aims at convincing them of the certainty of destruction should they longer presume on the forbearance of God, and thus provoke his anger the more by imagining that he can favor the practice of sin. No severer insult can be rendered against God than to rob him of his justice. Not that hypocrites would say this openly; however, they reshape God according to their deformed imagination, so that they continue to enjoy themselves on account of his forbearance. If they were thoroughly convinced that God loathes iniquity, they would unavoidably be tormented by constant anxiety on account of

---

[17]Cajetan, *In Sacrae Scripturae Expositionem*, 3:182.

[18]Selnecker, *Der gantze Psalter*, 1:226r-v.

their sins. Therefore, they display such careless indulgence that they impose a false character on God—they do not merely cut off his office as Judge but even mold him into the patron and approver of their iniquities. The psalmist reprehends them for abusing the goodness and clemency of God, in the way of cherishing a vain hope that they may transgress with impunity. He warns them that before long they will be dragged into the light and that those sins which they would have hidden from the eyes of God would be set in all their enormity before their view. He will set the whole list of their sins in distinct order . . . before their view and force them on their observation. . . .

And here what a remarkable proof we have of the grace of God in extending the hope of mercy to those corrupt people, who had so impiously profaned his worship, who had so audaciously and sacrilegiously mocked his forbearance and who had abandoned themselves to such scandalous crimes! In calling them to repentance, without all doubt he extends to them the hope of God being reconciled to them, so that they may have the courage to appear in the presence of his majesty. This is, without a doubt, a priceless clemency. He invites us to himself and into the bosom of the church—we who are such perfidious apostates and violators of his covenant, who had departed from the doctrine of godliness in which they had been brought up! Great as it is, we would do well to reflect that it is no greater than what we have ourselves experienced. We, too, had apostatized from the Lord, and in his singular mercy he has brought us again into his fold. COMMENTARY ON THE PSALMS.[19]

---

[19]CTS 9:278-79* (CO 31:506-7).

51:1-19 CREATE IN ME A CLEAN HEART

To the choirmaster. A Psalm of David, when Nathan the prophet went to him, after he had gone in to Bathsheba.

¹ Have mercy on me,ᵃ O God,
  according to your steadfast love;
according to your abundant mercy
  blot out my transgressions.
² Wash me thoroughly from my iniquity,
  and cleanse me from my sin!
³ For I know my transgressions,
  and my sin is ever before me.
⁴ Against you, you only, have I sinned
  and done what is evil in your sight,
so that you may be justified in your words
  and blameless in your judgment.
⁵ Behold, I was brought forth in iniquity,
  and in sin did my mother conceive me.
⁶ Behold, you delight in truth in the inward being,
  and you teach me wisdom in the secret heart.
⁷ Purge me with hyssop, and I shall be clean;
  wash me, and I shall be whiter than snow.
⁸ Let me hear joy and gladness;
  let the bones that you have broken rejoice.
⁹ Hide your face from my sins,
  and blot out all my iniquities.

¹⁰ Create in me a clean heart, O God,
  and renew a rightᵇ spirit within me.
¹¹ Cast me not away from your presence,
  and take not your Holy Spirit from me.
¹² Restore to me the joy of your salvation,
  and uphold me with a willing spirit.
¹³ Then I will teach transgressors your ways,
  and sinners will return to you.
¹⁴ Deliver me from bloodguiltiness, O God,
  O God of my salvation,
  and my tongue will sing aloud of your
    righteousness.
¹⁵ O Lord, open my lips,
  and my mouth will declare your praise.
¹⁶ For you will not delight in sacrifice, or I
    would give it;
  you will not be pleased with a burnt offering.
¹⁷ The sacrifices of God are a broken spirit;
  a broken and contrite heart, O God, you
    will not despise.
¹⁸ Do good to Zion in your good pleasure;
  build up the walls of Jerusalem;
¹⁹ then will you delight in right sacrifices,
  in burnt offerings and whole burnt offerings;
  then bulls will be offered on your altar.

a Or Be gracious to me b Or steadfast

OVERVIEW: Here in the most prominent of the penitential psalms, David serves as the exemplar par excellence of a repentant sinner before God. Commentators from across the spectrum of Reformation confessions agree that this psalm clearly teaches the doctrine of original sin and the need for redemption in the person of Jesus Christ. Despite various formulations of the relationship between divine sovereignty and human responsibility (e.g., Luther against Erasmus on the freedom of the will and the Reformed against the Remonstrants at the Synod of Dordrecht), the reformers, following Augustine, define original sin in contrast to Pelagian ideas about human nature. Pelagius argued that acts cannot weaken our nature, and because sin is indeed an act, our nature is unhindered by it; we are fully able to will and to do good. Such an idea the reformers stoutly resisted—even bristled at. It is the archenemy of gospel preaching, as Luther taught: "It has always interjected itself and sticks to the true preaching like muck on a wheel."[1]

---

[1] RCS NT 6:204.

Augustine agreed with Pelagius that sin is an act, not a substance; however, he corrected Pelagius, saying acts can indeed weaken our nature. Sin is the avoidance of relationship with God—true substance. Sin, therefore, necessarily weakens— even cripples—our nature. And so Augustine argued that human beings are wholly and irretrievably dependent on God's grace: absolutely no good deed is possible apart from his grace. Grace heals because we are disordered; grace assists because we are insufficient to the task. While Pelagius only allowed Jesus to be an example of holiness, Augustine—and the tradition that followed him—paired the gift of Jesus with the example of Jesus. Through the outpouring of his Spirit, Jesus enables us to follow his example. *That* is good news.[2]

This psalm, our interpreters remind us, must be understood and interpreted in Christ. Without his Spirit it is incomprehensible that because of the inheritance of Adam we are corrupt, so much so in fact that we do not even realize how sinful we are. Nevertheless, through the incarnation of Christ and the revelation of his Word, our God has condescended to us. We should seek to know God only through these revealed works, not his mysterious counsels. That is, our God is a God of mercy, not wrath. Jesus took on our very flesh, its substance—affirming the goodness of creation—to redeem and renew us. United to Christ we too are restored continually in the grace of the Holy Spirit.

TO UNDERSTAND THIS PSALM WE MUST KNOW CHRIST. MARTIN LUTHER: No one should expound this psalm—*Miserere mei, Deus*—except Paul. Whoever understands Paul also understands this psalm and this verse especially: "Against you alone have I sinned." That verse cannot be interpreted by anyone but Paul. And every passage of Scripture is impossible to be interpreted without knowledge of Christ.

Miserere mei wants to have all of Christ. Sadoleto hardly comes to political mercy in this psalm.[3] They are crass fools who are not only ignorant but also want to teach. TABLE TALK: KONRAD CORDATUS (1532).[4]

THE SUPERSCRIPTION MAKES CLEAR THE PSALM'S CONTENT AND CONTEXT. MOÏSE AMYRAUT: The title of this psalm quite clearly indicates its author as well as the occasion of its composition by David, so that it is surprising to find several exegetes who wonder about both. Add that they—the author and occasion included in the title—agree wonderfully with what is contained in the psalm itself, so that even if it bore no title, both the author and occasion of composition could be understood from reading the psalm itself. And so, I think that nothing needs to be said in the argument, except that this song was braided together from all these emotions which in so great a matter and in such great mental anguish, the pious man, having been established by this passage, was able to begin to feel deeply that his sins were gravely offensive to him. ARGUMENT OF PSALM 51.[5]

NATHAN CALLS DAVID OUT OF HIS LETHARGY. JOHN CALVIN: For a long period after his melancholy fall, David seems to have sunk into a spiritual lethargy, but when roused from it by the expostulation of Nathan, he was filled with self-loathing and humiliation in the sight of God and was anxious both to testify his repentance to all around him and leave some lasting proof of it to posterity. In the beginning of the psalm, having his eyes directed to the heinousness of his guilt, he encourages himself to hope for pardon by considering the infinite mercy of God. This he extols in high terms and with a variety of

---

[2]For Augustine's anti-Pelagian writings, see NPNF 5, especially "On Nature and Grace" (415) and "On the Grace of Christ and On Original Sin" (418), 121-51, 217-55.

[3]Luther is obliquely condemning Sadoleto's emphasis on grammar as the rule and norm of exegesis, in contrast to Luther's formulation of grammar as theology's handmaiden. See further Luther's above comment on Psalm 16, p. 119.
[4]WATR 3:217, no. 3198a (cf. no. 3198b; 1:151, no. 1609); citing Rom 3:4.
[5]Amyraut, *Paraphrasis in Psalmos Davidis*, 216.

expressions, as one who felt that he deserved multiplied condemnation. In the second part of the psalm, he prays for restoration to the favor of God, being conscious that he deserved to have been cast off forever and deprived of all the gifts of the Holy Spirit. He promises—should forgiveness be bestowed on him—to retain a deep and grateful sense of it. At the end, he declares it to be for the good of the church that God should grant his request. And, indeed, when the peculiar manner in which God had deposited his covenant of grace with David is considered, it could not but be felt that the common hope of the salvation of all must have been shaken on the supposition of his final rejection. COMMENTARY ON THE PSALMS.[6]

PROPHETICALLY THIS PSALM IS ABOUT THE CHURCH.

MARTIN LUTHER: This psalm can indeed be understood according to history, in the person of David. Nevertheless, according to the prophetic sense it should be received in the person of human nature, that is, the church of Christ. This is clear because this psalm teaches original sin and at the end it prays for the heavenly Zion. GLOSSA ON PSALM 51 (1513–1515).[7]

51:1-2 Show Mercy, O God; Cleanse Me

ON YOUR MERCIFUL NAME I DEPEND. RICHARD BAXTER: "O Lord our God, how excellent is your name in all the world!" Your glorious majesty is excellent, but that brings me nothing; your justice is excellent, but that brings me nothing. It is your mercy that must do me good, and therefore your other excellencies I adore, but this I invoke. To invoke your justice, I dare not; your glory, I cannot; but your mercy, I both dare and can. For why should I not dare, when fear gives me boldness? How should I not be able when weakness gives me strength? Why should I not dare, when you invite me to it? How should I not be able when you draw

me to it? Do you invite me, and shall I not come? Do you draw me, and shall I draw back? Can there be a patron so powerful as you? Can there be a suppliant so dejected as myself? Whom, then, is it more fit to ask for mercy than you, O God, who are the God of mercy? And for whom is it more fit to ask for mercy than for me who am a creature of misery? MEDITATIONS UPON PSALM 51.[8]

MISERY ASKS FOR MERCY. WOLFGANG MUSCULUS: David flees to no one other than God alone against whom he had sinned, in whose name he had already been rebuked by the prophet Nathan. God alone is the one who can remit sins and pacify a disturbed and anxious conscience. . . . He begs for mercy without any excuse or extenuation of sin and likewise without any mention of his past life. This is entirely consistent with a soul confessing its sin and in no respect justifying itself. He does not say, "Remember, O Lord, how righteously I walked in your sight before that sin; have regard for the rest of my righteousness. For even if I have sinned here, yet in other things I obeyed your will." He mentions none of these things but stands naked, devoid of all righteousness.

At this point . . . he also acknowledges that he is now a wretched and vile man who is liable to death. For whoever says, "Have mercy on me," what does he say other than that he is miserable and ruined? And in fact there is no greater calamity than that in which a transgression of the divine will debase us. We pity ourselves, and rightly so, as those who are paupers and affected miserably in our bodies. Because if we should see the misery of an adulterous and bloodthirsty person, even if he is the most powerful king of all, how much more does the calamity and occasion for mercy occur? Certainly if the sinner would not acknowledge this misery in himself, he will never say from his heart with David, "Have mercy on me, O God." For such a king, all those temporary things, on account of which the world assesses

---

[6]CTS 9:281-82* (CO 31:508).
[7]WA 3:284; citing Rom 3:4.

[8]Baxter, *Meditations and Disquisitions upon the one and fiftieth Psalme of David*, 1-2*.

human happiness, which cannot relieve the soul that acknowledges its sins, now disappear. Only the goodness of God is what he sighs for and which can comfort him in that misery. . . .

He not only acknowledges his sin, does not excuse himself and perceives that he is miserable, but also through confidence in the divine goodness flees to the mercy of God. Unless he had done this, all the rest would be in vain. More correctly they would produce nothing other than hopelessness— as is seen in the example of the traitor Judas, who acknowledged both his sin and his misery, and that with a momentous anxiety of heart, and he frankly confessed the enormity of his sin and even cast away the received money with great penitence. Nevertheless he did not find pardon for his sin, which he did not seek by faith, being devoid of the grace of God. COMMENTARY ON PSALM 51.[9]

SIN MUST BE FELT. MARTIN LUTHER: For a proper understanding of the fact that God hates sinners and loves the righteous, we must distinguish between the sinner who feels his sins and the sinner who does not feel his sins. God does not want the prayer of a sinner who does not feel his sins, because he neither understands nor wants what he is praying for. Thus a monk living in superstition often sings and mumbles, "Have mercy on me, O God." But because he lives with trust in his own righteousness and does not feel the uncleanness of his own heart, he is merely reciting syllables and neither understands nor wants the thing itself. Besides, he adds things that contradict his prayer. He prays for forgiveness, he prays for mercy; meanwhile, by this means or that he is looking for expiation of his sin and for satisfaction. Is this not actually an open mockery of God? It is just as though a beggar were constantly crying out for alms and when someone offered him some, he would begin to brag about his riches, that is, his poverty, and thus clearly show that he does not need the alms. LECTURES ON PSALM 51 (1532).[10]

THE POWER OF "HAVE MERCY." NIKOLAUS SELNECKER: Considering the law and our works as well as the help and power of all other creatures it could not be otherwise: we must despair and remain in eternal death and condemnation. For two extremes come together which cannot stand side by side: God and sinners. . . . There are two depths: the depth of sin and the height of righteousness, and yet both have to come together and the depth of sins assumed and set right by mercy.

Such, however, happens through the middle word (the one standing between the two extremes, God and me): "Have mercy." This middle word points to the Mediator, Jesus Christ, who brings together both extremes and reconciles God, his Father, to us through his intercession, benefit, sufferings, dying and perfect obedience. Thus, we poor sinners now may and can draw near to God, the Lord, and say, "Be gracious to me, Abba Father, for the sake of your Son, my Mediator and Advocate, Jesus Christ." For "have mercy" rests, stands and is founded on the Lord Christ alone. This is the basis and foundation. Paul calls him the same and says, "No other foundation can be laid than that which is laid, which is Jesus Christ." . . .

Now whoever wants to seek, find and keep grace must turn to this "have mercy" and know that God through his Son and for the sake of his merit wants to be gracious to us, have mercy on us and adopt us as his children and heirs. . . . Nothing shall discourage us or make us fainthearted: not our sin or our disobedience, or death, the devil, or the wrath of God, or any thought and affliction. But, rather, the more frightened the conscience is, the more frequent and fervent the crying shall be: "Lord, have mercy on me, be gracious to me, a poor sinner; for the sake of your Son Christ Jesus forgive me my transgression." Where this groaning and crying is— which cannot happen without faith—there one certainly has God's favor and mercy and must not fear wrath and disgrace. THE WHOLE PSALTER.[11]

---

[9]Musculus, *In Psalterium Commentarii*, 537-38.
[10]LW 12:315* (WA 40,2:333-34). These lectures were expanded

for publication—not without controversy—by Veit Dietrich in 1538; see further LW 12:vii-ix.
[11]Selnecker, *Der gantze Psalter*, 2:5v-6r; citing Rom 8:15 (cf. Gal 4:6); 1 Cor 3:11; Acts 10:43; 4:12; Sir 51:37; 1 Thess 5:9-10.

TRUE THEOLOGY ACKNOWLEDGES A MERCIFUL, NOT WRATHFUL, GOD. MARTIN LUTHER: God is served if you fear him and grasp Christ as the object of mercy. This is true theology about the true God and the true worship of God. It is false theology that God is wrathful to those who acknowledge their sins. Such a God is not in heaven or anywhere else but is the idol of a perverse heart. The true God says, "I do not want the death of the sinner, but rather that he would change course and live." This is proved also by the present example of David and his prayer. At the outset we reminded you that we should not only look at the example of David here but should change the psalm into a general teaching that applies to all people without exception. Thus the epistle to the Romans quotes as a general statement, "Every human being is a liar," and also says, "God has consigned all human beings to disobedience, so that he may have mercy on all." In the same way we said about David that he includes the death and life of the whole human race, not merely his own sin. Therefore God is the same sort of God to all human beings that he was to David, that is, one who forgives sins and has mercy on all who ask for mercy and acknowledge their sins. LECTURES ON PSALM 51 (1532).[12]

STAIN OF POLLUTION. GIOVANNI DIODATI: Sin has in it the stain of spiritual pollution and makes one liable to punishment; God blots it out, when notwithstanding the said stain he looks graciously on the soul by virtue of his Son's righteousness and satisfaction, which presents itself between the sinner and him, and together with that cancels the debt of the offense in his judgment, and so gives peace to the conscience. ANNOTATIONS ON PSALM 51:1.[13]

HERE THE LAW CONDEMNS; AT THE CROSS THE GOSPEL FORGIVES. NIKOLAUS SELNECKER: In this teaching we see what a big difference there is

between the law and the gospel. The law says, "As I find you, so I judge you. If you are a sinner and you recognize your sin, what you have earned is what you will get. According to your works you will be paid. You yourself then have to realize and confess that you deserve eternal punishment and are guilty of it." But the gospel says, "Just crawl to the cross! In the law there is neither rest nor peace. Your sins are forgiven before the judgment seat of Christ, not before the judgment seat of the law. The law has a judgment seat to condemnation; Christ has a mercy seat to life." Whoever comes here says, "Lord, I am a sinner, therefore be gracious to me; I am poor, therefore have mercy on me; I am condemned, therefore save me—you who are called Jesus, that is, Savior." THE WHOLE PSALTER.[14]

WE ARE RIGHTEOUS BECAUSE OF CHRIST. MARTIN LUTHER: Once Christians are righteous by faith and have accepted the forgiveness of sins, they should not be so smug, as though they were pure of all sins. For only then do they face the constant battle with the remnants of sin, from which the prophet here wants to be cleansed. They are righteous and holy by an alien or foreign holiness—I call it this for the sake of instruction—that is, they are righteous by the mercy and grace of God. This mercy and grace is not something human; it is not some sort of disposition or quality in the heart. It is a divine blessing, given us through the true knowledge of the gospel, when we know or believe that our sin has been forgiven us through the grace and merit of Christ and when we hope for steadfast love and abundant mercy for Christ's sake, as the prophet says here. Is not this righteousness an alien righteousness? It consists completely in the indulgence of another and is a pure gift of God, who shows mercy and favor for Christ's sake. LECTURES ON PSALM 51 (1532).[15]

A COMMON TERM FOR THE IMPUTATION OF CHRIST'S RIGHTEOUSNESS. GIOVANNI DIODATI: "Wash me" is a frequent term in Scripture to

---

Selnecker relies here on Luther's 1532 commentary on this psalm; see LW 12:319-20 (WA 40,2:339-40).
[12]LW 12:322* (WA 40,2:343-44); citing Ezek 33:11; Rom 3:4; Ps 116:11; Rom 11:32.
[13]Diodati, *Pious Annotations*, Tt4r*.

[14]Selnecker, *Der gantze Psalter*, 2:8v-9r.
[15]LW 12:328* (WA 40,2:352-53).

signify the lively application and imputing of Christ's blood to the sinful soul, whereby it is put into such an estate that God does no more abhor it as foul and impure but accepts it as beautiful and clean. ANNOTATIONS ON PSALM 51:2.[16]

WASH ME, O LORD, WASH ME THOROUGHLY.
GIROLAMO SAVONAROLA: According to the multitude of your compassions wash me thoroughly from my sin; for hitherto I have been cleansed imperfectly. Complete your work. Take away the whole body of sin. Take away the guilt. Increase the light. Inflame my heart with your love. Drive away fear, for perfect love casts out fear. Let the love of the world, the love of the flesh, the love of glory and self-love wholly depart from me. Thoroughly—and more and more—shall you wash me from my iniquity in which I have sinned against my neighbor, and from my sin with which I have offended against God. Wash me, so that you may remove not only the crime and guilt but also the fuel of sins. You shall wash me, truly, with the water of your manifold grace, with that water which whoever drinks it shall never thirst again: it shall be in him a well of water springing up into everlasting life. Wash me with the water of my tears. Wash me with the water of your Scriptures, so that I may be worthy to be numbered among those to whom you have already said, "You clean according to my Word." AN EXPOSITION OF THE PSALM *MISERERE*.[17]

51:3-6 *I Am Born in Iniquity; You Are Holy*

THE WORD TEACHES ORIGINAL SIN. JOHN CALVIN: The passage affords a striking testimony concerning original sin, which Adam brought on the whole human race. For this reason, it can also assist us in forming a correct description of it. The Pelagians, to avoid what they considered the absurdity of holding that all were ruined through

one man's transgression, maintained that sin descended from Adam only through the imitation of others. But the Bible, both here and in other passages, clearly asserts that we are born in sin, and that it exists within us as a disease fixed in our nature. David does not charge it on his parents or trace his crime to them but places himself before the judgment seat of God and confesses that he was formed in sin and that he was a transgressor before he emerged into the light. COMMENTARY ON THE PSALMS.[18]

OUR INHERITANCE FROM ADAM. PETER RIEDEMANN: The inheritance we all have from our father Adam is the inclination to sin. This means that by nature all of us have a tendency toward evil and toward taking pleasure in sin. This inheritance shows itself in all of Adam's children, in all who are born according to Adam. In people, it devours and consumes everything which is good and godly, so that no one may attain it again unless that person is born anew. Paul calls this inheritance the messenger of Satan, who strikes him on the head or buffets him with fists. He is speaking here of the sinful inclination that stirs in him as in all people. John states, "Whoever says he has no sin deceives himself and is not speaking the truth." He follows this with a discussion about the inheritance we have received from Adam, which he calls sin. In the book of Psalms, David says, "I was conceived and born in sin." Therefore, through Adam we all have become sinful and must be justified again through Christ if we want to have life with him. . . .

In this way we show people how far they have distanced themselves from God and submerged themselves in their sins. We show them also that all sin has its source and origin in embracing what is unrighteous. People embrace what they ought not to embrace and leave what they ought to accept. They love what they ought to hate and hate what they ought to love. Thus they are turned aside and led away from God by just those things which should show the way to God and teach them to know God.

---

[16]Diodati, *Pious Annotations*, Tt4r*.
[17]Savonarola, *An Exposition of the Psalm Miserere Mei Deus*, 14-15*.
[18]CTS 9:290* (CO 31:513).

Therefore, if anyone wants to come to God, that person must give up whatever was previously appropriated wrongly, that is, all that is temporal and transitory, and must depend on God alone. This is the true repentance which the Lord wants and expects of us. CONFESSION OF FAITH.[19]

To UNDERSTAND THE WORD WE MUST ACCEPT ORIGINAL SIN. MARTIN LUTHER: This doctrine of original sin is one of those outstanding doctrines which reason does not know but which, like others, is learned from the law and promises of God. Paul is the only one of the apostles to deal very seriously with this doctrine in particular. Perhaps the other apostles passed over it because this doctrine was being handed down by tradition. ... This doctrine was handed down by tradition, through Moses and David—and after them the apostle Paul—set it down in writing. Undoubtedly they drew this wisdom from the first commandment and from the promises given to Abraham and to Adam. Because these promise a blessing, they make clear that this nature is under a curse and under the kingdom of the devil, in which there is darkness, hate of God and mistrust.

This verse contains the reason why we all ought to confess that we are sinners, that all our efforts are damnable in the sight of God and that God alone is righteous. This teaching is most necessary in the church.... I can testify from my own example that I did not yet know this teaching when I had been a doctor of theology for many years. They used to discuss original sin, but they said that it was removed in baptism and that even outside baptism there was a light left in nature. If anyone followed this light, grace would inevitably be given to him.... Who does not see the contradiction between the statement that the natural powers are perfect and the statement that nature is corrupted by sin? The will is indeed a natural thing. But they do not argue merely about willing, but about willing good—and

this they call natural. Here is the error. Will remains in the devil, it remains in heretics; this, I admit, is natural. But that will is not good, nor does the intellect remain correct or enlightened. If we want to talk about natural powers on the basis of this psalm and on the basis of the Holy Spirit's manner of speaking, then we should call "natural" the fact that we are in sin and death and that we desire, understand and long for things that are corrupt and evil. This agrees with the present psalm and can be proved from it.

Let this be enough about the confession of original or innate sin, which is hidden from the whole world and is not revealed by our powers, reasonings or speculations, but is rather obscured, defended and excused by them. We need the Word of God from heaven to reveal this uncleanness or fault of our nature. With faith in this Word let us confess that this is the way things are, even though all nature should object, as object it must. This is the most difficult teaching of this psalm, yes, of all Scripture or theology; without it, it is impossible to understand Scripture correctly, as the dreams of modern theologians prove. LECTURES ON PSALM 51 (1532).[20]

THE DISTINCTION BETWEEN HUMAN NATURE AND ORIGINAL SIN. FORMULA OF CONCORD: We believe, teach and confess that there is a difference between original sin and human nature—not only as God originally created our nature pure, holy and without sin, but also as we now have our nature after the fall. Even after the fall this nature still is and remains a creature of God. The difference between our nature and original sin is as great as the difference between the work of God and the work of the devil.

We also believe, teach and confess that we must preserve this difference very carefully because the teaching that there is supposedly no difference between our corrupted human nature and original sin is contrary to the chief articles of our Christian faith on creation, redemption, sanctification and

---

[19]CRR 9:92-93, 94*; citing 2 Esdr 3:21-22; Jn 3:3-5; 2 Cor 12:7; 1 Jn 1:8-10; Ps 51:5; Rom 5:15-19; Gen 3:6; Mt 10:21-25; 1 Jn 2:15-17; Mt 10:5-10; Lk 14:33.

[20]LW 12:350-51* (WA 40,2:383-85); citing Rom 5:12-13; Ps 90:8.

the resurrection of our flesh, and it cannot coexist with them. For God created not only the body and soul of Adam and Eve before the fall but also our bodies and souls after the fall, even though they are corrupted. God also still recognizes them as his own work, as it is written, "Your hands fashioned and made me, together all around."

Furthermore, the Son of God assumed this human nature into the unity of his person—of course, without sin—and what he assumed was not another kind of flesh but our flesh. In this way he became our true brother. "Since the children share flesh and blood, he himself likewise shared the same things." And, "He did not [assume the nature of] the angels but of the descendants of Abraham; thus, he had to become like his brothers in every respect," apart from sin.

Therefore, Christ also redeemed human nature as his creation, sanctifies it as his creation, awakens it from the dead and adorns it in glorious fashion as his creation. But he did not create, assume, redeem or sanctify original sin. He will also not bring it to life in his elect. He will neither adorn it with glory nor save it. Instead, it will be utterly destroyed in the resurrection. From all this, it is easy to distinguish between the corrupted nature and the corruption which is embedded in this nature—through which this nature is corrupted.

On the other hand, we believe, teach and confess that original sin is not a slight corruption of human nature, but rather a corruption so deep that there is nothing sound or uncorrupted left in the human body or soul, in its internal or external powers. Instead, as the church sings, "Through Adam's fall is corrupted all human nature and essence."[21] The damage is so indescribable that it cannot be recognized by our reason but only from God's Word. The damage is such that only God alone can separate human nature and the corruption of this nature from each other. This separation will take place completely through death, at the resurrection, when the nature which we now have will rise and live eternally, without original sin—separated and severed from it. . . .

Concerning the Latin words *substantia* and *accidens*, since they are not biblical terms and are words unfamiliar to common people, they should not be used in sermons delivered to the common people, who do not understand them; the simple folk should be spared such words. But in the schools and among the learned these terms are familiar and can be used without any misunderstanding to differentiate the essence of a thing from that which in an accidental way adheres to the thing. Therefore, these words are properly retained in scholarly discussion of original sin. For the difference between God's work and the devil's work can be made most clear through these words because the devil cannot create a substance but can only corrupt the substance, which God has created, in an accidental way, with God's permission. ARTICLE 1: ORIGINAL SIN.[22]

TRIPARTITE REPENTANCE: FEEL REMORSE, REQUEST FORGIVENESS, DO RIGHTEOUSNESS. DIRK PHILIPS: Some now say that whenever whoremongers or adulterers have committed such sins, then accuse themselves, have remorse and promise amendment, then their sin is forgiven them by God already and they should not be separated. To this I reply in brief thus: The kingdom of God does not consist in words but in power, just as the apostle says. Therefore, true penitence does not consist of words alone but has three characteristics and signs by which it is recognized. First, one heartily laments before God the Lord, is remorseful over one's sins and is at all times troubled with it, as the prophet says: "My misdeed is ever before me." Second, out of a broken heart and a smitten conscience one confesses one's sins before God, asks for forgiveness, trusts firmly on the grace of God through Jesus Christ, and says with the prophet, "Be gracious to me, O God, according to your goodness; according to your great mercy blot out my sins. Wash me thoroughly from my misdeeds and cleanse me thoroughly

---

[21]See Selnecker's above comment on Ps 32, p. 251 n. 13.

[22]BoC 488-89, 491* (BSLK 770-72, 775-76); citing Job 10:8; Heb 2:14-17; Job 19:26-27.

from my sin! For I confess my sins and do not hide my misdeeds." Third, one should cease from sin and do righteousness, as the prophet says: "For to depart from wickedness is true worship which pleases the Lord; to cease from doing unrighteousness is the true sin offering."

Therefore now no penitence avails before God when one does not bring forth the fruits of repentance, just as John also indeed confessed when he said, "The ax is now laid to the root of the tree; every tree therefore that does not bear good fruit is cut down and thrown into the fire." THE ENCHIRIDION: THE BAN.[23]

REPENTANCE ACKNOWLEDGES OUR SIN AND GOD'S GRACE. MARTIN LUTHER: Here the doctrine of true repentance is set forth before us. There are two elements in true repentance: recognition of sin and recognition of grace; or—to use the more familiar terms—the fear of God and trust in his mercy. These two parts David sets forth before us in this prayer as in a beautiful picture for us to look at. At the beginning of the psalm we see him troubled by the knowledge of his sin and the burden of his conscience. At the end he consoles himself with trust in the goodness of God and promises that he will also instruct others so that they might be converted. So it is apparent that in this psalm the prophet wants to set down the true wisdom of divine religion in the right words with the right meaning, with the express purpose of teaching us the nature of sin, grace and total repentance. (There are also other psalms of this type, like Psalm 32 and Psalm 130.) David is a master in teaching this doctrine, but in such a way that in using this doctrine he remains a pupil with us; for all people— be they ever so illumined by the Holy Spirit—still remain pupils of the Word. They remain under and near the Word, and they experience that they can hardly draw out a drop from the vast ocean of the Holy Spirit. LECTURES ON PSALM 51 (1532).[24]

BE GRACIOUS TO ME. KATHARINA SCHÜTZ ZELL: You have recognized my helplessness, that I can do nothing but follow my sinful conception and birth, so you have given me another birth which should purify me through your Word which you send to me. Because of your ancient grace, you show me my sins and teach me what lies hidden in you: how people were corrupted in the root and there is nothing good in them but worthless sin and wrath, which, however, no one can confess or in truth understand without your Spirit. This is a great human stupidity: people always want to be and do something according to their former birth. . . . Therefore it is great wisdom in your eyes (but hidden to the sight of many) for a person to recognize and confess your true righteousness and his true sin. Ah, to do that is the real truth which you love, and you desire such truth, which is intimate and hidden with you. You give it to those you choose, and you reprimand the haughty who are not willing to confess the truth of their powerlessness. . . . Therefore I pray and weep before you with my whole heart, and ask you to be gracious to me according to your Word which you have spoken—that same Word abides eternally in heaven! THE *MISERERE* PSALM.[25]

51:7-12 Purge My Heart with Hyssop and Restore Me to Your Presence

A LEGAL METAPHOR. RUDOLF GWALTHER: "Remove my sin from me with hyssop." . . . That is, Proclaim me empty of my sins according to your promise and mercy which you have figured for us in the law with hyssop. And because he prays such a prayer to God, he wants it to be understood that the external ceremonies are unable to help; rather, they were only figures and representations of the things which were brought to completion in Christ. THE PSALTER.[26]

---

[23]CRR 6:247* (BRN 10:259); citing 1 Cor 4:20; Ps 32:5; 51:3; 32:3-5; 51:1; Sir 35:3; Ezek 18:27; 33:14-16; Mt 3:10.
[24]LW 12:305* (WA 40,2:317-18).

[25]Zell, *Church Mother*, 319-20*; citing Jn 3:31; 1 Pet 2:22-23; Rom 7:18; 1 Cor 2:7; Ps 119:21.
[26]Gwalther, *Der Psalter*, 90r, 91v; citing Ex 12:22; Lev 14:4; Num 19:18.

THE CLEANSING BLOOD OF CHRIST. JOHN
FISHER: If we turn to God and follow his commandments, forsaking our wretched life, having
faith and trust in his sacraments, we will without
doubt obtain forgiveness and mercy by virtue of
them. Perhaps someone will say, "We see what is
done in every sacrament. In the sacrament of
baptism the child is washed in the water, and a few
words spoken by the priest. In confirmation, the
forehead of the child is anointed with the holy
chrism in manner of a cross, with a few words
spoken by the priest. In the sacrament of penance,
after confession is heard and the satisfaction
enjoined, the priest also says a few words. What do
these have to do with the health of the soul? For
the words, as soon as they are spoken, vanish into
the air and nothing remains of them. The water as
well as the oil does not pierce from the body to the
soul." Perhaps someone will think this. It is true:
the water and oil have no strength from their own
nature by which they may enter into the soul or to
work in it good or evil. Nevertheless there is a
secret and hidden power given to them by the
merits of the passion of Jesus Christ and of his
precious blood, which on the cross was shed for
wretched sinners. This most holy and dear blood of
Jesus Christ, shed for our redemption, bought and
gave so great and plenteous power to the sacraments that as often as any creature shall use and
receive any of them, so often it is to be believed
they are sprinkled with the drops of the same most
holy blood, whose power pierces to the soul and
makes it clean from all sin.

But how do we know this? Truly he has shown
and revealed to us the hidden and unknown things
of his infinite wisdom. It was a custom in the old law
among the Jews to do away with sins by this manner.
If by touching a dead body or by any other thing they
were culpable and made unclean, immediately they
were made clean of that default with hyssop dipped
in the blood of certain beasts and sprinkled on them.
This manner and custom was given to the Jews by
Moses and ordained by the wisdom of God. Nevertheless at that time it was unknown what this matter
meant and signified. It was uncertain; it was hidden

what the wisdom of God wanted to be understood
by this aspersion or sprinkling of blood. And after
our blessed Lord Jesus Christ had shed his precious
blood and, as Saint Peter says, washed us from sin
with his blood, it was known to everyone what was
signified by the hyssop and by the aspersion of blood.
Hyssop is an herb of the ground that by its nature is
hot and has a sweet smell, signifying Christ who
humbled himself to death on the cross. . . . No one
may doubt this, that by the aspersion of beasts—before the incarnation—the effusion of the blood of
Christ for our redemption was signified and
represented. The blood of our Savior without doubt
is of incomparably more strength to do away with
our sins than the blood of beasts. And as often as the
holy sacraments be iterated and used according to the
commandment of Christ's church, so often is the
blessed blood of our Lord sprinkled abroad to
cleanse and put away sin.

Therefore let us all say with the holy prophet this
verse, "Sprinkle me, O Lord, with hyssop and I will
be clean." As we might say, "Lord, our faith is so clear
and undoubtful by the merit of the passion of your
Son our Lord Jesus Christ which by the effusion of
his blood has given such great efficacy and strength
to the holy sacraments of his church that when we
receive any of them we will be sprinkled and made
clean by the power of his precious blood as with
hyssop. This aspersion immediately follows the
water of grace that is infused in our souls by which
we are made whiter than snow." THE FOURTH
PENITENTIAL PSALM.[27]

FIXED INTO THE WHITENESS OF SNOW. JOHN
DONNE: Nothing in this world can send me home in
such a whiteness, no moral counsel, no moral
comfort, no moral constancy, as God's absolution by
his minister, the profitable hearing of a sermon and
the worthy receiving of a sacrament do. This is to be
as white as snow; in a good state for the present. But
David begs a whiteness above snow; for snow melts,
and then it is not white; our present sanctification
withers, and we lose that cheerful verdure which is

---

[27]Fisher, *Commentary on the Seven Penitential Psalms*, 1:94-96*.

the testimony of an upright conscience; and snow melted, snow water, is the coldest water of all; devout people departed from their former fervor are the coldest and most irreducible to true zeal and true holiness. Therefore David, who was metal tried seven times in the fire and desired to be such gold as might be laid up in God's treasury, might consider that in the transmutation of metals, it is not enough to come to a calcination or a liquefaction of the metal (that must be done) or to an ablution, to sever dross from pure, or to a transmutation, to make it a better metal, but there must also be a fixion, a setting thereof, so that it shall not evaporate into nothing or return to its former nature. Therefore he saw that he needed not only a liquefaction, a melting into tears, or only an ablution and a transmutation; those he had by this purging and this washing, this station in the church of God, and this present sanctification there. But he needed . . . an establishment, which the comparison of snow afforded not; that as he had purged himself with hyssop and so cleansed him, that is, enwrapped him in the covenant and made him a member of the true church; and there washed him so as that he was restored to a whiteness, that is, made his ordinances so effectual on him, as that then he delivers his soul into his hands at that time: so he would exalt that whiteness, above the whiteness of snow, so that nothing might melt it, nothing discolor it, but that under the seal of his blessed Spirit, he might ever dwell in that calm, in that assurance, in that acquiescence, that as he is in a good state this minute, he shall be in no worse, whenever God shall be pleased to translate him. SERMON 62: PREACHED UPON THE PENITENTIAL PSALMS.[28]

GOSPEL JOY. RUDOLF GWALTHER: By this joy David understands the joyous message of the gospel and the consolation of miserable consciences, which is proclaimed to us in Christ. That is what the angel calls it when he speaks to the shepherds: "I proclaim to you a great joy." THE PSALTER.[29]

THE JOY OF THE SPIRIT. JOHN CALVIN: The joy which he desires is what flows from hearing the Word of God, in which he promises to pardon our guilt and readmit us into his favor. It is this alone which supports the believer amid all the fears, dangers and distresses of his earthly pilgrimage. The joy of the Spirit is inseparable from faith. COMMENTARY ON THE PSALMS.[30]

CONSTANT RENEWAL IN THE PEACE OF THE LORD. MARTIN LUTHER: I understand this verse to be speaking of the increase of that peace and righteousness which conquers the feeling of God's wrath and of sin. Although the righteous truly have the forgiveness of sins, because they have trust in mercy and are in grace for Christ's sake, still the pangs of conscience and the remnants of sin that infest them do not stop. Hence it is a great power of the Holy Spirit to trust the grace of God and to hope that God is gracious and favorably disposed. Nor can this confidence be preserved without the most bitter struggles, aroused in our flesh by our daily occasions for trouble and sadness as well as by our inborn weakness and distrust. Even though today I may be of happy heart because of this hearing of joy, still something happens tomorrow to trouble me, when I remember that I did what I should have avoided or failed to do what I should have done. These storms and fluctuations never stop in the mind. Satan also keeps watch. When he notices that our hearts are not well fortified with the promises of God, he arouses other specters of wrath and trouble in us that melt our hearts like salt when it is thrown into the water. Therefore this prayer is necessary: "Turn away your face from my sins, and blot out all my iniquities." "All," he says, "whether past or present or future, for I sin daily. Blot out all of them, all, lest I fall into despair or forget your mercy." Here again you see that the forgiveness of sins is not in what I do but in the fact that by mercy God blots out, as Paul says about "the bond which is against us." LECTURES ON PSALM 51 (1532).[31]

---

[28]Donne, *Works*, 3:100-101*.
[29]Gwalther, *Der Psalter*, 91v; citing Lk 2:10-12.

[30]CTS 9:295-96* (CO 31:516).
[31]LW 12:376 (WA 40,2:419-20); citing Col 2:14.

THESE VERSES ARE FULFILLED IN BAPTISM.
JACOPO SADOLETO: This is the purpose of baptism.
For all these things are renewed in us: a pure heart,
a right spirit, eternal blessings, firm hope, participation in the divine. For through baptism we who
were born slaves will be made children of God.
INTERPRETATION OF PSALM 51.[32]

**THE MANY COMFORTS OF MISERABLE CON-
SCIENCES.** NIKOLAUS SELNECKER: Every poor
conscience, when it hears the beautiful promises of
God rejoices. "As surely as I live, I do not desire the
death of the sinner"; "Come to me, everyone"; "God
so loved the world"; "God takes pleasure in life and
is a God of the living"; "The one who believes in the
Son of God has eternal life." Or when it hears this
in the words of absolution, it rejoices. "I, in God's
stead by the command of Jesus Christ, release and
absolve you from all your sins in the name of
Christ Jesus your Lord and Savior and by his
merits." So also, in baptism: "I baptize you in the
name of God the Father, Son and Holy Spirit."
And in the Lord's Supper: "Take and eat, this is the
body of your Lord Jesus Christ whose body was
given for you for the forgiveness of your sins; drink,
this is the blood of your Lord Jesus Christ, which
was shed for you." Or if one reads the Word of
God and contemplates in it the glorious, sweet
promises, it is impossible that one should not have
and feel joy and delight in his heart and be
comforted by the fact that he is among the number
of believers and elect of God, a child and heir of
God and a coheir with the Son of God. Then all
fear, anxiety and hesitation disappears and that
person simply trusts the gracious promise of God
and believes the Word. THE WHOLE PSALTER.[33]

NOT BY HUMAN REASON. PHILIPP MELANCH-
THON: "And have sustained me with a willing spirit"
means, by freely and calmly obeying in our
affections, not murmuring against you, just as
Lawrence endured his torture with a cheerful

soul.[34] Others have philosophized much at this
point concerning the chief principle, because in this
way philosophy is denominated, but I omit those
disputations. For David does not preach only
about human reason, but for that reason he seeks
help from the Spirit of God and is called on
because human reason alone does not result in firm
assent or faith, ardent love, joy of heart and
tolerance. These virtues occur by these concurring
causes: the Word of God, the Holy Spirit and an
affirming will. COMMENTS ON THE PSALMS.[35]

51:13-17 *My Lips Will Publish Your Righteousness*

**HOW SHOULD *DAMÎM* BE UNDERSTOOD
HERE?** SEBASTIAN MÜNSTER: "Deliver me from
bloods," that is, from the retribution of Uriah's
blood and others' blood, whom I determined to kill.
The Chaldean translation has the following:
"Deliver me from the judgment of murder." THE
TEMPLE OF THE LORD: PSALM 51.[36]

DAVID WANTS TO LIVE. MOÏSE AMYRAUT:
Homicide and adultery, according to the law of
God, should be punished by death. ANNOTATIONS
ON PSALM 51:14.[37]

SAVING THE UNBELIEVER. JOHN CALVIN: Those
who have been mercifully recovered from their falls
will feel inflamed by the common law of charity to
extend a helping hand to their kindred. And in
general, all who have taken part in the grace of God
are constrained by religious principle, and by regard
for the divine glory, to do as much as they can to
bring others into the participation of grace as well.
The sanguine manner in which he expresses his

---

[34]Lawrence of Rome (c. 225–258), martyr during persecution of
Valerian in 258. Ambrose of Milan in a section on the virtue of
fortitude reports that Lawrence was martyred on a gridiron and
during the torture cried out, "Assumta est, versa et manduca,"
that is, "[This side] is done, turn it over and have a bite!" *De
officiis ministrorum* I.xli.214-16.
[35]MO 13:1117.
[36]Münster, *Miqdaš YHWH*, 1202.
[37]Amyraut, *Paraphrasis in Psalmos Davidis*, 220.

[32]Sadoleto, *Interpretatio in Psalmum Miserere mei*, unpaginated.
[33]Selnecker, *Der gantze Psalter*, 2:15v; citing Mk 2:5.

expectation of converting others is not unworthy of our notice. We conclude too soon that our attempts at reclaiming the ungodly are vain and ineffectual, and we forget that God is able to crown them with success. COMMENTARY ON THE PSALMS.[38]

REASON AND REPENTANCE. PHILIPP MELANCHTHON: In this passage an extraordinary teaching is delivered opposed to human judgments. Reason, when we are in calamities, judges that we are neglected and cast off by God. But the divine voice in the church teaches that there are other reasons for our afflictions, namely, that we may be called back to repentance, or that we may be strengthened or that we may be testimonies of the doctrine. Therefore he affirms that those afflicted ones who flee to God are truly received, heard and helped, and that fortitude in adversity is a worship pleasing to God. This necessary teaching about the cross is comprehended in this little verse, "the sacrifice to God is a contrite spirit." COMMENTS ON THE PSALMS.[39]

DRAW ME TO YOUR SALVATION. KATHARINA SCHÜTZ ZELL: Your glory is that you deal honorably and do not break your covenant and pledge to me on account of my shameful breach of that covenant and my rebellion. But you remember your word which you have sworn, regardless of all my wrongdoing, and you seek to concern yourself only with faith. Therefore you now send me your admonitions through people and in my heart, that I may humble myself and bewail my sins, that I may search into your Word, awake faith and show forth that you help without any work of mine: that is the way to salvation which you point out. THE MISERERE PSALM.[40]

GOD PREFERS A BROKEN HEART. ANDREAS VON KARLSTADT: The external sabbath has been instituted for the benefit of those who work, that they might renew or restore their strength and that

people and livestock—not only they but the householder—might be refreshed. However, God does not care much for external behavior and customs but merely that no one disadvantage or harm another. Therefore, the external celebration has not been commanded so rashly and seriously that work which might benefit another could not be done on the sabbath, or that we should suffer loss or disaster rather than do external work and so forfeit celebration. For God does not look to external things and sacrifices but to the internal ones. When these are upright, what follows externally is right, too, and everything a person does or leaves undone is right as well. Similarly, God prefers a broken heart—where that is found it matters little whether we fast or eat, drink or suffer thirst, sacrifice or not, celebrate or work, as long as we do not come to God while we are empty within. Although we might come empty-handed externally, it does not endanger us before God. REGARDING THE SABBATH AND STATUTORY HOLY DAYS.[41]

51:18-19 Show Mercy to Zion

JERUSALEM IS A SHADOW OF THE KINGDOM. SEBASTIAN MÜNSTER: David prays that Jerusalem and the worship of God in it would be restored and that on account of his sin those things which God had established in Jerusalem would not cease. And the prophet does not consider only the external edifice of the city and din of its ceremonies, but his mind's eye is fixed even more so on the kingdom of Christ, whose shadow he understands by the city of Jerusalem. Again, this is understood concerning the burnt sacrifice and whole burnt offering that were figures of the true sacrifice, that is, in righteousness. THE TEMPLE OF THE LORD: PSALM 51.[42]

ACT FAVORABLY TOWARD THE CHURCH, O LORD! GIROLAMO SAVONAROLA: When you have acted favorably in your good pleasure to Zion, you

[38]CTS 9:302* (CO 31:520).
[39]MO 13:1118.
[40]Zell, *Church Mother*, 323-24*; citing Ezek 16:59-63; 2 Sam 1; 13.

[41]CRR 8:327-28*.
[42]Münster, *Miqdaš YHWH*, 1202. Calvin follows Münster here; see CTS 9:307-8 (CO 31:523).

will accept the sacrifice of righteousness. You will accept it, I say, because you will consume it with the fire of your love. For in this way you accepted the sacrifice of Moses and the sacrifice of Elijah. For in this way you accept the sacrifices of righteousness when you bind with your grace the souls which are content to live justly.

What use is it to offer you sacrifices, when you do not accept them? O Lord, how many sacrifices do we daily offer you which are not pleasing to you but instead are abominable? For we offer you sacrifices not of righteousness but of our own formalism. Hence they are not acceptable to you. Where now is the glory of the apostles? Where is the constancy of the martyrs? Where are the fruits of the preachers? Where is the holy simplicity of the monks? Where are the virtues and good works of the first Christians? For then you accepted their sacrifices when you adorned them with your grace and virtues.

If, likewise, you should act favorably to Zion in your good pleasure, then you will accept the sacrifice of righteousness, because the people will begin to live rightly and to observe your commandments and to act justly and your blessing will be on them. Then the oblations of the priests and of the clergy will be acceptable to you, because, having forsaken worldly things, they will make themselves ready for the better life, and the unction of your blessing will be on their heads. Then the burnt offerings of the religious will be pleasing to you. Having forsaken the body and thrown off lukewarmness they will be perfected in every way with the fire of divine love.

Then bishops and preachers will offer young bulls on your altar, because being perfected in all virtue and filled with the Holy Spirit, they will not hesitate to offer their own souls for the sake of their flocks. For what is your altar but your cross, O good Jesus, on which you have been offered? What does the sportive young bull signify except our flesh? Therefore, then, they will offer young bulls on your altar when they offer their bodies on the cross, that is, to torture and to death for your name's sake. Then the church will flourish. Then it

will enlarge its borders. Then your praise will resound from the ends of the earth. Then joy and gladness will possess the whole world. Then the saints will exult in glory; they will rejoice on their beds, beholding us in the land of the living.

Make—I beseech you, O Lord!—for me a present *Now* of that *Then*, so that you may have pity on me according to your great mercy. May you support me in the sacrifice of righteousness, in the oblation of holiness, in the burnt offering of a religious life and in the blood-offering of your cross through which I may be worthy to pass over from this vale of misery to that glory which you have prepared for those who love you. Thanks be to God! An Exposition of the Psalm *Miserere*.[43]

Sacrifices of Repentance and Praise.

Martin Luther: The prophet sets forth a double sacrifice to us. The first is what he calls "a contrite heart," that is, when we feel a troubled spirit and a humbled heart which battles with thoughts of God's wrath and judgment. Here be careful not to add despair, but trust and believe in hope against hope. Christ is the physician of the contrite, who wants to lift up the fallen and "not to quench the dimly burning wick" but to cherish it. So if you are a wick, do not quench yourself, that is, do not add despair. If you are a "bruised reed," do not bruise yourself further or let Satan bruise you, but give yourself to Christ, who is a friend to human beings and who loves crushed and broken spirits. This is the first and most powerful sacrifice. Then, when you have thus acknowledged God to be the justifier of sinners, if you sing God even one song of thanks, you add another sacrifice, namely, a sacrifice of recompense or of thanksgiving for the gift you have received. This sacrifice is not merit but a confession and testimony of the grace which your God has bestowed on you out of sheer mercy. Thus the saints and the righteous in the Old Testament brought burnt offerings with the purpose not of being justified through them but of testifying that they had received mercy

---

[43]Savonarola, *An Exposition of the Psalm Miserere Mei Deus*, 75-77*.

and comfort. Thus a sacrificed ox is a witness of grace, or, so to speak, a "working voice" of gratitude or a manual gratitude through which the hand pours out gratitude as through words of actions. This is the second type of sacrifice.

The first sacrifice is a sacrifice of mortification that we be neither carried away by success nor crushed by failure but moderate our smugness with the fear of God and maintain our hope for mercy amid feelings of God's wrath and judgment. Thus we do not smash into heaven with our heads or into the earth with our feet. The second type of sacrifice is thanksgiving. This is not only a matter of the tongue, that we confess our faith and preach the name of the Lord, but of all the actions of life. It is called "a sacrifice of righteousness," which pleases God because the person is righteous and the sacrifice of humiliation and contrition has preceded. It observes the average between pride and despair—the physical average, that is, not the mathematical. In this weakness of ours it is impossible so to live that we never swerve to the right or to the left. Still an effort is required so that when we feel either smugness or despair, we do not succumb to it but resist it. Just as a target is assigned to an archer, so a place is given to those who do not miss the target completely, even though they do not hit the center of the mathematical point. For God it is enough that we battle against the smugness and pride of the flesh and against despair. Even though some happiness may be lacking in afflictions or some fear in prosperity, this is not imputed to the saints. For they have Christ as their Mediator. Through him it happens that they are regarded as truly holy even though they hardly have the first fruits of holiness. Those who in themselves are no more than first fruits become tithes through Christ.

Therefore the summary of this teaching is this. The afflicted should comfort themselves with the merit of Christ or the mercy of God. Those who are without afflictions should walk in the fear of God and cast out smugness. For this teaching we need the prayer which concludes this psalm, that the Lord might build his church. Then should follow sacrifices that are pleasing and acceptable to God. May God and our Redeemer Jesus Christ grant this to us all. Amen. Lectures on Psalm 51 (1532).[44]

Lord, Be Merciful to Your Creatures!
The Book of Common Prayer: O Lord, we beseech you, mercifully hear our prayers and spare all those who confess their sins to you, that they whose consciences by sin are accused, by your merciful pardon may be absolved through Christ our Lord. Amen. O most mighty God and merciful Father, you have compassion on all human beings, and you hate nothing that you have made. You do not desire the death of sinners but that they should rather turn from sin and be saved. Mercifully forgive us our trespasses, receive and comfort us, who be grieved and wearied with the burden of our sin. Your property is to have mercy; to you only it appertains to forgive sins. Spare us therefore, good Lord, spare your people whom you have redeemed. Enter not into judgment with your servants who be vile earth, and miserable sinners. But so turn your ire from us who meekly acknowledge our vileness and truly repent of our faults. Make haste to help us in this world, so that we may always live with you in the world to come. Through Jesus Christ our Lord. Amen. Ash Wednesday Liturgy.[45]

---

[44]LW 12:409-10* (WA 40,2:469-70); citing Rom 4:18; Is 42:3; Num 18:12-24.
[45]BCP 1549, 154*.

52:1-9 DO NOT BOAST; INSTEAD SEEK REFUGE IN OUR MIGHTY GOD

To the choirmaster. A Maskil[a] of David, when Doeg, the Edomite, came and told Saul, "David has come to the house of Ahimelech."

¹ Why do you boast of evil, O mighty man?
    The steadfast love of God endures all the day.
² Your tongue plots destruction,
    like a sharp razor, you worker of deceit.
³ You love evil more than good,
    and lying more than speaking what is right.
                                        Selah

⁴ You love all words that devour,
    O deceitful tongue.

⁵ But God will break you down forever;
    he will snatch and tear you from your tent;

he will uproot you from the land of the
    living.   Selah
⁶ The righteous shall see and fear,
    and shall laugh at him, saying,
⁷ "See the man who would not make
    God his refuge,
but trusted in the abundance of his riches
    and sought refuge in his own destruction!"[b]

⁸ But I am like a green olive tree
    in the house of God.
I trust in the steadfast love of God
    forever and ever.
⁹ I will thank you forever,
    because you have done it.
I will wait for your name, for it is good,
    in the presence of the godly.

a Probably a musical or liturgical term   b Or in his work of destruction

---

OVERVIEW: Our commentators do not lose sight of this psalm's background—Doeg's betrayal of David and the subsequent slaughter of priests—but they also find in this psalm relevant resonances for the contemporary church. Doeg and David are types for the wicked and the good, respectively. The wicked continue to choose cowardly conquests, oppressing the weak and defenseless; such actions will be met with the Lord's wrath. The good find shelter in God; despite their suffering, they find joy and comfort in God's enduring benevolence. We should not forget, Calvin reminds us, that while on earth the church consists of both the wicked and the good. The threshing of God's church is not our concern. Instead we must commend ourselves to his mercy in prayer and praise.

THE HORRIFIC CONTEXT OF THIS PSALM.
NIKOLAUS SELNECKER: The history of this psalm—as indicated in the title—stands in 1 Samuel 22; it is

horrible. David, when he fled from Saul, came to Ahimelech, the Lord's priest, and received from him in his time of need the Showbread for food and the sword of Goliath, whom he had defeated. All this Doeg an Edomite, the mightiest among Saul's shepherds, saw; he revealed it to Saul. On account of this Saul had the priest Ahimelech and still another eighty-four priests of the Lord along with him executed in a single day by the betrayer Doeg. Thus, this man of the royal court, Doeg, became a betrayer and murderer of the Lord's anointed. THE WHOLE PSALTER.[1]

52:1-4 Foolish Warriors, You Are Liars

DAVID DENIGRATES DOEG. RUDOLF GWAL-
THER: David calls Doeg a mighty man in a disparaging and derisive manner, because Doeg

---

[1]Selnecker, Der gantze Psalter, 2:21v.

boasts how he killed King Saul and executed the priests along with their families. It is as if he said, "How 'bravely' you have behaved and what a 'mighty' deed you have carried out, that you have slain poor, unarmed priests, their wives and innocent children, as well as their cattle." THE PSALTER.[2]

POWER AND GOODNESS ARE PARTNERS, NOT FOES. THE ENGLISH ANNOTATIONS: O Doeg, you make use of the power you have under Saul not to do good but to do mischief. This is contrary to God, whose constant goodness, even toward sinners, should be our example. The closer we come to him in power, we should do so in goodness also. ANNOTATIONS ON PSALM 52:1.[3]

THE SMALL BUT MIGHTY TONGUE. DAVID DICKSON: The tongue, when it is abused, is a world of wickedness, setting the world on fire, as it itself is set on fire from hell by Satan. Whatever mischief the devil can suggest or a wicked heart can devise is given vent by the tongue, and so the tongue is charged with devising mischief. The smooth communication of a wicked device does not hide the mischief from God's sight or extenuate the fault of the person but rather through its cunning and power helps the mischief. Moreover, when a person tells only part of a tale, the part which serves his own interests, but reserves that part which might declare the innocence of another, even if the first part of the tale is true, this is evil lying, a murdering and devouring speech full of deceit, as the speaker argues that Doeg's words were of this manner. COMMENTARY ON PSALM 52:2-4.[4]

52:5-7 God Will Vindicate the Righteous

THE CONSEQUENCES OF FALSE WORSHIP. RUDOLF GWALTHER: David meditates on the tent or tabernacle for this reason, that Doeg advised this murder in his heart while he was in the Lord's tabernacle, under the appearance of God's worship. And he wants to say this: "Because you have practiced such falsehood in the tabernacle of God, God will put you out from the same, yes, he will cast you out, so that you shall no longer be a member of his church and congregation." THE PSALTER.[5]

DUPLICITY EARNS DESTRUCTION, NOT PROSPERITY. DAVID DICKSON: As the wicked are instrumental for bringing temporal destruction on the godly, so are they instrumental in drawing everlasting destruction on themselves from God's hand. . . . Those who strive to settle themselves, to enlarge themselves, to root themselves in the earth and to prolong their standing in the world by wrong means—especially by harming the godly, their good name and cause—shall find the event quite contrary to their desire, design and expectation, as Doeg did, whose doom was destruction, for his evil offenses done at court against David and the Lord's ministers. COMMENTARY ON PSALM 52:5.[6]

DO NOT ROB GOD OF HIS GLORY. JOHN CALVIN: The two clauses, "made not God his strength" and "trusted in the abundance of his riches," stand mutually connected. None can be said sincerely to repose on God but he who has been emptied of all confidence in his own resources. As long as human beings imagine that they have something of their own in which they can boast, they will never resort to God. It is always the same thing: just in proportion as we arrogate to ourselves do we derogate from him. And it is not only wealth but any other earthly possession on which we put our trust that may prevent us from inquiring after the Lord. . . . Those who trust in riches and strengthen themselves in their substance defraud God of his just glory. COMMENTARY ON THE PSALMS.[7]

52:8-9 I Trust in and Wait for the Lord

A TREE IN STREAMS OF WATER. RUDOLF GWALTHER: Believers here are compared with an olive tree, because they are fruitful and always

[2]Gwalther, *Der Psalter*, 93r.
[3]Downame, ed., *Annotations*, 6F3r*.
[4]Dickson, *Other Fifty Psalms*, 15*; citing Jas 3:5-6.
[5]Gwalther, *Der Psalter*, 93r-v.
[6]Dickson, *Other Fifty Psalms*, 16*.
[7]CTS 9:316* (CO 31:528).

mature in their faith and confession of salvation. The Psalter.[8]

The Church on Earth Is a Mixed Body.

John Calvin: The passage puts us in possession of the grand distinction between the genuine children of God and those who are hypocrites. They are to be found together in the church, as the wheat is mingled with the chaff on the same threshing-floor; but the one class abides forever in the steadfastness of a well-founded hope, while the other is driven away in the vanity of its false confidences. Commentary on the Psalms.[9]

By Deliverance God Shows He Is Near Us.

Philipp Melanchthon: In the last verse the encouragement concerns thanksgiving and the celebration of divine goodness; he affirms that he gives thanks to God for this deliverance, and this will be celebrated in the assembly of the saints, so that in this example those strengthened are not broken in their trials but rather obey God, as well as seek and expect their deliverance according to the counsel of God. For God shows his presence in the church by many deliverances, and he witnesses that he hears our sighs and our prayers, so that others are invited to the faith, hope and prayer, and for the sake of these reasons he commands these kindnesses to be celebrated. Comments on the Psalms.[10]

---

[8]Gwalther, Der Psalter, 93v.
[9]CTS 9:319 (CO 31:530).

[10]MO 13:1122; citing Ps 9:13-14.

53:1-6 NO ONE DOES GOOD—NOT EVEN ONE

To the choirmaster: according to Mahalath. A Maskil[a] of David.

[1] *The fool says in his heart, "There is no God."*
They are corrupt, doing abominable iniquity;
there is none who does good.

[2] *God looks down from heaven*
on the children of man
to see if there are any who understand,[b]
who seek after God.

[3] *They have all fallen away;*
together they have become corrupt;
there is none who does good,
not even one.

[4] *Have those who work evil no knowledge,*
who eat up my people as they eat bread,
and do not call upon God?

[5] *There they are, in great terror,*
where there is no terror!
For God scatters the bones of him who encamps
against you;
you put them to shame, for God has rejected
them.

[6] *Oh, that salvation for Israel would come out*
of Zion!
When God restores the fortunes of his people,
let Jacob rejoice, let Israel be glad.

a Probably musical or liturgical terms   b Or *who act wisely*

OVERVIEW: The reformers recognize that this psalm is almost identical to Psalm 14; many simply refer their readers to their earlier exegesis. Those who do consider this psalm focus on the two points of divergence between Psalm 14 and Psalm 53: the title and the words of verse 5. Nevertheless, the reformers find that the teaching of the two psalms differs little. Thus they read David's words here as a lament over the sinful nature of humanity and a recognition of our need for redemption.

PSALM 14 AGAIN. CARDINAL CAJETAN: This psalm is the same as Psalm 14, almost word for word; only the fifth verse is different. Therefore we will pass over it briefly, referring you to what was written on Psalm 14—obviously both have the same material and development, as will be clear; only the fifth verse is different. COMMENTARY ON PSALM 53.[1]

BUT IT IS NOT REPEATED IN VAIN. RUDOLF GWALTHER: But it is not repeated without good reason, namely, that we would learn to judge the sinful, blasphemous nature of the godless and that we would not be frustrated by this, because we hear that God sees all this and will not allow it to pass unpunished. And he certainly protects and sustains his people in all times. THE PSALTER.[2]

Superscription: *According to the Māḥalat*

SAME LETTERS, DIFFERENT SPIRIT. MARTIN LUTHER: Because this psalm is an instruction [*eruditio*, i.e., *maśkil*] it compels us to understand it spiritually about spiritual idolatry, namely, those who, although they confess God with their mouths, nevertheless deny him in their hearts and actions, because they have a dead faith in God in their hearts. Also the difference in title from Psalm 14 indicates that this psalm should also be understood differently

---

[1]Cajetan, *In Sacrae Scripturae Expositionem*, 3:191. Luther and Calvin also highlight the similarity between Ps 14 and Ps 53; Calvin sees no reason to add additional comment. See WA 38:37 (cf. 3:297); CTS 9:320 (CO 31:531).

[2]Gwalther, *Der Psalter*, 94r.

from Psalm 14. Nevertheless according to the literal sense it speaks about the Jews. This sense has already been exegeted above in Psalm 14, so here we will disregard it. GLOSSA ON PSALM 53 (1513–1515).[3]

VARIOUS MEANINGS OF MĀHALAT. FELIX PRATENSIS: Different people expound the second term [māhalat] in this psalm's title in many different ways. Some translate it as "congregation"; others assert it to mean "choir"; others "infirmity" or "inheritance" (as we said in Ps 5). But others conclude it to be the name of a certain musical instrument. However, the Chaldean translator gives the following: "For praise over the retribution of the impious who disturbed the inheritance of the Lord, good knowledge by the hand of David." THE HEBREW PSALTER.[4]

53:5 The Lord Revenges His People

DIFFERENT WORDS, SAME MEANING. RUDOLF GWALTHER: Here this verse is stated with different words than it was in Psalm 14. . . . However, although the words are not the same, still at the root the meaning is one. Here the punishment which he promised in these descriptive words is carried out. And in the same way that he earlier spoke with the godless, he now turns his entire speech to the pious and shows them that although the godless effeminately and defiantly rage against them, still God will make them a curse and horror, even though there seems to be no danger at hand. For God is able to ridicule such "luminaries". . . . And as they presently disparage believers on account of their faith, thus God will put them to shame, so that they will be a laughingstock among all people. THE PSALTER.[5]

THE LITERAL SENSE HERE IS REDEMPTION FROM SIN. CARDINAL CAJETAN: According to the letter the salvation of the people by the Messiah was anticipated from Zion. And rightly, because in Jerusalem the Messiah saved the world. He explains how greatly and deeply this salvation was anticipated from the Messiah. God restores his people from captivity, not just from Babylon, not just from Egypt—instead this is simply and absolutely said about the captivity of his people, which is clearly their captivity to sin, according to the words of the angel: "He will prepare salvation for his people from their sins." "Let Jacob rejoice, let Israel be glad," so that from this twin joy—internal and external—you should understand the magnitude of this salvation. Amen. COMMENTARY ON PSALM 53.[6]

WE ARE NOTHING BEFORE GOD. NIKOLAUS SELNECKER: David here describes the misery, weakness, nothingness, sorrow and distress of all human nature. For this psalm is a penitential sermon and laments our whole being, birth, reason, sense, spirit, heart and will, and against all faculties of the soul and the body. . . . Because now this doctrine of our corrupt human nature is badly needed in the congregation of God, that it might be maintained forever, that we would recognize ourselves for what we are, consider and weep for our misery and nothingness and learn the proper *Nil sum*—"I am nothing and am good for nothing"—might not become proud or overconfident or trust in any merit or work of our own but live solely on the mere grace and mercy of God which he has shown us in his Son, therefore David, with diligence and at the suggestion and inspiration of the Holy Spirit, recorded this psalm twice, so that he might hammer this doctrine into us who are otherwise proud, who coddle, adorn and enhance ourselves and do not want to be nothing but rather be something before God. THE WHOLE PSALTER.[7]

---

[3]WA 3:296-97.
[4]Pratensis, *Psalterium*, 26v. Contemporary scholars speculate that *māhalat* is an instrument; see Kraus, *Psalms 1–59*, 27; Goldingay, *Psalms*, 2:151; Alter, *Book of Psalms*, 187.
[5]Gwalther, *Der Psalter*, 94r-v.

[6]Cajetan, *In Sacrae Scripturae Expositionem*, 3:192.
[7]Selnecker, *Der gantze Psalter*, 2:25r.

54:1-7 THE LORD GIVES LIFE

To the choirmaster: with stringed instruments. A Maskil[a] of David, when the Ziphites went and told Saul, "Is not David hiding among us?"

¹ O God, save me by your name,
  and vindicate me by your might.
² O God, hear my prayer;
  give ear to the words of my mouth.

³ For strangers[b] have risen against me;
  ruthless men seek my life;
  they do not set God before themselves.   Selah

⁴ Behold, God is my helper;
  the Lord is the upholder of my life.
⁵ He will return the evil to my enemies;
  in your faithfulness put an end to them.

⁶ With a freewill offering I will sacrifice to you;
  I will give thanks to your name, O LORD,
  for it is good.
⁷ For he has delivered me from every trouble,
  and my eye has looked in triumph on my
  enemies.

a Probably a musical or liturgical term   b Some Hebrew manuscripts and Targum *insolent men* (compare Psalm 86:14)

OVERVIEW: In this prayer of David following his betrayal by the Ziphites, our commentators recognize the significance of the sovereign will of God, which provides our only hope for deliverance and brings destruction to his enemies. The selections provided by Luther and Calvin provide an interesting juxtaposition, demonstrating two possible methods through which meaning can be drawn from the text for contemporary audiences. Luther applies a traditional hermeneutic and discerns three levels of meaning in the psalm, finding correspondence in the experiences of David, Christ and the church as they seek to enter the kingdoms established for them by God. Calvin, by contrast, distills principles from the experience of David and applies these to the present life of the church.

THE HISTORICAL CONTEXT OF THIS PSALM.

NIKOLAUS SELNECKER: This is a psalm of prayer against the enemies of God's church and the enemies of all those who fear God, that God would help and save them from the hand of tyrants and the mighty. The history which the title references stands in 1 Samuel 23 and 1 Samuel 26, when David fled before Saul and entered the

wilderness Ziph. Thus, the Ziphites—who were indeed from the tribe of Judah, just like David—came to Saul and told him that David was among them; if he wanted, they would surrender him into his hands. That is the hypocrite's way! The Ziphites wanted to earn Saul's gratitude, or they were afraid because they saw what happened to the city of Nob, which Saul struck with the edge of the sword—men, women, children, sucklings, oxen, donkeys and sheep (1 Sam 22).

And here we should note what happens when we seek the grace and favor of human beings and fear them—even if we are right. For certainly we deny the truth of God and betray Christ.... When we fear human beings more than God and conscience, it is time to despair, there is no more advice and help. THE WHOLE PSALTER.[1]

THROUGH TRIBULATION WE ENTER CHRIST'S KINGDOM.

MARTIN LUTHER: As David through many tribulations arrived at his kingdom, established for him by God, so it is fitting that Christ suffered and thus entered into his glory, established for him by God. So also it is fitting that we through many tribulations enter into the king-

---

¹Selnecker, *Der gantze Psalter*, 2:25v.

dom of heaven, promised to us. For everywhere in these histories David exhibits the figure of Christ, which also he understood in the Spirit; and so from these histories he composed prophecies about Christ. Indeed, David did not write this privately, as if composing these histories for himself, but he wrote whatever might be useful and suitable for all, especially concerning Christ. That is why it is not enough for you to be baptized and have your sins absolved; indeed, the kingdom is already yours, but it must be taken hold of through tribulation.

And because this psalm is in daily use, it is good to distinguish it in three senses. Therefore, the literal sense is about Christ; the allegorical sense, about the church against tyrants and heretics; the tropological sense, against the flesh, the world and the devil. And this in the Spirit, because superficially it could be understood about David. GLOSSA ON PSALM 54 (1513–1515).[2]

54:1-7 *Divine Deliverance*

ALL DELIVERANCE IS FROM GOD. JOHN CALVIN: As David was at this time placed beyond the reach of human assistance, he must be understood as praying to be saved by the name and the power of God, in an emphatic sense or by these in contradistinction to the usual means of deliverance. Though all help must ultimately come from God, there are ordinary methods by which he generally extends it. When these fail and every earthly stay is removed, he must then take the work into his own hands. It was in such a situation that David here fled to the saints' last asylum and sought to be saved by a miracle of divine power. Appealing to God as his protector, the one who judges his cause, David asserts his innocence. And it must strike us all that in asking for divine protection, it is indispensably prerequisite that we should be convinced of the goodness of our cause, as it would argue the greatest profanity in any person to expect that God

should patronize iniquity. David was encouraged to pray for deliverance by the goodness of his cause and the integrity of his conscience. He did not entertain a single doubt that on presenting this to God he would act the part of his defender and punish the cruelty and treachery of his enemies. COMMENTARY ON THE PSALMS.[3]

THE VALUE OF PRAYING OUT LOUD. DAVID DICKSON: In fervent prayer, the very voice has use, because it allows the supplicant to express his earnestness and faith in God, while also stirring him up and holding him fixed to his supplication. To God, the use of the voice demonstrates an immediate invocation, a sign of dependence and an expectation of a good answer from him. COMMENTARY ON PSALM 54:2.[4]

THE LORD'S POWER SUBVERTS HUMAN UNDERSTANDING. MARTIN LUTHER: What is the strength of God by which he saves us? It is that which is a stumbling block to the Jews and folly to the Gentiles. It is weakness, suffering, cross, persecution. These are the weapons of God, these the strengths and powers by which he saves and judges us and distinguishes us from those who think otherwise. For according to the apostle in 1 Corinthians 1, "The weakness of God is stronger than human beings, and the foolishness of God is wiser than human beings." And, "The gospel is the power of God to salvation to everyone who believes" (Rom 1). For this the world does not know that patience, humility, cross and persecution are strength and wisdom. Hence it is judged on this point and by its ignorance is distinguished from the saints, to whom Christ crucified is strength and wisdom. For through the cross and suffering that is both theirs and his they triumph over every force of the devil. Therefore this is truly God's power, and yet it is the weakness of human beings. For he has chosen what is weak to confound what is strong.

---

[2]WA 3:299; citing Acts 14:22.

[3]CTS 9:322* (CO 31:532).
[4]Dickson, *Other Fifty Psalms*, 23*.

Therefore they differ in this way:

The strength of God			endurance of the cross			the weakness of God		are truly
The strength of the world	}	is {	nonendurance of the cross	}	and {	the weakness of the world	}	the same.

FIRST PSALMS LECTURES (1513–1515).[5]

QUICK ANSWERS TO PRAYER. DAVID DICKSON: Fervent prayer often has a swift answer, and sometimes it is wonderfully swift, coming even before one finishes one's speech, as David experiences here. The light of faith is very clear, piercing through all clouds, and when God holds the light of the Spirit beside it, it can demonstrate the presence of God in an instant, ready to help in the greatest trials. COMMENTARY ON PSALM 54:4.[6]

HOW CAN DAVID REJOICE OVER DESTRUCTION? WOLFGANG MUSCULUS: David rejoiced concerning the destruction of his enemies—even already before this destruction happened.... He did not say this out of hatred or for his own advantage or in a spirit of vengeance. Otherwise whenever he could, he would have destroyed his enemies with his own hand. He considered it differently. He was anointed as the king over the people of the Lord. He loved the Lord the most and fell on his grace in many calamities and the irreconcilable hatred of Saul, by which he was being stubbornly sought out for death. Meanwhile in faith and hope he depended on the goodness of the Lord. He also experienced that grace everywhere. From which he gathered that the Lord was his helper and accordingly would continue to be.... He boasts about this protection and goodness of God toward him, while he boasts about his loved ones. In general he preferred to see the safety of Saul and the conversion of all his enemies rather than their destruction....

The saints themselves neither seek nor pursue their enemies with a private hatred, nor do they rejoice in the destruction of them according to the malice of human nature. Indeed, they depend on God and because they glory in his faithfulness and providence toward them, and above all things they thirst for the glory of the divine name. If it happens that they look with great joy on ... the destruction of their enemies themselves, it is because this declares that God is the protector of those who hope in him and the glory of his name is vindicated, which the impious in this world obscure. Thus the children of Israel sang praises to God when they saw the drowning of the impious pharaoh together with his army. Thus also we too will see with joy the destruction of those who stubbornly fight against the truth of Christ. COMMENTARY ON THE PSALMS.[7]

WE CAN REJOICE IN ALL GOD'S ACTS. DAVID DICKSON: The light of God's Word, made lively by God's Spirit, is able to show a person both the destruction of his wicked enemies and his own deliverance from them. As a person may rejoice in God's mercy, so also he may rejoice in God's justice against his enemies, provided that he is free from private revenge. COMMENTARY ON PSALM 54:7.[8]

THIS PSALM CAN BE USED AGAINST EXTERNAL AND INTERNAL ENEMIES. NIKOLAUS SELNECKER: The Christian church may use this psalm well against the Turks, Muscovites[9] and other foreign as well as internal enemies; through this use we cry out for help and deliverance. THE WHOLE PSALTER.[10]

---

[5]LW 10:250* (WA 3:301-2); citing 1 Cor 1:25; Rom 1:16.
[6]Dickson, *Other Fifty Psalms*, 24*.
[7]Musculus, *In Psalterium Commentarii*, 610; citing 2 Kings 7:2; Ps 91:8.
[8]Dickson, *Other Fifty Psalms*, 25*.
[9]By "Muscovites" Selnecker likely refers to the (Orthodox) Russian invasion of largely Protestant Livonia—present day Estonia and Latvia—that resulted in the Livonian War (1558–1583).
[10]Selnecker, *Der gantze Psalter*, 2:26v.

55:1-23 ALL OUR BURDENS WE CAST ON THE LORD

To the choirmaster: with stringed instruments.
A Maskil[a] of David.

¹ Give ear to my prayer, O God,
  and hide not yourself from my plea for mercy!
² Attend to me, and answer me;
  I am restless in my complaint and I moan,
³ because of the noise of the enemy,
  because of the oppression of the wicked.
For they drop trouble upon me,
  and in anger they bear a grudge against me.

⁴ My heart is in anguish within me;
  the terrors of death have fallen upon me.
⁵ Fear and trembling come upon me,
  and horror overwhelms me.
⁶ And I say, "Oh, that I had wings like a dove!
  I would fly away and be at rest;
⁷ yes, I would wander far away;
  I would lodge in the wilderness;   Selah
⁸ I would hurry to find a shelter
  from the raging wind and tempest."

⁹ Destroy, O Lord, divide their tongues;
  for I see violence and strife in the city.
¹⁰ Day and night they go around it
  on its walls,
and iniquity and trouble are within it;
  ¹¹ ruin is in its midst;
oppression and fraud
  do not depart from its marketplace.

¹² For it is not an enemy who taunts me—
  then I could bear it;
it is not an adversary who deals insolently
    with me—
    then I could hide from him.
¹³ But it is you, a man, my equal,
  my companion, my familiar friend.

¹⁴ We used to take sweet counsel together;
  within God's house we walked in the
    throng.
¹⁵ Let death steal over them;
  let them go down to Sheol alive;
  for evil is in their dwelling place and in
    their heart.

¹⁶ But I call to God,
  and the LORD will save me.
¹⁷ Evening and morning and at noon
  I utter my complaint and moan,
  and he hears my voice.
¹⁸ He redeems my soul in safety
  from the battle that I wage,
  for many are arrayed against me.
¹⁹ God will give ear and humble them,
  he who is enthroned from of old,   Selah
because they do not change
  and do not fear God.

²⁰ My companion[b] stretched out his hand
    against his friends;
  he violated his covenant.
²¹ His speech was smooth as butter,
  yet war was in his heart;
his words were softer than oil,
  yet they were drawn swords.

²² Cast your burden on the LORD,
  and he will sustain you;
he will never permit
  the righteous to be moved.
²³ But you, O God, will cast them down
  into the pit of destruction;
men of blood and treachery
  shall not live out half their days.
But I will trust in you.

a Probably a musical or liturgical term   b Hebrew *He*

OVERVIEW: Our Reformation commentators see David's petition in the midst of his intense sufferings as an affirmation that God hears the cries of his people, especially those who are afflicted and troubled, even when others ignore them. Some of our interpreters suggest that the psalmist's longing to fly away with wings like a dove should be read as the desire to flee sin and to be with Christ by the power of the Holy Spirit. Considering the reformers' christological interpretation, it is hardly surprising that they read David's distraught words about a close friend who has broken covenant and betrayed him as a prophetic reference to Judas's betrayal of Jesus, but they also note more generally the benefits—and dangers—of close friendships with others. Finally, for our commentators, this psalm affirms the twofold requirement that Christians should prepare for their own death while also steadfastly trusting in God.

WHAT IS THE CONTEXT OF THE PSALM?

SEBASTIAN MÜNSTER: This psalm seems to have been composed by David while he fled from Saul, his mortal enemy, on account of imminent danger, when he was protected in cities but wanted to have the wings of a dove, with which he could fly into the desert and into a safe place. Others expound it about Absalom's conspiracy when David with many others fled from Jerusalem. THE TEMPLE OF THE LORD: PSALM 55.[1]

55:1-8 *Listen to My Afflictions*

IN, THROUGH AND WITH CHRIST, RUN TO GOD. TILEMANN HESSHUS: Jesus Christ the Son of God brought all blessing to the world, revealing heavenly truth, refuting blasphemous errors, performing miracles, healing the sick, calling people to repentance, and offering and lavishing eternal salvation. By these great benefits he brought this grace from the heavens, even though princes and peoples had hated him most fervently. They slandered him with false charges and prepared ambushes to take his life. Therefore, in such orchestrated need, Christ, destitute of all human protection and help, fled to the eternal Father and pleaded for his help and defense in faith. By this example he teaches the entire church that there is no more salvific counsel nor safer refuge in danger and need than to plead with the eternal God by earnest prayer for his help, according to these words: "Call on me in the day of tribulation and I will rescue you, and you will glorify me."

"I am restless in my complaint and I am troubled." He uses an argument from an impulsive cause, because he is in great anguish and suffering. Our Lord Jesus Christ took on true human flesh with all its affections and properties. For he became like us through all things except sin. Therefore he experienced true terror, fear of heart and preservation, as he testified in the garden: "My soul is very sorrowful, even to death." It is as if he said, "There is such trembling and terror in my heart that it could kill me." Indeed Christ suffered the wrath of the eternal Father, incensed by our sin. Indeed he felt the burning wrath of God poured out on him. However, this suffering and terror in Christ was without sin. His natural emotions were preserved by God, so that he would avoid the destruction of his nature. In other saints—David, Abraham, Joshua, Jeremiah, Peter, Paul—great fear and terror often arise, too. "Fighting without," Paul says, "fear within." But these trepidations, lamentations and disturbances in the saints are not without sin and weakness. For these trepidations, lamentations and disturbances are joined with silent doubts and mutterings against God. But Christ in his trepidation displayed the most perfect faith and obedience in every way. COMMENTARY ON PSALM 55.[2]

RUN TO GOD. NIKOLAUS SELNECKER: These are words of a truly worried and hard-pressed conscience which is contested and afflicted from all directions and on all sides and has neither comfort nor advice nor help in this world except for God.

---

[1]Münster, *Miqdaš YHWH*, 1204.

[2]Hesshus, *Commentarius in Psalmos*, 233v-234r; citing Ps 50:15; Mk 14:34; 2 Cor 7:5.

He hears us even when nobody else wants to listen—when everyone stuffs their ears before our crying, shuts their doors and hides, so that we cannot find them, if we came. And if we were able to talk to them, they would not pay attention and would not listen to us, nor would they give advice or help, but leave us crying, moaning, lamenting, weeping, singing and saying whatever we want, as we often see with poor people who on account of their distress come to big cities. But God is different. Therefore we should run to God in our distress, like the centurion in Matthew 8, and tell him about our affliction and ask for help, so he himself will come and heal, comfort, strengthen, save and preserve us. The Whole Psalter.[3]

Soar on the Wings of the Contemplative Life. Martin Luther: This is the language of those who are in an active life and in the public eye; like Martha, troubled about many things, because with weariness they endure rebellion, opposition and envy from every side, as did Christ from the Jews. And therefore they sigh for a contemplative and quiet life of agreeable endeavors, and they crave to be set free from this bother. Where they cannot do this in the body, they are nevertheless in the wilderness and in solitude in their heart and desire, that is, separated from the rough and tumble of the affairs of an active life. Therefore they withdraw and take flight and tarry. These three are sought in order. First, they keep themselves aloof in attitude rather than in space. Second, they take flight, that is, they always withdraw more and more and eagerly. Third, they also keep it. But one to whom this cannot happen may grasp the following verse and say with Christ: "I waited for him who has made me safe."

But we must take note of the reasons why one should flee the active life and the circumstances of the one wishing to flee. First, there is the longing for wings, that is, for the contemplative life, not as from hatred of the active life and the duty of work but as from love of the contemplative life. The wings denote the acts and exertions of contemplation by which the mind is lifted up to God. And this so that one is not overpowered by the urge to seek the things that are his. . . . Second, like a dove, that is, not like the raven that flies from the ark to feed on carcasses. These are the ones who flee from being in charge and being of benefit to others so that they might enjoy the ease and pleasantness of life, as now the rich priests, having forsaken their priestly responsibilities, are gawking eagerly at gain and girls. The ravens shift the direction of their flight exclusively to what is advantageous for this life, whereas the dove, in its way, brings the branch of the greening olive, that is, the doctrine of godliness, to the ark of the church. Third, that the soul may not neglect something out of anger and the gall of bitterness but be like a dove, gentle and without gall. Otherwise there will never be a productive contemplation.

What follows is the same, "And I will fly." For one should love the contemplative life for this reason, that he may fly, not that he may be wanton, that is, swim in the slime of the flesh, nor that he may crawl on the ground like a greedy person, but fly in the sky. . . . He who has been a dove, the Holy Spirit, will teach him all these things, for he determined to appear and dwell in a dove. First Psalms Lectures (1513–1515).[4]

Fly to Christ. Viktorin Strigel: He adds to the complaint a vow concerning flight. . . . In the same way all saints long to be set free and be with Christ, that is, they desire to look on God more clearly and to be released from sin completely. For just as a traveler who is making a journey in the dark, and not familiar with the road or place, rejoices when in the morning the dawn begins to spread out its light, so all pious people, feeling the burden of sin and afflicted by various perils, long for companionship with God, and when their time of death comes, gladly they set aside the odious burden of doubts and the filth of sin, which is left

---

[3]Selnecker, *Der gantze Psalter*, 2:27r-v; citing Mt 8:5-13.

[4]LW 10:254-55* (WA 3:307-8); citing Mt 10:16; 1 Cor 13:5; Gen 8:7; Is 60:8; Mt 3:16.

in this impure lump of our present state, and they choose to be whole and forever burning with the love of God and happiness in him. HYPONĒMATA IN ALL THE PSALMS.[5]

55:9-11 Confound My Oppressors!

LIKE THE TOWER OF BABEL. RUDOLF GWALTHER: He says this according to that ancient example, that God would deal with them as he dealt with those building the tower of Babel; through the division of languages they would be thwarted. THE PSALTER.[6]

CONFUSED SPEECH IS DIVINE PUNISHMENT. NIKOLAUS SELNECKER: Here we learn that the confusion of speech and languages is a punishment of God. When God wants to punish, he lets foreign and twisted languages rise up, as we see with the Jews, Greeks and Romans. The Jewish land has Turkish, Slavic and other pagan, barbaric languages. The Jews themselves do not speak their true mother tongue, and they do not have the correct pronunciation, and they do not understand their tongue in holy Scripture, especially—as Theodoret and other ancient scribes testify—because they have their origin from Herod the Great, who was an Idumean. They are foreigners and not born ancient Jews from David's tribe. The Greeks, too, have lost their way of speaking, and their language is outrageously corrupted and adultered. The Latin language that formerly was magnificent, mighty and beautiful in Italy and among the Romans is now almost entirely snuffed out and only a little of it remains, so that we can still occasionally recognize or hear a Latin syllable or word, especially in Italian and French. And so the three most magnificent languages—Hebrew, Greek and Latin—are so corrupted that they can no longer be called mother tongues, because they are neither complete nor correct. Now instead they must be studied and learned with great diligence by Jews, Greeks and Latins just as much as by foreigners.

So we see with us, that truly the knowledge and study of language is declining rapidly. Educated people leisurely lose them one after the other; the youth are lazy, careless and study much too little. It is certainly worrisome that the old barbaric manner of speaking and writing ... will again trickle into schools and churches. Coquettes, churls and drunkards ... will again take their place and honor, with great disadvantage and detriment to the Christian church, as it has already begun. God help us! Perhaps our Lord God will come with a foreign, barbaric nation and punish us as we deserve, so that we must suffer unrestrained and unknown troops. Indeed, we will not even be able to understand them or speak with them; they will betray us, sell us off, torment us and hiss at us. THE WHOLE PSALTER.[7]

CITY HERE IS AMBIGUOUS. CARDINAL CAJETAN: By the term *city*, it is not clear whether the city of David from which he fled is meant, or the group of Saul which was against David. And this is the reason for the uncertainty: in Scripture we do not read about guards being placed in the city to keep David from escaping, but only in the house of David. Possibly, after Saul had ascertained that David had escaped through a window, he placed guards throughout the city, suspecting that he would not escape notice elsewhere in the city. If that is the right interpretation, then it is the guards of this sort with whom the prophet now deals. It is safer, however, to explain the word *city*—that is, the confederation of all those coming together with Saul against David—by stating that David himself is the enemy of the king. And along these lines, the three parts of the city (that is to say, the walls, the plaza and the center of it, which is mentioned twice) are to be taken metaphorically. You are to understand the whole group of them is wicked from top to bottom, and especially in their innermost hearts, and so twice the word *center* is repeated. COMMENTARY ON PSALM 55.[8]

[5]Strigel, *Hyponēmata*, 260.
[6]Gwalther, *Der Psalter*, 97v; citing Gen 11:1-9.
[7]Selnecker, *Der gantze Psalter*, 2:29r-v.
[8]Cajetan, *In Sacrae Scripturae Expositionem*, 3:196.

IMPIETY LEADS TO DISASTER. WOLFGANG MUSCULUS: How great is the curse, if with an impious magistrate in power, room is given to wicked people who not only disturb the city with their wicked behavior and evil nature, their violence, trickery and deceit, but also by their likeness to leaven corrupt the status and sincerity of their fellow citizens. Evil, as it is accustomed, creeps in like cancer until it spreads to all its surroundings and the entire city is infected. "A little yeast," Paul says, "corrupts the whole lump." Evil has its own beginning; it has its own progress by which it grows little by little until it's huge. It has fruitful and fertile soil, namely the minds of mortals—prone to all evil. So then, if anyone desires to be a sincere citizen, he must oppose the beginnings of evil and corruption. . . . Wherever impiety prevails and reigns, there peace and tranquility unavoidably will cease. "For there is no peace for the impious," says the Lord. "And the heart of the impious is like the churning sea." . . . What monstrous punishment such a city deserves! COMMENTARY ON THE PSALMS.[9]

55:12-15 Former Friends

WORDS ABOUT JUDAS'S BETRAYAL. MARTIN LUTHER: That Christ says "human being" and not "friend" or some other name indicates that Judas— according to human nature and appearance, which human beings see—was like himself and others; indeed, they were of one mind in all they did publicly. But inwardly he sees him to be the devil, as Jesus called him. He is speaking of him according to the human appearance, for it was certainly shameful that Christ was thus betrayed by his own disciple. Someone could say, "See, because he who was of one mind, a leader and associate betrayed Jesus, this would seem to be a strong argument that he was ungodly, because of the fact that one so close to him withdrew from him." And so Judas by his deed increased and strengthened the opinion of those who opposed Christ and offended others, and thus he magnified the hypocritical deceit over against him. Therefore the Lord speaks these words as if they could be spoken by someone else, like this: "See what this man does? And he was of one mind with him, he was a leader. What will other people do?" FIRST PSALMS LECTURES (1513–1515).[10]

THE VALUE OF FRIENDSHIP. JOHN CALVIN: We know that the Holy Spirit condemns all those who violate the sacred natural covenants that bind us together. One such covenant is the fellowship of all humanity. The nearer we are connected to someone, the more sacred the bond by which we are united. Because it was not unknown to the profane, we should understand that this principle does not happen by chance but by God's providence, so that proximity, relationship and common vocation join human beings together. Now the most sacred is the covenant of the pious. COMMENTARY ON THE PSALMS.[11]

FALSE AND FAITHFUL FRIENDS. NIKOLAUS SELNECKER: To have a good friend is a very precious treasure, but great danger is also involved. If a faithful friend remains with us to his grave, then nothing in this life can be called more precious and magnificent. "A faithful friend is a strong shelter and cannot be bought with gold or goods; he is a comfort of life." Like how David and Jonathan were with each other, and how it is written about Pylades and Orestes, when Pylades was willing to die for Orestes. These are true friends in times of distress who are given and added to those who fear God. . . .

Fairweather friends, needy friends and friends at table are more than plentiful. As long as they can enjoy something, they are friends. However, once things go badly—a person slides into disfavor, poverty and decline—the friendship is finished. "No goods, no courage; no money, no friends."

---

[9]Musculus, *In Psalterium Commentarii*, 617; citing 1 Cor 5:6 (cf. Gal 5:9); Is 57:20-21.

[10]LW 10:256-57* (WA 3:309); citing Jn 6:71.
[11]CO 31:540 (cf. CTS 9:336-37).

[*Nimmer gut, nimmer mut; Nimmer Gelt, nimmer Gesell.*] Needy friends are those who, if you show them complete love and favor, are pleased with you. You have to celebrate them and lift them up and approve of everything they do; carry them on your shoulders, say and do what they like to hear and see. But if you let yourself seem to disapprove of their behavior and plans, rebuke them and stop echoing their fiddling, or offend them out of human weakness and insult them a bit, then the friendship is absolutely over. You have poked the calf in its eye, and, as Sirach says, "If they know your murderous deeds, they'll tell everyone."

Friends at table are those coarse and barbaric platelickers and soupslurpers. They are good friends as long as you have enough beer, wine and food, as long as you pour their throats and bellies full, as long as you are always in a good mood with them; if you give them gifts and share with them, they will drain it and drink it up and wait for more. Just to please someone else they will bite off some of their glass, the pitcher or broken dishes and swallow it, break a plate in two over their head, mangle and cut their beard, puncture a hole through their ear, hang a string with a *groschen* from their beergut, jump over tables and benches, tumble like a monkey—yes, like a pig—yell and whoop, and want to be best friends. But they do not last, Sirach says, nor can they be trusted. May God protect us from such friends, who corrupt both body and soul. . . .

Such I say for this reason, that a good, faithful friend we should cherish highly and dearly; we should not trust a worldly person too much, not open up too quickly to make friends, but instead we should examine him and set him on the scales, so that we can recognize whether he is a friend in times of distress. It often takes two, three or even more years before you truly know someone else and what he holds under his shield. "So deceitful and unsearchable is the human heart," says Jeremiah. To enter into friendships thoughtlessly is a sign of a thoughtless mind. THE WHOLE PSALTER.[12]

DAVID DOES NOT WANT REVENGE BUT JUSTICE. JOHN CALVIN: He now denounces the whole faction, not the nation generally, but those who had taken a prominent part in the persecution of him. In imprecating this curse David was not influenced by any bad feeling toward them and must be understood as speaking not in his own cause but in that of God, and under the immediate guidance of his Spirit. This was no wish uttered in a moment of resentment or of reckless and ill-considered zeal which would justify us in launching maledictions against our enemies on every trivial provocation. The spirit of revenge differs widely from the holy and regulated fervor with which David prays for the judgment of God against the wicked, who had already been doomed to everlasting destruction. COMMENTARY ON THE PSALMS.[13]

55:16-21 God Will Humble False Friends

THE NEED FOR PREDETERMINED TIMES OF PRAYER. JOHN CALVIN: From the particular mention he makes of evening, morning and noon, we are left to infer that these must have been the stated hours of prayer among the godly at that time. Sacrifices were offered daily—in the morning and evening—in the temple, and by this the godly were taught to engage privately in prayer within their own houses. At noon also it was the practice to offer additional sacrifices. As we are naturally indisposed for the duty of prayer, there is a danger that we may be negligent and gradually omit it altogether, unless we restrict ourselves to a certain rule. By appointing fixed times for worship, God wants to remedy our infirmity. And the same principle should be applied to private prayers, as he shows from this passage as well as Daniel's example. Although today sacrifices have been abolished, nevertheless because we are not immune from that sluggishness which formerly required such an aid to be roused awake, we share this rule with the ancestors, that each one of us should appoint fixed

[12]Selnecker, *Der gantze Psalter*, 2:31v-32r; citing Sir 6:5-17; Jer 17:9.

[13]CTS 9:337* (CO 31:540-41).

times which we do not allow to slip by without prayer. COMMENTARY ON THE PSALMS.[14]

SEVERAL CHRISTOLOGICAL INTERPRETATIONS OF VERSE 17. MARTIN LUTHER: Cassiodorus explains "Evening and morning and noon I will speak" in this way. "I will speak in the evening, in which I was betrayed. I will declare in the morning, in which I was accused before Pilate. He will hear my voice at noon, when I am hanging on the cross." Augustine puts it this way: "In the evening," that is, concerning the past, "I will speak; in the morning," that is, concerning the future, "I will declare; at noon" that is, concerning eternity, "he will hear my voice." Another explanation: "In the evening," in which he died and was buried; "in the morning," in which he rose; "at noon," when he ascended into heaven. FIRST PSALMS LECTURES (1513–1515).[15]

ARMORED AGAINST DECEITFUL SPIRITS. DIRK PHILIPS: The bold and haughty spirits have nothing of the character and nature of Jesus Christ, but what they have, know and speak, that is from him who like lightning has fallen from heaven, because he was bold and untrue against his Creator and has not remained in the truth but has turned aside from it. He is a father of lies, an adversary of God, an opponent of his godly Word, a misleader of people, an Apollion, that is, a destroyer and killer of souls who also sends out his servants under a hypocritical appearance, who have the form of God's salvation but deny his power. Their words are sometimes smoother and softer than oil and butter, and yet they are bare swords, arrows and daggers.

We must be on guard against such spirits and not be afraid of them, but on the contrary we must arm ourselves with the armor of God, that is, with the breastplate of righteousness, with the helmet of salvation, with an evangelical, peaceful and God-saving walk, with the shield of faith and with the sword of the Spirit as well as a fiery prayer to God. Against such knights of Jesus Christ, all proud spirits are able to do nothing. For the weapons of this knighthood are powerful before God, as the apostle said, to break all pride which arises against the confession of Jesus Christ and to punish all disobedience with the sharpness of the divine Word, without regard to persons, not minding that the world, apostates and sectarians are against it.

While they rave and slander and their mouths are so full of curses that they cannot prove or subscribe to Scripture, we sit under the protection of the Most High . . . and remain under the shadow of the Almighty. We say to the Lord, "Our refuge, our fortress, our God in whom we hope." For he delivers us from the snare of the hunter and from harmful pestilence. He will cover us with his feathers; our refuge will be under his wings. His truth shields and protects us so that we do not fear before the terror of the night, for the arrows which fly in the day, for the pestilence which creeps in the dark, for the sickness which destroys at noon. A SHORT BUT FUNDAMENTAL ACCOUNT (1567).[16]

55:22-23 Cast Your Burden on God

FOLLY DRAWS DEATH NEAR. THE ENGLISH ANNOTATIONS: Those who by the course of nature might live twice as long shall die in the flower of their age. As by wickedness, so by folly and carelessness, a person may hasten his death and die before his time, in which case nevertheless, in justification of their own or other people's willful folly or carelessness, many will be apt to say that his or their time is come, which is foolish and impious. ANNOTATIONS ON PSALM 55:23.[17]

PREPARE DAILY FOR DEATH. RUDOLF GWALTHER: This should be understood concerning mad and wanton tyrants. They imagine how long

---

[14]CTS 9:338-39* (CO 31:541-42); citing Dan 9:3.
[15]LW 10:257* (WA 3:310). See further ACW 52:25; NPNF 8:215.

[16]CRR 6:516-17* (BRN 10:577-78); citing Lk 10:18; Jn 8:44; Rev 9:11; 2 Tim 3; Eph 6:13-18; 2 Cor 10:3-6.
[17]Downame, ed., *Annotations*, 6F4r*.

they will live and what great things they will accomplish; however, they will not even accomplish half of their dreamed-up goals. Believers, however, know that they are mortal. They prepare themselves every day and thus die well at the right time, whether it happens in youth or old age. THE PSALTER.[18]

TEACH US UNFAITHFUL CREATURES TO BE FAITHFUL! JOHANN ARNDT: Almighty, eternal God, the world is not to be trusted, your beloved Son himself was betrayed by his disciple Judas; everywhere in all places infidelity and injustice blossom. And nevertheless everyone wants to be innocent and pure; they offer good words out of a false heart. Therefore, I ask you that you would govern me with your Holy Spirit, so that I would not become impatient, but instead cling to your Word and promise, trust and hope in you, and carefully execute my office with devotion and diligence in good conscience; that I would learn to cast all my cares and concerns on you, who will not let me and all the righteous remain eternally in discord, even though the world makes much discord for us. I hope in you. And I will, with your help, break through all misery into eternal life, and laud and praise you and your Son and the Holy Spirit in eternity. Amen. THE WHOLE PSALTER OF DAVID, THE HOLY KING AND PROPHET: THIRD SERMON ON PSALM 55.[19]

---

[18]Gwalther, *Der Psalter*, 98r.

[19]Arndt, *Der gantze Psalter Davids des H. Königs und Propheten*, 478.

56:1-13 STEADFAST CONFIDENCE IN GOD

To the choirmaster: according to The Dove on Far-off Terebinths. A Miktam[a] of David, when the Philistines seized him in Gath.

¹ *Be gracious to me, O God, for man tramples*
 on me;
 all day long an attacker oppresses me;
² *my enemies trample on me all day long,*
 for many attack me proudly.
³ *When I am afraid,*
 I put my trust in you.
⁴ *In God, whose word I praise,*
 in God I trust; I shall not be afraid.
 What can flesh do to me?

⁵ *All day long they injure my cause;[b]*
 all their thoughts are against me for evil.
⁶ *They stir up strife, they lurk;*
 they watch my steps,
 as they have waited for my life.

⁷ *For their crime will they escape?*
 In wrath cast down the peoples, O God!

⁸ *You have kept count of my tossings;[c]*
 put my tears in your bottle.
 Are they not in your book?
⁹ *Then my enemies will turn back*
 in the day when I call.
 This I know, that[d] God is for me.
¹⁰ *In God, whose word I praise,*
 in the LORD, whose word I praise,
¹¹ *in God I trust; I shall not be afraid.*
 What can man do to me?

¹² *I must perform my vows to you, O God;*
 I will render thank offerings to you.
¹³ *For you have delivered my soul from death,*
 yes, my feet from falling,
 that I may walk before God
 in the light of life.

a Probably a musical or liturgical term   b Or *they twist my words*   c Or *wanderings*   d Or *because*

OVERVIEW: Our Reformation commentators reflect on David's repeated praise of God's Word; they see this as an affirmation of the importance of Scripture, which goes hand in hand with their own appeal to *sola Scriptura.* David's trust in God and his Word reflects, for them, the faith that followers of Christ are called to exhibit, even in the midst of anguish. Indeed, not only should Christians lean on God and find comfort in his Word, but also that trust should lead to an expression of praise and thanksgiving, for they—like David—should remember how they have been rescued and who has rescued them. In this way, the reformers point to the connection between the faith of the church and its expression of that faith.

Superscription: *To the Silent Dove?*

GOLDEN PSALMS WITH GOLDEN CONTENT.
NIKOLAUS SELNECKER: There are five psalms that follow one after the other with this title: "A golden treasure of David." (This title is discussed above in Ps 16). For it is as Jerome writes: the titles of the psalms are like keys with which we unlock the door and enter the correct understanding of the psalms. Thus, these psalms are called golden treasures on account of the beautiful teaching and consolation which is in them, as we will hear.

Ketem means the best Indian and Arabian pure gold, namely, a large nugget or piece of the purest gold, as the most precious gold was in India, where a piece of gold, wholly pure, dug up from the ground weighed almost half a centner [twenty-five kilograms]. From this word *miktām* is derived, that is, a treasure of the purest and best gold. It is magnificent and precious, dear and costly. This word is only used in the title of psalms. THE WHOLE PSALTER.[1]

THE DOVE IS DAVID. THE ENGLISH ANNOTATIONS: "The dumb dove in far countries," that is, David himself, who being chased by the fury of his enemies into a strange country, was a dumb dove, or, of the soul oppressed by a troop of foreigners. ANNOTATIONS ON PSALM 56.[2]

DOVE MIGHT INDICATE THE TUNE OR CONTEXT. JOHN CALVIN: The words "to the silent dove," some believe, formed the beginning of a well-known song at the time. Others have thought that David is here compared with a dove; this conjecture is borne out by the propriety of the metaphor in his present circumstances, especially because "in distant places" is added—he had been driven to an enemy's country by the fury of his persecutors. The meaning which some have attached to the word, translating it "a palace," is farfetched. COMMENTARY ON PSALM 56.[3]

THE DOVE IS CHRIST. MARTIN LUTHER: The "dove" concerning which the psalm is speaking is Christ, as is the case with Psalm 22, concerning "the doe of the dawn." And "silent" reveals why. "Of distances" . . . means that Christ was far removed from his land and inheritance, that is, the synagogue, as he says through Jeremiah: "I have left my inheritance." And he himself says, "I am going away, and you will seek me and die in your sin." FIRST PSALMS LECTURES (1513–1515).[4]

56:1-7 All Day I Am Oppressed

FEAR AND HOPE. JOHN CALVIN: David acknowledges his weakness, insofar as he was sensible of fear, but denies having yielded to it. Dangers might distress him but could not induce him to surrender his hope. He makes no pretensions to that lofty heroism which condemns danger, and yet while he allows that he felt fear, he declares his fixed resolution to persist in a confident expectation of the divine favor. The true proof of faith consists in this, that when we feel the solicitations of natural fear, we can resist them and prevent them from obtaining an undue ascendancy. Fear and hope may seem opposite and incompatible affections, yet it is proved by observation that the latter never comes into full sway unless there exists some measure of the former. In a tranquil state of the mind, there is no scope for the exercise of hope. At such times it lies dormant, and its power is displayed to advantage only when we see it elevating the soul under dejection, calming its agitations or soothing its distractions. This was the manner in which it manifested itself in David, who feared and yet trusted, was sensible of the greatness of his danger and yet quieted his mind with the confident hope of the divine deliverance. COMMENTARY ON THE PSALMS.[5]

GRASP HOLD THE WORD OF GOD! NIKOLAUS SELNECKER: We hear how everything depends on the Word of God. Whoever has it has everything. Whoever does not have it—or twists and distorts it, like the fanatical spirits, who say that they praise and honor God but do not do it according to his will and Word, as when the Sacramentarians say, "The bread is bread; the wine is wine."[6] Such is not the Word of God—reason knows this very well without it. But I want to exalt God's Word, which says, "Take, eat, this is my body, this is my blood." The papists say, "We need to become righteous and are saved through good works." This

---

[1]Selnecker, *Der gantze Psalter*, 2:36v; citing Jerome's prologue to his *Brevarium in Psalmos* (PL 26:824).
[2]Downame, ed., *Annotations*, 6F4r*.
[3]CTS 9:347-48* (CO 31:547).
[4]LW 10:259-60* (WA 3:314); citing Jer 12:7; Jn 8:21. While modern commentators still debate the meaning of this phrase, some second Calvin's conjecture that this is a popular song; see Kraus, *Psalms 1–59*, 526; Goldingay, *Psalms*, 2:183. Alter avoids any speculation about this "haunting" phrase, see Alter, *Book of Psalms*, 195.

[5]CTS 9:349-50* (CO 31:548).
[6]Selnecker is so irritated with people who, according to him, misinterpret the Eucharist that he does not finish his thought here.

is not the Word of God. Whoever wants to exalt the Word of God says, "We become righteous and are saved by faith alone, without the works of the law, out of grace, for the sake of Christ Jesus."

To this Word we should fully commend ourselves and insist on it, whatever the world will say. Flesh is flesh and to our Lord God it is hay and straw with all its pomp and power, and in the end it will be cast into the fire. What then should terrify us? The Turk, the pope, the emperor, the world and hell—what are all these before God? Scorn and derision, not worth mentioning, less than nothing. "I am the Lord your God, a jealous and mighty God." Blessed is the one who can correctly believe this and impress it on his weak heart. THE WHOLE PSALTER.[7]

EMPHATIC WORD ORDER. THE ENGLISH ANNOTATIONS: Some conceive that the order of the words is inverted, as if he intended "I will praise God for his word." But I conceive them in the order that we receive them as being more pregnant and emphatic, repeated also, in the same order, in verse 10. ANNOTATIONS ON PSALM 56:4.[8]

56:8-11 *In God I Trust*

RECALL GOD'S CATALOG. WOLFGANG MUSCU-LUS: In this argument for the care and providence of God . . . we see that God has enumerated all their affairs, and there is not anything that falls outside his care and providence. He does not simply say, "You have known my wanderings and you collect my tears, and you place them in your bottle, and you have written their number in your book." He speaks according to human custom, namely, for human beings it is the custom that those things for which they diligently care, they rank by number. Whatever they think and consider precious, they collect, and they place it in vessels; whatever they commit to memory, they commit to writing. Thus when he wishes to speak according

to his faith about his flights and escapes, in which he embraces his own calamity, he has exceedingly commended it to the care of God. . . .

Here in every affliction this passage must be especially noted against the thoughts of the flesh, which in those trials perpetually strive against our faith and interrupt crying out, "I have been cast away from the face of God; God turns his face away so that he does not see all the way to the end." Such thoughts are false and drive us toward impatience and hopelessness by the instigation of Satan. Indeed, faith retorts otherwise, namely, what we see here in David. COMMENTARY ON THE PSALMS.[9]

GOD'S CAREFUL GOVERNANCE. NIKOLAUS SELNECKER: These words are full of comfort. God counts our wanderings, how often, when, from where, to where we are chased. He also counts our tears and teardrops that flow down from our cheeks and collects them in his bag or pot and records them in his book, how many they are—he does not forget about them. Each teardrop of the pious flowing down is more precious to God than all the pearls in the whole world. This is a beautiful and glorious comfort beyond all measure for anxious and afflicted people. How often do pious, afflicted hearts weep? But such it is that a godfearing person can take comfort and say, "Now then, God does not forget me. He counts all of my tears and without his will not a hair shall fall from my head. He hears me and will surely save me and will drive back all my enemies and adversaries if I only cry out to him and pray. For as often as I call on him he answers me, and I truly become aware of his being my God and gladly helping me." These are beautiful words about a genuine prayer. THE WHOLE PSALTER.[10]

RELY ON THE WORD ALONE. JOHN CALVIN: The repetition adds an emphasis to the sentiment, intimating that though God delayed the sensible

---

[7]Selnecker, *Der gantze Psalter*, 2:38r-v; citing Is 40:6-8.
[8]Downame, ed., *Annotations*, 6F4v*, citing Isa 26:20.
[9]Musculus, *In Psalterium Commentarii*, 623.
[10]Selnecker, *Der gantze Psalter*, 2:39r.

manifestation of his favor and might seem to deal with him harshly in abandoning him to the word—giving him nothing more, he was resolved to glory in it with undiminished confidence. When in a spirit such as this we honor the Word of God, though deprived of any present experience of his goodness or his power, we "set to our seal that God is true." The repetition amounts to an expression of his determination that, notwithstanding all circumstances which might appear to contravene the promise, he would trust in it and persist in praising it both now, henceforth and forever.

How desirable is it that the Lord's people generally would accustom themselves to think in the same manner and find, in the Word of God, matters of never-failing praise amid their worst trials! They may meet many mercies calling for the exercise of thanksgiving, but can scarcely have proceeded one step in life before they will feel the necessity of reliance on the naked word. COMMENTARY ON THE PSALMS.[11]

WHY IS DAVID NOT AFRAID? MARTIN LUTHER: Because he hopes in God. On the contrary, a person who puts his hope in human beings or gold, what is there left for him but to fear what people may do to him, namely, by taking away gold, friendships, honors and other human goods? As a result, one person is afraid to tell the truth to another. And we do not praise speech in the Lord, but in human beings, for we speak those words which people want to hear, and also we hear those words which they want to speak. If we would disparage them and advise that the words of God should be either spoken or heard, those who are our friends would then become our enemies. Therefore we praise those words in human beings, that is, we hold them to be praiseworthy and good, or at least, by keeping silent and by hearing them we act as if we praised them. For whoever keeps silent and does not preach or does not hear the words of God will by that very fact be judged to have slandered. Therefore to praise the words of God is to preach and hear them gladly,

not indeed on their own account or because they come from a person—because every human being is a liar and speaks lies—but in God, that is, because the words of God are both true and righteous, I will not be ashamed of them. But why do we not do this? Because we have put our trust in human beings and human affairs, which must necessarily perish, if you have proclaimed the words of God. Therefore we are afraid that people may harm us. This person, however, can fear no one but God, because he puts his hope in God. For wherever there is hope, there is also fear and love and hatred and joy and sadness. FIRST PSALMS LECTURES (1513–1515).[12]

THANKS AND PRAISE TO GOD. MARTIN BUCER: He has called on God and received his help and become endowed with a confident and keen spirit—and that by relying on the word of divine promise. Consequently, he praised God and boasted and strengthened his trust so much that he would never fear human beings but would only think about giving thanks to God, to whom he would proclaim vows of praise and did not doubt that he himself would joyfully pay those vows in that church. HOLY PSALMS.[13]

56:12-13 Walk Before God

NEVER FORGET GOD'S DELIVERANCE. JOHN CALVIN: Contemplating the greatness of his danger, he considers his escape as nothing less than miraculous. It is our duty, when rescued from any peril, to retain in our recollection the circumstances of it, and all which rendered it peculiarly formidable. During the time that we are exposed to it, we are apt to err through an excessive apprehension; but when it is over, we too readily forget both our fears and the divine goodness manifested in our deliverance. COMMENTARY ON THE PSALMS.[14]

---

[11]CTS 9:356-57* (CO 31:552); citing Jn 3:33.

[12]LW 10:260-61* (WA 3:314-15).
[13]Bucer, *Sacrorum Psalmorum*, 236v.
[14]CTS 9:358-59 (CO 31:553-54).

DELIVERANCE AND THANKSGIVING ARE INSEPARABLE. TILEMANN HESSHUS: David concludes this psalm with thanksgiving. For David's prayers were not useless in such serious danger; instead he was rescued from heaven. Therefore he confesses that he owes this service to God, that he proclaim his goodness and lovingkindness. For the sweetest promise and divine command demand this from us: "Call on me in the day of tribulation, and I will rescue you, and you will glorify me." The vows of the pious are that they will celebrate God's omnipotence, clemency, wisdom, righteousness and lovingkindness. And here the prophet warns that they sin most gravely who, after they have been rescued out of great difficulties from heaven, shamefully neglect their debt of thanksgiving. To walk before God in the light of life is to delight in the tradition of the church in which God is present, to enjoy the ministry of the gospel, to hear pious sermons, to take hold of the sacraments, to offer worship to God along with other pious believers and to be a partaker of the most distinguished benefits which God regularly bestows on his church. COMMENTARY ON PSALM 56.[15]

---

[15]Hesshus, *Commentarius in Psalmos*, 238r; citing Ps 50:15.

57:1-11 FILL THE EARTH TO OVERFLOWING WITH YOUR GLORY

To the choirmaster: according to Do Not Destroy. A Miktam[a] of David, when he fled from Saul, in the cave.

¹ Be merciful to me, O God, be merciful to me,
    for in you my soul takes refuge;
in the shadow of your wings I will take refuge,
    till the storms of destruction pass by.
² I cry out to God Most High,
    to God who fulfills his purpose for me.
³ He will send from heaven and save me;
    he will put to shame him who tramples on
        me.   Selah
God will send out his steadfast love and his
    faithfulness!

⁴ My soul is in the midst of lions;
    I lie down amid fiery beasts—
the children of man, whose teeth are spears and
    arrows,
    whose tongues are sharp swords.

⁵ Be exalted, O God, above the heavens!
Let your glory be over all the earth!

⁶ They set a net for my steps;
    my soul was bowed down.
They dug a pit in my way,
    but they have fallen into it themselves.
                                               Selah

⁷ My heart is steadfast, O God,
    my heart is steadfast!
I will sing and make melody!
⁸ Awake, my glory![b]
Awake, O harp and lyre!
    I will awake the dawn!
⁹ I will give thanks to you, O Lord, among the
    peoples;
    I will sing praises to you among the
        nations.
¹⁰ For your steadfast love is great to the heavens,
    your faithfulness to the clouds.

¹¹ Be exalted, O God, above the heavens!
    Let your glory be over all the earth!

a Probably a musical or liturgical term   b Or my whole being

OVERVIEW: For our commentators, this psalm moves significantly, if not surprisingly, from personal lament to confidence in and praise of God. They find comfort in David's reflections on his own experiences, which affirm that the suffering of the righteous will only last for a while, like a passing storm. Indeed, the psalm culminates with David's praise to God, offering a stirring declaration of his assurance in God's faithfulness. Various elements of this psalm are interpreted by our commentators in light of Jesus Christ and his followers: the harp and lyre signify the two natures of Christ, the cave in which David hides refers to the grave of Christ, and the suffering of David is compared with the persecution of the church.

PSALM 56 AND PSALM 57 ARE SIMILAR.
NIKOLAUS SELNECKER: The whole psalm is rather similar to the previous one, almost the same words and meaning. On account of this we can use it also against tyrants and their poisonous councils and those who whisper in their ears; they turn the Word of God upside down. The Son of God himself used this psalm against his persecutors and praised God his Father, that he freed him from their accusations and lifted him up to a place of honor. THE WHOLE PSALTER.[1]

---

¹Selnecker, Der gantze Psalter, 2:40r.

Superscription: *Do Not Destroy!*

DELIVERANCE FROM DESPERATE SITUATIONS.
DAVID DICKSON: The inscription teaches us that
the godly may be involved in deadly danger, as
David was when he fled from Saul in the cave, and
still not perish. He was a man ready to be buried
alive, for the cave was a grave, and the army of Saul
at the mouth of the cave was a gravestone. If the
army of Saul knows that he is there and they keep
him in, he is gone. Yet God blinded them, brought
David out and so delivered him. COMMENTARY
ON PSALM 57.[2]

THESE WORDS ADDED TO CALM DAVID'S MEN.
SEBASTIAN MÜNSTER: Kimchi thinks that this—
"do not destroy"—is added to the title so that David
by these words would restrain his men, who tried to
convince and enrage him to destroy Saul while he
was defecating in the cave and sleeping in his camp.
THE TEMPLE OF THE LORD: PSALM 57.[3]

WHAT DOES 'AL-TAŠḤĒT MEAN? JOHN CALVIN:
We are left entirely to conjecture as to the meaning
of the word *miktām*, and equal uncertainty prevails
among interpreters regarding the reason of the
inscription given to the psalm, *'al-tašḥēt*, that is, "do
not destroy." Some are of the opinion that this
formed the beginning of a well-known song at the
time; others take it to be an expression uttered by
David in the desperate exigency to which he was
reduced, "O God! Do not destroy me." Others
conceive that the word is inscribed on the psalm in
praise of the high principle shown by David when
he prevented Abishai from slaying Saul, and they
are confirmed in their opinion by the fact that this
is the very expression which the inspired historian
represents him as having used. But as the prayers
which follow must have been offered up before he
gave any such injunction to Abishai, this explanation is not satisfactory. Thus we are left to adopt
one or the other of the two former suppositions,

either that the psalm was composed to the tune of
some song generally known at the time or that the
word expresses a brief prayer, which David notes
down as having been uttered in memorable circumstances and in circumstances of great danger.
COMMENTARY ON THE PSALMS.[4]

57:1-5 Prayer to and Praise for My Savior

LIKE A PASSING STORM. THE ENGLISH ANNO-
TATIONS: He compares the afflictions which God
lays on his children with a storm that comes and
goes. Tacitly encouraging himself thereby, as a
traveler on the way, that it is a thing not to be
wondered at (which therefore those who are wise
use to provide against before they set out) or likely
to last very long. ANNOTATIONS ON PSALM 57:1.[5]

TEMPORARY PERSECUTION. WOLFGANG
MUSCULUS: We are here admonished that where
the ungodly persecute the harmless, they envelop
themselves in greater shame, corresponding to their
violent persecutions of the innocent. This will
become evident in this psalm, where God will have
sent his salvation from heaven to the afflicted.
While God permits, the ungodly rule for some
time. By ruling, they oppress infants and the godly.
It is this way, so that they themselves may be held
in honor before human beings, and so that they
may be used for the sake of the righteous, and the
righteous for the sake of the unrighteous, which is
what happened to Saul and David. Truly, those
shadows only lasted for so long, until help was sent
from heaven. Now the righteous are freed, and the
ungodly persecutors of infants are wrapped in
shame. COMMENTARY ON THE PSALMS.[6]

SHAM CHARGES. PHILIPP MELANCHTHON: He
speaks about these slanderers when he says, "Their
teeth are spears and their tongues are sharp swords."
For being stripped of the reputation of righteousness

---

[2]Dickson, *Other Fifty Psalms*, 41*; citing 1 Sam 24.
[3]Münster, *Miqdaš YHWH*, 1206.

[4]CTS 9:359-60* (CO 31:554); citing 1 Sam 26:9. Kraus agrees with
  Calvin. See Kraus, *Psalms 1–59*, 529; Alter, *Book of Psalms*, 198.
[5]Downame, ed., *Annotations*, 6F4v*.
[6]Musculus, *In Psalterium Commentarii*, 619.

is a more bitter sorrow than to be stripped of life, just as the reputation of David was bespattered that he unjustly attempted to make himself king by transferring the kingdom from the royal family to himself. That crime was grave and plausible, and it terrified many among the people who were devoted to David so that they would not defend him, because a refutation of this was difficult. Thus frequently when the church differs from the highest authorities, it is called seditious and it is said it must be suppressed for the sake of the common peace. However, the hardest thing is for temperate people to sustain this sort of disgrace—that they are the sort that are seditious, hostile to civil concord and peace and would tear the church apart without well-founded and important reasons, because they are schismatics, firebrands of discord and war, and the destroyers of the human race. Second, the more heinous crime is the crime of heresy, because hypocrites clamor that we cause outrages, corrupt doctrine, abolish things necessary for the worship of God and invent idols, just as both of these crimes were hurled at the Son of God. Comments on the Psalms.[7]

57:6-10 My Heart Is Steadfast

Sing with Music. Wolfgang Musculus: The heart prepared for praising God is not idle. For the mouth speaks out of the abundance of the heart. Thus the one affected for the glory of God, which is in the heart, breaks forth into song and vocal praise of God; just as the heart filled with mourning and sadness boils up in wailing and tears, a joyful heart boils up in laughter and the face with cheerfulness. Thus it is fitting when he said, "God has prepared my heart; he has made it subject, I will recite and sing." He expressed exuberance and passion for praising God, namely, in that he does not simply desire to sing but also to sing with the lyre and stringed musical instruments, and that in the morning. And third, he does not sing in a hidden place but in the midst of the people. At this point, he also does this because he speaks with his tongue, lyre and stringed instruments, saying, "Rouse my glory, rouse the stringed instruments and lyre, I will rouse myself early." He considers the time in which he would restore peace, he had sought for the church of the Lord. Here he promises for himself that in the morning, with the greatest joy, he desires to seek the church of God, and in the middle of it and in the sight of all, to praise and extol the Lord with all his strength. Commentary on the Psalms.[8]

Christ's Two Natures Figured by These Instruments. Martin Luther: Christ is our psaltery and our harp, the psaltery because of his actions, the harp because of his sufferings, as Augustine suggests. For as the psaltery gets its sound from the top, so the activities of Christ and the powers of his miracles came from above by virtue of his divinity. On the other hand, as the sound of the harp comes from below, so the sufferings of Christ came from below, from his humanity and the weakness of his flesh. Augustine says that both are the body of Christ. Therefore he is the psaltery because he is God incarnate, and the harp because he is a deified, so to speak, human being. From this it is clear why this book is the most powerful psaltery, because it has so many references to the incarnation of God and the suffering of Christ. (For the rest see Ps 33 above.)

Therefore, to play on such a psaltery and harp is done, first, intentionally: by pondering and concerning oneself with the works and sufferings of Christ, which is the sweetest song for God and all the angels of God; second, in reality, by faith in Christ, like him to do heavenly deeds and suffer earthly evils, so that the flesh is the harp in the sufferings of Christ and the spirit is the psaltery in good works. And this is the psaltery and the harp tropologically. The church, however, in a similar way is both allegorically. Again holy Scripture is also both: the psaltery in a mystical sense, the harp literally and historically.

Hence Augustine puts it very briefly: "The divine flesh in action is the psaltery, and the human

---

[7]MO 13:1135-36.

[8]Musculus, *In Psalterium Commentarii*, 630.

flesh in suffering is the harp." Whence we also have the statement in Psalm 43, "To you, O God, I will give praise on the harp," namely, by approaching the altar in memory of the suffering. Also Psalm 33, "Give praise to the Lord on the harp." And thus he says also here, "Arise, psaltery," that is, "Christ, through whom and in whom the playing is done for me and in whom I will be praised." Therefore the playing is not done for the literal psaltery, because it does not have perceptive ears for actual hearing, but it is spiritual, and this only in Christ. FIRST PSALMS LECTURES (1513–1515).[9]

CALL ALL YOUR CREATION HOME TO YOU.
BOOK OF COMMON PRAYER (1549): Almighty and everlasting God, by whose Spirit the whole body of the church is governed and sanctified: receive our supplications and prayers, which we offer before you for every human estate in your holy congregation, that every member of the same, in their vocation and ministry, may serve you truly and godly through our Lord Jesus Christ.

Merciful God, who has made all human beings and who hates nothing that you have made, nor do you desire the death of a sinner but long that he should be converted and live, have mercy on all Jews, Muslims, pagans and heretics, and remove from them all ignorance, hardness of heart and contempt of your Word. And thus fetch them home, blessed Lord, to your flock that they may be saved among the remnant of the true Israelites, and be made one fold under one shepherd, Jesus Christ our Lord, who lives and reigns with you in the unity of the Spirit, one God, world without end. Amen. COLLECT FOR GOOD FRIDAY.[10]

GOD'S JUSTICE REPAYS HIS ENEMIES IN KIND.
JOHN BOYS: As the foes of David were cruel, a generation whose teeth are swords and jaws are knives to devour God's afflicted people, so likewise they are crafty . . . thinking to catch him in a pitfall,

as a bird or as a beast in a trap. The wicked bend their bow and make ready their arrows on the string, so that they can secretly shoot those who are upright in heart; whatever they cannot effect by power, they will attempt by policy. But the snare is broken, the net, which they laid secretly, caught themselves, and they who dug the pit have fallen into the middle of it. And here we may behold God's infinite justice, who never leaves the deeds of charity or the debts of cruelty unsatisfied. . . .

Mystically this hymn may be construed of Christ, who in the days of his flesh was assaulted by the tyranny of both temporal and spiritual enemies. His temporal enemies, Herod and Pontius Pilate, with the Gentiles and people of Israel, furiously raged and took counsel together against him. . . . His spiritual enemies also sought to swallow him up, his soul was among lions all the days of his life, at the hour of his death especially. . . . As David was in the cave, so Christ the son of David was in the grave. But it was impossible that the Lord of life should be beholden to death or that his flesh should see corruption. He therefore rose from the dead on this day. . . . According to this exposition, our church allotted this hymn to be read on this holy day: for in Christ's resurrection all his enemies' tyranny was passed over; in his resurrection his glory (which previously was obscure) appeared above all the earth. . . .

This also may be construed of the church, with respect to both its spiritual and temporal enemies. As for its ghostly foes, the devil is a roaring lion, and our sins are the whelps of lions, ready to devour us. And considering outward enemies, the church in this world is like Daniel in the lion's den, or as the suckling child playing on the hole of the asp. . . . Its oppression in the beginning was great by the persecution of tyrants, afterward greater by the conflict of heretics, but now greatest of all by the dangerous positions and practices of antichrists in the kingdom of popery, whose very Masses are sometime for massacres, and their sacred sacrifices offerings of blood. . . . The foes of David were set on fire: and who greater incendiaries than the papists? Their chief logic in their conference was "a

[9]LW 10:265-66* (WA 3:319-20); citing Ps 43:4; 33:2. See NPNF 8:228-29.
[10]BCP 1549, 52*.

faggot for the heretic," delighting so much in fire work that they burned God's people by the dozen, as so at Stratford the Bow near London, and bound them in chains by the score, as at Colchester in the bloody days of Queen Mary. Nay, their intent was on November 5, 1605, to burn, and that at one fire by the hundreds, and those not the meanest of the people but the very principals of our church and commonwealth, even the most meek king himself, together with the noble consort and all their royal retinue. . . .[11] The like of it was never done or heard of in Israel, or throughout the world, since the beginning. . . . Shall I call it a work done? No, beloved (as a reverend father of our church), it was the work of the Lord that it was not done. The snare was broken, we were delivered, and those who dug the pit for us fell into it. A work of such great might and mercy that it ought to be held in perpetual remembrance. . . . The fifth of November is the day we were delivered from the Babylonish and Romish tyranny. Let us be glad and rejoice therein, and sing as David in the second part of this hymn. EXPOSITION OF PSALM 57.[12]

57:11 Glory to God

A PRAYER FOR THE GENTILES. JOHN CALVIN: The psalmist concludes with a prayer that God would arise and not suffer his glory to be obscured or the audacity of the wicked to become intolerable by conniving longer at their impiety. The words, however, may be understood in another sense, as a prayer that God would hasten the calling of the Gentiles, of which he had already spoken in the language of prediction, and illustrate his power by executing not only an occasional judgment in Judea for the deliverance of distressed innocents but his mighty judgments over the whole world for the subjection of the nations. COMMENTARY ON THE PSALMS.[13]

LEARN TO SPEAK ABOUT GOD ACCORDING TO SCRIPTURE. NIKOLAUS SELNECKER: Here we should learn how we should speak of God, not only as he is in his essence but also how he has explained and revealed himself to us as kind, merciful and truthful. "When Scripture speaks about God, it does not speak about him only *in abstracto*, only according to his essence, but also *in concreto*, according to God clothed in his kindness and goodness," Dr. Johann Forster of blessed memory said.[14] We should not immediately think about the essential righteousness and the greatness of God's almighty majesty—before such thoughts the human heart is struck with horror and fear. Instead first we must contemplate how God is kind and merciful, and how he has manifested himself to us through his beloved Son and how he wants to have compassion on us, as he has promised us.

To God the Lord be praise and thanks! He is merciful to us; we trust and hope in him and are able to call on him, who redeems us from all misfortune and brings our sorrow to an end. He sends help from heaven, and casts our enemies, who trouble us, into the grave. He makes us righteous and holy in eternity. Amen. THE WHOLE PSALTER.[15]

---

[11]A group of English Catholics conspired to assassinate King James I (1566–1625) at the opening of parliament on November 5, 1605—the so-called Gunpowder Plot. The plan was uncovered, and around midnight on November 4, Guy Fawkes (1570–1606) was discovered guarding thirty-six barrels of gunpowder under the House of Lords. This intrigue is commemorated annually in Great Britain.
[12]Boys, *Exposition of Psalmes*, 106-12*.

[13]CTS 9:367* (CO 31:558).
[14]*In abstracto* refers to the attributes or essence of a thing apart from its existence. *In concreto* refers to a thing itself, where form, substance, essence and existence are manifest. See further Muller, *Dictionary of Latin and Greek Theological Terms*, 18, 76. On Forster, see above, p. 147.
[15]Selnecker, *Der gantze Psalter*, 2:42r.

58:1-11 GOD IS THE JUST JUDGE

To the choirmaster: according to Do Not Destroy. A Miktam[a] of David.

[1] *Do you indeed decree what is right, you gods?[b]*
  Do you judge the children of man uprightly?
[2] *No, in your hearts you devise wrongs;*
  your hands deal out violence on earth.

[3] *The wicked are estranged from the womb;*
  they go astray from birth, speaking lies.
[4] *They have venom like the venom of a serpent,*
  like the deaf adder that stops its ear,
[5] *so that it does not hear the voice of charmers*
  or of the cunning enchanter.

[6] *O God, break the teeth in their mouths;*
  tear out the fangs of the young lions, O Lord!

[7] *Let them vanish like water that runs away;*
  when he aims his arrows, let them be blunted.
[8] *Let them be like the snail that dissolves into slime,*
  like the stillborn child who never sees the sun.
[9] *Sooner than your pots can feel the heat of thorns,*
  whether green or ablaze, may he sweep them away![c]

[10] *The righteous will rejoice when he sees the vengeance;*
  he will bathe his feet in the blood of the wicked.
[11] *Mankind will say, "Surely there is a reward for the righteous;*
  surely there is a God who judges on earth."

a Probably a musical or liturgical term   b Or *you mighty lords* (by revocalization; Hebrew *in silence*)   c The meaning of the Hebrew verse is uncertain

OVERVIEW: This psalm of lament addresses unjust rulers. It cries out to God to bring swift and decisive vengeance on them for their predatory wickedness. And when it comes the righteous will rejoice. Whereas some contemporary Christians might flinch at the sharp imagery the psalmist employs in describing the godless, Selnecker finds solace in these similes—God's providence reigns. That the righteous will rejoice, "bathing his feet in the blood of the wicked" in response to God's judgment on the godless, at first blush seems unfitting for practitioners of Christian faith. However, our commentators emphasize that this rejoicing does not flow from a desire for revenge but for God to be glorified. Believers—like their God—do not delight in the death of a sinner, but they laud and praise God's justice.

THE FALSE DREAMS OF THE UNJUST. THEO-DORE BEZA: It can be gathered from this psalm that Saul—in order to have some pretext for his hatred against David—assembled a council of the nobles, to see to it that the absent man be condemned as a public enemy. Now there is no greater injustice than what prowls under the cloak of justice. Therefore, David, comforting himself and appealing to God, depicts those most corrupt judges in their own colors, as he had become most familiar with them. Not as a private citizen but as a prophet and king—appointed by God—he proclaims this sentence against them in the name of God himself. Now he uses the most fitting similes for such people's avarice and ambition. Although their primary purpose is to exalt themselves and their children by these tricks, nevertheless God often drags them away in the midst of their greed. In addition their progeny, contrary to what their ancestors imagined, either are gradually dissolved in the sight of all or are obliterated by some sudden fury. PARAPHRASE OF PSALM 58.[1]

---

[1]Beza, *Psalmes of Dauid*, 127* (*Psalmorum Davidis*, 254).

58:1-5 Wickedness Like Poison Pours Forth from Human Mouths

DENY YOURSELF AND TAKE CHRIST'S HAND.
MARTIN LUTHER: This judgment is to condemn oneself and in a way to justify oneself. And this is the beginning of righteousness . . . therefore this follows: teaching them this judgment, he says, "Indeed in your heart you work iniquities on earth." It is as if he were saying, "Thus you think and judge and feel about yourselves while on earth," that is, as long as you do not dwell in the heavens or in the kingdom of heaven in spiritual righteousness but still on earth and in carnal and earthly righteousness before human beings, you will always work iniquity, you will always sin and be sinners. As, on the contrary, according to John, "Everyone who is born of God does not sin," that is, that person is not in sin unless he should wish to be. But you are necessarily in sin as long as you are outside of Christ, and "your hands forge injustices." Therefore your heart must be condemned, your hands must be condemned, and the hand of Christ must be taken. It alone does justice, not your hand. For he alone does marvelous things, and he makes all the saints marvelous because he is marvelous in his saints. FIRST PSALMS LECTURES (1513–1515).[2]

THE STAIN OF ORIGINAL SIN. JOHN CALVIN: David adduces, in aggravation of their character, the circumstance that they were not sinners of recent date but persons born to commit sin. We see some people, otherwise not so depraved in disposition, who are drawn into evil courses through levity of mind, or bad example, or the solicitation of appetite, or other occasions of a similar kind; but David accuses his enemies of being leavened with wickedness from the womb, alleging that their treachery and cruelty were born with them. Although we are all born full of vices and depravity is instilled by birth in all Adam's posterity, so that we are able to do nothing right on account of our natural disposition, nevertheless we know that the majority of

humankind are restrained by a secret brake of God, lest they are cast headlong into the depths of iniquity. The corruption of original sin cleaves to the whole of humanity without exception. And yet experience proves that some are characterized by modesty and at least outward decency; the corruption of others is filled with mediocrity; while a third class are so depraved in disposition as to be intolerable members of society. Now, it is this excessive wickedness—too marked to escape detestation even amid the general corruption of humankind—which David ascribes to his enemies. He stigmatizes them as monsters of iniquity. COMMENTARY ON THE PSALMS.[3]

IMPIOUS POISON. KONRAD PELLIKAN: In this simile of very harmful poison David depicts the impious, who are also liars. For there is no medicine with which these shameless accusers can be opposed, whom no one would dare to admonish, and if they were admonished, they do not listen. They are full of the most deadly poison, in the form of an asp and with the breath of an adder, indeed, just by sight they cause death. For from the devil, their father, liars are born; they cannot be called back—at all—from their wickedness. COMMENTARY ON PSALM 58:4.[4]

THE DANGER OF SORCERY. HENRY AINSWORTH: Enchanters have this title here either because by sorcery they associate with serpents, making them tame and familiar, so that they do no harm; or because such people used to bind and tie bands or other things about the body, to heal or hurt by sorcery; or because by their conjuring art, they have society and fellowship with devils. ANNOTATIONS ON PSALM 58:5.[5]

58:6-9 Disarm and Sweep Them Away

THE GODLESS WILL BE FRUSTRATED. NIKOLAUS SELNECKER: This is a prayer, an imprecation

---

[2]LW 10:267* (WA 3:322-23); citing Jn 5:18.

[3]CTS 9:370-71* (CO 31:560).
[4]Pellikan, *Commentaria Bibliorum*, 4:105v; citing Jn 8:44.
[5]Ainsworth, *Annotations*, 2:528*; citing Deut 18:11.

and prophecy: the godless will become a mute, wanton, blasphemous, stark-raving mad people. Justly they will be pummeled in the jaw and their teeth—with which they have bitten and injured others, which are very sharp like lions' teeth—will be crushed and pulverized into dust. Consolation follows this prayer. There are five excellent similes, that the godless will not accomplish what they want, yes, they won't even accomplish half of it! THE WHOLE PSALTER.[6]

POTS AND THORNS. THE ENGLISH ANNOTATIONS: Of the drift and scope of the words in general, which concerns the suddenness of wicked people's destruction, of this there is no question at all, and this argument, here set out by a similitude, is often insisted on, not only by David in other psalms but also Job and others. The context reinforces this, and all interpreters understand it so. ANNOTATIONS ON PSALM 58:9.[7]

58:10-11 *The Righteous Rejoice in God's Righteousness*

THE RIGHTEOUS REJOICE IN THEIR SALVATION. THOMAS WILCOX: Those who are accounted righteous for the sake of Christ's righteousness shall rejoice, not only being glad for the overthrow of wickedness but also to give the praise and glory to God when they see the vengeance God cast on the wicked and ungodly. And this is not because the godly are carried forward with a desire of revenge, that they so rejoice in the destruction and overthrowing of the wicked, but because they conceive a wonderful joy when they see God's judgments executed,

whereby they know that their life is precious before God, for as there is mildness and gentleness in faithful people's hearts, so being led with a true zeal they take pleasure in the execution of God's judgments: and these affections are pure and right, because they are ruled according to God's will. EXPOSITION UPON PSALM 58.[8]

THE PROMISE OF PUNISHMENT REVEALS GOD'S RIGHTEOUSNESS. NIKOLAUS SELNECKER: This is a comfort and a promise, that God will redeem the pious and surely punish the wicked. The vengeance will be greater than anyone would have desired or imagined, so that, wherever a pious person asked for a drop of blood or vengeance, there will be so much that he could bathe in it. Not that pious persons would delight in the blood of the godless, but that they will see the punishment and recognize the sentence of God, who is still Judge on earth and cannot leave unpunished the wantonness of the wicked, as he cannot forget those who are his but must allow them to enjoy the fruits of their work, faithfulness and patience. As Paul says, "Your labor will not be in vain in the Lord." Indeed, for the pious, the punishment of the wicked is a mirror of the righteousness of God, so that they might trust in God even more boldly and fear him. "When the scorner is punished, the simple is made wise." May the eternal, good and merciful God help us graciously, so that we might recognize his sentences and his judgments, fear him, set our hope on him, persevere in patience and gentleness, as he demands of us, and that we might be saved through his Son, our Lord Christ Jesus. Amen. THE WHOLE PSALTER.[9]

---

[6]Selnecker, *Der gantze Psalter*, 2:44r.
[7]Downame, ed., *Annotations*, 6G1v*.

[8]Wilcox, *Godly Exposition upon the Psalmes*, 148*.
[9]Selnecker, *Der gantze Psalter*, 2:44v; citing 1 Cor 15:58; Prov 21:11.

59:1-17 SAVE ME FROM MY PURSUERS

To the choirmaster: according to Do Not Destroy. A Miktam[a] of David, when Saul sent men to watch his house in order to kill him.

[1] *Deliver me from my enemies, O my God;*
   protect me from those who rise up against me;
[2] *deliver me from those who work evil,*
   and save me from bloodthirsty men.

[3] *For behold, they lie in wait for my life;*
   fierce men stir up strife against me.
For no transgression or sin of mine, O Lord,
   [4] *for no fault of mine, they run and make ready.*
Awake, come to meet me, and see!
   [5] *You,* Lord *God of hosts, are God of Israel.*
Rouse yourself to punish all the nations;
   spare none of those who treacherously plot evil. Selah

[6] *Each evening they come back,*
   howling like dogs
   and prowling about the city.
[7] *There they are, bellowing with their mouths*
   with swords in their lips—
   for "Who," they think,[b] "will hear us?"

[8] *But you, O* Lord, *laugh at them;*
   you hold all the nations in derision.
[9] *O my Strength, I will watch for you,*
   for you, O God, are my fortress.

[10] *My God in his steadfast love[c] will meet me;*
   God will let me look in triumph on my enemies.

[11] *Kill them not, lest my people forget;*
   make them totter[d] by your power and bring them down,
   O Lord, our shield!
[12] *For the sin of their mouths, the words of their lips,*
   let them be trapped in their pride.
For the cursing and lies that they utter,
   [13] *consume them in wrath;*
   consume them till they are no more,
that they may know that God rules over Jacob
   to the ends of the earth. Selah
[14] *Each evening they come back,*
   howling like dogs
   and prowling about the city.
[15] *They wander about for food*
   and growl if they do not get their fill.

[16] *But I will sing of your strength;*
   I will sing aloud of your steadfast love in the morning.
For you have been to me a fortress
   and a refuge in the day of my distress.
[17] *O my Strength, I will sing praises to you,*
   for you, O God, are my fortress,
   the God who shows me steadfast love.

a Probably a musical or liturgical term b Hebrew lacks *they think* c Or *The God who shows me steadfast love* d Or *wander*

OVERVIEW: Our commentators picture David's flight from Saul as the occasion of this psalm, but it does not dictate the psalm's meaning for them. Selnecker pointedly maintains that the images of David's crossbearing and deliverance should be understood as spoken by the person of Christ. The reformers again probe the question of whether Christians may curse their enemies in the manner of the psalmist, reminding us that the Holy Spirit speaks these curses for the consolation of the church. The psalmist reveals faith in God's justice by making the seemingly contradictory request that his enemies would not be slain but consumed. Calvin understands this as a request that the Lord celebrate a triumph before the nations of the world: first parading and shaming his prisoners, then executing them. The enemies of the church may well be mightier—politically and physically—but the church's might is the radiant Sun of Righteousness, sovereign over the good and the wicked.

LISTEN TO CHRIST! MARTIN LUTHER: Such prayers and sufferings of Christ happened especially for us. But who considers that? What do you think the Son of God's fervent prayers and sufferings should indicate to us? If there were not to be some indescribable misery to come, without a doubt this indescribable orator would surely not have toiled so hard for us! But alas, we do not pay attention to such a priceless truth in all the psalms! FIRST PSALMS LECTURES (1513–1515).[1]

THE HISTORICAL AND CHRISTOLOGICAL CONTEXT OF THIS PSALM. NIKOLAUS SELNECKER: This is a psalm of prayer against the Saulists—as the title indicates. The history stands in 1 Samuel 19. Saul sent messengers to David's house to capture him and kill him in the morning. Michal, David's wife, revealed this to him, saying, "If you will not save your soul tonight, tomorrow you must die." So, Michal let him down through the window, so that he could escape and flee. He went to Samuel in Ramah, where he was sought anew by Saul's messengers and finally by Saul himself. There all of them prophesied and had to leave Saul in peace. From this story, the proverb came, "Is Saul also among the prophets?" So miraculously God protects his people; he brings the plots of the godless to nothing, putting them to shame....

Because such histories about David's crossbearing, suffering and deliverance are figures and images which signify the Lord Christ and his church—how, as several scribes point out excellently, Michal therefore placed an image in David's place in bed and a goatskin at the head of the bed, so that the true David signifies Christ and the true sacrifice—this psalm can and should be understood about and spoken in the person of the Lord Christ. THE WHOLE PSALTER.[2]

59:1-5 My Enemies Hound Me

COMPLAINTS OF AN INNOCENT MAN. WOLFGANG MUSCULUS: First, he begged the help of God so that he might be snatched from his malicious enemies, from men of blood rising up against him. Thus, he sets forth the greatness of the danger and the cruel attempts of those men.... It was the extremity of dangers to despair of life. And if this despair should be caused by an open attack, how much more would it be caused by the treachery and conspiracy of strong, malicious and cruel people.... The prophet wished to portray the desire, watchfulness and tumult of the servants of Saul, who were preparing themselves, working together and getting ready....

Second, he mixes his own innocence together with his complaints.... Third, he follows this by begging for help to come to him and for the vengeance of the wicked in the fourth and fifth verses.... Note his ardor of faith, because he says, "And you Lord, you who are the God of Hosts, the God of Israel." These are epithets beautifully suited for this purpose, because he pleads against those brave servants of Saul and against those alien from the people of God, those reprobate people, namely, the Israelites, who are called Gentiles here. COMMENTARY ON THE PSALMS.[3]

HOW TO IMPRECATE. PHILIPP MELANCHTHON: This question here is ... whether it is permitted to curse enemies, as is often done in the Psalms? I respond, if all four of these things are true. First, the cause which blasphemers protect must be condemned as severely as possible. Second, those propagators of blasphemies must be condemned because they sin "the sin unto death," that is, they tenaciously persevere in sin. Third, because without the help of God truth cannot conquer, it is necessary to seek it from God that he represses errors and the propagators of these errors. This is prayed for when one curses the impious, and yet it is an intensely pious and necessary prayer. Fourth,

---

[1]LW 10:272* (WA 3:329-30).
[2]Selnecker, *Der gantze Psalter*, 2:44v-45r; citing 1 Sam 19:11, 24.

[3]Musculus, *In Psalterium Commentarii*, 637-38.

such curses in the prophets should be read not only as human indignation but rather as the voice of the Holy Spirit, speaking the ultimate way of thinking about blasphemies and consoling the church so that it may know the truth that it will conquer, and God will repress and root out impious dogmas and the blasphemies of their propagators. Because this consolation is necessary for the church, it is often represented as curses, which have certainly been written more for consoling and strengthening the pious than for healing the impious who do not read them. COMMENTS ON THE PSALMS.[4]

BE CIRCUMSPECT IN PRAYING FOR DELIVER-ANCE.

THE ENGLISH ANNOTATIONS: It is the common course of all people who pretend to any piety or knowledge of God to pray to God against their enemies, if they have any. But it must be the care of all truly and solidly religious people to consider well first what enemies they pray against; whether they are such as David's enemies, who violently persecuted him without any just provocation. Yes, he sought peace and did his utmost to win them by his gentleness and the like, as he states in several places, and here particularly, as in the second, third and fourth verses. So we hope our prayers might be available, and at least not unacceptable. But if we make people our foes, by any proud, insolent or unjust actions, or if on apprehension of just provocation, we think to bear ourselves on God's protection of assistance before we ourselves have used all fair and charitable means of reconciliation (which God himself requires from our hands), we may sooner expect to make God our enemy by our prayers, than he will grant us our requests on such weak and ungodly grounds. ANNOTATIONS ON PSALM 59:1.[5]

EXTERNAL ACTS MUST REFLECT INTERNAL REALITIES.

MARTIN LUTHER: The psalmist goes by a direct and short way, he lays hold of the spirit by leaving out the long and manifold ceremonies of the flesh, or at least he fulfills the ceremonies spiritually at the same time. But those people are empty in spirit and wear themselves out and toil in a sheer round of ceremonies. Yet . . . they regard these as important but do not think of the spirit in this way. How many, I ask, do you see who perform their thumpings, genuflections, bowings, chants and prayers in their body alone, and their heart is never present? But is this not grieving the Spirit and serving God with the bare form without the spirit? And walking through the desert around the land of Edom and Mount Seir to the Red Sea? But it is not directing and acting in the spirit by a direct and short way. Therefore, he prays, "O Lord, direct my way in your sight." But these people lead their ways around in a circle in the sight of human beings, because the truth is not in their mouth, but only shadow and vanity in their body. For their heart is empty and without spirit. FIRST PSALMS LECTURES (1513–1515).[6]

DAVID DEMONSTRATES UNBELIEF AND BELIEF.

JOHN CALVIN: In using this language, the psalmist glances at the eagerness with which his enemies, as he had already said, were pressing on him, and states his desire that God would show the same haste in extending help as they did in seeking his destruction. With the view of conciliating the divine favor, he once more calls on God to be the witness and judge of his cause, adding "and behold." The expression is one which savors at once of faith and of the infirmity of the flesh. In speaking of God, as if his eyes had been hitherto shut to the wrongs which he had suffered and needed now for the first time to be opened for the discovery of them, he expresses himself according to the weakness of our human apprehension. On the other hand, in calling on God to behold his cause, he shows his faith by virtually acknowledging that nothing was hid from his providential cognizance. Though David may use language of this description, suited to the infirmity of sense, we must not suppose him to have doubted before

---

[4]MO 13:1144.
[5]Downame, ed., *Annotations*, 6G2r*.

[6]LW 10:276* (WA 3:333); citing Is 63:10; Num 21:4; Deut 2:1; Ps 5:8.

this time that his afflictions, his innocence and his wrongs were known to God. Now, however, he lays the whole before God for examination and decision. COMMENTARY ON THE PSALMS.[7]

59:6-13 Discipline These Dogs

WORDS LIKE SWORDS. WOLFGANG MUSCULUS: It is as if he should say, "So great are the evils brought toward me from a wicked heart that they also spit their words out from their mouth. These words speak about nothing else except killing me, so that even if the deeds and plans of those people do not succeed in their treachery, their plot still has a sufficient effect." COMMENTARY ON THE PSALMS.[8]

GOD'S LAUGH. JOHN CALVIN: When he says that God would laugh at his enemies, he employs a figure which is well-fitted to enhance the power of God, suggesting that when the wicked have perfected their schemes to the uttermost, God can, without any effort, and, as it were, in sport, dissipate them all. No sooner does God connive at their proceedings than their pride and insolence take occasion to manifest themselves. They forget that even when he seems to have suspended operation, he needs but nod, and his judgments shall be executed. COMMENTARY ON THE PSALMS.[9]

IMPRECATION FOR GOD'S GLORY. WOLFGANG MUSCULUS: At this point with the desire for the glory of God he prays for vengeance on his enemies, but of such a kind which tends toward the glory of God, which he expresses in frank words, saying, "That they may know that God rules over Jacob all the way to the ends of the earth." . . . He does not pray in any other way than that they are consumed by the fury of God so that they may not exist, than to the extent that it could occur for the glory of God. From these words—"so that they may not

exist"—we must conclude that they must be understood in such a way that these people are not the sort that to this point would fear his glory and power. COMMENTARY ON THE PSALMS.[10]

59:14-17 My Enemies' Howls and My Hallelujahs

DOES DAVID CONTRADICT HIMSELF? JOHN CALVIN: David may seem to contradict himself in praying for the utter destruction of his enemies, when immediately before he had expressed his desire that they might not be exterminated at once. What else could he mean when he asks that God would consume them in wrath, but that he would cut them off suddenly, and not by a gradual and slower process of punishment? But he evidently refers in what he says here to a different point of time, and this removes any apparent inconsistency, for he prays that when they had been set up for a sufficient period as an example, they might eventually be devoted to destruction. It was customary with victorious Roman generals first to lead the captives which had been kept for the day of triumph through the city, and afterwards, on reaching the capital, to give them over to the lictors for execution. Now David prays that when God had, in a similar manner, reserved his enemies for an interval sufficient to illustrate his triumph, he would on this consign them to summary punishment. The two things are not at all inconsistent: first, that the divine judgments should be lengthened out through a considerable period, to secure their being remembered better, and that then, on sufficient evidence being given to the world of the certainty with which the wicked are subjected in the displeasure of God to the slower process of destruction, he should in due time bring them forth to final execution, the better to awake, by such a demonstration of his power, the minds of those who may be more secure than others, or less affected by witnessing moderate inflictions of punishment.

He adds, accordingly, that they may know, even

---

[7]CTS 9:382* (CO 31:565-66).
[8]Musculus, *In Psalterium Commentarii*, 637-38.
[9]CTS 9:385* (CO 31:567-68).
[10]Musculus, *In Psalterium Commentarii*, 642.

to the ends of the earth, that God rules in Jacob. Some would insert the copulative particle, reading, that they may know that God rules in Jacob and in all the nations of the world, an interpretation which I do not approve and which does violence to the sense. The allusion is to the condign nature of the judgment, which would be such that the report of it would reach the remotest regions and strike salutary terror into the minds even of their benighted and godless inhabitants. He was more especially anxious that God should be recognized as ruling in the church, it being preposterous that the place where his throne was erected should present such an aspect of confusion as converted his temple into a den of thieves. COMMENTARY ON THE PSALMS.[11]

THE MIGHT OF THE SUN OF RIGHTEOUSNESS.
NIKOLAUS SELNECKER: What a magnificent thanksgiving this is! In it the previous words are

explained in the most beautiful way. "On account of your might I commend myself to you, for God is my shield. God reveals his goodness to me richly. Therefore I sing and jump; I boast in the might and power of God. Human beings have their might; I have *God's* might. Whenever they are punished, they howl in the darkness of night. But I sing in the morning, at the rising of the dear Sun, my Lord Jesus Christ—about my merciful God."

As Luther said:

Christ in eternity is my Protector and Redeemer
In death and life he is my lot and my salvation
Him I fear and adore, above all things I love
him alone
For this reason I believe: he will be my only
hope.

THE WHOLE PSALTER.[12]

---

[11]CTS 9:392-93* (CO 31:571-72).

[12]Selnecker, *Der gantze Psalter*, 2:47r.

60:1-12 TRAMPLE OUR OPPONENTS, LORD

To the choirmaster: according to Shushan Eduth. A Miktam[a] of David; for instruction; when he strove with Aram-naharaim and with Aram-zobah, and when Joab on his return struck down twelve thousand of Edom in the Valley of Salt.

[1] O God, you have rejected us, broken our defenses;
  you have been angry; oh, restore us.
[2] You have made the land to quake; you have
    torn it open;
  repair its breaches, for it totters.
[3] You have made your people see hard things;
  you have given us wine to drink that made
    us stagger.

[4] You have set up a banner for those who fear you,
  that they may flee to it from the bow.[b] Selah
[5] That your beloved ones may be delivered,
  give salvation by your right hand and
    answer us!

[6] God has spoken in his holiness:[c]
  "With exultation I will divide up Shechem
    and portion out the Vale of Succoth.
[7] Gilead is mine; Manasseh is mine;
  Ephraim is my helmet;
  Judah is my scepter.
[8] Moab is my washbasin;
  upon Edom I cast my shoe;
  over Philistia I shout in triumph."[d]

[9] Who will bring me to the fortified city?
  Who will lead me to Edom?
[10] Have you not rejected us, O God?
  You do not go forth, O God, with our armies.
[11] Oh, grant us help against the foe,
  for vain is the salvation of man!
[12] With God we shall do valiantly;
  it is he who will tread down our foes.

a Probably musical or liturgical terms b Or *that it may be displayed because of truth* c Or *sanctuary* d Revocalization (compare Psalm 108:10); Masoretic Text *over me, O Philistia, shout in triumph*

OVERVIEW: Our commentators generally agree that this psalm is about the fertile ministry of the church through the proclamation of the Word. When things seem to be in disarray, the Lord surely will bring order by his Word, for he is a God of order. Despite the scattered state of God's people, the Lord has unfurled a banner of refuge over them. Selnecker hones in on this imagery, expounding Old Testament cultic objects as symbols of redemption and restoration in Christ. The holy place of God, for the reformers, is wherever God speaks, wherever his Word resounds. We should not approach this holy place in a cold and clinical manner. Instead, we must read the Scriptures and hear them preached as the very words of God for us.

Superscription: *How to Understand Šûšān?*

UNSURE WHAT THIS TITLE MEANS. SEBASTIAN MÜNSTER: Concerning the testimonies of *šûšān*, the Hebrews have nothing certain that we can mention. THE TEMPLE OF THE LORD: Psalm 60.[1]

THE LAND AND FRUITS OF GOD'S PEOPLE. RUDOLF GWALTHER: These testimonies are the covenant and promises of God through which he promised this land generally to the people of Israel. They are called flowers, because they always bloom before God, never spoiled and bearing the promised fruit in season. THE PSALTER.[2]

[1]Münster, *Miqdaš YHWH*, 1208.
[2]Gwalther, *Der Psalter*, 105v-106r.

A Popular Song. John Calvin: *Šûšān-ʿēdût*—that is, the lily of witness or beauty—seems to have been the first words of some song which was commonly known at the time. Commentary on the Psalms.[3]

A Prophecy About the Church. Martin Luther: This psalm has a new title, because it is described neither as a song nor as a psalm but as a "testimony" [*ʿēdût*], like some others later on. Why? Perhaps because by this very word the psalmist forbids us to understand it in a physical sense. We are not to take it as a sign for a thing and a testimony for the setting forth of works. For a testimony is spoken with reference to something else, like John's testimony concerning Christ. Thus, this psalm is a testimony concerning a future rose, that is, a prophecy and sign of the church, for the psalm speaks about it and in its person. Indeed, the psalm itself is a testimony of the church. Thereby it witnesses to itself and to all concerning exclusively future good things, because it possesses no temporal goods. The fact that the psalmist speaks "for instruction" [*miktām*] certainly shows that the whole psalm is full of doctrine. First Psalms Lectures (1513–1515).[4]

How to Use This Psalm. Philipp Melanchthon: Therefore this is the use of the psalm, that we should first sustain ourselves by the promise which confirms that the church will remain, it will be victorious, and in this hope we should endure the toils of teaching. Second, by this example we should seek and expect help from God, so that we would not depend on human plans and protections, but in true dangers our minds would confidently lean on faith. Comments on the Psalms.[5]

60:1-3 *You Have Made Us Drink the Dregs of Your Rejection*

David Stirs Up God's People to Prayer. John Calvin: With the view of exciting both himself and others to a more serious consideration of the goodness of God, which they presently experienced, he begins the psalm with prayer; and a comparison is instituted, designed to show that the government of Saul had been under the divine reprobation. He complains of the sad confusions into which the nation had been thrown and prays that God would return to it in mercy and re-establish its affairs. Some have thought that David here attends to his own distressed condition; this is not likely. I grant that, before coming to the throne, he underwent severe afflictions, but in this passage he clearly speaks of the whole people as well as himself. The calamities which he describes are such as extended to the whole kingdom; and I have not the least doubt, therefore, that he is to be considered as drawing a comparison which might illustrate the favor of God, as it had been shown so remarkably, from the first, to his own government. With this view, he deplores the long-continued and heavy disasters which had fallen on the people of God under Saul's administration.

It is particularly noticeable, that though he had found his own countrymen his worst and bitterest foes, now that he sat on the throne, he forgets all the injuries which they had done him, and, mindful only of the situation which he occupied, associates himself with the rest of them in his addresses to God. The scattered condition of the nation is what he insists on as the main calamity. In consequence of the dispersion of Saul's forces, the country lay completely exposed to the incursions of enemies; not a person was safe in his own house, and no relief remained but in flight or banishment.

He next describes the confusions which reigned by a metaphor, representing the country as opened, or cleft asunder; not that there had been a literal earthquake, but that the kingdom, in its rent and shattered condition, presented that

---

[3]CTS 9:396* (CO 31:573).
[4]LW 10:280* (WA 3:338).
[5]MO 13:1148.

calamitous aspect which generally follows an earthquake. The affairs of Saul ceased to prosper from the time that he forsook God; and when he perished at last, he left the nation in a state little short of ruin. The greatest apprehension must have been felt throughout it; it had become the scorn of its enemies and was ready to submit to any yoke, however degrading, which promised tolerable conditions. Such is the manner in which David intimates that the divine favor had been alienated by Saul, pointing, when he says that God was displeased, at the radical source of all the evils which prevailed; and he prays that the same physician who had broken would heal. COMMENTARY ON THE PSALMS.[6]

THE WINE OF ASTONISHMENT. THE ENGLISH ANNOTATIONS: Called "the cup of trembling" in Isaiah 51:17, it is the same word here. A continual trembling, not in the act only but habitual, it is often the effect of long-practiced drunkenness. He means, therefore, that the evils had continued long. ANNOTATIONS ON PSALM 60:3.[7]

60:4-8 God's Holy Banner of Love

CHRIST AND HIS MINISTRY FIGURED TO US THROUGH OLD TESTAMENT ARTIFACTS.
NIKOLAUS SELNECKER: This is comfort and thanksgiving, that God always remembers his mercy and does not punish us according to the amount of our sins and according to the greatness of his wrath. In the preceding three verses, he lamented what a miserable condition the Jewish people were in and what an evil government there was; how it was torn apart in the times of Saul and heavily plagued by the Philistines; that they also did not cherish the ark of God, and beyond that there was much injustice, like it is and must be where God is not nearby and at home. However, now he says, God has kept all the same an excellent and comforting sign, banner and banderole, that

we have lifted high and boasted. For that reason we are sure and certain of God's grace. This sign is the tabernacle of Moses and the ark of the covenant with the mercy seat, which God brought out of the land and hand of the Philistines by great wonders. The people had to pray and call on God because of these things; thus, they were delivered from every distress and could meditate on the true banner of all people and the bloody banderole of our Prince of victory, Christ Jesus.

The tabernacle of Moses, regarding its color, was nothing other than a reminder of Christ's blood: scarlet or deep red points to the Lord Christ's blood. Roseate or the color of flame indicates the fervent love of the Son of God toward us. Violet, gold and blue point to his suffering, martyrdom, dying and all crossbearing. Finespun silky white indicates his righteousness with which he dresses and clothes his believers and establishes joy and comfort through his Spirit in their hearts.

The ark of the covenant is made from wood daubed with pitch and was decorated and overlaid with the purest gold. Above it was the golden crown or the place of reconciliation, surrounded in finery. On its corners there were loops and clasps or wooden rings overlaid with gold, with which the ark was lifted up by the Levites and could be carried here and there. In the ark the two tables of the Ten Commandments were placed, as well as manna and the rod of Aaron. And nowhere else but where this ark was could a public and common sacrifice and ecclesiastical service be celebrated and performed. Concerning the mercy seat God spoke with Moses; however, on the ark there stood two cherubim whose wings were touching as they faced one another.

All these things were a figure and reminder of our redemption. Christ the Son of God took on human nature, which indeed is a poor thing—sluggish and stubborn—like some pitch which we soil our hands with. But his divine nature and innocence is the purest, clearest, finest gold that cannot be consumed with fire. His divine nature adorned, graced, overlaid and sustained corrupted, human nature; it hovered over it, granted and brought pure mercy and reconcili-

---

[6]CTS 9:398-99* (CO 31:574-75).
[7]Downame, ed., *Annotations*, 6G2v-6G3r*.

ation and surrounded the entire person, internally and externally with his beauty, clarity, worthiness and righteousness. The rings with which the ark was carried around are God's Word and the preaching of the law and gospel, by which pious and faithful Levites, priests and teachers spread God's honor throughout the entire world and by which they praise the Lord Christ as the one who fulfilled the entire law through his obedience and suffering. He is the true, living manna, the bread and food of life. He is the recent Victor, who rose again from the dead and conquered all his enemies. Beside this sacrifice or without the Lord Christ no worship of God is valid. It does not please God, and he allows no work that does not direct and guide itself to this Mercy Seat and Victor, Christ, who is the Seat and eternal, essential Word of God his Father. Through him God the Father speaks with us. In him we find God. For his sake God answers us and accepts us into his mercy. The two cherubim indicate the entire preaching office and the consensus, unity and agreement of the teaching of the Old and New Testaments. For what the prophets preached concerning our righteousness, consolation, redemption, life and salvation, this the apostles and all true teachers preach until the end of the world. THE WHOLE PSALTER.[8]

GRACIOUS LOVE. JOHN CALVIN: In the previous verse he calls them "fearers of the Lord" and now his "beloved," implying that whenever God rewards those who fear and worship him, it is never without at the same seeing this as coming from his gracious love. And prayer is connected to that. For however great may be the favors which God has bestowed on us, modesty and humility will teach us always to pray that he would perfect what his goodness has begun. COMMENTARY ON THE PSALMS.[9]

THE AWESOME RESPONSIBILITY OF THE CHURCH'S MINISTRY OF THE WORD. MARTIN LUTHER: "God has spoken in his holy place," that is, in me, his people, which is his sanctuary. It is as if

he were saying, "I have the Word of God. And it is in me that he has spoken, that he speaks and that he will speak." "For it is not you who speak but the Spirit of your Father who speaks in you." Therefore "I will rejoice." For without joy this Word of God is not heard. . . . This psalm and all of divine Scripture are living and abiding, as Psalm 119 says: "Forever, O Lord, your Word and truth abide forever and ever." Therefore this must be understood as being for teaching to the present and to the end of the world. . . .

I think it is the first grace and a marvelous honor from God when it has been given to someone so to read and hear the words of Scripture as if he thought he was hearing them from God himself. How will such a person not bristle when he realizes that so great a majesty is speaking to him? As in Job 26: "And when we have heard scarcely a drop of his Word who will be able to behold the thunder of his greatness?" But we read and hear that Word so sluggishly, as if it were offered us by sheer accident or without anyone behind it. And we neither see nor feel how great he is who is speaking. Hence the church deservedly claims this happy boast, saying, "God has spoken in his holy place." "And therefore I will rejoice," he says, because the Word of God is a good and excellent word. FIRST PSALMS LECTURES (1513–1515).[10]

EARTHENWARE TO BE SHATTERED. THE ENGLISH ANNOTATIONS: Under the metaphor of this "vessel of dishonor," as the apostle says, is intimated the servile and abject condition of the conquered Moabites under David. If we take it of an earthen vessel, the meaning may be that he will break and bruise them in pieces (as indeed he did) like a potter's vessel. But in this place, he turns it to another purpose, as though David intended it of a vessel filled with the blood of the slain, wherein he would wash his feet. I do not like this interpretation, however, or the conceit that the whole country, through the number of the slain, should be as a great pan or bowl full of blood. If

---

[8]Selnecker, *Der gantze Psalter*, 2:50v-51r; citing 1 Chron 13; Is 11; Ex 25.
[9]CTS 9:402* (CO 31:576).

[10]LW 10:286, 287* (WA 3:342); citing Mt 10:20; Ps 119:89; Job 26:14.

the reader likes this better, however, he may hold this view. Annotations on Psalm 60:8.[11]

60:9-12 *The Lord Will Tread Down Our Foes*

Human Help Is Useless; All Aid Is From God. Johann Arndt: Four magnificent degrees or steps of divine help are described here. First, God is our Duke and Leader as well as our fortress, since the psalm says: "Who will lead me into a fortified city? Who will escort me to Edom?" It means to say this: Even if you subject the peoples under me, still I am indeed unable to keep them subjected by my own power, if you are not my fortress and fortified city and if you do not fortify my kingdom through your might, strength, wisdom and righteousness. To the prophet Jeremiah, God the Lord spoke: "I will make you a fortified city, an iron pillar and a bronze wall against the land." Thus God the Lord does to the dear magistrates whose rule he fortifies and protects. Here David acknowledges this, and thus he gives all high magistrates an example of the teaching, who the true fortress is, namely, God himself.

"Will you not do it, O God? Have you rejected us and do you not go out with our army?" This is the second degree of divine protection. God helps in the midst of crossbearing and helps in this way, so that at the same time he tests the righteous and punishes the godless. His help is also so secret and hidden that reason cannot grasp it. Here David complains: "O God, you do not go out with our army; it seems as if you are not among us!" If reason sees the enemies' great, terrifying swarm of troops, it thinks that God is with them. But God's armor and firepower are very different. He has a heavenly host. He has all of nature, which he armors for battle. He has fear and terror by which he defeats the enemies, so that he makes all human wisdom and reason into foolishness. He went with

the children of Israel through the Red Sea, but no one saw his footprints, Psalm 77 says.

The third degree of divine help is "Grant us help in times of need, for human help is no use!" God leads his poor little flock so mysteriously that he lets them fall into external troubles. And the holy church has no external might or power, thus it often seems as if the church will be eradicated and erased. First, God does this so that believers should not rely on worldly might and power, for that is contrary to faith. Second, God alone wants the glory, and we should say that God has done this, and confess that it is the Lord's work.... Thus, human help will not protect the church; it cannot do it. It is no use, if God does not grant help in times of need. God's strength must fight for us. God's might must sustain us. God's power must protect us. To this belong faith, prayer and patience. "You are Israel's consolation and its Savior in time of need."

Next follows the fourth degree of divine help: "With God we will do these deeds; he will trample over our enemies." Thus, God's strength and power must be in us, by us, with us, around us and over us; human help is nothing. The Whole Psalter of David, the Holy King and Prophet: Third Sermon on Psalm 60.[12]

Free Will. John Calvin: Even in our controversy with creatures like ourselves, we are not at liberty to share the honor of success with God; and must it not be accounted greater sacrilege still when human beings set free will in opposition to divine grace and speak of their concurring equally with God in the matter of procuring eternal salvation? Those who arrogate the least fraction of strength to themselves apart from God only ruin themselves through their own pride. Commentary on the Psalms.[13]

---

[11]Downame, ed., *Annotations*, 6G3r*; citing Ps 2:9; Ps 58:10.

[12]Arndt, *Der gantze Psalter Davids des H. Königs und Propheten*, 501-2; citing Jer 1:18; Ps 77:19; Jer 14:8.
[13]CTS 9:409* (CO 31:580).

61:1-8 LEAD ME TO THE ROCK

To the choirmaster: with stringed instruments. Of David.

^{1} Hear my cry, O God,
    listen to my prayer;
^{2} from the end of the earth I call to you
    when my heart is faint.
Lead me to the rock
    that is higher than I,
^{3} for you have been my refuge,
    a strong tower against the enemy.

^{4} Let me dwell in your tent forever!

Let me take refuge under the shelter of
    your wings!   Selah
^{5} For you, O God, have heard my vows;
    you have given me the heritage of those who
    fear your name.

^{6} Prolong the life of the king;
    may his years endure to all generations!
^{7} May he be enthroned forever before God;
    appoint steadfast love and faithfulness to
    watch over him!

^{8} So will I ever sing praises to your name,
    as I perform my vows day after day.

OVERVIEW: Our Reformation commentators here reflect on the significance of both temporal and eternal kingdoms. On the one hand, some suggest that the psalmist's prayer on behalf of the king signifies that Christians are called to be good citizens in this world and to pray for authorities. On the other hand, the reformers understand the eternally enthroned king as a prophetic foreshadowing of Christ's kingdom. Thus, they explore the various figures of Christ presented here: our rock, our tower of strength, our refuge. All of these things point to the mercy and grace of God in Christ.

DAVID'S KINGDOM FORESHADOWS CHRIST'S. RUDOLF GWALTHER: So much of this psalm deals with David and his kingdom, teaching both the rulers and the people that all prosperity comes from God whom we should cry out to in specific and general matters. Consequently, a foreshadow of Christ's kingdom is placed before us. It is an eternal kingdom; it should be enlarged and promoted by us with serious prayer. THE PSALTER.[1]

A PRAYER FOR THE AUTHORITIES. NIKOLAUS SELNECKER: This is a prayer for the magistrates and a good government, that God may sustain it for a long time and guard it against all enemies. And such prayer should constantly be offered by subjects and citizens. For indeed the beloved magistrates are a representative of God. And whoever despises the magistrates, priests, women and young children is—as the old proverb goes—an unrestrained scoundrel, a useless load of dirt. To me—as the least of all—this psalm has always been dear and precious because it treats magistrates so excellently and cheerfully.... Indeed, there is no life better and more glorious than to spend our life under upright magistrates. Therefore everyone is to pray diligently for the magistrates, as Paul commands in 1 Timothy 2, that we may lead a peaceful and quiet life in all godliness and honesty. THE WHOLE PSALTER.[2]

61:1-8 Draw Me into Your Presence

DAVID DEMONSTRATES WHAT OUR RESPONSE TO TRIALS SHOULD BE. JOHN CALVIN: Let those who may have been deprived of the hearing of the

---

[1]Gwalther, Der Psalter, 106v.

[2]Selnecker, Der gantze Psalter, 2:53r; citing 1 Tim 2:1-2.

Word and the distribution of the sacraments, so as, in a manner, to be banished out of the church, learn from the example of David to persevere in crying to God, even under these solitary circumstances. . . . Notice was taken already of the external trial to which he was subjected, in distance from the sanctuary, and of his rising above this, so as to direct his cry to God; and in the words before us, we have his confession that he was far from being stoically insensible, being conscious of a severe inward struggle with grief and perplexity of mind. It is the duty, then, of believers, when oppressed with heaviness and spiritual distress, to make only the more strenuous efforts for breaking through these obstacles in their approaches to God. His prayer is that God would bring him to that safety from which he seems to be excluded. By a rock or citadel he means, in general, secure protection, from which he complains of being shut out, as it was impossible to reach it unless he were raised by the hand of God. In looking round him, it seemed as if every place of shelter and safety were lifted up above his head and rendered inaccessible. He was cut off from all help, and yet, hopeless as deliverance appeared, he had no doubt of his safety, should God only extend his hand for interposition.

This is the plain meaning of the passage, when divested of figure: Although all other help might be withdrawn and the whole world closes off all means of escape, you, God, beyond all hope, will rescue me—a lesson which is eminently worthy of note. In looking for deliverance from God, we must not judge it by our own carnal perception; we should remember that he does not always work by apparent means but delivers us when he chooses by methods inscrutable to reason. For anyone who tries to prescribe God to any one particular line of procedure will do no less than willfully limit his almighty power. COMMENTARY ON THE PSALMS.[3]

THE PAINS OF EXILE. DAVID DICKSON: When the godly are driven from their country, from the fellowship of the saints and from the exercise of public ordinances, it is no wonder that they fall into perplexity of spirit, as David is here forced to flee and finds his heart overwhelmed within him. It is exile indeed to be secluded from the liberty of the public ordinances, and it is our home to be where God is publically worshiped. Indeed, David claims to be cast to the ends of the earth when he is debarred from the Temple of the LORD. That said, no matter how far a person is banished from the free association of the church and communion with God's people, he is still within cry of God. COMMENTARY ON PSALM 61:2.[4]

BY HIS GIFT AND EXAMPLE CHRIST IS MY REFUGE. MARTIN LUTHER: He established hope and a tower of strength by the example of his passion and resurrection: temptation is conquered and avoided in no other place or time or any other temporal thing except in Christ alone. Therefore fools who by fleeing or turning back seek victory over temptation should instead flee to Christ and be armored with his knowledge. GLOSSA ON PSALM 61 (1513–1515).[5]

DUAL MEANING. MOÏSE AMYRAUT: Because the tabernacle was a type for heaven, these words have a dual meaning: one according to the type, another according to the thing signified by the type. ANNOTATIONS ON PSALM 61:4.[6]

THE WINGS OF THE CHERUBIM. DAVID DICKSON: The ground of all spiritual consolation is in the mercy and grace of God offered to us in Christ, represented by the wings of the cherubim stretched out over the mercy seat. There, faith finds solid ground and a place of rest which is able to furnish abundant comfort. COMMENTARY ON PSALM 61:4.[7]

[3]CTS 9:411-12* (CO 31:581).

[4]Dickson, *Other Fifty Psalms*, 64*.
[5]WA 3:351.
[6]Amyraut, *Paraphrasis in Psalmos Davidis*, 253.
[7]Dickson, *Other Fifty Psalms*, 66*.

CHRIST HAS PURCHASED OUR INHERITANCE FOR US. RUDOLF GWALTHER: This inheritance is the land of Canaan, which God promised to the people of Israel as his hereditary, lawful possession. However, before David's time they were never able to capture it on account of their sins and unbelief. And here we should observe that this land was a figure and image of the eternal homeland in heaven, which Christ has acquired for us. THE PSALTER.[8]

IN VERSE 6 DAVID PROPHESIES CONCERNING CHRIST. JOHN CALVIN: David cannot be considered as using these words of rejoicing with an exclusive reference to himself. It is true that he lived to an extremely old age and died full of days, leaving the kingdom in a settled condition and in the hands of his son, who succeeded him; but he did not exceed the period of one man's life, and the greater part of it was spent in continued dangers and anxieties. There can be no doubt, therefore, that the series of years, and even ages, of which he speaks, extends prospectively to the coming of Christ, it being the very condition of the kingdom, as I have often remarked, that God maintained them as one people under one head, or, when scattered, united them again. The same succession still subsists in reference to ourselves. Christ must be viewed as living in his members to the end of the world. To this Isaiah alludes when he says, "Who shall declare his generation or age?" By these words he predicts that the church would survive through all ages, notwithstanding the incessant danger of destruction to which it is exposed through the attacks of its enemies and the many storms assailing it. So here David foretells the uninterrupted succession of the kingdom down to the time of Christ. COMMENTARY ON THE PSALMS.[9]

THIS IS ONLY ABOUT CHRIST. RUDOLF GWALTHER: "He will be enthroned eternally before God." . . . That is, he will reign eternally. Now this can only be understood about Christ, whose figure David was, about whom the angels testified that his kingdom will have no end. THE PSALTER.[10]

THE TRUE END OF EMPIRES. TILEMANN HESSHUS: The psalmist promises an act of thanksgiving for answering his prayer. He also teaches what should be the goal of all freedom and success in the state, and by which counsel God establishes, adorns and maintains kingdoms and polities. Alexander had no other goal for his state and conquests than to make his name great throughout the world—and not just to be held in great honor but also to be worshiped as a god. Sardanapalus sought nothing more than luxurious and obscene pleasures alone. Vitellius established his gullet and gluttony as the goal of his state. Vespasian established the glory and great power of wealth to be the goal of his labors. And so the majority of potentates in the world make wealth, glory and pleasures to be the greatest good and highest goal of their states. But the Holy Spirit teaches that the goal of the state should be something quite different: without a doubt, that we should sing psalms to the divine name and perform our vows to God. That is, we should acknowledge and glorify God's goodness, righteousness, lovingkindness, truth, omnipotence and wisdom. Yes, daily we should practice God's worship by prayer, faith, hope, endurance and similar sacrifices of righteousness. COMMENTARY ON PSALM 61.[11]

---

[10]Gwalther, *Der Psalter*, 107r, 107v.
[11]Hesshus, *Commentarius in Psalmos*, 249r. Sardanapalus was an Assyrian king—of uncertain historicity—in the histories of Ctesias, known for his decadence and opulent waste. Vitellius and Vespasian were the third and fourth Roman emperors, respectively, in the Year of Four Emperors (69). Vitellius was alleged to feast four times a day; Vespasian raised taxes and tributes empire-wide—even taxing public urinals (also called *pissoirs* or *vespasiennes*).

---

[8]Gwalther, *Der Psalter*, 107v.
[9]CTS 9:415* (CO 31:583).

62:1-12 MY SOUL AWAITS GOD'S SALVATION

To the choirmaster: according to Jeduthun. A
Psalm of David.

¹ *For God alone my soul waits in silence;*
  from him comes my salvation.
² *He alone is my rock and my salvation,*
  my fortress; I shall not be greatly shaken.

³ *How long will all of you attack a man*
  to batter him,
  like a leaning wall, a tottering fence?
⁴ *They only plan to thrust him down from his*
    high position.
  They take pleasure in falsehood.
They bless with their mouths,
  but inwardly they curse.   Selah

⁵ *For God alone, O my soul, wait in silence,*
  for my hope is from him.
⁶ *He only is my rock and my salvation,*
  my fortress; I shall not be shaken.

⁷ *On God rests my salvation and my glory;*
  my mighty rock, my refuge is God.

⁸ *Trust in him at all times, O people;*
  pour out your heart before him;
  God is a refuge for us.   Selah

⁹ *Those of low estate are but a breath;*
  those of high estate are a delusion;
in the balances they go up;
  they are together lighter than a breath.
¹⁰ *Put no trust in extortion;*
  set no vain hopes on robbery;
  if riches increase, set not your heart on them.

¹¹ *Once God has spoken;*
  twice have I heard this:
that power belongs to God,
  ¹² *and that to you, O* LORD, *belongs*
    steadfast love.
For you will render to a man
  according to his work.

OVERVIEW: For our Reformation interpreters,
David's trust in God and God's promises, which
he declares in the midst of suffering and uncertainty, is an impressive example of faithfulness.
The reformers hone in on the repeated lines, "For
God alone, O my soul, wait in silence, for my hope
is in him. He only is my rock and my salvation, my
fortress; I shall not be shaken." For some, this
serves as a reminder that while we constantly
pursue patience and trust in God, we will never
reach perfection in this life. For others, this points
to the fact that despite the ongoing reality of sin,
believers should have confidence in God's promise
of eternal salvation. Like David, we are to trust in
God alone—not in status or stuff. His unspeakable power and mercy strengthen, rule and
preserve us.

A POWERFUL ANTIDOTE FOR TEMPTATIONS.
THEODORE BEZA: Because of his son's conspiracy
David has been cast from his throne and with a
number of his troops has been forced to flee beyond
the Jordan (as can be inferred from verse 8). Struggling with grave temptation—without a doubt, on
account of so great and sudden an upheaval of everything in his life he was aroused to unlawful actions
or even despair—he decides that he will persevere in
boldly waiting on God's protection. And by his
example he confirms his companions. In fact he does
this with such great and vigorous courage that even
his very thoughts and words refute temptation, so
that whoever has this psalm ready will see that it
cannot easily be overcome with any sort of temptation. PARAPHRASE OF PSALM 62.[1]

---

[1]Beza, *Psalmes of Dauid*, 135* (*Psalmorum Davidis*, 268).

62:1-4 God Is My Rock and Salvation

IMPASSIONED PRAYER. JOHN CALVIN: The psalm is to be considered as beginning abruptly, in the usual style of compositions of an impassioned kind. Of this we have an instance in Psalm 73, where the prophet, who had been agitated with doubts, as we shall see more particularly afterwards, suddenly brings his mind to a fixed decision, and, cutting off all further subject of debate, exclaims, "Yet God is good to Israel." And so it is, I conceive, in the psalm before us. We know that the Lord's people cannot always reach such a measure of composure as to be wholly exempt from distraction. They would wish to receive the word of the Lord with submission and to be silent under his correcting hand; but inordinate affections will take possession of their minds and break in on that peace which they might otherwise attain in the exercise of faith and resignation. Hence the impatience we find in many; an impatience which they vent in the presence of God and which is an occasion to rid themselves of much trouble and disquietude....

The silence intended is, in short, that composed submission of believers, in the exercise of which they acquiesce in the promises of God, give place to his Word, bow to his sovereignty and suppress every inward murmur of dissatisfaction. COMMENTARY ON THE PSALMS.[2]

SILENT BEFORE HIS SHEARERS. MARTIN LUTHER: When David says, "My soul is silent before God," this is a Hebraic idiom. It means "The silence of my soul is toward God or for God." That is, "I am silent, and I subject myself to the godless, who entrust themselves to, trust and boast in human beings and lords. But I commend myself to God. I trust and boast in him, but so quietly and privately that they do not realize it and think me a fool because I do not join them in their ambition, flattery and greed." O, what a rare thing it is to have such a courtier! Yet Saul, the wicked king, had such

a courtier; David was like a rose among thorns in the midst of these rascals at court. Undoubtedly there can still be a righteous person at court, but he must also be among the thorns and always be prepared to be pricked. FOUR COMFORTING PSALMS FOR THE QUEEN OF HUNGARY (1526).[3]

DAVID'S SPEECH SHOWS HIS MODESTY. MOÏSE AMYRAUT: Here the prophet speaks about himself in the third person, because he begins to consider his future greatness. He bears a modest character, that in such occasions he changes his speech in this way. ANNOTATIONS ON PSALM 62:3-4.[4]

BEFORE GOD'S SPIRIT THE WICKED TREMBLE AND FALL. JOHN HOOPER: By the simile and metaphor of a tottering or quivering wall, the prophet declares how lightly and suddenly the Lord will destroy the persecutors of his people. For as the wall that is tottering and quivering with every wind and weather is easily and suddenly overthrown, so the wicked and tyrannical persecutors are suddenly destroyed—indeed, when they are most strong and valiant in their own deceits.... So by this we learn that the strength and persecution of the wicked is not permanent or strong but transitory and feeble. It is destroyed and vanquished with the presence of God's favor toward his people as often as it pleases him to punish the malice and mischief of the wicked.

But there is one lesson particularly to be noted in this simile of a trembling or tottering wall with which the prophet sets forth the fall and confusion of the wicked. It is this, that when the wicked persecute the godly and that the smallest resistance of the world is stirred up by God against them, he also strikes their hearts with such trembling and fear that one person in a good cause will be able to withstand ten such wicked persecutors whose conscience God has so seared that they are not able to bear the countenance of a human being. No, they are not even able to overcome the terror of

---

[2]CTS 9:417-18* (CO 31:584-85); citing Ps 73:1.

[3]LW 14:233* (WA 19:573).
[4]Amyraut, *Paraphrasis in Psalmos Davidis*, 255.

their own spirit, which testifies against them, that as in the past they have fought against God and his cause, so now God justly fights against them—both with the fear of hellfire toward their souls and with external adversities toward their bodies. Exposition upon Psalm 62.[5]

62:5-8 My Hope Is from God

David Fervently Repeats Himself. Nikolaus Selnecker: These two verses must have pleased and comforted David particularly well, for he sets them down twice, not as a tautology—as some say about Psalm 119's "tautological theology"—instead out of true passion in faith and solace. The Whole Psalter.[6]

Why Does David Repeat Himself? John Calvin: Here there may appear to be a slight inconsistency, because David encourages himself to do what he declared that he had already done. His soul was silent before God; and what is the necessity of this new silence, as if still under agitation of spirit? Here it is to be remembered that our minds can never be expected to reach such perfect composure as that there is no inward feeling of disquietude at all. The best we can reach is a situation like the sea before a light breeze, fluctuating sensibly, though not swollen into billows. Commentary on the Psalms.[7]

Two Ways to Understand This Repetition. John Hooper: The fifth and sixth verses are word for word the same as the first and second verses, except this word *greatly* is left out of these two verses. This word may be taken two ways, very comforting to the reader and hearer—if it be well observed and believed. The first way is that the prophet does not mean that the people of God will not fall, for that is against Scripture. For "the righteous person falls seven times in one day." Again, "If we say we have no sin in us, we

deceive ourselves and the truth is not it us." Now because sin dwells inseparably in a person—as it does in all human beings while they live on earth—there are faults before God on that person's part, in whom this sin dwells, yet God according to his mercy, for the sake of the blood and death of Christ, does not count these inseparable sins to be faults but loves the person, preserves him and will not impute any of those faults to his account, but in Christ will consider him justified and clean, as though he himself were so. And thus, the prophet says that because of God and because they are accepted into his favor through Christ the faithful do not fall. That is to say, their sins are not counted damnable or charged to their account for Christ's sake, as Saint Paul writes to the Romans.

Another way it may be understood is that Christians have a witness in their spirit by the Spirit of God, that they are elected, chosen and ordained by God to eternal salvation. No matter what the world, the flesh, the devil or sin might do, nevertheless they stand assured of God's election, grace, strength and fidelity, that they will never fall into damnation but rise again and be called from their faults—whatever they are. And yet this most sure and comforting knowledge will not give license or liberty to sin. Instead it will keep them in fear and love toward the strong and mighty God in whose hands they are; it will keep them from the great fall of eternal damnation from which they were delivered from the beginning with God. Thus, you may learn from this passage what perseverance is in the meditation and contemplation of God's most holy word and promises.

At first they seem to the flesh to be impossible things, as we see by Nicodemus, who was as ignorant as could be at the beginning, when he first came to the school of Christ. But when a person has been trained a while in it, he sees more sweetness in the promises of God, as we see by this prophet. For after he had born the cross of affliction a little while and learned the nature of God, how merciful he is to sinners, he said, "Although I fall,

---

[5]Hooper, *Certain Comfortable Expositions*, 58r-v*.
[6]Selnecker, *Der gantze Psalter*, 2:55r.
[7]CTS 9:422-23* (CO 31:587).

yet it shall not be greatly." But when he had tarried in the school of Christ and learned indeed what he was and how he was able to perform his mercy, he said plainly that no matter what sin, the devil, the world, the flesh, hell, heaven or earth would say against him, he will not fall. These two interpretations are to be observed. For whichever we use, we may find comfort and unspeakable consolation. Exposition upon Psalm 62.[8]

Pour Out Your Laments to God! Martin Luther: Strength fades, courage fails; God remains firm. In times of adversity and in times of prosperity, therefore, you should depend on God. If you are lacking something, well, here is good advice: "Pour out your heart before him." Voice your complaint freely, and do not conceal anything from him. Regardless of what it is, just throw it in a pile before him, as you open your heart completely to a good friend. He wants to hear it, and he wants to give you his aid and counsel. Do not be bashful before him, and do not think that what you ask is too big or too much. Come right out with it, even if all you have is bags full of need. Out with everything; God is greater and more able and more willing than all our transgressions. Do not dribble your requests before him; God is not a human being whom you can overburden with your begging and asking. The more you ask, the happier he is to hear you. Only pour it all out, do not dribble or drip it. For he will not drip or dribble either, but he will flood you with a veritable deluge. Four Comforting Psalms for the Queen of Hungary (1526).[9]

62:9-12 Place Your Trust in God, Not Human Beings

Human Beings Are Not a Source of Trust. Martin Luther: You have heard what God is, but now hear what human beings are. They are good for nothing, David says. If you

depend on them, you should know that you are depending on nothing at all, and that it will certainly fail you. Yes, he says, if we were to put them on a balance—human beings on one pan, vanity or nothing on the other—the human beings would be lighter than nothing. We Germans would render this Hebrew way of speaking thus: "Human beings amount to less than nothing." For what they call "vanity," we call "nothing." . . .

Here you may ask: "What? Are human beings worth nothing, even though they are a creature of God?" I answer: David is not speaking about the creature as such but about the use of the creature. That is, human beings are certainly a good thing, but they are not put to good use. Being a prince, a king or emperor is also a good thing, but it is not put to good use either. In what way? Because people try to put their trust in them and build on them. For such use they are worth nothing. Why? Because they are uncertain in their hearts and in their lives. Sand and water are a good thing too, but if I wanted to build a house on them, they would be worth nothing and less than nothing. When I drink water, however, or wash with it, then it is not worthless but a precious and useful thing; for this is what it was made for, this is its proper use. Thus also prince, king and emperor were made to keep peace in the land. For this purpose they are creatures of God and a good thing. But for me to trust in, they are worthless. . . . Trust belongs to God alone. You should not exchange gold for manure. Manure has its uses; but if it is palmed off as gold, it is worthless. You see that this psalm is talking only about faith, trust, confidence, reliance—all terms which are too sublime to apply to princes and other human beings. Nevertheless, the world consistently trusts in human beings and does not put its confidence in God. That is, it is nothing and it trusts in nothing. Four Comforting Psalms for the Queen of Hungary (1526).[10]

---

[8]Hooper, *Certain Comfortable Expositions*, 63v-64v*; citing Prov 24:16; 1 Jn 1:8; Rom 5:13.
[9]LW 14:237-38* (WA 19:578).

[10]LW 14:238-39* (WA 19:578-79). For Luther's understanding of the translation task, see his "Defense of the Translation of the Psalms" (1531), LW 35:209-32 (WA 38:9-17). See also Luther's comment on Ps 16 above, p. 119.

THE OPPRESSION OF WEALTH. WOLFGANG MUSCULUS: For the same reason, he also ascribes vanity to earthly riches . . . that is, in the resources acquired by oppression and plundering. For plundering is what is acquired by oppression. Thus, Isaiah 3 says, "The plundering of the poor person happens in your house." . . . Wealth is acquired by certain people through oppression and plundering, but it overflows for some people through a prosperous succession of other events. Wealth is permitted to some people to make them more distinguished, but it is given to others as vanity, so that they are unable to maintain lasting wealth when placed in necessity, or so that they place their confidence in the unworthy name of riches. Oppression and the plundering of some riches had been able to drive out the iniquity of riches as well as driving out their offensiveness to God and the thought of future punishment; truly, just as he established in this one matter, he maintained that riches are vanity—not only those which may be acquired by fraud and plundering but also those riches which will flow of their own accord. For he saw that these riches were like a fountain of oppression and plundering; wealth is admired and eagerly sought, because it is thought to bring much health and happiness. COMMENTARY ON THE PSALMS.[11]

"ONCE GOD HAS SPOKEN, TWICE HAVE I HEARD." SEBASTIAN MÜNSTER: That is, often God testified in the Law and the Prophets that he is most powerful and most merciful; he is the one who saves his people. All human beings are false and liars. Therefore human beings should fear nothing, nor should they seek salvation among themselves. THE TEMPLE OF THE LORD: PSALM 62.[12]

GOD'S POWER AND MERCY: OUR WINGS AND PILLARS. JOHN CALVIN: David does not thoughtlessly associate God's power with his clemency. They are the two wings which carry us up to God, the two pillars on which we rest, and no temptation might plunge us into a shipwreck. As often as fear is cast before anyone, then just let us call to remembrance the power of God, which is ready and eager to dispel all harm, and as this sentiment prevails in our minds, whatever is contrary to our salvation will be struck down. For what is to be feared, when the same God who covers us with the shadow of his wings rules the universe with his nod? When he holds Satan and all the wicked in secret chains? When he, in the end, controls all of their plans, pursuits and endeavors? COMMENTARY ON THE PSALMS.[13]

---

[11]Musculus, *In Psalterium Commentarii*, 652; citing Is 3:14.

[12]Münster, *Miqdaš YHWH*, 1209; citing Rom 3:4.
[13]CTS 9:431* (CO 31:592).

63:1-11 MY SOUL THIRSTS AND HUNGERS FOR THE LORD

A Psalm of David, when he was in the wilderness of Judah.

¹ *O God, you are my God; earnestly I seek you;*
  my soul thirsts for you;
my flesh faints for you,
    as in a dry and weary land where there is
      no water.
² *So I have looked upon you in the sanctuary,*
    beholding your power and glory.
³ *Because your steadfast love is better than life,*
    my lips will praise you.
⁴ *So I will bless you as long as I live;*
    in your name I will lift up my hands.

⁵ *My soul will be satisfied as with fat and rich food,*
    and my mouth will praise you with joyful lips,

⁶ *when I remember you upon my bed,*
    and meditate on you in the watches of the
      night;
⁷ *for you have been my help,*
    and in the shadow of your wings I will sing
      for joy.
⁸ *My soul clings to you;*
    your right hand upholds me.

⁹ *But those who seek to destroy my life*
    shall go down into the depths of the earth;
¹⁰ *they shall be given over to the power of the*
      sword;
    they shall be a portion for jackals.
¹¹ *But the king shall rejoice in God;*
    all who swear by him shall exult,
    for the mouths of liars will be stopped.

OVERVIEW: Here our commentators focus on David's desire to be in God's presence and to worship the one, true God despite being separated from the tabernacle and its communal cultic practices. Although David's particular circumstances were very different from those of the reformers, he still offers them an example of faithful confidence in the midst of suffering and questioning, which results in his praise of God, who alone can provide true food and drink. Some of our commentators emphasize that this is a wonderful example of how we worship by the Holy Spirit, who guides all of our praise and unites us to Christ. Others suggest that David's worship implies an affirmation of the Triune God and that his words show Christians how to seek God through pious prayer and avoid immoral speech, even when confronted by those who oppose or reject God.

YEARNING FOR GOD. CARDINAL CAJETAN: The psalm is divided into two parts: the laying out of

the subject matter, and the details of it, beginning there at "My soul thirsts." He makes two assertions in his proposal: first, "O God, you are my God." He proclaims that God is his God through an expression of worship, and so on. The second: "I shall seek you." He promises diligence in regard to those things which are of God by spelling out the love that is owed. As a result of his profession that God is his God, he in turn applies that love to seeking what things are of God. . . .

In reference to his seeking after God, first he expounds on the desire of the soul and body. "My soul thirsts for you." The soul wants to go to the sanctuary, worship through sacrifices and perform due rituals there. "My flesh yearns for you." The yearning of the flesh for God, understand, is an irrational yearning. By it, people are said to desire God to the extent that they desire good things for themselves that derive from God's goodness. But he does not forget carnal desire, in order to mark the need for things that are appropriate for the body, because desire is for those things which we lack. And this is meant to remind us that David in the desert suffered many discomforts of the body. COMMENTARY ON PSALM 63.[1]

Superscription: *Judah's Desert*

CUT OFF FROM THE TEMPLE, DAVID WORSHIPS IN THE TEMPLE OF HIS SPIRIT. SEBASTIAN MÜNSTER: "In the desert of Judah," that is, the desert Ziph in which David took refuge many times until eventually by the Ziphites' words he was betrayed to his enemy Saul. He sings about this also in Psalm 54. And because David especially sought to promote the glory of God and sought nothing so much as to glorify him with the saints, it was painful for him to be separated from the sanctuary of the Lord and from his sincere worshipers. Therefore, he cried out all these feelings in the desert. "At daybreak and in the morning I seek you, O Lord! To you I sigh; it is you whom I worship in this vast wilderness. And because I am not permitted to participate in your holy assembly, I meditate here in my spirit in my music, just as if I were in your sanctuary—as if I could see the ark of your mighty works and glory!" THE TEMPLE OF THE LORD: PSALM 63.[2]

63:1-8 *I Long for Your Rich Feasts*

THE LORD IS MY GOD. JOHN CALVIN: We may rely on the truth of the record he gives us of his exercise when under his trials; and it is apparent that he never allowed himself to be so far overcome by them as to cease lifting up his prayers to heaven, and even resting, with a firm and constant faith, on the divine promises. Apt, as we are when assaulted by the very slightest trials, to lose the comfort of any knowledge of God we may previously have possessed, it is necessary that we should notice this and learn, by his example, to struggle to maintain our confidence under the worst troubles that can befall us. David does more than simply pray; he sets the Lord before him as his God, so that he may throw all his cares unhesitatingly on his lap, deserted as he was by human beings—a poor outcast in the waste and howling wilderness. His faith persuaded him of the favor and help of God and kindled his heart to constant and ardent prayer, asking for the grace in which he hoped.

In saying that his soul thirsted and his flesh longed, he alludes to the destitution and poverty which he lay under in the wilderness, and intimates that though deprived of the ordinary means of subsistence he looked to God as his food and his drink, directing all his desires to him. When he represents his soul as thirsting and his flesh as hungering, we are not to seek for any nice or subtle design in the distinction. He means simply that he desired God, both with soul and body. For although the body, strictly speaking, is not of itself influenced by desire, we know that the feelings of the soul intimately and extensively affect it. COMMENTARY ON THE PSALMS.[3]

THE ONE AND ONLY GOD. NIKOLAUS SELNECKER: That there is one God, even the pagans know from nature—as Plato and Aristotle and others prove. However, that there is a single God in three, distinguishable persons, only those who have and accept God's Word know. Thus, it also stands here: "O God, you are my God," *'ĕlōhîm 'ēlî 'attāh.* "You persons, God the Father, Son and Holy Spirit, you are my God, my strength and help, might and power."

The most distinguished names of God in holy Scripture are these: Jehovah, Adonai, Elohim, Shaddai and Zebaoth. The word *Jehovah*, which we call the Tetragrammaton, is the name by which only the one, eternal, almighty majesty of God is called and it indicates the single divine essence—God the Father, God the Son and God the Holy Spirit. In our German Bibles, every time

---

[1]Cajetan, *In Sacrae Scripturae Expositionem*, 3:219.
[2]Münster, *Miqdaš YHWH*, 1210.

[3]CTS 9:433-34* (CO 31:594).

the word LORD is printed with capital letters, in Hebrew it is the word *Jehovah*, the one, eternal divine essence.[4] *Adonai* means "sustainer," the one who bears and sustains all things like a strong pillar; he is the Head of his church, and he protects and sustains it. Now this is the eternal Son of God. *Elohim* means a forceful, strong, powerful God—mighty and magnificent! And sometimes this name is also used for creatures like kings, princes and judges who perform a divine and mighty office, appointed by God. . . . *Shaddai* means strong and almighty, one whose goodness and power extend to all creatures. In him we have our being, we live and move. He has everything and can do everything and grant every good thing. And he loves his people with all his heart, as a mother loves and nourishes her nursing child. *Zebaoth* means a LORD of hosts, that is, of the dear angels, of all the heavens and the firmament and of his church or his believers, who all serve for God's glory and are always prepared and ready to serve God's glory.

Now because David calls God "Elohim" here, he is speaking about the one, eternal essence of God in three, distinguishable persons, and he distinguishes his prayer from all pagan and unchristian prayers. Then he speaks of God's will when he says, "You are my God." For it is required of us all that we not only know that there is one God or one Essence in three persons, but we must also believe and confess with confidence against all temptations, doubts, suspicions and fanaticism that the eternal God—the Father of our Lord Jesus Christ and the Son of God our Lord Christ Jesus and the Holy Spirit—are our God, my God and your God. He created me and you, nourishes us, sustains us, consoles us, strengthens us and redeems us, makes us righteous and holy. And he wants no person to be lost; instead, he wants all to be saved. For this actually means "You are my God according to the Word of God. *I am your*

God. That is, 'I care for you and love you, make you righteous and holy; you should entrust yourself to me with all confidence and have a refuge in me in all your times of need. I will help you.'" These words actually speak about the true knowledge of God. THE WHOLE PSALTER.[5]

FERVENT ZEAL FOR GOD'S WORSHIP. RUDOLF GWALTHER: By thirst he understands nothing other than his heartfelt and fervent desire which he holds toward the tabernacle of God and the external worship of God, and with which he pursues these things with other believers. So also he considers his soul and flesh, in order to show that all his powers together strive toward God and his worship. THE PSALTER.[6]

THE IMPORTANCE OF EVENING MEDITATION. MARTIN LUTHER: The evening's reflection and recall is especially helpful for the morning purity, just as, on the contrary, the evening's distraction is a particular hindrance to the morning meditation, because there the remnants of reflection make the day festive in the morning. Therefore it is most appropriate that when he had said "I have remembered," he immediately added, "I will meditate on you in the morning." For the more diligent the evening remembrance was, the easier is the morning meditation. But alas, how much the devil now subverts all of that through all stages, for drunkenness, frivolity, talkativeness, amusements and other monstrosities are now indulged in, especially in the evening, and for that reason people pray and celebrate that much worse in the morning and are very badly lacking. Note, however, that he attributes remembrance to the evening and meditation to the morning, and thus in a striking way shows us the difference. For because the vexation and the tickling of the flesh are wont to be aroused on the bed for the idle and especially for those who are drunk, remembrance is necessary, and not a perfunctory

---

[4]For more on the Tetragrammaton in early modern exegesis, see the overview for Ps 6 above, 51-52.

[5]Selnecker, *Der gantze Psalter*, 2:60v-61r; citing Acts 17:28.
[6]Gwalther, *Der Psalter*, 110v.

recall of God, but one must remain and go to sleep fixed on the meditation of God, so that it might somehow last also during sleep. FIRST PSALMS LECTURES (1513–1515).[7]

GOD'S HELP IMPLIES OUR COOPERATION.

JOHN DONNE: From this one word, that God has been my help, I make account that we have both these notions; first, that God has not left me to myself, but has come to my succor, and has helped me; and then, that God does not act apart from me; rather he has been my help, but he has left something for me to do with him and by his help. My security for the future, in this consideration of what is past, lies not only in this, that God has delivered me, but in this also, that he has delivered me by way of a help, and help always assumes an endeavor and cooperation in one who is helped. God did not elect me as a helper, or create me, or redeem me, or convert me by way of helping me; for he alone did all, and he had no use at all of me. God infuses his first grace, the first way, merely as a giver; entirely, all himself; but his subsequent graces, as a helper; therefore we call them auxiliary graces, helping graces, and we always receive them when we endeavor to make use of his former grace. SERMON 66: PREBEND SERMONS.[8]

UNITED IN CHRIST.

HENRY AINSWORTH: This shows love, constancy, humility and union in the Spirit. For as husband and wife cleaving together are one flesh, so "he who cleaves to the Lord is one spirit." And this union comes from the Lord, who says through the prophet, "As the girdle cleaves to the loins of a person, so I have tied to me the whole house of Israel, so that they might be my people." ANNOTATIONS ON PSALM 63:8.[9]

63:9-11 *The King Sings; Liars Are Silenced*

WHAT IS LYING? THE ENGLISH ANNOTATIONS: Swearing, such as is here understood, deliberate and conscientious swearing on weighty occasions to bear witness to the truth and so forth, is taken for the whole worship of God, because it presupposes a belief, first, of a God, and second, of a God who is privy to all the actions and intentions of human beings; and these two things are the foundation of all religion. So, that "to speak" here is opposed to "swearing" may properly imply absolute ungodliness and infidelity. For it is to be opposed, that whoever makes a practice of lying—which is a sin more immediately against God, because in his sight only, he has said in his heart that there is no God—feels no pang of conscience to tell an untruth with all security. Thus he may freely indulge himself a liberty of sinning in any other kind, when he sees his opportunity. ANNOTATIONS ON PSALM 63:11.[10]

JOY AND PRAISE.

KONRAD PELLIKAN: Because the pious consider nothing more majestic than God, their greatest joy is in God, and the fullest means of praising is to praise his goodness in order to stop up the mouth of those speaking vanities, those who are his enemies. Accordingly those who learn the nature of pious prayer and enjoy the contemplation of the divine works will learn that the pious may not rejoice in anything other than in the grace and favor of God, and in the divine praises, conscious of an innocent life, and in the exaltation of the truth and divine goodness, and so that with the greatest care every unjust, deceitful and lying speech may be shunned, by which they may remove injury to the pious and those beloved by God. COMMENTARY ON PSALM 63:11.[11]

---

[7]LW 10:305* (WA 3:361-62).
[8]Donne, *Works*, 3:168-69*.
[9]Ainsworth, *Annotations*, 2:537*; citing Gen 2:24; 1 Cor 6:16; Jer 13:11.

[10]Downame, ed., *Annotations*, 6G3v*.
[11]Pellikan, *Commentaria Bibliorum*, 4:109v.

64:1-10 HIDE ME FROM THE WICKED

To the choirmaster. A Psalm of David.

[1] *Hear my voice, O God, in my complaint;*
  preserve my life from dread of the enemy.
[2] *Hide me from the secret plots of the wicked,*
  from the throng of evildoers,
[3] *who whet their tongues like swords,*
  who aim bitter words like arrows,
[4] *shooting from ambush at the blameless,*
  shooting at him suddenly and without fear.
[5] *They hold fast to their evil purpose;*
  they talk of laying snares secretly,
thinking, "Who can see them?"
  [6] *They search out injustice,*
saying, "We have accomplished a diligent search."

For the inward mind and heart of a man
  are deep.

[7] *But God shoots his arrow at them;*
  they are wounded suddenly.
[8] *They are brought to ruin, with their own*
  tongues turned against them;
  all who see them will wag their heads.
[9] *Then all mankind fears;*
  they tell what God has brought about
  and ponder what he has done.

[10] *Let the righteous one rejoice in the LORD*
  and take refuge in him!
Let all the upright in heart exult!

OVERVIEW: That the psalmist begins by lamenting the plots of his enemies but ends by affirming God's might and care for the righteous, for the reformers, both foreshadows Christ's suffering and resonates with the challenges that Christians faced in their own time. They remind us that God is still sovereign over our suffering. This is a powerful prayer for believers in the midst of tumult and chaos.

THIS PSALM IS SIMILAR TO PSALM 55. NIKOLAUS SELNECKER: This is a psalm of prayer almost the same as Psalm 55. David prays against his betrayers and slanderers who construed him in the worst way with poisonous words and wicked tricks, like Doeg in Saul's court—spoken of above in Psalm 52—and like Absalom and Ahithophel or like Judas with the Lord Christ. THE WHOLE PSALTER.[1]

DAVID DID NOT PRAY IN VAIN. THEODORE BEZA: From this psalm, as well as from many others, it can be observed how David did not pour out so many complaints for nothing as well as how

great his persistence was. How great is the usefulness of these examples! Those to whom it has been given know not only that they must believe but also that they must suffer for Christ's sake. PARAPHRASE OF PSALM 64.[2]

64:1-10 *The Lord Is Good and Will Protect Me*

DAVID'S FEAR AND CONFIDENCE. JOHN CALVIN: He begins by saying that he prayed earnestly and with vehemence, stating at the same time what rendered this necessary. The voice is heard in prayer proportionally to the earnestness and ardor which we feel. He condescends on the circumstances of distress in which he was presently placed and takes notice of the dangers to which his life was exposed from enemies, with other points fitted to excite the favorable consideration of God. His praying that God would protect his life proves that it must have been in danger at this time. In the second verse, he intimates that his enemies were

---

[1]Selnecker, *Der gantze Psalter*, 2:66r.

[2]Beza, *Psalmorum Davidis*, 286 (cf. *Psalmes of Dauid*, 139).

numerous and that, without divine assistance, he would be unable to sustain their attacks. . . .

He solicits the compassion of God by complaining of the number that were banded against him. Still his language implies that he looked on the protection of heaven as amply sufficient against the greatest combination of adversaries. I may add that there is an implied plea strengthening his cause in prayer in what he says of the malice and wickedness of those opposed to him, for the more cruel and unjust the conduct of our enemies may be, we have proportionally better ground to believe that God will interpose on our behalf. COMMENTARY ON PSALMS.[3]

WHAT DOES IT MEAN TO "SHARPEN THEIR TONGUES"? NIKOLAUS SELNECKER: They stir up turmoil, tumult, war and bloodshed, and with words and works they provoke others to join in, as now many great potentates want to do against us or as some monk preached before the wise and mighty Emperor Charles V, that the mighty lords will never again have a merciful God unless they wash themselves up to their elbows in Lutheran blood. *That* is what it means to sharpen their tongues like a sword. THE WHOLE PSALTER.[4]

THE MERCILESS OPPRESSION OF THE WICKED. THE ENGLISH ANNOTATIONS: The more the wicked see God's children in misery, the more bold and impudent they are in oppressing them. If there is a danger in rejoicing too much at the fall of a wicked enemy, what may they expect at the hands of God one day, those who the more they prosper in their unjust oppression, the more they rage and malice against the oppressed. ANNOTATIONS ON PSALM 64:5.[5]

GOD'S WORD AND WORKS MUST BE ADJOINED. DAVID DICKSON: Not every spectator of God's works gives glory to God. It is only those who compare his word with his works and look through the veil of means and instruments that look on God, the righteous Judge of the world. COMMENTARY ON PSALM 64:9.[6]

THE FOURFOLD SENSE OF GOD'S WORK. MARTIN LUTHER: Briefly these things can be reduced to the fourfold sense concerning the works of God:

All of these are Christ at the same time	The work of God, literally, is the creation of the world and the deeds of the old law.
	The work of God, tropologically, is the righteousness of faith, not that righteousness proper to the law, signified by the righteousness of the law and nature.
	The work of God, allegorically, is the church, signified by the synagogue and other nations.
	The work of God, anagogically, is the church triumphing in glory.

FIRST PSALMS LECTURES (1513–1515).[7]

THE APPLICATION OF DAVID'S DELIVERANCE. JOHN CALVIN: The psalmist insists on the good effects that result from this judgment of God, rousing those who had formerly overlooked divine providence altogether to catch a spirit of inquiry, that they might consider and speak to one another of something that was entirely unknown to them before. Another desirable consequence which flows from the deliverance granted is that it affords joy, hope and holy triumph to the saints, who would be confirmed in expecting the same help from God which he had extended to his servant David. COMMENTARY ON PSALMS.[8]

---

[3]CTS 9:444-45* (CO 31:599-600).
[4]Selnecker, *Der gantze Psalter*, 2:66v. Selnecker is alluding to Luther's trial at the Diet of Worms (1521).
[5]Downame, ed., *Annotations*, 6G4r*; citing Prov 24:17.

[6]Dickson, *Other Fifty Psalms*, 82*.
[7]LW 10:312* (WA 3:369); see *quadriga* biographical sketch, 529.
[8]CTS 9:450* (CO 31:602).

65:1-13 PRAISE THE CREATOR OF HEAVEN AND EARTH!

To the choirmaster. A Psalm of David. A Song.

¹ Praise is due to you,ᵃ O God, in Zion,
   and to you shall vows be performed.
² O you who hear prayer,
   to you shall all flesh come.
³ When iniquities prevail against me,
   you atone for our transgressions.
⁴ Blessed is the one you choose and bring near,
   to dwell in your courts!
We shall be satisfied with the goodness of your
      house,
   the holiness of your temple!

⁵ By awesome deeds you answer us with
      righteousness,
   O God of our salvation,
the hope of all the ends of the earth
   and of the farthest seas;
⁶ the one who by his strength established the
      mountains,
   being girded with might;
⁷ who stills the roaring of the seas,

the roaring of their waves,
   the tumult of the peoples,
⁸ so that those who dwell at the ends of the
      earth are in awe at your signs.
You make the going out of the morning and the
      evening to shout for joy.

⁹ You visit the earth and water it;ᵇ
   you greatly enrich it;
the river of God is full of water;
   you provide their grain,
   for so you have prepared it.
¹⁰ You water its furrows abundantly,
   settling its ridges,
softening it with showers,
   and blessing its growth.
¹¹ You crown the year with your bounty;
   your wagon tracks overflow with abundance.
¹² The pastures of the wilderness overflow,
   the hills gird themselves with joy,
¹³ the meadows clothe themselves with flocks,
   the valleys deck themselves with grain,
   they shout and sing together for joy.

a Or Praise waits for you in silence   b Or and make it overflow

---

OVERVIEW: In meditating on David's words of praise and exaltation, the reformers seek to engender similar affections in their audiences. Our commenters find analogies in the Lord's care for his people in their time, recognizing the overwhelming value of his majesty, provision and power. As Calvin and Selnecker warn, however, the unspoken message of this psalm is that believers must be careful to recognize continually the guiding hand of the Lord in their lives. His abundant provision does not excuse human complacency; it also reveals the limits of human wisdom.

PRAISE FOR GOD'S ABUNDANT BENEFITS.
THEODORE BEZA: This psalm or hymn written to the praise of God, first, teaches that his benefits are never rightly acknowledged and praised anywhere except in his holy congregations. Second, it commands us to admire three very important things and to give thanks to God for them. The first, and by far the greatest, is that God gathers a church to himself in which he wants to be glorified, where he answers prayers, where he pardons sins—indeed, he never ceases to heap all kinds of blessings on the church and to guard it most powerfully. The second thing is that he sustains hu-

man society by establishing and maintaining governments in the midst of such great tumults. The third thing is that from heaven he so abundantly and generously supplies everything necessary for this life. Paraphrase of Psalm 65.[1]

Superscription: *A Variant in the Septuagint*

A Song from the Prophets or David?
Nikolaus Selnecker: The Greek text has a different title. It says that this psalm was a song of the prophets Jeremiah, Haggai[2] and Ezekiel, who sung it about the Babylonian captivity when everything was still and sorrowful. And it could indeed be the case that the holy people who lived at that time, like Jeremiah, Zephaniah, Ezekiel, Daniel and others composed this psalm about David and used it to remember their manifold sins and the innumerable mighty deeds of God. But not much depends on this. We will keep the normal and correct title, that it is a psalm of David, which he gave to his singers to sing and in this way to praise God for good and peaceful times. The Whole Psalter.[3]

65:1-4 We Orient Ourselves to You

Silence Is a Christian Trait.
Martin Luther: David adds this phrase "in silence." For this too pertains to being a Christian. When Christians pray and praise God, they should be able to be patient for a little while and to suffer, not cursing, grumbling or loathing God because things do not happen as quickly or go the way they want. Instead, it is as Psalm 4 says: "Be angry, do not sin, speak with your heart on your bed and be silent or remain still." . . . So, we learn to praise and thank

God, even if he is not there immediately whenever we would like him to be; instead we are patient and wait on him. . . . For this is still a small thing, that we praise and thank God, because he gives us what we want and lets things happen how we want. However, to praise and thank God rightly must happen in this way, that we keep quiet and remain firm and wait patiently on his help. He is such a God who will not be told the person, place and time, the what, when or how he will give, so that we learn to acknowledge and affirm correctly that he knows better how he should do what will be useful and beneficial for us than we ourselves! Sermon in Dessau Before the Prince of Anhalt (June 5, 1534).[4]

"Silence" Interpreted Metaphorically.
Sebastian Münster: "Praise awaits you." The text has a Hebraism: "to you silence is praise." Nevertheless *dumîyâ* ["silence"] is expounded by the Hebrews as *tôḥelet* ["expectation"], as we translated it. For it frequently happens in this book that "to be silent" is understood as "to await." The Temple of the Lord: Psalm 65.[5]

Affirmative Theology.
Martin Luther: In accordance with the ecstatic and negative theology, by means of which God is praised in a way beyond expression and by being silent because of the amazement and wonder induced by his majesty, so that now the worshiper feels that not only every word is less than his praise but also that every thought is inferior to his praise.[6] This is the true *kabbalah*, which is extremely rare. For as the affirmative way concerning God is imperfect, both

---

[1]Beza, *Psalmorum Davidis*, 289 (cf. *Psalmes of Dauid*, 140). That this psalm depicts and praises the ecclesial, political and agricultural estates was a common locus for the reformers; Luther and his adherents also explore it at length. For example, see further WA 37:425-28; Selnecker, *Der gantze Psalter*, 2:86r.
[2]The LXX title mentions only Jeremiah and Ezekiel.
[3]Selnecker, *Der gantze Psalter*, 2:69r.

[4]WA 37:428; citing Ps 4:5; Is 30:15.
[5]Münster, *Miqdaš YHWH*, 1211. Most of our commentators translated Ps 65:1 literally as "To silence is praise," though they acknowledged it could be interpreted metaphorically as "To you praise is due." Among English translations only the NASB and CEB use the former rendering. See further Alter, *Book of Psalms*, 221; Goldingay, *Psalms*, 2:272 n. 1; Kraus, *Psalms 60–150*, 27.
[6]Cataphatic theology affirms that positive statements may be made about God. Apophatic theology—more common in the Eastern traditions—insists that God is ineffable and cannot be described through human words. He can therefore only be represented negatively, that is, by understanding what he is not.

in understanding and in speaking, so the negative way is altogether perfect.... Nevertheless, I do not think that the letter of this psalm is speaking about this anagogy. Therefore our theologians are too rash when they argue and make assertions so boldly about matters divine. For, as I have said, the affirmative theology is like milk to wine in relation to the negative theology. This cannot be treated in a disputation and with much speaking, but must be done in the supreme repose of the mind and in silence, as in a rapture and ecstasy. This is what makes a true theologian. But no university crowns anyone like this, only the Holy Spirit. And whoever has seen this sees how all affirmative theology knows nothing. But this matter perhaps experiences more things than modesty. FIRST PSALMS LECTURES (1513–1515).[7]

GOODNESS TO THE CHURCH. JOHN CALVIN: God's goodness to his people is such as to afford constantly new matter of praise. It is diffused over the whole world but specially shown to the church. Besides, others who do not belong to the church of God, however abundantly benefits may be showered on them, see not where they come from, absorbing and consuming whatever God bestows on them in silence. COMMENTARY ON THE PSALMS.[8]

THE CALL OF THE NATIONS. MOÏSE AMYRAUT: According to my hypothesis, this verse should be understood as pointing to the call of the nations. ANNOTATIONS ON PSALM 65:2.[9]

THIS WAS THE PRAYER OF ALL THE SAINTS. NIKOLAUS SELNECKER: Here we see how the pious patriarchs and prophets and all the saints before the advent and incarnation of the Lord Christ prayed and with what they comforted themselves. "All flesh, namely, Jews and Gentiles from every nation and all sorts of people will come to you, and you will accept them all on account of your Son who will become human, and you will be merciful to them without any consideration of the person; you will answer their prayers and save them." THE WHOLE PSALTER.[10]

CITIZENRY OF THE WORD. VIKTORIN STRIGEL: He gives thanks to God for the ministry of the Word, by which the eternal church is gathered to God. For he calls the temple of God that society in which the word of the gospel resounds and where God is rightly called on. To be a citizen of this society is the highest and greatest thing on earth. Because God communicates himself to us by his Word, he consoles us and guides us by the Holy Spirit, lest, broken by temptations and difficulties, we lose hope. As in the time of David, God was living in a tabernacle, and afterwards in the temple of Solomon, so now God dwells in the entire earth, wherever the story of Christ's grace is spread. O magnificent goodness of God, who chose not only the Jews but also the Gentiles for eternal salvation, and called them to the fellowship of the true church! By thinking about the antithesis we can logically draw this conclusion: Whom he chose, he also called. Therefore, all who are not called are not elect. For this is certain, that the elect should not be sought anywhere outside the society of those who have been called, that is, of those who keep to the fundamentals and do not obstinately stand up for idols. And what are the benefits and blessings of the home and temple of God? God gave to his church the utmost blessings, his own Son Christ, faith that overcomes all dangers, true good works, the Holy Spirit, an understanding of Scripture, peace of conscience and other countless things. *HYPONĒMATA* IN ALL THE PSALMS.[11]

65:5-13 God's Care for Nature

AN AWESOME SERMON FOR ALL. NIKOLAUS SELNECKER: Here David asks that God would mercifully sustain us in the true teaching about our righteousness—how we are made righteous and

---

[7]LW 10:313* (WA 3:372).
[8]CTS 9:451-52* (CO 31:603).
[9]Amyraut, *Paraphrasis in Psalmos Davidis*, 263.
[10]Selnecker, *Der gantze Psalter*, 2:70r-v.
[11]Strigel, *Hyponēmata*, 289.

holy before God through faith in the Son of God. And he calls it an awesome righteousness, which Paul expounds in 1 Corinthians 1 and calls it a foolish sermon before the world, to the Jews a stumbling block and to the Greeks foolishness. For it is indeed awesome to hear, to speak and to believe that a poor sinner should be made righteous and eternally holy through faith in the Son of God without any merit and worthiness of his own. Thus, the whole doctrine of the gospel with all its articles and parts is an awesome sermon and at the same time terrifying to the unbelieving and the unrepentant. Thus the word stands here, awesome and terrifying. For it is indeed terrifying: whoever does not believe in the Son of God remains in God's wrath. But for believers there is nothing more blessed, comforting and pleasant than when they hear "whoever believes in the Son has eternal life." God is our salvation, he is our Jesus and our Savior, as it stands here: "God is our Jesus,"[12] a hope and confidence for all people in the entire world, Jews and Gentiles. If they believe in him, not one will be shut out regardless of who they are! For we must uphold this word *all*: "A confidence for *all*," as Christ also says, "Come to me *all*." THE WHOLE PSALTER.[13]

ONE GOD TO THE ENDS OF THE EARTH. JOHN DONNE: Here is a new mathematics; without change of elevation or parallax, I who live in this place and stand under this meridian, look up and fix myself on God, and those who are under my feet look up above themselves, and as different and distant as our locations are, we all fix at once on one God and meet in one center. But we do not do so on the sun or on one constellation or configuration in the heavens; when we see it, those Antipodes do not; but they and we see God at once. While various forms of religion lead us in different ways, by the very light and power of nature we meet in one God; and for so as much as may make God accessible to us and make us inexcusable toward him, there is light enough in this dawning of the day, reflection enough in this first meal, the knowledge of God, which we have in nature, that alone discharges God and condemns us; for, by that "He is," that is, he offers himself to be "the confidence of all the ends of the earth, and of them who are afar on the sea"; that is, of all humankind. SERMON 68: PREBEND SERMONS.[14]

PHILOSOPHY'S PURPOSE THWARTED BY OUR PRIDE. JOHN CALVIN: It would seem as if the more perspicacity human beings have in observing second causes in nature, they will rest in them the more determinedly instead of ascending by them to God. Philosophy ought to lead us upward to him, the more that it penetrates into the hidden things of God. However, this is prevented by the corruption and ingratitude of our hearts; and as those who pride themselves in their slyness avert their eye from God to find the origin of rain in the air and the elements, it was the more necessary to awaken us out of such a spirit. COMMENTARY ON THE PSALMS.[15]

THE LORD'S ABUNDANT MERCY. MARTIN LUTHER: "You visit the earth," that is, You mercifully give rain. If the Lord God grants a rain shower, it is his mercy, not our merit. We are knaves! You give plenty of grain, barley, eggs, chickens, strawberries, cherries, plums—this verse has an enormous manifest of goods in it! SERMON IN PRETZSCH (JULY 15, 1532).[16]

THE LORD'S UNSPEAKABLE BLESSING. TILEMANN HESSHUS: David gives thanks for this blessing from God: seasonable rain, fertile earth, the fruitfulness of the fields and an abundance of crops. It is no less a miracle that God in a single year brings forth such an abundance of crops from the earth, by which he nourishes the entire human

---

[12]Selnecker, recognizing Jesus' Hebrew name, translates *yišʿēnû* somewhat awkwardly here as "our Jesus," in order to emphasize the continuity of the Testaments and that salvation is through Christ alone.

[13]Selnecker, *Der gantze Psalter*, 2:71v-72r; citing 1 Cor 1:22-25.

[14]Donne, *Works*, 3:205-6*.

[15]CTS 9:463* (CO 31:609).

[16]WA 36:218.

race, than that he gave manna from heaven and fed people with spiritual food. If for one year rain did not fall on earth, no crops would grow—how great the misery in the world would be! Consequently, it is a dreadful crime that the world does not give thanks to God for such a remarkable blessing.

Clearly the benefits with which God manages and adorns this corporeal life are innumerable! Consequently David here briefly details the numerous benefits of God. "You crown the year with your bounty." That is, as a girl weaves together a garland from numerous flowers of different colors and fragrances, so also God fills the entire year with various different benefits. Or like how a wealthy patriarch, rich with an abundance of all sorts of things, constantly serves new and fresh platters of food. There are so many different kinds of grains, beans, wines, fruits, so many various types of animals, wild beasts, birds, fish, herbs and vegetables and harvests, that if you were to assign a certain type of good to each hour in a year, you are going to discover far more benefits of God than there are hours in a year. Consequently God crowns the year with his bounty, then repeats these universal benefits, so that there is an abundance of crops and animals! "Your footsteps are drenched with abundance." That is, wherever God is seen to be present, there his blessing produces an abundance of all things. Whether he walks in the desert or in the mountains or in the plains or in the valleys, blessing and great fruitfulness of the fields are left behind him. "The plains and valleys will rejoice!" That is, not only does God bless the earth, but also the valleys echo with the rejoicing and singing of human beings celebrating God's goodness. COMMENTARY ON PSALM 65.[17]

THE FIRST MUST BE LAST. NIKOLAUS SELNECKER: From this we should learn what our office and calling is, so that we would diligently perform it. For as they say, "The master's eye fattens the horse." That is, the lord of the house must be the servant himself, if he wants to find his house in order. The prince must be the councilor himself, if he does not want to come too late, when everything is already ruined. The manure which the landlord carries on his feet to the field fertilizes well. Sloth, laziness and negligence bring many a house into great suffering; indeed, a province and its people often perish because of it. THE WHOLE PSALTER.[18]

---

[17]Hesshus, *Commentarius in Psalmos*, 257r.
[18]Selnecker, *Der gantze Psalter*, 2:73v.

66:1-20 HOW AWESOME ARE THE LORD AND HIS DEEDS

To the choirmaster. A Song. A Psalm.

¹ Shout for joy to God, all the earth;
  ² sing the glory of his name;
  give to him glorious praise!
³ Say to God, "How awesome are your deeds!
  So great is your power that your enemies
    come cringing to you.
⁴ All the earth worships you
  and sings praises to you;
  they sing praises to your name."   Selah

⁵ Come and see what God has done:
  he is awesome in his deeds toward the
    children of man.
⁶ He turned the sea into dry land;
  they passed through the river on foot.
There did we rejoice in him,
  ⁷ who rules by his might forever,
whose eyes keep watch on the nations—
  let not the rebellious exalt themselves.   Selah

⁸ Bless our God, O peoples;
  let the sound of his praise be heard,
⁹ who has kept our soul among the living
  and has not let our feet slip.
¹⁰ For you, O God, have tested us;
  you have tried us as silver is tried.
¹¹ You brought us into the net;

you laid a crushing burden on our backs;
¹² you let men ride over our heads;
  we went through fire and through water;
yet you have brought us out to a place of
    abundance.

¹³ I will come into your house with burnt
    offerings;
  I will perform my vows to you,
¹⁴ that which my lips uttered
  and my mouth promised when I was in
    trouble.
¹⁵ I will offer to you burnt offerings of fattened
    animals,
  with the smoke of the sacrifice of rams;
I will make an offering of bulls and goats.   Selah

¹⁶ Come and hear, all you who fear God,
  and I will tell what he has done for my soul.
¹⁷ I cried to him with my mouth,
  and high praise was on[a] my tongue.[b]
¹⁸ If I had cherished iniquity in my heart,
  the Lord would not have listened.
¹⁹ But truly God has listened;
  he has attended to the voice of my prayer.

²⁰ Blessed be God,
  because he has not rejected my prayer
  or removed his steadfast love from me!

a Hebrew under   b Or and he was exalted with my tongue

OVERVIEW: Reflecting on God's historic acts of deliverance in this psalm, David exhorts the people of God to praise and worship the Lord. Our commentators urge a similar response from the church, calling on them to gather, worship and bear witness as the beneficiaries of God's mighty deeds. While David teaches a response aligned with the sacrificial system, the reformers recognize this institution as a shadow of true worship. Some identify the different sacrificial animals as types for distinct ministries in the church, while others remind us that all sacrifices figuratively anticipated the coming Messiah, who would alleviate the external demands of the law and make the spiritual sacrifices of the people of God sweet and acceptable.

KNOW THE LORD ACCORDING TO HIS WORD AND DEEDS. NIKOLAUS SELNECKER: This is a psalm of thanksgiving and exhortation to all people, that from his Word and great miracles and mighty deeds they should learn to acknowledge, honor and praise God as an almighty and merciful God. He is willing and able to save his people or the church of his Son—which he gathers to himself through the holy gospel and sanctifies through his Holy Spirit—from every distress, as he did in the Red Sea, and he continues to sustain and protect his people against all devils, the world, tyrants and evil spirits. And even until the end of the world he will continue to sustain and save them. He is always by them, presently. Yes, he dwells in them and governs them and protects them from all evil. THE WHOLE PSALTER.[1]

FOR THE CHURCH'S MEMORY. THEODORE BEZA: This psalm (as well as several others) seems to be written for the perpetual use of the church—even if their occasion was somewhat private—partly to renew the memory of so many past deliverances and partly to give thanks to God as often as the opportunity is presented, either privately or publicly. PARAPHRASE OF PSALM 66.[2]

66:1-7 Bless the Lord for Our Deliverance Through the Red Sea

PRAISE HIM, ALL YOU NATIONS! KONRAD PELLIKAN: David could desire nothing more holy for his faith than both what he hoped for and what he had received in the promises about his seed, the King of kings, who would reign over every nation for the greatest glory of God. This we now see abundantly fulfilled, that Christ the Lord, the Son of David, the leaders of every nation recognized as the eternal King and Head of all God's children. And so he repeatedly scurries to prayer with this, his very holy desire: to magnify the glory of God throughout the entire world. Thus he begins here with thanksgiving, not only that being offered by Judah but by the whole earth, by the church of believers scattered

across the globe. All the elect he exhorts to sing psalms gloriously about the divine Majesty, to hallow God's name with their mouths, hearts and voices. COMMENTARY ON PSALM 66:1.[3]

PROCLAIM HIS DEEDS! JOHN DONNE: Our duty itself is first *dicite*, "say." It is more than *cogitate*, to consider God's former goodness; more than *admirari*, to admire God's former goodness. Speculations and ecstasies are not sufficient services of God. *Dicite*, "Say to God!" To declare, manifest, publish your zeal is more than *cogitate*, consider it, think of it; but it is less than *facite*, to come to action. We must declare our thankful zeal to God's cause; we must not modify, nor disguise that. But for the particular ways of promoting and advancing that cause in matter of action, we must refer that to those to whom God has referred it. The duty is a commemoration of benefits.

Dicite. Speak of it, ascribe it, attribute it to the right author. Who is that? That is the next consideration, *Dicite Deo*, "Say to God." *Non vobis*, not to your own wisdom or power, *non sanctis*, not to the care and protection of saints or angels, *sed nomine eius da gloriam*, only to his name be all the glory ascribed. And then what falls within this commandment, this consideration is *opera eius*, the works of God. "How terrible you are in your works!" It is not *decreta eius, arcana eius*, the secrets of his state, the ways of his government, unrevealed decrees, but those things in which he has manifested himself to human beings: *opera*, his works. Consider his works and consider them as this commandment enjoins, that is, "How terrible God is in them!" Determine not your consideration on the work itself, for so you may think too lightly of it, that it is but some natural accident or some imposture and false miracle or illusion, or you may think of it with an amazement, with a stupidity, with a consternation, when you consider not from whom the work comes, consider God in the work. And consider that, though he be terrible in that work, yet, he is so terrible but so as the word of

[1]Selnecker, *Der gantze Psalter*, 2:74r.
[2]Beza, *Psalmes of Dauid*, 142* (*Psalmorum Davidis*, 293-94).

[3]Pellikan, *Commentaria Bibliorum*, 4:111r.

this text expresses this terribleness. The word is *nôrā³* and *nôrā³* is but *reverendus*. It is a terror of reverence, not a terror of confusion, that the consideration of God in his works should possess us with. Sermon 69: Prebend Sermons.[4]

Come and See! Wolfgang Musculus: Here the word *coming* has the force of "assembling." It indicates that the people should assemble to meditate on God's works. Indeed, they do not assemble in one place—that is neither useful nor possible—but instead they are unanimous in faith and piety with the people of God. "Come," he says, "and see the works of God!" He does not simply say, "Go and see the works of God," but "Come," that is, "Unite yourselves with the people of God and with us proclaim what the Lord has done for his people." And if he only speaks to Israelites, he uses the word *coming* for assembling and gathering the church of God for this purpose: to meditate on the works of God. And for what other purpose have ecclesiastical assemblies been established than to meditate on the works of God, by which faith and knowledge of God is nourished and matured? Indeed in those assemblies, the works of God are placed before the eyes of the mind for contemplation, so long as they are remembered, preached and glorified along with believers' rejoicing. And that is what he says: "See the works of God." Commentary on Psalm 66.[5]

Focus on God in the Scriptures, Not Yourself. John Donne: It is then his works on which we fix this commemoration, and this glorifying of God. But so that you focus not on the work itself but on God in the work, you must go as far as you can and not stop in yourselves or any other, until you come to God himself. If you consider the Scriptures to be his works, do not make Scriptures of your own; yet this is what you do, if you make them subject to your private interpretation. My soul speaks in my tongue, else I could make no sound; my tongue speaks in English,

else I should not be understood by the congregation. So God speaks by his Son, in the gospel; but then, the gospel speaks in the church, that everyone may hear. . . . And so, for a matter of action and protection, do not come home to yourselves, do not stay in yourselves, nor in a confidence of your own power and wisdom, but go forth into Egypt, go forth into Babylon, and look who delivered your predecessors (predecessors in affliction, predecessors in mercy), and know that God shall do the same things, which he did yesterday, today and forever. Sermon 69: Prebend Sermons.[6]

Pursue Christ In the Midst of Worldly Afflictions. Martin Luther: The Lord bestows on the saints so much grace that, triumphing even over all persecutors with an unimpaired faith in Christ and with an uninjured spirit, they may pass on into heaven. . . . For although according to the flesh they suffer and are hindered, yet according to the spirit they pass over freely and without any hindrance. Yes, that is marvelous: the waters on the right and on the left are like walls to them, because the adversities as well as the prosperities of the world move those who are strong in faith forward the more they are threatened by them. And so the way to heaven opens up to their souls through the midst of the whole world, through adversity and prosperity, through contempt and honor, through evil report and good report, as the apostle beautifully depicts this cross. Or both serve them as walls, for the saints immovably despise both. And so for the saints God turns the whole world and everything in it into a wasteland, in such a way that not a trace of desire for the world remains in them. Consequently, whoever wants to understand that story and all the others . . . let him think about the bodies of the children of Israel who crossed the Red Sea as if they were souls, and their steps as if they were thoughts, and their works in the midst of the sea, that is, in the world or their own flesh. This is truly the sea tropologically, as Psalm 114 says, "The sea saw and fled." That is, the world and the flesh withdrew from the faith of the

---

[4]Donne, *Works*, 3:227-28*.

[5]Musculus, *In Psalterium Commentarii*, 675.

[6]Donne, *Works*, 3:237*.

soul and the strength of the spiritual people. And all this because Moses struck the sea with a rod, that is, Christ instructed and chastised the world with the gospel. FIRST PSALMS LECTURES (1513–1515).[7]

GOD IS ALWAYS THE ULTIMATE AGENT. CARDINAL CAJETAN: When God governs the world through secondary causes without miraculous intervention, it appears that God does not interfere in the world but leaves people to control things as they can; but when God through the agency of miracles destroys or changes kingdoms, then it appears that he himself governs the world or that generation in which he does these things. And because at that time God destroyed those nations and gave their land to the people of Israel through the use of many miracles, which the prophet here alludes to in his mention of the Red Sea and the Jordan, therefore God is described as governing the world in his strength. And so that you may understand more clearly that they are going to be driven out, he says, "His eyes will keep watch on the nations; let not the rebellious exalt themselves." He calls those nations rebels, because "according to the truth" they continuously engaged in so many sins that they were truly rebellious against God, and idol worshipers. This agrees with what Genesis 15 says: "The iniquity of the Amorites is not yet complete." They were not exalted; in the end they are expelled, because they seek nothing but their own benefit. COMMENTARY ON PSALM 66.[8]

66:8-15 Bless the Lord by Your Vows and Sacrifices

THE REFINER'S FIRE. JOHN CALVIN: When visited with affliction, it is of great importance that we should consider it as coming from God and as expressly intended for our good. It is in reference to this that the psalmist speaks of their having been proved and tried. At the same time, while he considers God's trying his children in order to

purge away their sin, as dross is expelled from the silver by fire, he would intimate, also, that trial had been made of their patience. The figure implies that their testing had been severe; for silver is cast repeatedly into the furnace. They express themselves thankful to God, that, while proved with affliction, they had not been destroyed by it; but that their affliction was both varied and very severe appears not only from the metaphor but also from the whole context, where they speak of having been cast into the net, being reduced to straits, people riding over their heads and of being brought through shipwreck and conflagration. COMMENTARY ON THE PSALMS.[9]

MYSTICAL INTERPRETATION OF THE CEREMONIAL VICTIMS. MARTIN LUTHER: Burnt offerings and sacrifices are taken in a mystical sense, first, for the body itself, slaughtered and crucified through the Word of God and kindled by the fire of divine love and thus offered to God through true thanksgiving. For thus it results in the glory of God when it is all done for his sake. Romans 12, "Present your bodies." And thus all the sacrifices can be the same work or the whole body, as the *Rosegarden* says.[10] Thus the bulls are the bodies kept busy with work in the offices of the church, namely, by preaching, reproving, admonishing and thus threshing sinners. The rams are the bodies of those who are over others in administering the sacraments and grace and in praying, such as are the pastors of the churches. Therefore, he says here "with burnt offering of rams." The goats are the bodies of the saints in perpetual penitence imposed for sins. Thus there are here the three estates of the church, namely, the prelates who are the rams; the contemplative and the preachers who are the bulls; and the activists who are the goats. Therefore the

---

[7]LW 10:318* (WA 3:378-79); citing 2 Cor 6:8; Ps 114:3.
[8]Cajetan, *In Sacrae Scripturae Expositionem*, 3:226; citing Rom 2:2; Gen 15:16.

[9]CTS 9:472* (CO 31:613).
[10]Jan Mombaer, *Rosetum exercitiorum spiritualium et sacrarum meditationum* (Basel: Jakob Wolff, 1504), 155v. Born in Brussels, Jan Mombaer (1460–1501) was a prominent and widely respected monastic reformer in the low countries and France. Luther, Lefèvre and Ignatius of Loyola (1491–1556) commended Mombaer's influential devotional *Rosetum* (1494).

distinctive burnt offering of the prelates and officials is to perform and offer Masses....

Now the same work can be a burnt offering, a sacrifice or a victim, depending on the differing intention with which it is done.... But all of these are "of fatlings" when they are done from the innermost marrow of the heart and not only openly, as in the case of hypocrites and those who offer them with a lazy heart. Hence it is perfectly clear that the psalmist is here speaking about mystical things. For nowhere in the law are marrowy sacrifices mentioned.

The reason for them all: as the preacher by virtue of the act of preaching is called a "bull," which has two horns on its head, that is, he has and tills and threshes two Testaments in the soul, so also his words in a similar manner till and thresh and have two Testaments in bringing proof and so crush vices and sins. So also his works. Thus in Isaiah 5 and Micah 4 it is said of the church: "I will make your horn iron and your hooves I will make brass." Is not the church a remarkable bull which has an iron horn and brass hooves, that is, the invincible and victorious Word of preaching? FIRST PSALMS LECTURES (1513–1515).[11]

CHRIST MAKES OUR SACRIFICES WORTHY. JOHN CALVIN: The reason why God ordered victims to be offered as an expression of thanksgiving was, as is well known, to teach the people that their praises were polluted by sin and needed to be sanctified from without. However we might propose to ourselves to praise the name of God, we could only profane it with our impure lips, had not Christ once offered himself up as a sacrifice, to sanctify both us and our services. It is through him, as we learn from the apostle, that our praises are accepted. The psalmist, by way of commendation of his burnt offering, speaks of its incense or sweet savor. Although in themselves vile and loathsome, yet the rams and other victims, so far as they were figures of Christ, sent up a sweet savor to God.

Now that the shadows of the law have been abolished, attention is called to the true spiritual service. What this consists in is more clearly brought under our notice in the following verse, where the psalmist tells us that he would spread abroad the fame of the benefits which he had received from God. Such was the end designed, even in the outward ceremonies under the law, apart from which they could only be considered as an empty show. It was this—the fact that they set forth the praises of the divine goodness—which formed the very reason of the sacrifices, preserving them from insipidity.

In calling, as he does, on all the fearers of the Lord, the psalmist teaches us that if we duly feel the goodness of God, we will be inflamed with a desire to publish it abroad, that others may have their faith and hope confirmed, by what they hear of it, as well as join with us in a united song of praise. He addresses himself to none but such as feared the Lord, for they only could appreciate what he had to say, and it would have been lost labor to communicate it to the hypocritical and ungodly. COMMENTARY ON THE PSALMS.[12]

66:16-20 Tell Everyone What God Has Done

PRAY WITH AN UPRIGHT HEART. JOHN CALVIN: The psalmist next lays down the rule which must be attended to if we would pray properly and acceptably, guarding against that presumptuous exercise which overlooks the necessity of faith and penitence. We see with what audacity hypocrites and ungodly people associate themselves with the Lord's people, in compliance with the general calls of the Word to engage in prayer. To check this solemn mockery, the psalmist mentions integrity of heart as indispensable. I am aware that the words may be considered as an assertion of his own personal uprightness of conduct, as we find him frequently vindicating this by an appeal to the visible and practical proofs which God had shown of his favor to him. But his main object is evidently to enforce by the example of

---

[11]LW 10:320-21* (WA 3:380-81); citing Rom 12:1; Is 5:28; Mic 4:13.

[12]CTS 9:475-76* (CO 31:615); citing Heb 10:7.

his own exercise the common propriety of drawing near to God with a pure heart. COMMENTARY ON THE PSALMS.[13]

THEOLOGIANS MUST LEARN TO SPEAK GOD'S NAME IN REVERENT FEAR AT ALL TIMES. MARTIN LUTHER: It is as if he were to say, "You who fear the Lord understand well enough how much he would do for my soul in this matter, because I have cried to him and have extolled him with my tongue. For it is such a thing that others cannot understand it." We theologians commonly mention the holy name of God so irreverently, especially in our arguing and even in our praying, because we do not know how to extol with our tongue. And we argue so boldly about the Trinity of persons, even though their three names are exceedingly formidable and should never be uttered without a trembling of the heart. We argue about the formal and real distinction the way a cobbler argues about his leather. I believe that we would be better instructed by God inwardly if we would take these so holy names into our mouth with humility and reverence than when we move ahead foolhardily through our subtleties. For thus the saints, when they have taken God's name into their mouth, are inwardly so stunned by the majesty of him whom they have mentioned openly that they repent, as it were, for having taken his name into their mouth. This is what it means properly to extol with the tongue. . . .

But because we have learned from Aristotle to argue about things verbosely and boldly, we think that the same verbosity and boldness should be transferred to divine matters. It is for this reason that I have a hatred for those bold opinions of the Thomists, Scotists and others, for they so handle without fear the sacred name of God and extol it above the tongue but put it down under the tongue, that name with which we were signed, before which heaven and earth and hell tremble. FIRST PSALMS LECTURES (1513–1515).[14]

THE JEWS' CONTINUED REVERENCE FOR GOD'S NAME. MARTIN LUTHER: According to the old law the name of the Lord, the Tetragrammaton, was only pronounced in the temple. And so it continues even today that whenever the Jews speak about God, they speak in this way: "Thus says the Blessed Holy One." On account of this custom Caiaphas also says in the Gospel: "Are you the Christ, the Son of God, the Blessed?" GLOSSA ON PSALM 66 (1513–1515).[15]

SEEK GOD THROUGH PRAYER IN A HUMBLE AND INNOCENT CONSCIENCE. TILEMANN HESSHUS: He powerfully infuses here an essential doctrine. For by his example he displayed consolation to all who are in afflictions and miseries. He also taught in what way it is possible to obtain deliverance from God. But now he adds this essential doctrine: prayers to God must be poured out from a pure and unstained conscience. For God does not listen to sinners, and the speech of the impious is sin before God. If anyone therefore feels that his conscience is panged with some wicked deed, he should earnestly repent and seek pardon for his transgressions first, before he seeks either deliverance from dangers or assistance in toil or defense against enemies. For unless he has been reconciled to God, his prayers will not be heard. If anyone is not conscious of some wicked deed in himself, nevertheless he should acknowledge his weakness and beg for the remission of his sins through the Mediator. Then he should diligently beware lest he brave some forbidden help. He should not flee to the dark arts. He should not deviate from the truth. He should not unite himself with the impious. He should not mimic the deceits and crimes of the impious. Instead, he should walk in simplicity and uprightness, and wait on God's help and deliverance. COMMENTARY ON PSALM 66.[16]

---

[13]CTS 9:477* (CO 31:616).
[14]LW 10:322-23* (WA 3:382).

[15]WA 3:377-78; citing Mk 14:61. See overview for Ps 6, pp. 51-52; cf. also Beza's comment on p. 124.
[16]Hesshus, *Commentarius in Psalmos*, 259v.

67:1-7 LIFT THE VEIL AND REVEAL YOURSELF TO ALL PEOPLE

To the choirmaster: with stringed instruments. A Psalm. A Song.

¹ *May God be gracious to us and bless us*
and make his face to shine upon us,   Selah
² *that your way may be known on earth,*
your saving power among all nations.
³ *Let the peoples praise you, O God;*
let all the peoples praise you!

⁴ *Let the nations be glad and sing for joy,*
for you judge the peoples with equity
and guide the nations upon earth.   Selah
⁵ *Let the peoples praise you, O God;*
let all the peoples praise you!

⁶ *The earth has yielded its increase;*
God, our God, shall bless us.
⁷ *God shall bless us;*
let all the ends of the earth fear him!

OVERVIEW: The reformers recognize the historical context of this psalm: Israel, the blessed people of God, pray for the establishment of God's kingdom. Their exegesis, however, does not dwell on Jewish expectation. Instead, our commentators emphasize the final establishment of the kingdom that will be brought about through Christ. Their interpretation therefore takes on a New Testament key and calls on the church to respond to the Lord's abundant blessings in praise and thanksgiving while taking comfort in God's sovereign rule. Furthermore, in their exegesis they especially highlight the universalizing terminology of the psalm—the language concerning all people, places and nations refers to the extension of God's blessing, and thus his kingdom, to the Gentiles.

KINGDOM CARE FOR ALL. RUDOLF GWALTHER: This is an earnest prayer of the people of Israel, that God would awake his kingdom among them and that he would expand it through the entire world, among all nations. Notice also here what great benefit follows from this: we learn what we should most of all desire from God and that we too should be concerned for all other human beings. THE PSALTER.[1]

LONGING FOR CHRIST AND HIS KINGDOM. NIKOLAUS SELNECKER: This is a prophecy about Christ and his kingdom, that through the preaching of the gospel he will reign among all people and Gentiles, kingdoms and principalities of the whole earth, for the comfort, righteousness and salvation of all who will embrace such doctrine with faith. In this kingdom such worship will take place. The Gentiles will sing, rejoice, praise and glorify the grace and mighty deeds of God which he manifested to them through his Son, spiritually and bodily, and will thank God for it. They will fear him and serve him in all places of the world, so that worship would no longer be found only in Jerusalem, with circumcision and the sacrifices, but also in Gentile nations among everyone with thanksgiving, cheerfulness and the praise of God. In sum, this psalm is a wish and prayer for the promised Messiah to come in the flesh and for the blessed doctrine of the holy gospel to be sent out into all the world. THE WHOLE PSALTER.[2]

67:1-7 O Joyful Light!

HONOR GOD WITH HIS WORDS. THE ENGLISH ANNOTATIONS: All these forms and expressions are taken from that solemn form of blessing which was

---

[1]Gwalther, *Der Psalter*, 115v.

[2]Selnecker, *Der gantze Psalter*, 2:75v.

prescribed by God himself. The form being of God's own devising, holy people did not think that they could please God better than by using his own words, so far as they were agreeable to their occasions, as it was intended only as a form of blessing. As for prayer, we have great reason to think that the Lord's Prayer is the most acceptable prayer to God that we can use, although we may use others as our needs require. Yet to think better of any other prayers of our own devising, or to be so in love with our own forms, whether set or sudden, that we omit the forms of the Lord in our devotions, whether public or private, cannot be less than blasphemy or sacrilege in a high degree. . . . To return to the form prescribed in Numbers, it intends to teach us that the happiness of humanity consists of being admitted to the presence of God and his beatifical vision, the fruits of which are reaped even in this life. While we see only as through a glass, temporal and spiritual blessings demonstrate what we are to expect when we are admitted to behold him face to face. ANNOTATION ON PSALM 67:1.[3]

THROUGH SCRIPTURE GOD DAWNS OVER OUR LIVES. SEBASTIAN MÜNSTER: Our blindness is horrible, unless we are illuminated by divine rays of light. For what do we learn from human books, if there is no knowledge of sacred things, except darkness? No philosopher is able to show the true origin of the world or the way to eternal salvation! For this reason, those who lack the divine Scriptures live in error, ignorant of God *and* themselves, not knowing who they are and whence they came. THE TEMPLE OF THE LORD: PSALM 67.[4]

THE COVENANT FOR ALL PEOPLE. JOHN CALVIN: Here we have a clear prophecy of that extension of the grace of God by which the Gentiles were united into one body with the posterity of Abraham. The psalmist prays for some conspicuous proof of favor to be shown to his chosen people, which might attract the Gentiles to

seek participation in the same blessed hope. By the "way of God" is meant his covenant, which is the source or spring of salvation, and by which he revealed himself as a father to his ancient people, and afterwards more clearly under the gospel, when the Spirit of adoption was shed abroad in greater abundance. COMMENTARY ON THE PSALMS.[5]

PRAISE AND THANK GOD, OUR FRIEND! NIKOLAUS SELNECKER: This is a thanksgiving for the blessed Word and doctrine of the holy gospel.

> Now let the heathen thank and praise
> The Lord with gladsome voices
> Let all the world for joy upraise
> A song with mighty noises.[6]

For it is worthy of praise on praise that God has accepted us impure, idolatrous, blasphemous Gentiles, us poor, desperate, reprobate people in his grace for the sake of his Son and called us through his Word. Whoever does not want to give thanks here must be a child of the devil. Truly, we must confess that we were enemies of God, but now we are friends and children of God. Therefore we thank you, Lord God, from the depth of our hearts and say with the beloved Jacob: "Lord, I am all too humble compared with these great benefits, which you have shown unto me, a poor cripple." THE WHOLE PSALTER.[7]

TEACHING THE DIVINITY OF CHRIST. DAVID DICKSON: The Spirit who composed the Psalms did not degrade the promised Messiah, Jesus Christ, from his place in the Godhead in his future incarnation. Instead, it speaks of him and to him as God-blessed forever, that is, the true God to the Jewish church before his coming and the true God to the converted Gentiles after coming in the flesh, one with the Father and the Holy Spirit. Six times in this psalm he is called God. He is acknowledged to be the fountain of mercy and blessing to human

---

[3]Downame, ed., *Annotations*, 6H1r*; citing Num 6:24-26; Ps 4:6.
[4]Münster, *Miqdaš YHWH*, 1212-13.

[5]CTS 10:3 (CO 31:618), citing Jn 17:3.
[6]This is the first portion of the second verse from Luther's hymn "May God Bestow on Us His Grace" (1523), which is based on Ps 67; LW 53:232-34 (WA 35:418-19; cf. LSB no. 823).
[7]Selnecker, *Der gantze Psalter*, 2:77r.

beings, the one who manifests reconciliation with human beings, the object of all divine honor and praise, recognized to be God the Lord and understood as the Lawgiver to the converted Gentiles. COMMENTARY ON PSALM 67:4.[8]

SPIRITUAL JURISDICTION. JOHN CALVIN: The reference is not to that government of God which is general in its nature but to that special and spiritual jurisdiction which he exercises over the church. And, properly said, this means that God only governs in the real sense of the word those whom he has gathered under his sway by the doctrine of his law. The word *righteousness* is therefore inserted in commendation of his government. COMMENTARY ON THE PSALMS.[9]

ECSTATIC PRAISE TO THE LORD. MARTIN BUCER: For who does not earnestly praise and glorify that God—the eternal source of all goods— and acknowledge him? This God they know judges, that is, rules and controls all people, and indeed does so with the same equity and indulgence, so that those who trust in him and hand themselves over to be led by him never lack any good.... For this reason indeed there is gladness as well as clapping, concerning which he says, "Let the people glorify you, O Lord, let the whole earth glorify you." He repeats this verse about the burning zeal of glorifying God among all the nations so that he might magnify this happiness that the saints enjoy as the Lord speaks the law and his own Spirit leads them. The more the knowledge of God increases, the more the enjoyment of the same increases, and accordingly the highest delight of the soul, to which no greater desire can be imagined than to praise God everywhere, in which a soul of this sort lives eternally and blessedly. HOLY PSALMS.[10]

NOT MY WORD BUT GOD'S WORD. NIKOLAUS SELNECKER: From this pious teachers should take comfort, so that they might continue in their office

so much the more cheerful, although it might appear as if they achieve very little and as if all their speaking, admonitions and punishments fall to the ground or disappear into the air; they are despised, maligned and hated as it is in our time; and there is nothing more contemptuous than the pulpit itself and the one standing in it. Here we must not be deterred but must be mindful of the Word and the command of God, and think in this way. "God has commanded me to do this; therefore the Word is not mine but it is God's Word that I am supposed to preach and always to promote and convey. He will surely make it prosperous even if I do not see it immediately. And even if I do not perceive any improvement all my life and no one wants to turn to my sermons, I will nevertheless not cease doing it, or become lazy and careless; and I will commend the increase to God the Lord, who says: 'His word will not return to him void.'... When I baptize, I give new fruit to God and bring a fine child to his grace. When I preach, I praise God's name and speak a beautiful word of comfort a poor conscience can embrace or stir someone's heart who lives in coarse sins. When I administer the sacrament of the body and blood of Christ, I put the true body and the true blood of the Lord Christ into the mouth of many pious Christians, so that they will be united to him and elevated with him to eternal glory. When I go to sick persons, I hold before them the word and comfort of Christ and refresh their hearts with God's strength." All this is a superhuman and awesome work that will be a sweet comfort for all faithful teachers, motivating and cheering them that they might fulfill their office. THE WHOLE PSALTER.[11]

THE THREE IN ONE. MARTIN LUTHER: That he triplicates the word *God* reveals the Trinity in the Godhead; that he also says in the singular "May he bless" and "him" reveals the unity in the Godhead. GLOSSA ON PSALM 67 (1513–1515).[12]

[8]Dickson, *Other Fifty Psalms*, 98*; citing Rom 9:5.
[9]CTS 10:4* (CO 31:618).
[10]Bucer, *Sacrorum Psalmorum*, 254r.

[11]Selnecker, *Der gantze Psalter*, 2:78v-79r; citing Is 55:11; 1 Cor 15:58.
[12]WA 3:383.

68:1-35 GOD SCATTERS HIS ENEMIES

To the choirmaster. A Psalm of David. A Song.

¹ God shall arise, his enemies shall be scattered;
  and those who hate him shall flee before
    him!
² As smoke is driven away, so you shall drive
    them away;
  as wax melts before fire,
  so the wicked shall perish before God!
³ But the righteous shall be glad;
  they shall exult before God;
  they shall be jubilant with joy!

⁴ Sing to God, sing praises to his name;
  lift up a song to him who rides through the
    deserts;
his name is the LORD;
  exult before him!
⁵ Father of the fatherless and protector of widows
  is God in his holy habitation.
⁶ God settles the solitary in a home;
  he leads out the prisoners to prosperity,
  but the rebellious dwell in a parched land.

⁷ O God, when you went out before your people,
  when you marched through the wilderness,
                                    Selah
⁸ the earth quaked, the heavens poured down rain,
  before God, the One of Sinai,
  before God, the God of Israel.
⁹ Rain in abundance, O God, you shed abroad;
  you restored your inheritance as it languished;
¹⁰ your flockᵃ found a dwelling in it;
  in your goodness, O God, you provided for
    the needy.

¹¹ The Lord gives the word;
  the women who announce the news are a
    great host:
  ¹² "The kings of the armies—they flee,
    they flee!"
The women at home divide the spoil—
  ¹³ though you men lie among the sheepfolds—

the wings of a dove covered with silver,
  its pinions with shimmering gold.
¹⁴ When the Almighty scatters kings there,
  let snow fall on Zalmon.

¹⁵ O mountain of God, mountain of Bashan;
  O many-peakedᵇ mountain, mountain of
    Bashan!
¹⁶ Why do you look with hatred, O many-
    peaked mountain,
  at the mount that God desired for his abode,
  yes, where the LORD will dwell forever?
¹⁷ The chariots of God are twice ten thousand,
    thousands upon thousands;
  the LORD is among them; Sinai is now in
    the sanctuary.
¹⁸ You ascended on high,
  leading a host of captives in your train
  and receiving gifts among men,
even among the rebellious, that the LORD God
  may dwell there.

¹⁹ Blessed be the Lord,
  who daily bears us up;
  God is our salvation.   Selah
²⁰ Our God is a God of salvation,
  and to GOD, the Lord, belong deliverances
    from death.
²¹ But God will strike the heads of his enemies,
  the hairy crown of him who walks in his
    guilty ways.
²² The Lord said,
  "I will bring them back from Bashan,
I will bring them back from the depths of the
    sea,
²³ that you may strike your feet in their blood,
  that the tongues of your dogs may have their
    portion from the foe."

²⁴ Your procession isᶜ seen, O God,
  the procession of my God, my King, into the
    sanctuary—

²⁵ the singers in front, the musicians last,
   between them virgins playing tambourines:
²⁶ "Bless God in the great congregation,
   the Lord, O you^d who are of Israel's
      fountain!"
²⁷ There is Benjamin, the least of them, in the lead,
   the princes of Judah in their throng,
   the princes of Zebulun, the princes of
      Naphtali.

²⁸ Summon your power, O God,^e
   the power, O God, by which you have
      worked for us.
²⁹ Because of your temple at Jerusalem
   kings shall bear gifts to you.
³⁰ Rebuke the beasts that dwell among the reeds,
   the herd of bulls with the calves of the peoples.
Trample underfoot those who lust after tribute;

scatter the peoples who delight in war.^f
³¹ Nobles shall come from Egypt;
   Cush shall hasten to stretch out her hands to
      God.

³² O kingdoms of the earth, sing to God;
   sing praises to the Lord,   Selah
³³ to him who rides in the heavens, the ancient
      heavens;
   behold, he sends out his voice, his mighty
      voice.
³⁴ Ascribe power to God,
   whose majesty is over Israel,
   and whose power is in the skies.
³⁵ Awesome is God from his^g sanctuary;
   the God of Israel—he is the one who gives
      power and strength to his people.
Blessed be God!

a Or your congregation   b Or hunch-backed; also verse 16   c Or has been   d The Hebrew for you is plural here   e By revocalization (compare Septuagint); Hebrew Your God has summoned your power   f The meaning of the Hebrew verse is uncertain   g Septuagint; Hebrew your

---

Overview: The language, imagery and structure of this psalm—occasioned by David bringing the ark of the covenant to Zion—have posed a variety of difficulties for interpreters. Clearly imbued with the ethos of divine warfare and the celebration of God's victory over Israel's enemies, the complexity of this psalm provides our commentators with a rich field for figurative interpretation. Hesshus sets the scene by unfurling its tapestry of christological figures and tropes, while the discussion of the opening words and the meaning of the ark are also particularly noteworthy. The richest lines of this psalm are found in verse 18, which is quoted in Ephesians 4:8, though with a critical alteration: Whereas the psalm speaks of God in triumph *receiving* gifts, Paul has the ascended Christ *giving* gifts. As Luther points out, this "cardinal verse" in its fulfillment refers to the ascension and Pentecost. Bucer notes that Paul changed *received* to *giving* in order to clearly reveal the meaning: after Christ was received into heaven, gifts were given. Calvin adds that the gifts Christ received from the captives were distributed to those with whom he is united.

THE SCOPE AND SUMMARY OF CHRIST'S KINGDOM. TILEMANN HESSHUS: This psalm is an illustrious and excellent prophecy concerning the eternal and spiritual reign of the Messiah, through whom God demolished the tyranny of sin and death, overturned the power of Satan and assembled his church in the midst of the human race—his church is going to live with God in eternity. In this psalm the Holy Spirit eloquently and powerfully uses all sorts of figures and tropes, so that he might describe this kingdom most elegantly and gently draw the entire world to him with his arms outstretched, ready to embrace them.

The Holy Spirit observes that among the human race nothing is considered more contemptible, nothing is scorned more arrogantly than the spiritual kingdom of Christ. The human race is bewitched by deceptions, which befoul the kingdom of Christ with various blasphemies. For they consider the kingdom to be an impediment to them, on account of which they are less able to enhance and uphold their own dignity and eminence and wealth and honor. Tyrants especially hate the kingdom and persecute it with all their strength. For they think that it is the cause of all tumult and turmoil in politics. Nor for any reason are they able to preserve and protect peace, wherever room is made for the kingdom of Christ. The rabble scorn the kingdom most self-assuredly, because by it they gain no riches, but rather it preaches about being subjected to crossbearing, and it imposes that crossbearing on those who embrace it.

In order to refute therefore these profane and impious people's judgment and to invite the human race to accept this glorious King with his heavenly kingdom and innumerable benefits, the Holy Spirit describes with exceedingly eloquent and elegant words all the circumstances of this spiritual kingdom. He indicates how lofty the person of the Messiah is, who without a doubt is eternal and omnipotent God. He depicts his most ardent and merciful affections toward his subjects. He remembers his vast benefits. He discusses this kingdom's glory along with the glory of the old covenant. He describes the commanders and armies of this kingdom. He compares this kingdom with other empires of the world. He recounts the victory, triumphs and gifts of this kingdom, and he also shows the outcome of the battles: to the citizens of this kingdom he promises liberation and salvation, but to its enemies he proclaims their destruction. He prophesies about the destruction of the synagogue and about the blossoming of the church in the new covenant. He indicates that apostles should perform the ministry of the gospel with great authority and blessed success in these matters and establish everywhere distinguished churches. He threatens the antichrist and heretics with the wrath of God and destruction. He proclaims the greatness of Christ's kingdom, that even kings are going to be slaves to Christ and that the gifts of Christ are going to be carried to every nation and tribe. He also explains that the Messiah is going to pour out the Holy Spirit on his people, and he is going to adorn them with his extraordinary power.

And so, for such immeasurable blessings in Christ's kingdom we should give thanks to God. From this it is sufficiently clear that the whole body of Christian doctrine had been encompassed in this psalm. It mixes together everywhere both ardent prayers and remembrances for thanksgiving, in order to teach how this psalm should be used. COMMENTARY ON PSALM 68.[1]

68:1-6 *God Arises, Bringing Hope*

THE PSALM'S THESIS. JOHN CALVIN: In this verse the psalmist intimates, as it were by way of preface, the subject which he proposed to treat in the psalm and which related to the truth that God, however long he may seem to connive at the audacity and cruelty of the enemies of his church, will eventually arise to avenge it and will prove himself able to protect it by the mere extension of his hand. I agree with other interpreters in thinking that the sentiment is borrowed from Moses (Num 10). There can be little doubt that in dictating the form of prayer there referred to, he had an eye to the instruction and comfort of all succeeding ages and would teach the Lord's people confidently to rely for safety on the ark of the covenant, which was the visible symbol of the Divine presence. We may notice this difference, however, that Moses addressed the words to God as a prayer, while David rather expresses his satisfaction and delight in what he saw daily fulfilled before his own eyes. Some indeed read, "Let God arise," but they appear to misapprehend the scope of the psalmist. He means to say that observation attested the truth which Moses had declared of God's needing only to rise up that all his enemies might be scattered before his irresistible power. Yet I see no objections to the other reading, provided the idea now mentioned be retained and the words be considered as intimating that God needs no array of preparation in overthrowing his enemies and can dissipate them with a breath. We can conclude that when his enemies at any time become superior, this is due to an exercise of divine forbearance, and that rage as they may, it is only with his permission; the time being not yet come for his rising. This circumstance is full of the

---

[1]Hesshus, *Commentarius in Psalmos*, 262r.

sweetest consolation, as those who persecute the church are here spoken of as God's enemies. When he undertakes our defense, he looks on the injuries done to us as dishonors cast on his divine Majesty. COMMENTARY ON THE PSALMS.[2]

MYSTICAL UNDERSTANDING OF THE ARK.
NIKOLAUS SELNECKER: The ark of the covenant now is the church and people of Christ. The covenant is the spoken Word with the holy, most blessed sacraments of baptism and Christ Jesus' body and blood. The golden plates which adorned the ark are Christ himself, the true sin offering, the mercy seat who protects and shelters us from all danger and tyranny of the devil. THE WHOLE PSALTER.[3]

HOW SHOULD *YAH* BE UNDERSTOOD? JOHN CALVIN: As to the expression "in Yah, his name," there has been some difference of opinion.[4] We know that the letter *beth*, among the Hebrews, is often superfluous; therefore, it can be removed, "Yah is his name." Others translate it "in Yah is his name." I have no objection to this, though I prefer the translation which I have adopted. It is of less consequence how we construe the words, as the meaning of David is obvious. COMMENTARY ON PSALM 68.[5]

THE GOD OF BEING. SEBASTIAN MÜNSTER: The prophet says, "Sing psalms to the Lord according to his name, Yah." For this name, Yah, indicates his essence which makes and sustains all things, because it is from the verb *hyh* ["to be"] as well as YHWH. Further, although God dwells in the highest heavens, nevertheless even now he is the Father of all the afflicted, the defender of orphans and widows, and he gives a family to those who are single and childless. THE TEMPLE OF THE LORD: PSALM 68.[6]

PREPARE THE WAY OF THE LORD! GIOVANNI DIODATI: The terms are taken from what used to be done at the triumphal entrance of kings, whom they used to meet and make plain and mend the ways by which they are to come, if they be broken, ragged or stopped. So here is meant the preparation for the bringing of the ark, but especially the spiritual preparations for Christ's coming and reception into the world, which is a true wilderness, void of all goodness, justice and life. These preparations were made by his prophets, and especially by John the Baptist. ANNOTATIONS ON PSALM 68:4.[7]

THE COMFORT OF GOD AS FATHER. MARTIN LUTHER: You certainly ought to be of good cheer, because he, through faith, works a good conscience in you. Because of your faith, you may be forced here on earth to leave father, friend, life, goods and honor. You may have to become poor and wretched orphans and widows, suffering violence and injustice at the hands of all. Then you will find comfort in the knowledge that the Lord of creation is the Father of such orphans and the Avenger of such widows, that he is not distant, but near you, and that you need not seek him in Jerusalem or Rome. He resides in the midst of his Christians; there he is surely to be found. But he is not content just to dwell there. No, he also wants to be a God among them, a God to whom all hearts may flee, who freely gives all, does all, and is able to do all; in brief, who is all that you should have in a God. But this calls for faith. For the Father, the Judge, God, is present invisibly. His dwelling is holy; that is, it is set apart and can be seen only with the eyes of faith. If you believe that he is your Father, your Judge, your God, then this is what he is. PSALM 68: ABOUT EASTER, ASCENSION AND PENTECOST (1521).[8]

---

[2]CTS 10:6-7* (CO 31:620).

[3]Selnecker, *Der gantze Psalter*, 2:80r. Here Selnecker draws out the implicit intertestamental resonance between Christ's atoning work and the mercy seat through the word *hilastērion*—the LXX's translation for "mercy seat" (cf. Rom 3:25; Heb 9:5).

[4]*Yah* is rendered "Lord" here in the ESV text (cf. v. 18; Ps 118:14; Ex 15:2; 17:6; Is 12:2; 26:4; 38:11). Goldingay remarks that the relationship between *Yah* and YHWH is uncertain, though commentators generally assume *Yah* to be a variant of YHWH (as Münster argues). See Goldingay, *Psalms*, 2:316.

[5]CTS 10:9-10* (CO 31:621).

[6]Münster, *Miqdaš YHWH*, 1214.

[7]Diodati, *Pious Annotations*, Uu2r*; citing Is 40:3; Mal 3:1; Mt 3:3.

[8]LW 13:6 (WA 8:8).

68:7-14 *Abundance and Peace from the Lord*

FIGURES ENDED IN THE NEW TESTAMENT.
MARTIN LUTHER: The psalmist calls him a God of Mount Sinai and of Israel, thus outwardly identifying him with a certain place and a person. For at the time of figures, concerned with external things, the worship of God had to be connected outwardly with a place and a person. But in the New Testament, when the day of figures is ended and all are united in one faith, neither God nor his worship is any longer tied to one person or place; nor does his name any longer imply this. Today any believer is the child and servant of God, regardless of residence, whether he lives in Babylon or on Mount Sinai, whether he is Jew or Gentile. PSALM 68: ABOUT EASTER, ASCENSION AND PENTECOST.[9]

THE ABUNDANCE OF GOD'S FAVOR. JOHN CALVIN: Here David proclaims the everlasting course of the grace of God, which had been extended to the people from the time they entered the promised land. Indeed, it is called the inheritance of God, which he assigned to his children. Others understand the inheritance as the church, but this is not correct, for it is afterwards stated as being the place where the assembly of God dwells. The title is appropriately given to the land of Canaan, which was bequeathed to them through the right of inheritance by their Father in heaven. David takes notice of the fact that from the settlement of the seed of Abraham in it, God had never ceased to make the kindest fatherly provision for them, sending his rain in due season to prepare their food. Moreover, when the Hebrew uses *nĕdābāh*, for the freedom, or even the generosity, of the will, I agree with the interpreters who refer to the free and gracious will of God. COMMENTARY ON THE PSALMS.[10]

GOD VANQUISHES WITH HIS WORD AND SPIRIT. KONRAD PELLIKAN: Our God and Lord will give himself, that is, he sends proclamations of peace and salvation, which will conquer the entire world by the power of his strength and by the ministry of his heavenly hosts. And they will defeat this age not by worldly weapons but by his Word and by the outpouring of the Holy Spirit on believers, which no worldly power can oppose. COMMENTARY ON PSALM 68:11.[11]

PROCLAMATION OF VICTORY. RUDOLF GWALTHER: The Lord has given our wives and daughters reason and justification to sing new songs. The psalmist says this according to the common use of the Israelites among whom wives and daughters went around with victorious songs and instruments. However, through a higher understanding this should all be understood about Christ's victory: he defeated the devil and proclaimed this joyous news through his apostles throughout the entire world. THE PSALTER.[12]

HEBREW IDIOMS EXPRESS THE GLORY OF THE APOSTLES AND THE CHURCH. MARTIN LUTHER: What is the point of needlessly adhering so stiffly and stubbornly to the words, so that we cannot understand it at all? Whoever wants to speak German must not use Hebrew style. Rather he must see to it—once he understands the Hebrew author—that he concentrates on the sense of the text and thinks, "Dear man, how do Germans speak in such a situation?" Once he has the German words to serve the purpose, let him drop the Hebrew words and express the meaning freely in the best German he knows.

Thus, here in verse 13 we could easily have rendered the Hebrew woodenly, like this, "If you lie within the marked boundaries, then the wings of the doves will be covered with silver and their pinions with gleaming gold." But what German understands that? However, the preceding verse

---

[9]LW 13:9* (WA 8:10).
[10]CTS 10:13* (CO 31:623).

[11]Pellikan, *Commentaria Bibliorum*, 4:113r-v.
[12]Gwalther, *Der Psalter*, 120r; citing Ex 15:20-21; Eph 1:19-20.

sings of kings who make war and turn over the spoils to the women of the house. So the meaning of this verse is this: these kings have a fine, handsome and well-armed force in the field which, from the distance, looks like a dove whose feathers glisten white and red—as if they were silver and gold. These kings are the apostles who here and there in the world, gloriously aglow with the manifold wondrous gifts and miracles of the Holy Spirit, have taken the field against the devil and won many people away from him, turning them over as spoils to the mother of the house—the church—to govern and teach. DEFENSE OF THE TRANSLATION OF THE PSALMS (1531).[13]

GOD'S PEOPLE ARE A FLOCK OF DOVES. VIKTO-RIN STRIGEL: He compares the teachers of the gospel with multicolored doves because of the variety of their gifts. For one excels in the knowledge of tongues, another has the gift of interpretation, another skillfully makes judgments on controversies concerning dogmas. Finally, on some individuals the Holy Spirit bestows some gifts lavishly, for the building up of the church, as it is written in 1 Corinthians 12. For he alludes to the simplicity of the doves, as Christ says: "Be simple as doves." For the dove lacks animosity, it does not harm with its beak, it has harmless claws. And as hawks and ravens attack doves, so tyrants try to destroy pious teachers. Therefore, the church is an army of doves, which are exposed to all the darts and spears of tyrants. *HYPONĒMATA IN ALL THE PSALMS.*[14]

PROSPERITY AND PURITY. THE ENGLISH ANNOTATIONS: Mount Zalmon, they say, is always covered with snow, which is the case for many high hills. Always white then. Now whiteness, among all people, for several reasons, is emblematic of prosperity and purity. The meaning will then be that although the land, inheritance or people that are spoken of have been clouded and darkened by persecution and other sundry calamities, they are

now recovered through the manifold and miraculous defeats of their enemies to an estate of joyful peace and tranquility. ANNOTATIONS ON PSALM 68:14.[15]

68:15-18 *The Lord Ascends Leading Captivity Captive*

THE POWER AND SOLACE OF THE HEBREW LANGUAGE. MARTIN LUTHER: We have at times also translated quite literally—even though we could have rendered the meaning more clearly another way—because something important is intimated by these very words. Like here in verse 18, "You have ascended on high and have captured captivity." Here it would have been good German to say, "You have freed the captives." But this is too weak and does not give the excellent, rich meaning which is in the Hebrew, which says, "You have captured captivity." This does not imply merely that Christ freed the captives but also that he captured and led away *captivity*, so that it never again could or would take us captive. And so it is really an eternal redemption. Saint Paul likes to speak this way, as when he says, "Through the law I died to the law," again, "Through sin Christ condemned sin," and "Through Christ death has been put to death." These are the captives that Christ has captured and done away with. Death can no longer hold us, sin can no longer incriminate us, the law can no longer accuse our conscience. . . . Therefore out of respect for such doctrine and for the comforting of our conscience, we should keep such words, accustom ourselves to them and give room to the Hebrew language where it does a better job than our German can do. DEFENSE OF THE TRANSLATION OF THE PSALMS (1531).[16]

CHRIST ASCENDED; THE SPIRIT DESCENDED. MARTIN LUTHER: This is the cardinal verse of the entire psalm. . . . The psalmist here refers to the festivals of ascension and Pentecost. This is the import of his words: "All the miracles foretold here of the gospel and Christendom are traceable

---

[13]LW 35:213-14* (WA 38:11-12).
[14]Strigel, *Hyponēmata*, 303; citing 1 Cor 12:1-10; Mt 10:16.

[15]Downame, ed., *Annotations*, 6H2v*.
[16]LW 35:216* (WA 38:13); citing Heb 9:12; Gal 2:19; Rom 8:3.

to your ascent into heaven. For there you received all power and sent your Holy Spirit to the earth with his gifts, through which the gospel was proclaimed, the world converted and all that was predicted fulfilled." That he ascended on high implies, of course, that he first descended into hell, as Saint Paul expounds this in Ephesians 4. Therefore he said, "If I do not go away, the Holy Spirit will not come." It was necessary for him to rise from the dead and ascend into heaven before the Holy Spirit could come. PSALM 68: ABOUT EASTER, ASCENSION AND PENTECOST (1521).[17]

PAUL'S INTERPRETATION OF THIS PASSAGE. MARTIN BUCER: Saint Paul speaking about the exaltation of Christ and the distribution of the Holy Spirit in Ephesians 4 brings forth this verse, but instead of "you have received" he employed "you have given"—which nevertheless not even the common edition of the Greeks has. Thus it seems he desired to adduce the sense and not the words, so that God would receive gifts from human beings, that is, something given from mortals to him, before he would give gifts, in which some have been made apostles, others evangelists, others doctors and pastors, in turn they would bring forth the elect by the gospel in the place of gifts. And he has interpreted this passage rightly concerning Christ our Savior. David was entirely a type of Christ because the phrase "God ascending into heaven" in regards to David consists of him exercising his power and taking captive the nations that had previously been rebels and aliens to Israel and making them subject to him. But in regards to Christ it is much truer that God received him in heaven, that is, he revealed his own power far much more powerfully, when of course he called him back from the dead and seated him at his right hand. And then he did in fact take captives for his own Son, accordingly both by drawing and assigning so many to himself. These are most rightly spoken of as gifts offered to God, to whom they live entirely. HOLY PSALMS.[18]

UNION WITH CHRIST THROUGH HIS FLESH AND BLOOD. JOHN CALVIN: Considering the mysterious union between the Head and members [of the church], it is both truly and properly said that God who was revealed in flesh distributed to his people those gifts he received from the captives. No less applicable to Christ is what is said at the end of the verse, that God was the Victor, so that he could dwell among us. Because Christ did not depart from us so that he should be sought for far away, but rather so that he would fill all things, as Paul also says in Ephesians 4. And he also much more fully uncovered his divinity's power by his ascension into heaven, and although according to his flesh he does not move about on earth, nevertheless our souls feed on his flesh and blood spiritually. For physical distance does not oppose the fact that his flesh is indeed food for us and his blood is indeed drink for us. COMMENTARY ON THE PSALMS.[19]

68:19-27 Our Savior's Triumphant Procession

GOD'S VICTORY FOR US. MARTIN LUTHER: It would have been for nothing if he had assumed our burden and conquered death only for himself. But as matters stand, he presented us with his victory, conquering sin and death in our behalf, so that we, who were held captive by the evil spirit and lived in sin and death without any God and Lord, henceforth would have our own Lord and God, who reigns over us in such a manner that through him we were saved and escaped death. What more fervent wish does humanity entertain than deliverance from death? And now our God has become just such a Lord and God, who satisfies this ardent longing of all human beings for escape from death and for salvation. As this verse states, his kingdom means nothing else than accomplishing our salvation and being a God who snatches us from death. PSALM 68: ABOUT EASTER, ASCENSION AND PENTECOST (1521).[20]

---

[17]LW 13:20* (WA 8:20); citing Eph 4:8-9; Jn 16:7.
[18]Bucer, *Sacrorum Psalmorum*, 257r-v; citing Eph 4:8; 2 Cor 10:5;

Rom 15:16.
[19]CO 31:628-29 (cf. CTS 10:27); citing Eph 4:10.
[20]LW 13:22* (WA 8:22).

HAVE YOU CONFORMED YOUR LIFE TO YOUR SAVIOR'S? JOHN DONNE:

Be now content to consider with me how to this "God the Lord belonged the issues of death."[21] "That God the Lord," the Lord of life, could die, is a strange contemplation.... To us who speak daily of the death of Christ—"he was crucified, died and buried"—can the memory or the mention of our death be irksome or bitter? . . . It is good to dwell here, in this consideration of Christ's death, and therefore we transfer our tabernacle—our devotion—through some of these steps, which God the Lord made to his issue of death that day. Take in his whole day, from the hour that Christ ate the Passover on Thursday to the hour in which he died the next day. Make this present day that day in your devotion; consider what he did and remember what you have done. Before he instituted and celebrated the sacrament—which was after eating the Passover— he proceeded to the act of humility, to wash the disciples' feet; even Peter's who for a while resisted him. In your preparation to the holy and blessed sacrament, have you with a sincere humility sought a reconciliation with all the world, even with those who have been averse from it and refused that reconciliation from you? If so—and not otherwise—you have spent the first part of this, his last day, in conformity with him. After the sacrament, he spent the time till night in prayer, in preaching, in psalms. Have you considered that a worthy reception of the sacrament consists in continuation of holiness after as well as in preparation before? If so, you have in this also conformed yourself to him.

In this way Christ spent his time till night. At night he went into the garden to pray, and he spent much time in prayer. How much? Because it is literally expressed that he prayed there three times and that returning to his disciples after his first prayer and finding them asleep, said, "Could you not watch with me one hour?" it is collected that he spent three hours in prayer. I scarcely dare ask you where you went or how you disposed of yourself when it grew dark and after, last night. If that time was spent in holy recommendation of yourself to God and submission of your will to his, then it was spent in conformity with him. In that time and in those prayers were his agony and bloody sweat. I will hope that you did pray, not any ordinary and customary prayer but prayer that actually was accompanied with shedding of tears and dispositively in a readiness to shed blood for his glory in necessary cases, put you into conformity with him.

About midnight he was taken and bound with a kiss. Are you not too comfortable to him in that? Is not that too literally, too exactly your case? To have been taken and bound with a kiss? From there he was carried back to Jerusalem, first to Annas, then to Caiaphas and, as late as it was, there he was examined and buffeted and delivered over to the custody of those officers, from whom he received all that mockery and violence: the covering of his face, the spitting on his face, the blasphemous words and the smartness of blows which that Gospel mentions. In which compass fell that crowing of the rooster, which calls Peter to his repentance. How you passed all that time last night, you know. If you did anything then that needed Peter's tears and have not shed them, let me be your rooster. Do it now! Now your Master—in the unworthiest of his servants— looks back on you; do it now! Early in the morning, as soon as it was day, the Jews held a council in the high priest's house and agreed on their evidence against him, and then carried him to Pilate who was to be his judge. Did you accuse yourself when you awoke this morning? And were you content to admit even false accusations, that is, rather to suspect actions to have been sin which were not, than to smother and justify such as truly were sins? Then you spent that hour in conformity to him.

Pilate found no evidence against him. Therefore to appease himself and to pass a favor on to Herod, tetrarch of Galilee, who was at that time at Jerusalem—because Christ was a Galilean, he was under Herod's jurisdiction—Pilate sent him to Herod. And rather as a madman than a malefactor, Herod remanded him with scorns to Pilate to proceed against him. This was about eight o'clock.

---

[21]This is how older English versions rendered "and to God, the Lord, belong deliverances from death."

Have you been content to come to this inquisition, this examination, this agitation, this sifting, this pursuit of your conscience, to sift it, to follow it from the sins of your youth to your present sins, from the sins of your bed to the sins of your board, and from the substance to the circumstance of your sins? That is time spent like your Savior's.

Pilate would have saved Christ by using the privilege of the day on his behalf, because that day one prisoner was to be delivered, but they chose Barabbas. He would have saved him from death by satisfying their fury by inflicting other torments on him, scourging and crowning with thorns and loading him with many scornful and ignominious insults, but this did not redeem him. They demanded a crucifixion. Have you gone about to redeem your sin by fasting, by giving alms, by disciplines and mortifications, in the way of satisfaction to the justice of God? That will not serve; that is not the right way. We press an utter crucifixion of that sin that governs you, and *that* conforms you to Christ.

Around noon Pilate gave judgment. They made such haste to execution so that by noon he was on the cross. There now hangs that sacred body on the cross, rebaptized in his own tears and sweat and embalmed in his own blood alive. There are those bowels of compassion, which are so conspicuous, so manifested, so that you may see them through his wounds. There those glorious eyes grew faint in their light, so as the sun, ashamed to survive them, departed with his light too. And there that Son of God, who was never from us, and yet had now come anew to us, in assuming our nature, delivers that soul which was never out of his Father's hands into his Father's hands, by a new way, a voluntary emission of it. For to this God our Lord belongs these issues of death, so that, considered in his own contract, he must necessarily die. Yet at no breach or battery which they had made on his sacred body issues his soul, but he gave up the ghost. And as God breathed a soul into the first Adam, so this second Adam breathed his soul into God, into the hands of God. There we leave you, in that blessed dependency to hang on him who hangs on the cross. There bathe in his tears, there suck at his wounds, and lie down in peace in his grave till he vouchsafe you a resurrection and an ascension into that kingdom which he has purchased for you with the inestimable price of his incorruptible blood. Amen. SERMON 158: PREACHED AT WHITEHALL (1630).[22]

ONLY FAITH CONFESSES GOD AS KING. MARTIN LUTHER: No one can say "My God and my King" unless that person regards God with his eyes of faith, not only as a God, not only as a King, but as his God and his King, as the God and King of his salvation. Neither is it possible to recognize the ways and works of God in the absence of that faith. Faith renders him my God and my King and brings me to a realization that all my works are, after all, not mine but God's. Therefore the words "in holiness" are added. For many address him as "my God and my King" without any sincerity. Their words are permeated with hypocrisy, deceit and fraud, which defile them before God. But those who utter these words, "My God and my King," in holiness are truthful and sincere; they are the real believers. PSALM 68: ABOUT EASTER, ASCENSION AND PENTECOST (1521).[23]

THE SEPTUAGINT'S TRANSLATION AND ITS CONNECTIONS TO PAUL. HENRY AINSWORTH: The Greek version says, "in a trance," taking the Hebrew *rodem* to be from *radam*, though it is not found elsewhere in this form.... These things, applied to Christ's times and after, are very mystical. Benjamin, the least, is here put first; so in the heavenly Jerusalem, the "first foundation is a jasper," which was the last precious stone in Aaron's breastplate on which Benjamin's name was inscribed. In this tribe Paul excelled as a prince of God, though he was one of the last apostles; who was converted in a trance or ecstasy and in ecstasies he and other apostles saw the mysteries of Christ's kingdom. ANNOTATIONS ON PSALM 68:27.[24]

---

[22]Donne, *Works*, 6:292, 295-98*.
[23]LW 13:26* (WA 8:25).
[24]Ainsworth, *Annotations*, 2:549*; citing Rev 21:19; Ex 28:10, 20, 21; 1 Cor 15:8-10; Acts 9:3, 4; Acts 10:10, 11; 2 Cor 12:1-4.

68:28-31 *Trample the Violent*

PRAY FOR GROWTH IN FAITH. WOLFGANG
MUSCULUS: Because he prays for the success of this
prophecy, this is for us so that we should ardently
pray for increasing in the knowledge of Christ,
whom we apprehend by faith and in whom we
should hope for the future. Next, what that prayer
has [contained] in it must be observed: it has two
things. First, it gives glory to God for his work. It
does not say, "because we ourselves worked," but
"because you have worked in us." Second, it serves
the confidence of praying so that the God who is
about to act may be quickly believed for what is
sought. For who would deny the confirmation and
success of one's own work in this way when one
could help? This church sings on the day of
Pentecost, but it sings with the mouth of human
beings whose hearts neither acknowledge the work
of God nor ask for the confirmation of it in Christ.
Let us sing and say with our whole heart, "Confirm,
O God, what you have worked in Christ our Savior."
COMMENTARY ON PSALM 68.[25]

KINGS AS FRIENDS OF THE CHURCH. VIKTO-
RIN STRIGEL: He predicts that some kings and
rulers will be friends of the true church and of
eternal life and will support both teachers and
learners. And although religion has produced
riches, as someone has charmingly said, nevertheless the daughter, like an ungrateful cuckoo bird,
has devoured the mother. For bishops for so many
ages have not lived up to the idea of being an
overseer, that is, they have not taught the gospel,
nor have they administered the sacraments. They
have not even seen to it that the people are imbued
with true doctrine, but they were satraps in the
halls of kings, and although they were appointed to
tasks, those tasks did not fit with their calling.
Therefore, a bit of each is best, moderate opulence
and moderate poverty, while excess in either is the
worst. *HYPONĒMATA IN ALL THE PSALMS.*[26]

**THE CHURCH WILL NEVER HAVE EXTERNAL
PEACE.** JOHN CALVIN: When we find David, after
all the victories he had gained, still commending
himself and his people to the protection of God, it
should teach us to abandon the hope of ever seeing
the church placed in a state of perfect tranquility in
this world, exposed, as it is, to a succession of
enemies raised up by the malice of Satan and
designed by God for the trial and exercise of our
patience. In comparing their enemies with the
beasts here mentioned, and taking notice that they
delighted in war, it was no doubt his intention to
influence the minds of the people of God to the
contrary dispositions of clemency and mercy, as
being that frame of spirit in the exercise of which
they might expect to receive the Divine assistance.
The more violently their enemies raged and the
more lawless their attempts might prove, they had
only the more reason to expect the interposition of
God, who humbles the proud and the mighty ones
of this world. Therefore, since this prayer teaches
that God will be an adversary to all the violent, who
are carried away by the wicked desire to harm
others, whenever we are unjustly attacked, with a
tranquil mind we should flee to the power of God,
trusting most surely that he will scatter our enemies
for us. COMMENTARY ON THE PSALMS.[27]

68:32-35 *O Nations, Praise God's Voice, Power and Strength*

SELĀH, PART OF THE SPIRIT'S GRAMMAR.
MARTIN LUTHER: The word *selāh* has occurred three
times in this psalm. It is not usually read aloud in the
Psalter. Some think that this word is quite superfluous in the Psalms. Its real meaning is still obscure. I
believe that this word is a punctuation mark of the
Holy Spirit. Wherever we find it in the Psalter, the
Holy Spirit wants us to pause and ponder; there he
wants to touch and enkindle our heart for particularly
deep meditation. PSALM 68: ABOUT EASTER,
ASCENSION AND PENTECOST (1521).[28]

---

[25]Musculus, *In Psalterium Commentarii*, 709.
[26]Strigel, *Hyponēmata*, 308.

[27]CTS 10:41* (CO 31:634-35).
[28]LW 13:37 (WA 8:35).

THE CHURCH IS A FAMILY OF THUNDER.
RUDOLF GWALTHER: According to the letters this is said concerning peals of thunder. But it also depicts the preaching of the gospel which, like a thunderclap, moves the hearts of every human being. For this reason, John and James were called "sons of thunder" by Christ. THE PSALTER.[29]

OUR GOD AND ISRAEL'S IS THE SAME GOD.
MARTIN LUTHER: The appellation "the God of Israel" signifies that our God is none other than the one whom the Israelites once had. It is Christ, whom the Israelites once possessed and of whom we now also say: He who does these things is no longer only Israel's God but the God of the whole world. Nobody is strong in his own might; no one has the strength for successful resistance to evil. It is God alone who vouchsafes power and strength to all, namely, to all who are powerful and strong, so that he alone is blessed and he alone is God. PSALM 68: ABOUT EASTER, ASCENSION AND PENTECOST (1521).[30]

GOD IN OUR MIDST. JOHN CALVIN: The psalmist speaks of God's protection of his church. The plural number is used in speaking of the sanctuary, here as in other places, because the tabernacle was divided into three parts. He points, in short, to the ark of the covenant, as that which the believing people of God should recognize as a symbol of confidence, remembering the promise, "I will dwell in the midst of you," and thus resting with security under the wings of the divine protection and confidently calling on his name. Any right which Israel might have in distinction from others to trust in the guardianship of God rested entirely on that covenant of free grace by which they had been chosen to be God's peculiar heritage. Let it be remembered, however, that God continues to exert in behalf of his church still these terrible displays of his power of which the psalmist speaks. COMMENTARY ON THE PSALMS.[31]

---

[29]Gwalther, *Der Psalter*, 121r; citing Mt 3:17.
[30]LW 13:37 (WA 8:35).

[31]CTS 10:44* (CO 31:636).

69:1-36 SAVE ME FROM THE DEPTHS

To the choirmaster: according to Lilies. Of David.

¹ Save me, O God!
　　For the waters have come up to my neck.ᵃ
² I sink in deep mire,
　　where there is no foothold;
I have come into deep waters,
　　and the flood sweeps over me.
³ I am weary with my crying out;
　　my throat is parched.
My eyes grow dim
　　with waiting for my God.

⁴ More in number than the hairs of my head
　　are those who hate me without cause;
mighty are those who would destroy me,
　　those who attack me with lies.
What I did not steal
　　must I now restore?
⁵ O God, you know my folly;
　　the wrongs I have done are not hidden
　　　　from you.

⁶ Let not those who hope in you be put to
　　　　shame through me,
　　O Lord GOD of hosts;
let not those who seek you be brought to
　　　　dishonor through me,
　　O God of Israel.
⁷ For it is for your sake that I have borne
　　　　reproach,
　　that dishonor has covered my face.
⁸ I have become a stranger to my brothers,
　　an alien to my mother's sons.

⁹ For zeal for your house has consumed me,
　　and the reproaches of those who reproach
　　　　you have fallen on me.
¹⁰ When I wept and humbledᵇ my soul with
　　　　fasting,
　　it became my reproach.
¹¹ When I made sackcloth my clothing,
　　I became a byword to them.

¹² I am the talk of those who sit in the gate,
　　and the drunkards make songs about me.

¹³ But as for me, my prayer is to you, O LORD.
　　At an acceptable time, O God,
　　in the abundance of your steadfast love
　　　　answer me in your saving faithfulness.
¹⁴ Deliver me
　　from sinking in the mire;
let me be delivered from my enemies
　　and from the deep waters.
¹⁵ Let not the flood sweep over me,
　　or the deep swallow me up,
　　or the pit close its mouth over me.

¹⁶ Answer me, O LORD, for your steadfast love
　　　　is good;
　　according to your abundant mercy, turn to me.
¹⁷ Hide not your face from your servant;
　　for I am in distress; make haste to answer me.
¹⁸ Draw near to my soul, redeem me;
　　ransom me because of my enemies!

¹⁹ You know my reproach,
　　and my shame and my dishonor;
　　my foes are all known to you.
²⁰ Reproaches have broken my heart,
　　so that I am in despair.
I looked for pity, but there was none,
　　and for comforters, but I found none.
²¹ They gave me poison for food,
　　and for my thirst they gave me sour wine
　　　　to drink.

²² Let their own table before them become a
　　　　snare;
　　and when they are at peace, let it become
　　　　a trap.ᶜ
²³ Let their eyes be darkened, so that they
　　　　cannot see,
　　and make their loins tremble continually.
²⁴ Pour out your indignation upon them,
　　and let your burning anger overtake them.

[25] *May their camp be a desolation;*
  let no one dwell in their tents.
[26] *For they persecute him whom you have*
    struck down,
  and they recount the pain of those you have
    wounded.
[27] *Add to them punishment upon punishment;*
  may they have no acquittal from you.[d]
[28] *Let them be blotted out of the book of the living;*
  let them not be enrolled among the righteous.

[29] *But I am afflicted and in pain;*
  let your salvation, O God, set me on high!
[30] *I will praise the name of God with a song;*
  I will magnify him with thanksgiving.

[31] *This will please the LORD more than an ox*
  or a bull with horns and hoofs.
[32] *When the humble see it they will be glad;*
  you who seek God, let your hearts revive.
[33] *For the LORD hears the needy*
  and does not despise his own people who are
    prisoners.

[34] *Let heaven and earth praise him,*
  the seas and everything that moves in them.
[35] *For God will save Zion*
  and build up the cities of Judah,
and people shall dwell there and possess it;
  [36] *the offspring of his servants shall inherit it,*
  and those who love his name shall dwell in it.

a Or *waters threaten my life*   b Hebrew lacks *and humbled*   c Hebrew; a slight revocalization yields (compare Septuagint, Syriac, Jerome) *a snare, and retribution and a trap*   d Hebrew *may they not come into your righteousness*

OVERVIEW: While the reformers do not ignore the historical context of this psalm, their exegesis nevertheless subordinates this aspect of the text to its christological significance. Our commentators understand David here in his lament—frequently cited in the New Testament—as a type of Christ's suffering. Although some see him as a representative of the people of God, others focus on him as a type of the church as well. Through this typological lens, our commentators encourage their listeners to take refuge in God, be comforted in the knowledge of his sovereignty and rejoice as they await the reception of their heavenly inheritance.

A GOSPEL PSALM FOR US. NIKOLAUS SEL-NECKER: This psalm is a prayer of our Lord Jesus Christ, which he prayed to God his Father on the cross and in his deepest distress which he bore on account of our sins. And he speaks quite clearly about his suffering and grieves against those who crucified him and blasphemed him—those who gave him gall and vinegar to drink in his great thirst. He also prophesies . . . about the new covenant and the new worship of God. In summary, it is an entirely evangelical psalm, full of lament and full of consolation, full of weeping and full of rejoicing. Thus, in the New Testament this psalm is very often adapted to the Lord Christ himself as well as to his disciples and apostles. . . . This psalm is frequently used in the New Testament—more than almost any other psalm! THE WHOLE PSALTER.[1]

A PRAYER FOR THOSE WITH NO HOME. THEO-DORE BEZA: Because it is necessary for the members to be conformed to the Head, it follows that this psalm will be of the greatest use as long as the church sojourns on earth. PARAPHRASE OF PSALM 69.[2]

Superscription: *According to the Lilies*

DO NOT FORGET SUFFERING IN TIMES OF JOY. RUDOLF GWALTHER: Some understand by these lilies a particular zither which was used by the ancients. Others think that this psalm has this particular title because it was sung in May or spring when flowers begin to bloom. Thus during this joyful time we should remember crossbearing

---

[1]Selnecker, *Der gantze Psalter*, 2:88v.
[2]Beza, *Psalmorum Davidis*, 309 (cf. *Psalmes of Dauid*, 150).

and misery. And thus, by this, the Lord Christ may also be understood, as we indicated above in Psalm 45. The Psalter.[3]

69:1-5 Overcome by Mire, Floods and Lies, I Cry Out to the Lord

Metaphors of the Psalmist's Afflictions. John Calvin: Under the figure of waters, the psalmist represents his condition as so extremely distressing that it brought him even to the brink of despair. And yet we know that, so far from being a soft and effeminate person, he was one who encountered and overcame dreadful temptations with extraordinary courage. From this we may infer the bitterness of the distress with which he was at that time afflicted. Some understand the word *soul* as denoting "life," but this gives a very cold and unsatisfactory meaning. It rather signifies the heart. When a person falls into an abyss of water, he may prevent for some time the water from entering his body by stopping his mouth and his nostrils, but in the end, because it is impossible for a human being to live without breathing, suffocation will compel him to let in the waters, and they will penetrate even to the heart. David by this metaphor would intimate not only that the waters had covered and overwhelmed him but also that he had been forced to draw them into his body. . . .

Then he compares his afflictions with a deep sink of mire, where there is still greater danger. For if a person fixes his feet on a solid bottom, he may raise himself up, there having been many instances in which people, placing their feet on the bottom, have by a sudden spring emerged and escaped the peril of the waters. But when a person finds himself once sunk in some slough or muddy river, it is all over with him; he has no means of saving himself. The psalmist adduces additional circumstances in illustration of his afflicted condition. He declares that he was inundated by the flowing of the waters, an

expression indicating the disorder and confusion which his distresses and persecutions produced. Commentary on the Psalms.[4]

The Spirit Remains Steadfast. David Dickson: Though the flesh of the regenerate may be weak, the spirit remains ready and will never abandon calling on God, depending on him and holding fast to the covenant and the hope of deliverance. The flesh will make this a new ground of speech to God, because it is not able to speak anything, and a new ground of laying hold on God and hoping for help from him, because its hope is failing. Commentary on Psalm 69:3.[5]

Christ's Folly Is Our Sin. Martin Luther: He is saying this because when the Jews had crucified Christ, they thought that all had now been convinced that he was the worst kind of person and cursed by God and in every way ungodly and a liar. For the law says, "Cursed by the Lord is he who hangs on a tree." Therefore they rushed to this kind of death, so that they might show him to be hateful to God and might now conclude by the law's authority that he could not have perished by such a death unless he were unrighteous before God. Therefore they said, "He trusted in God. Let him deliver him, if he wants." As if they were to say: "It does not look as if he wanted him or had any desire for him. For 'cursed by the Lord is he who hangs on a tree.'" See, then, the people who do not know how he was cursed. And it is indeed true that he was cursed by the Lord, for the Father made him a curse for us, and he truly died because of our sins. Yet they did not know that these were their own sins, but God knew. For that reason, he says, "They do not know my offenses, but you know them." That is, they do not understand how they are mine, for I have made the sins of others mine. Nor did they understand that that curse could not swallow up the whole person, but because God was not able to bring him under any curse, only his flesh was

---

[3]Gwalther, *Der Psalter*, 124r-v. See above, p. 343.

[4]CTS 10:46-47* (CO 31:637-38).
[5]Dickson, *Other Fifty Psalms*, 117*.

swallowed up. Therefore he is at the same time cursed and blessed, at the same time alive and dead, at the same time grieving and rejoicing, so that he might absorb all evils in himself and bestow all blessings from himself. Blessed be our Lord, Amen! FIRST PSALMS LECTURES (1513–1515).[6]

69:6-13 *Zeal for Your House Consumes Me*

DAVID PRAYS THAT THE DEVOUT WOULD NOT BE DISCOURAGED. JOHN CALVIN: David declares that he is set forth as an example from which all the people of God may derive matter either of hope or despair. Although he was held in detestation and execrated by the great body of the people, there yet remained a few who were ready to bear just and impartial testimony to his innocence; knowing as they did that he was unrighteously afflicted by his persecutors, that he constantly reposed on the grace and goodness of God and that no temptations could discourage or prevent him from continuing steadfast in the practice of true godliness. But when they observed the distresses and calamities to which he was notwithstanding subjected, the only conclusion to which they were able to arrive was that all the pains and labor which he had taken in devoutly serving God were entirely thrown away. As all the instances in which God extends his succor to his servants are so many seals by which he confirms and gives us assurance of his goodness and grace toward us, the faithful must have been exceedingly discouraged had David been forsaken in the extremity of his distress. The danger of their being thus discouraged he now lays before God; not that God ever needs to be reminded of anything but because he allows us to deal familiarly with him at the throne of grace. The word *wait* is properly to be understood of hope, and the expression "to seek God" of prayer. The connecting of the two together teaches us the profitable lesson that faith is not an inactive principle, because it is the means of stirring us up to seek God. COMMENTARY ON THE PSALMS.[7]

A STRANGER TO MY BROTHERS. WOLFGANG MUSCULUS: There is one affection of mortals toward unknown persons and foreigners and another toward brothers, acquaintances, domestics, friends and family members. That distinction is innate to us by nature. Therefore it is asked, "How grave was that hatred and opprobrium which was undeservedly endured that he should have begun to be shunned and avoided by his brothers and the sons of his own mother (that is, brothers from the same womb)?" They were, of course, unwilling to risk mentioning David's name before the king and his courtiers; so also is everyone who is eager to consult his own safety, whatever may happen in the meantime—however undeserved—even to his own siblings.

We also see in this passage that saints are not free from brotherly affection and love, granted that, in common with all mortals, they quite desire this. For if that aversion of his brothers would not have grieved him, he certainly would not have complained about it. Nor would he have grieved unless he really had affection for them. COMMENTARY ON PSALM 69.[8]

CHRIST AND HIS FOLLOWERS ARE UNFASHIONABLE. MARTIN LUTHER: Although we do not read in the Gospel that they ridiculed Christ's fasting and goat-hair garment, yet the fact that they ridiculed and despised everything else he said and did, and even blasphemed some things, leads to the conclusion that they also ridiculed him in these matters. For when he preached poverty and said, "How difficult it is for a rich person to enter the kingdom of heaven," the Pharisees, who were greedy, heard this and mocked him. . . . Therefore just as in this matter, so also in abstinence and in clothing and in all things he was their opposite. But they loved to fare sumptuously and be clothed expensively like some carouser. Therefore, being perverse, they perverted everything.

But the same things happened and still happen to his members in our own time. They are regarded as fools by the world because they do not seek the things of this world, namely, feasting and a showy

---

[6]LW 10:364-65* (WA 3:426); citing Deut 21:23; Gal 3:13; Mt 27:43.
[7]CTS 10:52-53* (CO 31:640).

[8]Musculus, *In Psalterium Commentarii*, 714-15.

display of garments. This monster has made itself at home to the present day, so that a noble who does not choose to be a byword and reproach with Christ is forced to spend nearly his whole property and go into distress for clothing and drinking, so that he won't be different from anyone else in adornment and gluttony. And those who do not imitate them—if there are such—well understand this verse and can sing it: "I covered my soul with fasting, and it was made a reproach to me." For we hear the complaints of many, that those who avoid association with them are disparaged as if they were not human beings. So it happened without doubt also to Christ. And Saint Peter testifies that it happened also to the first Christians, saying in 1 Peter 4: "They are surprised that you do not now join them in the same wild profligacy." . . . They say, "You must conform; that is the style now." FIRST PSALMS LECTURES (1513–1515).[9]

THE GATE OF THE MAGISTRATE. DAVID DICKSON: It is a sore affliction to the godly to be condemned by the magistrates and judges, and yet the truly religious, even Christ and his followers, were, and are, subject to this exercise. Righteousness and truth are no worse for being condemned by civil judges, and God will not disclaim his cause because of this but instead will heed such complaints. When magistrates discountenance true religion, then it becomes a matter of derision to rascals and to every base villain without control, and table talk to every tippler. COMMENTARY ON PSALM 69:12.[10]

69:14-21 Answer Me!

THE LORD'S SWEET MERCY IS NOT SWEET TO EVERYONE. MARTIN LUTHER: Sweet and good is the mercy of God, namely, to those for whom their wretchedness is bitter and evil. But to those for whom their wretchedness is pleasing, the mercy of God is not good; indeed it is useless, because they scorn it, and this is so because there is a relationship between the greatness and variety of the mercy of God and our wretchedness. For grace does not abound except where sin and wretchedness abound. GLOSSA ON PSALM 69 (1513–1515).[11]

MERCY REQUIRES THAT WE SEE OURSELVES AS WE TRULY ARE. MARTIN LUTHER: For it is not possible to make the mercy of God large and good, unless a person first makes his miseries large and evil or recognizes them to be such. To make God's mercy great is not, as is commonly supposed, to think that God considers sins as small or that he does not punish them. Indeed, this especially means to reduce mercy. For how can one who regards evil as something small regard as something great the good by means of which the evil is removed? Hence our total concern must be to magnify and aggravate our sins and thus always to accuse them more and more, and earnestly judge and condemn them. The more deeply a person has condemned himself and magnified his sins, the more is he fit for the mercy and grace of God. FIRST PSALMS LECTURES (1513–1515).[12]

COMFORT IN GOD'S PROVIDENCE. JOHN CALVIN: Why is it that most people become dispirited when they see the wicked outrageously rushing on them, and their wickedness, like a flood of water, carrying everything before it, but they think that heaven is so obscured and overcast with clouds as to prevent God from beholding what is done on the earth? We should just take refuge in the providence of God, that contemplating it we may be assured beyond all doubt, that God will appear at the right time to help us. For he cannot, on the one hand, shut his eyes to our miseries, and it is impossible for him, on the other, to allow the license which the wicked take in doing evil to pass with impunity, without denying himself.

David, therefore, takes comfort from the consideration that God is the witness of his grief, fear, sorrows

---

[9]LW 10:366* (WA 3:427-28); citing Mk 10:23-24; Lk 18:26; 16:14; 8:53; Is 28:14; Prov 3:32-34; 9:12; Ps 1:1; Lk 16:19; 1 Pet 4:4.
[10]Dickson, *Other Fifty Psalms*, 121*.

[11]LW 10:367 n. 24 (WA 3:413).
[12]LW 10:368 (WA 3:428).

and cares; nothing being hidden from the eye of him who is the Judge and Governor of the world. Nor is it a vain repetition when he speaks so frequently of his reproach and shame. As he was subjected to such dreadful assaults of temptations as might have made the stoutest heart to tremble, it was indispensably necessary for his own defense to oppose them with a strong barrier for resistance. Nothing is more bitter to people of an ingenuous and noble spirit than reproach; but when this is repeated, or rather when shame and reproach are heaped on us, how needful is it then for us to possess more than ordinary strength, that we may not thereby be overwhelmed? For when succor is delayed, our patience is very apt to give way, and despair very easily creeps in on us. This shame and reproach may very properly be referred both to the outward appearance and to the actual feelings of the mind. It is well known that he was everywhere held in open derision; and the mockeries which he experienced could not but strike into him both shame and sorrow. For the same reason he subjoins that his enemies are before God or known to him; as if he had said, Lord, you know how, like a poor sheep, I am surrounded by thousands of wolves. COMMENTARY ON THE PSALMS.[13]

THEY EAT JUDGMENT TO THEMSELVES. PILGRAM MARPECK: For no greater punishment or vengeance can be found than to fall from one transgression and sin into another and still assume that one participates in the table fellowship of Christ. In truth they are and remain only at their own table, which has become a trap for them and from which they eat judgment to themselves, and not from the Lord's table. Although they have been invited or else appear at the wedding banquet with soiled garments, they will nevertheless not taste the Lord's Supper eternally, but rather eat their own meal from their own table perverted into a trap. They will be judged so that they will depart exiled and condemned. CONCERNING FIVE FRUITS OF TRUE REPENTANCE.[14]

A BANQUET OF GALL AND VINEGAR. THE ENGLISH ANNOTATIONS: Here David says that his affliction was so great that he had no comfort in his life and that no part of it was free of bitterness. His meat tasted of gall, and his drink was like vinegar. To feed one with gall was a common proverb among the Hebrews, and what the psalmist speaks proverbially and metaphorically of himself, Christ verified literally. ANNOTATIONS ON PSALM 69:21.[15]

69:22-28 Curse the Goods of the Wicked

PREPARE A TABLE OF MISFORTUNE FOR MY ENEMIES. JOHN CALVIN: David had complained that his enemies mingled his food with gall; and now he prays that their table may be turned into a snare for them and that the things which are for peace may be turned into a net for them. These expressions are metaphorical, and they imply a desire that whatever things have been allotted to them in providence for the preservation of life and for their welfare and convenience might be turned by God into the occasion or instrument of their destruction. From this we can conclude that things that are naturally and of themselves hurtful may become the means of furthering our welfare when we are in favor with God. This means on the other hand that when his anger is kindled against us, all those things which have a native tendency to produce our happiness are cursed and become so many causes of our destruction. It is an instance of the divine justice, which ought to deeply impress our minds with awe, when the Holy Spirit declares that all the means of preserving life are deadly to the reprobate, so that the very sun, which carries healing under its wings, breathes only a deadly exhalation for them. COMMENTARY ON THE PSALMS.[16]

PROPHECIES OF GOD'S PUNISHMENT. CARDINAL CAJETAN: See here the explanation for the punish-

---

[13]CTS 10:63-64* (CO 31:645-46).
[14]CRR 12:392.

[15]Downame, ed., *Annotations*, 6H3v-6H4r*; citing Jer 9:15; Jer 23:15; Mt 27:34.
[16]CTS 10:68* (CO 31:647-48); citing Tit 1:5; Mal 4:2.

ments: Because they persecuted him who in no respect and for no reason ought to have been persecuted, except that you, God, struck him, and it was your will to strike him. In this is implied the complete and utter innocence of Christ and the divine decree concerning the undeserved suffering of Christ. "On account of the wickedness of my people I struck him." . . . The continuation of the Jewish persecution of Christ is prophesied about, because not only did they persecute him but also they will tell their descendants that the persecution against the Christians must be continued. For this is "to speak of the pain of your martyred," not that the ones who have been martyred feel pain, but that they are martyred in pain. This happened in the case of Stephen, James and so on. These things refer to the punishment of the destruction of Jerusalem. . . .

The successive fall of reprobate Jews, along with their eternal punishment, is prophesied. "Add iniquity on their iniquity," that is, they will slip from crime into crime. "And they will not come into your righteousness," which is the righteousness of faith, the righteousness of grace according to election. And this is attributed to God when he says, "Add," because he "adds" by removing grace, which speaks to his permissive will. Commentary on Psalm 69.[17]

God Removes His Spirit from Stubborn Sinners. Tilemann Hesshus: Another punishment of Christ's enemies is to be deserted in sin and handed over to the power of Satan. This is the completely remarkable weakness of human beings: that no one can avoid all sin, no one can foresee all lapses, no one can rule himself. But it is a great happiness that when a human being has fallen into sin, by the inspiration of the Holy Spirit he returns to repentance. But when God removes his hand, deserts a human being, hands him over to his own passions and Satan's rage, then that person rushes headlong from crime to crime and immediately amasses sins and God's wrath until he finally rushes into eternal destruction. Nothing more severe can be said or imagined than this punishment. In this way

Cain, Saul, Absalom, Achitophel, Jeroboam, Ahab and Judas fell from one sin into another. And concerning Judas it is said: "Satan entered into him." In such people rage, hatred of God and savagery against the pious multiply, and they do not stop until they plunge into eternal destruction. That he says "Add to them iniquity upon iniquity" should not be understood as if God is the cause of sin or as if he forces human beings to sin. Instead it should be understood concerning the desertion and permission of God, that God removes his Spirit and hands them over to Satan, by whom they will be forced into every manner of sin.

"May they not come into your righteousness." That is, may they not repent and ask for the forgiveness of sins. For this is the righteousness of God, the righteousness of the gospel by which sinners become well, repenting. God does not refuse repentance to his enemies, but because so monstrous is the wickedness and insolence in the enemies of Christ and the gospel, that they want to crush Jesus Christ with his gospel, in which he most mercifully offers to everyone the forgiveness of sins and eternal life. "Come to me," he says, "all who are weary and heavy-burdened; I will restore you." . . . By no other way is it possible to come to the righteousness of God. Commentary on Psalm 69.[18]

Written Down and Blotted Out. John Calvin: This is indeed an improper manner of speaking, but it is one well adapted to our limited capacity. The book of life is nothing other than the eternal counsel of God, by which he has predestined his own people to salvation. God, it is certain, cannot be changed; and, further, we know that those who are adopted to the hope of salvation were written down before the foundation of the world. Because God's eternal election is incomprehensible to human understanding, it is said that those whom God openly and by manifest signs enrolls among his people, are written. On the other hand, those whom God openly rejects and casts out of his

---

[17]Cajetan, *In Sacrae Scripturae Expositionem*, 3:241; citing Is 53:9.

[18]Hesshus, *Commentarius in Psalmos*, 276r; citing Rom 1:18-32; Jn 13:27; Mt 11:28.

church are, for the same reason, said to be blotted out. COMMENTARY ON THE PSALMS.[19]

69:29-36 God Delights in His Praise

PROPHECY ABOUT A.D. 70. MOÏSE AMYRAUT: This prophetically handles the destruction of Jerusalem and its renewal which happened after [Roman] captivity in the year A.D. 70. ANNOTATIONS ON PSALM 69:35.[20]

UNDERSTAND THESE PLACE NAMES FIGURA-TIVELY. SEBASTIAN MÜNSTER: By "Zion," "Jerusalem" and "Judah" understand the church and its renewal. By "earth" think the believers who hold the true faith. Their seed and descendants will inherit the earth and will live by faith in God, which will restore any desert into paradise. THE TEMPLE OF THE LORD: PSALM 69.[21]

THE LAND OF ISRAEL IS A TYPE FOR OUR HEAVENLY INHERITANCE. JOHN CALVIN: Although that land was given to the chosen people to be possessed until the advent of Christ, we should remember that it was a type of the heavenly inheritance, and that, therefore, what is here written concerning the protection of the church has received a more true and substantial fulfillment in our own day. There is no reason to fear that the building of the spiritual temple, in which the celestial power of God has been manifested, will ever fall into ruins. COMMENTARY ON THE PSALMS.[22]

OUR PROMISED LAND: LIFE IN CHRIST. NIKOLAUS SELNECKER: These words speak of the fruit of the life and resurrection of our Lord Jesus Christ, namely, that Christ refreshes, consoles and redeems all who are tired and heavy-burdened, the suffering, the poor and the captured who acknowledge their sins and the wrath of God and who must therefore be cast headlong into the grave

where there is no water, into hell and eternal condemnation. Christ lifts them up so that they are no longer in darkness, in death and terror; instead, they live, they rejoice or, as Christ tells his believers and all his Christians until the end of the world: "Your hearts will live through me; I am your life and grant you life in eternity."

We all are by nature miserable, poor and captive. We are bound by the devil, strangled by death, conquered by sin, devoured by wrath. There is no counsel or help. There is only the Lord Jesus Christ for you! He defeats the devil, death, hell and destroys the entire kingdom of the devil, redeems us from sin, from the curse of the law and from eternal death. He also gives us his true righteousness and grants us the Holy Spirit, strengthens in us the covenant of grace and crafts in us a good, joyous conscience toward God, a brave, living heart. He renews our life, consoles, refreshes, sustains, guards and teaches us. He gives us eternal salvation, eternal peace, joy and happiness.

In short, he is our Emmanuel, our Redeemer, our Justifier, our Mediator and Savior, our Wisdom, Righteousness, Holiness and Redemption, as Paul says. Or, as the Lord himself says, he is our Way, Truth and Life. Whom now does he want to scare? Who now does not want to rejoice and praise God? To run to him, pray and be merry? God has helped. God is with us. God will continue to help and build us, that is, to sustain, guard, nourish and multiply his church. Against all enemies. "The Lord will rise over us and his glory will shine over us." The Lord is our eternal Light and our Sun who will never set again. For the Lord is our eternal Light, and the days of our suffering will have an end, and we are now completely and entirely in the grace of God. We are righteous and will possess the promised land, eternal life, forever, through the Lord Jesus Christ to whom be laud, honor and praise in eternity! Amen. THE WHOLE PSALTER.[23]

[19]CTS 10:73-74* (CO 31:650); citing Eph 1:4.
[20]Amyraut, Paraphrasis in Psalmos Davidis, 291.
[21]Münster, Miqdaš YHWH, 1216.
[22]CTS 10:80* (CO 31:653).
[23]Selnecker, Der gantze Psalter, 2:91r; citing 1 Cor 1:30; Jn 14:6; Is 60:2.

70:1-5 DO NOT DELAY, MY REDEEMER!

To the choirmaster. Of David, for the memorial offering.

¹ *Make haste, O God, to deliver me!*
  O LORD, make haste to help me!
² *Let them be put to shame and confusion*
  who seek my life!
Let them be turned back and brought to dishonor
  who delight in my hurt!
³ *Let them turn back because of their shame*

who say, "Aha, Aha!"

⁴ *May all who seek you*
  rejoice and be glad in you!
May those who love your salvation
  say evermore, "God is great!"
⁵ *But I am poor and needy;*
  hasten to me, O God!
You are my help and my deliverer;
  O LORD, do not delay!

OVERVIEW: The reformers commend the psalmist's reliance on the Lord in this time of distress and urge their audience to follow his example. As our commentators recognize, however, this psalm is nearly identical to the final verses of Psalm 40, and rather than commenting on it as a discrete text, many simply refer their readers to their earlier interpretations.

REPEATED FROM PSALM 40. RUDOLF GWAL-THER: This psalm is a portion of Psalm 40, from which it is taken word for word. Because Psalm 40 was composed during the time of a severe illness, it is easy to understand that this psalm too should be interpreted accordingly. THE PSALTER.[1]

Superscription: *For Remembrance*

KNOW YOURSELF! MARTIN LUTHER: With regard to the title, "For remembrance," this means remembrance of oneself. For whoever has forgotten himself has forgotten everything; whoever remembers himself remembers everything. Therefore he says "for remembrance" without qualification, for knowledge of self embraces all knowledge in itself. Thus blessed Augustine says about Psalm 70: "The sum total of all human knowledge is this: A person

must know that by himself he is nothing. Whoever does not remember himself remembers nothing." And in his *Confessions* he says the same thing: "When I found myself, I knew you; when I found you, I knew myself." Therefore, because it is the aim of this psalm that all should be turned toward self-knowledge, the title "For remembrance" is used fittingly. FIRST PSALMS LECTURES (1513–1515).[2]

70:1-5 *Deliver Me, O God!*

GOD'S TIME IS THE BEST TIME. THE ENGLISH ANNOTATIONS: A godly person in extreme distress may call earnestly on God to hurry his deliverance, and there is no hurt in that. Indeed, God is well pleased with our earnestness, and sometimes we reap the fruit of this in present help and deliverance according to our own desire and the intention of our prayers. In our earnestness, however, there must also be a resolution of patience and submission. With belief and assurance, we must understand that God's time, be it sooner or later, is our best time, even though present sense and weak flesh suggest the contrary. ANNOTATIONS ON PSALM 70:1.[3]

---

[1]Gwalther, *Der Psalter*, 125v; citing Ps 40:13-17.

[2]LW 10:394* (WA 3:449); citing *Confessions* 10.1. Augustine makes no such comment in his exposition of Ps 70; see NPNF 8:311-15.
[3]Downame, ed., *Annotations*, 6H4r*.

FLEE TO THE LORD IN PRAYER. NIKOLAUS SELNECKER: From this psalm we learn what we are to do when we are doing badly and many foes—highly learned and mighty people—are against us. We are to run to God in prayer, lament and hope that he is not going to leave us, nor does he desire to do so if only we have one good reason. We shall not grumble or chide back or take revenge or be impatient, because we are called a people of blessing. The best thing is to call on God and take comfort in this: God can and wants to help us in his time. THE WHOLE PSALTER.[4]

FOR GOOD REASON WE PRAY THIS EVERY HOUR. MARTIN LUTHER: Therefore this psalm, whose opening words we recite so often day and night, is to be commended to all priests so that they will not mumble it coldly and perfunctorily but help the church of God with this prayer with all their heart. For if the church were helped, we too would be saved, because it is our mother hen and we are its chicks. It is not without reason that the Holy Spirit decreed the opening words of this psalm as the beginning in every canonical hour.

Therefore remember to say, "O God—because there is no one else to help the church except you, our God—be pleased to deliver me, that is, help me, so that tyrants, heretics and those easily offended would not oppress me. And when I have been helped by you and have salvation for myself, I can easily come to the assistance of others with your help. Therefore, hasten to help me!" Truly we are not without tyrants and persecutors today who oppress the poor and do not judge the causes of widows and orphans. Because none but the rich and powerful can afford the ceremony and din of the court, the poor person who is drawn to court will have spent more than he ever had before justice would be done to him. Against them we must pray that those whom they persecute be patient. FIRST PSALMS LECTURES (1513–1515).[5]

---

[4]Selnecker, *Der gantze Psalter*, 2:91v.

[5]LW 10:391* (WA 3:446-47).

71:1-24 DO NOT FORSAKE ME

1 *In you, O Lord, do I take refuge;*
let me never be put to shame!
2 *In your righteousness deliver me and rescue me;*
incline your ear to me, and save me!
3 *Be to me a rock of refuge,*
to which I may continually come;
you have given the command to save me,
for you are my rock and my fortress.

4 *Rescue me, O my God, from the hand of the*
wicked,
from the grasp of the unjust and cruel man.
5 *For you, O Lord, are my hope,*
my trust, O Lord, from my youth.
6 *Upon you I have leaned from before my birth;*
you are he who took me from my mother's
womb.
My praise is continually of you.

7 *I have been as a portent to many,*
but you are my strong refuge.
8 *My mouth is filled with your praise,*
and with your glory all the day.
9 *Do not cast me off in the time of old age;*
forsake me not when my strength is spent.
10 *For my enemies speak concerning me;*
those who watch for my life consult together
11 *and say, "God has forsaken him;*
pursue and seize him,
for there is none to deliver him."

12 *O God, be not far from me;*
O my God, make haste to help me!
13 *May my accusers be put to shame and*
consumed;
with scorn and disgrace may they be
covered
who seek my hurt.
14 *But I will hope continually*
and will praise you yet more and more.

15 *My mouth will tell of your righteous acts,*
of your deeds of salvation all the day,
for their number is past my knowledge.
16 *With the mighty deeds of the Lord God I*
will come;
I will remind them of your righteousness,
yours alone.

17 *O God, from my youth you have taught me,*
and I still proclaim your wondrous deeds.
18 *So even to old age and gray hairs,*
O God, do not forsake me,
until I proclaim your might to another
generation,
your power to all those to come.
19 *Your righteousness, O God,*
reaches the high heavens.
You who have done great things,
O God, who is like you?
20 *You who have made me see many troubles*
and calamities
will revive me again;
from the depths of the earth
you will bring me up again.
21 *You will increase my greatness*
and comfort me again.

22 *I will also praise you with the harp*
for your faithfulness, O my God;
I will sing praises to you with the lyre,
O Holy One of Israel.
23 *My lips will shout for joy,*
when I sing praises to you;
my soul also, which you have redeemed.
24 *And my tongue will talk of your righteous*
help all the day long,
for they have been put to shame and
disappointed
who sought to do me hurt.

OVERVIEW: While David's lament to the Lord for refuge from his enemies again provides occasion for our commentators to muse on the righteousness of God and how it differs from human righteousness, the recurring motif of the human life cycle encourages the reformers to take a number of interesting exegetical directions. Thus Hesshus reads this lament as a cry of the church in its feeble senility, while Calvin meditates on the miracle of childbearing, undergirded by God's grace. Calvin and Hesshus also provide a stark juxtaposition in their consideration of the use of musical instruments in worship. For Calvin the harp and lyre are shadows from the old dispensation; for Hesshus these instruments awaken saints from drowsiness to praise.

SET YOUR HEART AND MIND ON GOD'S PRAISE. MARTIN LUTHER: The easier and more suited this psalm is to the intellect, the more fruitful and rich it is for the heart. All the psalms of praise and entreaty are of the highest feeling and adapted to the very seraphim. For to praise God and to pray are the ultimate and highest perfection, which require that vices are conquered and virtues are celebrated. For the impure cannot praise, because praise is not beautiful in the mouth of a sinner. FIRST PSALMS LECTURES (1513–1515).[1]

REQUEST FOR REVIVAL. TILEMANN HESSHUS: This psalm is the voice of the whole church, which groans to God in each member regardless of where they are. The church begs God for defense against enemies, deliverance from perils, consolation through the Holy Spirit, strength and might during times of hardship, and that it would not be discarded by God on account of senility and feebleness, but that it would be continually preserved in the world until final judgment, so that it would glorify God's immeasurable wisdom and righteousness throughout every generation in the world and recall the benefits of the Mediator. The church daily experiences that it becomes more sluggish and that

its strength is exhausted. Today there is not the same resilience of mind, the same strength of faith, such noble perseverance, such ardent love of God, such zeal and eagerness to confess the name of Christ as there was in the patriarchs, prophets, apostles and martyrs; today there is an unnatural infirmity in all the pious. Therefore, the senile, dying church begs that it not be discarded by God on account of its feebleness. For the church admits that it retains faith and hope in the greatest miseries and in great feebleness; it does not at any time neglect the confession of Christ's name and the proclamation of the truth! Also it admits that it is not crushed by hardship but instead gives glory to God. COMMENTARY ON PSALM 71.[2]

71:1-11 *Let Me Never Be Put to Shame*

THE RIGHTEOUSNESS OF GOD. VIKTORIN STRIGEL: Because I commented on these words sufficiently in Psalm 31 above, now I will only instruct the reader about the word *righteousness*, which he uses in some places in an active sense and in some places in a passive sense. The righteousness of God as revealed in the law is the will, whereby he wants right things and with his own particular joy takes pleasure in right things, and does not want things contrary to what is right, and with true indignation repels and destroys them. About this righteousness in Psalm 5 it is said, "Because you are not a God who wants iniquity, nor will a wicked person dwell with you, nor will the unjust remain before your eyes. You hate all who work iniquity. You will destroy those who speak a lie; the Lord will abhor a person of bloodshed and deceit."

The righteousness of God revealed apart from the law, about which the law and the prophets testify, is the free remission of sins and reconciliation with God and the reception into eternal life through the mediation of Christ. Therefore, he asks to be set free in the righteousness of God, not in the legal and active sense but in the evangelical and passive sense, as if he were saying, "Because I know

---

[1]LW 10:395* (WA 3:452); citing Sir 15:9.

[2]Hesshus, *Commentarius in Psalmos*, 279v.

for certain that I am righteous, not, though, by my own worth but by your righteousness, that is, imputed by you through the righteousness of your Son, I ask this additional thing, namely, liberation and glorification, according to the counsel of your wisdom." For those whom he justified, the same he has glorified, according to Romans 8.

That this interpretation is not imagined or falsified, the words of Dr. Luther bear witness in his commentary on Genesis 42: "Once," he said, "when I had to read and pray that passage of the psalm where it says, 'Free me in your righteousness,' I was wholly afraid, and I hated that word with my whole heart. Do not free me, I was thinking, by your righteousness, by which you are righteous in an active sense. Therefore, I should understand this righteousness, by which I will be justified, in a passive sense. . . . To me once it was very troubling when I came to those propositions: 'The righteousness of God,' 'the work of God,' 'your work,' 'your righteousness,' which if they are taken in the active sense are death but in the passive sense are life and salvation."[3] HYPONĒMATA IN ALL THE PSALMS.[4]

WE SHOULD BE GRATEFUL FOR OUR BIRTH.

JOHN CALVIN: David not only celebrates the goodness of God which he had experienced from his childhood but also those proofs of it which he had received previous to his birth. An almost similar confession is contained in Psalm 22, by which is magnified the wonderful power and inestimable goodness of God in human generation, the way and manner of which would be altogether incredible, were it not a fact with which we are quite familiar. If we are astonished at that part of the history of the flood, in which Moses declares that Noah and his household lived ten months amid the offensive nuisance produced by so many living creatures, when he could not draw the breath of life, have we not equal reason to marvel that the infant, shut up within its mother's womb, can live

in such a condition as would suffocate the strongest adult in half an hour? But we thus see how little account we make of the miracles which God works, in consequence of our familiarity with them.

The Spirit, therefore, justly rebukes this ingratitude by commending to our consideration this memorable instance of the grace of God, which is exhibited in our birth and generation. When we are born into the world, the mother may do her office, and the midwife may be present with her, and many others may lend their help, yet if God would not, so to speak, put his hand under us, receive us into his bosom, what would become of us? And what hope would there be of the continuance of our life? Yes, rather, were it not for this, our very birth would be an entrance into a thousand deaths. COMMENTARY ON THE PSALMS.[5]

PRAYER FOR THE CHURCH.

VIKTORIN STRIGEL: The main proposition of this psalm is not only a prayer but also a promise in accordance with the rule that all prayers of the Holy Spirit are promises. And think about how necessary this prayer is. Just as in the elderly all things are rather languid, so in this old age of the world the church has grown weaker and more squalid, because not only is it beset with the weakness of its age but also it is marred by punishments, which are heaped up on account of its sins, and the madness among the demons grows, because they know that soon judgment will be on them, in which their depravity will be made known before all angels and humanity. Let us seek, therefore, with our most ardent prayer, that God not cast away the remains of the aging church because of its foolish and shameful behavior, but because he knows that for old people there is need of rest, that he will show favor to the church as it is worn out by the feebleness of its age, according to the promise handed down in Isaiah 46: "You have been carried in my womb, you have been borne in my belly, I will carry you up to old age," that is, "In the last dark and gloomy times I will carry the aging church; I made it, I will carry it,

---

[3]LW 7:251 (WA 44:485-86).
[4]Strigel, *Hyponēmata*, 320.

[5]CTS 10:84-85* (CO 31:655-56); citing Ps 22:9-10; Gen 8:13.

I will bear it, and I will save it." Let us console ourselves with this promise, because in this upheaval and overturning of kingdoms we worriedly inquire where the church will continue.

The remaining two verses are easily understood by those who take into account the history of these times. For what devices has Satan not employed through his own tools—tyrants and hypocrites—to overcome and extinguish the light of doctrine that has once again been purified? He has started uprisings, he fueled civil wars, he conceived formulas of the adulterated reconciliation of dogmas, he has thrown our community into turmoil with disputations that are not necessary, and in short he has prepared and schemed up all things that had to do with wiping out the truth. But as waves dashed against the rocks flow down again, because the rocks themselves remain unmoved, so the attempts and machinations of Satan, ultimately speaking, have been and will be in vain, according to these words: "Behold, I am with you to the end of the age." *Hyponēmata in All the Psalms.*[6]

71:12-24 *From Youth to Old Age I Will Praise You*

Hope and Praise. Wolfgang Musculus: Verse 14 has two things. First, the psalmist wants constantly to hope, of course, for the help of the Lord. It is his self-control that said, "Hurry to help me." Although he longs for the help of God to come quickly, nevertheless he indicates that he will not despair, even if he is not delivered immediately. Flesh's nature is to demand that deliverance come quickly; however, it is the consideration of the spirit to hope for the time arranged by God. Second . . . he says, "And I will increase your praise above all!" This relates to the hope of deliverance. Here again he was moved by what he said, "I will hope continually." Because that relates to the desire to proclaim the praise of God, he indicates that he wants to magnify the praise of God and to have

material from which he could add praises to those which he had so far proclaimed; he could add new praise. . . . Daily the wicked hunt for new ways to add to their past sins, in the same way, by contrast, the pious with fervent longing daily hunt for new ways to add to the surplus of God's praise. *Commentary on the Psalms.*[7]

Human and Divine Righteousness. Martin Luther: In verse 19 at last the correct distinction between divine and human righteousness is depicted. For the righteousness of God reaches up to the heaven of heavens and causes us to reach up, too. It is righteousness even to the highest, namely, of reaching the highest. Not so human righteousness, but rather it reaches down to the lowest. This is so because one who exalts himself will be humbled, and one who humbles himself will be exalted. But now the whole righteousness of God is this: To humble oneself into the depth. Such a one comes to the highest, because he first went down to the lowest depth. Here he properly refers to Christ, who is the power of God and the righteousness of God through the greatest and deepest humility. Therefore he is now in the highest through supreme glory.

Therefore, whoever wants to relish the apostle and other Scriptures must understand everything tropologically: Truth, wisdom, strength, salvation, righteousness, namely, that by which he makes us strong, safe, righteous, wise. So it is with the works of God and the ways of God. All of them are Christ literally, and all of them are faith in him morally. First Psalms Lectures (1513–1515).[8]

Show Gratitude for the Lord. John Calvin: Our sense of the goodness of God should extend so far as to ravish us with admiration. For thus it will come to pass that our minds, which are often distracted by an unholy disquietude, will repose on God alone. If any temptation thrusts itself on us, we immediately magnify a fly

---

[6]Strigel, *Hyponēmata*, 321-22; citing Is 46:3-4.

[7]Musculus, *In Psalterium Commentarii*, 739.
[8]LW 10:401-2* (WA 3:458).

into an elephant; or rather, we rear very high mountains, which keep the hand of God from reaching us; and at the same time we basely limit the power of God. The exclamation of David, then, "Who is like you?" teaches us the lesson that we should force our way through every impediment by faith and regard the power of God, which is well entitled to be so regarded, as superior to all obstacles. All people, indeed, confess with the mouth that none is like God; but there is scarce one out of a hundred who is truly and fully persuaded that he alone is sufficient to save us. COMMENTARY ON THE PSALMS.[9]

THE RESURRECTION OF THE DEAD. NIKOLAUS SELNECKER: There is plenty enough unrest and crossbearing in the church that pious Christians nearly despair, become squeamish and do not know what they should begin to do. However, when the distress is at its greatest, the dear Sun, our Lord Christ Jesus, shines. He brings us back to life, consoles us and makes us strong. Yes, he pulls us out of the depths of the earth; when we are very dead, dead and eaten up by worms—in the ground—he awakes us again to eternal life. For these words I actually understand about the resurrection of the dead. These are very dear words about crossbearing and redemption in this life and true justice on the Day of Judgment. THE WHOLE PSALTER.[10]

INSTRUMENTS IN WORSHIP ARE NOW FORBIDDEN. JOHN CALVIN: In speaking of employing the psaltery and the harp in this exercise, he alludes to the generally prevailing custom of that time. To sing the praises of God on the harp and psaltery unquestionably formed a part of the training of the law and of the service of God under that dispensation of shadows and figures, but now they should not be used in public thanksgiving anymore. We are not, indeed, forbidden to use, in private, musical instruments, but they are banished out of the churches by the

plain command of the Holy Spirit, when Paul lays it down as an invariable rule that we must praise God and pray to him only in a known tongue. COMMENTARY ON THE PSALMS.[11]

STIR US TO GLORIFY THE LORD! TILEMANN HESSHUS: The church concludes its prayer with thanksgiving, so that it would demonstrate its certainty that it will be answered and that God is going to preserve the church continually, moreover, so that it would instruct the universal church to press on in these works of the church always and especially, so that it would proclaim God's praises in the world without end. By musical instruments the deeply grieved and drowsy mind is stirred up and in a way kindled. But in a sense it has become more excited and agitated. Therefore the ancients used them for religious ceremonies. For our hearts should be aflame in prayer and thanksgiving. Therefore they intimate that the church should not drowsily celebrate God's praises. The church gives thanks to God for his truth, that is, for the Word of God, by which the church is always instructed, and for his promises which are the church's solace.

The Holy One in Israel is Our Lord Jesus Christ, who is continually present with his people. He devoutly keeps his promises to us, sanctifies Israel and is with us every day until the consummation of this age. But not only should the charm of musical instruments be sought and considered, but also our lips and tongues should proclaim the blessings of God, so that among human beings the knowledge of God would be increased, others would be taught the truth and be invited to call on God, to believe, to hope and to persevere. Because this external proclamation of God's blessings and the church's deliverances is necessary among us, thus God demands that we not only confess with our mouth but also that we would believe with our heart and that thanksgiving would proceed from our heart. "My soul," he says, "which you have also redeemed, which you have released from the most burdensome fear, will sing to you!"

---

[9]CTS 10:96* (CO 31:661).
[10]Selnecker, *Der gantze Psalter*, 2:99v.

[11]CTS 10:98* (CO 31:662); citing 1 Cor 4:13.

Finally the church repeats . . . that it will glorify God's righteousness, so that it would teach all its posterity not only in times of peace—in safety we should confess the name of God, celebrate his glory and refute blasphemies—but all day, even in the most dangerous times, when tyrants demand our silence and threaten us most savagely. We should not grow weary in glorifying the divine name. We should not desire new dogmas or new religions; instead, we should only meditate on the righteousness of God. For this contains immeasurable and inexhaustible wisdom. COMMENTARY ON PSALM 71.[12]

---

[12]Hesshus, *Commentarius in Psalmos*, 282v-283r.

72:1-20 THE KING'S ETERNAL REIGN AND RIGHTEOUSNESS

Of Solomon.

¹ Give the king your justice, O God,
    and your righteousness to the royal son!
² May he judge your people with righteousness,
    and your poor with justice!
³ Let the mountains bear prosperity for the people,
    and the hills, in righteousness!
⁴ May he defend the cause of the poor of the
      people,
    give deliverance to the children of the needy,
    and crush the oppressor!

⁵ May they fear you[a] while the sun endures,
    and as long as the moon, throughout all
      generations!
⁶ May he be like rain that falls on the mown grass,
    like showers that water the earth!
⁷ In his days may the righteous flourish,
    and peace abound, till the moon be no more!

⁸ May he have dominion from sea to sea,
    and from the River[b] to the ends of the earth!
⁹ May desert tribes bow down before him,
    and his enemies lick the dust!
¹⁰ May the kings of Tarshish and of the coastlands
    render him tribute;
may the kings of Sheba and Seba
    bring gifts!
¹¹ May all kings fall down before him,
    all nations serve him!

¹² For he delivers the needy when he calls,
    the poor and him who has no helper.
¹³ He has pity on the weak and the needy,
    and saves the lives of the needy.
¹⁴ From oppression and violence he redeems
      their life,
    and precious is their blood in his sight.

¹⁵ Long may he live;
    may gold of Sheba be given to him!
May prayer be made for him continually,
    and blessings invoked for him all the day!
¹⁶ May there be abundance of grain in the land;
    on the tops of the mountains may it wave;
    may its fruit be like Lebanon;
and may people blossom in the cities
    like the grass of the field!
¹⁷ May his name endure forever,
    his fame continue as long as the sun!
May people be blessed in him,
    all nations call him blessed!

¹⁸ Blessed be the Lord, the God of Israel,
    who alone does wondrous things.
¹⁹ Blessed be his glorious name forever;
    may the whole earth be filled with his glory!
Amen and Amen!

²⁰ The prayers of David, the son of Jesse, are
    ended.

a Septuagint *He shall endure*   b That is, the Euphrates

OVERVIEW: The reformers understand this psalm to fit Christ and his reign better than Solomon, despite acknowledging that David probably composed this song for Solomon's coronation. The submission of worldly rulers to the eternal Ruler features prominently; indeed, wise rulers rely on the only wise God. Our commentators, longing for the peace that surpasses all understanding, see here intimations of that peace to come in Christ's kingdom. Delighting in the psalmist's vivid imagery, the reformers thicken it with canonical resonances. Selnecker interprets the mountain and hills as the gospel messengers of Isaiah 52 who proclaim, "Your God is King." Strigel connects the rain on mown grass to the dew on Gideon's fleece, considering various possible ruled interpretations. The arrival of wealthy and exotic magistrates points to the submission of all worldly power to Christ's reign. The final verse elicits a discussion of the (dis)order of the Psalms and the editorial function of the phrase "the prayers of David, the son of Jesse, are ended."

FIFTY FLORIN FOR WHOEVER CAN TRANSLATE PSALM 72 AND PSALM 73 BETTER THAN I! MARTIN LUTHER: To translate the Bible is a huge task. And although we have used a great deal of oil, nevertheless there will be those who want to make it better. They will harass me for one word; I could refute them in one hundred words, if they themselves tried to translate it. To the person who is able to translate Psalm 72 and Psalm 73 cleanly, I will give fifty florin—if they did not use our translation! TABLE TALK: KONRAD CORDATUS (1532).[1]

AUTHORSHIP UNCERTAIN; SUBJECT MATTER CERTAIN. SEBASTIAN MÜNSTER: Some hold the opinion that this psalm was composed by Solomon; others say that it was recited by David for Solomon. Neither opinion can be held for certain according to the title of this psalm. This, however, is certain according to the Hebrews, much written in this psalm is more truly said about Christ than about Solomon. THE TEMPLE OF THE LORD: PSALM 72.[2]

FOR SOLOMON'S CORONATION. RUDOLF GWALTHER: This psalm David composed and appointed for the entire people to sing, when he named his son, Solomon, as king and publicly instituted him as such. But because Solomon along with his kingdom was a type for the Lord Christ, many things here are reported by the inspiration of the Holy Spirit as chiefly about Christ alone. THE PSALTER.[3]

A CHRISTMAS PSALM. NIKOLAUS SELNECKER: This is a glorious prophecy about the Lord Christ

and his kingdom, that he is true God, whom the sun and moon will fear and all kings will worship and everyone will honor as long as sun and moon endure, in whom we should seek and find pure grace and righteousness and salvation. However, the beloved cross should also be part of this life, so that true believers in Christ must often suffer, shed their blood and die. But their death and blood will be dear and precious before God. It is indeed a proper Christmas psalm, when we sing beautiful hymns, like "From heav'n above to earth I come / To bear good news to ev'ry home" and "In Dulci Jubilo." THE WHOLE PSALTER.[4]

72:1-19 *Blessings on the King*

POLITICS REQUIRES GOD'S SPIRIT. JOHN CALVIN: From these words we learn that no government in the world can be rightly managed except under the conduct of God and by the guidance of the Holy Spirit. If kings would in themselves possess sufficient strength, there would have been no reason for David to have sought by prayer from another, that with which they were of themselves already provided. But in requesting that the righteousness and judgment of God may be given to kings, he reminds them that none are fit for occupying that exalted station, except insofar as they are formed for it by the hand of God. COMMENTARY ON THE PSALMS.[5]

SOLOMON, A TYPE FOR CHRIST. SEBASTIAN MÜNSTER: As Solomon had peace with all kinds and leaders, thus when Christ came, through the apostles, he published peace and righteousness throughout the world. THE TEMPLE OF THE LORD: PSALM 72.[6]

[1]WATR 2:642, no. 2763a (cf. pp. 642-43, no. 2763b).
[2]Münster, *Miqdaš YHWH*, 1219.
[3]Gwalther, *Der Psalter*, 128v; citing 1 Chron 28–29.
[4]Selnecker, *Der gantze Psalter*, 2:100r. Selnecker quotes the beginning of Luther's hymn "From Heaven Above to Earth I Come" and a medieval macronic Latin-German hymn, famously paraphrased as "Good Christian Men Rejoice." See LW 53:289-91 (WA 35:459; cf. LSB no. 358).
[5]CTS 10:102* (CO 31:664).
[6]Münster, *Miqdaš YHWH*, 1219.

MOUNTAINS SYMBOLIZE PREACHERS.

NIKOLAUS SELNECKER: We hold the simple understanding that the mountains and hills here mean all teachers of the Christian church, apostles and others until the end of the world, who faithfully taught the doctrine of the holy gospel: how we out of grace for Christ's sake, without the works of the law, are made righteous and holy through faith, as it stands in Isaiah 52: "How lovely on the mountains are the feet of the messengers who proclaim peace, who preach good news, who proclaim salvation; they say to Zion: Your God is King."

Nothing more beautiful could be said about the preaching office than what is written here. The beloved apostles and all other faithful preachers are called mountains and messengers, legates and servants of God, who first of all bring peace and a sure message that God wants to be at peace with us and no longer is angry or condemns us because of our sin. Afterwards they preach good things and bring righteousness; that is, they comfort, saying that God not only does not want to be angry any longer, but also he gives us his righteousness and all grace for his Son's sake. Third, they declare salvation and, as the psalm continues, they announce that God will keep his miserable people in justice and help the poor and break in pieces the blasphemers; that is, they promise that we who are weary and heavy-laden and have all kinds of inward and outward crosses, anxiety of conscience because of sins, illness and persecution in the world, shall be helped and counseled against the devil, death, world, sin and hell. God will be near, around, under, in and for us. He will minister to our needs, and himself be our Lord and King and protect and preserve to all eternity. . . . If God is for us, who will be against us? THE WHOLE PSALTER.[7]

RAIN SYMBOLIZES CHRIST'S REIGN. VIKTO-

RIN STRIGEL: There is no doubt that the prophet in this verse alludes to the story of Gideon. . . . But commentators apply this image taken from the story of Gideon in different ways. Some relate it to the birth of the Son of God from the Virgin, with the sense that Christ, the heavenly dew, so to speak, was conceived by the Holy Spirit in the womb of the Virgin Mary without the stain of sin. Though I do not reject this interpretation, because it is consistent with our faith, still I prefer to apply it to the reign of Christ.[8] For just as the grass, when sprinkled with dew, begins to spring up anew, so hearts, after hearing the gospel message, receive a fresh comfort, which is the beginning and foretaste of eternal life. We also have to take into account the imagery that is laid out in the same story. Before the birth of Christ, the Jewish synagogue was a fleece tinged by heavenly dew. Now the dry earth, that is, the nations, is watered by this dew. What shall I say about the wondrous and almost unbelievable victory of Gideon? Isaiah 9 compares it with the triumph of Christ. For just as Gideon led forth a weak army against an immense multitude of enemies and was crowned with a divine victory, so we, though pitiful and weak, follow the leadership and auspices of the Son of God, armed with the message of the gospel that we profess and a spark of faith shining amid our troubles, and conquer very powerful enemies, sin, death and the devil. But Dr. Luther illustrates this image best and very beautifully in his comments on Isaiah 9. Whoever wants can follow up on this there. *HYPONĒMATA IN ALL THE PSALMS.*[9]

THE RETURN OF RIGHTEOUSNESS FROM EXILE.

JOHN CALVIN: It was, indeed, the duty of Solomon to protect the righteous; but it is the proper office of Christ to make human beings righteous. He not only gives to every person his own, but also reforms their hearts through the agency of his Spirit. By this means he brings righteousness back,

---

[7]Selnecker, *Der gantze Psalter*, 2:104r-v; citing Is 52:7; Nah 1:15; Rom 10:15.

[8]On ruled reading, see above, *xlvi-lii.*

[9]Strigel, *Hyponēmata*, 327-28; citing Judg 6:11–7:25; LW 16:98-99 (WA 31,2:69-70).

as it were, from exile, which otherwise would be altogether banished from the world. The blessing of God follows, by which he causes all his children to rejoice as they see that under their King, Christ, every provision is made for their happiness. COMMENTARY ON THE PSALMS.[10]

WHO ARE THE KINGS OF SHEBA AND SEBA?

SEBASTIAN MÜNSTER: These are regions in fertile Arabia, whence also the queen of the south came, as the book of Kings testifies. It is indicated by this verse that as kings of great wealth came from far away to subject themselves to Solomon and to bring him gifts, so all the empires of the world are going to bow their head before Christ the Lord and come to him with gifts of whatever is very precious in the world and rejoice before Christ. THE TEMPLE OF THE LORD: PSALM 72.[11]

OPPRESSION MUST BE PREVENTED. THE

ENGLISH ANNOTATIONS: The effects of fraud and violence, the two noted engines of all mischief, are commonly felt most by those least able to bear them, the poor and needy. It is the case of many great and flourishing kingdoms that where the better sort are most at ease, the poorer people are most oppressed. As it is a commendation of a good king that he does not oppress others himself, so also a good and wise king will prevent the oppression of others. ANNOTATIONS ON PSALM 72:14.[12]

ONE DAY EVERY NATION WILL WORSHIP OUR

LORD. SEBASTIAN MÜNSTER: Rashi believes this verse should be understood in this way: "The king will live, and God will give him the gold of Sheba. Those who brought gold will pray for the salvation of the king." It is intimated by this little verse that as all the nations desire to honor King Solomon on account of his excellent wisdom, grace and dignity, so the entire world is going to worship Christ—who is the fountain and fullness of wisdom, knowledge, true riches and salvation—and pray for

his blessed kingdom's success and advance. THE TEMPLE OF THE LORD: PSALM 72.[13]

SPIRITUAL WEALTH. JOHN CALVIN: Christ, it is

true, does not reign to hoard up gold, but David meant to teach by this figure that even the nations which were most remote would yield such homage to him as to surrender to him themselves and all that they possessed. That the glory of the spiritual kingdom of Christ is being portrayed under images of outward splendor is not a new thing. David, in conformity with this usual style of Scripture, has here foretold that the kingdom of Christ would be distinguished for its wealth; but this is to be understood as referring to its spiritual character. COMMENTARY ON THE PSALMS.[14]

SCRIPTURE TEACHES THE TRINITY AND

UNITY OF GOD. KONRAD PELLIKAN: Let the sacred Divinity always be glorified by every creature and every nation. The Divinity is frequently revealed in Scripture by three names joined together, as here also and in the plural, so that not without reason even the Jews should consider the Trinity in the Divinity, not of nature and substance, majesty or deity—which is in the simplest and greatest unity; one not many—but of properties, which Christ the Lord explained and also ancient Jews taught by the names of Father, Son and Holy Spirit. COMMENTARY ON PSALM 72:18.[15]

HOW WONDROUS GOD'S INCARNATION!

NIKOLAUS SELNECKER: "Praise be to God the Lord, the God of Israel, who alone does wonders," which no angel or spirit has the power to do, which he does through his Son. Indeed, what greater wonder is there than that God became human? Than that Christ the Son of God redeemed us with his blood? These are not creaturely works, but rather only God's power and might. THE WHOLE PSALTER.[16]

---

[10]CTS 10:108* (CO 31:667).
[11]Münster, *Miqdaš YHWH*, 1219; citing 1 Kings 10:1.
[12]Downame, ed., *Annotations*, 6I2v*; citing Jas 5.
[13]Münster, *Miqdaš YHWH*, 1219.
[14]CTS 10:114* (CO 31:670).
[15]Pellikan, *Commentaria Bibliorum*, 4:119v.
[16]Selnecker, *Der gantze Psalter*, 2:108v.

72:20 *The End of David's Prayers*

THE LAST PSALM COMPOSED FOR THE PSALTER. MARTIN LUTHER: Although this psalm was composed by Solomon, nevertheless because it was the last of the entire Psalter—the majority of the psalms are David's—therefore it is said at the end of the book: "The prayers of David are finished." According to Augustine, too, this statement extends to the psalms that follow—see his fine tract on *mysteria*. GLOSSA ON PSALM 72 (1513–1515).[17]

FORMERLY THE PSALMS WERE IN DISARRAY. CARDINAL CAJETAN: The psalms were not arranged into the books of Psalms, which it now has, according to a certain order from the beginning; instead they were added in the order they were found. Accordingly they were strewn about and gathered together without order. For clearly it is obvious from the titles that Psalm 3 should be placed after Psalm 51 according to the proper order. That is why this psalm—with this title—is located in the middle of the Psalms. I believe . . . that this psalm is the last psalm of the entire Psalter and for this reason it had this title attached to it. COMMENTARY ON PSALM 72.[18]

REDACTORS OF THE PSALMS ADDED THIS. RUDOLF GWALTHER: This phrase was added by those who brought the psalms into one book. This does not mean that they thought that none of the following psalms were composed by David, but instead that this was the last one that he wrote and gave to the people. THE PSALTER.[19]

SOLOMON ADDED THIS. JOHN CALVIN: This was not without cause added by Solomon—if we may suppose him to have put the matter of this psalm into the form of poetical compositions—not only that he might avoid defrauding his father of the praise which was due to him but also to stir up the church the more earnestly to pour forth before God the same prayers which David had continued to offer even with his last breath. Let us then remember that it is our duty to pray to God, both with unfeigned earnestness and with unwearied perseverance, that he would be pleased to maintain and defend the church under the government of his Son. COMMENTARY ON THE PSALMS.[20]

A FITTING END TO THE SECOND BOOK OF THE PSALMS. NIKOLAUS SELNECKER: This was the last psalm which David composed shortly before his departure from this life, when his son Solomon should succeed him. This psalm belongs to the last words of David, which are in 2 Samuel 23. But that this psalm is not the last in the book of Psalms means nothing, for they were not organized in an orderly way, one after the other—as it surely should have been—but instead as they were found. And Ezra, as the rabbis say, restored and ordered the psalms in this way, as we now have them. We should let this short account suffice and in the name of God complete the second book of the Psalter. To God the Lord be praise and thanks for his mercy! May he help us further his honor.

> Without you, O Christ, O God, labor vanishes
>   into air,
>   Under miserable toil work sweats in vain.
> You yourself labor easily and happily.
>   So in the Psalms may you assist, my most
>   merciful Christ.
> And as people, neither in mind nor body, assist,
>   May you be the customary Physician for
>   my goodness.
> But as in other things, so also here, may your
>   righteous will be done,
>   And govern me, O Christ, at your command.

THE WHOLE PSALTER.[21]

---

[17]WA 3:461.
[18]Cajetan, *In Sacrae Scripturae Expositionem*, 3:250.
[19]Gwalther, *Der Psalter*, 130v-131r.
[20]CTS 10:119-20* (CO 31:672).
[21]Selnecker, *Der gantze Psalter*, 2:108v.

Map of Europe at the Time of the Reformation

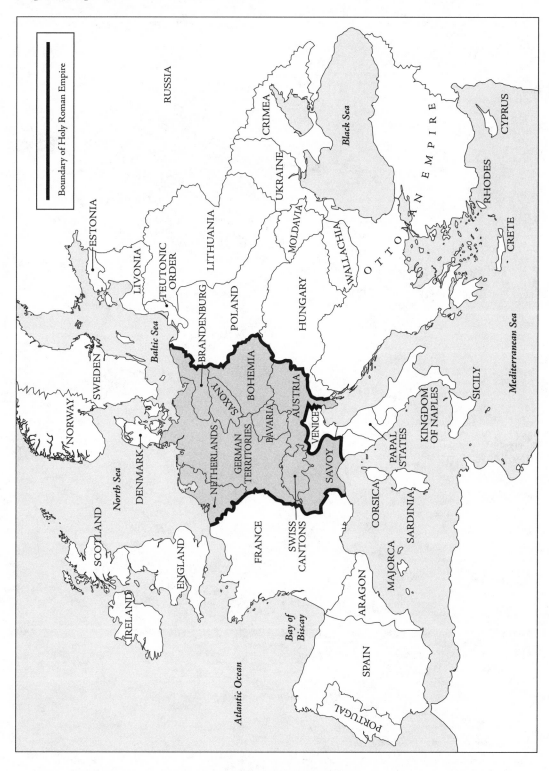

Timeline of the Reformation

	German Territories	France	Spain	Italy	Switzerland	Netherlands	British Isles
1337–1453		d. Nicholas of Lyra Hundred Years' War	b. Paul of Burgos (Solomon ha-Levi)(d. 1435)				Hundred Years' War
1378–1415		Western Schism (Avignon Papacy)		Western Schism			
1384							d. John Wycliffe
1414–1418					Council of Basel (1431–1437)		
1415				Council of Constance; d. Jan Hus; Martin V (r. 1417–1431); Council of Florence (1438–1445)			
1450	Invention of printing press						
1452				b. Leonardo da Vinci (d. 1519)			
1453				Fall of Constantinople			
1455–1485	b. Johann Reuchlin (d. 1522)						War of Roses; Rise of House of Tudor
1456	Gutenberg Bible						
1460				*Execrabilis*			
1466		b. Jacques Lefèvres d'Étaples (d. 1536)					
1467					b. Desiderius Erasmus (d. 1536)		b. John Colet (d. 1519)
1469	b. Antoius Broickwy von Königstein (d. 541)						
1470				b. Santes Pagninus (d. 1541)			b. John (Mair) Major (d. 1550)
1475				b. Michelangelo (d. 1564)			
1478	b. Wolfgang Capito (d. 1541)		Ferdinand and Isabella	b. Jacopo Sadoleto (d. 1547)			b. Thomas More (d. 1535)

	German Territories	France	Spain	Italy	Switzerland	Netherlands	British Isles
1480	b. Balthasar Hubmaier (d. 1528); b. Andreas Bodenstein von Karlstadt (d. 1541)						
1481–1530			Spanish Inquisition				
1482					b. Johannes Oecolampadius (d. 1531)		
1483	b. Martin Luther (d. 1546)						
1484	b. Johann Spangenberg (d. 1550)				b. Huldrych Zwingli (d. 1531)		
1485	b. Johannes Bugenhagen (d. 1554)						b. Hugh Latimer (d. 1555)
1486	r. Frederick the Wise, Elector (d. 1525); b. Johann Eck (d. 1543)						
1488	b. Otto Brunfels (d. 1534)						b. Miles Coverdale (d. 1568)
1489	b. Thomas Müntzer (d. 1525); b. Kaspar von Schwenckfeld (d. 1561)						b. Thomas Cranmer (d. 1556)
1491	b. Martin Bucer (d. 1551)		b. Ignatius Loyola (d. 1556)				
1492			Defeat of Moors in Grenada; Columbus discovers America; Explusion of Jews from Spain	Alexander VI (r. 1492–1503)			
1493	b. Justus Jonas (d. 1555)						
1494							b. William Tyndale (d. 1536)
1496	b. Andreas Osiander (d. 1552)					b. Menno Simons (d. 1561)	
1497	b. Philipp Melanchthon (d. 1560); b. Wolfgang Musculus (d. 1563) b. Johannes (Ferus) Wild (d. 1554)						
1498				d. Girolamo Savonarola	b. Conrad Grebel (d. 1526)		

	German Territories	France	Spain	Italy	Switzerland	Netherlands	British Isles
1499	b. Johannes Brenz (d. 1570)			b. Peter Martyr Vermigli (d. 1562)			
1500			b. Charles V (−1558)				
1501	b. Erasmus Sarcerius (d. 1559)						
1502	Founding of University of Wittenberg			Julius II (r. 1503–1513)		b. Frans Titelmans (d. 1537)	
1504					b. Heinrich Bullinger (d. 1575)		
1505	Luther joins Augustinian Order			b. Benedict Aretius (d. 1574)			
1506		b. Augustin Marlorat (d. 1562)		Restoration to St. Peter's begins			
1507				Sale of indulgences approved to fund building			
1508	b. Lucas Lossius (d. 1582)						
1509		b. John Calvin (d. 1564)					r. Henry VIII (−1547)
1510	Luther moves to Rome			b. Immanuel Tremellius (d. 1580)			b. Nicholas Ridley (d. 1555)
1511	Luther moves to Wittenberg						
1512				Sistene Chapel completed			
1512–1517				Fifth Lateran Council; rejection of conciliarism			
1513	Luther lectures on Psalms			r. Pope Leo X (−1521)			b. John Knox (d. 1572)
1515	Luther lectures on Romans	r. Francis I (−1547); b. Peter Ramus (d. 1572)					
1516		Est. French National Church (via Concordat of Bologna)		Concordat of Bologna		Publication of Erasmus's Greek New Testament	
1517	Tetzel sells indulgences in Saxony; Luther's Ninety-five Theses						
1518	Heidelberg Disputation; Luther examined by Eck at Diet of Augsburg			Diet of Augsburg			

	German Territories	France	Spain	Italy	Switzerland	Netherlands	British Isles
1519	Leipzig Disputation	b. Theodore Beza (d. 1605)	Cortés conquers Aztecs; Portuguese sailor Magellan circumnavigates the globe		Zwingli appointed pastor of Grossmünster in Zurich; b. Rudolf Gwalther (d. 1586)		
1520	Publication of Luther's "Three Treatises"; burning of papal bull in Wittenberg		Coronation of Charles V	Papal Bull v. Luther: *Exsurge Domine*			
1521	Luther excommunicated; Diet/Edict of Worms—Luther condemned; Luther in hiding; Melanchthon's *Loci Communes*	French-Spanish War (–1526)	French-Spanish War; Loyola converts	Papal excommunication of Luther			Henry VIII publishes *Affirmation of the Seven Sacraments* against Luther; awarded title "Defender of the Faith" by Pope
1521–1522	Disorder in Wittenberg; Luther translates New Testament						
1521–1525		First and Second Habsburg–Valois War					
1522	Luther returns to Wittenberg; Luther's NT published; criticizes Zwickau prophets; b. Martin Chemnitz (d. 1586)		Publication of Complutensian Polyglot Bible under Cisneros		Sausage Affair and reform begins in Zurich under Zwingli		
1523	Knight's Revolt	Bucer begins ministry in Strasbourg	Loyola writes Spiritual Exercises	r. Pope Clement VII (–1534)	Iconoclasm in Zurich		
1524–1526	Peasants' War						
1524	Luther criticizes peasants					Erasmus's disputation on free will	
1525	Luther marries; execution of Thomas Müntzer				Abolition of mass in Zurich; disputation on baptism; first believers' baptism performed in Zurich		
1526					Zurich council mandates capital punishment of Anabaptists	Publication of Tyndale's English translation of NT	

	German Territories	France	Spain	Italy	Switzerland	Netherlands	British Isles
1527	d. Hans Denck (b. c. 1500) d. Hans Hut (b. 1490) b. Tilemann Hesshus (d. 1588)			Sack of Rome by mutinous troops of Charles V	First Anabaptist executed in Zurich; drafting of Schleitheim Confession		
1528	Execution of Hubmaier						
1529	Second Diet of Speyer; evangelical "protest"; publication of Luther's catechisms; Marburg Colloquy; siege of Vienna by Turkish forces	Abolition of mass in Strasbourg			d. Georg Blaurock (b. 1492)		Thomas More appointed chancellor to Henry VIII
1530	Diet of Augsburg; Confession of Augsburg	d. Francois Lambert (Lambert of Avignon) (b. 1487)	Charles V crowned Holy Roman Emperor				
1531	Formation of Schmalkaldic League				d. H. Zwingli; succeeded by H. Bullinger		
1532		Publication of Calvin's commentary on Seneca; conversion of Calvin	b. Francisco de Toledo (d. 1596)				
1533	b. Valentein Weigel (d. 1588)	Nicholas Cop addresses University of Paris; Cop and Calvin implicated as "Lutheran" sympathizers	b. Juan de Maldonado (d. 1583)				Thomas Cranmer appointed as Archbishop of Canterbury; Henry VIII divorces
1534	First edition of Luther's Bible published	Affair of the Placards; Calvin flees d. Guillame Briçonnet (b. 1470)		Jesuits founded; d. Cardinal Cajetan (Thomas de Vio) (b. 1469)			Act of Supremacy; English church breaks with Rome
1535	Bohemian Confession of 1535; Anabaptist theocracy at Münster collapses after eighteen months						d. Thomas More; d. John Fisher

	German Territories	France	Spain	Italy	Switzerland	Netherlands	British Isles
1536	Wittenberg Concord; b. Kaspar Olevianus (d. 1587)				First edition of Calvin's *Institutes* published; Calvin arrives in Geneva (–1538); First Helvetic Confession	Publication of Tyndale's translation of NT; d. W. Tyndale	d. A. Boleyn; Henry VIII dissolves monasteries (–1541)
1537					Calvin presents ecclesiastical ordinances to Genevan Council		
1538					Calvin exiled from Geneva; arrives in Strasbourg (–1541)		
1539		Calvin publishes second edition of *Institutes* in Strasbourg		d. Felix Pratensis			Statute of Six Articles; publication of Coverdale's Wheat Bible
1540				Papal approval of Jesuit order			d. Thomas Cromwell
1541	Colloquy of Regensberg	French translation of Calvin's *Institutes* published	d. Juan de Valdés (b. 1500/1510)		d. A. Karlstadt; Calvin returns to Geneva (–1564)		
1542	d. Sebastian Franck (b. 1499)			Institution of Roman Inquisition			War between England and Scotland; James V of Scotland defeated; Ireland declared sovereign kingdom
1543	Copernicus publishes *On the Revolutions of the Heavenly Spheres*; d. Johann Eck (Johann Maier of Eck) (b. 1486)						
1545–1547	Schmalkaldic Wars; d. Martin Luther			First session of Council of Trent			
1546	b. Johannes Piscator (d. 1625)						
1547	Defeat of Protestants at Mühlberg	d. Francis I; r. Henri II (–1559)					d. Henry VIII; r. Edward VI (–1553)
1548	Augsburg Interim (–1552) d. Caspar Cruciger (b. 1504)						
1549	d. Paul Fagius (b. 1504)				Consensus Tigurinus between Calvin and Bullinger		First Book of Common Prayer published

	German Territories	France	Spain	Italy	Switzerland	Netherlands	British Isles
1550	b. Aegidius Hunnius (d. 1603)						
1551–1552				Second session of Council of Trent			Cranmer's Forty-Two Articles
1552	d. Sebastian Münster (b. 1488) d. Friedrich Nausea (b. c. 1496)						
1553	d. Johannes Aepinus (b. 1449)						Book of Common Prayer revised; d. Edward VI; r. Mary I (1558)
1554							Richard Hooker (d. 1600)
1555	Diet of Augsburg; Peace of Augsburg establishes legal territorial existence of Lutheranism and Catholicism b. Johann Arndt (d. 1621)	First mission of French pastors trained in Geneva				b. Sibbrandus Lubbertus (d. 1625)	b. Robert Rollock (d. 1599); d. Hugh Latimer; d. Nicholas Ridley d. John Hooper
1556	d. Pilgram Marpeck (b. 1495) d. Konrad Pellikan (b. 1478) d. Peter Riedemann (b. 1506)	Charles V resigns				d. David Joris (b. c. 1501)	d. Thomas Cranmer
1557					Michael Servetus executed in Geneva		Alliance with Spain in war against France
1558			d. Charles V				b. William Perkins (d. 1602); d. Mary I; r. Elizabeth I (–1603)
1559		d. Henry II; r. Francis II (–1560); first national synod of French reformed churches (1559) in Paris; Gallic Confession		First index of prohibited books issued	Final edition of Calvin's *Institutes*; founding of Genevan Academy	b. Jacobus Arminius (d. 1609)	Elizabethan Settlement
1560	d. P. Melanchthon	d. Francis II; r. Charles IX (1574); Edict of Toleration created peace with Huguenots			Geneva Bible		Kirk of Scotland established; Scottish Confession
1561-1563				Third session of Council of Trent			

	German Territories	France	Spain	Italy	Switzerland	Netherlands	British Isles
1561						Belgic Confession	
1562	d. Katharina Schütz Zell (b. 1497/98)	Massacre of Huguenots begins French Wars of Religion (–1598)					The Articles of Religion—in Elizabethan "final" form (1562/71)
1563	Heidelberg Catechism						
1564				b. Galileo (d. 1642)	d. J. Calvin		b. William Shakespeare (d. 1616)
1566	d. Johann Agricola (b. 1494)			Roman Catechism	Second Helvetic Confession		
1567						Spanish occupation	Abdication of Scottish throne by Mary Stuart; r. James VI (1603–1625)
1568						d. Dirk Phillips (b. 1504) Dutch movement for liberation (–1645)	British Bible
1570		d. Johannes Mercerus (Jean Mercier)		Papal Bull Regnans in Excelsis excommunicates Elizabeth I			Elizabeth I excommunicated
1571	b. Johannes Kepler (d. 1630)		Spain defeats Ottoman navy at Battle of Lepanto				b. John Downame (d. 1652)
1572		Massacre of Huguenots on St. Bartholomew's Day		r. Pope Gregory XIII (1583–1585)		William of Orange invades	b. John Donne (d. 1631)
1574		d. Charles IX; r. Henri III (d. 1589)					
1575	d. Georg Major (b. 1502); Bohemian Confession of 1575						
1576		Declaration of Toleration; formation of Catholic League		b. Giovanni Diodati (d. 1649)		Sack of Antwerp; Pacification of Ghent	
1577	Lutheran Formula of Concord						England allies with Netherlands against Spain
1578	Swiss Brethren Confession of Hesse d. Peter Walpot		Truce with Ottomans				Sir Francis Drake circumnavigates the globe

	German Territories	France	Spain	Italy	Switzerland	Netherlands	British Isles
1579			Expeditions to Ireland			Division of Dutch provinces	
1580	Lutheran Book of Concord						
1581			d. Teresa of Avila				Anti-Catholic statutes passed
1582				Gregorian Reform of calendar			
1583							b. David Dickson (d. 1663)
1584		Treaty of Joinville with Spain	Treaty of Joinville; Spain inducted into Catholic League; defeats Dutch at Antwerp			Fall of Antwerp; d. William of Orange	
1585	d. Josua Opitz (b. c. 1542)	Henri of Navarre excommunicated		r. Pope Sixtus V (–1590)			
1586							Sir Francis Drake's expedition to West Indies; Sir Walter Raleigh in Roanoke
1587	d. Johann Wigand (b. 1523)	Henri of Navarre defeats royal army					d. Mary Stuart of Scotland
1588		Henri of Navarre drives Henri III from Paris; assassination of Catholic League Leaders	Armada destroyed				English Mary defeats Spanish Armada
1589		d. Henri III; r. Henri (of Navarre) IV (–1610)	Victory over England at Lisbon				Defeated by Spain in Lisbon
1590		Henri IV's siege of Paris		d. Girolamo Zanchi (b. 1516)			Alliance with Henri IV
1592	d. Nikolaus Selnecker (b. 1530)						
1593		Henri IV converts to Catholicism					
1594		Henri grants toleration to Huguenots					
1595		Henri IV declares war on Spain; received into Catholic Church		Pope Sixtus accepts Henri IV into Church			Alliance with France
1596		b. René Descartes (d. 1650) b. Moïse Amyraut (d. 1664)					

	German Territories	France	Spain	Italy	Switzerland	Netherlands	British Isles
1598		Edict of Nantes; toleration of Huguenots; peace with Spain	Treaty of Vervins; peace with France				
1600	d. David Chytraeus (b. 1531)						
1601							b. John Trapp (d. 1669)
1602					d. Daniel Toussain (b. 1541)		
1603							d. Elizabeth I; r. James I (James VI of Scotland) (–1625)
1604	d. Cyriacus Spangenberg (b. 1528)						d. John Whitgift (b. 1530)
1605						b. Rembrandt (d. 1669)	Guy Fawkes and gunpowder plot
1606							Jamestown Settlement
1607							b. John Milton (d. 1674)
1608							
1610		d. Henri IV; r. Louis XIII (–1643)	d. Benedict Pererius (b. 1535)			The Remonstrance; Short Confession	
1611							Publication of Authorized English Translation of Bible (AV/KJV)
1612							b. Richard Crashaw (d. 1649)
1616							b. John Owen (d. 1683)
1617							b. Ralph Cudworth (d. 1689)
1618–1648	Thirty Years' War						
1618–1619						Synod of Dordrecht	
1620							English Puritans land in Massachusetts
1621							d. Andrew Willet (b. 1562)
1633	d. Christoph Pelargus (b. 1565)						Laud becomes Archbishop of Canterbury
1637	d. Johann Gerhard (b. 1582)						

	German Territories	France	Spain	Italy	Switzerland	Netherlands	British Isles
1638							d. Joseph Mede (b. 1638)
1640				Diodati's Italian translation of Bible published			
1642–1649							English civil wars; d. Charles I; r. Oliver Cromwell (1660)
1643–1649							Westminster Assembly
1643		d. Louis XIII; r. Louis XIV (–1715)					
1645							d. William Laud (b. 1573)
1648		Treaty of Westphalia ends Thirty Years' War					
1656	d. Georg Calixtus (b. 1586)						
1660							English Restoration; d. Oliver Cromwell; r. Charles II (–1685)
1662							Act of Uniformity
1664						d. Thieleman Jans van Bragt (b. 1625)	d. John Mayer (b. 1583)
1671							d. William Greenhill (b. 1591)
1677							d. Thomas Manton (b. 1620)
1678						d. Anna Maria von Schurman (b. 1607)	
1688							Glorious Revolution; r. William and Mary (-1702); d. John Bunyan (b. 1628)
1691							d. Richard Baxter (b. 1615)

BIOGRAPHICAL SKETCHES OF
REFORMATION-ERA FIGURES AND WORKS

For works consulted, see "Sources for Biographical Sketches," p. 539.

Johannes Aepinus (1499–1553). German Lutheran preacher and theologian. Aepinus studied under Martin Luther,* Philipp Melanchthon* and Johannes Bugenhagen* in Wittenberg. Because of his Lutheran beliefs, Aepinus lost his first teaching position in Brandenburg. He fled north to Stralsund and became a preacher and superintendent at Saint Peter's Church in Hamburg. In 1534, he made a diplomatic visit to England but could not convince Henry VIII to embrace the Augsburg Confession.* His works include sermons and theological writings. Aepinus became best known as leader of the Infernalists, who believed that Christ underwent torment in hell after his crucifixion.

Johann Agricola (c. 1494–1566). German Lutheran pastor and theologian. An early student of Martin Luther,* Agricola eventually began a controversy over the role of the law, first with Melanchthon* and then with Luther himself. Agricola claimed to defend Luther's true position, asserting that only the gospel of the crucified Christ calls Christians to truly good works, not the fear of the law. After this first controversy, Agricola seems to have radicalized his views to the point that he eliminated Luther's *simul iustus et peccator* ("at the same time righteous and sinful") paradox of the Christian life, emphasizing instead that believers have no need for the law once they are united with Christ through faith. Luther responded by writing anonymous pamphlets against antinomianism. Agricola later published a recantation of his views, hoping to assuage relations with Luther, although they were never personally reconciled. He published a commentary on Luke, a series of sermons on Colossians, and a massive collection of German proverbs.

Henry Ainsworth (1571–1622/1623). English Puritan Hebraist. In 1593, under threat of persecution, Ainsworth relocated to Amsterdam, where he served as a teacher in an English congregation. He composed a confession of faith for the community and a number of polemical and exegetical works, including annotations on the Pentateuch, the Psalms and Song of Songs.

Henry Airay (c. 1560–1616). English Puritan professor and pastor. He was especially noted for his preaching, a blend of hostility toward Catholicism and articulate exposition of English Calvinism. He was promoted to provost of Queen's College Oxford (1598) and then to vice chancellor of the university in 1606. He disputed with William Laud* concerning Laud's putative Catholicization of the Church of England, particularly over the practice of genuflection, which Airay vehemently opposed. He also opposed fellow Puritans who wished to separate from the Church of England. His lectures on Philippians were his only work published during his lifetime.

Alexander (Ales) Alesius (1500–1565). Scottish

Lutheran theologian. Following the martyrdom of his theological adversary Patrick Hamilton (c. 1504–1528), Alesius converted to the Reformation and fled to Germany. In 1535 Martin Luther* and Philip Melanchthon* sent him as an emissary to Henry VIII and Thomas Cranmer.* He taught briefly at Cambridge, but after the Act of Six Articles reasserted Catholic sacramental theology he returned to Germany, where he lectured at Frankfurt an der Oder and Leipzig. Alesius composed many exegetical, theological and polemical works, including commentaries on John, Romans, 1–2 Timothy, Titus and the Psalms.

Moïse Amyraut (1596–1664). French Reformed pastor and professor. Originally intending to be a lawyer, Amyraut turned to theology after an encounter with several Huguenot pastors and having read Calvin's* *Institutes*. After a brief stint as a parish pastor, Amyraut spent the majority of his career at the Saumur Academy. He was well known for his irenicism and ecumenicism (for example, in advocating intercommunion with Lutherans). Certain aspects of his writings on justification, faith, the covenants and especially predestination proved controversial among the Reformed. His doctrine of election is often called hypothetical universalism or Amyraldianism, stating that Christ's atoning work was intended by God for all human beings indiscriminately, although its effectiveness for salvation depends on faith, which is a free gift of God given only to those whom God has chosen from eternity. Amyraut was charged with grave doctrinal error three times before the National Synod but was acquitted each time. Aside from his theological treatises, Amyraut published paraphrases of almost the entire New Testament and the Psalms, as well as many sermons.

Jakob Andreae (1528–1590). German Lutheran theologian. Andreae studied at the University of Tübingen before being called to the diaconate in Stuttgart in 1546. He was appointed ecclesiastical superintendent of Göppingen in 1553 and supported Johannes Brenz's* proposal to place the church under civil administrative control. An ecclesial diplomat for the duke of Württemberg, Andreae debated eucharistic theology, the use of images and predestination with Theodore Beza* at the Colloquy of Montbéliard (1586) to determine whether French Reformed exiles would be required to submit to the Formula of Concord.* Andreae coauthored the Formula of Concord. He and his wife had eighteen children.

Benedict Aretius (d. 1574). Swiss Reformed professor. Trained at the universities of Bern, Strasbourg and Marburg, Aretius taught logic and philosophy as well as the biblical languages and theology. He advocated for stronger unity and peace between the Lutheran and Reformed churches. Aretius joined others in denouncing the antitrinitarian Giovanni Valentino Gentile (d. 1566). He published commentaries on the New Testament, as well as various works on astronomy, botany and medicine.

Jacobus Arminius (1559–1609). Dutch Remonstrant pastor and theologian. Arminius was a vocal critic of high Calvinist scholasticism, whose views were repudiated by the synod of Dordrecht. Arminius was a student of Theodore Beza* at the academy of Geneva. He served as a pastor in Amsterdam and later joined the faculty of theology at the university in Leiden, where his lectures on predestination were popular and controversial. Predestination, as Arminius understood it, was the decree of God determined on the basis of divine foreknowledge of faith or rejection by humans who are the recipients of prevenient, but resistible, grace.

Johann Arndt (1555–1621). German Lutheran pastor and theologian. After a brief time teaching, Arndt pastored in Badeborn (Anhalt) until 1590, when Prince Johann Georg von Anhalt (1567–1618) began introducing Reformed ecclesial policies. Arndt ministered in Quedlinberg, Brunswick, Eisleben and Celle. Heavily influenced by medieval mysticism, Arndt centered his theology on Christ's mystical union with the believer, out of which flows love of God and neighbor. He is best known for his *True Christianity* (1605–1609), which greatly influenced Philipp Jakob Spener (1635–1705) and later Pietists.

Articles of Religion (1562; revised 1571). The Articles underwent a long editorial process that drew from the influence of Continental confessions in England, resulting in a uniquely Anglican blend of Protestantism and Catholicism. In their final form, they were reduced from Thomas Cranmer's* Forty-two Articles (1539) to the Elizabethan Thirty-nine Articles (1571), excising polemical articles against the Anabaptists and Millenarians as well as adding articles on the Holy Spirit, good works and Communion. Originating in a 1535 meeting with Lutherans, the Articles retained a minor influence from the Augsburg Confession* and Württemberg Confession (1552), but showed significant revision in accordance with Genevan theology, as well as the Second Helvetic Confession.*

Anne Askew (1521–1546). English Protestant martyr. Askew was forced to marry her deceased sister's intended husband, who later expelled Askew from his house—after the birth of two children—on account of her religious views. After unsuccessfully seeking a divorce in Lincoln, Askew moved to London, where she met other Protestants and began to preach. In 1546, she was arrested, imprisoned and convicted of heresy for denying the doctrine of transubstantiation. Under torture in the Tower of London she refused to name any other Protestants. On July 16, 1546, she was burned at the stake. Askew is best known through her accounts of her arrests and examinations. John Bale (1495–1563), a bishop, historian and playwright, published these manuscripts. Later John Foxe (1516–1587) included them in his *Acts and Monuments*, presenting her as a role model for other pious Protestant women.

Augsburg Confession (1530). In the wake of Luther's* stand against ecclesial authorities at the Diet of Worms (1521), the Holy Roman Empire splintered along theological lines. Emperor Charles V sought to ameliorate this—while also hoping to secure a united European front against Turkish invasion—by calling together another imperial diet in Augsburg in 1530. The Evangelical party was cast in a strongly heretical light at the diet by Johann Eck.* For this reason, Philipp Melanch-

thon* and Justus Jonas* thought it best to strike a conciliatory tone (Luther, as an official outlaw, did not attend), submitting a confession rather than a defense. The resulting Augsburg Confession was approved by many of the rulers of the northeastern Empire; however, due to differences in eucharistic theology, Martin Bucer* and the representatives of Strasbourg, Constance, Lindau and Memmingen drafted a separate confession (the Tetrapolitan Confession). Charles V accepted neither confession, demanding that the Evangelicals accept the Catholic rebuttal instead. In 1531, along with the publication of the Augsburg Confession itself, Melanchthon released a defense of the confession that responded to the Catholic confutation and expanded on the original articles. Most subsequent Protestant confessions followed the general structure of the Augsburg Confession.

Robert Bagnall (b. 1559 or 1560). English Protestant minister. Bagnall authored *The Steward's Last Account* (1622), a collection of five sermons on Luke 16.

Thomas Bastard (c. 1565–1618). English Protestant minister and poet. Educated at Winchester and New College, Oxford, Bastard published numerous works, including collections of poems and sermons; his most famous title is *Chrestoleros* (1598), a collection of epigrams. Bastard was alleged to be the author of an anonymous work, *An Admonition to the City of Oxford*, which revealed the carnal vices of many clergy and scholars in Oxford; despite denying authorship, he was dismissed from Oxford in 1591. Bastard was recognized as a skilled classical scholar and preacher. He died impoverished in a debtor's prison in Dorchester.

Johann (Pomarius) Baumgart (1514–1578). Lutheran pastor and amateur playwright. Baumgart studied under Georg Major,* Martin Luther* and Philipp Melanchthon* at the University of Wittenberg. Before becoming pastor of the Church of the Holy Spirit in 1540, Baumgart taught secondary school. He authored catechetical and polemical works, a postil for the Gospel readings throughout the church year, numerous hymns and a didactic play (*Juditium Salomonis*).

Richard Baxter (1615–1691). English Puritan minister. Baxter was a leading Puritan pastor, evangelist and theologian, known throughout England for his landmark ministry in Kidderminster and a prodigious literary output, producing 135 books in just over forty years. Baxter came to faith through reading William Perkins,* Richard Sibbes* and other early Puritan writers and was the first cleric to decline the terms of ministry in the national English church imposed by the 1662 Act of Uniformity; Baxter wrote on behalf of the more than 1700 who shared ejection from the national church. He hoped for restoration to national church ministry, or toleration, that would allow lawful preaching and pastoring. Baxter sought unity in theological, ecclesiastical, sociopolitical and personal terms and is regarded as a forerunner of Noncomformist ecumenicity, though he was defeated in his efforts at the 1661 Savoy Conference to take seriously Puritan objections to the revision of the 1604 Prayer Book. Baxter's views on church ministry were considerably hybrid: he was a paedo-baptist, Nonconformist minister who approved of synodical Episcopal government and fixed liturgy. He is most known for his classic writings on the Christian life, such as *The Saints' Everlasting Rest* and *A Christian Directory*, and pastoral ministry, such as *The Reformed Pastor*. He also produced *Catholick Theology*, a large volume squaring current Reformed, Lutheran, Arminian and Roman Catholic systems with each other.

Thomas Becon (1511/1512–1567). English Puritan preacher. Becon was a friend of Hugh Latimer,* and for several years chaplain to Archbishop Thomas Cranmer.* Becon was sent to the Tower of London by Mary I and then exiled for his controversial preaching at the English royal court. He returned to England upon Elizabeth I's accession. Becon was one of the most widely read popular preachers in England during the Reformation. He published many of his sermons, including a postil, or collection of sermon helps for undertrained or inexperienced preachers.

Belgic Confession (1561). Written by Guy de Brès (1523–1567), this statement of Dutch Reformed faith was heavily reliant on the Gallic Confession,* although more detailed, especially in how strongly it distances the Reformed from Roman Catholics and Anabaptists. The Confession first appeared in French in 1561 and was translated to Dutch in 1562. It was presented to Philip II (1527–1598) in the hope that he would grant toleration to the Reformed, to no avail. At the Synod of Dordrecht* the Confession was revised, clarifying and strengthening the article on election as well as sharpening the distinctives of Reformed theology against the Anabaptists, thus situating the Dutch Reformed more closely to the international Calvinist movement. The Belgic Confession in conjunction with the Heidelberg Catechism* and the Canons of Dordrecht were granted official status as the confessional standards (the Three Forms of Unity) of the Dutch Reformed Church.

Theodore Beza (1519–1605). French pastor and professor. Beza was compatriot and successor to John Calvin* as moderator of the Company of Pastors in Geneva during the second half of the sixteenth century. He was a noteworthy New Testament scholar whose *Codex Bezae* formed the basis of the New Testament section of later English translations. A leader in the academy and the church, Beza served as professor of Greek at the Lausanne Academy until 1558, at which time he moved to Geneva to become the rector of the newly founded Genevan Academy. He enjoyed an international reputation through his correspondence with key European leaders. Beza developed and extended Calvin's doctrinal thought on several important themes such as the nature of predestination and the real spiritual presence of Christ in the Eucharist.

Bishops' Bible (1568). Anglicans were polarized by the two most recent English translations of the Bible: the Great Bible (1539) relied too heavily on the Vulgate* and was thus perceived as too Catholic, while the Geneva Bible's* marginal notes were too Calvinist for many Anglicans. So Archbishop Matthew Parker (1504–1575) commissioned a new translation of Scripture from the original languages with marginal annotations (many of which, ironically, were from the Geneva Bible). Published under royal warrant, the Bishops' Bible became the official translation for the Church of England. The 1602 edition provided the basis for the King James Bible (1611).

Georg Blaurock (1492–1529). Swiss Anabaptist. Blaurock (a nickname meaning "blue coat," because of his preference for this garment) was one of the first leaders of Switzerland's radical reform movement. In the first public disputations on baptism in Zurich, he argued for believer's baptism and was the first person to receive adult believers' baptism there, having been baptized by Conrad Grebel* in 1525. Blaurock was arrested several times for performing mass adult baptisms and engaging in social disobedience by disrupting worship services. He was eventually expelled from Zurich but continued preaching and baptizing in various Swiss cantons until his execution.

Bohemian Confession (1535). Bohemian Christianity was subdivided between traditional Catholics, Utraquists (who demanded Communion in both kinds) and the *Unitas Fratrum*, who were not Protestants but whose theology bore strong affinities to the Waldensians and the Reformed. The 1535 Latin edition of this confession—an earlier Czech edition had already been drafted—was an attempt to clarify and redefine the beliefs of the *Unitas Fratrum*. This confession purged all earlier openness to rebaptism and inched toward Luther's* eucharistic theology. Jan Augusta (c. 1500–1572) and Jan Roh (also Johannes Horn; c. 1490–1547) presented the confession to King Ferdinand I (1503–1564) in Vienna, but the king would not print it. The *Unitas Fratrum* sought, and with slight amendments eventually obtained, Luther's advocacy of the confession. It generally follows the structure of the Augsburg Confession.*

Bohemian Confession (1575). This confession was an attempt to shield Bohemian Christian minorities—the Utraquists and the *Unitas Fratrum*—from the Counter-Reformation and Habsburg insistence on uniformity. The hope was

that this umbrella consensus would ensure peace in the midst of Christian diversity; anyone who affirmed the 1575 Confession, passed by the Bohemian legislature, would be tolerated. This confession was, like the Bohemian Confession of 1535, patterned after the Augsburg Confession.* It emphasizes both justification by faith alone and good works as the fruit of salvation. Baptism and the Eucharist are the focus of the sacramental section, although the five traditional Catholic sacraments are also listed for the Utraquists. Though it was eventually accepted in 1609 by Rudolf II (1552–1612), the Thirty Years' War (1618–1648) rendered the confession moot.

Book of Common Prayer (1549; 1552). After the Church of England's break with Rome, it needed a liturgical manual to distinguish its theology and practice from that of Catholicism. Thomas Cranmer* drafted the Book of Common Prayer based on the medieval Roman Missal, under the dual influence of the revised Lutheran Mass and the reforms of the Spanish Cardinal Quiñones. This manual details the eucharistic service, as well as services for rites such as baptism, confirmation, marriage and funerals. It includes a matrix of the epistle and Gospel readings and the appropriate collect for each Sunday and feast day of the church year. The 1548 Act of Uniformity established the Book of Common Prayer as *the* authoritative liturgical manual for the Church of England, to be implemented everywhere by Pentecost 1549. After its 1552 revision, Queen Mary I banned it; Elizabeth reestablished it in 1559, although it was rejected by Puritans and Catholics alike.

The Book of Homilies (1547; 1563; 1570). This collection of approved sermons, published in three parts during the reigns of Edward VI and Elizabeth I, was intended to inculcate Anglican theological distinctives and mitigate the problems raised by the lack of educated preachers. Addressing doctrinal and practical topics, Thomas Cranmer* likely wrote the majority of the first twelve sermons, published in 1547; John Jewel* added another twenty sermons in 1563. A final sermon, *A Homily against Disobedience*, was appended to the canon in 1570. Reprinted regularly, the *Book of Homilies* was an important resource in Anglican preaching until at least the end of the seventeenth century.

John Boys (1571–1625). Anglican priest and theologian. Before doctoral work at Cambridge, Boys pastored several parishes in Kent; after completing his studies he was appointed to more prominent positions, culminating in his 1619 appointment as the Dean of Canterbury by James I. Boys published a popular four-volume postil of the Gospel and epistle readings for the church year, as well as a companion volume for the Psalms.

Thieleman Jans van Braght (1625–1664). Dutch Radical preacher. After demonstrating great ability with languages, this cloth merchant was made preacher in his hometown of Dordrecht in 1648. He served in this office for the next sixteen years, until his death. This celebrated preacher had a reputation for engaging in debate wherever an opportunity presented itself, particularly concerning infant baptism. The publication of his book of martyrs, *Het Bloedigh Tooneel of Martel-aersspiegel* (1660; *Martyrs' Mirror*), proved to be his lasting contribution to the Mennonite tradition. *Martyrs' Mirror* is heavily indebted to the earlier martyr book *Offer des Heeren* (1562), to which Braght added many early church martyrs who rejected infant baptism, as well as over 800 contemporary martyrs.

Johannes Brenz (1499–1570). German Lutheran theologian and pastor. Brenz was converted to the reformation cause after hearing Martin Luther* speak; later, Brenz became a student of Johannes Oecolampadius.* His central achievement lay in his talent for organization. As city preacher in Schwäbisch-Hall and afterward in Württemberg and Tübingen, he oversaw the introduction of reform measures and doctrines and new governing structures for ecclesial and educational communities. Brenz also helped establish Lutheran orthodoxy through treatises, commentaries and catechisms. He defended Luther's position on eucharistic presence against Huldrych Zwingli*

and opposed the death penalty for religious dissenters.

Guillaume Briçonnet (1470–1534). French Catholic abbot and bishop. Briçonnet created a short-lived circle of reformist-minded humanists in his diocese under the sponsorship of Marguerite d'Angoulême. His desire for ecclesial reform developed throughout his prestigious career (including positions as royal chaplain to the queen, abbot at Saint-Germain-des-Prés and bishop of Meaux), influenced by Jacques Lefèvre d'Étaples.* Briçonnet encouraged reform through ministerial visitation, Scripture and preaching in the vernacular and active study of the Bible. When this triggered the ire of the theology faculty at the Sorbonne in Paris, Briçonnet quelled the activity and departed, envisioning an ecclesial reform that proceeded hierarchically.

Otto Brunfels (c. 1488–1534). German Lutheran botanist, teacher and physician. Brunfels joined the Carthusian order, where he developed interests in the natural sciences and became involved with a humanist circle associated with Ulrich von Hutten and Wolfgang Capito.* In 1521, after coming into contact with Luther's* teaching, Brunfels abandoned the monastic life, traveling and spending time in botanical research and pastoral care. He received a medical degree in Basel and was appointed city physician of Bern in 1534. Brunfels penned defenses of Luther and Hutten, devotional biographies of biblical figures, a prayer book, and annotations on the Gospels and the Acts of the Apostles. His most influential contribution, however, is as a Renaissance botanist.

Martin Bucer (1491–1551). German Reformed theologian and pastor. A Dominican friar, Bucer was influenced by Desiderius Erasmus* during his doctoral studies at the University of Heidelberg, where he began corresponding with Martin Luther.* After advocating reform in Alsace, Bucer was excommunicated and fled to Strasbourg, where he became a leader in the city's Reformed ecclesial and educational communities. Bucer sought concord between Lutherans and Zwinglians and Protestants and Catholics. He emigrated to England, becoming a professor at Cambridge. Bucer's greatest theological concern was the centrality of Christ's sacrificial death, which achieved justification and sanctification and orients Christian community.

Johannes Bugenhagen (1485–1558). German Lutheran pastor and professor. Bugenhagen, a priest and lecturer at a Premonstratensian monastery, became a city preacher in Wittenberg during the reform efforts of Martin Luther* and Philipp Melanchthon.* Initially influenced by his reading of Desiderius Erasmus,* Bugenhagen grew in evangelical orientation through Luther's works; later, he studied under Melanchthon at the University of Wittenberg, eventually serving as rector and faculty member there. Bugenhagen was a versatile commentator, exegete and lecturer on Scripture. Through these roles and his development of lectionary and devotional material, Bugenhagen facilitated rapid establishment of church order throughout many German provinces.

Heinrich Bullinger (1504–1575). Swiss Reformed pastor and theologian. Bullinger succeeded Huldrych Zwingli* as minister and leader in Zurich. The primary author of the First and Second Helvetic Confessions,* Bullinger was drawn toward reform through the works of Martin Luther* and Philipp Melanchthon.* After Zwingli died, Bullinger was vital in maintaining adherence to the cause of reform; he oversaw the expansion of the Zurich synodal system while preaching, teaching and writing extensively. One of Bullinger's lasting legacies was the development of a federal view of the divine covenant with humanity, making baptism and the Eucharist covenantal signs.

John Bunyan (1628–1688). English Puritan preacher and writer. His *Pilgrim's Progress* is one of the best-selling English-language titles in history. Born to a working-class family, Bunyan was largely unschooled, gaining literacy (and entering the faith) through reading the Bible and such early Puritan devotional works as *The Plain Man's Pathway to Heaven* and *The Practice of Piety*. Following a short stint in Oliver Crom-

well's parliamentary army, in which Bunyan narrowly escaped death in combat, he turned to a preaching ministry, succeeding John Gifford as pastor at the Congregational church in Bedford. A noted preacher, Bunyan drew large crowds in itinerant appearances and it was in the sermonic form that Bunyan developed his theological outlook, which was an Augustinian-inflected Calvinism. Bunyan's opposition to the Book of Common Prayer and refusal of official ecclesiastical licensure led to multiple imprisonments, where he wrote many of his famous allegorical works, including *Pilgrim's Progress, The Holy City, Prison Meditations* and *Holy War*.

Jeremiah Burroughs (c. 1600–1646). English Puritan pastor and delegate to the Westminster Assembly. Burroughs left Cambridge, as well as a rectorate in Norfolk, because of his nonconformity. After returning to England from pastoring an English congregation in Rotterdam for several years (1637–1641), he became one of only a few dissenters from the official presbyterianism of the Assembly in favor of a congregationalist polity. Nevertheless, he was well known and respected by presbyterian colleagues such as Richard Baxter* for his irenic tone and conciliatory manner. The vast majority of Burroughs's corpus was published posthumously, although during his lifetime he published annotations on Hosea and several polemical works.

Cardinal Cajetan (Thomas de Vio) (1469–1534). Italian Catholic cardinal, professor, theologian and biblical exegete. This Dominican monk was the leading Thomist theologian and one of the most important Catholic exegetes of the sixteenth century. Cajetan is best-known for his interview with Martin Luther* at the Diet of Augsburg (1518). Among his many works are polemical treatises, extensive biblical commentaries and most importantly a four-volume commentary (1508–1523) on the *Summa Theologiae* of Thomas Aquinas.

Georg Calixtus (1586–1656). German Lutheran theologian. Calixtus studied at the University of Helmstedt where he developed regard for Philipp

Melanchthon.* Between his time as a student and later as a professor at Helmstedt, Calixtus traveled through Europe seeking a way to unite and reconcile Lutherans, Calvinists and Catholics. He attempted to fuse these denominations through use of the Scriptures, the Apostles' Creed, and the first five centuries, interpreted by the Vincentian canon. Calixtus's position was stamped as syncretist and yielded further debate even after his death.

John Calvin (1509–1564). French Reformed pastor and theologian. In his *Institutes of the Christian Religion*, Calvin provided a theological dogmatics for the Reformed churches. Calvin's gradual conversion to the cause of reform occurred through his study with chief humanist scholars in Paris, but he spent most of his career in Geneva (excepting a three-year exile in Strasbourg with Martin Bucer*). In Geneva, Calvin reorganized the structure and governance of the church and established an academy that became an international center for theological education. He was a tireless writer, producing his *Institutes*, theological treatises and Scripture commentaries.

Wolfgang Capito (1478?–1541). German Reformed humanist and theologian. Capito, a Hebrew scholar, produced a Hebrew grammar and published several Latin commentaries on books of the Hebrew Scriptures. He corresponded with Desiderius Erasmus* and fellow humanists. Capito translated Martin Luther's* early works into Latin for the printer Johann Froben. On meeting Luther, Capito was converted to Luther's vision, left Mainz and settled in Strasbourg, where he lectured on Luther's theology to the city clergy. With Martin Bucer,* Capito reformed liturgy, ecclesial life and teachings, education, welfare and government. Capito worked for the theological unification of the Swiss cantons with Strasbourg.

Thomas Cartwright (1535–1606). English Puritan preacher and professor. Cartwright was educated at St. John's College, Cambridge, although as an influential leader of the Presbyterian party in the Church of England he was continually at odds with the Anglican party,

especially John Whitgift.* Cartwright spent some time as an exile in Geneva and Heidelberg as well as in Antwerp, where he pastored an English church. In 1585, Cartwright was arrested and eventually jailed for trying to return to England despite Elizabeth I's refusal of his request. Many acknowledged him to be learned but also quite cantankerous. His publications include commentaries on Colossians, Ecclesiastes, Proverbs and the Gospels, as well as a dispute against Whitgift on church discipline.

Mathew Caylie (unknown). English Protestant minister. Caylie authored *The Cleansing of the Ten Lepers* (1623), an exposition of Luke 17:14-18.

John Chardon (d. 1601). Irish Anglican bishop. Chardon was educated at Oxford. He advocated Reformed doctrine in his preaching, yet opposed those Puritans who rejected Anglican church order. He published several sermons.

Martin Chemnitz (1522–1586). German Lutheran theologian. A leading figure in establishing Lutheran orthodoxy, Chemnitz studied theology and patristics at the University of Wittenburg, later becoming a defender of Philipp Melanchthon's* interpretation of the doctrine of justification. Chemnitz drafted a compendium of doctrine and reorganized the structure of the church in Wolfenbüttel; later, he led efforts to reconcile divisions within Lutheranism, culminating in the Formula of Concord*. One of his chief theological accomplishments was a modification of the christological doctrine of the *communicatio idiomatium*, which provided a Lutheran platform for understanding the sacramental presence of Christ's humanity in the Eucharist.

David Chytraeus (1531–1600). German Lutheran professor, theologian and biblical exegete. At the age of eight Chytraeus was admitted to the University of Tübingen. There he studied law, philology, philosophy, and theology, finally receiving his master's degree in 1546. Chytraeus befriended Philipp Melanchthon* while sojourning in Wittenberg, where he taught the *Loci communes*. While teaching exegesis at the University of Rostock Chytraeus became acquainted with Tilemann Heshusius,* who strongly influenced Chytraeus away from Philippist theology. As a defender of Gnesio-Lutheran theology Chytraeus helped organize churches throughout Austria in accordance with the Augsburg Confession.* Chytraeus coauthored the Formula of Concord* with Martin Chemnitz,* Andreas Musculus (1514–1581), Nikolaus Selnecker* and Jakob Andreae.* He wrote commentaries on most of the Bible, as well as a devotional work titled *Regula vitae* (1555) that described the Christian virtues.

John Colet (1467–1519). English Catholic priest, preacher and educator. Colet, appointed dean of Saint Paul's Cathedral by Henry VII, was a friend of Desiderius Erasmus,* on whose classical ideals Colet reconstructed the curriculum of Saint Paul's school. Colet was convinced that the foundation of moral reform lay in the education of children. Though an ardent advocate of reform, Colet, like Erasmus, remained loyal to the Catholic Church throughout his life. Colet's agenda of reform was oriented around spiritual and ethical themes, demonstrated in his commentaries on select books of the New Testament and the writings of Pseudo-Dionysius the Areopagite.

Gasparo Contarini (1483–1542). Italian statesman, theologian and reform-minded cardinal. Contarini was an able negotiator and graceful compromiser. Charles V requested Contarini as the papal legate for the Colloquy of Regensburg (1541), where Contarini reached agreement with Melanchthon* on the doctrine of justification (although neither the pope nor Luther* ratified the agreement). He had come to a similar belief in the priority of faith in the work of Christ rather than works as the basis for Christian life in 1511, though unlike Luther, he never left the papal church over the issue; instead he remainied within it to try to seek gentle reform, and he adhered to papal sacramental teaching. Contarini was an important voice for reform within the Catholic Church, always seeking reconciliation rather than confrontation with Protestant reformers. He wrote many works, including a treatise detailing the ideal bishop, a manual for lay church leaders, a political text on right governance, and brief commentaries on the Pauline letters.

John Cosin (1594–1672). Anglican preacher and bishop. Early in his career Cosin was the vice chancellor of Cambridge and canon at the Durham cathedral. But as a friend of William Laud* and an advocate for "Laudian" changes, he was suspected of being a crypto-Catholic. In 1640 during the Long Parliament a Puritan lodged a complaint with the House of Commons concerning Cosin's "popish innovations." Cosin was promptly removed from office. During the turmoil of the English Civil Wars, Cosin sojourned in Paris among English nobility but struggled financially. Cosin returned to England after the Restoration in 1660 to be consecrated as the bishop of Durham. He published annotations on the Book of Common Prayer* and a history of the canon.

Council of Constance (1414–1418). Convened to resolve the Western Schism, root out heresy and reform the church in head and members, the council asserted in *Sacrosancta* (1415) the immediate authority of ecumenical councils assembled in the Holy Spirit under Christ—even over the pope. Martin V was elected pope in 1417 after the three papal claimants were deposed; thus, the council ended the schism. The council condemned Jan Hus,* Jerome of Prague (c. 1365–1416) and, posthumously, John Wycliffe. Hus and Jerome, despite letters of safe conduct, were burned at the stake. Their deaths ignited the Hussite Wars, which ended as a result of the Council of Basel's concessions to the Bohemian church. The council fathers sought to reform the church through the regular convocation of councils (*Frequens*; 1417). Martin V begrudgingly complied by calling the required councils, then immediately disbanding them. Pius II (r. 1458–1464) reasserted papal dominance through *Execrabilis* (1460), which condemned any appeal to a future council apart from the pope's authority.

Miles Coverdale (1488–1568). Anglican bishop. Coverdale is known for his translations of the Bible into English, completing William Tyndale's* efforts and later producing the Great Bible commissioned by Henry VIII (1539). A former friar, Coverdale was among the Cambridge scholars who met at the White Horse Tavern to discuss Martin Luther's* ideas. During Coverdale's three terms of exile in Europe, he undertook various translations, including the Geneva Bible*. He was appointed bishop of Exeter by Thomas Cranmer* and served as chaplain to Edward VI. Coverdale contributed to Cranmer's first edition of the Book of Common Prayer.*

William Cowper (Couper) (1568–1619). Scottish Puritan bishop. After graduating from the University of St. Andrews, Cowper worked in parish ministry for twenty-five years before becoming bishop. As a zealous Puritan and advocate of regular preaching and rigorous discipline, Cowper championed Presbyterian polity and lay participation in church government. Cowper published devotional works, sermon collections and a commentary on Revelation.

Thomas Cranmer (1489–1556). Anglican archbishop and theologian. Cranmer supervised church reform and produced the first two editions of the Book of Common Prayer.* As a doctoral student at Cambridge, he was involved in the discussions at the White Horse Tavern. Cranmer contributed to a religious defense of Henry VIII's divorce; Henry then appointed him Archbishop of Canterbury. Cranmer cautiously steered the course of reform, accelerating under Edward VI. After supporting the attempted coup to prevent Mary's assuming the throne, Cranmer was convicted of treason and burned at the stake. Cranmer's legacy is the splendid English of his liturgy and prayer books.

Richard Crashaw (1612–1649). English Catholic poet. Educated at Cambridge, Crashaw was fluent in Hebrew, Greek and Latin. His first volume of poetry was *Epigrammatum sacrorum liber* (1634). Despite being born into a Puritan family, Crashaw was attracted to Catholicism, finally converting in 1644 after he was forced to resign his fellowship for not signing the Solemn League and Covenant (1643). In 1649, he was made a subcanon of Our Lady of Loretto by Cardinal Palotta.

John Crompe (d. 1661). Anglican priest. Educated at Cambridge, Crompe published a commentary on the Apostles' Creed, a sermon on Psalm 21:3 and an exposition of Christ's passion.

Caspar Cruciger (1504–1548). German Lutheran theologian. Recognized for his alignment with the theological views of Philipp Melanchthon,* Cruciger was a scholar respected among both Protestants and Catholics. In 1521, Cruciger came Wittenberg to study Hebrew and remained there most of his life. He became a valuable partner for Martin Luther* in translating the Old Testament and served as teacher, delegate to major theological colloquies and rector. Cruciger was an agent of reform in his birthplace of Leipzig, where at the age of fifteen he had observed the disputation between Luther and Johann Eck.*

Jakob Dachser (1486–1567). German Anabaptist theologian and hymnist. Dachser served as a Catholic priest in Vienna until he was imprisoned and then exiled for defending the Lutheran understanding of the Mass and fasting. Hans Hut* rebaptized him in Augsburg, where Dachser was appointed as a leader of the Anabaptist congregation. Lutheran authorities imprisoned him for nearly four years. In 1531 he recanted his Radical beliefs and began to catechize children with the permission of the city council. Dachser was expelled from Augsburg as a possible insurrectionist in 1552 and relocated to Pfalz-Neuberg. He published a number of poems, hymns and mystical works, and he versified several psalms.

Jean Daillé (1594–1670). French Reformed pastor. Born into a devout Reformed family, Daillé studied theology and philosophy at Saumur under the most influential contemporary lay leader in French Protestantism, Philippe Duplessis-Mornay (1549–1623). Daillé held to Amyraldianism—the belief that Christ died for all humanity inclusively, not particularly for the elect who would inherit salvation (though only the elect are in fact saved). He wrote a controversial treatise on the church fathers that aggravated many Catholic and Anglican scholars because of Daillé's apparent demotion of patristic authority in matters of faith.

John Davenant (1576–1641). Anglican bishop and professor. Davenant attended Queen's College, Cambridge, where he received his doctorate and was appointed professor of divinity. During the Remonstrant controversy, James I sent Davenant as one of the four representatives for the Church of England to the Synod of Dordrecht.* Following James's instructions, Davenant advocated a *via media* between the Calvinists and the Remonstrants, although in later years he defended against the rise of Arminianism in England. In 1621, Davenant was promoted to the bishopric of Salisbury, where he was generally receptive to Laudian reforms. Davenant's lectures on Colossians are his best-known work.

Defense of the Augsburg Confession (1531). See *Augsburg Confession*.

Hans Denck (c. 1500–1527). German Radical theologian. Denck, a crucial early figure of the German Anabaptist movement, combined medieval German mysticism with the radical sacramental theology of Andreas Bodenstein von Karlstadt* and Thomas Müntzer.* Denck argued that the exterior forms of Scripture and sacrament are symbolic witnesses secondary to the internally revealed truth of the Sprit in the human soul. This view led to his expulsion from Nuremberg in 1525; he spent the next two years in various centers of reform in the German territories. At the time of his death, violent persecution against Anabaptists was on the rise throughout northern Europe.

Stephen Denison (unknown). English Puritan pastor. Denison received the post of curate at St. Katherine Cree in London sometime in the 1610s, where he ministered until his ejection from office in 1635. During his career at St. Katherine Cree, Denison waded into controversy with both Puritans (over the doctrine of predestination) and Anglicans (over concerns about liturgical ceremonies). He approached both altercations with rancor and rigidity, although he seems to have been quite popular and beloved by most of his congregation. In 1631, William Laud* consecrated

the newly renovated St. Katherine Cree, and as part of the festivities Denison offered a sermon on Luke 19:27 in which he publicly rebuked Laud for fashioning the Lord's house into a "den of robbers." Aside from the record of his quarrels, very little is known about Denison. In addition to *The White Wolf* (a 1627 sermon against another opponent), he published a catechism for children (1621), a treatise on the sacraments (1621) and a commentary on 2 Peter 1 (1622).

David Dickson (1583?–1663). Scottish Reformed pastor, preacher, professor and theologian. Dickson defended the Presbyterian form of ecclesial reformation in Scotland and was recognized for his iteration of Calvinist federal theology and expository biblical commentaries. Dickson served for over twenty years as professor of philosophy at the University of Glasgow before being appointed professor of divinity. He opposed the imposition of Episcopalian measures on the church in Scotland and was active in political and ecclesial venues to protest and prohibit such influences. Dickson was removed from his academic post following his refusal of the oath of supremacy during the Restoration era.

Veit Dietrich (1506–1549). German Lutheran preacher and theologian. Dietrich intended to study medicine at the University of Wittenberg, but Martin Luther* and Philipp Melanchthon* convinced him to study theology instead. Dietrich developed a strong relationship with Luther, accompanying him to the Marburg Colloquy (1529) and to Coburg Castle during the Diet of Augsburg (1530). After graduating, Dietrich taught on the arts faculty, eventually becoming dean. In 1535 he returned to his hometown, Nuremberg, to pastor. Later in life, Dietrich worked with Melanchthon to reform the church in Regensburg. In 1547, when Charles V arrived in Nuremberg, Dietrich was suspended from the pastorate; he resisted the imposition of the Augsburg Interim to no avail. In addition to transcribing some of Luther's lectures, portions of the Table Talk and the very popular *Hauspostille* (1544), Dietrich published his own sermons for children, a manual for pastors and a summary of the Bible.

Giovanni Diodati (1576–1649). Italian Reformed theologian. Diodati was from an Italian banking family who fled for religious reasons to Geneva. There he trained under Theodore Beza;* on completion of his doctoral degree, Diodati became professor of Hebrew at the academy. He was an ecclesiastical representative of the church in Geneva (for whom he was a delegate at the Synod of Dordrecht*) and an advocate for reform in Venice. Diodati's chief contribution to the Italian reform movement was a translation of the Bible into Italian (1640–1641), which remains the standard translation in Italian Protestantism.

John Donne (1572–1631). Anglican poet and preacher. Donne was born into a strong Catholic family. However, sometime between his brother's death from the plague while in prison in 1593 and the publication of his *Pseudo-Martyr* in 1610, Donne joined the Church of England. Ordained to the Anglican priesthood in 1615 and already widely recognized for his verse, Donne quickly rose to prominence as a preacher—some have deemed him the best of his era. His textual corpus is an amalgam of erotic *and* divine poetry (e.g., "Batter My Heart"), as well as a great number of sermons.

John Downame (c. 1571–1652). English Puritan pastor and theologian. See *English Annotations.*

Daniel Dyke (d. 1614). English Puritan preacher. Born of nonconformist stock, Dyke championed a more thorough reformation of church practice in England. After the promulgation of John Whitgift's* articles in 1583, Dyke refused to accept what he saw as remnants of Catholicism, bringing him into conflict with the bishop of London. Despite the petitions of his congregation and some politicians, the bishop of London suspended Dyke from his ministry for refusing priestly ordination and conformity to the Book of Common Prayer.* All of his work was published posthumously; it is mostly focused on biblical interpretation.

Johann Eck (Johann Maier of Eck) (1486–1543). German Catholic theologian. Though Eck was not an antagonist of Martin Luther* until the dispute over indulgences, Luther's Ninety-five Theses (1517) sealed the two as adversaries. After their debate at the Leipzig Disputation (1519), Eck participated in the writing of the papal bull that led to Luther's excommunication. Much of Eck's work was written to oppose Protestantism or to defend Catholic doctrine and the papacy; his *Enchiridion* was a manual written to counter Protestant doctrine. However, Eck was also deeply invested in the status of parish preaching, publishing a five-volume set of postils. He participated in the assemblies at Regensburg and Augsburg and led the Catholics in their rejection of the Augsburg Confession.

English Annotations (1645; 1651; 1657). Under a commission from the Westminster Assembly, the editors of the English Annotations—John Downame* along with unnamed colleagues—translated, collated and digested in a compact and accessible format several significant Continental biblical resources, including Calvin's* commentaries, Beza's* *Annotationes majores* and Diodati's* *Annotations.*

Desiderius Erasmus (1466–1536). Dutch Catholic humanist and pedagogue. Erasmus, a celebrated humanist scholar, was recognized for translations of ancient texts, reform of education according to classical studies, moral and spiritual writings and the first printed edition of the Greek New Testament. A former Augustinian who never left the Catholic Church, Erasmus addressed deficiencies he saw in the church and society, challenging numerous prevailing doctrines but advocating reform. He envisioned a simple, spiritual Christian life shaped by the teachings of Jesus and ancient wisdom. He was often accused of collusion with Martin Luther* on account of some resonance of their ideas but hotly debated Luther on human will.

Paul Fagius (1504–1549). German Reformed Hebraist and pastor. After studying at the University of Heidelberg, Fagius went to Strasbourg where he perfected his Hebrew under Wolfgang Capito.* In Isny im Allgäu (Baden-

Württemberg) he met the great Jewish grammarian Elias Levita (1469–1549), with whom he established a Hebrew printing press. In 1544 Fagius returned to Strasbourg, succeeding Capito as preacher and Old Testament lecturer. During the Augsburg Interim, Fagius (with Martin Bucer*) accepted Thomas Cranmer's* invitation to translate and interpret the Bible at Cambridge. However, Fagius died before he could begin any of the work. Fagius wrote commentaries on the first four chapters of Genesis and the deuterocanonical books of Sirach and Tobit.

John Fary (unknown). English Puritan pastor. Fary authored *God's Severity on Man's Sterility* (1645), a sermon on the fruitless fig tree in Luke 13:6-9.

William Fenner (1600–1640). English Puritan pastor. After studying at Cambridge and Oxford, Fenner ministered at Sedgley and Rochford. Fenner's extant writings, which primarily deal with practical and devotional topics, demonstrate a zealous Puritan piety and a keen interest in Scripture and theology.

First Helvetic Confession (1536). Anticipating the planned church council at Mantua (1537, but delayed until 1545 at Trent), Reformed theologians of the Swiss cantons drafted a confession to distinguish themselves from both Catholics and the churches of the Augsburg Confession.* Heinrich Bullinger* led the discussion and wrote the confession itself; Leo Jud, Oswald Myconius, Simon Grynaeus and others were part of the assembly. Martin Bucer* and Wolfgang Capito* had desired to draw the Lutheran and Reformed communions closer together through this document, but Luther* proved unwilling after Bullinger refused to accept the Wittenberg Concord (1536). This confession was largely eclipsed by Bullinger's Second Helvetic Confession.*

John Fisher (1469–1535). English Catholic bishop and theologian. This reputed preacher defended Catholic orthodoxy and strove to reform abuses in the church. In 1521 Henry VIII honored Fisher with the title *Fidei Defensor* ("defender of the faith"). Nevertheless, Fisher opposed the king's divorce of Catherine of Aragon (1485–1536) and the independent establishment of the Church of England; he was convicted for treason and executed. Most of Fisher's works are polemical and occasional (e.g., on transubstantiation, against Martin Luther*); however, he also published a series of sermons on the seven penitential psalms. In addition to his episcopal duties, Fisher was the chancellor of Cambridge from 1504 until his death.

John Flavel (c. 1630–1691). English Puritan pastor. Trained at Oxford, Flavel ministered in southwest England from 1650 until the Act of Uniformity in 1662, which reaffirmed the compulsory use of the Book of Common Prayer. Flavel preached unofficially for many years, until his congregation was eventually allowed to build a meeting place in 1687. His works were numerous, varied and popular.

Giovanni Battista Folengo (1490–1559). Italian Catholic exegete. In 1528 Folengo left the Benedictine order, questioning the validity of monastic vows; he returned to the monastic life in 1534. During this hiatus Folengo came into contact with the Neapolitan reform-minded circle founded by Juan de Valdés.* Folengo published commentaries on the Psalms, John, 1–2 Peter and James. Augustin Marlorat* included Folengo's comment in his anthology of exegesis on the Psalms. In 1580 Folengo's Psalms commentary was added to the Index of Prohibited Books.

Formula of Concord (1577). After Luther's* death, intra-Lutheran controversies between the Gnesio-Lutherans (partisans of Luther) and the Philippists (partisans of Melanchthon*) threatened to cause a split among those who had subscribed to the Augsburg Confession.* In 1576, Jakob Andreae,* Martin Chemnitz,* Nikolaus Selnecker,* David Chytraeus* and Andreas Musculus (1514–1581) met with the intent of resolving the controversies, which mainly regarded the relationship between good works and salvation, the third use of the law, and the role of the human will in accepting God's grace. In 1580, celebrating the fiftieth anniversary of the presentation of the

Augsburg Confession to Charles V (1500–1558), the *Book of Concord* was printed as the authoritative interpretation of the Augsburg Confession; it included the three ancient creeds, the Augsburg Confession, its Apology (1531), the Schmalkald Articles,* Luther's *Treatise on the Power and Primacy of the Pope* (1537) and both his Small and Large Catechisms (1529).

Sebastian Franck (1499–1542). German Radical theologian. Franck became a Lutheran in 1525, but by 1529 he began to develop ideas that distanced him from Protestants and Catholics. Expelled from Strasbourg and later Ulm due to his controversial writings, Franck spent the end of his life in Basel. Franck emphasized God's word as a divine internal spark that cannot be adequately expressed in outward forms. Thus he criticized religious institutions and dogmas. His work consists mostly of commentaries, compilations and translations. In his sweeping historical *Chronica* (1531), Franck supported numerous heretics condemned by the Catholic Church and criticized political and church authorities.

Leonhard Frick (d. 1528). Austrian Radical martyr. See *Kunstbuch*.

Gallic Confession (1559). This confession was accepted at the first National Synod of the Reformed Churches of France (1559). It was intended to be a touchstone of Reformed faith but also to show to the people of France that the Huguenots—who faced persecution—were not seditious. The French Reformed Church presented this confession to Francis II (1544–1560) in 1560, and to his successor, Charles IX (1550–1574), in 1561. The later Genevan draft, likely written by Calvin,* Beza,* and Pierre Viret (1511–1571), was received as the true Reformed confession at the seventh National Synod in La Rochelle (1571).

Geneva Bible (originally printed 1560). During Mary I's reign many English Protestants sought safety abroad in Reformed territories of the Empire and the Swiss Cantons, especially in Calvin's* Geneva. A team of English exiles in Geneva led by William Whittingham (c. 1524–1579) brought this complete translation to press in the course of two years. Notable for several innovations—Roman type, verse numbers, italics indicating English idiom and not literal phrasing of the original languages, even variant readings in the Gospels and Acts—this translation is most well known for its marginal notes, which reflect a strongly Calvinist theology. The notes explained Scripture in an accessible way for the laity, also giving unlearned clergy a new sermon resource. Although controversial because of its implicit critique of royal power, this translation was wildly popular; even after the publication of the Authorized Version (1611) and James I's 1616 ban on its printing, the Geneva Bible continued to be the most popular English translation until after the English Civil Wars.

Johann Gerhard (1582–1637). German Lutheran theologian, professor and superintendent. Gerhard is considered one of the most eminent Lutheran theologians, after Martin Luther* and Martin Chemnitz.* After studying patristics and Hebrew at Wittenberg, Jena and Marburg, Gerhard was appointed superintendent at the age of twenty-four. In 1616 he was appointed to a post at the University of Jena, where he reintroduced Aristotelian metaphysics to theology and gained widespread fame. His most important work was the nine-volume *Loci Theologici* (1610–1625). He also expanded Chemnitz's harmony of the Gospels (*Harmonia Evangelicae*), which was finally published by Polykarp Leyser (1552–1610) in 1593. Gerhard was well-known for an irenic spirit and an ability to communicate clearly.

Anthony Gilby (c. 1510–1585). English Puritan translator. During Mary I's reign, Gilby fled to Geneva, where he assisted William Whittingham (c. 1524–1579) with the Geneva Bible.* He returned to England to pastor after Elizabeth I's accession. In addition to translating numerous continental Reformed works into English—especially those of John Calvin* and Theodore Beza*—Gilby also wrote commentaries on Micah and Malachi.

Bernard Gilpin (1517–1583). Anglican theologian and priest. In public disputations, Gilpin defended Roman Catholic theology against John Hooper (c. 1495-1555) and Peter Martyr Vermigli.* These debates caused Gilpin to reexamine his faith. Upon Mary I's accession, Gilpin resigned his benefice. He sojourned in Belgium and France, returning to pastoral ministry in England in 1556. Gilpin dedicated himself to a preaching circuit in northern England, thus earning the moniker "the Apostle to the North." His zealous preaching and almsgiving roused royal opposition and a warrant for his arrest. On his way to the queen's commission, Gilpin fractured his leg, delaying his arrival in London until after Mary's death and thus likely saving his life. His only extant writing is a sermon on Luke 2 confronting clerical abuses.

Glossa ordinaria. This standard collection of biblical commentaries consists of interlinear and marginal notes drawn from patristic and Carolingian exegesis appended to the Vulgate*; later editions also include Nicholas of Lyra's* *Postilla*. The *Glossa ordinaria* and the Sentences of Peter Lombard (c. 1100–1160) were essential resources for all late medieval and early modern commentators.

Conrad Grebel (c. 1498–1526). Swiss Radical theologian. Grebel, considered the father of the Anabaptist movement, was one of the first defenders and performers of believers' baptism, for which he was eventually imprisoned in Zurich. One of Huldrych Zwingli's* early compatriots, Grebel advocated rapid, radical reform, clashing publicly with the civil authorities and Zwingli. Grebel's views, particularly on baptism, were influenced by Andreas Bodenstein von Karlstadt* and Thomas Müntzer.* Grebel advocated elimination of magisterial involvement in governing the church; instead, he envisioned the church as lay Christians determining their own affairs with strict adherence to the biblical text, and unified in volitional baptism.

William Greenhill (1591–1671). English Puritan pastor. Greenhill attended and worked at Magdalen College. He ministered in the diocese of Norwich but soon left for London, where he preached at Stepney. Greenhill was a member of the Westminster Assembly of Divines and was appointed the parliament chaplain by the children of Charles I. Oliver Cromwell included him among the preachers who helped draw up the Savoy Declaration. Greenhill was evicted from his post following the Restoration, after which he pastored independently. Among Greenhill's most significant contributions to church history was his *Exposition of the Prophet of Ezekiel*.

Catharina Regina von Greiffenberg (1633–1694). Austrian Lutheran poet. Upon her adulthood her guardian (and half uncle) sought to marry her; despite her protests of their consanguinity and her desire to remain celibate, she relented in 1664. After the deaths of her mother and husband, Greiffenberg abandoned her home to debtors and joined her friends Susanne Popp (d. 1683) and Sigmund von Birken (1626–1681) in Nuremberg. During her final years she dedicated herself to studying the biblical languages and to writing meditations on Jesus' death and resurrection, which she never completed. One of the most important and learned Austrian poets of the Baroque period, Greiffenberg published a collection of sonnets, songs and poems (1662) as well as three sets of mystical meditations on Jesus' life, suffering and death (1672; 1683; 1693). She participated in a society of poets called the Ister Gesellschaft.

Rudolf Gwalther (1519–1586). Swiss Reformed preacher. Gwalther was a consummate servant of the Reformed church in Zurich, its chief religious officer and preacher, a responsibility fulfilled previously by Huldrych Zwingli* and Heinrich Bullinger.* Gwalther provided sermons and commentaries and translated the works of Zwingli into Latin. He worked for many years alongside Bullinger in structuring and governing the church in Zurich. Gwalther also strove to strengthen the connections to the Reformed churches on the Continent and England: he was a participant in the Colloquy of Regensburg (1541) and an opponent of the Formula of Concord.*

Hans Has von Hallstatt (d. 1527). Austrian Reformed pastor. See *Kunstbuch*.

Henry Hammond (1605–1660). Anglican priest. After completing his studies at Oxford, Hammond was ordained in 1629. A Royalist, Hammond helped recruit soldiers for the king; he was chaplain to Charles I. During the king's captivity, Hammond was imprisoned for not submitting to Parliament. Later he was allowed to pastor again, until his death. Hammond published a catechism, numerous polemical sermons and treatises as well as his *Paraphrase and Annotations on the New Testament* (1653).

Peter Hausted (d. 1645). Anglican priest and playwright. Educated at Cambridge and Oxford, Hausted ministered in a number of parishes and preached adamantly and vehemently against Puritanism. He is best known for his play *The Rival Friends*, which is filled with invective against the Puritans; during a performance before the king and queen, a riot nearly broke out. Haustead died during the siege of Banbury Castle.

Heidelberg Catechism (1563). This German Reformed catechism was commissioned by the elector of the Palatinate, Frederick III (1515–1576) for pastors and teachers in his territories to use in instructing children and new believers in the faith. It was written by theologian Zacharias Ursinus (1534–1583) in consultation with Frederick's court preacher Kaspar Olevianus* and the entire theology faculty at the University of Heidelberg. The Heidelberg Catechism was accepted as one of the Dutch Reformed Church's Three Forms of Unity—along with the Belgic Confession* and the Canons of Dordrecht—at the Synod of Dordrecht,* and became widely popular among other Reformed confessional traditions throughout Europe.

Niels Hemmingsen (1513–1600). Danish Lutheran theologian. Hemmingsen studied at the University of Wittenberg, where he befriended Philipp Melanchthon.* In 1542, Hemmingsen returned to Denmark to pastor and to teach Greek, dialectics and theology at the University of Copenhagen. Foremost of the Danish theologians, Hemmingsen oversaw the preparation and publication of the first Danish Bible (1550). Later in his career he became embroiled in controversies because of his Philippist theology, especially regarding the Eucharist. Due to rising tensions with Lutheran nobles outside of Denmark, King Frederick II (1534–1588) dismissed Hemmingsen from his university post in 1579, transferring him to a prominent but less internationally visible Cathedral outside of Copenhagen. Hemmingsen was a prolific author, writing commentaries on the New Testament and Psalms, sermon collections and several methodological, theological and pastoral handbooks.

Tilemann Hesshus (1527–1588). German Lutheran theologian and pastor. Hesshus studied under Philipp Melanchthon* but was a staunch Gnesio-Lutheran. With great hesitation—and later regret—he affirmed the Formula of Concord.* Heshuss ardently advocated for church discipline, considering obedience a mark of the church. Unwilling to compromise his strong convictions, especially regarding matters of discipline, Hesshus was regularly embroiled in controversy. He was expelled or pressed to leave Goslar, Rostock, Heidelberg, Bremen, Magdeburg, Wesel, Königsberg and Samland before settling in Helmstedt, where he remained until his death. He wrote numerous polemical tracts concerning ecclesiology, justification, the sacraments and original sin, as well as commentaries on Psalms, Romans, 1–2 Corinthians, Galatians, Colossians and 1–2 Timothy, and a postil collection.

Christopher Hooke (unknown). English Puritan physician and pastor. Hooke published a treatise promoting the joys and blessings of childbirth (1590) and a sermon on Hebrews 12:11-12. To support the poor, Hooke proposed a bank funded by voluntary investment of wealthy households.

Richard Hooker (c. 1553–1600). Anglican priest. Shortly after graduating from Corpus Christi College Oxford, Hooker took holy orders as a priest in 1581. After his marriage, he struggled to find work and temporarily tended sheep until Archbishop John Whitgift* appointed him to the Temple Church in London. Hooker's primary work is *The Laws of Ecclesiastical Polity* (1593), in which he sought to establish a philosophical and logical foundation for the highly controversial Elizabethan Religious Settlement (1559). The Elizabethan Settlement, through the Act of Supremacy, reasserted the Church of England's independence from the Church of Rome, and, through the Act of Uniformity, constructed a common church structure based on the reinstitution of the Book of Common Prayer.* Hooker's argumentation strongly emphasizes natural law and anticipates the social contract theory of John Locke (1632–1704).

John Hooper (d. 1555). English Protestant bishop and martyr. Impressed by the works of Huldrych Zwingli* and Heinrich Bullinger,* Hooper joined the Protestant movement in England. However, after the Act of Six Articles was passed, he fled to Zurich, where he spent ten years. He returned to England in 1549 and was appointed as a bishop. He stoutly advocated a Zwinglian reform agenda, arguing against the use of vestments and for a less "popish" Book of Common Prayer.* Condemned as a heretic for denying transubstantiation, Hooper was burned at the stake during Mary I's reign.

Rudolf Hospinian (Wirth) (1547–1626). Swiss Reformed theologian and minister. After studying theology at Marburg and Heidelberg, Hospinian pastored in rural parishes around Zurich and taught secondary school. In 1588, he transferred to Zurich, ministering at Grossmünster and Fraumünster. A keen student of church history, Hospinian wanted to show the differences between early church doctrine and contemporary Catholic teaching, particularly with regard to sacramental theology. He also criticized Lutheran dogma and the Formula of Concord*. Most of Hospinian's corpus consists of polemical treatises; he also published a series of sermons on the Magnificat.

Caspar Huberinus (1500–1553). German Lutheran theologian and pastor. After studying theology at Wittenberg, Huberinus moved to Augsburg to serve as Urbanus Rhegius's* assistant. Huberinus represented Augsburg at the Bern Disputation (1528) on the Eucharist and images. In 1551, along with the nobility, Huberinus

supported the Augsburg Interim, so long as communion of both kinds and regular preaching were allowed. Nevertheless the people viewed him as a traitor because of his official participation in the Interim, nicknaming him "Buberinus" (i.e. scoundrel). He wrote a number of popular devotional works as well as tracts defending Lutheran eucharistic theology against Zwinglian and Anabaptist detractions.

Balthasar Hubmaier (1480/5–1528). German Radical theologian. Hubmaier, a former priest who studied under Johann Eck,* is identified with his leadership in the peasants' uprising at Waldshut. Hubmaier served as the cathedral preacher in Regensberg, where he became involved in a series of anti-Semitic attacks. He was drawn to reform through the early works of Martin Luther*; his contact with Huldrych Zwingli* made Hubmaier a defender of more radical reform, including believers' baptism and a memorialist account of the Eucharist. His involvement in the Peasants' War led to his extradition and execution by the Austrians.

Aegidius Hunnius (1550–1603). German Lutheran theologian and preacher. Educated at Tübingen by Jakob Andreae (1528–1590) and Johannes Brenz,* Hunnius bolstered and advanced early Lutheran orthodoxy. After his crusade to root out all "crypto-Calvinism" divided Hesse into Lutheran and Reformed regions, Hunnius joined the Wittenberg theological faculty, where with Polykarp Leyser (1552–1610) he helped shape the university into an orthodox stronghold. Passionately confessional, Hunnius developed and nuanced the orthodox doctrines of predestination, Scripture, the church and Christology (more explicitly Chalcedonian), reflecting their codification in the Formula of Concord.* He was unafraid to engage in confessional polemics from the pulpit. In addition to his many treatises (most notably *De persona Christi*, in which he defended Christ's ubiquity), Hunnius published commentaries on Matthew, John, Ephesians and Colossians; his notes on Galatians, Philemon and 1 Corinthians were published posthumously.

Jan Hus (d. 1415). Bohemian reformer and martyr. This popular preacher strove for reform in the church, moral improvement in society, and an end to clerical abuses and popular religious superstition. He was branded a heretic for his alleged affinity for John Wycliffe's writings; however, while he agreed that a priest in mortal sin rendered the sacraments inefficacious, he affirmed the doctrine of transubstantiation. The Council of Constance* convicted Hus of heresy, banned his books and teaching, and, despite a letter of safe conduct, burned him at the stake.

Hans Hut (1490–1527). German Radical leader. Hut was an early leader of a mystical, apocalyptic strand of Anabaptist radical reform. His theological views were shaped by Andreas Bodenstein von Karlstadt,* Thomas Müntzer* and Hans Denck,* by whom Hut had been baptized. Hut rejected society and the established church and heralded the imminent end of days, which he perceived in the Peasants' War. Eventually arrested for practicing believers' baptism and participating in the Peasants' War, Hut was tortured and died accidentally in a fire in the Augsburg prison. The next day, the authorities sentenced his corpse to death and burned him.

George Hutcheson (1615–1674). Scottish Puritan pastor. Hutcheson, a pastor in Edinburgh, published commentaries on Job, John and the Minor Prophets, as well as sermons on Psalm 130.

Abraham Ibn Ezra (1089–c. 1167). Spanish Jewish rabbi, exegete and poet. In 1140 Ibn Ezra fled his native Spain to escape persecution by the Almohad Caliphate. He spent the rest of his life as an exile, travelling through Europe, North Africa and the Middle East. His corpus consists of works on poetry, exegesis, grammar, philosophy, mathematics and astrology. In his commentaries on the Old Testament, Ibn Ezra restricts himself to *peshat* (see *quadriga*).

Valentin Ickelshamer (c. 1500–1547). German Radical teacher. After time at Erfurt, he studied under Luther,* Melanchthon,* Bugenhagen* and Karlstadt* in Wittenberg. He sided with Karlstadt against Luther, writing a treatise in Karlstadt's defense. Ickelshamer also represented the Wittenberg guilds in opposition to the city council. This guild committee allied with the peasants in 1525, leading to Ickelshamer's eventual exile. His poem in the Marpeck Circle's *Kunstbuch** is an expansion of a similar poem by Sebastian Franck.*

John Jewel (1522–1571). Anglican theologian and bishop. Jewel studied at Oxford where he met Peter Martyr Vermigli.* After graduating in 1552, Jewel was appointed to his first vicarage and became the orator for the university. Upon Mary I's accession, Jewel lost his post as orator because of his Protestant views. After the trials of Thomas Cranmer* and Nicholas Ridley,* Jewel affirmed Catholic teaching to avoid their fate. Still he had to flee to the continent. Confronted by John Knox,* Jewel publicly repented of his cowardice before the English congregation in Frankfurt, then reunited with Vermigli in Strasbourg. After Mary I's death, Jewel returned to England and was consecrated bishop in 1560. He advocated low-church ecclesiology, but supported the Elizabethan Settlement against Catholics and Puritans. In response to the Council of Trent, he published the *Apoligia ecclesiae Anglicanae* (1562), which established him as the apostle for Anglicanism and incited numerous controversies.

Justus Jonas (1493–1555). German Lutheran theologian, pastor and administrator. Jonas studied law at Erfurt, where he befriended the poet Eobanus Hessus (1488–1540), whom Luther* dubbed "king of the poets"; later, under the influence of the humanist Konrad Muth, Jonas focused on theology. In 1516 he was ordained as a priest, and in 1518 he became a doctor of theology and law. After witnessing the Leipzig Disputation, Jonas was converted to Luther's* cause. While traveling with Luther to the Diet of Worms, Jonas was appointed professor of canon law at Wittenberg. Later he became its dean of theology, lecturing on Romans, Acts and the Psalms. Jonas was also instrumental for reform in Halle. He preached Luther's funeral sermon but had a falling-out with Melanchthon* over the Leipzig Interim. Jonas's most influential contribution was translating Luther's *The Bondage of the Will* and Melanchthon's *Loci communes* into German.

David Joris (c. 1501–1556). Dutch Radical pastor and hymnist. This former glass painter was one of the leading Dutch Anabaptist leaders after the fall of Münster (1535), although due to his increasingly radical ideas his influence waned in the early 1540s. Joris came to see himself as a "third David," a Spirit-anointed prophet ordained to proclaim the coming third kingdom of God, which would be established in the Netherlands with Dutch as its *lingua franca*. Joris's interpretation of Scripture, with his heavy emphasis on personal mystical experience, led to a very public dispute with Menno Simons* whom Joris considered a teacher of the "dead letter." In 1544 Joris and about one hundred followers moved to Basel, conforming outwardly to the teaching of the Reformed church there. Today 240 of Joris's books are extant, the most important of which is his *Twonder Boek* (1542/43).

Andreas Bodenstein von Karlstadt (Carlstadt) (1486–1541). German Radical theologian. Karlstadt, an early associate of Martin Luther* and Philipp Melanchthon* at the University of Wittenberg, participated alongside Luther in the dispute at Leipzig with Johann Eck.* He also influenced the configuration of the Old Testament canon in Protestantism. During Luther's captivity in Wartburg Castle in Eisenach, Karlstadt oversaw reform in Wittenberg. His acceleration of the pace of reform brought conflict with Luther, so Karlstadt left Wittenberg, eventually settling at the University of Basel as professor of Old Testament (after a sojourn in Zurich with Huldrych Zwingli*). During his time in Switzerland, Karlstadt opposed infant baptism and repudiated Luther's doctrine of Christ's real presence in the Eucharist.

David Kimchi (Radak) (1160–1235). French Jewish rabbi, exegete and philosopher. Kimchi wrote an important Hebrew grammar and dictionary, as well as commentaries on Genesis, 1–2 Chronicles, the Psalms and the Prophets. He focused on *peshat* (see *quadriga*). In his Psalms commentary he attacks Christian interpretation

as forced, irrational and inadmissible. While Sebastian Münster* censors and condemns these arguments in his *Miqdaš YHWH* (1534–1535), he and many other Christian commentators valued Kimchi's work as a grammatical resource.

John Knox (1513–1572). Scottish Reformed preacher. Knox, a fiery preacher to monarchs and zealous defender of high Calvinism, was a leading figure of reform in Scotland. Following imprisonment in the French galleys, Knox went to England, where he became a royal chaplain to Edward VI. At the accession of Mary, Knox fled to Geneva, studying under John Calvin* and serving as a pastor. Knox returned to Scotland after Mary's death and became a chief architect of the reform of the Scottish church (Presbyterian), serving as one of the authors of the Book of Discipline and writing many pamphlets and sermons.

Antonius Broickwy von Königstein (1470–1541). German Catholic preacher. Very little is known about this important cathedral preacher in Cologne. Strongly opposed to evangelicals, he sought to develop robust resources for Catholic homilies. His postils were bestsellers, and his biblical concordance helped Catholic preachers to construct doctrinal loci from Scripture itself.

Kunstbuch. In 1956, two German students rediscovered this unique collection of Anabaptist works. Four hundred years earlier, a friend of the recently deceased Pilgram Marpeck*—the painter Jörg Probst—had entrusted this collection of letters, tracts and poetry to a Zurich bindery; today only half of it remains. Probst's redaction arranges various compositions from the Marpeck Circle into a devotional anthology focused on the theme of the church as Christ incarnate (cf. Gal 2:20).

François Lambert (Lambert of Avignon) (1487–1530). French Reformed theologian. In 1522, after becoming drawn to the writings of Martin Luther* and meeting Huldrych Zwingli,* Lambert left the Franciscan order. He spent time in Wittenberg, Strasbourg, and Hesse, where Lambert took a leading role at the Homberg Synod (1526) and in creating a biblically based plan for church reform. He served as professor of theology at Marburg University from 1527 to his death. After the Marburg Colloquy (1529), Lambert accepted Zwingli's symbolic view of the Eucharist. Lambert produced nineteen books, mostly biblical commentaries that favored spiritual interpretations; his unfinished work of comprehensive theology was published posthumously.

Hugh Latimer (c. 1485–1555). Anglican bishop and preacher. Latimer was celebrated for his sermons critiquing the idolatrous nature of Catholic practices and the social injustices visited on the underclass by the aristocracy and the individualism of Protestant government. After his support for Henry's petition of divorce he served as a court preacher under Henry VIII and Edward VI. Latimer became a proponent of reform following his education at Cambridge University and received license as a preacher. Following Edward's death, Latimer was tried for heresy, perishing at the stake with Nicholas Ridley* and Thomas Cranmer.*

William Laud (1573–1645). Anglican archbishop, one of the most pivotal and controversial figures in Anglican church history. Early in his career, Laud offended many with his highly traditional, anti-Puritan approach to ecclesial policies. After his election as Archbishop of Canterbury in 1633, Laud continued to strive against the Puritans, demanding the eastward placement of the Communion altar (affirming the religious centrality of the Eucharist), the use of clerical garments, the reintroduction of stained-glass windows, and the uniform use of the Book of Common Prayer.* Laud was accused of being a crypto-Catholic—an ominous accusation during the protracted threat of invasion by the Spanish Armada. In 1640 the Long Parliament met, quickly impeached Laud on charges of treason, and placed him in jail for several years before his execution.

John Lawson (unknown). Seventeenth-century English Puritan. Lawson wrote *Gleanings and Expositions of Some of Scripture* (1646) and a treatise on the sabbath in the New Testament.

Jacques Lefèvre d'Étaples (Faber Stapulensis) (1460?–1536). French Catholic humanist, publisher and translator. Lefèvre d'Étaples studied classical literature and philosophy, as well as patristic and medieval mysticism. He advocated the principle of *ad fontes*, issuing a full-scale annotation on the corpus of Aristotle, publishing the writings of key Christian mystics, and contributing to efforts at biblical translation and commentary. Although he never broke with the Catholic Church, his views prefigured those of Martin Luther,* for which he was condemned by the University of Sorbonne in Paris. He then found refuge in the court of Marguerite d'Angoulême, where he met John Calvin* and Martin Bucer.*

Edward Leigh (1602–1671). English Puritan biblical critic, historian and politician. Educated at Oxford, Leigh's public career included appointments as a Justice of the Peace, an officer in the parliamentary army during the English Civil Wars and a member of Parliament. Although never ordained, Leigh devoted himself to the study of theology and Scripture; he participated in the Westminster Assembly. Leigh published a diverse corpus, including lexicons of Greek, Hebrew and juristic terms, and histories of Roman, Greek and English rulers. His most important theological work is *A Systeme or Body of Divinity* (1662).

John Lightfoot (1602–1675). Anglican priest and biblical scholar. After graduating from Cambridge, Lightfoot was ordained and pastored at several small parishes. He continued to study classics under the support of the politician Rowland Cotton (1581–1634). Siding with the Parliamentarians during the English Civil Wars, Lightfoot relocated to London in 1643. He was one of the original members of the Westminster Assembly, where he defended a moderate Presbyterianism. His best-known work is the six-volume *Horae Hebraicae et Talmudicae* (1658–1677), a verse-by-verse commentary illumined by Hebrew customs, language and the Jewish interpretive tradition.

Lucas Lossius (1508–1582). German Lutheran

teacher and musician. While a student at Leipzig and Wittenberg, Lossius was deeply influenced by Melanchthon* and Luther,* who found work for him as Urbanus Rhegius's* secretary. Soon after going to work for Rhegius, Lossius began teaching at a local gymnasium (or secondary school), *Das Johanneum*, eventually becoming its headmaster. Lossius remained at *Das Johanneum* until his death, even turning down appointments to university professorships. A man of varied interests, he wrote on dialectics, music and church history, as well as publishing a postil and a five-volume set of annotations on the New Testament.

Sibrandus Lubbertus (c. 1555–1625). Dutch Reformed theologian. Lubbertis, a key figure in the establishment of orthodox Calvinism in Frisia, studied theology at Wittenburg and Geneva (under Theodore Beza*) before his appointment as professor of theology at the University of Franeker. Throughout his career, Lubbertis advocated for high Calvinist theology, defending it in disputes with representatives of Socinianism, Arminianism and Roman Catholicism. Lubbertis criticized the Catholic theologian Robert Bellarmine and fellow Dutch reformer Jacobus Arminius*; the views of the latter he opposed as a prominent participant in the Synod of Dordrecht.*

Martin Luther (1483–1546). German Lutheran priest, professor and theologian. While a professor in Wittenberg, Luther reinterpreted the doctrine of justification. Convinced that righteousness comes only from God's grace, he disputed the sale of indulgences with the Ninety-five Theses. Luther's positions brought conflict with Rome; his denial of papal authority led to excommunication. He also challenged the Mass, transubstantiation and communion under one kind. Though Luther was condemned by the Diet of Worms, the Elector of Saxony provided him safe haven. Luther returned to Wittenberg with public order collapsing under Andreas Bodenstein von Karlstadt;* Luther steered a more cautious path of reform. His rendering of the Bible and liturgy in the vernacular, as well as his hymns and sermons, proved extensively influential.

Georg Major (1502–1574). German Lutheran theologian. Major was on the theological faculty of the University of Wittenberg, succeeding as dean Johannes Bugenhagen* and Philipp Melanchthon.* One of the chief editors on the Wittenberg edition of Luther's works, Major is most identified with the controversy bearing his name, in which he stated that good works are necessary to salvation. Major qualified his statement, which was in reference to the totality of the Christian life. The Formula of Concord* rejected the statement, ending the controversy. As a theologian, Major further refined Lutheran views of the inspiration of Scripture and the doctrine of the Trinity.

John (Mair) Major (1467–1550). Scottish Catholic philosopher. Major taught logic and theology at the universities of Paris (his alma mater), Glasgow and St Andrews. His broad interests and impressive work drew students from all over Europe. While disapproving of evangelicals (though he did teach John Knox*), Major advocated reform programs for Rome. He supported collegial episcopacy and even challenged the curia's teaching on sexuality. Still he was a nominalist who was critical of humanist approaches to biblical exegesis. His best-known publication is *A History of Greater Britain, Both England and Scotland* (1521), which promoted the union of the kingdoms. He also published a commentary on Peter Lombard's *Sentences* and the Gospel of John.

Juan de Maldonado (1533–1583). Spanish Catholic biblical scholar. A student of Francisco de Toledo,* Maldonado taught philosophy and theology at the universities of Paris and Salamanca. Ordained to the priesthood in Rome, he revised the Septuagint under papal appointment. While Maldonado vehemently criticized Protestants, he asserted that Reformed baptism was valid and that mixed confessional marriages were acceptable. His views on Mary's immaculate conception proved controversial among many Catholics who conflated his statement that it was not an article of faith with its denial. He was intrigued by demonology (blaming demonic influence for the Reformation). All his work was published posthumously; his Gospel commentaries were highly valued and important.

Thomas Manton (1620–1677). English Puritan minister. Manton, educated at Oxford, served for a time as lecturer at Westminster Abbey and rector of St. Paul's, Covent Garden, and was a strong advocate of Presbyterianism. He was known as a rigorous evangelical Calvinist who preached long expository sermons. At different times in his ecclesial career he worked side-by-side with Richard Baxter* and John Owen.* In his later life, Manton's Nonconformist position led to his ejection as a clergyman from the Church of England (1662) and eventual imprisonment (1670). Although a voluminous writer, Manton was best known for his preaching. At his funeral in 1677, he was dubbed "the king of preachers."

Augustin Marlorat (c. 1506–1562). French Reformed pastor. Committed by his family to a monastery at the age of eight, Marlorat was also ordained into the priesthood at an early age in 1524. He fled to Geneva in 1535, where he pastored until the Genevan Company of Pastors sent him to France to shepherd the nascent evangelical congregations. His petition to the young Charles IX (1550–1574) for the right to public evangelical worship was denied. In response to a massacre of evangelicals in Vassy (over sixty dead, many more wounded), Marlorat's congregation planned to overtake Rouen. After the crown captured Rouen, Marlorat was arrested and executed three days later for treason. His principle published work was an anthology of New Testament comment modeled after Thomas Aquinas's *Catena aurea in quatuor Evangelia*. Marlorat harmonized Reformed and Lutheran comment with the church fathers, interspersed with his own brief comments. He also wrote such anthologies for Genesis, Job, the Psalms, Song of Songs and Isaiah.

Pilgram Marpeck (c. 1495–1556). Austrian Radical elder and theologian. During a brief sojourn in Strasbourg, Marpeck debated with Martin Bucer* before the city council; Bucer was declared the winner, and Marpeck was asked to leave Strasbourg for his views concerning paedobaptism (which he compared to a sacrifice to Moloch). After his time in Strasbourg, Marpeck travelled throughout southern Germany and western Austria, planting Anabaptist congregations. Marpeck criticized the strict use of the ban, however, particularly among the Swiss brethren. He also engaged in a Christological controversy with Kaspar von Schwenckfeld.*

Johannes Mathesius (1504–1565). German Lutheran theologian and pastor. After reading Martin Luther's* *On Good Works*, Mathesius left his teaching post in Ingolstadt and traveled to Wittenberg to study theology. Mathesius was an important agent of reform in the Bohemian town of Jáchymov, where he pastored, preached and taught. Over one thousand of Mathesius's sermons are extant, including numerous wedding and funeral sermons as well as a series on Luther's life. Mathesius also transcribed portions of Luther's Table Talk.

John Mayer (1583–1664). Anglican priest and biblical exegete. Mayer dedicated much of his life to biblical exegesis, writing a seven-volume commentary on the entire Bible (1627–1653). Styled after Philipp Melanchthon's* *locus* method, Mayer's work avoided running commentary, focusing instead on textual and theological problems. He was a parish priest for fifty-five years. In the office of priest Mayer also wrote a popular catechism, *The English Catechisme, or a Commentarie on the Short Catechisme* (1621), which went through twelve editions in his lifetime.

Joseph Mede (1586–1638). Anglican biblical scholar, Hebraist and Greek lecturer. A man of encyclopedic knowledge, Mede was interested in numerous fields, varying from philology and history to mathematics and physics, although millennial thought and apocalyptic prophesy were clearly his chief interests. Mede's most important work was his *Clavis Apocalyptica* (1627, later translated into English as *The Key of the Revelation*). This work examined the structure of

Revelation as the key to its interpretation. Mede saw the visions as a connected and chronological sequence hinging around Revelation 17:18. He is remembered as an important figure in the history of millenarian theology. He was respected as a mild-mannered and generous scholar who avoided controversy and debate, but who had many original thoughts.

Philipp Melanchthon (1497–1560). German Lutheran educator, reformer and theologian. Melanchthon is known as the partner and successor to Martin Luther* in reform in Germany and for his pioneering *Loci Communes*, which served as a theological textbook. Melanchthon participated with Luther in the Leipzig disputation, helped implement reform in Wittenberg and was a chief architect of the Augsburg Confession.* Later, Melanchthon and Martin Bucer* worked for union between the reformed and Catholic churches. On account of Melanchthon's more ecumenical disposition and his modification of several of Luther's doctrines, he was held in suspicion by some.

Johannes Mercerus (Jean Mercier) (d. 1570). French Hebraist. Mercerus studied under the first Hebrew chair at the Collège Royal de Paris, François Vatable (d. 1547), whom he succeeded in 1546. John Calvin* tried to recruit Mercerus to the Genevan Academy as professor of Hebrew, once in 1558 and again in 1563; he refused both times. During his lifetime Mercerus published grammatical helps for Hebrew and Chaldean, an aid to the Masoretic symbols in the Hebrew text, and translated the commentaries and grammars of several medieval rabbis. He himself wrote commentaries on Genesis, the wisdom books, and most of the Minor Prophets. These commentaries—most of them only published after his death—were philologically focused and interacted with the work of Jerome, Nicholas of Lyra,* notable rabbis and Johannes Oecolampadius.*

Ambrose Moibanus (1494–1554). German Lutheran bishop and theologian. Moibanus helped reform the church of Breslau (modern Wroclaw, Poland). He revised the Mass, bolstered pastoral care and welfare for the poor, and wrote a new evangelical catechism.

Thomas More (1478–1535). English Catholic lawyer, politician, humanist and martyr. More briefly studied at Oxford, but completed his legal studies in London. After contemplating the priesthood for four years, he opted for politics and was elected a member of Parliament in 1504. A devout Catholic, More worked with church leaders in England to root out heresy while he also confronted Lutheran teachings in writing. After four years as Lord Chancellor, More resigned due to heightened tensions with Henry VIII over papal supremacy (which More supported and Henry did not). Tensions did not abate. More's steadfast refusal to accept the Act of Supremacy (1534)—which declared the King of England to be the supreme ecclesial primate not the pope—resulted in his arrest and trial for high treason. He was found guilty and beheaded with John Fisher (1469–1535). Friends with John Colet* and Desiderius Erasmus,* More was a widely respected humanist in England as well as on the continent. Well-known for his novel *Utopia* (1516), More also penned several religious treatises on Christ's passion and suffering during his imprisonment in the Tower of London, which were published posthumously.

Sebastian Münster (1488–1552). German Reformed Hebraist, exegete, printer, and geographer. After converting to the Reformation in 1524, Münster taught Hebrew at the universities of Heidelberg and Basel. During his lengthy tenure in Basel he published more than 70 books, including Hebrew dictionaries and rabbinic commentaries. He also produced an evangelistic work for Jews titled *Vikuach* (1539). Münster's *Torat ha-Maschiach* (1537), the Gospel of Matthew, was the first published Hebrew translation of any portion of the New Testament. Despite his massive contribution to contemporary understanding of the Hebrew language, Münster was criticized by many of the reformers as a Judaizer.

Thomas Müntzer (c. 1489–1525). German Radical preacher. As a preacher in the town of

Zwickau, Müntzer was influenced by German mysticism and, growing convinced that Martin Luther* had not carried through reform properly, sought to restore the pure apostolic church of the New Testament. Müntzer's radical ideas led to expulsions from various cities; he developed a highly apocalyptic theology, in which he heralded the last days that would establish the pure community out of suffering, prompting Müntzer's proactive role in the Peasants' War, which he perceived as a crucial apocalyptic event. Six thousand of Müntzer's followers were annihilated by magisterial troops; Müntzer was executed.

John Murcot (1625–1654). English Puritan pastor. After completing his bachelor's at Oxford in 1647, Murcot was ordained as a pastor, transferring to several parishes until in 1651 he moved to Dublin. All his works were published posthumously.

Simon Musaeus (1521–1582). German Lutheran theologian. After studying at the universities of Frankfurt an der Oder and Wittenberg, Musaeus began teaching Greek at the Cathedral school in Nuremberg and was ordained. Having returned to Wittenberg to complete a doctoral degree, Musaeus spent the rest of his career in numerous ecclesial and academic administrative posts. He opposed Matthias Flacius's (1505–1575) view of original sin—that the formal essence of human beings is marred by original sin—even calling the pro-Flacian faculty at Wittenberg "the devil's latrine." Musaeus published a disputation on original sin and a postil.

Wolfgang Musculus (1497–1563). German Reformed pastor and theologian. Musculus produced translations, biblical commentaries and an influential theological text, *Loci Communes Sacrae Theologiae* (*Commonplaces of Sacred Theology*), outlining a Zwinglian theology. Musculus began to study theology while at a Benedictine monastery; he departed in 1527 and became secretary to Martin Bucer* in Strasbourg. He was later installed as a pastor in Augsburg, eventually performing the first evangelical liturgy in the city's cathedral. Though Musculus was active in the pursuit of the reform agenda, he was also concerned for ecumenism, participating in the Wittenberg Concord (1536) and discussions between Lutherans and Catholics.

Friedrich Nausea (c. 1496–1552). German Catholic bishop and preacher. After completing his studies at Leipzig, this famed preacher was appointed priest in Frankfurt but was run out of town by his congregants during his first sermon. He transferred to Mainz as cathedral preacher. Nausea was well connected through the German papal hierarchy and traveled widely to preach to influential ecclesial and secular courts. Court preacher for Ferdinand I (1503–1564), his reform tendencies fit well with royal Austrian theological leanings, and he was enthroned as the bishop of Vienna. Nausea thought that rather than endless colloquies only a council could settle reform. Unfortunately he could not participate in the first session of Trent due to insufficient funding, but he arrived for the second session. Nausea defended the laity's reception of the cup and stressed the importance of promulgating official Catholic teaching in the vernacular.

Melchior Neukirch (1540–1597). German Lutheran pastor and playwright. Neukirch's pastoral career spanned more than thirty years in several northern German parishes. Neukirch published a history of the Braunschweig church since the Reformation and a dramatization of Acts 4–7. He died of the plague.

Nicholas of Lyra (1270–1349). French Catholic biblical exegete. Very little is known about this influential medieval theologian of the Sorbonne aside from the works he published, particularly the *Postilla litteralis super totam Bibliam* (1322–1333). With the advent of the printing press this work was regularly published alongside the Latin Vulgate and the *Glossa ordinaria*. In this running commentary on the Bible Nicholas promoted literal interpretation as the basis for theology. Despite his preference for literal interpretation, Nicholas also published a companion volume, the *Postilla moralis super totam Bibliam* (1339), a commentary on the spiritual meaning of the biblical text. Nicholas was a major conversation partner for many reformers though many of them rejected his exegesis as too literal and too "Jewish" (not concerned enough with the Bible's fulfillment in Jesus Christ).

Johannes Oecolampadius (Johannes Huszgen) (1482–1531). Swiss-German Reformed humanist, reformer and theologian. Oecolampadius (an assumed name meaning "house light") assisted with Desiderius Erasmus's* Greek New Testament, lectured on biblical languages and exegesis and completed an influential Greek grammar. After joining the evangelical cause through studying patristics and the work of Martin Luther,* Oecolampadius went to Basel, where he lectured on biblical exegesis and participated in ecclesial reform. On account of Oecolampadius's effort, the city council passed legislation restricting preaching to the gospel and releasing the city from compulsory Mass. Oecolampadius was a chief ally of Huldrych Zwingli,* whom he supported at the Marburg Colloquy (1529).

Kaspar Olevianus (1536–1587). German Reformed theologian. Olevianus is celebrated for composing the Heidelberg Catechism and producing a critical edition of Calvin's *Institutes* in German. Olevianus studied theology with many, including John Calvin,* Theodore Beza,* Heinrich Bullinger* and Peter Martyr Vermigli.* As an advocate of Reformed doctrine, Olevianus oversaw the shift from Lutheranism to Calvinism throughout Heidelberg, organizing the city's churches after Calvin's Geneva. The Calvinist ecclesial vision of Olevianus entangled him in a dispute with another Heidelberg reformer over the rights of ecclesiastical discipline, which Olevianus felt belonged to the council of clergy and elders rather than civil magistrates.

Josua Opitz (c. 1542–1585). German Lutheran pastor. After a brief stint as superintendent in Regensburg, Opitz, a longtime preacher, was dismissed for his support of Matthias Flacius's (1520–1575) view of original sin. (Using Aristotelian categories, Flacius argued that the formal essence of human beings is marred by original sin,

forming sinners into the image of Satan; his views were officially rejected in Article 1 of the Formula of Concord.*) Hans Wilhelm Roggendorf (1533–1591) invited Opitz to lower Austria as part of his Lutheranizing program. Unfortunately Roggendorf and Opitz never succeed in getting Lutheranism legal recognition, perhaps in large part due to Opitz's staunch criticism of Catholics, which resulted in his exile. He died of plague.

John Owen (1616–1683). English Puritan theologian. Owen trained at Oxford University, where he was later appointed dean of Christ Church and vice chancellor of the university, following his service as chaplain to Oliver Cromwell. Although Owen began his career as a Presbyterian minister, he eventually departed to the party of Independents. Owen composed many sermons, biblical commentaries (including seven volumes on the book of Hebrews), theological treatises and controversial monographs (including disputations with Arminians, Anglicans, Catholics and Socinians).

Santes Pagninus (c. 1470–1541). Italian Catholic biblical scholar. Pagninus studied under Girolamo Savonarola* and later taught in Rome, Avignon and Lyons. He translated the Old Testament into Latin according to a tight, almost wooden, adherence to the Hebrew. This translation and his Hebrew lexicon *Thesaurus linguae sanctae* (1529) were important resources for translators and commentators.

Paul of Burgos (**Solomon ha-Levi**) (c. 1351–1435). Spanish Catholic archbishop. In 1391 Solomon ha-Levi, a rabbi and Talmudic scholar, converted to Christianity, receiving baptism with his entire family (except for his wife). He changed his name to Paul de Santa Maria. Some have suggested that he converted to avoid persecution; he himself stated that Thomas Aquinas's (1225–1274) work persuaded him of the truth of Christian faith. After studying theology in Paris, he was ordained bishop in 1403. He actively and ardently persecuted Jews, trying to compel them to convert. In order to convince Jews that Christians correctly interpret the Hebrew Scriptures, Paul wrote

Dialogus Pauli et Sauli contra Judaeos, sive Scrutinium Scripturarum (1434), a book filled with vile language toward the Jews. He also wrote a series of controversial marginal notes and comments on Nicholas of Lyra's* *Postilla*, many of which criticized Nicholas's use of Jewish scholarship.

Christoph Pelargus (1565–1633). German Lutheran pastor, theologian, professor and superintendent. Pelargus studied philosophy and theology at the University of Frankfurt an der Oder, in Brandenburg. This irenic Philippist was appointed as the superintendent of Brandenburg and later became a pastor in Frankfurt, although the local authorities first required him to condemn Calvinist theology, because several years earlier he had been called before the consistory in Berlin under suspicion of being a crypto-Calvinist. Among his most important works were a four-volume commentary on *De orthodoxa fide* by John of Damascus (d. 749), a treatise defending the breaking of the bread during communion, and a volume of funeral sermons. He also published commentaries on the Pentateuch, the Psalms, Matthew, John and Acts.

Konrad Pellikan (1478–1556). German Reformed Hebraist and theologian. Pellikan attended the University of Heidelberg, where he mastered Hebrew under Johannes Reuchlin. In 1504 Pellikan published one of the first Hebrew grammars that was not merely a translation of the work of medieval rabbis. While living in Basel, Pellikan assisted the printer Johannes Amerbach, with whom he published some of Luther's* early writings. He also worked with Sebastian Münster* and Wolfgang Capito* on a Hebrew Psalter (1516). In 1526, after teaching theology for three years at the University of Basel, Huldrych Zwingli* brought Pellikan to Zurich to chair the faculty of Old Testament. Pellikan's magnum opus is a seven-volume commentary on the entire Bible (except Revelation) and the Apocrypha; it is often heavily dependent upon the work of others (esp. Desiderius Erasmus* and Johannes Oecolampadius*).

Benedict Pererius (1535–1610). Spanish Catholic theologian, philosopher and exegete. Pererius entered the Society of Jesus in 1552. He taught philosophy, theology, and exegesis at the Roman College of the Jesuits. Early in his career he warned against neo-Platonism and astrology in his *De principiis* (1576). Pererius wrote a lengthy commentary on Daniel, and five volumes of exegetical theses on Exodus, Romans, Revelation and part of the Gospel of John (chs. 1–14). His four-volume commentary on Genesis (1591–1599) was lauded by Protestants and Catholics alike.

William Perkins (1558–1602). English Puritan preacher and theologian. Perkins was a highly regarded Puritan Presbyterian preacher and biblical commentator in the Elizabethan era. He studied at Cambridge University and later became a fellow of Christ's Church college as a preacher and professor, receiving acclaim for his sermons and lectures. Even more, Perkins gained an esteemed reputation for his ardent exposition of Calvinist reformed doctrine in the style of Petrus Ramus,* becoming one of the first English reformed theologians to achieve international recognition. Perkins influenced the federal Calvinist shape of Puritan theology and the vision of logical, practical expository preaching.

Dirk Philips (1504–1568). Dutch Radical elder and theologian. This former Franciscan monk, known for being severe and obstinate, was a leading theologian of the sixteenth-century Anabaptist movement. Despite the fame of Menno Simons* and his own older brother Obbe, Philips wielded great influence over Anabaptists in the Netherlands and northern Germany where he ministered. As a result of Philips's understanding of the apostolic church as radically separated from the children of the world, he advocated a very strict interpretation of the ban, including formal shunning. His writings were collected and published near the end of his life as *Enchiridion oft Hantboecxken van de Christelijcke Leere* (1564).

Johannes Piscator (1546–1625). German Reformed theologian. Educated at Tübingen (though he wanted to study at Wittenberg),

Piscator taught at the universities of Strasbourg and Heidelberg, as well as academies in Neustadt and Herborn. His commentaries on both the Old and New Testaments involve a tripartite analysis of a given passage's argument, of scholia on the text and of doctrinal loci. Some consider Piscator's method to be a full flowering of Beza's* "logical" scriptural analysis, focused on the text's meaning and its relationship to the pericopes around it.

Felix Pratensis (d. 1539). Italian Catholic Hebraist. Pratensis, the son of a rabbi, converted to Christianity and entered the Augustinian Hermits around the turn of the sixteenth century. In 1515, with papal permission, Pratensis published a new translation of the Psalms based on the Hebrew text. His *Biblia Rabbinica* (1517–1518), printed in Jewish and Christian editions, included text-critical notes in the margins as well as the Targum and rabbinic commentaries on each book (e.g., Rashi* on the Pentateuch and David Kimchi* on the Prophets). Many of the reformers consulted this valuable resource as they labored on their own translations and expositions of the Old Testament.

Quadriga. The *quadriga*, or four senses of Scripture, grew out of the exegetical legacy of Paul's dichotomy of letter and spirit (2 Cor 3:6), as well as church fathers like Origen (c. 185–254), Jerome (c. 347–420) and Augustine (354–430). Advocates for this method—the primary framework for biblical exegesis during the medieval era—assumed the necessity of the gift of faith under the guidance of the Holy Spirit. The literal-historical meaning of the text served as the foundation for the fuller perception of Scripture's meaning in the three spiritual senses, accessible only through faith: the allegorical sense taught what should be believed, the tropological or moral sense taught what should be done, and the anagogical or eschatological sense taught what should be hoped for. Medieval Jewish exegesis also had a fourfold interpretive method—not necessarily related to the *quadriga*—called *pardes* ("grove"): *peshat*, the simple, literal sense of the text according to grammar; *remez*, the allegorical sense; *derash*, the moral sense; and *sod*, the mystic sense related to Kabbalah. Scholars hotly dispute the precise use and meaning of these terms.

Petrus Ramus (1515–1572). French Reformed humanist philosopher. Ramus was an influential professor of philosophy and logic at the French royal college in Paris; he converted to Protestantism and left France for Germany, where he came under the influence of Calvinist thought. Ramus was a trenchant critic of Aristotle and noted for his method of classification based on a deductive movement from universals to particulars, the latter becoming branching divisions that provided a visual chart of the parts to the whole. His system profoundly influenced Puritan theology and preaching. After returning to Paris, Ramus died in the Saint Bartholomew's Day Massacre.

Rashi (Shlomo Yitzchaki) (1040–1105). French Jewish rabbi and exegete. After completing his studies, Rashi founded a yeshiva in Troyes. He composed the first comprehensive commentary on the Talmud, as well as commentaries on the entire Old Testament except for 1–2 Chronicles. These works remain influential within orthodox Judaism. Late medieval and early modern Christian scholars valued his exegesis, characterized by his preference for peshat (see quadriga).

Remonstrance (1610). See *Synod of Dordrecht*.

Johannes Reuchlin (1455–1522). German Catholic lawyer, humanist and Hebraist. Reuchlin held judicial appointments for the dukes of Württemberg, the Supreme Court in Speyer and the imperial court of the Swabian League. He pioneered the study of Hebrew among Christians in Germany, standing against those who, like Johannes Pfefferkorn (1469–1523), wanted to destroy Jewish literature. Among his many works he published a Latin dictionary, an introductory Greek grammar, the most important early modern Hebrew grammar and dictionary (*De rudimentis hebraicis*; 1506), and a commentary on the penitential psalms.

Urbanus Rhegius (1489–1541). German Lutheran pastor. Rhegius, who was likely the son of a priest, studied under the humanists at

Freiburg and Ingolstadt. After a brief stint as a foot soldier, he received ordination in 1519 and was made cathedral preacher in Augsburg. During his time in Augsburg he closely read Luther's* works, becoming an enthusiastic follower. Despite his close friendship with Zwingli* and Oecolampadius,* Rhegius supported Luther in the eucharistic debates, later playing a major role in the Wittenberg Concord (1536). He advocated for peace during the Peasants' War and had extended interactions with the Anabaptists in Augsburg. Later in his career he concerned himself with the training of pastors, writing a pastoral guide and two catechisms. About one hundred of his writings were published posthumously.

Lancelot Ridley (d. 1576). Anglican preacher. Ridley was the first cousin of Nicholas Ridley,* the bishop of London who was martyred during the Marian persecutions. By Cranmer's* recommendation, Ridley became one of the six Canterbury Cathedral preachers. Upon Mary I's accession in 1553, Ridley was defrocked (as a married priest). Ridley returned to Canterbury Cathedral after Mary's death. He wrote commentaries on Jude, Ephesians, Philippians and Colossians.

Nicholas Ridley (c. 1502–1555). Anglican bishop. Ridley was a student and fellow at Cambridge University who was appointed chaplain to Archbishop Thomas Cranmer* and is thought to be partially responsible for Cranmer's shift to a symbolic view of the Eucharist. Cranmer promoted Ridley twice: as bishop of Rochester, where he openly advocated Reformed theological views, and, later, as bishop of London. Ridley assisted Cranmer in the revisions of the Book of Common Prayer.* Ridley's support of Lady Jane Grey against the claims of Mary to the throne led to his arrest; he was tried for heresy and burned at the stake with Hugh Latimer.*

Peter Riedemann (1506–1556). German Radical elder, theologian and hymnist. While traveling as a Silesian cobbler, Riedemann came into contact with Anabaptist teachings and joined a congregation in Linz. In 1529 he was called to be a minister, only to be imprisoned soon after as part of

Archduke Ferdinand's efforts to suppress heterodoxy in his realm. Once he was released, he moved to Moravia in 1532 where he was elected as a minister and missionary of the Hutterite community there. His *Account of Our Religion, Doctrine and Faith* (1542), with its more than two thousand biblical references, is Riedemann's most important work and is still used by Hutterites today.

Nehemiah Rogers (1593–1660). Anglican priest. After studying at Cambridge, Rogers ministered at numerous parishes during his more than forty-year career. In 1643, he seems to have been forced out of a parish on account of being a Royalist and friend of William Laud.* Rogers published a number of sermons and tracts, including a series of expositions on Jesus' parables in the Gospels.

Robert Rollock (c. 1555–1599). Scottish Reformed pastor, educator and theologian. Rollock was deeply influenced by Petrus Ramus's* system of logic, which he implemented as a tutor and (later) principal of Edinburgh University and in his expositions of the Bible. Rollock, as a divinity professor and theologian, was instrumental in diffusing a federalist Calvinism in the Scottish church; he lectured on theology using the texts of Theodore Beza* and articulated a highly covenantal interpretation of the biblical narratives. He was a prolific writer of sermons, expositions, commentaries, lectures and occasional treatises.

Jacopo Sadoleto (1477–1547). Italian Catholic Cardinal. Sadoleto, attaché to Leo X's court, was appointed bishop in 1517, cardinal in 1536. He participated in the reform commission led by Gasparo Contarini.* However, he tried to reconcile with Protestants apart from the commission, sending several letters to Protestant leaders in addition to his famous letter to the city of Geneva, which John Calvin* pointedly answered. Sadoleto published a commentary on Romans that was censored as semi-Pelagian. His insufficient treatment of prevenient grace left him vulnerable to this charge. Sadoleto emphasized grammar as the rule and norm of exegesis.

Heinrich Salmuth (1522–1576). German

Lutheran theologian. After earning his doctorate from the University of Leipzig, Salmuth served in several coterminous pastoral and academic positions. He was integral to the reorganization of the University of Jena. Except for a few disputations, all of Salmuth's works—mostly sermons—were published posthumously by his son.

Edwin Sandys (1519–1588). Anglican bishop. During his doctoral studies at Cambridge, Sandys befriended Martin Bucer.* Having supported the Protestant Lady Jane Grey's claim to the throne, Sandys resigned his post at Cambridge upon Mary I's accession. He was then arrested and imprisoned in the Tower of London. Released in 1554, he sojourned on the continent until Mary's death. On his return to England he was appointed to revise the liturgy and was consecrated bishop. Many of his sermons were published, but his most significant literary legacy is his work as a translator of the Bishop's Bible (1568), which served as the foundational English text for the translators of the King James Bible (1611).

Erasmus Sarcerius (1501–1559). German Lutheran superintendent, educator and pastor. Sarcerius served as educational superintendent, court preacher and pastor in Nassau and, later, in Leipzig. The hallmark of Sarcerius's reputation was his ethical emphasis as exercised through ecclesial oversight and family structure; he also drafted disciplinary codes for regional churches in Germany. Sarcerius served with Philipp Melanchthon* as Protestant delegates at the Council of Trent, though both withdrew prior to the dismissal of the session; he eventually became an opponent of Melanchthon, contesting the latter's understanding of the Eucharist at a colloquy in Worms in 1557.

Michael Sattler (c. 1490–1527). Swiss Radical leader. Sattler was a Benedictine monk who abandoned the monastic life during the upheavals of the Peasants' War. He took up the trade of weaving under the guidance of an outspoken Anabaptist. It seems that Sattler did not openly join the Anabaptist movement until after the suppression of the Peasants' War in 1526. Sattler interceded with Martin Bucer* and Wolfgang Capito* for imprisoned Anabaptists in Strasbourg. Shortly before he was convicted of heresy and executed, he wrote the definitive expression of Anabaptist theology, the Schleitheim Articles.*

Girolamo Savonarola (1452–1498). Italian Catholic preacher and martyr. Outraged by clerical corruption and the neglect of the poor, Savonarola travelled to preach against these abuses and to prophesy impending judgment—a mighty king would scourge and reform the church. Savonarola thought that the French invasion of Italy in 1494 confirmed his apocalyptic visions. Thus he pressed to purge Florence of vice and institute public welfare, in order to usher in a new age of Christianity. Florence's refusal to join papal resistance against the French enraged Alexander VI (r. 1492–1503). He blamed Savonarola, promptly excommunicating him and threatening Florence with an interdict. After an ordeal by fire turned into a riot, Savonarola was arrested. Under torture he admitted to charges of conspiracy and false prophecy; he was hanged and burned. In addition to numerous sermons and letters, he wrote meditations on Psalms 31 and 51 as well as *The Triumph of the Cross* (1497).

Leupold Scharnschlager (d. 1563). Austrian Radical elder. See *Kunstbuch*.

Leonhard Schiemer (d. 1528). Austrian Radical martyr. See *Kunstbuch*.

Hans Schlaffer (c. 1490–1528). Austrian Radical martyr. See *Kunstbuch*.

Schleitheim Articles (1527). After the death of Conrad Grebel* in 1526 and the execution of Felix Manz (born c. 1498) in early 1527, the young Swiss Anabaptist movement was in need of unity and direction. A synod convened at Schleitheim under the chairmanship of Michael Sattler,* which passed seven articles of Anabaptist distinctives—likely defined against both magisterial reformers and other Anabaptists with less orthodox and more militant views (e.g., Balthasar Hubmaier*). Unlike most confessions, these articles do not explicitly address traditional creedal interests; they explicate instead the Anabaptist view of the sacraments, church discipline, separatism, the role of ministers, pacifism and oaths. Throughout the document there is a resolute focus on Christ's example. The Schleitheim Articles are considered the definitive statement of Anabaptist theology, particularly regarding separatism.

Schmalkald Articles (1537). In response to Pope Paul III's (1468–1549) 1536 decree ordering a general church council to solve the Protestant crisis, Elector John Frederick (1503–1554) commissioned Martin Luther* to draft the sum of his teaching. Intended by Luther as a last will and testament—and composed with advice from well-known colleagues Justus Jonas,* Johann Bugenhagen,* Caspar Cruciger,* Nikolaus von Amsdorf (1483–1565), Georg Spalatin (1484–1545), Philipp Melanchthon* and Johann Agricola*—these articles provide perhaps the briefest and most systematic summary of Luther's teaching. The document was not adopted formally by the Lutheran Schmalkald League, as was hoped, and the general church council was postponed for several years (until convening at Trent in 1545). Only in 1580 were the articles officially received, by being incorporated into the *Book of Concord* defining orthodox Lutheranism.

Anna Maria van Schurman (1607–1678). Dutch Reformed polymath. Van Schurman cultivated talents in art, poetry, botany, linguistics and theology. She mastered most contemporary European languages, in addition to Latin, Greek, Hebrew, Arabic, Farsi and Ethiopian. With the encouragement of leading Reformed theologian Gisbertus Voetius (1589–1676), van Schurman attended lectures at the University of Utrecht—although she was required to sit behind a wooden screen so that the male students could not see her. In 1638 van Schurman published her famous treatise advocating female scholarship, *Amica dissertatio . . . de capacitate ingenii muliebris ad scientias*. In addition to these more polemical works, van Schurman also wrote hymns and poems, including a paraphrase of Genesis 1–3. Later in life she became a devotee of Jean de Labadie (1610–1674), a former Jesuit who was also expelled from the Reformed church for his separatist

leanings. Her *Eucleria* (1673) is the most well known defense of Labadie's theology.

Kaspar von Schwenckfeld (1489–1561). German Radical reformer. Schwenckfeld was a Silesian nobleman who encountered Luther's* works in 1521. He traveled to Wittenberg twice: first to meet Luther and Karlstadt,* and a second time to convince Luther of his doctrine of the "internal word"—emphasizing inner revelation so strongly that he did not see church meetings or the sacraments as necessary—after which Luther considered him heterodox. Schwenckfeld won his native territory to the Reformation in 1524 and later lived in Strasbourg for five years until Bucer* sought to purify the city of less traditional theologies. Schwenckfeld wrote numerous polemical and exegetical tracts.

Scots Confession (1560). In 1560, the Scottish Parliament undertook to reform the Church of Scotland and to commission a Reformed confession of faith. In the course of four days, a committee—which included John Knox*—wrote this confession, largely based on Calvin's* work, the Confession of the English Congregation in Geneva (1556) and the Gallic Confession.* The articles were not ratified until 1567 and were displaced by the Westminster Confession (1646), adopted by the Scottish in 1647.

Second Helvetic Confession (1566). Believing he would soon die, Heinrich Bullinger* penned a personal statement of his Reformed faith in 1561 as a theological will. In 1563, Bullinger sent a copy of this confession, which blended Zwingli's and Calvin's theology, to the elector of the Palatinate, Frederick III (1515–1576), who had asked for a complete explication of the Reformed faith in order to defend himself against aggressive Lutheran attacks after printing the Heidelberg Confession.* Although not published until 1566, the Second Helvetic Confession became the definitive sixteenth-century Reformed statement of faith. Theodore Beza* used it as the organizing confession for his *Harmonia Confessionum* (1581), which sought to emphasize the unity of the Reformed churches. Bullinger's personal confession was adopted by the Reformed churches of Scotland (1566), Hungary (1567), France (1571) and Poland (1571).

Obadiah Sedgwick (c. 1600–1658). English Puritan minister. Educated at Oxford, Sedgwick pastored in London and participated in the Westminster Assembly. An ardent Puritan, Sedgwick was appointed by Oliver Cromwell (1599–1658) to examine clerical candidates. Sedgwick published a catechism, several sermons and a treatise on how to deal with doubt.

Nikolaus Selnecker (1530–1592). German Lutheran theologian, preacher, pastor and hymnist. Selnecker taught in Wittenberg, Jena and Leipzig, preached in Dresden and Wolfenbüttel, and pastored in Leipzig. He was forced out of his post at Jena because of suspicions that he was a crypto-Calvinist. He sought refuge in Wolfenbüttel, where he met Martin Chemnitz* and Jakob Andreae.* Under their influence Selnecker was drawn away from Philippist theology. Selnecker's shift in theology can be seen in his *Institutio religionis christianae* (1573). Selnecker coauthored the Formula of Concord* with Chemnitz, Andreae, Andreas Musculus (1514–1581), and David Chytraeus.* Selnecker also published lectures on Genesis, the Psalms, and the New Testament epistles, as well as composing over a hundred hymn tunes and texts.

Short Confession (1610). In response to some of William Laud's* reforms in the Church of England—particularly a law stating that ministers who refused to comply with the Book of Common Prayer* would lose their ordination—a group of English Puritans immigrated to the Netherlands in protest, where they eventually embraced the practice of believer's baptism. The resulting Short Confession was an attempt at union between these Puritans and local Dutch Anabaptists ("Waterlanders"). The document highlights the importance of love in the church and reflects optimism regarding the freedom of the will while explicitly rejecting double predestination.

Richard Sibbes (1577–1635). English Puritan preacher. Sibbes was educated at St. John's College, Cambridge, where he was converted to reforming views and became a popular preacher. As a moderate Puritan emphasizing interior piety and brotherly love, Sibbes always remained within the established Church of England, though opposed to some of its liturgical ceremonies. His collected sermons constitute his main literary legacy.

Menno Simons (c. 1496–1561). Dutch Radical leader. Simons led a separatist Anabaptist group in the Netherlands that would later be called Mennonites, known for nonviolence and renunciation of the world. A former priest, Simons rejected Catholicism through the influence of Anabaptist disciples of Melchior Hoffmann and based on his study of Scripture, in which he found no support for transubstantiation or infant baptism. Following the sack of Anabaptists at Münster, Simons committed to a nonviolent way of life. Simons proclaimed a message of radical discipleship of obedience and inner purity, marked by voluntary adult baptism and communal discipline.

Henry Smith (c. 1550–1591). English Puritan minister. Smith stridently opposed the Book of Common Prayer* and refused to subscribe to the Articles of Religion,* thus limiting his pastoral opportunities. Nevertheless he gained a reputation as an eloquent preacher in London. He published sermon collections as well as several treatises.

Cyriacus Spangenberg (1528–1604). German Lutheran pastor, preacher and theologian. Spangenberg was a staunch, often acerbic, Gnesio-Lutheran. He rejected the Formula of Concord* because of concerns about the princely control of the church, as well as its rejection of Flacian language of original sin (as constituting the "substance" of human nature after the fall). He published many commentaries and sermons, most famously seventy wedding sermons (*Ehespiegel* [1561]), his sermons on Luther* (*Theander Luther* [1562–1571]) and Luther's hymns (*Cithara Lutheri* [1569–1570]). He also published an analysis of the Old Testament (though he only got as far as Job), based on a methodology that anticipated the logical bifurcations of Peter Ramus.*

Johann Spangenberg (1484–1550). German

Lutheran pastor and catechist. Spangenberg studied at the University of Erfurt, where he was welcomed into a group of humanists associated with Konrad Muth (1470–1526). There he met the reformer Justus Jonas,* and Eobanus Hessius (1488–1540), whom Luther* dubbed "king of the poets." Spangenberg served at parishes in Stolberg (1520–1524), Nordhausen (1524–1546) and, by Luther's recommendation, Eisleben (1546–1550). Spangenberg published one of the best-selling postils of the sixteenth century, the *Postilla Teütsch*, a six-volume work meant to prepare children to understand the lectionary readings. It borrowed the question-answer form of Luther's *Small Catechism* and was so popular that a monk, Johannes Craendonch, purged overt anti-Catholic statements from it and republished it under his own name. Among Spangenberg's other pastoral works are *ars moriendi* ("the art of dying") booklets, a postil for the Acts of the Apostles and a question-answer version of Luther's *Large Catechism*. In addition to preaching and pastoring, Spangenberg wrote pamphlets on controversial topics such as purgatory, as well as textbooks on music, mathematics and grammar.

Georg Spindler (1525–1605). German Reformed theologian and pastor. After studying theology under Caspar Cruciger* and Philipp Melanchthon,* Spindler accepted a pastorate in Bohemia. A well-respected preacher, Spindler published postils in 1576 which some of his peers viewed as crypto-Calvinist. To investigate this allegation Spindler read John Calvin's* *Institutes*, and subsequently converted to the Reformed faith. After years of travel, he settled in the Palatinate and pastored there until his death. In addition to his Lutheran postils, Spindler also published Reformed postils in 1594 as well as several treatises on the Lord's Supper and predestination.

Michael Stifel (1486–1567). German Lutheran mathematician, theologian and pastor. An Augustinian monk, Stifel's interest in mysticism, apocalypticism and numerology led him to identify Pope Leo X as the antichrist. Stifel soon joined the reform movement, writing a 1522 pamphlet in support of Martin Luther's* theology. After Luther quelled the fallout of Stifel's failed prediction of the Apocalypse—October 19, 1533 at 8AM—Stifel focused more on mathematics and his pastoral duties. He was the first professor of mathematics at the University of Jena. He published several numerological interpretations of texts from the Gospels, Daniel and Revelation. However, Stifel's most important work is his *Arithmetica Integra* (1544), in which he standardized the approach to quadratic equations. He also developed notations for exponents and radicals.

Viktorin Strigel (1524–1569). German Lutheran theologian. Strigel taught at Wittenberg, Erfurt, Jena, Leipzig and Heidelberg. During his time in Jena he disputed with Matthias Flacius (1520–1575) over the human will's autonomy. Following Philipp Melanchthon,* Strigel asserted that in conversion the human will obediently cooperates with the divine will through the Holy Spirit and the Word of God. In the Weimar Disputation (1560), Strigel elicited Flacius's opinion that sin is a substance which mars the formal essence of human beings. Flacius's views were officially rejected in Article 1 of the Formula of Concord*; Strigel's, in Article 2. In 1567 the University of Leipzig suspended Strigel from teaching on account of suspicions that he affirmed Reformed Eucharistic theology; he acknowledged that he did and joined the Reformed confession on the faculty of the University of Heidelberg. In addition to controversial tracts, Strigel published commentaries on the entire Bible (except Lamentations) and the Apocrypha.

Johann Sutell (1504–1575). German Lutheran pastor. After studying at the University of Wittenberg, Sutell received a call to a pastorate in Göttingen, where he eventually became superintendent. He wrote new church orders for Göttingen (1531) and Schweinfurt (1543), and expanded two sermons for publication, *The Dreadful Destruction of Jerusalem* (1539) and *History of Lazarus* (1543).

Swiss Brethren Confession of Hesse (1578). Anabaptist leader Hans Pauly Kuchenbecker penned this confession after a 1577 interrogation by Lutheran authorities. This confession was unusually amenable to Lutheran views—there is no mention of pacifism or rejection of oath taking.

Synod of Dordrecht (1618–1619). This large Dutch Reformed Church council—also attended by English, German and Swiss delegates—met to settle the theological issues raised by the followers of Jacobus Arminius.* Arminius's theological disagreements with mainstream Reformed teaching erupted into open conflict with the publication of the *Remonstrance* (1610). This "protest" was based on five points: that election is based on foreseen faith or unbelief; that Christ died indiscriminately for all people (although only believers receive salvation); that people are thoroughly sinful by nature apart from the prevenient grace of God that enables their free will to embrace or reject the gospel; that humans are able to resist the working of God's grace; and that it is possible for true believers to fall away from faith completely. The Synod ruled in favor of the Contra-Remonstrants, its Canons often remembered with a TULIP acrostic—total depravity, unconditional election, limited atonement, irresistible grace, perseverance of the saints—each letter countering one of the five Remonstrant articles. The Synod also officially accepted the Belgic Confession,* Heidelberg Catechism* and the Canons of Dordrecht as standards of the Dutch Reformed Church.

Richard Taverner (1505–1575). English Puritan humanist and translator. After graduating from Oxford, Taverner briefly studied abroad. When he returned to England, he joined Thomas Cromwell's (1485–1540) circle. After Cromwell's beheading, Taverner escaped severe punishment and retired from public life during Mary I's reign. Under Elizabeth I, Taverner served as justice of the peace, sheriff and a licensed lay preacher. Taverner translated many important continental Reformation works into English, most notably the Augsburg Confession* and several of Desiderius Erasmus's* works. Some of these translations—John Calvin's* 1536 catechism, Wolfgang

Capito's* work on the Psalms and probably Erasmus Sarcerius's* postils—he presented as his own work. Underwritten by Cromwell, Taverner also published an edited version of the Matthew Bible (1537).

Thomas Thorowgood (1595–1669). English Puritan pastor. Thorowgood was a Puritan minister in Norfolk and the chief financier of John Eliot (1604–1690), a Puritan missionary among the Native American tribes in Massachusetts. In 1650, under the title *Jews in America, or, Probabilities that Americans be of that Race*, Thorowgood became one of the first to put forward the thesis that Native Americans were actually the ten lost tribes of Israel.

Frans Titelmans (1502–1537). Belgian Catholic philosopher. Titelmans studied at the University of Leuven, where he was influenced by Petrus Ramus.* After first joining a Franciscan monastery, Titelmans realigned with the stricter Capuchins and moved to Italy. He is best known for his advocacy for the Vulgate and his debates with Desiderius Erasmus* over Pauline theology (1527–1530)—he was deeply suspicious of the fruits of humanism, especially regarding biblical studies. His work was published posthumously by his brother, Pieter Titelmans (1501–1572).

Francisco de Toledo (1532–1596). Spanish Catholic theologian. This important Jesuit taught philosophy at the universities of Salamanca and Rome. He published works on Aristotelian philosophy and a commentary on Thomas Aquinas's work, as well as biblical commentaries on John, Romans and the first half of Luke. He was also the general editor for the Clementine Vulgate (1598).

Daniel Toussain (1541–1602). Swiss Reformed pastor and professor. Toussain became pastor at Orléans after attending college in Basel. After the third War of Religion, Toussain was exiled, eventually returning to Montbéliard, his birthplace. In 1571, he faced opposition there from the strict Lutheran rulers and was eventually exiled due to his influence over the clergy. He returned to Orléans but fled following the Saint Bartholomew's Day Massacre (1572), eventually becoming pastor in Basel. He relocated to Heidelberg in 1583 as pastor to the new regent, becoming professor of theology at the university, and he remained there until his death.

John Trapp (1601–1669). Anglican biblical exegete. After studying at Oxford, Trapp entered the pastorate in 1636. During the English Civil Wars he sided with Parliament, which later made it difficult for him to collect tithes from a congregation whose royalist pastor had been evicted. Trapp published commentaries on all the books of the Bible from 1646 to 1656.

Immanuel Tremellius (1510–1580). Italian Reformed Hebraist. Around 1540, Tremellius received baptism by Cardinal Reginald Pole (1500–1558) and converted from Judaism to Christianity; he affiliated with evangelicals the next year. On account of the political and religious upheaval, Tremellius relocated often, teaching Hebrew in Lucca; Strasbourg, fleeing the Inquisition; Cambridge, displaced by the Schmalkaldic War; Heidelberg, escaping Mary I's persecutions; and Sedan, expelled by the new Lutheran Elector of the Palatine. Many considered Tremellius's translation of the Old Testament as the most accurate available. He also published a Hebrew grammar and translated John Calvin's* catechism into Hebrew.

William Tyndale (Hychyns) (1494–1536). English reformer, theologian and translator. Tyndale was educated at Oxford University, where he was influenced by the writings of humanist thinkers. Believing that piety is fostered through personal encounter with the Bible, he asked to translate the Bible into English; denied permission, Tyndale left for the Continent to complete the task. His New Testament was the equivalent of a modern-day bestseller in England but was banned and ordered burned. Tyndale's theology was oriented around justification, the authority of Scripture and Christian obedience; Tyndale emphasized the ethical as a concomitant reality of justification. He was martyred in Brussels before completing his English translation of the Old Testament, which Miles Coverdale* finished.

Juan de Valdés (1500/10–1541). Spanish Catholic theologian and writer. Although Valdés adopted an evangelical doctrine, had Erasmian affiliations and published works that were listed on the Index of Prohibited Books, Valdés rebuked the reformers for creating disunity and never left the Catholic Church. His writings included translations of the Hebrew Psalter and various biblical books, a work on the Spanish language and several commentaries. Valdés fled to Rome in 1531 to escape the Spanish Inquisition and worked in the court of Clement VII in Bologna until the pope's death in 1534. Valdés subsequently returned to Naples, where he led the reform- and revival-minded Valdesian circle.

Peter Martyr Vermigli (1499–1562). Italian Reformed humanist and theologian. Vermigli was one of the most influential theologians of the era, held in common regard with such figures as Martin Luther* and John Calvin.* In Italy, Vermigli was a distinguished theologian, preacher and advocate for moral reform; however, during the reinstitution of the Roman Inquisition Vermigli fled to Protestant regions in northern Europe. He was eventually appointed professor of divinity at Oxford University, where Vermigli delivered acclaimed disputations on the Eucharist. Vermigli was widely noted for his deeply integrated biblical commentaries and theological treatises.

Vulgate. In 382 Pope Damasus I (c. 300–384) commissioned Jerome (c. 347–420) to translate the four Gospels into Latin based on Old Latin and Greek manuscripts. Jerome completed the translation of the Gospels and the Old Testament around 405. It is widely debated how much of the rest of the New Testament was translated by Jerome. During the Middle Ages, the Vulgate became the Catholic Church's standard Latin translation. The Council of Trent recognized it as the official text of Scripture.

Peter Walpot (d. 1578). Moravian Radical pastor and bishop. Walpot was a bishop of the Hutterite community after Jakob Hutter, Peter Riedemann* and Leonhard Lanzenstiel. Riedemann's *Confession of Faith* (1545; 1565) became a vital authority for Hutterite exegesis, theology and morals. Walpot added his own *Great Article Book* (1577), which collates primary biblical passages on baptism, communion, the community of goods, the sword and divorce. In keeping with Hutterite theology, Walpot defended the community of goods as a mark of the true church.

Valentin Weigel (1533–1588). German Lutheran pastor. Weigel studied at Leipzig and Wittenberg, entering the pastorate in 1567. Despite a strong anti-institutional bias, he was recognized by the church hierarchy as a talented preacher and compassionate minister of mercy to the poor. Although he signed the Formula of Concord,* Weigel's orthodoxy was questioned so openly that he had to publish a defense. He appears to have tried to synthesize several medieval mystics with the ideas of Sebastian Franck,* Thomas Müntzer* and others. His posthumously published works have led some recent scholars to suggest that Weigel's works may have deeply influenced later Pietism.

Hieronymus Weller von Molsdorf (1499–1572). German Lutheran theologian. Originally intending to study law, Weller devoted himself to theology after hearing one of Martin Luther's* sermons on the catechism. He boarded with Luther and tutored Luther's son. In 1539 he moved to Freiburg, where he lectured on the Bible and held theological disputations at the Latin school. In addition to hymns, works of practical theology and a postil set, Weller published commentaries on Genesis, 1–2 Samuel, 1–2 Kings, Job, the Psalms, Christ's passion, Ephesians, Philippians, 1–2 Thessalonians and 1–2 Peter.

John Whitgift (1530–1604). Anglican archbishop. Though Whitgift shared much theological common ground with Puritans, after his election as Archbishop of Canterbury (1583) he moved decisively to squelch the political and ecclesiastical threat they posed during Elizabeth's reign. Whitgift enforced strict compliance to the Book of Common Prayer,* the Act of Uniformity (1559) and the Articles of Religion.* Whitgift's policies led to a large migration of Puritans to Holland. The bulk of Whitgift's published corpus is the fruit of a lengthy public disputation with Thomas Cartwright,* in which Whitgift defines Anglican doctrine against Cartwright's staunch Puritanism.

Johann Wigand (1523–1587). German Lutheran theologian. Wigand is most noted as one of the compilers of the *Magdeburg Centuries*, a German ecclesiastical history of the first thirteen centuries of the church. He was a student of Philipp Melanchthon* at the University of Wittenburg and became a significant figure in the controversies dividing Lutheranism. Strongly opposed to Roman Catholicism, Wigand lobbied against innovations in Lutheran theology that appeared sympathetic to Catholic thought. In the later debates, Wigand's support for Gnesio-Lutheranism established his role in the development of confessional Lutheranism. Wigand was appointed bishop of Pomerania after serving academic posts at the universities in Jena and Königsburg.

Thomas Wilcox (c. 1549–1608). English Puritan theologian. In 1572, Wilcox objected to Parliament against the episcopacy and the Book of Common Prayer,* advocating for presbyterian church governance. He was imprisoned for sedition. After his release, he preached itinerantly. He was brought before the courts twice more for his continued protest against the Church of England's episcopal structure. He translated some of Theodore Beza* and John Calvin's* sermons into English, and he wrote polemical and occasional works as well as commentaries on the Psalms and Song of Songs.

Johann (Ferus) Wild (1495–1554). German Catholic pastor. After studying at Heidelberg and teaching at Tübingen, this Franciscan was appointed as lector in the Mainz cathedral, eventually being promoted to cathedral preacher—a post for which he became widely popular but also controversial. Wild strongly identified as Catholic but was not unwilling to criticize the curia. Known for an irenic spirit—criticized in fact as *too* kind—he was troubled by the polemics between all parties of the Reformation. He preached with great lucidity, integrating the liturgy, Scripture and doctrine to exposit Catholic worship and teaching for common people. His sermons on John were pirated for publication without his knowledge; the Sorbonne banned them as heretical. Despite his popularity among clergy, the majority of his works were on the Roman Index until 1900.

Andrew Willet (1562–1621). Anglican priest, professor, and biblical expositor. Willet was a gifted biblical expositor and powerful preacher. He walked away from a promising university career in 1588 when he was ordained a priest in the Church of England. For the next thirty-three years he served as a parish priest. Willet's commentaries summarized the present state of discussion while also offering practical applications for preachers. They have been cited as some of the most technical commentaries of the early seventeenth century. His most important publication was *Synopsis Papismi, or a General View of Papistrie* (1594), in which he responded to many of Robert Bellarmine's critiques. After years of royal favor, Willet was imprisoned in 1618 for a month after presenting to King James I his opposition to the "Spanish Match" of Prince Charles to the Infanta Maria. While serving as a parish priest, he wrote forty-two works, most of which were either commentaries on books of the Bible or controversial works against Catholics.

John Woolton (c. 1535–1594). Anglican bishop. After graduating from Oxford, Woolton lived in Germany until the accession of Elizabeth I. He was ordained as a priest in 1560 and as a bishop in 1578. Woolton published many theological, devotional and practical works, including a treatise on the immortality of the soul, a discourse on conscience and a manual for Christian living.

Girolamo Zanchi (1516–1590). Italian Reformed theologian and pastor. Zanchi joined an Augustinian monastery at the age of fifteen, where he studied Greek and Latin, the church fathers and the works of Aristotle and Thomas Aquinas. Under the influence of his prior, Peter Martyr Vermigli,* Zanchi also imbibed the writings of the Swiss and German reformers. To avoid the

Inquisition, Zanchi fled to Geneva where he was strongly attracted to the preaching and teaching of John Calvin.* Zanchi taught biblical theology and the *locus* method at academies in Strasbourg, Heidelberg, and Neustadt. He also served as pastor of an Italian refugee congregation. Zanchi's theological works, *De tribus Elohim* (1572) and *De natura Dei* (1577), have received more attention than his commentaries. His commentaries comprise about a quarter of his literary output, however, and display a strong typological and Christological interpretation in conversation with the church fathers, medieval exegetes, and other reformers.

Katharina Schütz Zell (1497/98–1562). German Reformed writer. Zell became infamous in Strasbourg and the Empire when in 1523 she married the priest Matthias Zell, and then published an apology defending her husband against charges of impiety and libertinism. Longing for a united church, she called for toleration of Catholics and Anabaptists, famously writing to Martin Luther* after the failed Marburg Colloquy of 1529 to exhort him to check his hostility and to be ruled instead by Christian charity. Much to the chagrin of her contemporaries, Zell published diverse works, ranging from polemical treatises on marriage to letters of consolation, as well as editing a hymnal and penning an exposition of Psalm 51.

Huldrych Zwingli (1484–1531). Swiss Reformed humanist, preacher and theologian. Zwingli, a parish priest, was influenced by the writings of Desiderius Erasmus* and taught himself Greek. While a preacher to the city cathedral in Zurich, Zwingli enacted reform through sermons, public disputations and conciliation with the town council, abolishing the Mass and images in the church. Zwingli broke with the lectionary preaching tradition, instead preaching serial expository biblical sermons. He later was embroiled in controversy with Anabaptists over infant baptism and with Martin Luther* at the Marburg Colloquy (1529) over their differing views of the Eucharist. Zwingli, serving as chaplain to Zurich's military, was killed in battle.

SOURCES FOR
BIOGRAPHICAL SKETCHES

General Reference Works

Allgemeine Deutsche Biographie. 56 vols. Leipzig: Duncker & Humblot, 1875–1912; reprint, 1967–1971. Accessible online via deutsche-biographie.de/index.html.

Baskin, Judith R., ed. *The Cambridge Dictionary of Judaism and Jewish Culture.* New York: Cambridge University Press, 2011.

Bettenson, Henry and Chris Maunder, eds. *Documents of the Christian Church.* 3rd ed. Oxford: Oxford University Press, 1999.

Betz, Hans Dieter, Don Browning, Bernd Janowski and Eberhard Jüngel, eds. *Religion Past & Present: Encyclopedia of Theology and Relgion.* 13 vols. Leiden: Brill, 2007–2013.

Haag, Eugene and Émile Haag. *La France protestante ou vies des protestants français.* 2nd ed. 6 vols. Paris: Sandoz & Fischbacher, 1877–1888.

Hillerbrand, Hans J., ed. *Oxford Encyclopedia of the Reformation.* 4 vols. New York: Oxford University Press, 1996.

Kolb, Robert, and Timothy J. Wengert, eds. *The Book of Concord: The Confessions of the Evangelical Lutheran Church.* Translated by Charles Arand et al. Minneapolis: Fortress, 2000.

McKim, Donald K., ed. *Dictionary of Major Biblical Interpreters.* Downers Grove, IL: InterVarsity Press, 2007.

Müller, Gerhard, et al., ed. *Theologische Realenzyklopädie.* Berlin: Walter de Gruyter, 1994.

Neue Deutsche Biographie. 28 vols. projected. Berlin: Duncker & Humblot, 1953–. Accessible online via deutsche-biographie.de/index.html.

New Catholic Encyclopedia. 15 vols. New York: McGraw-Hill, 1967; 2nd ed., Detroit: Thomson-Gale, 2002.

Oxford Dictionary of National Biography. 60 vols. Oxford: Oxford University Press, 2004.

Stephen, Leslie, and Sidney Lee, eds. *Dictionary of National Biography.* 63 vols. London: Smith, Elder and Co., 1885–1900.

Terry, Michael, ed. *Reader's Guide to Judaism.* New York: Routledge, 2000.

Wordsworth, Christopher, ed. *Lives of Eminent Men connected with the History of Religion in England.* 4 vols. London: J. G. & F. Rivington, 1839.

Additional Works for Individual Sketches

Akin, Daniel L. "An Expositional Analysis of the Schleitheim Confession." *Criswell Theological Review* 2 (1988): 345-70.

Bald, R. C. *John Donne: A Life.* Oxford: Oxford University Press, 1970.

Doornkaat Koolman, J ten. "The First Edition of Peter Riedemann's 'Rechenschaft.'" *Mennonite Quarterly Review* 36, no. 2 (1962): 169-70.

Fishbane, Michael A. "Teacher and the Hermeneutical Task: A Reinterpretation of Medieval Exegesis." *Journal of the American Academy of Religion* 43, no. 4 (1975): 709-21.

Friedmann, Robert. "Second Generation Anabaptism as Illustrated by the Walpot Era of the Hutterites." *Mennonite Quarterly* 44, no. 4 (1970): 390-93.

Frymire, John M. *The Primacy of the Postils: Catholics, Protestants, and the Dissemination of Ideas in Early Modern Germany.* Leiden: Brill, 2010.

Furcha, Edward J. "Key Concepts in Caspar von Schwenckfeld's Thought, Regeneration and the New Life." *Church History* 37, no. 2 (1968): 160-73.

Greaves, Richard L. *Society and Religion in Elizabethan England.* Minneapolis: University of Minnesota, 1981.

Greiffenberg, Catharina Regina von. *Meditations on the Incarnation, Passion and Death of Jesus Christ.* Edited and translated by Lynne Tatlock. The Other Voice in Early Modern Europe. Chicago: University of Chicago Press, 2009.

Grendler, Paul. "Italian biblical humanism and the papacy, 1515-1535." In *Biblical Humanism and Scholasticism in the Age of Erasmus.* Edited by Erika Rummel, 225-276. Leiden: Brill, 2008.

Heiden, Albert van der. "Pardes: Methodological

Reflections on the Theory of the Four Senses." Journal of Jewish Studies 34, no. 2 (1983): 147-59.

Hendrix, Scott H., ed. and trans. *Early Protestant Spirituality*. New York: Paulist Press, 2009.

Hvolbek, Russell H. "Being and Knowing: Spiritualist Epistelmology and Anthropology from Schwenckfeld to Böhme." *Sixteenth Century Journal* 22, no. 1 (1991): 97-110.

Kahle, Paul. "Felix Pratensis—a Prato, Felix. Der Herausgeber der Ersten Rabbinerbibel, Venedig 1516/7." Die Welt des Orients 1, no. 1 (1947): 32-36.

Kelly, Joseph Francis. The Ecumenical Councils of the Catholic Church: A History. Collegeville, MN: Liturgical Press, 2009.

Lake, Peter. *The Boxmaker's Revenge: 'Orthodoxy', 'Heterodox' and the Politics of the Parish in Early Stuart London*. Stanford, CA: Stanford University Press, 2001.

Lockhart, Paul Douglas. *Frederick II and the Protestant Cause: Denmark's Role in the Wars of Religion, 1559–1596*. Leiden: Brill, 2004.

Lubac, Henri de. Medieval Exegesis: The Four Senses of Scripture. 3 vols. Translated by Mark Sebanc and E. M. Macierowski. Grand Rapids: Eerdmans, 1998–2009.

Norton, David. A Textual History of the King James Bible. New York: Cambridge University Press, 2005

Packull, Werner O. "The Origins of Peter Riedemann's Account of Our Faith." *Sixteenth Century Journal* 30, no. 1 (1999): 61-69.

Papazian, Mary Arshagouni, ed. *John Donne and the Protestant Reformation: New Perspectives*. Detroit: Wayne State University Press, 2003.

Pragman, James H. "The Augsburg Confession in the English Reformation: Richard Taverner's Contribution." *Sixteenth Century Journal* 11, no. 3 (1980): 75-85.

Rashi. Rashi's Commentary on Psalms. Translated by Mayer I. Gruber. Atlanta: Scholars Press, 1998.

Spinka, Matthew. John Hus: A Biography. Princeton, NJ: Princeton University Press, 1968.

———. John Hus at the Council of Constance. New York: Columbia University Press, 1968.

———. John Hus and the Czech Reform. Hamden, CT: Archon Books, 1966.

Steinmetz, David C. "The Superiority of Pre-Critical Exegesis." Theology Today 37, no. 1 (1980): 27-38.

Synder, C. Arnold. "The Schleitheim Articles in Light of the Revolution of the Common Man: Continuation or Departure?" *Sixteenth Century Journal* 16, no. 4 (1985): 419-30.

———. "The Confession of the Swiss Brethren in Hesse, 1578." In *Anabaptism Revisited: Essays on Anabaptist/Mennonite Studies in Honor of C. J. Dyck*. Edited by Walter Klaassen, 29-49. Waterloo, ON; Scottdale, PA: Herald Press, 1992.

Todd, Margo. "Bishops in the Kirk: William Cowper of Galloway and the Puritan Episcopacy of Scotland." *Scottish Journal of Theology*, 57 (2004): 300-312.

Van Liere, Frans. An Introduction to the Medieval Bible. New York: Cambridge University Press, 2014.

Voogt, Gerrit. "Remonstrant-Counter-Remonstrant Debates: Crafting a Principled Defense of Toleration after the Synod of Dordrecht (1619–1650)." *Church History and Religious Culture* 89, no. 4 (2009): 489-524.

Wengert, Timothy J. "'Fear and Love' in the Ten Commandments." *Concordia Journal* 21, no. 1 (1995): 14-27.

Wilkinson, Robert J. Tetragrammaton: Western Christians and the Hebrew Name of God. Leiden: Brill, 2015.

BIBLIOGRAPHY

Primary Sources and Translations Used in the Volume

Ainsworth, Henry. *Annotations on the Pentateuch or the Five Books of Moses, the Psalms of David and the Song of Solomon.* 2 vols. Glasgow: Blackie and Son, 1846. Digital copy available online at archive .org. First published as *The Book of Psalmes: Englished both in Prose and Metre.* Amsterdam: Giles Thorp, 1612. Digital copy online at EEBO.

Alesius, Alexander. *Priumus Liber Psalmorvm, ivxta Hebraeorvm et Divi Hieronymi svppvtationem.* Leipzig: Georg Hantzsch, 1554. Digital copy online at www.gateway-bayern.de.

Amyraut, Moises. *Paraphrasis in Psalmos Davidis una cum annotationibus et argumentis.* Saumur: Isaac Desbordes, 1662. Digital copy online at books.google.com.

Arminius, Jacobus. *The Works of James Arminius.* 3 vols. Translated by James Nichols and W. R. Bagnall. Auburn, NY: Derby, Miller and Orton, 1853. Digital copy online at archive.org.

Arndt, Johann. *Der gantze Psalter Davids des Heiligen Königs und Propheten: In 462. Predigten außgelegt und erklärt.* Frankurt am Main: Johann David Zunner and Johann Görlin, 1621. Digital copy online at www.gateway-bayern.de.

Baxter, Richard. *Meditations and Disquisitions upon the one and fiftieth Psalme of David: Miserere mei Deus.* London: Edward Griffin, 1638. Digital copy online at EEBO.

Beza, Theodore. *Psalmorum Davidis et aliorum prophetarum, libri quinque.* Geneva: Henri Estienne, 1579. Digital copy online at www.e-rara.ch.

———. *Psalmorum sacrorum libri quinque.* 2nd ed. Geneva: Jean Berjon, 1580. Digital copy online at www.e-rara.ch.

———. *The Psalmes of Dauid.* Translated by Anthonie Gilbin. London: Richard Yardley and Peter Short, 1590. Digital copy online at EEBO.

Bibliotheca Reformatoria Neederlandica. 10 vols. Edited by S. Cramer and F. Pijper. The Hague: Martinus, Nijhoff, 1903–1914. Digital copy online at babel.hathitrust.org.

[Bishop's Bible (1568).] *The holie Bible conteynyng the olde Testament and the newe.* London: Richard Iugge, 1568. Digital copy online at archive.org.

The Book of Common Prayer (1549). In *The Two Liturgies, A.D. 1549 and A.D. 1552.* Edited by Joseph Ketley, 9-158. Cambridge: Cambridge University Press, 1844. Digital copy online at books.google.com.

Boys, John. *An Exposition of the Proper Psalms used in our English Liturgy.* London: Felix Kingston, 1616. Digital copy online at EEBO.

Bucer, Martin. *Sacrorum Psalmorum libri quinque.* Strasbourg: Andlanus, 1529. Digital copy online at www.gateway-bayern.de.

Bugenhagen, Johannes. *In librvm Psalmorvm interpretatio.* Strasbourg: Johannes Knoblouch, 1524. Digital copy online at www.gateway-bayern.de.

Cajetan, Cardinal (Thomas de Vio). *Opera omnia qvotqvot in Sacrae Scripturae expositionem reperiuntur.* 5 vols. Lyons: Jean and Pierre Prost, 1639. Digital copy online at www.gateway-bayern.de.

Calvin, John. *Commentarius in librum Psalmorum.* Ioannis Calvini Opera quae supersunt omnia 31–32. Edited by G. Baum, E. Cunitz and E. Reuss. Brunswick: C. A. Schwetschke, 1891. Digital copy online at archive-ouverte.unige.ch/unige:650.

———. *Commentary on the Book of Psalms.* 5 vols. Calvin Translation Society 8–12. Translated by James Anderson. Edinburgh: Calvin Translation Society, 1845–1849. Digital copy online at archive.org.

Crashaw, Richard. *The Complete Works of Richard Crashaw, Canon of Loretto.* Edited by William B. Turnbull. London: John Russell Smith, 1858. Digital copy online at books.google.com.

Dachser, Jakob. *Gsang büchlin: Darinn der gantze Psalter Davids sampt andern Gaistlichen gesangen mit jren Melodeyen begriffen mit fleiß übersehen und Corrigert.* Augsburg: Philip Ulhart, 1557. Digital copy online at www.gateway-bayern.de.

Dickson, David. *A Brief Explication of the First Fifty Psalms.* London: Ralph Smith, 1653. Digital copy online at EEBO.

———. *A Brief Explication of the Other Fifty Psalms.* London: Ralph Smith, 1653. Digital copy online at EEBO.

Diodati, Giovanni. *Pious Annotations upon the Holy Bible.* London: Nicolas Fussell, 1651. Digital copy online at EEBO.

Donne, John. *The Works of John Donne.* 6 vols. Edited by Henry Alford. London: John Parker, 1839. Digital copies online at books.google.com.

———. *The Poems of John Donne.* Edited by Herbert J. C. Grierson. Oxford: The Clarendon Press, 1912. Digital copy online at books.google.com.

Downame, John, ed. *Annotations upon All the Books of the Old and New Testament.* London: Evan Tyler, 1657. Digital copy online at EEBO.

Erasmus, Desiderius. *Expositions on the Psalms.* Collected Works of Erasmus 63–65. Toronto: University of Toronto Press, 1997–2010.

Fisher, John. *Commentary on the Seven Penitential Psalms.* 2 vols. Edited by J. S. Phillimore. London: Manresa Press, 1914. Digital copy online at archive.org.

Folengo, Giovanni Battista. *In Psalterium Davidis Israelitarum regis et vatis divinissimi.* Basel: Michael Isingrinius, 1543. Digital copy online at books.google.com.

[*Geneva Bible* (1560).] *The Bible and Holy Scriptures conteyned in the Old and Newe Testament.* Edited by William Whittingham. Geneva: Rouland Hall, 1560. Digital copy online at EEBO.

Gwalther, Rudolf. *Der Psalter: Grundtlich und eigentlich verteütschet und mit neuwen Summarien erkläret.* Zurich: Christoph Froschauer, 1558. Digital copy online at www.gateway-bayern.de.

Hesshus, Tilemann. *Commentarius in libros Psalmorum.* Helmstadt: Lucius, 1586. Digital copy online at www.gateway-bayern.de.

Hooper, John. *Certeine comfortable Expositions of the constant Martyr of Christ, M. John Hooper, Bishop of Gloucester and Worcester, written in the time of his tribulation and imprisonment, upon the XXIII, LXII, LXXIII and LXXVII psalms of the prophet David.* London: Henrie Middleton, 1580. Digital copy online at EEBO.

Jewel, John. *The Works of John Jewel, Bishop of Salisbury.* 4 vols. Edited by John Ayre. Cambridge: Cambridge University Press, 1845–1850. Digital copy online at archive.org.

Joris, David. *The Anabaptist Writings of David Joris, 1535–1543.* Edited and translated by Gary K. Waite. Classics of the Radical Reformation 7. Scottsdale, PA: Herald Press, 1994.

Karlstadt, Andreas Bodenstein von. *The Essential Carlstadt: Fifteen Tracts by Andreas Bodenstein (Carlstadt) from Karlstadt.* Edited and translated by E. J. Furcha. Classics of the Radical Reformation 8. Scottdale, PA: Herald Press, 1995.

———. *Von den zweyen höchsten gebotten der lieb Gottes und des nechsten.* Strasbourg: Schwan, 1524. Digital copy online at www.gateway-bayern.de.

Knox, John. *A Fort for the afflicted: Wherin are ministred many notable & excellent remedies against the stromes of tribulation.* London: Thomas Dawson, 1580. Digital copy online at EEBO.

Lefèvre d'Étaples, Jacques. *Quincuplex Psalterium: Gallicum, Rhomanum, Hebraicum, Vetus, Conciliatum.* Paris: Henry Stephen, 1513. Digital copy online at www.gateway-bayern.de.

Luther, Martin. *D. Martin Luthers Werke, Kritische Gesamtausgabe: [Schriften].* 73 vols. Weimar: Hermann Böhlaus Nachfolger, 1883–2009. Digital copy online at archive.org.

———. *D. Martin Luthers Werke, Kritische Gesamtausgabe: Tischreden.* 6 vols. Weimar: Hermann Böhlaus Nachfolger, 1912–1921. Digital copy online at archive.org.

———. *Dr. Martin Luther's sämmtliche Werke.* 2nd ed. 26 vols. Frankfurt and Erlangen: Heyder & Zimmer, 1862–1885. Digital copy online at babel.hathitrust.org.

———. *Luther's Works* [American edition]. 82 vols. projected. St. Louis: Concordia; Philadelphia: Fortress, 1955–86; 2009–.

Melanchthon, Philipp. *Philippi Melanthonis Opera quae supersunt omnia.* 28 vols. Corpus Reformatorum 1–28. Edited by C. G. Bretschneider. Halle: C. A. Schwetschke, 1834–1860. Digital copy online at archive.org and books.google.com.

Moibanus, Ambrosius. *Der XXIX Psalm Davids von der gewalt der stimme Gottes inn den lüfften.* Wittenberg: Hans Lufft, 1536. Digital copy online at www.gateway-bayern.de.

Münster, Sebastian. *Miqdaš YHWH: 'esrîm wĕ'arba' sifrê hammikhtav haqqadôsh 'im 'āthîqathô kol.* Basel: Michael Isinginius and Henricus Petrus, 1546. In English the title is *The Temple of the Lord: The Twenty-Four Books of Holy Scripture with All Its Antiquity.* Digital copy online at www.e-rara.ch.

Musculus, Wolfgang. *In Sacrosanctum Davidis Psalterium commentarii.* Basel: Johann Herwagen, 1551. Digital copy online at www.gateway-bayern.de.

Pellikan, Konrad. *Commentaria Bibliorum.* 7 vols. Zurich: Christoph Froschauer, 1532–1539. Digital copy online at www.e-rara.ch.

Philips, Dirk. *The Writings of Dirk Philips 1504–1568.* Edited by Cornelius J. Dyck, William E. Keeney and Alvin J. Beachy. Classics of the Radical Reformation 6. Scottdale, PA: Herald Press, 1992.

Pratensis, Felix. *Psalterium ex hebreo diligentissime ad verbum fere translatum.* Venice: Peter Liechtenstein, 1515. Digital copy online at www.gateway-bayern.de. Another edition was also consulted— Haguenau: Thomas Anselm, 1522.

Rempel, John D., ed. *Jörg Maler's Kunstbuch: Writings of the Pilgram Marpeck Circle.* Classics of the Radical Reformation 12. Kitchener, ON: Pandora, 2012.

Riedemann, Peter. *Peter Riedemann's Hutterite Confession of Faith: Translation of the 1565 German Edition of* Confession of Our Religion, Teaching and Faith by the Brothers Who Are Known as the Hutterites. Edited and translated by John J. Friesen. Classics of the Radical Reformation 9. Scottdale, PA: Herald Press, 1999.

Rollock, Robert. *An exposition upon Some Select Psalmes of David.* Translated by Charles Lumsden. Edinburgh: Robert Waldegrave, 1600. Digital copy online at EEBO.

Sadoleto, Jacob. *Interpretatio in Psalmum Miserere mei.* Rome: Francisci Minitii Calvi, 1525. This work is unpaginated. Digital copy online at www.gateway-bayern.de.

Savonarola, Girolamo. *An Exposition of the Psalm* Miserere Mei Deus. Translated by F. C. Cowper. Milwaukee: The Young Churchman, 1889. Digital copy online at archive.org.

Schaff, Philip. *The Creeds of Christendom: With a Critical History and Notes.* 3 vols. New York: Harper & Row, 1877; reprint, Grand Rapids: Baker, 1977. Digital copy online at ccel.org.

Selnecker, Nikolaus. *Der gantze Psalter des Königlichen Propheten Davids*. 3 vols. Nuremberg: Christoph Heußler, 1565–1566. Digital copy online at www.gateway-bayern.de.

Simon, Menno. *The Complete Works of Menno Simon*. Edited by Joseph F. Summers. Translated by I. Daniel Rupp and Piebe Swart. Elkhart, IN: John F. Funk and Brother, 1871. Digital copy online at archive.org.

Strigel, Victorinus. Ὑπομνήματα: *In omnes Psalmos Davidis, ita scripta, ut a piis amantibus consensum expressum in scriptis Proheticis, Apostolicis, & Scriptoribus vetustis ac purioribus utiliter legi possint* Leipzig. Ernst Voeglin, 1563. Digital copy online at www.gateway-bayern.de.

Weigel, Valentin. *Valentin Weigel Sämtliche Schriften*. 14 vols. Stuttgart-Bad Cannstatt: Frommann-Holzboog, 1996–.

Weller, Hieronymus von Molsdorf. *Brevis enarratio aliquot Psalmorum: Libellus de modo concionandi, pro studiosis theologiae*. Wittenberg: Johannes Crato, 1558. Digital copy online at www.gateway-bayern.de.

Wilcox, Thomas. *A Right Godly and Learned Exposition, upon the whole Booke of Psalmes*. London: Thomas Dawson, 1586. Digital copy online at EEBO.

Zell, Katharina Schütz. *Den Psalmen Misere, mit dem Khünig David bedacht, gebettet, und paraphrasirt*. Strasbourg: Samuel Emmel, 1558.

———. *Church Mother: The Writings of a Protestant Reformer in Sixteenth-Century Germany*. Edited and translated by Elsie Anne McKee. Chicago: University of Chicago Press, 2006.

Zwingli, Huldrych. *Huldreich Zwinglis Sämtliche Werke*. 14 vols. Corpus Reformatorum 88–101. Edited by E. Eglis et al. Berlin: C. A. Schwetschke, 1905–1959; reprint, Zurich: Theologischer Verlag Zürich, 1983. Digital copies online at www.irg.uzh.ch.

———. *Zwingli and Bullinger*. Edited and translated by G. W. Bromiley. Library of Christian Classics 24. Philadelphia: Westminster Press, 1953.

Other Works Consulted

Alter, Robert. *The Book of Psalms: A Translation with Commentary*. New York: Norton, 2007.

Arnold, Bill T. and H. G. M. Williamson, eds. *Dictionary of the Old Testament: Historical Books*. Downers Grove, IL: InterVarsity Press, 2005.

Athanasius. "Letter to Marcellinus." In *On the Incarnation*. Edited and translated by Penelope Lawson, 97–119. Crestwood, NY: St. Vladimir's Seminary Press, 1993.

Augustine. *The Literal Meaning of Genesis*. Translated by John Hammond Taylor. Ancient Christian Writers 41–42. Mahwah, NJ: Paulist, 1982.

———. *The Confessions of St. Augustine*. Translated by Rex Warner. New York: Mentor-Omega, 1963.

Beckwith, Carl L., ed. *Ezekiel, Daniel*. Reformation Commentary on Scripture, Old Testament 12. Downers Grove, IL: IVP Academic, 2012.

Bell, Dean Phillip, and Stephen G. Burnett, eds. *Jews, Judaism and the Reformation in Sixteenth-Century Germany*. Brill: Leiden, 2006.

Beutel, Albrecht, ed. *Luther Handbuch*. Tübingen: Mohr Siebeck, 2005.

Biblia Sacra cum Glossa oridinaria, novisque additionibus. 6 vols. Venice: Magna Societas, 1603. Digital copies online at lollardsociety.org.

Billings, J. Todd. *Rejoicing in Lament: Wrestling with Incurable Cancer and Life in Christ*. Grand Rapids: Brazos Press, 2015.

———. *The Word of God for the People of God: An Entryway to the Theological Interpretation of Scripture*. Grand Rapids: Eerdmans, 2010.

Blaising, Craig A., and Carmen S. Hardin, eds. *Psalms 1–50*. Ancient Christian Commentary on Scripture, Old Testament 7. Downers Grove, IL: InterVarsity Press, 2008.

Bokedal, Tomas. "The Rule of Faith: Tracing Its Origins." *Journal of Theological Interpretation* 7, no. 2 (2013): 233-55.

Bray, Gerald. *Biblical Interpretation: Past and Present*. Downers Grove, IL: InterVarsity Press, 1996.

———. ed. *Galatians, Ephesians*. Reformation Commentary on Scripture, New Testament 10. Downers Grove, IL: IVP Academic, 2011.

Brown, Peter. *Augustine of Hippo: A Biography*. Berkeley and Los Angeles: University of California Press, 1967.

Bultmann, Christoph. "Luthers Betrachtung der Juden nach Psalm 109 und der evangelische Anspruch auf Schriftgemäßheit." *Luther* 85, no. 3 (2014): 179-93.

Burnett, Stephen G. "Reassessing the 'Basel-Wittenberg Conflict': Dimensions of the Reformation-Era Discussion of Hebrew Scholarship." In *Hebraica Veritas?: Christian Hebraists and the Study of Judaism in Early Modern Europe*. Edited by Allison Coudert and Jeffrey S. Shoulson, 181-201. Philadelphia: University of Pennsylvania Press, 2004.

———. "The Strange Career of the *Biblia Rabbinica* Among Christian Hebraists, 1517–1620." In *Shaping the Bible in the Reformation: Books, Scholars and Their Readers in the Sixteenth Century*. Edited by Bruce Gordon and Matthew McLean, 63-84. Leiden: Brill, 2012.

Buschart, W. David, and Kent D. Eilers. *Theology as Retrieval: Receiving the Past, Renewing the Church*. Downers Grove, IL: IVP Academic, 2015.

Calvin, John. *Institutes of the Christian Religion (1559)*. Edited by John T. McNeill. Translated by Ford Lewis Battles. Library of Christian Classics 20–21. Philadelphia: Westminster, 1960. Latin text available in CO 2 (1864). Digital copy online at archive-ouverte.unige.ch/unige:650.

———. "The Forms of Prayers and Songs of the Church (1542): Letter to the Reader." Translated by Ford Lewis Battles. *Calvin Theological Journal* 15, no. 2 (1980): 160-65.

Cassiodorus. *Explanation of the Psalms*. 3 vols. Translated and annotated by P. G. Walsh Ancient Christian Writers 51–53. Mahweh, NJ: Paulist Press, 1990–1991.

Castellio, Sebastian. *Psalterium reliquaque sacrarum literarum Carmina et Precationes*. Basel: Oporinus, 1547. Digital copy online at www.gateway-bayern.de.

Childs, Brevard S. "Does the Old Testament Witness to Jesus Christ?" In *Evangelium Schriftauslegung Kirche: Festschrift für Peter Stuhlmacher zum 65. Geburtstag*. Edited by Jostein Ådna, Scott J. Hafemann and Otfried Hofius, 57-64. Göttingen: Vandenhoeck & Ruprecht, 1997.

———. "The Sensus Literalis of Scripture: An Ancient and Modern Problem." In *Beiträge zur Alttestamentlichen Theologie: Festschrift für Walther Zimmerli zum 70. Geburtstag*. Edited by Herbert Donner, Robert Hanhart and Rudolf Sment, 80-93. Göttingen: Vandenhoeck & Ruprecht, 1977.

Chung-Kim, Esther and Todd R. Hains, eds. *Acts*. Reformation Commentary on Scripture, New Testament 6. Downers Grove, IL: IVP Academic, 2014.

Cicero. *Tusculan Disputations*. Translated by J. E. King. Loeb Classical Library 141. Cambridge: Harvard University Press, 1927.

The Commission on Worship for the Lutheran Church–Missouri Synod, ed. *Lutheran Service Book*. St. Louis: Concordia, 2006.

Eck, Johann. *Warhafftige handlung wie es mit herr Lenhart Käser zu Schärding verbrent ergangen ist: Wider ain falsch erdicht unnd erlogen büchlin*. Ingolstadt: Apian, 1527. Digital copy online at www.gateway-bayern.de.

Edwards, Mark U., Jr. *Luther's Last Battles: Politics and Polemics, 1531–46.* Ithaca, NY: Cornell University Press, 1983.

Ellis, Brannon E. *Calvin, Classical Trinitarianism and the Aseity of the Son.* Oxford: Oxford University Press, 2012.

Erasmus, Desiderius, and Martin Luther. *Luther and Erasmus: Free Will and Salvation.* Translated and edited by E. Gordon Rupp and Philip S. Watson. Library of Christian Classics 17. Louisville, KY: Westminster John Knox Press, 1969.

Fairbairn, Donald L. *Life in the Trinity.* Downers Grove, IL: IVP Academic, 2009.

Farmer, Craig S., ed. *John 1–12.* Reformation Commentary on Scripture, New Testament 4. Downers Grove, IL: IVP Academic, 2014.

Fast, Heinold and John H. Yoder. "How to Deal with Anabaptists: An Unpublished Letter of Heinrich Bullinger." *Mennonite Quarterly Review* 33, no. 2 (1959): 83-95.

Frend, W. H. C. *The Donatist Church.* 3rd ed. Oxford: Clarendon, 1985.

Frymire, John M. *The Primacy of the Postils: Catholics, Protestants and the Dissemination of Ideas in Early Modern Germany.* Leiden: Brill, 2010.

Ganoczy, Alexandre. *La Bibliothèque de l'Académie de Calvin.* Geneva: Droz, 1969.

———. *The Young Calvin.* Translated by David Foxgrover and Wade Provo. Philadelphia: Westminster, 1987.

George, Timothy. *Theology of the Reformers.* Revised ed. Nashville: B & H Academic, 2013.

Goldingay, John. *Psalms.* 3 vols. Baker Commentary on the Old Testament Wisdom and Psalms. Grand Rapids: Baker Academic, 2006.

———. *Do We Need the New Testament?* Downers Grove, IL: IVP Academic, 2015.

Graham, W. Fred. *The Constructive Revolutionary: John Calvin and His Socio-Economic Impact.* Richmond, VA: John Knox Press, 1971.

Greene-McCreight, Kathryn. "Literal Sense." In *Dictionary for Theological Interpretation of the Bible.* Edited by Kevin J. Vanhoozer, 455-56. Grand Rapids: Baker Academic, 2005.

———. "Rule of Faith." In *Dictionary for Theological Interpretation of the Bible.* Edited by Kevin J. Vanhoozer, 703-704. Grand Rapids: Baker Academic, 2005.

Haile, H. G. *Luther: An Experiment in Biography.* Garden City, NY: Doubleday, 1980.

Hall, Christopher A. *Reading Scripture with the Church Fathers.* Downers Grove, IL: InterVarsity Press, 1998.

———. *Worshiping with the Church Fathers.* Downers Grove, IL: IVP Academic, 2009.

Helmer, Christine. "Luther's Trinitarian Hermeneutic and the Old Testament." *Modern Theology* 18, no. 1 (2002): 49-73.

Hobbs, R. Gerald. "Conrad Pellican and the Psalms: The Ambivalent Legacy of a Pioneer Hebraist." *Reformation & Renaissance Review* 1, no. 1 (1999): 72-99.

———. "How Firm a Foundation: Martin Bucer's Historical Exegesis of the Psalms." *Church History* 53, no. 4 (1984): 477-91.

Kapic, Kelly M. "Faith, Hope and Love: A Theological Meditation on Suffering and Sanctification." In *Sanctification: Explorations in Theology and Practice.* Edited by Kelly M. Kapic, 212-31. Downers Grove, IL: IVP Academic, 2014.

Klaassen, Walter. "Bern Debate of 1538: Christ the Center of Scripture." *Mennonite Quarterly Review* 40, no. 2 (1966): 148-56.

Kraus, Hans-Joachim. *Psalms 1–59: A Commentary.* Continental Commentaries. Translated by Hilton C. Oswald. Minneapolis: Augsburg, 1988.

————. *Psalms 60–150: A Commentary.* Continental Commentaries. Translated by Hilton C. Oswald. Minneapolis: Augsburg, 1989.

Kreitzer, Beth, ed. *Luke.* Reformation Commentary on Scripture, New Testament 3. Downers Grove, IL: IVP Academic, 2015.

Lubac, Henri de. *Medieval Exegesis: The Four Senses of Scripture.* 3 vols. Translated by Mark Sebanc and E. M. Macierowski. Grand Rapids: Eerdmans, 1998–2009.

Luther, Martin. *Von Er Lenhard keiser ynn Beyern umb des Euangelii willen verbrandt: Eine selige geschicht.* Wittenberg: Hans Lufft, 1528. Digital copy online at www.gateway-bayern.de.

Luy, David J. Dominus Mortus: *Martin Luther on the Incorruptibility of God in Christ.* Minneapolis: Fortress Press, 2014.

Major, Georg. *Psalterium Davidis.* Magdeburg: Michael Lotther, 1547. Digital copy online at www.gateway-bayern.de.

Manetsch, Scott M. *Calvin's Company of Pastors: Pastoral Care and the Emerging Reformed Church, 1536–1609.* Oxford: Oxford University Press, 2012.

Marlorat, Augustin. *Liber Psalmorum Davidis, cum catholica expositione Ecclesiastica.* Geneva: Henri Estienne, 1562. Digital copy online at www.e-rara.ch.

Mattox, Mickey L. "Luther's Interpretation of Scripture: Biblical Understanding in Trinitarian Shape." In *The Substance of Faith: Luther's Doctrinal Theology for Today.* Edited by Paul R. Hinlickey, 11-57. Minneapolis: Fortress, 2008.

Meijering, E. P. *Melanchthon and Patristic Thought: The Doctrines of Christ and Grace, the Trinity and the Creation.* Leiden: Brill, 1983.

Mombaer, Jan. *Rosetum exercitiorum spiritualium et sacrarum meditationum.* Basel: Jakob Wolff, 1504.

Moibanus, Ambrosius. *Wie in Schlesien zur Olsen über die Stadt ain unerhört, wunderbarlich und grawsam ungewitter mit feür regnen und erschrocklichem wunderwürckenden wind kommen ist allen Gots förchtigen wolzuwissen.* Augsburg: Philipp Ulhart, 1536. Digital copy online at www.gateway-bayern.de.

Muller, Richard A. "Biblical Interpretation in the Era of the Reformation: The View from the Middle Ages." In *Biblical Interpretation in the Era of the Reformation: Essays Presented to David C. Steinmetz in Honor of His Sixtieth Birthday.* Edited by Richard A. Muller and John L. Thompson, 3-22. Grand Rapids: Eerdmans, 1996.

————. *Dictionary of Latin and Greek Theological Terms: Drawn Principally from Protestant Scholastic Theology.* Grand Rapids: Baker Academic, 1985.

Muller, Richard A., and John L. Thompson. "The Significance of Precritical Exegesis: Retrospect and Prospect." In *Biblical Interpretation in the Era of the Reformation: Essays Presented to David C. Steinmetz in Honor of His Sixtieth Birthday.* Edited by Richard A Muller and John L. Thompson, 335-45. Grand Rapids: Eerdmans, 1996.

Myers, Benjamin. *Salvation in My Pocket: Fragments of Faith and Theology.* Eugene, OR: Cascade Books, 2013.

Oberman, Heiko A. *Forerunners of the Reformation: The Shape of Late Medieval Thought.* Translations by Paul L. Nyhus. New York: Holt, Rinehard and Winston, 1966.

————. *The Roots of Anti-Semitism in the Age of the Renaissance and Reformation.* Translated by James I. Porter. Philadelphia: Fortress Press, 1984.

Ozment, Steven E. *The Serpent and the Lamb: Cranach, Luther and the Making of the Reformation.* New Haven, CT: Yale University Press, 2011.

Pak, Sujin G. *The Judaizing Calvin: Sixteenth-Century Debates over the Messianic Psalms.* Oxford: Oxford University Press, 2010.

———. "Luther, Bucer and Calvin on Psalms 8 and 16: Confessional Formation and the Question of Jewish Exegesis." *Nederlands archief voor kerkgeschiedenis* 85, no. 1 (2005): 169-86.

Parker, T. H. L. *Calvin's Preaching*. Louisville, KY: Westminster John Knox Press, 1992.

Pelikan, Jaroslav. *The Christian Tradition*. 5 vols. Chicago: University of Chicago Press, 1971–1989.

Plass, Ewald, ed. *What Luther Says: An Anthology*. 3 vols. St. Louis: Concordia, 1959.

Pliny the Elder. *The Natural History*. 10 vols. Translated by H. Rackham. Cambridge, MA: Harvard University Press, 1947. Digital copy available online at archive.org.

Pratensis, Felix. *Psalterium Sextuplex: Hebraeum cum tribus Latinis videlicet Divi Hieronymi, R. P. Sanctis Pagnini et Felicis Pratensis, Graecum Septuaginta interpretum cum Latina vulgata*. Leiden: Sebastian Gryphius, 1530. Digital copy online at books.google.com.

Reuchlin, Johannes. *De rudimentis Hebraica*. Pforzheim: Thomas Anselm, 1506. Digital copy online at www.gateway-bayern.de and gallica.bnr.fr.

———. *In septem psalmos poenitentiales hebraicos*. Tübingen: Thomas Anselm, 1512. Digital copy online at www.gateway-bayern.de.

Rittgers, Ronald K. *Reformation of Suffering: Pastoral Theology and Lay Piety in Late Medieval and Early Modern Germany*. Oxford: Oxford University Press, 2012.

Saebø, Magne, ed. *Hebrew Bible, Old Testament: The History of Its Interpretation*. 3 vols. Göttingen: Vandenhoeck & Ruprecht, 1996–2015.

Sattler, Michael. *The Legacy of Michael Sattler*. Translated and edited by John H. Yoder. Classics of the Radical Reformation 1. Scottdale, PA: Herald Press, 1973.

Selderhuis, Herman J. *Calvin's Theology of the Psalms*. Grand Rapids: Baker Academic, 2007.

———. ed. *The Calvin Handbook*. Grand Rapids: Eerdmans, 2009.

Smith, Mahlon H., III. *And Taking Bread . . . : Cerularius and the Azyme Controversy of 1054*. Paris: Beauchesne, 1978.

Soulen, R. Kendall. *The Divine Name(s) and the Holy Trinity*. Louisville, KY: Westminster John Knox, 2011.

Stec, David, trans. *The Targum of Psalms*. Collegeville, MN: Liturgical Press, 1987.

Tetz, Martin. "Zum Psalterverständnis bei Athanasius and Luther." *Lutherjahrbuch* 79 (2012): 39-61.

Tremellius, Immanuel. *Testamenti Veteris Biblia Sacra sive Libri Canonici priscae Iudaeorum Ecclesiae a Deo traditi*. London: Henry Middleton, 1580. Digital copy online at EEBO.

Virgil. *The Aeneid*. Translated by Robert Fitzgerald. New York: Vintage Classics, 1990.

Wels, Volkhard. "Melanchthon's Textbooks on Dialectic and Rhetoric as Complementary Parts of a Theory of Argumentation." In *Scholarly Knowledge: Textbooks in Early Modern Europe*. Edited by Emidio Campi, 139-56. Geneva: Droz, 2008.

Wesselschmidt, Quentin F., ed. *Psalms 51–150*. Ancient Christian Commentary on Scripture, Old Testament 8. Downers Grove, IL: InterVarsity Press, 2007.

Williams, George H. *The Radical Reformation*. 3rd ed. Kirksville, MO: Sixteenth Century Journal Publishers, 1992.

Zachman, Randall C. *John Calvin as Teacher, Pastor and Theologian: The Shape of His Writings and Thoughts*. Grand Rapids: Baker Academic, 2006.

Author and Writings Index

Subject Index

Abimelech, as kingly title, 269

Abraham, 39, 47, 256

Absalom, 30, 36, 39, 333, 401

Adam, 69-70, 74, 203, 251, 365, 382

Adonai, 51-53, 441

affliction. *See* trials

ʿalmût, 81-82, 310, 351

ʾal-tašḥēt, 414

ambition, human, 311-12

"amen," meaning of, 323-24

angels, 74-76
as protectors of the church, 271-72

anger
dealing with, 40-41
effects of, 294

animals
humanity as, 256, 369
as subject to humans, 78
typology of wild, 181

anthropopathic language, 89, 99-101, 280

antichrist, 94, 123

apostles, as Christ's cavalry, 344

ark, of the covenant, 112, 138, 155, 157, 196, 200, 222, 235, 252, 356-58, 428, 460-62

Asaph, 371

ascension, of Christ, 356-58, 464-65

atheism, 88-89, 108

authority, of Christ, 21, 26

Baal, 225

Balaam, 35

baptism, 114, 225, 228
apart from faith, 48
of Christ, 17
purpose of, 388
as salvation, 184, 254-55

beauty, of the church, 348

beggars, and the church, 320-21

believers, sin nature of, 151-52

blessings
of Christ, 75-76
contemplation of, 79
disregarding God's, 134-35

equating earthly and heavenly, 130-31
given unequally, 297-98
from God, 35, 50, 55, 77-78, 445-46, 448-49

boasting, human, 393

body, metaphors of the human, 277-78

bribes, accepting, 116

brides, encouragement to, 349

bulwark. *See* refuge

Canaan, as heavenly inheritance, 294-95, 433, 477

cave, of David, 416

ceremony, external, 423

cherubim, 138
typology of, 432

childbearing, miracle of, 481-82

choirs, 38

Christ Jesus, 96, 111, 113, 116-17, 124-26, 141, 146-48, 154-56, 182-83, 199-200, 209, 212, 223, 237, 252, 255, 288, 326, 371-72, 378, 401, 409, 428-29, 477
betrayal of, 319-20, 322-23, 404
blood of, 386
as bridegroom, 147-48
as the church, 242
as divine, 24-26, 28, 76, 457-58
as example, 1, 8-9, 310-11, 315, 422
as fountain, 13, 328
as fulfillment of prophecy, *xlviii-xli, li,* 2-4, 17-18, 45, 73, 77, 118, 128, 134, 164, 166-69, 224, 238, 366, 406
as intercessor, 4, 155, 302
as king, 17-19, 23, 161-62, 196
lips of, 344
as lower than angels, 74-76
mission of, 79

as promise of woman's seed, 250
prophecy about, 67, 109, 137, 196, 237
quoting Psalms, 1, 237-38, 240, 343, 413
as redeemer, 153
as rock, 315-16
as savior, 19, 52, 63, 184, 224
as shepherd, 130, 186-91, 194-95
as substance of typology, 83, 112, 114, 130, 433, 463
suffering of, 77, 136, 142-43, 169-73, 175-79, 240, 243, 246, 301, 416, 466-67, 475-76
as Sun of Righteousness, 147, 368, 425
as the temple, 48, 198-99
two natures of, 1, 17, 26, 100, 415-16
union with, 10, 302, 327, 341-43, 347-48, 442, 465
and virgin birth, 174

church, the, 121, 161, 182, 197, 199, 206, 209, 246, 283, 298, 379
attendance in, 325-26, 452
authority of God over, 458
as bride of Christ, 342-43, 347-48
cherishing, 361-62
as city of God, 353
as doves, 464
as example, 269, 271
faithfulness of, 207-9, 407
as fountain, 350-51
as God's house, 193-94, 231
as heaven, 157
as Jew and Gentile, 141, 349, 463
as lilies, 343, 471-72
as living for God, 283
as reigning with Christ, 368

as set apart, 212
as spiritual Israel, 17, 23, 196, 198, 201, 209, 224, 265, 336
suffering of, 177, 242, 290, 302, 320, 331
as the temple, 200
unbelievers in, 114-15, 392, 394
unity of, 48, 84, 270, 369

city of David, 403

cleansing of believers, 386-87

clouds, as majesty of God, 372

comfort for believers, 40, 59-60, 69, 243-45, 297, 317, 321, 330, 352-53, 361, 363, 388, 437, 462, 474-75

commandments, the ten, 239

confidence in God, 34, 149, 190, 218, 221, 337, 354-55
boasting in, 238-39

conscience, 56, 58, 102, 128-29, 145, 149-50, 177, 189, 286
guilty, 109, 140, 176, 183, 253-54, 304, 387-88
keeping a good conscience, 39-41, 63-64, 66, 68, 113, 124, 139-40, 210, 281-82, 284
nature of, 62-63

consolation. *See* comfort

contemplation. *See* meditation

contentment with earthly possessions, 193

contrition, metaphor of, 340

conversion, of unbelievers, 223

counsel, spiritual 105, 123, 265

covenant, of God
with all people, 457
with the church, 151, 207, 216, 336
meaning of, 205

creation
as fallen, 70

Scripture Index